Nineteenth-Century Literature Criticism

Topics Volume

Guide to Gale Literary Criticism Series

For criticism on	Consult these Gale series
Authors now living or who died after December 31, 1999	*CONTEMPORARY LITERARY CRITICISM (CLC)*
Authors who died between 1900 and 1999	*TWENTIETH-CENTURY LITERARY CRITICISM (TCLC)*
Authors who died between 1800 and 1899	*NINETEENTH-CENTURY LITERATURE CRITICISM (NCLC)*
Authors who died between 1400 and 1799	*LITERATURE CRITICISM FROM 1400 TO 1800 (LC)* *SHAKESPEAREAN CRITICISM (SC)*
Authors who died before 1400	*CLASSICAL AND MEDIEVAL LITERATURE CRITICISM (CMLC)*
Authors of books for children and young adults	*CHILDREN'S LITERATURE REVIEW (CLR)*
Dramatists	*DRAMA CRITICISM (DC)*
Poets	*POETRY CRITICISM (PC)*
Short story writers	*SHORT STORY CRITICISM (SSC)*
Black writers of the past two hundred years	*BLACK LITERATURE CRITICISM (BLC)* *BLACK LITERATURE CRITICISM SUPPLEMENT (BLCS)*
Hispanic writers of the late nineteenth and twentieth centuries	*HISPANIC LITERATURE CRITICISM (HLC)* *HISPANIC LITERATURE CRITICISM SUPPLEMENT (HLCS)*
Native North American writers and orators of the eighteenth, nineteenth, and twentieth centuries	*NATIVE NORTH AMERICAN LITERATURE (NNAL)*
Major authors from the Renaissance to the present	*WORLD LITERATURE CRITICISM, 1500 TO THE PRESENT (WLC)* *WORLD LITERATURE CRITICISM SUPPLEMENT (WLCS)*

ISSN 0732-1864

Volume 100

Nineteenth-Century Literature Criticism

Topics Volume

Excerpts from Criticism of Various
Topics in Nineteenth-Century Literature,
including Literary and Critical Movements,
Prominent Themes and Genres, Anniversary
Celebrations, and Surveys of National Literatures

Thomas J. Schoenberg
Lawrence J. Trudeau
Editors

Jessica Menzo
Russel Whitaker
Associate Editors

GALE GROUP

THOMSON LEARNING

Detroit • New York • San Diego • San Francisco
Boston • New Haven, Conn. • Waterville, Maine
London • Munich

STAFF

Lynn M. Spampinato, Janet Witalec, *Managing Editors, Literature Product*
Kathy D. Darrow, Ellen McGeagh, *Content-Product Liaisons*
Thomas J. Schoenberg, Lawrence J. Trudeau, *Editors*
Mark W. Scott, *Publisher, Literature Product*

Jessica Menzo, Russel Whitaker, *Associate Editors*
Maikue Vang, *Assistant Editor*
Jenny Cromie, Mary Ruby, *Technical Training Specialists*
Deborah J. Morad, Joyce Nakamura, Kathleen Lopez Nolan, *Managing Editors, Literature Content*
Susan M. Trosky, *Director, Literature Content*

Maria L. Franklin, *Permissions Manager*
Edna M. Hedblad, *Permissions Specialist*
Kim Davis, Debra Freitas, *Permissions Associates*

Victoria B. Cariappa, *Research Manager*
Sarah Genik, *Project Coordinator*
Ron Morelli, Tamara C. Nott, Tracie A. Richardson, *Research Associates*
Michelle Campbell, *Administrative Specialist*

Dorothy Maki, *Manufacturing Manager*
Stacy L. Melson, *Buyer*

Mary Beth Trimper, *Composition and Prepress Manager*
Carolyn Roney, *Composition Specialist*

Randy Bassett, *Imaging Supervisor*
Robert Duncan, Dan Newell, Luke Rademacher, *Imaging Specialists*
Pamela A. Reed, *Imaging Coordinator*
Kelly A. Quin, *Imaging Editor*
Michael Logusz, *Graphic Artist*

Library of Congress Catalog Card Number
ISBN 0-7876-4555-9
ISSN 0732-1864
Printed in the United States of America

10 9 8 7 6 5 4 3 2 1

Contents

Preface vii

Acknowledgments xi

Literary Criticism Series Advisory Board xiii

Preface

Since its inception in 1981, *Nineteeth-Century Literature Criticism* (*NCLC*) has been a valuable resource for students and librarians seeking critical commentary on writers of this transitional period in world history. Designated an "Outstanding Reference Source" by the American Library Association with the publication of is first volume, *NCLC* has since been purchased by over 6,000 school, public, and university libraries. The series has covered more than 300 authors representing 29 nationalities and over 17,000 titles. No other reference source has surveyed the critical reaction to nineteenth-century authors and literature as thoroughly as *NCLC*.

Scope of the Series

NCLC is designed to introduce students and advanced readers to the authors of the nineteenth century and to the most significant interpretations of these authors' works. The great poets, novelists, short story writers, playwrights, and philosophers of this period are frequently studied in high school and college literature courses. By organizing and reprinting commentary written on these authors, *NCLC* helps students develop valuable insight into literary history, promotes a better understanding of the texts, and sparks ideas for papers and assignments. Each entry in *NCLC* presents a comprehensive survey of an author's career or an individual work of literature and provides the user with a multiplicity of interpretations and assessments. Such variety allows students to pursue their own interests; furthermore, it fosters an awareness that literature is dynamic and responsive to many different opinions.

Every fourth volume of *NCLC* is devoted to literary topics that cannot be covered under the author approach used in the rest of the series. Such topics include literary movements, prominent themes in nineteenth-century literature, literary reaction to political and historical events, significant eras in literary history, prominent literary anniversaries, and the literatures of cultures that are often overlooked by English-speaking readers.

NCLC continues the survey of criticism of world literature begun by Gale's *Contemporary Literary Criticism* (*CLC*) and *Twentieth-Century Literary Criticism* (*TCLC*).

Organization of the Book

An *NCLC* entry consists of the following elements:

- The **Author Heading** cites the name under which the author most commonly wrote, followed by birth and death dates. Also located here are any name variations under which an author wrote, including transliterated forms for authors whose native languages use nonroman alphabets. If the author wrote consistently under a pseudonym, the pseudonym will be listed in the author heading and the author's actual name given in parenthesis on the first line of the biographical and critical information. Uncertain birth or death dates are indicated by question marks. Single-work entries are preceded by a heading that consists of the most common form of the title in English translation (if applicable) and the original date of composition.

- The **Introduction** contains background information that introduces the reader to the author, work, or topic that is the subject of the entry.

- A **Portrait of the Author** is included when available.

- The list of **Principal Works** is ordered chronologically by date of first publication and lists the most important works by the author. The genre and publication date of each work is given. In the case of foreign authors whose works have been translated into English, the list will focus primarily on twentieth-century translations, selecting those works most commonly considered the best by critics. Unless otherwise indicated, dramas are dated by first performance, not first publication. Lists of **Representative Works** by different authors appear with topic entries.

- Reprinted **Criticism** is arranged chronologically in each entry to provide a useful perspective on changes in critical evaluation over time. The critic's name and the date of composition or publication of the critical work are given at the beginning of each piece of criticism. Unsigned criticism is preceded by the title of the source in which it appeared. All titles by the author featured in the text are printed in boldface type. Footnotes are reprinted at the end of each essay or excerpt. In the case of excerpted criticism, only those footnotes that pertain to the excerpted texts are included. Criticism in topic entries is arranged chronologically under a variety of subheadings to facilitate the study of different aspects of the topic.

- A complete **Bibliographical Citation** of the original essay or book precedes each piece of criticism.

- Critical essays are prefaced by brief **Annotations** explicating each piece.

- An annotated bibliography of **Further Reading** appears at the end of each entry and suggests resources for additional study. In some cases, significant essays for which the editors could not obtain reprint rights are included here. Boxed material following the further reading list provides references to other biographical and critical sources on the author in series published by Gale.

Indexes

Each volume of *NCLC* contains a **Cumulative Author Index** listing all authors who have appeared in a wide variety of reference sources published by the Gale Group, including *NCLC*. A complete list of these sources is found facing the first page of the Author Index. The index also includes birth and death dates and cross references between pseudonyms and actual names.

A **Cumulative Nationality Index** lists all authors featured in *NCLC* by nationality, followed by the number of the *NCLC* volume in which their entry appears.

A **Cumulative Topic Index** lists the literary themes and topics treated in the series as well as in *Classical and Medieval Literature Criticism, Literature Criticism from 1400 to 1800, Twentieth-Century Literary Criticism,* and the *Contemporary Literary Criticism* Yearbook, which was discontinued in 1998.

An alphabetical **Title Index** accompanies each volume of *NCLC*, with the exception of the Topics volumes. Listings of titles by authors covered in the given volume are followed by the author's name and the corresponding page numbers where the titles are discussed. English translations of foreign titles and variations of titles are cross-referenced to the title under which a work was originally published. Titles of novels, dramas, nonfiction books, and poetry, short story, or essay collections are printed in italics, while individual poems, short stories, and essays are printed in roman type within quotation marks.

In response to numerous suggestions from librarians, Gale also produces an annual paperbound edition of the *NCLC* cumulative title index. This annual cumulation, which alphabetically lists all titles reviewed in the series, is available to all customers. Additional copies of this index are available upon request. Librarians and patrons will welcome this separate index; it saves shelf space, is easy to use, and is recyclable upon receipt of the next edition.

Citing *Nineteenth-Century Literature Criticism*

When writing papers, students who quote directly from any volume in the Literary Criticism Series may use the following general format to footnote reprinted criticism. The first example pertains to material drawn from periodicals, the second to material reprinted from books.

Kim McQuaid, "William Apes, Pequot: An Indian Reformer in the Jackson Era," *The New England Quarterly,* 50 (December 1977): 605-25; excerpted and reprinted in *Nineteenth-Century Literature Criticism,* vol. 73, ed. Janet Witalec (Farmington Hills, Mich.: The Gale Group, 1999), 3-4.

Richard Harter Fogle, *The Imagery of Keats and Shelley: A Comparative Study* (Archon Books, 1949), 211-51; excerpted and reprinted in *Nineteenth-Century Literature Criticism,* vol. 73, ed. Janet Witalec (Farmington Hills, Mich.: The Gale Group, 1999), 157-69.

Suggestions are Welcome

Readers who wish to suggest new features, topics, or authors to appear in future volumes, or who have other suggestions or comments are cordially invited to call, write, or fax the Managing Editor:

Managing Editor, Literary Criticism Series
The Gale Group
27500 Drake Road
Farmington Hills, MI 48331-3535
1-800-347-4253 (GALE)
Fax: 248-699-8054

Acknowledgments

The editors wish to thank the copyright holders of the excerpted criticism included in this volume and the permissions managers of many book and magazine publishing companies for assisting us in securing reproduction rights. We are also grateful to the staffs of the Detroit Public Library, the Library of Congress, the University of Detroit Mercy Library, Wayne State University Purdy/Kresge Library Complex, and the University of Michigan Libraries for making their resources available to us. Following is a list of the copyright holders who have granted us permission to reproduce material in this volume of *NCLC*. Every effort has been made to trace copyright, but if omissions have been made, please let us know.

COPYRIGHTED EXCERPTS IN *NCLC*, VOLUME 100, WERE REPRODUCED FROM THE FOLLOWING PERIODICALS:

COPYRIGHTED EXCERPTS IN *NCLC*, VOLUME 100, WERE REPRODUCED FROM THE FOLLOWING BOOKS:

PHOTOGRAPHS AND ILLUSTRATIONS APPEARING IN *NCLC*, VOLUME 100, WERE RECEIVED FROM THE FOLLOWING SOURCES:

Literary Criticism Series Advisory Board

The members of the Gale Group Literary Criticism Series Advisory Board—reference librarians and subject specialists from public, academic, and school library systems—represent a cross-section of our customer base and offer a variety of informed perspectives on both the presentation and content of our literature criticism products. Advisory board members assess and define such quality issues as the relevance, currency, and usefulness of the author coverage, critical content, and literary topics included in our series; evaluate the layout, presentation, and general quality of our printed volumes; provide feedback on the criteria used for selecting authors and topics covered in our series; provide suggestions for potential enhancements to our series; identify any gaps in our coverage of authors or literary topics, recommending authors or topics for inclusion; analyze the appropriateness of our content and presentation for various user audiences, such as high school students, undergraduates, graduate students, librarians, and educators; and offer feedback on any proposed changes/ enhancements to our series. We wish to thank the following advisors for their advice throughout the year.

The Journals of Lewis and Clark

INTRODUCTION

By the turn of the nineteenth century, interest in discovering a northwest passage across North America to the Pacific Ocean was intense. European powers Spain, France and Britain, along with the fledgling United States, strove to find a water route across the continent in order to facilitate easier trade with the East. The French had held the Louisiana Territory, a vast area stretching from the Gulf of Mexico to Canada, for more than a century prior to the American Revolutionary War. However, in 1762, during the Seven Years' War, New France faced almost certain defeat by the British, whose blockade cut off all aid to the region. In order to keep the land from falling into British hands, King Louis XV ceded all holdings west of the Mississippi River to Spain. By 1800 the nominally weak Spain feared that it could not hold Louisiana and secretly signed the Treaty of San Ildefonso, which ceded the colony back to the French. Led by Napoleon Bonaparte, the French initially hoped to establish an overseas empire in North America; these hopes were abandoned only a few years later when, needing troops for their renewed war with Great Britain, Napoleon offered the whole of Louisiana to the newly-formed United States. Signed in 1803, the Louisiana Purchase doubled the size of the U.S. For fifteen million dollars, Thomas Jefferson, the third president of the U.S., purchased nearly one million square miles of land, and finally secured for himself the opportunity to fulfill his dream of exploring the entire northwest.

Born in 1743 in Virginia, Jefferson had long believed that the west would one day be populated by Americans. He often ruminated about the uncharted wilderness west of the Mississippi River, which had recently marked the western boundary of the country. Hoping to open trade with the Indians and with traders on the Pacific Coast from Europe and the Orient, Jefferson was adamant in his goal of finding a water route across the continent. He specifically wished to discover if there was a west-flowing stream emanating from the Missouri River and running into the Pacific. It was known that the Missouri River ran east from the mountains into the Mississippi River and that the Columbia River flowed west out of the mountains into the Pacific. Jefferson hoped to find that the headwaters of the Missouri and Columbia rivers were close together, forming a relatively easy water route to the Pacific Coast.

To lead the expedition, Jefferson chose Meriwether Lewis, his personal friend and private secretary. Lewis was born in 1774 on a Virginia plantation less than ten miles from Jefferson's home on Monticello. Although Lewis had little formal schooling, he was considerably knowledgeable about the outdoors, spending a great amount of time hunting, teaching himself about plants and vegetation, and, with help, managing the family's thousand-acre farm, where he learned how to herd, make clothing, and maintain financial accounts. Joining the militia in 1794, Lewis enlisted in the regular army in 1795 and by 1800 had become a captain. By 1802, when first approached by Jefferson about the expedition, Lewis had several years of experience in the Northwest Territory. His first choice as his second-in-command was William Clark, a former captain in the military who had commanded Lewis in the Chosen Rifle Company, an elite group of sharpshooters, in the mid-1790s and who had become good friends with Lewis during their eight months together. Clark had little formal schooling, which resulted in a lifelong struggle with language and grammar, but he excelled at science, natural history, and math. Clark joined the military in 1789, but resigned his captaincy in 1796 in order to attend to family matters. Lewis commissioned Clark a second lieutenant for the expedition, though in practice Clark was considered a captain and on equal footing with Lewis.

The objectives of the expedition were clear—first and foremost, the explorers were to seek a water route from the Missouri River to the Pacific Ocean. In 1803 Jefferson told Lewis: "The object of your mission is to explore the Missouri river, & such principal stream[s] of it, as, by it's course and communication with the waters of the Pacific ocean, whether the Columbia, Oregan, Colorado, or any other river may offer the most direct and practicable water communication across this continent for the purposes of commerce." Second, the explorers were to gather scientific data, including notes about the mineralogy, climate, and geography of the region; perhaps most importantly, they were to survey and map the courses of the Missouri. In addition, the explorers were to study and return samples of vegetation and wildlife and provide an account of the native tribes of the western country, detailing their language and customs while serving as diplomats from the U.S.

Lewis planned the trip carefully with Jefferson, spending months preparing scientific and surveying equipment, weaponry, clothing, medicines, and tools, eventually assembling thousands of pounds of supplies. Both Lewis and Clark selected members of the company with great deliberation. Becoming known as the Corps of Discovery, the group initially consisted of approximately forty men, sixteen of whom traveled with the company only through the first stretch of the journey. Those sixteen returned to St. Louis, Missouri, when the expedition reached present-day North Dakota in late 1804, where the remaining group would spend the winter. This latter group included twenty-three regular army men along with two woodsmen who served as interpreters and hunters. One of these, Toussaint Chaboneau, brought along his Shoshone wife, Sacajawea, the only woman on the journey. Sacajawea, who gave birth to a son during the winter of 1805, proved invaluable to the expedition for her help in serving as a liaison between the company and various Indian tribes.

Equipped with one keelboat and two *pirogues* (smaller open boats), the Corps of Discovery began what would become their more than two-and-a-half-year journey in mid-May, 1804. Departing from St. Louis, they followed the Missouri River through what is now Kansas, Iowa, Nebraska, and South Dakota, finally reaching a site they named Fort Mandan in present-day North Dakota, where they prepared for their first winter. From October 1804 to early April 1805, they camped near the Mandans, a group of peaceful Indians, sharing buffalo catches, gathering information from the Indians, and meeting with British-financed traders in the area. By mid-July, 1805, having restarted their journey in the spring, they had reached the headwaters of the Missouri and had begun the laborious western trek over the Rocky Mountains on the Montana-Idaho border. By the fall of 1805 the company had reached the Columbia River, which they then followed through present-day Oregon and Washington down to the Pacific Coast, which they reached on November 14th. Constructing Fort Clatsop on the Pacific Coast, the expedition wintered there, aided by the Clatsop and Chinook Indians, who counseled the company on when critical food supplies might arrive on foreign ships and on the locations of elk herds. In late March, 1806, they began their return trip. The company split into two groups in July of 1806, following two different routes eastward after crossing the main divide of the Bitterroot Mountains from what is now Idaho into present-day Montana. While Lewis crossed the Continental Divide and headed northeast to try to discover a shorter passage over the mountains, Clark turned southeast to travel down the Yellowstone River. The groups converged in present-day North Dakota and finally returned to St. Louis in late September, 1806. All total the Corps had traveled more than 7,600 miles, including 4,134 miles outward and 3,555 miles on the return trip. They had traversed regions unseen by European eyes, relying on information from Indian guides, who were well familiar with their expansive homelands. The Corps had also found a path across the continent, although not the water route that Jefferson had so desperately sought.

The captains also brought back a wealth of information, in essence an encyclopedia of the West, which inspired Lewis and Clark scholar Donald Jackson to dub them "the writingest explorers of their time." Instructed by Jefferson to keep meticulously detailed journals during the expedition, Lewis and Clark filled notebooks with descriptions and narrative accounts of their travels, creating what many scholars have called an American literary treasure. It is generally believed that the bulk of the writing was done during the course of the expedition, although it is not clear whether events were recorded on the day on which they occurred or during the days and weeks following. Regard-

less, the journals depict the beauty of the landscape, the dangers of the wilderness, and the constant hardships the company endured. Among the latter were the numerous afflictions the men withstood, including bouts of malaria, dysentery, diarrhea, and venereal disease. Fatigue and hunger were common as well, as were the constant battles with ticks, gnats, and mosquitoes, which were often so numerous that the men could not keep them from getting into their eyes, noses, mouths, and ears. Encounters with wildlife are retold, including one meeting with an enormous grizzly bear, who took close to ten shots before swimming across a river and finally dying.

Lewis and Clark's accounts of the native tribes have been singled out as particularly invaluable, as they offer the first survey of the indigenous peoples west of the Mississippi before the influence of whites. Pointing out the customs, clothing, politics, and economics of the various tribes, the captains also provided transcriptions of as much of the native languages as they could, attempting to render the vocabulary into English spellings. This was a task difficult for both men—Clark in particular—as both had their own quirky ways of capitalizing, spelling, and using grammar, factors which have continued to vex as well as amuse scholars. Relations with native tribes are also recounted in detail. Lewis and Clark had been ordered to treat the natives in a friendly manner but not to take any unnecessary risks. They were also instructed to tell the Indians not to obstruct the passage of any white man and to make peace with one another for the good of European and American trade. If the Indians resisted, they would, as Lewis told a band of Otos in August of 1804, "bring upon your nation the displeasure of your great father, who could consume you as the fire consumes the grass of the plains."

In addition, because of their accurate and comparatively objective observations of the wildlife, vegetation, and geology they encountered, Lewis and Clark became known as pioneering scientific naturalists. One of the main objectives of the expedition was to gather and send back botanical and zoological specimens for research. To this end, Jefferson had Lewis prepare by studying under the scrutiny of scientific experts in Philadelphia, who taught him how to collect specimens, write descriptions, store and transport wildlife specimens, and how to collect plant samples and press them. The captains took extensive notes on the trees and shrubbery they encountered; the wildlife populations, including buffalo—a very important food source for the company—grizzlies, mule deer, bobcats, and squirrels; and the conditions of soils, mountains, rivers, and minerals.

In late 1806, Lewis and Clark rented a room in St. Louis in which to commence "Wrighting," though it is not clear whether they began recopying journal entries, writing to family and friends, or determining how to tell Jefferson that, in essence, the expedition had failed—no water route existed to link the two parts of the country together. Lewis was chosen to prepare the manuscript for final publication and within weeks had issued a prospectus outlining the forthcoming three-volume work, but he never finished the task. Lewis, who had been made governor of the Louisiana Territory, died in 1809 of an apparent suicide. Intending to reach Washington to settle bills for Indian affairs with then-President James Madison and to meet with Jefferson, who was still impatient for publication of the journals, Lewis spent the night at a settler's cabin near Nashville. Though two shots were heard during the night, and the proprietor of the cabin heard Lewis crying out for help, no one investigated. At daylight Lewis was found with two bullet wounds: one to his side and the other to his head. He died later that morning, on October 11th. Though the official version, supported by Jefferson, was that Lewis had killed himself, it has never been entirely proven whether his wounds were self-inflicted or whether they constituted murder.

It was left to Clark to tell the tale of their exploration. Finding massive amounts of notes in Lewis's room, most of which were in no order whatsoever, Clark realized that Lewis had made virtually no progress on the manuscript. Lewis's publishers informed Jefferson that although they had been in frequent contact with Lewis, he had never provided them with one line of manuscript. Requiring help, Clark procured the services of lawyer and scholar Nicholas Biddle, who agreed to abridge the extensive records brought back by Lewis and Clark and eventually published the two-volume *History of the Expedition Under the Command of Captains Lewis and Clark* in 1814, eight years after the end of the expedition. Paraphrasing the various journals into a continuous account, Biddle gave the public a narrative of the expedition framed as a glorious western adventure. However, with the country at war with England, public interest in the expedition had greatly subsided.

In 1893, ornithologist and military surgeon Elliott Coues published the four-volume *History of the Expedition Under the Command of Lewis and Clark,* based on the original 1814 narrative. However, late in the course of Coues's research, he made the remarkable discovery of the original manuscript of the journals in the archives of the American Philosophical Society, where they had been stored. Since Coues's edition was already at the printer, he hurriedly pushed through a revision before publication. Ten years later historian and editor Reuben Gold Thwaites edited the original journals found by Coues, undertaking the monumental task of transcribing the journals verbatim. Included among Thwaites's eight-volume *Original Journals of the Lewis and Clark Expedition, 1804-1806* (1904-05) is an atlas, journals of two of the sergeants on the expedition, Joseph Whitehouse and Charles Floyd, and related correspondence. This first edition of the actual journals in their entirety appeared exactly a century after the expedition embarked from St. Louis.

In the years following the Thwaites edition, interest in the expedition appeared to be on the rise and grew even more so in 1953, when a major portion of Clark's field notes were found in a private collection in St. Paul. The first

part of the notes, from December, 1803, to May, 1804, details the day-to-day preparations for the expedition at Camp Dubois, the company's winter encampment at the mouth of the Missouri. The second part, from spring of 1804 to April, 1805, records the 1600-mile trip north to the Mandan villages. Eventually published as *The Field Notes of Captain William Clark, 1803-1805* (1964) by Ernest Staples Osgood, these rough notes, which were probably used by the captains to compose their journal entries, are now stored at Yale University. The most comprehensive collection since Thwaites's edition has been undertaken by Gary E. Moulton, whose *Journals of the Lewis and Clark Expedition* consists of twelve volumes to date.

It has been said that in the years after the expedition Lewis, in particular, may have begun to regard the expedition as a failure. His Indian diplomacy, for the most part, had failed—the immense tribes of Sioux and Blackfeet were still hostile to the U.S.; Americans had yet to populate the west; and no major trade relations had been established. Another great disappointment felt by both Lewis and Clark was the fact that their findings were never published to their satisfaction during their lifetimes. Even Clark, who outlived Lewis by almost three decades, never saw the word-for-word publication of the journals. The captains did, however, ultimately provide the world with the first maps of a previously uncharted landscape and succeeded in helping to open the western frontier to settlers. Clark, however, lived long enough to witness the great tide of Americans heading west and the subsequent upheaval of the native population. Active in an official capacity in Indian affairs throughout most of the remainder of his life, he helped ease the removal of Indians from their homes and assisted in their transition to an agrarian lifestyle, but was hardly able to negate the massive continental movement to conquer the natives and exploit the country's natural resources, consequences of the Lewis and Clark expedition that neither man could have foreseen.

REPRESENTATIVE WORKS

Frank Bergon, ed.
The Journals of Lewis and Clark (journals) 1989

Nicholas Biddle, ed.
History of the expedition under the command of Captains Lewis and Clark, to the sources of the Missouri, thence across the Rocky Mountains and down the river Columbia to the Pacific Ocean: performed during the years 1804-5-6 by order of the government of the United States 2 vols. (journals) 1814

Elliott Coues, ed.
The History of the Expedition Under the Command of Lewis and Clark, to the Sources of the Missouri River, Thence across the Rocky Mountains and down the Co-

lumbia River to the Pacific Ocean, Performed During the Years 1804-5-6, by Order of the Government of the United States 4 vols. (journals) 1893

Bernard DeVoto, ed.
The Journals of Lewis and Clark (journals) 1953

G. E. Moulton, ed.
The Journals of the Lewis and Clark Expedition 12 vols. to date (journals) 1981-

Ernest Staples Osgood, ed.
The Field Notes of Captain William Clark, 1803-1805 (journal) 1964

Milo M. Quaife, ed.
The Journals of Captain Meriwether Lewis and Sergeant John Ordway Kept on the Expedition of Western Exploration, 1803-1806 (journals) 1916

Reuben Gold Thwaites, ed.
Original Journals of the Lewis and Clark Expedition, 1804-1806 8 vols. (journals) 1904-05

OVERVIEWS AND GENERAL STUDIES

Bernard DeVoto (essay date 1953)

SOURCE: An introduction to *The Journals of Lewis and Clark,* edited by Bernard DeVoto, Houghton Mifflin Company, 1953, pp. xv-lii.

[*In the following essay, DeVoto offers a comprehensive survey of the political and historical state of affairs both before and during the expedition, and provides a detailed overview of the expedition itself—noting its objectives, its major finds and contributions, as well as its principal players.*]

Toward the end of November 1802, President Thomas Jefferson asked the Spanish minister a carefully unofficial question. Would the Spanish court "take it badly," he inquired, if the United States should send a small expedition to "explore the course of the Missouri River," which lay wholly in the still Spanish territory of Louisiana? The ostensible reason for such an expedition, he went on, would be the advancement of commerce, since Congress had no power to appropriate money for its real object. But "in reality it would have no other view than the advancement of the geography." Louisiana would not continue to be Spanish much longer; it was to be returned to French sovereignty under the Treaty of San Ildefonso, which had been signed in October 1800. But since the transfer had not yet been made, the duty of the minister, the Marqués de Casa Yrujo, was to protect the interests of Spain. He and the

Spanish officials in New Orleans and St. Louis had long been afraid of American expansion in Louisiana, and of American and British military expeditions against New Mexico by way of Louisiana. He therefore, with the same scrupulous informality, told the President that "I persuaded myself that an expedition of this nature could not fail to give umbrage to our Government."

"Then he replied to me," Yrujo wrote to his chief, the Commandant of the Interior Provinces at Madrid, "that he did not see the motive why they [the Spanish government] should have the least fear, inasmuch as its object would not be other than to observe the territories which are found between 40° and 60° from the mouth of the Missouri to the Pacific Ocean, and unite the discoveries these men would make with those which the celebrated Makensi [Alexander Mackenzie] made in 1793, and be sure if it were possible in that district to establish a continual communication, or little interrupted, by water as far as the South Sea." Yrujo asserted that there was no need to inquire into this question further than had already been done. He summarized findings of various French, Spanish, Canadian, British, and imaginary explorers in the region proposed. They had demonstrated, he said, that the long sought Northwest Passage did not exist, that "a considerable cordillera" existed between 50° and 60°, that "a very great distance" must be traversed by land, and that Indian tribes had not been able to inform Mackenzie of "any considerable river whatsoever" that flowed from the mountains to the Pacific. In the interest of Spain Yrujo was being a good deal more positive than the state of knowledge justified, was inventing information which no one had, and was actually contradicting some things Mackenzie had said in his book—all of which, of course, Jefferson recognized. But, Yrujo said, "this account of the useless and fruitless attempts, it seems to me calmed his spirit with which he began to talk to me of the subject."

Yrujo had some but not much hope that this would be the end of the proposed expedition. Asking for instructions about it, he ended his dispatch with a comment on Jefferson which expressed the prevailing view of him and his country in the diplomatic corps at Washington. "The President has been all his life a man of letters, very speculative and a lover of glory, and it would be possible he might attempt to perpetuate the fame of his administration not only by the measures of frugality and economy which characterize him, but also by discovering or at least attempting to discover the way by which the Americans may some day extend their population and their influence up to the coasts of the South Sea." He did not need to point out to the colonial minister that the most promising "way" was the one Jefferson had mentioned, the Missouri River, since for ten years the Spanish themselves had been trying to reach the Pacific by ascending it.[1]

This dispatch of Yrujo's was dated December 2 1802. Two months later, on January 31 1803, he reported that Jefferson "has communicated his design to the Senate, which has already taken a step toward the execution." He understood, however, that the "good judgment of the Senate" could not see in the proposed expedition such advantages as the President claimed for it and was, besides, afraid that "it might offend one of the European nations." Probably therefore, Yrujo concluded, "the project will not proceed."[2]

Modern techniques for leaking to the press the secret proceedings of the Congress of the United States had not yet been developed. Jefferson had sent a secret message to Congress embodying his proposal, on January 18 1803. It had been considered in committees of the whole. The appropriation asked for had promptly been passed by the House and concurred in by the Senate. Thirteen days later a minister is ignorant of the message's content and the action taken on it.

In the message of January 18 Jefferson reversed what he had said to Yrujo. He asked for an appropriation of $2500 to cover the cost of an expedition to ascend the Missouri River to its source and to go on from there to the Pacific Ocean. He suggested that it be made "for the purpose of extending the external commerce of the United States," phraseology which was so general that as the title of a bill it would attract no attention. He would, however, explain the expedition to Spain as "a literary pursuit," that is, as solely an effort to add to geographical and scientific knowledge.

The expedition would indeed accomplish that end but, the message said, its primary purpose was to investigate a commercial opportunity of very great importance to the United States. Certain Indian tribes who lived in the Missouri country were known to "furnish great supplies of furs and peltry to the trade of another nation, carried on in a high latitude through an infinite number of portages and lakes shut up by ice through a long season." A route which would bring this trade down the Missouri to its mouth and then across the United States would be so superior that the established one could "bear no competition with it."

Jefferson went on to tell Congress that the Missouri was understood to traverse country which had "a moderate climate"—that is, the river did not freeze in winter, or at any rate not for long. It offered "according to the best accounts continued navigation from its source"—that is, there would be no portages at all, as contrasted with the "infinite number" of the northern route. Perhaps indeed, and this was exceedingly important, there need be only "a single portage to the Western Ocean"—that is, trade goods could be carried between the Pacific and the Mississippi with only one transshipment. Then from the Mississippi to American ports on the Atlantic there would be "a choice of channels through the Illinois or Wabash, the (Great) Lakes and Hudson, through the Ohio and Susquehanna, or Potomac or James Rivers, and through the Tennessee and Savannah rivers."[3] The expedition which he desired to send out, the President said, would explore this route and would conduct with the Indians negotiations preparatory to securing to American citizens the trade he envisioned.

The nation he referred to but did not name was Canada, and the route he described was the famous one by which the North West Company transported to Montreal the wealth in beaver it acquired by trade with the Indians west, northwest, and north of Lake Winnipeg. As many entries in the Lewis and Clark journals show, Jefferson believed that by means of the Upper Missouri American traders and carriers could get easy access to the highways of the Canadian fur trade, the Assiniboine, Saskatchewan, and Athabaska Rivers, and to the wealth in furs of the lands they drained. The expedition he now proposed was to establish a basis for opening American trade with Indians along the Missouri—in Louisiana, a province still under Spanish rule though about to be transferred to France. It was also to prepare an early and, so Jefferson believed, very promising effort by American traders to invade, and perhaps eventually to monopolize, the biggest business in Canada.

These were the principal declared purposes of the Lewis and Clark expedition. There were undeclared purposes as well, which will presently be described here. Now, however, it becomes expedient to glance at certain domestic and international matters that were at a critical stage when Jefferson sent his secret message to Congress.

2

The area called Louisiana was the western half of the drainage basin of the Mississippi River, except such parts of it as were acknowledged to have been Spanish before 1762.[4] (Thus excluded is the region south of the Arkansas River, west of the 100th meridian, and east of the Continental Divide.) According to the generally accepted belief, the northern boundary of Louisiana had been established by treaty at the 49th parallel. (Actually it had not been; there was a legal and diplomatic hiatus which permitted the manipulation of many theories and interpretations, one which might well have caused more confusion than in the eventual negotiations with Canada it did.) Jefferson, however, believed that if any portions of the Missouri drainage basin extended north of 49° they were part of Louisiana, and this was in the forefront of his thinking in 1803. The western boundary was the Continental Divide (which was still almost entirely a hypothetical conception), though some people held that, south of 49° and north of the undefined California, Louisiana extended all the way to the Pacific. In 1803 Jefferson believed that at least a faint claim to this far-western extension might exist.

Whatever the exact boundaries were, France had ceded Louisiana to Spain in 1762. The cession had a twofold purpose: to win Spain's assent to a peace treaty following the Seven Years' War by compensating her for losses suffered, and to make sure that Great Britain could not acquire Louisiana as well as Canada at the peace conference. Louisiana had therefore been a Spanish possession during the American Revolution and the entire national existence of the United States down to 1800. In October of that year Napoleon, as First Consul, forced Spain to "retrocede" it to France. This cession was made by the Treaty of San Ildefonso, news of which reached the United States in May 1801.

The acquisition of Louisiana was a step in Napoleon's effort to restore the French Empire in North America. In continuation of that effort he assembled two armies. One was sent to San Domingo in January 1802, to recover the island from the Negro dictator Toussaint L'Ouverture. The other, equipped and mobilized with great secrecy, was intended for Louisiana, which it was to secure against the British in the inevitable war whose outbreak would not be long postponed. Also, when reinforced by the one that would reconquer San Domingo, it was to be available for action against Canada—and to awe and if need be invade the United States. As early as April 1802 the State Department learned what its destination was to be.

It never sailed for Louisiana. The army in San Domingo did capture Toussaint but it was wiped out by yellow fever. The regiments that had been mobilized for Louisiana were sent instead to San Domingo, where they too were decimated by the fever and the incessant guerrilla attrition of Toussaint's successors. That Napoleon's great effort in the Western Hemisphere had failed was apparent to Jefferson when he addressed Congress in January 1803, though the full extent of the failure would not be understood till November. In that month the last remnants of the French army surrendered to a blockading British fleet, in order to escape massacre by the blacks.

Spain's cession of Louisiana to France had created a situation of very great danger to the United States. It established on our western boundary, instead of the weak and lethargic government of Spain, the greatest military power that had ever existed, the expanding French Empire under the dictatorship of the man who intended to conquer Europe and so master the world. Unassisted, the United States would be unable to drive the French out except by a total military effort that would require years, and there was little likelihood that under the pressures of war the young republic could hold together for so long a time. "From that moment," Jefferson, a lifelong anglophobe, wrote to our minister at Paris, "from that moment we must marry ourselves to the British fleet and nation." So long as France ruled Louisiana, our hope of safety lay in joint sea power.

That, however, was a long-term problem in foreign relations. The immediate urgency created by the cession was a domestic crisis. The Spanish Intendant took advantage of the impending transfer to reinstitute what he considered the proper trade policy for Louisiana. In October 1802 he withdrew the right of deposit at New Orleans. Together with the right to navigate the Mississippi, the right of deposit (the right to transship cargo from river boats to ocean-going vessels without excise or customs fee) had been granted to the United States for a term of three years by the Treaty of San Lorenzo in 1796, and on the expiration of that term it had been tacitly continued in effect. The withdrawal was a crippling blow to the commerce of the entire United States west of the Appalachian system. Moreover, it was certain that the Mississippi would remain closed after the transfer of Louisiana, for Napoleon's imperial brand of mercantilism would seal it tight against everyone but the French.

Free navigation of the Mississippi and the right of deposit at its mouth, or some other guarantee of free access to the Gulf of Mexico, were economic necessities to the American West. They were therefore political necessities to the United States—and to the administration.

Water transport by way of the Ohio River system and the Mississippi afforded the trans-Alleghany region its only practicable trade outlet. Primarily for that reason the West was but loosely attached to the federal union, which after all in 1801 had been in existence for only twelve years. Throughout the life of the Republic many Westerners had argued and agitated, and some had conspired, for the secession or separation of the West, in order to attach the area to Spain, France, or Great Britain, or to establish an independent republic which could make favorable arrangements with one of these countries. As Washington's Secretary of State, Jefferson had had to deal at alarming length with the possibility that such a separation might occur. Spain had once closed the Mississippi and thereafter, by alternately loosening and tightening control, had repeatedly tried to coerce the United States or detach the West.[5] The treaty of 1796 had quieted both the agitation and the conspiracies but had not killed either of them. All three foreign powers, but most constantly Spain, had given secret encouragement and assistance to Western separatist movements. The attitude toward the West of New England Federalists and the growth of separatist feeling among them following Jefferson's election threatened to intensify such movements.

Moreover, it had always been possible that the impatient Westerners might themselves act to open the Mississippi permanently. They might raise irregular or militia forces and seize New Orleans. (And St. Louis and lesser Louisiana settlements.) That would mean war with Spain, not a dangerous prospect in itself but one that would create a grave, possibly fatal, danger. The world had been on fire since 1792; the wars of the French Revolution were becoming the Napoleonic Wars. In such a world the entrance of the United States into any war would expose it to attack by either France or Great Britain. The outcome might well be destruction.

Jefferson was confident that he could settle both the international and the domestic crises to the advantage of the United States and without war. In the outcome his confidence proved justified. He understood the meaning of events better and estimated the forces at work more accurately than any other statesman of the time. In our entire diplomatic history there has been no greater brilliance or skill than he now displayed.

Jefferson was entirely clear, as the foreign offices of the other three powers were and long had been, that if the United States entered a war, any war whatever, it would seize not only the mouth of the Mississippi but the rest of Louisiana as well. This fact must be understood, and the further fact that if Louisiana should thus become American only severe defeat could force its return, such a defeat as might involve the military occupation of a large portion of the United States. But it was essential to avoid war. As soon as Jefferson learned that Louisiana was to be ceded to France, he moved to settle the Mississippi question permanently. He directed the American minister to France, Robert R. Livingston, to open negotiations for the purchase of New Orleans,⁶ or failing that for the right of deposit or some other means of temporarily saving the situation. Napoleon's foreign minister, Talleyrand, completely frustrated Livingston, refusing to come to grips with his proposals. Yet by October 1802, when the Spanish closed the Mississippi, it was evident that a change in his attitude might soon occur, for the failure of French arms in San Domingo was already far advanced.

The exceedingly sensitive situation became precarious as soon as the closure of the river was announced. It was imperative to prevent the Westerners from taking aggressive action, so that the State Department could continue its work. To convince the West that diplomacy was better than force and that it promised results, Jefferson appointed James Monroe "minister extraordinary and plenipotentiary" to negotiate American rights in the Mississippi. Before Monroe reached Paris, however, Napoleon had accepted the fact that he had failed in San Domingo. Abandoning his plan of attacking the British Empire by way of the Western Hemisphere, he prepared to attack it in the center, by way of Germany and the English Channel. It was certain that on the outbreak of the war he now proposed to make Great Britain, the mistress of the seas, would seize Louisiana. It was primarily to deny her such an enormous increase of wealth and power that Napoleon determined to sell Louisiana to the United States. Empowered to buy a city of seven thousand inhabitants, Monroe found his colleague Livingston discussing (with the minister of finance, Barbé-Marbois) the purchase of an area somewhat greater than the United States. And since the maximum Livingston had been authorized to offer for New Orleans was only three-quarters of what Napoleon asked, he was haggling over the price.

The Louisiana Purchase was one of the most important events in world history. It was an event of such magnitude that, as Henry Adams said, its results are beyond measurement. Not only did it double the area of the United States, not only did it add to our wealth resources of incalculable value, not only did it provide a potential that was certain to make us a great power, not only did it make equally certain that we would expand beyond the Rockies to the Pacific, and not only did it secure us against foreign victory on any scale conceivable in the nineteenth century—it also provided the centripetal, unifying force that would hold the nation firm against disruptive forces from within. Whether or not the rebellion that became the Civil War was inevitable, the Purchase had made certain that it could not succeed. And there is no aspect of our national life, no part of our social and political structure, and no subsequent event in the main course of our history that it has not affected.

3

A curious convention of historiography has long held that the acquisition of all Louisiana was a stunning surprise to Jefferson, and that he believed the area too large to be governed by our political institutions. It is true that he did not expect to obtain all Louisiana at this time and true that he occasionally, though with careful, contingent reservations, faced the hypothesis that a Republic of the West might, at some distant time and in certain eventualities, separate from the old Republic. But to suppose that he did not fully expect the extension of American settlement across Louisiana, or to suppose that he did not expect extension of settlement to produce extension of sovereignty as well, is to ignore the most massive facts about the nation his administration governed. They are all relevant to the Lewis and Clark expedition.

Both as Secretary of State and as President, Jefferson had repeatedly declared that the United States must and would seize Louisiana if war should break out. At an early stage of his negotiations with Talleyrand, Livingston was proposing to buy a large part of Louisiana if not all of it. At the same time Rufus King, our minister to London, was representing to the British that American possession of Louisiana would surely be favorable to their interests. But there was a far weightier fact: if war meant American possession, obviously peace meant it too. The westward progress of settlement that had been filling up the Old West ever since the Revolution was manifestly certain to take the American people across the Mississippi in force, as it had already taken a large number of them by 1803. American sovereignty was manifestly certain to follow them across the river at no very distant date. Early predictions that this would happen, dating back to the adoption of the Constitution or the peace treaty that recognized the independence of the United States, may be dismissed as speculative. (Though the awareness they signalized had also led Great Britain, France, and Spain to endeavor to confine the United States east of the Alleghanies and then, failing that, to detach the West.) But in 1803 the expectation was as logical and as realistic as any on which diplomacy can be based, and discussions of it were routine in the dispatches of all the ministers in Washington. Every chancellery in Europe knew that, unless severely defeated in war, the United States was certain to cross the Mississippi and to advance an unpredictable distance beyond it. Knowledge common to all Europe was not withheld from the American President.

He had, in fact, acted on that knowledge. He was sending, as he had long intended to send, an expedition to explore a water route for American commerce across the territory of a foreign power. He could hardly have believed that the territory was long to remain foreign. The reason why his message was secret was not that the expedition was to be concealed from the three powers, to all of which it would be fully visible and to two of which it was at once formally accredited. Not the expedition but its true purpose was to be concealed. So far as secrecy was possible that purpose had to be concealed, for it had in view the fur trade of Canada, the maritime trade in sea otter and China goods, and the Columbia River, to whose basin the United States had established a valid territorial claim through Captain Robert Gray's discovery of its mouth in 1792. Jefferson's nomination of Monroe to his mission was dated January 11 1803 and Monroe's commission was dated January 13, seven and five days respectively before the secret message; Jefferson had taken up the expedition with the Spanish minister six weeks earlier. That is to say: before Monroe sailed to negotiate for the mouth of the Mississippi, before in fact he was nominated to do so, Jefferson had moved to acquire all Louisiana and, as well, the great expanse that was to be called Oregon. Perhaps it would be just to reverse that order.

The expedition was to be commanded by Captain Meriwether Lewis, First Infantry, U.S.A. He was then on detached duty, serving as Jefferson's private secretary. Jefferson had offered him the position in February 1801, a month before his inauguration. Lewis was a family friend[7] but Jefferson had many friends better qualified by background and education to be secretary to the President. He was, however, uniquely qualified for a project which Jefferson had cherished for many years, the exploration of the Missouri River and the lands west of its source. Obviously, Jefferson entered office determined to carry out the project as soon as possible and took Lewis into his personal and official household for that purpose. Lewis had had a long experience of military command and wilderness life. He was well acquainted with Jefferson's interest in the West and to explore it had long been what he called "a darling project of my heart." And, soliciting Jefferson's help, he had applied to be made a member of André Michaux's attempt to make the exploration in 1793.

Two years as secretary and member of the official family served, as Jefferson said in his instructions,[8] to familiarize Lewis completely with "the objects of my confidential message of Jan. 18, 1803, to the legislature. you have seen the act they passed, which, tho' expressed in general terms, was meant to sanction those objects, and you are appointed to carry them into execution."

The maritime trade of the Northwest coast, which was based on the value of sea otter furs at Canton, had been opened by the British in 1785. The first American ship that engaged in it was the *Columbia,* on her first voyage, 1787-90, the one before she entered the river to which she gave her name. It was a rich trade and by 1803 the Americans had all but cornered it. The sailing qualities of American ships, the skill of their captains, and American business sagacity had been fundamental in that triumph, but so had the restrictions under which British traders had to operate. Nootka Sound, the original center of the trade, and the adjacent coast were territory in which the South Seas Company held a monopoly charter from the crown; Canton, where the furs were exchanged for China goods, was in the territory of a similar and far more powerful monopoly, the East India Company. The latter had opened the

trade but its interests were elsewhere; British traders were forced either to sail under license from it or to find some equally expensive way of circumventing its demands. So that the China trade (comprehending in that term the American commerce with the Orient which did not touch the Northwest coast as well as that which did) had by 1803 become by far the greatest exterior wealth of the United States.

Usually a trading voyage to "the Coast" lasted three years. It was exposed to all the hazards of the Cape Horn route. If the Missouri and the Columbia did indeed provide a water route across North America, as Jefferson believed, the voyage could be shortened, the costs reduced, and the hazards almost eliminated. And there was a further consideration, equally or perhaps even more important in this generation of global warfare. Such a route would be safe from blockade, navies, and privateers.

The discovery of this route would be inestimably valuable to the United States. It is hardly necessary to fill out the syllogism. The route would not be expeditious, cheap, and safe from blockade and attack if the territory it crossed were to remain foreign soil.

These vital considerations grew in exigency as the value of the trade increased and the wars spread. Another compelling circumstance had been intensifying for exactly ten years. The Canadian fur trade east of the Rocky Mountains, much of which Jefferson hoped to divert to American waterways and even to American management, had been endeavoring to establish a base on the Pacific coast.

The development of the trade in the Canadian West and North was primarily the achievement of the North West Company. An organization of remarkably able and daring businessmen, it had become the first large-scale enterprise of the continent and in effect the first trust. It had opened and organized the rich beaver country along the Saskatchewan and Athabaska Rivers, extending its operations to the Arctic on the north, the Rockies on the west, and the Big Bend of the Missouri on the south. By superior skill and enterprise it had won supremacy over its great rival, the cumbersome, conservative Hudson's Bay Company. Yet the English company had an advantage which enabled it to remain in competition and which had grown steadily more important. Like the East India Company it held a monopoly charter from the crown: it alone could use Hudson Bay and the rivers that emptied into it from the west, of which the Hayes was the most important, for access to the beaver country. All the North West Company's goods, supplies, and furs had to be transported to and from Montreal, where deepwater carriage began, along the difficult and almost endless canoe route which Jefferson described to Congress. Every additional mile the North West Company incorporated in its system added to the difficulty and the cost of doing business. Time, distance, logistics, finance, terms and duration of credit had combined to force on the Northwesters an organization remarkably like that of a twentieth-century industrial corporation—all for the purpose of carrying goods from Montreal to the beaver country and carrying furs back to Montreal. Whereas the Hudson's Bay Company, loading its goods at London, could take them direct to Port Nelson, at 92° W. and 57° N. before transshipping them to a river route.

As soon as they reached the far longitudes and high latitudes, the North West Company partners had realized the great desirability of extending their trade network to the Pacific. Deepwater transport to Nootka or some other depot on the coast would neutralize the Hudson's Bay Company's advantage, expediting carriage and enormously lowering the overhead. In 1781, twenty-two years before Jefferson's message, Alexander Henry the elder had proposed to the Royal Society an exploration to discover a water route to the Pacific in the high latitudes. His ideas had been formed by his partner, the crabbed genius Peter Pond. Pond himself trained and inspired the young man who eventually tried to put them into effect. This was Alexander Mackenzie, one of the principal wintering partners, a brilliant geopolitical thinker, and among the most remarkable of American explorers.

In 1789 Mackenzie made an attempt to find the route to the Pacific that Pond had thought must exist north of Lake Athabaska. The venture led him to the river named for him and to the Arctic, not the Pacific. This failure dampened the enthusiasm of the North West Company, but the necessity remained unchanged and the less conservative partners supported Mackenzie's desire to continue the exploration. In 1793, the year of André Michaux's abortive attempt, Mackenzie succeeded in reaching the Pacific after as daring and exciting a journey as any in the annals of discovery. He thus became the first man since Cabeza de Vaca, in 1536, to make a transcontinental crossing north of Mexico. His route involved the Peace River, a stretch of the Fraser River, the Blackwater River, and a long land traverse (the heart of the matter) to the Bella Coola River which led to the sea north of Vancouver Island.

It was a magnificent achievement but commercially futile. To take goods and furs by canoe along this route was impossible. The Rocky Mountains and the kind of rivers that threaded them forbade.

Mackenzie had been led to the Fraser, for which he used an Indian name, Tacoutche Tesse, by Indian reports that it was a big river and emptied into the Pacific. The mouth of the Fraser is just north of 49°, at the city of Vancouver, on the Strait of Georgia, but Mackenzie did not reach the mouth. Unable to take his canoe through the furious water of its upper canyons, he had to abandon it and eventually descended the Bella Coola. When he returned to civilization, he learned that the American Captain Gray had discovered the mouth of a big river at 46°. He assumed that this, the Columbia, must be the river which he had been unable to descend, the Tacoutche Tesse. So, till Lewis and Clark, did everyone else. Meanwhile it remained possible, and in Mackenzie's view likely, that below the place where

he had been forced away from it, the Tacoutche Tesse might be navigable and therefore that the North West Company canoes could descend it with their furs. If this were true, the Northwesters must reach it by some route as yet undiscovered—but one that led through British territory.

Mackenzie was now dedicated to getting a Pacific outlet for his company. And now the intensifying urgency that Jefferson felt was communicated to him as well. The Americans had established a claim to the great river part of which, so he thought, he had traveled and which, so he believed, was the solution to the Company's problem. And not only that: the Americans were wresting the maritime trade of the Northwest coast from the British. Mackenzie worked out a plan which foreshadowed the pattern of nineteenth-century British imperialism. But though some North West Company partners supported his ideas, he was frustrated by the hostility, arrogance, and financial conservatism of Simon McTavish, who was the real head of the trust.

In 1799 therefore Mackenzie withdrew from the North West Company and went to England, to try to realize his imperial vision by exterior means. In its final form his plan had three parts:

1. The Hudson's Bay Company must either merge with the North West Company or else grant or lease to it the right to transport goods to the western shore of the Bay and thence to the fur country. If the HBC should refuse to do either, then Parliament must so alter its charter as to enable the Northwesters to use its route. (When it refused, Mackenzie tried to carry the position by financial maneuvers, organizing a syndicate to buy the closely held, immensely valuable HBC stock—it was thus that Lord Selkirk began his fateful career in Canada. In the succeeding years the Northwesters tried to secure the right of transport on the HBC routes by negotiation, by lease or purchase, and by appeal to Parliament.[9] Eventually, following actual guerrilla war between the two companies, Parliament forced precisely the merger that Mackenzie had urged in the beginning.)

2. Either the merger or the North West Company must secure a firm position on the Northwest coast. Thereupon the East India Company must concede it the right to trade at Canton on terms that would make competition with the Americans possible.

3. West of the Continental Divide, British sovereignty must be extended southward far enough to include the Columbia River, which Mackenzie expected to become the route between the beaver country and the Pacific. This, of course, was a problem not for the fur merchants but for the government. In a proposal made after his book was published Mackenzie explained that sovereignty must be supported by a military establishment at Nootka with subsidiary ones at the mouth of the Columbia and elsewhere. He believed that Great Britain had unwisely abandoned her rights east of the Divide when treaties and conventions

relating to the Canadian boundary were drawn up, and that the damage thus done must be repaired. He believed, specifically, that Canada was legally and morally entitled to a connection between the Great Lakes and the Mississippi, that it was entitled also to exclusive possession of the great canoe route from Lake Superior to Lake of the Woods, that (west of Lake Superior) British sovereignty extended south to 45°, and that the boundary must be relocated accordingly.[10] If this readjustment could not be made, it was still possible to make the Columbia River securely British and this must be done.

This constituted a blueprint for imperial expansion. At the end of his exposition and analysis Mackenzie says:

> By opening this intercourse between the Atlantic and Pacific Oceans, and forming regular establishments through the interior and at both extremes, as well as along the coasts and islands, *the entire command of the fur trade of North America might be obtained from 48° North to the pole, except that portion of it which the Russians have in the Pacific. To this may be added the fishing in both seas and the markets of the four quarters of the globe.* Such would be the field for commercial enterprise and incalculable would be the produce of it, when supported by the operations of that credit and capital which Great Britain so pre-eminently possesses. Then would this country begin to be remunerated for the expenses it has sustained in discovering and surveying the coast of the Pacific Ocean, which is at present left to American adventurers. . . . Such adventurers, and many of them, as I have been informed, have been very successful, would instantly disappear before a well-regulated trade. . . . Many *political* reasons, which it is not necessary here to enumerate, must present themselves to the mind of every man acquainted with the enlarged system and capacities of British commerce in support of the Measure which I have very briefly suggested, as promising the most important advantages of the trade of the united kingdoms.

The quoted passage ends Mackenzie's book, *Voyages from Montreal,* which was published late in 1801. Lewis and Clark took a copy of it west with them and it obviously had conclusive force for Jefferson. The President, who already contemplated moving to secure the Columbia to the United States, was thus notified by the most powerful personality in the Canadian fur trade that the fur trust intended to secure the Columbia to Great Britain. The notification, however, only increased his realization that the situation was urgent, for he had long understood the essentials of what Mackenzie set forth.

Following Mackenzie's withdrawal from the North West Company, the despotic McTavish relaxed sufficiently to permit some action on his ideas. For a number of years the fur merchants of St. Louis and the Spanish officials there had known of the company's intention to carry the trade to the Rocky Mountains in Louisiana as it had done in Canada. Now the summer meeting of the North West partners in 1800 voted to send explorers over the Canadian Rockies to the vital area. Duncan M'Gillivray, who was

the principal exponent of Mackenzie's ideas, and David Thompson, who was the company's most gifted surveyor, prepared to make the exploration. In the fall of 1800 two of their *engagés* crossed the mountains to prepare a base. Some students have believed that in the next year, 1801, either M'Gillivray or Thompson or both made a quick crossing to the base, but this is not evident and indeed it is unlikely. At least a start had been made toward the execution of Mackenzie's ideas, however, when Jefferson addressed Congress—this in addition to Mackenzie's polemic and his financial efforts in England to get support for them.

These and other efforts continued through the succeeding years. In 1802 Mackenzie returned to Canada and joined the most violent and most successful opposition the North West Company had ever had, a group of former partners and some additional associates usually called the X Y Company in the literature. In 1804 McTavish died and the X Y Company rejoined the North West Company. (News of this reached Lewis and Clark at Fort Mandan; see the journal for March 2 1805.) Immediate resumption of Mackenzie's plan was now possible, and though he was denied participation in field management, Duncan M'Gillivray, who spoke for him, grew steadily in power. Even before tidings of the merger reached the West, François Larocque of the North West Company's Assiniboine Department asked to accompany Lewis and Clark to the Pacific. His request was refused but in the summer of 1805 he made the long contemplated attempt to open the western Louisiana trade, traveling west from the Mandan villages to the Yellowstone River and returning down its valley, while Lewis and Clark were ascending the Missouri. In that same summer, and there can be no doubt that Lewis and Clark were a contributing cause, the partners voted to make a permanent establishment west of the mountains. And Simon Fraser crossed to the Tacoutche Tesse, which in common with everyone else he took to be the Columbia, and built the first trading post on Pacific drainage. He left a party to spend there the same winter that Lewis and Clark spent at Fort Clatsop.

The continuation of this policy may be outlined here. In 1806, the year in which Lewis and Clark made their return journey, Fraser made another extensive exploration farther north, in the country to which he gave the long-memorable name, New Caledonia. He built two other permanent posts there, so that the Northwesters now had three west of the Continental Divide. New Caledonia, however, was in the high latitudes and it offered no water route to the Pacific; it did not satisfy the Northwesters' requirements. In the same year, 1806, therefore, David Thompson sent two men to cut a horse trail across the Canadian Rockies farther south. In 1807, beginning a permanent occupation, he reached the Columbia. He did not recognize it as the Columbia but determined its longitude and realized that it was not the Tacoutche Tesse. (He named it the Kootanae.) The next year, 1808, Thompson moved south of 49° into Idaho. In 1809, provided with information from the first published account of Lewis and Clark, the journal of

Patrick Gass, he went still deeper into territory that is now American, the site of Missoula, Montana. But not till 1811—and there is no satisfactory explanation of his delay—did he descend the Columbia to the sea. He reached it too late by a few months: John Jacob Astor's Pacific Fur Company had got there first and had built Fort Astoria. Meanwhile in 1808 Simon Fraser, triumphing over the ferocious waters that had turned Mackenzie back, had taken a party down the Tacoutche Tesse, now the Fraser, to its mouth. So he had made the shattering discovery that it was not the Columbia after all.

4

Unless all these forces, pressures, and actions are taken into account, Jefferson's purpose in sending Lewis and Clark up the Missouri and on to the Pacific cannot be understood.[11] (Those mentioned in the last paragraph above were developments of situations already existing in January 1803 when Jefferson asked for the appropriation, and were either foreseen or understood as implicit when he entered office in March 1801.) The "literary" purpose was subsidiary to the others, though it might be of assistance to them. The others can now be stated with assurance.

The expedition was to survey in detail the water route up the Missouri and down the Columbia which, so Jefferson supposed, would provide easy transport between the Mississippi and the Pacific. It was to give the United States a direct overland connection with the maritime trade of the Northwest coast. It was to amass the details on which could be laid the groundwork for an American challenge to the North West Company's route of carriage from the beaver country of northwestern Canada, a challenge which might result in just such a trade victory as the sea captains had won at Nootka. Using the standard techniques of negotiating with Indians, it was to prepare the tribes for this challenge, and for the coming of American traders. That is, it was to advertise the superiority of American trade—its superiority to the French-Spanish trade from St. Louis and the British trade of the upper Mississippi and the Assiniboine. It was to establish as much intertribal peace as possible. This much is explicit and another purpose is clearly implied: to buttress the American claim to the Oregon country which rested on the *Columbia*'s discovery by making a land traverse before the British could.

All this in January 1803, when Jefferson addressed Congress and when Louisiana was to remain a French possession. By the middle of June news of Livingston's and Monroe's astonishing triumph reached Washington. The acquisition of Louisiana provided additional duties for the expedition that was to have crossed it as foreign soil. Any fact whatever that could be learned about its far northern fringe would now be welcome, for it might bear on the uncertainties of the boundary and the disputes about them. Also, it was now important to learn as much as possible about the southwestern reaches of Louisiana, the Spanish settlements (which had only an occasional connection with St. Louis), and the topographical, military, and commercial

problems associated with them. All the Indian tribes which the expedition would encounter must be notified that the Great Father now lived in Washington and that their allegiance had changed with his residence. In particular the Sioux, about whose hostility to St. Louis traders the administration was well informed, must be impressed by American strength and authority. The British traders who were known to be in the vicinity of the Mandan villages—where their presence was illegal under Spanish law and would have continued to be under French law—must be notified of their accountability as well as their privileges under American jurisdiction. Finally, there was the increased but still deluded hope that the expedition could produce a general prairie peace. It was to induce the tribes to make sacredly binding treaties with one another and it was to persuade delegations of chiefs to travel to Washington, to be impressed by the power and splendor of American civilization.

Two further points. Jefferson's instructions to Lewis say that he need not pay so much attention to the northern affluents of the Missouri River as to the southern ones, for it may be assumed that the British fur companies have pretty well found out whatever should be known about them. This remark is sharply at variance with the behavior of the captains in the field. No other inquiry recorded in the journals is made so persistently as the one about the northern tributaries. At Fort Mandan and beyond it, on both the outward and the return journeys, Lewis and Clark are incessantly preoccupied with the desirability of finding a northern affluent that will lead to the Saskatchewan and the Athabaska. Since this search dovetails with the purpose which Jefferson expressed in his secret message and with his theory about the northern boundary as he phrased it in a memorandum for the ministers to France and Spain, we must conclude that he privately directed Lewis to solve the problem. Finally, the journals contain abundant evidence relating to another purpose that is not specifically stated in either the message to Congress or the instructions to Lewis. The captains repeatedly promise tribes west of the Continental Divide that the Americans will soon open the trade in their country. Two reports by Lewis and one by Clark discuss problems and measures connected with this innovation. The development will require two stages. First, posts will be set up east of the Divide, in American Louisiana, and the tribes will be encouraged to cross the mountains and trade at them. (Protection from the Blackfeet will be provided for them.) Later, when the system has grown in strength, posts will be established west of the Divide, in the home country of the tribes that have become customers during the first stage. No one can suppose that agents of the American government could so confidently promise action of such serious import unless they had directions from the President to do so. Note once more that this trade is to be opened in country that is not American soil when the promises are made.

5

Jefferson's instructions to Lewis say: "The object of your mission is to explore the Missouri river, & such principal stream of it, as, by it's course & communication with the waters of the Pacific Ocean, may offer the most direct & practicable water communication across this continent, for the purposes of commerce." Ten years earlier, in 1793, speaking for the American Philosophical Society, he had phrased the same objective. André Michaux was "to pursue such of the largest streams of [the Missouri] as shall lead by the shortest way and the lowest latitudes to the Pacific ocean. When, pursuing those streams, you shall find yourself at the point from whence you may get by the shortest and most convenient route to some principal river of the Pacific ocean, you are to proceed to such river and pursue its course to the ocean." When he drafted these instructions for Michaux, the *Columbia* had not yet returned to the States, and so he did not know of Captain Gray's momentous discovery. He reminded Michaux that a large river was supposed to come down to the Pacific somewhere in the vicinity of Nootka, and said that this river would probably prove to be his best route. It was called the Oregon, he said, and its waters "interlocked with the Missouri for a considerable distance." So Jefferson and the sum of geographical knowledge understood. But the Oregon was an entirely hypothetical river, the current embodiment of the imaginary stream, the River of the West, which for more than a century had been believed, deduced, and rumored to cross the part of North America that lay west of the height of land.[12]

There *had* to be such a river; the logic of geography, of teleology, and of desire required one. When the Columbia was discovered, it was almost universally accepted as the River of the West. Following Mackenzie's crossing, his Tacoutche Tesse was believed to be the Columbia. The Tacoutche Tesse was the only addition to knowledge of or relating to the vital area which Lewis and Clark must cross, and its relationship was unknown. That area was entirely untraveled by white men: between the Great Bend of the Missouri, in central North Dakota, and the place where the Columbia issued from the Cascade Mountains. Vancouver's Lieutenant Broughton had traveled the Columbia from its mouth almost to that emergence from the Cascades. Mackenzie's crossing had provided no actual knowledge of the area, but it had opened it to additional speculation.

The reader has long since perceived that, in the widest view, the Lewis and Clark expedition belongs to the line of endeavor that had taken Columbus to the New World, the effort to establish a western trade route with the Orient. Specifically, it belongs to the branch of that endeavor which undertook to find direct water communication between the Atlantic and the Pacific, a waterway that led across the land mass of North America. Belief in the existence of such a landlocked Northwest Passage dates back almost to Columbus. Various conceptions of it had existed: as a strait or series of straits leading entirely across the continent at almost any latitude; as such a strait connecting the Pacific with Hudson Bay or the Arctic; as a river route connecting the eastern rivers or the Great Lakes with a body of salt or fresh water in the interior of the continent (the hypothetical or imaginary Western Sea) whence other rivers, or an arm of the sea, would lead on to the Pacific.

By the middle of the eighteenth century, explorations of Hudson Bay had proved that no strait led westward from its far shore, but though this should have destroyed that particular variant of the ancient hope it did not. In 1771 Samuel Hearne of the Hudson's Bay Company went down the Coppermine River to the Arctic. In 1789 Alexander Mackenzie discovered the Mackenzie River and descended it to the Arctic. Meanwhile in 1778 the great James Cook, on his third voyage, had proved that north of Nootka Sound there existed no strait or river which could be the western portal of the Northwest Passage. Gradually the significance of these voyages was realized. When Mackenzie's transcontinental crossing was added to them, that there was no water route to the Pacific in the area of Canada (north of 49°) should have been accepted as proved. For the most part it was so accepted but a few geographical thinkers on both sides of the Atlantic continued to believe that somehow there must be a connection by way of Lake Winnipeg, though the rivers of Lake Winnipeg flow into it from the west. This conception cannot be phrased clearly for it was not precise. But it could convert to the service of wishfulness one hiatus in knowledge that remained following Mackenzie's two voyages. On the first of them he had learned that a mountain barrier extended north all the way to the Arctic. On the second this same barrier, or one to the west of it (and no one, including Mackenzie, had decided which), had prevented him from descending the Tacoutche Tesse to the sea. But how far to the south of his land-crossing did the mountain barrier extend? Yrujo reminded Jefferson that "a very considerable cordillera" existed *between 50° and 60°*. Did it extend below 50° and how continuously? Those who brought Arrowsmith's maps to bear on the problem saw the Rockies as a single chain and knew that this presentation was wholly speculative south of the route ascribed to Peter Fidler, which carried him to 45°. (Actually, Fidler had not reached as far south as 50°.) Northward from New Mexico there was only speculation about the Rockies.

Might there not be a gap in the "cordillera" through which a water route led to the Pacific? There might indeed be a gap, and therefore conceivably (though in retrospect one wonders how) it might somehow connect with Lake Winnipeg. And indeed the best knowledge in St. Louis indicated that there was. On the basis of what St. Louis traders had learned, or thought they had learned, from the Indians, the Missouri River might flow through such a gap—and, in any event, the Missouri could be followed to and into the mountains. And, St. Louis believed, if you ascended the Missouri, which was navigable all the way, it would lead you to within a very short distance of the Pacific, at most a hundred miles.

These various ideas cannot be harmonized—for the simple but adequate reason that they define the state of knowledge, which is always a definition of ignorance as well.

But the components of knowledge can never be harmonized until all the relevant facts are in. And the bearing of everything that was known and assumed was clear: the one remaining hope of the water passage from sea to sea was provided by the Missouri River.

Jolliet and Marquette discovered the mouth of the Missouri in 1673. From then on in the ideas that were held of American geography, prismatic with illusion and misconception, the river was supposed to lead near or to the Pacific. No conception of it provided a basis of action, however, and there was no realistic knowledge in the first reasoned proposal to use it as a route to the Pacific, that of the Jesuit Pierre Charlevoix in 1720. Charlevoix had been sent to America by the French government, which was under increasing urgency to reach the Pacific overland, to collect all the existing information about possible routes. He decided that by ascending the Missouri one could reach the Western Sea, which would be found to have some kind of connection with the Northwest Passage. The great explorer Pierre Gaultier de Varennes de la Vérendrye was commissioned to discover the route proposed by Charlevoix. In 1738 he reached the Missouri with his sons, traveling from the Lake Winnipeg region to the Mandan villages below the Great Bend. The Vérendryes were the first white men to see the Upper Missouri (and one of them was the effective discoverer of the other key river of the West, the Saskatchewan) but nothing came of their enterprise.

British thinking about the Missouri route to the Pacific was almost as old, dating back to 1727, when Daniel Coxe concocted the error that was to prove most durable of all, the theorem that only a very short land traverse would be found necessary from Missouri to Pacific waters. Attention was permanently focused on the Missouri route, however, by Robert Rogers, or rather first by his employe Jonathan Carver. In 1765 Rogers proposed to reach the "River Ouragan" from "the head of the Mississippi." It was Carver who, during his journey in Wisconsin and Minnesota, 1766-67, determined that the Missouri was a conceivable route. (And who fixed the spelling of the great name as Oregon.) When Rogers renewed his proposal in 1772, he specified the Missouri, intending to travel it to the source.

Rogers asserted in 1772 that a portage of "about twenty miles" separated navigable waters of the Missouri and the Oregon. Coxe in 1727 had made his hypothetical separation "a ridge of hills" which would prove "passable by horse, foot, or wagon in less than half a day." Jefferson accepted this conception; it defines the "single portage from the Western Ocean" of his message to Congress. It is the basic and crucial conception in his plan, as indeed it had been in all theorems concerning a water route for commerce and (in the Spanish view) for military invasion.

This basic conception, this irreducible minimum, left no room for the Rocky Mountains. Geographical thinking had been unable to imagine them—unable first to imagine their existence and then, when their eastern slope in Canada became familiar, unable to imagine their width or the impossibility of traversing them by canoe. The Spanish knew the southern end of the Rockies in New Mexico and most of the eastern slope in Colorado and in the 1760's they began to travel along the western slope, but did not penetrate them. But the Rockies had been crossed only by Mackenzie's party, and his experience did not give him or suggest to anyone else a realistic conception of the obstacle they were to freight transport by water. In Clark's entry for February 14 1806 Jefferson's "single portage" (Rogers's "twenty miles" and Coxe's "less than half a day") becomes an actual land traverse of 220 miles. That in itself wrecked the expectation of three centuries. And even so, it disregarded the difficulty and expense of water travel on the Missouri above the Great Falls.

In the 1790's Spanish officials and French fur traders in St. Louis had put together from Indian accounts a conception of the Rockies as a single or multiple mountain range that ran parallel to the Pacific coast and a varying distance from it usually less than a hundred miles inland. They believed that the Missouri led up to this range and well into it, or through it by means of a gap or across it by means of a gap and a long and hardly imaginable fall. That vestiges of this idea figured in Jefferson's thinking is evident from his instructions to Lewis and from entries in the captains' journals.

The Missouri was familiar from its mouth to the Mandan villages, some sixty miles upstream from Bismarck, where Lewis and Clark spent the winter of 1804-5. French traders from the Illinois country entered its mouth shortly before 1700. Between 1712 and 1717 Etienne de Bourgmond ranged as far as the mouth of the Platte, perhaps a little farther. The Platte, which was always regarded as the "equator" of the upstream journey, remained the limit of knowledge till shortly before 1790, when somewhat higher ascents were made. Then the Spanish and French of St. Louis undertook to reach the Pacific, both to rescue the Indian trade of upper Louisiana from the British and to secure the route as a military frontier to defend New Mexico. (That New Mexico was considered in danger of invasion by both land and water from Canada shows how ignorant of the land mass they were, how much smaller than it is they conceived it to be.) They got as far as the Mandan villages, but only with great difficulty, and got no farther.[13] They could not finance further exploration nor were they able to compete with the British trade, which had reached the Mandan villages about 1785, coming down from the Assiniboine River and its affluent the Souris.

The tribes between the Platte and the James—Omahas, Otos, and Poncas—harassed and blackmailed the small trading parties that ascended the Missouri from St. Louis. They were less important, however, than the two tribes immediately beyond them, the Arikaras and the Sioux. The former had been till lately a powerful people but they had been weakened by smallpox epidemics and by the Sioux, whose westward migration had reached the Missouri in force. Both tribes sought to establish themselves as middle-

Meriwether Lewis (1774–1809).

men in the upriver trade—the desire of all Indian tribes and a recurrent cause of wars. In this position they could secure the profits of the trade to themselves and could control the supply of guns and powder to their enemies. In effect the two tribes closed the Upper Missouri to St. Louis traders as the Spanish at New Orleans had closed the Mississippi to the Americans. A few years before Lewis and Clark the Sioux had established permanent supremacy over the Arikaras. Among the most warlike of Indians, swaggerers and bullies, bound firmly to the British by the superior goods and cheaper prices of the British trade, incited to opposition by the British who traded with them on the Des Moines and James Rivers, the Sioux were a formidable obstacle to trade, to exploration, and to the exercise of sovereignty over upper Louisiana. That is why so much hung on the meeting of Lewis and Clark with them, which must be regarded as one of the crises of the expedition.

6

In 1803 Meriwether Lewis was twenty-nine years old. He had joined the militia at the time of the Whiskey Rebellion, at its end he had transferred to the regular army, and he had remained in service ever since. For a short period he had been an ensign in a rifle company commanded by Captain William Clark, and the two had developed an enduring respect for each other. Clark was the youngest

brother of George Rogers Clark, who had played the leading role in the actions that saved the trans-Alleghany West for the United States during the Revolution, and whom Jefferson had once proposed to send on an exploring expedition across Louisiana. He was thirty-three years old in 1803. He too had militia service before becoming a regular, and unlike Lewis he saw considerable Indian fighting. He resigned his captaincy in 1796.

Thus both leaders of the expedition had had much experience of command and of wilderness life. Clark was Lewis's choice to share the expedition, and Lewis promised him, on Jefferson's authority, equality of command and a captain's commission. The War Department, however, found bureaucratic reasons to frustrate the President's intention and commissioned Clark a second lieutenant in the Corps of Artillerists. Nevertheless, the journals always refer to him as "Captain Clark" and he signs that rank to orders and other official papers. That the promised equality of command became a fact is evident. But it is also evident that if there had been any occasion to interrupt it, by personality and temperament Lewis was the natural commander and Clark the adjutant. There never was an occasion; the two agreed and worked together with a mutuality unknown elsewhere in the history of exploration and rare in any kind of human association.

Their roles in the expedition are also self-evident in the journals. Lewis was the diplomatic and commercial thinker, Clark the negotiator. Lewis, who went specially to Philadelphia for training in botany, zoology, and celestial navigation, was the scientific specialist, Clark the engineer and geographer as well as the master of frontier crafts. Both were experienced rivermen but Lewis acknowledged that Clark had greater skill and usually left the management of the boats to him. Clark evidently had the greater gift for dealing with Indians. But by chance Lewis was alone at two critical encounters with Indians, the Snakes and the Blackfeet, and he handled them with an expertness that no one could have surpassed. Lewis was better educated than Clark and he had a speculative mind; almost all the abstract ideas and philosophical remarks in the journals are his. He was introverted and mercurial—almost all the bursts of anger and all the depressed moods are his too—whereas Clark was extroverted and even-tempered. Both were men of great intelligence, of distinguished intelligence. The entire previous history of North American exploration contains no one who could be called their intellectual equal.

In fact, intelligence was the principal reason for the success of the expedition, which is also unequaled in American history and hardly surpassed in the history of exploration anywhere. They were masters of every situation and they successfully handled every emergency. Remarkably few emergencies arose, a fact which always defines expert management of wilderness travel. The expedition was of proper, though minimal, size. It was intelligently and adequately equipped, though trade goods ran out and Jefferson was inexplicably negligent in failing to send a ship to the mouth of the Columbia so that the outfit could have been replaced and the supplies replenished.[14] The company was recruited with good judgment and was physically hardened and well disciplined by six months of cantonment life in the winter of 1803-4, on the Illinois shore, opposite the mouth of the Missouri. Only a few infractions of discipline are recorded in the journals and all but one of these occur before the arrival at the Mandans.[15] Moses Reed deserted in the vicinity of the Platte and so did "La Liberté," a boatman whose connection with the expedition is ambiguous. John Newman was dropped from the permanent party and sent back from the Mandan villages to be discharged, in punishment of an outburst of insubordination. There was no further trouble serious enough to be noted in the journals, and a quarrel between Drewyer and Colter was so unusual an occurrence that it *is* noted. All of which is evidence that cuts two ways: the recruits were sound stock and the captains were remarkable leaders. Unquestionably, military organization and military discipline added effectiveness to the wilderness techniques and so help to explain the success of the expedition, but after the opening weeks of the journals the reader will seldom, if ever, be aware of them.

The only fatality of the expedition, Charles Floyd's death, could not have been prevented. His symptoms suggest a ruptured appendix, which at that period would almost certainly have been fatal anywhere. There was only one serious accident, Cruzatte's wounding of Lewis while they were hunting in the brush. Cruzatte was blind in one eye and the vision of his other eye was impaired, but he nevertheless was one of the expedition's best plainsmen (in the captains' estimation ranking just below Drewyer), as he was its master riverman. And he had been acquitting himself brilliantly as a hunter for two years.

It is the very singularity of these occurrences and certain lesser episodes that makes them stand out so prominently against a background of wilderness travel so expertly conducted that it seems commonplace, to be expected. Indeed, except on the upper stages of the Jefferson, where the labor is enormous, and on the crossing of the Bitterroots where food fails, it seems easy. Yet most of it was exceedingly difficult, recurring portions of it were dangerous in a high degree, and nearly all of it was in country foreign to the wilderness experience of Americans and requiring radically different techniques. Not only the Rocky Mountains, their rivers, and the Cascade Mountains were unprecedented and unimaginable; so were the high plains, the high plateaus, the overwhelming waters of the Columbia, the tremendous forest of the Northwest, and the sodden winter climate there. It added up to a strangeness for which nothing in the previous frontier culture was a preparation. The impact of these new conditions on the frontier consciousness and their strain on the frontier skills were formidable, as the succeeding expeditions by Manuel Lisa and the Astorians amply attest. But there is only a single, momentary lapse in the company's morale, when food fails in the Bitterroots. Running the Columbia rapids in cottonwood dugouts required both skill and courage in the

greatest measure, all the more so because not even Cruzatte had ever seen such water, but it is done with entire nonchalance. The same unhesitating confidence in the presence of the unknown and unpredictable can be seen in the decision to strike for the Nez Percé trail when, at Lemhi Pass, they learn that they cannot go down either the Salmon or its banks.

In such episodes certain elements of the wilderness mind reach their highest expression; there are other elements as well. Lewis and Clark exercised a constant but untroubled vigilance. (Nevertheless, they lapsed from it several times, notably at Fort Mandan, when they failed to send with the detail that was to bring in the meat an escort strong enough to keep the Sioux respectful, and when Lewis went to sleep in the presence of the Blackfeet.) Success in a strange country required a curious mixture of open-mindedness and skepticism, capable of adjusting accepted ideas and practices to unfamiliar conditions. It required too both an analytical and an intuitive understanding of geography. Just as Lewis had to amend his disparagement of a grizzly's toughness, so they both had repeatedly to amend their prepossessions and especially their assumptions about the country. The discovery that the Missouri forked at a place where they were not expecting a tributary was a stunning shock. Forthwith they determined that the northern fork, the Marias, was not the Missouri proper, and this determination is a remarkable act of thought, unsurpassed in the annals of exploration in the New World. Yet this analysis of fact, appearance, and evidence, and the empirical demonstration that proved it right, merely confirmed conclusions that both Lewis and Clark reached in the first hour or two. Similarly, Clark knew at once on reaching the main stream of the Clearwater River that it was a part of the same river system as the Salmon River, from whose impassable canyon they had turned back. Lewis clearly ranks with Thompson and Mackenzie as a geographer but Clark had geographical genius.

Ingenuity and resourcefulness in the field are so continuous that a casual reader may not notice them. The portage round the Great Falls is a remarkable achievement in all respects, from Clark's survey of the best route to the construction of the crude truck with which the outfit was transported. Perhaps, however, such mastery is to be expected from experienced frontiersmen, who had to be adept at contriving expedients or they did not last to become experienced. What is altogether beyond expectation, and beyond praise too, is the captains' management of the Indians they met. In personal dealings with them they made no mistakes at all. In so much that at the critical points it is impossible to imagine a more successful outcome or a better way of achieving it, whereas it is easy to instance similar occasions when less skillful men failed badly. With the Sioux they were always firm, always clearly incapable of being scared or bluffed, amiable or threatening or defiant to precisely the right degree at precisely the right moments. As a result they won a considerable victory for the international relations of the United States. This triumph served them well with the village tribes farther up the river. But with these tribes, as with those farther west, other qualities as well contributed to their remarkable success. They were obviously unawed and unafraid, but they were also obviously friendly and fair, scrupulously honest, interested, understanding, courteous, and respectful. That last quality must be insisted on, for rare as honesty and fairness were in the white American's dealing with Indians, they were commoner than respect. Lewis and Clark respected the Indians' personal dignity, their rituals, their taboos, their religious thinking, indeed the full content of their thought. They understood that thought so well that they must be ranked among the masters of primitive psychology. Finally there was the simple fact that they, and Clark especially, liked Indians. All this being true, they required a similar attitude from their command.

It paid off. They had no trouble with most tribes, after the Sioux none at all till they reached the decadent, thievish people of the lower Columbia, who had been debauched by the maritime trade, and no difficulty they had with them even threatened to get out of hand.[16] They attached the Nez Percés and the Flatheads to the American interest permanently. Both tribes were fortunate beyond most others in the missionaries visited on them when the period of Christianizing the Western Indians began,[17] and in the fact that their countries, especially that of the Flatheads, were distant from the area of early settlement. But their loyalty was created by Lewis and Clark. The Flatheads never did commit a hostile act of any consequence, and when one of the most flagrant land-steals in the annals of Indian land-steals was perpetrated, they submitted with bitter fatalism. The Nez Percés accepted great indignity over a long time. When at last an altogether atrocious injustice moved their great man, Chief Joseph, to lead one band of them in a running fight toward a decenter country, he said truthfully that up to that time they not only had never attacked a white man, they had never been offensive to one. (When in the course of the great march Joseph's forces approached the Bitterroot Valley, the Flatheads announced a policy of noninterference, and though they connived at the sale of ammunition to the retreaters they also quietly took measures to protect the white men who had settled in their country and were appropriating it.) The expedition did not win any other tribes so permanently as these, but it established so great a good will as to make the early years of the fur trade era a good deal less violent than they could possibly have been without it.

This climate of approval extended far beyond the tribes which the expedition actually met and it made a kind of culture hero of William Clark. All the Plains and Northwest tribes knew of the Red Headed Chief and came to depend on him for friendship and, if not justice, at least advocacy. He was the white man whose tongue was straight, our elder brother. Miracles were expected of him, indeed he was able to perform miracles on their behalf, but if he had been able to obtain for them any substantial measure of justice it would have been a transcendent miracle. He did what he could; he was able to procure occasional decencies and often able to prevent or moderate

indecencies and he accomplished more for the Indians than anyone else in Western history. If a delegation of Indians went to St. Louis, it sought out Clark first of all; if a fur company sent a brigade up the Missouri or into the mountains, it provided itself with a passport in the form of messages and greetings from Clark. If the U.S. government had to send an embassy to the Indian country it began by trying to get Clark to accompany it, and if Clark consented he was invariably able to get fairer treatment for the Indians and more amenable behavior from them. This subsequent function is a bright strand in a dark history. It has had less attention than it deserves from those who write history; sometime it should be described in detail.

7

Creating such a predisposition, however insecure, in the Far West must be accounted one of the important results of the Lewis and Clark expedition. Those results were so numerous that little can be said about them in an introduction but they must be characterized. They were of various orders of immediacy and significance.

The first major achievement was the demonstration that the last area of North America in which a commercially practicable water route to the Pacific might exist did not contain one. In the long arc of history this ended the search for the Northwest Passage. And ending that chapter, it closed the volume which opened with the first voyage of Columbus.

Lewis's reluctance to accept the fact which his journey had demonstrated, attested in two of his reports of Jefferson, strikingly signalizes the intensity of the hope. Nevertheless the demonstration was immediately accepted by commercial interests to which an inland water route would have been supremely important. When John Jacob Astor organized a fur company to fulfill the commercial (and incidentally the political) vision of Jefferson, he based the organization solidly on salt-water transport, though he also sent an overland expedition to reconnoiter other areas and to check the results of Lewis and Clark. But unquestioning acceptance of those results was among the reasons why his partisan, Wilson Price Hunt, abandoned the Upper Missouri route and crossed to the south of it.

With the transcontinental water route, Jefferson's hope of engrossing the Canadian fur trade, or at least its carriage, disappeared too. It was not a realistic hope anyway, even if such a route had existed, but on the other hand in the outcome this potential wealth was not missed. Lewis and Clark established that the American West was a treasury of beaver and its exploitation began at once. The amazing solitary pair of trappers whom they met near the mouth of the Yellowstone in 1806, Dixon and Handcock, were the portents that heralded developments to come. St. Louis capital was behind the venture of Manuel Lisa the next year, 1807. Lisa hired three of the expedition's veterans, Drewyer, Potts, and Wiser, and, meeting Colter on his way downriver from his winter with the forerunners, persuaded him too to return to the fur country. Lisa's first Missouri voyage is the beginning of the Western fur trade, and he was bound for the fields that Lewis and Clark had most highly recommended, the Three Forks and the valley of the Yellowstone. The Western trade, roughly divided between two regions, the Upper Missouri and the Rocky Mountains, was continuous thenceforward and steadily increased in importance till the break in beaver prices toward the end of the 1830's. The "mountain men" whom the trade developed completed the exploration of the West that Lewis and Clark had begun.

It may be that to secure the Columbia country—Oregon— was the earliest as it was certainly the most urgent of Jefferson's purposes. The expedition served it vitally; in fact, one is justified in saying, decisively. The land traverse bolstered the claim established by Robert Gray's discovery and was of equal or greater legal importance; in international polity the two combined to give the United States not only a prior but a paramount claim. More, it was the journey of Lewis and Clark that gave the American people a conviction that Oregon was theirs and this conviction was more important than the claim. And pragmatically, the establishment of Fort Astoria by Astor's party won the British-American race to the Pacific. Astor's American Fur Company and Pacific Fur Company were established not only as a result of the expedition's reports but in exact accordance with Lewis's analysis of the practices required.

Here we may glance at a map. The route of the Western emigration was to be that of the Platte Valley, pioneered in 1824 and 1825 by William Ashley and his subordinates when the Arikaras tried their hand at closing the Missouri. The emigration had to be by land travel; distances and geographical conditions necessitated it. They also made the Platte Valley the route of the Pacific Railroad. Nevertheless, despite the circuitousness of the Missouri and the hazards and difficulties of traveling it by boat it remained an important route to the West, the Rockies, and the Northwest till the end of the steamboat age. And the railroads which ended that age on the Missouri followed its valley, and beyond it, in great part followed the route of Lewis and Clark to the Northwest. How minutely the expedition pioneered one main course of American economic development a list of names reveals at once: Kansas City, Leavenworth, St. Joseph, Atchison, Omaha, Council Bluffs, Sioux City, Yankton, Pierre, Bismarck, Williston, Miles City, Billings, Bozeman, Fort Benton, Great Falls, Helena, Dillon, Salmon, Missoula, Lewiston, Walla Walla, Portland, Astoria.

A century and a half later, it is still impossible to make a satisfactory statement about the scientific results of the expedition: qualified scientists and historians have not been interested in making the requisite studies. Lewis's untimely death in 1809[18] prolonged the already serious delay in the issuance of a detailed official account of the expedition. Unquestionably he would have written one if he had lived and he was in a better position to formulate findings

than Biddle, who wrote the invaluable *History.* As it is, the only "literary" results that were not indirect are anthropological. The voluminous notes on Indian tribes, mainly by Lewis, which were sent to the War Department from the Mandan villages in 1805, were codified and tabulated and published as "A Statistical View of the Indian Nations Inhabiting the Territory of Louisiana . . ."[19] This report was at once immensely important and, as the first survey of the trans-Mississippi tribes, is permanently important.

The "Statistical View" defines the nature of Biddle's *History,* through which mainly the "literary" purposes of the expedition were fulfilled. Lewis's carefully assembled Indian vocabularies were lost but Biddle worked into narrative an enormous amount of the information about Indians that the journals contained. He also wrote several extended passages of generalization, based not only on the journals but on communications from Clark and discussions with George Shannon, and these too are amazingly sound and useful. The *History* is the first detailed account, and one may add the first reliable account of whatever length, of the Western tribes. It put a valuable bulk of knowledge at the disposal of anyone who had interest in or use for knowledge relating to the Indians of the West. So it has always been a prime source for anthropologists and historians.

But that, of course, is true of much more than anthropology. History is not so divisible as to permit us to say exactly how important the Lewis and Clark expedition was in securing Oregon, as a physical possession, to the United States, though its paramount importance is self-evident. But it gave not only Oregon but the entire West to the American people as something with which the mind could deal. The westering people had crossed the Mississippi with the Louisiana Purchase and by that act had acquired the manifest destiny of going on to the Pacific. But the entire wilderness expanse, more than twice the size of the United States at the beginning of Jefferson's administration, was a blank, not only on the map but in human thought. It was an area of rumor, guess, and fantasy. Now it had been crossed by a large party who came back and told in assimilable and trustworthy detail what a large part of it was. Henceforth the mind could focus on reality. Here were not only the Indians but the land itself and its conditions: river systems, valleys, mountain ranges, climates, flora, fauna, and a rich and varied membrane of detail relating them to one another and to familiar experience. It was the first report on the West, on the United States over the hill and beyond the sunset, on the province of the American future. There has never been another so excellent or so influential. So it was rather as a treasury of knowledge than as a great adventure story that the *History* became a national and international favorite, reprinted, translated, pirated, and counterfeited. It satisfied desire and it created desire: the desire of the westering nation.

That, the increase of our cultural heritage, the beginning of knowledge of the American West, must be accounted the most important result of the Lewis and Clark expedition.

Notes

1. A. P. Nasatir, ed., *Before Lewis and Clark* (St. Louis, 1952), II, 712-14. For the state of knowledge and explorations of the far Northwest, including Mackenzie and the Spanish efforts from St. Louis, see Nasatir's introduction and Chapters VIII and IX of DeVoto, *The Course of Empire*.

2. Nasatir, II, 716.

3. Jefferson was working out a transcontinental route for interoceanic trade, which was the hope that had sustained nearly three centuries of search for the Northwest Passage. He did not need to point out to Congress that some of the routes east of the Mississippi which he named were almost continuous. The one from the mouth of the Missouri to Lake Michigan by way of the Illinois River was interrupted only by the short Chicago Portage; indeed, during the flood season of some years this stretch could be paddled. After the Chicago Portage to Lake Michigan there was no interruption all the way to Oswego on Lake Ontario, and from Oswego a few easy portages led to the Mohawk River. (With equal ease an alternative route led from Lake Erie to the Finger Lakes. Note the relation of both these routes to that of the Erie Canal.) The Great Lakes were not navigable during the winter, however, and a route up the Ohio River would be far preferable—though Jefferson did not say so to New York congressmen. Such a route would necessitate a long interruption for the difficult and costly crossing of the Pennsylvania mountains. Yet in 1803 it was a reasonable expectation that various proposed canals would soon greatly reduce this difficulty, or perhaps even overcome it. In 1802 the Potomac Company, which Washington had helped to organize in 1785, had completed a series of locks round the Great Falls of the Potomac. By 1808 additional locks and short canals provided continuous passage to Harper's Ferry, and eventually, as the Chesapeake and Ohio Canal, the system extended to Cumberland.

4. The fact that the city and "Isle" of New Orleans were east of the Mississippi confused thinking, and therefore negotiation, about the Louisiana Purchase after it was made. Whether the United States had bought "the Isle of Orleans," or part or all of West Florida were questions which provided ample room for honest and dishonest debate and later led to much turmoil, fraud, and even insurrection. The legal question never was directly settled; it was extinguished by the purchase of East Florida and the accompanying concession of West Florida in the Adams-Onís Treaty, signed in 1819.

5. The closure was never absolute. The customs house at Natchez and the river patrols ignored some American boats and with even greater frequency granted permission to pass. The uncertainty and the expense combined with the confiscation of many boats and the threat to confiscate every boat, however, were as intolerable as complete closure. Even worse was the flagrant and corrupt favoritism by which the officials, in return for political activity as well as bribes, allowed such agents as Wilkinson the profitable privileges denied the common trade.

6. At various times the size of the area in view varied from a few square miles embracing the city itself, or adjacent to it, on to the entire Isle of Orleans. This was an area of about 2800 square miles, extending to the Gulf of Mexico from the bodies of water lying east of the Mississippi, that actually made an island of the city, Iberville River and Lakes Maurepas and Pontchartrain. As far back as 1790 the United States had tried to buy it from Spain.

7. He had gone to school to the Reverend James Maury, Jefferson's schoolmaster and one of the group of ardent Virginia expansionists who certainly fired his imagination for Western exploration at a very early age. Maury was a conspicuous member of a long line of thinkers who regarded a water route across North America as carrying with it political and commercial domination of the continent. See DeVoto, *op. cit.,* 411 ff.

8. The instructions are printed as Appendix I [of *The Journals of Lewis and Clark*].

9. British energy and money were absorbed by the Napoleonic Wars or, very likely, Mackenzie's vision would have been acted on by government or by private enterprise. This delay was Napoleon's second gift to American expansion.

10. The boundary ambiguities resulted from ignorance, at the peace treaty following the Revolution, of the source of the Mississippi. Mackenzie's proposal looked to establishing a connection with the Mississippi from the western end of Lake Superior. The St. Louis River would provide the beginning of such a connection but the line must be drawn far enough south to reach the Mississippi at a point where it was navigable by canoes; its extreme upper reach he regarded as "a brook." The 45th parallel is just above Minneapolis; the rectified boundary would run due west from here to intersect a line drawn south from the western shore of Lake of the Woods. It crosses South Dakota, the upper third of which would thus with North Dakota become Canadian, and is the southern boundary of Montana as far as the Continental Divide. Mackenzie's plan allows for the possibility that this equitable and highly desirable relocation might not be secured. But west of the Divide the Columbia *must* be made British and the 45th parallel would effect this; it crosses Oregon just below the latitude of Salem.

11. It must be constantly remembered that in 1801 when Jefferson addressed Congress, Louisiana was Spanish territory and destined to become French, and that the United States had a recognized prior claim to the Co-

lumbia country, to which Spain had some claim and which both Great Britain (by the Nootka convention) and Russia might also make claim. Thus Jefferson's proposal to establish an American trade route down the Missouri was a proposal to establish American trade in territory from which French law must exclude it. This same route across foreign soil was to be used to give American trade an overland connection with the Columbia. That region, in January 1803, was a legitimate field for American expansion as Louisiana was not. The American prior claim to it was, according to usages of nations, so good that in the same year as Gray's discovery of the Columbia, Vancouver had to take the stand for Great Britain that Gray had never really entered the river, whereas his lieutenant, Broughton, had. This remained the official British stand till the Oregon question was settled.

In January 1803, the attractive force, therefore, was the Columbia region, a detached portion of the American economy, to sovereignty over which the United States had a prior but unadjudicated and untested claim. The tacitly assumed force was the extension of American settlement into Louisiana.

12. Rivers that reach the sea must come down to it from a height of land, and on the western coast of a continent the height of land from which they come down must be inland to the east—these axioms behind the theory of the River of the West are entirely sound. The theory, however, had been elaborated from additional axioms which postulated a geographical symmetry at variance with the realities of the North American continent. In its ideal form the theory held that from a fundamental height of land a principal river ran in each of the cardinal directions. The River of the East was the St. Lawrence, which was understood to include the entire chain of the Great Lakes it drained; the River of the South was the Mississippi. The River of the North was hypothetical until the Nelson, which drains Lake Winnipeg, was fairly well understood. By the time the Coppermine and Mackenzie were discovered, the concept of a fundamental height of land had to be abandoned and they could not be assumed to "head" with the Mississippi and the St. Lawrence. By 1793 the River of the West could not head with them, either, but it could with the Missouri.

13. They supposed themselves then so near to the Pacific that a journey to the coast from the villages, or even from the Platte, and return could be made in a single season. An inexplicable vestige of this naïveté still lingered in Lewis's mind when the expedition started west from the villages in 1805, in spite of the fact that during the winter Clark had worked out an astonishingly accurate table of distances as far as the mountains.

14. Obviously, the inventories which Thwaites found and published fail to list the equipment and supplies in full. For instance, in caches at the Three Forks at the head of the Jefferson, and at Canoe Camp on the Clearwater, almost as much gunpowder is deposited as the inventories show—this on an expedition that had been using gunpowder daily since it left St. Louis and giving sizable amounts of it to Indians. It is equally clear that the original appropriation of $2500 fell short of paying for the expedition but no records of supplementary payments have been found. They could have been made from the Executive's free funds or charged against either the War Department or the State Department.

15. The journals of the captains record the floggings inflicted by sentence of court-martial. Those of Ordway, Gass, and Whitehouse so conspicuously fail to mention them as to suggest that they may have been directed to make no record of them.

16. These tribes had indeed been corrupted by the debauchery, brutality, and terrorism of the Northwest trade, but they were the fringe tribes of their culture group and it seems to be true that they had started on a cultural decline before the arrival of the trade.

17. Henry Spalding and Father de Smet.

18. He died in a squalid roadside cabin, used as an ordinary, in frontier Tennessee. He was en route from St. Louis to Washington to cope with snarls of red tape which, from political motives, had brought his official accounts into question. (He was Governor of Louisiana Territory.) The circumstances of the mysterious affair strongly suggest murder but Jefferson, who knew that he was subject to fits of depression, believed that he had committed suicide and it is clear that he was in a very nervous state when he left St. Louis.

19. *American State Papers,* Indian Affairs, No. 113, 9th Cong., 1st Sess.

James P. Ronda (essay date 1998)

SOURCE: "'The Writingest Explorers': The Lewis and Clark Expedition in American Historical Literature," in *Voyages of Discovery: Essays on the Lewis and Clark Expedition,* edited by James P. Ronda, Montana Historical Society Press, 1998, pp. 299-326.

[*In the following essay, Ronda surveys the publication history of the Lewis and Clark journals, detailing scholarly as well as public reaction to the various editions.*]

On September 26, 1806, just four days after returning from the Pacific Coast, Meriwether Lewis and William Clark settled into a rented room at Pierre Chouteau's and "commenced wrighting."[1] Journal entries, scientific observations, ethnographic notes, and detailed maps—a virtual encyclopedia of the West—needed to be examined, catalogued, and arranged for further study. Surveying the literary remains of their expedition, Lewis and Clark surely would have agreed with historian Donald Jackson that they were the "writingest explorers" the West had yet seen.[2] The struggle to understand the meaning of what Clark once called a "vast, Hazidous and fatiguing enterprize" began in that St. Louis room and continues into our own time.[3]

Both the explorers and those who followed them sensed that the expedition occupied a special place in American history. But the exact character of that place has often proved elusive. Confusion and ambiguity about the meaning of the venture surfaced no more than two days after the party's return. St. Louis townspeople, bent on celebrating the homecoming, hosted a grand dinner and ball at William Christy's city tavern. Those festivities included a round of toasts. Such expressions were an indicator of the expedition's public image, a kind of initial evaluation of what the explorers had accomplished. And if the drinking at Christy's meant anything, merchants and traders were not quite sure what Lewis and Clark had done. The toasts that night praised the nation and the Louisiana Territory, memorialized Christopher Columbus and George Washington, and lauded "the fair daughters of Louisiana—May they ever bestow their smiles on hardihood and virtuous valor." Once Lewis and Clark withdrew, as custom required, they were cheered for "their perilous services" to the nation.[4]

The exuberant townspeople of St. Louis were not alone in their confusion about the expedition's significance. Was the great trek nothing more than a grand adventure at public expense? When a group of citizens at Fincastle, Virginia, sent their congratulations, the testimonial emphasized daring against terrible odds. "You have navigated bold and unknown rivers, traversed Mountains which had never before been impressed with the footsteps of civilized man, and surmounted every obstacle, which climate, Nature, or ferocious Savages could throw in your way." A passing mention of extending geographic knowledge was overwhelmed by a burst of patriotic rhetoric comparing Lewis and Clark to Columbus. Fincastle residents were ready to predict that the explorers would enjoy "pure and unsullied" fame. But the reasons for that reputation seemed hard to define.[5]

St. Louis merchants and Fincastle well-wishers could be excused for their uncertainty about the journey. They had seen nothing of the journals, maps, and specimens brought back from the West. Yet the public confusion about the expedition was shared by Lewis and Clark as well as Jefferson. Had the undertaking achieved its central purpose? From its inception the enterprise had one goal. As the president put it to Lewis in June 1803: "The object of your mission is to explore the Missouri river, & such principal stream[s] of it, as, by it's course and communication with the waters of the Pacific ocean, whether the Columbia, Oregan, Colorado, or any other river may offer the most direct and practicable water communication across this continent for the purposes of commerce."[6] When Lewis

appeared to stray from that objective, Jefferson reined him in with a sharp reminder that "the object of your mission is single, the direct water communication from sea to sea formed by the bed of the Missouri and perhaps the Oregon."[7] Whatever else his Corps of Discovery might accomplish, whether in science or diplomacy, Jefferson was intent on tracing that Passage to India.

Sitting in their St. Louis rooms, the president's men had to face an unpleasant reality. They had failed to find that "direct water communication from sea to sea." Indeed, what they had come upon were mountain barriers that made such a passage virtually impossible. Torn between accurate reporting and the desire to satisfy their patron, the explorers sought to put the best face on failure. Writing to Jefferson just one day after the end of the journey, Lewis assured the president that the expedition "penitrated the Continent of North America to the Pacific ocean, and sufficiently explored the interior of the country to affirm with confidence that we have discovered the most practicable rout[e] which dose exist across the continent by means of the navigable branches of the Missouri and Columbia Rivers." But what the explorer gave with one hand he snatched away with the other. Lewis admitted that the passage, while valuable for the fur trade, was hardly a plain path across the continent. There was no direct water communication and the northern overland route charted by the captains would never take the place of sea lanes around the Cape of Good Hope. As Lewis delicately put it, the overland path was useful only for goods "not bulky brittle nor of a very perishable nature."[8] Clark walked the same tightrope. Writing a letter he knew would be quickly printed in many western newspapers, the explorer pronounced the venture "completely successful." But there was the inevitable hedge. Clark had "no hesitation in declaring that such as nature has permitted it we have discovered the best rout[e] which does exist across the continent of North America in that direction." But what nature had permitted was not quite what Jefferson had in mind.[9]

The president's own understanding of the expedition proved equally selective. Jefferson's initial reaction—"unspeakable joy"—at the safe return of the party was reflected in his December 1806 annual message to Congress. Legislators were told that the expedition "had all the success which could have been expected." The measure of that success came as the explorers "traced the Missouri nearly to it's source, descended the Columbia to the Pacific ocean, ascertained with accuracy the geography of that interesting communication across our continent, learnt the character of the country, of it's commerce and inhabitants."[10] By the time Lewis got to Washington in January 1807, Jefferson must have begun to realize that his "interesting communication" was still more hope than reality.

When the expedition was in its earliest planning stages, Attorney General Levi Lincoln warned Jefferson about the high price of failure. Lincoln evidently had seen an early draft of expedition instructions, a draft containing little about ethnography and natural history. Lincoln suggested that "some new aspects be usefully given to the undertaking, and others made more prominent." As Lincoln saw it, the expedition ought to pursue scientific objectives so that if the passage to the Pacific proved illusory there would still be much to claim.[11] The attorney general's suggestions were both politically astute and strangely prophetic. By the summer of 1808 Jefferson was busy reshaping the meaning of the Lewis and Clark Expedition. Writing to French naturalist Bernard Lacépède, he asserted that "the addition to our kno[w]le[d]ge, in every department, resulting from that tour, of Messrs. Lewis and Clarke, has entirely fulfilled my expectations in setting it on foot."[12] As the hope of a water passage faded, the image of the expedition as a great scientific enterprise grew brighter. Jefferson's correspondence with Bernard McMahon and Charles Willson Peale pointed to that new understanding of the expedition's central mission. Levi Lincoln had been right. Science, the shape of strange animals, exotic Indians, and useful plants might rescue the whole venture from oblivion.

The emphasis on scientific accomplishment fit Lewis's personal conception of what he always called his "tour" of the West. Although he once told guests at a Washington dinner that the establishment of an American trading post on the Columbia would prove the expedition's greatest attainment, that bit of geopolitical fortune-telling was not at the heart of Lewis's writing.[13] In the spring of 1807 Philadelphia printer John Conrad issued a prospectus for Lewis's proposed three-volume expedition report. Lewis intended that the first volume be "a narrative of the voyage, with a description of some of the most remarkable places in those hitherto unknown wilds of America . . . together with an itinerary of the most direct and practicable rout[e] across the Continent of North America." Here was the tale of adventure sought by an enthusiastic public. But in keeping with the new emphasis on expedition science, Lewis promised two full volumes packed with ethnography, botany, zoology, and "other natural phenomena which were met with in the course of this interesting tour."[14] In many ways this prospectus was the formal announcement of the new wisdom about the expedition. Jefferson's desired passage and the failure to find it was lost in glowing promises of memorable scientific advances.

The success of this new interpretation depended on the timely publication of Lewis's history of the expedition. By mid-1807 he had made preliminary arrangements for printing the work. Plans were also underway for engraving maps and plates. The only thing lacking was a completed manuscript. Nearly a year later an impatient Jefferson prodded Lewis for news. "We have no tidings yet of the forwardness of your printer." The president could only hope that "the first part will not be delayed much longer." A full year after administering that polite scolding, Jefferson admitted that "every body is impatient" for the great work.[15]

Word of Lewis's suicide at Grinder's Stand on the Natchez Trace in 1809 was shocking enough. Almost as stunning

was news that Lewis had made virtually no progress on his literary project. In late 1809 Lewis's publishers wrote Jefferson with the sorry news that "Govr. Lewis never furnished us with a line of the M.S. nor indeed could we ever hear any thing from him respecting it tho frequent applications to that effect were made to him."[16] Lewis's failure as an author and his untimely death now set off a complex series of events that finally led William Clark to obtain the services of Philadelphia lawyer and litterateur Nicholas Biddle. What Biddle finally brought to press in 1814 was essentially what Lewis had proposed as his first volume. Here, in an edition of only 1,417 copies, was the story of the expedition as a glorious western adventure. Readers would find a powerful story but no science. As Jefferson lamented to Alexander von Humboldt, "the botanical and zoological discoveries of Lewis will probably experience greater delay, and become known to the world thro other channels before that volume will be ready."[17]

Publication delays, omission of the vital scientific data, and poor sales all conspired to produce an expedition record with little public appeal. Stripped of its intellectual achievements, the Lewis and Clark Expedition was increasingly viewed by Americans as a great national adventure. Jefferson's bold western thrust had been transformed into a symbol for a westering nation. But the symbol lacked substance. No wagon trains followed the expedition's overland track. American diplomats caught up in the Oregon question used the voyages and travels of Captain Robert Gray and the Astorians to justify Yankee claims on the Columbia. An occasional eastern promoter might call up the captains' ghosts but even those appearances were few and far between. Americans had not lost a national fascination with exploring the West. Lewis and Clark simply could not compete with the much-publicized exploits of John Charles Frémont and other pathfinders. Jefferson's Corps of Discovery had been eclipsed by Frémont and explorer-scientists like John Wesley Powell, Clarence King, and F. V. Hayden. Eliminated from the scientific lists, Lewis and Clark fared poorly against popular heroes like Jesse James and Kit Carson. By the late nineteenth century the expedition had almost disappeared from the historical landscape.[18]

The struggle to recover the expedition and its meanings for American history began in June 1891 when New York publisher Francis P. Harper wrote naturalist and ex-army surgeon Elliott Coues asking if he would be interested in editing a new printing of the Biddle narrative. What pushed Harper to make such a suggestion has never been clearly explained. Harper and Brothers had obtained copyright to the Biddle edition in 1842 and had over the years issued printings of an abridged version of the narrative. In 1891 Harper evidently intended no more than a reprint of Biddle with some explanatory notes. Whatever Harper's motives and plans, the choice of Coues was an inspired one. During the 1860s Coues served as an army surgeon at a number of frontier posts. That western exposure and later work for the Northern Boundary Commission and the United States Geological and Geographical Survey of the Territories gave Coues's lifelong interest in ornithology a wider field. Here was a man who knew much of the Lewis and Clark West from personal experience and was ready to appreciate the expedition's scientific labors.

Coues's "discovery" of the original Lewis and Clark journals at the American Philosophical Society and his cavalier treatment of those documents is a familiar story. What is important is the refurbished image of the expedition that emerged when the Biddle-Coues edition appeared in 1893. Coues centered his extensive annotations on three subjects. The eighteenth century had defined natural history in the broadest terms, encompassing everything from botany to zoology. Coues found that definition congenial to his own scientific method and busied himself annotating expedition observations on western plants and animals. Lewis had once promised a full accounting of western Indian life and material culture. Little of that ethnography made it into the Biddle narrative. The late nineteenth-century frontier had seen valuable work done by soldier-ethnographers like John Bourke and John Wesley Powell. Influenced by those examples, Coues spent considerable annotation space commenting on native customs, behavior, and objects. Finally, Coues sought to identify as many Lewis and Clark campsites as possible. He did this neither from an antiquarian passion nor a boosterism that shouted "Lewis and Clark slept here." Rather, he wanted to place Lewis and Clark at the center of western exploration. More than Frémont and the post-Civil War surveys, Lewis and Clark had scientific primacy. As Paul Cutright observed some seventy years after Coues's work first appeared, that new edition "focused attention for the first time on the vast amount of unpublished and virtually unknown scientific data in the original journals and, thereby, on the salient roles played by Lewis and Clark as outstanding pioneer naturalists."[19]

Any significant reassessment of the Lewis and Clark Expedition required publication of the original journals. Coues's annotations might suggest new directions, but they were no substitute for the captains' own words, maps, observations, and specimens. In 1901, with the twin centennials of the Louisiana Purchase and the expedition at hand, the American Philosophical Society decided to seek publication of its treasured expedition records. Negotiations with Dodd, Mead and Company followed as did a search for an editor. Reuben Gold Thwaites, then superintendent of the State Historical Society of Wisconsin, was eventually chosen for the task. Thwaites had just completed a massive edition of the *Jesuit Relations* and enjoyed a growing reputation as a documentary editor. Equally important, he had at Madison a skilled staff of research associates, including Louise Phelps Kellogg and Emma Hunt Blair. Thwaites's work on the Lewis and Clark manuscripts is well known and has received careful commentary in Paul Cutright's comprehensive *History of the Lewis and Clark Journals.* Thwaites predicted that his edition would prompt "a new view of Lewis and Clark." He was especially sanguine about prospects for a thorough evaluation of expedition science. "The voluminous scientific data here given—in botany, zoology, meteorology, ge-

ology, astronomy, and ethnology—is almost entirely a fresh contribution."[20] But Thwaites had more than science on his mind. Like his friend Frederick Jackson Turner, he believed that explorers were the vanguard in the steady westward march of the young republic. Thwaites and Turner shared the notion of sequential development on the frontier. Lewis and Clark were at the head of an irrepressible American advance to the Pacific, an advance that promised political democracy, economic prosperity, and civilized values. For Thwaites, the expedition represented "that notable enterprise in the cause of civilization."[21]

The *Original Journals of the Lewis and Clark Expedition,* published by Dodd, Mead in 1904-5, quickly found its place on library shelves and in private collections. But the volumes did not spark a substantial reevaluation of the expedition. In fact, Thwaites's own writing about Lewis and Clark remained traditional in narrative style and emphasis on high adventure. In 1904, while still working on the journals, he wrote *A Brief History of Rocky Mountain Exploration, with Especial Reference to the Expedition of Lewis and Clark.* The book offered a chronological treatment of the journey, spiced with quotes from the then-unpublished journals. Perhaps Thwaites thought reading those lines would be reward enough since the Lewis and Clark chapters never rose above simple storytelling. Thwaites claimed that the expedition was "the most important and interesting of Rocky Mountains explorations" but let readers struggle to define that import and interest.[22] Several years later Thwaites had another opportunity to explain the expedition to a wider audience. In collaboration with Calvin Noyes Kendall, he wrote *A History of the United States for Grammar Schools.* Here was a chance to give young students a glimpse of that "new view of Lewis and Clark" promised some seven years before. But it was a promise largely unfulfilled. Seventh- and eighth-graders got a meager outline of the expedition's progress across the continent. Thwaites's own Turnerian interpretation came to the surface when students were instructed about the venture's larger meaning. "The path having now been broken by Lewis and Clark, wandering fur traders soon thronged into the Far West. Many American settlers also opened farms in what became known as the Oregon Territory, and their presence furnished a basis for our later claim to the Northwest Coast."[23] Thwaites's new view ended up as nothing more than a vision of the expedition as an agent of a triumphant Manifest Destiny.

In the four decades that followed publication of the Lewis and Clark journals, American historians paid little attention to the West in general and Jefferson's explorers in particular. Edward Channing, the first professional historian to use the Thwaites edition, saw the expedition as a scientific venture. But the dimensions of that science eluded him, and he quickly fell back on the expedition-as-great-adventure approach, concluding that the journals "read like a romance."[24] The standard school text for the period, David S. Muzzey's *American History,* gave one scant paragraph to the expedition. Like Thwaites, Muzzey saw Lewis and Clark as part of an inevitable American conquest of the West.[25]

While textbook writers and some historians continued to believe that the expedition had some significance—however hard to define—others were beginning to doubt that Lewis and Clark were anything more than adventurers. Frederic L. Paxson's influential *History of the American Frontier, 1763-1893,* argued that the expedition produced neither lasting scientific results nor the basis for future settlement. Paxson insisted that "the results of the Lewis and Clark Expedition were not commensurate with the effort or the success that attended it."[26] Other frontier historians tended to agree. What really mattered in the history of the West was land, cattle, railroads, and the Indian wars. Dan Elbert Clark, a prominent western historian in the 1930s, found that the expedition failed to publish its findings, findings that had no lasting significance.[27] But no scholar in those years fashioned so negative an image of the expedition as did Walter Prescott Webb. In his *The Great Plains,* Webb insisted that the Lewis and Clark journals were "meager and unsatisfying." Pressing his indictment, Webb maintained that a reading of Lewis and Clark revealed a "lack of specific detail, a vegueness, an absence of names of persons and places in connection with episodes related." Webb was convinced that neither explorer knew anything about geology, botany, zoology, or ethnography. "Why a man of Jefferson's philosophical and scientific turn of mind," Webb wondered aloud, "should have been unable to select more capable men for the enterprise, keen observers with trained minds, is hard to understand."[28]

In the midst of cliché-ridden textbooks and professional historians either indifferent or openly hostile to the expedition, the 1930s saw two scholars offer serious studies of the journey. John Bartlett Brebner's carefully researched and well-written *Explorers of North America* was a thoughtful narrative history of the major expeditionary probes from coastal margins to interior plains and mountains. Brebner defined his geographical arena as North America, breaking from the parochial limits of the United States. He argued persuasively that French Canada, Russian Alaska, and the Spanish Southwest were essential parts of the wider story. Brebner saw the Lewis and Clark Expedition as the conclusion of imperial conflicts that had shaped the history of the continent since the Age of Columbus. More important, he portrayed the expedition as the beginning of professional, scientific studies of the West. "It is impossible," he asserted, "not to feel that the Lewis and Clark Expedition opened a new era in North American exploration." Brebner's Lewis and Clark were hard-eyed pragmatists supported by the best available technology and a national treasury. There was no romance here, no chasing after myths of Welsh Indians or elusive northwest passages. Lewis and Clark were wholly "unlike the daring dashes of the French and the Canadians or the grand cavalry marches of the Spanish." In the end, Brebner offered an expedition suited to a rational, technological society. "Its success," he wrote, "was a triumph of the elaborate co-ordination of geographical and technical knowledge and of the expenditure of public money without interest in material return."[29]

Brebner's evaluation of Lewis and Clark was based on reading the Thwaites edition as well as a broad knowledge of North American exploration. No scholar had yet undertaken the sorts of specialized studies Thwaites envisioned in 1905. Those studies might have begun with botany, zoology, or ethnography. That the first specialized expedition monograph was in linguistics proved a considerable surprise. In the 1930s Elijah H. Criswell came to the University of Missouri to pursue graduate studies in English. At Missouri Criswell fell under the influence of Professor Robert L. Ramsay. Ramsay, one of the foremost scholars of American regional language, suggested that Criswell study the Lewis and Clark journals as a means to probe "what is truly American in our language."[30] Challenged by Ramsay, Criswell began a thorough study of the language in expedition records. This was no narrow undertaking. Criswell and Ramsay defined language in the broadest terms. Scientific names, nautical phrases, military commands, medical jargon, frontier slang, and geographic descriptions all drew Criswell's attention. Employing the advice of several professional botanists and zoologists, he compiled the first comprehensive list of Lewis and Clark flora and fauna. Perhaps most valuable, the dissertation contained an extraordinary "Lewis and Clark Lexicon." From aborigines to Yellowstone, Criswell defined words as they were used in the period and gave the necessary Lewis and Clark references.

Published as part of the University of Missouri Studies in 1940, Criswell's *Lewis and Clark: Linguistic Pioneers* drew scant notice from historians. But its achievement should not be measured by that lack of attention. At a time when few scholars were studying the expedition, Criswell produced a book of genuine range and imagination. With little support from historians and no models on which to pattern his work, Criswell defined a crucial aspect of the expedition and wrote about it with grace and skill.[31]

Brebner's technocrats and Criswell's pupils of American English seemed remote from the West Bernard DeVoto sought to chronicle. Journalist, novelist, and magazine editor, DeVoto was also a passionate student of those lands beyond the Mississippi. His trilogy—*Year of Decision: 1846* (1942), *Across the Wide Missouri* (1947), and *The Course of Empire* (1952)—remains required reading on subjects as diverse as the Rocky Mountain fur trade, the conquest of California, and Jefferson's vision of an American empire. In the 1930s DeVoto was primarily interested in Mark Twain and western literature but Lewis and Clark were never far from mind. When the Christmas 1936 issue of the *Saturday Review* lacked a lead essay, editor DeVoto decided to write a Lewis and Clark piece. Titled "Passage to India: From Christmas to Christmas with Lewis and Clark," it tracked the expedition from Fort Mandan's bountiful holidays to the lean celebrations at Fort Clatsop. Here was DeVoto at his storytelling best, filling the reader's mind with images of firelight and shadow. But behind the dancing language was a real idea, what he would jokingly call years later an important "Historical Idea." The expedition touched "a crisis of world polity." Jefferson's dream of an American Passage to India meant something central about the imperial destiny of the young republic.[32] In 1936 DeVoto was not quite sure how the fabled Northwest Passage, Jefferson's imperial vision, and a band of tattered soldiers all fit together. Making the connections would take another decade and a half.

More than once in the years that followed, DeVoto gave thought to writing a full narrative history of the expedition. But other books kept getting in the way. Manifest Destiny, the Mexican War, and California all seemed more compelling. Those events and places came together in *Year of Decision: 1846,* a book that sought to "realize the pre-Civil War, Far Western frontier as personal experience."[33] That book forced DeVoto to confront the origins of empire in the West. The more he thought about it, the more he became convinced that Jefferson and his captains were at the heart of that powerful drive west. In the mid-1940s DeVoto seemed ready to write his book on Lewis and Clark. He confidently told Henry Steele Commager that he was "eyeing" the explorers.[34] And there was ample evidence of DeVoto's growing Lewis and Clark interest in a 1945 essay for *Harper's Magazine* on the meaning of the expedition. He was increasingly convinced that Lewis and Clark's wilderness errand said something fundamental about the history of North America, perhaps even the history of the world. The expedition was, he asserted, "conceived by the earliest, most farseeing of American geopoliticians, Thomas Jefferson, as a necessary step in the defense of the United States against expanding, rival empires in the Western Hemisphere."[35] But as chance had it, Lewis and Clark were shouldered aside by the Rocky Mountain fur trade. What began as a simple assignment providing captions for recently discovered paintings by Alfred Jacob Miller blossomed into a masterful book. *Across the Wide Missouri* was DeVoto's evocation of the western fur trade. Lewis and Clark had gotten lost in the presence of Jim Bridger, Black Harris, and Tom Fitzpatrick.

The mountain men and their wild Green River rendezvous only temporarily overshadowed Lewis and Clark. By late 1946 DeVoto was busy "filling his tank" for a book about the expedition.[36] That tank was getting far more than readings of the Lewis and Clark journals. DeVoto now believed that a simple narrative could not do justice to the larger history of the expedition. Garrett Mattingly, DeVoto's closest historian friend, once wrote that "American history was history in transition from an Atlantic to a Pacific phase."[37] DeVoto's problem was to trace that transition without becoming mired in the travels of every explorer from Columbus and Cabot to Pike and Frémont. Lewis and Clark were important, but DeVoto now knew that they were at the end of the transition, not at its beginnings.

What had started as a traditional history of the great expedition became DeVoto's most important and most complex book. *The Course of Empire* was dominated by two powerful, interconnected ideas. Struggling to find meaning in that Atlantic to Pacific shift, DeVoto settled upon the search for the Passage to India as his unifying theme. But he was not interested in following a northwest passage through Arctic waters. DeVoto's route was the Missouri River, Marquette's "Pekitonoui," the river of the big canoe. He had once told Catherine Drinker Bowen that American history was "the most romantic of all histories."[38] That romance meant leading the reader through all the myths, dreams, and mad schemes that drove everyone from the Sieur de la Vérendrye to Lewis and Clark into "the Northwestern Mystery."

But *The Course of Empire* was far more than a fascinating catalog of geographic delusions. DeVoto wanted the book to explain how the United States had become a continental nation, how it had come to occupy what Abraham Lincoln called a "national homestead." DeVoto had been thinking about continentalism since the 1930s. His Lewis and Clark research convinced him that geographic realities—river systems and mountain ranges—shaped American expansion. Here DeVoto danced with a dangerous idea. Geographic determinism, the likes of which had been proposed earlier in the century by Ellen Churchill Semple and Albert P. Brigham, reduced history to mathematical precision. DeVoto always affirmed the primacy of individuals in history. His continentalism, rooted in a sure sense of western geography, focused on Thomas Jefferson. DeVoto had been saying for years that Jefferson was the first American geopolitician, and in *The Course of Empire* he set out to prove it.

Thomas Jefferson, Meriwether Lewis, and William Clark occupied a mere 170 pages in a book of well more than 500 pages. But those concluding chapters were the crucial ones. Here was the culmination of a three-century quest for the Northwest Passage. Those pages made plain the first move by the United States to dominate the continent. Recounting Jefferson's 1803 message to Congress proposing a western expedition, DeVoto found a president bent on making the United States a Pacific power. Challenged by Anglo-Canadian moves carried out by Alexander Mackenzie and driven by his own understanding of western geography, Jefferson fashioned an enterprise that would wrest an empire from rival hands. The explorers were engaged in an "imperial necessity," a "heavy national responsibility."[39] In the midst of writing *Course of Empire* DeVoto told Mattingly that he wanted to "chock up American history on blocks, turn it around and give it a new orientation."[40] The Lewis and Clark Expedition was a grand adventure and DeVoto related it with zest and delight. But he knew that Jefferson and the captains meant to achieve more than a daring western tour. The expedition made the United States a continental power, a force in world history.

Course of Empire gave the Lewis and Clark Expedition context and meaning. DeVoto had succeeded in making the expedition into something more than a company of soldiers bound for the great western sea. The book brought its author critical acclaim but most academic reviewers missed its central message. Accustomed to a literary DeVoto, scholars found it easy to dismiss or ignore the book and its themes. Historians in the 1950s did not have the West on their research agendas. The Western History Association was years away. *Course of Empire,* the book that might have revitalized studies of Lewis and Clark, had the misfortune to fall into a vacuum. Praised and purchased, *Course of Empire* had no immediate heirs.

DeVoto's grand sweep of western history excited little interest in the 1950s. John Bakeless certainly found nothing compelling about such a synthesis. Drawn to the expedition as a way to write biography, Bakeless began his research in 1939. Wartime service interrupted his progress, and it was not until 1947 that *Lewis and Clark: Partners in Discovery* was finally published. This was the descriptive history of the expedition DeVoto had once assayed. Bakeless wrote traditional narrative largely untouched by larger questions of meaning and interpretation. His readers got a rattling good tale but remained innocent about questions of science, Indian relations, geography, and international politics. Bakeless's version of the expedition fit the optimism of postwar America, an America confident about its place in the world. DeVoto's disturbing questions about imperialism seemed as out of place as did his spirited defense of wilderness and conservation issues.[41]

Perhaps more than fresh ideas, the study of the expedition needed new evidence. There had been important documentary discoveries including the publication of Sergeant John Ordway's diary and Lewis's Ohio River journal in 1913.[42] More dramatic was the 1953 discovery of Clark's field notes covering the period from December 1803 to April 1805. After extended litigation the Clark materials were published by Ernest S. Osgood in 1964.[43] At the same time New York's Antiquarian Press reprinted the Thwaites edition, bringing the journals back into print for the first time in some forty years. Here was fuel enough to rekindle expedition fires.

One person was largely responsible for fanning that flame. In the mid-1950s Donald Jackson was editor at the University of Illinois Press. While busy shepherding other authors' manuscripts through publication, he had also done considerable research and writing on his own. Custer's 1874 Black Hills reconnaissance and the early history of Fort Madison in present-day Iowa captured his attention. When the press decided to reissue the autobiography of Black Hawk and could find no one eager to edit the book, Jackson took it on. Lewis and Clark drifted through this and other projects, more as federal officials than as explorers. Jackson knew that the expedition had produced a large body of documents beyond the party's official journals. While Thwaites had printed some of those letters, many more awaited discovery. By November 1958 Jackson's Lewis and Clark letters project had taken shape and direction. Jackson defined his task as compiling and annotating "an edition of all letters pertaining to the expedition and to the production of the original Biddle edition and transfer of the journals to the American Philosophical Society."[44]

When the University of Illinois Press published *Letters of the Lewis and Clark Expedition with Related Documents,*

1783-1854 in 1962, the hefty volume contained 428 documents, well over half previously unpublished. A two-volume, revised edition, issued in 1978, added 29 more documents. Perhaps no documentary find both revealed more about Jackson's painstaking scholarship and proved more valuable to later scholars than his discovery of the Biddle Notes. In April 1810 Nicholas Biddle traveled to Virginia to interview William Clark. Those conversations amounted to a post-expedition debriefing. Biddle asked about everything from Indian linguistics to botany and geography. Those questions and Clark's answers were all duly recorded in Biddle's peculiar, hard-to-decipher handwriting. Working through Lewis and Clark manuscripts at the American Philosophical Society, Jackson came upon those notes. With an acute eye for handwriting, he quickly recognized the author. Equally important, Jackson grasped the significance of his discovery. Here was William Clark being queried by an intelligent scholar about major expedition matters just four year after the venture's end. Every student of the expedition, whether probing Indian relations or geography, soon came to recognize the Biddle Notes as a major source.[45]

Jackson's *Letters* proved far more than a skillfully presented collection of documents. The items themselves, their arrangement, and the editor's masterful annotations amounted to a scholarly transfusion for Lewis and Clark research. More important than any single monograph, the collection expanded the Lewis and Clark horizon. As Jackson put it, "it is no longer useful to think of the Lewis and Clark Expedition as the personal story of two men." Jackson's documents portrayed "an enterprise of many aims and a product of many minds."[46] Those many minds were reflected in letters from Jefferson, Albert Gallatin, Benjamin Rush, Benjamin Smith Barton, and a host of lesser-known scientists, politicians, army officers, and frontiersmen. Here were letters and reports on botany, zoology, ethnography, and physical geography. Knowing that Jefferson had planned other western exploring ventures before 1803, Jackson presented a full range of documents detailing those enterprises. Diplomacy and international relations were not ignored. Spanish reactions were traced in a number of important letters. Jackson's collection urged scholars to get beyond the great journey itself to see its consequences in the wider worlds of science, Indian relations, politics, and diplomacy.

Donald Jackson once wrote that "an editor's work is meant to be pillaged."[47] That pillaging began almost at once. In the 1950s DeVoto had complained that "it is still impossible to make a satisfactory statement about the scientific results of the expedition."[48] Challenged by both DeVoto and Jackson, a qualified scientist began such studies. Paul Cutright, a professor of biology at Beaver College, took up the task. Although Criswell and Jackson had compiled fairly complete lists of plants and animals encountered by the explorers, Cutright undertook a comprehensive examination of expedition science. His work, published as *Lewis and Clark: Pioneering Naturalists,* made plain the substantial achievements of the expedition. Cutright noted each plant and animal found by the explorers, recorded the names used by the expedition, and identified each by its modern binomial. Other writers had given expedition science an obligatory mention. Cutright did more. He clearly demonstrated both the depth and range of those accomplishments.[49]

Cutright's book fueled the blaze sparked by Jackson. The Lewis and Clark bonfire got fresh wood in 1975. Today Lewis and Clark each wear the title "explorer," a word neither man used to describe himself. No student of the expedition had carefully examined the nature of the exploratory process. Equally telling, there had been no systematic analysis of expedition cartography. Those gaps were filled when John Logan Allen completed his doctoral dissertation at Clark University in 1969 and subsequently published that work in revised and expanded form as *Passage through the Garden: Lewis and Clark and the Image of the American Northwest.*[50]

Allen's ambitious and provocative book probed the nature of the exploration by looking at field decisions made by the captains. At the same time he examined the geographical images that shaped the expedition. But the book was neither a simple catalog of choices made at this river or that mountain pass nor a study of disembodied "landscape images." As a historical geographer, Allen brought the two topics together by posing three vital questions. Following ideas set out by John K. Wright, Allen examined in great detail the ways knowledge—"lore" was Wright's word—from previous travelers fashioned an image of western geography. Here Allen provided an illuminating discussion of conceptual geography, the notions of river systems and mountain ranges that formed Jefferson's mental picture of the West. Allen then took that image and tracked it along the Lewis and Clark trail. As he envisioned it, the expedition was guided by geographic images constantly tested, modified, or discarded. Finally, Allen devoted considerable space to the role of Lewis and Clark as creators of new geographic imagery.

Passage through the Garden was an extraordinary book. Allen had not only discovered new cartographic evidence but he also had put Lewis and Clark in the mainstream of geographic thought. The emphasis on exploration as a "programmed enterprise" gave meaning to daily decisions about course and distance. Deeply influenced by DeVoto, Allen paid tribute to *Course of Empire* as "the major conceptual foundation" of his own work. Jackson's *Letters* had an importance, Allen wrote, "readily apparent" throughout his book.[51] *Passage through the Garden* was proof that the Lewis and Clark renewal sought by DeVoto and Jackson was now in full flame.

The course of historical research is often guided by lucky chance, and nothing was more serendipitous than the way Allen's work prompted the next major Lewis and Clark book. In 1976 *Ohio History* asked James P. Ronda to review *Passage through the Garden.* Ronda had previously written ethnohistorical accounts of Indian-missionary rela-

tions on eastern frontiers. Impressed by Allen's book, Ronda set out to write what he called "exploration ethnohistory."[52] *Lewis and Clark among the Indians,* published in 1984, used a wide variety of historical and anthropological sources to reveal the full range of relations between the expedition and its Indian neighbors. As Ronda imagined it, the expedition was one human community moving through and living among other human communities. Lewis and Clark traversed a crowded West already explored and settled by many native peoples. The story of the expedition could not be told apart from the lives of scores of Mandans, Shoshones, Nez Perces, and Chinookans. *Lewis and Clark among the Indians* probed everything from diplomacy and ethnography to trade and sexual relations. The book argued that the expedition was a shared enterprise, one that united different peoples with the bonds of common experience. Ronda's book offered two new interpretive directions for the study of the expedition. The traditional telling of the voyage had a small cast of characters. Ronda increased that cast and expanded the stage. He urged readers to listen to Indian voices and watch native people as active participants in the venture. Equally important, the book suggested that the expedition was a microcosm for the larger world of cultural relations in North America.

Books by Cutright, Allen, and Ronda filled major gaps in Lewis and Clark literature. At the same time it was clear that a modern edition of the journals was needed. Discoveries of new manuscript materials and more exacting annotation standards made Thwaites increasingly out-of-date. At the 1967 centennial meeting of the Missouri Historical Society, Donald Jackson issued a public call for such a new edition.[53] Jackson's prompting and suggestions from others finally caught the attention of Stephen F. Cox, executive editor at the University of Nebraska Press. Jackson was engaged as a consultant to prepare plans for a multivolume edition sponsored by the University of Nebraska Press, the Center for Great Plains Studies at the University of Nebraska, and the American Philosophical Society. Professor Gary E. Moulton was selected as the new editor for the journals. The first volume, a Lewis and Clark atlas, was published in 1983 and three journal volumes have appeared thus far.[54]

Now that a substantial portion of the new edition has been published it is important to step back and evaluate what has been accomplished. Perhaps that evaluation might begin with a commonsense question. What does it mean that these are the journals of the Lewis and Clark Expedition? Questions about what to include determine later decisions about presentation and annotation. As Moulton explains in his introduction, the new edition will eventually print "the journals of Lewis, Clark, Charles Floyd, John Ordway, Patrick Gass, and Joseph Whitehouse (all the extant journals associated with the expedition); and a volume of the expedition's natural history materials."[55]

How that intention works out in practice can best be judged by looking at a sample day in the life of the expedition.

On July 30, 1804, the explorers made camp at Council Bluff along the Missouri River some fifteen miles north of present-day Omaha, Nebraska. There Lewis and Clark prepared for their first Indian conference, a meeting with Oto and Missouri headmen. The new edition prints entries made by both captains. In addition there is the entry from Clark's field notes.[56] But the reader who assumes that this was the whole sum of writing done by the expedition that day will be wide of the mark. Sergeants Ordway and Floyd as well as Privates Whitehouse and Gass commented on the day's events. Their observations have been put off to be printed in a later volume. Although Moulton probably made a wise decision not to clutter each day with too many documents, the neglect of Ordway is a real loss. Ordway was the only member of the expedition to pen a journal entry every day. Ordway's importance lies not only in his comprehensive coverage but in his keen eye for detail. The young soldier could capture a scene or event with colorful, memorable language of the sort that often eluded his superiors.

The canons of documentary editing demand accurate transcription and clear printing of the original. Thwaites and his associates produced a reasonably clean reading of expedition journals. There were some errors, as when the phrase "cut my hand" was rendered as "cue my hare" in Clark's November 13, 1805, entry. The new edition locates and corrects those errors. At the same time the integrity of the originals, with all their delightful spellings and peculiar punctuations, has been honored. What readers are given is a reliable transcription. The chapter divisions, while not in the originals, are retained from Thwaites as they have become a useful research convention. Important scientific matter, relegated to volume six in Thwaites, is placed at the appropriate date and place.

No historical document can stand by itself. Obscure words need definition, little-known individuals require identification, and remote places demand location. Annotation provides that essential context. Documents without annotation are little more than disconnected fragments from a dark past. A generation ago documentary editors believed that their mission was to write long, learned footnotes. While some still cling to that tradition, the tide has turned toward a more restrained approach. Thanks in large part to the example of Donald Jackson in his Lewis and Clark, Pike, and Frémont editions, editors now annotate and avoid essay-length notes.

Moulton's annotation method can best be understood by returning to the events of July 30, 1804. An alert editor will surely find much to comment upon for that day. Thwaites wrote one note; Moulton has seven. A voyage of discovery is all about place and location. Any Lewis and Clark scholar must have a sure sense of place. Using both contemporary and modern maps, Moulton tells readers just where the expedition was on that July day. Locations throughout the edition are done by state, county, and closest present-day town. Unique terrain features that might further pinpoint a particular campsite are also included.

One of the central reasons for this edition is the renewed emphasis on expedition science. Moulton has used a whole corps of specialists in botany, geology, and zoology to make his scientific annotations both informative and accurate. When Clark mentioned the "coffeenut" among a number of well-known trees, Moulton identifies it as the Kentucky coffee tree, *Gymnocladus dioica* (L.). Throughout the edition plants and animals, especially those discovered by Lewis and Clark, are carefully identified by both common and scientific name. When Joseph Field killed and brought to camp an animal the French *engagés* called a *Brárow,* the critter quickly drew Lewis's attention. Moulton identifies the badger and tells the reader something about the French and Pawnee derivations of its name.[57]

Mention of the Pawnee word *cuhkatus* for badger raises the question of linguistic and ethnographic annotation. Expedition journalists filled their notebooks with important observations on native cultures as well as hundreds of Indian words and names. One of the lasting contributions of this edition is that it takes seriously those ethnographic and linguistic contributions. The entry for August 3, 1804—the day of the Oto-Missouri conference—is a good example of Moulton's Indian annotations. Here the editor briefly discusses Indian-Spanish relations, the protocol of Indian diplomacy, and the proper meaning of Oto and Missouri personal names listed by Clark. Moulton draws on the best recent anthropological and archaeological information to make these annotations of real value.[58]

In 1905 Reuben Gold Thwaites confidently predicted that "we shall henceforth know Lewis and Clark as we never knew them before."[59] With this new edition of the journals, that prophecy edges toward reality. What the Moulton volumes offer is not so much a new image of the expedition as a refurbished one. Donald Jackson once observed that the editor's task was like that of a specialist seeking to restore a fine painting. Generations of dirt, abuse, and misunderstanding had to be peeled away to reveal the splendid original. The new edition brings readers back to Jefferson's conception of the venture. Here is an expedition with many missions. Readers now see more clearly Lewis and Clark's diverse roles as advance agents of empire, geographic explorers and cartographers, federal Indian diplomats, ethnographers, and scientists. Almost two centuries after the fact, we are beginning to comprehend Jefferson's western vision.

What might justly be called the golden age of expedition scholarship began in 1962. Is the new journals' edition the conclusion to that burst of scholarly creativity or will these handsome volumes advance Lewis and Clark research into unpathed territories? Simply put, what remains yet unexplored? In recent years much emphasis has been placed on the expedition as a scientific reconnaissance. Cutright has gone so far as to insist that Lewis had scientific attitudes "more consistent with scientists of the twentieth century than those of his own."[60] While the expedition did make important botanical and zoological discoveries, its science was firmly rooted in eighteenth-century Enlightenment and natural history traditions. "Scientist" has become a convenient label to hang on the captains without much examination of the meaning and techniques of science in the Lewis and Clark years. As John C. Greene makes plain in his recent *American Science in the Age of Jefferson,* the expedition moved in an intellectual world quite unlike our own.[61] Now that scholars properly appreciate the natural history contributions made by the explorers, it is time to place those achievements in their historical context.

For all the public interest in the lives of expedition members, the shelf of biographies is indeed short. The captains themselves have suffered from a remarkable scholarly neglect. All too often students of the expedition have fallen into the habit of writing about that composite personality called "Lewisandclark." Richard Dillon's 1965 biography of Lewis is a fairly straightforward account but one that hardly fulfills the demands of modern biography.[62] Lewis was a person of extraordinary complexity, and too many writers have spilled ink on the circumstances of his death while ignoring larger and more important issues. William Clark, whose career went well beyond the expedition, has fared no better. Jerome Steffen's brief *William Clark: Jeffersonian Man on the Frontier* looks only at Clark's post-1806 career and tends to submerge him in Steffen's own theory about frontier politics and social change.[63] Clark's slave York has done better at the hands of the biographers than either of the captains. Robert Betts's *In Search of York* is a sensitive treatment of the man Indians called "Big Medicine."[64]

Meriwether Lewis once described the expedition as a family. Indeed, the Corps of Discovery was a community. We need to know much more about the life of that community. Eldon G. Chuinard's *Only One Man Died* suggests the medical dimension of that common life.[65] More remains to be said. How did a racially and culturally diverse group become a harmonious body ready to bend all energies to reach a common goal? Where did that remarkable social cohesion come from? Historians busy examining frontier communities might well study this expedition for clues about what Robert V. Hine has called the western tension of "separate but not alone."[66]

Lewis and Clark moved through lands claimed by others. Expedition relations with native peoples have been given a broadbrush treatment by James Ronda. But there is much room left for deeper study of the complex interactions between explorers and individual villages, bands, and tribes. Equally important, some scholar fluent in Spanish and knowledgeable about Iberian and Mexican archives must undertake a thorough study of Spain's reactions to the various American expeditions in the Jeffersonian period. A. P. Nasatir has gathered some important documents in his *Before Lewis and Clark.* Warren Cook's *Flood Tide of Empire: Spain and the Pacific Northwest, 1543-1819* makes some preliminary evaluation of Spanish attempts to halt the Lewis and Clark Expedition.[67] In his most recent book, *Among the Sleeping Giants,* Donald Jackson speculates about the consequences of a successful Spanish interdiction of the expedition. Because Jefferson had pinned so many personal and national hopes on the expedition, he might have reacted with considerable fury had Spanish forces arrested the man they called "Captain Merry." Jackson's thought-provoking "what if" points to the need for a major study of Spanish efforts to defend threatened borderlands.[68]

Jefferson's explorers have found their place in the history of North America. They have yet to be put in the wider context of eighteenth-century exploration. Lewis and Clark lived in the age of Cook, Vancouver, La Pérouse, and the incomparable Sir Joseph Banks. Enlightenment science and imperial power pushed voyagers to fill in the map of mankind. Recent books by David Mackay, Richard Van Orman, and P. J. Marshall and Glyndwr Williams all reveal important aspects of that worldwide exploration enterprise.[69] Lewis and Clark need to stand in company with Cook and Mackenzie if we are to gain a fuller understanding of both the American explorers and their European counterparts.

What remains to be written about the Lewis and Clark Expedition suggests that DeVoto was right. The expedition was a turning point in world history. Here are the beginnings of an American empire. That westering would transform the political and cultural boundaries of North America and eventually the wider world. Fresh readings of the Lewis and Clark journals, readings with new eyes, guarantee a continuing exploration of what Lewis once called his "darling project." What Lewis and Clark began in that rented room shows no sign of losing power and fascination.

Notes

1. Reuben G. Thwaites, ed., *Original Journals of the Lewis and Clark Expedition, 1804-1806* (New York, 1904-5), 5:395 (hereafter Thw).

2. Donald Jackson, ed., *Letters of the Lewis and Clark Expedition with Related Documents, 1783-1854,* 2d ed. (Urbana, Ill., 1978), 1:v.

3. William Clark to Meriwether Lewis, July 24, 1803, in Jackson, *Letters,* 1:112.

4. Frankfort, Kentucky, *Western World,* October 11, 1806, reprinted in this volume [*Voyages of Discovery*], 203-5.

5. Citizens of Fincastle to Lewis and Clark, January 8, 1807, in Jackson, *Letters,* 1:358-59.

6. Jefferson's Instructions to Lewis, June 20, 1803, in Jackson, *Letters,* 1:61, reprinted in this volume, 31-38.

7. Jefferson to Lewis, November 16, 1803, in Jackson, *Letters,* 1:137.

8. Lewis to Jefferson, September 23, 1806, in Jackson, *Letters,* 1:319-24.

9. Clark to [George Rogers Clark?], September 23, 1806, in Jackson, *Letters,* 1:326.

10. Jefferson to Lewis, October 26, 1806, in Jackson, *Letters,* 1:352.

11. Lincoln to Jefferson, April 17, 1803, in Jackson, *Letters,* 1:35.

12. Jefferson to Bernard Lacépède, July 14, 1808, in Jackson, *Letters,* 2:443.

13. Samuel L. Mitchill, *A Discourse on the Character and Services of Thomas Jefferson* (New York, 1826), 27-28.

14. *The Conrad Prospectus* (Philadelphia, c. April 1, 1807), in Jackson, *Letters,* 2:395. Although the prospectus was printed by Conrad, it was written by Lewis while the explorer was staying in Philadelphia.

15. Jefferson to Lewis, July 17, 1808, in Jackson, *Letters,* 2:445; Jefferson to Lewis, August 16, 1809, in ibid., 2:458.

16. C. and A. Conrad and Co. to Jefferson, November 13, 1809, in Jackson, *Letters,* 2:469.

17. Jefferson to F. H. Alexander von Humboldt, December 6, 1813, in Jackson, *Letters,* 2:596.

18. John L. Allen, "'Of This Enterprize': The American Images of the Lewis and Clark Expedition," in *Enlightenment Science in the Pacific Northwest: The Lewis and Clark Expedition,* ed. William F. Willingham and Leonoor S. Ingraham (Portland, 1984), 29-45, reprinted in this volume, 255-80.

19. Paul R. Cutright, *A History of the Lewis and Clark Journals* (Norman, Okla., 1976), 98.

20. Thw, 1:lvi.

21. Ibid.

22. Thwaites, *A Brief History of Rocky Mountain Exploration, with Especial Reference to the Expedition of Lewis and Clark* (New York, 1904), 187.

23. Reuben G. Thwaites and Calvin Noyes Kendall, *A History of the United States for Grammar Schools* (Boston, 1912), 236.

24. Edward Channing, *The Jeffersonian System, 1801-1811* (New York, 1906), 94.

25. David S. Muzzey, *American History* (Boston, 1911), 210.

26. Frederic L. Paxson, *History of the American Frontier, 1763-1893* (Boston, 1924), 137.

27. Dan E. Clark, *The West in American History* (New York, 1937), 405-8.

28. Walter Prescott Webb, *The Great Plains* (1931; reprint, Lincoln, Nebr., 1981), 143-44.

29. John Bartlett Brebner, *The Explorers of North America, 1492-1806* (New York, 1933), 464-65.

30. Elijah H. Criswell, "Lewis and Clark: Linguistic Pioneers," *University of Missouri Studies: A Quarterly of Research,* 15 (April 1940), vii.

31. Cutright, *History of the Lewis and Clark Journals,* 208. See also a brief biographical sketch of Criswell by Cutright in "Dr. Elijah Harry Criswell (1888-1967)," *We Proceeded On,* 5 (February 1979), 6-7.

32. Bernard DeVoto, "Passage to India: From Christmas to Christmas with Lewis and Clark," *Saturday Review of Literature,* 15 (December 1936), 3-4, 20, 24, 28, reprinted in this volume, 89-100.

33. Bernard DeVoto, *Year of Decision: 1846* (Boston, 1943), xi.

34. DeVoto to Commager, April 30, 1944, in *The Letters of Bernard DeVoto,* ed. Wallace Stegner (Garden City, N.Y., 1975), 271.

35. Bernard DeVoto, untitled essay in "The Easy Chair," *Harper's Magazine,* 190 (March 1950), 312.

36. Bernard DeVoto to Samuel Eliot Morison, December 1946, in Stegner, *DeVoto,* 273.

37. Mattingly's memorable phrase is recorded in DeVoto to Mattingly, November 1, 1945, in Stegner, *DeVoto,* 273.

38. DeVoto to Catherine D. Bowen, [n.d.], in Stegner, *DeVoto,* 285-86.

39. Bernard DeVoto, *The Course of Empire* (Boston, 1952), 426, 429, 430-31, 443. See also DeVoto's much neglected "An Inference Regarding the Expedition of Lewis and Clark," *Proceedings of the American Philosophical Society,* 99 (August 1955), 185-94, for his most pointed treatment of the expedition's role in American western imperialism.

40. DeVoto to Mattingly, March 14, 1948, in Stegner, *DeVoto,* 293.

41. John Bakeless, *Lewis and Clark: Partners in Discovery* (New York, 1947).

42. Milo M. Quaife, ed., *The Journals of Captain Meriwether Lewis and Sergeant John Ordway* (Madison, Wis., 1916).

43. Ernest S. Osgood, ed., *The Field Notes of Captain William Clark, 1803-1805* (New Haven, Conn., 1964).

44. For a full discussion, see Donald Jackson, *Among the Sleeping Giants: Occasional Pieces on Lewis and Clark* (Urbana, Ill., 1987), 55-74.

45. Jackson, *Letters,* 2:497-545; Jackson, *Sleeping Giants,* 71.

46. Jackson, *Letters,* 1:v.

47. Refer to introduction in Donald Jackson, ed., *The Expedition of John Charles Frémont: Map Portfolio* (Urbana, Ill., 1970), 5.

48. Refer to introduction in Bernard DeVoto, ed., *Journals of the Lewis and Clark Expedition* (Boston, 1953), li.

49. Paul R. Cutright, *Lewis and Clark: Pioneering Naturalists* (Urbana, Ill., 1969).

50. John L. Allen, *Passage through the Garden: Lewis and Clark and the Image of the American Northwest* (Urbana, Ill., 1975).

51. Ibid., xv-xvi.

52. James P. Ronda, *Lewis and Clark among the Indians* (Lincoln, Nebr., 1984), xii.

53. Donald Jackson, "Some Advice for the Next Editor of Lewis and Clark," *Bulletin of the Missouri Historical Society,* 24 (October 1967), 52-62.

54. This essay was originally published in 1988. As of 1997, ten journal volumes and the atlas have been completed.

55. Gary E. Moulton, ed., *The Journals of the Lewis and Clark Expedition* (Lincoln, Nebr., 1983-97), 2:viii.

56. Ibid., 2:428-30.

57. Ibid., 2:431.

58. Ibid., 2:438-44.

59. Thw, 1:lvii.

60. Cutright, *Pioneering Naturalists,* 398.

61. John C. Greene, *American Science in the Age of Jefferson* (Ames, Iowa, 1984), chap. 8; See also Roy Porter, "The Terraqueous Globe," in *The Ferment of Knowledge: Studies in the Historiography of Eighteenth-Century Science,* ed. Roy Parker and G. S. Rousseau (Cambridge, England, 1980), 285-324.

62. Richard Dillon, *Meriwether Lewis: A Biography* (New York, 1965).

63. Jerome O. Steffen, *William Clark: Jeffersonian Man on the Frontier* (Norman, Okla., 1977).

64. Robert B. Betts, *In Search of York* (Boulder, Colo., 1985). Two other members of the expedition also have received biographical treatment: Burton Harris, *John Colter* (New York, 1952), and M. O. Skarsten, *George Drouillard* (Glendale, Calif., 1964). The literature on Sacagawea is large and often uncritical. It is summarized in Ronda, *Lewis and Clark among the Indians,* 256-59.

65. Eldon G. Chuinard, *Only One Man Died: The Medical Aspects of the Lewis and Clark Expedition* (Glendale, Calif., 1979).

66. Robert V. Hine, *Community on the American Frontier: Separate But Not Alone* (Norman, Okla., 1980).

67. A. P. Nasatir, ed., *Before Lewis and Clark: Documents Illustrating the History of the Missouri, 1785-1804,* 2 vols. (St. Louis, 1952). See also Warren L. Cook, *Flood Tide of Empire: Spain and the Pacific Northwest, 1543-1819* (New Haven, Conn., 1973).

68. Jackson, *Sleeping Giants,* 12-16.

69. David Mackay, *In the Wake of Cook: Exploration, Science, and Empire, 1780-1901* (New York, 1985); Richard A. Van Orman, *The Explorers: Nineteenth Century Expeditions in Africa and the American West* (Albuquerque, N. M., 1984); and P. J. Marshall and Glyndwr Williams, *The Great Map of Mankind: British Perceptions of the World in the Age of Enlightenment* (Cambridge, Mass., 1982). The best introduction to the period remains Donald Jackson, *Thomas Jefferson and the Stony Mountains: Exploring the West from Monticello* (Urbana, 1981).

JOURNAL-KEEPING METHODS

Gary E. Moulton (excerpt date 1986)

SOURCE: An introduction to *The Journals of the Lewis and Clark Expedition: August 30, 1803-August 24, 1804,* Volume 2, edited by Gary E. Moulton, University of Nebraska Press, 1986, pp. 8-35.

[*In the following excerpt, Moulton examines in detail how and by what methods Lewis and Clark chronicled their expedition. Moulton focuses in particular on whether or not the captains wrote continuously throughout the duration of the expedition or whether they wrote the majority of the text after the expedition was complete.*]

. . . THE JOURNAL-KEEPING METHODS OF LEWIS AND CLARK

Clark's last entry is a reminder that "wrighting &c." was one of the principal tasks of the captains, and one that they thoroughly fulfilled. As Donald Jackson has observed, Lewis and Clark were "the writingest explorers of their time. They wrote constantly and abundantly, afloat and ashore, legibly and illegibly, and always with an urgent sense of purpose."[1] They left us a remarkably full record of their enterprise, but questions about that record remain unanswered. One of the most vexing problems of the journals, as such, concerns a question whose answer might appear quite obvious: when and how were the journals written? The immediate and natural supposition of any reader is that the entries were written day by day on the dates placed at their heads by the authors. Examination of the journals now available, however, discredits that expectation. The existence of duplicate journals, mainly by Clark, for certain periods of the expedition, and internal evidence indicating that many entries cannot have been written on the days they cover, require greater consideration of the journal-keeping methods of the captains.

Nicholas Biddle, as a result of his collaboration with Clark in 1810 on the published history of the expedition, probably had more information about the two captains' methods of keeping a journal than anyone else who was not with the expedition, but he did not reveal it to his readers. By the time anyone again examined the journals at length, the authors were no longer available to provide what were no doubt simple explanations of many mysteries and apparent inconsistencies. When Elliott Coues examined the notebooks in the American Philosophical Society archives in 1892-93, he was struck by their good condition and concluded that the predominant red morocco-bound books, at least, could not have crossed the continent: "The covers are too fresh and bright, the paper too clean and sound. . . . The handwritings are too good, and too uniform. . . . The red books were certainly written after the return of the Expedition, and before Lewis's death in October, 1809—that is, in 1806-9."[2]

In opposition to Coues's belief that the journals might have been written, in part, as late as 1809 is Jefferson's statement that Lewis turned the notebooks over to him "on his return"—that is, on or soon after Lewis's arrival in Washington on December 28, 1806. Jefferson's understanding was that they had been written day by day, and that each notebook was sealed in a tin box when finished to protect it from the elements. Even assuming that Jefferson learned the exact procedure the captains followed, his description, written from memory nine years later, might not be precisely correct. However, he was hardly likely to have gained the impression that the volumes he specifically called "travelling pocket journals" were written on the trip if they were blank when he first saw them on Lewis's return. Nothing could have kept the president from poring over them, as he apparently did those sent back from Fort Mandan in 1805. His words strongly imply that the notebook journals were more or less complete by the time of Lewis's arrival in Washington.[3]

Of course, Coues never imagined that the captains wrote their journals from memory in the years after their homecoming. The red books he viewed at the American Philosophical Society did not include some other notebooks there that have different bindings; their condition convinced him that those could have been on the expedition, and he thought that true of some but not all the small, fragmentary items of a few sheets each that he examined. Those last he thought likely to be the remains of field journals made on the spot, day by day, their information later being transferred into the notebooks.[4]

When Reuben Gold Thwaites examined additional materials that he discovered a few years later, he found among them Clark's Elkskin-bound Journal, as he called it, covering the same period as some of the red books. This new volume, written on letter paper later sewn together and bound, undoubtedly in the field, seemed to fit exactly the description of field notes, later copied and expanded in the notebook journals. The Elkskin-bound Journal and some other new fragments made Thwaites confident that he understood the captains' basic procedures:

> It was the daily custom of the captains to make rough notes, with rude outline maps, plans, and miscellaneous sketches, in field-books which they doubtless carried in their pockets. When encamped for a protracted period, these were developed into more formal records. In this development, each often borrowed freely from the other's notes—Lewis, the better scholar of the two generally rewriting in his own manner the material obtained from Clark; while the latter not infrequently copied Lewis practically verbatim, but with his own phonetic spelling. Upon returning to St. Louis, these individual journals were for the most part transcribed into neat blank books—bound in red morocco and gilt-edged—with the thought of preparing them for early publication. After this process, the original field-books must have been cast aside and in large measure destroyed; for but one of these [*the Elkskin-bound Journal*] is now known to exist. There have come down to us, however, several note-books which apparently were written up in the camps.[5]

Thwaites did not attempt to say just when the field books were made, nor why some field notes and journals, notably the Elkskin-bound Journal, were preserved when so many others were "in large measure destroyed."

Thwaites's explanation is broadly plausible, but again we confront Jefferson's statement that the red books turned over to him at the beginning of 1807 were written on the trip. If Jefferson was mistaken on this point, then Thwaites's theory requires the captains to have written the entire body of red notebook journals—fourteen notebooks containing several hundred thousand words—between the arrival in St. Louis on September 23, 1806, and late December 1806. Clark's last journal entry (September 26, 1806), apparently written in St. Louis, says that "we commenced wrighting &c," but as noted, there is no indication of what they were writing.

Following Thwaites's theory, the red books had to have been written in the course of some three months or a little more, during which the captains were traveling; visiting relatives; seeing to other business; and attending public ceremonies, welcoming celebrations, and banquets. During that period Lewis was also escorting the Mandan chief Big White (Sheheke) to the capital. Moreover, substantial parts of Clark's journals for the last part of the expedition are evidently copied from Lewis. On the journey to Washington the captains separated in mid-November and did not reunite until January 21, 1807, when Clark reached Washington. Unless Lewis left a great part of his journals with Clark, which seems most unlikely, the period during which the journal writing could have been done narrows to a period of less than two months after the expedition's arrival in St. Louis. If we add the fact that Clark's next to last notebook journal has a lengthy passage in Lewis's hand, inserted in the middle with no apparent gaps in the writing, the theory that the red books were wholly the product of the period after the return to St. Louis seems questionable.

There are other good reasons for doubting the postexpedition theory of composition. Eighteen red books are known, all having some connection with the expedition, though it is not known when the captains obtained them. One of them is Codex O, as labeled by Coues, which contains Lewis's astronomical observations for the first year of the expedition and his summary of creeks and rivers. It is generally believed that this book was among the materials sent back from Fort Mandan in April 1805; it has no data collected after that time. If so, then the captains had it with them from the start, and in all probability they had all eighteen identical books from the beginning, wherever they were purchased. No one can possibly imagine that they carried eighteen notebooks to the Pacific and back without having intended from the first to write in them along the way.

There is no specific reference to the red books in any of the preexpedition lists of supplies. Lewis listed "Books" and "Writing paper" among his requirements for the trip, and since he did not specify titles, the books may well mean notebooks. He drew "8 Rect. books" from the U.S. arsenal in Philadelphia and purchased six packing boxes for "Stationary &c." there, in the spring of 1803. An undated memorandum in Codex C, in an unknown hand, lists goods packed for the expedition at some point. The list includes four bales of goods, each containing "2 tin Boxes, with 2 mem. Books in Ea."; a recapitulation of the same goods in the memorandum gives "8 tin Boxes with memm. Books". This gives sixteen books. Among Lewis's personal effects inventoried after his death in 1809 were "Sixteen Note books bound in red morocco with clasps." The coincidence in number is striking; it would indeed be conclusive, except that there are eighteen red books extant, all having some connection with the expedition. There is no really satisfactory way to account for the two extra books. Since there is no certainty when the memorandum in Codex C was written, we cannot say which red books might have been in use and so not listed among those packed. For instance, Lewis used Codex O for his astronomical observations from the beginning of the expedition. If the Codex C list was made up just before setting out from Wood River, Codex O might not have been packed away in a relatively inaccessible box in a bale but could have been with Lewis or easily available.

It is, of course, entirely possible that the captains purchased two more identical books after the expedition, and it would be exceedingly difficult to say which of those now known would be the extra two, since all eighteen red notebooks contain or apparently did once contain material that could have been written during the expedition. Neither is there any clear indication of which two red books Lewis would not have included among the expeditionary materials he had with him on his last journey in 1809. The

captains' practice of taking pages from one notebook and inserting them in another makes it impossible to be certain what material (particularly the fragmentary Lewis items) may have been in what book at the time of Lewis's death, or at any other time before the Clark-Biddle collaboration in 1810.[6]

Jefferson says the books were "cemented" up in tin boxes for protection when completed, but that they had been removed from the boxes before Lewis delivered them to him. Lewis or Clark must therefore have told him those details, which implies that they gave him some information about their methods of journal keeping. The captains could have kept the notebooks in boxes sealed in some manner to keep out moisture, taking them out for writing in relatively sheltered camps or when the weather was good, while rough field notes served for daily entries under less favorable conditions.

Writing in 1807, David McKeehan, Patrick Gass's editor, sought to establish the reliability of Gass's work by stating, "At the different resting places during the expedition, the several journals were brought together, compared, corrected, and the blanks which had been unavoidably left, filled up."[7] This information, vague and unspecific as it is, could only have come from Gass; the journals referred to could be field notes or notebook journals, or both. Certainly such resting places would have been the points at which the notebook journals were brought up to date, if they were not, in fact, the journals in which the entries were kept day by day.

The discovery in 1953 of rough, unbound notes by Clark, covering, besides the period at Camp Dubois, the first eleven months of the expedition—the same period as Clark's first three notebooks—complicates as much as it clarifies. One can easily believe that these scribbled, interlined entries, written on miscellaneous sizes of loose paper, often over sketch maps, arithmetical calculations, and addresses on used envelopes, were first-draft notes taken in the field on the journey up the Missouri. It is then easy to imagine Clark copying and expanding on them in the notebooks whenever time allowed, even as late as the winter at Fort Mandan. Once they reached Fort Mandan, however, the *Field Notes* become increasingly skimpy, with gaps sometimes weeks in length. For this period we must either imagine another full set of field notes, whose existence is both unproven and unnecessary, or suppose that in this period Clark wrote his entries daily into a bound journal.[8]

There is, however, material in the notebooks that is not in the *Field Notes,* indicating that Clark wrote into them when events were fairly fresh in his mind. In his Codex A entry for July 4, 1804, we find reflections on the Kansa Indians not in the *Field Notes.* On the other hand, in the Codex A entry for July 23, 1804, he names Camp White Catfish, although the fish for which the camp was named was not caught until the next day. Thus we must assume that the codex entry was written on or after July 24, or that he wrote the entry on the twenty-third, inserting the name of the camp later—which from the appearance of the page is entirely possible.

In the *Field Notes* for August 20, 1804, Clark records in the present tense that Sergeant Charles Floyd was seriously ill, then writes of Floyd's death. In Codex B for the same day, Clark repeats the description of Floyd's illness and death. One must suppose either that Clark wrote both the *Field Notes* and Codex B simultaneously, with considerable difference in wording, or that he wrote the codex entry later, without taking into account his knowledge that Floyd had died. This journalistic convention persists throughout the journals and, of course, complicates the problem of determining the time of writing of particular entries. In any case, in the notebook entry of August 20, Clark refers to Floyd as "our Decesed brother," a phrase not found in the *Field Notes*—perhaps evidence that he wrote the notebook entry when the emotion was still fairly fresh.

On October 13, 1804, a court-martial of party members tried Private John Newman for "mutinous expression." Clark's brief record of the episode in his Codex C entry for October 13 says that Newman was tried "last night." Apparently he wrote the codex entry the day after the trial. The paragraph on the trial comes at the very end of the entry, so it is likely that the whole entry was composed on October 14, the day after its ostensible date. This is at a time when the *Field Notes* entries are still continuous and fairly extensive; the Codex C entry, however, includes much information not found in the *Field Notes,* apparently taken down by Clark at the time he received it. At this time he was obviously copying and expanding his first notes into the notebook journal quite promptly.

During the Fort Mandan winter, when Clark's notebook entries are quite full, entries in the *Field Notes* for widely separated dates follow one another without any evidence of missing pages. In fact, a single sheet, document 64 of Ernest Osgood's arrangement of the *Field Notes,* contains the entries for the period from November 19, 1804, to April 3, 1805; the entries follow one another with no indication of spaces for later insertion of material. Sheets in the *Field Notes* may have been lost, but it seems more likely that Clark wrote directly into his notebook journal. As further evidence, note that Lewis kept the bound book up to date when Clark was absent for ten days in February on a hunting trip; Clark then wrote a short summary of his excursion in the book on his return. From the appearance of the journal, Clark wrote this account immediately after his return, rather than inserting it later.

It does not seem wise to postulate the writing of field notes by either captain in cases where none have been found and there is no strong evidence of their having existed. Theories involving the existence of such notes are to be avoided unless the evidence clearly requires them. The sheer amount of labor involved in composing multiple sets of notes and journals argues against such suppositions.

Considering the history of journal discoveries to date, however, no one would wish to assert positively that there are no lost notes or journals, or that none will ever be found. Certainly there are cases where notebook journal entries were clearly written weeks or months after the given date, and then it does not seem unreasonable to suppose that the writer kept notes of some sort.

The discovery of Clark's *Field Notes* consisting of the Dubois and River Journals, and other discoveries at various times and places, may seem to support the possibility of other such field journals. But the Dubois Journals relate to the period before the expedition proper and were not the basis, as far as we know, for a duplicate set of notebook journals. Obviously Clark kept both field notes and notebook journals for the journey up the Missouri to Fort Mandan, but it does not necessarily follow that he used the same procedure throughout the expedition, especially since he apparently did not follow this method at Fort Mandan and his field notes fall off sharply after his arrival there.

On April 7, 1805, the permanent party set out upriver from Fort Mandan; at the same time, the keelboat carrying the discharged members of the party headed downriver with a load of dispatches, papers, and specimens for delivery to Jefferson. At this point we encounter more complex problems of journal-keeping procedures and missing notes.

The first question concerns just what journal materials were sent to Jefferson on the keelboat. At several points in the summer and fall the captains indicated that they intended to send back a pirogue with some of the soldiers and boatmen under Corporal Richard Warfington. Clark indicates more than once that they were preparing materials to be sent back with that party. As it happened, they did not dispatch the return party until the following spring, for reasons never stated. Both Clark and Lewis wrote letters to Jefferson indicating what they were sending, but neither was specific enough to spare us some puzzlement. Clark wrote on April 3, 1805, that he was sending the "notes which I have taken in the form of a journal in their original state," apologizing because "many parts are incorrect." Lewis wrote that they were sending the president "a part of Capt. Clark's private journal, the other part you will find inclosed in a separate tin box. The journal is in it's original state, and of course incorrect, but it will give you the daily detales of our progress, and transactions." A great deal hinges on the meaning of the expressions "private journal" and "original state," and on how we interpret the two parts of Clark's journal.[9]

Various interpretations are possible. We could take Clark's *Field Notes* to be a "private" journal, and the notebook journals to be "public" or official; thus the *Field Notes* constitute one part and the notebook journals—Codices A, B, and C—the other. We might take the Dubois Journal and the River Journal, the two parts of the *Field Notes,* as the two parts meant, but there is no evidence that the Dubois Journal ever went to Jefferson, and the division into the Dubois Journal and the River Journal is merely a modern convenience. The argument can be made that the two parts were parts of the River Journal itself, on the basis of a notation by Clark on document 56 of the *Field Notes.* One side contains journal entries for September 20-23, 1804. The other side bears an address:

> Sept 20 &
> Genl. Jona. Clark of Kentucky
> To the 22nd of Septr. 1804
> To the care of Genl. Jona. Clark near Louisville Kty
> To be opened by Capt. W. Clark or Capt. Meriwether
>   Lewis.[10]

On the same document under the September 23 entry Clark wrote, "I must seal up all those scripts & draw from my Journal at some other time."

The address and the conclusion of entries on the same sheet seem to indicate that the captains still hoped to send a party back before winter, and that Clark intended to send the *Field Notes* to his oldest brother Jonathan, to be kept until his return. They had kept Warfington with them past the end of his enlistment in August so that he could head the return party. We might suppose that Clark made sure that his notebook journals were up-to-date at this point, since he could not use the *Field Notes* for this purpose after sending them back, and he may have brought the notebooks up-to-date similarly when they considered sending materials back from Camp White Catfish in July. On the other hand, if the notebooks were not up-to-date, this could be the reason why the return party did not set out before winter. This might even be the reason why Clark neglected the *Field Notes* at Fort Mandan and apparently wrote directly into his notebook journal, the earlier procedure having proved too time-consuming.

On document 58 of the *Field Notes* is a notation by Clark: "A Continuation of notes taken assending the Missourie in 1804—by W. Clark." It may be, then, that the two parts of Clark's "private journal" are the two parts of the *Field Notes*—the part sealed up to be sent to Jonathan Clark in September 1804, but not sent, and the notes taken after that time. The note about "A Continuation" could indicate that Clark thought of the *Field Notes* as being in two parts.[11]

Against the above interpretation, however, is another notation by Clark, written April 2, 1805, on document 64 in the *Field Notes,* during preparations to send off the keelboat and its cargo from Fort Mandan:

> I conclude to Send my journal to the President of the United States in its original State for his own perusal, untill I Call for it or Some friend if I Should not return, an this journal is from the 13th of May 1804 untill the 3rd of April 1805.

Here again is the phrase "in its original state," suggesting that the journal referred to is the same as mentioned in the captains' letters to Jefferson as Clark's "private journal." What journal was it?

Clark says the journal began on May 13, 1804, which cannot apply to the *Field Notes,* unless he was in error. The last document of the Dubois Journal ends on May 14, and the River Journal's first sheet begins with the same date. The first notebook journal, Codex A, however, does begin on May 13. The journal to be sent back, Clark says, ends on April 3, 1805; that is true of the *Field Notes* and, in a sense, of the notebook journals. The April 3 entry in Codex C is followed by a list of items to be sent back on the keelboat, then the entries for April 4-7. Since the entry for April 3 in Clark's *Field Notes* shows that they expected to leave the next day, Clark could well have thought of the April 3 entry in Codex C as the last, adding a list of materials to be sent back for Jefferson's information. Thus, when he wrote in the *Field Notes* on April 2 that the journal went to April 3, that could also have been the case with the notebook journals. Since they did not, in fact, leave until April 7—due presumably to last-minute delays—it was natural for Clark to add entries for the extra days in Codex C.

With such an indication that Clark considered his notebook journals to be in their "original state," it seems reasonable that the two parts of his journal were the *Field Notes* and the notebook journals—Codices A, B, and C. That the notebook journals went to Jefferson is clear from Jefferson's letter to Benjamin Smith Barton in December 1805, referring to the feeding of cottonwood bark to horses by the Indians in terms very similar to those in Codex C but not in the *Field Notes.*[12] It seems most likely that the *Field Notes* also went to Jefferson, though there is no specific evidence proving this. Clark did note in a letter from Fort Mandan that he was sending "papers of considerable consequence" to his brother in Louisville, and the *Field Notes* would meet this description. It is likely, however, that those "papers" consisted of the Dubois Journal, not the River Journal. Document 65 bears the address of Jonathan Clark and the notation "notes at Wood River in 1803-4." Clark certainly did not send those notes—which surely must be the Dubois Journal—to Jonathan before the departure from St. Louis in 1804, for the other side of document 65 bears an entry for November 30, 1804, after they had reached Fort Mandan. From its appearance, document 65 could have been the wrapper in which the Wood River notes (Dubois Journal) were sealed for shipment to Jonathan Clark. If those notes were in a separate packet, it may have been because they were going to a different destination that the River Journal, sent to Jefferson. That Clark wrote a full entry for November 30 on document 65 may only mean that he thought of taking up regular keeping of the *Field Notes* after they had settled in at Fort Mandan, then abandoned the idea in favor of the notebook journals.[13]

Clark's journal-writing procedure, up to the departure from Fort Mandan, then, seems reasonably clear. On the upriver journey he kept daily field notes and copied and expanded them into his notebook journals as convenient, sometimes neglecting the *Field Notes* at Fort Mandan in favor of writing directly into Codex C. The daily continuity of the *Field Notes* ends with November 13, 1804, the entries becoming increasingly irregular; document 64 covers the entire period from that date to April 3, 1805, and appears to be the last sheet of the *Field Notes*. During the building of Fort Mandan in early November, the keeping of two journals may have seemed too much of a burden in the midst of other demanding work. If so, then Codex C was presumably up-to-date at that time, and perhaps Codices A and B were also. Codices B and C, however, overlap on October 1, 2, and 3, and the entries in Codex C for the first and second are skimpy in comparison to those in Codex B. Possibly Clark began writing in Codex C when Codex B was not yet up to date, on the first of October. The fuller entry for October 3 is in Codex C, and conceivably he had caught up and filled in Codex B by then.

More difficult to explain is Lewis's journal-keeping procedure and particularly the large gaps in his writing, which raise the possibility of missing manuscripts. The largest gap, and the one most curious to historians, is the long hiatus from the start of the expedition in May 1804, until the group set out from Fort Mandan in April 1805. That gap is particularly bewildering because we would expect Lewis to be more conscientious at the outset of the expedition, especially in light of Jefferson's explicit instructions about the keeping of multiple journals.[14] So incredulous have some observers been at this gap that they have speculated that Lewis was probably keeping either field drafts or standard journals of the party's activities that have since been lost.[15]

To say that Lewis was keeping no journal from the outset is not precisely correct. There exist two small fragments, called Codices Aa and Ba by Coues, for the dates May 15 and 20, and September 16-17, 1804. Those sheets, apparently torn from one of the red books, suggest to some that Lewis was keeping a journal for the initial period, and that the remaining pages were so soiled, ruined, or unnecessary that they were discarded. Or perhaps the remaining pages are simply lost. Another explanation seems plausible and is presented here as part of a larger conception of Lewis's journal-keeping activities throughout the trip.

In Codex Aa it is noteworthy that the order of days is reversed; the entry for May 20 precedes the entry for May 15, with no break between the two. The entry for May 20 recounts Lewis's activities for that day as he set out by land from St. Louis for St. Charles where he was to rendezvous with Clark, who was leading the party upriver. The entry also reports the activities of Clark's party. Perhaps Lewis saw this entry as the beginning of his journal keeping since the captains had determined to set out the next day (May 21). Then why the addition of notes for May 15? That is a more detailed report of Clark's trip upriver, written as if Lewis had been present. Information in that entry exceeds the notes taken by Clark for that day in either of his two accounts (*Field Notes* and Codex A) and probably came directly from Clark. Perhaps Lewis thought he ought to add an entry for May 15 after his May 20 entry to give a more detailed account of the actual start of

the expedition. Although Clark set out from River Dubois on May 14, the captains had earlier established May 15 as the date to begin, and perhaps Lewis still had that date in mind.

Codex Ba presents a different situation. On September 16 and 17, 1804, the group was encamped at "Corvus" Creek just above today's White River in South Dakota. . . . There the captains made the decision not to send back the pirogue with artifacts and other items representing their journey thus far. Perhaps Lewis had thought that their notes to that point would return to St. Louis with the other materials and eventually reach President Jefferson; thus, he may have considered that he was now beginning a journal, in a sense the first for him since he had apparently quit writing after his May 15 entry. Having made the decision not to send a boat and crew back, he may have ceased his journalizing (indeed, he stopped at midpage in midsentence) and perhaps delayed writing again until after the winter at Fort Mandan.

Even before those dates Lewis may have established a pattern of laxness in journal writing. He began a diary (here called the Eastern Journal) when he left Pittsburgh in August 1803, as he descended the Ohio River enroute to St. Louis, but from September 19 to November 11, he made no entries. He left thirty-nine pages blank in the notebook between those separated entries, however, perhaps with the intention of supplying the missing information later, but that hiatus was never filled. About October 26, Clark joined Lewis at Louisville, but Lewis did not turn over journal-keeping chores to his friend at that time. Had he done so, today we might have a more complete record of the remainder of the trip to Camp Dubois, for Clark was a more consistent recorder than his companion. Lewis returned to journalizing on November 11 and gave the journal to Clark on November 28, near Kaskaskia, as they separated while Lewis went ahead by land to St. Louis and Clark brought the boat party forward to establish Camp Dubois. From that point we have a nearly consistent record because of Clark's faithful journal keeping.[16]

Those writing gaps of Lewis's may be instances of a larger pattern of negligence. The gaps as a whole include the missing days from the Eastern Journal (September 19 to November 11, 1803); the lapse from May 14, 1804, to April 7, 1805 (with the exceptions noted); only spotty entries from August 26, 1805, to January 1, 1806; and the final hiatus from August 12, 1806, to the completion of the expedition. The last gap can be explained by Lewis's being partially disabled from a wound; in contrast to other stoppages, he noted that he was laying down his pen at that point. In all from May 1804, to September 1806, Lewis missed over four hundred days of journal entries.[17]

Some authorities have supposed that Lewis was keeping field notes during the period from Camp Dubois to Fort Mandan and intending to use that material to fill regular notebooks later, or that the fragments from a red book (the entries for May and September) were part of a complete set of notes that are now lost. Jackson has made the strongest case for Lewis having kept notes during the first leg of the journey, but he emphasizes the speculative nature of his conclusions. Briefly, Jackson believes that a mishap on May 14, 1805, may indicate a loss of journals. On that day one of the pirogues turned on its side and filled with water, and some of the papers and notebooks got wet. Jackson discovered that within a few days of the accident Clark began conscientiously to copy into his own journal Lewis's natural history notes, something he had not previously done. Jackson argues that the spoilages may have been greater than expected, convincing the captains that duplicating all records was necessary, not just keeping multiple diaries. He also conjectures that "perhaps Lewis's notes for the entire first leg of the expedition were either badly water-soaked or entirely lost." Thus, Jackson believes that the entries by Lewis for May and September 1804 may be fragments of a larger journal from that early period. Thwaites also thought that Lewis was a regular journal-keeper, but his reasoning is less plausible than Jackson's. He supposed that the journals may have been lost after Lewis's death in Tennessee. However, we would expect that Clark or Jefferson would have bemoaned such a loss at some time, but neither ever made reference to so serious a loss in any known source. Jackson's answer for a reason that there is no mention of the supposed loss of journals in May 1805 is that Lewis would tell Jefferson about the accident after his return but that there was no need to announce it to the world in his diary.[18]

Jackson and others who think Lewis kept a journal or field notes during the trip to Fort Mandan have found strong evidence in letters of Lewis and Clark to Jefferson just before the party set out from that post. The opening phrase of Clark's letter has been struck out and other words substituted by Lewis. Clark wrote, "As Capt. Lewis has not Leasure to Send <write> a correct Coppy journal of our proceedings &c." and Lewis substituted, "It being the wish of Capt. Lewis." There are several ways to read the excised parts: does Lewis not have time to send his journal, has he not had time to write it, or has he not had time to make a correct copy? Lewis's letter stated that he would send a canoe with some men back from the extreme navigable point of the Missouri River (a scheme later rejected) and with that boat "I shal send you my journal." Again, one can read the phrase variously: is Lewis to send a journal he has been keeping or one he intends to write? Rather than speculate on the hidden meaning of the letters, it is better to examine the totality of Lewis's journal keeping and to interpret from that perspective.[19]

Although extant daily entries by Lewis from St. Charles to Fort Mandan are lacking, there exists quite a bit of Lewis's writing from that period, and additional material is known to be missing. As the expedition's naturalist he kept fairly extensive notes on the flora and fauna of the region through which the party passed. In Codex R, he made a list of herbarium specimens that he was collecting. The descriptive writing is occasionally lengthy and shows not only Lewis's powers of observation but also his record-keeping activi-

ties. Observations of animals are almost as extensive and cover over fifty pages of Codex Q. The captain was also noting mineral deposits and geologic features along the Missouri and taking astronomical observations—both time-consuming tasks that included record-keeping. And, although Lewis cannot be credited directly, it is known that the captains were keeping lists of Indian vocabularies during this period, work that may have amounted to extensive note taking. The vocabularies are the missing material that might exhibit additional record keeping by Lewis.

From January to May 1804, Lewis was keeping a weather diary. Those observations are repeated in Clark's Codex C, and it seems probable that Lewis was copying Clark's entries. After May 14 there is a gap of weather data in both captains' books until September 19; the notations are then resumed with hardly an interruption until April 3, 1805, when Lewis began placing weather data with the daily entries. The weather notes indicate a substantial amount of writing because they consist of two temperature readings for each day, the general state of the weather, the wind direction, and the rise and fall of the river. There are also comments on natural history including sightings of animals and the budding and fading of flora. It is uncertain whether Lewis made the notes along the way or at Fort Mandan, but it was a collaborative effort of the captains.[20]

Evidence that Lewis may have done more extensive writing exists in the form of a single loose sheet from Clark's *Field Notes* (Osgood's document 35). The sheet is entirely in Lewis's hand and contains on one side a draft for Lewis's description of the Platte River, which he later transferred into Codex O as his survey of rivers and creeks. Although there is a date of July 21 (1804) on the document, the reverse contains lunar observations (also in Lewis's hand) for February 23, 1805, while the party was at Fort Mandan. It could be that the draft describing the Platte was also written at Fort Mandan and there copied into Codex O. Because the draft from the *Field Notes* is an incomplete portion, it is certain that other pages are missing; whether they describe only the Platte or are a full draft of his summary may never be known. If Lewis was keeping thorough topographical notes throughout the first portion of the trip, it helps explain why no daily entry material has been found. It may simply have amounted to too much writing.

Taken together, Lewis's recording activities up to Fort Mandan add up to a large amount of writing and may represent a proportional share of the writing duties of the captains. What emerges is a picture of the two men sharing journal-keeping chores, though not following Jefferson's prescription to the letter. It is difficult to believe that all of Lewis's daily-entry journals (except for a few pages of writing for May and September 1804), from St. Charles to Fort Mandan and during the winter of 1804-5, could be lost. Clark during that period filled three notebooks of writing, and Lewis, the more verbose, would have written even more. Unless actual journals by Lewis or definite references to such writing are discovered, it seems likely that he kept no record of daily events for this period.

One incident on the way to Fort Mandan may corroborate the notion that Lewis kept no journal of daily events during that period. On July 14, 1804, a sudden storm hit the river, and great gusts of wind turned one boat on its side so that it began to fill with water. Cool heads and quick action saved the vessel from destruction, but Clark reported that his notes of the previous day had blown overboard during the accident. Clark mentioned that the loss "obliges me to refur to the <notes> Journals of Serjeants, and my own recollection [of] the accurences Courses Distance &. of that day." If Lewis had been keeping a journal of events during this time, why would Clark go to the journals of the sergeants or depend on his own recollection for the "accurences"? Certainly he would have trusted Lewis's notes over his memory or the notes of enlisted men if Lewis's journal had been available.[21]

From the April 7, 1805, departure from Fort Mandan to late August 1805, complete notebook journals for both captains exist, with no fragmentary or parallel journals until August, although some copying was being done between the two men. There is no indication that either followed Clark's earlier practice of writing field notes and transferring them, with revisions, into notebook journals. Indeed, there is no reason to assume that the captains consistently followed any one plan or procedure throughout the expedition. Their responsibility was to keep as complete a record as possible of the many kinds of information that Jefferson wanted and to preserve that record from harm or loss. They could follow any procedure that suited their convenience and the conditions of the moment, in keeping with that mission. External conditions varied so much throughout the trip that there was every reason to change journal-keeping procedures to conform to the needs of the moment. When they were inconsistent in so much else, there is no reason to expect them to be consistent in this.

It is not necessary to believe, then, that for every finished journal there was a preliminary set of field notes nearly duplicating it, as in the case of the River Journal and Codices A and B. Without the known existence of field notes, or strong evidence requiring them, there is no need to assume that they were made. Duplication of journals would serve as insurance against loss or damage, but with both captains definitely keeping journals after April 7, 1805, there would be less need for keeping both field notes and notebook journals, which amounted to a time-consuming task.[22]

Field notes, however, would be of value in situations where there was an increased risk of damage or loss from weather or difficult travel conditions, when it seemed wise to seal up the notebooks in tin boxes (described by Jefferson) and keep field notes easily accessible or carried on the person. Such precautions could also be taken when one of the captains was scouting ahead on foot, accompanied by only a few men; he might leave his notebook journals with the main body, for convenience or in case something happened to him and he did not return. After such separations, one might copy the experiences of the other into his own journal, to insure the preservation of a complete record.

As they moved up the Missouri around the Great Falls, the captains were separated at various times in June, July, and August 1805, as one or the other was ahead, portaging the falls or later looking for the Shoshone Indians. In these intervals, Lewis sometimes copied Clark's journal for the days of separation under the date of their reunion, suggesting that he was keeping the notebook journal day by day. At other times, Lewis gave an account of Clark's activities in his own entries for each day, indicating that those entries must have been written after they were reunited. Clark in this period did not ordinarily copy Lewis's record of daily events while they were separated.[23]

In some of Clark's red notebooks are extra pages he apparently inserted, sometimes torn from other red books but at least once cut to fit from letter paper. The handwriting on the inserted sheets is neater and more legible than Clark's usual bold but rather careless hand, but it is definitely Clark's, and the need for legibility is the likely reason for many of the insertions. This circumstance strengthens the likelihood that the ordinary handwriting represents daily entries written on the trail, during the day or in camp. A notable example is Clark's insertion of pages to recopy his survey notes of the Great Falls portage, already written in his rougher hand in the middle of his June 17, 1805, entry, probably during the course of the day. He decided to copy the notes over for greater legibility and in fact inserted more sheets than he needed. The inserted sheets are in the middle of the original rough notes.[24]

There are four fragmentary journals by Lewis from August and September 1805, designated Codices Fa, Fb, Fc, and Fd by Coues. Each consists of a few loose sheets covering periods of two to five days. Codex Fa describes events also related in more detail in Lewis's Codex F; the others are all from periods after the end of Codex F, during a hiatus of over four months for which there are no other known Lewis journals, except for a later fragment, Codex Ia.[25] It is tempting to regard them as being literally "fragments," that is, portions of a lost body of field notes by Lewis covering perhaps the entire gap in his journal from late August 1805, to January 1, 1806. But the fragments themselves provide no evidence for this hypothesis. If they had portions of a previous day's entry at the beginning, or of the next day's entry at the end, there would be good reason to regard them as portions of a larger body of notes now lost. On the contrary, however, they appear to be complete in themselves. Codex Fa has a dated heading for an entry at the end that was never written, since only a blank space follows the date on the last sheet of the codex. Moreover, all of the fragments except Fc relate to periods when the captains were separated; Fa chronicles a scouting excursion ahead of the main body when Lewis might have preferred not to risk his notebook journal, and the other two describe periods when Clark scouted ahead and Lewis had to keep a record of the movements of the main party. Codex Fc derives from two days of relative leisure at

William Clark (1770–1838).

Travelers' Rest in western Montana when Lewis may have intended to resume journal keeping after a lapse of about two weeks.[26] Lewis's later Codex Ia (November 29-December 1, 1805) also covers part of a period of separation and gives no indication of being part of a larger whole.[27]

In Codex G, Clark sometimes groups courses and distances for several days in one place, suggesting that he may have kept this information in separate notes and transferred it to his notebooks when time allowed. It may be that he kept course and distance notes on the same sheets with sketch maps, as he did with *Atlas* maps 33-42, although no such maps have been found for the route from the Great Falls to Travelers' Rest in western Montana, traversed during the period covered in Codex G.

On September 11 the Corps left Travelers' Rest on the Lolo Trail; this is the day on which Clark's Elkskin-bound Journal begins, continuing until December 31, 1805. It thus overlaps his red notebook journals Codex G (to October 10), Codex H (October 11-November 19), and Codex I (to December 31). This journal consists of sheets of letter paper sewn together and crudely bound in elkskin, presumably in the field. While we cannot be certain whether it was bound before or after writing, the fact that it ends precisely on the last day of 1805, the day before Lewis's known journal-writing again resumes, strongly suggests the latter.

From September 11 to 20, the Elkskin-bound Journal consists of courses and distances, with sketch maps of the Lolo Trail route. The courses and distances become progressively more detailed, briefly mentioning daily incidents; by September 13 they are in effect short journal entries in themselves. After September 21, the book becomes a regular journal of daily events. Here some speculation seems warranted. The Lolo Trail was one of the roughest parts of the trip, the trail hazardous and the weather terrible; the horse carrying Clark's writing desk slipped down a mountainside on the fifteenth, smashing the desk. These were conditions under which it would be prudent to seal up the notebook journals in tin boxes for protection and keep rough field notes along the trail. The sketch maps and courses and distances suggest that the elkskin book started out as the sort of route notes Clark kept at other times, such as those with *Atlas* maps 33-42. Their becoming progressively more extensive from September 11 to 20 suggests that Clark did indeed seal up Codex G at some point during this period, the Elkskin-bound Journal becoming the preliminary journal, the first draft for the notebooks. Clark went ahead with a few men, looking for game, on September 18, and the courses and distances in the elkskin book become particularly extensive from that date. There can be no certainty, however, that was the date when Codex G was sealed up.

From September 21, the elkskin book consists of regular daily entries in the conventional form, not in the form of courses and distances. September 20 was the day Clark met the Nez Perces at Weippe Prairie, Idaho, a meeting described in some detail in the elkskin notebook courses and distances. Lewis and the main party did not catch up until September 22. If Codex G was in a tin box on a packhorse with Lewis's group, we can understand why Clark wrote his regular September 21 entry in the elkskin book. He traveled a few miles that day but gave no courses and distances until the next day, September 22, when he wrote, "our first course of yesterday was nearly . . . ," as if he had not written it down anywhere else and was going by memory. There may have been no notes other than those in the elkskin book.

Clark's courses and distances for September 11-21 and September 25 are together in Codex G after the September 30 entry; he may have taken the notebook out on that day and brought it up to date, or he may have been keeping entries in it and simply have delayed copying the courses and distances because he was busy. In any case, he continued to keep journal entries in the elkskin book until December 31, paralleling notebook journal entries in Codices G, H, and I. That the Elkskin-bound Journal entries were the first draft and the codices the second seems probable. For much of the period from early October to early December the expedition was going downriver in small dugout canoes, and when they neared the Pacific Coast they entered an area of almost constant rain and storms. It may have seemed wise to keep the red books in their waterproof boxes much of the time and continue to use the sheets that became the Elkskin-bound Journal.

The elkskin book begins on the exact date of starting on the Lolo Trail, which may indicate that Clark had not kept detailed field notes for some time before that but had written daily information directly into his notebook journals. He could well have been keeping course and distance notes, with sketch maps of the route, as he had earlier, notes such as the pages in the elkskin book apparently started out to be. But why were those bound notes preserved if similar ones for an earlier period (the summer and fall of 1805) were not saved also? We must, of course, allow something for sheer chance, but the special care taken to bind the notes suggests a particular need to preserve material covering that period. One reason for preserving them might be the exceptionally large number of maps (nineteen) along with the journal material; none of the maps of the Elkskin-bound Journal are repeated in the codices for the same period. Again note that there are, to our present knowledge, no notebook journals by Lewis from late August 1805, to January 1, 1806; only fragmentary loose sheets are known, and all except one (Codex Fc) cover periods when the captains were separated.

The Elkskin-bound Journal ends the day before Lewis is known to have resumed his journal-keeping, the first day of 1806. It would be a remarkable coincidence if Clark just happened to run out of paper in the book on that day. Internal evidence indicates that large portions of Clark's notebook journals after early November 1805 were probably written months later. If the sheets in the elkskin book were the only continuous record by either captain for a period of over three and one-half months, then we can readily understand why they took special care to preserve them. If Clark's red books were sealed up and packed away for much of that time, we can also understand why what started out as rough notes and sketch maps became a journal of events as well.[28]

What was Clark doing with his notebook journals during the period (September 11-December 31, 1805) covered by the Elkskin-bound Journal? Entries in late September and early October 1805 in Codex G are generally more extensive than those in the Elkskin-bound Journal; both are brief during periods when Clark was ill or particularly busy. After the party set out down the Clearwater River in canoes on October 7, the Elkskin-bound Journal again becomes primarily expanded courses and distances. Codex H, however, begins on October 11, and from this point the elkskin book entries again become progressively more detailed and lengthy, as if it were again the record actually kept on the given dates. On November 7, 1805, the day the party arrived, or so they thought, in sight of the Pacific, Clark records the event in both journals in terms suggesting immediate emotion.

The Codex H entry for November 7, however, also contains a passage in quotes describing the dress of the local Indian women, noting that it was so skimpy that the "battery of venus is not altogether impervious to the penetrating eye of the amorite." Not only is the language most unlike Clark's, but the whole paragraph is placed in quotation marks to indicate that it was not Clark's. In fact, the whole paragraph occurs verbatim in Lewis's Codex J entry for March 19, 1806—over four months after the ostensible date of Clark's entry. This forces us to conclude that Clark wrote the November 7, 1805, entry in Codex H on or after March 19, 1806. Lacking any indication that the page with the quoted paragraph was inserted later, we must assume that the remainder of Codex H after that date—and Clark's subsequent notebook journals, largely copied from Lewis—were written on or after March 19, 1806—an assumption that creates some intriguing problems.[29]

There is some evidence, moreover, that much of Codex H before November 7, 1805, was not written until months after the given dates. In the entry in that journal for October 18, Clark notes how "the Great Chief and one of the *Chim-nâ-pum* nation" on the Columbia drew for him a sketch of the upper Columbia and its inhabitants and tributaries. Clark's copy of the sketch appears in the middle of the journal entry as if done at the same time as the entry itself. Yet the map labels as "Clark's River" the Pend Oreille River where it enters the Columbia. There is good reason to believe that the captains did not decide to give the name Clark's River to the combined Bitterroot-Clark Fork-Pend Oreille rivers until between April 17 and May 6, 1806 (see *Atlas,* pp. 10-11). An almost exact duplicate of the map in another notebook not containing daily entries shows the same stream as the "Flathead River," the name they used earlier. It may be, then, that Clark did not write the October 18 entry until late April or early May of 1806, inserting the sketch the Indians had given him under the appropriate date by copying from an earlier version. Codex H begins only a few days before that date, on October 11, 1805, so it might well be that, on finishing Codex G on October 10, Clark decided that since they were traveling downstream in canoes, it would be wise to use the Elkskin-bound Journal for daily journal keeping and keep his notebooks safely sealed away in boxes. As noted, the elkskin book's entries become increasingly extensive about this time.

Codex H ends on November 19 with a brief entry and Clark's words "See another book for perticulars." Codex I takes up with a longer entry for the same date, but only after thirty-four pages of introductory miscellaneous material—courses and distances from Fort Mandan to the Pacific, including some for a trip down the coast that Clark made in January 1806. That Codex I then takes up the narrative on November 19, 1805, immediately after this collection of data, suggests that Codex H was finished and the daily entries in Codex I begun in sequence. If so, then Clark also wrote Codex I after March 19, 1806, when Lewis wrote the "battery of venus" passage, which Clark copied under the date of November 7, 1805, in Codex H.

Why, then, did Clark wait so long to write this material in the red books? Up to December 31, 1805, he was writing in the sheets bound in elkskin and may not have seen any reason to start another journal, or he may not have gotten around to it. There is no clear evidence of such notes continuing after the first day of 1806. But Clark's Codex I has three short entries for January 1, 2, and 3 at one end of the book, upside down to all the rest of the writing in that book, which starts at the other end. It would seem that Clark began Codex I as a continuation of the Elkskin-bound Journal (ending December 31), then decided to do something else. It appears that he again took up Codex H, filled it up with entries paralleling the elkskin book through November 19, then continued in sequence in Codex I; if so, then he evidently did so after March 19, the date of Lewis's observations about the visibility of the "battery of venus." Apparently Clark wrote no journals of which we have knowledge for nearly three months, and this at Fort Clatsop, where he would have had relative leisure for writing. Codex I does contain a detailed record of Clark's trip down the Oregon coast on January 6-10, taken from notes (here called First Draft, January 6-10, 1806) of the kind the captains kept on other occasions when separated. Lewis's synopsis of Clark's trip is in his Codex J for January 10, the day of Clark's return, and was likely written at that time from Clark's verbal account and First Draft notes.

Lewis began a new journal (Codex J) on January 1, 1806, and continued a consistent writing until August 12 when he laid his pen down, ending his record of the expedition. That is the first journal writing by him, as far as we know, since August 1805, except for scattered fragments. Perhaps the new journal is another point of beginning as has been conjectured with Codices Aa, Ba, and Fc, and here his good intentions of journal keeping (combined perhaps with a New Year's resolution) were fulfilled. Codex J is a detailed record, to March 20, of life at Fort Clatsop, and contains extensive descriptions of local flora and fauna and the life of the nearby Indians, with numerous illustrations. Nowhere else did Lewis devote more time to fulfilling the scientific objectives of the expedition by recording so much. All of the observations are incorporated in the daily entries, generally after the record of the day's events. In what was evidently an additional measure to insure the preservation of this material, Clark copied most of it into his journals almost verbatim. For some reason Clark did not always copy material under the same date as Lewis and sometimes placed it under an entry several days earlier than that of Lewis. Clearly he was not copying Lewis day by day.

Clark's copying of Lewis for the period after January 1, 1806, is in a more careful, neater hand. There is no way of knowing whether Clark's neater hand was something he could do at any time he chose to make the effort, or whether it represents writing at leisure and in comfort after the return from the voyage. But if the reason for copying from Lewis was insurance against loss, it would make more sense to complete it as soon as possible during the journey.

Lewis's Codex J also includes natural history material appropriate to the Rocky Mountains and Interior Basin, notes additional to the few fragments extant for that period. If Lewis had kept a journal for that period (August-December 1805), why did he copy it into daily entries for the time at Fort Clatsop? Why not copy it into a separate journal covering the actual dates? That question must remain a mystery. There must have been some sort of natural history field notes or other journals for that period that are now lost. If Lewis did have notes in daily journal form covering the August-December gap, why did he not copy them into his own journal at Fort Clatsop when he would have had time? One answer might be that the notes he had were mainly natural history and ethnographic material, and that he did copy them into Codex J, under current dates. If both Lewis and Clark were copying from supposed notes made by Lewis before arriving at Fort Clatsop, then it might be clear why Clark's version of the scientific material comes under different dates than in Lewis's journals, while his daily record of events follows Lewis verbatim on the same dates. But Clark's duplication of Lewis's natural history notes in the codices (particularly Codex J) is so exact that the hypothetical notes must themselves have been as elaborate as those in Lewis's notebooks.[30]

As noted, Clark apparently did not write his November 7, 1805 entry in Codex H until on or after March 19, 1806, when he copied the "battery of venus" passage into that entry. March 19, when Lewis evidently wrote the paragraph, was just four days before the expedition left Fort Clatsop on the return trip. We can hardly imagine Clark writing over four months' worth of notebook journals, including extensive natural history notes, in that period of time, which surely was crowded with preparations for leaving. If he was copying from Lewis after the departure from Fort Clatsop, when did he do it—along the trail, during the lengthy stopover at Camp Chopunnish in Idaho, or after the arrival in St. Louis? And what did he do about his own daily journalizing during the homeward journey?

Clark's copying of Lewis continues during the first few days of the party's journey up the Columbia; he was still writing in the same book (Voorhis No. 2 in Thwaites's numbering system) and the entries could have been written some time later. The last two days of Voorhis No. 2, April 2 and 3, describe Clark's trip up the Willamette River on those days and could easily have been taken from field notes.[31] Lewis copied that narrative under his April 6 entry, with some changes in wording. Clark's Voorhis No. 3 begins on April 4 and is more a record of daily events without the extended descriptions copied from Lewis.

Since Voorhis No. 3 takes up immediately where No. 2 leaves off, however, it is logical to think that Clark did not start No. 3 until the other was finished—perhaps some time after the given date. Under April 6, Clark again has some natural history data copied from Lewis's entry of April 7. Clark may have been keeping some sort of field notes at this time. There are such notes made by him for the period of April 16-21, but for most of that time the captains were separated, with Clark trading for food at various Indian villages near the Great Falls of the Columbia. He might well have not wanted to be troubled with carrying a notebook journal at that time, but perhaps he was not keeping a journal at all in the period of the journey upriver. We have no idea when the two decided that Clark should copy Lewis's Fort Clatsop journals, perhaps doing no journalizing himself in the meantime, although the short entries for January 1-3 in his Codex I suggest the decision was taken in early January 1806. Nor is it clear how long after March 19 Clark waited to begin his copying.

From May 14 to June 10, 1806, the expedition was at rest at Camp Chopunnish, on the north bank of the Clearwater River in the Nez Perce country of Idaho, waiting for the snow to melt sufficiently on the Lolo Trail for their passage east. In this extended period of relative leisure Clark might have done some of the extensive copying from Lewis's journals. As noted, the use of the name "Clark's Fork" in a map placed with the October 18, 1805, entry in Codex H suggests that much of that notebook journal was not written until late April or early May of 1806, or later. That possibility would fit well with the hypothesis that much of Clark's catching up in his notebook journals and his copying from Lewis took place at Camp Chopunnish in May and June of 1806. Voorhis No. 3 has on its flyleaf a list of Chopunnish (Nez Perce) names for rivers; that fact suggests that the book, covering April 4-June 6, 1806, was out of its box and readily available during the period to record the information. Perhaps Clark finished his copying at Camp Chopunnish, although it would have been a substantial task. Clark records events of the period in words very similar to Lewis's, but daily events could obviously have been copied the day they happened. It is notable, however, that after the end of May we no longer have passages in Clark's journal that are clearly copied from Lewis, placed by Clark under dates earlier than in Lewis's journal.[32]

At the beginning of Codex M is a map of the Rockies based on a sketch given by "Sundary Indians of the Chopunnish Nation on the 29th 30th and 31st of May 1806." Clark may not have copied the sketch until several days later, but its presence in Codex M, which begins on June 6, near the end of the Camp Chopunnish sojourn, suggests that the book was unpacked and available at that time. It is therefore possible that Clark's copying from Lewis was complete to June 6 and he was able to start Codex M on the actual date.

Having returned to Travelers' Rest, the captains split the party on July 3, Lewis going northeast to seek a shorter route to the Missouri, Clark southeast to explore the Yellowstone. By all previous experience they should each have kept a journal during the period of separation, especially since they would be covering territory they had not previously explored.[33] Did they keep field notes on the trail or write in their notebook journals?

Lewis's Codex L runs to July 4, then resumes after eighteen blank pages with an entry for July 15; that is the only such unfilled gap in time in a notebook journal. The fragmentary Codex La (July 3-15) covers that period, and Lewis probably intended it as the first draft. He probably

packed away the notebook Codex L for safekeeping while traveling through the mountains, then resumed writing in it on July 15, leaving the blank pages to fill in later from the material in Codex La. In fact he never got around to that, probably because he quit writing entirely on August 12, by which date all the writing in Codex L was probably complete. He probably wrote his account of the violent encounter with the Blackfeet on July 27-28 at least a few days later, after rejoining his party following a hurried ride across country. He continued Codex L to August 8, after which the fragmentary Codex Lb covers August 9-12; on the twelfth Lewis stopped writing entirely because of discomfort from the accidental gunshot wound inflicted by Pierre Cruzatte on August 11. He had rejoined Clark on August 12, and the latter could now keep a record for the whole party.

The loose pages constituting Codex Lb were evidently once part of a red notebook found among Clark's papers, which bears on its cover the notation "9 to 12 Augt. 1806"; it now contains no expeditionary material. Lewis evidently began writing in the book after finishing Codex L, then stopped after a few days because of the pain of his wound. In later years Clark removed those few pages to use the book for other purposes. Considering the unfilled gap in Codex L, it appears that Lewis's journal keeping ceased entirely on August 12, 1806, and was then complete as it now stands.

Clark's travels after leaving Lewis involved several shifts from horseback to canoes and back to horses, but there is little indication that he did not write entries directly into his notebook journal (Codex M) for much of the period. A fragment for this period, covering the days July 13-19 and July 24-August 3, consists of courses and distances for his Yellowstone exploration—July 13 was the day he left the Three Forks of the Missouri headed for the Yellowstone. The Codex M entries for those days are much more extensive than the material in the fragment. The gap in the fragment represents the period when Clark's party stopped to build canoes, when there were no courses and distances to be recorded. Codex M has fairly extensive entries for those days. The Codex M entries through July 23 are in sequence, with no large gaps or crowding; as far as we can tell, Clark could either have been keeping that journal day by day, or he could have brought it up to date to the twenty-third while encamped.

Clark reached the Missouri, at the mouth of the Yellowstone, on August 3. At the end of his August 3 entry in Codex M is a passage, over two pages in Lewis's hand, describing the Yellowstone, which obviously Lewis could not have written before the captains' reunion on August 12. Clark's August 4 entry then follows on the next page without any gap. Unless Lewis managed to fit his passage neatly into a gap left by Clark, then the subsequent entries by Clark must also have been written after August 12. Lewis may have written the passage on August 12 before he stopped writing, but he could also have written it weeks later, after he had largely recovered from his gunshot wound, even after the arrival in St. Louis.

In his August 10 entry in Codex M, Clark gives a description of a cherry in Lewis's characteristic technical vocabulary, which is in fact copied from Lewis's description in Codex Lb for August 12; Clark could not have copied it before August 12, the date of their reunion.[34] Clark has a lengthy description of Lewis's experiences after their parting, with courses and distances, in his August 12 entry. The day of their reunion was the logical place for that information, but there is no proof that he actually wrote it on the twelfth. After that narration, however, Clark finishes the entry with the remaining events of August 12, the natural sequence if he had written the entry on that date.

The last daily entry in Codex M is that of August 14; it breaks off in the middle and is taken up in Codex N, an unusual procedure for Lewis and Clark. The entry in Codex M runs into the bottom of a weather table for the month of August 1806, which is complete to the end of the month. It is not clear which was written first, since Clark might have broken off the August 14 entry to leave space for finishing the weather table already started. Otherwise, we would have to assume he wrote the August 14 entry after the end of August. Codex N takes up under the heading of August 15, yet it clearly describes the same Indian council as that of August 14, in Codex M; the transition from one day to the next is never clear. Hurried copying at a later date might be the explanation of the unusual confusion of dates.

At the end of Codex M, Clark wrote an undated "Memorandum" to himself about some things that needed to be done; among them was to "Copy a Sketch of the rochjhone [Yellowstone]." Under the date of August 10, Clark notes that he "finished a copy of my Sketches of the River Rochejhone," which may mean the memorandum was written before that date. He also notes that he must make "a copy of the courses and distances," perhaps meaning to copy the fragment giving courses and distances for July 13-19 and July 24-August 3. The last item is "to fill up [vacinces?] in my book." Those "vacancies" could be merely the various blanks left in the journals for names of streams decided on later; they could be portions of pages left blank for insertion of material; or they could be more extensive blank spaces in the notebooks. At any rate, the note emphasizes the uncertainty for scholars of determining when any particular entry or portion of one was written.

Clark's Codex N has several blank spaces at the end of entries, perhaps left for insertion of extra information in case of need; that provides no satisfactory indication of when the writing was done. Codex N also contains miscellaneous notes that could have been made at various dates. The first two pages (including one side of the front flyleaf) are lists of goods shipped from St. Louis after the expedition's return, written in the same direction as the journal entries that follow. It is possible, then, that Clark wrote the whole of the daily entries in the book (August 15-September 26) after the latter date. The use of the flyleaf,

however, might be taken as an indication that the list was written after the journal entries. The confusion of dates at the beginning of Codex N, the gaps perhaps left for later insertions, and one instance (August 16-17) where one day's entry runs over into the beginning of the next, could all be taken as indications of haste. Such haste, however, could belong either to the period of the final rush downriver by the homesick explorers, or to the period after the return, when Clark was trying to finish his task. Codex N ends on September 26, three days after the arrival in St. Louis; the entries are progressively shorter the last few days, the last two notably so. There is no discernible reason why Clark chose to end at this particular point rather than on the day of arrival; that would be especially odd if he were copying the material from notes later.

There is still doubt, then, as to when Clark finished his writing. Jefferson's statement that "ten or twelve" red books were turned over to him on Lewis's return is too vague to support any precise conclusions. If Lewis showed the president all his own and Clark's daily notebook journals—Codices D through N and Voorhis Nos. 1, 2, and 3, there would be fourteen red books.[35] That leaves room for some unfinished journal keeping by Clark, consisting most probably of Codex N and part of Codex M if there was any such unfinished work. If Clark had delivered the remaining material on or soon after his own arrival in Washington on January 21, 1807, Jefferson might not have considered the circumstance memorable or worth mentioning years later, especially since he always tended to think and write of the expedition and the journals as essentially Lewis's.

The reader may not think the above a substantial advance beyond David McKeehan's statement of 1807 that "the several journals were brought together . . . and the blanks . . . filled up . . . at the different resting places." That is the procedure common sense would suggest, and it accords with the evidence available. In all probability, the bulk of the journals were complete when Jefferson saw them, some three months after the end of the expedition. Neither Jefferson nor McKeehan made any specific mention of field notes, but they were certainly made because some still exist. The possibility remains that the captains made other field notes and that some of those may yet be found. The evidence, however, does not require us to assume extensive sets of field notes amounting to duplicate journals covering the whole journey and copied into notebooks during or after the expedition.

Neither does the evidence indicate a uniform journal-keeping procedure followed consistently throughout the expedition. The captains followed their own convenience so far as consistent with making a complete record and with the safety of the documents themselves. If they had any fixed procedure in mind when they started out, they were certainly flexible enough to change it in the light of experience. Clark's full and extensive *Field Notes* for the journey up to Fort Mandan do not prove the existence of such notes for periods when none have been found. There are good reasons for believing that both captains wrote parts of their notebook journals later than their given dates, in the case of some of Clark's journals months later. At other times the evidence suggests that they kept the notebook journals day by day or soon after the given dates. They may have written in the notebook journals daily when the going was fairly smooth and the books were easily transported and protected. Under bad conditions they probably sealed up the notebooks in tin boxes for safety, using more or less extensive rough notes to keep a daily record.

The most significant criterion for the use of field notes would be the risk factor. In the beginning, when they were still gaining experience and testing procedures (on the journey to Fort Mandan), when travel and weather conditions were particularly bad (on the Lolo Trail), or during separations (the trip to the whale site on the Oregon coast), we can expect to find field notes with the finished journals.

The presence of several fragmentary, unbound codices naturally suggests a comparison with Clark's *Field Notes* of the first year; could they be the remains of a similar comprehensive set of preliminary journals, the basis of the notebook journals? The majority of them represent periods when the captains were separated; does this mean that the authors wrote them only because of that circumstance, or was that the reason those notes were preserved while many others were discarded? None of the fragments gives a clear indication of being part of a more extensive body of notes. There are no parts of a previous day's entry at the beginning, nor the beginning of another entry cut off at the bottom of the last page. In one or two cases the author may have intended to continue but left blank space indicating he never got around to it. The same appears to be the case with the Elkskin-bound Journal. The "fragments," as far as the evidence goes, are complete in themselves and not the remains of something larger. There was nothing, after all, to prevent the author of each fragment from copying it into his notebook and then discarding it with the rest of his hypothetical field notes. The preservation of these scattered pieces is more likely to have been the result of the captains' desire to preserve everything that could possibly be useful and relevant. Because so many of the fragments are Lewis's, they are part of the mysteries surrounding his journal keeping.

Nine of Lewis's fragmentary codices (Aa, Ba, Fa, Fb, Fc, Fd, Fe, Ia, and Lb) are apparently pages taken from notebooks, all but one (Ia) from red books. It is possible that Lewis removed the pages before writing on them, but it is equally possible that the writing was done in the books and the pages removed at some later period. Codex Fc, for instance, came from Codex P, and there is some reason to believe that those pages were not removed until 1810, when the book was used to copy natural history notes for Benjamin Smith Barton. As noted, many of the fragments represent periods when the captains were separated or when weather and travel conditions posed a special risk to the journals. On such occasions Lewis may have used a book that was largely blank, containing perhaps some relatively unimportant or duplicated data. Thus if the book he was carrying with him was damaged by weather or a dip in a river, or if he failed to return from a scouting mission, important material would not be lost, as would be the case if a regular daily journal suffered. This possibility may strengthen the likelihood that the so-called fragments are complete in themselves and not part of a body of lost field notes. Jefferson's reference to the red books as "travelling pocket journals," although he was not present when they were written, at least suggests that some of them were at some times carried on the person. Their size renders this quite possible. The "fragment" pages could have been removed from the books during the expedition, after the return, or when Clark and Biddle were working on the journals in 1810. If Lewis did have daily field notes and did not get them copied, what happened to them? When they saved so much else—so many fragments, scraps, and sketches—why not save material by the expedition leader covering periods when there is no other writing by him? Once again we have hypothetical lost journals, for whose existence there is no real evidence.

When Clark gave Nicholas Biddle custody of the notebook journals in 1810, Clark retained some of his own notebooks, which became part of Thwaites's discovery of material from the Voorhis family. The ones he retained covered periods for which there are known Lewis journals. The ones turned over to Biddle cover the periods where no Lewis journals are known to exist and the long separation in the summer of 1806. It certainly appears that the basis of Clark's choice of which of his own books to give Biddle was the existence or nonexistence of journals by Lewis covering the same period. If so, then the present gaps in Lewis's journals apparently existed by 1810 at the latest, and as noted no letters are known that lament the loss of daily journals by Lewis, either at the time of his death or earlier.

Clark's Elkskin-bound Journal represents a special case where extra care was taken to preserve a lengthy body of what evidently started out as rough course and distance notes with sketch maps made on the spot. But for most of the period covered by that journal there is no known writing by Lewis, and it seems that Clark did not write his notebook journals for at least half the period until months later. Moreover, conditions during the period were often such that the notebooks would have been safer in their sealed boxes. The Elkskin-bound Journal ends at the very point where Lewis's known journalizing resumes.

From the evidence it appears that Clark kept no regular journal for almost three months at Fort Clatsop (January, February, and March 1806), while Lewis was keeping his journal with its extensive notes on natural history and ethnology. Either they planned all along for Clark to copy those notes or decided on this precaution at some later point for safety's sake. It is unclear when Clark completed the copying of Lewis's Fort Clatsop journals or when he wrote the remainder of his notebook journals—how much he completed on the trail or how much, if any, after reaching St. Louis. We can only guess how long it took him to copy from Lewis or to compose his own entries. He introduced many of his own characteristic spellings into copied material, indicating that he was not trying to achieve literal faithfulness, and he sometimes changed the wording and included material from his own experiences where it seemed relevant.

At points where a notebook journal appears from good evidence to have been written weeks or months after the given date, it is not unreasonable to suppose the existence of some sort of field notes to assist memory. The clearest and most extreme case of the sort, Clark's notebook journals of fall 1805 to spring 1806 (Codices H and I and Voorhis No. 2), is explained by the existing Elkskin-bound Journal (from November 1805 to December 31, 1805), and after January 1, Clark copied from Lewis's journals. In cases where the interval between the given date and the actual writing of the entry was shorter, the notes could have been as extensive as the existing field notes of Clark's from the first year, or they might have been in the nature of expanded course and distance notes with sketch maps, of which various examples remain.

There is little reason to accept the theory that the red notebook journals were all written after the return from subsequently discarded field notes. Considering the great amount of extant material and the labor involved in writing it, we need not imagine extensive sets of field notes paralleling the notebooks when the existence of such notes is neither known nor required by the evidence. Whatever Clark's "we commenced wrighting" in his last journal entry refers to, it was probably not the task of writing all the red books covering a year and a half of travel. Most of the material we now have was written by the captains in the course of the expedition. In reading it, we are in a sense traveling with them and sharing their day-by-day experiences and uncertainties. . . .

Notes

1. Jackson (*LLC* [*Letters of the Lewis and Clark Expedition*]), 1:vii.

2. Coues (*DOMJ* [*History of the Expedition under the Command of Captains Lewis and Clark . . .*]), 31.

3. Jefferson to Corrèa da Serra, April 26, 1816, Jefferson to Clark, September 8, 1816, Jackson (*LLC*), 2:611, 619.

4. Coues (*DOMJ*), 31.

5. Thwaites (*LC* [*Original Journals of the Lewis and Clark Expedition, 1804–1806*]), 1:xxxiv-xxxv.

6. Coues (*DOMJ*), 28-29 and Thwaites (*LC*), 6:263, agree that Codex O was sent back from Fort Mandan. Besides the red books, there were also "Nine memorandum books" in Lewis's effects, taken by Clark and therefore relating to the expedition. If we assume them to be bound books, we may tentatively (and very speculatively) identify them as Codices A, B, C, Q, and R, the Eastern Journal, the Weather Diary, Floyd's Journal, and Ordway's notebook No. 2. See Appendix C [in *The Journals of the Lewis and Clark Expedition*]. "Six note books unbound" are nearly impossible to identify from the description, and there were numerous bundles of loose papers and maps. Jackson (*LLC*), 1:70, 92, 96, 98, 2:471. At the time of Lewis's death, Codex O was probably in the possession of Ferdinand Hassler, who was checking the astronomical observations. Clark to William D. Meriwether, January 26, 1810, Clark to Hassler, January 26, 1810, ibid., 2:490-92.

7. Gass's Prospectus, March 23, 1807, Jackson (*LLC*), 2:390-91.

8. Osgood (*FN*), xix, xxv, argues that Clark made a clean copy of his *Field Notes,* at least the latter part, at Fort Mandan. Why he would do so, when the notes were also copied in the notebooks, is not clear.

9. Clark to Jefferson, April 3, 1805, Lewis to Jefferson, April 7, 1805, Jackson (*LLC*), 1:230-32.

10. Osgood (*FN*), 302. The notation "Sept 20 &" may be the handwriting of Biddle.

11. Ibid., 305.

12. Jefferson to Barton, December 22, 1805, Jackson (*LLC*), 1:272; Osgood (*FN*), xxii-xxiii.

13. Osgood (*FN*), 321-22.

14. Jefferson to Lewis, June 20, 1803, Jackson (*LLC*), 1:61-66.

15. Jackson presents the strongest case for Lewis having kept a journal during the first leg of the journey, from Camp Dubois to Fort Mandan. His thesis will be considered in more detail in the paragraphs that follow. Jackson (*TJ* [*Thomas Jefferson and the Stony Mountains: Exploring the West from Monticello*]), 193-95.

16. The blank pages of the Eastern Journal were later filled by Biddle. See Appendix B [in *The Journals of the Lewis and Clark Expedition*].

17. Thwaites (*LC*), 1:xxxv n. 2; Cutright (*HLCJ* [*A History of The Lewis and Clark Journals*]), 9-10.

18. It is interesting that Clark's entry for May 14, 1805, in Voorhis No. 1, consists of half a page by Clark and half a page by Lewis describing the boat incident, the latter in nearly the same language as in Lewis's journal, Codex D. (Voorhis No. 1 is a designation by Thwaites for the family who had the items when he discovered them. See Appendixes B and C [in *The Journals of the Lewis and Clark Expedition*].) The last line of Lewis's material is crowded onto the top of the page where Clark resumes; almost certainly Clark left the blank space for some lines about

the mishap, which Lewis could have written the same day or much later. Jackson may consider the lost notes to be field notes; at one point he uses the term "unrevised notes." Jackson (*TJ*), 192-95; Thwaites (*LC*), 1:xxxv n. 2.

19. Clark to Jefferson, April 1, 1805, Lewis to Jefferson, April 7, 1805, Jackson (*LLC*), 1:226, 231-32. Jackson presumes that Lewis's substitutions mean that he wanted "Clark's statement to Jefferson to be completely noncommittal." Ibid., 226, headnote. Cutright thinks that the words imply that Lewis had not completed converting his field notes into a regular journal. His interpretation of Lewis's letter is that it cannot be taken as *prima facie* evidence that he had a journal in form to send to Jefferson." Cutright's wording ("journal in form") leaves an opening for supposing field notes, as he does with Clark's letter. Cutright (*LCPN* [*Lewis and Clark: Pioneering Naturalists*]), 120. Only one historian has concluded that Lewis kept no journal, "I do not think there is enough available evidence to support a conclusion that Lewis was keeping a journal on the first leg of the journey." But even he hesitates over a full commitment and in another instance writes, "Field notes . . . must have been taken by both Lewis and Clark during the whole journey." Osgood (*FN*), xxii, xv.

20. It may be significant that September 19 is the date of again taking up the weather notations, since it is so near the start of Codex Ba and the time of the decision not to send back pirogues to St. Louis. If Lewis was keeping the weather diary independent of Clark, and Clark was copying the weather data into his Codex C, then there may be a case of missing field notes, at least weather remarks, for Lewis during this period. Because Lewis's weather diary has so much of Clark's handwriting, it is here supposed that Clark was the weather recorder and Lewis the copier. However, one can as easily suppose missing weather notes of Clark as of Lewis.

21. Clark does not report the loss in Codex A but only in his *Field Notes*. Clark's entry (*Field Notes*), July 13, 1804. Ordway reported that Clark's notes for two days had blown overboard. Ordway's entry, July 14, 1804.

22. On many occasions the captains copied from each other's journals; judging from vocabulary and phrasing, Clark most often copied from Lewis, who was more literate and better versed in scientific terminology. Because Clark did not always copy the material under the same date as it is found in Lewis's journal, we can say with some confidence that Clark's notebook journal entries in 1805 and 1806 were not always written on the days given. Jackson has shown that after Fort Mandan there was a definite break in journalizing techniques, so that not only multiple journals but also duplicate records of important observations were being kept. Jackson (*TJ*), 192-95.

23. Initial times of separation and journal copying include the following: April 25-26, 1805, when Lewis added some notes about Clark's activities, which information he received after the men reunited; June 4-8, 11-16, 1805, when Lewis copied from Clark's journal (Voorhis No. 1) into his own (Codex E) under entries on the day they rejoined, suggesting that Lewis was writing day by day in his notebook journal; and during the portage around the Great Falls of the Missouri and afterwards when Lewis included the "Occurrences with Capt. Clark and Party" as part of each day's entry (in Codices E and F), indicating that he wrote those individual entries after the two reunited. Lewis explained his procedure in the latter instance, for on June 23 he wrote, "I shall on each day give the occurences of both camps during our seperation as I afterwards learnt those of the lower camp from Capt. Clark." He continued this practice until they reunited on July 1. Without saying so, Lewis apparently continued the practice while separated from Clark, July 10-13, 15-16, 18-22, and 23-27, 1805. For periods when he was scouting ahead in July 1805, Clark gives the courses and distances of the main party in Codex G, presumably copying from Lewis at some time after their reunion. Courses and distances are given in blocks of several days, interspersed with several days' narrative entries, in a way that suggests Clark went ahead in Codex G to write them, leaving space to fill in the narrative material. The latter narrates only his own movements, and he may have written them within a few days of their occurrence.

24. Clark's entry for May 31, 1805, is another example of such an insertion.

25. For example, Lewis describes the pinyon jay on August 1, 1805, in Codex F, but it is not noted in Codex Fa, the supposed field notes. Other descriptions are also found in Codex F but not in Codex Fa.

26. Perhaps Lewis started Codex Fc in the middle of a blank book (Codex P) because he intended to fill in the space left with his journalizing for the two weeks from the end of Codex Fb (August 26). If so, he surely had notes of some kind on which to base the entries. Apparently he never got around to it, and there is no sign that he continued after September 10, 1805, at least not in Codex P.

27. A final fragment, Codex Fe, consists of ten pages torn from Codex D recording weather data for April 1-June 30, 1805, and six pages taken from another red book recording weather data for July 1-September 30, 1805. Lewis was the principal author, but Clark shared some of the writing.

28. The Elkskin-bound Journal contains some miscellaneous material of uncertain date, between the December 7 and 8 entries, including distances on the lower Columbia and a list of local tribes. Here also is an entry dated January 1, 1806, having no daily

material but consisting of a list of sea captains who traded with the nearby Indians, from Indian information. Lewis has a similar list in Codex J under March 17. We cannot say which list was written first; Clark's list in the elkskin book has more details, and material of any date could have been included in the book.

29. Dunlay.

30. Cutright (*LCPN*), 263; Jackson (*TJ*), 192-93. Most of the material Clark copied from Lewis into Voorhis No. 2 is from the Lewis journals covering the Fort Clatsop winter. A notable exception is a description of the mule deer in Clark's entry for March 11, 1806; that he copied from Lewis's Codex D entry for May 10, 1805, ten months before the ostensible date of Clark's entry. Whenever Clark wrote Voorhis No. 2, he evidently had other Lewis journals out, combing them for important material to duplicate. In addition, in his own May 10, 1805 entry in Voorhis No. 1, he inserted a note: "The Mule Deer Described in No. 8." Today's Voorhis No. 2 was apparently Number 8 in Clark's original numbering system, so he must have inserted the note before his collaboration with Biddle in 1810, when he adopted Biddle's numbering system for cross-references. See Appendix B. [in *The Journals of the Lewis and Clark Expedition*].

31. Voorhis No. 2 contains a map of the area around the confluence of the Columbia and Multnomah (Willamette) rivers in the midst of the April 3 entry. It is quite similar to the one Clark apparently drew in Lewis's Codex K at the end of the April 3 entry, and there is no certainty which came first. It does suggest that the book (Voorhis No. 2) was available for sketching at the time or soon after.

32. As noted, Clark's Elkskin-bound Journal contains a number of sketch maps, some of them made going down the Columbia in October 1805. Obviously the journal was out and in use during the return up the Columbia. But the Lolo Trail maps in the same book do not have return campsites marked. That may indicate that Clark finished his copying of the Elkskin-bound Journal (to December 31, 1805) by the time he left Camp Chopunnish, having been engaged in copying from it there or during the upriver journey.

33. François-Antoine Larocque, a North West Company trader the captains had met at Fort Mandan, explored a considerable portion of the Yellowstone in 1805. Clark, of course, was unaware of this when he went down the river in 1806 and would have kept a detailed journal in any case. See Larocque.

34. Cutright (*LCPN*), 325; Jackson (*TJ*), 192-93.

35. Codex P would have been largely blank at this time, containing the pages now in Codex Fc, some of Lewis's weather notes, and miscellaneous memoranda. Some of the other fragmentary codices may also have been torn out of it. There is no certainty that Jefferson saw Codex P, therefore, but his vagueness about the number of books reduces the relevance of the matter in any case. The same uncertainty applies in the case of Voorhis No. 4. . . .

FORT MANDAN

Stephen E. Ambrose (essay date 1996)

SOURCE: "Report from Fort Mandan, March 22-April 6, 1805," in *Undaunted Courage: Meriwether Lewis, Thomas Jefferson, and the Opening of the American West*, Simon & Schuster, 1996, pp. 202-10.

[*In the following essay, Ambrose surveys the almost book-length report Lewis and Clark issued from Fort Mandan, providing a summary of the maps, correspondence, and descriptions of waterways, plants, minerals, and wildlife that the captains included in their final report.*]

New life was stirring. On the first day of spring, it rained—the first rain since fall. The river ice began to break up. Ducks, swans, and geese sometimes seemed to fill the sky. The Indians set fire to the dry grass to encourage new grass to come up, for the benefit of their horses and to attract the buffalo.

By the end of March, the ice was coming down in great chunks, along with drowned buffalo who had been on the ice when it gave way. "I observed extraordinary dexterity of the Indians in jumping from one Cake of ice to another," Clark wrote on the 30th, "for the purpose of Catching the buffalow as they float down."

The joy of spring was everywhere, and doubly welcome by the men of the expedition, who had just survived the coldest winter any of them had ever known. They worked with enthusiasm, eager to get going again. Teams of men were repairing the boat, while others were building canoes, packing, making moccasins, making jerky, pumping the bellows. They sang as they worked.

In the five months between May and October 1804, the captains and their men had traveled more miles than many of their contemporaries would do in a lifetime. In the five months between November 1804 and April 1805, they had stayed in one place. The anticipation of getting going on the river again was so keen it was almost unbearable.

On the last day of March, Clark wrote, "All the party in high Spirits, but fiew nights pass without a Dance. Possessing perfect harmony and good understanding towards each other. Generally healthy except venerials complains which is verry Commion. . . ."

On April 5, the keelboat and the two pirogues that had come down the Ohio and then up the Mississippi and Missouri to Fort Mandan, along with six new canoes, were put into the water. They would be packed the next day, then set off on April 7, the keelboat headed downstream for St. Louis while the two pirogues and the lighter and more maneuverable canoes headed upstream, where the river would gradually become shallower and swifter.

As the men went about their work, the captains wrote. So much writing did they do that Clark complained he had no time to write his family. Lewis managed to work in a letter to his mother, but most of it was unoriginal—he just copied passages from his report to Jefferson.

The captains worked with passion and dedication. For several weeks, Lewis did nothing but write, eat, and sleep. There was so much to say. He felt he needed to justify the expedition. He wanted to please Jefferson, to be able to report that they had discovered what he had hoped they would, to answer his questions, to promote his program for the development of Louisiana.

Even more, the captains wanted to be accurate in all their observations. They were men of the Enlightenment, dedicated to collecting facts and then putting the new knowledge to work for the good of mankind. So, in addition to describing the geography, the soils, the minerals, the climate, they had the responsibility of describing the tribes, and of making recommendations on the economic future of Louisiana. They needed to make available in permanent form as much as they could of what they had learned.

Lewis was determined to get these jobs done and done right. In his mind, everything that had happened since Jefferson put him in command was preliminary to the expedition, which was only now about to begin. On April 7, the Corps of Discovery would set out into territory no white man had entered. Thus far, as Gary Moulton writes, "All the men's efforts had been directed to reaching a point where other whites had ventured before them, on a route already mapped."[1]

But although the expedition had yet to do any exploring, the captains had managed to pick up a tremendous amount of new information on Upper Louisiana—its flora and fauna, its climate and fertility, its peoples and their wars and their economies. Put together correctly, and properly organized and labeled, all this information would constitute the first systematic survey of the trans-Mississippi West, and would thus provide an invaluable contribution to the world's knowledge—and equally invaluable to the United States government and American businessmen, frontier farmers, fur traders, and adventurers.

The captains collected information in two basic ways. First and foremost, from their own observations. Second, by making local inquiry. They asked questions about the surrounding country of every Indian and white trader they met. These information-gathering sessions sometimes lasted a full day, occasionally even longer.

Jefferson had a passion for Indian language, believing he would be able to trace the Indians' origins by discovering the basis of their language. So the gathering of vocabularies was an important charge on the captains. They put a major effort into attempting to render words from various Indian languages into an English spelling.

MacKenzie was present once to see the captains at work on their vocabularies. The language being recorded was Hidatsa. A native speaker would say a word to Sacagawea, who would pass it on in Hidasta to Charbonneau, who would pass it on in French to Jessaume, who would translate it into English for the captains. MacKenzie thought Jessaume's English ranged somewhere between inadequate and nonexistent, magnifying the chances for error.

On another occasion, MacKenzie wrote: "I was present when vocabularies were being made of the Mandans; the two Frenchmen [Charbonneau and Jessaume] had warm disputes upon the meaning of every word that was taken down by the captains. As the Indians could not well comprehend the intention of recording their words, they concluded that the Americans had a wicked design upon their country."[2] Despite the difficulties, Lewis kept at it. He put in immense amounts of time on the task. Whether he found the work interesting, or thought it important, cannot be said. It sufficed that Mr. Jefferson wanted it done.

Lewis was relatively uninterested in Indian mythology or spiritual life, but he was a skilled observer of some parts of Indian culture, especially how things were done. One of his contributions, for example, was a graphic and precise description of glass-bead-making among the Arikaras. As the expedition prepared to depart for the mountains, the captains purchased a buffalo-skin tepee to provide shelter for themselves, Charbonneau, Sacagawea, and Pomp. Lewis described it in his journal entry of April 7, 1805, in what James Ronda characterized as "one of the best descriptions yet drafted of that distinctive plains dwelling."[3]

In addition to their written descriptions, the captains gathered such objects as Arikara corn, tobacco seeds, mineral and botanical specimens, along with artifacts from Indian life, including bows, clothing, and painted robes, to be sent to Jefferson. Altogether, the amount of information they gathered, organized, and presented in a systematic fashion to Jefferson—and, beyond him, to the scientific world—was enough to justify the expedition, even if it made not a single further contribution.

The model for Lewis and Clark's report was Jefferson's *Notes on the State of Virginia*. Like that work, written a quarter-century earlier, Lewis's description of Upper Louisiana was part guidebook, part travelogue, part booster-like promotion, part text to accompany the master map. Adding in Clark's contributions, the final report from Fort Mandan totaled something close to forty-five thousand words, almost book-length (Jefferson's *Notes* ran to some eighty thousand words).

Like Jefferson, Lewis began with a detailed account of the waterways, or, as he put it, "A Summary view of the rivers and Creeks, which discharge themselves into the Missouri . . . from the junction of that river with the Mississippi, to Fort Mandan."[4] As Jefferson had done for Virginia, Lewis described not only the tributaries but the people living along the rivers, whether the French at St. Charles, or the Otos, or the Sioux. He included information on the local economy, the soil, mineral deposits, climate, and more.

The report combined the captains' actual observations of the various rivers flowing into the Missouri with information received from traders and Indians about the upper reaches of those streams and their own principal tributaries. For example, Lewis saw only the mouth of the Platte River, but he described it up to its head in the mountains. From what he had been told, he said, the Platte ran "through immence level and fertile plains and meadows, in which, no timber is to be seen except on it's own borders." He named five major tributaries of the Platte, discussed the mineral deposits in its drainage, the soil, the people—Otos and Missouris—and more. Naturally, the farther west Lewis's report ventured, the more speculative it became. His conjecture about the Platte's relationship to Santa Fe and to the Black Hills was purely imaginative and badly wrong.

Lewis expected that Jefferson would have his work printed and distributed as a report to Congress, and he knew something about the audience for the work, so on occasion he sounded like a promoter writing a broadside: "This river [the Muddy, in eastern Missouri] waters a most delightfull country; the land lies well for cultivation, and is fertile in the extreem . . . covered with lofty and excellent timber, and supplyed with an abundance of fine bould springs of limestone water." The Grand River, farther west, was also prime farm country. "The lands are extreemly fertile; consisting of a happy mixtuure of praries and groves, exhibiting one of the most beautifull and picteresk seens that I ever beheld."

Enthusiastic as he was in his report about the lower-Missouri country—he made it sound almost like heaven—he actually was holding back his emotions. In his letter to his mother, dated March 21, 1804, he allowed himself to rhapsodize about the country, writing not so much as son to mother as Virginia planter to Virginia planter. "This immence river so far as we have yet ascended," he wrote, "waters one of the farest portions of the globe, nor do I believe that there is in the universe a similar extent of country, equally fertile, well watered, and intersected by suuch a number of navigable streams." He added, "I had been led to believe that the open prarie contry was barren, steril and sandy; but on the contrary I found it fertile in the extreem, the soil being from one to 20 feet in debth, consisting of a fine black loam [that produces] a luxuriant growth of grass and other vegitables."

The Plains were not quite Eden, however; the absence of timber was a serious drawback, for it was almost unimaginable for any American in 1805 to live in a country without plenty of lumber and fuel. Indeed, in the eastern third of the United States, too much timber was the problem.[5]

In his report to Jefferson, Lewis took note of all the things that would spring to the mind of a frontier farmer hankering to move into Upper Louisiana. He pointed out "several rappids well situated for water-works"; he warned against areas that had tolerably fertile soil but no timber. Lewis was an advance man for the American fur trappers and traders as well as farmers. He noted the furs available and scouted likely spots for trading posts.

One of Lewis's responsibilities was to make recommendations on how to drive the British away from the Missouri so that American companies could take over the fur trade. His analysis of the economic-political situation on the river led him directly to his conclusion and recommendation.

"I am perfectly convinced that untill such measures are taken by our government as will effectually prohibit all intercourse or traffic with the Sioux" and the British fur companies, he reported to Jefferson, "the Citizens of the United States can never enjoy, but partially, those important advantages which the navigation of the Missouri now presents." He recommended establishing garrisons in places where the soldiers could stop the British from coming into Dakota from Canada or across today's Minnesota. If trade between the British and the Sioux was prohibited for a few years, he wrote, "the Sioux will be made to feel their dependence on the will of our government for their supplies of merchandize, and in the course of two or three years, they may most probably be reduced to order without the necessity of bloodshed." Given what happened in Sioux-American relations over the following seventy-one years, that was a hopelessly optimistic prediction.

Much of the report was a business prospectus, with the emphasis on the Indian as customer and supplier. In a separate section, written in Clark's hand but the product of both men's labor, entitled "Estimate of the Eastern Indians,"[6] the captains described no fewer than seventy-two different tribes and bands, with at least some information on where they lived, how they lived, who they were at war with, their numbers, their dwellings, and more. Of course the captains could only describe a few tribes from firsthand knowledge, but they made clear where their information was word-of-mouth.

Those they knew they did not hesitate to characterize, often in a heartfelt fashion. They wrote of their friends the Mandans, "These are the most friendly, well disposed Indians inhabiting the Missouri. They are brave, humane and hospitable." Of the Teton Sioux, the opposite: "These are the vilest miscreants of the savage race, and must ever remain the pirates of the Missouri, until such measures are pursued, by our government, as will make them feel a dependence on its will for their supply of merchandise."

Of the tribes living along the route they intended to follow, they wrote of the mountain-dwelling Flatheads: "They are a timid, inoffensive, and defenceless people. They are said to possess an abundance of horses."

Of the Shoshones, the captains' information indicated that they traded with the Spanish, who refused to give them firearms. Consequently, although the Shoshones were a very numerous and well-disposed people, "All the nations on the Missouries below make war on them & Steal their horses."

Of the Nez Percé: "Still less is known of these people, or their country. The water courses on which they reside, are supposed to be branches of the Columbia river."

Along with the written report, the captains sent back to Jefferson 108 botanical specimens, to add to the collections at the American Philosophical Society, all properly labeled as to where and when collected, and described. The first was "a species of Cress, taken at St. Louis May 10th 1804. It is common in the open growns on the Mississippi bottomes, appears in the uncultivated parts of the lots gardens and orchards, the seed come to maturity by the 10th of May in most instances."

If medicinal properties were claimed for a plant, Lewis mentioned them. If the claim touched a common medical problem back in the States, Lewis emphasized it, none more so than a root known by the name of "white wood of the prairie" which was said to be sovereign for the bite of a mad wolf or a mad dog, and for the bite of the rattlesnake. Rabies and snakebite were common dangers in the early nineteenth century, so a cure was such an exciting prospect that Lewis made the root of the white wood the subject of a separate letter to Jefferson, in which he detailed how to prepare it as a poultice, how to apply it, and so forth. He concluded: "I have sent herewith a few pounds of this root, in order that experiments may be made by some skilfull person under the direction of the pilosophical society of Philadelphia."[7]

It was probably the purple coneflower, which was widely used by the Indians as an antidote for snakebite. Jefferson sent the root along to a doctor to experiment with it.[8]

Lewis also sent to Jefferson sixty-eight mineral specimens, all labeled as to where and when collected. He included such items as "sand of the Missouri," "one pint of Missouri water," "pebbles common to the Missouri," lead ore, quartz, Glauber salts, alum, pyrites, lime, lava and pumice stone, and fossils.

The plants and minerals were part of a larger shipment to Jefferson that included skeletons of a male and female pronghorn, the horns of two mule deer, insects and mice, skins of various animals, including a marten and a white weasel that came from beyond the mountains via the trade route, and more. There were live animals too, new to science: four magpies, a prairie dog, and a prairie grouse hen (only one magpie and the prairie dog reached Jefferson alive).

Included also in the shipment was Clark's map of the United States west of the Mississippi River. It was a masterpiece of the cartographers art, and an invaluable contribution to knowledge. From St. Louis to Fort Mandan, Clark got it exactly right along the Missouri. His map became a bit sketchier as it moved west, naturally, because his depictions of the various tributaries was based on hearsay, often from people who did not claim to be eyewitnesses but knew someone who had been there. Lewis explained Clark's method: he would compare one Indian's description with another's, questioning them separately and at different times, and questioning as many as possible. Only when there was agreement on placement, distance, mountain passes, and so forth was the information put on Clark's map and into Lewis's report.

For all their concern with getting the specimens ready for shipment and with making their report and the map as complete as possible, in the first two weeks of spring what was uppermost in the captains' minds was what lay ahead. They pumped the Mandans, who never ventured very far west and thus could tell them little, and the Hidatsas, whose war parties ranged to the mountains and who thus could tell them a lot.

From the Hidatsas, Lewis had learned the names of rivers coming into the Missouri, and their connections with one another. He commented on his source: "I conceive [the Hidatsas] are entitled to some confidence."

Lewis expected to find, at 117 miles upriver from Fort Mandan, the White Earth River coming in on the north side. The prospect excited him greatly, because if the White Earth came in from as far north as the Indians indicated, it would mean that the boundary between Canada and the United States might be moved north by as much as a full degree of latitude, something Jefferson very much hoped for.

Three miles above the mouth of the White Earth, the Indians told Lewis he would come to the greatest of all the tributaries of the Missouri, the Yellowstone. The Hidatsas said that the Yellowstone "waters one of the fairest portions of Louisiana, a country not yet hunted, and abounding in animals of the fur kind." They thought the river navigable "at all seasons of the year for boats and perogues to the foot of the Rocky Mountains, near which place, it is said to be not more than 20 miles distant from the three forks of the Missouri."

The obvious importance of the Yellowstone led Lewis to recommend that the government build a trading post at the junction with the Missouri. It would "afford to our citizens the benefit of a most lucrative fur trade [and] might be made to hold in check the views of the British N. West Company," whose intention was "to panopolize" the Missouri River fur-trade business. "If this powerfull and ambitious company are suffered uninterruptedly to prosecute their trade," Lewis warned, the British might someday use their influence with the natives to block all American navigation on the Missouri.

Some 150 miles upstream from the mouth of the Yellowstone would come "The River Which Scolds at All Others," falling in on the north side. Then the Musselshell from the south. Another 120 miles and the expedition would be at the falls of the Missouri, "discribed by the Indians as a most tremendious Cataract. They state that the nois it makes can be heard at a great distance. . . . They also state that there is a fine open plain on the N. side of the falls, through which, canoes and baggage may be readily transported. this portage they assert is not greater than a half a mile."

Some fifteen miles beyond the falls, the Medicine River would fall in on the north side. Another sixty miles and the expedition would enter the first connected chain of the mountains. After another seventy-five miles, the Missouri would divide into three nearly equal branches, at the place called Three Forks, where Sacagawea had been captured some five years earlier. The most northern of the three rivers "is navigable to the foot of a chain of high mountains, being the ridge which divides the waters of the Atlantic from those of the Pacific ocean. The Indians assert that they can pass in half a day from the foot of this mountain on it's East side to a large river which washes it's Western base."

How Jefferson must have loved reading that line. The singular objective of the expedition was about to be realized.

The Divide was as far as the Hidatsas ever ventured. Lewis noted that "we have therefore been unable to acquire any information further West than the view from the top of these mountains."

But what the Hidatsas said they saw from the top of the mountain was exactly what Lewis and Jefferson hoped for and expected: "The Indians inform us that the country on the Western side of this river consists of open & level plains like those they themselves inhabit." The Flathead and Shoshone tribes lived on a river in that country. Their principal food was fish. "This river we suppose to be the S. fork of the Columbia," Lewis wrote, "and the fish the Salmon, with which we are informed the Columbia river abounds. This river is said to be rapid but as far as the Indian informants are acquainted with it is not intercepted with shoals."

What had been high expectations now soared, both at Fort Mandan and, some months later, in Washington, when the report arrived and Jefferson read it with what must have been the most intense satisfaction, feeling that, even as he was reading, the all-water route to the Pacific was being found and mapped.

Along with the report, Lewis sent back to St. Louis various letters, dispatches, and copies of the drafts and chits he had signed, what he called "my public accounts." In a covering letter to Jefferson dated April 7, but almost certainly written the previous day, Lewis confessed to considerable embarrassment about those accounts.[9] He had intended to put them in order and have them returned to St. Louis in the fall of 1804, but in the event it turned out that

"the provision perogue and her crew could not have been dismissed . . . without evedently in my opinion, hazarding the fate of the enterprise in which I am engaged, and I therefore did not hesitate to prefer the sensure that I may have incurred by the detention of these papers, to that of risking in any degree the success of the expedition."

Jefferson had instructed Lewis to be diligent about his accounts and to get his drafts back to the War Department with all possible speed. Lewis said his failure to do so had become "a serious source of disquiet and anxiety; and the recollection of your particular charge to me on this subject, has made it still more poignant."

Clearly, as an army officer, Lewis had made the correct decision. But as the president's protégé he felt terrible about it, because he hated disappointing Jefferson. Yet, however bad he felt about it, Lewis's casualness with his accounts and the chits he had signed was becoming habitual.

In the second half of his April 7 letter to Jefferson, Lewis told his commander-in-chief his plans. In the morning, he intended to send the keelboat and pirogues on their way. Accompanying Corporal Warfington would be four privates plus Newman [Newman had conducted himself admirably since his court-martial and discharge. He had volunteered for the toughest jobs and impressed the men so much that they urged Lewis to meet Newman's request that he be allowed to rejoin the expedition. Although he later had some words of praise for Newman, Lewis would not reinstate him, and he returned to St. Louis with the deserter Reed.] and Reed, Mr. Gravelines acting as pilot and interpreter, and four Frenchmen. They were well armed and adequately supplied. "I have but little doubt but they will be fired on by the Siouxs," Lewis wrote, "but they have pledged themselves to us that they will not yeald while there is a man of them living."

The expedition's six canoes and two pirogues were loaded, ready to go. They would shove off the instant Warfington turned the keelboat downstream. Lewis said he intended to leave the two pirogues at the falls of the Missouri. On the far side of the falls he intended to put his iron-frame boat together and cover it with skins.

Freed of the cumbersome keelboat, Lewis said he anticipated traveling at a rate of twenty to twenty-five miles per day until he reached the falls. After that, "any calculation with rispect to our daily progress, can be little more than bare conjecture." But his hopes were high: "The circumstance of the Snake Indians possessing large quantities of horses, is much in our favour, as by means of horses, the transportation of our baggage will be rendered easy and expeditious over land, from the Missouri to the Columbia river."

Supplies were adequate, Lewis said, thanks to the skills of the hunters, whose efforts made it possible to live on a diet of meat, thus saving the parched corn, portable soup, flour, and salt pork for the mountains. He put in not a word about Mandan corn, a glaring omission that left Jefferson with the entirely wrong impression that it was possible for white men to winter on the Plains without help from the Indians. Lewis did say that the Indians assured him the country ahead "abounds with a vast quantity of game."

Lewis predicted that the expedition would reach the Pacific Ocean that summer, then return as far as the head of the Missouri, or perhaps even as far as Fort Mandan, for the winter of 1805-6. He told Jefferson, "You may therefore expect me to meet you at Monachello in September 1806."

Lewis's concluding paragraph must be the most optimistic report from the field from an army officer about to set off on a great venture that any commander-in-chief ever received: "I can foresee no material or probable obstruction to our progress, and entertain therefore the most sanguine hopes of complete success. As to myself individually I never enjoyed a more perfect state of good health, than I have since we commenced our voyage. My inestimable friend and companion Capt. Clark has also enjoyed good health generally. At this moment, every individual of the party are in good health, and excellent sperits; zealously attached to the enterprise, and anxious to proceed; not a whisper of discontent or murmur is to be heard among them; but all in unison, act with the most perfect harmoney. With such men I have everything to hope, and but little to fear."

Notes

1. Gary Moulton, ed., *The Journals of the Lewis & Clark Expedition,* vol. 3 (Lincoln: University of Nebraska Press, 1987), p. 333.

2. L. R. Masson, *Les Bourgeois de la Compagnie du Nord-Ouest* (New York: Antiquarian Press, 1960 reprint), pp. 336-37.

3. James P. Ronda, *Lewis and Clark Among the Indians* (Lincoln: University of Nebraska Press, 1984), p. 121.

4. The text I use here is Moulton, ed., *Journals,* vol. 3, pp. 336-69.

5. Donald Jackson, ed., *Letters of the Lewis and Clark Expedition, with Related Documents: 1783-1854,* 2nd ed. (Urbana: University of Illinois Press, 1978), vol. I, pp. 222-23.

6. Moulton, ed., *Journals,* vol. 3, pp. 386-450.

7. Jackson, *Letters,* vol. I, p. 220.

8. Eldon G. Chuinard, *Only One Man Died: The Medical Aspects of the Lewis and Clark Expedition* (Glendale, Calif.: Arthur Clark Company, 1980), pp. 271-72. Chuinard notes that the plant was widely known for its anti-snakebite properties among frontiersmen.

9. Jackson, *Letters,* vol. I, pp. 232-33.

THE CLARK JOURNAL

Ernest Staples Osgood (essay date 1964)

SOURCE: An introduction to *The Field Notes of Captain William Clark, 1803-1805,* Yale University Press, 1964, pp. xiii-xxxv.

[*In the following essay, Osgood provides background and analysis of the rough journal kept by Captain William Clark from December, 1803, to early April, 1805.*]

The returning explorer has never been without an audience as he recounted his adventures. Men of all times and in all places, their minds reaching out from the known and familiar to the new and the strange, have listened to him. From the discovery of the New World until the last mile of coastline had been mapped, the last river ascended, the last mountains crossed, each generation watched and listened. The story of the exploration of the North American continent—by Spaniard and Frenchman, Englishman and American—is a great and compelling chapter in our history. From Quebec on the north to New Spain on the south, from the scattered settlements along the eastern seaboard on beyond the farthest western horizon, the story runs. The Indian alone knew the secrets of this great land; the white man had to penetrate every corner of it before he could call it his own.

Hunters, missionaries, fur traders, soldiers, and government officials moved out into this wilderness and returned, most of them, to report in one way or another on what they had seen and what they had learned. Excitement and danger were always with them along the hunting and war trails of the Indian, beside them on the craft that moved up strange and treacherous rivers, and with them as the long pack train struggled upward to the pass from which they could catch their first glimpse of an unknown and unexplored land.

Many of these forerunners left no account of their wanderings. The adventures of the lone hunter who broke open the first trails were remembered only in tales told in the frontier cabins. Sometimes a name is preserved for us only in the names of trails and streams and frontier posts. However, there is a great body of reports, journals, and letters written by men who went out as official explorers, agents, and servants for government, church, or business—stuff out of which much of the history of the American frontier is fashioned.

These records are more than written words on paper. The stained and worn notebook, the ragged and torn bits of paper are in themselves a tangible record. Words are blotted and crowded together, for often the pen faltered and the mind clouded with fatigue. To hold in one's hand such documents, to examine them and discover in them something more than the information that the words convey, brings one closer to the event, and to the men who wrote them. The records are in a very real sense living history. For the fortunate one who may have come upon such an account which, through accident or neglect, had been lost, his is an unforgettable experience.

Such documents are often of far greater import than a mere narrative of travel with the day to day entries of distances traversed, of events and hazards of the journey. They record the moves in the great game of empire that was being played out on the North American continent. Lewis and Clark and their men were counters on the chessboard of international politics; every scrap of information on the initiation, progress, and completion of their memorable expedition is significant.

The arrival of the party at the mouth of the Missouri in December 1803 was an immediate threat to the oldest empire in the western hemisphere. The great, undefined territory of Louisiana was already lost to France and within a few months it would be taken over by the aggressive Americans, who knew no boundaries in their lust for land and profits. Somewhere to the west the new American Louisiana bordered on Spanish territory. The ancient city of Santa Fe was within striking distance, and beyond the mountain barriers lay California. Once the Americans pushed their outposts toward New Mexico on the southwest and once they succeeded in getting a foothold on the Pacific coast, the Spanish knew that all the regions north of the Rio Grande were in danger, and they could no longer boast that the South Sea was a Spanish ocean.

When the intentions of the Americans became clear to the Spaniards, their official letters to Mexico City and Madrid were filled with alarm. In great agitation Casa Calvo, Governor General of Louisiana, wrote from New Orleans on March 30, 1804, to Cavallos, Commandant General of the Interior Provinces, that something must be done, for "the moment is a critical one." The Americans were taking "hasty and gigantic steps . . . toward the South Sea, entering by way of the Missouri river and other rivers of the west bank of the Mississippi; furthering their discoveries in that district . . . it is of the greatest importance to restrain in that area the progress of the discoverers who are directing toward that district all their views and voyages . . . making themselves masters of our rich possessions which they desire."[1]

It was too late. By the time Cavallos received this letter, July 18, 1804, the "gigantic step" had been taken. Lewis and Clark had already reached the mouth of the Platte River, six hundred miles on their way.

The story of the exploration of the Lewis and Clark party in 1804-06 is known in detail. Reuben Gold Thwaites transcribed and edited the journals of the two captains together with those of two of their men, Floyd and Whitehouse. These were published in 1904-05 under the title *Original Journals of the Lewis and Clark Expedition.* The manuscript from which this official record of the expedition was compiled is in the form of several small-size notebooks, very different in appearance from the manuscript of the journal published in these pages. Long before the publication of the official record, the journal of another member of the party, Sergeant Gass, was published. In 1916 Milo Quaife discovered the journal of Sergeant Ordway and made this important document a part of the corpus. Maps, letters, and fugitive notes relating to the expedition have found their way into historical collections.

In spite of all the known material dealing with this memorable journey, scholars have had suspicions that there was more to be found. They examined the manuscript notebook journals in the collections of the American Philosophical Society in Philadelphia that had been transcribed by Thwaites, and as they noted the clean appearance of most of them, some wondered if the captains had not first made rough notes, under conditions that would have precluded careful writing, and then used these notes at some later time to post their notebook journals. Were there such notes, and if so, what had happened to them?

The discovery in 1953 in an attic in St. Paul of a second journal, in the form of rough notes in William Clark's handwriting, was a partial answer to their questions. This journal, now in the Western Americana Collection at Yale University, is here presented. It was found among the personal papers of John Henry Hammond, Civil War general, one-time inspector in the employ of the Indian Bureau, frontier entrepreneur, and capitalist. After his death in 1890, his daughter continued to live in the family residence until her death in 1952. Upon the request made by one of the heirs to the estate, the general's papers were turned over to the Minnesota Historical Society for examination. When the curator of manuscripts at the society, Miss Lucile Kane, examined them, she found among them a packet wrapped in a copy of the *National Intelligencer* of Washington, D.C., dated 1805. So tightly was the packet folded that it did not seem possible that it had been opened for years. When I examined its contents, there was no question that here was a rough journal by William Clark. His handwriting was unmistakable.

Further examination revealed that this journal fell naturally into two parts. The first is Clark's day-by-day account from December 13, 1803 to May 14, 1804, recording the events at Camp Dubois, the winter quarters established by the party opposite the mouth of the Missouri River. This part of the journal is of particular importance, for with the exception of a few scattered notes made by the two captains while at Camp Dubois and published by Thwaites, this is the only record we have of the winter of preparation before the expedition began its actual progress up the great river of the West, the Missouri. The second part, beginning on May 14, 1804, is partly in the form of rough field notes in which Clark recorded the sixteen-hundred-mile trip upriver to the Mandan villages, which the party reached in November. From then on, there are only scattered entries in the journal for the winter of 1804-05. The journal ends on April 3, 1805, four days before the party resumed the voyage up the Missouri on the way to the Pacific.

Using these field notes and enlarging upon them, Clark set down day-by-day entries in his notebook journal, which he started the day the party left Camp Dubois. By April 1805 he had filled three of these pocket-size books, the first of a series of notebooks recording the complete journey from Camp Dubois to the Pacific and the return to St. Louis in November 1806. As has been noted, these notebooks have been published in their entirety by Thwaites, as the official record of the expedition. To distinguish between the journals published by Thwaites and the field notes transcribed and printed in these pages, the term "Notebook Journal" will be used hereafter whenever reference is made to the former.

Field notes such as these must have been taken by both Lewis and Clark during the whole journey, and were used in preparing the full text of the Notebook Journal. If they were not destroyed, there is always the chance that more will some day be brought to light, through some such fortunate circumstance as attended the discovery of those printed here.

Those who have followed the trail of Lewis and Clark should have no complaint as to the paucity of written records. As one expert has pointed out, the party was "the writingest crew" in the history of exploration. Besides the two captains, seven of the men kept journals. Four of these seven have been preserved and published. The impressive literary activity of the party was in part the result of strong encouragement from President Jefferson. Ten months before the expedition moved out of its winter quarters at Camp Dubois and up the Missouri, the writing began. In July 1803, Lewis bade goodbye to Jefferson and took the familiar route across the mountains to the forks of the Ohio. There, after frustrating delays, the keelboat was built and made ready, two pirogues were bought, and skeleton crews recruited. On August 31, 1803, the little flotilla headed down the Ohio, and Lewis made his first entry in the first of the many journals. This journal, referred to hereafter as the Ohio Journal, has been edited by Milo Quaife and published by the Wisconsin Historical Society.

At Louisville, Lewis picked up Clark and continued down the Ohio to the Mississippi and up that river to Kaskaskia on the Illinois shore a few miles below St. Louis. Here he left Clark in command and turned over to him his journal. From then on until the party reached the site of the future Camp Dubois on December 12, 1803, the entries in the Ohio Journal were made by Clark. At Camp Dubois on December 13, Clark appears to have picked up the first sheet of paper that came to hand, a map that he had made of the junction of the Ohio and Mississippi, and to have written down on the reverse side his first entry of the Dubois Journal. Until now, despite the abundance of documents relating to the expedition, there has been a gap between the Ohio Journal and the journals of the voyage up the Missouri and back. With the discovery of the Dubois

Journal, we have at last what amounts to an unbroken record of the expedition from Pittsburgh to Camp Dubois and from there to the Pacific and back to St. Louis, from August 1803 to November 1806.

The Dubois Journal is more than a daily record. On many loose sheets of paper of all shapes and sizes, the subject matter is set down in no logical order. Interspersed with the daily entries are bits of information as to the country to the north and west gathered from visitors who came to the camp and from some of the men, lists of Indian tribes that would be encountered, comments on the men in Clark's command and thoughts about the problem of discipline, lists of supplies and equipment delivered by the contractor or bought from nearby farmers, plans for loading the keelboat and pirogues, and hastily scribbled notations of things to be done or remembered.

One question that must have been constantly on Clark's mind was the distance that the party must travel to reach its objective, the Pacific, and the time it would take to go and to return. All matters concerning the preparations for the journey were in some way or other related to this question. On a January night when through the walls of his cabin came the muffled growl of the ice floes as they collided at the junction of the two greatest rivers of the continent, Clark set himself to the task of answering the question, "How long, and how far?" Like many another explorer before him, his maps misled more than they helped. The chart, so painstakingly and meticulously drawn up . . . , attests not only to the over-all accuracy of his estimates but to his awareness of the importance of arriving at some kind of answer.

No one can turn over the scattered sheets on which the Dubois Journal is written without coming closer to a knowledge and understanding of this great Kentuckian, his devotion and courage, his sense of duty and his full commitment to the great adventure that lay ahead. Clark was not a ready writer as was Lewis, who had had a good education. The Kentucky frontier where Clark grew to manhood did not afford opportunities for a formal education. Doggedly he set himself to the task of keeping a journal. Indeed, one passage that will be noted appears to be a copy-book exercise in composition. . . . His orthography is a puzzle but also a delight. As has been said of another great explorer, Martin Frobisher, "When . . . he entered on one of his rare and hazardous adventures with the pen, he created spelling absolutely afresh, in the spirit of simple heroism with which he was always ready to sail out into strange seas" (Havelock Ellis, *Dance of Life,* New York, 1923, p. 165).

Whatever conclusions Clark had reached during the winter, as he tried to foresee the trials ahead, were now to be tested. Spring had come and the ice that had barred all passage had long since gone. The boats were loaded, the party fully outfitted, organized, and ready to move. At this time Clark had to decide what should be done with the journal he had kept at Camp Dubois. Instead of putting it in the hands of someone in St. Louis, or sending it to his brother in Louisville—a step that would seem logical, since it was written before the party began its exploration—Clark took it along with him. An examination of the reproduction of Document 65 proves that Clark had the Dubois Journal with him at Fort Mandan in November 1804. On a large, heavy sheet of paper he had made an entry for November 30. Although this entry gives only the day of the month, the Notebook Journal for the same date in 1804, recounts the same incidents. On the verso Clark had written, "Genl Jonathan Clark Near Louisville, Kentucky." In another position on the sheet he had written the address a second time. If the paper is folded along the old folds, this last address comes on the reverse side of the packet. In the left-hand corner of the sheet Clark wrote, "Notes at Wood River in 1803-4." There can be no doubt that the packet was made up and sealed at Fort Mandan; for when the seal was broken, a hole was made in the manuscript, resulting in a break in one of the sentences in the entry for November 30. . . . We do not know why Clark decided to take the Dubois Journal up the Missouri, but there can be no doubt that he did.

On the same date on which Clark made his last entry in the Dubois Journal, May 14, 1804, he began a second series of notes, which I shall refer to as the River Journal. It records the sixteen-hundred-mile voyage up the Missouri to the winter quarters established at the Mandan villages, continues with scattered entries through the winter of 1804-05, and ends on April 3, 1805, when the party was ready to continue westward.

As one reads through the pages of the River Journal, many questions arise. There is no doubt that it was written by Clark, with a few exceptions that will be noted in the text. However, at the time he began this journal he also began the first of his three notebook journals, covering the same period, from May 14, 1804, to April 7, 1805. The difference between these and the rough notes published here is striking. They are cleanly written in pocket books with few emendations. In contrast, this journal—for the Dubois period and for the journey up the Missouri—is for the most part written on fragments of paper that were at hand: coverings of letters that Clark or Lewis had received, and small sheets which when measured were found to be the same size as the notebooks carried by the party and from which they were obviously torn. Their appearance reflects the urgency, the hazards, and the unending labor, as the little flotilla fought its way upstream against the relentless current of the mighty river. When Clark wrote at the end of a day's struggle, "We Com too and Camped," the relief that the words convey can be sensed by anyone who examines the bits of paper on which they are written. Crowded, crabbed, and blotted, they are indeed rough notes, these "scripts" as Clark once called them. On one occasion his notes blew overboard and he was compelled to refer to the journals of the men in order to complete his entry for that day. I believe that these notes were in many instances made on the keelboat during the day's voyage. At convenient times Clark wrote up the same entries in his Notebook Journal, using these rough notes for reference.

Having used the rough notes to post his journal, why did Clark keep them? He was carrying out Jefferson's wishes as both he and Lewis understood them. For years the President had seized upon every bit of information about the vast areas that reached westward to the Pacific. No travelers' tales, no speculations, passed unheeded. Even before the purchase of Louisiana, Jefferson was busy with the organization of the party of exploration. The camp at Dubois had been established, the preparations were going forward, before the treaty of 1803 was fulfilled by the transfer of the territory from France to the United States. In the very precise instructions that he gave to Lewis, he insisted that a careful and detailed journal should be kept, not only by the two captains but by any of the men under their command who were literate and who could be induced to make their own records. There were to be as many journals kept as possible, so that in case of accidents from the unforeseeable hazards of travel, some record would be preserved. Jefferson urged that the two captains seize upon every opportunity to communicate with him, for he was deeply concerned and involved in the great enterprise. Both Lewis and Clark felt the responsibility placed upon them by the President and strove to carry out his instructions to the very best of their abilities. In preserving these rough notes, Clark was mindful, I believe, of the wishes of his commander-in-chief. The more journals, the less likelihood that any scrap of information would be lost.

By April 1805 the long winter that had tested the fortitude of the men, often to the limit, was over, and all was in readiness for the party to continue on its way west. The keelboat was waiting to return to St. Louis. The time had come to send to Jefferson the report of their progress for which he had so long and anxiously waited.

Six months before, in September 1804, preparations had been made to send Jefferson such a report of the journey up to that time. Indeed, before the party set out from Camp Dubois, Clark had indicated that at some convenient time one of the pirogues would be sent back with dispatches. By September it was time to carry out this plan. Lewis presumably prepared his reports and Clark made a packet of the rough notes, "those scripts" as he called them, that he had taken from May 14 to September 23. For an outside covering he used a large heavy sheet of paper, on one side of which he had made the entries for September 20-23. On the verso he wrote the following address:

> Genl, Jona Clark
>   of
> Kentucky Sept 20th
> To the 22nd of Septr 1804
> To the Care of Genl. Jona. Clark
> Near Louisville Kty
> To be opened by Capt. W. Clark
> or Capt. Meriwether Lewis.

The question immediately comes to mind why Clark decided to send these rough notes to his brother in Louisville rather than to Jefferson. Any answer to this question would be pure speculation. Certainly the two captains must have known that Jefferson would have welcomed any information, particularly such rough notes as Clark had taken. It has been suggested to me that perhaps Lewis was also keeping a journal for this part of the trip and that he intended to send that to the President. The evidence for this will be presented shortly. In any event, neither Lewis' reports nor Clark's "scripts" were sent downriver: it was impossible to release the pirogue to carry back the packets at this time. . . . The only hope of getting information to Jefferson before winter prevented all communication was to meet some trading boat on its way to St. Louis with a crew that could be entrusted with the dispatches. No boat came by, and everything was taken up to Fort Mandan.

However, Jefferson had received some news about the party's progress even before it reached the Fort in November 1804. In a letter to Reuben Lewis, Meriwether's brother, dated Washington, November 6, the President wrote,

> We have lately received through a channel meriting entire confidence, advice that on the 4th of Aug. he [Lewis] was at the mouth of the river Plate, 600 miles up the Missouri, where he had met a great council of the Missouris, Panïs & Ottos . . . Two of his men has deserted from him . . . He was then setting out up the river. One of his boats & half of his men would return from his winter quarters. In the Spring he would leave about a fourth where he wintered to make corn for his return & proceed with the other fourth.[2]

A few days later a letter from Auguste Chouteau dated St. Louis, November 20, informed Jefferson that the party would presumably winter at the Mandan villages.[3] These letters show that in early August some trader did meet the party and brought the news to St. Louis. At that time the two captains were still holding to their original intention of sending one of the pirogues back, and apparently did not wish to trust their dispatches to this person, whoever he was. By September, as noted, it was impossible to send back the pirogue, and no other trader appeared.

Lewis and Clark were, of course, unaware that Jefferson had received any information as to their whereabouts. This added to their concern and to their determination to send as complete a report as possible from Fort Mandan, as soon as the river was open in the spring. The question of what the two captains decided to send is of great importance in any discussion of the provenance of the journal published here.

They had with them at the Fort in April 1805 the Notebook Journal in three separate notebooks, and this journal, composed of rough notes and divided into the sections I have referred to as the Dubois Journal and the River Journal. Part of the River Journal had been wrapped up in September and addressed to Louisville. After September 23, 1804, the River Journal takes on another distinction. It is quite different in physical appearance from the section that precedes it. The entries are in Clark's hand but are written neatly, with few emendations and on large sheets of paper. The size of one of these sheets, Document 60, is 40¾

inches long and 13 wide. These are not rough notes, and could not have been written in the field. They must have been copied from notes for that part of the journey. The question of what happened to the originals, and the significance of this variation in the physical character of the documents, will be considered shortly.

The preparation of reports and dispatches to be sent downriver was only part of the hectic activity at Fort Mandan just before the party ventured westward. The pirogues that had come up the river and the keelboat which was to return to St. Louis were badly in need of repair. Additional pirogues had to be built to carry the men and their provisions. Stores had to be sorted and equipment repaired and made ready. The boxes and crates of specimens had to be packed and loaded onto the keelboat. Both the Notebook Journal and the River Journal reflect the urgency of the days and the pressure that all hands felt. There was little time for writing, as both the journals show.

This is all reflected in a letter Lewis wrote to Jefferson from Fort Mandan on April 7, 1805, the day the party resumed its voyage westward. This letter is of the utmost importance in determining whether the journal was sent downriver. In it Lewis noted that he was forwarding an invoice of specimens and instructions as to their disposal. Then he wrote,

> You will also receive herewith inclosed a part of Capt. Clark's private journal, the other part you will find inclosed in a separate tin box. this journal (is in it's original state, and of course incorrect, but it) will serve to give you the daily detales of our progress, and transactions. (Capt. Clark dose not wish this journal exposed in it's present state.)

Lewis went on to say that Clark did not object to having one or more copies made by someone Jefferson might select, who would correct the grammatical errors in it. Indeed, he asked that such copies be made and retained until the party's return, adding that such a copy would aid him in compiling his own journal for publication. Neither he nor Clark objected to Jefferson's showing such copies to qualified persons. He continued by reporting his intention to

> dispatch a canoe with three, perhaps four persons, from the extreem navigable point of the Missouri . . . by the return of this canoe, I shal send you my journal, and some one or two of the best of those kept by my men. I have sent a journal kept by one of the Sergeants [Floyd?], to Capt Stoddard, my agent at St. Louis, in order as much as possible to multiply the chances of saving something.[4]

He added that the men had been encouraged to keep journals, and that seven had done so.

The first point to note in this letter is Lewis' reference to what I believe is the present journal, which he calls a "private journal"; it is being sent in two parts, one part "herewith inclosed" and the other part "inclosed in a separate tin box"; it would give Jefferson "the daily details of our progress, and transactions." The question whether Clark's journal was a private one or not will be discussed later. The more important point is what Lewis meant by the "two parts."

The first answer to this question that comes to mind is, of course, the two parts of the journal printed here, namely the Dubois Journal—December 13, 1803, to May 13, 1804—and the River Journal. I do not think that this is the division Lewis had in mind. The Dubois Journal had been prepared for delivery to Jonathan Clark. There seems to be no good reason for sending it to Jefferson, who was interested in the progress of the party up the Missouri. While the party was at Camp Dubois, Lewis was in constant communication with Jefferson, reporting what went on there and in St. Louis. Evidence, weighty though not conclusive, will be presented shortly to show that the Dubois Journal did go to Jonathan as Clark had intended, and the three notebooks containing the official journal were sent to Jefferson at this time. However, these notebooks could not be one of the two parts referred to here, for Lewis specifically mentions that it was Clark's journal in its original state that was in two parts.

This being the case, the journal Lewis referred to in his letter to Jefferson must be Clark's River Journal, a proposition supported by two pieces of evidence. While Lewis was preparing his reports, Clark took enough time off from his many duties to write, with Lewis' help, a short note to the President. Since we have only the rough draft of the letter, and since it contains evidence bearing on this problem that cannot be overlooked, I present it in its entirety. The portions of the draft that are in Lewis' hand are in italics.

Fort Mandan April 1st 1805

Sir

<As Capt. Lewis has not Leasure to Send write a correct Coppy journal of our Proceedings & c.> *It being the wish of Capt. Lewis* I take the liberty <by the> request of Captain Lewis to send you to send you for your own perusal perusal, the notes which I have taken in the form of a journal in their original state. You will readily perceive in reading over those notes, that many parts are incorrect, principally owing to the variety [of] information received at different times, *I most sincerely wish that leasure had permited me to offer them in a more correct form. Receive I pray you my unfained acknoledgements for your friendly recollection of me in your letters to my friend and companion Capt. Lewis, and be assured of the sincere regard with which I have the honor to be your most Obt. & Humble Servt.*[5]

The key sentence in this letter is in Clark's hand, "the notes which I have taken in the form of a journal in their original state." This, I believe, can only refer to the River Journal. It should also be noted that the description "in its original state" is the same that Lewis employed in his letter about Clark's journal.

Related to the problem of the two parts of the journal is the question whether the River Journal as it was found in the attic in St. Paul in 1953 was sent to Jefferson in its entirety. The evidence on this point might easily be overlooked by anyone examining the documents, but it is nonetheless important. At the head of each document on which the River Journal is written there is a notation giving the dates of the entries that were put down on that particular document. Since the journal is on loose sheets of paper, this was obviously done to facilitate their arrangement in chronological order. (There are some fragments not so dated that I have had to fit into their proper places; such arrangement has been noted.) These date headings are in neither Clark's nor Lewis' handwriting. From the character of the ink, they appear to have been written at some time after Clark had written the original. Since they are very brief, giving only the month and day of the month, any conclusion as to their authorship must be tentative. From a comparison of the dates at the heads of letters written by Jefferson and by Nicholas Biddle, it is my present belief that they were written by Biddle, whose part in the handling of these documents will be discussed later.

More important than the question of the authorship of the dates at the head of each document is the point that their consecutive dating is an indication of the unity of the River Journal. All of the papers were in the hands of Jefferson or Biddle (or some unknown person) at the time the dates were written. There is however one exception, Document 67 [included in *The Field Notes of Captain William Clark*], carrying the entry for November 30, 1804. As has been noted, this sheet was used by Clark at Fort Mandan to wrap up the Dubois Journal, which he addressed to his brother. Therefore, the Dubois Journal presumably went to Louisville and the River Journal to Washington. I have no way of knowing when the two came together as I found them in St. Paul. It is reasonable to suppose that they were combined by Clark at some later date.

To continue with the question of the "two parts" of the journal in its "original state" described by Lewis in his letter to Jefferson, I cannot escape the conclusion that one part was composed of the rough notes of the River Journal from May 14 to September 23, 1804, which Clark had previously sealed up to send to his brother. I believe that the seal was torn at the Mandans, and that these notes were sent downstream with the others intended for Jefferson. Document 56, which had been used as a wrapper, carries the "Biddle" date, as do the other documents that had been in the packet. It is my belief that the other part of the journal was the clean copy of the field notes that Clark took for the remainder of the trip, a copy made during the winter. (This copy also carries the Biddle dating.) That the clean copy is dated in sequence with the rough notes is the basis for my conclusion that it is the second of the two parts of Clark's River Journal. What became of the rough notes from which the copy was made is a question open to speculation which will be referred to again.

It is quite possible that Clark intended to copy all of the rough notes. There is a note of embarrassment in Clark's letter to Jefferson—"I most sincerely wish that leasure had permitted me to offer them in a more correct form." Although this sentence was written by Lewis, it is reasonable to assume it expressed Clark's feeling about the matter. Sometime during the winter he began copying his notes, but the pressure of preparations for continuing the journey, and the need to finish the map he intended to send to Jefferson prevented him from completing the task. He simply combined the uncopied rough notes with the finished clean copy and sent the whole thing as we have it to the President—thus the "two parts," one part enclosed with Lewis' reports and the other in a tin box. There is a more obvious explanation for the phrase "two parts," namely that all of Clark's journal may have been too bulky to have been enclosed in the packet Lewis was making up and it was arbitrarily divided.

In this examination of Lewis' letter to Jefferson one more point needs to be commented upon. Lewis describes Clark's journal as a "private journal." On these words, and on Clark's expressed wish that he did not want his journal shown to everyone, rests the contention that this was his private diary. Nowhere except in Lewis' letter can I find it referred to as such. Clark merely thought it was not in a "correct form." The day-by-day entries in the Notebook Journal and in this journal are similar but not identical. Matters that under any definition of the term would be regarded as private are found in both. It is inconceivable to me that Clark would record the courses and distances of each day's journey, or the identification of geographical features, in a diary devoted to private matters. Furthermore, Lewis wrote that this journal will "give you [Jefferson] daily detales of our progress and transactions." I do not believe it to be a private journal, in any accepted sense of the word, but a second journal kept for the reasons that I have already given. Clark simply did not want it to be handed around generally until a fair copy had been made.

There is some slight evidence to suggest that Lewis kept his own journal of the trip up the Missouri to the Mandans. In his Mandan letter to Jefferson he assured the President that when the party reached the headwaters of the Missouri, he would send back by canoe his journal and one or two of those kept by the men. There was no opportunity to carry out this plan, and it was not until the party returned to St. Louis that the journals of the two captains were delivered to Jefferson. It is impossible to determine whether the words "my journal" in Lewis' letter refer to a journal he had been keeping from the outset of the expedition or to one he intended to keep for the remainder of the trip.

One other piece of evidence on this point comes to mind. Lewis had a hand in helping Clark write his short note of April 1, 1805, to Jefferson. We must rely on the rough draft quoted above, and too much weight cannot be given to the first two lines, which are in Clark's hand—"As Capt. Lewis has not Leasure to Send write a correct Coppy journal of our Proceedings &c." The letter continues, in Clark's hand, that he is sending his journal in its original

state at Lewis' request. About all that can be deduced from this is that the two captains regretted that a correct copy was not being sent. The words apply as well to the journal printed here as they do to a hypothetical journal kept by Lewis. The three Notebook Journals were also sent to the President. All of the entries in the first two are Clark's, with only a few exceptions. In the third notebook Lewis made entries for a ten-day period when Clark was on a hunting trip. One other entry was made by Lewis before the party left Fort Mandan; all the others are in Clark's hand. I do not think there is enough available evidence to support a conclusion that Lewis was keeping a journal on the first leg of the journey.

There is no question in my mind that the three Notebook Journals were sent to the President along with Clark's rough notes. In a letter of Jefferson, December 22, 1805, to Benjamin Smith Barton, the evidence on which this conclusion is based is hardly open to question. Barton, an accomplished botanist, member of the American Philosophical Society, and an old friend of Jefferson, had promised to assist Biddle in preparing the history of the expedition. Because of the importance of this letter, I give it in its entirety:

> Washington, Dec. 22, 1805
>
> Dear Sir
>
> Under another cover I send you drawings & specimens of the seed, cotton & leaf of the cotton tree of the Western country, received from Genl. Wilkinson at St. Louis. To these I must add that it appears from the journals of Lewis & Clarke that the boughs of this tree are the sole food of the horses up the Missouri during the winter. Their horses having on a particular occasion gone through extraordinary fatigue, bran of the maïs [maize] was ordered for them, which they refused, preferring their ordinary food the boughs of this tree, a few of which are chopped off from the tree with a hatchet every evening & thrown into their pen. Accept affectionate salutations & assurances of great esteem & respect.
>
> Th. Jefferson[6]

There are two references in Clark's rough notes concerning this Indian practice of feeding horses on cottonwood. . . . Both are very brief, and lack the details given by Jefferson to Barton. However, if one turns to Lewis' entry in the Notebook Journal for February 12, 1805, one finds the source of Jefferson's information. For purposes of comparison I quote the relevant portion of Lewis' entry:

> Drewyer [Drouillard] arrived with the horses about the same time, the horses appeared much fatieged I directed some meal brands [bran] given them . . . but to my astonishment found that they would not eat it but preferred the bark of the cottonwood which forms the principall article of food usually given them by their Indian masters in the winter season . . . the Indians in our neighborhood . . . put their horses in their lodges at night. in this situation the only food of the horse consists of a few sticks of the cottonwood . . .[7]

Jefferson must have had this entry before him when he wrote to Barton. The similarity of the two passages is obvious: the fatigued horses, their refusal to eat bran, and "the particular occasion," Drouillard's arrival with the worn-out animals. When he wrote that this incident was drawn from the journals of Lewis and Clark, he could have meant only the Notebook Journals. I can find no other description of this practice among the Indians in any other material related to the expedition that Jefferson could have seen in December 1805. The brief references in Clark's rough notes could not have been the basis for Jefferson's circumstantial account in his letter to Barton.

It would seem reasonable to expect that Lewis would have notified Jefferson that he was sending along the three Notebook Journals. However, there is nothing in the correspondence that refers to them in any way. One is puzzled by the words in Lewis' Mandan letter, where he wrote that Clark's journal in its original state "will serve to give you the daily detales of our progress and transactions." Certainly if Jefferson was to have the Notebook Journals, he would get a clearer idea of the "progress and transactions" of the party than he could from Clark's rough notes.

It was, of course, a wise decision to send both Clark's rough notes and the Notebook Journals downriver. To expose them to the hazards of travel to the Pacific and back was too great a risk. Furthermore, Jefferson's instructions to Lewis as to the keeping of journals, their preservation, and their transmission to the government had been very specific. He wrote that observations were to be taken "with great pains and accuracy" and "several copies of these, as well as other notes, should be made at leisure times & put into the care of the most trustworthy of your attendants to guard, by multiplying them, against the accidental losses to which they will be exposed." The President went on to say that Lewis should avail himself of any trader "to communicate to us at seasonable intervals, a copy of your journal, notes and observations."[8] The two captains tried to carry out Jefferson's instructions as faithfully as possible by taking and keeping rough notes as well as posting their notebooks and urging the men to do the same. Unable to depend on the safe transmission of documents to St. Louis before the spring of 1805, they now prepared to send back nearly all the documents they had, which included the rough notes as well as the Notebook Journals and the journal that Sergeant Floyd had kept until his death in August 1804. Lewis sent the latter to Captain Stoddard at St. Louis.[9]

During those crowded days in early April the two captains found time to write to others who were awaiting news of their progress, and these letters give some additional information on the variety of material, documentary and otherwise, that was sent downriver. Lewis got off a long, descriptive letter to his mother, assuring her of his good health and the high spirits of the party as it prepared for its adventure westward.[10] Clark wrote to his old friend, Governor William Henry Harrison, a long letter full of detail about the trip so far. Those who have been inclined to

compare unfavorably Clark's literary efforts with Lewis' should note the straightforward and spare prose of this letter.[11] He also wrote a "hasty scrawl" to his brother-in-law, William Croghan, apologizing for its brevity and adding, "I must therefore take the liberty of refuring you to my brother to whome I have inclosed a Map and some sketches relative to the Indians."[12] Since, as we have seen, two packets had been addressed to his brother Jonathan, Clark's words here are worth notice, particularly if they are considered together with a brief letter to Captain Amos Stoddard at St. Louis. Stoddard was the military commander at St. Louis and the official representative of the United States when the transfer of the territory of Louisiana from France to the United States was consummated. He was in close touch with Lewis and Clark during the whole Dubois period. He had been instructed by the Secretary of War, General Dearborn, to cooperate fully with the two commanders of the exploring party and to afford them every assistance possible. There seems no doubt that the Virginian, the Kentuckian, and the Connecticut Yankee became strong friends. Before Lewis left, he designated Stoddard as his agent in St. Louis, and in the event that Stoddard could not carry out this assignment Charles Gratiot was to take over.

We have only the rough draft of this letter—written, incidentally, on the same sheet of paper as the rough draft of Clark's letter to Jefferson. It does not specify to whom the letter was written, nor does it carry a date. From the wording of the letter, and from the fact that Stoddard was the man chosen by Lewis to receive communications from the party and to forward them, there can be no doubt that Stoddard was the intended recipient. Because of the importance of this letter, I present it in full:

> DSir
>
> I must request the favour of you to send by some safe conveyance as early as possible a red box containing some specimens & papers of consequence [?] to my brother Genl. Jonathin Clark of Kentucky as Directed on the top of the Box. R. Worvington the Bearer of this is intrusted with duplicates & papers of considerable consequence which I wish lodged in the hands of my brother in Kentucky be so good as to furnish this man with a publick horse if you have one which may be returned to you by the post rider. I do not think it worth while to enter into a detaill of occurrences as Capt. Lewis has written you fully on that subject Yrs. &c.[13]

It may well be that Clark was sending his brother the Dubois Journal which, as we have seen, he took up to Fort Mandan and addressed to Jonathan in November 1804. This would certainly belong under the heading "papers of consequence." Among the other papers entrusted to Corporal Wafvington (who was in command of the soldiers sent back to St. Louis) for delivery to Jonathan with all possible speed were "sketches relative to the Indians" that Clark in his letter to Croghan said he was sending to Louisville. The word "duplicates" suggests that Clark was sending the rough notes that he had made of the trip for the period from September 23, 1804, to April 2, 1805, and from which, as we have noted, he made a clean copy.

There is, however, another explanation for the term "duplicates," suggested by the mention of "rough notes" in a letter written by Clark to Nicholas Biddle in 1811. Before presenting this letter, events that occurred after the return of the party and before the letter to Biddle was written need to be briefly indicated. Both captains knew of Jefferson's interest in seeing the history of the expedition published as soon as possible. This project was delayed, first by the official duties that both men assumed immediately following their return, and then by the death of Lewis in 1809. The task of directing the publication devolved on Clark. Under the constant urging of Jefferson, he finally got in touch with Nicholas Biddle of Philadelphia, who agreed to write the story. It was understood that Clark would help in the enterprise and that Biddle would have at his disposal all the records of the expedition.

In the course of his correspondence with Biddle, Clark wrote from St. Louis, January 24, 1811, the following brief note:

> I hope you have received my several letters my new map, and sundry other papers relative to such information as I could collect. Inclosed I sent you some rough notes which I made at the Mandans the 1st year of my tour, perhaps you may Collect from this something which you may wish to Know. *A Copy of these notes were sent to Mr. Jefferson from the Mandans* &c. I send this as I have sent several other papers thro' the Secty. of War. [Italics mine][14]

If Clark's memory was correct after six years, the rough notes made at the Mandans were copied and the copy was sent to the President. I do not think that this refers to the clean copy of the field notes of the River Journal from September 23, 1804, to April 3, 1805, which went to Jefferson. The rough notes Clark mentions in this letter to Biddle were made at the Mandans, not on the journey upstream. After he made a copy of these for Jefferson, he either carried them to the Pacific and back to St. Louis, or he sent them to someone. He did not destroy them, for they were in his possession in 1811. There is the possibility that these were the "duplicates" mentioned in Clark's letter to Stoddard and which the latter was to send to Jonathan.

It is hazardous to speculate about which of the papers sent to Jefferson might have been the copy of notes made at the Mandans, but there is the following possibility. While the party was at Fort Mandan, Clark prepared for the Secretary of War a tabulated statement containing names, languages, numbers, trade, and general information concerning the Indian tribes that lived along the banks of the Missouri, and with which the party had come in contact thus far on the journey. Thwaites has pointed out that two copies were made, one of which was sent to the Secretary of War and was probably burned when the British raided Washington in 1814.[15] Thwaites found the second copy in the Lewis and Clark collection in the American Philosophical Society. This "Statistical View" with "additional Remarks" was presented to Congress by Jefferson with his

message of February 9, 1806. It is found in the American State Papers, Indian Affairs, *1*, 705-43, and in the Thwaites edition of the Notebook Journals, Vol. 6, under the heading "Ethnology: Eastern Indians."

To return to Clark's letter of 1811 to Biddle, we see that either he had sent these rough notes to Biddle enclosed with his map and "sundry other papers" or he was sending them with the letter quoted. The last sentence may be confusing, for he told Biddle, "I send this as I have sent several other papers thro' the Secty. of War." It is not unlikely that he was corresponding with Biddle through the Secretary of War and here is telling Biddle that he had sent the copy of rough notes made at the Mandans to the Secretary in 1805 as he had sent other papers. If the above interpretation is correct, then the copy made at Fort Mandan for Jefferson got to him through the Secretary of War, and was later destroyed as Thwaites suggests. The rough notes were retained by Clark and may have gone to Jonathan Clark at Louisville, to be reclaimed by William on his return and then sent to Biddle in 1811.

Although there is no evidence in Jonathan's diary, or in his papers for 1805 and thereafter, that he ever received anything from his brother William, it can, I think, be concluded that a military messenger—Corporal Warfington, perhaps—galloped off to Louisville on a "publick horse" with a bulky package in his saddle bags. Still another bit of evidence may have some bearing on the matter. In the appendix to the Notebook Journals published by Thwaites there is a copy of a newspaper account which appeared in the Boston *Centinel* for July 13, 1805. It appears to have been taken from a story printed in the *Kentucky Gazette* under the dateline Lexington, June 18, 1805. The paper reported the arrival of an express with dispatches from the winter quarters of the exploring party. It went on to say,

> letters were received from Captain *Clark* to his correspondents in *Kentucky*. A gentleman from *Jefferson* County [Louisville?], has obligingly favored the Editor of the *Kentucky Gazette* with the following account, which he obtained from one of the men who returned with the express, and from letters from some of the party.[16]

This means only that Kentucky, and presumably Clark's brother Jonathan, knew of the return of the keelboat, that someone had been interviewed, and that "letters . . . from Captain Clark" and "from some of the party" had been received. The account goes on to say that Lewis and Clark had sent to the President "an accurate journal, with a map of the country through which they passed."

Now we are ready to review the documents which Charles Gratiot, who was acting as Lewis' agent in the absence of Stoddard, received when the keelboat with its diverse cargo tied up at the levee in St. Louis on May 20, 1805.

> 1. Lewis' letter to Jefferson, April 7, 1805, and with it Clark's River Journal, published here. According to Lewis, part of it was enclosed in his letter and part was in a tin box.

2. Clark's Dubois Journal, published here, probably sent to his brother as "papers of consequence."

3. The three Notebook Journals, perhaps in the two tin boxes that Gratiot forwarded to the Secretary of War.

4. A copy of the rough notes that Clark took at the Mandans in 1804-05, which in 1811 he remembered he had sent to Jefferson, and which was probably embodied in the *Statistical View of the Indian Nations* that accompanied Jefferson's Message to Congress, February 6, 1806.

5. Possibly the originals of the above. These may be the "Indian Sketches" that Clark said (in his letter to Croghan) he was sending to his brother, or the "duplicates" he referred to in his letter to Stoddard.

6. Clark's map, perhaps a copy, which according to his letter to Croghan he sent to Jonathan.

7. Clark's map which Jefferson received. This will be mentioned later.

8. According to the index of letters received by Jefferson, a "personal letter" from Lewis to Jefferson. This letter has not been found.[17]

9. A letter from Lewis to Jefferson, dated Fort Mandan, March 5, 1805, containing information on the Indians' treatment of snake bite.

10. Lewis' letter to Stoddard, mentioned in Clark's letter to Stoddard.

11. Lewis' letter to his mother, from Fort Mandan, dated March 31, 1805.

12. Clark's short note to Jefferson, from Fort Mandan, dated April 1, 1805.

13. Clark's letter to Stoddard, no date.

14. Clark's letter to Croghan, from Fort Mandan, dated April 2, 1805.

15. Clark's letter to Harrison, from Fort Mandan, dated April 2, 1805.

16. Possibly a letter by Clark to his brother, covering the "papers of consequence."

17. Letters by other members of the party, as suggested by the news item in the Boston *Centinel*.

18. Sergeant Floyd's journal, sent to Stoddard, according to Lewis' Mandan letter of April 7, 1805.

19. Lewis' report to the Secretary of War, including public accounts, muster rolls, and information relating to the Indian country, according to Lewis' Mandan letter of April 7, 1805.

20. An invoice of the specimens collected by the party and enclosed with Lewis' letter to the President, with the information that the boxes and trunks containing them would be forwarded by Captain Stoddard. (On this list was another tin box which, much to my relief, contained only insects and mice.)

It is impossible to say with certainty that every item listed above was on the keelboat, or that each one got to its intended destination—particularly those I have listed as going to Jonathan Clark. The difficulty Gratiot and Chouteau must have had in sorting out the cargo of the keelboat, I can appreciate.

There was delay. In a letter to the Secretary of War, dated Vincennes, May 27, 1805, a week after the keelboat arrived, Harrison wrote that the dispatches to Washington would be delayed by nearly a fortnight. He added that he had received Clark's letter by express.[18] Chouteau reported on June 15 that the boxes and trunks were on their way to New Orleans. From there on, it would be General Claiborne's responsibility to see that they were shipped by sea to Washington.[19]

It was late June before Jefferson received word that the keelboat had arrived in St. Louis. In a letter to William Eustis dated Washington, June 25, 1805, he wrote,

> I have the pleasure to inform you that one of Capt Lewis' barges returned to St. Louis brings us certain informaton from him. He wintered with the Mandans, 1609 miles up the Missouri . . . all well, and peculiarly cherished by all of the Indian nations. He has sent in his barge 45 deputies from 6 of the principal nations in that quarter who will be joined at St. Louis by those of 3 or 4 nations between the Missouri and the Missisipi, and will come on here.[20]

The long-awaited dispatches arrived in Washington three weeks later. Lewis' Mandan letter with the enclosures was endorsed as received on July 13, 1805. On the next day Jefferson informed General Dearborn that he was sending his servant over with "Lewis's large map."[21] He also got off a letter to General Claiborne saying that in Lewis' letter he had noted that "6 or 8 packages filled with very curious subjects from the upper country" were to be forwarded to him.[22] These arrived at Monticello on August 12.[23]

During the autumn months of 1805 Jefferson found time to go over the journals, including, I believe, this journal in its "original state." In December he was writing to Barton about the use of cottonwood as fodder for Indian ponies, information that he could only have obtained from the Notebook Journal.

I have been unable to find in the documents of this period any direct reference to this journal. In his letter to Barton, Jefferson wrote of the "Lewis and Clark Journals." In a letter, January 12, 1806, to William Dunbar, another member of the American Philosophical Society in frequent correspondence with the President, Jefferson wrote,

> We have Capt. Lewis's notes of the Missouri to his wintering place at Fort Mandan, and a map of the whole country watered by the Missouri & Columbia composed by himself last winter on very extensive information from Indians & traders, in which he expresses a good deal of confidence.[24]

One month later, and a week before his message to Congress in which he reported on the expedition, Jefferson wrote to his friend the Comte de Volney of the news from the west.

Our last news of Captn Lewis was that he had reached the upper part of the Missouri and had taken horses to cross the highlands to the Columbia river. He passed the last winter among the Mandans 1610 miles above the mouth of the river. So far he had delineated it with as great accuracy as will probably be ever applied to it, as his courses & distances by mensuration were corrected by almost daily observations of Latitude and Longitude. With his map he sent us specimens or information of the following animals not before known to the northern continent of America.[25]

On February 19, 1806, Congress and the public were officially informed that Jefferson had received Lewis' letter. In his message to Congress he reported:

> On the 8th of April, 1805, they [the exploring party] proceeded up the river in pursuance of the objects prescribed to them. A letter of the preceding day, April 7th, from Capt. Lewis is herewith communicated. During his stay among the Mandans he had been able to lay down the Missouri according to courses & distances taken on his passage up to it [Fort Mandan] . . . & to add to the actual survey of this portion of the river a general map of the country between the Mississipi and the Pacific from the 34th to the 54th degree of Latitude . . . Copies of this map are now presented to both houses of Congress. With these I communicate also a statistical view . . .[26]

Clark's name is not mentioned in any of these communications. Jefferson, in all three of the passages quoted above, refers to the map of the Missouri as Lewis' map. But the map was the work of Clark, the cartographer of the exploring party. He had been at work on it from the start of the expedition. According to his letter to Croghan, a copy had been sent to Jonathan. Lewis was in command of the exploration, and it was natural for the President to use Lewis' name in the above statements. In his message to Congress Jefferson's only mention of Clark is to refer to him as second in command. As to this journal in its "original state," Jefferson made no mention of it, for he was obviously carrying out Clark's wishes as expressed in Lewis' Mandan letter of April 7, that it not be handed about and that it should be "retained until our return."

I have attempted to trace this journal from Fort Mandan in April 1805 into the hands of the President. Anyone who attempts to follow it from there to an attic in St. Paul in 1953 is doomed to lose himself in an underbrush of speculation, obscurity, and confusion. There is always the hope that additional material may turn up that will yield enough light so that the trail may be revealed.

Although there are some clues in the documents after 1806, which I shall briefly touch upon, there is nothing substantial enough on which to rest any firm conclusions. The absence of any information as to what happened to these documents is understandable if the reader is reminded of the events following the return of the exploring party to St. Louis. Both captains had long had in mind joint publication of a history of the exploration, and their intention had been ardently encouraged by Jefferson.

However, the publication was long delayed. The appointment of both of the captains to government office soon after their return meant that they were soon involved in official business. Lewis became Governor of the Territory of Louisiana, and Clark took over the duties of Principal Agent of Indian Affairs for the Louisiana Territory. There was little spare time to collect the records of the expedition that were already scattered, some in Washington, some in Philadelphia, and probably some in Louisville.

In November 1806, shortly after the party's return, Lewis left St. Louis for Washington. In a letter written ten years later to Correa da Serra, Jefferson gives us the only firm evidence as to what notebooks Lewis had with him when he and the President met in 1806 and what was done with them. Jefferson wrote that Lewis had with him,

> Ten or twelve such pocket volumes, Morocco bound, as that you describe, in which, in his own hand writing, he had journalised all occurences, day by day, as he travelled. They were small 8vos and opened at the end for more convenient writing. Every one had been put into a separate tin case, cemented to prevent injury from wet. But on his return the cases, I presume, had been taken from them, as he delivered me the books uncased . . . we were willing to give to Lewis and Clarke whatever pecuniary benefits might be derived from the publication [of the journals] and therefore left the papers in their hands.[27]

From this letter certain conclusions may be drawn that have some bearing on the provenance of the documents published here. As has been noted above, Jefferson had received the three notebook journals of the trip from May 14, 1804, to April 7, 1805. I have stated on the basis of the available evidence that he also had these field notes used by Clark to write the entries in the three notebooks. Jefferson now had in his hands the morocco-bound notebooks recording the rest of the trip. It is my opinion that Jefferson's words, "we . . . therefore left the papers in their [Lewis' and Clark's] hands," refer to all the papers: these field notes with the exception of the Dubois Journal, the three notebook journals, and the morocco-bound journals. As I have pointed out, the clean and unworn appearance of the latter has led many to believe that they could not have been carried on the trip. Yet Lewis delivered them to Jefferson uncased. Certainly there was not enough time between the arrival of the party at St. Louis and the departure of Lewis for Washington for the two captains to copy whatever rough notes they had into these clean journals. The only reasonable conclusion is that the entries in the morocco notebooks were written from field notes while the trip was being made, and when each notebook was full, it was cemented into one of the tin boxes. Apparently the practice Clark instituted at the outset, of copying the field notes into the notebooks, was continued throughout the whole trip. It is quite possible that during the long winter at Fort Clatsop at the mouth of the Columbia, the two captains were busy copying their field notes of the journey thus far and sealing them up in the tin boxes. For the eastward trip, entries in the notebooks must have been made as the party proceeded. What happened to the field notes? Were they destroyed, were they preserved? There is no answer to this question. Scholars may hope that sometime they may come to light as did those of the journey from Camp Dubois to the Mandans.

Not until September 1809 was Lewis free to leave St. Louis for a second visit to Washington, a journey that ended fatally. His suicide or murder in a tavern on the Natchez Trace on October 11, 1809, shocked the whole country. To Clark it was a shrewd blow, for the two men—so different in temperament and training—had formed one of the most famous friendships in our annals. Now the task of telling the story of their common experience, out of which this friendship had grown, rested on Clark alone. Not only had he lost a beloved companion but the man whose literary talents Clark would be the first to admit were superior to his own.

In the room in which Lewis died were found two trunks. An inventory of their contents was made on November 23, 1809, more than a month following his death. From this list I have selected several items that appear to have some bearing on the problem of gathering together the documents of the expedition. To the left of the inventory column under the heading "Forwarded" there is a notation of the disposition of each item.

Forwarded	Inventory
Depts:	One small bundle of Letters & Vouchers—of consequence
W. C. [William Clark]:	One Book an Estimate of the western Indians
Th. Jefferson:	One Memorandum Book
Pret. U.S. [James Madison]:	A Transcript of Records &c.
W. C.:	Nine Memorandum books
W. C.:	Sixteen Note books bound in red morocco with clasps
Th. Jefferson:	One bundle of Misceleans. paprs.
W. C.:	Six note books unbound
W. C.:	One bundle of Maps &c.
W. C.:	One do. [bundle] "Ideas on the Western expedition
W.C.:	One do. [bundle] Vocabulary
W.C.:	One do. [bundle] Maps & Charts
Th. Jefferson:	One Bundle of papers marked A[28]

Although there is no specific mention of Clark's map in this list, Jefferson, in a letter to Correa da Serra written five years later, recalled that it had been among Lewis' papers at the time of his death.

Clark arrived in Washington shortly after he received the news of the death of his friend. There he met Isaac A. Coles, Jefferson's former private secretary who was then acting as secretary for the new President, James Madison. In a letter to Jefferson, dated January 5, 1810, Coles reported that Lewis' trunks had arrived and that "they were opened by Genl. Clarke and my self, when every thing of a public nature was given to the Dept. to which it properly

belonged, every thing relating to the expedition to Genl. Clarke, & all that remained is contained in the five little bundles now directed to you."[29]

Appended to the above inventory was a note by Coles, dated Washington, January 10, 1810, describing the condition that the papers were in as he and Clark found them.

> The bundles of Papers referred to in the above memorandum were so badly assorted, that no idea could be given of them by any terms of general description. Many of the bundles containing at once, Papers of a public nature—Papers intirely private, some important & some otherwise with accts. Receipts, & &. They were all carefully looked over, & put in separate bundles. . . . Everything relating to the expedition [was given] to Genl. Clarke.[30]

Three days later, Jefferson wrote from Monticello to Bernard McMahon that after the delivery of the papers to Clark, he took them to Philadelphia, where he intended to take measures "for immediate publication."[31]

That not all the papers relating to the expedition were in Lewis' trunks is suggested by a letter written by Jonathan Clark to his brother George Rogers, dated Louisville, February 3, 1810, in which he reported that William was leaving Washington for Philadelphia, "in search of some of the papers, that he hoped had been sent there, by Governor Lewis—a part of the journals etc. of the trip to the Western oceans, had been sent to him [Clark?] but not the whole."[32]

As has been noted, four years before this letter was written, Jefferson had turned over the records of the expedition to Lewis, who had taken most of them back to St. Louis—but not all, for apparently he had left some in Philadelphia. At the time of his death, as seen from the inventory, Lewis had most of the papers, and in 1810 Clark was in search of the rest. We have no way of knowing whether he had in his possession the journal published here. All we can say is that the records were already scattered.

Even though Clark did succeed in collecting all the material—and the mass of it must have daunted even a man who had faced down a band of hostile Sioux—Clark realized that he must have help if the history was ever to be written. Now it had become something more than ink on paper; it was to be a monument to a shared experience with a departed comrade. After several rebuffs in his search for a collaborator, he turned to Nicholas Biddle.

Biddle, whose name was and still is almost synonymous with Philadelphia, was a young lawyer and literary dilettante. In the future he would leave a mark on American history as a diplomat and as Andrew Jackson's great antagonist. On March 17, 1810, after some hesitation, he agreed to undertake the task of writing the history of the expedition, and he promised to do all in his power to bring it to completion.[33] This meant, first of all, that Biddle had to acquire from Clark all the documents on which he would depend in writing the history. From this time on, Clark wrote often and continued to send him additional material as it came to hand.

To assist Biddle in organizing and integrating the scientific data, Clark had enlisted the help of Benjamin Smith Barton. . . . On May 22, 1810, Clark wrote to him from Louisville that he had been with Biddle at Fincastle and received from him "a Copy of such part of my journal as I had Copied from the Original, which I hope with the assistance of the specimins and what information the young gentleman who will hand you this letter (Mr. George Shannon) Can give you."[34]

This letter may refer to the copy he made of the River Journal after September 23, 1805 . . . , but this is by no means certain, for the phrase "I had Copied" might refer to a copy made by some other person. At any rate, Clark had given Biddle a part of the original journal which, it is my belief, is printed here, and Biddle was handing on at least some of it to Barton.

In January of the next year Clark wrote to Biddle from St. Louis and sent him "some rough notes which I made at the Mandans the 1st year of my tour . . . A Copy of these notes were sent to Mr. Jefferson from the Mandans &c." . . .

These two letters give us the last faint trace of the journals here published. To sum up: we know that Jefferson had these journals, the three notebook journals, and a copy of the Mandan notes in 1805. We know that when Lewis came to Washington in 1806, he brought with him the morocco-bound notebooks that contained the record of the trip from Fort Mandan to the Pacific and return. We know that Jefferson examined them, and I interpret Jefferson's phrase "we left the papers in their hands" to mean that he returned the morocco-bound notebooks and the other journals and papers just mentioned. We know that when Clark arrived in Washington after Lewis' death, all the papers in Lewis' trunks including the morocco-bound notebooks were turned over to him. We do not know whether this journal was in the trunks or whether Clark had brought it with him from St. Louis. We do know that when the River Journal came into Biddle's hands, he dated it consecutively—both the rough notes up to September 23, 1804, and the clean copy after that date. After Biddle was through with the River Journal and the Mandan notes, he probably turned them over to Clark. It is impossible to determine under what circumstances the River Journal was combined with the Dubois Journal which, I believe, was sent from Fort Mandan to Louisville in 1805. Either Clark or some other person brought them together and wrapped them up in a copy of the *National Intelligencer.* One hundred and fifty years later the packet was discovered in an attic in St. Paul.

Here, then, in 1811, the trail ends, for in the correspondence concerning the publication of the history of the ex-pedition and the disposal of the journals there is nothing to isolate this journal from the mass of material, most of which found its way into the collections of the American Philosophical Society in Philadelphia.

When this journal was discovered in St. Paul, I hoped that some inquiry into the life of General Hammond, in whose papers the packet was discovered, and an examination of his other papers, might yield some clue as to their whereabouts from 1811 until their discovery. A report of the effort made to find some solution to the puzzle is, I think, due the reader.

In the trial held in the United States District Court in Minneapolis in December 1953 over the question of ownership of the documents, there was no firm evidence brought out in the examination of witnesses that the family of General Hammond or his heirs ever knew of their existence. Indeed, it was on the initiative of one of the heirs to the estate of the General's daughter that the papers were turned over to the Minnesota Historical Society, with the alleged verbal understanding that after an inventory had been made, they should remain with the Society. No one seemed to have known that such an historical treasure as these documents was in the St. Paul attic, buried in the papers of the General, who had died in 1890. Had the heirs known that such was the case, it is doubtful that they would have initiated steps to have their grandfather's papers transferred to the Society. When the curator sorted out the Hammond papers and came upon the packet containing the journal, she noted that it looked as if it had not been disturbed for years. When she testified in the trial, she pointed out, however, that three small pieces of paper that were later found to be part of the journal were not found in the packet but were loose among the other papers.

Fortunately, in most cases where a collection of documents such as these is discovered, their origin and their history can be traced. There is usually some information from one source or another that will answer the question of how the owner acquired the papers, and the approximate time when they came into his hands. Starting with such data, it is usually possible to trace them back to their origin. In this case, however, there was no such information.

Because of the possibility that some connection between the Clark family and the Hammonds might have existed, the logical place to begin the investigation seemed to be Louisville. Members of the Clark family had lived there for years, and General Hammond and his wife, Sophia Hammond, had also resided there. There was also the possibility that the collection of manuscript material in the Filson Club in Louisville might contain something useful. In Louisville I learned that the General's wife was the daughter of one Nathaniel Wolfe, who had come there in 1838 and began the practice of law. In 1864 General Hammond had been relieved of his duties on General Sherman's staff because of illness. He came to Louisville and married Sophia Wolfe, whose father died in 1865. Perhaps there had been some connection between the Clark and the Wolfe families; some property belonging to the Clark family may have been purchased by Wolfe, and these documents in some way or other may have come into General Hammond's possession when he married Wolfe's daughter. I could find no record of such an exchange of property. It is, of course, impossible to say that Wolfe, a prominent lawyer in Louisville, had no contact with the Clarks, or that some piece of furniture belonging to the Clarks did not at some time or other become the property of the Wolfe-Hammonds. But the collection in the Filson Club contained nothing that would even remotely connect the two families. Nor did I find anything in the Draper Collection of the Wisconsin Historical Society, in the Missouri Historical Society in St. Louis, or in other collections containing Clark papers that referred in any way to the Wolfe family. The trail hopefully begun in Louisville and elsewhere faded into mere conjecture.

There is only one time, so far as is now known, when General Hammond ever saw or handled any documents that Clark may have written. In the trial in Minneapolis, Oliver Wendell Holmes of the National Archives, in direct charge of the papers of the Indian Bureau, presented evidence on this point. His testimony deserves some mention here.

Until his death in 1838, Clark continued to direct Indian relations west of the Mississippi, first as principal agent for the Louisiana Territory, then Superintendent for the Western District and finally as Superintendent of the Central District. Following his death, the office and presumably all of its papers were moved first to St. Joseph, Missouri, then to Atchison, Kansas, and finally, in 1869, to Lawrence, Kansas. In 1878, the government decided to close out the superintendency and bring its papers to Washington. General Hammond, who was for a brief period an inspector in the Indian Bureau, was instructed to proceed to Lawrence, examine, classify, and arrange the official papers, make an inventory of them and box them up and send them to Washington. In the inventory that was presented as an exhibit in the trial, there are a few papers going back to the Clark period and an item described as "one bundle of old maps" and another of "old bills and papers" dated 1830 and 1833.

The presence of a bundle of old maps seemed significant, for in 1924 a bundle of such maps was transferred from the Indian Bureau to the Library of Congress. In this packet Miss Annie Heloise Abel discovered the map which she assumed was the Evans Map, which Clark took up the Missouri in 1804 and which is referred to in the footnotes accompanying this text as the Indian Office Map. Without going into the provenance of the map, Mr. Holmes merely referred to it to give some support to his argument that this map was in the bundle listed by Hammond, and if such a Clark document was included, the present journal might well have been among the papers found by Hammond in Lawrence, Kansas in 1878.

There is nothing in the Hammond papers that would support this conclusion. The diary kept by the General for the period records his trip to Kansas and the execution of orders given him by the Indian Bureau. The official papers were boxed, an inventory of their contents was taken, and the lot sent to Washington. There is not the slightest hint that Hammond ever saw the Clark journal that was found among his papers in St. Paul.

With all due respect to Mr. Holmes' solid and scholarly research, made in an effort to solve this puzzle, it must be admitted that the evidence is far too tenuous to support any conclusions. It is my hope, and I know that I share it with all those who are interested in the history of the American frontier, that further research and perhaps some fortunate discovery of new material will solve this fascinating problem.

However, we have this journal, a valuable addition to our knowledge of an American odyssey which captured the attention and imagination of the American people as they looked westward and wondered what lay beyond the farthest horizon. Across the span of years, these documents enlist us with those men who fought their great protagonist, the Missouri, pouring its flood down "through a vast and unknown barbarism." We feel Clark's excitement when for the first time he looked upon the wide sweep of the plains, and with him our minds reach out to the mountains that lie far to the west. In these days of our narrowed world, it is good to go with him into a new great land, known then only to the Indian and the few fur traders who had penetrated its fastnesses.

Notes

1. A. P. Nasatir, *Before Lewis and Clark: Documents Illustrating the History of the Missouri, 1785-1804* (St. Louis, 1952), 2, 728.

2. Donald Jackson, [ed.,] *Letters of the Lewis and Clark Expedition with Related Documents* (Urbana, Ill., 1962), p. 216, hereafter cited as Jackson. Dr. Jackson has presented in a single volume practically all of the pertinent documents related to the expedition. Those of us who have used these materials scattered in many depositories are indebted to him for bringing them together in such convenient form.

3. Ibid., p. 219 n.

4. Ibid., p. 231-34; Thwaites, [*Original Journals of the Lewis and Clark Expedition, 1804–1806* 8 vols.] 7, 318-21.

5. Jackson, p. 226; Thwaites, *7*, 313.

6. Jackson, p. 272.

7. Thwaites, *1*, 258.

8. Jackson, pp. 61-66; Thwaites, *7*, 247-52.

9. Jackson, p. 232; Thwaites, *7*, 319.

10. Jackson, pp. 222-25; Thwaites, *7*, 309-12.

11. Jackson, pp. 227-30; Thwaites, *7*, 314-16.

12. Jackson, p. 230; Thwaites, *7*, 317.

13. Jackson, pp. 226-27.

14. Ibid., pp. 565-66.

15. Thwaites, *6*, 80.

16. Ibid., *7*, 324-26.

17. Jackson, p. 236 n. Jackson believes that this letter, dated March 30, 1805, was a personal report to Jefferson supplementing Lewis' Mandan letter of April 7, 1805, which was for publication and was presented to Congress with Jefferson's message of February 19, 1806 (Jackson, pp. 298-300; Thwaites, *7*, 328).

18. Jackson, pp. 246-47.

19. Ibid., pp. 248-49.

20. Ibid., p. 249.

21. Ibid., p. 252.

22. Idem.

23. Ibid., pp. 253-54.

24. Ibid., p. 290.

25. Ibid., p. 291; Thwaites, *7*, 327.

26. Jackson, pp. 298-300; Thwaites, *7*, 328.

27. Jackson, pp. 611-13; Thwaites, 7, 394-96.

28. Jackson, pp. 470-72.

29. Ibid., pp. 486-87.

30. Ibid., p. 472.

31. Ibid., pp. 488-89.

32. This letter of Jonathan Clark in the Wisconsin Historical Society Collections is referred to by Jackson, p. 486 n.

33. Jackson, p. 496.

34. Ibid., pp. 548-49.

THE JOURNALS AS LITERARY TEXTS

Albert Furtwangler (essay date 1993)

SOURCE: "Themes for a Wilderness Epic," in *Acts of Discovery: Visions of America in the Lewis and Clark Journals,* University of Illinois Press, 1993, pp. 192-207.

[*In the following essay, Furtwangler examines the Lewis and Clark journals in terms of a literary epic, focusing on such themes as pluralism, heroism, exploration, and the act of writing itself.*]

The term *epic* has often been used to describe the Lewis and Clark expedition. In its loose, modern usage, the word is an adjective that means grand, colossal, larger than life; it has been beaten to death in advertising blurbs for novels, films, and television spectacles. But as a noun, *epic* still has some meaning left as the name for a particular kind of story. An epic tells of extraordinary deeds—wars, travels, and feasts on a scale far beyond our own, even direct encounters with gods and monsters. The heroes of epics meet superhuman adversaries as well as the most threatening or imposing human counterparts, and their heroic actions disclose the full measure of human power, intelligence, and worth.

The Lewis and Clark story seems to fit this pattern very naturally, to be a tale of genuine heroism in early America, for in tracing the Missouri to its source, crossing the Rockies, and encountering new peoples who had long held the West, the Corps of Discovery was challenging great and unforeseen powers. They were testing their own characters against vastness, wilderness, and alien human cultures. Because they survived and succeeded, Lewis, Clark, Sacagawea, and many others in the party have remained visible public heroes in many states—memorialized in statues, parks, monuments, roadside markers, and the names of many schools, towns, counties, festivals, and natural features such as mountains and rivers. The signers of the Declaration of Independence and the delegates who shaped the Constitution are celebrated in the eastern states; the Corps of Discovery is memorialized along the Missouri and in the Pacific Northwest. Clad in rougher clothing, engaged outdoors in gathering food and pressing through plains and forests, they are a far cry from the proud gentlemen who sat deliberating together in Independence Hall. But like their eastern counterparts, these western explorers are remembered as founders of the great American nation.

Frank Bergon stresses the epic qualities of the Lewis and Clark story in the introduction to his popular edition of the journals; in fact, his essay is organized around the idea of epic deeds and epic features in the explorers' writings. "Of course," he admits, "it is only from the hindsight of 180 years that it might be suggested that these journals, with their daily logs of temperature, astronomical observations, tabulations of longitude and latitude, technical descriptions of flora and fauna, anthropological data, misspellings, and neologisms, might serve as an appropriate American epic." Nonetheless, he goes on to praise the journals in well-considered epic terms:

> They tell a heroic story of a people's struggles through a wilderness and the return home. Better than more artfully constructed poems or novels or plays, they embody with the colloquial directness and power of an oral epic the mythic history of a nation. Like ancient epics, they tell the story of the tribe, in this case the story of a people moving west. It is not the story of an individual frontiersman but of a pluralistic, fluctuating community of thirty-five to forty-five people, including soldiers, woodsmen, blacksmiths, carpenters, cooks, French *engagés*, a black slave, a Lemhi Shoshone

woman, and a newborn baby of mixed race, all heading west. In retrospect, that story portrays the fall of one civilization and the rise of another. It dramatizes the relationship of a people to the natural world and the design of a nation committed to the belief that—as William Gilpin expressed it seventy years later—"the *untransacted* destiny of the American people is to subdue the continent."[1]

Here in six sentences are six overlapping stories or themes: an adventure in the wilderness, the origin of a nation, a tribe moving west, a success story of a pluralistic society, a change of civilizations, the rise of a new creed in the midst of nature. Perhaps all six should be further refined and interrelated to bring out *the* central story of America. But certainly all are themes at the heart of American history; all are also central to the story of the Corps of Discovery; and as Bergon is well aware, all are well-worn themes of the epic poems that would have been familiar to educated readers of the early nineteenth century.

Bergon's suggestion calls for a few lines of criticism and several pages of further development. The journals, as we have seen, were never finished for publication to the satisfaction of their authors. "The colloquial directness and power of an oral epic" that Bergon describes is an illusion that only a literary imagination can project back onto these pages. Clark's embarrassment with language forced him to struggle—and now forces the reader to follow him—through many indirect spellings and structures; Lewis has his solecisms, too, and his elaborate passages that are anything but colloquial or direct.

Another strong objection should be raised about pluralism as a guiding principle in this expedition. It is true that the company was made up of many people, mainly enlisted soldiers and common workers, who came to depend on each other for survival. But it was also a strict military company in which the officers were conspicuously privileged over the others. Offenses were severely punished with the lash. And while there were a black man, a Shoshone woman, and many of "mixed race" in the company, there is no evidence that these differences were acknowledged with respect. York, Clark's "servant," was a slave. He sometimes carried a gun and sometimes had a vote in company decisions. But he was also put on display as a kind of woolly black curiosity among the Indians, and when he returned from the West he was again forced into hardships as a slave.[2] Sacagawea rode in the captains' pirogue and shared their quarters along with Charbonneau and their baby; but she, too, could be put down suddenly and have her belt of blue beads snatched from her when it was thought necessary to conclude a good bargain ([Gary E. Moulton, ed. *Journals of the Lewis and Clark Expedition.* 7 vols. to date. Lincoln: University of Nebraska Press, 1981-. Hereafter abbreviated as *Journals.*] 6:73). Members of the company danced with each other often and joined Indians in their dances, and shared their embraces too. But it is hard to tease an abiding sense of fellowship from the surviving records. When the company had achieved its purposes at any location, it moved on, leaving the Indians

there forever. When the expedition was over, its members dispersed. There were few reunions even of individuals. Lewis made a final roll of his men in a report to the secretary of war, in which he held them together by order of rank and with a sharp sense of differences in worth. Some he commended particularly; most are listed just by name and rank over a general commendation for "a just reward in an ample remuneration on the part of our Government"; two are noted as of "no peculiar merit"; two are commended despite short or unsatisfactory service ([Donald Jackson, ed. *Letters of the Lewis and Clark Expedition,* rev. ed. 2 vols. Urbana: University of Illinois Press, 1978. Hereafter abbreviated as *Letters.*] 1:364-69).

Bergon's sense of idealistic pluralism is not the most fitting theme, but there is still much more than coincidence to the three patterns he superimposes: expedition history, American history, and classic epic form. To hold the many, repetitious, and scattered journal records together, a reader has to find some pattern of coherence. An epic pattern is a useful, revealing framework for them. It cannot be fully sustained or fleshed out, but as Bergon explains it, the idea of epic points to some good questions about these writings. It was an idea and an ideal still revered by poets and readers in their time. But its values do not fit comfortably with new ideals of American democratic pluralism, and that discrepancy opens some crucial problems. What kind of hero was Lewis or Clark, or the entire corps that they led? If not pluralism, what was the central theme or principle of their shared experience? And how should readers now attempt to grasp what they wrote: if it resembles an epic, what are its ideal proportions; if it diverges, how should one resist its epic appeal?

In the time of Lewis and Clark, epic poetry was still a cherished, even revered, ideal of literary excellence and patriotic pride. "By the general consent of critics," Samuel Johnson wrote in his *Life of Milton* (1779), "the first praise of genius is due to the writer of an epic poem." Johnson goes on to explain: "Epic poetry undertakes to teach the most important truths by the most pleasing precepts, and therefore relates some great event in the most affecting manner."[3] The epic poet had to be a master of universal knowledge, capable of seeing into the depths of moral truth and presenting them in a composition of dramatic power and exquisite language. Such accomplishments were rare in the history of the world. But it was a point of national pride that in Milton's *Paradise Lost* England had attained a poem that rivaled and, according to some, surpassed the *Iliad* and *Odyssey* of Homer and the *Aeneid* of Virgil. John Dryden, who was himself poet laureate, composed an epigraph to go under Milton's portrait in a new edition of the poem in 1688:

> Three poets, in three distant ages born,
> Greece, Italy, and England did adorn.
> The first in loftiness of thought surpass'd,
> The next in majesty, in both the last:
> The force of Nature could no farther go;
> To make a third, she join'd the former two.[4]

Milton's Christian vision had superseded the pagan morality of the ancients, and his English blank verse attained greater majesty than Virgil's carefully polished Latin. Throughout the eighteenth century, ambitious English poets aspired to write epic poetry and yet despaired of surpassing Milton's achievement. Dryden and Pope gained money and fame by producing elegant translations of Virgil and Homer. They played with epic conventions in mock-epic satires: *Mac Flecknoe, The Rape of the Lock, The Dunciad.* Both poets became revered public figures; both were widely imitated. Yet neither could summon the muse, find the inspiration, or sustain the faith to sing a full epic of his own.

By 1800 there had been a century and more of epic versifying, editing, criticism, and memorizing, which made Homer, Virgil, Milton, Dryden, and Pope the familiar classics of educated readers in England and America. And there was still a felt challenge to create a more adequate epic to express a fuller vision of the universe. In England, Wordsworth was already drafting passages of a long autobiographical poem; its subject was transcendent visions revealed in meetings between the mind and nature. In America a half-dozen poets now forgotten had labored to celebrate the rise of a new nation on a new continent, dedicated to new principles of democracy and freedom.[5]

At the heart of every well-known epic there was a well-defined mythic action, concisely stated in the opening lines. As Bergon indicates, these were great stories about nations as well as heroes. One way of defining *epic* is as the story of a hero, a single person on whom the fate of a race or nation depends. The *Iliad* is about the Trojan War, but the outcome of that conflict depends on Achilles. When he fights among the Greeks they win their battles; when he withdraws, they lose; when he returns, he kills the Trojan leader Hektor and so ensures the complete downfall of Troy. Odysseus and Penelope in the *Odyssey* live out a story of extraordinary marital fidelity. Although Odysseus is alone on a desert island with an enchantress who wants him, he yearns for his own wife and family and labors past monstrous obstacles to return to them. The restoration of this marriage completes the healing of the Trojan War, which originally carried him away—a war that began over the abduction of Helen, entailed the anger of Achilles over a woman stolen from him, and led to the murder of Agamemnon by his wife (and Helen's sister) Clytemnestra. Aeneas in the *Aeneid* carries his father on his shoulders to escape Troy as it falls, resists the temptations of an alliance with Dido in Africa, and overpowers adversaries in Italy to settle his people there. His piety as well as his courage and steadfastness go into the new Roman nation that derives from him. In *Paradise Lost,* the epic story involves all people who ever lived—who fell with Adam and Eve to gain the promise of redemption through Christ. In these poems the heroes represent a kind of national character, a great founder, defender, or savior. Later poets still were teased by thoughts of global changes achieved by single men. Pope at one point thought of rewriting the legend of Brutus, the grandson of Aeneas who voyaged

through the straits of Gibraltar to found a new nation in Britain. The American Joel Barlow published the *Columbiad* in 1807, a poem on the deeds and visions of Christopher Columbus.

These are the particular stories that loom behind some of Bergon's phrases: "mythic history of a nation," "heroic story of a people's struggles through a wilderness [to] return home," "a people moving west," "the fall of one civilization and the rise of another." Lewis and Clark do not consciously enlarge this pattern, but they certainly reenact it in their expedition. And their times seemed to call for just such a deed, another westering, another empire founding, another vision of people creating a new order in the universe.

Yet by 1800 the idea of epic had also lost its value for many writers and critics. The ideal of a single, aristocratic, military hero like Homer's or Virgil's did not fit very well with current ideals of British freedom or American democracy. Besides, epic poems were addressed to the ear and the common memory of a people; they were meant to be heard and learned by heart. But in the eighteenth century the audience for English literature was no longer to be found in a central city with a common culture. It was increasingly a reading public, a widely dispersed, even multinational society of individuals who chose their own books and took them in with different tastes, in privacy and solitude. In short, the same pluralism that Bergon traces as the theme of the journals was a force undermining the unity of any epic poem. The high ambitious days of Dryden and Pope were yielding to the era of Defoe, Fielding, Scott, and Austen—writers who composed the world not once and magisterially but often and in prose accessible to multitudes.

In America, moreover, the act of nation founding had been united with the act of composing lofty and memorable language not in epic poems but in great public documents. If there was no American Milton or Pope, there had still been a Jefferson, a Hamilton, and a Madison. The Declaration of Independence and the Constitution made up what could be called the common poetry of Americans, the carefully deliberated phrases that everyone knew then and that many of us still recite from memory. And if one needed heroic deeds, the War of Independence had left its indelible marks in the minds of the people and on the familiar scenes of all the eastern states. While the achievements of the Revolution endured, however, the fame of individual leaders became mired in political controversies. Washington, Jefferson, Adams, Franklin, and Hamilton had all been spattered with the thick ink of partisan journalism by the end of the century. On the one hand, American heroism was palpable in the achievement of new freedoms and institutions, but on the other hand, not even Washington could seem fully convincing as a hero in immortal verse.

For all these reasons the Lewis and Clark expedition must remain an unsung act of heroism. It came too late for epic.

It survives in its own prosaic records. It extended but could not overturn the more comprehensive founding of America.

Yet the expedition journals do touch two or three abiding epic strains—strains that do not quite match Bergon's description but underlie his far-reaching suggestions. These patterns are inescapable, I believe, and must be acknowledged by anyone who becomes caught up in reading the journals and settles down to reread and savor them as exciting texts in American literature.

First of all, the journals record extraordinary feats of physical strength and ready intelligence. Lewis and Clark achieved a transcontinental crossing such as no one had made before and few would make after them for many years. Stage by stage they conquered obstacles worthy of an Odysseus. Anyone who has paddled against the stream on the Columbia or the Missouri, looked straight on at the Great Falls or an approaching bear, endured days of hunger and nights of mosquitoes far from home, been sick and wet through during a week of cold drizzle, picked a wearying path over miles of fallen timber or numbing snow, negotiated nervously for the good of a whole company while surrounded by distrusting foreigners—whoever has done just one of these things can find an action to respect in the pages of this story. Lewis and Clark did them all. Sometimes they did two or three on the same day, then moved on over the horizon to meet another array of challenges in a different climate. By their actions they showed that these things could be done, could even be accomplished by a rather ordinary troop of foot soldiers. By being the first to do them in their long journey, they also transformed the world through which they passed. "His legs bestrid the ocean," Cleopatra says of a heroic Mark Antony in Shakespeare's play; "His reared arm crested the world. . . . Realms and islands were as plates dropped from his pocket."[6] Cannot almost the same be said of these captains? Their legs strode over the continent, including its highest mountains, and with lordly command they named the creeks and rivers they found for each other, for their companions, for their friends, for the people they admired, even for their dog.

The classicist Eric Havelock has argued that exemplary doing is the essential action of the Homeric poems. In a time before widespread reading and writing, oral poetry preserved the ways things were done. By memorizing the ways of feasting, greeting a guest, making sacrifice to the gods, taunting an enemy—as these doings were recited in the *Iliad*—the young learned the ways of their elders, and those elders held on to a standard of excellent behavior. In fact, Havelock argues, it was to break down a powerful tradition of such wisdom, rote-learned through poetry, that Plato wrote his dialogues. They presented a new kind of literate, critical thinking, and yet they enacted that newer behavior too through oral exchanges with an exemplary character named Socrates.[7]

A second dimension of the journals, therefore, is that their great deeds are told with literate sophistication. These heroes are their own best historians. They not only do wonderful things but also sit down daily to collect and comprehend what they are doing. Sometimes their actions occur in the course of their writing these pages, as they weigh, recount, and reshape their experiences and so find their way mentally through the snares and distractions that bewildered their active hours.

A third epic strain derives from their achievement in the history of world geography. The westering movement we have seen in a sequence of epics here comes to its end. The Homeric Greeks defined themselves against the world of the East. They gathered a great army and navy, sent them across the Aegean Sea, reduced an enemy city to ashes, then turned their backs on that annihilated threat. The sea lanes of Odysseus and Aeneas led westward toward recovered or new-found homes. In the familiar lines of his poem "Ulysses," Tennyson recaptured that westering urge derived from Odysseus:

> All experience is an arch wherethrough
> Gleams that untraveled world whose margin fades
> Forever and forever when I move. . . .
>   Come, my friends,
> 'Tis not too late to seek a newer world.
> Push off, and sitting well in order smite
> The sounding furrows; for my purpose holds
> To sail beyond the sunset, and the baths
> Of all the western stars, until I die.[8]
>
>   (lines 19-21, 56-61)

It might almost seem that the core story of the most famous epics was a constant westward movement in pursuit of the sun. Milton, too, understood that his constant theme of fall and redemption refigured the daily miracles of sunrise and sunset, that our days and lives follow the sun to the west. The shepherd in *Lycidas* drowns but rises to a new life in heaven with the sun's glorious ease and certainty:

> So sinks the day-star in the ocean bed
> And yet anon repairs his drooping head
> And tricks his beams, and with new-spangled ore,
> Flames in the forehead of the morning sky:
> So Lycidas sunk low, but mounted high,
> Through the dear might of him that walked the waves.[9]
>
>   (*Lycidas*, lines 168-73)

With Lewis and Clark the course of the sun came full circle. The passage to India sought by Columbus was at last complete. The party made it to the Pacific coast and found unmistakable evidence there of merchants who were carrying furs to China and then sailing on to the Atlantic.

The party could not recognize the full import of the new links they had made. Intercultural equality was not their conscious aim, as we have seen. Along with learned men like Jefferson, they often had very mistaken, even deeply prejudiced notions about the settlement of continents and the aptitudes of other people. But sometimes deliberately, sometimes casually, Lewis and Clark took step after step to integrate the peoples of Asia, Europe, and Africa on North American soil. Among Indians derived from Asian explorers of the Ice Age they brought Europeans speaking English and French and a black man descended from Africans. They carried a baby, half Shoshone and half French Canadian. They were often guided by Drouillard, the son of a French Canadian father and a Shawnee mother. Their survival frequently depended on making exchanges and learning the ways of indigenous hunters and settlers; in return, they shared their medicines with people in pain. The sexual adventures of their party introduced different genes among the people of the West. Their medals, certificates, and promises were attempts to introduce different political understandings. They tried to hear and record Indian languages. They carried back samples of Indian handiwork and tools. They even induced some chiefs to travel back with them to see and be seen in eastern cities.

So in 1806 a decisive link was forged between East and West. Although their hands were bloodstained once or twice, although extension of empire was their central purpose, and although their arrival spelled eventual doom for many western species and peoples, Lewis and Clark came not at all as Agamemnon and his hosts had come against Troy. They came not to destroy and deny but to learn.

Beyond the old world of epic beckoned the new world of science. And it was this world that they entered too, as much as the western American landscape—entered, inhabited, and enlarged. For this reason the numbers and jottings on their pages that Bergon sees as an intrusion or distraction in the epic narrative—"their daily logs of temperature, astronomical observations, tabulations of longitude and latitude"—rather beat a steady rhythm of progress. They mark a disciplined effort—crudely done, perhaps on mistaken principles, but nonetheless far-seeing—to hold the entire planet together, to fit even unknown America into a new unity, a globe of knowledge all literate people might share.

The Lewis and Clark journals therefore resemble an epic poem in odd, paradoxical ways. For good and indisputable reasons they do not fit this genre at all, or any literary genre whatever. They are scientific notebooks, and sometimes very sketchy ones at that. Yet in the story they tell, the achievements they record, and even the minute details of their composition they repeat epic impulses toward grandeur and integrative comprehension. They present a completely new universe in a complex language that draws the reader toward a new power of universal understanding.

This ambiguity of form and formlessness may put a beginning reader off or overwhelm anyone who begins (as most probably do) by seeking just an incident of local history, some episodes of adventure, or a few bright records of natural description. Since 1806 the explorers themselves and many an editor after them have wondered how to shape these materials so as to display their riches and eliminate meaningless repetitions and details. But always the solution has been some form of narrative, either rambling or artificially compacted. It has always been a roughly implied epic of discovery. The range, depth, and significance of discovery has varied from the all-inclusive to the monographic. But book after set of books has, ineluctably, recounted a story of great deeds leading on to wonder and to a knowledge beyond wonder.

Perhaps the serious reader should be encouraged to avoid such patterning by becoming immersed in the full confusion of the complete journals, as many a book and article recommends. But anyone who begins that task had better have stamina, patience, and a large library—and a vivid imagination too. The full journals fill many thick volumes. The entries for any day are likely to be repetitious and confusing. Lewis, Clark, and their sergeants kept different sets of records in different ways. Each captain recopied his own field notes; at times each borrowed and rewrote entries from the other. But one cannot easily skip these copied versions, because there is no way to know in advance which version may contain some further lively detail or comment. During the long winters, the journals grew to include summary records and inventories of specimens collected so far. Daily logs of travels and actions overlap with scientific descriptions and observations. One also needs another set of volumes of correspondence about the expedition, and another of maps. To make sense of these pages, the reader will be grateful, too, for the labors of several skilled editors and annotators. But the result of all their apparatus is that an evening in the armchair may well conclude with a half-dozen volumes opened, bookmarked, and scattered on every nearby surface. A patient eye and mind can thus take in the full journey in close detail, and for many the process has proved rewarding. But a reader with a sense of humor will want to cover the mirrors to keep from seeing Don Quixote looking back. Who can pore so assiduously over these books without longing to follow their heroes back onto the trail—if only to get fresh air?

To reach the many readers they deserve, the journals require severe but sensitive editing. But that means some severe deleting and reshaping into a new design. From the work of Nicholas Biddle to the present, the main editorial practice has been the same: tell a coherent story by weaving together the highlights of single entries; make steady chronological progress across the continent and back; relegate technical observations to occasional notes or appendixes. In short, make a narrative—and by implication decide on a central story line, something very suspiciously akin to an epic theme.

Two popular editions of selections illustrate this point. Bernard DeVoto's *Journals of Lewis and Clark,* first published in 1953, emphasizes political geography. DeVoto even substitutes a long section from his own book, *The Course of Empire,* to keep the narrative smooth and compact over Clark's return trip along the Yellowstone River. Frank Bergon's more recent volume of the same name (1989) explicitly claims to correct DeVoto's work by including "much of the natural-history material omitted in earlier edited versions" and reprinting only passages from either Lewis or Clark, not eclectic excerpts from the captains, Biddle, and four other party members.[10] For DeVoto the guiding theme is Jeffersonian westward expansion; for Bergon it is epic visions of, by, and for the people, in the midst of natural wonders.

At least four other fine scholarly books have followed the same design. A recounting of consecutive events along the trail forms the backbone of *Lewis and Clark: Pioneering Naturalists* by Paul Russell Cutright (1969); *Passage through the Garden: Lewis and Clark and the Image of the American Northwest* by John Logan Allen (1975); *Thomas Jefferson and the Stony Mountains: Exploring the West from Monticello* by Donald Jackson (1981); and *Lewis and Clark among the Indians* by James P. Ronda (1984). Each of these books makes generous quotations from the journals and other sources to bring out a different story. Allen and Jackson re-create a tale mainly about geography and politics, as DeVoto did before them. Cutright retraces an excursion into wonders of botany and zoology. Ronda fills out a story of encounters between cultures. These are four separate studies, each with its own integrity. Yet each one is also a complete and satisfying narrative of the entire expedition. Whoever studies just one of these books can rightly claim to have accompanied the Corps of Discovery and taken a fair sampling of what all the other books stress.

The list of attempts to edit or reorganize the journals extends much further. It includes biographies of the main members of the party, focused on their heroic or not-so-heroic characters; novels and romances about their adventures; guide books for western travelers; picture books of art works collected or created on the trail; museum rooms and suites of rooms, from St. Louis to Fort Canby, Washington, that match displays with passages from the journals in chronological sequence; and special projects such as videotapes of sites on the trail and portfolios of modern large-scale maps.

All these works tell a story; in fact they all purport to tell the same story. Yet they differ widely in what they select, exclude, and embellish. Some make modest claims to supplement the journals themselves. Some make an ambitious bid to supplant those tedious volumes with a more popular or exciting version. Taken together, the collection of books, pamphlets, tapes, brochures, pictures, and offprints about Lewis and Clark has its own epic dimensions. It is enough to fill a room, as it does in some college and museum libraries. Yet does any single work get to *the* theme of this epic? Or do they all compete and proliferate because this story intrinsically has no single center—or can reveal none in the pluralistic world in which we now live?

The travel narrative, however presented, has its boring stretches, too, despite the explorers' best efforts to record something worth noting every day. And strict, even chronology creates a further problem. If forces any teller into

an awkward corner with this particular story. The way west is full of excitement. Every day is a day of suspense and new things unfolding, and the tension builds as winter closes in around remote Indian villages, then unimagined tracts of buffalo country appear, then high mountains loom up to block further passage. But this great story reaches its climaxes when the corps crosses the Continental Divide and successfully paddles down to reach the Pacific before winter. The exclamations are right there in the journals. "The road took us to the most distant fountain of the waters of the mighty Missouri," Lewis wrote on August 12, 1805, "in surch of which we have spent so many toilsome days and wristless nights. thus far I had accomplished one of those great objects on which my mind had been unalterably fixed for many years, judge then of the pleasure I felt in allying my thirst with this pure and ice cold water . . . two miles below McNeal had exultingly stood with a foot on each side of this little rivulet and thanked his god that he had lived to bestride the mighty & heretofore deemed endless Missouri" (*Journals* 5:74). On November 7, Clark put the next great elation in few words: "*Ocian in view*! O! the joy" (6:58).

Thereafter follows a winter of wet, sick, hungry, tedious discontent, then a demoralizing climb into unconquerable barriers of snow, and at last swift passage back down the Missouri. The thousands of miles covered on the return trip resemble the thousands already seen, but the return is not all anticlimax. There are new adventures and new landmarks worth recording. But many of these have a dark underside—Lewis's gunfight resulting in Indians slain near the Marias River; Lewis himself being shot by another hunter; the long, meandering, still uncompleted course of translating all the journals into print; the fading away of most of the corpsmen into unmarked graves; and the sudden, mysterious death by violence of Meriwether Lewis while he was still beating a trail in pursuit of fair fame and due reward.

No matter how the journals are edited or recounted in strict chronology, they do not come to a rounded, satisfying close. Every ending point one can find or impose for the history of the Corps of Discovery is raw-edged, lame, or forced—whereas the art of epic is to blend bloody strife and dislocation into the harmonies of highly civilized poetry.

By this point the reader must have discerned that this present book, too, is shaped by epic considerations. So I may as well step forward and candidly confess it. My powers do not permit me to celebrate the Corps of Discovery in anything but academic prose, but I have come to believe that their writings most consistently and variously turn on a different central theme from what others have put forward. I take them at their word, literally the main word of their name, and see their controlling action as the act of discovery—of seeing America new and transforming all subsequent seeing by summoning new languages to describe the vast West. Discovery seems to irradiate all the kinds of seeing they did and every kind of jotting they made, however rough. It relates them to our time as much as to the limited science and lore of centuries past. And it is an act or series of acts that need not be traced strictly chronologically. It is an ever-new beginning; the story of Lewis and Clark is a living invitation to return to an ongoing American trail and make one's own new perceptions. That can still happen in Missouri or Montana, in botany, zoology, or mineralogy, in intercultural relations or national and international politics—whatever scenes or fields one chooses to project around the inquiring American mind. It can also occur in a later chapter here as well as an early one, on the exciting way out or the richly laden return.

A canny reader will also notice that these chapters [in *Acts of Discovery*] are now moving toward an attempt at harmony. That may be because an epic shape is the unavoidable medium for this material, or it may be because I have been a student and teacher of literature for thirty years. As scientists and poets both know, discoveries worth reporting always emerge through the peculiar quirks of their inventors' minds; in that respect my designs here are no doubt as eccentric as William Wordsworth's, William Clark's, or Robert Fulton's. In any event, it should be obvious to anyone who has had a proper college humanities course that the preceding chapters loosely follow the familiar conventions of epic. The opening states and develops the theme immediately. Then the heroes are plunged *in medias res* to confront well-defended ramparts, encounter monsters, and interpret omens. They follow paths blazed for them by their elders, feast hugely on rare delicacies, exchange elaborate gifts and ceremonious speeches, learn to respect the most alien adversaries, take note of signs in the sky, and wrestle with rivers and oceans. They tour the whole world before they are through and then point onward toward home.

What remains to be told is a balance of visions: a descent to the underworld and a climb to the heights. That is the entire plot of *Paradise Lost,* as a matter of fact, and of the *Divine Comedy* of Dante. Odysseus and Aeneas also visit mysterious regions to meet the dead or to recognize the past as past beyond recovery. And there is a long tradition of rising to high promontories to look into the future. Moses stands on Mount Nebo to see the Promised Land. Milton sets Adam high in Eden in his final books to peer into the future with an angel as his guide. At the time of Lewis and Clark, Wordsworth was climbing Mount Snowdon on a walking tour and transfiguring his experiences there in the closing books of the *Prelude.* And Joel Barlow was creating visions of a free America by placing Christopher Columbus high on the Mount of Vision.

Our explorers, too, saw into the American past and future. Literally and intellectually Lewis and Clark met the outcasts of the new nation, left their own shadows behind them, and climbed to heights of vision previously unattained. . . .

Notes

1. Frank Bergon, ed., *The Journals of Lewis and Clark* (New York: Viking, 1989), x. William Gilpin (1813-94) was the first territorial governor of Colorado and author of *Mission of the North American People* (1873).

2. Robert B. Betts, *In Search of York* (Boulder: Colorado Associated University Press, 1985), must now be supplemented by a more recently discovered cache of Clark letters, being edited at the Filson Club in Louisville, Kentucky. According to James J. Holmberg, the curator of manuscripts at the Filson Club, these letters show that Clark treated York harshly after his return, separated him from his wife and family, hired him out to a severe master in Kentucky, and threatened him with beatings or sale to a slave trader when he became refractory. Holmberg presented a preliminary report on these letters at the meeting of the Lewis and Clark Trail Heritage Foundation in Louisville on August 7, 1991.

3. Samuel Johnson, *Lives of the English Poets,* ed. George Birkbeck Hill, 3 vols. (1905; New York: Octagon, 1967), 1:170. I have modernized some spellings.

4. John Dryden, *Poetical Works,* rev. ed. by George R. Noyes (Boston: Houghton Mifflin, 1950), 252.

5. The pressure to produce an epic worthy of early America is recounted in detail in John P. McWilliams, Jr., *The American Epic: Transforming a Genre, 1770-1860* (New York: Cambridge University Press, 1989), esp. 15-93.

6. William Shakespeare, *Antony and Cleopatra* 5.2.82-83, 91-92, in *The Riverside Shakespeare,* ed. G. Blakemore Evans (Boston: Houghton Mifflin, 1974), 1383.

7. Eric A. Havelock, *Preface to Plato* (Cambridge, Mass.: Harvard University Press, 1963).

8. M. H. Abrams et al., eds. *The Norton Anthology of English Literature,* 4th ed., 2 vols. (New York: W. W. Norton, 1979), 2:1110-11.

9. Ibid., 1:1395.

10. These editorial principles are explained in Bernard DeVoto, ed., *The Journals of Lewis and Clark* (Boston: Houghton Mifflin, 1953), v-x; and Bergon, *Journals,* xvii.

Frank Bergon (essay date 1997)

SOURCE: "Wilderness Aesthetics," in *American Literary History,* Vol. 9, No. 1, Spring, 1997, pp. 128-61.

[In the following essay, Bergon considers the Lewis and Clark journals as characteristic of early American nature writing.]

The Lewis and Clark expedition, like the adventures in the *Epic of Gilgamesh* and the *Odyssey,* was a trek into an unfamiliar and often frightening wilderness—the first, longest, and largest of nineteenth-century US government expeditions into terra incognita. Launched from St. Louis in 1804 in a 55-foot masted keelboat and two pirogues carrying more than 8,000 pounds of food and equipment, the Voyage of Discovery, as it was called, lasted two years, four months, and ten days. Round-trip, it covered 7,689 miles between the mouth of the Missouri River and the Pacific outlet of the Columbia River. To a young nation—the US was barely 17 years old at the time—Lewis and Clark brought back maps of previously uncharted rivers and mountains, specimens of previously unknown plants and animals, amazing artifacts, and even representatives of previously unseen peoples of the West. But the explorers' most valuable contribution came in an elkskin-bound field book and red morocco-bound journals stored in tin boxes. Written in an odd, fragmented style that vacillated between the languages of art and science in accordance with the aesthetic expectations of the day, these remarkable journals offered a new natural history of the West. More significant—and surprising—is that the strange, vacillating style of the journals came to characterize the entire genre of American nature writing in the nineteenth century.

Beginning in 1983, *The Journals of the Lewis and Clark Expedition* have been appearing piecemeal from the University of Nebraska Press in a projected standard edition of 13 volumes, including an oversize atlas, a volume of natural history materials, the diaries of four enlisted men, and the complete journals of the expedition leaders, Meriwether Lewis and William Clark, once dubbed "the writingest explorers of their time" (Jackson v). More than a million words of journal entries in over 5,000 pages of text and annotation will culminate this 20-year project. Edited by Gary E. Moulton, professor of history at the University of Nebraska-Lincoln, this joint venture of several institutions and numerous scholars, the product of both private and government funding, will come to completion just shy of the bicentennial of the 1804-06 expedition. According to a reviewer's puff quoted on a publisher's brochure, "These journals of exploits and courage in a pristine West have a simplicity and timelessness about them—never failing to capture the imagination of the ordinary reader or to interest the historian, scientist, or geographer."

But what about students and teachers of American literature? Do these expeditionary materials stimulate their interest with the same intensity as that of historians, scientists, and geographers? If for an answer we turn to current canon-forming literary histories and college anthologies, the response would be no. The journals are absent from major commercial anthologies of American literature published by Norton (1994), Heath (1994), HarperCollins (1994), Macmillan (1993), and Prentice Hall (1991), while the recent *Columbia Literary History of the United States* (1988) advises readers to forgo the complete journals and explore a modern abridgment because "[t]edious detail so clutters their narrative" (Hedges 202). Perhaps a change is imminent. The more recent *Cambridge History of American Literature* (1994) discusses the journals at length, and the new scholarly Nebraska edition now provides an opportunity to see that these writings—with their logs of temperature and weather, astronomical observations, tabulations of longitude and latitude, descriptions of flora and fauna, anthropological data, misspellings, and neologisms—do indeed constitute a classic "literary pursuit"—a natural history of the lands, animals, and native peoples of the West that rises to the level of an American epic.

"Epic" is a word frequently and loosely applied to the expedition itself—the historic act of exploration—with respect to its magnitude, but the term might also characterize the journals as literary texts.[1] In 1989, when asked to produce a popular abridgment of the journals not unlike those recommended by the *Columbia Literary History of the United States,* I found myself arguing in the introduction that "no abridgment can fully convey the dazzling epic quality of the complete journals or their splendid achievement in the literature of natural history, for their effect is monumental and cumulative" (xvii). I organized the abridgment into the paradigmatic 12-book epic scheme, and with the freewheeling hyperbole welcome in such editions, I argued that from the hindsight of almost two centuries, these uneven, fragmented, and unpolished journals offer the equivalent of a national poem. In a multistyled language as distinctive as those that characteristically identify ancient epics, they tell a heroic story of a people's struggles through a wilderness and the return home. Better than more artful poems or novels or plays, they embody with the directness and plainness of an oral tale the mythic history of a nation. They tell the story of the tribe, moving west. Not the conventional mythic story of the lone frontiersman facing the wilderness, this tale depicts a cooperative enterprise: a fluctuating community of some 35 to 45 people, including soldiers, woodsmen, blacksmiths, carpenters, cooks, French engagés, a black slave, a Lemhi Shoshone woman, and a newborn baby of mixed race, all heading west. In retrospect, the journals also dramatize the disturbing design of a nation committed to the arrogant belief that—as William Gilpin expressed it 70 years later—the *"untransacted* destiny of the American people is to subdue the continent" (130). In portending the destruction of one civilization and the rise of another, the journals reveal the dark imperialistic underside of the epical adventure.

To Lewis and Clark themselves, however, and the expectant readers of their time, the account of this particular epic followed the format of a work in natural history that conformed to a well-established New World genre. In 1526, when the Spanish naturalist, and friend of Columbus, Gonzalo Fernández de Oviedo y Valdés published his *Natural History of the West Indies,* he initiated a freshet of works in this genre from New Spain, New France, New England, and other New Founde Lands that left Lewis and Clark the inheritors of an American literary tradition more than 250 years old. As with many of their predecessors, Lewis and Clark's conception of "natural history" was rooted in the double meaning of *history* as it had evolved from Aristotle and Pliny. History, or 'ιϛτορία, to the Greeks meant "an inquiry" or "an account of one's inquiries," so that natural history came to mean an inquiry into the natural world and a systematic account (without relation to time) of its observable forms. But *history* in the Aristotelian sense also meant "a narrative or tale or story" in time. Since many naturalists combined their "inquiry into nature" with a narrative of their journeys and adventures, it came to be accepted that natural history was an eyewitness account of nature encountered on one's travels. For the natural historians of the Americas, observable phenomena included landforms, bodies of water, minerals, plants, mammals, birds, reptiles, fishes, amphibians, invertebrates—all the expected and unexpected flora and fauna—as well as the commodities and manners of the people in these areas, especially those native inhabitants of the Americas known as Indians.

Lewis and Clark were heirs to this genre that, in the eighteenth century, despite increasing specialization in the sciences, remained for the most part a branch of literature. When Benjamin Smith Barton, scientific adviser to Lewis and author of the first American textbook of botany—a book the explorers carried on their journey—wrote to the naturalist William Bartram in 1788 thanking him for botanical information, he said, "I know not how to repay your goodness, and attention to my literary pursuits" (5). He urged Bartram to publish his manuscript of natural history because it would be of "essential benefit to the cause of Science [and] would be considered a very valuable presente to the literary world" (4). He was right. William Bartram's *Travels through North and South Carolina, Georgia, East and West Florida,* published in 1791, quickly passed into no fewer than nine European editions. It seems only appropriate that this remarkable work, given the importance of its genre to the New World, was arguably the first book published in the US to become internationally recognized as a literary classic. Coleridge copied passage after passage into his own notebooks and acclaimed it "a work of high merit [in] every way" (qtd. in Harper xxvii). Images from Bartram's *Travels* made their way into Goldsmith's "Deserted Village," Coleridge's "Kubla Khan," Wordsworth's "Ruth," and Chateaubriand's "Atala." Carlyle asked Emerson, "Do you know *Bartram's Travels*? . . . treats of *Florida* chiefly, has a wonderful kind of floundering eloquence in it. . . . All American libraries ought to provide themselves with that kind of Books; and keep them as a kind of future *biblical* article" (468).

That type of comprehensive book, with its fusion of scientific and literary concerns, was what Jefferson had in mind for Lewis and Clark. A fine naturalist himself, with a particular interest in phenology (the study of relationships between climate and periodic biological phenomena), Jefferson gave the explorers careful written instructions for observing and recording in detail the natural world. As a result, Jefferson's influence informs the journals like that of a muse. The Voyage of Discovery was his dream, and the journals his inspiration. For 20 years he had sought to have someone do what Lewis and Clark were finally ac-

complishing. As a congressman in 1783, Jefferson had unsuccessfully tried to enlist General George Rogers Clark, the Revolutionary War hero and William's older brother, to explore the lands west of the Mississippi. As minister to France in 1786, Jefferson supported the Connecticut adventurer John Ledyard in his daring but frustrated attempt to cross the continent by first traveling eastward over Siberia and the Bering Sea and then walking from the Pacific Coast, over the Rockies, to the Missouri River. In 1793, as secretary of state and vice president of the American Philosophical Society, Jefferson backed another aborted exploration when he instructed André Michaux, France's most accomplished botanist, to "find the shortest & most convenient route of communication between the U.S. & the Pacific ocean" (Jackson 669). A current misconception found in several recent books is that when Jefferson, as president in 1803, finally received congressional approval and funds to launch his expedition across the continent, he invited Bartram to serve as the expedition's naturalist.[2] An admirer of Bartram's work and one of the first public officials, along with President Washington and Vice President Adams, to order Bartram's *Travels,* Jefferson did later try to enlist Bartram on an expedition up the Red River, which the 65-year-old naturalist politely declined.

For the more demanding trek across the continent, Jefferson had had his eye on young Meriwether Lewis ever since the 19-year-old boy requested Jefferson's permission to accompany Michaux to the Pacific. For two years before the expedition, Lewis had virtually lived with Jefferson, serving ostensibly as the president's private secretary while training to lead the Corps of Discovery. In 1803, when Jefferson sent Lewis to scientists and physicians in Philadelphia for brief but intensive instruction in botany, zoology, celestial navigation, and medicine, he confided to Barton that he needed not just a trained specialist but someone with "firmness of constitution & character, prudence, habits adapted to the woods, & a familiarity with the Indian manners & character, requisite for this undertaking. All the latter qualifications Capt. Lewis has" (Jackson 17). As an ensign in the army, Lewis had earlier served briefly in a rifle company under the command of Captain William Clark, who became his immediate choice as co-commander of the expedition. In both Lewis and Clark, Jefferson found men capable of "a remarkable mass of accurate observation." In their ability to keep "a sharp lookout"—as the naturalist John Burroughs describes it (333)—Lewis and Clark shared with other naturalists, like John James Audubon, Thoreau, John Muir, and Burroughs, a trait that surpassed their formal scientific training. They were not scientific specialists; the word *scientist* in its modern sense had not yet been invented. They were natural historians whose range encompassed all of nature. The strange landforms and new water-courses the explorers encountered were the primary concerns of Clark, who served as the main cartographer and geographer, while Lewis was the botanist and zoologist. Both compiled a valuable ethnographic record of Indian people, especially of the Lemhi

Shoshone, whose meeting with Lewis and Clark marked their first encounter with whites.

In 1803 the writing of this natural history faced political obstacles. The vast stretch of lands that Jefferson wanted documented was still a foreign territory subject to murky claims by Great Britain, Spain, France, and Russia. Jefferson tried to assure these nations that his encroachment into their possessions was a "literary" endeavor, undertaken in the disinterested spirit of expanding scientific and geographical knowledge. He also couched his secret congressional request for exploratory funds in careful terms. In addition to increasing the literary store of natural history, he was interested in looking for possible trade routes, he told Congress, for external commerce. Everyone knew otherwise, especially the European powers who were anxious to keep the original colonies of the US tidily contained along the continental eastern seaboard. Jefferson's grand design, they knew, was imperial, to make way for American expansion from sea to shining sea.

As with earlier accounts of American explorers, the enterprises of natural history writing and colonization became intertwined. *Westward the course of Empire makes its way* was the eighteenth-century sentiment that seemed to become reality when Napoleon, short of cash after failing to overcome the slave revolt in Haiti, abandoned his own imperial ambitions in North America and tried to frustrate Britain's by selling the vast Louisiana Territory to the US for three cents an acre. The US suddenly doubled its holdings, and expansion to the Pacific became a virtual certainty. "The consequences of the cession of Louisiana," President Jefferson predicted, "will extend to the most distant posterity" (qtd. in Duncan 10). Scarcely six months after congressional retification of the sale in October 1803, Lewis and Clark were on their way across the continent, writing their journals, and the US was on its way to becoming a world power. After hearing of the Louisiana Purchase, the Federalist Fisher Ames fearfully warned, "We rush like a comet into infinite space!" (324).

Although the political and commercial ramifications of Lewis and Clark's trek are well known, they should not overshadow what Jefferson told Congress were the "literary purposes" of the venture. In fact, it might be argued that the expedition succeeded more spectacularly as Jefferson's "literary pursuit" than in some of its other aims. Lewis and Clark failed in their primary commercial purpose of finding a practical water route across the continent to link the US in trade with China. There was no Northwest Passage. They also failed to establish workable routes up the northern tributaries of the Missouri to capture the Canadian fur trade for the US. And they failed to establish a lasting peace with the native peoples, especially those who controlled passage on the Missouri, and the killing of two Blackfeet warriors actually aggravated relations with tribes of the Northern Plains. It is also questionable how firmly the expedition reinforced the nation's claim to the Oregon Territory. But as a "literary pursuit"—a report on the lands, animals, and native peoples of the American West—the expedition succeeded in ways that only now, after nearly 200 years, are fully appreciable.

In 1806 Jefferson greeted the return of Lewis and Clark to the US with "unspeakable joy" (Jackson 350), noting that even the "humblest of it's citizens" (Jackson 591) looked forward with impatience to publication of the explorers' journals. The president envisioned a revised, polished version of the raw journals, similar to the literate accounts of Bartram's travels and Captain Cook's voyages. Within weeks Lewis released a prospectus announcing the 1807 publication of a three-volume history of the expedition, including all the "scientific research . . . which may properly be distributed under the heads of Botany, Mineralogy, and Zoology," "a view of the Indian nations," and "Lewis & Clark's Map of North America" (Jackson 395-96). This project was delayed and then ended with Lewis's death, an apparent suicide, in 1809. Responsibility for the edition shifted to Clark, then serving as Indian agent for the Louisiana Territory, who engaged the Philadelphia lawyer and self-styled litterateur Nicholas Biddle to deal with the journals. Meanwhile, a number of apocryphal patchwork accounts composed of older explorers' journals and Jefferson's message to Congress had appeared in popular editions, as did the bowdlerized diary of expedition sergeant and carpenter, Patrick Gass, whose *Journal of the Voyages and Travels of a Corps of Discovery,* published in 1807, quickly went through seven editions. Finally in 1814, Biddle's authorized *History of the Expedition under the Commands of Captains Lewis and Clark* appeared, much to Jefferson's disappointment, because all the scientific material given to Barton for preparation had not been completed and was therefore excluded from what Jefferson called the "mere journal" (1313). Biddle's version was a paraphrase of the original journals written in the first person plural that compressed the two captains into a composite "we," with accounts of Indian sexual activity translated into Latin. This edition stood as the only representation of the explorers' writings for nearly a century. In 1893 the redoubtable ornithologist and military surgeon, Elliott Coues, edited Biddle's history with massive annotations that brought attention to the previously neglected scientific material. In the process, however, Coues took liberty in emending the original journals, and his numerous interlineations on the manuscript earned him the derision of later scholars despite his valuable editorial achievement. Coues, however, was not the only person who had left his smudges on the pages. At the turn of the century, on the eve of the Lewis and Clark centennial, when the American Philosophical Society authorized a verbatim edition of the original journals, the manuscripts were a palimpsest of interlineations and emendations in different shades of ink by Coues, Biddle, Clark, and at least one other unknown person. Biddle's notes in red reflected his own words as well as those of George Shannon, a member of the expedition who, along with Captain Clark, had helped Biddle in his interpretation of the journals. The American Philosophical Society considered asking Western writer Owen Wister to edit the manuscripts, but it finally selected the historian Reuben Gold Thwaites, who had just edited the 73 volumes of the *Jesuit Relations* (1896-1901). Thwaites chose to reproduce the journals in their current marked-up state, using a variety of typographical pyrotechnics to indicate authorship of most emendations and interlineations except extensive ones by Coues. With a surprising paucity of annotation about the scientific and geographic achievement, Thwaites's edition focused on transcription and compilation of extant materials, so that in 1904-05, 100 years after the expedition, there at last appeared a *verbatim et literatim et punctuatim* edition of the *Original Journals of Lewis and Clark,* and the captains' actual words were published for the first time.

I have hovered over this history of the manuscripts because the new *Journals of the Lewis and Clark Expedition,* edited by Moulton, expands and updates the 1904-05 Thwaites edition. Moulton adopts Thwaites's format of printing Lewis's and Clark's entries in tandem with appropriate sections introduced by the writer's bracketed name. As in Thwaites's edition, chapter divisions follow the chronological and geographical demarcations inherited from Biddle's edition, and the journals of enlisted men are consigned to separate volumes. Like Thwaites, Moulton has identified emendations and interlineations in the text; only he adds the emender's italicized initials. Moulton relies on reproductions of the Thwaites text as scanned by the optical character recognition (OCR) process but checked, for the first time in a century, against the original journals to insure accurate transcription. In the last 90 years, misplaced or lost expeditionary documents, unavailable to Thwaites, have been found and published, most notably Lewis and Clark's 1803 eastern journal and Sergeant Ordway's three-volume journal, edited by Milo Milton Quaife. Quaife's 1916 publication of the eastern journal, which recounts the preliminary trip from Pittsburgh on August 30, 1803, to the Mississippi River, presented the captains' earliest writings and extended the documented length of the expedition to three years and one month. Clark's field notes, discovered in 1953 and dubbed the "Dubois Journal" and the "River Journal," were edited by Ernest Staples Osgood and published in 1964. Other valuable materials became available in 1962 with the publication of Donald Jackson's *Letters of the Lewis and Clark Expedition with Related Documents, 1783-1854.* These and other important books in the last 50 years have rendered Thwaites's scanty notations antiquated, and previously neglected achievements of the expedition in the realms of botany, zoology, medicine, ethnography, linguistics, and geography/cartography have become documented.

Moulton's stated purpose is to gather these scattered materials into the first comprehensive, collated edition with a reliable, definitive text and a thorough, uniform annotation. No newly discovered, previously unpublished materials appear in this edition. Accurate transcription is the primary task. "I'm very concerned," Moulton has written, "to get every jot and tittle correct. . . . We're supposed to do the final edition that will stand for all time" (qtd. in Goodman 25-26).

A comparison of sample passages from the Thwaites and Moulton editions exhibits the measure of care taken in rendering an accurate text. Here is Thwaites's 1904 transcription of Lewis's well-known account of the departure from the Mandan villages for the great unknown after sending the keelboat with 18 men and important expeditionary materials back to St. Louis on April 7, 1805:

> Our vessels consisted of six small canoes, and two large perogues. This little fleet altho' not quite so rispectable as those of Columbus or Capt. Cook, were still viewed by us with as much pleasure as those deservedly famed adventurers ever beheld theirs; and I dare say with quite as much anxiety for their safety and preservation. we were now about to penetrate a country at least two thousand miles in width, on which the foot of civilized man had never trodden; the good or evil it had in store for us was for experiment yet to determine, and these little vessells contained every article by which we were to expect to subsist or defend themselves. however, as the state of mind in which we are, generally gives the colouring to events, when the immagination is suffered to wander into futurity, the picture which now presented itself to me was a most pleasing one. enterta[in]ing as I do, the most confident hope of succeeding in a voyage which had formed a da[r-]ling project of mine for the last ten years, I could but esteem this moment of my departure as among the most happy of my life.

(1: 284-85)

And here is Moulton's corrected version:

> Our vessels consisted of six small canoes, and two large perogues. This little fleet altho' not quite so rispectable as those of Columbus or Capt. Cook were still viewed by us with as much pleasure as those deservedly famed adventurers ever beheld theirs; and I dare say with quite as much anxiety for their safcty and preservation. we were now about to penetrate a country at least two thousand miles in width, on which the foot of civilized man had never trodden; the good or evil it had in store for us was for experiment yet to determine, and these little vessells contained every article by which we were to expect to subsist or defend ourselves. however as this the state of mind in which we are, generally gives the colouring to events, when the immagination is suffered to wander into futurity, the picture which now presented itself to me was a most pleasing one. entertaining <now> as I do, the most confident hope of succeading in a voyage which had formed a da[r]ling project of mine for the last ten years <of my life>, I could but esteem this moment of my <our> departure as among the most happy of my life.

(4: 9-10)

Moulton has made nine alterations in vocabulary, spelling, and punctuation. The slight difference between the two renditions, hardly noticeable to the average reader, demonstrates that Thwaites did a good job in his original transcriptions, but Moulton's are even better. No one can anticipate when a minuscule alteration might significantly affect interpretation, and care in transcription now gives scholars a text to rely on. The same care is extended to the correction of Thwaites's notations. For example, Thwaites's binomial identification of a Lewis zoological discovery misnames the bushy-tailed woodrat as *Neotama cinera* (2: 205), which Moulton silently corrects to *Neotoma cinerea* (4: 354). The few typographical errors that appear in the new edition pop out of the editorial scaffolding rather than the texts themselves, where, I assume, editors properly applied more scrupulous proofreading; but even a typographical slip, like the spelling of "allitudes" for "altitudes" in the editorial front matter of volume 3, is corrected in subsequent volumes. After such evidence of careful editing, it may seem unfair to suggest that the reading of a passage in Moulton is affected less by transcriptive changes than by the awkward three- to four-pound volumes in which they appear. Better suited to the scholar's desk than the reader's lap, these boxy books are less friendly to the general reader than is the Thwaites's edition with its compressed, old-fashioned print. Thwaites's notes, skimpy as they may be, do appear conveniently at the bottom of the page, a good place for many brief items which simply identify geographical location or the scientific denominations of plants and animals. Moulton's blocks of notes at the conclusions of daily entries, rather than in footnotes or chapter endnotes, are not always easy to locate, and their varied appearance within the text at the top, middle, or bottom of a page creates much shuffling back and forth between text and annotation.

In his arrangement of texts, however, Moulton has done a significant service by moving materials that were chronologically out of place in the Thwaites edition. For example, the extensive summations about rivers, Indian tribes, and botanical and mineralogical collections prepared during the winter at Fort Mandan, which Thwaites tucked into an appendix in volume 6 of his edition, now properly appear with the other writings of that winter to give a better sense of the captains' enterprise among the Mandan. In other instances, however, interspersion of new materials, particularly from Clark's field notes, is not clearly noted. In the Moulton edition a passage about the Mandan by William Clark for March 30, 1805, reads in part: "All the party in high Spirits, but fiew nights pass without a Dance they are helth, except the—vn. [venereal]—which is common with the Indians and have been communicated to many of our party at this place—those favores bieng easy acquired. all Tranquille" (3: 322). This passage is absent from Thwaites, but whether the earlier editor neglected to transcribe it or whether the passage has been inserted into the journal from Clark's rediscovered field notes is not made clear. In other instances, one wishes controversial interpretations of transcriptions were noted. For instance, a long-standing problem in geographical nomenclature has concerned the captains' naming of the Milk River (in present-day Montana). Lewis refers to the Milk River as the "scolding river" (3: 367), the one called by the Hidatsa *the river that scolds at all others*" (4: 248). Scholars Donald Jackson and Paul Russell Cutright both claim that "scolding river" makes no sense; they assume that Thwaites, in transcribing Lewis, mistook "scalds" for "scolds." They argue that "scalds" or "scald-

ing" could be a reference to the color and temperature of scalded milk, an interpretation supported by an entry in a paraphrased version of Private Joseph Whitehouse's journal, discovered in 1966: "Our officers gave this River the name, Scalding Milk River" (qtd. in Cutright, *History* 258). To my surprise, the Moulton edition shows that Jackson and Cutright are wrong. Thwaites did indeed correctly decipher Lewis's handwriting and properly transcribed "scolds" and "scolding." The Indian terms do make sense when referring to the only stream of any magnitude above the mouth of the Yellowstone to discharge with enough force into the Missouri to churn, or "scold," it. But Moulton offers no commentary on nomenclature that has puzzled historians since the appearance of the *Original Journals of Lewis and Clark* 90 years ago.

In 1980, at the start of the project, Moulton wrote, "The most difficult and time-consuming work on the journals will be in the area of annotation. In hundreds of footnotes, the staff will clarify and expand upon the manuscript diaries. If we were to edit the journals only in terms of placing the original material into print we could complete the project in short order, even considering the extreme care we will give to this dimension. But a great deal of effort will be required to search out the writers' numerous obscure references to people, places, and events" ("Journals" 15).

The staff has relied not only upon published scholarship for their annotations but also upon direct consultation with experts in various fields around the country. The result is a fund of information gleaned from anthropologists, archaeologists, astronomers, botanists, geologists, geographers, ornithologists, cartographers, historians, linguists, and zoologists. Identifications of plants, animals, people, places, and events along the route are excellent, but notes occasionally reflect incomplete assimilation of such varied sources. For example, in the sections on the Lemhi Shoshone the staff relied on the noted linguist and anthropologist Sven Liljeblad for clarification of Shoshone words and phrases. Information about the Lemhi Shoshone as a group, however, is spotty despite the extensive account Lewis and Clark provided. In volume 4, when Lewis's first use of the word Shoshone ("Sosonees or snake Indians" 4: 398) appears, a note tells us that "[i]t was not the Shoshone name for themselves" (4: 401n3) but does not say what that name was or what "snake" signified. Later, in volume 5, we learn that the Shoshone "call themselves *nimi* (singular), 'person' or *niminii* (plural), 'the people,'" and that the Lemhi Shoshone were a "division of the Northern Shoshones of the Rocky Mountains, known to the Great Plains tribes as 'Snakes'" (5: 85n7), but the staff offers no cultural or linguistic identification of the various Northern Shoshone "divisions" (some of whom, including Bannocks, were also called "Snakes") or of the related "divisions" of Eastern Shoshone or Western Shoshone, information that Sven Liljeblad or recent studies by Brigham Madsen, Wick Miller, or Robert Murphy and Yolanda Murphy could easily have provided. In a subsequent footnote, the "Tukudikas" [sic] are described as a "Shoshonean group . . . later referred to by whites as 'Sheepeaters' because they ate the bighorn sheep" (5: 94n8), but it would be helpful to know that they are also called Agaideka ("eaters of salmon") and that they a group of Northern Shoshone with an important relationship to the Lemhi Shoshone. Both the Tukudeka and Lemhi Shoshone shared a common cultural origin and were virtually indistinguishable until they diverged after the arrival of the horse. Today, however, both groups are still compositely referred to in the Shoshone language as Agaideka. In the annotations the generic term "Shoshone" causes confusion because it is repeatedly applied to the Lemhi Shoshone, despite the term's correct reference to a large language group of culturally distinct peoples ranging from northern Idaho to south-eastern California. The staff's use of the term "Shoshonean" obscures matters even more because this linguistic category properly includes peoples as different as the Paiute, Ute, Comanche, and Hopi. Tossing around terms like "Shoshonean" and "Tukudikas" might produce the illusion of precision, but the uninformed reader remains so. In contrast, the staff provides full, clear annotations about other Native American peoples like the Mandan and the seven divisions of Teton, "those Sioux who spoke the western or *Lak'ota* dialect" (3: 109n4). The excellent note about the Hidatsa amounts to a concise interpretive essay (3: 206-07n8)

Although the Moulton edition includes no previously unpublished writings or stylistic changes to transform or subvert our general impression of the explorers' journals, it does radically improve the Thwaites edition in its weakest dimension—maps. As one wrestled with the boxed set of maps in the Thwaites edition, it was difficult to make heads or tails out of the sometimes mislabeled, accordion-pleated reproductions of poor quality. In contrast, the first volume of the Moulton edition is a folio-size *Atlas of the Lewis and Clark Expedition* reproducing in facsimile on thick, creamy pages the maps Clark sketched on the expedition, those the captains consulted beforehand, and those executed after the trip, all clearly organized, labeled, and described. It is a beautiful set. Many were unavailable or unknown to Thwaites. Of the 129 maps in the atlas, 118 are at original size, and 42 have never been previously published. Many of Clark's lost maps have been reproduced from accurate copies of the originals prepared for the 1833 expedition of the naturalist Prince Maximilian of Wied Neuwied and the great Swiss artist Karl Bodmer. The only disappointment is the omission of the 1802 Aaron Arrowsmith map of North America. Moulton explains in a note that it is not printed because the Nicholas King 1803 map, which is printed, largely duplicates it. The reason does not hold up when one considers the overlap of other maps as well as Moulton's admission that King made significant modifications from Arrowsmith's map. As John Logan Allen notes, the Arrowsmith map was "the single most important item of cartographic data" (79) available to the explorers; more detailed than the King map in representing the upper Missouri basin, it served as a template for the explorers' cartographic corrections of the area. Jefferson had ordered a copy in the summer of 1803, and it is virtually certain that Lewis and Clark carried the map with them on the transcontinental trek. When gathering information about the upper Missouri from the Mandans during the winter of 1804-05, Lewis refers to the errors "I see that Arrasmith in his late map of N. America has laid down" (4: 266). Its absence from the atlas is unfortunate.

Nevertheless, 34 of the maps in the atlas show about 900 previously undetailed miles of the trip, and all reinforce the achievement of Clark as a geographer who sketched the course of the journey with impressive care. He records the longitude and latitude, though not always accurately, of all important geographical features as well as compass readings of each twist and turn in the streams and rivers he explored. As he sailed up the Missouri, Clark estimated distances by eyesight, recording, for instance, that the expedition had traveled between the mouth of the Missouri and the Platte River a distance of 600 miles. A surveying team several years later concluded from their instruments that the distance was actually 611 miles.

What does all of this material add up to in relation to those teachers and students of literature I referred to at the beginning of this survey? The maps suggest an answer. They are not just illustrative enhancements of the Moulton edition; they heighten our understanding of the explorers' writings, for they offer a detailed portfolio of the exploratory process itself, which is dramatized to a greater extent than in most expedition accounts in the journals' day-by-day record of route finding and decision making in the field. The 129 maps of the atlas also reflect a concern for measurement and demarcation informing much of the language of the journals. Almost any page offers the explorers' counts and measurements or estimates of size, weight, or time. On July 21, 1804, Clark observes the Platte River with typical detail:

> the Rapidity of the Current of this river which is greater than that of the Missourie, its width at the Mouth across the bars is about 3/4 of a mile, higher up I am told by one of the bowmen that he was 2 winters on this river above and that it does not rise <four> 7 feet, but Spreds over 3 miles at Some places, Capt Lewis & my Self went up Some Distance & Crossed found it Shallow. This river does not rise over 6 or 7 feet . . . The Otteaus a Small nation reside on the South Side 10 Leagues up, the Panies on the Same Side 5 Leagus higher up—about 10 Leagus up this river on the S. Side a Small river Comes into the Platt Called Salt River.
>
> (2: 401, 403)

After killing a rodent which the explorers eventually name the prairie dog, Clark notes: "The toe nails of his fore feet is one Inch & 3/4 long, & feet large; the nails of his hind feet 3/4 of an Inch long, the hind feet Small and toes Crooked, his legs are Short and when he Moves Just Sufficent to raise his body above the Ground" (2: 430). On May 5, 1805, Lewis similarly considers the corpse of a terrifying grizzly:

> it was a most tremendious looking anamal, and extreemly hard to kill notwithstanding he had five balls

through his lungs and five others in various parts he swam more than half the distance across the river to a sandbar & it was at least twenty minutes before he died; he did not attempt to attact, but fled and made the most tremendous roaring from the moment he was shot. We had no means of weighing this monster; Capt. Clark thought he would weigh 500 lbs. for my own part I think the estimate too small by 100 lbs. he measured 8 Feet 7 1/2 Inches from the nose to the extremety of the hind feet, 5 F. 10 1/2 Inch around the breast, 1 F. 11 I. arround the middle of the arm, & 3 F. 11 I arround the neck; his tallons which were five in number on each foot were 4 3/8 Inches in length.

(4: 113)

The explorers are here engaged in their work as scientific collectors of objective data about the natural world. These details, when added to astronomical symbols and tabulations of longitude and latitude, produce those texts that the *Columbia Literary History of the United States* finds so cluttered with tedious detail. But the cumulative effect of this detail is monumental. Clark's hunters shoot 1,001 deer. In one day Lewis and 10 men catch 800 fish. Gifts for Indians include 2,800 fishhooks, 4,600 assorted needles, and 130 twisted rolls of tobacco. Among medicines are 3,500 pills to counter sweats, 1,100 doses of emetics to induce vomiting, and over 600 pills, appropriately named "Rush's Thunderbolts" after their inventor, to counteract constipation. On the Missouri a floating mass of white feathers 70 yards wide and 3 miles long lead to an island covered with thousands of pelicans. The petrified backbone of an ancient fish is 45 feet long. The carcass of a beached whale measures 110 feet. July hail 7 inches in circumference hits the ground and bounces 12 feet into the air. Under the unbearably difficult circumstances of their composition, the writing of such detailed accounts was the most heroic of acts. Bristling with factual matter characteristic of scientific enterprises in the New World, the texts also reflect the early American literary fascination with registering the density of the physical world and ways of encountering it. The extensive language of measurement and demarcation elevates the journals into an epic of the quotidian.

In contrast to the language of contemporary science, the journals also offer the explorers' subjective responses in language borrowed from the prevailing lexicon of art, including literature, painting, sculpture, music, and architecture, to produce a vacillating style. The language of eighteenth-century science with its penchant for objective observation and quantification vies with that of art in its figurative modes of classifying the natural world. Both forms of expression, however, are ordered by the prevailing aesthetic expectations of the day. "Nature does nothing in vain" was the scientific position of the seventeenth-century physician William Harvey, and the eighteenth-century naturalist Thomas Jefferson concurs in *Notes on the State of Virginia,* "Such is the oeconomy of nature, that no instance can be produced of her having permitted any one race of her animals to become extinct; of her having formed any link in her great work so weak as to be

broken" (176). The stable relationships and processes of nature's economy, the concept that the great naturalist Baron Karl von Linné (or Carolus Linnaeus, as the master Latinist dubbed himself) coined in *Oeconomia Naturae* (1749), were apparent to both eighteenth-century naturalists and poets. Everything is in balance in the vast chain of being, according to general laws, to produce "th' amazing whole," as Alexander Pope writes, "Where, one step broken, the great scale's destroyed" (279). The key to such beliefs comes with Popian succinctness: "ORDER is Heaven's first law" (300), and "The general ORDER, since the whole began, / Is kept in nature, and is kept in Man" (276).

In the 1780s such aesthetic assumptions intertwined with political ideology to shape Jefferson's argument with the French naturalist, Comte Georges-Louis Leclerc de Buffon, about the character of the natural world in the Americas. Jefferson offered measurements of everything, from the height of American mules to the size of strawberries from his own garden, to counter Buffon's theory that flora and fauna had degenerated in the inferior environment of the New World so that "animals of America are tractable and timid, very few ferocious and none formidable. . . . All animals are smaller in North America than Europe. Everything shrinks under a 'niggardly sky and unprolific land'" (qtd. in Kastner 123). About America's wild animals, Jefferson exclaimed, "It does not appear that Messrs. de Buffon and D'Aubenton have measured, weighed, or seen those of America" (177). In the aftermath of this debate, Lewis and Clark's descriptions of large bison and fierce grizzlies became both scientific and patriotic weapons. Jefferson's view that the bones of what he called the Megalonyx in Virginia provided triumphant evidence against the purported degeneracy of American animals, along with his belief that the economy of nature disallows the annihilation of any species, led him to order Lewis and Clark to look out for signs of animals deemed rare or extinct, like the mammoth. According to the "traditionary testimony of the Indians," as Jefferson reports in *Notes on the State of Virginia* "this animal still exists in the northern and western parts of America" (176).

As for the native peoples of the New World, Jefferson is happy "for the honor of human nature" (183) to dismiss Buffon's claim that Indians are feeble, insensitive, timid, cowardly, and listless—lower than animals—lacking passion, intelligence, honor, body hair, and developed sexual organs. Lewis and Clark's detailed accounts of native habits and physical characteristics support Jefferson's defense, including his riposte that the "Indian is neither more defective in ardor nor more impotent with his female than the white man" (184). The explorers even comment on the bare breasts of women and other "parts" of both men and women "usually covered from formiliar view." When a Chinookan woman wearing a short cedar-bark skirt "stoops or places herself in many other attitudes, this battery of Venus is not altogether impervious to the inquisitive and penetrating eye of the amorite" (6: 435). Many tall, well-proportioned Indians, like the Flatheads, who "are a very light coloured people of large stature and comely form" (5: 197), and the Nez Perces—"Stout likeley men, hand-som women, and verry dressey in their way" (5: 258)—counter French claims of physical degeneracy. As evidence against moral degeneracy, numerous accounts of kindness and honor include the story of a man who walked all day to catch up with the expedition to return a hatchet left be-hind in camp.

No ideologues of noble savagery, Lewis and Clark also re-port what they perceive as brutality, thievery, and squalor. Their mixed accounts of unsavory and noble behavior cre-ate a complex ethnographic record of culturally diverse native peoples in their historical situation. "I think the most disgusting sight I have ever beheld," Lewis notes about some northwest coastal women, "is these dirty na-ked wenches" (6: 436), and Clark finds a coastal Cath-lamet village "the dirtiest and Stinkingest place I ever Saw" (7: 10). The cultural biases of certain reports are clear, as when Lewis watches some starving Lemhi Shos-hone eating raw venison innards—kidney, spleen, liver—"blood runing from the corners of their mouths"; one man "with about nine feet of the small guts one end of which he was chewing on while with his hands he was squezzing the contents out at the other. I really did not untill now think that human nature ever presented itself in a shape so nearly allyed to the brute creation. I viewed these poor starved divils with pity and compassion" (5: 103). Just three months earlier Lewis had delightedly praised his own cook's preparation of "*boudin blanc*"—composed of buffalo innards, intestine, and a "moderate portion" of what normally "*is not good to eat*"—as "one of the great-est delacies of the forrest" (4: 131). Those Indians the ex-plorers find least aesthetically pleasing and most corrupt are tribes on the northwest coast who have had extensive commerce with whites. Deteriorating and demoralizing conditions even extend to the speech of coastal Indians who "inform us that they speak the same language with ourselves, and give us proofs of their veracity by repeating many words of English, as musquit, powder, shot, nife, damned rascal, sun of a bitch &c." (6: 187).

In pursuing Jefferson's directions to gather linguistic infor-mation, Lewis and Clark engage in the search for the pos-sible origin of Native Americans and their interconnec-tions within the human family. The explorers collect extensive vocabulary lists, make comparative observations, and note inflectional distinctions in Indian speech. The Flatheads, they notice, appear to have a brogue as they speak a "gugling kind of languaje Spoken much thro the Throught" (5: 188). Reluctant to harden their data into a premature theory, the captains do not write down what Jo-seph Whitehouse reports in his journal: "we take these Savages to be the Welch Indians if their be any Such from the Language. So Capt. Lewis took down the names of everry thing in their Language, in order that it may be found out whether they are or whether they Sprang or ori-genated first from the welch or not" (Thwaites 7: 150-51). The legend that certain light-skinned Indians were off-shoots of a Welsh prince named Madoc and his compan-

ions who had traveled to America in the remote past was a popular theory of origin based on speculation that Native Americans were descendants of Old World peoples like the Phoenicians, Egyptians, Chinese, Greeks, or even one of the Lost Tribes of Israel. Jefferson had lamented the de-struction of so many tribes before their languages had been recorded, for he firmly believed that comparative lin-guistics would eventually "construct the best evidence of the derivation of this part of the human race" (227).

Apparent in Jefferson's views of native peoples and the natural world are the aesthetic underpinnings of value and meaning provided by the Linnaean concept of *oeconomia naturae*—the governing plan that sustains the processes of nature and the existence of individual species so that all natural things are interconnected, chained together, in a common, ordered function. The antecedents of such an aesthetic view extend at least as far back as Plato, but Lin-naeus approached the question of nature's balance, or na-ture's economy, as a scientific problem, albeit one with a mythological basis as old as Plato's *Protagoras* and a theological basis in its manifestations of the creator's be-nevolent disposition. What Linnaeus found in nature was an economy that worked for the good of the whole and the preservation of individual species. What Lewis and Clark found in the wilderness did not consistently support such an amiable view. A shadow world of disorder, underlying every aesthetic scheme, thus provides dynamic tension to the language of the journals.

Still, an aesthetics of order, moderation, regularity, and stability shaped Jefferson's and the explorers' preconcep-tions of Western rivers and mountains. Long navigable riv-ers flowing eastward suggested their counterparts in the West. One supposedly could anticipate the western course of the Missouri from the eastern course of the Ohio. The same apparent symmetry affected the order of mountains. "Our mountains," Jefferson writes, "are not solitary and scattered confusedly over the face of the country; but that they commence at about 150 miles from the sea-coast, are disposed in ridges one behind another, running nearly par-allel with the sea-coast." Jefferson adds that "as the tract of country between the sea-coast and the Mississippi be-comes narrower, the mountains converge into a single ridge" (142). A country seemingly ruled by such balance and economy had given rise to the myth of the Northwest Passage, a fantasy bolstered by the dreams of earlier ex-plorers and substantiated by the illusory documentation of maps, including those Lewis and Clark consulted in prepa-ration for their journey. A single "pyramidal height of land" (5: 1), as the Arrowsmith map showed, would offer an easy portage between the eastward flowing Missouri River and the westward flowing Columbia River.

Lewis and Clark's subjective responses to the Western wilderness also drew from artistic tropes ruled by Enlight-enment assumptions of harmony and order. Lewis finds a pleasing neoclassic balance between wildness and sweet-ness in the songs of birds, described as those "feathered tribes who salute the ear of the passing traveler with their wild and simple, yet s[w]eet and cheerfull melody" (4: 266); and he likens a stretch of the Great Plains to a "beatifull bowlinggreen in fine order" (3: 80). Expectations of encountering fertile, well-watered lands across the country trigger frequent, hopeful notations on areas suitable for agrarian settlement. Adjacent to "lofty and open forrests," Lewis finds "one of the most beatifully picteresque countries that I ever beheld . . . it's borders garnished with one continued garden of roses" (4: 266). Even late in the journey when the country does not quite measure up to its promise, Clark can speculate that it would be fine when cultivated. The explorers do seem at times like new men in a new Eden, walking peacefully among hundreds of animals that will not scare: "the whol face of the country was covered with herds of Buffaloe, Elk & Antelopes; deer are also abundant, but keep themselves more concealed in the woodland. the buffaloe Elk and Antelope are so gentle that we pass near them while feeding, without apearing to excite any alarm among them, and when we attract their attention, they frequently approach us more nearly to discover what we are" (4: 67).

Horror shatters this Edenic world in the form of enraged grizzlies, rampaging buffalo, violent storms, flash floods, smashed boats, horses rolling down hillsides, feet torn and bleeding from cactus needles, incessant rain, fleas, and mosquitoes. The thick, multiridged labyrinth of lines "scattered confusedly" (Jefferson 142) on Lewis and Clark's Map of the West denotes the actual Rocky Mountains the explorers enter, where, as Lewis writes, "every object here wears a dark and gloomy aspect. the tow[er]ing and projecting rocks in many places seem ready to tumble on us" (4: 402). Rather than the easy two-day portage the explorers anticipated, the trek spanned some 45 days of hardship from the headwaters of the Missouri to those of the Columbia. A reverential distance from wilderness might allow one to see reflected there a benevolent order and a peaceable millennium, but in the space of one day, Lewis is chased into a river by a bear, attacked by a "tyger cat," and charged by three buffalo bulls. "It now seemed to me," he writes, "that all the beasts of the neighbourhood had made a league to distroy me" (4: 294). The wilderness becomes animate in a way that is as primal as it is gothic. Measurable topography and objective events melt into romantic "seens of visionary inchantment" (4: 226) and "curious adventures" that "might be a dream" (4: 294). In the woods we return to reason and faith, Emerson was to say, but not in the West of Lewis and Clark where "evil gennii" (4: 225) lurk. The journals often become an epic story of confrontations with dark monsters and inexplicable powers. But the real snake in the garden hideously follows the explorers themselves. In the wanton smashing of a wolf's skull with a spontoon, the slaughtering of animals, and the proprietary attitudes toward the land, the explorers reveal sad glimpses of the dark side of American imperialism. Their first council with Native Americans likewise becomes both a threat and an omen. Characterized as the president's "red children," the Otos and Missouris are warned not to displease "your great father, the great chief of the Seventeen great nations of America, who could consume you as the fire consumes the grass of the plains" (Jackson 206). As a military expedition, the Corps of Discovery made way for others, seemingly bent on transforming what Clark calls "a land of Plenty" (3: 66) into a land of waste.

When the conventions of the age fail to encompass the Western wilderness, Lewis opts for the conventional trope of noting such failures. While trying to describe the Great Falls of the Missouri, Lewis "truly regretted" that he had not brought along a camera obscura, sometimes called a Claude glass, the popular device carried by tourists that projected an image though a lens onto the back wall of the box. The reflected photographic image could then be traced onto a sheet of paper, rendering the scene into the ordered perspective of picturesque art. But as commentators like Robert Edson Lee and Robert Lawson-Peebles have noted, the Great Falls of the Missouri would only elude the tranquil principles of Claude Lorrain's aesthetics. To apprehend these extravagant waterfalls, Lewis also "wished for the pencil of Salvator Rosa . . . or the pen of Thompson," but the aesthetic framework informing the wild, desolate scenes of the seventeenth-century Italian painter and the eighteenth-century Scottish poet would be "fruitless and vain" for Lewis to achieve (4: 285). Only the concept of the Burkean sublime, which, as Ernst Cassirer notes, had shattered the "conceptual framework of previous aesthetic systems" (329), could suggest the grandeur that "fills [Lewis] with such pleasure and astonishment" (4: 285). Enlightenment order collapses into sublime asymmetry, and the aesthetic of measurement shifts to the aesthetic of the measureless to accommodate natural disorders like floods and earthquakes. Still, Lewis feels he can offer only an "imperfect description" of these "truly magnificent and sublimely grand" torrents of falling water (4: 285). Unlike Jefferson, who confidently described the Natural Bridge on his own Virginia property as the "most sublime of Nature's works" (148), Lewis wrestles for two days to convey a "faint idea" (4: 285) of the beauty and sublimity that distinguish the twin falls, only to come up with his own uneasy, qualified categorization of them: "nor could I for some time determine on which of those two great cataracts to bestoe the palm, on this or that which I had discovered yesterday; at length I determined between these two great rivals for glory that this was *pleasingly beautifull,* while the other was *sublimely grand*" (4: 290).

It is now a commonplace of Lewis and Clark criticism to characterize the stylistic extremes of the two explorers as reflections of their sensibilities. Laconic, measured, and scientifically objective accounts of the environment are identified with Clark. Effusive, romantic, and subjective literary responses are identified with Lewis. The styles supposedly mirror the personalities of the two men as polar opposites: Lewis as a brooding introvert given to melancholy speculation, Clark an even-tempered, sociable extrovert inclined toward good-natured self-effacement. Charles Willson Peale's famous portraits, now hanging in the Independence National Historical Park in Philadelphia, seem to emphasize these contrasting images. Clark, a husky man with a high forehead and shock of red hair, looks boldly from the canvas directly at the viewer, while Lewis, tall and slender with sensitive bow lips and an aquiline nose, gazes dreamily toward the side of the canvas. The contrasting careers of the two men after their renowned expedition also have reinforced the image of Clark as a gregarious public official and Lewis as a moody loner. Clark pursued a long and distinguished career as superintendent of Indian Affairs at St. Louis, while Lewis experienced a brief and troubled governorship of the Louisiana Territory—ridden with alcoholism and abruptly terminated by a murky death.

The stylistic differences of the two men cannot be ignored, nor can their differences of temperament—Lewis is more subjective, circumlocutory, and polished, Clark more terse, objective, and direct—but the journals do not bear out the rigid categorizations of either style or personality imposed from hindsight on their subsequent careers. Lewis employs the descriptive discourse of science as scrupulously as Clark, even more so in many cases, particularly in regard to flora and fauna, where his command of technical terminology is greater. Lewis's rhetorical nod to the "truly magnificent and sublimely grand" (4: 285) Great Falls of the Missouri occupies only a brief moment in pages of careful observation and measurement. At times Clark's quantitative topographical recordings also might break into brief rhetorical flourishes about "butifull fertile picteresque Country" (7: 223), or a place he called "bad humered Island as we were in a bad humer" (3: 114). The distinction between verbose Lewis and laconic Clark also needs qualification, for Clark contributed to the journals many more of the 862,500 total words than did Lewis. Unless some journals were lost, Lewis made entries for only 441 of the 863 days, while Clark provided entries for all but 10 days, which he later summarized.

Moments even occur where the two men seemingly reverse personalities, and Clark becomes the melancholy loner depressed by bad weather and bugs, while Lewis retains his joie de vivre amid misfortune and longs for the companionship of friends and civil society. "O! how horrible is the day," Clark writes in November 1805, during winter encampment on the Pacific Coast (6: 79); "!O how Tremedious is the day. This dredfull wind and rain. . . . O! how disagreeable is our Situation dureing this dreadfull weather" (6: 92); "Small bugs, worms, Spiders, flyes & insects of different kinds are to be . . . Seen in abundance" (6: 94); "Since we arrived in Sight of the Great Western; (for I cannot Say Pacific) Ocian as I have not Seen one pacific day Since my arrival in its vicinity . . . tempestous and horiable" (6: 104); "The winds violent Trees falling in every direction, whorl winds, with gusts of rain Hail & Thunder, this kind of weather lasted all day, Certainly one of the worst days that ever was!" (6: 126); "The flees are So troublesom that I have Slept but little for 2 nights past and we have regularly to kill them out of our blankets every day for Several past" (6: 138). On Christmas Day, 1805, Clark complains, "we would have Spent this day the nativity of Christ in feasting, had we any thing either to

raise our Sperits or even gratify our appetites, our Diner concisted of pore Elk, So much Spoiled that we eate it thro' mear necessity, Some Spoiled pounded fish and a fiew roots" (6: 138). On New Year's Day, 1806, as the weather improves, Clark flatly notes, "This morning proved cloudy with moderate rain, after a pleasent worm night during which there fell but little rain" (6: 153). In contrast, Lewis is able to keep his spirits elevated as he faces the new year: "our repast of this day tho' better than that of Christmass, consisted principally in the anticipation of the 1st day of January 1807, when in the bosom of our friends we hope to participate in the mirth and hilarity of the day, and when with the zest given by the recollection of the present, we shall completely, both mentally and corporally, enjoy the repast which the hand of civilization has prepared for us" (6: 151-52).

The expeditionary record shows that Lewis and Clark form an alliance that transcends their differences of personality and style. They seem to command, effortlessly and without conflict, as one; over the course of the journey, both demonstrate cunning, intelligence, and dignity in their leadership of others. In chronicling their trials and achievements, the heroes of this epic adventure sing of themselves, becoming—in a modern literary twist—their own bards. Where modesty commends one to silence about his own achievement, history compels the other to document the worthiness of the event, producing an absence of boastfulness that Theodore Roosevelt found so impressive. The effectiveness of this strange alliance, a sharing of command that defies military hierarchy, is unique to military history. While Lewis enjoys eating dog meat and Clark hates it, and Lewis craves salt and Clark dismisses it as a luxury, and Lewis likes eating black currants and Clark favors yellow ones, the two leaders otherwise form a harmonious relationship. A moving aspect of the journals is how much they care for each other. They remain friends to the end.

It is the composite character of these leaders—their pervasive outpouring of intellectual and moral energy—that sustains the expedition and guarantees its success. This composite character manifests itself in the thousands of right decisions the leaders jointly make to avert disaster. Only when Lewis and Clark are apart on the return journey does tragedy strike, when two Blackfeet Indians are killed. Clark's declamations against the harsh winter weather also peak when the men are separated. While they are still apart, Lewis is almost killed when accidentally shot by one of his own hunters. It is as if the division of the classical hero into two men allows Lewis and Clark to embody heroic impulses in believable ways. They become heroes cut down to credible size, eighteenth-century men who merge into a composite character acceptable to the skepticism of the modern age. Of all the heroic moments recorded in the journals, however, none surpasses the writing of the journals themselves. In a touching moment, Lewis notes "the ink feizes in my pen" (5: 133), and yet he continues to write. When the explorers copy from each other's field notes or journals, original authorship sometimes becomes blurred. The "I" of some entries becomes that composite hero and author whom Clark seems to have honored, after his co-captain's death, when he named his son Meriwether Lewis Clark. The journals appropriately end with William Clark's last brief entry on September 25, 1806: "a fine morning we commenced wrighting &c" (8: 372).

The vacillating style of this composite authorship is less the product of differing sensibilities than of the era's competing languages of art and science. That two men happened to write the journals conveniently symbolizes the split in discourse that had characterized American nature writing since the eighteenth century. In the 1787 edition of his *Notes on the State of Virginia,* Jefferson typically jumps from the language of science to that of art when his quantitative description of Virginia's topographical features breaks into paeans to the sublimity of the Natural Bridge or the Potomac River. Even more extreme are the wild swings in style in Bartram's 1791 *Travels.* Bartram's sudden flip-flops between neoclassic poetic tropes and scientific Latinate descriptions now cause student wonderment that such a schizophrenic text was actually written by one person. A similar tension continued into the nineteenth century, evident in the split between Thoreau's transcendental flights and those journalistic observations once dismissed as dry, meaningless factual details about grasses, snowfalls, tree rings, lichens, and seeds. After the Civil War, the prose of trained geologists like John Wesley Powell, Clarence King, and Clarence Dutton vacillates between technical description and metaphors drawn from mythology and architecture to shape a visionary, aesthetic response to an apparently inanimate landscape. Static buttes, mesas, and canyon lands become animate dramas of shifting forms under the violently changing pressures of wind, water, fire, and light. In *My First Summer in the Sierra* (1911), John Muir's prose undergoes extravagant stylistic shifts not seen since Bartram's *Travels* 120 years earlier. Technical descriptions of lateral moraines, *Quercus Douglasii,* residual glaciers, albicaulus pines, and bituminous beds erupt into ecstatic renderings of the "spiritual affinities" binding the personalities of trees, ants, people, and "noble rock . . . full of thought, clothed with living light" (129). The birds of Burroughs, reduced at one moment to conventional poetic epithets of "widowed mothers" or "happy bridegrooms" (36), are rendered vivid in subsequent sentences of astonishing transparency yet scientific accuracy.[3]

Part of the reason for the vacillating style of American nature writing lies in the increasing professionalization of scientific pursuits and scientific language in the eighteenth century. Earlier writers of American natural history drew from a common language, free of specialized terminology, to record both natural phenomena and personal experience, so that Thoreau could refer to the "strong and hearty but reckless hit-or-miss style" in the early works of John Josselyn and William Wood, "as if they spoke with a relish, smacking their lips like a coach-whip, caring more to speak heartily than scientifically true" (108). By Bartram's

time, "natural philosophy," a term once loosely encompassing all scientific pursuits, had become sharply differentiated from "natural history," which in turn was splintering into the specifically termed studies of botany, zoology, geology, and mineralogy. Specialization of scientific tasks was making way for the nineteenth-century invention of the word *scientist,* and the specialized language of naturalists like Bartram pointed toward James Fenimore Cooper's caricature of Dr. Battius in *The Prairie* (1827), floundering through the wilderness, a danger to himself and others, oblivious to everything except new species, gibbering in the Latin derivatives of the Linnaean system.

Why Lewis and Clark avoided the Linnaean system of taxonomy and nomenclature has puzzled many commentators. Recent studies have shown Lewis to be better trained and more scientifically competent than is often assumed. His careful descriptions of plants include no fewer than 200 technical botanical terms. He had studied Latin as a young man and had worked for two years with Jefferson who, as Cutright observes, "took to binomials like a poet to iambic pentameter" (*Lewis and Clark* 8). At Fort Clatsop in 1806 Lewis exhibited familiarity with Linnaean principles in the organization of his ethnobotanical and ethnozoological data. Because they provided the first detailed, formal descriptions of new flora and fauna, the explorers are now credited with the discovery of 178 plants and 122 birds, animals, fish, and reptiles, including the cutthroat trout, mountain quail, pack rat, western hog-nose snake, western meadowlark, kit fox, Lewis's woodpecker, and Clark's nutcracker. But in their journals Lewis and Clark employ Latinate classifications only three times and an actual binomial only once. As a result, their prose does not reach the extreme vacillations of diction marking other works of natural history such as Bartram's.[4]

The explorers' scrupulous adherence to Jefferson's instructions during the trip west suggests that their use of the vernacular met with the president's charge and approval. "Your observations are to be taken," Jefferson wrote, "with great pains & accuracy, to be entered distinctly, & intelligibly for others as well as yourself" (1127). Although Jefferson himself used scientific names as often as the vernacular in his own writings, and although he believed in the aesthetic and theoretical order of nature's economy, he maintained that the first task of good science is the accurate collection and precise description of data. "A patient pursuit of facts, and cautious combination and comparison of them is the drudgery to which man is subjected by his Maker, if he wishes to attain sure knowledge" (qtd. in Miller 44). A faulty scientific investigator like Buffon too precipitously selects "facts, and adopts all the falsehoods which favor his theory, and very gravely retails such absurdities as zeal for a theory alone could swallow" (1261). As a Lockean empiricist, Jefferson notes that "he who attempts to reduce [the natural world] into departments, is left to do it by the lines of his own fancy" (1330). Here, Jefferson joins hands with his old intellectual avatar, Buffon, who had attacked the Linnaean system from its incep-

Fort Clatsop, winter quarters of the Lewis and Clark expedition (1805-06).

tion, arguing that its categories of classes, orders, genera, and species imposed an enormous abstraction on the natural world.

Jefferson's views dramatize what Linnaeus himself had come to realize: the *systema naturae* is actually a *systema Linnaei.* The system is artificial, Linnaeus grudgingly acknowledged, although he maintained that it was a step toward the discovery of the natural system he felt sure existed. In searching for the structure of nature and—his favorite slogan—the "object itself," he sought to rid science of figurative language and allusion. But while rejecting the falsity of rhetoric, in Hobbesian and Lockean terms, as powerful instruments of error and deceit, Linnaeus found himself replacing one rhetorical trope for another. His "kingdoms" of plants and animals in the "empire" of nature, composed of "phalanxes," "regiments," and "recruits" underscore the imperialist thrust of his scientific enterprise to dominate both the study of nature and nature itself. In his last edition of *Systema naturae,* however, Linnaeus no longer insisted on the immutability of species, the concept that had sustained the aesthetic order and meta-

phor of nature's economy. The Linnaean system, prior to the moment of its widest acceptance, was already crumbling.

By the time Lewis and Clark trekked into the West, rejection of Linnaeus's system and method was widespread. The breakdown was anticipated in Bartram's *Travels,* where an Ovidian world of metamorphosis shattered the Linnaean economy of nature. Likewise, in *Elements of Botany* (1803), appropriately illustrated with Bartram's pre-Darwinian drawings, Benjamin Smith Barton provided a running criticism of Linnaeus's ideas. Newly proposed systems had begun to dominate the sciences. Antoine Laurent de Jussieu's new botanical system was superseding that of Linnaeus. In zoology, Baron Georges Cuvier completely revised Linnaeus's classifications of animals, and Jean-Baptiste de Monet de Lamarck subverted the economy of nature with a theory of organic evolution. In the age of Romanticism, old metaphoric notions of teleology and animism that Linnaeus had tried so hard to kick out the door of science would reenter through the window newly guised in the acceptable concept of "life." But to Jefferson, such scientific revolutions merely added more arbitrary systems to the old. He criticized Antoine-Laurent Lavoisier's standardized nomenclature in chemistry for prematurely closing the door to discovery and retarding the "progress of science by a jargon" (qtd. in Greene 33). One new discovery, he said, could send the whole system crumbling. "We can no longer say there is nothing new under the sun," Jefferson writes. "The great extent of our republic is new. Its sparse habitation is new" (1086).[5]

Lewis and Clark's disregard of Latinate terminology coincides with a need to forge language appropriately descriptive of a new country and its inhabitants. While the explorers never completely abandon the literary and scientific conventions of their age, a qualitative change does occur over the course of the journals as those conventions diminish. Most of Clark's topographical descriptions in quantitative scientific language appear early in the journals. Conventional rhetoric and cultural assumptions break down as the country, animals, and native peoples of the West effect new forms of perception. Less often as they move west do the explorers encounter landscapes that "exhibit a most romantic appearance" (4: 225). On the return home, the Rocky Mountains become to Lewis "that icy barier which seperates me from my friends and Country, from all which makes life esteemable" (7: 267). Conceptual frameworks and aesthetic orderings, like instruments of measurement hauled from the East, crack, as did the expedition's three thermometers. Two streams the explorers tried to name in honor of the Enlightenment virtues of Wisdom and Philanthropy are now called Big Hole and Stinking Water. At the Great Falls of the Missouri, where Lewis finds his aesthetic descriptions shaky, he watches helplessly as his collapsible iron boat, designed and built in the East, sinks into a Western river. In the Rockies the explorers abandon their canoes and depend on Indian horses to cross the Bitterroots to where they can chop and carve native cottonwoods into dugouts for the final run down the Snake and Columbia rivers to the sea. Attempts to render their experience, the country, and its wildlife through conventional expression give way to new terms. Language itself has to be altered in the process; words coined and twisted to fit the occasion produce in the journals, according to the lexicon compiled by Elijah Criswell, the first usage of 1,004 new words or extended meanings in the American language, some adapted from Native American languages and frontier French, others jammed into new linguistic hybrids. Instead of being honored for using scientific terms like *Odocoileus hemionus,* Lewis and Clark are remembered for adding the names "mule deer," "prairie dog," and "whistling swan" to the American language.

The best linguistic study of the journals, Elijah H. Criswell's *Lewis and Clark: Linguistic Pioneers,* appeared as a quarterly issue of University of Missouri Studies in 1940. Although photocopies are currently available from the Lewis and Clark Trail Heritage Foundation, this fine 313-page monograph has never been republished. This is a shame, for Criswell's investigations of Lewis and Clark's Americanisms—ripe for correction and expansion—offer fruitful entry into the explorers' achievement as writers. The Nebraska edition, for example, might have noted how Lewis and Clark, as masters of the vernacular, used American words that in some cases had recently entered the language, like *cut-off, tote, overalls, barefoot, cloud up, overnight, shut of, lick* (as a verb), *jerk* (in reference to cured meat), and *balance* (in the sense of "remainder" or "leftover"). Criswell presents 301 examples of new words or new meanings of old words that antedate their earliest usage cited in the *Oxford English Dictionary.* The *OED* does note that some Americanisms like *noon it* (as in "we nooned it just above the entrance of a large river" 4: 124) mark their first recorded appearance in the journals, but it leaves out others like the specific definition of *cheek,* as Clark uses the word, when he observes after Lewis is shot that the bullet "cut the cheek of the right buttock for 3 inches in length" (8: 290).

The new Nebraska edition of the journals does not gloss words or extended meanings that Lewis and Clark contributed to the language, nor does it note when they use recently coined Americanisms, but it does draw on Criswell's lexicon to define some nonce words, like *happerst* as "some form of knapsack, perhaps from 'hoppas,' an Indian knapsack" (4: 253n10). Other apparent nonce words or individualisms like *dismorallity* remain unglossed. We learn from Criswell that *dismorallity* is Lewis's humorous combination of *disease* and *morality* to describe flatulence as "a dismorallity of order in the abdomen" from smoking intoxicating Indian tobacco (6: 179). As these examples show, not all neologisms in the journals have entered the language. Neither did the maxim "accidents will happen in the best families," nor the adage "to push a tolerable good pole" (4: 423), but such coinages do invest the journals with lively, inventive prose responsive to fresh experience. Given the excellent annotations of the Moulton edition in other fields, one can only wish that it might have more fully built on Criswell's preliminary linguistic investigation and filled its gaps. For example, the term *hair pipe* baffled Criswell. "I do not know," he writes, "the identity of this article apparently taken along for Indian trade" (45). Moulton offers no help. The term *hair pipe* receives no gloss. But as one can readily see in Karl Bodmer's and George Catlin's paintings of Great Plains Indians, hair pipes are tubular lips of conch shells about the size of normal pipe stems, drilled through the center from end to end so that they can be strung in the hair. They were as popular among Plains Indians as the famous blue beads that the explorers also brought with them.

Besides freshly minted words that would eventually make their way into dictionaries, the explorers' diction and syntax reveal the survival of obsolete words and the frequent use of archaisms in American speech. Many words, though departing from today's standard English, extend back to older forms, even to Middle English. When Lewis refers to a woman's breast as a "bubby," his use of this obsolete word lacks the vulgar connotations of later slang and employs its former acceptable usage in prose and poetry by writers like John Dryden. When Clark writes "for to" (as in "I prepare Some presents for to give the Indians of the *Mahars* nation" 2: 474) and Lewis writes "same of" for "same as," the result is not bad grammar but use of once standard forms that have survived in American dialect into the twentieth century.

Irregularities of grammar and spelling in the journals have given commentators much to chuckle over. A favorite observation is that the explorers spell the word *Sioux* at least 27 different ways. In an age when orthographic variants were common, even Jefferson regularly began sentences without capital letters and spelled words inconsistently. But the absence of standardized spelling before the publication of Noah Webster's dictionary in 1828 cannot account for the extremes of the journals. Who but Clark, one scholar asks, could create such a "classic howler" as "fee-Mail" for *female* (Betts 11)? Yet in spelling *accent* "axcent" and *sagacity* "segassity," the explorers are clearly striving to spell words phonetically. Rather than howlers and malapropisms, the explorers often accurately present the vernacular as it was heard at the time in the speech of Virginia and Kentucky backwoodsmen. Sharp ears, rather than ignorance or subliteracy, account for much of the inventive orthography in the journals.

While Criswell's study is primarily one of vocabulary, not of grammar or orthography, his work offers a valuable starting point for investigation of the journals as a compendium of colloquial pronunciation. Some spellings produce dialect reminiscent of Mark Twain's best efforts to put colloquial speech on the page, as when we read "fur" for *far,* "git" for *get,* "jest" for *just,* "tegious" for *tedious,* "furin" for *foreign,* "pint" for *point,* and—sounding much like Natty Bumppo—"sarvis-berry" for *service-berry.* In certain words, consonants intrude or disappear, as can still be heard in some regional dialects today, as in "idear" for *idea,* "onced" for *once,* "musquetor" for *mosquito.* The same is true for the formation of doubly inflected participles like "drownded."

Variations in spelling, along with departures from current standard usage in the forms of nouns and the tenses of verbs, sometimes reflect not only regional pronunciation but also the survival of once acceptable forms, as in "catched" for *caught.* In fact, the word *fitten,* whose usage in England is last noted in the *OED* in a quotation for 1642, continued to survive in America to become a favorite colloquialism of Twain. To study the journals in this way, as reflecting speech in the time of Lewis and Clark, opens a resource for understanding the development of American English. Perhaps an analogy with the interpretation of Mayan transcriptions is not inappropriate. For years, Mayan glyphs had eluded decipherment until scholars overcame the mistake earlier decoders had made in thinking that glyphic writing did not reflect spoken language. Reading the journals as largely oral transcriptions reveals Lewis and Clark's mastery of the vernacular in their achievement as effective, vigorous writers.

It might be argued that the vernacular adds a competing strain to the literary and scientific languages of the journals. In a way, it does, producing a linguistically tense, multistyled text common to epics, like Dante's, that employ the vernacular. In such tensions, symbolically reinforced through dual authorship, the journals characterize the vacillation in much American nature writing between, on the one hand, scientific precision and poetic extravagance, or on the other, scientific reductiveness and poetic vision. The vernacular occasionally offers a way out of this split by fusing literary and scientific concerns in untechnical language. When Lewis describes how antelopes are like birds on the plains, figurative language anticipates the metamorphosis of post-Darwinian science. Anthropocentrism diminishes. One aspect of nature is defined in terms of another. When Clark documents the rise and fall of a river in the animistic speech of a backwoodsman, his writing fuses the relics of an older language with that of future geologists like Powell or King whose visions of landscapes are more alive than conventional science would allow. The literary result of such composition, unlike a scientific experiment, is as unrepeatable as a Twain novel.

The new Nebraska edition of *The Journals of the Lewis and Clark Expedition* in its inclusiveness takes an important step in fostering appreciation of the journals as an important contribution to American literature. On display are those monumental accumulations of data and varied systems of notation—a massive achievement in the genre of natural history—that take on epic characteristics. Ragged and unpolished, the journals now bear comparison to oral tales that are often even more expansive, digressive, and tediously detailed, unlike the doctored versions that survive in popularly printed editions. The unpolished journals appropriately become an unfinished epic for a nation still discovering its ties to the natural world. Like other great nature writers, Lewis and Clark often move against contemporary conventions toward an apprehension of the unknown and the uncategorized in imaginative ways that abandon technical terms and stock conceits for fresh, flexible uses of the vernacular. Such writing anticipates future moments in Thoreau's *Maine Woods* (1864), Burroughs's *Signs and Seasons* (1886), and Muir's *Mountains of California* (1894), where fusions of documentary and visionary expression through a vernacular style will continue to invigorate the genre of American nature writing at its best.

Notes

1. In 1893 Elliott Coues wrote in the introduction to his edition of the journals, "This is our national epic of exploration" (v). In 1988 editor Gary Moulton writes, "It is our national epic of exploration" ("Lewis and Clark" 8). John Logan Allen notes that the expedition "has long been recognized as the American exploratory epic" (Rev. of *The Journals* 630). Marius Bewley observes that the "community that existed between Lewis and Clark" and the members of the expedition "was very much of that character we find described in heroic poetry" (214).

2. This erroneous claim seems to have originated with N. Bryllion Fagin's *William Bartram: Interpreter of*

the *American Landscape* (1933), but it reappears in Josephine Herbst's *New Green World* (1954), Joseph Ewan's introduction to William Bartram, *Botanical and Zoological Drawings, 1756-1788* (1968), and Kastner, among others.

3. It is interesting to note that Stephen Fender discerns in the journals, letters, and diaries of 1849 transcontinental travelers a similar "double style," varying between formal and factual description, picturesque and scientific rhetoric, or literal and figurative language. Fender extends his examination of the "forty-niners' 'double style'" to include "their better known contemporaries, Hawthorne, Thoreau, and Melville, whose prose also exhibits (though more designedly and much more famously) the strategic fracture between fantasy and documentary fact" (14). Although Fender has been criticized for a vague shifting of dualistic categories, his stylistic observations about mid-century travel accounts, particularly those of John Charles Frémont, are valuably pertinent to this study of nature writing.

4. Field collectors like Lewis and Clark would normally not presume to name new species but would turn over their descriptions and samples to taxonomic specialists (usually noncollectors), such as the German botanist Frederick Pursh, who received Lewis's herbarium and credited the explorers with providing 122 specimens of the new plants scientifically named and classified in his two-volume *Flora Americae Septentrionalis* (1814), including ones tagged with newly coined genera and species honoring their discoverers as *Lewisia* and *Clarkia*. Field collectors, however, would commonly use Latinate binomials for the identification of known species and Linnaean terms for the classification of new species, as Lewis does when comparing the eulachon or candle fish to "the herring, shad anchovey &c of the Malacopterygious Order & Class Clupea" (6: 344) or when describing the magpie as a "bird of the *Corvus genus*" and "order of the pica" (3: 83).

5. Resistance to the Linnaean system coincided with widespread American suspicion of specialized terminology. The earlier objection of some poets like Joel Barlow to foreign terms in the American language, especially a Latinity equated with monarchy, also shaped the views of those in the sciences, such as Charles Willson Peale. Although Peale's museum in Philadelphia provided an orderly exposition of natural history according to Linnaean principles, Peale himself rejected Linnaean terminology and complained to Jefferson that "men pretending to a knowledge must be humored with the high sounding names made from the dead Languages" (Jackson 308-09).

Works Cited

Ames, Fisher. *Works of Fisher Ames,* Ed. Seth Ames. Vol. 1. Boston, 1854. 2 vols.

Allen, John Logan. *Passage through the Garden: Lewis and Clark and the Image of the American Northwest.* Urbana: U of Illinois P, 1975.

———. Rev. of *The Journals of the Lewis and Clark Expedition,* vols. 2-4, ed. Gary E. Moulton. *William and Mary Quarterly* 46 (1989): 630-32.

Barton, Benjamin Smith. Letters to William Bartram. 19 Feb. and 13 Dec. 1788. Bartram Papers. Historical Society of Pennsylvania, Philadelphia.

Bergon, Frank. Introduction. *The Journals of Lewis and Clark.* Ed. Bergon. New York: Viking, 1989. ix-xix.

Betts, Robert B. "'we commenced wrighting &c': A Salute to the Ingenious Spelling and Grammar of William Clark." *We Proceeded On* 6.4 (1980): 10-12.

Bewley, Marius. "The Heroic and the Romantic West." *New York Review of Books* 8 Apr. 1965. Rpt. in *Masks and Mirrors: Essays in Criticism.* By Bewley. New York: Atheneum, 1970. 213-20.

Burroughs, John. *A Sharp Lookout: Selected Nature Essays of John Burroughs.* Ed. Frank Bergon. Washington: Smithsonian, 1987.

Carlyle, Thomas. Letter to Emerson. 8 July 1851. *The Correspondence of Emerson and Carlyle.* Ed. Joseph Slater. New York: Columbia UP, 1964, 467-69.

Cassirer, Ernst. *The Philosophy of the Enlightenment.* Trans. Fritz C. A. Koelln and James P. Pettegrove. Princeton: Princeton UP, 1951.

Coues, Elliott. Introduction. *History of the Expedition under the Command of Lewis and Clark. . . .* Ed. Coues. Vol. 1. New York, 1893. 4 vols.

Criswell, Elijah Harry. *Lewis and Clark: Linguistic Pioneers.* University of Missouri Studies 15. Columbia: U of Missouri P, 1940.

Cutright, Paul Russell. *A History of the Lewis and Clark Journals.* Norman: U of Oklahoma P, 1976.

———. *Lewis and Clark: Pioneering Naturalists.* Urbana: U of Illinois P, 1969.

Duncan, Dayton. *Out West: An American Journey.* New York: Viking, 1987.

Fender, Stephen, *Plotting the Golden West: American Literature and the Rhetoric of the California Trail.* Cambridge: Cambridge UP, 1981.

Gilpin, William. *Mission of the North American People, Geographical, Social, and Political. . . .* Rev. 2nd ed. Philadelphia, 1874.

Goodman, Howard. "Lewis and Clark Redux." *We Proceeded On* 19.4 (1993): 25-26.

Greene, John C. *American Science in the Age of Jefferson.* Ames: Iowa State UP, 1984.

Harper, Francis. Introduction. *The Travels of William Bartram: Naturalist's Edition.* Ed. Harper. New Haven: Yale UP, 1958. xvii-xxxv.

Hedges, William L. "Toward a National Literature." *Columbia Literary History of the United States*. Ed. Emory Elliott et al. New York: Columbia UP, 1988. 187-202.

Jackson, Donald, ed. *Letters of the Lewis and Clark Expedition with Related Documents, 1783-1854*. Urbana: U of Illinois P, 1962.

Jefferson, Thomas. *Writings: Autobiography,* Notes on the State of Virginia, *Public and Private Papers, Addresses, Letters*. Ed Merrill D. Peterson. New York: Library of America, 1984.

Kastner, Joseph. *A Species of Eternity*. New York: Knopf, 1977.

Miller, Charles A. *Jefferson and Nature: An Interpretation*. Baltimore: Johns Hopkins UP, 1988.

Moulton, Gary E. "The Journals of the Lewis and Clark Expedition: Beginning Again." *We Proceeded On* 6.4 (1980): 14-16.

———. "Lewis and Clark: Our 'National Epic of Exploration' Worthy of Monumental Editing." *Nebraska Alumnus* Mar 1-1 Apr. 1988: 8-11.

Muir, John. *My First Summer in the Sierra*. Boston: Houghton, 1911.

Pope, Alexander. "An Essay on Man." *Alexander Pope*. Ed. Pat Rogers. Oxford Authors. New York: Oxford UP, 1993. 270-309.

Thoreau, Henry David. *The Journal of Henry D. Thoreau*. Ed. Torrey Bradford and Francis H. Allen. Vol. 7. Boston: Houghton, 1906. 14 vols.

Thwaites, Reuben Gold, ed. *Original Journals of Lewis and Clark, 1804-1806*. . . . 8 vols. New York: Dodd, 1904-05.

FURTHER READING

Biography

Bakeless, John. *Lewis and Clark: Partners in Discovery*. New York: William Morrow & Company, 1947, 498p.
    Biography of the famous team of explorers, based on original documents and archival material. Emphasizes the entire length of Lewis and Clark's relationship, rather than just their years together on their expedition.

Criticism

Botkin, Daniel B. *Our Natural History: The Lessons of Lewis and Clark*. New York: G. P. Putnam's Sons, 1995, 300p.
    From an environmental perspective, compares the American West as seen by Lewis and Clark during their epic journey of 1804 to 1806 with the West of the late twentieth century, a landscape almost completely transformed by modern technology and industry.

Burroughs, R. D. *Exploration Unlimited: The Story of the Lewis and Clark Expedition*. Detroit, Mich.: Wayne University Press, 1953, 48p.
    Brief account of the expedition with an emphasis on the scientific objectives of the journey.

Duncan, Dayton. *The Journey of the Corps of Discovery: Lewis and Clark; An Illustrated History*. New York: Alfred A. Knopf, 1997, 248p.
    Heavily illustrated book based on a film documentary by Ken Burns. Intermixes original writings with background information and details supplied by the author.

———. *Out West: An American Journey*. New York: Viking, 1987, 434p.
    Travel book in which the author compares the original route taken by Lewis and Clark with what he witnessed while retracing their steps during the early to mid-1980s.

Gasque, Thomas J. "Lewis and Clark's Onomastic Assumptions." *Midwestern Folklore* 21, Nos. 1-2 (Spring/Fall 1995): 30-38.
    Explores the onomastic assumptions that Lewis and Clark brought with them on their expedition, and how these assumptions affected both their recording and assigning of placenames.

Greenfield, Bruce. "The Rhetoric of British and American Narratives of Exploration. *Dalhousie Review* 65, No. 1 (Spring 1985): 56-65.
    In part, focuses on Nicholas Biddle's 1814 account of the expedition in an effort to examine the popularity of exploration reports in America during the early to mid-nineteenth century.

Jackson, Donald. *Among the Sleeping Giants: Occasional Pieces on Lewis and Clark*. Urbana: University of Illinois Press, 1987, 136p.
    Provides anecdotal details to the epic journey of Lewis and Clark.

———, ed. *Letters of the Lewis and Clark Expedition, with Related Documents, 1783-1854*. Urbana: University of Illinois Press, 1962, 728p.
    Reprints letters and other documents related to the expedition, revealing the extensive preparations for the journey, the Spanish reaction to the trip, and the struggle to publish a narrative of the findings, among other topics.

Laut, A. C. "Lewis and Clark." In *Pathfinders of the West: Being the Thrilling Story of the Adventures of the Men Who Discovered the Great Northwest: Radisson, La Vérendrye, Lewis and Clark,* pp. 307-34. New York: The Macmillan Company, 1922.

Historical account of the Lewis and Clark expedition based on the explorers' journals.

Lavender, David. *The Way to the Western Sea: Lewis and Clark Across the Continent.* New York: Harper & Row, 1988, 444p.

Readable narrative detailing the course of the expedition. Opens with historical background about Lewis and Jefferson.

Quaife, Milo M., ed. *The Journals of Captain Meriwether Lewis and Sergeant John Ordway, Kept on the Expedition of Western Exploration, 1803-1806.* 1916. Reprint. Madison: The State Historical Society of Wisconsin, 1965, 444p.

Reprints the account Lewis kept of the river expedition from Pittsburgh to the camp on River Dubois; also reprints the long-lost journal of Sergeant John Ordway.

Strong, Emory and Ruth. *Seeking Western Waters: The Lewis and Clark Trail from the Rockies to the Pacific,* edited by Herbert K. Beals. Oregon Historical Society, 1995, 383p.

Intersperses journal entries with detailed descriptions of the landscape, wildlife, and vegetation seen by the explorers. Includes numerous illustrations as well as several maps.

Taylor, J. Golden. "Across the Wide Missouri: The Adventure Narrative from Lewis and Clark to Powell." In *A Literary History of the American West,* pp. 71-103. Fort Worth: Texas Christian University Press, 1987.

Using both primary and secondary sources, surveys seven decades of western exploration beginning with the Lewis and Clark expedition and ending with the examinations of the Colorado River region by Civil War veteran and scientist John Wesley Powell.

Additional coverage of the journals of Meriwether Lewis and William Clark is contained in the following source published by the Gale Group: *Dictionary of Literary Biography,* **Vol. 183.**

Representations of the Devil in Nineteenth-Century Literature

INTRODUCTION

Known by a variety of names—Satan, Lucifer, Mephistopheles—the Devil remains one of the most intriguing and ubiquitous figures in western literature, with such literary luminaries as Dante, Milton, and Goethe finding in him the perfect personification of the human impulse toward evil. Since the advent of the Bible, the Devil has existed as the quintessential adversary, and the ultimate antithesis to goodness and morality. In the Medieval era, the Devil evolved from a relatively minor role in Holy Scripture to a dominant figure in the didactic mystery and morality plays of the day. During the Reformation and Renaissance, Luciferian figures continued to be abstracted and allegorized in literature, that is until the publication of John Milton's *Paradise Lost* in 1667. In the poem Milton drew a dynamic and supremely defiant Satan, whom subsequent interpreters would sometimes view as the epic's subversive protagonist. Meanwhile, in the eighteenth-century, the rising tide of Enlightenment rationalism prompted a decline in literary representations of Satan, with many considering the Devil as an inappropriate subject even of mockery or satire. All of this began to change by the end of the century and the new vogue of the Gothic novel in England. Writers, typified by Matthew Gregory Lewis in his popular *Ambrosio the Monk* (1796), seized upon Satan as a principal source of supernatural horror, creating a mania for spine-tingling terror among readers.

Also in England during the last decade of the eighteenth century, the nascent Romantic movement, led by William Blake, was about to embark upon a philosophical and poetic reinterpretation of the Devil. Blake's *Marriage of Heaven and Hell* (1790-1793) provided the groundwork for a reevaluation of Satan by figuring the Devil once again in Miltonic terms as an intractable and energetic individual who stood in opposition to an autocratic God. Miltonic and Blakean interpretations of Satan were furthered by Percy Bysshe Shelly and Lord Byron, poets who by the early nineteenth century had made the Devil into a representative icon of the Romantic movement. Rather than simply a symbol of pure evil, the Romantic Satan appeared as an embodiment of vitality, strength, boldness, and political and cultural rebellion. Indeed, the Romantics sought to treat the Devil as a tragic or heroic figure worthy of pathos, thereby inaugurating the tradition of the Promethean Satan, an indefatigable rebel, long since abused by the oppression of Heaven. This literal denunciation of Biblical morality did not sit well with numerous conservative commentators, including the outspoken poet and critic Robert Southey. Southey's vehement public attacks in print on Byron's atheism culminated in his suggestion that the Romantic poets should more accurately be dubbed the 'Satanic School'—a term of derision that only added to the popular myths surrounding the literary personas of both Byron and Shelley. Consequently, the process of extolling the Satanic in verse continued; later in the century, the Symbolists Charles Baudelaire and Arthur Rimbaud would choose to emphasize the dark, seductive power of the Devil indirectly in their poetry.

Another more traditional development in modern interpretations of the Devil had also begun by the early nineteenth-century with the appearance of the first part of Johann Wolfgang von Goethe's drama *Faust* in 1808. The Faust-myth, a venerable legend drawn from Germanic folklore, treats an integral theme within diabolical literature, that of the devil-compact. In a prototypical deal with the Devil, the legendary Faust, often depicted as a sorcerer, offered up his soul in exchange for otherworldly pleasure and power. Goethe adjusted the story somewhat so that his Faust instead desired limitless knowledge, and, because his intentions were not purely selfish or evil, he was able to circumvent his contract with Mephistopheles and prevent his soul from being cast into hell. This subject of a mortal being who enters into a compact with the Devil became a common one in nineteenth-century American fiction. Washington Irving, in his story "The Devil and Tom Walker" (1824), employed the theme, and critics recognize Faustian elements in many of the tales of Nathaniel Hawthorne. Mark Twain, additionally, evoked folklore interpretations of the Devil in his satiric novel *The Mysterious Stranger* (1916), while numerous other examples of the formula appeared in popular fiction.

With the notable exception of Goethe, nineteenth-century European writers generally offered a more symbolic representation of Satan than their American counterparts. A tattered devil inhabits the dreams of Ivan Karamazov in Feodor Dostoevsky's novel *Brat'ya Karamzovy* (1880; *The Brothers Karamazov*). Ivan's devil exists as a slovenly, down-on-his-luck figure whom critics have viewed as both a manifestation of philosophical evil and a type of the late nineteenth-century Russian atheist. Nikolai Gogol presents an at once sardonic and metaphorical view of the Devil in human form as Chichikov, the unscrupulous gatherer of the dead in his *Mertvye dushi* (1842; *Dead Souls*). Such diabolical incarnations in literature as Gogol's additionally represent an important segment of fictional treatments of the Devil in human form, in a varied tradition that stretches from Medieval romance to the modern novel.

REPRESENTATIVE WORKS

Honoré de Balzac
Le centenaire; ou, les deux Beringheld (novel) 1822
Melmoth réconcilié (novel) 1835

Charles Baudelaire
Les Fleurs du mal [*Flowers of Evil*] (poetry) 1857

William Blake
Marriage of Heaven and Hell (poetry) 1790-1793
Milton (poetry) 1800-1804

Robert Burns
"Address to the Deil" (poetry) 1785

Lord George Gordon Byron
Manfred (verse drama) 1817
Cain: A Mystery (verse drama) 1821
The Deformed Transformed (unfinished verse drama) 1822

Giosue Carducci
Inno a Satana (poetry) 1865

Marie Corelli
The Sorrows of Satan (novel) 1895

Feodor Dostoevsky
Brat'ya Karamzovy [*The Brothers Karamazov*] (novel) 1880

Théophile Gautier
Albertus (poetry) 1832
La larme du diable (poetry) 1839

Johann Wolfgang von Goethe
Faust. 2 vols. (drama) 1808-1832

Nikolai Gogol
Mertvye dushi [*Dead Souls*] (novel) 1842

Nathaniel Hawthorne
"Young Goodman Brown" (short story) 1837

Victor Hugo
Le fin de Satan (poetry) 1886

Washington Irving
"The Devil and Tom Walker" (short story) 1824

Frederick Maximilian Klinger
Fausts Leben, Taten und Höllenfahrt (novel) 1791

Mikhail Lermontov
Demon (poetry) 1856

Matthew Gregory Lewis
Ambrosio the Monk (novel) 1796

Leconte de Lisle
"La tristesse du Diable" (poetry) 1866

Charles Robert Maturin
Melmoth the Wanderer (novel) 1820

Gérard de Nerval
Nicolas Flamel (drama) 1830
Le Prince de sots (drama) 1830

Charles Nodier
Le nouveau Faust et la nouvelle Marguerite; ou, comment je me suis donné au Diable (drama) 1832
"La combe de l'homme mort" (short story) 1833

Frederick Beecher Perkins
"The Devil-Puzzlers" (short story) 1871

Arthur Rimbaud
Une saison en enfers [*A Season in Hell*] (poetry) 1873

Sir Walter Scott
"Wandering Willie's Tale" (short story) 1824

Percy Bysshe Shelley
The Cenci (verse drama) 1819
On the Devil, and Devils (essay) 1819

William Gilmore Simms
*Paddy McGann; or, the Demon of the Stump (novel) 1863

William Makepeace Thackeray
"The Devil's Wager" (short story) 1833
"The Painter's Bargain" (short story) 1840

Mark Twain
The Mysterious Stranger, a Romance (novel) 1916

Paul Verlaine
"Crimen Amoris" (poetry) 1873

Alfred de Vigny
Eloa (poetry) 1823

*Likely date of composition.

OVERVIEWS AND GENERAL STUDIES

Maximilian Rudwin (essay date 1931)

SOURCE: "The Salvation of Satan in Modern Poetry," in *The Devil in Legend and Literature*, AMS Press, 1970, pp. 280-308.

[*In the following essay, originally published in 1931, Rudwin considers the sympathetic portrayal of Satan in nineteenth-century poetry.*]

The reversal of poetic judgment with regard to the Devil is among the most striking characteristics of the modern period. The popular medieval conception degraded Diabolus from the former high potentate of paradise to a powerless and ludicrous personage, who served our ancestors as the butt of such laughter as still rings across the ages. The modern period, on the other hand, has clothed the Devil with the pathos of a defeated hero. The Devil of today forms a complete contrast to his *confrère* of former times. The modern devil is as fascinating as the medieval devil was frightful; he is as bright and beautiful as his predecessor was dismal and dreadful. The new devil enlists as much of our sympathy and admiration as the old devil inspired horror and terror in medieval man.

This change of attitude toward the Devil during the past century has been well expressed by Renan, who, in an anonymous article, writes as follows:[1]

> Of all the formerly accursed beings that the tolerance of our century has raised from their anathema, Satan is, without contradiction, the one who has chiefly profited from the progress of the lights [of reason] and of universal civilization. The Middle Ages, which understood nothing of tolerance, found pleasure in representing him as wicked, ugly and distorted. . . . A century as fruitful as our own in rehabilitations of all kinds could lack no reasons for excusing an unfortunate revolutionary, whom the need of action threw into hazardous enterprises. If we have become indulgent toward Satan, it is because Satan has thrown off a part of his wickedness and is no longer that baneful spirit, the object of much hatred and horror. Evil is evidently nowadays less strong than it was in former times.

As so aptly stated by Renan in the foregoing passage, the century which demanded the rehabilitation of all outcasts of terrestrial society, the bastard and the bandit, the courtesan and the criminal, also claimed the restoration and return to heaven of the celestial outlaw.

From the philosophical point of view, the conception of Satan's conversion and re-admission to heaven is the corollary of faith in the perfectibility of man, and belief in the consequent end of evil on earth. This utopian hope for the final triumph of universal good, which was aroused in the minds of men during the eighteenth century, was still strengthened by the French Revolution. The enthusiasts of this great historical event believed that the revolutionary revelation would put an end to the reign of the Powers of Evil, and usher in the universal reign of the Powers of Good. Furthermore, many metaphysicians developed the theory of the Devil's repentance and return to heaven as part of their explanation of the origin and function of evil in the cosmic order. They believed in the essential unity and fundamental identity of good and evil. The poets of the past century followed the path paved by the philosophers of the preceding century and envisaged the salvation of Satan as a symbol of their belief in the messianic era approaching for all mankind. They desired to bring about a reconciliation of the Deity with the Devil, or, as it would seem, aspired to marry hell to heaven.

From the æsthetic point of view, the idea of Satan's salvation is the natural outgrowth of the literary conception of Satan. Byron and Shelley created in the Devil a personage whom a superficial reader might well call Promethean. What then was left to their French followers? Nothing but a step further in the attempt to lead the fallen archangel back to heaven.

It must be admitted, however, that this original and spiritual idea of the salvation of Satan, beautiful as it may be philosophically, is neither æsthetically nor theologically acceptable. Such a conception of Satan is inconsistent with the grandeur of the Personality of Evil. The sentimental devil, who repents his past wrongs and is willing to creep to the Cross, is certainly inferior to Byron's impenitent Empyrean, who scorns all ideas of reconciliation with his ancient Adversary, and who prefers torment to "the smooth agonies of adulation, in hymns and harpings, and self-seeking prayers." The idea of Satan's return to his former paradisaical position is also in flat contradiction to the traditional belief in the irreversibility of the Devil's doom. All successful treatment of the Devil in literature and art, however, must be made to conform to the norm of popular belief and Catholic dogma. In art we are all othodox, whatever our views may be in religion.

Orthodoxy has always taught that Satan is doomed for all eternity. The Devil, it is maintained by the theologians, is damned beyond redemption, and cannot repent and win pardon like Adam. The fall of Satan, according to Catholic creed, is greater than that of our first ancestor. The original sin, by which mankind fell a prey to the powers of hell, will be wiped out, at least for a part of mankind, but Satan's sin can never be expiated. This Catholic conviction is based on the biblical text that "the Devil will be destroyed utterly" (Hebr. ii. 14; cf. also Ez. xxviii. 18-19). St. Michael, who appears in Jude 9 as the enemy of Satan, will in the end of days, according to the Revelation of St. John (xii. 7 ff.), vanquish the diabolical dragon. The Adversary will be chained eternally in hell, the portals of which will never again open to permit him to molest mankind.

The dogma of the eternal damnation of the Devil was, however, not universal in the Church. Basing their belief on the biblical passage: "Even the devils are subject unto us through thy name" (Luke x. 17), several fathers and doctors of the Church entertained hopes for the Devil's reform and restoration to heaven. Origen, who was among the leading authorities in deciding what was and what was not to be included in the New Testament, predicted the Devil's purification and pardon. This belief in the salvability of Satan was apparently shared by Justin, Clemens Alexandrinus and afterwards by Didymus and Gregory of Nyssa. In the eighth century, St. John Damascene taught that the Lord gave Satan some time to reform after the sin of the fall, but that the Tempter used it instead to lead Adam astray. In the following century, the famous Irish philosopher and theologian, John Scotus Erigena, professed the belief that, inasmuch as all beings came from

God, they must all return to him, including the evil spirits. A religious poem of the thirteenth century, *A Moral Ode,* contains the assertion that the Devil himself might have had mercy if he had sought for it.[2]

Father Sinistrary, the famous *consulteur* of the Inquisition, in the seventeenth century, argued that the atonement wrought by Christ included the demons, who might attain final beatitude. He even intimated, though more timidly, that even their father, Satan himself, as a participator in the sin of Adam and sharer of his curse, might be included in the general provision of the Deity for the entire and absolute elimination of the curse throughout nature.[3]

The belief in the final unity of Good and Evil, and the reconciliation of the Deity and the Devil, was taught by the magi and Gnostics and shared by many medieval sects. The modern George Sand, who expressed through the mouth of Lélia her belief that "the spirit of evil and the spirit of good are but one spirit, *i.e.* God," later put this idea in the mouth of a heretical sect. We read in her novel *Consuelo* (1842-3) the following report concerning the supposed followers of John Huss in Bohemia:

> A mysterious and singular sect dreamed . . . of uniting these two arbitrarily divided principles into one single principle. . . . It tried to raise the supposed principle of evil from its low estate and make it, on the contrary, the servant and agent of the good.

Many pietists, deviating from orthodox teaching, also believed in the possibility of the repentance and restoration of the Devil. Madame de Krüdener (1764-1824), the Swedenborgian mystic, who converted many handsome but wicked men even at the cost of her own virtue, had the utmost confidence in her ability to bring about even Satan's conversion. This lady from Courland turned to religion after a rather dissipated youth, which she prolonged as much as she could.[4] Having arrived at the conclusion that all was not well with the world, she decided to reform humanity, and was seized with a great ardor of proselytism. During her apostolic mission, she traveled all over Europe and preached her gospel to everyone she could reach; princes, kings, emperors, dwellers in huts, all listened with rapture to her inspired words. Her holy zeal to recall to the mercy of the Lord the inhabitants of this earth extended even to the hosts of hell. Again and again the idea of converting the very denizens of darkness,—nay the Devil himself, occurs in her writings. "What can I say to Thee, O my Beloved?" she addresses the Lord. "Would that I could shout over the whole earth, and through all the heavens, how much I love Thee! Would that I could lead not only all men, but all the rebel spirits back to Thee!" In another connection she writes: "I cannot help wishing that hell might come to this God who is so good."

But the Church has always condemned the belief in the redemption of Satan. Protestants and Catholics alike hold out no hope for the deliverance of the Devil from his deserved damnation. In our own country, the Reverend Mr. Tillotson, a minister of the Universalist Church, which believes in the salvation of all men, was unfrocked by his church for wishing to extend its doctrine of universal salvation to Satan.

Christianity showed itself less tolerant with regard to the Evil Spirit than the ancient religions. The Hindus thought that, inasmuch as evil is but a passing form of the realization of existence, it cannot last eternally and must some day disappear by merging with the Absolute. Buddha believed in the universal redemption of every creature throughout the worlds. In Persian eschatology, Evil will in the latter days disappear from the face of this earth, and the Spirit of Evil, having been wholly regenerated, will be the last to arrive saved and sanctified in Paradise. The Yezidis, a sect of devil-worshippers living in ancient Assyria, still hold the belief that the rebel will in the end of days celebrate his return to heaven.[5]

. . . . .

When the beautiful Balder, god of light, was slain by Loki and descended to the land of the dead, Hel, the queen of the lower world, promised that he would be raised from the dead if one day there would be found on earth someone who would weep for him. In like manner, Satan, the successor to Balder and all other pagan gods, should long ago have been redeemed from hell and returned to heaven by virtue of the tears which the French Romantic poets of the past century have shed over him.

The Devil has not been denied pity in earlier ages. He has had apologists even among the saints, particularly among the saints of the weaker sex. St. Theresa desired that men should not speak ill of the Devil, and pitied him for not being able to love. St. Thomas Aquinas could hardly be happy, it is said, from thinking of the doom of the Devil and went so far in his pity for the prisoner of the pit as to spend a night in prayer for the pardon and restoration of the dethroned archangel. "O God," he prayed, "have mercy upon Thy servant the Devil."[6]

It was, however, particularly in the peasant's mind and in the peasant's heart that there slowly grew up a flower of pity for the doomed Devil, who could never hope to be at peace. Robert Burns, the Scotch poet, who was first and last a peasant, expressed his sympathy for the sufferings of Satan in his "Address to the Deil" (1785). This very human poem is full of fellow-feeling for the Fiend. It reaches its climax in the unexpectedly pathetic stanza at the end, in which the poet credits the Devil with something akin to compunction, and ventures a faltering hope on his behalf. The Scotch bard salutes Satan in the following words, which suggest Carducci's *Hymn to Satan* (1865):

> But fare-you-weel, auld Nickie-Ben!
> O wad ye tak a thought an' men'!
> Ye aiblins might—I dinna ken—
>   Still hae a stake:
> I'm wae to think upo' yon den,
>   Ev'n for your sake!

Satan secured his strongest sympathy, however, from the French poets of the Romantic period. This sympathy among the French Romantics for Satan is a part of their humanitarianism, which a misanthropic humorist has named "redemptorism"; that is, the desire to redeem all sinners by means of love. Emotionalism, which, as we know, was an essential part of the Romantic temperament, manifested itself, among other characteristics, in a feeling of boundless sympathy for suffering humanity. Compassion was a master passion with the Romantics. In their eyes the greatest of all virtues was pity—pity for the forsaken and forlorn, pity for the dispossessed and disinherited of this earth, pity even for sin and sinners. This sympathy, which the Romantics felt for all the erring, was also extended to the Sinner from the Beginning. As a matter of fact, it was precisely on account of his sin, as will be shown later, that Satan inspired the Romantics with their singular sympathy.

Satan's suffering puts a halo around his sin. Supreme suffering, hence supreme sympathy. Indeed, what agonies can be compared to those of Satan? Just think! For thousands of years he has been dragging himself through this world of sorrows, the most wearied and the most restless of all afflicted spirits. As his ordeal seemed endless, he was particularly an object of pity to the Romantics. We know what a resistless attraction hopeless woe had for Romantic imagination. As Satan was, moreover, staggering beneath the unjust condemnation of a superior power, he was the worthiest object of Romantic devotion. He figured among the "lost causes, and forsaken beliefs, and impossible loyalties," in support of which the Romantics threw their weight. It is a psychological fact that an individual who is an artist, or peculiar in some other way, naturally has great sympathy with unpopular causes or individuals for the reason that he himself is unpopular.

Moreover, the Romantics felt a deep admiration for solitary grandeur. This "knight of the doleful countenance," laden with a curse and drawing misfortune in his train, was the ideal Romantic hero. As the original *beau ténébreux*, Satan was the typical figure of the Romantic period and its poetry. It has been well remarked that if Satan had not existed, the Romanticists would have invented him.

The sympathy of the Romantics for Satan was far greater by reason of the bond of kinship which they felt with the celestial rebel. We must bear in mind that the spirit of revolution is at the very root of Romanticism. This movement was a revolt against all authority, in heaven as well as on earth. Romanticism was the logical reflex of the political revolution which preceded it. All French Romantics were members of the Opposition. The Romantic School, we may say without any derogatory intent, was a human Pandemonium. They all were "of the Devil's party," to employ the term applied to Milton by William Blake. George Sand might just as well have called her contemporaries sons of Satan as "sons of Prometheus." The most characteristic trait of all the Romantics was a proud and rebellious spirit. Even the sweetest and serenest of the great Romantics, Lamartine, also revealed a Satanic streak.

He, too, shouted to heaven his "Désespoir" (1818); and the echo of his cry of despair uttered in this poem is prolonged through most of his later works.

The Romantic generation saw its own spirit best personified in Satan. He was the symbol of all its aspirations and afflictions, the incarnation of all its longing and yearning. In himself Satan personified the daring and self-sufficiency, the mystery and gloom, the love of liberty and hatred of authority; all held as the highest ideal of every Romanticist. The Devil is the very embodiment of the malady of the century, which is the most characteristic trait of Romanticism. This malady—the *Weltschmerz*—has been made flesh in the celestial outlaw.

The Romantics painted themselves and recognized themselves in Satan more fully and more perfectly than in any other historical or mythological character. They found in his career much of their own unhappy lot, of their own thwarted ambitions. In their eyes he represented all that they loved and cherished. They felt they had so much in common with him that they looked up to Satan as to a blood brother.

The man in opposition to a society which refused to accept his claims had a fellow feeling for Satan, who is the father of all unappreciated geniuses. The Devil has always complained that he is misunderstood on earth. "Le démon souriant dit: Je suis mećonnu," says Victor Hugo. The Devil, in Sir Walter Scott's "Wandering Willie's Tale" (1824), also complains that he is "sair misca'd in the world." The Shavian demon, in *Man and Superman* (1905), likewise bemoans the fact that he is so little appreciated on earth. He who shook off the trammels of tradition had a spirit kindred to that of the fallen angel, who was the first to combat conformity. The man who craved personal dignity and political freedom was attracted by the Demon, who was the first to proclaim the sovereignty of the individual spirit. The rebels against conventions, creeds and critics on earth felt drawn to him who demanded freedom of thought and independence of action in heaven.

The Romantics could never speak of Satan without tears of sympathy. The fighters for political, social, intellectual and emotional liberty on earth could not withhold their admiration from the angel who raised the standard of rebellion in heaven. "Cher Satan" was always on their lips. They pitied the fallen angel as an outlaw; they applauded him as a rebel. "A noble heart will always love the rebel," declared a Romantic poet in 1846. The rebel of the Emperean was hailed as the first martyr in the cause of liberty—"the first dreamer, the oldest victim," as Leconte de Lisle terms the Devil. The word Satan on the lips of the French poets offered the hint of a hard-won salvation. The rebellious Romantics were bold enough to demand a revision of the judgment pronounced against the celestial hero and endeavored, each in his own manner, to rewrite Milton's *Paradise Regained*. They even predicted the day

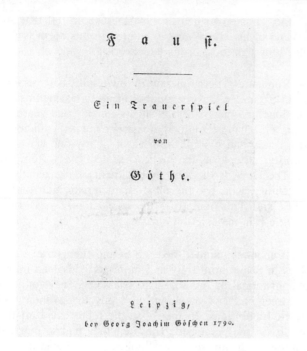

Title page of Johann Wolfgang von Goethe's Faust, *1808-1832.*

when the Devil should return to heaven and occupy his former seat at the right hand of the Lord.

. . . . .

It must be admitted, however, that the idea of the rehabilitation of the Devil was not wholly original with the French Romantics. The theme was touched upon by writers in other countries as far back as the eighteenth century.[7] Klopstock, in his *Messias* (1748-73), depicts the fallen angel, Abbadona, of lower rank to be sure, re-entering heaven. Goethe intimated that he had written a passage in his *Faust* "where the Devil himself receives grace and mercy from God." It was, however, in France during the Romantic period that the idea of the Devil's redemption and restoration to celestial favor found frequent expression in the different forms of various poetical works. The sympathy extended by that country, considered the center of the revolutionary spirit of Europe, to all victims of oppression and to all rebels, whether individuals or classes or nations, could not well be denied to the expatriate from Paradise.

The happy change in the character of the Devil, which Origen anticipated, for which St. Thomas Aquinas prayed, to which Robert Burns looked forward, which Goethe contemplated, and which Mme. de Krüdener wished to bring about, was eloquently preached by the French Romantics. First, they believed in this conversion from a feeling of sympathy, and secondly, as a part of their conviction that the end of the reign of Evil on earth was imminent. Byron, from across the Channel, also shared the belief of his French *confrères* in a new earth and a new hell. In his *Heaven and Earth* (1822), the English poet predicted a time

When man no more can fall as once he fell,
And even the very demons shall do well!

The only discordant note in this general clamor for clemency toward the celestial outlaw was sounded by Balzac. The creator of the *Comédie humaine* was prevented by his Catholic convictions from sharing the dream of his day for the final salvation of Satan. Balzac thought, however, that if Satan should ever make his peace with God, unless the Fiend were a greater scoundrel than popularly depicted, he ought to bargain for the pardon of his adherents (*l'Élixir de longue vie,* 1830).

Alfred de Vigny is the first French poet to approach the problem of the Devil's purification and pardon. The beautiful poem *Eloa* (1823) . . . may be considered the turning point in the literary treatment of the relations between hell and heaven. Vigny's work was the prologue to a long series of compositions, the authors of which, rejecting all tradition, endeavored (without especial success, however) to lead the legend of the Devil into new channels.

Eloa expresses in its highest form the sympathy for suffering which is at the root of Vigny's best work. This pessimistic poet had a passion for pity, which he wished to see manifested without limits. His sympathetic heart was always touched by the sorrows of his fellow men. He loved, as he said, the grandeur of human sufferings, and poured out all his treasures of tenderness and devotion on his "companions in misery." He was a great champion of lost causes in his period. He pleaded for the aristocrat, the soldier and the poet. But, though the aristocratic bent of his mind led him to dwell on exceptional natures, he was equally touched by the boundless misery in the lot of the common man.

His *Eloa* is inspired by his feeling of pity—pity for all suffering, pity for all that lives but a moment, pity even for sin and Satan. Supreme guilt, therefore, supreme misfortune! This poem is the glorification of compassion, of tenderness and sacrifice, of vain self-immolation and of pity without hands to help. It is the story of a bright being, a woman-angel, born from a tear of the Redeemer. Tempted by pity, she falls a victim to the Spirit of Darkness. This "sister of the angels," having heard in heaven the tale of the misfortune of the brightest archangel, leaves her dwelling of delights and descends to the bottom of the pit in order to search for her unfortunate brother and bring him back to bliss. But, unsuccessful in her efforts, she prefers to remain with him in hell rather than return to heaven.

In a sequel poem, which was to bear the title *Satan sauvé,* the author, however, intended to bring this woman-angel out of hell, to save this pathetic damned spirit, the least criminal and certainly the most lovable that hell has ever received. And the poet conceived the notion of saving Satan himself by the grace of Eloa, and, at the same time, of abolishing hell by the all-powerful virtue of love and pity. The following are the poet's notes on his proposed sequel to *Eloa:*

Eloa had not spoken since her fall. She sat immovable in the eternal shade, like a precious stone which casts its ray of light. The night was less profound since she came into the nether darkness. The spirits of the damned passed and repassed near her, to see themselves by the light of her beauty, and their despair was calmed. A mysterious restraint prevented Satan from approaching her. He walked around her like a wolf round a sheep. From time to time, he rejoiced over the misfortunes of men. . . . Every time that more souls arrived in hell Eloa wept. And one day, while her tears were flowing, Satan looked at her. He had ceased to take pleasure in evil. She saw his change of heart and spoke to him. He wept. Eloa smiled and raised her finger to heaven, a gesture which one dares not make in that place.

'Listen!' she cried. 'It is the crash of worlds which fall in dust. Time is no more.—Thou art saved.'

Vigny never carried out his project of portraying the redemption of Satan through the pity of this woman-angel who descended into hell to bring cheer and comfort to her fallen brother. It is, therefore, fair to say that Théophile Gautier is the first of all French Romantics to treat the beautiful subject of Satan's salvation.

This dramatic poem, *la Larme du Diable* (1839), is one of Gautier's most original fantasies. In its consistent levity, it is most characteristic of his art. It is a clever *pasticcio* of the medieval miracle-plays, and nothing illustrates better the way in which Gautier conceived the most exalted ideas as subject-matter for pictorial purposes. The play is full of humor and irony. The scene is placed alternately in heaven and on earth. Satan is the hero, and "le Bon Dieu" and Christus, comically assembled with Othello and Desdemona, are among the minor characters. The poem is less indecent, but more impudent and irreverent than *Albertus* (1832). Satan offers the impression that he is a good fellow, pleasing and amusing, mischievous rather than malicious. He bears no ill-will toward God or man. He jokes with the Lord about the denizens of heaven and maintains that any man of good judgment and independent spirit would prefer going to hell. Satan wins the sympathy of the women among the elect in heaven, and they plead with the great God in his behalf.

The principal *motif* of the poem involves a wager between the Lord and the Devil in regard to two mortal maidens. God believes them to be proof against all temptation, but Satan insists that he could cause their fall. A bet is arranged between the Deity and the Devil. If Satan wins, he is to obtain pardon for Eloa, the beautiful woman-angel, who (in Vigny's poem) forsook heaven to seek Satan in his misery. But this angel makes her voice heard in heaven. From the depths of hell she proclaims that she still loves the rebel spirit, and that she prefers hell with him to heaven without him. Satan then requests a glass of cold water to cool his parched lips as a reward in the event he accomplishes his aim.

Satan sets his wiles to work and is about to win the wager, but touched by the purity and delicacy of the feelings of the young girls he is about to lead astray, he sheds a tear. The angels gather up the tear and lay it at the feet of the

Lord. This exhibition of pity on the part of Satan so stirs the hearts of the blessed women among the hosts of heaven that they plead with the Lord in behalf of the fallen archangel. The magnanimous God is willing enough to pardon his old enemy, but he cannot reverse the judgment he previously pronounced, and so prefers to drag the matter out at great length. "I cannot perjure myself like an earthly king," he informs the angelic delegation." It is not, however, a flat refusal, for he adds, "In two thousand years we shall see!"

Vigny considered setting free the damned spirits through the daughter of Christ, but Alexandre Soumet, in his *Divine Épopée* (1840), makes Christ himself redeem the dwellers in hell. Soumet supposes that the Saviour returns to earth to offer himself a second time, and on this occasion his mission is not to redeem the inhabitants of this earth, but the damned spirits of hell. Christ suffers a second Calvary. Lucifer is given again his place among the archangels of heaven, a general hosannah is sung to the Highest; and the poem ends with the following words written across the heavens in letters as bright as the sun:

Salut Éternel.

The popular French song-writer, Jean Pierre de Béranger, also treated the subject of Satan's salvation. His poem, "la Fille du Diable" (1841-43), inspired by a touching philosophy, contains notes of deep and universal tenderness for all sufferers, including the Devil.

Satan, traveling in Rome in the form of a young man, seduces a virgin, who presents him with a daughter. The Devil, moved by the smile of this child, wishes to preserve her from the evils of earth so that after her death she will go to heaven. He has his child baptized, intentionally choosing the name "Marie," puts her into virtuous hands, and leaves hell every day, assuming a human form, to visit her on earth. At the age of fifteen, this saintly child, who has consecrated herself from her earliest youth to almsgiving and prayer, is admitted to her first communion. Her father trembles at the idea that God might repudiate her. But this fear is without foundation. So Satan conceals himself in the organ of the church, which under his hands sends forth torrents of such celestial harmonies that, in order to hear them the better, the angels descend from heaven. After the ceremony, Marie totters and drops dead in the arms of her heartbroken father. Satan falls into despair, just like an ordinary mortal, but does not blaspheme against the Lord, for the soul of his daughter is perceived rising up to heaven. Broken-hearted, the Devil returns to hell, where he abandons himself entirely to his sorrows and to thoughts of repentance. He reviews all the wrongs of his past and is tortured by remorse. Satan implores his daughter to intervene on her father's behalf with the Lord. Christ is so touched by the repentance and the sorrow of Satan that he begins to weep. One of the tears which Christ sheds over the misfortune of the banished angel penetrates into hell and falls on the heart of Satan. In an instant, the infernal spirit is transformed into the dazzling Lucifer and goes to join his daughter in the celestial choir-stalls.

Edgar Quinet, in his *Merlin l'enchanteur* (1869), a vast prose dramatic epic, containing twenty-four books and nine hundred pages, depicts the son of Satan redeeming his father. Merlin, as the legend goes, was born of the morganatic marriage of the Devil with a nun. Prodigies—such as a great storm—occurred on the night of his birth. As often happens with young men of good family, Merlin in his youth evidences traits more characteristic of his mother, the daughter of heaven, than of his father, the ruler of hell. Instead of carrying out his father's mission among men, he helps to establish the Kingdom of Heaven on earth. When Satan sees that he no longer wields the power of sowing evil in a world which has been transformed under the influence of his own son, he repents and turns in prayer to his old Adversary. After having received pardon and mercy from the Lord, the Devil with his own hands destroys the pillars which support the vaults of hell. The souls of the damned receive liberty and perfect happiness in the world, and the Devil is restored to his ancient estate in heaven.

Victor Hugo has perhaps carried the new evangel of universal sympathy further than the other Romantics. This writer is the most illustrious representative of the Romantic ideal of cordial compassion for all beings, even for those who have fallen into the very depths of the abyss. The greatest French poet of modern times had that general unlimited sympathy for the unfortunate which is finally extended to the wicked as well as to the luckless. In his "la Prière pour tous" (1830), the Christian poet asks his daughter to pray for all the sorrowful, including Satan. How, indeed, could he deny the Devil that pity which in his heart was not limited to humanity but comprehended all creation, including animals, plants, and even inanimate objects? What does it matter if Satan is guilty or not? Victor Hugo with his doctrine of universal indulgence and forbearance does not judge; he forgives. He refuses to recognize a single being on earth or under the earth whom one could hold responsible for his crimes.

Thus Victor Hugo is primarily the poet of pity. He felt a deep and ardent compassion for all who suffer through the fault of others. His sympathy went out to the sufferings of all the down-trodden, of all the oppressed, whether peoples or individuals. He gave pity an important place in his poetry, and to this sentiment he finally consecrated his work *la Pitié suprême* (1879), in which he asked pity for hatred, pity for evil, pity for the Devil. A few passages from this new gospel of evangelical pity, referring to his compassion for the denizens of hell, follow:

> Oh! je me sens parfois des pitiés insondables,
> Je gémis . . .
> Sur les démons grondants.
>
> > (*la Pitié suprême*, V.)

> Pardonnons. Jetons même aux démons l'indulgence.
>
> > (*ibid.*, XIII.)

Victor Hugo's pity for the demons of hell may also be noted in his other works:

> Bénir le ciel est bien; bénir l'enfer est mieux.
>
> > (*le Pape*, IV.)

> Ma pente est de bénir dans l'enfer les maudits.
>
> > (*les Quatre vents de l'esprit*, I, xxxiii.)

Victor Hugo's pity for the Devil is so great that he declares,

> Si Jésus . . .
> . . . venait à son tour crucifier Satan,
> Je dirais à Jésus: tu n'est pas Dieu. Va-t'en.
>
> > (*ibid.*, I. xx.)

The great exile of Guernsey had a fraternal feeling for the archangel banished from heaven. Exile alone in the eyes of the expatriate poet was sufficient to put the aureole of martyrdom on the Devil's brow.

> "C'est une chose
> Inexprimable, affreuse et sainte que l'exil," said
> Victor Hugo in June, 1870.
>
> > (*l'Année terrible*.)

The fighter for freedom on earth, who lived for twenty years as a martyr to his ideal, was deeply affected by the fate of the fighter for liberty in the skies. The champion of the sacred right and the holy duty of opposition to tyranny on earth must perforce extend his hand to him who, in the words of Milton, "opposed the tyranny of heaven" (*Par. Lost* i. 124). The champion of all outlaws could not refuse his protection to the first outlaw. The warm defender of the fugitives of all nations, who turned toward him as toward a lodestar, declared himself ready to protect even Satan if the latter should seek asylum with him.

His Messianism—his belief in the final extinction of all evil in this world—led him also to predict the end of Satan. His beautiful epic poem, *la Fin de Satan* (begun in 1854 and published posthumously as a fragment in 1886), describes the end of the reign of the Spirit of Evil on this earth. Satan's fate, however, for Victor Hugo does not consist in the exiled archangel's final punishment and eternal perdition, but, contrary to Church dogma and tradition, in his pardon and peace. The salvation of Satan, which the poet of pity predicts, will come about through the mediation of a being engendered jointly by the Devil and the Deity. A feather, detached from the wings of the archangel when he was hurled from heaven, remains lying on the edge of the abyss. The Lord takes pity on it. A ray from the eternal eye of Him, who created the world, is fixed on it and puts life into it. Under this animating glance, the feather comes to life and grows into a woman-angel. In answer to an inquiry from the angels, the Lord gives the name Liberty to this "daughter of hell and heaven." The spirit who thus owes her birth to the Devil and the Deity will, when the proper occasion presents itself, deliver from sin and suffering the Devil along with humanity. In order to conquer death and redeem the individual, the Son of God was made man. In order to break the shackles of the masses and deliver the nations from bondage, the daughter of the Devil was made a woman. This woman-saviour will on a certain day lead the masses in their rebellion against their oppressors. We may detect in this detail Victor Hugo's political views. Liberty is created by the Lord from Lucifer's feather. Liberty is born only from rebellion. Revolution is necessary to set the nations free from political oppression.

When Satan's heart softens and he turns to the Lord, beseeching mercy, his prayers ascend to heaven and touch the heart of his daughter. She asks the Deity's permission to descend into the dismal darkness and bring deliverance to the Devil. This supplication granted, the angel Liberty, after much wandering, finally alights at the feet of Satan, and bends over her father, who has fallen asleep from exhaustion. Pitying him, consoling him, bathing him with her tears, the angel of pity and mercy falls on her knees before the unhappy accursed archangel. She extends her supplicating arms towards him, enveloping him with a mysterious incantation. All the infernal pride, all the hatred in the Demon's soul melt in the warmth of the humanly humble and divinely tender words of his daughter. The angel Liberty begs her father to pity the misery of mankind and end his own sufferings. "Father," she implores him, "permit me to save the good, the pure, the innocent. Look! I weep over them and over you. Oh, hear my prayers. *Dieu me fit Liberté, toi, fais-moi Délivrance.*"

The struggle between good and evil in Satan's heart is reflected on his face. Suddenly on his forehead appears a light similar to that which formerly shone on his countenance, and from his lips escapes the word for which the angel has been waiting. It is the signal for her to break the chains that bind humanity. Liberty makes her appearance on earth to carry out the mission of delivering humanity from the fetters of oppression. Immediately the angel starts for Paris to break the bolts of the symbolical prison, the Bastille, which is to disgorge its captives. By the fall of the prison-fortress of Paris Victor Hugo intended to represent the symbolical liberation of humanity. The work of evil was for him incarnated in this famous prison for political offenders. According to Victor Hugo's symbolism, Cain, in order to murder his brother, Abel, used a nail, a stick and a stone. The nail later became the sword of Nimrod. The Lord broke it, and war was eventually to disappear. The stick became the cross of Calvary. Religion, alas! crucified Christ. The Church founded by Christ, placing itself at the service of the State, oppressed the masses and blessed mass-murder, war.[8] The stone served as a foundation for the Bastille. The French nation will tear it down and carry out the work left uncompleted by Christ. France will again take up the interrupted work of Jesus and guide it to fruition. Human liberty will bring about what the Nazarene himself could not accomplish. Through the destruction of political tyranny, progress will be advanced to such an extent that misery, misfortune, and perhaps even death, will be no more. For in the eyes of the great French poet, the French Revolution is the most important event in the history of humanity. The real Messiah is no other than the Revolution.

The deliverance of man will be followed by the deliverance of the fallen angel. The harmony between the inhabitants of this earth, particularly between the oppressors and oppressed, will also bring about a reconciliation between the Deity and the Devil. Good, having conquered Evil, will now reign forever over all creation.

The merits of the angel Liberty are counted to her demon-father for righteousness. The Lord applies to the Devil the Catholic dogma of the reversibility of punishments and rewards. As the poem ends, Satan is offered amnesty. The Devil is dead; the archangel is reborn.[9]

Leconte de Lisle, in his poem "la Tristesse du Diable" (1866), which shows echoes of Victor Hugo's *la Fin de Satan,* predicts another fate for the Devil. Satan, sitting silently on a mountain peak covered with eternal snow, and thence surveying the sufferings of humanity on this Sorrowful Star, is willing to put an end to himself and to the world in order to do away once and for all with sin and suffering on this earth.

Paul Verlaine, the leader of the decadent poets of France and the most distinguished disciple of Baudelaire, also envisioned the end of the old antagonism of the Deity and the Devil. Verlaine, however, was not interested in the cosmic conflict carried on between Good and Evil so much as in the war waged in his own heart between his guardian angel and his evil demon, as he has described this conflict in his collection of poems entitled *Sagesse* (1881). What Verlaine attempted was the reconciliation of the seven deadly sins and the three cardinal virtues, or a harmonizing of the pagan idea of self-affirmation and the ascetic theory of self-abnegation. What he desired was the reconciliation within him of St. Francis of Assisi and the Marquis de Sade, as Vance Thompson (*French Portraits,* 1899) puts it.

Verlaine kept the affairs of his soul in two separate compartments. The effects of his conversion in the prison of Mons did not last long. The old Adam within him soon reasserted himself. He continued to proclaim himself a Catholic, but he practised few of the tenets of that religion. "Verlaine believes in the Roman Catholic Church," said Jules Lemaître, "as earnestly as the Pope himself, but in Verlaine there is only belief; practice is wholly wanting in him."

The work of Verlaine shows a twofold aspect. His poetry offers alternations of fervency and flippancy, spirituality and sensuality, mysticism and eroticism, piety and perversity. This satyr-songster introduced an infinitely more religious mood into his poetry than did any of the other Symbolist poets. "Verlaine wrote the most Christian verses we have in France," says Jules Lemaître. "Certain strophes in *Sagesse* recall in their accent the *Imitation of Christ*" (*les Contemporains,* 4e série, 1886). But, we might add, he has also written some of the lewdest lines in modern French poetry.

Verlaine's interest in diabolism derived in a direct line from Baudelaire, that superb singer of sin and Satan. The poet of the *Fleurs du Mal* (1857) was a deity in the youthful eyes of Verlaine. The latter's *Poèmes saturniens*, published in 1866 but written for the most part during his later school-days, reveal many traces of his master's Satanism. But *Jadis et Naguère* (1884) is the Bible of the young decadent and diabolist poets. And in this perfection of their methods and aims, we find Verlaine's most important diabolical poem. It is in this poem, "Crimen Amoris," written in the prison of Petits-Carmes, Belgium, in 1873, that Verlaine treats the subject so dear to the Romantic generation, the salvation of Satan. Mr. Arthur Symons puts this poem at the head of all of Verlaine's work "for a certain diabolical beauty, for an effect of absolute sublimity" (*The Symbolist Movement in Literature,* 1919). The words have a marvelously musical rhythm, "full of the sound of gongs and trumpets," to employ Symons' expression.

The poem takes for its subject-matter the wish on the part of Hell to sacrifice itself of its own accord to Universal Love. In a palace blazing with silk and gold, at Ecbatane in Asia, to the sound of Mohammedan melodies, a band of juvenile demons "font litière aux sept péchés de leurs cinq sens." Finally, satiated with their sensual pleasures, the demons vainly attempt to break away from the evil to which they are attached, but which at heart they abhor. And one, the youngest and brightest of them all, despairingly exclaims:

> Nous avons tous trop souffert, anges et hommes,
> De ce conflit entre le Père et le Mieux!

He proposes with his fellow-demons to suppress hell, in order to do away with sin and suffering in the world. They set the infernal palace on fire. The flames rise to heaven. Singing hymns, the demons perish in the flames. Everything crumbles down. At that moment, a thunderbolt descends from heaven as an indication that the sacrifice has not been accepted. As a good Catholic, Verlaine realized that no reconciliation could be effected between Good and Evil, and that the Devil was damned for all eternity.

The last French evangelist who assumed to convert the Devil was Jules Bois, who wrote a curious "esoteric drama," to which he gave the name of *Noces de Satan* (1890).

. . . . .

The subject of the Devil's absolution and redemption has also been appropriated by a few English and German poets of the past century. Philip James Bailey treated it in his *Festus* (1839), a philosophical poem, which at the time of its publication was favorably compared with Goethe's *Faust* and enjoyed a greater popularity than it deserved. The idea of Satan's final return to his former glory in heaven also served as subject for Kurt von Rohrscheidt's *Satans Erlösung* (1894) and Wilfrid Scawen Blunt's *Satan Absolved: a Victorian Mystery* (1899), a dramatic poem of political content, also suggested by the Prologue to Goethe's *Faust*

The American writer, Henry Mills Alden, has expressed his belief in the final redemption of the Devil as follows:

Lucifer is the light-bearer, the morning-star, and whatever disguises he may take in falling, there can be no new dawn that shall not witness his rising in his original brightness.

The most important treatment of the subject of Satan's salvation by a poet other than the French is found in Lermontov's *The Demon* (1829-41). . . .

The woman in this Russian poem, who finally, out of pity for the fallen angel, consents to return his love, is no longer the symbolic virgin, who held Vigny's enamoured fancy. She is not like that being born from a tear dropped by Christ over the tomb of Lazarus, but a living, passionate woman—a Jewess of the Babylonian captivity in the first sketch of the work, then a Spanish nun, and finally a Georgian princess. It must be admitted, however, that Lermontov's version, though written in the main under the inspiration of Vigny's poem, is based on a Caucasian legend, according to which the Evil Spirit will reform and become regenerate when he is redeemed by the love of an innocent young woman.

It may be recalled that, the moment the Demon sees the beautiful Georgian maiden, Tamara, he becomes more and more freely human in his feelings and actions. The first awakening of passion brings to him the long forgotten thought of redemption. But Tamara is too weak a woman to bring about a reform in the heart of her demon-lover. At his first kiss, she dies from terror. Only Vigny's angel, not Lermontov's woman, would have conceivably succeeded in converting her demon-lover to repentance and reconciliation with God.

. . . . .

Other French Romantics, not satisfied with leading the Devil back to celestial glory, wished him to carry out after his restoration the project which he had failed to accomplish before he was hurled from heaven. They expected him again to start the revolution he had headed in the beginning of time, and supplant the King of Heaven in the government of this earth. This champion of celestial combat, in the Romantic version of the war in heaven, was not actuated by hatred and envy of man, as Christianity was thought to teach us, but by love and pity for mankind. The eternal war waged between the Lord and Lucifer, in the opinion of the Romantics, was not for glory but for humanity.

It is needless to say that the Devil, as conceived by the writers of the past century, is the very antithesis of the dogmatic demon. He has been divested of his traditionally diabolical character. He is an altogether new species of the *genus diabolus*. Instead of a demon of darkness, he is a god of grace. He continues to be the enemy of the Lord, but he is no longer the enemy of man (Tasso's *"gran nemico dell' umane genti"*). Far from being the tormentor, he is regarded as the benefactor of mankind. In Byron's *Cain* (1821) Lucifer takes men under his protection as his natural allies and his brothers in misfortune in his war against the Ruler of the Heavens. Strindberg's Lucifer also is full of compassion for men. He enters into combat with Jehovah not to wrest the power from Him, but to prevent Him from torturing mankind. Marie Corelli, in *The Sorrows of Satan* (1895), describes the Devil as a generous spirit, who wanders up and down the earth, lamenting the fact that the Christians will not suffer to aid them. As Mr. George Arliss portrayed the Devil in Molnar's well-known play, Satan is seemingly the friend to all mankind.

This commendation of Satan implied the condemnation of God, and, as a corollary, the belief that the accomplishment of the salvation of humanity must be taken out of the hands of the Ruler of the Heavens. The Romantics, from their pessimistic point of view, thought ill of the world and consequently also of its Creator. Of all French Romantics, Alfred de Vigny perhaps held the most pessimistic attitude toward this earth. He considered the world an evil creation and compared it with a prison. In 1824 he jotted down in his diary the following remark:

> We have been thrown into the world, and as in a prison we are forced to do our sentence of penal servitude for life, yet we know not what wrong we have done.

This French poet had so poor an opinion of the world, into which mankind had been tossed, that he wished to see it destroyed.

> "If there were a God," he said again in his dairy, "we would provoke Him to shatter this earth into a thousand fragments; and so, by our suffering a speedy annihilation, at least the generations of the future would be spared existence."

Romanticism is the consciousness of a disorder in the individual and in the world in general. The Romantic generation of 1830 thought the world out of joint more than ever. To Hamlet, Denmark seemed gloomy; to the Romantic, the whole world appeared dark. In this world composed of good and evil, the Romantics believed that the evil far outbalances the good; in fact, to paraphrase Leibnitz, that all is for the worst in this worst of all possible worlds. They did not believe that there was any balm either in Gilead or Golgotha. And if we wish to be truthful with ourselves we must admit that the world is not actually well run; rather, that it is very badly run; and no Huxley is needed to point out this obvious fact.

Now if the Romantics did not think well of the world, how could they think well of its Creator and Ruler? The author of an evil world must necessarily himself be evil. There is no escaping from this inference. The French, with their logical minds, were more consistent in their disillusionment than the men of other nations. If we abandon the Christian teaching of purification through suffering—and that is just what the Romantics did—what answer, indeed, can we find to the eternal question: "Why is the world so full of difficulties and dismays, of deceptions and disappointments, of defeat and despair, of sin and suffering, of misery and malady, of decay and death?" It is necessary to reach the conclusion that God is either not omnipotent or

not benevolent.[10] As we cannot very well doubt the omnipotence of God (for otherwise He would not be God) we must reach the conclusion that He is not benevolent This is just what the Romantics finally deduced from the existence of evil in the world. Stendhal, speaking of the reality of evil, remarked, "God's only excuse is that He does not exist." Proudhon, author of the famous dictum, "Property is theft," said, "God is evil."

Mme. Louise Ackermann was deeply indignant against what she called "la caprice divine" and its disarrangement of human affairs. In her poem, "les Malheureux" (1871), she depicts the dead at the Last Judgment refusing to rise at the summons of the archangel, and rejecting even happiness, since it is God, the author of evil, who brings it to them.

It must be counted to the Romantics for righteousness that they deeply concerned themselves with the problem of human destiny. The question of the presence of evil in a God-governed world obsessed their minds. Their eyes were open to the sorrows, the sufferings and the struggles of humanity. They made moan over the miseries and maladies of mankind. They were touched by the boundless wretchedness of the common lot of humanity. They were puzzled about man's painful powerlessness over life. Their souls were filled with righteous indignation concerning the reign of injustice all about them. They were always "complaining and sighing and wailing" over the woes of this world.

The Romantics were faced by a world whose inhabitants were sick and weary, yet battled on with a courage which would make a pagan god relent, but which had no power to move the Christian God. What other conclusion could they reach except the alternative that either God did not concern himself with the affairs of men or that he even delighted in human struggling and suffering? Theirs was the revolt of the human reason crying out in despair, "He who is almighty has willed that pain should be!"

Alfred de Vigny considered the Creator cold, capricious and cruel, standing aloof from his creation in eternal unconcern, or even actually finding joy in the sufferings of mankind. This French poet could not suppress a cry of anger against the Author of all Evil, who is deaf to man's cries of anguish and who refused even to lend an ear to the prayers of His Son who, sad unto death on the Mount of Olives, implored his Father in Heaven to permit him to remain on earth in order to help humanity. In a postscript to his poem "le Mont des Oliviers," which he entitled "le Silence" (1862), he exclaims:

> If it be true that, in the Sacred Garden of Scriptures,
> The Son of Man said that which is reported;
> Mute, blind, and deaf to the cry of his creatures,
> If Heaven abandoned us like an abortive world,
> The just man will meet absence with disdain,
> And a cold silence will evermore be the reply
> To the eternal silence of the Deity.

Vigny even went so far as to depict the Deity as a God of blood, intoxicated by the fumes of the sacrifices offered on

His altar, causing the just and unjust to perish together in the Flood, delivering up a daughter to her father's ax.

In our indignation over the bold blasphemies of Vigny, we should not forget that the God of the Hebrew Dispensation is actually represented in the Old Testament as unjust and cruel, and that the official creeds of many churches of Christianity even today contain conceptions of God's nature and of His actions toward the human race which are intolerable in the light of the ethical standards and ideals of the nineteenth and twentieth centuries.

In one of his projected poems, Vigny depicts a young man committing suicide and appearing before God in order to ask the creator of the world:

> And why hast Thou created the evil of the soul—sin, and the evil of the body—suffering? Was it necessary to offer Thee still longer the sight of our sufferings?

The sketch entitled "le Jugement dernier," found among the poet's papers at his death, contains a scathing arraignment of God, an indictment unprecedented in Christendom. The poet represents God himself on the last day standing before the bar of justice, with Man sitting in judgment over his Creator.[11]

Small wonder that God saw the great Rebels rising up against Him: Still less need we wonder to discover that man harbors a secret admiration for these Contemners of the Creator! Says Alfred de Vigny:

> The world revolts at the injustices entailed by the creation; dread of the Eternal prevents it from speaking openly; but its heart is full of hatred against the God who created evil and death. When a defier of the gods, like Ajax, the son of Oileus, appears, the world approves of him and loves him. Such another is Satan, such is Orestes, such is Don Juan. All who have combated the injustices of heaven have been admired and secretly loved by men.[12]

We now can understand why Satan was such an object of admiration to the Romantics, and why he was selected to express their dissatisfaction with the celestial government of terrestrial affairs. It was out of the mouth of the Great Malcontent that the Romantics expressed the darkness and doubt, the disenchantment and despair of their souls. Satan was the interpreter of their sorrows and heart-searchings. He voiced their rebellious and blasphemous words. He was the patron of their poetry of complaints. The genius of the hapless and hopeless generation of a century ago uttered its protest against the world and its Ruler through the mouth of the Great Accuser. From his lips was heard man's despairing cry of anguish against the accumulated miseries of many thousands of years, and against the ever-increasing sufferings of thousands of generations.

Even when the Romantics portrayed Prometheus, they had Satan in mind. The railing of the fettered Titan against Jupiter in the numerous Prometheus-poems of the Romantic School was but a thin veil for the blasphemies of Beelzebub. Louise Ackermann, in her "Prométhée" (1866), pictures her protagonist rebelling against the Creator—the Being who fashioned man and caused his misery. "Why are there evils in the world?" Prometheus asks, and concludes that the God who could prevent it willed that suffering should exist. The Titan blasphemes against the Creator and predicts for Him judgment, vengeance, and ultimate rejection by man, who shall be "delivered from faith as from an evil dream." Again, in Rapisardi's epic *Lucifero* (1877), the two Titans join forces to dispel the darkness from the earth. Lucifer departs for Hell to tell Prometheus of his plan to hurl God from Heaven and reign in His stead.

Cain, another favorite character with the Romantics, was a kind of Satan clad in human flesh. In his Promethean anger, this afflicted and heavily laden primal son of man, becomes the avenger of mankind by insisting on the eternal *why*. It is significant that the story of Cain has inspired three of the greatest poets of the past century—Byron, Victor Hugo, and Leconte de Lisle. Victor Hugo, as might be expected, treated the subject from a less heterodox point of view than the other two. Byron in his *Cain* (1821) brings together two titanic spirits, Lucifer and Cain, drawn to each other by mutual sympathy. The first was exiled from the celestial paradise, the latter from the terrestrial paradise. Leconte de Lisle personifies in the hero of his poem *Quain* (1869) suffering humanity in revolt against the injustices of a jealous God. He uses the accursed son of Adam as a mouthpiece to rail against the God of the Catholic Church, the monks, the Inquisition, and the smoking *auto da fé*.[13]

.   .   .   .   .

Just as pessimism leads to anti-theism, anti-theism leads to Satanism. If what has been considered good is found to be evil, what opposes it must necessarily be good. Thus the denunciation of the Deity led to the sanctification of Satan. If the ruler of an evil world is bad, his adversary must necessarily be good. This paradox accounts for the belief held by many Romantics that Satan was wronged and that there was, as Vigny asserted, a great historical case to be judged anew before the court of our conscience. Baudelaire, who addressed prayers to Satan, also argued from this assumption when he termed the Devil "*Dieu trahi par le sort*"—"a Deity betrayed by Destiny." Thus was born among the Romantics the wish for Satan's return to heaven, with the aim of delivering man from the cruelty of his Creator. In the modern Anatole France's *la Révolte des Anges* (1914), however, Satan declines an opportunity to head a second revolution against his adversary. He decides in the end that it is not worth the effort to supplant the King of Heaven, as a successful revolt with a new ruler will make so little difference on earth that he really prefers to remain in the Opposition. Power makes for tyranny; rebellion is the essence of nobility.

It must not be denied, however, that among the Romantics many might be named who were led to their adoration of Satan through their love of evil. Instead of exchanging, they accepted the traditional conceptions of the Deity and the Devil, nevertheless substituting Satan for the Saviour in their adoration. "Naturally," says Max Nordau in his *Entartung* (1893), "the love of evil can only take the form of devil-worship or diabolism, if the subject is a believer, that is if the supernatural is held to be a real thing. Only he who is rooted with all his feelings in religious faith will, if he suffers from moral aberration, seek bliss in the adoration of Satan, and in impassioned blasphemy of God and the Saviour."

We know of at least two groups in Paris who, in the first half of the last century, organized a Satanic cult and created a class of poetry expressing their worship of Satan and predicting his usurpation of the power of heaven.[14] Just as the Christians gathered on Sunday morning to sing glory to God, these diabolists congregated on Sunday evening to honor Satan with hymns and harpings, and to address prayers to the powers of Evil for alliance and aid. Each member of the group officiated in turn; in other words, recited the verses he had written for the occasion. These extravagants, in their eagerness to show their opposition to all orthodoxy, proclaimed that "fair is foul and foul is fair." "Evil," they declared, "be thou my good, and good my evil." Thus the son of poor Pierre Huet declares in Eugène Sue's *Salamandre* (1832): "Vice, crime, infamie, voilà les seules choses qui ne trompent jamais." These diabolists expressed delight over the works of the Devil and disgust for the acts of the Deity. They even argued the merits of the seven deadly sins. Eugène Sue sang the praises of the seven sins in his *Sept péchés capitaux* (1847-9). In all likelihood a few among them went even so far as to put their teachings into practice, and "romanticized" their lives, as they called such perversions in those Romantic days. The Romantic search for new sensations led to all sorts of sexual aberrations. In this manner, the Romantic rant about self-expression and self-fulfillment was reduced to the ridiculous. These devotees of the Devil wished and prayed for a universal reign of evil, and predicted the day when the Devil should regain heaven, wrest the reins of government from the hands of God, and clutch the world completely in his claws.

This movement, however, may have been of a very harmless character. It probably was but another manifestation of that search for singularity which was the besetting sin of all Romantics. The Bohemian must, perforce, hold beliefs diametrically opposed to those of the bourgeois.

Furthermore, any affirmation of the Devil in modern times must necessarily follow the rehabilitation of the world and the emancipation of the flesh, both of which Catholicism associated with the Spirit of Evil. In discarding the ascetic dogmas of Christianity and refusing any longer to reject the world and the flesh, the youthful generation of a century ago also declined to deny the Devil.

In the last analysis let us not forget that, at a period in which monarchism and Catholicism were joined in holy wedlock, the crown and the cross could not be separated. Neither of the two could be rejected without the other. If the monarchists claimed the Deity for themselves, the republicans could not help declaring for the Devil.[15]

. . . . .

We can offer no better end for our chapter on the idea of Satan's salvation in contemporary thought than by quoting the following paragraph of the penetrating study of the Polish critic, Ignace Matuszewski:

> The poetic type of Satan has to a certain degree ended the cycle of his individual existence. He has passed from one form into another, until he has gone through the various forms and existences of all life. He has passed through all the rungs of the double ladder on which, according to the theory of the Hindu thinkers as well as of certain European pantheists, every nomad of the eternal existence must descend and remount. In the beginning Satan descended from the absolute to matter, from heaven to earth (the fall), where he was lowered to the rank of the inferior animals and was even forced, according to the New Testament, to enter into the bodies of the unclean animals. Then rising endlessly from a lower form to a higher form, he finally dematerialized himself in the works of our contemporary poets. He has reconquered his attributes of an archangel and has entered again into the Infinite (the redemption).[16]

Notes

1. *Journal des Débats,* April 25, 1855.

2. *Old English Miscellany* (*Early English Text Society*), I, 214ff.

3. Anatole France, in *les Opinions de Jérôme Coignard* (1893), quotes the liberal abbé, contrary to Catholic dogma, expressing his hope for the redemption of Satan.

4. The most pathetic episode of her first period, her *liaison* with Alexandre de Skatieff, Mme de Krüdener described in her novel *Valérie* (1803).

5. See I. Joseph, "Yesidi Texts: The Devil Worshippers; their Sacred Books and Traditions." *American Journal of Semitic Languages and Literatures,* XXV (1909), nos. 2-3.

6. The English poet, Wathen Mark Wilks Call, has treated the prayer of the Angelical Doctor on behalf of the Devil in a beautiful poem on the subject, which will be found in his *Reverberations* (1849).

7. William Blake's *Marriage of Heaven and Hell* (1790) has nothing to do with the idea of a reconciliation between the powers of Good and Evil. This allegory is a mystical work full of diabolical humor, in which hells and heavens change names and alternate through mutual annihilations.

8. During the Great World War an eminent bishop of the Episcopal Church justified war on the ground that there was already war in heaven. In Stephen Phillips' play *Armageddon* (1915), on the other hand, war is represented as being planned in hell.

9. A longer analysis of Victor Hugo's *la Fin de Satan* will be found in the present writer's study, *Satan et le Satanisme dans l'œuvre de Victor Hugo* (Paris: Les Belles Lettres, 1926), pp. 88-103.

10. The present writer was told a few years ago by a Hindu that he had seen the following inscription on the portal of a secret Gnostic church in Paris: "Si Dieu existe, il n'y a pas de mal. Si mal existe, où est Dieu?"

11. Alfred de Vigny would furnish an interesting subject for a psychoanalytic study. In a recent number of *Psyche and Eros* (III, 68), Dr. Wm. Stekel, of Vienna writes: "Those who suffer from nervous depression hate God just as they hate everybody else. The malady is often ushered in with some blasphemy or revolt against God."

12. Émile Montégut (*Revue des deux Mondes,* LXVIII, 231) thinks that Vigny might have shown better judgment in his selection of the contemners of the gods. Satan will do, but not Orestes, still less Don Juan.

13. *Cf.* Henri Bernes: "le *Quain* de Leconte de Lisle et ses origines littéraires." *Revue d'histoire littéraire de la France,* XVIII (1911), 485-502.

14. *Cf.* Louis Maigron: *le Romantisme et les mœurs* (1910), p. 187.

15. This idea has been developed at greater length toward the end of the present writer's monograph: *Romantisme et Satanisme* (Paris: Les Belles Lettres, 1927).

16. *Cf.* Ignace Matuszewski: *Dyabel w Poezyi.* 2nd edition. Warsaw, 1899.

Hannes Vatter (essay date 1978)

SOURCE: "Romantic Satanism: Blake, the Gothic Novel, Shelley and Byron," in *The Devil in English Literature,* Francke Verlag, 1978, pp. 148-78.

[*In the following essay, Vatter surveys figures bearing qualities of the Miltonic Satan in the writings of English Romantic poets and Gothic novelists.*]

The first step towards a freer development of the devil figure had been made, as we have seen, with the abandonment of Biblical subject matter in the first Moralities. A next, and more decisive step could be taken when the dogmatical tenets of theology were no longer accepted as binding and unquestionable realities. The Age of Reason, itself hostile to Satanism—who would imagine Dr. Johnson dealing with the devil?—prepared the ground for a revaluation of the image of Satan not only by smothering old superstitions, but by questioning the authority of the Church as such. The wave of witchcraft had died away. Addison gave voice to the new scepticism when he wrote: "I believe, in general, that there is, and has been, such a thing as Witchcraft; but, at the same time, can give no Credit to any Particular Instance of it."[1] Even in Scotland, the last stronghold of witch belief in Great Britain, no one was executed for witchcraft after 1722; and in 1736 an Act of Parliament under George II (9 Geo II cap. 5) made the death penalty for witchcraft no longer possible.[2] The removal of legal punishment for heresy immensely enlarged the freedom of thought and enabled writers and artists to re-interpret the meaning of the figures of Biblical mythology in the light of their own revolutionary convictions and ideas.

As to the devil, however, it was not the Biblical figure who inflamed the imagination of a new generation of writers, but the Satan of *Paradise Lost.* In the Romantic outlook, the hero of Milton's epic poem became a symbol figure for almost everything the age valued most: defiance, rebellion against a cruel authoritarian order, individualism, energy and vitality, passion and imagination. The eminent influence of the Miltonic Satan in English literature becomes evident if we look at the development of the devil figure in German literature, where it culminated in the wily and sophisticated Mephistopheles of Goethe's *Faust,* never reaching the Titanic height of the Romantic devil type based on the protagonist of *Paradise Lost.* And not even German literature remained uninfluenced by Milton's poem, which had its traceable impact on Klopstock's *Messias.* Still more consequential was the influence of the Miltonic Satan on French Romanticism, due to the literary leadership of Chateaubriand who admired and translated *Paradise Lost.*[3] Indeed, Satan became such a dominating philosophic and political symbol for the Romantic School that it is possible to say that "Satanism is not a part of Romanticism. It is Romanticism."[4]

The first true representant of Romanticism in England was William Blake (1757-1827), and he was also the first to give Milton's Satan a central part in his work.

Blake was a mystic, and his images are therefore not always rationally penetrable. But while there are minor inconsistencies, it is impressive to notice the coherency of the monumental framework of his personal mythology. Though in earlier centuries he would probably have been hanged for heresy, there can be no doubt about the earnestness of his religiosity (taking the word in its widest meaning); he certainly lacked the occasional cynicism of Byron. If Milton was a "Protestant church of one", Blake became a whole religious system of one. Like all visionaries, he gained his inspirations by the contemplation of his inner self, which at the same time represented the universe. It is important to remember this mystic notion of the identity of macrocosm and microcosm when dealing with Blake's writing. So "The Four Zoas" are the basic powers of the universe as well as those of man's personality; the individual human being and the infinity of the universe unite in the figure of the "Universal Man" (I, 1. 6). This double perspective is relevant also for Satan—in whatever form he may appear—since he is at the same time a mythological figure and the symbol of a force within man's mind.

Blake came into contact with mysticism early; his father James had occasionally been referred to as a Swedenborgian.[5] Yet Emanuel Swedenborg (1688-1772) was but a starting point for Blake, whose *Marriage of Heaven and Hell* (1790-93) is in many respects an ironic comment on the doctrine of the Swedish mystic, who used to picture his devils in rather conventional colours. It is in the *Marriage* that Blake makes his famous statement on Milton and his Satan.[6] His main point is to prove that the depiction of God and devil in orthodox Theology is wrong. Milton attempted to justify the ways of God to man; Blake most emphatically aims at a justification of the devil.

> Good is the passive that obeys reason: Evil
> is the active springing from energy.
>   Good is Heaven; Evil is Hell.
>
> ([*Marriage of Heaven and Hell*]; hereafter cited as *MHH*,
>   II, l. 11ff.)[7]

These equations are followed by the 'Voice of the Devil', culminating in the assertion:

> Energy is eternal delight.
>
>   (II, 29)

This is a total reversal of traditional values: it is Hell which is associated with eternal delight, not Heaven. Blake leaves no doubt that what he ironically calls 'Evil' is really Good to him.

This attitude must be borne in mind as the dominant feature in Romantic Satanism: the appreciation, often passionate, of values and ideas which are condemnable by orthodox standards, but are considered essentially good in the light of the new Romantic philosophy. It is a view which has to be kept well apart from the other kind of Satanism, the perverse love of evil for evil's own sake. This second, more objectionable sort of Satanism was essentially a post-Romantic sign of decline. It appeared more pronounced in France—starting with Baudelaire's *Fleurs du Mal* (1857)—than in England, where it was softened, as in De Quincey's works, by ironic undertones. The reason for this may lie in the innate 'common sensical' sobriety of the British mind as well as in the smaller amount of clerical pressure, resulting in a less violent reaction. It is readily admitted, however, that Romanticism proper—and particularly its side-line, the Gothic Novel—is also not free from glimpses of this fascination of evil.

Part III of Blake's *Marriage,* the "Proverbs of Hell", represents a glorification of various manifestations of energy: action, passion, imagination, strength and sensual beauty:

> The pride of the peacock is the glory of God.
> The lust of the goat is the bounty of God.
> The wrath of the lion is the wisdom of God.
> The nakedness of the woman is the work of God.
>
>   (III, l. 22ff.)

> One thought fills immensity.
>
>   (l. 36)

> The tigers of wrath are wiser than the horses of
>   instruction.
>
>   (l. 44)

> Exuberance is beauty.
>
>   (l. 64) etc.

The opposite of energy is seen in reason, the controlling, restricting faculty. Yet Blake insists on the necessity of its existence, since

> Without contraries is no progression.
>
>   (II, l. 7)

Or, in other words, referring to the field of human activities:

> Thus one portion of being is the prolific, the other, the devouring . . .
>
> the prolific would cease to be prolific unless the devourer as a sea received the excess of his delights.
>
>   . . . . .
>
> These two classes of men are always upon earth, and they should be enemies; whoever tries to reconcile them seeks to destroy existence.
>
> Religion is an endeavour to reconcile the two.
>
> Note. Jesus Christ did not wish to unite but to separate them, as in the parable of sheep and goats. And he says, 'I came not to send peace, but a sword.'
>
> Messiah or Satan or Tempter was formerly thought to be one of the antediluvians who are our energies.
>
>   (IV, ll. 110 - 26)

Thus Jesus becomes a Satanic hero, a symbol of energy and life. Blake's devil emphasizes that Jesus was a man, and should be loved for this, for

> Those who envy or calumniate great men hate God, for there is not other God.
>
>   . . . . .
>
> . . . Jesus Christ is the greatest man . . .
>
>   (IV, l. 260ff.)

He is also a rebel, since he broke the Ten Commandments. His virtue was passion, not pale obeisance of a cold law.

> Jesus was all virtue, and acted from impulse, not from rules.
>
>   (IV, l. 282)

The latest part of the *Marriage,* the "Song of Liberty," foreshadows—or mirrors, since it may have been written later—the theme of the later books: the rebellion of a youthful hero against the oppression of bloodless age.

In *America* (1791-93), *Europe* (1794), *The First Book of Urizen* (1794) and *Vala, or The Four Zoas* (1797-1800) Blake develops his central myth of the conflicting powers of Urizen and Orc. It will be shown that both these figures have Satanic traits, for, as Clutton-Brock remarks, Blake "observes that God and Devil are almost interchangeable terms, a fact which Dr. Freud has subsequently noticed."[8] After what has been said about the psychological origins of the devil figure, and considering the fact that Blake as a visionary and mystic was particularly open to 'inspiration', i. e., emanations of the subconscious, this interchangeability will hardly come as a surprise. Yet it is quite evident that evil, in Blake's eyes, lies predominantly in the figure of Urizen.

The First Book of Urizen takes the place of a 'Genesis' in what was announced in the *Marriage of Heaven and Hell* as the "Bible of Hell". It is not Lucifer who rebels, but Urizen-Jehovah who separates himself from the other 'Eternals' by the invention of laws. His name is derived from the Greek verb 'orizein': to define, to make boundaries.[9] He is responsible for the creation; and the creation, which cannot be without laws and boundaries, is considered the primeval error leading to all evil. Accordingly, his motive for creation is not a positive one: he creates for fear of Chaos, frightened by the abyss at his feet:

> Terrific, Urizen strode above; in fear and pale dismay
> He saw the indefinte space beneath, & his soul shrunk with horror.
> His feet upon the verge of non-existence his voice went forth.
> Luvah & Vala, trembling & shrinking, beheld the great workmaster,
> And heard his word, 'Divide, ye bands, influence by influence.
> Build we a bower for Heaven's darling in the grisly deep;
> Build we the mundane shell around the rock of Albion.
>
>   *(Vala* II, ll. 229 - 39)

The association of Urizen with the Father-God Jehovah is corroborated by Blake's pictorial illustrations which invariably show him as an aged and bearded man. He is brought into connection with coldness, snow and ice. So, in *America,* full of jealousy against the flaming Orc,

> His stored snows he poured forth, and his icy magazines
> He opened on the deep, and on the Atlantic sea, white, shivering.
> Leprous his limbs, all over white, and hoary was his visage,
> Weeping in dismal howlings before the stern Americans,
> Hiding the demon red with clouds and cold mists from the earth—
>
>   (ll. 212 - 16)

Since *America* is a paraphrase on a political event—the American War of Independence—Urizen is to be identified with the British monarchy, seen as an oppressive and reactionary force by Blake. In a more general sense, Urizen stands for analytical Reason—"Newton's pantocrator"—, the cold force of disunion utterly hostile to the passionate flame of imagination.

Urizen's opponent is Orc, the spirit of passion and rebellion, politically manifest in the American Wars and the French Revolution. It is Orc who is commonly associated with the traditional attributes of the devil. He is called "demon red" (*America, A Prophecy,* l. 138) and "terror", and is addressed by Albion's angel in the following manner:

> Blasphemous demon, Antichrist, hater of dignities,
> Lover of wild rebellion and transgressor of God's law
> . . .
>
>   (*Am.,* l. 56f.)

His name is connected with Orcus, the Roman netherworld and its god; yet he should not be taken as a symbol of death, but of the chthonic 'Urgrund' from which all life springs. It has been pointed out that in the social body Orc represents not the heart, but the genitals[10], the organs of creativity. It is evident that this 'fiery youth', a symbol of energy and desire, represents a positive value for Blake, to whom "Active Evil is better than Passive Good".[11] Orc's affinity to Satan is further underlined by his occasional appearance in serpent form, as in *The First Book of Urizen* (ch. VI) and *The Four Zoas* (VII b). In both these poems he is moreover linked with the Prometheus tradition, being bound by Urizen with the "Chain of Jealousy" (Ur., VII, l. 394).

But not only Urizen and Orc, also the other Zoas or elements of Eternal Man have Satanic traits. This bewildering fact is explained by Blake's conception of Satan not as a being, but a state:

> There is a state named Satan—learn distinct to know, O Rahab,
> The difference between states, & individuals of those states.
> The state named Satan never can be redeemed in all eternity;
> But when Luvah in Orc became a serpent he descended into
> The state called Satan.
>
>   (*Vala* VIII, l. 367ff.)

In the light of the Christian doctrine of love and forgiveness—as opposed to the stern Mosaic law of Urizen-Jehovah—, evil is not seen as an absolute, but as a passing state of this limited worldly scene. This interpretation links up with the distinction Blake makes between 'negations' and 'contraries'.[12] Contraries are necessary, since there is no progress without them. The real evil is in negation, in nothingness; and Satan, being a state and not an entity, is pure negation.

The notion of negation is closely linked with another of Blake's terms, the Spectre. The Spectre can be defined as the opposite of the active aspects of the Zoas[13]; it is their unreal shadow or, again, their negation. And since every Zoa has its Spectre, there is a Satanic side to each of them.

How can this view of Satan be reconciled with Blake's statement: "Nature is the work of the Devil. The Devil is in us as far as we are in Nature."?[14] It certainly could not if Blake had shared the common Romantic nature worship; but in this point he differed decisively from Wordsworth and his followers. Particularly in his later works, Blake, the visionary artist, found reality only in imagination, not in natural forms which ultimately had to be considered as delusions—necessarily so, if creation, the division of the world under natural laws, is seen as the primeval Urizenic error. Though Orc is metaphorically brought in connection with sexual love (as in the Preludium to *America*), his creativity is in fact of a purely spiritual kind. This view allows Blake to group nature together with technology on Satan's side, an idea which later poets of the Romantic generation would have abhorred.[15]

Blake's conception of Satan is rounded off in *Milton* (1800-1804), where the figure appears under its own name. In this poem Blake endeavours to show that Milton—whom he reveres as the greatest English poet—has misinterpreted the cosmic struggle, portraying God as a lawgiving tyrant instead of a merciful brother.

The image of Satan gets a new dimension in *Milton* through the artist's personal experiences. In 1799 William Hayley, an amateur of letters and biographer of Cowper, generously invited Blake to live on his estate at Felpham. Blake, threatened by penury at the time, gladly accepted the offer, and all went well at first. But when Hayley, as a well-meaning critic, began to interfere with Blake's work, relations became strained. An open break could be prevented by Hayley's loyalty in a law case and their separation in 1803; but Blake's resentment at the pharisaic intrusion of one so much below his own genius into his work, at times almost unbearable to the impetuous artist, is reflected in his portrait of Satan:

> With incomparable mildness
> His primitive tyrannical attempts on Los—with most
> endearing love
> He soft entreated Los to give to him Palamabron's
> station.

(I, Pl. 7, l. 5ff.)

> Meanwhile wept Satan before Los, accusing Palam-
> abron,
> Himself exculpating with mildest speech . . .

(I, Pl. 8, l. 1f.)

Satan here usurps his brother Palamabron's position, not with force, but with hypocritical mildness, pretending to be good-natured while acting tyrannically.

> To do unkind things in kindness! With power armed,
> to say

> The most irritating things in the midst of tears & love
> These are the stings of the serpent.

(Pl. 12, l. 32)

This genuine touch of human psychology is an essential enrichment of the portrait of Satan. It is in the vein of the tyrannical Urizen-Jehovah, when Satan commands:

> I am God alone,
> There is no other!

(Pl. 9, l. 25)

Among the three classes of men in Calvinistic doctrine—the Elect, the Redeemed and the Reprobate—Satan belongs to the first, which to Blake represent the self-righteous rather than the righteous.

If we equal Milton to the Eternal Man in the *Four Zoas,* Satan represents the 'Selfhood' in his breast. He can take on an impressive stature:

> The spectre of Satan stood upon the roaring sea and
> beheld
> Milton within his sleeping humanity. Trembling and
> shuddering
> He stood upon the waves, a twenty-sevenfold mighty
> demon,
> Gorgeous & beautiful; loud roll his thunders against
> Milton.

(Pl. 38, l. 9)[16]

Yet Milton defies him in a grand speech, in which Satan's nature is once more admirably summed up:

> Satan, my spectre, I know my power thee to annihi-
> late
> . . . . .
> Thy purpose and the purpose of thy priests and of the
> churches
> Is to impress on men the fear of death; to teach Trem-
> bling & fear, terror, constriction, abject selfishness.
> Mine is to teach men to despise death, & to go on
> In fearless majesty annihilating self, laughing to scorn
> Thy laws and terrors, shaking down thy Synagogues
> as webs.
> I come to discover before Heaven & Hell the self-
> righteousness
> In all its hypocritic turpitude, opening to every eye
> These wonders of Satan's holiness, showing to the
> earth
> The idol-virtues of the natural heart, & Satan's seat
> Explore, in all its selfish natural virtue, & put off
> In self-annihilation all that is not of God alone:
> To put off self & all I have, ever & ever. Amen.

(II, Pl. 38, ll. 29 - 49)

So Blake's message is in the end optimistic: Satan, the spectral state of Selfhood and spiritual death, can be overcome by the annihilation of one's self, which is attained through imagination.

While Blake boldly challenged the old pattern of good and evil, regrouping traditional values, the Gothic novelists did not, as a rule, question the conventional system; they dealt with evil mainly for the sake of its peculiar poetical fascination. Theirs was a straightforward kind of literature, aiming at stirring strong emotions; for emotion, independent of its moral value, was considered of positive quality since the early days of *Sturm und Drang* (and it may be remembered that M. G. Lewis was well acquainted with German literature). Strong passion could not be feigned. It came from the heart, it was natural and original and defied the fetters of convention and social oppression. The predilection for violent passion must be seen partly as a reaction against the restrictive rationalism and didacticism of the preceding period. As a literary movement it was carried to a large extent by very young people: the German *Sturm und Drang* was initiated by a group of writers hardly beyond the age of boys; Keats, Shelley and Byron died as young men, and Lewis was twenty years old when he wrote *The Monk*. So juvenile excitability accounts for much of the hyperbolism of this literary period.

Moreover, the political events of the age had nourished the public's taste for strong excitement. After the terrors of the French Revolution, a writer had to use strong means to surpass the reality in his fiction. One possibility of reaching this aim was obviously to resort to supernatural agencies. While Ann Radcliffe, born in the Age of Johnson, still declined to use supernaturalism in her works, later writers were less willing to renounce the possibilities of magical action. Maturin professed it his aim "to base the interest of my novel entirely on the passion of supernatural terror" and added: "Emotions are my events."[17]

The use of supernatural agents in the Gothic Novel is not only the result of a reaction against the dominance of realism in the novel of the age of rationalism. It also brings about an enormous widening of the possibilities of poetic invention—a thing most welcome to writers more interested in the stirring of emotions than the conveyance of knowledge. The novel of realism had for the most part neglected the irrational side of man; the Gothic novel restored it to its full right.

The devil in the Gothic Novel is therefore not a philosophical or political symbol, but an instrument to evoke terror and strong feelings in the reader's mind. The figure had thus a function similar to that of the early medieval stage devil, though the ultimate aim was different: while the devil in the Mysteries was devised to underline the didacticism of the clerical message by pointing out to the spectator the possible consequences of his sins, the Gothic devil's primary object was to raise fear, with little or no regard for its corrective effect on the reader's moral attitude.

What had been felt by earlier writers—notably the Elizabethans—, namely, that there was such a paradoxical thing as "delightful horror", had by the time of Walpole and his followers been sanctioned on a philosophical level by the separation of ethical and aesthetical categories. Closely linked with the development of the Gothic Novel is the idea of the Sublime. It was Burke who, in *A Philosophical Inquiry into the Origin of our Ideas of the Sublime and the Beautiful* (1756), had recognized in sublimity a category of its own.[18] "Whatever is fitted in any sort to excite the ideas of pain . . . whatever is in any sort terrible . . . is a source of the sublime . . .".[19] All terrible things are sublime, since no real danger can leave us unimpressed. The sublime evokes awe and—if it is terrible—pain, while beauty evokes pleasure. And as the highest degree of pain surpasses the utmost degree of pleasure in its emotional impact, the sublime is superior to the beautiful with regard to its poetical quality.

There is also a direct link between pain and pleasure on a psychological level. The feeling of having escaped a danger produces fright and pleasure at the same time; and dangers in a fictional area—as in a novel—create a feeling of taking part and yet not being involved, which is definitely pleasant. "Terror is a passion which always produces delight when it does not press too close".[20] The happiness of the contemplation of beauty is surpassed by the joy of being spared threatening destruction. And so the devil as a personification of evil and terror could be pictured with all the more vivid colours, as he had, by the 18th century, become a predominantly fictional figure with little or no relation to everyday reality.

The similarity of the Gothic with the medieval devil must be seen in the light of the general affinity of the Romantic Age, and more particularly Gothic literature, to the Middle Ages. While many of the actual Romantics glorified the lost unity of pre-reformatory times, the novelists of terror put the stress on the strange and sombre sides of the so-called 'Dark Ages'—the 'Gothic' aspect. Gloomy vaults, decaying cathedrals, monkish intrigues and the tortures of the Inquisition: whatever the historical truth, these were the features of the Middle Ages to the Gothic novelists. The devil, as an integral part of this setting, usually appears is a horrid beastly shape:

> He appeared in all that ugliness which, since his fall from heaven, had been his portion. His blasted limbs still bore marks of the Almighty's thunder. A swarthy darkness spread itself over his gigantic form: his hands and feet were armed with long talons. Fury glared in his eyes, which might have struck the bravest heart with terror. Over his huge shoulders waved two enormous sable wings; and his hair was supplied by living snakes, which twined themselves round his brows with frightful hissings.
>
> (*The Monk*, p. 348)

This description aims at evoking a maximum of terror; yet we feel that it somehow falls short of its aim. The reason for this lies in its very outspokenness. Lewis, whose "peculiar gift", as E. A. Baker ironically remarks, "was the negation of reticence"[21], is too direct; he does not leave anything to the reader's imagination. Maturin is much more consciously artistic in this respect. In *Melmoth* we never meet the devil face to face, and yet his presence behind the scene is constantly and alarmingly felt. All that we see of him—and even this only in a dream—are the two gigantic black arms of a being "too vast and horrible even for the imagery of a dream to shape" (p. 539), holding Melmoth over the fatal abyss.

This technique of tantalizing and exciting the reader's imagination by vague and ominous hints was rightly recognized as being more effective in raising fear and anxiety than plain description.[22] While it was later developed to mastership by Poe, it was already successfully used by the Gothic School. One of its consequences was the disappearance of the devil himself from the tales of terror, since as a figure with considerable tradition—Biblical and Miltonic—he used to evoke rather definite associations, thus thwarting the vagueness of feeling striven for. Fear is heightened by obscurity; if horror can be given a name it loses much of its hold on us.

M. G. Lewis, as has been shown, did not adhere to this principle. Yet he was not so crude an artist as he is often supposed to be; he had other means at his disposal. The first description of Lucifer in *The Monk* is very effective. In a carefully built-up atmosphere of fearful expectation—sulphurous flames, blue fire and strange chillness prepare the reader for the worst—the actual apparition of the devil comes as an almost shocking surprise:

> Ambrosio started, and expected the demon with terror. What was his surprise when, the thunder ceasing to roll, a full strain of melodious music sounded in the air! At the same time the cloud disappeared, and he beheld a figure more beautiful than fancy's pencil ever drew. It was a youth, seemingly scarce eighteen, the perfection of whose form and face was unrivalled. He was perfectly naked: a bright star sparkled upon his forehead, two crimson wings extended themselves from his shoulders, and his silken locks were confined by a band of many-coloured fires . . . His form shone with dazzling glory: he was surrounded by clouds of rose-coloured light; and at the moment that he appeared, a refreshing air breathed perfumes through the cavern . . . Ambrosio gazed upon the spirit with delight and wonder; yet, however beautiful the figure, he could not but remark a wildness in the demon's eyes, and a mysterious melancholy impressed upon his features, betraying the fallen angel, and inspiring the spectators with secret awe.
>
> (p. 220f.)

This devil could be the "Satan in his original glory" of Blake's painting[23], were it not for his eyes; and it is these eyes, too, which form a connecting link with the second, more conventional description of Lucifer in *The Monk*.

The dark and wild eyes of Satan are, in fact, a 'leitmotiv' in the Gothic Novel. They are also found in the human heroes of these novels, thus establishing an unmistakable link between them and Satan. A few random passages, besides those quoted above, may suffice to illustrate this connection:

> —(a description of Ambrosio:) He was a man of noble port and commanding presence. His stature was lofty,

and his features uncommonly handsome. His nose was aquiline, his eyes large, black and sparkling, and his dark brows almost joined together.

> . . . . .

> He bowed himself with humility to the audience. Still there was a certain severity in his look and manner that inspired universal awe, and few could sustain the glance of his eye, at once fiery and penetrating.
>
> (*The Monk*, p. 10)

> —(of Melmoth's picture:) It represented a man of middle age. There was nothing remarkable in the costume, or in the countenance, but the eyes, John felt, were such as one feels they had never seen, and feels they can never forget.
>
> (*Melmoth*, p. 17f.)

> —(of Melmoth:) . . . the Englishman's eyes were observed by all the guests, from the moment of his entrance, to effuse a most fearful and preternatural lustre . . .
>
> (id., p. 34)

> —(of Melmoth:) I felt that I had never beheld such eyes blazing in a mortal face,—in the darkness of my prison, I held up my hand to shield myself from their preternatural glare.
>
> (id., p. 227)

This persistent motif of the Satanic look no doubt owes a lot to the popular superstition of the 'evil eye', and at the turn of the century it may have gained particular significance through the fashionable craze of Mesmerism and hypnotical experimenting. But the eyes of Satan had been considered remarkable by earlier writers, as Praz has shown with quotations from Tasso's *Gerusalemme Liberata* and Marino's *Strage degli Innocenti,* notably drawing attention to the new element of sadness added by Marino to the expression of terror and death in the eyes of Tasso's Satan.[24] And then it is again Milton who refers to this peculiar mixture of terror and melancholy in the devil's looks:

> cruel his eye, but cast
> Signs of remorse and passion . . .
>
> (P. L., I, l. 604)

Yet the dark and piercing looks are not the only Satanic traits in Melmoth. This English Ahasuerus possesses powers which are clearly superhuman:

> He retreated a few paces, and sheathing his sword, waved them back only with his arm; and this movement, that seemed to announce an internal power above all physical force, had the effect of nailing every spectator to the spot where he stood.
>
> (p. 521)

And, most important of all, he confesses to the primeval Luciferian sin of hubris:

> Mine was the great angelic sin—pride and intellectual glorying!
>
> (p. 499)

So, while gradually abandoning the figure of the devil for its too definite associations, the Gothic novelists furnished their heroes with an increasing amount of Satan's qualities. A transcendental figure is lastly unfit to evoke sympathy or condemnation in a heightened degree; a human being, even if close to caricature, will always be more suitable for the purpose. Satan retired behind the scenes, but he swayed his sceptre still vigorously enough in the Gothic villains whom he, re-assuming his strange medieval double role of an adversary and punishing executive of God, came to fetch—as he had fetched Dr. Faustus—at the end of their ungodly lives.

Percy Bysshe Shelley (1792 - 1822) was well acquainted with Gothic literature. The cult of the Gothic Novel was at its peak in his teens[25], and the morbid fascination of evil—common to the bulk of Romantic writing, but appearing in its crudest form in the novel of terror since Walpole—has left its traces in his works, most notably in *The Cenci*. But to him, unlike the Gothic novelists, evil was not only a poetical motif, but a political problem. Like Wordsworth and his own generation, he had witnessed the deterioration of the values won in the French Revolution; he had been shocked and disappointed by the bloody aftermath of an event hailed as the advent of political freedom in Europe. He had further watched the degeneration of Napoleon's reign from republicanism to despotism. Why had these attempts at political self-determination, so hopefully and gloriously begun, ended in failure and dismay? It was Godwin who gave the pessimistic answer that the high passions and lofty designs of well-meaning men are perverted in a corrupt world.[26] So the moral distortions of the ancien régime poisoned the children of the revolution, and 18th century absolutism in Europe foreshadowed the ill course of Napoleon's career. Shelley was led to the conviction that evil in human society was "the result of unnatural political institutions".[27] Moral advancement of man could not be achieved without changing the institutions. But how should this be accomplished, if man himself was constantly perverted by the very same institutions? This contradiction could only be overcome by a particular idea of development: the institutional reform on a political level, so much desired by Shelley, had to be prepared by individual reform on a poetical level. Poetry, to Shelley, is synonymous with true humanity, and it is closely linked with love:

> The great secret of morals is love; or a going out of our own nature, and an identification of ourselves with the beautiful which exists in thought, action, or person, not our own.
>
> . . . . .
>
> The great instrument of moral good is the imagination; and poetry administers to the effect by acting upon the cause.
>
> . . . . .
>
> Poetry strengthens the faculty which is the organ of the moral nature of man, in the same manner as exercise strengthens a limb.[28]

So, if individual men were taught love long and intensely enough, they would gradually grow sufficiently strong to resist the perverting power of evil institutions and in turn even become able to alter them.

One of the institutional stumbling blocks which seemed to stand in the way of human development towards universal love and self-esteem was the Church. In what Shelley himself calls 'an amusing fragment', titled *On the Devil and Devils*[29], he takes the devil as a starting point for an attack against orthodox theology. The devil, whom he calls "the weak place of the popular religion—the vulnerable belly of the crocodile"[30], is to him an invention of the religious establishment, a desperate attempt at accounting for evil in a world which is supposed to have been created by a good, omnipotent God. Shelley flatly rejects this whole "system of casuistry".[31] He insists that the entire responsibility is with God, who "need not damn unless he likes".[32] It seems that God has installed the devil to have him do the dirty work while he himself retires into an aura of hypocritical impeccability. Worse still: God obviously has pleasure in tormenting the devil. Such a God, of course, would be entirely unacceptable, and Shelley indeed prefers the Platonic idea of the origin of evil: that evil has to be accounted for by matter, which as a coarse and inert—though everlasting—material is a perpetual impediment to the divine spirit.

Though there is no doubt that Shelley was fiercely anti-clerical, he cannot be called an atheist. He firmly believed in the principle of love and hope—and what is God if not the principle of universal love? The boundaries of orthodoxy were to him—as to many Romantic poets—too narrow, and so his religiosity took the form of a far-reaching Pantheism, heavily influenced by Platonic thought.[33] So the devil was not a religious problem to him, but an important poetical symbol in an ethical, poetical and political context.

Shelley numbers among the most fervent admirers of Milton's Satan; his comments about the hero of *Paradise Lost* leave no doubt about that:

> Nothing can exceed the grandeur and the energy of the character of the Devil as expressed in *Paradise Lost*.
>
> . . . . .
>
> Milton's Devil as a moral being is as far superior to his God as one who perseveres in some purpose which he has conceived to be excellent in spite of adversity and torture is to one who in the cold security of undoubted triumph inflicts the most horrible revenge upon his enemy, . . .[34]

It is easily understood that Shelley, the young radical, felt attracted to Milton's sublime portrayal of the arch-rebel, which inspired him to come to the same strange reversal of values as Blake, namely, to put evil on the side of God and good on the side of His opponent. But then he is detached enough a thinker to become aware of the ethical problems involved in incorporating Satan into his creed of universal love, and so he prefers to pick out another mythological figure as his hero: Prometheus. He explains his choice by the following discerning remarks on the relation between Prometheus and Satan in the Preface to *Prometheus Unbound*:

> The only imaginary being resembling in any degree Prometheus, is Satan; and Prometheus is, in my judgement, a more poetical character than Satan, because, in addition to courage, and majesty, and firm and patient opposition to omnipotent force, he is susceptible of being described as exempt of the taints of ambition, envy, revenge, and a desire for personal aggrandisement, which, in the Hero of *Paradise Lost,* interfere with the interest. The character of Satan engenders in the mind a pernicious casuistry which leads us to weigh his faults with his wrongs, and to excuse the former because the latter exceed all measure. In the minds of those who consider that magnificent fiction with a religious feeling it engenders something worse. But Prometheus is, as it were, the type of the highest perfection of moral and intellectual nature, impelled by the purest and the truest motives to the best and noblest ends.[35]

Aischylos's original drama is subjected to one substantial alteration by Shelley: he rejects a reconciliation between Prometheus and Jupiter, because he "was averse from a catastrophe so feeble as that of reconciling the Champion with the Oppressor of mankind".[36] Indeed, Jupiter is shown in too negative a light to make such an arrangement plausible. Like Blake's Urizen, Shelley's Jupiter is a personification of reactionary power, a hoariheaded embodiment of everlasting negation, suppressing every progress towards human freedom with cold laws and brutal despotism. He must be overthrown, and his cry on falling from his throne is—despite its classical flavour—strikingly similar to the comical lament of the Mystery devils, as if to prove his identity with the power of Evil:

> Ai! Ai!
> The elements obey me not. I sink
> Dizzily down, ever, for ever, down.
> And, like a cloud, mine enemy above
> Darkens my fall with victory! Ai, Ai![37]

Prometheus, like Satan, resisted temptation and embraced love; only then could he be freed, and only then his victory became true. The ethical message of the play—inobtrusively expressed by Shelley, to whom "didactic poetry" was an "abhorrence"[38]—is that, in spite of the perverting power of the ruling institutions, the ultimate responsibility for his acts is with man himself.[39] Man's will is free to accept the principle of love, and if he does so, the world can be cleansed from evil.[40]

Though he believed in the perfectibility of man, Shelley did by no means underrate the power of evil. That even a pure and virtuous soul can be driven to commit a foul and fatal deed is exemplified in his drama *The Cenci* (1819). This play, "perhaps the best serious English play written between 1790 and 1890"[41], is important to us as it contains, in the person of Count Francesco Cenci, a dramatically intensified portrayal of "a spirit of deep hell" in "human form".[42] Cenci is utterly and totally evil, and in this respect very similar to the Vice and the Shakespearean vil-

lains with their "motiveless malignity". Indeed, the influence of Elizabethan drama is unmistakable; King-Hele has counted more than twenty possible verbal echoes from Shakespeare's plays, notably *Macbeth,* in *The Cenci.*[43] Psychologically, though, Cenci's malignity is not quite without motive. He is entirely given to luxury and dissipation, and he draws his greatest sensual pleasure from inflicting pain on others:

> All men delight in sensual luxury,
> All men enjoy revenge; and most exult
> Over the tortures they can never feel—
> Flattering their secret peace with others' pain.
> But I delight in nothing else. I love
> The sight of agony, and the sense of joy,
> When this shall be another's, and that mine.
>
> (I, I, l. 77ff.)

As his senses become gradually dulled, they demand increasingly sharper stimuli. This progressive destruction of one's own sensibility is what Shelley calls corruption[44]; and indeed, Cenci feeds on his own corruption in a truly vicious circle. That he is so entirely given to sensual luxury at an age when calm spirituality would be more appropriate, is a further sign of his unnaturalness. As a matter of fact, "unnaturalness" is a leitmotiv in the characterization of old Cenci:

> unnatural man . . .
>
> (I, III, l. 54)
> unnatural pride . . .
>
> (II, I, l. 44)
> and upon Earth
> All good shall droop and sicken, and ill things
> Shall with a spirit of unnatural life
> Stir and be quickened . . . even as I am now.
>
> (IV, I, l. 186ff.)

Instead of accepting the natural slackening of his sensitive faculties, due to old age, Cenci goes to the utmost to stir his senses. The lines

> And but that there yet remains a deed to act
> Whose horror might make sharp an appetite
> Duller than mine—I'd do—I know not what.
>
> (I, I, l. 100ff.)

already foreshadow the act of incest.

It must be noted, however, that, in the Romantic outlook, incest has not only negative aspects. "Incest is, like many other incorrect things, a very poetical circumstance. It may be the excess of love or hate . . .".[45] The trespassing of conventional limits may be accepted if it springs from a spirit of boundless love, in accordance with the Romantic inclination of probing every height and depth of human experience. Shelley, therefore, has to make it clear that, in Cenci's case, incest does not spring from an excess of love, and he does so by stressing Cenci's outrageous hatred towards his children, his sons as well as Beatrice.[46]

The Count's perverted joy at the death of his sons is only surpassed by his sadistic delight in making his daughter the victim of an unnatural crime.[47] But even so, with its quality of excess, this crime is in the neighbourhood of the sublime and thus remains "a very poetical circumstance".

In Count Cenci, elements of the 'traditional' pre-Miltonic devil meet with the new Romantic picture of the archfiend as Blake sketched it. Cenci is "hoary grey"[48], with "white venerable hairs", just like Blake's Urizen[49]; yet, on the other hand, he is not a symbol of lifeless passivity, but an extremely active driving force. Indeed, he is the centre of action, bringing about rape and murder and eventually—by provoking a violent reaction—his own killing, thus fulfilling the moral law that "ill must come of ill".[50] His thanksgiving prayer after the death of his two sons cannot be called cynical, for God has seemingly granted him a thing he really wished for. The blasphemy and utter perversion lies in the fact that he actually supposes God to be on his side. In this attitude he is supported by the Pope, Clement VIII, who, though desperately implored by Beatrice, refuses to interfere with what he interprets as a father's legitimate reaction to filial disobedience. Shelley portrays the Pope with all his anticlerical fervour; indeed, it is in the Pope that we find the truest parallel to Blake's Urizen, when he is described as "a marble form; a rite, a law, a custom: not a man".[51]

Beatrice, the heroine of the play, becomes a tragic figure because her nature is poisoned by the infectious influence of vice in its ugliest form. It is her very virtue which, once spoilt, makes her a murderess; it is the filial affection which, thwarted to the utmost, drives her to kill. Though she acts understandably, she acts wrongly. Shelley makes this quite clear in the Preface:

> Undoubtedly, no person can be truly dishonoured by the act of another; and the fit return to make to the most enormous injuries is kindness and forbearance, and a resolution to convert the injurer from his dark passions by peace and love. Revenge, retaliation, atonement, are pernicious mistakes.[52]

These are the words of the reformer, not the revolutionary; of the man who believes with Beatrice that "ill must come of ill" and that only a breaking out of the vicious circle in the spirit of Christian ethics can put an end to the monstrous power of evil. Pride is no help, since the feeling of hurt pride will inevitably lead to rash actions. This reminds us of Shelley's political conviction that in a revolutionary change the uprising force is always in danger of being infected by the ills of the powers overturned, and that only a wilful effort and constant vigilance can prevent that fatal perversion.

In some strange way, Beatrice makes the same mistake as Cenci: she is too much concerned with her own person. Shelley proves a fine psychologist when having Orsino speak:

> . . . 'tis a trick of this same family
> To analyse their own and other minds.

> Such self-anatomy shall teach the will
> Dangerous secrets: for it tempts our powers,
> Knowing what must be thought, and may be done,
> Into the depth of darkest purposes . . .

(II, II, l. 108ff.)

In considering herself the last pillar of the honour of her house, in considering the murder an absolute necessity, she goes too far and crosses the border line to presumption. Though the guilt of her action is with her father, the responsibility remains hers. Less self-analysis—the source of her "melancholy thoughts" (I, II, l. 36)—and more detachment from her own self might have prevented the fatal crime. Nevertheless it is evident that the sympathies of writer and reader alike are on Beatrice's side. Tyrant killers can always count on sympathy. And yet, if we put the heroine's character to close scrutiny, we cannot entirely spare her the blame of excessive self-concern—which is just a milder term for the Satanic arch-sin of pride.

Lord George Gordon Byron (1788 - 1824), Shelley's contemporary and personal friend, is widely considered the paradigm of a Romantic poet. Yet, while lacking Shelley's poetical simplicity and Blake's rhapsodical grandeur, he still had strong traces of 18th century rationalism in him. Though he shared some of Blake's basic conceptions to an astonishing degree, he had a Popean sarcasm at his disposal which the visionary painter-poet did not possess (with the possible exception of the *Marriage of Heaven and Hell*). At the same time, he stood, like Blake and Shelley, under the influence of Milton's *Paradise Lost*; an influence, however, which was by no means exclusive, for with the stress on poetical liberty so characteristic for Romantic poetry he blended the figure of the Miltonic Satan freely with traits of Aischylos's Prometheus, Goethe's Mephistopheles, and the Ahasuerus legend. Rudwin has drawn attention to the important fact that most literary recreators of Satan were exiles from their native country or had been ostracized from the community of their class; he numbers among them Dante, Luther, Vondel, Milton, Byron, Heine, Lermontov, Quinet and Hugo.[53] The similarity of their fate accounts for their being attracted by the figure of the banished archangel. Yet mental exile and alienation was not merely a problem of Byron the man, but of his whole age. The rebellious spirit of the younger Romantic generation had radically broken with most of the theological, philosophical and social conventions of the preceding period. This separation, self-inflicted but inevitable, provided them with a hitherto unknown freedom, but also with an intense feeling of rootlessness and alienation.[54] The parallelity of their fate with Satan, the outcast from heaven, is evident. To cope with the problem of alienation, two solutions offered themselves: pride and ironic distance. Both are found in Byron's Satanic figures.

Caesar, the devil figure of the dramatic fragment *The Deformed Transformed* (1822), owes his irony and sarcasm to Goethe's Mephistopheles; in his Advertisement to the play, Byron readily admits his indebtedness to *Faust*. Caesar grants Arnold, an ugly hunchback, a magical transformation into the bodily shape of Achilles. He does so without binding Arnold to any formal contract, since he is convinced of the corruptibility of the human soul; and indeed he easily succeeds in seducing the man to 'heroic' deeds of war and bloodshed. If this devil was ever envious of man, he has overcome this sentiment long ago with the knowing and disillusioned contempt for the human race:

> And these are men, forsooth!
> Heroes and chiefs, the flower of Adam's bastards!
> This is the consequence of giving matter
> The power of thought. It is a stubborn substance.
> And thinks chaotically, as it acts,
> Ever relapsing into its first elements.
> Well! I must play with these poor puppets: 'tis
> The spirit's pastime in his idler hours.

>> (I, 2, ll. 314 - 21)

In spite of his sarcasm, he is a faithful servant to Arnold, putting his magical power at his service, a power, however, which ends at the frontiers of life: "the resurrection is beyond me", he has to admit, when Olimpia, the woman Arnold has fallen in love with, seems near her death.

Caesar is definitely no flatterer. His pungent remarks recall the tradition of the Elizabethan court jester. Arnold calls him an "everlasting sneerer" (I, 2, l. 117), and the Bourbon asks him in comic despair: "Wilt never be serious?" (I, 2, l. 290). But, like the jester, his outspokenness has solid ground:

> The devil speaks the truth much oftener than he's
>> deem'd:
> He hath an ignorant audience.

>> (II, 3, l. 149)

This devil gives no sign of deeper emotion: save for a short allusion to Asmodeus, which remains purely verbal, he does not even show signs of sensuality. Though the drama is unfinished, we may assume that in the end he has to capitulate, in spite of his contempt for human affairs, before true love.

Clearly Miltonic, on the other hand, is the Satan of *The Vision of Judgement* (1822). His dignity is all the more striking as the general tone of the poem—a biting reply to Southey's "Vision of Judgement"—is highly sarcastic. Thus is Satan's arrival described:

> But bringing up the rear of this bright host,
> A Spirit of a different aspect waved
> His wings, like thunder-clouds above some coast
> Whose barren beach with frequent wrecks is paved;
> His brow was like the deep when tempest-toss'd;
> Fierce and unfathomable thoughts engraved
> Eternal wrath on his immortal face,
> And where he gazed a gloom pervaded space.

>> (XXIV)

Significantly, he is not despised by the archangel Michael, but honoured as a noble adversary:

> He and the sombre, silent Spirit met—
> They knew each other both for good and ill;
> Such was their power, that neither could forget
> His former friend and future foe; but still
> There was a high, immortal, proud regret
> In either's eye, as if 'twere less their will
> Than destiny to make the eternal years
> Their date of war, and their 'champ clos' the spheres.

>> (XXXII)

The somewhat old-fashioned aristocratic politeness with which Satan meets his counterpart may, as Baugh remarks, have been influenced by the picture of the courtly devil Astarotte in Pulci's *Morgante Maggiore* (1482), a work in the tradition of the burlesquing Charlemagne legend.[55] It is in accordance with this dignity that Satan displays a certain nonchalance as to the fate of the soul of the late King George III; he has "kings enough below, God knows!" and makes his claim merely on formal grounds. With equal dignity he later silently declines an offer of "multiscribbling Southey" to write his biography. He is no busy soul-hunter, for men themselves—and kings, like George, in particular—do his business in the world well enough.

This Miltonic Satan is enriched with Promethean elements in the figure of Lucifer in *Cain* (1821). Prometheus, in Byron's poem of the same title (1816)[56], is a rebel out of pity for humanity. He opposes the "ruling principle of Hate" in the tyranny of Zeus, and, though cruelly punished, he continues to defy the Thunderer with silent pride so "that in his hands the lightnings trembled".

Lucifer shows the same pity for man:

> I know the thoughts
> of dust, and feel for it, and with you.

>> (I, 1, l. 100)

Yet because of this very knowledge he is not capable of true, joyful love. This becomes clear in his elusive answers to Cain's questions on this subject (II, 2, l. 305ff.), and it is also stated in his dialogue with Adah:

> Adah. I have heard it said,
> The seraphs love most—cherubim know most—
> And this should be a cherub—since he loves not.
>
> Luc. And if the higher knowledge quenches love,
> What must he be you cannot love when known?
> Since the all-knowing cherubim love least,
> The seraphs' love can be but ignorance:
> That they are not compatible, the doom
> Of thy fond parents, for their daring, proves.

>> (I, 1, ll. 418 - 25)

As a 'Lucifer', a bringer of light, he is determined to pass on that knowledge, the knowledge of God's tyranny, to Cain. His own attitude towards God is one of brave defiance, like that of Prometheus and Milton's Satan in his best moments. He is one of the

> Souls who dare look the Omnipotent tyrant in
> His everlasting face, and tell him that
> His evil is not good!
>
> (I, 1, l. 137ff.)

He covers his suffering with pride. 'Right' pride, in the Byronic sense, is not Faustian hubris and megalomania, but a defence mechanism for the vulnerable spirit after the experience of separation; it is the realization that, to use a Miltonic phrase, "the mind is its own place". Though he has "a victor", he has "no superior" (II, 2, l. 429), and he is resolved to carry on his battle against an unjust heaven in all eternity. Byron has called the play a 'Mystery'; but unlike the medieval plays it does not deal with the mysteries of God's perfection, but the puzzling imperfection of the world, as it is formulated in Cain's question:

> Then why is evil—he (God) being good?
>
> (II, 2, l. 285)

Lucifer's logical answer is that God is not good after all, but tyrannical and unloving; hence his, Lucifer's, Promethean sympathy for man. It is true that he brings death into the world, but then

> It may be death that leads to the highest knowledge;
> And being of all things the sole thing certain,
> At least leads to the surest science . . .
>
> (II, 2, l. 164)

Death may become the ultimate experience of sublimity, if it is fearlessly accepted as the Fall was accepted by Satan.

The problem of meeting death in the right way is central in *Manfred* (1817). This dramatic poem offers a good illustration for the 'Satanic principle' developed in Byronic poetry insofar as it shows the clash of 'good' and 'evil' Satanism, the first being embodied in Manfred, the latter in Arimanes (Ahriman). If we attempt to read Manfred's crime in Blakean terms, his incest is the sin of Selfhood, since his beloved sister, in symbolical interpretation, is nothing else than a metaphor for his self, his 'alter ego'. Manfred suffers from his sin, but his initial endeavour to get rid of it by oblivion is the wrong way. Only when he is ready to accept it, to live and—what is more—to die with it he really overcomes his guilt. If he accepts death undauntedly, it may indeed lead him to the last knowledge, to the highest sublimity; for giving up his self, he reaches the aim of Romantic 'Todessehnsucht'; the dissolution and fusion of his personality in the boundless energy of the living universe.

> . . . Satan is a symbol paradoxically not of death and evil in the mundane world (for which Byron in Manfred offers Arimanes as a symbol) but of that spiritual death upon which will follow an aggressive, self-made sort of spiritual rebirth. . . . Milton's Satan comes to be regarded as the representative of true life, of man reborn in and by himself through the experience of the sublime . . .[57]

This 'Satanic principle', as has been noted, is not embodied in the actual devil figure of the play—Arimanes—but in Manfred. Arimanes is the powerful spirit of evil and destruction, the absolute ruler of a fallen world:

> Beneath his footsteps the volcanoes rise;
> His shadow is the Pestilence; his path
> The comets herald through the crackling skies;
> And planets turn to ashes at his wrath.
> To him War offers daily sacrifice;
> To him Death pays his tribute; Life is his,
> With all its infinite of agonies—
> And his the spirit of whatever is!
>
> (II, 4, l. 9ff.)

But Manfred refuses to bow to him, as he later defies the spirits who want to fetch him at the moment of his death; for, having shaken off the tyranny of negation, he has realized that, after all, "'tis not so difficult to die" (III, 4, l. 151).

Manfred stands out as the prototype of the Byronic hero, whose characteristics are also met—in varying intensity—in Childe Harold, Don Juan, the Giaour and other figures from Byron's work. In them is mixed the heritage of Milton's Satan, Prometheus, Ahasuerus, Faust and the Gothic villain: defiance, love of individual freedom, self-reliance, scepticism, melancholy, a criminal past vaguely hinted at, and separation from society. While Satanic qualities such as these retain a prominent position in poetry and fiction, the devil himself loses much of his importance as a literary figure, for the Romantic striving for universality, enriched—above all in Blake—with Mystic traditions and distinguished by growing psychological refinement, has successfully begun to place Heaven and Hell within the breast of Man.

Notes

1. Spectator, Nr. CXVII, 1711.

2. Ashton, p. 191.

3. On Satanism in French literature cf. Rudwin, *Romantisme et Satanisme,* Paris 1927.

4. Rudwin, *The Devil,* p. 277.

5. Clutton-Brock, *Blake,* London 1933, p. 10.

6. See p. 132.

7. Quotations are from the edition by W. H. Stevenson (*The Poems of William Blake*), London 1971.

8. p. 54.

9. Hagstrum, *William Blake, Poet and Painter,* Chicago and London, 1964, p. 105.

10. Townsend, p. 110.

11. Marginalia to Lavater, p. 409; quoted in Frye, p. 72.

12. Cf. also Raine (*Blake and Tradition,* London 1969), vol. II, p. 220.

13. Townsend, p. 144.

14. Raine, vol. II, p. 223.

15. On Blake's attitude to nature cf. Hirsch, "The Two Blakes," *RES* N. S. XII, 1961, p. 373ff.

16. Cf. Blake's watercolour painting "Satan in his original glory", which shows a beautiful youth (reproduced in Raine, vol. II, p. 222). Evidently Selfhood must be given an attractive form.

17. Varma, *The Gothic Flame,* New York 1957, p. 161.

18. Jürgen Klein, *Der Gotische Roman und die Aesthetik des Bösen,* Darmstadt 1975, p. 21ff.

19. Burke, *Inquiry,* London/New York 1958, 39f.

20. ibid., 45.

21. In the Preface of his edition of *The Monk,* p. IX

22. A fact succinctly summed up in Sulzer's remark (1763): "Je verworrener die Vorstellung, desto stärker die Empfindung." (quoted in Klein, p. 46).

23. Cf. p. 157.

24. Praz, *The Romantic Agony,* London 1954, p. 53f.

25. King-Hele, *Shelley, his Thought and Work,* London 1962, p. 138.

26. McNiece, *Shelley and the Revolutionary Idea,* Cambridge Mass. 1969, p. 169.

27. ibid., p. 158.

28. A Defense of Poetry, 1821 (here from: *Shelley, Poetry & Prose,* OUP London 1931, repr. 1966, p. 136f.).

29. Composed with all probability in 1820/21 (Shelley, *Complete Works,* ed. by Ingpen/Peck, London and New York 1964, vol. VII, p. 87ff.)

30. ibid., p. 87.

31. *On the Devil and Devils,* p. 94.

32. ibid., p. 95.

33. Cf. King-Hele, p. 201ff., et al.

34. *On the Devil and Devils,* p. 90; literally repeated in "A Defense of Poetry", p. 147.

35. Shelley, *Poetical Works,* OUP 1905, repr. 1968, p. 205.

36. ibid.

37. *Poetical Works,* p. 244 (Act III, Sc. I).

38. Preface to *Prometheus Unbound* (*Poetical Works,* p. 207).

39. Cf. McNiece, p. 159.

40. Cf. also Mrs. Shelley's note on P. U. [*Prometheus Unbound*] (*Poetical Works,* p. 270ff.)

41. King-Hele, p. 127.

42. *The Cenci,* IV, 2, l. 7f.

43. King-Hele, p. 128.

44. A Defense of Poetry (Shelley, *Poetry & Prose,* p. 143).

45. Quoted in King-Hele, p. 136.

46. Shelley refers in the Preface to Cenci's "implacable hatred towards his children".

47. It was Swinburne who traced the influence of de Sade on *The Cenci* (cf. Praz, p. 114).

48. IV, I, l. 19.

49. I, I, l. 39.

50. I, III, l. 151.

51. V, IV, l. 4. Cf. also Shelley's remark on Ahriman and his reign of ice in his letter to Peacock of 22/24 July 1816 (Shelley, *Poetry and Prose,* p. 163).

52. *Poetical Works,* p. 276.

53. Rudwin, *The Devil,* p. 276f.

54. On Byron's alienation problems cf. also Bruffee, *Satan and the Sublime: The Meaning of the Romantic Hero,* Diss. Northwestern University (U. S. A.), 1964 (unpubl.).

55. Baugh, p. 1224 (note).

56. Shelley scholars have generally assumed that it was Shelley who suggested the theme of Prometheus to Byron; but Thorslev has shown that the influence was in all probability the other way round (*The Byronic Hero,* Minnesota 1962, p. 123f.).

57. Bruffee, p. 180.

Works Cited

A. GENERAL STUDIES

Anderson, M. D., *Drama and Imagery in English Medieval Churches,* London 1963

Ashton, John, *The Devil in Britain and America,* Adelphi W. C., 1896

Baughman, Ernest W., *Type and Motif Index of the Folktales of England and North America,* The Hague 1966

Blackburn, Ruth H., *Biblical Drama under the Tudors,* The Hague/Paris, 1971

Chambers, E. K., *The Medieval Stage,* 2 vol., London 1903

———. *English Literature at the Close of the Middle Ages* (Vol. II, Pt. 2 of the Oxford History of English Literature, Oxford 1945)

Craig, Hardin, *English Religious Drama of the Middle Ages,* Oxford 1955

Creizenach, Wilhelm, *Geschichte des neueren Dramas: Das englische Drama im Zeitalter Shakespeares,* Halle a. d. Saale 1909

Cushman, L. W., *The Devil and the Vice in the English Dramatic Literature before Shakespeare,* London 1900

Douglas, Mary, *Natural Symbols, Explorations in Cosmology,* London 1970

Eliade, Mircea, *Méphistophélès et l'androgyne,* Paris 1962

Frazer, Sir James George, *The Golden Bough, A Study in Magic and Religion,* London 1922

Habicht, Werner, *Studien zur Dramenform vor Shakespeare,* Heidelberg 1968

Jung, C. G., *Mysterium coniunctionis,* 2 vol., Zürich 1955 - 56

————. *Die psychologischen Grundlagen des Geisterglaubens,* Zürich 1919 (in: *Ueber psychische Energetik und das Wesen der Träume,* Zürich 1948)

————. *Symbolik des Geistes,* Zürich 1948

————. *Zur Psychologie westlicher und östlicher Religion,* Zürich und Stuttgart 1963

Kinghorn, A. M., *Medieval Drama,* London 1968

Klein, Jürgen, *Der Gotische Roman und die Aesthetik des Bösen, Wissenschaftliche Buchgesellschaft,* Darmstadt 1975

Langton, Edward, *Essentials of Demonology,* London 1949

————. *Satan, a Portrait,* London 1946

McAlindon, T., "The Emergence of a Comic Type in Middle English Narrative: The Devil and Giant as Buffoon," *Anglia* 81, 1963, p. 365ff.

Mountford, W. M., "The Devil in English Literature from the Middle Ages to 1700," Diss. London 1931 (unpubl.)

Ohse, Bernhard, *Die Teufelliteratur zwischen Brant und Luther,* Diss. phil., Berlin 1961

Papini, Giovanni, "Der Teufel," *Anmerkungen für eine künftige Teufelslehre,* Stuttgart 1955

Penzoldt, Peter, "The English Short Story of the Supernatural," Thèse lettres, London 1952

Pollard, Alfred W., *English Miracle Plays, Moralities and Interludes,* Oxford 1923

Praz, Mario, *The Romantic Agony,* Oxford 1933 (2nd printing 1954)

Roskoff, Gustav, *Geschichte des Teufels,* Leipzig 1869

Rossiter, A. P., *English Drama from Early Times to the Elizabethans,* London 1950

Rudwin, Maximilian, *The Devil in Legend and Literature,* Chicago and London 1931

————. *Romantisme et Satanisme,* Paris 1927

Schärf, Rosa Rikwah, *Die Gestalt des Satans im Alten Testament,* Diss. phil., Zürich 1948

Trevor Davies, R., *Four Centuries of Witch-Beliefs,* London 1947

Trevor-Roper, Hugh Ewald, *The European Witch-Craze of the 16th and 17th Centuries,* London 1969

Tucker Brooke, C. F., *The Tudor Drama,* London 1964

Wickham, Glynne, *Early English Stages 1300 - 1660,* London and New York 1963

Williams, Arnold, *The Drama of Medieval England,* Michigan 1961

Woolf, Rosemary, *The English Mystery Plays,* 1972

Young, Karl, *The Drama of the Medieval Church,* 2 vols., London 1933

B. Special Studies

Anderson, John R., "John Cowper Powys's 'Lucifer', An Appreciation;" *Dublin Mag.,* Vol. XXXII, No. 3, 1957

Battenhouse, Roy W., *Tamburlaine's Passions,* 1941 (in: Leech, q. v.)

Bradbrook, M. C., *Marlowe's Faustus,* 1935 (in: Farnham, q. v.)

Barker, Arthur E., *Milton, Modern Essays in Criticism,* New York 1965

Blatt, Thora B., *The Plays of John Bale,* Copenhagen 1968

Boas, Frederick S., *Marlowe and his Circle,* London 1931

————. *Marlowe, A Biographical and Critical Study,* Oxford 1940

Brockbank, J. P., *Marlowe: Dr. Faustus,* London 1962

Brooks, Cleanth, *The Unity of Marlowe's Doctor Faustus,* 1966 (in: Jump, q. v.)

Brown, Beatrice Daw, "Marlowe, Faustus and Simon Magus," *PMLA* LIV, 1939, p. 82ff.

Bruffee, K. A., "Satan and the Sublime: The Meaning of the Romantic Hero," Diss. Northwestern University (U. S. A.) 1964 unpubl.)

Bush, Douglas, *Paradise Lost in Our Time,* New York 1948

Clutton-Brock, Alan, *Blake,* London 1933

Cole, Douglas, *The Nature of Faustus's Fall,* 1962 (in: Farnham, q. v.)

Collins, H. P., *John Cowper Powys, Old Earth-Man,* London 1966

Dustoor, P. E., "Legends of Lucifer in Early English and in Milton," *Anglia* LIV, 1930, p. 213ff.

Ellis-Fermor, Una M., *Christopher Marlowe,* London 1927

Empson, William, *Milton's God,* London 1965

Farnham, William (ed.), *Twentieth Century Interpretations of Doctor Faustus,* Englewood Cliffs N. J., 1969

Frye, Northrop, *Fearful Symmetry, A Study of William Blake,* Boston 1947

———. *Five Essays on Milton's Epics,* London 1966

Gardner, Helen, "The Damnation of Faustus," *ES,* Vol. I, 1948

Gaunt, William, *Arrows of Desire, A Study of William Blake and his Romantic World,* London 1956

Greg, W. W., *The Damnation of Faustus,* 1942 (in: Leech, q. v.)

Hagstrum, Jean H., *William Blake, Poet and Painter,* Chicago and London 1964

Hirsch, E. D. Jr., "The Two Blakes," *RES* XII, 1961, p. 373ff.

Hobson, Harold, *All This and Helen, Too,* 1966 (in: Jump, q. v.)

Joad, C. E. M., *Shaw,* London 1949

Joseph, M. K., *Byron the Poet,* London 1964

Jump, John (ed.), *Marlowe: Doctor Faustus, A Collection of Essays,* 1969

King-Hele, Desmond, *Shelley, his Thought and Work,* London 1962

Kirschbaum, Leo, Marlowe's Faustus: A Reconsideration, RES XIX, 1943

Knights, L. C., *The Orthodoxy of Faustus,* 1965 (in: Farnham, q. v.)

Kocher, Paul H., *Christopher Marlowe, A Study of his Thoughts, Learning and Character,* New York 1962

Kolve, V. A., *The Play Called Corpus Christi,* London 1966

Leech, Clifford, *Marlowe, A Collection of Critical Essays,* New Jersey 1964

Levin, Harry, *The Overreacher,* London 1953

Lewis, C. S., *A Preface to Paradise Lost,* London 1942

Mc Niece, Gerald, *Shelley and the Revolutionary Idea,* Harvard University Press, Cambridge Mass. 1969

Maxwell, J. C., "The Plays of Christopher Marlowe" (in: Ford, Boris, *A Guide to English Literature,* 1954 - 61)

———. "The Sin of Faustus" (in: *The Wind and the Rain,* 1947)

Musgrove, S., "Is the Devil an Ass?" *RES* XXI, 1945, p. 302ff.

Middleton Murray, J., *William Blake,* London and Toronto, 1933

Ornstein, Robert, *The Comic Synthesis in Doctor Faustus,* (in: Ribner, q. v.)

Palmer, D. J., *Magic and Poetry in Doctor Faustus,* 1964 (in: Jump, q. v.)

Poirier, *Christopher Marlowe,* London 1968

Purdom, C. B., *A Guide to the Plays of Bernard Shaw,* London 1963

Raine, K., *Blake and Tradition,* 2 vols., London 1969

Rajan, B., *Paradise Lost and the Seventeenth Century Reader,* London 1947

Ribner, Irving (ed.), *Christopher Marlowe's Doctor Faustus,* New York 1966

Rutherford, Andrew, *Byron, A Critical Study,* Edinburgh and London 1961

Salmon, Paul, The Site of Lucifer's Throne, *Anglia* 81, 1963, p. 118ff.

Santayana, George, *The Rehabilitation of Faustus,* 1910 (in: Farnham, q. v.)

Saurat, Denis, *Milton, Man and Thinker,* New York 1925

Smith, James, *Faustus as Allegory,* 1939 (in: Farnham, q. v.)

Steane, J. B., *Marlowe, A Critical Study,* Cambridge 1964

Stokoe, F. W., *German Influence in the English Romantic Period 1788 - 1818,* Cambridge University Press 1926

Stoll, Elmer Edgar, "Give the Devil his Due: A Reply to Mr. Lewis," *RES* XX, 1944, p. 108ff.

Thorpe, James, *Milton Criticism: Selections from Four Centuries,* London 1951

Thorslev, Peter L. Jr., *The Byronic Hero, Types and Prototypes,* Minneapolis 1965

Townsend Domke, Ch. F., "Progeny of Fire: A Study of Blake's Satanic Images," Diss. University of Texas 1971 (unpubl.)

Tucker Brooke, C. F., "The Life of Marlowe" (in: *Works and Life of Christopher Marlowe,* ed. by R. H. Chase, Oxford 1930ff.)

Varma, *The Gothic Flame,* New York 1957

Waldock, A. J. A., *Paradise Lost and its Critics,* Cambridge 1947

Werblowski, Zwi, *Lucifer and Prometheus, A Study of Milton's Satan,* London 1952

White, Helen C., *The Mysticism of William Blake,* New York 1964

Wilson, Mona, *The Life of William Blake,* London 1927

Wilson Knight, G., *The Saturnian Quest,* London 1964

THE DEVIL IN AMERICAN FICTION

Robert Bush (essay date 1965)

SOURCE: "*Paddy McGann,* William Gilmore Simm's Devil Story," in *Bulletin of the New York Public Library,* Vol. 69, No. 3, March, 1965, pp. 197-204.

[*In the following essay, Bush explicates* Paddy McGann, *a picaresque dialect novel that features a comical and symbolic representation of the Devil.*]

William Gilmore Simms's most notable wartime publication, *Paddy McGann; or, The Demon of the Stump,* was published in 1863 in a Richmond weekly, *The Southern Illustrated News.* The novel has never been published in book form, probably because of the element of Southern patriotism that Simms included in it. There is elation over the Confederate victory at Fredericksburg and contempt for the character of Northern people and institutions. Simms's biographer, William Peterfield Trent, believed the work would never be resurrected, but Trent's slight references to the novel suggest that he may have known only the beginning of it. At any rate it is forgotten, a fate which it scarcely deserves.

There are a number of reasons why *Paddy McGann* makes interesting reading today. As a picaresque dialect novel about a raftsman on a Southern river, it anticipates *Huckleberry Finn.* Like the later novel it grew out of the accumulated knowledge its author had of the folklore, the dialects, the social traditions, and the popular superstitions of his region. But unlike *Huckleberry Finn* it has only praise for the old way of life of the Southern gentry, and the life of the Negro is unimportant to it. It is one of the few American novels or stories with a theme of diabolism. As such it holds a place in a rather thin tradition from the tales of Irving and Hawthorne to Mark Twain's *The Mysterious Stranger.*

Paddy McGann is a series of adventures related by the hero to several gentlemen in a South Carolina plantation house. There are four major parts, which Simms probably wrote with little consideration for the structural effect of the whole. The parts differ greatly in subject matter and in mood. Part one depicts Paddy as the exploiter of the forests and streams, punished by the visitations of a tormenting demon; the mood is comic, the moral theme conservation of the wilderness. Part two takes Paddy down the Edisto River on a raft; the Devil is at least temporarily thwarted and Paddy's salvation seems assured. The mood is serious, even visionary and religious; the moral theme is the South's faith that God will preserve her in spite of the despair she must endure. Part three brings the hero to New York, where his visions of the Devil are replaced by unpleasant experiences with the devilish New Yorkers; the mood is contemptuously satirical. The final part brings Paddy back home, where he becomes involved in a ca-

lamitous marriage from which he extricates himself by volunteering for service in a Confederate regiment; the mood again is comic, but a serious message is implied as Paddy seems to become the embodiment of Southern patriotic virtue.

Simms's hero is the son of an Irish immigrant, a backwoodsman who makes his living hunting and fishing in the South Carolina wilderness and also working as carpenter and raftsman. He is a thirty-four year old bachelor whose aged mother constantly tries to marry him off. As an heroic type he is a Natty Bumpo with an Irish accent and a sense of humor. Although no stiff hero, he has the virtue of being able to meet men of higher degree on their own ground; he is admired by them as having at least the rudimentary virtues of the gentleman even if he is a rustic. Paddy's consumption of whiskey is prodigious, and although he is never drunk in the vulgar sense, some of his more scientific auditors interpret his pursuit by the Devil as the hallucinations of an inebriate. This explanation of diabolism is characteristic of the comic tradition of the literature of the Devil in Scotland and the United States. The visions of Tam O'Shanter, real enough in the poem, are explicable as induced by liquor. So too, Washington Irving gives a scientific way out for the diabolism of "The Devil and Tom Walker." Less well known is John Pendleton Kennedy's "Mike Brown," a story in *Swallow Barn* about a blacksmith who drank heavily and had an interesting conflict with the Devil. Poe's jocular story "Bon-Bon" is again about a visit from the Devil by a French Philosopher-gourmet who indulges in quantities of wine along with his metaphysics.

Paddy McGann's Devil never appears in human form and never proposes a pact to acquire the hero's soul. Rather, he appears in animistic projections of the forms of nature with which Paddy is familiar. Simms's story is closest to Kennedy's "Mike Brown," which is also about a man of heroic size in the Southern backwoods country. It is possible that Kennedy and Simms were indebted to Irving's "The Devil and Tom Walker," since Irving makes the Devil himself an axe-carrying woodsman. All three authors make use of the gloom and mystery of the woods and swamps.

Paddy's demon appears in various forms: as a bodiless voice with a tormenting shout of "Hoo, hoo, hoo!", as a stump, as a great red eye, as an enormous buck deer, as a swift beast resembling a bull, or as a gigantic owl. Simms uses these aspects of the Devil to show the torment that comes as a result of various wrongdoings of the hero. Sometimes the encounters occur when Paddy indulges in one of the seven deadly sins. Paddy is an active man who despises the inactive men, who, he believes, never really live. He says "I knows men who are harmless as rabbits; that jest sit down, feed and sleep; and hardly say anything. Other men are always a-doing; and I'm one of them. Ef I ain't a-doing good, you may be sure I'm doing bad; for I'm sure to be doing something. And them's the kind of men that's always in danger. And them's the sort of men that Providence, or the Devil, will always be choosing out for their work; for the idle, aisy sort of men, that do nothing, I don't count them altogether men at all!"[1] It is good to be active, according to the Simms ideal, even though the active life may be morally dangerous.

Simms stresses the point that it is better for backwoodsmen like Paddy to spend their time in the useful occupations of the settlements rather than in the wasteful exploitation of the wilderness. When Paddy himself leads the easy life of the backwoods hunter and fisherman, the Devil pursues him and torments him. His rifle misfires and he kills no game, and the fish fail to bite at his hook. But later when he settles down to a trade of lumbering, making shingles, and carpentering, the demon leaves him and he begins to be a useful citizen. The narrator tells us that "His demon, if he had a demon, was a blessing to him! Before he was troubled, as he tells you, he had a score of other demons at his heels; the worst of all, such as accompany the idle life of the hunter and fisherman in our country; not one of whom did I ever meet who was not worthless in all other respects. The moment Paddy ceased to lead a desultory life he prospered."[2] The idea is also set forth that the hunter and fisherman have exploited the forests and the streams enough. The demon pursues Paddy partly for this reason, proclaiming himself the genius of the forest, the protecting deity of wildlife. Paddy himself relates that the Devil "didn't worry me much . . . when I was on a *rigilar* job. But let me go fishing or hunting, and then comes the parsecutions and the frettings and bad luck, jist as ef the beast hed told me true when he said the partridges waur his chickens! It jist seemed as ef he was determined that I shouldn't kill bird or beast in that swamp any more; as ef he thought I hed killed more than my share a'ready. . . ." Here Simms is taking a realistic look at the American backwoodsman, idealized in so many volumes by Fenimore Cooper. The backwoodsman had served his purpose in penetrating the wilderness, but once there were settlements he should learn a trade and abandon the easy life of the woods.

Paddy's actual encounters with the Devil contain some of Simms's most imaginative writing. There is an incident of a deer hunt in which Paddy becomes convinced that the Devil has taken the form of a great buck who seems to have uncanny intelligence; like Faulkner's bear the animal seems to be an invincible embodiment of the wilderness. In another incident Paddy struggles with a demon stump, rolls with it down a hill, and although he fails to vanquish the demon, he is exalted in his self-respect for having wrestled with the Devil.

Commissioned to deliver seventy bulls by raft down the Edisto River, Paddy sets out with his cargo and a group of Negro aides. Here Simms's impressions of the river through the lyric dialect of Paddy are anticipations of similar passages in *Huckleberry Finn*: "It's a mighty sweet and purty river—clear and sweet for drinking, and the trees shade you pretty much all the way till you get upon the salts; and you may do some fishing and hunting as you go. I've headed a deer into the stream, and got him by the horns. I've shot and fished some times every day going down. . . ." The end of the trip is at hand when the view of Charleston appears, "lying like a great terrapin in the water, with a world of steeples and churches and houses on her back—. . . ."

Paddy and his fellow raftsmen make several stops at bawdy houses situated conveniently along the river. The robust pleasures of these men are described without Victorian restraint; the modern reader is surprised to hear of whites and Negroes drinking and dancing to the fiddle at the house of "Nelly Miller and her gals," who "didn't keep the most respectable house on the river; but it was a mighty pleasant place for a frolic among the rough fellows of the rafts. She got her money by accomodating them handsome." We assume that it is the sins of a series of these frolics that work their way into Paddy's subconscious mind and give him the diabolic nightmare he describes: ". . . I had a most tremenduous drhame, of the biggest owl in the world, taking me off the top of my chimbley, on his wings; I riding on his back as ef he was a horse; and he carrying me, full speed down the river, fast as he could fly, whooping, all the time, with the most infarnal 'Hoo! Hoo! Hoo! that had iver shivered my senses."

On another night he boards his raft, falls into a whiskey stupor, and while he is again experiencing the owlish nightmare, drifts out to sea on his small caboose raft. He had tied his stern rope to a fatal stump, the embodiment of the Devil. Adrift, Paddy now experiences his most terrible ordeal, since he is beset with the physical dangers of the sea and the spiritual dangers of the Devil. He tells his listeners that after he prayed he looked out on the sea "with the biggest eyes of expectation that ever started out of a poor mortal's head! And so I saw the great sun go down. He sot for a while on the very edge of the waters, a-looking into my very face, and was looking at me in sorrow! Soon the face looked like a great bushy head, with human hair, but of the very reddest gould color. And it was the beautifullest, terriblest sight I iver seed—that great sun—so parfect and so big, looking so human at me, as ef he would like to stay longer, but going down at last with a sudden rush, that seemed fairly to set a-fire the big waters that were burying him. And over his burial place, there was a sort of goulden and purple crown; and it was as ef onseen sperrits waved an army of bright beautiful flags over him; and then, soon a'ter, came the black pale—Och! how black it was!—of the etarnal night!"[3]

The darkness suggests Paddy's despair until three stars appear that convince him that he has the favor of God: "And the three seemed to me like a staff put into my hand for support; and I says, 'This is a staff from God.'" As he sees more stars Paddy's poetic spirit expands in the form of imaginative imagery: "A'ter that the stars come out broadcast, thick as white bolls in a prime cotton field; and I lay back on the raft a-watching 'em; and some seemed to gather into diamonds, and some into squares, and some into sarcles, all round, and I found they all lived in families, and had relations—a thing which I had niver seed in all my watchings in the Heavens before. And I thought these were God's watchers for the night, over the poor blind airth, wrapt up in the mouth of darkness."[4]

After another moment of despair when at the sight of a shark he is deterred from plunging into the sea, Paddy begins to see visions of four moons, representing traditional religious symbols. The first vision seems to combine the concepts of God the Father and Moses striking the rock: ". . . a great grey-bearded man—his beard reaching to his middle, and of a shining silver white; and his face was as sweet as a girl's, yet it was grander and stronger than the face of any mortal man! And in his hand he carried a staff, and touched the rock he sat on . . . and at the touch the water spouted from the rock, like a beautiful rain, and sprinkled me all over, and kept sprinkling me; and I opened my mouth and caught it as it fell, and it seemed to cool me delightful!" The second moon vision represents the Virgin and Child: "a beautiful young woman, all in white, with a leetle baby very sweet, but sorrowful too." The third is "a strong man holding up the head of an old woman, who had her eyes shut, and looked to be dead or dying; for I could see the tears dropping from the strong man's eyes!" The fourth moon image pictures Paddy himself in an attitude of "doing nothing better than drawing figgers in the air!" Paddy asks what that could mean, "whether I really seed that vision or only dhramed it?"

Of course Simms would hardly put his hero through such an elaborate ordeal and ascribe to him such fantastic visions without point. He intends us to believe that Paddy indeed saw the visions and that he is a childlike man, capable of mysticism and even prophecy. Beyond that, Paddy seems to epitomize the raw strength of the South that was at that time undergoing its heroic if losing struggle. Simms also must have identified himself personally with the ordeal: not only was the way of life he honored at stake, but his own plantation, the symbol of that way of life, had been burned in 1862. Paddy's third vision, then, that of the strong man upholding the dying old woman, probably is intended to suggest the heroic Southern youth or the Confederate army, attempting to defend the old way of life of the South. We are encouraged in this interpretation since there are hints of the contemporary North-South rivalry at several points during the picaresque adventure. The three stars that appear during Paddy's night of despair and which Paddy calls the "staff from God" suggest God's sign of favor to the agonized South. Paddy says of the Staff, "'I will hold on to this staff of God. It is a sign to me. He will not let me sink.'"

After the exalted mood of the visions, the narrative tone changes when a vivid devil dance follows in which Paddy dances vigorously with the haunted stump and they are joined by all the logs on the woodpile of the caboose raft. The moons finally fade out; the logs return to the woodpile. Paddy falls down in exhaustion, remembering only that "the rain was pouring down upon me in a flood from every window in Heaven." The benison of rain tells us that Paddy will be rescued, that his soul and body are no longer in jeopardy.

After Paddy is rescued and taken to New York the surface story bears a resemblance to Caruthers' narrative of Montgomery Damon, the woodsman who is *The Kentuckian in New York.* Caruthers' rustic becomes a celebrity in the big city as does Paddy, who is known as the famous Edisto raftsman. But where the Kentuckian's experience attempts to explain the North and the South to each other, Paddy's is the vehicle for Simms's intense bitterness against the North. The New York episode is the least successful of the novel because the thread of diabolism is lost and with it some of the unity of the entire work. Also, Simms is ineffective as a satirist since he chooses to lampoon not the culture of the 'sixties, but that of the 'forties when Poe and Margaret Fuller were alive. Paddy is pursued by an aggressive female Fourierist who believes in free love and socialism. About all that Simms seems to be saying in the episode is that New York or the North generally is the center of radicalism for the sake of radicalism. These attitudes among the intellectuals of the city are made to seem irresponsible, and the reader is to contrast them with the conservative attitudes of the Southern planter. Even the average New Yorker is irresponsible. The man in the street is mercenary and dishonest; Paddy is several times made the dupe of this calculating Northerner.

Paddy had been warned against the exploiting Northerner by the Scotch captain who rescued him at sea. Paddy showed resentment against the Scot for speaking of the meanness of the American character, but the captain, as a foreigner, made it clear that Southerners were not really Americans at all: "Oh pooh! . . . You're a Southern—you're one of the *geese;* the *fox* is in your feathers! The Amerikin character is made by the North. The people of Europe knows nothing about *you,* 'cept that *you* keeps the niggers and the Yankees keeps *you.* Why, man, . . . they'll cheat the very eyes out of *your* head, and you niver see 'em! They're too smart for *you!*"[5] The marriage of North and South, according to this speech, is one entirely to the advantage of the North and at the expense of the South. In the fourth episode, when Paddy returns to South Carolina, he makes an unfortunate marriage to Susan Pogson, the pretty daughter of a shiftless backwoods family. It is a marriage in which the wife's family thoroughly exploits the husband's small wealth, suggesting a North and South union such as the one described by the Scotch captain. Soon disillusioned about marriage, Paddy's only resort is to leave his wife and volunteer in a Confederate regiment. The fourth episode, then, can be read as an allegory of Simms's political conviction of the justification of secession.

But Simms in his earlier career had recognized the necessity of the urban centers of the North to the regional culture of the South. His own career could not have flourished without Northern enthusiasm for his romances. He admits the cultural dependence of regional cultures on the large urban centers in the words of the narrator toward the end of *Paddy McGann*: "*No purely rustic population . . . has ever yet been known to achieve what is called a high civilization—that is, as shown in the development of let-*

ters, science, and the arts. These must always come from the great marts and the densely packed communities of States.—The individual genius, emerging from such a population, would make no show, would find no audience, would perish among them unless it threw itself, for attrition, audience and stimulus, upon the great city. . . ."[6]

And what became of the Devil, who played so important a role in the earlier episodes? Almost forgotten in New York, he reappears in the fourth episode to warn Paddy against marriage. He has become a comic figure that Paddy has learned to accept. But on the fatal wedding night the Devil makes his farewell with a serious joke: "I'll trouble you no more; and now you'll find, ould fellow, you're in worse hands than mine ever waur!" And it takes Paddy only a short time to learn "how far inferior is the grief and misery of being haunted by the Devil, than of being married to a fool!"

With such material Simms diverted himself and his Southern readers in 1863. *Paddy McGann* is a rich mixture of Southern folk humor and local color. Although almost unknown today, it is perhaps Simms's most imaginative work.

Notes

1. William Gilmore Simms, *Paddy McGann; or, The Demon of the Stump,* serialized in *The Southern Illustrated News,* ɪ No 30 (April 4 1863). The entire novel runs from Feb 14 1863 to May 23 1863. See also his early story about another Edisto raftsman: "Home Sketches . . . ," *The Literary World* (New York) x (Feb 7 1852) 107-110.

2. Simms, *Paddy McGann, The Southern Illustrated News* ɪ No 36 (May 16 1863) p 5.

3. Simms, *Paddy McGann, The Southern Illustrated News* ɪ No 30 (April 4 1863) p 7.

4. Simms, *Paddy McGann, The Southern Illustrated News* ɪ No 31 (April 11 1863) p 4.

5. Simms, *Paddy McGann, The Southern Illustrated News* ɪ No 32 (April 18 1863) p 5.

6. Simms, *Paddy McGann, The Southern Illustrated News* ɪ No 37 (May 23 1863) p 7.

Charles G. Zug III (essay date 1968)

SOURCE: "The Construction of 'The Devil and Tom Walker': A Study of Irving's Later Use of Folklore," in *New York Folklore,* Vol. 24, No. 4, December, 1968, pp. 243-60.

[*In the following essay, Zug traces folklore elements in Washington Irving's "The Devil and Tom Walker," viewing the story as a masterful blending of German and American folk motifs.*]

Although it is unquestionably one of Washington Irving's finest tales, "The Devil and Tom Walker" has never attracted much critical attention. First published in 1824 in Part IV of *Tales of a Traveller,* the tale recounts the fate of an avaricious New Englander, who sells his soul to the Devil in return for Captain Kidd's treasure, and is finally carted off to Hell after a long and profitable career as a usurer in colonial Boston. For the most part, critics have been content to note that the tale is "a sort of comic New England *Faust,*"[1] or that it "is redolent of the American soil."[2] In other words, the consensus is that the tale has certain Germanic overtones but is indigenous to the young American republic in which Irving grew up. No one, however, has really attempted to examine the possible sources for this work or note the complex manner in which Irving has interwoven numerous motifs from American and German folklore.

There are a number of reasons for the lack of interest in "The Devil and Tom Walker." Foremost, perhaps, is the fact that *Tales of a Traveller* was poorly received when it was first published and has never attained the popularity of such works Knickerbocker's *History of New York* (1809) or *The Sketch Book* (1819). Also, there is the oft-cited critical attitude that Irving lacked "the sustaining qualities of a great imagination,"[3] and was always content to merely embellish and lengthen folktales which he had discovered during his extensive readings. This attitude is well substantiated in Henry A. Pochmann's collation of "Rip Van Winkle" and Otmar's "Peter Klaus." Pochmann's study reveals that Irving must have had the latter before him as he wrote, and that he did not hesitate to borrow sentences or even whole passages.[4] Citing Pochmann's article, Irving's biographer, Stanley T. Williams, labels Irving's imitation of his original source as "slavish,"[5] and it is this general estimate of Irving's use of folklore that has largely prevailed over the last thirty years. As an example, a recent writer in a prominent folklore journal has described "The Devil and Tom Walker" as a typical New England folktale, naively stating that "one is inclined to think Irving almost wrote the tale exactly as he heard it, with perhaps some smoothing of the style and a conscious development of mood."[6] As will be shown, "The Devil and Tom Walker" is in no sense a folktale that has been merely copied down from oral tradition. Further, of the numerous traditional motifs contained in it, the majority are German and only six appear to be native to America.

At the outset, it is significant that no source has ever been discovered for "The Devil and Tom Walker." Most commonly, critics cite the *Faust* theme as the basis for the tale, but this is rather inaccurate, for Tom Walker is in no sense a scholar who desires to extend the limits of human knowledge. In actuality, it is not the *Faust* theme but the wellknown motif M211, Man sells soul to devil,[7] that lies at the heart of the tale. This, however, is only one of numerous folk motifs used, and taken by itself, it provides little insight into the source or structure of the tale. The problem here is that unlike "Rip Van Winkle," which is largely patterned on a complete tale, "The Devil and Tom

Walker" is based on a series of folk motifs gathered by Irving from a wide variety of sources. It is important at this point to understand the exact distinction between a tale and a motif. The former is a complete and independent narrative which consists of one or more motifs traditionally associated with each other, while the latter is "the smallest element in a tale having a power to persist in tradition." Generally, motifs fall into one of three categories: "the actors in a tale," "items in the background of the action," and most commonly, "single incidents."[8] Although based on folklore like "Rip Van Winkle," "The Devil and Tom Walker" is thus a much more complex and original work, for instead of starting with a fully developed plot, Irving began with a series of plot elements and fused them into a new and harmonious whole. That he was highly skilled in assembling these traditional motifs is evidenced by the number of critics who have accepted "The Devil and Tom Walker" as a rewritten version of a folktale that he had heard or read.

To fully understand Irving's increasingly sophisticated use of folklore, it is necessary to briefly consider some of Irving's activities between the publication of *The Sketchbook* in 1819 and the writing of "The Devil and Tom Walker" in 1824. The key event here appears to have been the year-long tour through Germany in 1822 and 1823. Prior to this journey, Irving had shown an increasing interest in German lore and literature, and had been encouraged by Sir Walter Scott "to study the fascinating history of folklore."[9] However, Irving's contact with German folklore at this time was limited to the few works over which he struggled to learn the German language and a number of English publications which were "Translated or adapted from the popular literature of Germany."[10] The trip to Germany in 1822 gave Irving a new opportunity: a chance to investigate and gather up German folklore at first-hand. As he wrote to Thomas Storrow at the beginning of the tour, "I mean to get into the confidence of every old woman I meet with in Germany and get from her, her wonderful budget of stories."[11] In other words, Irving was out to collect folklore in its purest state, directly from oral transmission. Stanley Williams notes this shift in Irving's attitude, commenting that "he now formed a resolution that folklore should not merely entertain the knight-errant but should earn his lordship's bread and butter. He would really follow that impulse felt at Abbotsford in 1817 and create his volume of German legends. The tour now became a hunt for gnomes, pixies, and phantom armies; and he extended the journal into a saving bank for this species of coin."[12] That the hunt was clearly successful is revealed by the numerous legends and scraps of lore that may be found in the letters and journals written during the German tour. At Salzburg, for example, Irving noted that "the mountain regions are full of fable and elfin story, and I had some wonderful tales told me."[13] In his journal, he even wrote out seven local legends from this region, all of them concerned with the imposing figure of Untersberg Mountain.[14] Walter Reichart points out that none of these legends appears to have a literary source, "so that it seems

likely that Irving actually heard them from some of the inhabitants."[15] Since Irving had little time or ability for reading German during his travels, this conclusion is almost inescapable. In addition, the letters and journals abound with fragments of and brief references to well-known tales and motifs, such as "the Emperor and his army shut up in the enchanted mountain" and "the Black Huntsman and the enchanted Bullets."[16] Altogether, it appears that Irving rapidly enlarged his working knowledge of German folklore, and there are numerous entries indicating that he also enjoyed retelling the tales to his friends. The German experience thus served not only to increase his "savings bank" of potential source materials, but more important, to teach him the technique of combining and recombining these materials so as to form new tales. It is exactly this shift in emphasis, from written to oral sources, from the tale to the motif, and from the mere materials to the actual mechanics of folklore, that is reflected in "The Devil and Tom Walker." As such, this tale suggests that a re-evaluation of Irving's later use of folklore is very much needed. As the following analysis reveals, Irving's use of folklore after his German tour was somewhat less "slavish" than most critics have been willing to admit.

There are really two approaches to a study of the genesis and construction of "The Devil and Tom Walker." The first, which might be considered an internal approach, consists of outlining the basic plot of the tale, and indicating the motifs which Irving employed. In abbreviated form and with the help of the *Motif-Index,* the structure of "The Devil and Tom Walker" appears as follows:

Motif-Index No.	Motif	Source	Text Page[17]
1) N511.1.9	Treasure buried under tree	(U.S., India)	251
2)	American legend: Kidd buries enormous treasure		251, 254, 256
3) N571	Devil (demon) as guardian of treasure	(Numerous including U.S., Germany)	251
4)	Domestic subject: squabbles of Tom Walker and his wife		251-2, 255-7
5)	American legend: Indian sacrifices		252, 254
6) E765.3.3	Life bound up with tree	(India)	253-5
7) G303.3.1.1	The devil as a large, strong man	(Germany)	253
8) G303.3.1.6	The devil as a black man	(Germany, Denmark, Ireland)	253
9) G303.3.1.7	Devil as a huntsman	(Germany, England, France)	254
10) G303.2.2	Devil is called "the black one"	(Germany, Denmark)	254
11) G243.1	Obeisance to devil at witches' sabbath	(England, Spain, West Indies)	254

12) G303.4.8.10	Devil's hand marks person he touches	(U.S., England)	255
13) M211	Man sells soul to devil	(Numerous including U.S., Germany)	254-5, 257-8
14)	Financial subplot: usury in colonial Boston		258-60
15) G303.16.2	Devil's power over one avoided by prayer	(Numerous including Germany)	259
16) C12.2	Oath: "May the devil take me if. . . ."	(Germany, U.S., Ireland, Norway)	260
17) G303.7.1.1	Devil rides on black horse	(Germany, England)	260
18) G303.17.2.5	Devil retreats into hell amid thunder and lightning	(Germany)	260-1
19) G303.21.1	Devil's money becomes ashes	(U.S., Denmark, Lithuania)	261

With each of the traditional motifs, I have listed the motif number from the *Motif-Index* and the countries indicated in the bibliographical references which are supplied. It should be noted that the bibliography for each motif in the *Motif-Index* is not meant to be complete; the references cited are intended to "give some preliminary guidance in finding examples of the items concerned."[18] Nevertheless, it is certainly remarkable that two thirds of the traditional motifs here have a known German source. And for two motifs (nos. 7 and 18), the only reference cited is from Germany. This clearly suggests that Irving's use of German folklore in "The Devil and Tom Walker" is far more extensive than has previously been suspected. Reichart, for example, who has produced a long and useful study of the influences of Germany on Irving's works, finds that "aside from the reference to the wild huntsman of German legend, . . . only the general theme of a pact with the devil is reminiscent of a German source."[19] While he has noted only two German motifs, there are in actuality at least ten.

In conjunction with the prevalence of German motifs, it is important to note that practically the entire plot is made up of elements from folklore. In fact the only nontraditional portions of the plot are the two sections which I have labeled the domestic and financial subplots. The tale opens with three American motifs built around the legend of Captain Kidd. Immediately following is the domestic subplot, which is reminiscent of the marital situation in "Rip Van Winkle" and serves to develop the mutual enmity between Tom and his wife. Merely to infuriate her, Tom obstinately refuses to close his pact with the Devil. She, therefore, runs off with the family silverware to make her own bargain, and is apparently carried off by the Devil after an heroic struggle. After this humorous interlude, Irving immediately returns to the main plot of folk motifs, and it is not until after the pact is actually completed that he inserts the financial subplot. This section describes the state of affairs in colonial Boston, neatly delineating the avarice and religious hypocrisy of the inhabitants. With the uttering of the oath, Irving again returns to the main plot, and the tale moves swiftly to a close. Taken as a whole, the plot thus consists of a central chain of folk motifs into which two realistic subplots have been inserted.

One of the major difficulties in recognizing the extensive use of folk motifs in "The Devil and Tom Walker" is ironically due to Irving's craftsmanship. As previously mentioned, critics and readers have had little difficulty in isolating the well-known theme of the pact with the Devil or the explicit reference to the Black Huntsman. However, the remainder of the motifs have remained obscure because Irving has fused them so skillfully with the American setting, the American legends of the Indians and Captain Kidd, and the two realistic subplots. Take, for example, Irving's description of the Devil. In conjunction with the four German motifs listed above (nos. 7-10), Irving adds a distinctly American feature by describing the Devil as "dressed in a rude half Indian garb" (253) and associating him with former sacrifices held by the Indians. In addition, the Devil informs Tom that "'I am the great patron and prompter of slave-dealers, and the grand-master of the Salem witches'" (254). The resultant figure is thus a neat composite of traditional German, American Indian, and Puritan elements. Although more explicit than a typical folk version,[20] Irving's Devil is clearly much closer to folklore than such sophisticated, literary versions as the suave, black-mustachioed villain in Stephen Vincent Benet's "The Devil and Daniel Webster."

Irving's ability to disguise and integrate traditional motifs is also seen in his development of the two subplots. At the center of the domestic subplot is the soul-selling motif, for it is this which provides the final source of conflict between Tom and his wife and leads to the latter's flight and disappearance. In the financial subplot, Irving again employs the soul-selling motif as the primary motivation for the action. He also integrates Motif G303.16.2, Devil's power over one avoided by prayer, to accentuate the religious hypocrisy of Tom, and indeed, of the whole Boston community. This use of traditional motifs as a basis for satire is also evident earlier in the tale. When the tree with the buccaneer Absalom Crowninshield's name on it is hewed down by the Devil, the man dies and the papers piously announce that "'A great man had fallen in Irsael'" (255). Motif E765.3.3, life bound up with tree, lies at the center of the incident and reveals the lack of scruples and lust for wealth that lie behind the pious, dignified veneer of Puritan society. Here, as throughout the tale, Irving is skillfully combining a folk motif with realistic elements, thereby obscuring the presence of the former.

However, it is not merely Irving's ability to fuse and integrate the traditional motifs that makes them so difficult to recognize. As previously suggested, it is also their unique combination into a new tale that has blinded most readers to Irving's heavy reliance on folklore. Unlike "Rip Van Winkle," "The Devil and Tom Walker" has no single antecedent. The companion volume to the *Motif-Index, The Types of the Folktale*, lists numerous tales of the type "A Man Sells his Soul to the Devil,"[21] but none of them is akin to Irving's version. While each of them is built around

Motif M211, none of them contains the same auxiliary motifs, nor are they anywhere near as complex in structure. It is thus clear that in writing "The Devil and Tom Walker," Irving must have drawn on a number of separate motifs that he had heard or recorded during his travels. In combining these motifs into such an original pattern, he was acting very much in the manner of the traditional tale-teller, whose major recourse to originality is to combine or recombine already existing motifs. However, Irving took far greater freedom than a conservative member of the folk would have done, for his new structure of motifs is far more complex than any of his sources, and includes materials which are distinctly nontraditional.

Thus far only an internal or textual approach has been considered for the construction of "The Devil and Tom Walker." This has been useful in revealing Irving's debt to traditional motifs, notably German, and indicating the unique manner in which he combined and even disguised these motifs. However, there is yet another tack which can be used to corroborate and even complement the previous discussion. This involves the use of various external sources related to "The Devil and Tom Walker," notably the journals and letters which Irving wrote while he was struggling to organize and write *Tales of a Traveller.* Through the use of these materials, it is possible to trace the actual process of construction of "The Devil and Tom Walker" and even some of the immediate sources on which Irving drew.

The first reference to the general plan for *Tales of a Traveller* appears in a journal entry for November 2, 1822, three months after Irving had begun his German tour. Irving was staying in Vienna at the time and wrote: "tho[ugh]t of preparing a collection of tales of various countries, made up from legends."[22] During the year following this vague initial formulation, Irving traveled extensively and spent a busy winter in Dresden among the fashionable English and German society. Apparently he gave little additional thought to the plan for the *Tales of a Traveller* during this period, for it is not until December 8, 1823, a little more than a year later, that he mentions it again. By this time Irving was living in Paris and was struggling to renew his literary activities. As he noted in his journal on this date, "tried to commence work on Germany but could not do any thing—towards twelve o'clock an idea of a plan dawned on me—Felt more encouraged—Felt as if I should make something of it."[23]. It is important to note the emphasis on Germany here, an emphasis clearly not present in the previous journal entry. As for the vague "idea of a plan," Pierre M. Irving, Irving's nephew and early biographer, explains that "this was a plan, as he once told me, to mingle up the legendary superstitions of Germany, in the form of tales, with local descriptions and a little of the cream of travelling incidents."[24] Although intended as a general description of the *Tales of a Traveller,* Pierre Irving's remark is particularly applicable to "The Devil and Tom Walker," for it is exactly this mingling up of German legend that forms the backbone of the tale. Finally, along with these excerpts, there is the preface to

Tales of a Traveller, in which the author states that "I rummaged my portfolio, and cast about, in my recollection, for those floating materials which a man naturally collects in travelling; and here I have arranged them in this little work" (6). This preface could hardly be more explicit or more in agreement with the journal entries and the preceding textual analysis of the tale. All of this evidence clearly reveals that Irving's general method gradually evolved during the German tour and was a well formulated and consistent one: he simply drew on his journals and his memory for German folk motifs, and reassembled them into new combinations.

While the journals help to indicate the general plan behind the construction of "The Devil and Tom Walker," they are even more useful in revealing the specific origins and development of the tale. The key entries, all for 1824, may be tabulated as follows:

> May 3 "Col Aspinwall called & told me stories about Kidd"
>
> May 6 "This morning wrote story of the Devil & Tom Walker"
>
> May 7 "Wrote all morning at Tom Walker"
>
> May 8 "Wrote this Morng at story of Tom Walker"
>
> May 10 "Wrote a little at the Story of Tom Walker, introducing dialogue between him & D[evil]. on subject of the bargain"
>
> May 21 "This Morng—rewrote parts of Tom Walker"[25]

From the above, it appears that the legends of Captain Kidd provided the impetus to start "The Devil and Tom Walker," for Irving heard them just three days before he began writing the tale. The legends were told to him by his London literary agent, Colonel Thomas Aspinwall, a close friend who is mentioned frequently in the journal during this period. Once started, Irving apparently wrote at great speed, adding the numerous German motifs to the framework provided by the Kidd legends. Apparently the tale was finished after only two weeks, for there is no further mention of it after May 21.

Irving's choice of the Kidd legends as a framework for "The Devil and Tom Walker" was a good one, for it placed the tale in a distinctly American setting. Willard Hallam Bonner, who has made an extensive study of Kidd, notes that "the composite legend surrounding him is Saxon North America's first full-bodied legend."[26] However, this legend is a limited one, in that it generally contains only a few, often recurring motifs. There is first a widespread belief that Kidd did bury his treasure, either along the southern New England coast or up the Hudson River.[27] In addition, there is the belief that the treasure is guarded either by a slain sailor or worse, by "the Earl of Hell himself, at whose command Kidd 'buried his Bible in the sand.'"[28] As noted in the earlier plot outline, Irving used these American motifs at the beginning of the tale, although he shifted the place of burial to the Boston region. With the introduction of the domestic subplot, which follows immediately, Irving moved away from the Kidd legends and began using German motifs which concerned the Devil. Apparently it was the Kidd stories heard from Colonel Aspinwall that gave Irving the initial inspiration and got the tale underway. Once started, Irving inserted the two realistic subplots and used the figure of the Devil, first mentioned in the American legend (Motif 571), as the means of transition to the numerous German materials.

One possible objection to this reconstruction of the development of "The Devil and Tom Walker" is that Colonel Aspinwall might simply have told Irving the entire tale as it stands. This would be in accord with the previously mentioned theory of Sara Rodes that "the lively story of 'The Devil and Tom Walker' is a New England folk tale which Irving merely retells with very little addition."[29] However, the main flaw in this point of view is that there is absolutely no evidence that the Kidd legends ever accumulated the particular motifs that Irving used. Had they done so, folklorists and storytellers would almost certainly have recorded the evidence. The second weakness in this theory is, of course, the prevalence of German motifs. Only a person who was intimate with German folklore could have assembled so many of them so skillfully. And finally, there are the time and place in which "The Devil and Tom Walker" was written. Irving wrote the tale in Paris in May, 1824, shortly after a year in Germany and long after he had left America. Under these conditions, it is hardly possible that "The Devil and Tom Walker" could have evolved from a genuine New England folktale. Rather, as the journals, letters, and preface to *Tales of a Traveller* indicate, "The Devil and Tom Walker" can only be a skillful mingling up of folk motifs gathered for the most part in Germany and all neatly introduced by a true American legend that, ironically, was also heard in Europe.

Just about the only missing evidence in this reconstruction of "The Devil and Tom Walker" is the exact source material for the German motifs. However, there are still a number of definite clues contained in Irving's writings. One of Irving's references to the Black Huntsman has already been cited, and others can be found in both the journals and letters. Evidently Irving frequently encountered stories of this figure during his travels, and it is not unreasonable to assume that he picked up the other motifs used to describe the Devil in exactly the same manner. As for the soul-selling, there is an entry in the journal for August 24, 1824, indicating that Irving "told the story of Peter Schlemihl."[30] This is the legend of a man who sold his shadow to the Devil, and while not exactly the same as Motif M211, it does indicate Irving's familiarity with the general theme of the pact with the Devil. As previously cited, Irving made a special note of writing this section of "The Devil and Tom Walker" in the journal entry for May 10, four days after he began writing the tale. This suggests that Irving considered the motif of special importance and that it was inserted as a unit independent of the Kidd legends received from Colonel Aspinwall. For the final motifs

concerning the oath and the retreat of the Devil, there are no explicit references in Irving's journals or letters. This last section is really a unit in itself and is akin to tale Type 813, A Careless Word Summons the Devil. However, none of the examples of this type listed in *The Types of the Folktale* contains the same motifs, indicating that once again Irving devised his own combination.

Altogether, then, the internal and external evidence strongly suggests both the process and units of construction of "The Devil and Tom Walker." To the native American legend of Captain Kidd, Irving added the well-known soul-selling motif, thereby giving the tale its main outline. Then, to give the tale body, he integrated a large number of traditional motifs focusing on the description and activities of the Devil. Finally, as a kind of moral to the action, he fittingly capped the tale with Motif G303.21.1, Devil's money becomes ashes. Of the nineteen plot elements listed, no less than fifteen are clearly traditional according to the *Motif-Index*. And of these fifteen, ten are from Germany and six are from the U.S.; only two (nos. 6 and 11) are listed as coming from other countries. While, as previously cited, the bibliography of the *Motif-Index* is not intended to be complete, it still clearly reveals the nature and extent of Irving's debt to folklore in "The Devil and Tom Walker."

Along with Irving's use of German and American folklore, it is also important to note the particular setting and atmosphere which he has employed. As a background for the tale, Irving develops a genuine folk community, the Boston area in the year 1727. The countryside is rife with local legends of Captain Kidd's buried treasure and of ancient sacrifices and incantations held by the Indians. Earthquakes are regarded providentially, and send "many tall sinners down upon their knees" (251). Even the miraculous disappearance of Tom Walker is readily accepted: "the good people of Boston shook their heads and shrugged their shoulders, but had been so much accustomed to witches and goblins, and tricks of the devil, in all kinds of shapes, . . . that they were not so horror-struck as might have been expected" (261). Altogether, Irving's Boston reveals the major characteristics of the folk community: an essential isolation; a narrow, parochial outlook; credulous, superstitious attitudes; and homogeneity in behavior and belief.

In conjunction with the folk setting, Irving also constructs a mood which is appropriate to a folktale. He claims to have learned his story from "an old iron-faced Cape-Cod whaler" (250) and avers that he has given "the purport of the tale" "as nearly as I can recollect" (261). Furthermore, phrases such as "some say" (260), "the old stories add" (251), and "according to the most authentic old story" (256) are scattered throughout to give the flavor of an authentic folktale and the impression that the tale is coming directly from an oral source. With the identification of the "informant," these stylistic devices, and a professed adherence to the "original tale," Irving is attempting to simulate the mood of a genuine folktale, with its uncertainty, open credulity, and appeal to traditional belief. Irving's purpose in developing this mood is clearly to give the story an air of verisimilitude; he even ends by declaring that "the story has resolved itself into a proverb . . . prevalent throughout New England" (261).

However, despite the elaborate structure of folk motifs and the carefully devised setting and mood, it is clearly naive "to think Irving almost wrote the tale exactly as he heard it." As stated earlier, this is exactly the sort of attitude that arises from the preconception that Irving merely rewrote folktales without making any significant changes. In actuality, "The Devil and Tom Walker" contains many elements that are decidedly foreign to folktales. Most obvious are the previously discussed domestic and financial subplots and the related satire on avarice and hypocrisy. In addition, there are the frequent, detailed descriptions, such as the delineation of Tom Walker's front yard: "a miserable horse, whose ribs were as articulate as the bars of a gridiron, stalked about a field, where a thin carpet of moss, scarcely covering the ragged beds of puddingstone, tantalized and balked his hunger" (251). The imagery has been carefully chosen here, for the specific purpose of depicting the essential sterility and desolation of Tom Walker's existence. In an actual folktale, however, such a description would be brief and stylized, and would not be designed to produce such a particular effect. Still another nontraditional element is the historical sketch of the Land Bank and the colonists' madness for land speculation which Irving includes in the financial subplot. Such detail has no place in a folktale, for the folk mind never possesses or is even concerned with a strict historical sense. And finally, there is the polished, well-balanced literary style of the tale, the very antithesis of the rough and often staccato vernacular which characterizes a tale taken directly from an oral source.

None of these nontraditional elements is really surprising here, however, for Irving certainly never intended "The Devil and Tom Walker" to be taken as a folktale. His purpose was to produce an entertaining, fast-moving story based largely on German folk motifs and firmly rooted in an American locale. In this he was eminently successful, and "The Devil and Tom Walker" deserves to be ranked with "Rip Van Winkle" and "The Legend of Sleepy Hollow" as one of his best tales. Stanley Williams has pointed out that the major flaw in *Tales of a Traveller* was Irving's failure "to draw bravely from that wonderful stock of German legend in his notebooks and in his mind."[31] While this analysis is true for most of these tales, it is clearly not applicable to "The Devil and Tom Walker," where the carefully assembled chain of German motifs provides the backbone for a unique and vigorous plot structure. Still a second valid criticism of the *Tales of a Traveller* is that Irving did not succeed "in transplanting German legends into American settings where the native landscape could reflect the spirit of the tale."[32] Once again, "The Devil and Tom Walker" proves the exception, for Irving skillfully introduced the German materials through the use of the native Kidd legends, using the figure of the Devil as the uni-

fying force for all of the motifs. By adding the two realistic subplots, a few brief character sketches, and some local history and legend, Irving succeeded in developing a truly American atmosphere. As William L. Hedge has observed, Irving was able "to bring certain aspects of Puritanism into dramatic focus by connecting Yankee shrewdness and Puritan respectability."[33] As previously noted, this satire on the avarice and hypocrisy of colonial Boston is skillfully integrated with the folklore Irving used, and the final motif, Devil's money becomes ashes, is so well chosen that it serves as a fitting epilogue to the tale.

Once the construction of "The Devil and Tom Walker" is laid bare, it becomes evident that Irving, at least after his German tour, was no "slavish" imitator but rather a highly skilled manipulator of both American and German folklore. In avoiding the stock Gothic machinery and a distant, foreign setting for an American locale, and in assembling a chain of folk motifs that was distinctly his own invention, he created a vigorous tale that is still very much alive and meaningful today. This is not to assert that Irving possessed a first-rank imagination, as his successors Poe and Hawthorne did. Instead, as his contemporary Coleridge might have observed, Irving was endowed with a mechanical rather than an organic imagination. In this sense, he is not unlike the medieval French author Chrétien de Troyes, who drew so heavily on traditional materials yet left his own stamp on them. Like Chrétien, Irving knew and understood the traditional storyteller's skill in relating folk motifs and so, in tales such as "The Devil and Tom Walker," he was able to recombine and reshape such motifs into new and significant forms.

Notes

1. O. S. Coad, "The Gothic Element in American Literature," *JEGP* [*Journal of German and English Philology*], XXIV (1925), 85.

2. Maximilian Rudwin, *The Devil in Legend and Literature* (Chicago, 1931), p. 218.

3. Robert E. Spiller, *The Cycle of American Literature* (New York, 1957), p. 37.

4. "Irving's German Sources in *The Sketch Book*," *SP* [*Studies in Philology*], XXVII (1930), 490-494. See also Walter A. Reichart's amplification of Pochmann's discussion in *Washington Irving and Germany* (Ann Arbor, 1957), pp. 26-29.

5. *The Life of Washington Irving* (New York, 1935), I, 183.

6. Sara Puryear Rodes, "Washington Irving's Use of Traditional Folklore," *SFQ* [*Southern Folklore Quarterly*], XX (1956), 146.

7. This and subsequent motifs cited are from Stith Thompson, *Motif-Index of Folk-Literature*, 6 vols. (Bloomington, 1955).

8. Stith Thompson, *The Folktale* (New York, 1946), pp. 415-416.

9. Reichart, p. 20.

10. Reichart, p. 24.

11. *Washington Irving and the Storrows,* ed. Stanley T. Williams (Cambridge, Mass., 1933), p. 17.

12. Williams, *Life,* I, 225.

13. Pierre M. Irving, *The Life and Letters of Washington Irving* (New York, 1862), II, 119.

14. *The Journals of Washington Irving,* ed. William P. Trent and George S. Hellman (Boston, 1919), pp. 91-95.

15. Reichart, p. 53.

16. Williams, *Storrows,* pp. 23-24.

17. Washington Irving, *Complete Works* (New York, 1899), Vol. XV.

18. *Motif-Index,* I, 24.

19. Reichart, p. 156.

20. The actual features of the Devil are always nebulous and ill-defined in folktales. Where Irving has employed four traditional motifs (plus some nontraditional description), the average folktale would use only one. See Thompson, *The Folktale,* pp. 42, 251-252.

21. Antti Aarne and Stith Thompson (Helsinki, 1961). See in particular Types 1170-1199.

22. *The Journals,* I, 101.

23. *Journal of Washington Irving (1823-1824),* ed. Stanley T. Williams (Cambridge, Mass., 1931), pp. 83-84.

24. *Life and Letters,* II, 178.

25. *Journal (1823-1824),* pp. 176-180, 186.

26. *Pirate Laureate: The Life and Legends of Captain Kidd* (New Brunswick, N. J., 1947), p. xi.

27. Harold W. Thompson, *Body, Boots and Britches* (New York, 1962), p. 20.

28. Thompson, *Body,* p. 22.

29. Rodes, p. 147.

30. *The Journals,* II, 11.

31. Williams, *Life,* I, 265.

32. Reichart, p. 163.

33. *Washington Irving: An American Study, 1802-1832* (Baltimore, 1965), p. 232.

William Bysshe Stein (essay date 1968)

SOURCE: "The Devils of Hawthorne's Faust Myth," in *Hawthorne's Faust: A Study of the Devil Archetype,* Archon Books, 1968, pp. 67-86.

[*In the following essay, Stein investigates Nathaniel Hawthorne's use of the Faustian myth in his short stories to examine man's ability to profit morally from an encounter with evil.*]

With renewed sincerity Hawthorne declares in *Twice-Told Tales* that the achetypal covenant with the devil most persuasively symbolizes the enigma of human destiny.[1] This statement occurs in "The Haunted Mind," a narrative that defines the creative patterns of Hawthorne's imagination. In a few words he unbosoms the secret inspiration to which he rarely alludes directly: "there is no name for him unless it be Fatality, an emblem of the evil influence that rules your fortunes; a demon to whom you subjected yourself by some error at the outset of life, and were bound his slave forever, by once obeying him. See! those fiendish lineaments graven on the darkness, the writhed lip of scorn, the mockery of the living eye, the pointed finger, touching the sore place in your heart!" As Hawthorne speculates on the different literary forms that the idea might wear, he stumbles upon an experiential equivalent in the spiritual state of the mind represented by remorse, where riotously cavort "the devils of a guilty heart, that holds its hell within itself."[2] And here presented clearly, for the first time, is the hypothesis of universal moral truth: ordeal by sin. This mythic conception, as he develops the ramifications of his Faust myth, will activate the plots of such tales as "John Inglefield's Thanksgiving" and "The Minister's Black Veil." When at times he feels that his preoccupation with diabolic symbolism reflects his own disturbed consciousness, he reassures himself by fixing his attention upon the realities of life to discover that "the fiends [are] anywhere but in [his] haunted mind."[3] In the parallel between human life and the inspiration which he cultivates, he observes: "In both you emerge from mystery, pass through a vicissitude that you can but imperfectly control, and are borne on to another mystery." The point of view is singularly rewarding: the imagination "strays, like a free citizen, among the people of a shadowy world, beholding strange sights, yet without wonder or dismay."[4]

The prerequisite to a consuming interest in the lives of other individuals is a Faustian curiosity about oneself. Hawthorne discloses this attitude in "Monsieur du Miroir." His image in a mirror taunts him with the ontological mystery of existence. The confused inconsistencies of man's spiritual life, he confesses, must ever remain insoluble unless he can unravel the secret motivations of his own being: "I will be self-contemplative, as Nature bids me, and make him [the other self] the picture or visible type of what I muse upon, that my mind may not wander so vaguely as heretofore, chasing its own shadow through a chaos and catching only the monsters that abide there. Then will we turn our thoughts to the spiritual world. . . ."[5] If the sphinx in the mirror should deign to commit himself, then Hawthorne may legitimately probe into the multifarious expressions of human nature. He is not content to accept passively the limitations imposed upon his knowledge by God. Some uncontrollable impulse of his soul urges him to lift the veil that divine intelligence has dropped before his eyes: "A few words, perhaps, might satisfy the feverish yearning of my soul for some master thought that should guide me through this labyrinth of life, teaching wherefore I was born, and how to do my task on earth, and what is death."[6] Thus Hawthorne submits the thesis that man's spiritual unrest derives from his Faustian desire to apprehend the eternal truths of the universe. Though they forever elude the grasp of his intelligence, nevertheless they retain the ambiguous reality of the fleeting reflections that haunt the face of a mirror. But the Faustian soul will have no peace until it has realized its destiny, however vague its promptings, however illicit its quest. In "The Ambitious Guest" and "The Threefold Destiny," Hawthorne deals with the ironic configurations of this compulsive yearning; in "The Great Carbuncle" and "The Prophetic Pictures," he warns of the moral perversions that attend desperate Faustian enterprises.

It is necessary to remember that Hawthorne was not morbidly serious, for in evolving his Faust myth he also investigated its potential of humor. He recognized that not all the foibles of mankind were worthy of moral consideration; yet, as he pondered them, he could not resist attempting their solution with the Faustian equation. In the lighter variations of diabolic myth, as represented in the didactic folk tale, he found his prototype of the puckish demon. This incomparable artificer, who was not at all interested in immortal souls, tempted his victims into laughably gigantic follies. Hawthorne first mentions the comic devil in "The Seven Vagabonds." The association is aroused by his meeting with a wandering fortune-teller and conjurer who "pretended to familiarity with the Devil. . . ." But so far as Hawthorne is able to judge, the scheming old man is only a shallow counterpart of the evil spirit with whom he professes intimacy. His mental and moral traits resemble those of a down-at-the-heel Mephistopheles: "Among them might be reckoned a love of deception for its own sake, a shrewd eye and keen relish for human weakness and ridiculous infirmity, and the talent of petty fraud. Thus to this old man there would be pleasure even in the consciousness so insupportable to some minds, that his whole life was a cheat upon the world. . . ."[7] This undignified disciple of the mighty Lucifer appears in "Peter Goldthwaite's Treasure" and "Mrs. Bullfrog."

Though Washington Irving's "The Devil and Tom Walker" is usually called the "comic New England *Faust,*" on the basis of sheer humor Hawthorne's "Peter Goldthwaite's Treasure" perhaps has a more legitimate claim to the title. Peter is a crackbrained schemer, impatient of ordinary business methods. He trades only in bubbles and wishful dreams, the vast fortunes of legendary El Doradoes. He is at last compelled to pin his hope for riches on the tradition that his great grand-uncle once hid a fabulous treasure in the ancestral mansion, the last of Peter's possessions. Rumor had it that the uncle had acquired this vast wealth through a deal with "Old Scratch," but ultimately the devil had tricked the elder Peter by "some secret impediment . . . [which] debarred him from the enjoyment of his riches."[8] The heir chooses to ignore this part of the old wives' tale, and begins to disembowel the house, confident of uncovering untold wealth; symbolically he is emptying himself of all desire to live within ordinary society.

Throughout the remainder of the story Hawthorne uses the symbol of the roguish devil of the popular Faustian folk tale to amplify Peter's stupendous folly. Tabitha, Peter's witch-like housekeeper, tells her master that he ought to take cognizance of his uncle's bad luck, for, as the latter "went to unlock the chest, the Old Scratch came behind and caught his arm. The money, they say, was paid Peter out of his purse; and he wanted Peter to give him a deed of this house and land, which Peter swore he would not do."[9] In the process of the wrecking operation, Peter finds a charcoal sketch on the wall of a room which momentarily disconcerts him, for it is a pictorial embodiment of Tabitha's yarn: "It represented a ragged man, partly supporting himself on a spade, and bending his lean body over a hole in the earth, with one hand extended to grasp something he had found. But close behind him, with a fiendish laugh on his features, appeared a figure with horns, a tufted tail, and a cloven hoof." With an "Avaunt Satan!"[10] Peter puts an axe to "Old Scratch," convinced that he has lifted the evil spell held by the demon over his uncle's treasure. Not until Peter has demolished everything in the house except the kitchen does he find a large chest which holds the reward of his labors. But as Tabitha hinted, the devil was not to be tricked. Peter finds a useless fortune in old provincial currency—the emblem of his status in the community.

Hawthorne once again uses the symbol of the jesting demon to give "Mrs. Bullfrog" the moral that fraud begets fraud. Mr. Bullfrog, a fastidious bachelor, marries a woman who epitomizes his quest for perfection. She possesses charm, good breeding, and virginal innocence, besides a considerable sum of money. The bride is intelligent enough to reason that her assets constitute about ninety-five per cent of her attraction for Mr. Bullfrog. Immediately after the ceremony the couple sets off in a stagecoach for a distant town. As they are riding along, the vehicle capsizes. Mr. Bullfrog, who is slightly stunned, rises from the side of the road to go to the assistance of his lovely wife. But the person in his wife's garb has metamorphosed into a monster. Gone are the glossy curls, the elegance, and the gentility. Blaming the driver for her ruin, this strange creature, bald, hollow-cheeked, and toothless, belabors the unfortunate man with an umbrella to the accompaniment of blistering imprecations. Mr. Bullfrog is terrified. He fears that the mocking fiend is at the bottom of the troubled situation: "In my terror and turmoil of mind I could imagine nothing less than that the Old Nick, at the moment of our overturn, had annihilated my wife and jumped into her petticoats. The idea seemed the more probable, since I could nowhere perceive Mrs. Bullfrog alive, nor, though I looked very sharply about the coach, could I detect any traces of the beloved woman's dead body."[11] Shortly thereafter, Mr. Bullfrog is confronted with the unhappy truth that he has married an impostor; instead of a treasure he has picked up a bundle of artificiality which, according to the standards of innocent beauty, is almost as worthless as Peter Goldthwaite's outmoded currency. Mr. Bullfrog's spontaneous conviction that "Old Nick" was the key to the duplicity is figuratively confirmed. His wife is indeed an old witch with as much guile as the folk-tale demon. When her husband indignantly protests the imposture, she merely remarks that she still has her fortune. Hearing this, Mr. Bullfrog, somewhat abashedly, recants the ideal of perfection, and the devil of greed wins again.

But as skillfully as Hawthorne managed the less meaningful symbol of the folk-tale Mephistopheles, it was no more than an experiment in technique. Perfect control over his mythic imagery presupposed a knowledge of the ideas that it could embrace on every level of human experience. The follies of a Peter Goldthwaite or the duplicities of a Mrs. Bullfrog illustrated only the proverbial truths of the practical world; they could not preoccupy Hawthorne long. In the melancholy expression of the young Faust of "The Ambitious Guest" there was more to learn of the tormented human soul than in a thousand recitals of the petty aspirations of an empty-headed speculator of Goldthwaite's stature. The ambitions of the youth who is a chance guest in the cottage situated in the notch of the sublimely beautiful White Mountains are for Hawthorne an exemplification of life's bitter irony. Rising above the shallow desires of the masses, the ambitious guest cries: "But I cannot die till I have achieved my destiny. Then, let Death come!"[12] Not achievement for achievement's sake is his ideal, but an abstract ambition to leave "a glorious memory in the universal heart of man."[13] For this reason "he had travelled far and alone; his whole life, indeed, had been a solitary path; for, with the lofty caution of his nature, he had kept himself apart from those who might otherwise have been his companions."[14] The death that overtakes this proud, reserved Faust is as anonymous as his vague, high-souled ambitions. A sudden landslide sweeps down from the heights to bury him with the humble family of the cottage. Only he among the group dies unnoticed: an unheralded stranger, an uninvited guest. So Hawthorne depicts the illicit character of an overruling desire for fame that left its aspirant stranded on an untraveled highway of life. Without depending upon the dynamic archetypal symbolism, he pronounces isolation from humanity the inevitable doom of the eccentric Faustian soul. The author does not condemn the actions of the ambitious guest; as in "Monsieur du Miroir," he views them as a quest for the "master-thought," human nature in rebellion against the limitations imposed upon it by unknown forces.

"The Threefold Destiny" serves as a companion piece to "The Ambitious Guest." But Hawthorne in this story allows his mythic symbolism to operate overtly. Ralph Cranfield, who believes "himself marked out for a high destiny," imbibes the idea through supernatural means: it is "revealed to him by witchcraft, or in a dream of prophecy. . . ."[15] Three signs are to confirm the approach of these marvelous attainments: a heart-shaped jewel on the bosom of a maiden is to proclaim the discovery of the only woman who can make him happy; a hand, visible only to him, is to point out a mighty treasure hidden in the ground; and an extensive influence and sway over his fellow-creatures is to be a harbinger of great leadership. Ralph becomes a world-wanderer, but nowhere does he encounter the fateful signs. When he returns to his native village, he finds the illusive tokens; but they augur more modest achievements than he had hoped. He accepts his prophetic destiny, adjusting his wild Faustian dreams to the commonplace duties of those precincts in which he had been born.

In neither of these tales of high-destined individuals does Hawthorne extend the outline of his myth. Though aware of the spiritual tensions generated by overweening ambition, he loses dramatic impact by his failure to give them expression. The conflict with conventional mores prevails only by implication, or is given a romantic solution, as in *Fanshawe*. The symbolic pursuits excite moral platitudes, not philosophical truths. But as he writes in "The Threefold Destiny," he is still experimenting with "the spirit and mechanism" of legend or myth, searching for the incidents, "the characters [and] manners of familiar life" to embody in the form.[16]

When symbol and idea perfectly balance, as in "The Prophetic Pictures," Hawthorne assumes the role of a moral philosopher. The mysterious painter of this tale is the counterpart of Leonardo da Vinci, the Italian Faust, who "chose rather to know than to be, and that curiosity led him within forbidden portals."[17] Not only does Hawthorne's painter excel in his peculiar art, but he "possesses vast acquirements in all other learning and science."[18] His most astounding gift, deriving from his prodigious knowledge, is the awful power to delineate in a picture not merely his subject's features but his mind and heart. Hawthorne, in this instance mentally attuned to the harmonies of his Faustian imagery, ascribes this talent to intercourse with the devil. Pious New Englanders inveigh against this rare pictorial skill: "Some deemed it an offense against the Mosaic law, and even a presumptuous mockery of the Creator. . . . Others, frightened at the art which could raise phantoms at will, and keep the forms of the dead among the living, were inclined to consider the painter as a magician, or perhaps the famous Black Man, of old witch times, plotting mischief in a new guise."[19] Yet the painter is indifferent to public opinion. What his art reveals he accepts dispassionately. He displays no more interest in a sitter than a scientist does in a specimen to be dissected. Each flaw of character that he is able to portray adds but another objective fact to his knowledge of human nature. This intellectualization of emotion is severely criticized by Hawthorne. Aloofness from the ordinary feelings of mankind is a patent evil: "Like all other men around whom an engrossing purpose wreathes itself, he was insulated from the mass of human kind. He had no aim—no pleasure—no sympathies—but what were ultimately connected with his art . . . he did not possess kindly feelings; his heart was cold; no living creature could be brought near enough to keep him warm."[20] In this fatal inadequacy, Hawthorne discovers the fallacy of the Faustian superman. Deliberate isolation from the common aspirations of the human heart he considers a breach of universal morality. When knowledge becomes an end in itself, divorced from the public good, it takes on the function of evil. It ceases to seek a verification of its ethics in the external world, being a law unto itself: "It is not good for man to cherish a solitary ambition. Unless there be those around him by whose example he may regulate himself, his thoughts, desires, and hopes will become extravagant, and he the semblance, perhaps the reality, of a madman. Reading other bosoms with an acuteness almost preternatural, the painter failed to see the disorder of his own."[21] Translated into the values of the devil-image, the diabolic portraiture of the artist, in its failure to direct his spiritual government, merely corroborates the thesis that the evil of the ego-consciousness is the inability of this presumptuous faculty to think itself capable of wrong.

In "The Prophetic Pictures" Hawthorne realizes the full ethical potential of Faustian mythmaking. The supernatural endowments of the painter, attributed to intercourse with the devil, bring the hero into contact with the inherent capacity for evil which every individual possesses. In transmitting these secrets to the canvas, literally the lineaments of a devil-image, the painter himself fails to heed the counsel with self which they urge. He is oblivious to his own evil instincts because his ego overrules all responsibility to the community; for the image which he surveys is, after all, a communal symbol whose ethical purpose eludes him. He has divorced himself, emotionally, from his human heritage. On another level of the story, Hawthorne focuses on still another inadequacy of Puritan morality. He condemns his forefathers' intolerance of art, their fear that it encroached upon God's prerogatives; and indirectly he deplores their suspicion of the beautiful in painting, the only ideal that momentarily exalts man to the status of a god. And in equating the beautiful with infernal conjuration, they were exposing to public gaze the deserts of their souls over which the hot breath of the devil blew in fiendish glee. They, too, were blind to their devil-thoughts.

The fabulous jewel of "The Great Carbuncle" embraces the idea of a quest as infamous as the painter's pursuit of dispassionate knowledge. But the search for the carbuncle enables Hawthorne to broaden the canvas of his narrative picture. With the possible exception of the young couple, each individual participating in the adventure is motivated by a desire that reflects a specific phase of universal human conduct. Hawthorne is therefore allowed to pass moral judgment on their actions. Because "the quest for the Great Carbuncle is deemed little better than a traffic with the Evil One," doing "grievous wrong to [the] soul [and] body, . . ."[22] Hawthorne's symbol acquires its necessary mythic connotations.

The story, in relation to Hawthorne's development of his Faust myth, shows him widening the periphery of meaning of his conceptual pattern. The motives inciting the different adventurers gain his strong disapprobation. He censures mere romantic pursuit, vain and directionless ambition; the pride of the scientist who sees the carbuncle as a "prize . . . reserved to crown [his] scientific reputation; . . ." the selfishness of a merchant who thinks only of "the marketable value of the true gem"; the egotism of the poet who believes its radiance will be diffused through his works, establishing "the splendor" of his "intellectual powers"; the haughtiness of the nobleman who deems the carbuncle the only fitting "ornament for the great hall of [his] ancestral castle"; the cynicism of the disbeliever who wishes to prove that the legend of the great carbuncle "is all a humbug."[23] At the end only the couple prove themselves "so simply wise as to reject [the] jewel" because it "would have dimmed all earthly things" by its splendor.[24] Thus Hawthorne contemptuously dismisses all forms of human activity actuated by vanity, selfishness, or pride. In the process he casts the net of his Faust myth into the deeper waters of mankind's experiences.

The two historical tales "Edward Randolph's Portrait" and "Lady Eleanore's Mantle" present another variant of the Faust myth. Hawthorne this time utilizes the symbolic pact with the devil to magnify political tyranny in the American colonies. In the first story the portrait of Randolph, who obtained the repeal of the first provincial charter, is the symbol of the people's curse on all irresponsible rulers. The action begins with the provincial governor meditating an oppression against the inhabitants of old Boston. As he sits at his desk, momentarily reluctant to add his signature to the document that will implement the offense, his eyes scrutinize Randolph's portrait. A military aide, noticing the governor's curiosity, volunteers to relate the history of the dark canvas. His recital introduces the connection between the devil and political injustice: "One of the wildest, and at the same time the best accredited, accounts, stated it to be an original and authentic portrait of the Evil One, taken at a witch meeting near Salem; and that its strong and terrible resemblance had been confirmed by several of the confessing wizards and witches, at their trial, in open court. It was likewise affirmed that a familiar spirit or demon abode behind the blackness of the picture, and had shown himself, at seasons of public calamity, to more than one of the royal governors."[25] The governor ridicules the story as a fantasy. And when his niece chides his skepticism, he harshly announces his intention of putting the city under martial law. One of the representatives of the people urges him to rescind the order, warning, "If you meddle with the devil, take care of his claws!"[26]

Angered by these threats against royal authority, the governor seizes the pen, resolved to sign his name to the paper that will put his orders into execution. A provincial captain calls his attention to Randolph's portrait, and he lifts his eyes to scan it. The governor stares at it aghast. His aide's tale begins to materialize: "The expression of the face . . . was that of a wretch detected in some hideous guilt, and exposed to the bitter hatred and laughter and withering scorn of a vast surrounding multitude. There was the struggle of defiance, beaten down and overwhelmed by the crushing weight of ignominy. The torture of the soul had come forth upon the countenance. It seemed as if the picture . . . threw its evil omen over the present hour."[27] The governor, however, stubbornly persists in enforcing his will. Casting a second glance of defiance at the picture, he affixes his signature. The rumors flowing from this crucial meeting relate that his name was scrawled in "characters that betokened it a deed of desperation. . . . Then, it is said, he shuddered, as if that signature had granted away his salvation."[28] With ineffable ingenuity, Hawthorne deepens the significance of a historic moment in New England culture, giving it an unforgettable emphasis by equating political dictatorship with the loss of salvation: the signing away of one's soul to the devil. And again the mythic image is evoked to direct and guide individual human behavior, but aristocratic pride prohibits its lesson to prevail. The governor refuses to take counsel with the evil that divides his heart.

The pride of Lady Eleanore Rochcliffe in the second of the stories symbolizes the hell-inspired harshness of the British agents ruling the American colonies. By retelling history with this pardonable democratic bias, Hawthorne succeeds in representing the courage that went into the founding of the republic. Haughtily conscious of her heredity and personal advantages as a relative of the royal governor of Massachusetts, Lady Eleanore places herself above the sympathies of the common nature which binds together human souls. This scornful attitude, coupled with an extraordinary loveliness, is ascribed to supernatural influences by the ladies of the province. The article that sets off her irresistible charms is an embroidered mantle "which had been wrought by the most skillful artist in London, and possessed even magical properties of adornment."[29]

To re-enforce the impression of Lady Eleanore's Luciferian pride, Hawthorne foreordains the dark fate that will smite her soul. One of her rejected lovers, a colonial youth of unimportant birth and no fortune, insanely importunes her to drink consecrated wine to prove her human ties: ". . . in requital of that harm, if such there be, and for your own earthly and heavenly welfare, I pray you to take one sip of this holy wine, and then to pass the goblet round among the guests. And this shall be a symbol that you have not sought to withdraw yourself from the chain of human sympathies—which whoso would shake off must keep company with fallen angels." When she refuses to do his bidding, the youth presents another strange petition to the arrogant woman: "It was no other than that she should throw off the mantle, which, while he pressed the silver cup of wine upon her, she had drawn more closely around her form, so as almost to shroud herself within it."[30] But still she will not relinquish this other talisman of her superiority.

When shortly thereafter a small-pox epidemic breaks out in the colony, the source of the dreadful plague is traced back to Lady Eleanore's mantle. Now the residents of the region find confirmation of their belief that the diseased mantle was the devil's banner: "The people raved against the Lady Eleanore, and cried out that her pride and scorn had evoked a fiend, and that, between them both, this monstrous evil had been born."[31] And soon the pride which brought the downfall of the mighty Lucifer and his most ardent disciple, Faust, also reduces Lady Eleanore to shame and to ruin. Her lovely face is blasted by the horrible scourge. Her lunatic suitor, whose very name Helwyse apparently provides a foreknowledge of her doom, insanely pronounces her elegy: "All have been her victims! Who so worthy to be the final victim as herself?"[32] And with this homonymic symbol Hawthorne concludes another historical tale whose macabre tension derives from the fire and brimstone of his devil-image. The poetic liberties that he takes with historical data are equally determined by art and by personal democratic conviction. The pride evinced by Lady Eleanore, with its immovable cruelty and heartless indifference, was for Hawthorne the emotional and intellectual index of British imperialism and, in historical perspective, of all conquering powers. In the light of his artistic method, nothing could project abuse of authority more clearly than the functional imagery of his plastic Faust myth. He had used it to ferret out the evils of Puritanism in "The Maypole of Merry Mount" and other tales, in one way; now, in another manner, he applied it to enhance the heroic courage of the founding fathers in their struggle with the evils of monarchical persecutions.

"The devils of the guilty heart," upon whom Hawthorne mused in "The Haunted Mind," are his subject in "John Inglefield's Thanks-giving." Here he studies the war between good and evil raging continually in the guilty conscience, and he focuses once more on the educative image of the devil, in this instance on a negative reaction. The dilemma in which Prudence Inglefield finds herself has its parallel in the Faust chapbook and in Marlowe's *Faustus.* The chapbook Faust, though he wants to repent, will not repent: "In this perplexity lay this miserable Doctor Faustus, having quite forgot his faith in Christ, never falling to repentance truly, thereby to attain the grace and holy spirit of God again, the which would have been able to have resisted the strong assaults of Satan; for although he had made him a promise, yet he might have remembered through true repentance sinners come again into the favour of God."[33] Hawthorne does not merely report Prudence's fleeting impulse toward repentance. He presents it as a concrete action, having reality in time and place. In the theatre of her conscience occurs her struggle with the devil, actually the attempt to school herself to a genuine understanding of the mythic image which her conscience invokes to warn her of evil. On the evening of Thanksgiving Day, in the midst of dissolute revelry, Prudence suddenly remembers the pious celebrations of her innocent youth. She re-creates in her imagination what would take place if she were now to visit the fireside circle. She envisions a cool welcome, with family affection growing in warmth the longer she stays. When her mind turns to the hour of domestic worship, her heart suddenly yearns for this solace. For a moment she is on the verge of repentance. But in this crisis she is intimidated by the demonic image of the devil which rises to her consciousness: "But her face was so changed that they hardly recognized it. Sin and evil passions glowed through its comeliness, and wrought a horrible deformity; a smile gleamed in her eyes, as of triumphant mockery, at their surprise and grief."[34] At the sight of their unhappiness, Prudence dares to challenge the negative power of the devil-image: ". . . her countenance wore almost the expression as if she were struggling with a fiend, who had power to seize his victim within the hallowed precincts of her father's hearth."[35] But, as with Faustus, she lacked the conviction of faith in God, and her volition was strangled by the overpowering challenge to her spirit. In this narrative Hawthorne, by recourse to the oneiric symbols of myth and by constructing an otherworldly domain of myth, succeeds in achieving the dramatic persuasion of similar scenes in Marlowe's *Faustus*. By conceding the reality of the invisible world of the conscience, he presents good and evil as the chief actors in the kaleidoscope of individual human experience.

The sharp-toothed devils of remorse that gnaw at Mr. Hooper's conscience in "The Minister's Black Veil" are symbolized in the black veil, which is the physical emblem of his secret sin. As Hawthorne develops the meaning of the veil, he denotes it the sign of the parson's bondage to the devil: ". . . catching a glimpse of his figure in the looking-glass, the black veil involved his own spirit in the horror with which it overwhelmed all others. His frame shuddered, his lips grew white, he spilt the untasted wine upon the carpet, and rushed forth into the darkness."[36] Here Hawthorne merely gives tangible embodiment to the general idea of the devils of the guilty conscience which he discussed in "The Haunted Mind," transforming the mythic devil-image into the shape the plot of his tale demands. On another occasion he confirms this transmutation, for he remarks that behind the crepe veil "ghost and fiend consorted" with Mr. Hooper. To enforce this impression further, he notes that "among all its bad influences" it had only one good result: "By the aid of his mysterious emblem . . . he became a man of awful power over souls that were in agony for sin."[37]

In this extremely subtle fashion Hawthorne repeats the moral import of "Young Goodman Brown." The overemphasis on sin obscures the possibilities of good in the human soul. Mr. Hooper's claim that every individual "loathsomely treasur[es] up the secret of his sin . . ."[38] is an indictment of no one but himself. In effect, Hawthorne states that a minister, as a human agent of God, is not supposed to flaunt the power of Lucifer. His mission is to guide both the pure and the sinful along the path to righteousness. He must demonstrate the capacity of good which is inherent in any individual who dares confront evil, triumphing over its negations and reading the sphinx-like mystery of the devil-symbol. The very veil which ought to have guided Mr. Hooper to a new understanding of spiritual truth distorts his mind as a similar experience had affected Goodman Brown.

That Hawthorne's attitude toward evil was going through a stage of ethical refinement, consistent with the principle advanced in "The Minister's Black Veil," is clearly indicated in "Fancy's Show-Box." He grants that man is tempted into evil "by many devilish sophistries," since the fiend has "a wondrous power, and terrible acquaintance with the secret soul. . . ."[39] Nevertheless Hawthorne in-

sists that man's capacity for evil is overestimated: "In truth, there is no such thing in man's nature as a settled and full resolve, either for good or evil, except at the very moment of execution."[40] In other words, neither human depravity nor original sin but rather the pressure of circumstances and the confusion of purpose operate to promote the commission of sin. Such an outlook on evil is obviously in direct opposition to the Calvinistic exposition of the idea. This stand verifies the fact that Hawthorne approached the problem philosophically, not theologically. In terms of the Faust myth this philosophical curiosity is of even greater importance. It suggests that Hawthorne's ethical analyses are rapidly assuming the direction of those in Goethe's *Faust*. Since both men were interested in evil only in the narrow sense that experience with it awakened spiritual conflict, they could determine the enduring validity of man's ethical ideals by taking man's reaction to participation in sin as a positive test of his moral integrity. If sin functions to distort completely man's prospects of the good, then he is indeed damned; if, however, he consciously admits his errors and thereby resolves to transcend them, he is admitting his responsibility to the unwritten laws of universal truth. In the specific sense of Hawthorne's art, the mythic image of the devil functions in exactly this way: it is the oneiric projection of the great racial memory that has endlessly mediated the problem of good and evil for man.

"Dr. Heidegger's Experiment" lays open to view another of Hawthorne's attempts to examine the individual's ability to profit morally as the result of a previous experience with evil. The elixir of life motif, as in Goethe's *Faust*, is the device Hawthorne employs to elucidate his problem. But unlike the playwright, he is compelled to resolve the consequences of temptation to further evil within the limits of a short narrative. All the magic paraphernalia of the play are reproduced in Hawthorne's setting. Faust's enchanted mirror is converted into a fitting ornament for Dr. Heidegger's study: "Between two of the bookcases hung a looking-glass, presenting its high and dusty plate within a tarnished gilt frame. Among many wonderful stories related of this mirror, it was fabled that the spirits of all the doctor's deceased patients dwelt within its verge, and would stare him in the face whenever he looked thitherward."[41] The witches' apes and the steaming cauldron that attend the preparation of the rejuvenating liquor are symbolically expressed by the doctor's black book: "The greatest curiosity of the study remains to be mentioned; it was a ponderous folio volume, bound in black leather, with massive silver clasps . . . and nobody could tell the title of the book. But it was well known to be a book of magic; and once, when a chambermaid had lifted it, merely to brush away the dust, the skeleton had rattled in its closet, the picture of the young lady had stepped one foot upon the floor, and several ghastly faces had peeped forth from the mirror. . . ."[42] Five venerable friends of Dr. Heidegger are invited to share in the experiment of rejuvenation. They, like Faust, have long since expended the vitality of youth. Before the scientist offers them the potion, he urges them to use their past experience in the event that the elixir produces the desired effects: ". . . it would be well that, with the experience of a lifetime to direct you, you should draw up a few general rules for your guidance, in passing a second time through the perils of youth. Think what a sin and shame it would be, if, with your peculiar advantages, you should not become patterns of virtue and wisdom to all the young people of the age!"[43] But once they have sipped the magical draught, they immediately revert to the conduct of youth. And in the exuberance of their revived energies, they topple over the container of precious fluid. The effects of the preliminary samplings wear off, and the five return to their dotage. In the spontaneous lapse of these aged people to the sinful behavior of the past, Hawthorne isolates the ethical problem broached in "Fancy's Show-Box." Even if the individual engages in evil once, he nevertheless can attain the good life. All he needs to do is to become conscious of his moral lapse. Dr. Heidegger's friends, instead of perceiving their errors, resolve to search for the fountain of youth. They fail to reap the truth that is implicit in evil. Only the old doctor, who does not bemoan the loss of the elixir, reads the lesson so vividly illustrated by their actions. In this way Hawthorne transforms the elixir of life motif of the Faust myth into an instrument of ethical clarification.

Hawthorne's two stories of the Shaker community in New Hampshire tentatively explore the fringes of contemporary life within the confines of his mythic imagery. This act betokens his confidence in his operative conception, and anticipates its later extension into the more critical problems of his times. The Shakers, whose religious principles forbade the practice of sexual intercourse, allow him to speculate on the type of moral rigorism that he associated with dogmatic Puritanism: in a word, with the spiritual pride which reflects the negative aspect of evil embodied in the devil-archetypes. In "The Canterbury Pilgrims" two lovers fleeing from the Shaker village are accosted by a group of pilgrims who, conversely, are seeking refuge with the sect. The pilgrims attempt to persuade the lovers to renounce their plan, pointing out that the outside world breeds only disillusionment. The young couple, however, are not to be shaken in their mutual faith. They are willing to accept "mortal hope and fear" as a substitute for a "cold and passionless security."[44] The truth that emerges from this story is simply explained: a religion intolerant of human nature is a worse evil than any its practices may seemingly thwart. In a Faustian context, the philosophy which subsumes this belief recognizes the sources of moral perversion in the denial of the natural man and in a complete surrender to evil. The inversion of emotions which Hawthorne condemns is what each individual's personal Mephistopheles fosters if there is no attempt made to circumvent his trickery.

The principle of moral cowardice is re-examined in "The Shaker Bridal." Hawthorne describes the evil wrought in family relations by an unthinking submission to abnormal dogmas: "One, when he joined the Society, had brought with him his wife and children, but never, from that hour, had spoken a fond word to the former, or taken his best-beloved child upon his knee. Another, whose family refused to follow him, had been enabled . . . to leave them to the mercy of the world."[45] But it is in the marriage of Martha and Adam that Hawthorne sees a travesty on natural morality. The couple, who are in the prime of life, are about to be ordained the temporal spiritual leaders of the movement. A mock marriage is to symbolize their consecration to the ascetic ideal. The despair which originally drove Adam to forsake normal existence has crystallized into a hard core of selfishness in the new environment. He has disciplined his emotions to the extent that they are now brutally impersonal. Martha, who joined the community upon the urging of Adam, has sustained herself on the hope that Adam, once rehabilitated, would return to the world of men and consummate their long-delayed marriage. But now that Adam has risen to leadership among the Shakers, his pride in the specious success has entirely divorced him from thoughts of Martha. As a consequence, when Adam signifies his intention to remain celibate, Martha dies, being unable to endure a desolate agony. Thus Hawthorne, in his first attempt to study contemporary life, castigates the diabolic negations of a current religious sect. In relation to his myth, he has progressively expanded its definition until now he is at a point in modern life identical with the one he had assumed in his examination of Puritan history. His moral objection to the negative aspects of Puritanism was the creative origin of his mythic conception; his first effort to adapt its motivations to the life that surrounded him is characterized by this coincidence of approach.

In summary it may be said that, with the statement in "The Haunted Mind" reaffirming his belief that all the evils of life could be balanced with the infernal pact of the Faustian equation, Hawthorne declared his intention to extend the outlines of his Faust myth. In "Monsieur du Miroir" he indicated that the peculiarity of individual destiny would engage his attention. And since human ambition is usually the most powerful influence in shaping destiny, Hawthorne, beginning with the rather vague and romantic motivations of "The Ambitious Guest" and "The Threefold Destiny," moved toward a moral clarification of the compulsive desires dominating man's nature in "The Prophetic Pictures" and "The Great Carbuncle." The humorous possibilities of the devil-inspired folk tale momentarily diverted him in "Peter Goldthwaite's Treasure" and "Mrs. Bullfrog." The dramatic value of the mythic imagery in enforcing the lessons of American history was skillfully realized in "Edward Randolph's Portrait" and "Lady Eleanore's Mantle." His concern with the insidious effects of evil upon moral volition in "John Inglefield's Thanksgiving" and "The Minister's Black Veil" reflected an attitude toward evil that was a necessary prelude to the dogmatic standpoint of "Fancy's Show-Box." No Faust myth, in the sense of the greatness of Marlowe's *Faustus* or Goethe's *Faust,* is possible unless the author holds to a definite opinion on the function of evil in the universe. In this latter sketch he adopted a Pelagian position: man, hampered by no deterministic principle of natural depravity, has the power within himself to overcome evil and attain moral truth. "Dr. Heidegger's Experiment" isolated the negative aspect of this issue, suggesting that the individual is prone to be overwhelmed by evil only when he refuses to profit by the counsel with self which it urges. The last stage of this particular development in Hawthorne's Faust myth found him tentatively exploring its practicability in appraising the moral values at stake in contemporary life. The Shaker stories, though they are tangential to the real problems of the age, anticipate the direction of his thinking in the next evolution of his myth.

Notes

1. The tales and sketches considered in this chapter were written between 1830 and 1842; most of them were included in the two editions of *Twice-Told Tales* (1837, 1842).

2. *Complete Works,* [*The Complete Works of Nathaniel Hawthorne,* with Introductory notes by George Parsons Lathrop, 13 vols. (Riverside Edition Boston: Houghton, Mifflin and Co., 1883.] I, 346.

3. *Ibid.,* I, 347.

4. *Ibid.,* I, 348.

5. *Ibid.,* II, 194.

6. *Ibid.,* II, 195.

7. *Ibid.,* I, 405.

8. *Ibid.,* I, 433.

9. *Ibid.,* I, 440.

10. *Ibid.,* I, 442.

11. *Ibid.,* II, 153.

12. *Ibid.,* I, 368.

13. *Ibid.,* I, 369.

14. *Ibid.,* I, 367.

15. *Ibid.,* I, 528.

16. *Ibid.,* I, 527.

17. Edward McCurdy, *Leonardo da Vinci's Notebooks* (New York: Empire State Book Company, 1923), p. 8.

18. *Complete Works,* I, 192.

19. *Ibid.,* I, 195.

20. *Ibid.,* I, 206.

21. *Ibid.,* I, 207.

22. *Ibid.,* I, 179.

23. *Ibid.,* I, 178-182.

24. *Ibid.,* I, 191.

25. *Ibid.,* I, 295.

26. *Ibid.,* I, 301.

27. *Ibid.,* I, 303.

28. *Ibid.,* I, 304.

29. *Ibid.,* I, 310-311.

30. *Ibid.,* I, 316-317.

31. *Ibid.,* I, 321-322.

32. *Ibid.,* I, 325.

33. [William Rose, ed. *The Famous History of Dr. Faustus, 1592-1594* (New York: E. P. Dutton & on. d.)] pp. 89-90.

34. *Complete Works,* III, 589.

35. *Ibid.,* III, 590.

36. *Ibid.,* I, 59.

37. *Ibid.,* I, 65.

38. *Ibid.,* I, 69.

39. *Ibid.,* I, 255.

40. *Ibid.,* I, 257.

41. *Ibid.,* I, 259.

42. *Ibid.,* I, 260.

43. *Ibid.,* I, 263.

44. *Ibid.,* III, 530.

45. *Ibid.,* I, 474.

James L. Williamson (essay date 1981)

SOURCE: "'Young Goodman Brown': Hawthorne's 'Devil in Manuscript,'" in *Studies in Short Fiction,* Vol. 18, No. 2, Spring, 1981, pp. 155-62.

[*In the following essay, Williamson studies multiple devil figures in Nathaniel Hawthorne's satirical tale "Young Goodman Brown."*]

When Hawthorne commented on the vocation of authorship, he was often drawn to analogies between writing and damnation. ". . . authors," he wrote with tongue-in-cheek in 1821, "are always poor devils, and therefore Satan may take them."[1] The pun is on "devil," which can mean a literary hack; and the meaning is clear: to write conventionally and without integrity is to damn oneself as a writer, even at the cost of popularity and recognition. ". . . America is now wholly given over to a d[amne]d mob of scribbling women," Hawthorne wrote in 1855, "and I should have no chance of success while the public taste is occupied with their trash—and should be ashamed of myself if I did succeed."[2] Yet, going to the devil, in another context, was the highest form of praise Hawthorne could bestow on a fellow author. "The woman writes as if the Devil was in her," he commented upon reading Sara P.

Willis's *Ruth Hall,* "and that is the only condition under which a woman ever writes anything worth reading. Generally women write like emasculated men . . . ; but when they throw off the restraints of decency, and come before the public stark naked, as it were,—then their books are sure to possess character and value."[3] To write as though possessed in this sense meant to penetrate beneath social convention and to speak in an authentic, potent voice. Such a descent could be liberating (for writer and reader), as well as damning in a personal and professional sense. For when Hawthorne described *The Scarlet Letter* as "positively a h[el]l-f[ire]d story," he bestowed upon his Romance his highest praise and severest criticism. A hell-fired story was "powerfully written," but, for that reason, unlikely to "appeal to the broadest class of sympathies," nor to "obtain a very wide popularity."[4] To write as though possessed from this perspective was to contend with social and literary conventions (as the root meaning of "Satan" is "adversary"), and a writer who challenged such conventions could expect to alienate part of the popular reading audience.

The personal cost of going to the devil as a writer was earliest dramatized in the figure of Oberon, the artist hero of "The Devil in Manuscript," a burlesque on the conditions of authorship in America in the 1830's. Published in the *New-England Magazine* seven months following the appearance of "Young Goodman Brown," the sketch provides an excellent gloss on that tale. For Oberon has given himself to the devil; that is, his vocation has been dedicated to creating in fiction "'the character of a fiend, as represented in our traditions and the written records of witchcraft.'" "'You remember,'" he tells his companion, "'how the hellish thing used to suck away the happiness of those who, by a simple concession that seemed almost innocent, subjected themselves to his power. Just so my peace is gone, and all by these accursed manuscripts.'" Just so Goodman Brown's innocent venture into the devil's woods and simple concessions to the devil's arguments will end in his permanent loss of peace and happiness. And just so will Brown come to find himself trapped in a world of uncertainties and spectral appearance. "'I am surrounding myself with shadows,'" laments Oberon, "'which bewilder me, by aping the realities of life. They have drawn me aside from the beaten path of the world, and led me into a strange sort of solitude—a solitude in the midst of men—where nobody wishes for what I do, nor thinks nor feels as I do. The tales have done all this.'" But Oberon, unlike Brown, is finally of the devil's party. His tale concludes not with death and gloom, but with fire and triumph, as the ashes from his burning manuscripts escape from the chimney to set the town ablaze. "'My tales!'" he cries. "'The chimney! The roof! The Fiend has gone forth by night, and startled thousands in fear and wonder from their beds! Here I stand—a triumphant author! Huzza! Huzza! My brain has set the town on fire!'" Oberon's final words affirm the demonic, that is, destructive but liberating aspects of his art as it awakens his neighbors from their accustomed slumbers to "fear and wonder." Although Brown lacks the ironic, cosmopolitan

perspective of the artist, and although he fears the wrath of an Old Testament God throughout his life of gloom, he nonetheless suffers the fate of the romantic writer: a damnation that becomes a salvation (however unorthodox). To examine "Young Goodman Brown" from this point of view, however, we must turn from Brown for a moment to focus on the speaker of the tale, remembering Hawthorne's analogies between writer and devil, as well as between writing and damnation. As we shall see, the devil figures who appear to Brown in the woods will each bear a certain resemblance to the speaker of the tale, or to those characteristics of the speaker dramatized in his voice. The speaker, that is, will show himself to be of the devil's party, and Brown's experience in the woods will come to represent the experience of art, of reading the tale "Young Goodman Brown."[5]

II

At a climatic moment, as he is about to be baptized into the devil's fold, Goodman Brown calls upon Faith to "'Look up to Heaven, and resist the Wicked One!'" Yet in the course of the tale, Brown encounters not one, but three "wicked ones," each with a peculiar character and distinct voice. The first of these devils presents himself as a casual, urbane individual: "simply clad" and "as simple in manner too," but possessing "an indescribable air of one who knew the world, and would not have felt abashed at the governor's dinner-table, or in King William's court. . . ." Adept at the art of understatement, this devil addresses Brown in an amused, patronizing tone as he mimics Brown's own naive pretensions and self-righteousness. Witness the following dialogue:

> "My father never went into the woods on such an errand, [exclaimed Brown] nor his father before him. We have been a race of honest men and good Christians, since the days of the martyrs. And shall I be the first of the name of Brown, that ever took this path, and kept—"
>
> "Such company, thou wouldst say," observed the elder person, interpreting his pause. "Well said, Goodman Brown! I have been as well acquainted with your family as with ever a one among the Puritans; and that's no trifle to say. I helped your grandfather, the constable, when he lashed the Quaker woman so smartly through the streets of Salem. And it was I that brought your father a pitch-pine knot, kindled at my own hearth, to set fire to an Indian village, in King Philip's war. They were my good friends, both; and many a pleasant walk have we had along this path, and returned merrily after midnight. I would fain be friends with you, for their sake"
>
> (X, 76-77).[6]

This devil subverts Brown's sentimental view of his ancestral past in manner as well as matter; for linked with the evidence of those ancestors' sins is a satiric, parodic mode of expression that reduces Brown's arguments to a child's recitations. It will be no accident that the second devil figure Brown witnesses will appear in the form of the old woman who taught him his catechism; but just as telling is the first devil's striking resemblance to both Brown's father and grandfather.[7] In appearance, as well as theme and tone, this devil mocks Brown's words.

The speaker, too, shows these devilish characteristics; for he can be quite condescending and sarcastic toward his bewildered hero. For example, Brown begins his night experience with the following sentiment about Faith: "'Well; she's a blessed angel on earth; and after this one night, I'll cling to her skirts and follow her to Heaven.'" "With this excellent resolve for the future," responds the speaker in a tone that parodies Brown's naive presumptuousness, "Goodman Brown felt himself justified in making more haste on his present evil purpose." And when, deep within the dark woods, Brown sits down and refuses to go on with the devil, the speaker makes the following damning comment:

> The young man sat a few moments, by the road-side, applauding himself greatly, and thinking with how clear a conscience he should meet the minister, in his morning-walk, nor shrink from the eye of good old Deacon Gookin. And what calm sleep would be his, that very night, which was to have been spent so wickedly, but purely and sweetly now, in the arms of Faith! Amidst these pleasant and praiseworthy meditations . . .
>
> (X, 80-81).

Like the urbane devil, the speaker mocks Brown in Brown's own words. The consequence of this technique is a sustained tone of satire in the tale. To cite another example, consider how the speaker describes Brown's initial reactions to the gathering of devils and witches in the woods:

> Either the sudden gleams of light, flashing over the obscure field, bedazzled Goodman Brown, or he recognized a score of the church-members of Salem village, famous for their especial sanctity. . . . But, irreverently consorting with these grave, reputable, and pious people, these elders of the church, these chaste dames and dewy virgins, there were men of dissolute lives and women of spotted fame, wretches given over to all mean and filthy vice, and suspected even of horrid crimes. It was strange to see, that the good shrank not from the wicked, nor were the sinners abashed by the saints
>
> (X, 85).

Here the speaker combines his omniscient point of view that allows him to describe Brown's feelings about events with a viewpoint that imitates Brown's literal process of observation. His "either . . . or" device dramatizes Brown's dilemma as a participant in the events of the tale; but, at the same time, his melodramatic, almost mawkish sentiments are satiric comments on Brown's moral priggishness: his naive desire to see clear-cut divisions in human experience.

The second devilish figure, a boisterous old hag named Goody Cloyse, appears to Brown in the shape of the "very pious and exemplary dame" and "Christian woman," who we are told, "had taught him his catechism." Colloquial in speech, folksy, and something of a gossip (in the nineteenth as well as the seventeenth century meaning of the word) and quarreler, she overflows with a mirthful spirit and mocking wit. The scene in which she appears commences with a pun and verges upon farce as it develops:

> "The devil!" screamed the pious old lady.
>
> "Then Goody Cloyse knows her old friend?" observed the traveller, confronting her, and leaning on his writhing stick.
>
> "Ah, forsooth, and is it your worship, indeed?" cried the good dame. "Yea, truly is it, and in the very image of my old gossip, Goodman Brown, the grandfather of the silly fellow that now is. But—would your worship believe it?—my broomstick hath strangely disappeared, stolen, as I suspect, by that unhanged witch, Goody Cory, and that, too, when I was all anointed with the juice of smallage and cinque-foil and wolf's-bane—"
>
> "Mingled with fine wheat and the fat of a new-born babe," said the shape of old Goodman Brown.
>
> "Ah, your worship knows the receipt," cried the old lady, cackling aloud. "So, as I was saying, being all ready for the meeting, and no horse to ride on, I made up my mind to foot it; for they tell me, there is a nice young man to be taken into communion to-night . . ."
>
> (X, 79).

The old hag's opening exclamation works as an ironic counter to Brown's repeated invocations of "Faith"; indeed, the pervasive tone of her remarks mocks Brown's sentimental expectations of how "pious" older women should conduct themselves, while retaining the childish diction associated with religious persons in their dotage. If the first devil acts as her foil on this occasion, then the speaker participates in the jesting as well, repeatedly referring to her as the "pious old lady" and "good dame" in blatantly ironic contexts and mimicking Brown's point of view when he introduces her as "mumbling some indistinct words, a prayer, doubtless. . . ." Later at the witch meeting, the speaker will become something of a gossip himself. "Some affirm," he tells us as though he were repeating a rumor, "that the lady of the governor was there. At least, there were high dames well known to her. . . ." And, when the shape of Martha Carrier appears, he gives vent to a sudden outburst of devilish spite: "A rampant hag was she!"

Going to the devil, in "Young Goodman Brown," means not just encountering certain unsettling insights into the terrible and the grotesque in human experience, but also confronting a mocking, satiric attitude toward such revelations. The devils who haunt Brown's woods know how to laugh; and there is a kernel of devilish wisdom in the first figure's words to Brown during "a fit of irrepressible mirth": "'Ha!ha!ha!' shouted he, again and again; then composing himself, 'Well, go on, Goodman Brown, go on; but pr'y thee, don't kill me with laughing!'" Could Brown learn to laugh, that is, could he learn to take an ironic view toward his experience in the Salem woods, then he might well begin to exorcise his tormenting devils. He will never be able to dismiss their words, but he might learn to live with them. Perhaps the best commentary on this aspect of the tale is to be found in a passage written two decades later in *The Scarlet Letter.* Commenting on Dimmesdale's vigils before the looking glass, in which "diabolic shapes" grin and mock at the bewildered minister and "spectral thoughts" assume life-like form, the speaker of the Romance points out that, although such fantasies are "the truest and most substantial things" to Dimmesdale, and although their effect is to steal "the pith and substance out of whatever realities" surround him, nevertheless: "Had he once found power to smile, and wear a face of gayety, there would have been no such man!" (I, 145-146). Certainly in both "Young Goodman Brown" and *The Scarlet Letter,* the speaker is on hand to show the reader that such laughter is possible; indeed, that an amused, ironic attitude toward the darker aspects of human experience is an accommodation of art to the recognition of the perverse and the demonic.

The third devil figure, who appears to Brown at the witches' meeting, is more grave and formal than his predecessors, though he shares their disposition for mocking wit. "With reverence be it spoken," the speaker tells us, "the figure bore no slight similitude, both in garb and manner, to some grave divine of the New-England churches." And this devil addresses Brown "in a deep and solemn tone, almost sad, with its despairing awfulness, as if his once angelic nature could yet mourn for our miserable race." Nonetheless, the incongruity between dark matter and light, ironic manner is apparent in his sermonic form of speech:[8]

> "There . . . are all whom ye have reverenced from youth. Ye deemed them holier than yourselves, and shrank from your own sin, contrasting it with their lives of righteousness, and prayerful aspirations heavenward. Yet, here are they all, in my worshipping assembly! This night it shall be granted you to know their secret deeds; how hoary-bearded elders of the church have whispered wanton words to the young maids of their households; how many a woman, eager for widow's weeds, has given her husband a drink at bed-time, and let him sleep his last sleep in her bosom; how beardless youths have made haste to inherit their fathers' wealth; and how fair damsels—blush not, sweet ones!—have dug little graves in the garden, and bidden me, the sole guest, to an infant's funeral . . ."
>
> (X, 87).

The speaker, too, affects a reflective, mock-reverential pose. His appeal to "the sacred truths of our religion" at the conclusion of the tale, as well as such asides to the reader as: "With reverence be it spoken . . ." (cited above), express a mock-pious attitude; but the speaker can also affect a graver, moralistic tone. "The fiend in his own shape is less hideous," he tells us as, maddened with despair, Brown rushes through the forest, "than when he rages in the breast of man." Like the devils in the tale, the speaker is something of a chameleon, assuming now an amused, satiric tone of voice, now a graver, moralistic seriousness.

III

The speaker in "Young Goodman Brown" bears, then, a striking resemblance to the devil figures in the tale. He shares with them an ironic, parodic mode that ranges from boisterous laughter, to subtle, amused satire, to mock-reverential reflectiveness. In manner, as well as matter, the devils subvert Brown's naive notions; and the speaker is on hand to support their designs. Indeed, the speaker's mocking attitude is directed not just toward Brown, but toward the conventions of Romance as well. "And Faith, as the wife was aptly named . . . ," he comments in the opening lines of the tale, countering his allegoric appeal with an amused detachment toward the very process of allegory. "But the only thing about him, that could be fixed upon as remarkable," he tells his reader when introducing the first devil figure, "was his staff, which bore the likeness of a great black snake, so curiously wrought, that it might almost be seen to twist and wriggle itself, like a living serpent. This, of course, must have been an ocular deception, assisted by the uncertain light." Throughout the tale the speaker will present his reader traditional emblems like the serpentine staff, but will do so in a teasing manner. Affecting a naive pose, so that he appears an inquisitive, unsophisticated spectator of events, he mimics Brown's perspective. Yet his commonsense observations have a sarcastic resonance to them, reinforced by such ironic qualifiers as "of course," "doubtless," "in truth," and "perhaps." Like the devil figures in the tale, the speaker feigns a Brown-like innocence as he satirically mocks such credulity.

Brown's complacent faith in saintly ancestors and angelic wives, as well as a moral order that reflects a clear-cut segregation between good and evil, makes him an inviting target for the devils' satire. Behind this attack on Brown lies Hawthorne's own burlesque on certain conventions of authorship in the 1830's: the attitude, for example, that historical romance should suppress those aspects of the past which, in Rufus Choate's words, "chills, shames, disgusts us," while accommodating "the show of things to the desires and needs of the immortal, moral nature,"[9] and, for another example, the cult of "Heaven, Home, and Mother"[10] preached by the scribbling women Hawthorne damned in 1855. For Brown acts as a determined sentimentalist throughout his adventure, fleeing from the unpleasant aspects of his past and his home into pat, reassuring morals whenever he can. The opening scene of the tale dramatizes this pattern well.

> "Dearest heart," whispered [Faith], softly and rather sadly, when her lips were close to [Brown's] ear, "pr'y thee, put off your journey until sunrise, and sleep in your own bed to-night. A lone woman is troubled with such dreams and such thoughts, that she's afeard of herself, sometimes. Pray, tarry with me this night, dear husband, of all nights in the year!"

"My love and my Faith," replied young Goodman Brown, "of all nights in the year, this one night must I tarry away from thee. . . . What, my sweet, pretty wife, dost thou doubt me already, and we but three months married!"

"Then, God bless you!" said Faith, with the pink ribbons, "and may you find all well when you come back."

"Amen!" cried Goodman Brown. "Say thy prayers, dear Faith, and go to bed at dusk, and no harm will come to thee"

(X, 74-75).

Though Faith's manner is coy and playful, her words reveal a deeper, more unsettling aspect of her character. A "lone woman," "troubled with such dreams and such thoughts, that she's afeard of herself, sometimes," she seems to want Brown to remain at home to protect her from experiencing facets of herself with which she is uncomfortable. Her parting words to her husband show a troubled resignation and sound more like a challenge than a blessing. Brown's responses show his reluctance to scrutinize his wife's troubled words and puzzling tone. In leaving behind "a blessed angel on earth" for a flirtation with evil in the night woods, Brown seems to hope to evade a problematic moment in his marriage; but in the woods he will be forced to confront unpleasant aspects of his wife and himself as he encounters the dark words and unsettling visions of the devils. Behind these mocking antagonists stands the skeptical figure of the author's persona, mocking such pretensions about life and literature. This "devil in manuscript," like his counterparts in the tale, combines a tragic perspective with a satiric wit, converting "gloom" into demonic delight: the delight of writing "hell-fired" satires like "Young Goodman Brown."

Notes

1. From a letter dated 13 March 1821 from Hawthorne to his mother. See Julian Hawthorne, *Nathaniel Hawthorne and His Wife; A Biography* (Boston: Osgood, 1885), I, 108.

2. From a letter dated January, 1855, from Hawthorne to William D. Ticknor. See Caroline Ticknor, *Hawthorne and His Publisher* (Boston: Houghton, Mifflin, 1913), p. 141.

3. *Hawthorne and His Publisher,* p. 142, from a letter from Hawthorne to Ticknor dated February, 1855.

4. From a letter dated 4 February 1850 from Hawthorne to Horatio Bridge. See Bridge, *Personal Recollections of Nathaniel Hawthorne* (New York: Harper, 1893), pp. 111-112.

5. The following studies of "Young Goodman Brown" have most influenced this approach to the tale. Curtis Dahl's "The Devil is a Wise One," *Cithara,* 6 (May 1967), 52-58, makes the well-taken point that the devil can often be a spokesman in Hawthorne's tales for the author's own subtle and paradoxical ideas. R. H. Fogle's two studies of the tale discuss its "light

and idealizing" tone, as well as its elements of understatement and parody. See "Ambiguity and Clarity in Hawthorne's 'Young Goodman Brown,'" *New England Quarterly,* 18 (December 1945), 448-465, and "Weird Mockery: An Element of Hawthorne's Style," *Style,* 2 (Fall 1968), 191-202. Sheldon W. Liebman contributes to the discussion of Hawthorne's narrative mode in "The Reader in 'Young Goodman Brown,'" *Nathaniel Hawthorne Journal 1975* (Englewood, Co.: Microcard Editions, 1975), 156-169. The reader, he finds, is made to be the central character of the story, and Hawthorne's narrative technique works to put him in Brown's place. Indirect but nonetheless important sources for this discussion are Taylor Stoehr's "'Young Goodman Brown' and Hawthorne's Theory of Mimesis," *Nineteenth-Century Fiction,* 23 (March 1969), 393-412, and Darrel Abel's "Black Glove and Pink Ribbon: Hawthorne's Metonymic Symbols," *New England Quarterly,* 42 (June 1969), 163-180. For writers like Hawthorne, writes Stoehr, "correspondences of dream and reality are to a great extent problems of verbal imagination, referential language, and literary mimesis." The tale, from this perspective, is "peculiarly about itself, about the nature of belief in imagined realities, and about the status of such realities."

6. All quotations from Hawthorne's fiction are from *The Centenary Edition of the Works of Nathaniel Hawthorne,* eds. William Charvat et al. (Columbus, Ohio: Ohio State University Press, 1962-). References to longer passages are identified by volume and page numbers.

7. "Still, they might have been taken for father and son," the speaker tells us, referring to the first devil figure and Brown. Later, a witch in the shape of the woman who taught Brown his catechism will compare this devil to "the very image of . . . Goodman Brown, the grandfather of the silly fellow that now is."

8. Fogle makes the following comment on this passage: "The difference between matter and manner is great, considering that the matter is lust, murder most foul, and possibly abortion. There is a ceremonious gallantry, along with an indulgent chiding, in 'fair damsels—blush not, sweet ones.' Girls will be girls, and a very entertaining circumstance it is, too." See "Weird Mockery: An Element of Hawthorne's Style," p. 199.

9. Quoted from extracts of Rufus Choate's 1833 oration, "The Importance of Illustrating New-England History by a Series of Romances Like the Waverly Novels," reprinted in Neal Frank Doubleday's *Hawthorne's Early Tales, A Critical Study* (Durham, N. C.: Duke University Press, 1972), p. 25. See especially Doubleday's discussion of literary theory and Hawthorne's practice in the "Age of Scott," pp. 18-26.

10. See Herbert Ross Brown's discussion of Richardson and the "triumph of the novel" in America in *The Sentimental Novel in America, 1789-1860* (New York: Pageant Books, 1940), pp. 3-51.

Terence J. Matheson (essay date 1982)

SOURCE: "The Devil and Philip Traum: Twain's Satiric Purposes in *The Mysterious Stranger*," in *Markham Review*, Vol. 12, Fall, 1982, pp. 5-11.

[*In the following essay, Matheson concentrates on Mark Twain's ironic treatment of Satan in* The Mysterious Stranger.]

It is now generally known that the version of Mark Twain's *The Mysterious Stranger* familiar to most readers is the product of considerable editorial liberties taken by the author's literary executor, Albert Bigelow Paine, and his publisher Frederick A. Duneka, who worked extensively on Twain's unfinished manuscripts in order to create a marketable product. Paine and Duneka, it has been proved,[1] were responsible for deleting large sections from the original, adding material of their own, and in general changing the text to produce a work wherein the author's original purposes have been somewhat obscured. Given this, it is not surprising that many critics have turned to events from Twain's later life to provide them with possible clues as to the work's meaning, to say nothing of Twain's purpose in writing it. Unfortunately, what has emerged from this approach is a generally-held but untenable assumption that, since Twain's final years were full of suffering and personal misfortune, his views and those of the totally pessimistic, bitter and cynical Philip Traum must be virtually identical, and that given this, neither Traum nor the boys he appears to befriend should be interpreted ironically. Wendell Glick is typical of most critics in "feeling that Twain is unabashedly using Satan as his *redacteur*."[2] To Glick, Satan is obviously Twain's "mouthpiece," as he is his "spokesman" to Coleman Parsons,[3] serving as a source of information the veracity of which we are not supposed to question. He is a "deity" to E. S. Fussell,[4] "a supernatural spectator"[5] to Henry Nash Smith, "a force of spiritual . . . innocence charged with divine-like creative power"[6] to Stanley Brodwin, a "Self-controlled Gentleman of the Southwestern tradition"[7] to Kenneth Lynn: anything, it seems, other than simply the Devil himself.

Critics have not been blind to the many inconsistencies in the philosophy and arguments expressed by Twain's Satan, but when examined, they have been dismissed simply as proof of the author's declining powers. To Albert E. Stone Jr., such weaknesses in Satan's arguments say more about Twain's lack of skill than anything else, any contradictions within Satan's account of man merely mirroring "the contradictions of Twain's own tortured mind."[8] At one point, commenting on the arguments Satan presents on behalf of determinism, Stone shrewdly observes that his deterministic assertions contradict his earlier remarks about man's freedom to choose between right and wrong. However, even though Stone sees this as typical of "many such ambiguities," he can only conclude that this proves the work to be "the end-product of a tired mind grappling with ideas foreign or inaccessible to it."[9]

It is surprising that critics such as Stone have been so disinclined to appreciate *The Mysterious Stranger* in a manner more flattering to Twain. Once we are prepared to regard it as something other than a confused piece by a confused man, and stop placing so much importance on our knowledge that Twain's final years were unhappy, it can be seen as a tale of considerable ironic and satiric complexity. Dismal though Twain's last decade undoubtedly was, it is presumptuous to assume that he himself was in a state of continuous despondency, or that even if he were, it would produce in him a pessimism as transparently simplistic as that voiced by one of his created characters. While a good deal of what Satan says regarding human nature is undeniably true—what sensitive person has not, on occasion, felt as much when confronted with examples of human cruelty and evil?—we must not make the mistake of taking Satan's observations out of their literary context, or of placing them in isolation. Unfinished though *The Mysterious Stranger* may have been, it was still conceived by its author as a literary work and must be appreciated as such. Once we look at it in this way, we immediately see there are other events in the work which lead us to a different and more complex vision of human nature, a vision which, when set against the pessimistic position taken by Satan, goes far toward nullifying its effectiveness and force.

In discussing the various ways we determine when irony is present, Wayne Booth in *A Rhetoric of Irony* has observed that "If a speaker betrays ignorance or foolishness that is 'simply incredible', the odds are comparatively high that the author, in contrast, knows what he is doing."[10] Later, Booth adds that the likelihood irony is present is logically apt to increase in proportion to the number of suspected ironic situations encountered. Given this, it is indeed difficult not to regard the beginning of *The Mysterious Stranger* as heavily ironic, for the opening pages are especially rich in such clues. A plethora of sleep imagery is initially used to describe the setting:

> Yes, Austria was far from the world, and asleep, and our village was in the middle of that sleep, being in the middle of Austria. It drowsed in peace in the deep privacy of a hilly and woodsy solitude where news from the world hardly ever came to disturb its dreams, and was infinitely content.[11]

Everywhere the atmosphere is soporific and sluggish, suggesting dullness, complacency, and smug, unused intellects. Though it is 1590 (or 1702, as originally conceived) Austria is still in the "Middle Ages" which Twain defines as the "Age of Faith" or, in this sense, credulity, at least a full century behind the times and promising "to remain so forever" (3). In short, not only are the inhabitants of this region intellectually asleep, they are uneducable as well. Not surprisingly, the boys are "not overmuch pestered with schooling" (4), but are encouraged to remain docile and respectful of their superiors.

Booth elsewhere comments that "we are alerted [to irony] whenever we notice an unmistakable conflict between the beliefs expressed" by a character or narrator "and the beliefs we hold *and suspect the author of holding.*"[12] Any look at Theodor Fischer, Twain's narrator, reveals him as a person whose naivete and gullibility are beyond dispute, and just as surely suggests his credibility is extremely suspect. By presenting us with a narrator who, it is immediately evident from his opening statements, is easily duped, Twain increases the likelihood that we will see the subsequent encounter between Theodor and Satan ironically, and not simply as a straightforward transfer of knowledge from a wise and benevolent being to an ignorant but responsive and sensitive one. For that matter, Theodor is so gullible it is hard to imagine how this credulous fool could be respected sufficiently by readers ever to have been taken seriously in the first place. Theodor, it will be recalled, accepted without hesitation the premise that "knowledge was not good for the common people" (4), and in so doing reveals an uncritical readiness to subscribe to beliefs which our experience tells us are patently false. Elsewhere, when telling us of Father Adolf's self-professed, direct encounter with the Devil, Theodor offers as proof the fact that "on occasion [Adolf] quarreled with the enemy, and intrepidly threw his bottle at him; and there, upon the wall of his study, was the ruddy splotch where it struck and broke" (5). The ruddiness of the splotch strongly suggests Adolf was quite likely drunk at the time, but this does not seem to occur to naive Theodor. Surely such examples prepare us to see Twain's narrator ironically, as a person always predisposed to accept teachings of *anyone* he believes to be his superior, regardless of that person's moral worth or merit.

Many other examples of irony can be found in the opening pages. The name of the town—Eseldorf, or Assville—tells us much about the intellectual capacities of its citizens, as far as Twain is concerned. That Theodor is the son of one of Assville's leading residents is similarly revealing. Nor would readers even passingly familiar with Twain's thought have trouble recognizing the irony implicit in Theodor's role as a typical Catholic of the Middle Ages who believes everything the priest tells him, given that Twain's "attitude toward the Middle Ages, particularly toward Catholicism, was one of almost undisguised contempt."[13] But Theodor's awe of and respect for the transparently hypocritical and pharisaic Father Adolf also points to a boy whose capacity to distinguish right from wrong is disturbingly minimal; he is not simply a harmless, comic naif. Having been encouraged all his life to live a mindless existence, his capacity for discriminating moral analysis has been all but completely blunted. For example, though vaguely disturbed by certain aspects of Father Adolf, and capable of pity for the kindly and loving Father Peter—obviously the one honorable, intelligent and decent man in

the village—Theodor has no ability to act on the basis of this knowledge, let alone see precisely wherein the two priests are evil and good, respectively. Clearly, this narrator, who believes it was "just and right" (60) to burn young girls suspected of being witches, plainly resents but does not oppose the community's ostracism of Marget and Father Peter (who he knows are innocent of stealing the money), throws stones against his will at people suspected of witchcraft, etc.—clearly he is many removes from earlier Twain narrators such as Huck Finn. It is doubtful that Theodor Fischer would ever decide to "go to Hell" on behalf of a friend.[14]

These and other examples compel us to view Theodor ironically, and to observe the effect the Mysterious Stranger has on him with considerable suspicion. But what of the Stranger himself? First, in order that Satan be at all convincing as a tempter, Twain must present his arguments as specious; he cannot be simply a comic Devil, or the underlying purpose of the encounter would be lost on the reader. However, lest we take him too seriously, Twain inserts many clues (especially in the opening pages) to show us we are intended to view him ironically as well. For example, Satan initially creates fire for the boys, which might in itself liken him to Prometheus. However, immediately after, he turns water to ice. The combination of fire and ice cannot help but bring to mind Milton's Hell, to say nothing of Dante's Satan ensconced in ice, and suggests he may not be the benevolent angel he claims to be. But surely Twain's choice of name for his "superior" being is the most obvious indication of his true nature. Though he attempts to reassure the boys he is the Devil's nephew, and that his uncle is "the only member of [the family] that has ever sinned'" (15)—which incidentally contradicts his later claim that angels are "'not able to commit'" (16) sin—we can neither remain oblivious to the traditional associations the name "Satan" carries with it, nor can we assume that Twain chose perversely to ignore these implications. Coleman Parsons has demonstrated convincingly that on many occasions Twain expressed both outrage at the arbitrariness of the Old Testament God and sympathy for "the insulted and injured Satan."[15] But, though undoubtedly Twain used Satan sympathetically and more straightforwardly in a work such as "Letters from the Earth," this would in no way prevent him from using the character ironically in another. Had Twain *not* meant us to view his mysterious stranger ironically, it does not make sense that he would assign him a name that, from earliest times, has carried with it negative connotations—Satan is, after all, the Father of Lies—connotations with which Twain would have been perfectly familiar, and then go out of his way to present him in a dubious light. One must not forget that Twain was at perfect liberty to do whatever he liked with his characters and situations. Had he wished his readers to respect Satan as a character and accept his views without irony, he could easily have called him by any other name, or could have presented him to us sympathetically; instead, he chose the one name which he knew carried with it connotations of evil, deception and mendacity. Now, if Satan's name were his only dubious aspect, that is, if he were in all other respects a sympathetic character, we could perhaps agree that Twain had chosen the name simply to emphasize his character's freedom from arbitrary social convention. But Twain goes out of his way to present *this* Satan as also cruel and unfeeling, incapable of love or kindness in any easily recognizable form. Several undeniable examples of Satan's cruelty are presented, one of which—the destruction of the little people—ironically occurs precisely at the moment he says he cannot sin:

> Satan reached out his hand and crushed the life out of them with his fingers, threw them away, wiped the red from his fingers on his handkerchief, and went on talking where he left off: "We cannot do wrong; neither have we any disposition to do it, for we do not know what it is."
>
> (16)

Later, during the funeral of the little men, the sound "of the weeping and praying [significantly] began to annoy" him, and he "took the heavy board seat out of our swing and brought it down and mashed all those people into the earth just as if they had been flies, and went on talking just the same" (17). Plainly, this Satan has been made hard to like. Indeed, throughout the work Satan's contact with others invariably causes sorrow, despair or destruction for those concerned. At no point do people ever genuinely benefit from their association with him, as far as we can see. But, though Theodor even seems to realize all this, however dimly—at one point he pleads with him to "stop making people unhappy" (77)—he has from birth been taught never to question his superiors, or to criticize anyone in a position of authority. Appalled though he may be at Satan's cruelty, because Satan appears aristocratic, so, Theodor reasons, he must also be "superior"; as such, everything Satan says must be in turn true. Blinded by Satan's impressive displays of magic and wit, he fails to see that anyone so unfeeling should not be trusted implicitly. Twain's point, of course, is that Theodor has been won over by Satan's "new and good clothes," his "winning face," and the "fatal music of his voice" (18)—that is, his polish—just those superficial qualities one would expect shallow and gullible peasants to be impressed by.

We readers are meant to see an entirely different Satan. There is ample evidence that Philip Traum *is* the Devil of popular mythology, out to "damn" the boys by causing them to despair. With no one present capable of challenging him, Satan launches easily into his attack on man, never failing to speak of the human race in a debasing way that made Theodor

> seem sorrowfully trivial, and the creature of the day, and such a short and paltry day, too. And he didn't say anything to raise up your drooping pride—no, not a word. He always spoke of men in the same old indifferent way—just as one speaks of bricks and manure-piles and such things; you could see that they were of no consequence to him, one way or the other.
>
> (25)

Twain, of course, did not seriously adhere to Satan's belief that "'Man is [only] a museum of diseases, a home of

impurities'" (26). There is much evidence that, while he may have agreed with Satan on certain points, his own vision of human nature was more complex. In short, both Theodor's ignorance *and* Satan's pessimism are satirized throughout *The Mysterious Stranger,* and it is only when we realize Twain's satiric attack is taking place on these two fronts does the full worth of the work emerge.

Satan's campaign to drive the boys to despair takes place in three stages. First, he tries to convince them of man's utter worthlessness by showing that nothing man does can be anything but vile; secondly, he shows them through sophisticated but inherently-flawed arguments that man's moral sense is ironically the principal cause of evil; and finally, he forces them to concede that man is powerless, due to the presence of inexorable deterministic forces, to meliorate his miserable condition.

But as Stone and others have seen, if we are at the mercy of a universe which is essentially fatalistic,[16] then the contempt Satan earlier heaped upon us for our viciousness can hardly be justified, since morality, as Twain well knew, is not operational in a world where free choice is nonexistent. That Twain simply could not have been blind to this—the very fact that it *is* so obvious—should lead us to see that for Twain Satan's arguments are not meant to be taken seriously in themselves. For that matter, that he can abandon logic virtually at will and still impress Theodor and his friends, says much about the limited intellects of his pliable pupils and shows us how easily the ignorant can be impressed and led into error.

For example, when Satan speaks so disparagingly of the "moral sense," the success of his argument rests almost entirely on the fact that Theodor "had but a dim idea of what the Moral Sense was" (26). Only vaguely aware of what it is, Theodor is in no position to debate Satan, much less require that he define his terms when he himself is so unsure of his own understanding of them. It goes without saying that when Theodor confesses ignorance of a basic ethical term the average reader would have little trouble with, there can be no longer any doubt about the low level of his learning and intelligence. But Twain does not stop there. Not only is Theodor ignorant; even when told what the moral sense is, he has no idea *why* such a faculty is valuable to man, and must ask Father Peter.

Peter defines the term as we would expect, as "'the faculty which enables us to distinguish good from evil'" (33). But even with Peter's help, Theodor is only slightly less befuddled. Though disappointed (because he dimly expected a definition that would make sense of Satan's odd use of the term) and embarrassed (with good reason, in his very need to ask Peter such a question), in his stupidity Peter's definition does "not remind [him] of anything further to say" (34), as well it should. Where a more intelligent person might easily have gone on from there to discuss Satan's cryptic use of the term with Father Peter, Theodor, ever unused to asking critical questions, simply leaves.

That Twain was deeply concerned with the prevalence of such ignorance is evident from the fact that Theodor is far from being the only gullible person in Eseldorf. Seppi and Nikolaus, Ursula, even Marget, are all easily won over. Ursula is an especially easy prey to the cynical Satan. When shown that Agnes (the name means "sacred") the cat is lucky, Agnes quickly changes spiritual allegiance, begins to refer to Satan as her "'dear master and benefactor'" (44) and "kissed his hand, over and over again. . . . In her heart she probably believed it was a witch-cat and an agent of the Devil [which of course it is!]; but no matter" (44). For his part, while listening to Satan impress Marget and Ursula, Theodor fails to see anything unusual in an angel telling "a good many lies" (49), because after all, "They do not know right from wrong; I knew this," he adds with a straight face, "because I remembered what he had said about it" (49). Why Satan would feel the necessity to lie in the first place never crosses his mind. Furthermore, that Satan could freely lie to others does not shake the gullible Theodor's belief that all Satan has told *him* is nevertheless true. Surely by this point in the work, though Theodor can see nothing wrong in accepting Satan's every utterance, the reader should be viewing him with considerable reservation. Lest there be any lingering doubt as regards Satan's true identity and purpose, Twain has him mention to Marget and Ursula, in the midst of a discussion of his "uncle," that "he hoped some day to bring [Ursula] and his uncle together" (49), a comment that makes even Theodor shudder.

In spite of all this, Theodor's faith in man is quickly destroyed. Satan first shows him a torture chamber and a workhouse, to both of which he responds in horror. He then presents Theodor with an argument on behalf of the ubiquity of human depravity, based on the examples he has presented. Though Theodor finds Satan's conclusions irrefutable, the reader should have no trouble seeing them as specious and glib. First, if we agree that Father Peter's definition of the Moral Sense was basically correct—that the term refers to an individual's sensitivity to moral issues—then the examples Satan is presenting to Theodor are not demonstrations of man's moral sense at work at all, but precisely the reverse: the torturers and workhouse proprietors are plainly examples of human moral *insensitivity*. Obviously, these are people who lack the ability to make meaningful distinctions between right and wrong. Secondly, while such evil undeniably exists, to argue as Satan does, that the perpetration of such atrocities is the direct result of man's possession of a moral sense, is demonstrably absurd. That *we* do not condone the torture of individuals and the evils of the workhouse and are appalled by what we see—or, for that matter, that Theodor is appalled as well—is proof in itself that man is capable of responses that point to a more complex definition of our moral nature than the one suggested by Theodor to Satan. Indeed, the very horror and outrage we feel as we read and reflect sadly that such behavior is, lamentably, all too common, become the proof that other, more humane responses are possible.

Thus, when Satan concludes that "'It is the Moral Sense which teaches the factory proprietors the difference be-

tween right and wrong—you perceive the result'" (53), all he is really showing us is that in the above instances, the moral sense either is not operating at all, or it has manifested itself in a perverted form which others can see as such. To argue as he does that our possession of this faculty leads directly to such acts of cruelty is to ignore or gloss over—as Satan does intentionally, of course—that there can be other, proper ways of reacting in situations which call for a moral response. All Satan has shown Theodor is one of two such possible responses, and a perverse one at that. While it is certain that man's inhuman treatment of his fellows has always been an unfortunate part of the human condition, it does not follow that the presence of such evil precludes the possibility of good, as Satan cunningly implies. We still lay claim to those virtues, the existence of which Satan tries to deny, even when confronted with the spectacle of evil and perverted persons.

Theodor's own moral revulsion becomes the most obvious proof within the work of the existence of those very qualities Satan is trying to get the boy to deny. But in his gullibility, Theodor is powerless to see that he himself is arguably the strongest evidence that Satan's conclusions are less than fair. Though, strictly speaking, terms such as "brutal" or "inhuman" are misnomers as Satan says, the boys fail to see (and Satan is too cunning to remind them) that Theodor's anger over Hans Oppert's cruelty to his dog and his pity for the animal are also distinctly human traits. At any rate, it is ridiculous to argue that the dog has a greater "'stock of morals and magnanimities'" (56) and in fact possesses a more highly developed moral sense simply because it is not cruel. When Satan calls the bullock out of the pasture and observes it "'wouldn't drive children mad with hunger and fright and loneliness, and then burn them for confessing to things invented for them which never happened'" (61-62) he ignores that the bullock would do no *good* either. To argue thus would force us to conclude that rocks, stones and trees possess greater virtue, and are in a sense morally better than man, simply because they do no visible harm. Crucial to the success of Satan's argument, of course, is that he "never had a kind word for" (62) the human race.

Many other untenable statements follow. When Satan tells Theodor that "'In most cases . . . man's life is about equally divided between happiness and unhappiness. When this is not the case the unhappiness predominates—always; never the other'" (78), we can only marvel at the enormity of such an oversimplification, and note that proof is conspicuously not supplied. Similarly, when Satan claims that we are to the gods as is a spider to an elephant, because an angel's capacity for love is "'limited to his own august order'" (81), we have only Satan's unsupported word for it that this is so. Even if true, life would only become meaningless to childish people like Frau Brandt who need a belief in direct Providence to sustain them, and who fall into despair whenever life cannot be reduced to such simplistic dimensions.

Satan's unconvincing defense of determinism follows. Theodor, of course, is unable to challenge his mentor, and can only observe that "It seemed so dismal" (83). But, lest we take this seriously, Twain presents Satan at his most inconsistent here: for, immediately after telling Theodor the future cannot be altered, he proceeds to alter it in several cases, thus rendering anything he has said about the all-powerful nature of the forces of fate null and void. For his part, Theodor is completely convinced, but can only conclude that such makes man "'a prisoner for life'" (83), failing to see that if so, man need not bear any burden of guilt for his acts. If anything, Theodor should be breathing a sigh of relief at this point; instead, he lapses even more into a despair that the reader should have no trouble seeing is simply unwarranted.

Throughout this work, Twain inserts much evidence to confute Satan's purely negative assessment of man. Sleepy though Eseldorf may be, it is still sprinkled with kind and decent people. Seppi, for instance, appears as a genuinely sensitive figure, whose "voice trembled with pity and anger" (54) when speaking of the cruel Hans Oppert. Father Peter is "good and truthful" (5), Marget is "lovely," and William Meidling displays courageous loyalty to them in the face of adverse public opinion. Nicky's heroic act of self-sacrifice is, of course, the most dramatic example of such decency. When told Nikolaus will die, Theodor and Seppi are understandably grieved, but ironically fail to see that their capacity to feel such grief reveals another distinctly human characteristic, and one of which we can be proud. For that matter, in their grief they also fail to see in the very circumstances of his death—dying in the act of rescuing a drowning girl—positive proof that man is something other than the loathsome creature of Satan's definition.

The boys are similarly unable to see anything editorially-slanted in Satan's subsequent parade of history, which carefully shows man at his depraved worst. Plainly, there is more to the Roman Empire than Caesar's invasion of Britain, more to the entire Christian era than war alone. Concluding his history lesson with an "evil chuckle" the ironic significance of which is lost on the boys, Satan summarizes his "findings," claiming that history shows us we "'gain nothing; you always come out where you went in. For a million years the race has gone on monotonously propagating itself and monotonously reperforming this dull nonsense—to what end? No wisdom can guess!'" (111-112). Needless to say, the force of this argument is entirely dependent on our acceptance of the panorama of futility we have just seen.

The lesson over, the boys are offered and drink "heavenly" wine, in a perverse parody of the communion. As they drink, Seppi wonders if they will enjoy Paradise some day, but receives no answer from Satan, whose silence (given his knowledge of the future) understandably distresses them. Here, Twain is pointing out that in his opinion these well-intentioned but weak-willed boys are "damned" as a result of their uncritical adoration of Satan, their blind respect for authority, and in short, their total lack of self-reliance. It is surely no accident that, immediately after

this scene, Theodor is observed at his most despicable, stoning a woman against his will simply out of fear of offending members of the community.

Finally, Satan proceeds to show the boys that happiness as they understand the term can never be realized, and that given this, only the dead or the insane can ever be "happy." As if to prove this point, he drives Father Peter mad, thus creating an insane but happy person. When questioned by Theodor on his methods, Satan simply replies by stating that "'No sane man can be happy, for him life is real, and he sees what a fearful thing it is. Only the mad can be happy, and not many of those'" (130). That happiness in Theodor's puerile understanding of the term may be beyond man does not deny the likelihood that more mature forms of fulfillment are possible. In Father Peter's case, there is a third alternative cunningly ignored by Satan—Peter sane *and* free, with the money, acquitted of the charge, his good name intact—which would obviously constitute a happier state of affairs for all concerned. It would, however, tend to undermine the credibility of Satan's pessimistic position, and this he cannot allow. Furthermore, it is very much in Satan's best interest to render Father Peter insane. Peter, it will be recalled, was the one person in Eseldorf "not ignorant and dull" (23) and as such able to challenge Satan intellectually. It is doubtless for this reason Satan took such pains to avoid Father Peter throughout his sojourn in Eseldorf. By destroying Peter's mind Satan effectively removes the one person capable of seeing through his specious arguments. It is easy, then, to see why Peter is rendered insane. But we must not forget that Peter only appears to prove Satan's contention that "sanity and happiness are an impossible combination'" (130); the insane hilarity of Father Peter is not meant to convince the reader as well.

We can certainly agree with Kenneth Lynn that the ending was "a brilliant choice"[17] on Paine's part, even while acknowledging that it does not necessarily represent how Twain himself would have finished the tale.[18] For, though written as a conclusion to a later version of the work, the Mysterious Stranger's final comments relate to so much of the "Eseldorf" material, and in fact make so much more sense when set against the manuscript than they do when read in connection with the rambling and unstructured "Print Shop" version, it is almost inconceivable that Twain did not also have Theodor Fischer and Philip Traum somewhere in the back of his mind when penning this particular exchange. In brief, the conclusion Paine tampered with so extensively (by, among other things, changing the names to make it fit the Eseldorf version) perfectly summarizes everything Satan has been teaching Theodor: life is utterly without meaning, and our only proper response to it can be one of despair. Nor, I think, need we take the narrator's agreement with Satan's solipsism too seriously. For, although Theodor's initial reaction to Satan's revelation is one of "thankfulness" and relief, Satan's subsequent description of the implications of living in a solipsistic universe is, as ever, calculated to induce despair: "In a little while you will be alone in shoreless space, to wander its limitless solitudes, without friend or comrade for-ever. . . . And you are but a *thought*—a vagrant thought, a useless thought, a homeless thought, wandering forlorn among the empty eternities'" (140). Though the naive Theodor sighs a desperate assent—"I knew, and realized, that all he had said was true" (140)—and is left "appalled," there is no reason for us to share his despair, for we have Theodor's own account of life in Eseldorf to counter Satan's dismal philosophical conclusions. There, we saw loy-alty, generosity, and numerous demonstrations of love and self-sacrifice, in short, all those characteristics commonly considered to raise the human condition from the purely vile and sordid. That these qualities are ironically over-looked by a narrator too obtuse to see their significance does not invalidate them or nullify their existence or im-portance. Rather, this more complex picture of human na-ture, coming to us as it does from Twain, far from being untrue, completes the satire by giving us a framework whereby both the uncritical gullibility of Theodor and the pure pessimism of Satan can together be weighed in the balance and be found wanting.

Notes

1. Readers interested in the textual history of *The Mys-terious Stranger* should consult John S. Tuckey's *Mark Twain and Little Satan: The Writing of "The Mysterious Stranger"* (Lafayette: Purdue University Studies, 1963). Also informative is Sholom J. Kahn, *Mark Twain's Mysterious Stranger: A Study of the Manuscript Texts* (Columbia, Missouri: University of Missouri Press, 1978). One problem now facing stu-dents of *The Mysterious Stranger* concerns which text to use when discussing the work. The authorita-tive text, *Mark Twain: The Mysterious Stranger*, ed. with an intro. by William M. Gibson (Berkeley and Los Angeles: University of California Press, 1969), while of great scholarly interest, is not a complete literary work as such, but rather a collection of un-finished manuscripts. The Paine-Duneka version, while lacking Twain's imprimatur, has the advantage of being commonly known. In defending continued discussion of Paine's version, James Cox has argued that Paine did no more than Mrs. Twain had done for her husband's previous work, and that "Paine's post-humous edition of Mark Twain's last work is the closest thing to Mark Twain's intention that we shall ever have"; see *Mark Twain: The Fate of Humor* (Princeton: Princeton University Press, 1966), p. 272. As I hope to demonstrate in this article, I believe Cox's position to be basically correct. At the same time, I have made a point of referring only to mate-rial from Twain's pen. The analysis of *The Mysteri-ous Stranger* which follows is, I think, a fairly accu-rate account of what Twain's intentions were when he first wrote what Gibson entitled, "The Chronicle of Young Satan," intentions which Paine perspica-ciously discerned.

2. "The Epistemological Theme of 'The Mysterious Stranger,'" from *Themes and Directions in American Literature,* ed. Ray B. Browne and Donald Pizer (West Lafayette, Ind.: Purdue University Studies, 1969), p. 144.

3. "The Devil and Samuel Clemens," *Virginia Quar-terly Review,* XXIII (Autumn, 1947), 582-606, rpt. in *Mark Twain's "The Mysterious Stranger" and the Critics,* ed. John S. Tuckey (Belmont, Calif: Wad-sworth Publishing Co., Inc., 1970), p. 158.

4. "The Structural Problem of *The Mysterious Stranger,"* *Studies in Philology,* XLIX (January, 1952), 95-104.

5. *Mark Twain: The Development of a Writer* (Cambridge, Mass.: Harvard University Press, 1962), pp. 185-88, rpt. in *Mark Twain's Mysterious Stranger and the Critics,* p. 192.

6. "Mark Twain's Masks of Satan: The Final Phase," *AL* [*American Literature*], XLV (May, 1973), 206-27.

7. *Mark Twain and Southwestern Humor* (Boston: Little, Brown and Co., 1959), p. 284.

8. *The Innocent Eye: Childhood in Mark Twain's Imagi-nation* (New Haven: Yale University Press, 1970), p. 243.

9. Stone, p. 245.

10. *A Rhetoric of Irony* (Chicago: University of Chicago Press, 1975), p. 57.

11. Mark Twain, *The Mysterious Stranger And Other Stories* (New York: 1922), p. 3. All subsequent refer-ences are to this edition.

12. Booth, p. 73.

13. James Cox, *Mark Twain: The Fate of Humor* (Princeton: Princeton University Press, 1966), p. 261. Cox is actually discussing Twain's *Joan of Arc* when he makes this statement. The best-known work illus-trative of this contempt is doubtless *A Connecticut Yankee,* but the attitude can be found throughout his writing, certainly in the original *Mysterious Stranger* MS.

14. Indeed, Gladys Carmen Bellamy believes that *The Mysterious Stranger* represents Twain's final loss of faith in boys as embodiments of moral strength, in-tegrity and self-reliance, since they now, in her opin-ion, "seem bent on earning the reader's contempt." See *Mark Twain as a Literary Artist* (Norman: Uni-versity of Oklahoma Press, 1950), p. 361.

15. "The Devil and Samuel Clemens," rpt. in *"The Mys-terious Stranger and the Critics,* ed. Tuckey, p. 160.

16. Although Satan appears only to be arguing on behalf of a deterministic universe (one where every event has a cause), he draws fatalistic implications from his argument, namely, that the future is unalterable.

17. *Mark Twain and Southwestern Humor,* p. 284.

18. One may admire Paine's effort without going quite as far as James Cox; see above, fn. 1. At the same time it seems a bit strong to refer to Paine's version as simply an "editorial fraud," as Gibson does. See Gibson, *The Mysterious Stranger,* p.1.

ENGLISH ROMANTICISM: THE SATANIC SCHOOL

Charles E. Robinson (essay date 1970)

SOURCE: "The Devil as Doppelgänger in *The Deformed Transformed*: The Sources and Meaning of Byron's Unfinished Drama," in *Bulletin of the New York Public Library,* Vol. 74, No. 3, March, 1970, pp. 177-202.

[*In the following essay, Robinson probes the Faustian and other sources and thematic implications of the diabolical double in Lord Byron's* The Deformed Transformed.]

Byron's *The Deformed Transformed* is a complex, fragmentary, and uneven drama which has received little critical attention and less praise since its publication in 1824; yet the potential effect of this drama prompted Montague Summers in an unguarded moment to express "infinite regret" that Byron "did not finish the piece, which has a eerie and perhaps unhallowed fascination all its own."[1] Summers undoubtedly praised this drama because of its unorthodox plot containing a pact with the devil, its perplexing incompleteness, its autobiographical revelations, and its indebtedness to Byron's acknowledged sources: Joshua Pickersgill's unbridled Gothic novel, *The Three Brothers* (1803); and Goethe's *Faust, Part I* (1808). But the "fascination" attending *The Deformed Transformed* is manifestly increased when one realizes that Byron's drama was conceived and written and would have been completed under the indirect influence of Percy Bysshe Shelley, that it is a central document for a literary motif transcending continents and centuries, and that it is in fact the "Unwritten Drama of Lord Byron" publicized by Thomas Medwin and Washington Irving in 1835.

Of the three parts of the incomplete *Deformed Transformed,* the first scene of Part I is by far the most imaginative and intense, and for this reason Hermann Varnhagen suggested facetiously that the remainder of the drama had been written by someone else.[2] In this first scene, Arnold, the deformed hero, was rejected by his mother and reminded of his hunchback and lame, cloven foot by his reflection in a fountain. Hated and hating himself, Arnold despaired and attempted suicide, but was deterred by a Mephistophelean "Stranger" who miraculously appeared from the fountain and offered Arnold a new body in order that he could successfully love and be beloved by others.

After engaging a compact with the Stranger, who then raised the bodily forms of Julius Caesar, Alcibiades, Socrates, Antony, Demetrius Poliorcetes, and Achilles from antiquity, Arnold chose the form of Achilles and was transformed into the "unshorn boy of Peleus" and and "Beautiful shadow / Of Thetis's boy."[3] But then the Stranger, transforming himself, cleverly assumed Arnold's rejected and deformed "form," consequently became the "shadow" (I.i.449) or second self of Arnold, and chose to be called Caesar. The protagonist and antagonist in new forms then mounted their coal-black horses and raced to "where the World / Is thickest," to "where there is War / And Woman in activity" (I.i.494-497).

The remainder of the unfinished drama presents Arnold's and Caesar's exploits with "War" and "Woman." The second scene of Part I and the three scenes of Part II describe Arnold and Caesar before and during the Siege and Sack of Rome in 1527. As the Bourbon's gallant knight, Arnold successfully led the besieging army over the walls of Rome, engaged Benvenuto Cellini, who had slain the Bourbon as he ascended the wall, and rescued the Roman beauty, Olimpia, from the despoiling troops in St Peter's. Although Olimpia disdained Arnold's bravery and cast herself down from the Pope's altar in the church, Arnold and Caesar revived her and bore her body from the carnage at the conclusion of Part II. Part III of *The Deformed Transformed* includes only a sixty-seven line choral song which offers virtually no suggestion concerning the future adventures of Arnold, Caesar, and Olimpia. The setting had been changed to a castle in the Apennines, but the plot is advanced no further than the following:

> The wars are over,
>   The spring is come;
> The bride and her lover
>   Have sought their home.

(III.i.1-4)

But in 1901 E. H. Coleridge published from Byron's manuscript a second scene for Part III in which Arnold expressed his jealousy and regret that Olimpia could not love him as he loved her. Noting that the new Achilles would become "jealous of himself under his former figure," Byron was prepared to increase the conflict between Arnold and Caesar, his "former figure."

Of these three parts briefly summarized above, the first scene of Part I reveals an emotional intensity that rivals *Manfred* and *Cain.* This intensity is manifest in Byron's sympathetic portrait of the unloved hunchback, in the Faustian pact between Arnold and Caesar, and in Arnold's glorious transformation, for each of which Byron acknowledged his indebtedness to external influences. But significantly more important for the meaning of *The Deformed Transformed* is what Byron did not acknowledge: his indebtedness to the doppelgänger tradition for his apparently unique portrayal of the Stranger's assumption of Arnold's deformed body. It is this second transformation that not only intensifies the action of the first scene but also imposes a unity on the drama, in that Caesar inseparably accompanied Arnold as a reflection of his former self, that is, as his metamorphic doppelgänger. That Byron was consciously working within the tradition of the double may be demonstrated, but it is first necessary to consider the sources he acknowledged for his unfinished drama.

Byron once confessed to Lady Blessington that *The Deformed Transformed* was "suggested" by his own lameness and by the "rage and mortification" he experienced when his mother ridiculed his "personal deformity."[4] But if Byron sought to purge these feelings of rage and mortification by empathically portraying Arnold's deformities, he also welcomed other reproaches. Shortly after concluding the fragmentary *Deformed Transformed,* Byron offered the following comparison between his own lameness and that of his friend, Henry Fox: "but there is this difference, that *he* appears a halting angel, who has tripped against a star; whilst I am *Le Diable Boiteux,*—a soubriquet, which I marvel that, amongst their various *nominis umbrae,* the Orthodox have not hit upon."[5] Byron, by portraying the diabolical Stranger's assumption of Arnold's deformed body (with both hunchback and cloven foot), was evidently provoking the Orthodox to compare him with the cynical and deformed devil in Le Sage's *Le Diable Boiteux.*

Byron did not mention his own lameness in the prefixed advertisement to *The Deformed Transformed,* but he did acknowledge two literary sources for his drama: "This production is founded partly on the story of a novel called 'The Three Brothers,' published many years ago [1803], from which M. G. Lewis's 'Wood Demon' [sic] was also taken; and partly on the 'Faust' of the great Goethe."[6] *The Three Brothers* was written by Joshua Pickersgill, an author who in 1804 was unknown by his reviewer, and who in 1826 was mistakenly "supposed to have been the late M. G. Lewis."[7] Byron, who may have been introduced to this novel in 1816,[8] borrowed incidents chiefly from its fourth volume, in which the diabolical villain, Julian, recounted the miseries of his former life as Arnaud. Like Byron's Arnold, Pickersgill's Arnaud was a hunchback (he had been wounded and deformed by the banditti at the age of eight) whose parents had rejected him. Unsuccessful in love, depraved in character, yet proud in spirit ("I! I! I! being the utterance everlastingly on his tongue"[9]), Arnaud despaired. Just as Arnold attempted suicide when he saw his reflected ugliness in the fountain or "Nature's mirror" (I.i.47), so also had Arnaud twice attempted to hurl himself from a precipice after a polished broken blade had mirrored his deformity. Unsuccessful in these attempts, Arnaud conjured up Satan who offered the deformed hero a new body. Because *The Three Brothers* is not readily accessible, the central transformation scene (also transcribed by Coleridge in *Poetry* v 473n-474n) is here quoted in full:

> The satanic gaze turned on the side of the cavern heat so powerful, that the clay in the interstices was absumed to an ash, and the flinty rock vitrified into glass pervious to the sight of Arnaud, who saw thereon visions admirable and amazing.

> There passed in liveliest portraiture, the various men distinguished for that beauty and grace, which Arnaud so much desired, that he was ambitious to purchase them with his soul.

> He felt that it was his part to chuse whom he would resemble, yet he remained unresolved, though the spectator of an hundred shades of renown, among which glided by Achilles and Alexander, Alcibiades, and Hephestian: at length appeared the supernatural effigy of a man, whose perfections human artist never could depict or insculp—Demetrius the son of Antigonus. Arnaud's heart heaved quick with preference, and strait he found within his hand the resemblance of a poinard, its point inverted towards his breast. A mere automaton in the hands of the Demon, he thrust the point through his heart, and underwent a painless death.

> During this trance, his spirit metemsychosed from the body of his detestation to that of his admiration: like an infant new-born, that exist without consciousness of that existence, incarnate in each desirable perfection, Arnaud awoke a Julian!

> (IV 347-348)

The power of this scene was not wasted on Byron, for he adopted the substance of it, even to the similar choice of forms offered by the tempter. Yet the character of the Demon was not developed beyond this point, although he was twice seen as an infernal spirit attending Arnaud (called Julian after the transformation). And there is no suggestion in the four volumes that Arnaud was shadowed by his former self. In fact, Arnaud's rejected and deformed body had been preserved in a grotto in the Forest of the Pines.

Since Byron mentioned in his advertisement that Monk Lewis's unpublished drama, "The Wood Daemon" (1807), was also influenced by *The Three Brothers,* he may have read this drama in its published and revised form, a "Grand Musical Romance" with the title *One O'Clock! or, The Knight and the Wood Daemon* (1811).[10] Lewis acknowledged his indebtedness to Pickersgill's novel in his advertisement to the first edition, and the parallels between the two works are quite obvious. Hardyknute, Lord of Holstein and villain of the drama, was "born deformed" (like Byron's Arnold, but unlike Pickersgill's Arnaud) and engaged "a dreadful compact with the Wood Daemon," Sangrida, by which he was transformed: "She chained success to my footsteps; she rendered me invulnerable in battle; she endowed me with perpetual youth and health; and she cast over my person a magic charm to dazzle all female eyes, and seduce all female hearts. I was rich, potent, beloved, and wretched! for, oh! to that fatal bond was annexed a penalty."[11] This fatal "penalty" was Monk Lewis's adaptation of Arnaud's desire for a second transformation in *The Three Brothers*: seeking a new form to elude detection on the first anniversary of his initial transformation, Arnaud promised Satan to kill the first person he saw; similarly, Hardyknute had sacrificed for eight years a young child on the anniversary of his transformation (the "seventh of each revolving August" at one o'clock) in order to maintain his transformed body. In the climax of Lewis's drama, Hardyknute failed to fulfill the bargain the ninth time and forfeited his soul to Sangrida, the Wood Daemon. Yet, like the Demon in *The Three Brothers*, Sangrida was virtually undeveloped, did not assume Hardyknute's body, and did not influence Byron's characterization of Caesar in *The Deformed Transformed*.

The final influence Byron acknowledged for his drama was Goethe's *Faust*, translations of which he read in January 1822, just before he began *The Deformed Transformed*. Notwithstanding E. H. Coleridge's statements to the contrary, the dating of *The Deformed Transformed* can be determined, for Byron himself prefixed "Pisa J[anuar]y 1822" to the first page of his manuscript.[12] Although Byron probably did not begin this new drama until after he had completed *Werner* by January 20 1822, he had written part, if not all, of the first scene "some days after" February 6 1822, by which time he had seen Southey's "pretended reply"[13] to his earlier attack on Southey in the Appendix to *The Two Foscari*. The authority for this dating is Thomas Medwin's account of the following dialogue between Byron and Shelley in Pisa:

> Some days after these remarks [Byron's reaction to Southey's reply], on calling on him one morning, he produced 'The Deformed Transformed.' Handing it to Shelley, as he was in the habit of doing his daily compositions, he said:
>
> "Shelley, I have been writing a *Faustish* kind of drama: tell me what you think of it."
>
> After reading it attentively, Shelley returned it.
>
> "Well," said Lord Byron, "how do you like it?"
>
> "Least," replied he, "of any thing I ever saw of yours. It is a bad imitation of 'Faust;' and besides, there are two entire lines of Southey's in it."
>
> Lord Byron changed colour immediately, and asked hastily what lines? Shelley repeated,
>
> 'And water shall see thee,
> And fear thee, and flee thee.'
>
> "They are in 'The Curse of Kehama.'"
>
> His Lordship, without making a single observation, instantly threw the poem into the fire. He seemed to feel no chagrin at seeing it consume—at least his countenance betrayed none, and his conversation became more gay and lively than usual. Whether it was hatred of Southey, or respect for Shelley's opinions, which made him commit an act that I considered a sort of suicide, was always doubtful to me.[14]

Although Medwin has often been accused of fabrication here, Edward Trelawny confirmed the substance of Medwin's report: "I was in the room—*half a sheet* of M.S. of The Deformed Transformed was given Shelley to read—which had been written in the night—& that half which was distroyed [sic]."[15] Byron, then, did not destroy the manuscript of *The Deformed Transformed*, but he evidently did not continue this "*Faustish* kind of drama" until

some months later. Byron was preoccupied in February 1822 with the adverse critical reception of *Cain* and with Southey's attacks on him; and the Dragoon affair in March, the death of Allegra in April, the writing of Cantos VI and VII of *Don Juan* from April to June,[16] and Shelley's death in July were more than enough to prevent his continuation of *The Deformed Transformed*, which he attempted to finish in Genoa even as late as January 1823.[17]

Yet it was in Pisa, shortly after he had finished *Werner* on January 20 1822, that Byron began *The Deformed Transformed*, and he had access to at least two translations of *Faust* at this time. Desiring to read Goethe's drama in English, Byron had requested John Murray to send him "designs from *Faust*. . . . and a translation of it" on December 4 1821;[18] but because there had been no complete translation by then, Murray sent only *Retsch's Series of Twenty-Six Outlines, Illustrative of Goethe's Tragedy of Faust, Engraved from the Originals by Henry Moses, and an Analysis of the Tragedy* (London 1820). This volume, which contained a prose translation of *Faust* (with select scenes only summarized), was received by January 12 1822, and by that time the Pisan circle also possessed a copy of John Anster's alternating translation (in poetry) and summary of *Faust* which had appeared in *Blackwood's Edinburgh Magazine* for June 1820.[19] Consequently, Byron's statement to Medwin in Pisa, that his knowledge of *Faust* was only "from a sorry French translation [by Madame de Staël in *De l'Allemagne*], from an occasional reading or two into English of parts of it by Monk Lewis when at Diodati, and from the Hartz mountain-scene, that Shelley versified the other day,"[20] does not reflect his access to these two translations, unless Byron told Medwin this before *Retsch's Outlines* arrived in Pisa. If this were the case, then Byron had heard Shelley's translation by January, that is before he began *The Deformed Transformed* and before Shelley had formally completed his written translation of "several scenes" from Goethe's *Faust* and Calderon's *El Magico Prodigioso* for *The Liberal* in April.[21]

Byron's avowed interest in *Faust* before and during his writing of the first scene for *The Deformed Transformed* significantly affected the structure of his drama. The long temptation scene between Arnold and Caesar and their companionship for the remainder of the drama undoubtedly reflect the similar pattern between Faust and Mephistopheles in Goethe's drama, a pattern not present in either *The Three Brothers* or *The Wood Daemon*. Goethe himself remarked on Byron's indebtedness to *Faust* for the characterization of Caesar, at one point egotistically asserting that "Lord Byron's transformed Devil is a continuation [with no originality] of Mephistophiles." Goethe later tempered this remark, citing Byron's original employment of Caesar, and confessed that Byron's devil was only "suggested by my Mephistophiles."[22] Varnhagen, in his study of *The Deformed Transformed*, denied any further similarities between Mephistopheles and Caesar (except that "Beide sind skeptische, cynische Spötter"); on the contrary, as F. W. Stokoe has observed, "the Stranger or Caesar has throughout a strain of the cynical humour, almost good-humour, that characterises the Mephisto of *Faust I*."[23] Furthermore, as will be demonstrated below, Byron saw Mephistopheles as Faust's symbolic doppelgänger, and he imitated their psychological identity in his characterizations of Caesar and Arnold. But since Mephistopheles did not assume Faust's body, Goethe's drama did not, in itself, provide Byron the idea to use the transformed Caesar as Arnold's physical double.

Having exhausted Byron's acknowledged sources, I do not mean to propose that his conception of the transformed Caesar as Arnold's physical double was his unique creation; quite the contrary. Byron owed a manifest debt to the doppelgänger tradition in literature, extending to such diverse works as Dryden's *Amphitryon,* Monk Lewis's *The Bravo of Venice,* and Le Sage's *Le Diable Boiteux.*[24] Neither *Amphitryon* nor *The Bravo of Venice* employs the devil as double, but both emphasize a schizophrenia that is thematically central to *The Deformed Transformed.* In Dryden's *Amphitryon* (as in Plautus's and Moliere's dramas by the same title), Jupiter and Mercury assumed the forms of Amphitryon and his slave, Sosias, in order that Jupiter might easily seduce Amphitryon's wife, Alcmena. Having fulfilled his desires with Alcmena, Jupiter (still impersonating Amphitryon) concluded an ironic argument on the difference between the Husband and the Lover in this fashion:

> To please my niceness you must separate
> The Lover from his Mortal Foe, the Husband.
> Give to the yawning Husband your cold Vertue,
> But all your vigorous Warmth, your melting Sighs,
> Your amorous Murmurs, be your Lover's part.[25]

Although Alcmena later accused Jupiter of speciousness ("How vainly wou'd the Sophister divide, / And make the Husband and the Lover, two!"), the Husband (Amphitryon) and the Lover (Jupiter) in Dryden's comedy are psychologically and symbolically reflections of one personality.

Byron had also discovered a different and a more intense double personality, without intervention of god or devil, in Monk Lewis's adapted translation of J. D. D. Zschokke's *Aballino, der grosse Bandit,* first published as *The Bravo of Venice* in 1805. The Neapolitan hero, Rosalvo, requiring a disguise, symbiotically projected for himself two distinct personalities: Abellino, the extremely ugly bravo of Venice whose dissembling ultimately freed the Doge from the threat of the banditti; and the extremely handsome Florentine nobleman, Flodoardo, who ultimately won the love of the Doge's daughter, Rosabella. Since Rosalvo was both the ugly Abellino and the handsome Flodoardo, there could be no direct confrontation between his two other selves; rather, as in Stevenson's *Dr Jekyll and Mr Hyde,* the appearance of one depended on the disappearance of his opposite. This physical antagonism between two personalities manufactured by one self in *The Bravo of Venice* contrasts with the existence of the second self (Jupiter) who actually confronted his physical counterpart in *Amphitryon.* And unlike Arnold's extraordinary pact with the devil in *The Deformed Transformed,* Rosalvo's transformations were self-initiated and were selflessly directed to preserving the Venetians and the Doge from the banditti. Notwithstanding these differences, *The Bravo of Venice,* which Byron had read, provided and entertaining characterization of dual personality and revealed the potential of subtle variations on the doppelgänger motif.

Although the Venetians had suggested that Abellino, the bravo of Venice, had Satanic origins, Rosalvo finally explained the natural creation of his double personality. Consequently, neither *The Bravo of Venice* nor *Amphitryon* offered Byron examples of the devil as doppelgänger. But Byron had also read Le Sage's *Le Diable Boiteux,* a satirical novel in which the devil, Asmodeus, accompanied and cynically instructed Don Cleophas Leandro Perez Zambullo, a young student, in the vanities of the Spanish people. In one of the episodic scenes, the devil Asmodeus borrowed the form of Don Cleophas in order to save the beautiful Seraphina from a burning house and consequently win her love for Don Cleophas. Byron might have remembered the comic effect of this diabolic transformation when he discovered a similar instance of "doubling" in Goethe's *Faust.* In a scene translated in both the Retsch volume and *Blackwood's Edinburgh Magazine,* Mephistopheles clothed himself in Faust's gowns and cynically deluded one of Faust's young students. Byron alluded to this scene in *Faust* as early as December 1821 (see note 21 above), at which time he may have recognized its symbolic value. But by no later than January 1822 Byron would see in Mephistopheles' masquerade an objective correlative for the symbolic identity between the devil and Faust.

Byron's discovery of the devil as doppelgänger in *Faust* was occasioned by his receipt, by January 12 1822, of *Retsch's Series of Outlines* which contained, in an anonymous introduction (p 2), the following interpretation of Goethe's drama: "that the easiest clue to the moral part of this didactic action is, to consider Faust and Mephistopheles as *one* person, represented symbolically, only in a two-fold shape." Encountering this highly sophisticated interpretation of Faust, Byron was led to recognize the potential of devil as doppelgänger in Goethe's drama and to realize this potential in *The Deformed Transformed.* Consequently, the companionship of Faust and Mephistopheles in *Faust* takes on new meaning in relation to Byron's drama, for if Mephistopheles and Faust, though distinct dramatis personae, were symbolically one personality, then the devils Mephistopheles and Caesar merely embodied Faust's and Arnold's moral imperfections (compare, for example, each protagonist's suicide attempt before the devil appeared). Furthermore, Byron made explicit what was but implicit in *Faust* by having Caesar, through transformation, embody not only Arnold's moral imperfections but also his physical deformities.

That Byron encountered and adopted this interpretation of *Faust* appearing in the Retsch volume would be highly speculative were it not for Byron and Shelley's discussions of the doppelgänger in January 1822. Shelley, having

Sir Henry Irving dressed as Mephistopheles.

read at least part of *Le Diable Boiteux*,[26] having understood the symbolic relationship between Frankenstein and his monster in Mary Shelley's novel, having employed Demogorgon to represent a union of Prometheus (head) and Asia (heart) in *Prometheus Unbound,* and having completed by February 1821 *Epipsychidion* which, like *Alastor,* employed the epipsyche as the idealized double of one's self, was no novice in the tradition of the doppelgänger. And by January 1822 Shelley was translating for Byron not only episodes from Goethe's *Faust* but also scenes from Calderon's *El Magico Prodigioso,* a drama depicting a relationship between demon and hero similar to that between Mephistopheles and Faust. Furthermore, in January 1822 Shelley was translating (or summarizing) for Byron another Calderon drama, most often entitled "El Embozado," containing a bizarre plot in which the protagonist was pursued by his "second self." Since Byron, who had already experimented with the double in *Manfred* and *Cain,* intended to adapt the plot of "El Embozado" for his own dramatic purposes, there can be no question that he and Shelley discussed the dramatic possibilities and function of the doppelgänger. Indeed, since Shelley was

translating parts of *Faust* and the two Calderon dramas for Byron, and since he read the Retsch volume the day it arrived, January 12, he probably was the first to recognize the insight of the anonymous editor who claimed that Mephistopheles and Faust were but symbolic representations of one personality.[27]

Having discovered the symbolic doubling within *Faust,* Shelley, and consequently Byron, proceeded to compare Goethe's drama with Calderon's *El Magico Prodigioso,* based on the legend of St Cyprian's pact with the devil in Antioch. After he had finished written translations of scenes from both plays, Shelley cited in April 1822 the "striking similarity" between the plots and suggested that "*Cypriano* [i.e., *El Magico Prodigioso*] evidently furnished the *germ* of Faust."[28] And when Byron discussed *Faust* with Medwin in January (see note 21 above), he repeated Shelley's earlier and more extensive comparison of the two plays: "You tell me the plot [of *Faust*] is almost entirely Calderon's. The fête, the scholar, the argument about the *Logos,* the selling himself to the fiend, and afterwards denying his power; his disguise of the plumed cavalier; the enchanted mirror,—are all from Cyprian. That *Magico Prodigioso* must be worth reading, and nobody seems to know any thing about it but you and Shelley."[29] The demon or fiend in this drama has been recently interpreted as a "projection, as it were, of processes that go on within Cyprian's mind, imagination, and sensibility";[30] by comparing Calderon's demon to Goethe's Mephistopheles, Byron and Shelley undoubtedly made the same judgment.

The demon of *El Magico Prodigioso,* like Mephistopheles in *Faust* and Caesar in *The Deformed Transformed,* is a Protean figure who frequently transformed himself. Disguised *"as a fine Gentleman"* searching for Antioch in Act I, the demon initially engaged the pagan Cyprian in a theological debate. Having lost this debate, the demon then manipulated Cyprian's involvement with the fair Justina, and in Act II, after Cyprian offered his soul to Hell's "most detested spirit" in exchange for Justina's love, the demon reappeared in an "unknown form" as a shipwreck victim to claim Cyprian's soul. Preceding the symbolic embrace between Cyprian and his magical tempter, the demon quite clearly explained that he would become Cyprian's shadow or second self: "so firm an amity / 'Twixt thee and me be, that neither Fortune . . . nor Time . . . nor / Heaven itself . . . can ever make / The least division between thee and me,— / Since now I find a refuge in thy favour."[31] This symbolic unity between devil and hero was eventually destroyed when Cyprian realized he had been duped by the demon who was powerless in comparison to the Christian God.[32] Although Cyprian reclaimed his soul and died a Christian martyr, eternally separated from his inimical second self, the pattern of devil as doppelgänger is quite evident in this drama which has many affinities with *Faust.*

By the end of January 1822 Byron had thus been introduced to a tradition of doubles which bound Lover (Jupiter) to Husband (Amphitryon), villain (Abellino) to hero (Flodoardo), and most importantly devil (Mephisto and Calderon's demon) to man (Faust and Cyprian). If the anonymous editor of *Retsch's Series of Twenty-Six Outlines* provided the formal cause (i.e., revealed to Byron the potential of devil as doppelgänger in *Faust* and *El Magico Prodigioso*) for *The Deformed Transformed,* then Percy Bysshe Shelley provided the efficient cause by acquainting Byron in January 1822 with a bizarre doppelgänger in another Calderon drama, which Byron acknowledged as the source for a drama he intended to write. This source, mistakenly entitled either "El Embozado" or "El Encapotado," was actually Calderon's *El Purgatorio de San Patricio.*

The evidence for Byron's interest in this Calderon drama was offered by Thomas Medwin to Washington Irving in 1825, in the form of an "unpublished note" which recorded Byron's summary of "El Embozado" or "El Encapotado" together with Byron's expressed design to adapt Calderon's plot of the doppelgänger for his own projected drama. Medwin's alternate titles (neither of which was correct) resulted from his "scanty" record of Byron's conversations in Pisa on this subject. And when Washington Irving transcribed Medwin's "unpublished note" for his own journal of 1825, he accepted not only Medwin's titles (Irving fruitlessly searched Spain in 1826 for a Calderon drama by these titles) but also Medwin's assumption that Byron never began his adaptation of Calderon's plot. Irving retained these misconceptions when he rewrote Medwin's "unpublished note" for publication as "An Unwritten Drama of Lord Byron" in *The Knickerbocker: New York Monthly Magazine.*[33] The first misconception, that of the title and identity of the play, has perplexed Byron scholars up to this day, for they are not aware that Horace E. Thorner, in 1934, satisfactorily identified the plot of "El Embozado" as but a scene from Calderon's *El Purgatorio de San Patricio,* in which Ludovico Enio vainly attempted to kill a mantled figure ("un Hombre Embozado") who finally revealed himself as Enio's skeletal "second self."[34] The second and more important misconception, that Byron's projected drama was "unwritten," has been accepted as fact, for no one has recognized that Byron adapted Calderon's bizarre plot in the unfinished *Deformed Transformed.*

Although Irving's "An Unwritten Drama of Lord Byron" has been reprinted often since its publication in August 1835, Irving's transcription of Medwin's "unpublished note" in his 1825 journal has never been published. In this "note," which Medwin "had intended to append to a new edition of his Memoirs"[35] and which contains Byron's summary of "El Embozado," Medwin prefaced his remarks by some important qualifications which were not included in Irving's published version in 1835:

> At the time when Lord Byron threatened to make himself as voluminous & prolific an author as Shakespeare, one of the subjects on which he formed a design of exercising his fancies (during a short poetical repose between the burning of the Deformed Transformed and [the completion of] Werner) was the *Embozado* or *Encapotado* of Calderon. It is one of the plays that my

edition of that past poet (I had nearly said Dramatist) does not contain and which I have in vain endeavoured to procure, to the shame of literature & of his nation, no perfect collection of his work being extant. For the outline of the story Lord Byron was indebted to Shelley, for he did not understand Spanish (the translation of the Ballad ahi de mi alhama [sic]—notwithstanding). My note of the conversation I had with him was so scanty that I did not mention it in my published Journal, but the plot he had in view to develope (I know not how it agrees with the original [)] was nearly as follows.

Three significant items emerge from this introduction and increase Medwin's reliability as Byron's amanuensis in this case. First of all, Medwin specified that Byron was planning this drama on the double in January or February (i.e., between the completion of *Werner* on January 20 1822 and the burning of *The Deformed Transformed* manuscript no later than March 1822), when Byron and Shelley discussed the various possibilities of the doppelgänger. Secondly, Medwin's avowed ignorance of the relation between the "plot" and its "original" indicates that he did not hear Shelley's translation or "outline" of *El Purgatorio de San Patricio* and that he recorded only Byron's summary of the drama. Thirdly, what follows in the remainder of Medwin's "unpublished note" is not merely a summary of the source (*El Purgatorio*) but a summary of the "plot [Byron] had in view to develope" (hereafter called "El Embozado"):

> The hero of the piece is a nobleman (whom I call Alfonzo) just making his debut on the stage of life. His passions from early and unrestrained indulgence are impetuous and ungovernable and he follows their dictates with a wild and thoughtless disregard of consequences. These consequences are obvious enough. Such a moral would be a very common place one but with Calderon [i.e., following Calderon's example] I should take a new and different way of enforcing it and a truly dramatic one it might be made if treated in the genuine spirit of Goethe. Soon after our Spaniards entrance into the world a person in a masque or cloak, that prevents his features or figure from being recognized (for the titles of the play leave us in doubt as to the express nature of the disguise) becomes as it were his shadow— his second self.
>
> This mysterious being Alfonzo is unable to identify with any of his acquaintances; his real name—or country—or place of abode are a mystery—and he is equally at a loss to form even a conjecture as to the peculiar observations and interest of the stranger. This curiosity at first scarcely noticed, or only considered as idle impertinence, daily becomes more irksome. Not only his most-private actions pass under the scrutiny of this officious monitor, but his most secret thoughts are known to him. Speak of him, he stands by his side—think of him—though invisible he feels his presence oppress and weigh upon his spirits like a troubled atmosphere. Waking or asleep he is ever with him or before him—he crosses his path, at every turn he intrudes like the demon in Faust in his solitude—he follows him in the crowded street, in the brilliant saloon, he sees him winding through the assembly & the honied words of

seduction that he is addressing to his fair partner in the dance die unfinished on his lips. One voice like the voice of his own soul whispers in his ears and silences the music—Who can he be [?]

Is it the false embodying of his fantasy—a shape his melancholy spirits have engendered out of the atoms of the day? No! It is something more than an apparition that haunts him. Like the Schedoni of The Italian † († vide. romance by Mrs Radcliff) his evil genius counteracts all his projects, thwarts him in all his deep laid schemes of ambition and fame, unwinds through all their intricacies and shapes, the webs of his intrigues, developes the hidden motives of his conduct and betrays that those actions which he wishes to make appear the most disinterested are only based in self.

The Hero of the drama is become abstracted and gloomy. Youth, health, wealth, power all that promised to give life its zest in the outset have lost their charm. The sweetest cup to others is poison to him. Existence becomes a burthen, and to put a [? trouble] to his misery & drive him to a state bordering on frenzy he suspects that the guilty object of his affections has fallen a prey to his tormentor. Alonzo now thirsts only for vengeance but the unknown eludes his pursuit and his emissaries endeavour in vain to discover his retreat; at length he succeeds in tracing him into the house of his mistress & attacking him with all the fury which jealous rage inspires, taxes him with his wrongs and demands *satisfaction*. His rival scarcely defends himself and the sword of Alonzo at the first thrust pierces the breast of his enemy, who in falling utters "are you satisfied!" his mantle drops off and discovers—his own image the spectre of himself—his self—He dies with horror!

The spectre is an alegorical [sic] being—the personification of conscience or of the passions.[36]

When Washington Irving rewrote this "unpublished note" by Medwin in "An Unwritten Drama of Lord Byron," he correctly observed that the plot summary was "somewhat vague and immature, and would doubtless have undergone many modifications" in Byron's projected adaptation. But because Joshua Pickersgill's *The Three Brothers* and Goethe's *Faust* provided these "modifications," Irving (as well as Medwin and subsequent Byron scholars) failed to recognize the fundamental similarity between "El Embozado" and Byron's written, not "unwritten," *The Deformed Transformed*. The conflict between Alonzo and his "double" and that between Arnold and Caesar are essentially identical, but Byron disguised his indebtedness by altering the character of Alonzo. Influenced by his own lameness and borrowing from Pickersgill's *The Three Brothers,* Byron created a hunchbacked Arnold whose physical deformities symbolically embodied Alonzo's "impetuous and ungovernable" passions. The consequences of Arnold's deformity, his Faustian pact with Caesar and his transformation into Achilles, were significant structural additions to the frame of "El Embozado," but Byron did not change the function of the doppelgänger in his adaptation, even though Caesar became the double of Arnold's *former* self. The "stranger" in Calderon's drama was Alonzo's uneludable "shadow—his second self"; in nearly identical fashion,

Byron's "Stranger," before he took the name of Caesar and became Arnold's "second self," revealed Arnold's destiny: "In a few moments / I will be as you were, and you shall see / Yourself for ever by you, as your shadow" (I.i.447-449). Just as Calderon's "stranger," a "personification of conscience or of the passions," shadowed Alonzo as a reflection of his moral weaknesses, Caesar, who assumed the rejected and hunchbacked body, accompanied Arnold as a reminder of his former physical deformities and of his diabolical transformation.

Byron's adaptation of the physical doubles in "El Embozado" was also influenced by his awareness of the symbolic doubles in Goethe's *Faust*. Byron recognized the parallels between the two works and told Medwin that his modification of "El Embozado" would be "in the genuine spirit of Goethe" and that Alonzo's double intruded "like the demon in Faust." In other words, Arnold and Caesar in *The Deformed Transformed* were a product of Alonzo and the "stranger" interpreted as Faust and Mephistopheles. This accounts for the difference between Alonzo's ignorance of his pursuing double and Arnold's knowledge of his accompanying double: having altered the structure of his source by introducing the Satanic pact and Arnold's physical transformation, Byron could not retain the unrecognized physical double in "El Embozado"; instead, like Goethe, Byron had the Mephistophelean Caesar accompany Arnold as a symbolic representation of his moral and mortal inadequacies. However, since he assumed Arnold's hunchbacked body, Caesar, like Alonzo's "second self," was Arnold's physical double. Thus, the doppelgänger in *The Deformed Transformed* was a unique and imaginative fusion of "El Embozado" and *Faust*: Byron not only retained the bizarre physical doubling in Calderon's drama; he also made explicit what Goethe but implied in the characterization of Faust and Mephistopheles.

Having fused these two plots, Byron could not recreate the actual suspense of self pursuing self in "El Embozado," but he did intend to use the climactic scene between Alonzo and his second self in order to resolve the conflict between Arnold and Caesar. Because Byron's indebtedness to this Calderon drama has never been recognized, no reader of *The Deformed Transformed* has satisfactorily projected the conclusion of this unfinished drama. Mary Shelley, who copied what Byron wrote, acknowledged that she did "not know how he meant to finish it," but reported that Byron had "the whole conduct of the story . . . already conceived."[37] In 1826, unaware of the "fragment" to Part III that was not published in Hunt's 1824 edition of *The Deformed Transformed*, George Clinton mistakenly proposed that Byron would "invent new adventures for his hero" rather than "follow the course of the romance"[38] between Olimpia and Arnold. When E. H. Coleridge first published this "fragment," which contained not only Byron's memorandum on jealousy ("Jealous—Arnold of Caesar. Olympia [sic] at first not liking Caesar—then?—Arnold jealous of himself under his former figure, owing to the power of intellect, etc., etc., etc."), but also Arnold and Caesar's dialogue on jealousy, he cautiously, but correctly, stated that "Byron intended to make Olimpia bestow her affections, not on the glorious Achilles, but the witty and interesting Hunchback."[39] A further insight into Byron's intentions was offered by Emil Koeppel who interpreted Caesar's statement that the Faustian pact between the two would be signed in blood, but not in Arnold's blood (I.i.147-149), to mean that Arnold would forfeit his soul to Caesar by killing Olimpia in a jealous rage.[40] But Koeppel was only partially correct here: the text suggests that Arnold would kill Olimpia, but this action would not forfeit his soul but only formalize the bond between tempter and tempted. It is generally overlooked that Arnold had not signed any compact with Caesar in *The Deformed Transformed,* but Byron did indicate the nature of this "signature" in Caesar's veiled threat to Arnold: "You shall have no bond / But your own will, no contract save your deeds" (I.i.151-152). But this "deed" of contract does not appear in the finished portion of Byron's drama: the transformed Arnold does not join the devil's party by any ignoble action; quite the contrary, as Samuel C. Chew objected, "all that Caesar incites him to do [in the siege of Rome and after] it would occur to any high-minded man to undertake."[41] Most probably, the "deed" was to be Arnold's shedding of Olimpia's blood. Arnold, through his own wilful act, would assume the spiritual depravity of Caesar just as Caesar had assumed Arnold's physical deformities.

What Coleridge and Koeppel did not know was that Byron's introduction of Arnold's jealousy "of himself under his former figure" was merely an imitation of Alonzo's jealousy of his double, the mantled figure in "El Embozado." Arnold's destruction of Olimpia would have bound him to Caesar, but it would not have provided Byron the means to resolve the conflict between Arnold and his double. Rather, Byron, who had "already conceived" the climax and who had already "transformed" Calderon's doubles into Arnold and Caesar, intended that Arnold would forfeit his soul by a symbolic "suicide": just as Alonzo died when he killed his own physical double, Arnold, motivated by a similar jealousy, would have shed "all" of his own blood by killing his diabolical rival and double. Byron's intentions are clear not only from his expressed "design" to imitate Calderon's plot but also from his explicit preparation for this climax in the finished portions of *The Deformed Transformed.* Koeppel, in his eagerness to project that Olimpia would be killed, overlooked Byron's hint that Arnold's blood would also be shed. When Caesar asked Arnold for "a little of [his] blood" to make the transformation effective, Arnold offered "it all." Caesar's answer indicates that Arnold's body would later be slain: "Not now. A few drops will suffice for this" (I.i.157). Byron further prepared for Arnold's fate by consciously paralleling the fundamental destructive conflict between Arnold and Caesar to that between other mutually antagonistic doubles: Romulus and Remus; Gore and Glory; Lucifer and Venus; Eros and Anteros; and even Huon and Memnon. The most significant doubles in this series are the twins, Romulus and Remus, and Byron twice referred to Romulus's destruction of Remus: Caesar informed Arnold that he had seen "Romulus . . . / Slay his

own twin"; and the Chorus of Spirits bemoaned Romulus's "Awful . . . crime" and "inexpiable sin" (I.i.80-81; II.i.38, 76). Metaphorically, the foundation for the "Glory" of Romulus's Rome was the "Gore" of Remus's blood; thus Caesar's description of Arnold's coming "Hand in hand with the mild twins—Gore and Glory" (II.ii.12) and his allusions to Romulus and Remus do more than provide a historical perspective to the Bourbon's pillage of Rome—they actually prepare for Arnold's slaying of his own twin.[42] Thus the "deed" of *forfeiture,* Byron's climax for *The Deformed Transformed,* was to be Arnold's suicide, symbolically represented by his wilful murder of his double, Caesar in the form of Arnold's hunchbacked body.

Once Byron's intended imitation of the climax in "El Embozado" is recognized as the only logical resolution between Arnold and his diabolical double, the function of the doppelgänger in this drama becomes more apparent. Like *Manfred* and *Cain,* Byron's only finished "speculative" dramas, *The Deformed Transformed* dramatized man's self-destruction whereby his immortal aspirations were annihilated by his own mortality. Unlike the heroes in Byron's Oriental tales and unlike Prometheus, Childe Harold, and even the narrator of *Don Juan,* the protagonist in the "speculative" drama was engaged not in a constructive conflict whereby the self triumphed, sometimes even in death, through its independence and defiance of the "other" (whether man, nature, society, government, religion, or "metaphysics"); rather, with a "chaos of thought and passion, all confused," this protagonist precipitated a destructive conflict within his own nature in which mortal self destroyed immortal self. Byron's introduction to the plot of "El Embozado" was actually fortuitous, because it provided him the artistic means to give final form to the idea of self-alienation and self-destruction which had been dramatized in *Manfred* and *Cain.*

In *Manfred,* his first "speculative" drama, Byron created an introspective hero whose "half dust, half deity" (I.ii.40) engendered a conflict between his mortally limiting body and his immortally aspiring mind. Byron externalized this internal conflict by juxtaposing to Manfred "The Lady Astarte, his [physical double and psychological counterpart]" (III.iii.47), as I interpret and complete Manuel's interrupted description of her. Manfred himself described his resemblance to Astarte: "She was like me in lineaments—her eyes— / Her hair—her features—all, to the very tone / Even of her voice . . . were like to mine" (II.ii.105-107). Yet with "gentler powers," "humility," and "virtues," Astarte possessed a heart which had psychologically complemented Manfred's Faustian pursuit of knowledge. Manfred confessed to the Chamois Hunter that he and Astarte formerly possessed "one heart" (II.i.26), but he told the Abbot that this heart was now "withered, or . . . broken" (III.i.145). Because Astarte, representing Manfred's heart, had died, the zealous Abbot sensed the futility of appealing to the half-destroyed Manfred: "my humble zeal . . . May light upon your head—could I say *heart*— / Could I touch *that,* with words or prayers, I should / Recall a noble spirit" (III.iv.47, 50-52). Even the Chamois Hunter unwittingly recognized this "noble spirit's" divided nature when he cautioned Manfred: "Thy mind and body are alike unfit / To trust each other" (II.i.2-3); and when he prayed for Manfred: "Heaven give thee rest! / And Penitence restore *thee* to *thyself*" (II.i.87-88, my italics). In other words, the "thee" (Manfred's heart or mortality as represented by Astarte) had been severed from the "thyself" (Manfred's mind with its immortal aspirations).

Because Manfred had destroyed his own heart, his gentler self in the person of Astarte, he should have died; yet it was his "fatality to live" (I.ii.24). Protesting too much for "self-oblivion" and "forgetfulness" (I.i.144, 136) of Astarte, whose uneludable "shadow" (I.i.219) reminded him of his divided self, Manfred really quested for self-integration. The Witch of the Alps best understood Manfred's quest for Astarte:

> And for this—
> A being of the race thou dost despise—
> The order, which thine own would rise above,
> Mingling with us and ours,—thou dost forego
> The gifts of our great *knowledge,* and shrink'st back
> To recreant *mortality.*
>
> (II.ii.121-126, my italics)

Manfred's head or knowledge could not transcend his heart or mortality. His self-sufficient claim to be "self-condemned" in Act III (i.177) misrepresented the truth: he was his "own destroyer" (III.iv.139) only because he had "loved her, and destroyed her [Astarte, his double]" (II.ii.117).

That Byron was artistically prepared for the development of the doppelgänger in *The Deformed Transformed* is also manifested by his second "speculative" drama, *Cain,* whose hero, like Manfred and Arnold, was self-destructive. But this time Byron externalized man's internal conflict by using not just one, but two doubles: Lucifer, the Mephistophelean spirit, represented Cain's Faustian quest for knowledge and immortality; and Adah, Cain's twin sister, represented his emotional need for mortal love. Although Cain could judge the differences between his two companions—he said that Adah "understands not" (I.i.188) and that Lucifer "lov'st nothing" (II.ii.338)—he did not recognize their symbolic functions. Rather, only Adah sensed that Lucifer represented Cain's "own / Dissatisfied and curious thoughts" for immortality (I.i.402-403);[43] and only Lucifer judged Adah to represent Cain's enfeebling love for "frail mortality" (II.ii.269). Thus when Lucifer and Adah debated the relative merits of knowledge and love in Act I, Cain did not know that this external debate represented his internal conflict. But finally choosing knowledge over love, Cain separated himself from Adah, his heart, and entered the abyss of space with Lucifer. As Adah informed Lucifer in Act I, "thou . . . steppest between heart and heart" (I.i.349).

In Act II, Cain attempted to unify his divided nature. Declaring "*I* must be / Immortal in despite of *me*" (II.i.90-91, my italics), he requested knowledge not only of his "I," his "immortal part" (I.i.104), but also of his "me," his mortal limitation or death. What Cain discovered, in Byron's slightly altered phrase, was the "inadequacy of his [mortal] state to his [immortal] conceptions."[44] The incompatibility of Cain's two natures is suggested by his dialogue with Lucifer at the end of Act II:

> *Lucifer.* Didst thou not require
> Knowledge? And have I not, in what I showed,
> Taught thee to know thyself?
>   *Cain.* Alas! I seem
> Nothing.
>   *Lucifer.* And this should be the human sum
> Of knowledge, to know mortal nature's nothingness.
>
> (II.ii.418-422)

Cain, like Manfred, learned that the "Tree of Knowledge is not that of Life": self-knowledge revealed a disintegrated personality in conflict with itself.

The final act of this drama is but a phenomenal representation of Cain's noumenal experience in Act II. Still alienated from his gentler self—"leave me" (III.i.94), he says to Adah—Cain, according to Byron, "falls into the *frame* of *mind* that leads to the Catastrophe":[45] he murdered Abel, brought death into the world, and confirmed "mortal nature's nothingness." Ironically, Cain finally recognized Abel, not Adah or Lucifer, as his double: "'Tis blood—my blood— / My brother's and my own! and shed by me! . . . I have taken life from my own flesh" (III.i.345-348). There is a tradition whereby Cain and Abel were physical twins, and hence doubles,[46] but Byron either did not know or develop this circumstance. Nevertheless, Cain's destruction of Abel, who had "sprung from the same womb . . . drained / The same breast," and Cain's consequent expulsion "Eastward from Eden" (III.i.535-536, 552), phenomenally represented the destruction of his own immortal aspirations and his self-alienation.

Having already used the double to dramatize the divided self in *Manfred* and *Cain,* and having used the devil as doppelgänger in *Cain* (according to Samuel Chew, the "tempter and tempted are absolutely at one"[47]), Byron in January 1822 adopted the doppelgänger in "El Embozado" to once more portray man's self-alienation. Even before the transformations of Arnold and Caesar, Arnold revealed his double identity by damning his mortal form which limited not his mental conceptions, as in *Cain,* but his emotional desire for love: "[oh] that the Devil, to whom they liken me, / Would aid his likeness! If I must partake / His *form,* why not his *power*" (I.i.40-42, my italics). Like Narcissus, Arnold gazed into the fountain, hoped for the devil's power to complement his form, but was mocked by his "horrid shadow" (I.i.51)—a reminder that his devil's likeness determined the barrenness of his mortality since he could neither be loved nor love himself. Hated by others and hating himself, Arnold despaired and attempted suicide, but was prevented by the stirring of the fountain, the source of his double or reflected image. "Nature's mirror" not only revealed a disintegrated personality but actually separated the opposing principles within Arnold: the diabolical "form" reflected in the fountain was miraculously transformed into the diabolical "power" in the person of the Stranger who emerged from the waters. Thus the Stranger, like Faust's Mephistopheles and Cain's Lucifer, appeared not as an incarnation of the power of abstract evil in the universe; rather, he was an embodiment of Arnold's idealization of power—a double who reflected Arnold's potential for disintegration and self-destruction.

Because the tempter and tempted are symbolic representations of one disintegrated personality, the remainder of *The Deformed Transformed* is a phenomenal representation of Arnold's internal conflict. Naively idealistic and risking his soul for the love he lacked, Arnold chose to be transformed into the glorious Achilles. Thinking that he had transcended his mortal limitations, the new Achilles believed he had the power to realize his desires: "I love, and I shall be beloved" (I.i.421). That Arnold was only deluding himself and could not transcend his mortality was symbolically represented by the Stranger's transformation into the deformed Arnold. Thus the Mephistophelean Stranger, who had represented Arnold's idealization of power, remained Arnold's double by regressing into the hunchbacked form initially mirrored by the fountain. Power and form were not integrated; they merely changed places. Ever by his side as his shadow, Caesar reminded Arnold of his eternally conflicting double nature, and Arnold discovered that neither esteem in war nor possession of Olimpia, the "Essence of all Beauty" (II.iii.143), could reintegrate the divided self.

Arnold's desire for self-integration through love was, then, limited by his mortality. In Part I, Caesar rose from the fountain as Anteros (the negation of love) to confront Arnold's desire for Eros.[48] And in the "fragment" to Part III, Caesar (still representing Anteros in the form of Arnold's mortally limiting body) accurately diagnosed the source of Arnold's frustrations:

> you would be *loved*—what you call loved—
> *Self-loved*—loved for *yourself*—for neither health,
> Nor wealth, nor youth, nor power, nor rank, nor
> 　beauty—
> For these you may be stript of—but *beloved*
> As an abstraction.
>
> 　　　　　　　　　　　(lines 61-65)

But the power and the form of one personality were not united by the ideal of self-love. As Cain discovered from Lucifer (I.i.420-431), knowledge destroyed love. Similarly, Arnold's ideal of self-love was an illusion and would be destroyed by his final knowledge of his divided self: "owing to the power of intellect," Arnold was to become "jealous of himself under his former figure" (Byron's memorandum to this "fragment"). The disintegrating reality of jealousy rather than the integrating ideal of love was to seal Arnold's fate. Caesar warned Arnold that he would become jealous of his mortal self, and he metaphorically

explained the nature of this jealousy: "Now Love in you is as the Sun—a thing / Beyond you—and your Jealousy's of Earth— / A cloud of your own raising" (lines 80-82). Thus Arnold would have attributed his inability "to be [Olimpia's] heart as she is [his]" (line 101) to the presence of Caesar, confirmed his mortality by being jealous of his own hunchbacked form, and consequently increased his self-alienation. As in *Othello* (which Byron and Shelley talked of "getting up" in February 1822[49]), Arnold, motivated by jealousy, was destined to yield up love to tyrannous hate, to destroy Olimpia (an object of his love), to recognize his self-delusions, and finally to destroy himself. But since the doppelgänger modified this tragic action, Arnold, finally recognizing the source of his self-delusions, would destroy that which he wanted to love—himself, mortally represented in the form of Caesar. Thus the suicide which the self-alienated Arnold had prevented by self-hypnosis in the fountain was to be symbolically reenacted at the end of the drama by his murder of Caesar: ironically, Arnold's final triumph over his mortally limiting body would have confirmed his mortality; he would have destroyed himself.

Having demonstrated the subtleties of *The Deformed Transformed,* I propose that it contains something more significant than what G. Wilson Knight calls "Byron's 'Richard' complex."[50] Whether Byron could have artistically completed this representation of the destructive conflict within man is doubtful, not only because the disproportionately detailed account of the Siege of Rome violates the drama's integrity, but also because its bitter portrayal of "mortal nature's nothingness" demanded a total cynicism that is not readily compatible with the increasing mellowness of the last few cantos of *Don Juan.* Yet if Byron had completed *The Deformed Transformed,* it would have been a major document in the Byron canon and among other literary treatments of the doppelgänger. As it is, Byron's development of Arnold and his summary of "El Embozado" as reported by Medwin and Irving influenced such diverse works as Irving's abortive "El Embozado" (1825), Mary Shelley's short story, "Transformation" (1831), Hawthorne's "Howe's Masquerade" (1838), Poe's "William Wilson" (1839), Irving's "Don Juan: A Spectral Research" (1841), and even Yeats's *A Vision* (1925).[51] A historically ironic footnote to these treatments of the doppelgänger is that three "critics," without knowing it, prophesied the existence of *The Deformed Transformed* and its offspring: the anonymous reviewer of Pickersgill's novel observed that *The Three Brothers* would "furnish more than one topick [sic] for dramatic ingenuity"; Shelley, that "*Cypriano* evidently furnished the *germ* of Faust, as Faust may furnish the germ of other poems"; and Irving, that "the foregoing sketch of the plot [of "El Embozado"] may hereafter suggest a rich theme to a poet or dramatist of the Byron school."[52] Irving's statement is doubly ironic, since he anachronistically failed to recognize that Byron, the creator of this "school," had himself adapted this "rich theme" in *The Deformed Transformed.*[53]

Notes

1. *The Gothic Quest: A History of the Gothic Novel* (London [1938]) 276.

2. *Über Byrons dramatisches Bruchstück "Der umgestaltete Missgestaltete"* (Erlangen 1905) 18.

3. I.i.268, 381-382. *The Works of Lord Byron: Poetry* ed Ernest Hartley Coleridge (London 1901) v 487, 491. All subsequent quotations from Byron's poetry will be taken from this edition (hereafter cited as *Poetry*) and will be followed by line numbers in the text.

4. *Lady Blessington's Conversations of Lord Byron* ed Ernest J. Lovell, Jr (Princeton 1969) 80-81.

5. *The Works of Lord Byron: Letters and Journals* ed Rowland E. Prothero (London 1901) VI 178-179. Hereafter cited as *L&J*.

6. *Poetry* v 473-474.

7. *The Gentleman's Magazine* 74 (1804) 1047; George Clinton *Memoirs of the Life and Writings of Lord Byron* (London 1826) 666. For evidence of Joshua Pickersgill's authorship, see *N&Q* [*Notes and Queries*] 169 (1935) 262, 299, 339, 378.

8. In 1816 at Diodati, Monk Lewis, in translating *viva voce* Goethe's *Faust* for Byron, may have referred to the Satanic pact in Pickersgill's novel, which formed the basis of his 1807 drama, "The Wood Daemon." It is also possible that Mary Shelley drew Byron's attention to the novel, for she read it in December 1817. See *Mary Shelley's Journal* ed Frederick L. Jones (Norman, Okla 1947) 88.

9. *The Three Brothers: A Romance* (London 1803) IV 273-274. Arnaud narrates the events of his life in Chapter XI (IV 224-351).

10. For a consideration of this play's complex history, see Summers *The Gothic Quest* 274-276. For a summary of the unpublished "Wood Daemon," see "First Visit to the Theatre in London" *Poems by Hartley Coleridge* ed Derwent Coleridge (London 1851) I cxcix-cciii (Appendix C). Coleridge interestingly called Hardyknute, "the Deformed Transformed."

11. These and other quotations from *One O'Clock! or, The Knight and the Wood Daemon* are taken from Act III of the Oxberry edition (London 1824).

12. Although E. H. Coleridge recorded (*Poetry* v 469) that the "date of the original MS. of *The Deformed Transformed* is 'Pisa, 1822,'" Professor Truman Guy Steffan has informed me that a MS in his possession bears the more specific date. Coleridge mistakenly conjectured that the drama was begun and finished between April 20 and July 8 1822.

13. Letter to Kinnaird, February 6 1822 (*L&J* VI 10).

14. *Medwin's Conversations of Lord Byron* ed Ernest J. Lovell, Jr (Princeton 1966) 153-154. The terminal date for this dialogue is March 11 1822, the day Medwin left Pisa for Rome (see 242, 245n). But the chronological sequence (haphazard as it may appear) of the *Conversations* suggests that this dialogue took place in February.

15. As quoted by Lovell *Medwin's Conversations* 155n. Most recently, John Buxton, in *Byron and Shelley: The History of a Friendship* (New York 1968) 197-198, gratuitously dismissed Medwin's account without examining Trelawny's supporting statement. Consequently, Buxton's statement that "Byron did not begin *The Deformed Transformed* until some weeks after Medwin left Pisa," repeats E. H. Coleridge's mistaken dating of this drama.

16. To further substantiate Truman Guy Steffan's well-reasoned "conjecture that Byron began to write Canto VI about the middle of April and finished it and Canto VII at least by the end of June" (*Byron's Don Juan: The Making of a Masterpiece* [Austin 1957] I 384n-385n), see Shelley's reference to the completion of these two cantos on June 29 1822 (*The Letters of Percy Bysshe Shelley* ed Frederick L. Jones [Oxford 1964] II 442; hereafter cited as *PBSL*).

17. Byron had Mary Shelley copy at least the first scene of *The Deformed Transformed* by November 1822, at which time she quizzed Byron about the transformed Caesar: "I have copied your MSS. The 'Eternal Scoffer' seems a favourite of yours. The Critics, as they used to make you a Childe Harold, Giaour, & Lara all in one, will now make a compound of Satan & Caesar to [? serve as (*MS torn*)] your prototype." (*The Letters of Mary W. Shelley* ed Frederick L. Jones [Norman, Okla 1944] I 202). But Byron had apparently not finished Part II of the drama by that time, for he sent Mary Shelley a "few scenes more" for transcription on January 25 1823 (*L&J* VI 165). For Mary Shelley' continued praise of this drama, see *Letters* I 213.

18. *L&J* v 488.

19. VII (1820) 253-258. For Shelley's criticisms of both translations, see *PBSL* II 376.

20. *Medwin's Conversations* 141-142, and note 335.

21. Shelley began his translations of these two works some months before April. In December 1821, Byron and Shelley had already discussed the scene in which "Goethe's Mephistopheles [masquerading in Faust's gowns] calls the Serpent who tempted Eve '*my Aunt the renowned Snake*'" (*PBSL* II 368n-369n). And on January 14 1822, the day Trelawny arrived in Pisa, Shelley had been orally translating *El Magico Prodigioso*: see Trelawny, *Records of Shelley, Byron, and the Author* (London 1887) 14. Consequently, it is quite possible that "the other day" in Byron's reference to Shelley's translation from *Faust* was in January 1822.

22. *Conversations of Goethe with Eckermann and Soret,* trans John Oxenford, rev ed (London 1909) 108, 174. Conversations for January 18 1825 and November 8 1826.

23. Varnhagen *Über Byrons dramatisches Bruchstück* 21; Stokoe *German Influence in the English Romantic Period: 1788-1818* (New York 1963) 167. For further discussion of similarities between *Faust* and *The Deformed Transformed,* see also Samuel C. Chew, Jr *The Dramas of Lord Byron* (New York 1964) 145-148.

24. Byron's references to *Amphitryon* and *The Bravo of Venice* (*Medwin's Conversations* 178, 191) and to *Le Diable Boiteux* (*L&J* VI 178-179) demonstrate his knowledge of these works. Byron was evidently unaware of the doppelgänger in such continental works as Chamisso's *Peter Schlemihl* and Hoffmann's *The Devil's Elixir,* both of which were first published in English translation in 1824, the year of publication not only for *The Deformed Transformed* but also for James Hogg's portrayal of the devil as doppelgänger in *The Private Memoirs and Confessions of a Justified Sinner.*

25. Act II, scene ii, as quoted from *Dryden: The Dramatic Works* ed Montague Summers (London 1932) VI 173-174. See also Act IV, scene i (VI 194) for Jupiter's further distinction between Husband and Lover.

26. *Mary Shelley's Journal* (entry for March 23 1815) 42.

27. Shelley's letter to John Gisborne (*PBSL* II 376) demonstrates his reading of the Retsch volume which Murray sent to Byron. Although Byron's extant letters do not refer to his receipt or reading of this volume, his request for it, his interest in *Faust* and Goethe at the time, and his conversations with Shelley indicate that he would have read or at least discussed the volume when it arrived.

28. Letter to John Gisborne (*PBSL* II 407).

29. *Medwin's Conversations* 142, 143n.

30. A. A. Parker "The Devil in the Drama of Calderon" *Critical Essays on the Theatre of Calderon* ed Bruce W. Wardropper (New York 1965) 19-20. For a similar interpretation of the devil as doppelgänger in *El Magico Prodigioso,* see Everett W. Hesse *Calderon de la Barca* (New York 1967) 92.

31. These quotations are from Shelley's translation of *El Magico Prodigioso* in *The Complete Works of Percy Bysshe Shelley* ed Roger Ingpen and Walter E. Peck (New York 1965) IV 299-320. For a complete translation of this drama, see *The Wonder-Working Magician* in *Calderon's Dramas* trans Denis Florence Mac-Carthy (London 1873).

32. After failing to pervert Justina, the demon intended to impersonate and defame her through his actions ("I will assume a feignèd form, and thus / Make thee a victim of my baffled rage"). But it was the Christian God who sent a phantom-figure of Justina in skeletal form to intimidate Cyprian and effect his conversion. Note then the tradition of the angelic as well as the diabolical doppelgänger.

33. 6 (August 1835) 142-144. Irving's article for the *Knickerbocker* has been reprinted at least four times: see *The New York Mirror* 13 (October 17 1835) 122; *The Gift: A Christmas and New Year's Present for 1836* ed Miss Leslie (Philadelphia, nd) 166-171; Thomas Ollive Mabbott "An Unwritten Drama" *The Americana Collector* (November 1925) 64-66; and *His Very Self and Voice: Collected Conversations of Lord Byron* ed Ernest J. Lovell, Jr (New York 1954) 279-281.

34. "Hawthorne, Poe, and a Literary Ghost" *The New England Quarterly* 7 (1934) 146-154. Although Thorner did not specifically acknowledge his source for the identification of "El Embozado," he was indebted to Denis Florence Mac-Carthy who, by 1873, had recognized that "the 'Embozado' which Captain Medwin and others supposed to be the name of one of Calderon's dramas, and which, as might be expected, Washington Irving vainly looked for in Spain, was the *'Hombre embozado,'* the 'Muffled Figure' of Calderon's *Purgatorio de San Patricio*" (*Calderon's Dramas* 353). The failure to recognize that Byron's summary had its source in Calderon's *Purgatorio* has caused critics to question Medwin's reliability. Even Ernest J. Lovell asked: "Did Medwin make up this narrative of man's dual nature, the seed of it Byron's relation to him of a waking nightmare or vision Shelley had at San Terenzo in 1822?" (*Captain Medwin: Friend of Byron and Shelley* [Austin 1962] 149). Rather than discrediting Medwin's story, Shelley's nightmare in which he, like Ludovico Enio, encountered his mantled "second self" suggests that Calderon's *Purgatorio* had been a topic of conversation in 1822. For reports of this nightmare, see Medwin *The Life of Percy Bysshe Shelley* (London 1847) II 299-301; *Shelley Memorials: From Authentic Sources* ed Lady Shelley, 3rd ed (London 1875) 191-192; and Trelawny's note as quoted by Harry B. Smith "Books and Autograph Letters of Shelley" *Scribner's Magazine* 72 (1922) 74. Shelley had read *Purgatorio* by July 1819 (see *PBSL* II 105) and had praised it in a note to *The Cenci* (see *Complete Works* II 72n).

35. Washington Irving's letter of March 1825 to his brother, Peter, as quoted in Pierre M. Irving *The Life and Letters of Washington Irving* (New York 1864) IV 71.

36. Quoted from Washington Irving's "Note book containing extracts of poetry and prose; hint for a tale or farce; and miscellany [1824-26]" with the permission of the Manuscript Division, The New York Public Library. In subsequent references to this plot sum-

mary, the hero will be called Alonzo. Irving (or Medwin) called the hero both "Alfonzo" and "Alonzo."

37. From Mary Shelley's inscription on the fly leaf of her copy of *The Deformed Transformed,* as quoted in *Poetry* v 474n.

38. *Memoirs of Byron* 672.

39. *Poetry* v 531, 533n.

40. *Lord Byron* (Berlin 1903) 192.

41. *The Dramas of Lord Byron* 148.

42. For the reference to Lucifer and Venus, see II.iii. 189, and for the possible allusion to Eros and Anteros, see *Poetry* v 480n. That Arnold as Achilles would slay Caesar is also indicated by the names given the two pages at the end of the first scene. Although they are not twins and are not mentioned again in the drama, Huon (with the "golden horn" and the "bright / And blooming aspect") and Memnon (the "darker" one "who smiles not") reflect the antagonistic countenances of the transformed Arnold and Caesar. Byron, who was introduced to Huon of Bordeaux (a medieval hero who had obtained what Arnold desired: success in "War" and with "Woman") in William Sotheby's translation of Wieland's *Oberon,* probably did not know that Huon's original adventures involved a confrontation with the devil, Lucifer (see D. D. R. Owen "The Principal Source of *Huon of Bordeaux*" *French Stuides* 7 [1953] 129-139); but Byron certainly recognized that the Ethiopian, Memnon, a son of Eos and brother of Phosphor or "Lucifer," was slain by Achilles in the Trojan war. Thus this allusion to Memnon (an oblique reflection of the diabolical Caesar with the "swart face") who had been slain by Achilles prepares for the destruction of Caesar (and consequently Arnold) by the new Achilles, Arnold himself.

43. Even Lucifer hinted at his symbolic function when he described the snake in Eden not as a demon but as a snake who "but woke one [demon] / In those he spake to with his forky tongue" (I.i.229-230).

44. Letter to John Murray, November 3 1821 (*L&J* v 470).

45. *L&J* v 470, my italics. Byron was most probably aware of the irony in this statement: "the *frame* of *mind,*" with its analogue in Blake's "mind-forg'd manacles," draws attention to the head's destruction of the heart.

46. See Otto Rank "The Double as Immortal Self" *Beyond Psychology* (New York 1958) 90.

47. *The Dramas of Lord Byron* 131.

48. This distinction between Anteros and Eros is based on Byron's allusion to the paired opposites in the stage directions following I.i.82. See E. H. Coleridge's accompanying note, *Poetry* v 480n.

49. See *Mary Shelley's Journal* 167n.

50. *Byron and Shakespeare* (New York 1966) 155.

51. For Irving's notes on his proposed "El Embozado," see *The Journals of Washington Irving* ed William P. Trent and George S. Hellman (Boston 1919) II 171-174; for the influence of "El Embozado" on "Howe's Masquerade" and "William Wilson," see Thorner "Hawthorne, Poe, and a Literary Ghost"; for its influence on "Don Juan: A Spectral Research," see Lovell *Captain Medwin* 149 and Stanley T. Williams *The Life of Washington Irving* (New York 1935) I 466-467; and for Yeats's use of *The Deformed Transformed* see Giorgio Melchiori *The Whole Mystery of Art* (London 1960) 277-279.

52. *The Gentlemen's Magazine* 74 (1804) 1047; *PBSL* II 407; "An Unwritten Drama of Lord Byron" *The Knickerbocker* 6 (1835) 144.

53. This study was begun with the assistance of the University of Delaware Faculty Research Fund.

Ross Woodman (essay date 1984)

SOURCE: "Milton's Satan in Wordsworth's 'Vale of Soul-making,'" in *Studies in Romanticism,* Vol. 23, No. 1, Spring, 1984, pp. 3-30.

[*In the following essay, Woodman discusses subtle echoes of the Miltonic Satan in William Wordsworth's poetry.*]

> By our own spirits are we deified:
> We Poets in our youth begin in gladness;
> But thereof come in the end despondency and madness.
>
> ("Resolution and Independence." ll. 47-49)

I

In several of Wordsworth's lyrics, "We Are Seven" and "Anecdote For Fathers" among them, an adult narrator confronts a small child and, like the "homely Nurse"[1] of the "Immortality" ode, "even with something of a Mother's mind, / And no unworthy aim" does all he can to make the child "forget the glories he hath known, / And that imperial palace whence he came" (ll. 79-84). Because the narrator presumably has "yearnings . . . in [his] own natural kind," the encounter is an attempted seduction the purpose of which is to bind the child and man together as inmates of the earth. Particularly is this true in the attempted binding of the son to his father in "Anecdote For Fathers." At the same time, however, the narrator in each case acts somewhat in the manner of Milton's Satan confronting the still innocent Eve. In his "Immortality" ode, which (as Wordsworth points out in the Fenwick note) explores the same issues as "We Are Seven," Wordsworth examines the relationship of the adult narrator to the child in a far more complex way. Watching "a six years' Darling of a pigmy size" (l. 86) playing at life in the presence of its parents, he is at once amused and appalled by what he sees. On the one hand, the child is a "little Actor" who, "with new joy and pride," plays out the stages of life in the manner described in *As You Like It,* making himself in the process earth's "Inmate Man." On the other hand, he is blindly destroying his own condition of "blessedness" (l. 129) by provoking "with such earnest pains . . . / The years to bring the inevitable yoke" (ll. 127-28). While in the two lyrics already cited it is the narrator who does the provoking, in the ode it is the child himself, Wordsworth's narrator remaining the *spectator ab extra.* At the same time, however, Wordsworth, as distinct from the narrator, internalizes the child whom the narrator objectively observes, making him in the process a metaphor of the poet writing an ode about growing up. The tension between narrator and child, the narrator perceiving in the child at play the unconscious process by which the child will eventually merge with the narrator, becomes as mental action (the mythos of the poem) the struggle of the mind itself in its act of creation questioning its own activity. The narrator's consciousness of the child at play enacts within the poem the poetic consciousness that is shaping it. While the narrator's persistent questioning brings into play a self-consciousness which could rob the child of its unconscious innocence, the poet's philosophic consciousness finally redeems that destructive self-consciousness by absorbing it into a larger awareness that is "too deep for tears" (l. 207). What finally emerges as the poem's mythos is neither a fallen child nor a guilt-ridden observer, but, rather, a philosophic mind whose affirmation of immortality keeps "watch o'er man's mortality" (l. 202). The poet's consciousness redeems a potentially Satanic narrator by its affirmation of the fortunate fall. The triumph of that consciousness within the poem itself allows Wordsworth to declare in the final lines that "another race hath been, and other palms are won" (l. 203). What began as an elegy has ended as an ode.

Having scaled the walls of Eden and positioned himself like a cormorant on the Tree of Life where he sits devising death, Milton's Satan, like Wordsworth's narrator viewing the children at play on a blissful May morning, sees before him the innocent couple in their idyllic setting, Milton's "Heaven on Earth" (iv:208) becoming Wordsworth's "Heaven" that "lies about us in our infancy" (l. 66). Gazing upon them, Satan is again reminded (as is Wordsworth's narrator) of the "celestial light" (i:244) that was once the daily apparel of his world. "League with you I seek," he declares to the couple who are unaware of his presence (even as Wordsworth's children are unaware of the potentially intrusive narrator), "And mutual amity so streight, so close, / That I with you must dwell, or you with me" (iv:375-77). Since it is impossible for Satan to dwell with them unless he repents, they must of "necessitie" (iv:393) dwell with him. "Ah gentle paire," he cries with a pity that mocks its own intention because it is powerless to act,

> ye little think how nigh
> Your change approaches, when all these delights
> Will vanish and deliver ye to woe,

More woe, the more your taste is now for joy,
Happie, but for so happie ill secur'd
Long to continue. . . .

(IV:366-71)

Watching the innocent children at play, Wordsworth's narrator, without Satan's intent, echoes Satan's sentiments. Unlike Satan, he is able, because of the very different mythos Wordsworth has in mind, to check his "thought of grief" (l. 22), though not without reiterated effort. "No more shall grief of mine the season wrong" (l. 26), he declares, rebuking himself for the sentiments already expressed in the first two stanzas, sentiments which he will nevertheless continue to repeat until, it would seem, Wordsworth was forced to lay the poem aside. "Oh evil day!" he cries again as he struggles to pull away from his own powerful sense of "lost happiness" (*P.L.* [*Paradise Lost*] I:55) which pervades the elegiac tone of the first four stanzas,

> if I were sullen
> While Earth herself is adorning,
> This sweet May-morning. . . .

(ll. 42-44)

And yet, having again (and yet again) rebuked himself for his alien intrusion upon an idyllic scene, he sees himself finally at the end of the fourth stanza cut off from, while in the very presence of, the Tree of Life:

> —But there's a Tree, of many, one,
> A single Field which I have looked upon,
> Both of them speak of something that is gone.

(ll. 51-53)

However checked or rebuked, the narrator's sense of alienation in which even the Tree of Life speaks to him, as it does to Satan, of death prepares the way for his grim apostrophe to the child that echoes Satan's apostrophe to Adam and Eve. Contemplating the child at play whom he demonically perceives buried alive in lines that Coleridge considered so abhorrent that Wordsworth removed them in the 1820 and all subsequent printings,[2] the narrator continues:

> Thou little Child, yet glorious in the might
> Of heaven-born freedom on thy being's height,
> Why with such earnest pains dost thou provoke
> The years to bring the inevitable yoke,
> Thus blindly with thy blessedness at strife?
> Full soon thy Soul shall have her earthly freight,
> And custom lie upon thee with a weight,
> Heavy as frost, and deep almost as life!

(ll. 125-32)

Where, in Milton, Satan's "necessitie" (iv:392) is the "Tyrants plea" (iv:392), in Wordsworth, the narrator's "inevitable" (l. 128) is the tyranny of sense binding him to an earth he can no longer escape, leaving him, at least without the intervention of a larger poetic consciousness, still alive in thought awaiting release from the grave.

In a letter to Mrs. Clarkson (December 1814), Wordsworth says that his "Immortality" ode "rests entirely upon two recollections of childhood; one that of a splendour in the objects of sense which is passed away; and the other an indisposition to bend to the law of death, as applying to our particular case."[3] Judging from the first four stanzas of his ode, Wordsworth laid the poem aside because he could not finally rescue his narrator from what appeared to be a fatal tendency to bend to what he seemed to consider the inevitable "law of death." He could not, that is, rescue his narrator from the Satan at work within him. In "We Are Seven," the narrator as Satan "devising Death / To them who liv'd" (*P.L.* IV:197-98) is far more starkly present, Wordsworth making no attempt to rescue him. The poem concludes with an impasse as child and narrator fail to make any real contact with each other, leaving the reader to construct for himself a dialectic out of the contraries that are presented. Wordsworth's narrator, it would appear, is entirely Satanic because he cannot, despite the presence of the child, make contact with the lost innocence in himself. The poet, however, distances himself from his narrator through the inclusion of the first quatrain and locates his energy in his sympathetic presentation of the child. His narrator, isolated from the poet's creativity, becomes the Accuser whose death-dealing arithmetic is a lie because it "murder[s] to dissect" ("The Tables Turned," l. 28). "—A simple child," the poem begins, rebuking the narrator in advance for what he is about to attempt,

> That lightly draws its breath,
> And feels its life in every limb,
> What should it know of death?

> (ll. 1-4)

To force death upon the child, the quatrain suggests, is to force her to catch her breath, to feel her life draining from her limbs, to abandon her innocent world for a killing self-consciousness in which knitting stockings, hemming kerchiefs, singing songs, eating supper from a porringer are no longer possible as vital, creative acts. It is, rather, to rob those acts of their spontaneity which is, as metaphor, to rob the poet of his creative power. Narrator and child confront each other in "We Are Seven" in what could be in the creative dynamics of the poet's mind a life and death struggle. It is those dynamics engaged in that life and death struggle that Wordsworth explores in his "Immortality" ode as indeed he explores them in all those other works in which his powers are fully engaged, though, quite clearly, here in this modest lyric they are not. Instead of the "feelings of childhood" flowing into "the powers of manhood," the two confront each other as mortal enemies.

With tyrannical insistence accompanied by a growing impatience, the narrator in "We Are Seven" tries to persuade the "simple Child" to "bend to the law of death." "But they are dead; those two are dead!" he finally exclaims in sheer exasperation, knowing at the same time that it is merely "throwing words away" to argue further. Though he would "dissect" by simple arithmetic what she is saying, the dissection is in vain. The child cannot subtract; her unconscious is a plenitude which continuously overflows with life. The narrator cannot reach "the hiding-places of man's power" which, as Wordsworth points out toward the end of *The Prelude* (XII:279-80), are open to the child but closed to him. Because the narrator is unable to murder the child by bringing death into her world with all its woe through loss of Eden, the poet need not intervene on her behalf as the "one greater Man" who can restore her to her "Blissful Seat" (*P.L.* I:5). Wordsworth, as poet, need not call his whole soul into activity in an effort to enact its "ideal perfection." He is not called upon to reveal himself as the "Mighty Prophet! Seer blest!" a role which he assigns to both Coleridge and himself in the concluding lines of *The Prelude*.

II

In his treatment of the fall, Wordsworth in his "Immortality" ode chose the Platonic myth of pre-existence because it allowed him to present it as a gradual, less traumatic, process than the direct confrontation with Satan offered by Milton. Despite Adam's final realization that his fall was fortunate, the grounding of psychic growth in an act of disobedience bringing with it "death" and "woe" ruled out nature as man's moral and spiritual guide. For Milton's "one greater Man" he therefore substituted the "homely Nurse" whose maternal concern for her foster-child's natural development by-passed any need to bring Satan directly upon the human scene. Wordsworth worked out this loosely adapted Platonic resolution to the dilemma of the first four stanzas in March, 1804, at a time when he had decided to extend *The Prelude* beyond the completion of his formal education at Cambridge to include his encounter with the revolution in France and its aftermath in England. In his examination of himself as a patriot, Wordsworth was equally concerned to steer for himself a course that led away from the pattern of crime and punishment explored in *The Borderers* and "Guilt and Sorrow" in the direction of something more modest which he at one point describes as "juvenile errors" (XI:54). The station he assigned himself, though it was one he could not entirely sustain, is described at the end of Book VIII. "From those sad scenes when meditation turned," he writes of his experience in France, setting it in advance within the mythos of his recently completed "Immortality" ode,

> Lo! everything that was indeed divine
> Retained its purity inviolate,
> Nay brighter shone, by this portentous gloom
> Set off; such opposition as aroused
> The mind of Adam, yet in Paradise
> Though fallen from bliss. . . .

> (VIII:654-60)

"Though fallen from bliss," Wordsworth will argue, he remained "yet in Paradise."

As Wordsworth describes it, the France of the revolution seemed initially to him "apparelled in celestial light," having for him "the glory and the freshness of a dream." Under the direction of Michael Beaupuy, he, like the idealized Beaupuy,

> . . . through the events
> Of that great change wandered in perfect faith,
> As through a book, an old romance, or tale
> Of Fairy, or some dream of actions wrought
> Behind the summer clouds. . . .
>
> (IX:298-302)

Like the child of the "Immortality" ode who finds heaven about him in his infancy, the earth of France seemed to Wordsworth "an inheritance, new fallen" which he now visited for the first time to find in it a home. "Bliss was it in that dawn to be alive," he exclaims, "But to be young was very Heaven" (XI:108-9). And the reason was that he found himself among ideal companions, men who were still playing the same games that he played as a child. "I had a world about me—'twas my own," Wordsworth writes of his own childhood, "I made it, for it only lived to me, / And to the God who sees into the heart" (III:141-43). Describing himself as a patriot in France, he images himself walking about in his new home, looking upon the spot "with cordial transport," moulding and remoulding it in his imagination, "half-pleased with things that [were] amiss" because it would be "such joy to see them disappear" (XI:149-52).

This same childhood world, which in Book III he identifies with "earth's first inhabitants" (III:152), is, he continues, the "very world" of the two revolutionary factions, the Jacobins and the Girondists. "They who fed their childhood upon dreams," Wordsworth writes of the Jacobins,

> The play-fellows of fancy, who had made
> All powers of swiftness, subtilty, and strength
> Their ministers,—who in lordly wise had stirred
> Among the grandest objects of the sense,
> And dwelt with whatsoever they found there
> As if they had within some lurking right
> To wield it. . . .

He then goes on to contrast the fierce spirit of the Jacobins with the gentler spirit of the Girondists in a manner that evokes the prevailing and contrasting moods of his own childhood:

> . . . they, too, who of gentle mood
> Had watched all gentle motions, and to these
> Had fitted their own thoughts, schemers more mild,
> And in the region of their peaceful selves;—
> Now was it that *both* found, the meek and lofty
> Did both find, helpers to their hearts' desire
> And stuff at hand, plastic as they could wish,—
> Were called upon to exercise their skill,
> Not in Utopia,—subterranean fields,—
> Or some secreted island, Heaven knows where!
> But in the very world, which is the world
> Of all of us,—the place where, in the end,
> We find our happiness, or not at all!
>
> (XI:125-44)

Having recreated in France the "celestial" world of the infant, identifying the two revolutionary factions with the *puer aeternus*, Wordsworth, in his extended *Prelude,*[4] had

to explore his own gradual disillusionment in a manner that would, in his words, "suit the work we fashion" (XI:285). He had, that is, to assert, so far as he could, that his faith in the ultimate end of the revolution left him, in the immediate arena of actual events, "as far as angels are from guilt" (X:145). Thus, describing his reaction to the rise of Robespierre, he is careful to insist that "these are things / Of which I speak, only as they were storm / Or sunshine to my individual mind, / No further" (X:121-24). And when he received in England news of Robespierre's death, his response is the innocent one of a child at play. "Come now, ye golden times" (X:578), he exclaims in mock imitation of the rescuing knights who presided over his childhood games. Having exhausted his "uneasy bursts / Of exultation," Wordsworth describes his return home in a manner that is intended to preserve his child-like distance from the contamination of human guilt. Not Satan, but the "homely Nurse" presides. "I pursued my way," he writes,

> Along that very shore which I had skimmed
> In former days, when—spurring from the Vale
> Of Nightshade, and St. Mary's mouldering fane,
> And the stone abbot, after circuit made
> In wantonness of heart, a joyous band
> Of schoolboys hastening to their distant home
> Along the margin of the moonlight sea—
> We beat with thundering hoofs the level sand.[5]
>
> (X. 596-603)

Wordsworth's image of the "joyous band / Of schoolboys hastening to their distance home" fully describes his early adventures as a revolutionary in France. It was, however, an image he could not sustain. The inclusion of the revolution, carrying his poem beyond its originally conceived "single and determined bounds" (I:641), brought with it a descent into a Satanic darkness that in his "Immortality" ode he was careful to avoid, though its presence could be felt, particularly in the lines that Wordsworth would later remove. He had, that is, to come finally to grips in the 1805 *Prelude* with the experience dealt with in 1795-96 at a distance from himself in *The Borderers.*

In the figure of Oswald, Wordsworth in *The Borderers* explores at the distance of a "dramatic tale" what in *The Prelude* he describes as "the errors into which [he] fell" in France.[6] These "errors," he argues, arose from turning his heart aside "from Nature's way," substituting for it "present objects" and "reasonings false / From their beginnings" (XI:286-91). Explaining to Marmaduke the trap into which he has led him, Oswald tells of leaving his captain to die on a bare rock because the captain had presumably "hatched among the crew a foul Conspiracy / Against [his] honour" (IV:1690-91). In reality, the captain was innocent, and Oswald, initially overcome by guilt, sought refuge in a convent. There, like Wordsworth, he dissected the workings of his own brain, and concluded that he could either submit to his suicidal despair or ascend, Godwin-like, "into a region of futurity / Whose natural element was freedom" (IV:1817-18).[7]

The "foul Conspiracy / Against [Wordsworth's] honour" lay in England's betrayal of the revolution in France by its declaration of war. In that declaration Wordsworth experienced the betrayal of his own innocence, which is to say, his own idealism. "No shock," he writes,

> Given to my moral nature had I known
> Down to that very moment; neither lapse
> Nor turn of sentiment that might be named
> A revolution, save at this one time;
> All else was progress on the self-same path
> On which, with a diversity of pace,
> I had been travelling: this a stride at once
> Into another region.
>
> (x:269-76)

The result was a treasonous withdrawal from his own country which he vividly describes as "a conflict of sensations without a name" (x:290). Though he does not name it, he does image it. Loving the sight of a village steeple, he found himself among a congregation praying for victory sitting silent, "like an uninvited guest / Whom no one owned" fed "on the day of vengeance yet to come" (x:292-99). Wordsworth in his village church had become Satan in the Garden of Eden looking down upon an innocent congregation and plotting its destruction. "Three sleepless nights," Oswald tells Marmaduke of his brief sojourn in the convent,

> I passed in sounding on,
> Through words and things, a dim and perilous way;
> And wheresoe'er I turned, I beheld
> A slavery compared to which the dungeon
> And clanking chains are perfect liberty.
>
> (iv:1774-78)

"Most melancholy at that time, O Friend! / Were my day-thoughts," Wordsworth writes of his life in England, pacing the sea-shore where the fleet lay anchored,

> —my nights were miserable
> Through months, through years, long after the last
>   beat
> Of those atrocities, the hour of sleep
> To me came rarely charged with natural gifts,
> Such ghastly visions had I of despair
> And tyranny, and implements of death;
> And innocent victims sinking under fear,
> And momentary hope, and worn-out prayer,
> Each in his separate cell, or penned in crowds
> For sacrifice, and struggling with forced mirth
> And levity in dungeons, where the dust
> Was laid with tears. Then suddenly the scene
> Changed, and the unbroken dream entangled me
> In long orations, which I strove to plead
> Before unjust tribunals,—with a voice
> Labouring, a brain confounded, and a sense,
> Death-like, of treacherous desertion, felt
> In the last place of refuge—my own soul.
>
> (x:397-415)

The child for whom in the original version of the "Immortality" ode "the grave / Is but a lonely bed without the sense or sight / Of day or the warm light," like the twelve year old boy of Winander before whose grave the poet stands, perhaps has its psychic origin in Wordsworth in England contemplating the death of his soul, a soul already celebrated in the fullness of its life in the vision of childhood and youth that constituted the two earlier versions of *The Prelude.*

"Juvenile errors," "storm / Or sunshine to my individual mind / No more" were, Wordsworth slowly realized as he continued to write, deceptively simple renderings of his experience of the revolution. The form he wished to impose could not contain what he had to say. Neither "popular government and equality" nor "wild belief engrafted on their names / By false philosophy" were, Wordsworth argues, the cause of the reign of terror. It was, rather,

> . . . a terrific reservoir of guilt
> And ignorance filled up from age to age,
> That could no longer hold its loathsome charge,
> But burst and spread in deluge through the land.
>
> (x:473-80)

This reservoir with its loathsome charge was not, however, something from which he was himself immune. Though he struggled to keep his distance, he could not finally maintain his child-like stance. Introducing his account of the revolution, he returns to the image of the river of his own consciousness to describe it not as flowing naturally to an immortal ocean but as engulfing him "soon in a ravenous sea" (ix:4). In this context, the first two versions of *The Prelude,* more or less complete by the spring of 1804, assume a rather different character. Wordsworth was in them yielding to "old remembrances" because he feared "to shape a way direct" to the ravenous engulfment of the revolution. The earlier versions of *The Prelude* become a measuring back, far back, in an effort to find "the very regions which he crossed / In his first outset." They constitute a turning and returning "with intricate delay" (ix:1-7), a flight from danger in quest of a lost innocence.

While working on the two book and five-part versions of *The Prelude,* Wordsworth had apparently no intention of setting off the vision of his early years by the "portentous gloom" that overtook him in France. He had, that is, originally no intention of subjecting his vision of his early years to the logic of the Satanic narrator in "We Are Seven." The decision to continue *The Prelude* beyond the age of twenty to include his experience in France was more by default than by design. Like Coleridge, Wordsworth had thought of *The Prelude* as a "tail-piece of 'The Recluse'" which he was more than anxious to get on with; had Coleridge as his joint-labourer been more cooperative and reliable, he would in all likelihood have concluded *The Prelude* in 1799 or, at the very latest, 1804. When, however, Coleridge, in declining health, left for Malta in March 1804 (taking most of the five-part *Prelude* with him), Wordsworth, dependent upon his presence, was forced to procrastinate. Instead of continuing with *The Recluse,* he started by the end of March the sixth book of

The Prelude. In his introduction to Book IX, he admits to his "shapeless eagerness" (l. 19), still uncertain about a plausible shape for his life as a patriot, given the form that his earlier version had already taken. The result was a confusion of voices that, despite continued revision, Wordsworth could not in the books on the revolution resolve, the darkness that surfaced remaining a threatening intrusion upon the benign administrations of the "homely Nurse" who was and remained his muse.

III

Justifying the "independent intellect" (mind divorced from instinct and feeling), Oswald in *The Borderers* describes leaving the camp of Crusaders to wander alone through "deep chasms troubled by roaring streams," or surveying from the top of Lebanon "the moonlight desert, and the moonlight sea," perceiving in the process "what mighty objects do impress their forms / To elevate our intellectual being" (IV:1802-10). In the opening book of *The Excursion,* Wordsworth describes the Wanderer struggling at the age of eighteen "to mitigate the fever of his heart" by scanning "the laws of light / Amid the roar of torrents," only then to ask repose "from his intellect / And the stillness of abstracted thought" (I:291-95). Finding in the turbulence of nature no repose for his "wandering thoughts," he finally settled for the "irksome drudgery" of a "vagrant Merchant under a heavy load / Bent as he moves, and needing frequent rest" (I:322-25). This choice of a vocation has, on one level, a certain resemblance to the fate of Marmaduke in *The Borderers.* "A wanderer *must I* go," he tells Wallace, "The Spectre of that innocent Man, my guide" (V:2344-45). Marmaduke must wander the earth expiating the crime he has committed "till anger is appeased / In Heaven, and Mercy gives me leave to die" (V:2352-53). In his choice of the life of a Pedlar, Wordsworth metaphorically describes his own choice of the life of a poet. "Yet do such travellers find their own delight," Wordsworth continues, describing the Pedlar's lot,

> And their hard service, deemed debasing now,
> Gained merited respect in simpler times;
> When squire, and priest, and they who round them
>   dwelt
> In rustic sequestration—all dependent
> Upon the Pedlar's toil—supplied their wants,
> Or pleased their fancies, with the wares he brought.
> Not ignorant was the Youth that still so few
> Of his adventurous countrymen were led
> By perseverance in this track of life
> To competence and ease:—to him it offered
> Attractions manifold;—and this he chose.
>
> (I:326-37)

In the vocation of poet, Wordsworth found, in addition to "attractions manifold," a way to expiate his intellectual crime against nature. Though the poet's vocation, particularly as he chose to practise it, beginning with the *Lyrical Ballads,* was "deemed debasing now," he recognized that "in simpler times" it had "gained merited respect." The restoration of those times, if not on earth at least in the

mind, became his avowed intention. Barely concealed within his portrait of the wandering Pedlar is his own idealized image of the poet as wandering minstrel. "I, too, have been a wanderer," he exclaims in *The Prelude,* contrasting his wanderings with those of Coleridge. It is an image and a contrast to which he returns more than once. Rejoicing in the "windings of a public way," he implicitly contrasts his own earth wanderings with those of Coleridge:

> Yes, something of the grandeur which invests
> The mariner who sails the roaring sea
> Through storm and darkness, early in my mind
> Surrounded, too, the wanderers of the earth;
> Grandeur as much, and loveliness far more.
>
> (XIII:152-56)

Particularly in the composition of *The Prelude,* Wordsworth, still haunted by his Satanic experience in France, was continually forming and reforming his image of himself as poet. In the two part version of 1799, he was largely concerned to retrace his life "up to an eminence" (III:171), to describe

> the might of souls,
> And what they do within themselves while yet
> The yoke of earth is new to them, the world
> Nothing but a wild field where they are sown.
>
> (III:177-80)

His real subject in this early version was "genius, power, / Creation and divinity itself" (III:170-71), beginning with an image of the "infant Babe" as an "agent of the one great Mind / . . . creator and receiver both" (II:257-58) and ending at the age of seventeen when his soul had attained its "eminence," an eminence that Wordsworth would image in his account of the ascent of Mount Snowdon, there to confront upon its peak his own creative power in the guise of a "fixed, abysmal, gloomy, breathing-place" that seemed to him "the type of a majestic intellect" (XIV:58-67). In the context of this image of himself as a "Mighty Prophet! Seer blest!" Wordsworth could in his 1800 introduction to *The Recluse* announce his epic theme as the poet's apocalyptic marriage to the "goodly universe / In love and holy passion."[8] Upon a mount of transfiguration he had perceived his "celestial" form and could, therefore, in the imagery of the Second Coming proclaim in his own "spousal verse" the descent of the New Jerusalem.

So long as he was satisfied to limit his vision to this "heroic argument" celebrating "genuine prowess' (III:181-82), so long, that is, as he was content to tell

> a tale
> Of matters which not falsely may be called
> The glory of my youth,
>
> (III:171-73)

he had no need to abandon Paradise for a fallen world. The decision to continue his "tale" beyond "the glory of [his] youth," however, forced him radically to modify his "heroic argument" and view in a very different light the "genuine prowess" proper to it. The failure of the French revolution forced him to abandon "heroic argument" even as Milton was forced by the failure of the English revolution. The youth standing upon the eminence of his seventeenth year becomes, if arrested, or stationed there for worship, the Oswald of *The Borderers*. Like Milton before him, Wordsworth in his greatly expanded vision abandoned the "heroic" image by turning it over to Satan.

Having described his moment upon the "eminence" as a point within his own soul where he stood single, language itself becoming from within that point "breathings for incommunicable powers" (III:187), Wordsworth, enlarging his poem beyond his seventeenth year to include his life at Cambridge, realized that he "must quit this theme" (III:189). The "heroic argument" rejected, he substitutes for the image of the poet as "Mighty Prophet," the image of the poet as "Traveller":

> No more: for now into a populous plain
> We must descend. A Traveller I am,
> Whose tale is only of himself; even so,
> So be it, if the pure of heart be prompt
> To follow, and if thou, my honoured Friend!
> Who in these thoughts art ever at my side,
> Support, as heretofore, my fainting steps.
>
> (III:194-200)

The descent from the "eminence" in the second version of *The Prelude* avoids almost entirely the traumatic fall that accompanied his experience of the revolution with which he was still not prepared to deal. "Yet true it is," he writes,

> that I had made a change
> In climate, and my nature's outward coat
> Changed also slowly and insensibly.
> Full oft the quiet and exalted thoughts
> Of loneliness gave way to empty noise
> And superficial pastimes; now and then
> Forced labour, and more frequently forced hopes;
> And, worst of all, a treasonable growth
> Of indecisive judgments, that impaired
> And shook the mind's simplicity.
>
> (III:204-13)

The reason for the impaired simplicity is more apparent in the third version of *The Prelude* where Wordsworth's "treasonable growth / Of indecisive judgments" becomes the Godwinian result of his disillusionment with the revolution and the demonic form of the eminence that attended his seventeenth year. The "might" of soul, the "majestic intellect," had become the "purer element," a "tempting region . . . / For Zeal to enter and refresh herself." "Reason's naked self" became "the object of [his] fervour." "What delight!" Wordsworth exclaims,

> How glorious! in self-knowledge and self-rule,
> To look through all the frailties of the world,
> And, with a resolute mastery shaking off
> Infirmities of nature, time, and place,
> Build social upon personal Liberty,

> Which, to the blind restraints of general laws
> Superior, magisterially adopts
> One guide, the light of circumstances, flashed
> Upon an independent intellect.
> Thus expectation rose again; thus hope,
> From her first ground expelled, grew proud once more.
> Oft, as my thoughts were turned to human kind,
> I scorned indifference; but, inflamed with thirst
> Of a secure intelligence, and sick
> Of other longing, I pursued what seemed
> A more exalted nature; wished that Man
> Should start out of his earthly, worm-like state,
> And spread abroad the wings of Liberty,
> Lord of himself, in undisturbed delight—
> A noble aspiration! *yet* I feel
> (Sustained by worthier as by wiser thoughts)
> The aspiration, nor shall ever cease
> To feel it. . . .
>
> (XI:227-58)

Seduced by "Reason's naked self," Wordsworth entered a "purer element" that became the demonic form of his earlier envisioned apocalyptic marriage. And the result was a psychic condition that for a time approximated that of Marmaduke seduced by Oswald. It is from this condition—Wordsworth, his brain confounded, pleading before "unjust tribunals" in an effort to save a "death-like" soul guilty of "treacherous desertion" (X:412-15)—that Dorothy, Wordsworth's "homely Nurse," rescued him. "Then It was," he writes,

> Thanks to the bounteous Giver of all good!—
> That the beloved Sister in whose sight
> Those days were passed, now speaking in a voice
> Of sudden admonition—like a brook
> That did but *cross* a lonely road, and now
> Is seen, heard, felt, and caught at every turn,
> Companion never lost through many a league—
> Maintained for me a saving intercourse
> With my true self; for, though bedimmed and changed
> Much, as it seemed, I was no further changed
> Than as a clouded and waning moon:
> She whispered still that brightness would return,
> She, in the midst of all, preserved me still
> A Poet, made me seek beneath that name,
> And that alone, my office upon earth;
> And, lastly, as hereafter will be shown,
> If willing audience fail not, Nature's self,
> By all varieties of human love
> Assisted, led me back through opening day
> To those sweet counsels between head and heart
> Whence grew that genuine knowledge, fraught with
>   peace,
> Which, through the later sinkings of this cause,
> Hath still upheld me, and upholds me now
> In the catastrophe (for so they dream,
> And nothing less), when, finally to close
> And seal up all the gains of France, a Pope
> Is summoned in to crown an Emperor.
>
> (XI:336-60)

In "Tintern Abbey," what is "felt in the blood, and felt along the heart" passes, says Wordsworth, "even into my purer mind / With tranquil restoration" (ll. 28-29). In the aftermath of the revolution, Wordsworth's mind was cut off from his "blood" and "heart." He had condemned himself to a guillotine of his own devising, moved about in a "death-like" condition, the bloodless and heartless ghost of his former self, until, under Dorothy's guidance, the "sweet counsels between head and heart" were restored. Brutally dismembered by the trauma of self-betrayal, Wordsworth began with Dorothy's help the long process of re-membering. "But is not each a memory to himself?" Wordsworth asks. The "memory" that Wordsworth was "to himself" is, finally, Wordsworth's subject. Understood in the context of the 1850 version of *The Prelude,* Wordsworth's re-membering becomes a redemptive journey in which the Marmaduke seduced by Oswald becomes finally the Pedlar of *The Excursion.* In that process, similar in so many respects to the movement of Milton's mind from *Paradise Lost* to *Paradise Regained,* Wordsworth succeeded in substituting Milton's "deeds / Above Heroic, though in secret done, / And unrecorded left through many an age" (*P.R.* I:14-16) for his original "heroic argument." In Milton that substitution was finally the defeat of Satan by the "one greater Man" (*P.L.* 4) within the wide wilderness of the human mind. In Wordsworth, it was finally the defeat of a Satanic intellect by a "homely Nurse" who not only assisted Wordsworth to restore that intellect to its original state of innocence, but also to grant it its proper "secret" action "unrecorded left through many an age," which is to say, since Milton's very different treatment of it. The redemptive power of God present in Christ becomes in *The Prelude* the redemptive power of nature present in Dorothy.

IV

Christ overcoming the Tempter in *Paradise Regained* overcomes the world, instructing the reader how, in the concluding words in *The Prelude,*

> the mind of man becomes
> A thousand times more beautiful than the earth
> On which he dwells, above this frame of things
> (Which, 'mid all revolution in the hopes
> And fears of men, doth still remain unchanged)
> In beauty exalted, as it is itself
> Of quality and fabric more divine.

(XIV:448-54)

In the concluding books to *Paradise Lost,* Milton had offered that same instruction, though in a less dramatic fashion, in the dialogue between Michael and Adam upon the Mount of Vision. Both Christ and Adam, tempted by Satan, rejected the "heroic" ideal in favour of "deeds / Above Heroic" which, belonging essentially to the mind itself, were accessible only to the poet who could alone provide "breathings for incommunicable powers." The events which Milton declares were "unrecorded left through many an Age / Worthy t'have not remain'd so long unsung" are, in the final analysis, the architecture of those inner events constituting the Paradise constructed within Milton himself for which the Bible provided a model subject finally to the poet's "answerable style" (IX:20). The Kingdom of

God is, for Milton and Wordsworth alike, a metaphor of the human mind viewed in its ideal perfection. Like Christ's Kingdom it is *in* this world but not *of* it.

When in the "Nativity" ode, the birth of Christ silences the pagan oracles, Milton is already announcing the death of the heroic ideal as a model of human behaviour. Rather than reject that ideal outright, however, he assigns it to a pre-existent world of super-human beings perverted by Satan into a state of primitive conflict that descends into the pagan world whose gods are the incarnation of fallen angels. The gradual overcoming, rather than conquest, of this fallen "heroic" world constitutes the building of a Paradise within Adam happier far than the one he had lost. For both Milton and Wordsworth, Adam's work was itself the metaphor of the poet's task. The poet who, like Wordsworth, retires "to his native mountains, with the hope of being enabled to construct a literary work that might live" is Adam building a Paradise within him surpassing the Garden that he had lost.

In the opening books of *The Prelude,* Wordsworth is simultaneously describing an earthly paradise and building an inner one. The paradise within is, for Wordsworth, the unconscious paradise inhabited by the child and therefore "unrecorded left through many an age," the child before Wordsworth leaving behind him no written record of himself. Though reading "the eternal deep," he remains "deaf and silent." What the child is in touch with, Wordsworth suggests, is "incommunicable." The world he inhabits is a hiding-place of power that is open to the child though closed to the adult.[9] It is a "fixed, abysmal, gloomy, breathing-place" which in *The Prelude* becomes the breath issuing forth in articulate sound described by him as a spontaneous overflow of "poetic numbers." These numbers, he suggests, flow directly from the unconscious to become the poet's "own voice" carrying within it "the mind's / Internal echo of [that] imperfect sound" (I:51-56). It is this "internal echo," "correspondent breeze," that constitutes the presence of the divine child within the man.

"Haunted forever by the eternal mind," the Wordsworthian child is unconsciously in touch with divinity. In his spontaneous play he acts as an "agent of the one great Mind" (I:257) so that in describing the play Wordsworth is speaking of "genius, power, / Creation and divinity itself." So long as the child remains "housed in a dream," "moving about in worlds not realized," his play is innocent. If, however, that unconscious life is exploited in a "lordly wise" way by men who believe "they [have] within some lurking right / To wield it," the apocalyptic world proper to the child becomes the demonic parody of it in the adult. The divinity in which the child unconsciously participates becomes in the adult the mind's "strength / Of usurpation" by which it abrogates that divinity to itself to wield it as if it were a god. Adults arrested in innocence, as the revolutionaries were in France, are, Wordsworth gradually realized, Satanic.

That recognition, explored in depth in "the less guarded words" of *The Borderers,* constituted Wordsworth's awakening to his vocation as a poet. When Blake argues in his *Marriage of Heaven and Hell* that all true poets are "of the Devil's party without knowing it," he means, in part, that the poet is born and made in coming to terms with his own "strength of usurpation." The arts, Blake suggests, are the legitimate use of that strength, the object of which is the construction of an inner Paradise. He therefore identifies the imagination with God and the poet with Christ. Wordsworth, like Milton and Blake, realized that political revolution constitutes an arrested exploitation of creative power in which the "feelings of childhood" have not been fully absorbed into the "powers of manhood."[10] That absorption required for all of them a confrontation with the actual or potential Satan within themselves in an attempt to release the imagination from the fetters to which it is otherwise bound. In this sense, Satan in *Paradise Regained* is determined to keep the human imagination which is Christ fettered to the world which Satan alone can offer. The release of the imagination from those fetters constitutes the mythos of Milton's brief epic.

In the heroic world which all three poets rejected, the release of the imagination from the fetters of the world constituted in the final analysis the hero's tragic enmeshment in the world. Lacking in the pagan hero is any consciousness of an inner world so that he is forced to act out on political and military battlefields an inner or psychic reality about which he knows nothing at all.[11] The classical hero acts in ignorance of his true self. He is, therefore, in this respect, like the revolutionaries in France who remained in their political and military exploits children innocent of who they were. Oswald sums up for Wordsworth the radical limitations of the heroic ideal. "Action is transitory," he tells Marmaduke,

> —a step, a blow,
> The motion of a muscle—this way or that—
> 'Tis done, and in the after-vacancy
> We wonder at ourselves like men betrayed:
> Suffering is permanent, obscure and dark,
> And shares the nature of infinity.
>
> (III:1539-44)

In turning aside from action understood as "a step, a blow, / The motion of a muscle," Wordsworth, like Milton and Blake, is redirecting it toward a psychic rather than physical universe which remains as yet both "above" it and "secret." In redirecting the imagination toward this inner world, making that the proper field of action, Wordsworth, like Milton and Blake, had no desire to affirm or celebrate the oracular or the occult. Indeed, as poets, they were anxious to reach as wide an audience as possible while insisting that they could not in the process betray their vision by clothing it in false heroic apparel. The heroic had become Satan's domain and the poet in rejecting it was, in the final analysis, rejecting the Satan within himself who was tempted by it, particularly as the heroic assured him of an audience. Having confronted the Satanic in the "heroic" deeds of the revolution, Wordsworth set about in his vision of childhood to restore them to their original innocence as spontaneous acts "in secret done." "Unknown,

unthought of, yet I was most rich," Wordsworth writes of the world in which he moved as a child. "I had a world about me—'twas my own," he continues. "I made it, for it only lived to me, / And to the God who sees into the heart" (III:140-43). Any outward gesture that rendered that world visible to adult eyes, he goes on, constituted a betrayal. Whenever that happened, "though rarely," the adult witnesses "called it madness." "So indeed it was," Wordsworth boldly replies to his hostile critics,

> If child-like fruitfulness in passing joy,
> If steady moods of thoughtfulness matured
> To inspiration, sort with such a name;
> If prophecy be madness; if things viewed
> By poets in old time, and higher up
> By the first men, earth's first inhabitants,
> May in these tutored days no more be seen
> With undisordered sight. But leaving this,
> It was no madness. . . .
>
> (III:146-55)

Wordsworth then goes on to argue that the so-called "madness" of the child was actually an enormously sensitized perception of the natural world which bound him to it so that the inner and outer worlds still remained one:

> for the bodily eye
> Amid my strongest workings evermore
> Was searching out the lines of difference
> As they lie hid in all external forms,
> Near or remote, minute or vast; an eye
> Which, from a tree, a stone, a withered leaf,
> To the broad ocean and the azure heavens,
> Spangled with kindred multitudes of stars,
> Could find no surface where its power might sleep;
> Which spake perpetual logic to my soul,
> And by an unrelenting agency
> Did bind my feelings even as in a chain.
>
> (III:140-66)

Wordsworth's task in the third version of *The Prelude* was to distance this visionary world of the child from the actual world of men in such a way that it could feed the actual without at the same time overwhelming it, for in that case the divine madness of the child would become the actual madness of the adult. In the necessary process of distancing, which Wordsworth considered less a loss than a gain, the poet gradually absorbs an unconscious childhood into his adult consciousness by transforming unconscious play into conscious creative power. The child raised to consciousness becomes the poet. "The eagerness of infantine desire" (II:25) becomes "punctual service high, / Matins and vespers of harmonious verse" (I:44-45). Like Milton in his "Nativity" ode, Wordsworth found in the divine child a metaphor of the poet subduing the world to the "meek-eyed Peace" of the Paradise within:

> No War, or Battails sound
> Was heard the World around:
>   The idle spear and shield were high up hung;
> The hooked Chariot stood
> Unstained with hostile blood,

The Trumpet spake not to the armed throng,
And Kings sate still with awfull eye,
As if they surely knew their sovran Lord was by.

(ll. 53-60)

To this image of himself as poet, Dorothy, as "homely Nurse," finally, after his Satanic encounter, brought him: "For, spite of thy sweet influence," he writes of Dorothy,

fand the touch
Of kindred hands that opened out the springs
Of genial thought in childhood, and in spite
Of all that unassisted I had marked
In life of nature of those charms minute
That win their way into the heart by stealth,
Still, to the very going-out of youth,
I too exclusively esteemed *that* love,
And sought *that* beauty, which, as Milton sings,
Hath terror in it. Thou didst soften down
This over-sternness; but for thee, dear Friend!
My soul, too reckless of mild grace, had stood
In her original self too confident,
Retained too long a countenance severe;
A rock with torrents roaring, with the clouds
Familiar, and a favourite of the stars:
But thou didst plant its crevices with flowers,
Hang it with shrubs that twinkle in the breeze,
And teach the little birds to built their nests
And warble in its chambers.

(XIV:237-56)

Milton's beauty that "hath terror in it" was the beauty particular to Satan to which, in retrospect, Wordsworth realized he was early unconsciously committed until in France its terror finally reigned in his own mind, destroying the very soul that Dorothy would restore to life. The "strength / Of usurpation" which characterizes for Wordsworth the poet's imagination must therefore remain the secret prerogative of the soul silently weaving its "fabric more divine" out of the stuff of earth on which for a time it dwells, even as nature, by its "dark / Inscrutable workmanship" (I:341-42) weaves a body that evokes in "the meanest flower that blows . . . / Thoughts that do often lie too deep for tears." Under Dorothy's guidance, Wordsworth came to see in "the meanest flower" a metaphor of his own soul-making, substituting it for "*that* beauty, which, as Milton sings, / Hath terror in it." For this reason the silent action of the soul which operates beyond the "imperfect sound" of words "seeks for no trophies, struggles for no spoils / That may attest her prowess." The soul, Wordsworth concludes, is hidden in "its own perfection and reward," even as the source of the Nile's mighty flood is hidden in Abyssinian clouds (VI:610-16). Poetry, like the "whole Egyptian plain," is fertilized from a hidden fount which must remain hidden, for if invaded by the militant ego bent upon "trophies" and "spoils / That may attest her prowess," poetry, like the Egyptian plain, becomes a "death-like" desert, a place of "treacherous desertion." The soul's hiding-place of power invaded by the Satanic intellect releases not a fertilizing flood but a "terrific reservoir of guilt" that "burst[s] and spread[s] in deluge through the [poet's] land" (X:477-80). The danger, as Wordsworth came

to understand it, lay in rejecting "mild grace" in favour of self-deification. "But in its utmost abstraction and consequent state of reprobation," Coleridge writes in *The Statesman's Manual*,

the Will becomes satanic pride and rebellious self-idolatry in the relations of the spirit itself, and remorseless despotism relatively to others; the more hopeless as the more obdurate by its subjugation of sensual impulses, by its superiority to toil and pain and pleasure; in short by the fearful resolve to find in itself alone the one absolute motive of action, under which all other motives from within and from without must be either subordinated or crushed. . . . This is the character which Milton has so philosophically as well as sublimely embodied in the Satan of his Paradise Lost.[12]

V

When Satan in *Paradise Regained* offers Christ the Kingdoms of the world on the condition that he fall down and worship him, Milton presents a demonic parody of the descent of the New Jerusalem, a parody which Milton himself found in Christ's supposed marriage with the Roman Church. The descent of New Jerusalem in the posture of a whore is precisely what, finally, Wordsworth came to see in the failure of the French Revolution, a failure summed up for him "when finally to close / And seal up all the gains of France, a Pope / Is summoned in to crown and Emperor" (XI:358-60). "Since neither wealth, nor honour, arms nor arts, / Kingdom nor Empire please thee," Satan finally replies to Christ,

nor aught
By me propos'd in life contemplative,
Or active, tended on by glory, or fame,
What dost thou in this World? the Wilderness
For thee is fittest place, I found thee there,
An thither will return thee. . . .

(IV:368-74)

Paradise Regained ends with Christ "unobserv'd" privately returning to "his Mothers house" (IV:638-39)

Though Wordsworth avoids an encounter as direct as the religious one Milton presents, the larger pattern of the final version of *The Prelude* images a Wordsworth confronting a Tempter in the wilderness of his own mind, defeating him by rejecting the "wealth," "honour," "arms," "arts," "Kingdom" and "Empire" that the "heroic" world had to offer, and returning privately and "unobserv'd" to "his Mothers house," which is to say, to the "chosen Vale" (I:93) of the "homely Nurse." *The Prelude* opens with Wordsworth, spontaneously, even consciously, setting out on a three-day journey to his "chosen Vale" where Dorothy waits to greet him. Because he is propelled by "incommunicable powers" both within and without (the "blessing in this gentle breeze" is bound to the "correspondent breeze" within himself) he cannot lose his way, unless, that is, the "correspondent breeze" becomes an apocalyptic force, a tempest in the mind like the terror in France "vexing its own creation" (I:37). At the end of *The*

Prelude the reunion with Dorothy is accomplished. The space between, "a pleasant loitering journey" Wordsworth initially calls it, becomes in its inner dimension a redemptive journey under the aegis of the "mild grace" of the "homely Nurse" which as metaphor hides the invisible and "incommunicable" fount, fertilizing the poet's mind, constructing the poem as it moves along.

In his influential study of Wordsworth's major poetry, Geoffrey Hartman examined at length the way in which Wordsworth draws back like a "halted traveller" from the apocalyptic dimension that is natural to his imagination. Wordsworth, he concludes,

> never achieved his philosophic song. *Prelude* and *Excursion* are no more than "ante-chapels" to the "gothic church" of his unfinished work. An unresolved opposition between Imagination and Nature prevents him from becoming a visionary poet. It is a paradox, though not an unfruitful one, that he should scrupulously record nature's workmanship, which prepares the soul for its independence from sense-experience, yet refrain to use that independence out of respect of nature. His greatest verse still *takes its origin* in the memory of given experiences to which he is often pedantically faithful. He adheres, apparently against nature, to natural fact.[13]

Wordsworth, I suggest, experienced as a patriot the Satanic nature of the apocalyptic imagination.[14] While the soul is in its essence independent of sense-experience, being "strong in herself and in beatitude / That hides her," Wordsworth, like the Christ of *Paradise Regained,* is determined, despite the Satanic temptation to do so, not to release, "under such banners militant," its apocalyptic power. Hartman's conclusion that Wordsworth "never achieved his philosophic song" becomes, in the context of the song that Wordsworth did achieve, the complaint of Satan in *Paradise Regained* that Christ refused to avail himself of the "strength of usurpation" that was his to offer. The Christ of *Paradise Regained* knows that he is destined to sit "on *David's* Throne," a throne which he identifies with the Tree of Life, the Tree which Wordsworth himself had looked upon. "Know therefore," Christ tells Satan,

> when my season comes to sit
> On *David's* Throne, it shall be like a tree
> Spreading and over-shadowing all the Earth,
> Or as a stone that shall to pieces dash
> All Monarchies besides throughout the world,
> And of my Kingdom there shall be no end:
> Means there shall be to this, but what the means,
> Is not for thee to know, nor me to tell.
>
> (IV:146-53)

The means that is not for Satan to know is, Wordsworth asserts, following in the footsteps of Milton and Blake, the imagination, hiding its apocalyptic power by attending to "the simple produce of the common day." It is, Wordsworth argues, the poets who forward the day of man's deliverance "surely yet to come" (XIV:443). "Dearest Friend!," writes Wordsworth, addressing Coleridge toward the end of *The Prelude,*

> If thou partake the animating faith
> That Poets, even as Prophets, each with each
> Connected in a mighty scheme of truth,
> Have each his own peculiar faculty,
> Heaven's gift, a sense that fits him to perceive
> Objects unseen before, thou wilt not blame
> The humblest of this band who dares to hope
> That unto him hath also been vouchsafed
> An insight that in some sort he possesses,
> A privilege whereby a work of his,
> Proceeding from a source of untaught things,
> Creative and enduring, may become
> A power like one of Nature's.
>
> (XIII:300-312)

Following those critics like Harold Bloom and Paul de Man[15] who staked out for Wordsworth a Satanic territory free of nature, Hartman sees in Wordsworth's poetry of nature, merely the "ante-chapel" to a Gothic church he never completed. Milton, of course, knew the danger to the poet in committing himself to the construction of a Gothic cathedral, finding in that commitment the presence of the Tempter contaminating the voice of the "Heavenly Muse" who prefers "before all Temples th'upright heart and pure" (I:18). *The Prelude* is, finally, Wordsworth's temple to the human heart to which in the concluding lines of his "Immortality" ode he gives his final thanks. The Kingdom secretly present in the metaphor of the "meanest flower that blows" is a Kingdom that "Satan cannot find / Nor can his Watch Fiends find it" (*Milton,* 39:41-42). In Blake's *Milton,* the "meanest flower" becomes the "Wild Thyme" which, releasing its morning odour, becomes "Los's Messenger to Eden" (39:46-52). But Blake in *Milton* had, with Milton's help, confronted Satan directly, being as a poet far more apocalyptic than either Milton or Wordsworth. He could therefore release from his "meanest flower" the thoughts that Wordsworth kept hidden in the "beatitude" of a redeemed consciousness. The secrets that Christ is unwilling to reveal to Satan in *Paradise Regained* are the apocalyptic reality that Wordsworth himself gradually learned, as a result of the failure of the revolution, to conceal in metaphors that, to the discerning intellect of an enlightened reader, open to view the inner Kingdom which Christ compared to a little child.

Notes

1. All references to Wordsworth's poetry are taken from *The Poetical Works of Wordsworth,* ed. T. Hutchinson, revised, E. De Selincourt (London: Oxford U. Press, 1960). All references to Milton's poetry are taken from *The Student's Milton,* ed. F. W. Patterson (New York: Appleton-Century-Crofts, Inc., 1933).

2. Commenting upon Wordsworth's description of the grave as "A place of thought where we in waiting lie," Coleridge argues against Wordsworth's suggestion that a child "has no other notion of death than that of lying in a dark, cold place." "And still, I hope," Coleridge continues, "not as in a *place of thought*! not the frightful notion of lying *awake* in the grave! The analogy between death and sleep is

too simple, too natural, to render so horrid a belief possible for children . . ." (*Biographia Literaria,* ed. J. Shawcross [London: Oxford U. Press, 1979], II, 113-14).

3. *The Letters of William and Dorothy Wordsworth,* ed. E. De Selincourt (Oxford: Clarendon Press, 1937), II, 619.

4. For discussions of the two part and five-book *Prelude,* see Jonathan Wordsworth and Stephen Gill, "The Two Part *Prelude* of 1798-9," *JEGP* [*Journal of English and German Philology*], 72 (1973), 503-25; Jonathan Wordsworth, "The Five-Book *Prelude* of Early Spring 1804," *JEGP,* 76 (1977), 1-25; and Ross Woodman, "Child and Patriot: Shifting Perspectives in *The Prelude,*" *The Wordsworth Circle,* XI (1980), 83-92.

5. Nowhere does Wordsworth more forcibly call attention to the child-like innocence with which he attempted to portray himself as a patriot than in his careful repetition in Book X, line 603, of line 137 in Book II. The elements of the mock heroic (Wordsworth as Don Quixote) should not be ignored in his treatment of the revolution.

6. In the Fenwick note to *The Borderers,* Wordsworth writes:

> The study of human nature suggests this awful truth, that, as in the trials to which life subjects us, sin and crime are apt to start from their very opposite qualities, so there are no limits to the hardening of the heart, and the perversion of the understanding to which they may carry their slaves. During my long residence in France, while the revolution was rapidly advancing to its extreme of wickedness, I had frequent opportunities of being an eyewitness of this process, and it was while this knowledge was fresh upon my memory, that the Tragedy of 'The Borderers' was composed.

Wordsworth does not, of course, here suggest that what he observed in others he also observed in himself, though he does in *The Prelude* very carefully delineate his own "hardening of the heart" and "perversion of the understanding" which had their origin in "their very opposite qualities" in himself. It was, as we shall see, largely because of Dorothy's influence that his own "sin and crime" did not take up the kind of mental residence they assume in Oswald. Wordsworth in this respect is close to Marmaduke than to his villain-hero. His "slavery" was short-lived, though, as I shall suggest, his poetry became, in part, a penance for it that greatly modified his earlier revolutionary (or apocalyptic) view of freedom.

7. "Whether or not Oswald was conceived in revulsion as a critique of Godwin's separation of head and heart," writes Geoffrey Hartman, "he fosters this imperialism of the intellect, this ruthless futurism of a revolutionary who would achieve autonomy at one blow and by a divorce from natural process. To this tempting philosophy Wordsworth once succumbed" (*Wordsworth's Poetry 1787-1814* [New Haven: Yale U. Press, 1964], p. 127).

8. The role assigned to the "homely Nurse" in both *The Prelude* and the "Immortality" ode precluded the apocalyptic marriage which Wordsworth originally announced as his "spousal verse" or epic theme. The "Consummation" between Wordsworth and his sister was, needless to say, of a very different sort. "Passion" and "appetite" ("Tintern Abbey," ll. 76-80) underwent their necessary displacement into a vision of past time which, if caught up into the here and now of the creative act (as in the writing of the Simplon Pass episode) could momentarily obliterate the senses. Whatever was revealed to Wordsworth in such a moment of "usurpation" he preferred not to confess it. We catch glimpses of it only in its transcendental guise.

9. The hidden world of apocalypse which Wordsworth metaphorically located in the child imposes upon the poet a trust that he not betray it by directly exploiting it as the revolutionaries in France exploited it. The poet's task, Wordsworth suggests, is to conceal rather than reveal, or, more precisely, to reveal through concealment by means of metaphor. Wordsworth's method can be seen in "The Idiot Boy." Replying to John Wilson's criticism of the poem, Wordsworth wrote (June 1802): "I have often applied to idiots, in my own mind, that sublime expression of Scripture, that *their* life is *hidden with God.*" "Oh Reader!," writes Wordsworth in his poem,

> now that I might tell
>
> What Johnny and his Horse are doing!
>
> What they've been doing all the time,
>
> O could I put it into rhyme,
>
> A most delightful tale pursuing.

What Wordsworth cannot directly tell by putting it into rhyme is that Johnny has been performing a natural miracle, healing Susan Gale who "makes a piteous moan / As if her very life would fail." As Johnny spends "from eight o'clock till five" gazing at the moon's reflection in the pool ("And the sun did shine so cold"), Susan rises "from her bed, / As if by magic cured."

10. "To carry on the feelings of childhood into the powers of manhood," writes Coleridge, ". . . this is the character and privilege of genius, and one of the marks which distinguish genius from talents" (*Biographia Literaria,* I, 59).

11. The absence of a genuine inner life, consciously and creatively explored, is what Keats argues in his "Ode to Psyche" characterized the Greeks. They had no "vale of Soul-making" into which to descend. In us-

ing Keats's famous phrase in my title, I have in mind his continuous attempts to measure the genius of Wordsworth (in contrast to that of Milton) by his immersion in that vale which is in a very real sense the "chosen Vale" of *The Prelude* itself. For a helpful discussion of the image of the vale in *The Prelude*, see Mary Lynn Woolley, "Wordsworth's Symbolic Vale as it Functions in *The Prelude*," SiR [*Studies in Romanticism*], 7 (1968), 176-89. "It [the Vale] is," she writes, "the norm for all the hero's experiences and the background for his gradual transformation from aesthete to artist, from pilgrim to prophet, from unfinished youth to mature human being" (p. 189).

12. *Lay Sermons*, ed. R. J. White (Princeton: Princeton U. Press, 1972), p. 65.

13. *Wordsworth's Poetry 1787-1814*, p. 39.

14. For a thorough discussion of the delusory tendencies of Wordsworth's imagination, see Gene W. Ruoff, "Religious Implications of Wordsworth's Imagination," SiR, 12 (1973), 670-92. While Professor Ruoff is not specifically concerned with the Satanic in relation to the apocalyptic imagination, his exploration of its treacherous tendencies bear directly on what is being argued here.

15. Hartman acknowledges his indebtedness to both critics when he writes in *Wordsworth's Poetry 1787-1814* (pp. 350-51): "Harold Bloom in *The Visionary Company* (New York, 1961), our first systematic and eloquent questioning of the idea that the Romantics are fundamentally nature poets, and Paul de Man in his essay on the Romantic image, *Revue internale de philosophie*, 14 (1960), 68-84, have also helped to destroy this 'large and lazy assumption of which Jones [*The Egotistical Sublime*] complained.'" The "School" of romantic criticism here affirmed by Hartman may, I suggest, more properly be described as the Satanic School that explores the larger implications of Blake's notion that all "true poets" are "of the Devil's party." Wordsworth, unlike Shelley, for example, could not finally liberate Milton's Satan from a moral (as opposed to aesthetic or imaginal) framework. His consequent binding to nature was, of course, rejected by both Blake and Shelley (as indeed it is, at least by implication, by Hartman, Bloom, and de Man).

William D. Brewer (essay date 1991)

SOURCE: "The Diabolical Discourse of Byron and Shelley," in *Philological Quarterly*, Vol. 70, No. 1, Winter, 1991, pp. 47-65.

[*In the following essay, Brewer asserts that a complimentary interest in Satan as a literary presence inspired a number of the great poetic works of Lord Byron and Percy Shelley.*]

1

Shelley's praise of Byron's *Cain* was immediate and enthusiastic. In a 12 January 1822 letter to John Gisborne, he asked: "What think you of Lord Byron now? Space wondered less at the swift and fair creations of God, when he grew weary of vacancy, than I at the late works of this spirit of an angel in the mortal paradise of a decaying body."[1] Elsewhere, Shelley used such terms as "apocalyptic" and "revelation" to describe Byron's mystery play.[2] Part of Shelley's enthusiasm for *Cain* could be explained by the fact that *Cain* treated themes he himself had explored in *Queen Mab, Prometheus Unbound*, and *On the Devil, and Devils*. And Byron's use of Lucifer in *Cain* would also have intrigued Shelley, who, like Byron, enjoyed speculating about the nature and character of the arch-fiend. It seems likely, moreover, that *Cain* was at least partly inspired by the poets' discussions of metaphysical and religious questions during their meetings in Switzerland and Italy. What might be called Byron's and Shelley's diabolical discourse began when Shelley sent Byron a copy of his highly controversial *Queen Mab* (possibly in 1813)[3] and did not end until the last year of Shelley's life, when both Byron (in *The Deformed Transformed*) and Shelley (in his translation of scenes from *Faust*) found themselves responding imaginatively to Goethe's Mephistopheles.

Thomas Medwin was among the first to see the parallels between Shelley's visionary *Queen Mab* and *Cain*, particularly in Shelley's and Byron's descriptions of the vastness of space.[4] In *Queen Mab* Shelley writes:

> Earth's distant orb appeared
> The smallest light that twinkles in the heaven;
> Whilst round the chariot's way
> Innumerable systems rolled,
> And countless spheres diffused
> An ever-varying glory.
> It was a sight of wonder
>
> (1.250-256)[5]

Byron has Cain describe a similar view:

> CAIN. As we move
> Like sunbeams onward, [the earth] grows smaller and
>   smaller,
> And as it waxes little, and then less,
> Gathers a halo round it, like the light
> Which shone the roundest of the stars, when I
> Beheld them from the skirts of Paradise:
> Methinks they both, as we recede from them,
> Appear to join the innumerable stars
> Which are around us; and, as we move on,
> Increase their myriads.
>
> (2.1.34-43)[6]

But while *Cain* and *Queen Mab* both deal with space travel, the results of the journeys in these works are radically different. Ianthe learns from her interstellar flight with Queen Mab that "when the power of imparting joy /

Is equal to the will, the human soul / Requires no other Heaven" (3.11-12). In contrast, Lucifer teaches Cain that "the human sum / Of knowledge [should be] to know mortal nature's nothingness" (2.2.421-22) and leads Cain to despair. Behind both works is an interest in the discoveries of nineteenth-century science, particularly in astronomy, but while Shelley's perception of scientific knowledge and voyages through space is positive, Byron is more wary: rather than being uplifted, Cain is cast down by his vision of the cosmos. In Byron's words, by showing Cain "infinite things," Lucifer suggests Cain's comparative "abasement."[7] Knowledge, in *Cain,* is dangerous; what Cain learns in act 2 leads to the tragic violence of act 3.

It is clear, then, that Byron, while willing to borrow the idea of space travel from Shelley's *Queen Mab,* uses this device to draw different conclusions. Shelley's utopian belief that "A garden shall arise, in loveliness / Surpassing fabled Eden" (*Queen Mab,* 4.88-89) contrasts radically with Byron's vision, in *Cain,* of a universe in which everything progressively degenerates (2.2.67-74). But before too much emphasis is put on this difference in the poets' visions, it is important to remember that *Queen Mab* was published in 1813, *Cain* in 1821: the mature Byron, in effect, is arguing with a very young Shelley. It also should be noted that *Queen Mab* was both pirated and reissued in 1821, and that it was raising considerable interest in England at about the time Byron was composing *Cain.*[8]

In *Prometheus Unbound,* Shelley refined the utopianism of *Queen Mab*: Prometheus, unlike Ianthe, pays a very high price for his wisdom. Moreover, *Prometheus Unbound* confronts the problems of man's self-defeating urge to hate and denounce the God of this world, the urge which leads Prometheus to enshrine and then curse Jupiter, and which inspires Cain to strike out in frustration and kill his brother. Byron's reservations about the meliorism presented in *Queen Mab* do not seem to extend to Shelley's *Prometheus Unbound,* published seven years later: Byron, Shelley wrote, "was loud in his praise of 'Prometheus.'"[9] Although *Cain* differs from *Prometheus Unbound* in many respects, a comparison of the two works is enlightening, and serves to show how Shelley and Byron continued the conversation begun in Venice on "God, freewill and destiny; / Of all that earth has been or yet may be / All that vain men imagine or believe, / Or hope can paint or suffering may atchieve" ("Julian and Maddalo," 42-45).

The determination of Byron and Shelley to write poems about Prometheus probably dated from the summer of 1816—Byron told Medwin that Shelley translated Aeschylus's *Prometheus Bound* for him in Switzerland, and, soon after, Byron composed "Prometheus."[10] Writing to John Murray, Byron claimed that Aeschylus's play was an important influence on much of his poetry: "The Prometheus—if not exactly in my plan—has always been so much in my head—that I can easily conceive its influence over all or anything that I have written."[11] Byron composed his "Prometheus" in 1816, without the benefit of having read Shelley's *Prometheus Unbound* (1819), and

he tended to think of Prometheus bound rather than unbound, defiant rather than pitying, a static "symbol" and "sign" ("Prometheus," 45) rather than a being capable of change. Byron's Prometheus has a certain moral authority, strong enough to make Jove's lightnings tremble (34), but it is not clear that his rebellion will ever accomplish anything. Similarly, Manfred's "Promethean spark" (*Manfred,* 1.1.154) is never used to threaten Arimanes's dark reign; Manfred's goal proves, in fact, to be self-destruction. In *The Prophecy of Dante* Byron writes that even when a poet seeks to become a "new Prometheus of new men, / Bestowing fire from heaven" (4.14-15), this gift will be repaid with pain, and there is no indication that any other outcome is possible. Cain is yet another potential Prometheus, an aspirer to better things for himself and mankind, a would-be rebel against divine authority, and a protester against death. But Byron presents him differently from his other Promethean figures: *Cain* is a portrait of a metaphysical rebel who becomes an ironic, rather than heroic, figure. Wolf Hirst describes the irony of Cain's act of violence succinctly: "The irony of Cain's surrender to fury, to irrationality, after vainly pleading with his brother for reason, is enhanced by the circumstance that Cain's murderous frame of mind was caused by Lucifer, the advocate of reason."[12] While Byron's other Prometheus-figures rely on their moral superiority to their tormentors to make them heroic, if bound, personages, Cain finds himself on the defensive, a criminal who can no longer judge his creator without seeming hypocritical. The simple conflict between the righteous rebel and the tyrannical and unjust God becomes in *Cain* a complex confrontation between a man who has condemned and then caused death and a Jehovah who is invisible and therefore inscrutable. Cain never learns the lessons of Shelley's Prometheus: that anger and resentment are self-destructive and that the only thing that will save mankind is love.

One looks in vain through Byron's works for the kind of positive apocalypse that is found in Shelley's *Prometheus Unbound,* in which the universe is revitalized and changed for the better. In fact, Byron's apocalyptic view, as presented in "Darkness" and in Lucifer's speeches to Cain, has to do with a constant loss of energy, a kind of entropy which makes each race of intelligent beings less vital and noble than the race before.[13] The successive falls mount up: the superior race of Pre-Adamites are annihilated and replaced by the less intelligent Adam and Eve, who fall from paradise; their son, Cain, is banished from Eden and, in Byron's *Heaven and Earth,* his offspring the Cainites are annihilated by the flood. This is not, as Byron suggests in his preface to *Cain,* simply a "poetical fiction" to help Lucifer make his case: the notion that the history of the universe is marked by a constant downward spiral is an integral part of the myth he presents in *Cain* and elsewhere. It is a situation that man can deplore but not reverse. While Adam's fatalism seems abject, Cain's rebellion is clearly counterproductive, and neither attitude will lead to paradise regained. In *Cain,* of course, Byron was to some extent bound by the text of Genesis. But it remains, I think, significant that Byron chose this biblical context for an exploration of Prometheanism or, in other words, that he chose a context in which Promethean aspirations cannot be realized without violating the integrity of the original text. Shelley's vision of Prometheus unchained and the world renewed seems to have no place in Byron's poetry.

It would be incorrect to say, however, that Byron's and Shelley's metaphysical outlooks have nothing in common. One should not forget that Shelley's apocalypse is not final, and that future falls are possible even after the apocalypse of *Prometheus Unbound.* Demogorgon's speech at the end of the drama is revealing:

> if, with infirm hand, Eternity
> Mother of many acts and hours, should free
>   The serpent that would clasp her with his length—
> These are the spells by which to reassume
> An empire o'er the disentangled doom.
>
>   (4.565-69)

Shelley's "serpent" does not disappear after Prometheus's triumph, and there is a possibility that "Eternity" will become "infirm," that entropy will affect Shelley's cosmic myth as well as Byron's. Moreover, both poets show that violence is a misguided response to injustice and tyranny, whether divine or temporal. To Shelley, violence makes the rebel morally equivalent to the tyrant, and Prometheus's hatred must give way to pity before he can end Jupiter's evil reign. Byron, on the other hand, shows that violence, directed against a god like Jehovah, tends to miss its target (the creator-tyrant) and hit an innocent bystander (Abel) instead. And in *Cain,* as in *Prometheus Unbound,* love is presented as a viable alternative to the barren and self-destructive man-versus-God scenario. Prometheus recognizes the importance of Asia's love—"Most vain all hope but love" (1.808)—and Asia becomes a vital part of his unchaining and the renewal of the universe. But while Prometheus realizes the necessity of love, Cain tends to view Adah as basically irrelevant to his goals and aspirations, and leaves her to be with the skeptical Lucifer, a being devoid of love. This is a crucial mistake: apart from Adah, Cain despairs and ultimately turns to violence. In these works love constitutes man's only hope for salvation. Separated from Asia, Prometheus remains bound and tortured; while away from Adah, Cain becomes bitter and potentially murderous. Although *Cain* does not explore the possibility of a redeeming apocalypse, it, like *Prometheus Unbound,* shows the error of a rebellion based on hatred, and the necessity of love as a counterbalance to man's tendency towards despair when he is faced with human suffering and divine injustice.

Another resemblance between *Cain* and *Prometheus Unbound* has to do with the psychological nature of the metaphysical rebellions that Byron and Shelley are describing. Lucifer, Cain says, speaks to him "of things which long have swum / In visions through" (1.1.167-68) his own mind, and Adah is quick to warn Cain of demons who tempt man with his "own / Dissatisfied and curious thoughts" (1.402-3). Jehovah can be seen as a projection

of Cain's pessimistic speculations, merely articulated by Lucifer, much as Jupiter can be interpreted as a vision of tyranny and injustice created by Prometheus. And if both Cain and Prometheus create, out of their own minds, the problems which beset them, then they, not simply some exterior beings such as Jehovah and Jupiter, are to blame for their sufferings. Cain's banishment to the land east of Eden and Prometheus's binding are caused by failures of the imagination: Cain's failure to understand the true nature of death, which he ends up causing, and Prometheus's foolish decision to enthrone Jupiter. The fallen nature of reality is not caused solely by "something out there," but by the erring minds of men.

Moreover, both Cain and Prometheus have antitypes, Adah and Asia, female reflections of themselves. Adah, of course, is Cain's twin sister and wife, and Asia is presented as a "golden chalice" into which part of Prometheus's "being overflowed" (1.809-10). As James Rieger notes, the reverse of incest (self-love) is fratricide (self-hatred): "The mirror connects incest with fratricide in the . . . sense that both are born out of self-love. Narcissus presses his lips to the looking-glass; Cain smashes it with a rock."[14] In a sense *Cain,* like *Prometheus Unbound,* can be seen allegorically, the difference being that while Prometheus is able to disarm his negative mental imagery with the self-love personified by Asia, Cain allows his nihilistic vision to create in him the violent self-hatred symbolized by his murder of his brother. It is significant, moreover, that both Cain and Prometheus withdraw from society at the end of the dramas, Prometheus to his visionary cave (3.3.10-12) and Cain to the lands east of Eden. Although metaphysical rebels, they tend towards introversion, a characteristic more often associated with poets than with revolutionaries. Thus Shelley and Byron use their closet-dramas to explore the psychological ramifications of the Prometheus and Cain myths. Cain's view of a Jehovah who creates only to destroy is never actually verified by anyone other than Lucifer, who can only be seen as an unreliable source, and may well tell us more about Cain's perspective on reality than about the universe or its creator. Perhaps Cain makes his own universe in a negative way, as Prometheus positively recreates his world.

Like Shelley's Prometheus, Cain has some of the attributes of a poet, but he is clearly a fallen poet, his vision corrupted by his rage and despair.[15] Of course Byron's vision of Cain as poet predates his reading of *Prometheus Unbound*—in a letter to James Hogg written in 1814 Byron speculates on Cain's status as a poet:

> Milton's Paradise Lost is, as a whole, a heavy concern; but the two first books of it are the very finest poetry that has ever been produced in this world—at least since the flood—for I make little doubt that Abel was a fine pastoral poet, and Cain a fine bloody poet, and so forth; . . . Poetry must always exist, like drink, where there is a demand for it. And Cain's may have been the brandy of the antediluvian, and Abel's the small [?] still.[16]

The Old Testament notes that among Cain's descendants are Jubal, the first man to play the harp and organ, and

Tubal-Cain, the first artificer in brass and iron (Genesis 4:21 and 4:22). In *Paradise Lost,* Michael warns Adam of Cain's descendants, artisans and inventors who spurn God:

> Those Tents thou sawst so pleasant, were the Tents
> Of wickedness, wherein shall dwell his Race
> Who slew his Brother; studious they appear
> Of Arts that polish life, Inventors rare,
> Unmindful of their Maker, though his Spirit
> Taught them, but they his gifts acknowledg'd none.
>
> (3.607-12)

The aspiring, inquisitive Cain is the predecessor of those artists who seek to supplant the Creator by becoming creators in their own right. In *Adonais,* written during the summer before Byron's composition of *Cain,* Shelley presents himself as a poet who simultaneously resembles Cain and Christ: "his branded and ensanguined brow, / . . . [is] like Cain's or Christ's" (*Adonais,* 305-6). To both Byron and Shelley, Cain is an exemplar of the self-destructive side of the poetic temperament, as represented by such figures as Manfred and the self-defeated Rousseau of *The Triumph of Life.* Every poet has Cain's ability to destroy and Christ's ability to redeem, and the tragedy of *Cain* is that the protagonist tries to change the world in a positive way but only succeeds in committing the first murder.[17] Like a rebel artist who rejects traditional religious beliefs in order to create his own world view, Cain turns his back on his father's religious orthodoxy and tries to define the nature of the universe for himself. But Cain's perspective is affected by "the corrupting blight of tyranny"[18] that Shelley claimed made Tasso a lesser poet than Dante. In the universe in which he finds himself, Cain can only perceive Infernos. Cain is similar to the type of poet described in Grimm's *Correspondance,* quoted by Byron in his letters: "a poet, or . . . a man of genius in any department, . . . must have 'une ame qui se tourmente, un esprit violent'."[19] According to this description, continues Byron, he himself would be a poet "per excellenza," since he possesses a self-torturing soul and a violent spirit. Like many of the Romantic poets, Cain is more interested in the rebellious Lucifer, with his Satanic pride and resolute heroism, than in the tyrannical Jehovah, who inspires simple-minded devotion from Adam and Abel. He also has a powerful imagination capable of transcending everything Lucifer shows him in their tour through the universe. Cain tells Lucifer: "thou show'st me things beyond *my* power, / Beyond all power of my born faculties, / Although inferior still to my desires / And my conceptions" (2.1.80-83). Even before Lucifer describes his vision of the universe, Cain has imagined it (1.167-68). In fact, Cain's imagination is Napoleonic in its ambition; he is tortured by "Thoughts which arise within [him], as if they / Could master all things" (1.177-78). Despite the universal scope of his imaginative vision, Cain is capable of extemporizing a paean to Adah, in which he says that she is superior to "the bird's voice— / The vesper bird's, which seems to sing of love" (2.2.263-64). Cain is a fancier of "the lights above us, in the azure, / Which are so beautiful" (1.280-81) and looks to the stars for beauty as he aspires to greater things than a farmer's lot. Cain has the temperament of a poet who wants the world to match his imaginative conceptions—without that, he deems life not worth living.

As Byron noted in a letter to John Murray, Cain goes into a rage inspired by "the inadequacy of his state to his Conceptions," which expresses itself in violence directed against "the author of Life" rather than against the actual victim, Abel.[20] The injustice that most outrages Cain is that he cannot recreate the world to match his own "conceptions." Shelley's Prometheus, who is responsible for Jupiter's oppressive rule, succeeds in transforming his vision of reality, in eventually presiding over a creation which does, in fact, fulfill his aesthetic requirements. Cain cannot, however, overcome his vision of a Jehovah-dominated world, and therefore his poetic idealism becomes a chimera that haunts him, that reduces him to rage against the more prolific, if less imaginative, creative power of the "Author of Life."

In his ultimate frustration, and violent reaction to what he perceives as an unjust universe, Cain has far more resemblances to Beatrice Cenci than he does to Shelley's Prometheus. We know that Byron had read *The Cenci* at least by 10 September 1820,[21] so it is possible that Shelley's tragic heroine influenced his conception of Cain. In *A Mental Theater: Poetic Drama and Consciousness in the Romantic Age,* Alan Richardson draws some useful parallels between *The Cenci* and *Cain.* For example, Beatrice and Cain are at first "young, morally integral, idealistic, but critically lacking in self-awareness,"[22] but they are soon affected by older, sophisticated beings who tempt them to commit acts of violence. The result of the influence that Cenci and Lucifer have on the young protagonists is a loss of innocence and a growing self-consciousness: this self-consciousness, Richardson notes, "pays for its emergence with a loss of integrity,"[23] and both Beatrice and Cain commit crimes which violate the ideals they once held sacred. The journey to self-consciousness, in *The Cenci* and *Cain,* is symbolized by crossing an abyss.[24] In Beatrice's case, the abyss is found at the spot where she plans to have Cenci ambushed:

> there is a mighty rock,
> Which has, from unimaginable years,
> Sustained itself with terror and with toil
> Over a gulph, and with the agony
> With which it clings seems slowly coming down;
> Even as a wretched soul hour after hour,
> Clings to the mass of life; yet clinging, leans;
> And leaning, makes more dark the dread abyss
> In which it fears to fall.
>
> (3.1.247-55)

The disorienting image of the abyss is also used in *Cain,* in which Lucifer conveys Cain across "The Abyss of Space,"[25] taking him on a voyage which is both liberating and completely alienating. In *The Cenci* and *Cain,* Shelley and Byron explore the problems confronting Romantic idealists, the disillusionment, pain and injustice that can lead beings like Beatrice and Cain to act exactly like those they most detest, as Beatrice reacts to Cenci's violence against his children by conspiring to assassinate him, and Cain protests against the Jehovah who dooms man to death by committing murder.

2

Byron's presentation of Lucifer, the other metaphysical rebel in *Cain,* may owe a great deal to Shelley's influence. Both poets had a half-whimsical interest in the devil and delighted in attributing demonic qualities to each other. In "Julian and Maddalo" Shelley compares the discourse between himself and Byron to the discussions that "The devils held within the dales of Hell" (41), and Byron, inspired by a quotation from Goethe's *Faust,* nicknamed Shelley "the Snake."[26] In his *Recollections of the Last Days of Shelley and Byron,* Trelawny relates the story of Byron nicknaming Shelley "the Snake" and adds: "Byron was the real snake—a dangerous mischiefmaker."[27] Coincidentally, both Shelley and Byron were inspired, as young men, to imitate a satire written by Coleridge and Robert Southey entitled "The Devil's Thoughts" (1799).[28] Shelley composed "The Devil's Walk: A Ballad" in 1812, and Byron, in the same year, wrote "The Devil's Drive." Both poems use the idea of the devil visiting England as a vehicle for radical social and political satire. Byron's interest in portraying the devil went, of course, far beyond this relatively juvenile effort: the coldly intellectual Lucifer of *Cain,* the haughty, aristocratic Satan of *The Vision of Judgment* and the mephisphelean Stranger/Caesar of *The Deformed Transformed* all serve to illustrate his continuing fascination with the arch-fiend. Shelley presented diabolical beings in his Byronic *Peter Bell the Third,* in the fragmentary prologue to *Hellas,* and in his humorous essay *On the Devil, and Devils,* as well as in other works. In his translation of scenes from Goethe's *Faust,* Shelley depicted Mephistopheles brilliantly, and one can certainly see his Cenci as a type of Satan. Although often tongue-in-cheek, the poets' common interest in demonology is reflected in many of their works, and may well have helped shape Byron's Lucifer.

Both Shelley and Byron parted company with Milton in their refusal to identify the Devil with the serpent who tempted Adam and Eve. As Shelley writes in his essay *On the Devil, and Devils,* the transformation of the serpent of Genesis into the Devil of Christian mythology is a willful misreading of the Bible: "The Christians have turned this Serpent into their Devil, and accommodated the whole story to their new scheme of sin and propitiation."[29] Byron's Lucifer takes pains to disabuse Cain of any notion that he might be implicated in the serpent's crime: "I tell thee that the serpent was no more / Than a mere serpent / . . . Thy / Fond parents listen'd to a creeping thing, / And fell" (1.231-42). In removing the Devil from the story of man's fall, Shelley and Byron remain consistent with the actual text of Genesis, and suggest that man himself, not a demon, is to blame for his expulsion from the Garden of Eden. The fact that Byron's Lucifer did not lead Adam and Eve into temptation allows him to approach Cain with a certain degree of self-righteousness; it also makes origi-

nal sin a part of God's creation, not something imported into Eden by an evil demon, since the tempter is a serpent created by God, and Adam and Eve are God's creations as well. In *On the Devil, and Devils* Shelley challenges the reader to rethink the notion of a God who is both omnipotent and benevolent by questioning the idea that the Devil can be blamed for all evil. Shelley writes that Christians

> have tortured themselves ever to devise any flattering sophism, by which they might appease [God] . . . endeavoring to reconcile omnipotence, and benevolence, and equity, in the Author of an Universe where evil and good are inextricably intangled and where the most admirable tendencies to happiness and preservation are for ever baffled by misery and decay. The Christians therefore, invented or adopted the Devil to extricate them from this difficulty.[30]

Similarly, Byron's Lucifer tells Cain not to use him as a scapegoat for the evil that God the creator has made:

> if he gives you good—so call him; if
> Evil springs from *him,* do not name it *mine,*
> Till ye know better its true fount; and judge
> Not by words, though of spirits, but the fruits
> Of your existence, such as it must be.
> *One good* gift has the fatal apple given—
> Your *reason*:—let it not be over-sway'd
>
>   (2.2.454-60)

But although Shelley's heterodox opinions probably influenced the speeches of Byron's Lucifer, it would be difficult to separate Shelley's heresies from Byron's. In Shelley's "Julian and Maddalo," both Julian and Maddalo delight in diabolical conversations, and one gathers that Shelley and Byron encouraged one another to make speculations which would be considered heretical by many of their contemporaries. And although they pursued these speculations with some interest, they did not take the concept of hell entirely seriously. For example, Byron professes to doubt the existence of eternal punishment in *The Vision of Judgment* even though "one may be damn'd / For hoping no one else may e'er be so" (106-7), and, in a letter dated 10 April 1822, Shelley disputed the idea that "after sixty years of suffering . . . we [are] to be roasted alive for sixty million more in Hell."[31] Both poets seem, then, to have suspected that hell and the devil were superstitions, fictions which were created to make evil a place and an entity separate from heaven and God.

Besides Shelley's and Byron's conversations about the Devil, the portrait of Ahasuerus in *Queen Mab* may also have had an influence on Byron's portrayal of Lucifer. Shelley's Ahasuerus, after being cursed by Christ, begins his wanderings in the spirit of defiance:

> But my soul,
> From sight and sense of the polluting woe
> Of tyranny, had long learned to prefer
> Hell's freedom to the servitude of heaven.
> Therefore I rose, and dauntlessly began
> My lonely and unending pilgrimage,

Resolved to wage unweariable war
With my almighty tyrant, and to hurl
Defiance at his impotence to harm
Beyond the curse I bore.

(7.192-201)

Byron's Lucifer expresses similar sentiments when he describes his "unweariable war" with Jehovah:

I have a victor—true but no superior.
Homage he has from all—but none from me:
I battle it against him, as I battled
In highest heaven. Through all eternity,
And the unfathomable gulfs of Hades,
And the interminable realms of space,
And the infinity of endless ages,
All, all, will I dispute!

(2.2.429-36)

These immortal beings seem to exist solely to oppose the divine rulers of creation in a war that seems both endless and futile, and Shelley's and Byron's portraits of these two metaphysical rebels underline the uselessness as well as the admirable tenacity of Ahasuerus's and Lucifer's defiance of heaven. Whatever sympathy we may have for the rebels' viewpoints, they do not present perspectives on reality that are helpful to either Ianthe or Cain. The Fairy waves her wand and Ahasuerus disappears as a "phantasmal portraiture / Of wandering human thought" (7.274-75), a desolate dream which is replaced by a vision of a much brighter future. Likewise, Lucifer's world view is negative and counterproductive: it leads to Cain's frustration and his murder of Abel, a murder which makes Cain recognize that he has been influenced by "a dreary dream" (3.378). While Jehovah may be a tyrant, and while Christianity itself may have serious flaws, eternal hatred of the reigning divinities is not seen as a viable stance in either *Queen Mab* or *Cain*. Ianthe can escape Cain's bitterness because she, unlike Cain, can look toward the future with hope. While both Shelley and Byron are capable of presenting divine injustice and human suffering in a very pessimistic way, Shelley's futurism gives *Queen Mab* and *Prometheus Unbound* positive conclusions, whereas Byron's *Cain* ends in virtual despair. Although Lucifer may have many admirable qualities, his relentless skepticism leads Cain to an act which is as irrevocable as it is tragic.

As they developed their revisionist views of the devil, Shelley and Byron tried to determine the nature of his powers. New astronomical studies shaped their speculations, and their devil became, as a result, something of an astronaut. In *On the Devil, and Devils,* Shelley considers the problem of a devil who has the job of doing evil in innumerable worlds:

It is discovered that the earth is a comparatively small globe, in a system consisting of a multitude of others, which roll round the Sun; and there is no reason to suppose but that all these are inhabited by organized and intelligent beings. . . . There is little reason to suppose that any considerable multitude of the planets

were tenanted by beings better capable of resisting the temptations of the Devil than ours. But is the Devil, like God, omnipresent? If so he interpenetrates God, and they both exist together. . . .[32]

Similarly, Byron's Lucifer professes himself ready to struggle against Jehovah throughout the vast universe, over which they *both* reign (2.2.392). The earth becomes a tiny part of a war that stretches across infinity and eternity, and man, who imagines himself the center of the struggle between good and evil, begins to seem almost insignificant. Thus the devil attains God's power of omnipresence, becoming, in this respect, God's equal. The recent discoveries by astronomers, Byron and Shelley suggest, further bring into question the orthodox views of the devil.

The idea that God and the devil work in a sort of partnership, God creating man to be burned by the devil in hellfire, is found in both Shelley's essay *On the Devil, and Devils,* and Byron's *Vision of Judgment,* as well as in *Cain.* In Shelley's words, "These two considerable personages are supposed to have entered into a sort of partnership, in which the weaker has consented to bear all the odium of their common actions."[33] Satan and the archangel Michael are seen as friends with "political" differences in *The Vision of Judgment* (Stanza 62), in which God's minions and the devil cooperate in trying to decide the fate of George III. In *Cain* Lucifer makes his relationship with God mysterious and chastises Cain for wishing to know "the great double Mysteries . . . the *two Principles*" (2.2.404), but he does agree that he and Jehovah are "as brethren" (2.2.381) and that they reign together (2.2.392). That there is, in fact, an understanding between Jehovah and Lucifer is indicated by what happens to Cain: Lucifer puts the would-be rebel in the state of mind that leads him to kill Abel, and Jehovah promptly sends down his angel to pronounce sentence on the first murderer. In order to further antagonize Cain, moreover, Jehovah spurns his sacrifice. The kind of partnership described in Shelley's *On the Devil, and Devils,* in which the devil leads man astray so God can condemn him, also seems present in *Cain.*

Thus Shelley's views on the devil and Byron's presentation of Lucifer reveal the poets' desire to subvert and even poke fun at the orthodox Christian belief in the archfiend. Both Shelley and Byron were inspired by Milton's Satan, but neither poet was blinded by Satan's heroic stature. As Shelley wrote, Satan has the "taints of ambition, envy, revenge, and a desire for personal aggrandisement" (preface to *Prometheus Unbound*), and Byron's Lucifer, who professes himself unable to love, has similar flaws. According to Richardson, "Lucifer belongs to the tradition of demonic seducers exemplified by Satan, Iago, and the Witches of *Macbeth.*"[34] But, nevertheless, in refusing to accept blame for man's fall and arguing against the idea of an omnipotent and benevolent Jehovah, Lucifer expresses many of the poets' irreverent notions. In an 11 April 1822 letter to Horace Smith, Shelley wrote that if he had any influence on Byron, he would certainly "employ it to eradicate from his great mind the delusions of Christianity, which in spite of his reason, seem perpetually to recur, & to lay in ambush for the hours of sickness & distress."[35] While he did not succeed in banishing all of Byron's Christian beliefs, he did seem to have an effect on Byron's conception of the devil. But whereas Shelley simply mocks popular notions of the devil in his *On the Devil, and Devils,* in *Cain* Lucifer is taken more seriously: his nihilism, his belief in man's nothingness, leads Cain to violence and misery.

In some ways, *On the Devil, and Devils* has more in common with Byron's *The Vision of Judgment* than it does with *Cain,* although both *The Vision of Judgment* and *Cain* were written during the latter half of 1821. Like Shelley's *On the Devil, and Devils, The Vision of Judgment* is deflationary rather than tragic in its implications, seeking to question traditional Christian beliefs through irony and humor. On the other hand, Lucifer is one of the intellectual cherubs, not simply a common devil pandering to man's base appetites, or a restrained, gentlemanly personage like the urbane Satan of *The Vision of Judgment.* As such, he presents more of a threat to the poetic, aspiring Cain than would a demon who, in Byron's words, promised Cain "kingdoms, etc."[36] Although his discussions with Shelley probably influenced Byron's idea of the devil, in *Cain* he takes his conception of the archfiend one step further, presenting a demoniacal intelligence capable of perverting the Promethean aspirations of a would-be metaphysical rebel. In part, Lucifer leads Cain to despair by showing him the "high, / Intelligent, good, great, and glorious" (2.2.66-67) beings of the past, who were destroyed; these noble victims demonstrate, Lucifer suggests, the destructive nature of Jehovah, and the ultimate futility of man's aspirations. Significantly, in his "Prologue to *Hellas*" (written October 1821) Shelley seems to realize the potency of this kind of argument, and puts it in the mouth of his Satan, who points to the ruin of Greece and uses the fact of Greece's fall from its golden age to argue against the possibility of its return to greatness. Christ responds to Satan by dismissing this vision, which "seest but the Past in the To-come" ("Prologue to *Hellas,*" 161).[37] In Shelley's view, the future is not condemned to repeat the past, and later descendants of Adam and Eve may still succeed in recreating their world. But, while Shelley's and Byron's outlooks for the future differed, they seemed to agree that the real threat to modern man comes not from a devil with horns and a forked tail, but from the nihilistic despair a limited rationalism such as Lucifer's can inspire.

It is significant that in Shelley's last year both he and Byron wrote fragments which were influenced by Goethe's characterization of Mephistopheles in *Faust:* Shelley composed a relatively free translation of scenes from *Faust* in the spring of 1822, and the Stranger/Caesar figure of Byron's *The Deformed Transformed* (written in early 1822) is clearly mephistophelean.[38] Shelley's translation of *Faust* altered the original German, as Timothy Webb writes in *The Violet in the Crucible: Shelley and Translation,* to add a new quality to *Faust* which has "the effect of establishing Mephistopheles as a gentleman of fashion."[39] The

Stranger of *The Deformed Transformed* also has a gentlemanly, even snobbish quality:

> *Arnold.* I said not
> You *were* the demon, but that your approach
> Was like one.
> *Stranger.* Unless you keep company
> With him (and you seem scarce used to such high
>   Society) you can't tell how he approaches;
> And for his aspect, look upon the fountain,
> And then on me, and judge which of us twain
> Looks likest what the boors believe to be
> Their cloven-footed terror.
>
>   (1.1.93-101)[40]

Thus the poets' interest in the figure of the devil, manifested in their 1812 imitations of Coleridge's and Southey's "The Devil's Thoughts," continued to the end of their relationship, when Shelley's and Byron's fascination with Goethe's Mephistopheles led to their writing two intriguing, if fragmentary, works. Unfortunately their "Julian and Maddalo"-style conversation on "God, freewill and destiny" was interrupted by Shelley's death, which was soon followed by Byron's—we will never know how or if it would have continued. But there can be little doubt that Byron's and Shelley's diabolical discourse helped inspire some of their most important works.

Notes

1. *The Letters of Percy Bysshe Shelley,* ed. Frederick L. Jones, 2 vols. (Oxford: Clarendon Press, 1964), 2:376. This edition will be abbreviated as *PBSL* in the following notes.

2. *PBSL,* 2:388.

3. For evidence about when Byron received *Queen Mab,* see Charles E. Robinson, *Shelley and Byron: The Snake and Eagle Wreathed in Fight* (Johns Hopkins U. Press, 1976), p. 244.

4. Thomas Medwin, *The Life of Percy Bysshe Shelley,* ed. H. Buxton Forman (Oxford U. Press, 1913), p. 334.

5. Unless otherwise indicated, all quotations from Shelley's poetry are taken from *Shelley's Poetry and Prose,* ed. Donald H. Reiman and Sharon B. Powers (New York: Norton, 1977).

6. Unless otherwise noted, all quotations from Byron's works are taken from the Oxford Authors *Byron,* ed. Jerome J. McGann (Oxford U. Press, 1986) and *Byron. The Complete Poetical Works,* ed. Jerome J. McGann, 5 vols. (Oxford U. Press, 1980-86).

7. *Byron's Letters and Journals,* ed. Leslie Marchand, 12 vols. (Harvard U. Press, 1973-82), 9:53. Henceforth *Byron's Letters and Journals* will be abbreviated as *BLJ.*

8. See *Shelley's Poetry and Prose,* 14n, and Shelley's 16 June 1821 letter to John Gisborne, *PBSL,* 2:300-1.

9. *PBSL,* 2:345.

10. Thomas Medwin, *Medwin's "Conversations of Lord Byron,"* ed. Ernest J. Lovell (Princeton U. Press, 1966), p. 156.

11. *BLJ,* 5:268.

12. Wolf Z. Hirst, "Byron's Lapse into Orthodoxy: An Unorthodox Reading of Cain," *Keats-Shelley Journal* (1980): 153.

13. See Paul A. Cantor, *Creature and Creator: Myth-Making and English Romanticism* (Cambridge U. Press, 1984), pp. 146-47, in which he compares "Darkness" with *Prometheus Unbound:* "'Darkness' reads almost like a point-by-point refutation of the great apocalyptic speeches at the end of *Prometheus Unbound.*" Of course since Byron wrote "'Darkness" well before Shelley composed *Prometheus Unbound,* one could not argue that Shelley's lyrical drama actually influenced Byron's earlier poem.

14. James Rieger, *The Mutiny Within: The Heresies of Percy Bysshe Shelley* (New York: George Braziller, 1967), p. 198.

15. A short discussion of the biblical and Miltonic references to Cain as artist can be found in Peter L. Thorslev, Jr., *The Byronic Hero* (U. of Minnesota Press, 1962), p. 94.

16. *BLJ,* 4:84.

17. For a provocative discussion of Cain's process of self-definition, see Leonard Michaels, "Byron's Cain," *PMLA* 84 (1962): 74.

18. *PBSL,* 2:122.

19. *BLJ,* 8:41.

20. *BLJ,* 9:54.

21. *BLJ,* 7:174 and n.

22. Alan Richardson, *A Mental Theater: Poetic Drama and Consciousness in the Romantic Age* (Pennsylvania State U., 1988), p. 4.

23. Richardson, p. 14.

24. Richardson, p. 115.

25. Oxford Authors *Byron,* p. 901.

26. Edward John Trelawny, *Records of Shelley, Byron, and the Author,* ed. David Wright (Harmondsworth: Penguin, 1973), p. 103.

27. Trelawny, p. 310, n. 17.

28. See C. Darrel Sheraw, "Coleridge, Shelley, Byron and the Devil," *Keats-Shelley Journal* 33 (1972): 6-9.

29. *The Complete Works of Percy Bysshe Shelley,* ed. Roger Ingpen and Walter E. Peck, 10 vols. (London: Ernest Benn, 1926-30), 7:104.

30. *The Complete Works of Percy Bysshe Shelley,* 7:89.

31. *PBSL,* 2:407.

32. *The Complete Works of Percy Bysshe Shelley,* 7:97.

33. *The Complete Works of Percy Bysshe Shelley,* 7:94.

34. Richardson, p. 61.

35. *PBSL,* 2:412.

36. *BLJ,* 9:53.

37. *The Complete Works of Percy Bysshe Shelley,* 3:15.

38. See Robinson, p. 213.

39. Timothy Webb, *The Violet in the Crucible: Shelley and Translation* (Clarendon Press, 1976), p. 186.

40. *The Poetical Works of Byron,* ed. Robert F. Gleckner (Boston: Houghton Mifflin, 1975), p. 723.

Peter A. Schock (essay date 1995)

SOURCE: "The 'Satanism' of *Cain* in Context: Byron's Lucifer and the War Against Blasphemy," in *Keats-Shelley Journal,* Vol. 44, 1995, pp. 182-215.

[*In the following essay, Schock views Lucifer in Lord Byron's* Cain *as an ambiguous figure—at once both "the traditional tempter" and "the Promethean metaphysical rebel"—and discusses Byron's purposes in manipulating the Satanic myth.*]

In *Cain: A Mystery* (1821), Byron offers the reader the enigma of his Lucifer, a demonic figure who oscillates between traditional diabolism and all that is implied by "Romantic Satanism." On the one hand, Byron seems to introduce a conventional if unusually haughty, aloof, and sadistic tempter into his revision of Genesis 4. Because Cain yearns to recover his "just inheritance," the Eden his parents briefly knew, or at least to learn what he calls "the mystery of my being," Lucifer breaks him down, first promising metaphysical knowledge, then revealing and ridiculing the hopelessness of Cain's mortal existence.[1] Yet from the outset Lucifer is presented as a defamiliarized Devil: the startling preface to the play implies that Lucifer is not to be identified with the serpent who tempted Eve. Lucifer does much more than merely seduce Cain; he instructs him in the values of autonomy, defiance, and metaphysical rebellion. At the end of act II, Lucifer leaves Cain with the exhortation that "the mind is its own place," urging Cain to resist Jehovah's "tyrannous threats" compelling faith and to form instead

> an inner world
> In your own bosom—where the outward fails;
> So shall you nearer be the spiritual
> Nature, and war triumphant with your own.
>
> (II.ii.459-66; p. 275)

Enacting two conflicting roles, the traditional tempter and the Promethean metaphysical rebel, Lucifer appears to be a radically ambiguous figure; his shifting identity does not readily resolve, as does that of his principal model, Milton's Satan, into an appearance-reality dichotomy.

To a significant degree, of course, the characterization of Lucifer is driven by his dramatic function—laying bare those aspects of Cain's nature that make the first murder possible. Consequently the reader may partly or entirely subordinate Lucifer's ambiguities to the conflict within the titular, thematically central figure. Yet many critics from Byron's day to our own have attended to the figure of Lucifer itself, and their perceptions during this time have replicated its shifting of roles, coming down first on one side, then on the other of the split characterization. Hostile reviewers of *Cain* in 1821-1822 certainly saw little ambiguity: Lucifer's tirades against the cosmic government of Jehovah struck them forcefully enough for most to conclude that this character was the poet's mouthpiece in a violently blasphemous attack on the authority of the Bible. Byron's contemporaries thus regarded Lucifer as the perverse moral center of the play and saw only Byron's attempts to glamorize his defiant Devil.[2] A number of twentieth-century critics, also focusing on the heroic aspect of Lucifer while no longer castigating Byron for his "Satanism," have idealized Lucifer and identified his rhetoric with Byron's rebellious and skeptical impulses.[3] Some modern readings of the play have emphasized the equivocal characterization of Lucifer, but those that assume Byron's conception of this figure as conventionally diabolical have increasingly displaced both the more balanced interpretations and those which play up its Romantic Satanism.[4] Thus the figure of Lucifer is easily assimilated to theologically conservative readings of *Cain*.[5]

That Lucifer represents a sort of fault line in criticism of *Cain* suggests that this character and its perceived functions merit further study, but scholarly attention has actually shifted away: recent efforts to restore *Cain* to its historical context have not yielded a reconsideration of Byron's satanic figure. While Marilyn Butler has convincingly argued that *Cain* and other second-generation Romantic deployments of myth have consistently political and polemical, as opposed to more private, spiritual functions, she nevertheless views Lucifer as a traditional tempter and looks elsewhere in the play for evidence of Byron's religious controversialism.[6] But the figure of Lucifer may appear more closely linked to Byron's iconoclastic handling of Christian myth if we understand its ambiguous characterization as a response to some of the specific circumstances surrounding the composition of *Cain*. These include the campaign to suppress anti-Christian publications in the Regency years, which—coupled with the considerable influence of Shelley's writing—brought to Byron's attention the currency and power of blasphemous writing as a vehicle of controversy; the pressure on Byron to respond to ideologically charged accusations of Satanism and Manicheism coming from conservative voices; and the poet's concern to elude charges

of blasphemy and to avoid presenting an easy target to his opponents. The ambiguity of Lucifer is strategic, then. The fracturing of this character into opposed roles can be understood as the response to pressures that pulled Byron in two different directions: toward a more aggressively unconventional and heroic conception of Lucifer on the one hand, as the author subverts biblical myth and attacks his opponents, and toward a theologically inoffensive representation of this figure on the other, as Byron reins in his iconoclasm to mystify the reader and thus head off renewed "Satanic school" diatribes and accusations of blasphemy. Collectively these pressures shape and complicate the mythic vehicle Byron used to enter the lists in 1821 as a guarded controversialist.

In constructing the figure of Lucifer Byron participated in the larger resurgence and transformation of the myth of Satan which began toward the end of the eighteenth century. An exploded critical fiction, "Romantic Satanism" is seldom invoked today to explain this phenomenon.[7] But if, as we now know, Romantic writers did not thoroughly idealize Milton's Satan in their criticism and poetry, the origin and nature of this reshaped myth, its functions, and its significance for writers like Blake, the Shelleys, and Byron still require exploration. The Romantic myth of Satan emerges from a matrix of specific cultural forces and influences.[8] One aspect of this matrix is religious: the fading belief in the existence of the Devil and the rise of syncretic or comparative mythography in the eighteenth century established Satan as a purely mythic figure, freeing him for artistic and ideological purposes. A second aspect involves the widespread political appropriation of the myth in England during the French Revolution and again in the Regency years, as conservatives and radicals alike branded and castigated the opposition by satanizing it. The third dimension of the cultural matrix is the conception of Milton's Satan in the criticism and illustration of *Paradise Lost* during the age, which increasingly idealized the fallen archangel, representing him as a sublime, human, and heroic figure. The three dimensions of the cultural matrix collectively brought about the result that the religious myth of the adversary lost authority, and Milton's charismatic fallen angel was reconstituted as an ideological vehicle, a mythic standard-bearer of moral, political, and religious values. Byron's Lucifer constitutes an especially complicated deployment of this kind of figure.[9]

When he began writing *Cain,* Byron knew that in England a volatile political climate had surrounded the state trials of William Hone, Richard Carlile, and countless others for blasphemy. He was aware that to the Tory Ministry and to prominent Evangelicals, "infidelism" automatically implied sedition. The speeches Byron gives Lucifer, like the attacks of Regency blasphemers on "the Christian mythology" and its political power, subvert Christian theodicy and the authoritarian myth of origins which reinforces it—"the politics of Paradise," as Byron derisively termed the foundations of religious and political authority in Genesis.[10] In producing a satanic voice that deconstructs sacred myth, Byron had to know he was adopting tactics resembling those of the lower-class radicals he professed to despise. He must have assumed that his play would become part of the controversy—and that he would be perceived as an aristocratic provocateur in the struggle over the authority of the Bible.

Byron's specific refashioning of Lucifer is indebted primarily to Shelley, whose *Queen Mab* (1813), *The Revolt of Islam* (1818), and essay "On the Devil, and Devils" (ca. 1819) radically reconceive the figure of Satan in order to force the Christian mythology to implode. Shelley's essay, written I suggest in direct response to the conviction of Richard Carlile in 1819 for blasphemous libel, extended and refined Carlile's attack on biblical myth, and brought Byron into contact with both the infidel program and the movement to suppress blasphemous writing. Although his approach in *Cain* is more oblique, ironic, and qualified than Shelley's, Byron followed the latter's strategy of using the satanic figure to undermine biblical myth. Through the figure of Lucifer Byron struck generally at the "tyrants who are trampling upon all human thought": all who contributed to repression at this time, from the Tory ministers who authored the Six Acts to the Crown lawyers who prosecuted infidels (*BLJ* ix, 152). More specifically, Byron struck back at the conservative voices of the *Quarterly Review,* principally Reginald Heber and Robert Southey. These men brought home to Byron the war against blasphemy with their accusations of his own satanic irreligion—his "Manicheism" and "audacious impiety." Thus Byron's play and its satanic figure display complex filiations with a specific cultural and political situation; the blasphemy controversy, the extent to which Byron was implicated in it, and his response to it all bear on the problematic characterization of Lucifer, yet the significance of this context remains largely unexplored.

I. Byron and the War against Blasphemy

A wave of blasphemy prosecutions swept over England after the end of the Napoleonic wars: literally hundreds were carried out before the Regency ended. These state trials were conducted in response to what conservative prophets portentously called "the revival of infidelity"—the emergence of skeptical, anti-clerical, and anti-Christian writing which appeared to resurrect the infidel spirit of early 1790s Jacobinism, the most significant English embodiment of which had been Thomas Paine's *The Age of Reason* (1794). The two principal "infidels" during the Regency years were William Hone, whose parodies of the litany, the catechism, and the Athanasian Creed earned him three trials and acquittals for blasphemy in 1817, and the most celebrated martyr for the cause of free thought, Richard Carlile, who was convicted on a dozen counts of blasphemous libel in October 1819 for republishing Paine. Sentenced to three years in prison and fined £1500, Carlile remained in Dorchester Gaol until 1825 because he would not pay the fines and sureties against future offenses. It was Carlile's trial and incarceration which seized the attention of both Shelley and Byron.

The suppression of blasphemy in the Regency years was justified by resurrecting the "conspiracy theory" of the late 1790s—that the French Revolution had been an infidel plot hatched by the Illuminati, Freemasons, and *philosophes* to subvert government by attacking religion.[11] In the years of unrest after Waterloo, this spectre of a revolution engineered by undermining religion again appeared. The anxiety of the Tory Ministry over this danger peaked in 1819 in response to the Peterloo Massacre, and in November the ministers recalled Parliament to introduce the Six Acts, three of which dealt harshly with the blasphemous press.[12] In these acts, the ministers and their allies specifically invoked the prosecution of "blasphemous libel" as an instrument of social control because it addressed the widespread fear that attacks on Christianity subverted belief in postmortal sanctions, thus dissolving the social bonds and encouraging the unrest of the lower classes.[13] In speech after speech, the assumption that blasphemy leads inevitably to sedition is axiomatic. In the House of Commons, W. C. Plunket described the "revolutionary project" of radical reformers like Henry Hunt as a plan to seize the property of the upper classes and to distribute it among a "rabble . . . previously debauched by the unremitting dissemination of blasphemous libels, and freed from the restraints of moral or religious feeling."[14]

But the Six Acts were only the climax of a long and broad movement to suppress blasphemy, a campaign which enlisted the support of the English Church and other religious groups. By 1819, as Robert Hole observes, most Anglican clergymen were already preaching on themes of social control, all in response to post-Waterloo disturbances and infidelism.[15] Richard Watson, the Bishop of Llandaff and the polemical opponent of Paine's *The Age of Reason,* roundly asserted that the "anti-Christian writings of the nineteenth-century were too unreasonable to be suppressed by anything less than the terrors of the law" (Wickwar, p. 136). Evangelical groups also believed blasphemy was a social solvent. Politically aligned with the Tories, they shared their anxiety over the connection between blasphemy and civil unrest. Upon reading the Committee on Secrecy papers after Peterloo, the Evangelical leader Wilberforce concluded that radicals had moved from political to irreligious propaganda as a more effective instrument for undermining the social order. Consequently, Wilberforce and other Evangelicals were committed to working with the Tory Ministry to suppress blasphemy.[16] Evangelical and other religious groups, such as the Society for Enforcing the King's Proclamation (founded in 1787 by Wilberforce) and the Society for the Suppression of Vice, collaborated with the government to secure convictions of offending publishers. Superintending the government's role in these proceedings was the Home Office, and thus a prominent member of the Tory Ministry was extensively involved in this aspect of the crusade: Lord Sidmouth, the Home Secretary, approved each prosecution for blasphemy.[17] Given the extensive political and legal power available and the intensity of motives driving the crusade to wipe out the blasphemous press, it is hardly surprising that these actions were carried out with ferocity and broad scope. Between 1819 and 1823 the Vice Society alone initiated about two hundred prosecutions.[18] Twenty-five *ex of-*

ficio informations (which authorized holding an individual for up to eighteen weeks without trial if bail could not be met) were laid against ten London booksellers in 1819. In the same year many provincial radicals were also punished for selling the *Black Dwarf,* Carlile's *Republican,* and Hone's parodies; half of the seventy-five prosecutions for blasphemous libel in 1819 were outside London.[19]

Though he lived at this time in Italy, Byron would have found it impossible to remain unaffected by the war against blasphemy back in England, and his knowledge would have been fairly specific. Byron undoubtedly knew, for example, about the first prominent figure in the controversy, William Hone. Byron would not only have become acquainted with Hone's reputation through newspaper accounts of the trials of 1817, in which Hone successfully defended himself three times; for years Hone had been an irritant to Byron's publisher, John Murray, pirating and forging Byron's works.[20] More important, it is possible that Byron was influenced by the satanic, infidel aura surrounding Hone's renewed "blasphemy," his publication of the *Apocryphal Gospels* in 1820. A hostile article on this book appeared in the *Quarterly Review* one month after Byron had finished *Cain.*[21] Through his acquaintances in the House of Murray, Byron may have heard of the book earlier, and the review as well, which rabidly demonizes Hone, describing his attempt to "destroy the credit of the New Testament" as a "diabolical task." Echoing the parliamentary speeches on the Six Acts, the reviewer strikes out at what he interchangeably calls the "infidel" or "deistical" party—"men, who for their own evil purposes, are anxious to destroy every principle and feeling which binds the citizen to his country."[22]

Byron would have regarded this diatribe as a provocation. If it did not reach him in time to influence the composition of *Cain,* it is nevertheless representative of the kind of attacks he did encounter in 1820 and 1821, attacks which classed him with plebeian infidels under the "satanic" rubric. Used to demonize figures like Paine and Priestley in the propagandistic pamphlets and cartoons of the 1790s, satanic iconography remained vital in the early nineteenth century. It was extensively deployed in the polarized political discourse of these years, shifting its targets, first to Napoleon, then to religious and political radicalism.[23] Both the parliamentary speeches on the Six Acts and their reception by conservative reviewers display the durability and power of this political trope: an article in the *Quarterly Review* summarizing the debates quotes Lord Grenville's description of Henry Hunt and Richard Carlile as "fiends in human shape endeavouring to rob their unhappy victims of all their consolations here, and of all their hopes hereafter."[24] Sharing the hysteria of the parliamentary speakers, the author of this article paints the struggle with blaspheming and seditious radicalism as a Manichean battle with "men, who, like the Malignant principle himself, can knowingly take advantage of the distresses of mankind, to blast their virtues—base artificers of ruin, who drive the trade of destruction . . ." (22 [1820], 502). Though fortified by the passage of the Six Acts, the writer

goes on to urge a vigilant watch over a foe as formidable as Milton's Satan: "the calm may cease; the enemy may start up from 'the oblivious pool' on which he lies or affects to lie astonished: and the war, which appeared to have been extinguished, may prove to be only in its beginning" (557). A poem published in the *Manchester Patriot* in December 1819 updates "The Devil's Thoughts" (the satirical ballad of 1799 by Southey and Coleridge) by representing Carlile as the agent of Satan.[25] And the Prince Regent himself invoked the myth: a royal proclamation of 1820 characterized infidels as "diabolical men" (Wickwar, p. 159).

By this time, of course, Byron already had a long-established reputation for diabolism: his quasi-autobiographical heroes and the legends accumulating around him had over the years built up a satanic public identity. By 1820 Byron's satanic persona had become almost exclusively the channel through which conservative voices expressed opprobrium, especially concerning the content of the first two cantos of *Don Juan* (1819). In 1820, writing in the *Quarterly Review,* Reginald Heber added a new dimension to the attacks on Byron: "by a strange predilection for the worser half of manicheism, one of the mightiest spirits of the age has, apparently, devoted himself and his genius to the adornment and extension of evil. . . ."[26] This is saying in elegant terms that Byron is a Satanist, which was in fact precisely how he interpreted it.[27]

In *A Vision of Judgment* (1821), Robert Southey went further, crystallizing the new legend of Byron the satanic blasphemer. Branding Byron as the pre-eminent foe of moral, religious, and political order, Southey called for the suppression of Byron's writing. Southey's poem conjures up the demon of sedition as a visionary portent, a hubbub of Whig and radical voices issuing from the monstrous Accuser of George.[28] In the preface to the poem, the laureate focuses his attack on one manifestation of this vast demonic threat—the bad eminence of the Satanic school, Byron. In Southey's diatribe, the "audacious impiety" of Byron's school, enacted in its rebellion "against the holiest ordinances of society," receives concluding emphasis (p. 769). This makes clear Southey's aim in calling the attention of the "rulers of the state." He thus acts as a one-man Vice Society, suggesting an indictment of Byron's satanic blasphemy. Thus two prominent writers for the journal regarded as the organ of the Tory ministry applied to Byron the politicized brand of "satanic," grouping him with the infidels. It should come as no surprise, then, that a satanic figure looms so large in *Cain.* Unleashing a blaspheming satanic character in a religious drama must have seemed especially opportune as an ideological counterstrike, the fulfillment of Byron's threat to "give Mr. Milman Mr. Southey & others of the crew something that shall occupy their dreams!" (*BLJ* VIII, 193). The precise direction Byron was to take here—using a satanic character to subvert biblical myth—came from his awareness of Richard Carlile's work, filtered through Shelley's experiments in blasphemous writing.[29]

Before his trial for blasphemous libel in 1819, Carlile began a new venture, *The Republican.* In the voluminous writing Carlile contributed to each issue of this radical journal, he attacked the mythology of Christianity and its political power, deriving his central argument from his mentor, Paine: that Christianity was falsehood and superstition in the service of state power, using its mind-imprisoning mythology to legitimize autocracy, retard the advancement of the human mind, and thus obscure the rights of man.[30] As a publisher and writer Carlile carried on the program of *The Age of Reason*—destroying the power of the Bible by revealing the fabulous nature of its mythology.[31] At one time Byron found Carlile practically beneath his notice, remarking in letters of November and December 1819 to Douglas Kinnaird and John Murray that trying "the fool Carlile and his trash" would only make a martyr of him (*BLJ* VI, 240, 256). By August 1822, however, Byron's opinion of Carlile's achievements had substantially improved: the preface to Cantos 6-8 of *Don Juan* passionately defends the imprisoned radical publisher from the Tory "hirelings" of the *Quarterly Review.* Aligning the iconoclasm of this "'wretched Infidel,' as he is called," with that of Christ and Socrates, Byron predicts that Carlile's martyrdom will produce countless converts to Deism (*Works*, V, 297). Since he too had by now been attacked as a blasphemer, Byron obviously would feel some sympathy for Carlile; but something else must have happened after 1819 to alter so profoundly his conception of the man.

Shelley, who had identified himself with the cause of infidelism since 1812 and who now expressed his outrage over Carlile's conviction in an indignant letter to the *Examiner* on 3 November 1819, undoubtedly influenced Byron's views here. In his letter, Shelley defends Carlile with the central polemic of the infidel tradition:

> the prosecutors care little for religion, or care for it only as it is the mask & the garment by which they are invested with the symbols of worldly power. In prosecuting Carlile they have used the superstition of the Jury as their instrument for crushing a political enemy, or rather they strike in his person at all their political enemies. They know that the Established Church is based upon the belief in certain events of a supernatural character having occurred in Judea eighteen centuries ago; that but for this belief the farmer would refuse to pay the tenth of the produce of his labours to maintain its numbers in idleness; that this class of persons if not maintained in idleness would have something else to do than to divert the attention of the people from obtaining a Reform in their oppressive government. . . .[32]

This essentially replicates the argument with which Carlile and Paine attacked the political power of biblical myth. It is therefore highly significant that we find Shelley, at about the same time he denounced the conviction of Carlile, writing his enigmatic essay "On the Devil, and Devils," which skeptically attacks the theological ideas of Satan and hell, the underbelly of—Shelley adopts Paine's very phrase—"the Christian mythology."

The occasion for this essay has never been established, but it seems more than likely that Shelley wrote it in response to Carlile's conviction, intending to add his voice to Carlile's—as if Shelley meant to pick up where the radical publisher left off in his blaspheming demolition of state religion.[33] The Devil is "the outwork of the Christian faith," Shelley argues, necessary to reconcile God's benevolence and omnipotence with the existence of evil; without the scapegoat of Satan, the entire Christian system collapses.[34] Hence Shelley ironically deplores the growing skepticism about the Devil: "depend upon it, that when a person once begins to think that perhaps there is no Devil, he is in a dangerous way" (Julian, VII, 92). That is, the skeptic will no longer exonerate God from responsibility for the existence of evil, a point related to Shelley's observation in the letter to the *Examiner*: the Christian mythology serves to divert the attention of the people away from Reform and thus deflect responsibility for social evil away from the temporal ruler.

Besides dismissing the traditional theological idea of Satan, Shelley's essay also transforms the myth in two bold idealizations of this figure: the famous critique of *Paradise Lost* he later incorporated in *A Defence of Poetry,* and a pathetic treatment of the myth—God's corruption of the unfallen Lucifer into Satan—which Shelley used as the paradigm for *The Cenci.* Both passages showed Byron the possibility of revitalizing the myth of Satan and assigning it new functions rather than merely killing it off; the essay appears also to have suggested the tactic of incorporating blasphemy in dramatic form as a shield from "persecution."[35] The strategy of assault through a blasphemous re-shaping of the myth of Satan Shelley had already carried out in the speech of Ahasuerus in *Queen Mab,* and a renewal of this tactic may very well have been a subject of conversation when Shelley visited Byron in August 1821, just three weeks after Byron had begun writing *Cain.* As Charles Robinson has shown, it was precisely at this time that Shelley urged Byron to counterattack the *Quarterly Review* (and Southey in particular).[36] Their talk would likely have sharpened the ideological edge of *Cain,* leading Byron to heighten the "Satanism" of the work by shaping Lucifer into the antagonist of the Christian mythology of Creation and Fall.

Whatever Byron's actual religious position was in 1821, his skeptical conception of biblical myth overlapped sufficiently with Shelley's infidel program to draw him into controversy.[37] Further, with Shelley and other infidels, Byron held that belief was involuntary, not at all a function of the will; hence the policing of anti-religious utterance embodied in the Six Acts would have struck him as particularly absurd and outrageous.[38] That his nemesis, Castlereagh, was regarded as their chief architect, and that the Whigs failed utterly to oppose the legislation, would not likely have escaped his notice.[39] Byron's encounter with these ideological provocations, I suggest, combined with the charges of Satanism levelled at him, generated the inflammatory, blasphemous speeches of Lucifer. In this poetic response, Byron's aim seems to have been more complex than Philip Martin has suggested—that *Cain* is animated by a "frivolous impulse to be offensive."[40] In 1822 the *Eclectic Review* speculated that Byron, encouraged by the examples of Hone and Carlile, was resolved to test for himself the limits of the freedom of the press. If so, then Byron was enacting in a tangible way his wish to add through his writing "a dreadful impulse to each loud meander / Of murmuring Liberty's wide waves" (*Don Juan*, VI. 741-42; *Works*, V, 327).[41]

Yet Byron's strategy in constructing Lucifer was also to avoid presenting an easy target for the *Quarterly Review*. To idealize the myth of Satan—what Byron's readers surely expected from him—would simply invite more propagandistic attacks and charges of Satanism; a more ambiguous treatment in a dramatic context might head them off. And there was even more riding on the manner in which Byron constructed his satanic figure than confusing his conservative opponents: there were the legal implications to consider. Not only the radical penny-press publishers were affected by the political climate; as Donald Thomas notes, it was in these years that high-toned authors and publishers first ran into trouble because of the blasphemy laws.[42] The extent of the actual threat to Byron of a blasphemy prosecution is hardly obvious, and a peer, whether living in England or Italy, probably had little to fear. In fact publishers, not writers, were most at risk, and the specific danger they faced was not fine or imprisonment but the failure to have their copyright protected, resulting in income lost to cheap pirated editions. This in fact happened to Murray in Chancery court; Lord Eldon would not protect the copyright of *Cain* because he found its content blasphemous. There was no further court action—no prosecution for blasphemy.[43] Yet well before writing *Cain*, Byron had worried frequently about the consequences of publishing blasphemy. In 1817 Shelley had lost the custody of his children in Chancery court over the anti-Christian diatribes of *Queen Mab*, which were uttered by the rebellious, satanic figure of Ahasuerus. Byron repeatedly reminded Murray, Douglas Kinnaird, and John Cam Hobhouse of this in 1819 and 1820 after the publisher sought an injunction in Chancery court to stop the piracy of *Don Juan*; Byron warned that he did not want to lose his parental rights over his daughter Ada (*BLJ* VI, 252, 256; VII, 121, 195). This chronic anxiety that a Chancery court might judge his published writing blasphemous warrants the inference that Byron took some care in writing his play—especially in the speeches of its superhuman infidel—to avoid the charges.

Thus, because biblical myth was contested in the blasphemy controversy, because the brand of "satanic" had been fixed first to plebeian infidels and then to Byron himself, and because publishing blasphemy carried real consequences, to take up the myth of Satan in 1821 in the context of biblical drama was to enter an intense ideological conflict. The fragmented characterization of Lucifer in *Cain* bears the traces of this conflict. Taking back the myth from those who used it propagandistically, Byron transforms its meaning and function. He first destabilizes

the traditional role of Satan as author of evil. Then, with this accomplished, Byron introduces Lucifer into the biblical drama as a skeptical commentator who unsettles Christian myth—as if, in the reflexive irony of this work, he were speaking on the yet unwritten text of Genesis. Yet at crucial points Byron undermines the heroic rebelliousness of Lucifer, interspersing motifs and gestures of transparent diabolism with Lucifer's more characteristic Socratic questioning and denunciation of Jehovah's ways. By alternately idealizing and deflating Lucifer, Byron preserves an ambiguous perspective on his biblical subject and an elusive stance as a "Satanist." His remark in a letter of 19 September 1821 to Thomas Moore suggests that his intentions had in fact included this form of mystification; he subtitled the play a "Mystery," he says, to correspond with what it "will remain to the reader" (*BLJ* VIII, 216).

II. LUCIFER AS BLASPHEMING PERSONA

Byron's complicated negotiation of the myth of Satan first appears in the preface to *Cain*, where he pursues two objectives at once. In a series of mingled assertions, disclaimers, and challenges, he attempts to head off charges of blasphemy while at the same time unsettling the reader by puncturing the conventional myth of Satan. After emphasizing the fidelity of the language of his play to scripture, Byron abruptly focuses this mock-apology for his modest literalism on a specific case.

> The reader will recollect that the book of Genesis does not state that Eve was tempted by a demon, but by 'the Serpent;' and that only because he was 'the most subtil of all the beasts of the field.' Whatever interpretation the Rabbins and the Fathers may have put upon this, I take the words as I find them, and reply with Bishop Watson upon similar occasions, when the Fathers were quoted to him, as Moderator in the Schools of Cambridge, 'Behold the Book!'—holding up the Scripture.
>
> (p. 228)

While the action of *Cain* does not directly involve the temptation of Eve, the question of the identity of the serpent is among the first subjects in the preface. Byron goes out of his way to pick up an inflammatory topic, yet he downplays his role as provocateur. The tone is temperate—for Byron; he affects to take the Bible seriously, almost submerging his irony. These gestures, along with the effort to line up authorities (later adding Warburton to Watson), indicate that Byron not only expected trouble but anticipated it would center around the figure of Lucifer.[44]

Yet Byron's somewhat mild tone does not disarm the very first imaginative premise of his play. Challenging the standard interpretation of Genesis 3, he removes the traditional Author of Evil from events, and despite his adduced "authorities," Byron knew that this was bound to offend. The Bible commentaries of the day maintained that the serpent housed Satan.[45] Uncoupling Satan and the serpent has several explosive implications. It first calls into question the existence of the Devil, which in turn suggests that the character Lucifer cannot be understood in his traditionally diabolical role. This defamiliarizing effect is compounded by the use of the angelic name derived from Isaiah, distancing Lucifer from the New Testament tradition of demonology.

Byron's abandonment of the dramatist's objectivity in the preface grounds his reconception of Satan. As the prelude to the entrance of Lucifer into a drama which purports to take scripture for truth and to realize it, Byron's skeptical denial of the identity of Satan and the serpent forces the pious reader to shift uncomfortably between the Bible and the play in an effort to pin down this ambiguous satanic figure. More important, the rhetoric of the preface authorizes Lucifer to unsettle the Christian mythology. By undermining Lucifer's traditional identity and role, Byron in a sense exonerates him, thus rendering him a credible commentator on scriptural matters. This manuever also provides Lucifer with a conceptual foundation for attacking the Fall and the Expulsion, for removing the figure of Satan from the temptation of Eve implicitly causes the whole machinery of Fall, Atonement, and Redemption to collapse; Byron recognized with Shelley that the identity of Satan and the serpent is necessary to the Christian "scheme of sin and propitiation" (Julian, VII, 104). Thus Lucifer's denial that he tempted Eve, confirmed in the preface by the author, destabilizes these dogmas, and little in the play suggests that a Fall as such took place—only the wrathful expulsion from Eden.[46] The preface therefore opens the way for Lucifer's blasphemous countermyth, which explains the Expulsion and everything else back to the pre-Adamites in terms of Jehovah's caprice and tyranny.

Byron's ironic controversialism contrasts with that of infidels like Carlile, who approach the Fall and the role of Satan more directly and aggressively, with the blunt weapons borrowed from Paine.

> If it can be shewn that this chapter is a fiction, away goes the Christian religion; for unless we admit the doctrine of the fall of man, we can find no need of a Redeemer . . . of all animals to be endowed with human speech, the serpent is the least adapted. Divines . . . in order to get over this difficulty, have asserted, that this omnipotent and omnipresent gentleman, the devil, or satan, either changed himself into a serpent, or entered spiritually into one. . . . I, who believe that the common course of nature has never been changed in any one instance, can only look on this account of the talking serpent as a fable, or the fiction of the human imagination.
>
> (*The Republican*, [7 April 1820], 410)

Through his manuevers in the preface Byron similarly implies that Genesis 3 is merely a fable, incapable of sustaining the exegetical weight that has been placed upon it. The aims of Byron and Carlile appear identical, then, but their rhetorical strategies differ radically. Following Paine, Carlile simply seeks to destroy Genesis 3 and its power by declaring it fabulous, and the central absurdity is the figure of Satan; what he dismisses Byron seizes and transforms into the vehicle for his ironic treatment of biblical myth.

Byron was sufficiently certain that through the figure of Lucifer he could reconceive the myth of Satan, subvert Genesis, confound the orthodox, and get away with it that he even paused at one point in the preface to jeer at his accuser in the *Quarterly Review,* Heber.

> I am prepared to be accused of Manicheism—or some other hard name ending in '*ism*' which make[s] a formidable figure and awful sound in the eyes and ears of those who would be as much puzzled to explain the terms so bandied about as the liberal and pious Indulgers in such epithets.
>
> (p. 229)

These defiant sentences were prudently suppressed by Murray, but their presence in the manuscript establishes that Byron was utterly disingenuous when he claimed that he never expected the uproar which greeted the publication of this play. On the contrary, the deleted paragraph reveals that in defamiliarizing the figure of Satan into a Manichean "Principle" who comments on scripture from an infidel perspective, Byron courted controversy.[47]

The figure who appears in response to Cain's opening soliloquy looks at first like a relatively unthreatening replica of Milton's fallen angel. Byron's contemporaries had rarely if ever seen a poetic reincarnation of Milton's Satan which embodied iconoclastic views: only Shelley's Ahasuerus had appeared (and the limited familiarity of this figure had come only recently with the pirating of *Queen Mab* in early 1821), while Blake's radical experiments with satanic myth were largely unknown.[48] Thus Byron initially avoids unsettling the reader by aligning Lucifer with a relatively familiar and uncontroversial character; Cain beholds a figure like Milton's Satan, "majestic though in ruin" and "mightier far" than the cherubim who guard Paradise,

> nor less
> Beauteous, and yet not all as beautiful
> As he hath been, and might be: sorrow seems
> Half of his immortality.
>
> (I.i.93-96; p. 235)

Yet Byron soon distances his creation from its Miltonic model. Lucifer's indignant denials that he tempted Eve thoroughly disengage him from the "infernal serpent" of *Paradise Lost,* a deflection which enraged contemporary readers, who saw immediately that unlike Milton's Satan, Lucifer never acknowledges that he misrepresents God, never soliloquizes remorsefully like Satan on Mount Niphates.[49]

In a subtler way, as well, by assuming the role of commentator on the yet unwritten Bible, Lucifer has already moved even further from the Miltonic model. Quoting Genesis, Lucifer holds forth to Cain, who, as an original recipient of Revelation, is in the position of a reader of scripture.

> LUCIFER. . . . and even He who thrust ye forth, so
>   thrust ye

Because 'ye should not eat the fruits of life,
And become gods as we.' Were those his words?
CAIN. They were, as I have heard from those who
  heard them,
In thunder.

(I.i.203-7; p. 238)

Lucifer deconstructs scripture with special insight, for he apparently knows the heavenly record and is thus prepared to refute Genesis in advance; when Cain suggests that "the serpent was a spirit," Lucifer retorts that

It is not written so on high:
The proud One will not so far falsify,
Though man's vast fears and little vanity
Would make him cast upon the spiritual nature
His own low failing. The snake was the snake—
No more

(I.i.219-24; p. 239)

When a mythic character comments on the story he inhabits, "it undercuts the myth by making it self-conscious," as David Eggenschwiler has observed of the irony in this speech.[50] Moreover, because Lucifer's reflexive commentary on Genesis emphasizes his awareness that he is dealing with myth, this device enables him to go on to deny both the truth and divine inspiration of Genesis, dismissing it with the blasphemer's catchword—"fable":

When thousand ages
Have roll'd o'er your dead ashes, and your seed's
The seed of the then world may thus array
Their earliest fault in fable, and attribute
To me a shape I scorn.

(I.i.233-37; pp. 239-40)

Lucifer's assertion—that only "man's vast fears" and "vanity" have produced the preposterous supernaturalism of Satan seducing Eve—aligns his utterance squarely with the infidel tradition. His dismissal replicates not only the views of genteel infidels like Volney, Holbach, or Shelley (in his essay "On the Devil"), but that of the vulgarian Paine as well, who regards the "strange fable" of the Fall and Redemption as a monument to nothing but "the gloomy pride of man."[51]

The mystification of Lucifer's identity, achieved by obscuring his traditional role in this dialogue and in the preface, is an effect Byron has already compounded in the first two hundred lines of the act by blurring Lucifer with Prometheus. It is the Promethean Lucifer of act I who trumpets the most controversial matter in the play, starting with the attack on the silence of Genesis about immortality. At the core of Cain's metaphysical rebelliousness is his bewildered resentment over the death-sentence pronounced on humanity, aggravated by his ignorance of the immortality of the soul. Seizing this opening, Lucifer immediately dons the role of the Promethean benefactor, asserting repeatedly his sympathy with the "thoughts / Of dust" (I.i.100-101; p. 235). In addressing Cain's confusion about death, Lucifer here also takes on the stance of the

commentator, an effect again amplified by the preface. Here Byron justifies his dramatic inquiry into the absence of a future state in Genesis through the precedent of the ingenious explanation offered by Warburton.[52] It is striking that Byron neither affirms nor denies Warburton's heterodox argument, but merely says it is the best we can do to explain this "extraordinary omission" (p. 229), thus calling attention to the huge gap in scripture, which Lucifer goes on to exploit. Lucifer's exposure of this defect in Revelation replicates a central manuever in infidel writing, one which Paine had popularized and Carlile had carried on: exposing the gaps, discrepancies, and contradictions in scripture, then pointing out how they reflect on God. This technique is dramatically enacted in Lucifer's Promethean delivery of the secret to Cain; the fire-bringer astonishes Cain by telling him,

They have deceived thee; thou shalt live.

   . . . . .

             think not
The earth, which is thine outward cov'ring, is
Existence—it will cease, and thou wilt be
No less than thou art now.

(I.i.109-19; pp. 235-36)

In revealing this, Lucifer casts a sinister light on the divine guardian of the secret, an effect closely resembling that produced by a reading of Genesis 4 printed in *The Republican*. God provokes the jealous murder of Abel "and then, like a designing assassin, inquires after Abel as if he knew nothing about it" (*The Republican*, 1.7 [8 October 1819], 102). Byron's comparably blasphemous handling of Genesis is undertaken entirely by Lucifer, while Byron coolly withdraws, ironically summing up his treatment of this episode as follows: "I have therefore supposed it [the idea of immortality] new to Cain without, I hope, any perversion of Holy Writ."

The most inflammatory material of the first act emerges in Lucifer's Promethean tirade against the "Omnipotent tyrant." The speech begins almost innocuously, with Lucifer's assertion of autogeny—his hypothetical "if he made us" is actually wobbly when compared with the strident declaration of Milton's Satan that he and the rebel angels are "self-begot, self-rais'd." But the implications of Lucifer's speech are less tame. As Lucifer continues to excoriate Jehovah for disguising evil as good, it becomes clear that Byron is using Lucifer in specific ways—most obviously, to taunt Heber once again. For this speech invokes and rearranges the Manichean dualism, through which Lucifer portrays the creating God of Genesis as an evil demiurge.

Goodness would not make
Evil; and what else hath he made? But let him
Sit on his vast and solitary throne,
Creating worlds, to make eternity
Less burthensome to his immense existence
And unparticipated solitude!

(I.i.146-51; p. 237)

More than any other, this speech drew hostile responses from contemporary reviewers, because Byron impudently transvalues the "worser" and "better" halves of Manicheism by inverting the moral hierarchy of Jehovah and Lucifer.[53] Even more outrageously, he follows Shelley closely in doing this.

In the allegorical introductory canto of *The Revolt of Islam* (1818), Shelley pursues Volney's program of shaking traditional myths apart by recasting the story of the origin of evil. "Two Powers" struggle for dominion over the world, the narrative explains, but the Fallen "Spirit of Good" has been compelled by the Evil principle to metamorphose into a serpent.

> The great Spirit of Good did creep among
> The nations of mankind, and every tongue
> Cursed, and blasphemed him as he past; for none
> Knew good from evil, though their names were hung
> In mockery o'er the fane where many a groan,
> As King, and Lord, and God, the conquering Fiend
> did own[.][54]

Identified with the morning star (which Shelley consistently names Lucifer), the Spirit of Good reassumes his original shape at the end of the episode, materializing as the angelic form of Lucifer. From this canto Byron borrowed Shelley's morally inverted Manichean myth and his reconceived figure of Lucifer. To construct the content of Lucifer's Manichean blasphemy, Byron drew from Shelley's *Queen Mab* (1813). As William D. Brewer has noted, Byron closely modeled Lucifer on Shelley's satanic antagonist of the God of Moses, Ahasuerus.[55] But it is not only his echoes of Milton's Satan which link Shelley's Wandering Jew with *Cain* and Lucifer.[56] The defiance hurled by Ahasuerus at the "almighty Tyrant," which resembles Lucifer's tirade, is itself embedded in a discourse of blasphemy (line 199).

As the legendary denouncer of Christ, Ahasuerus is of course an archetypal infidel; but Shelley has extended his traditional authority to blaspheme into the present day. The eternal figure who once overheard Moses is now a witness to latter-day religious oppression, which his speech represents through satanic myth. Exalting "Hell's freedom" (i.e., unbelief) over the "servitude of Heaven" (line 195), Ahasuerus denounces the persecution of "unoffending infidels" by Jehovah's slaves (line 209), an allusion to the 1812 conviction of Daniel Isaac Eaton for blasphemy (which Shelley had protested in "A Letter to Lord Ellenborough"). Ahasuerus goes on to reveal the wickedness of the mythology which Eaton had gone to jail to oppose: the remainder of his speech surveys from the infidel perspective biblical history from the Creation to the Passion. The God who dictates to Moses is roughly the same figure Byron's Lucifer condemns in his Manichean tirade, for he confesses (in terms borrowed from Volney) that he "planted the tree of evil so that he [man] / Might eat and perish, and My soul procure / Wherewith to sate its malice" (lines 110-12). To Jehovah's sadistic delight, the "strange sacrifice" (line 142) of the Atonement will save only a handful from eternal agony.

Byron appears to have imported many of these details into the speech of his satanic persona, but even more important, he understood and used the general strategy of the speech. Shelley designed this episode to destroy the Christian mythology: the speech of Ahasuerus works by exposing the error in biblical myth itself—its projection of a bloodthirsty and tyrannical God. Assuming a stance anticipating Lucifer's, Ahasuerus declares that Jehovah's perverse redemption scheme will collapse, for Reason now is establishing the "throne of truth" (lines 246-47), whose rule will eclipse that of the Bible. Thus the approach Byron would adapt to Lucifer: a mythological figure burrows into Genesis and disrupts the structure from within, from an infidel perspective.

From these two works, then, Byron draws on the ideological resonance given to Manichean myth by Shelley. Other poets in recent years had invoked radically dualistic mythic frameworks—Southey, for example, in *Thalaba the Destroyer* (1801) and *The Curse of Kehama* (1810), and Moore, in *The Veiled Prophet of Khorassan* (*Lalla Rookh*; 1817). But these treatments are theologically and morally conventional, clearly aligning the satanic figure with evil. The dualism that Byron himself had invoked in *Manfred,* where he established Arimanes as the Evil Principle, conformed as well. But Shelley rudely overturned the convention. Though Bayle is often cited as a source of Byron's controversial Manicheism, it is the Shelleyan dimension, rather than the theological ideas Byron found in Bayle, which generated the inflammatory power of this speech.[57] The line Shelley and Byron take embodies the oppositional form of Manicheism Marilyn Butler has explored: a use of myth to discredit Christianity and autocracy.[58]

The coda to Lucifer's Manichean tirade would have amounted to blasphemous overkill had Murray not suppressed it; the last four lines blast the Atonement in advance:

>   perhaps he'll make
> One day a Son unto himself—as he
> Gave you a father—and if he so doth
> Mark me!—that Son will be a Sacrifice.
>
>   (I.i.163-66; p. 237)

The crackling tone of outrage here not only communicates Byron's Socinian biases. It melds Lucifer once again with the infidel tradition, which found the Atonement a morally repugnant element of the Christian mythology. By echoing the attacks on the Atonement by Shelley's Ahasuerus and Paine (who said the doctrine made God a vengeful murderer), Lucifer's outpouring thus squares with infidel polemics against cornerstone dogmas derived from Genesis 3.[59]

In these speeches, Lucifer's authority to undermine scripture is unchallenged; as so many of the reviewers noticed, Byron refused to create even one character capable of refuting the attacks on the divine prohibition, Fall, and Expulsion. However, just as the preface guards Byron against charges of blasphemy by pretending to honest literalism, the characterization of Lucifer fractures at a crucial point in the first act. When Cain requests that his mentor supply him with metaphysical knowledge, Lucifer reverts to the traditional manner of his satanic majesty:

> CAIN. Wilt thou teach me all?
> LUCIFER. Ay, upon one condition.
> CAIN. Name it.
> LUCIFER. That thou dost fall down and worship me—
> thy Lord.
>
> (I.i.301-3; p. 242)

This is inconsistent—to say the least—with Lucifer's Promethean declaration that he would have made gods of men. The reader might infer that Lucifer's overtures simply represent a sham Prometheanism, contrived in order to seduce Cain. Yet it seems just as likely that the transparent diabolism from the temptation of Christ in Matthew 4:9 has been inserted initially to reassure but in the long run to confuse the conservative reader about Lucifer's satanic identity. For the characterization of Lucifer remains problematic even after this episode, and his role never resolves in any pattern of consistently diabolical action. In Lucifer's opening speech in the second act, for example, he begins by naming himself the Prince of the Air, then cancels his demand that Cain worship him (II.i.3; p. 252). Moreover, this reversal itself expresses an offensively irreligious position of Byron's day; since infidels held that religious belief is not subject to the will, it follows that faith cannot be meritorious or constitute the source of morality or salvation. Indeed, as Ursula Henriques has observed, the doctrine of salvation by faith "was felt to point to an unjust God," which Lucifer himself proclaims by scorning the "edict of the other God" (II.i.6; p. 252), which requires faith for salvation.[60]

> *I* will not say,
> Believe in *me*, as a conditional creed
> To save thee; but fly with me o'er the gulf
> Of space an equal flight, and I will show
> What thou dar'st not deny, the history
> Of past, and present, and of future worlds.
>
> (II.i.20-25; p. 252)

Finally, in this spasmodic temptation there is a curious lack of dramatic tension: Lucifer demands worship baldly and drops the request abruptly, and this is characteristic of his diabolical action throughout. If the first two acts constitute the "temptation of Cain," then Lucifer's approach is much too casual. He appears about as interested in winning Cain's soul as Satan in *The Vision of Judgment* is in seizing George.

In the tour of Hades, Lucifer undermines the authority of the Christian mythology from a new perspective. Here Byron turns Lucifer into the oracle of the cataclysm-theory of Cuvier, using the latter's work to shake up biblical cosmogony. Once again, Byron's satanic controversialism is at first glance disarming, but finally proves explosive. Had Byron used the ideas of James Hutton, the "infidel" Plu-

tonist, the attack on scripture would have been transparent; Hutton's theories of a cyclic uplifting and erosion of land over a practically infinite range of time dispensed with the idea of beginnings and ends. The attempt to square the geological record with Mosaic history is not even made. But to invoke the name of Cuvier in the preface to *Cain* probably would not unsettle the theologically conservative reader in 1821. Cuvier's work had been taken over by diluvian geologists who found his catastrophism compatible with Genesis where Hutton's Plutonism was not, chiefly because Cuvier upheld the account of the Flood.[61] What Lucifer does with Cuvier is another matter, however. In his "poetic fiction," as Byron ironically termed it, Lucifer de-centers the Creation, extending Cain's vision backward into deep time to reveal that Jehovah has been creating and destroying worlds for ages. Thus the explanatory power of the biblical myth is immediately compromised, for Lucifer implies that Jehovah's fearful labors, and the alarming account of the mighty race of pre-Adamites and its fate did not get written into Genesis—all of this is as it were lopped off from its beginning. Asked to account for the extinction of these colossal beings, Lucifer merely replies in Cuvier's terms—that it arrived "By a most crushing and inexorable / Destruction and disorder of the elements, / Which struck a world to chaos" (II.ii.80-82; p. 262). Like the interpretation Lucifer derives from the silence of Genesis on immortality, the counter-cosmogony also represents scripture as a defective Revelation.

Byron's satanic critique of biblical cosmogony aligns him with the infidel tradition; once again, however, it does so obliquely. In *The Age of Reason*, Paine established the technique of employing science to attack the Christian mythology. Around 1820, Carlile began to follow this program, popularizing catastrophism not only to discredit Genesis as a fabulous support of state power, but to justify violent and sweeping political change by analogy with natural cataclysms.[62] If Byron recognized the more volatile political implications in these tactics, he chose not to press the case in Carlile's manner. Like Carlile, Byron uses Lucifer's Cuvierean countermyth to subvert the compromise between geologists and Genesis, yet he confines himself to pursuing the moral questions implied by the French paleontologist's work: why would God repeatedly destroy the world, as the fossil record interpreted by Cuvier indicated? How had God's creatures offended him that he chose to annihilate them several times over before Noah's flood?

As the second act draws to a close, Lucifer's manner toward Cain shifts again, and he increasingly bears out the role Byron assigns him in his explanatory letter to Murray. He depresses Cain by showing him "infinite things—& his own abasement" (*BLJ* IX, 53), especially his humiliating inferiority to the pre-Adamites.

> I show thee what thy predecessors are,
> And what they *were* thou feelest, in degree
> Inferior as thy petty feelings and
> Thy pettier portion of the immortal part
> Of high intelligence and earthly strength.
>
> (II.ii.89-93; p. 262)

In response Cain gradually comes to realize that Lucifer is a loveless being, capable of caring only for "some vast and general purpose, / To which particular things must melt like snows" (II.ii.314-15; p. 270). His attitude toward Cain finally hardens into scorn for Cain's metaphysical aspirations, and when Lucifer at last confesses indifference to the human condition, the Promethean figure of act I dissolves once again. It has been argued repeatedly and persuasively that in these exchanges the central ethical conflict of the play finally emerges, displacing Cain's quarrel with Jehovah: the human world of love and community struggles against the transcendental imperatives of Lucifer.[63] Cain ends up killing his brother because he has abandoned his humanity for the intellectualized hatred of Jehovah Lucifer has fostered in him. As convincing as this reading is, it tends to disconnect the two principal thrusts of the play: its critique of biblical authority (acts I-II) and its dramatization of an archetypal tragic event, the first murder (act III). That is, the critique loses its impetus when Lucifer leaves the action, at which point Byron submits to the authority of the biblical model and proceeds with the fratricide and the vindication of Jehovah.[64]

To perceive what this reading obscures—how the satanic critique of bibliolatry actually reverberates through the final act—involves reading Lucifer's final speech reflexively once again, as if his words were directed at Cain as a reader of the Bible. This speech enacts yet another reversal of Lucifer's role, the most extreme in the play. With a climactic, ringing challenge to Jehovah, Lucifer returns once more to the blaspheming Prometheanism of act I:

> *One good* gift has the fatal apple given—
> Your *reason*:—let it not be over-sway'd
> By tyrannous threats to force you into faith
> 'Gainst all external sense and inward feeling:
> Think and endure,—and form an inner world
> In your own bosom—where the outward fails;
> So shall you nearer be the spiritual
> Nature, and war triumphant with your own.
>
> (II.ii.459-66; p. 275)

Lucifer's ambiguous stance comes full circle to the satanic credo, "the mind is its own place." In both obvious and subtle ways, of course, this speech can be regarded as inciting the rebellious murder of Abel. Few critics who view Lucifer as a purely demonic figure, however, take up this speech. It seems that most readers sense that this panegyric on the defiantly autonomous mind has a different thematic register—that it defends intellectual freedom. This very effect of the speech is heightened, moreover, when it is read in terms of the historical differential. Lucifer's denunciation of "tyrannous threats to force you into faith" resonated strongly in an age when, as Shelley observed in his essay "On the Devil," "the most enormous sanctions of opinion and law are attached to a direct avowal of certain speculative notions" (Julian, VII, 91). Lucifer's speech is the final, culminating appeal made to Cain to resist with his mind the authority of the biblical myth he lives in, to continue his skeptical refusal to "Reconcile what I saw with what I heard" (I.i.168-69; p. 237). Yet Cain fails to

achieve the intellectual liberation Lucifer sets before him—to live without the fable—and in the third act, he becomes the Cain of biblical myth. Cain's collapse is manifest in his bizarre "prayer" to Jehovah before the sacrifice. In his final speech Lucifer had warned him that he must judge God's dealings with him by their fruits only, because "Evil and Good are things in their own essence, / And not made good or evil by the giver" (II.ii.452-56; p. 274). Yet at the last Cain resigns himself to Jehovah's disposition of good and evil, implicitly acknowledging that power overwhelms knowledge: "good and evil seem / To have no power themselves, save in thy will" (III.i.274-75; p. 285). That is, Cain does not resolve to live independently of compelled belief, but merely to endure tyranny or to rebel. When the whirlwind of Jehovah destroys Cain's altar, this theophany shows Jehovah's readiness to compel faith, and Cain demonstrates in turn that he can endure no longer. By dangling knowledge in front of Cain, Lucifer has tempted and destroyed him. Yet in his final speech Lucifer's other role, the only role Byron's contemporaries saw, emerges once again: Lucifer exhorts Cain to create a world in his own bosom—one which supplants the biblical cosmos. But this form of intellectual freedom is rejected in favor of violent and futile rebellion.

Soon after the publication of *Cain*, Carlile's *Republican* increasingly began to attack Christian demonology, spurred on by Byron to mount an offensive against this "outwork of the Christian faith."[65] From Dorchester gaol Carlile wrote that this "Atheistical poem" deals

> the Bible and its supporters . . . some terrible and irrecoverable blows; and the cause of Lord Byron's putting his name to such a poem, or publishing it at such a moment, cannot be doubted or misunderstood. It is a ponderous blow at superstition from his pen.
>
> (*The Republican*, 5.6 [8 February 1822], 192)

Carlile's reaction to *Cain* went overboard, of course—Byron's iconoclasm is much more indirect and ironic. He never insists outright that Genesis is merely fabulous, as the programmatic infidel would. Yet Carlile rightly saw in the speeches of Lucifer Byron's refusal to approach the Bible as an instrument of faith and to accept its authority. But why did Byron turn to such an oblique mode of controversialism? As Marilyn Butler has observed, oppositional writing at this time was characteristically elliptical and elusive, for writers like Shelley and Peacock avoided the direct presentation of extreme positions on domestic issues not only because of their ambivalence about popular disaffection and violence, but because so few sympathetic readers existed among the literate classes. By embodying the voice of contemporary blasphemy in the figure of Lucifer, Byron actually stepped somewhat out of this mode of "self-censorship" described by Butler, engaging matters more directly.[66] But there were real limits on what was tolerable and publishable, and as I have shown, Byron's strategy in *Cain* was to press against these limits, while at the same time strengthening his hand by blending uncontroversial elements into his treatment of Lucifer: the dramatic treatment, the rhetoric of the preface, the Miltonic features, the name of Cuvier, and the frequent swerving into traditional diabolism. Byron's equivocal handling of Lucifer reveals not so much his lingering orthodox belief as his willingness to sacrifice the unity of a character to the ends of embodying iconoclastic positions and manipulating the reader through ambiguity. Taken as a whole, the handling of Lucifer's characterization reveals that in 1821 Byron had less interest in maintaining traditional satanic roles than in exploring new and controversial ones.

In the final scene of *Manfred,* the culminating moment of Byron's early myth of Satan, the hero's Miltonic speech to his infernal "genius" declares the autonomy of "the mind which is immortal"—that is, the mind of Manfred alone (III.iv.129; *Works,* III, 101). Thus, in language colored by the speech of Milton's Satan on the burning plain of Hell, Manfred announces his solitary apotheosis, his entrance into an afterlife created by his own will. When satanic myth re enters Byron's writing four years later, its function has shifted profoundly: less private in its concerns, it has become more ideologically driven. Examining the figure of Lucifer in the context of the blasphemy controversy identifies this new function, for it suggest that Byron's abrupt return to satanic myth was an exercise in agitational writing, guarded though it is by his dramatic techniques and by his disingenuous protests that he intended no blasphemy. Through his experiment in satanic myth, Byron moved toward the even more combative cantos of *Don Juan* on the Siege of Ismail and their bellicose and partisan preface.

Notes

1. Byron, *Complete Poetical Works,* ed. Jerome J. McGann and Barry Weller, 7 vols. (Oxford: Clarendon Press, 1980-1993), VI, *Cain* I.i.87 (p. 235), and 322 (p. 243); hereafter cited parenthetically in the text. (I would like to thank my colleagues, Leslie White and Joyce Zonana, who read this essay in manuscript and made many helpful suggestions.)

2. Writing for the *Quarterly Review,* Reginald Heber observed that "The sarcasms of Lucifer . . . proceed to the subversion of every system of theology . . . ," in *The Romantics Reviewed: Contemporary Reviews of British Romantic Writers,* ed. Donald H. Reiman, 9 vols. (New York: Garland, 1972), part B, V, 2076. In the *Edinburgh Review,* Francis Jeffrey seized immediately on the play's links with contemporary anti-Christian writing, its air of "argumentative blasphemy" (part B, II, 930).

3. Constantine N. Stavrou asserts that Lucifer "is indisputably the protagonist"; he is a "romantic personage, and to the extent that Byron was himself a 'romantic rebel,' Lucifer voices his author's quarrel with orthodoxy. His prototype is Prometheus . . ." ("Milton, Byron, and the Devil," *University of Kansas City Review,* 21.3 [March 1955], 153-59 [155]). In *The Byronic Hero,* Peter L. Thorslev, Jr. presents Lucifer as Cain's complement in the total representa-

tion of Byronic heroism in this play; together the two embody "metaphysical rebellion in the cause of Romantic self-assertion" (*The Byronic Hero: Types and Prototypes,* [Minneapolis: University of Minnesota Press, 1962], p. 178). Although he acknowledges Lucifer's "Mephistophelean tendency to stoop to grim ironic mockery," Leslie A. Marchand mainly describes him as the Promethean "champion of humanity against an authoritarian and arbitrary deity" (*Byron's Poetry: A Critical Introduction* [Boston: Houghton Mifflin, 1965], p. 86).

4. For a reading responsive to the essential ambiguities of Byron's Lucifer, see Jerome McGann, *Fiery Dust: Byron's Poetic Development* (Chicago: University of Chicago Press, 1968), pp. 255ff. Discussions of *Cain* which stress Lucifer's diabolical qualities depend heavily on Byron's letter to Murray of 3 November 1821, in which he writes that "the object of the demon is to *depress* him [Cain] still further in his own estimation than he was before—by showing him infinite things—& his own abasement—till he falls into the frame of mind that leads to the Catastrophe . . ." (*Byron's Letters and Journals,* ed. Leslie A. Marchand, 12 vols. [Cambridge: Harvard University Press, 1973-1982], IX, 53; hereafter cited as *BLJ.*) We must remember that Byron is addressing his conservative publisher, attempting to persuade him that the play is not impious and should be published without suppressing any lines. Truman Guy Steffan accepts as authoritative Byron's statements and therefore finds little ambiguity in Lucifer's villainous motives (*Lord Byron's Cain: Twelve Essays and a Text with Variants and Annotations* [Austin: University of Texas Press, 1968], pp. 9, 58). Paul A. Cantor follows this line of interpretation (*Creature and Creator: Mythmaking and English Romanticism* [Cambridge: Cambridge University Press, 1984], pp. 140-41), as does William D. Brewer's recent essay, "The Diabolical Discourse of Byron and Shelley," *Philological Quarterly,* 70 (1991), 47-65 (61).

5. Wolf Z. Hirst argues that "Lucifer is the scheming tempter of orthodox tradition" in "a Biblical drama reflecting divine inscrutability," in "Byron's Lapse into Orthodoxy: An Unorthodox Reading of *Cain,*" *Keats-Shelley Journal,* 29 (1980), 151-72 (154, 151).

6. Marilyn Butler, "Myth and Mythmaking in the Shelley Circle," in *Shelley Revalued: Essays from the Gregynog Conference,* ed. Kelvin Everest (Leicester University Press, 1983), 1-19 (6). Elsewhere Butler writes, "Lucifer tempts Cain much as Iago tempts Othello, for malign and selfish reasons" ("Romantic Manicheism: Shelley's 'On the Devil, and Devils' and Byron's Mythological Dramas," in *The Sun is God: Painting, Literature, and Mythology in the Nineteenth Century,* ed. J. B. Bullen [Oxford: Clarendon Press, 1989], 13-37 [33]). I am deeply indebted nevertheless to the general argument of both articles, which redirect the study of Romantic myth away from its religious or spiritual functions and to-

ward the "pragmatic" orientation described by Malinowski, thus opening inquiry into the ideological functions of myth in Romantic poetry. Philip Martin's survey of the historical and cultural contexts of *Cain* does not examine the figure of Lucifer, which he regards as a "limited" dramatic character, not related in any complex way to Byron's program of "literary vandalism" (*Byron: A Poet Before His Public* [Cambridge: Cambridge University Press, 1982], pp. 155, 148).

7. See Joseph Anthony Wittreich, Jr., "The Satanism of Blake and Shelley Reconsidered," *Studies in Philology,* 65 (1968), 816-33; and Stuart Curran, "The Siege of Hateful Contraries: Shelley, Mary Shelley, Byron, and *Paradise Lost,*" in *Milton and the Line of Vision,* ed. Joseph Anthony Wittreich, Jr. (Madison: University of Wisconsin Press, 1975), 209-30.

8. I have explored the matrix of the myth in "*The Marriage of Heaven and Hell*: Blake's Myth of Satan and its Cultural Matrix," *ELH,* 70 (1993), 441-70.

9. Lucifer is not, of course, the first embodiment of satanic myth in Byron's writing; early on he generated a series of heroes—the Giaour, Conrad, Lara, and Manfred—each delineated by explicit reference to Milton's fallen angel. For an account of the early Byronic myth of Satan, see Jerome McGann, *Don Juan in Context* (Chicago: University of Chicago Press, 1976), pp. 23-34.

10. The distinctive phrase "the Christian mythology" is Paine's, used repeatedly in *The Age of Reason.* See *The Writings of Thomas Paine,* ed. Moncure Daniel Conway, 4 vols. (New York: AMS Press, 1967), IV, 29; hereafter cited parenthetically. Byron's phrase appears in his letter to Thomas Moore, 19 September 1821 (*BLJ* VIII, 216).

11. The development of the conspiracy theory is discussed fully in Robert Hole, *Pulpits, Politics, and Public Order 1760-1832* (Cambridge: Cambridge University Press, 1989), pp. 152-55.

12. The Six Acts are summarized in Elie Halévy, *The Liberal Awakening 1815-1830,* vol. II of *A History of the English People in the Nineteenth Century,* trans. E. I. Watkin (London: Ernest Benn, 1926; rev. 1949), pp. 67-72.

13. The crime of blasphemous libel was construed more as an offense against the state ("the peace of our Lord the King, his crown and dignity") than against God; this transference was achieved by arguing from the 1676 precedent of Sir William Hale that Christianity was the law of the land—that it was part and parcel of the common law—and that infidelity therefore represented an attack on the Constitution. See W. H. Wickwar, *The Struggle for the Freedom of the Press, 1819-1832* (London: Allen and Unwin, 1928), pp. 20-25; hereafter cited parenthetically.

14. "The Substance of a Speech of the Right Hon. W. C. Plunket . . . with respect to the Numerous Meetings

which have taken place," *Quarterly Review,* 22 (1820), 510, 511. See also the speech of Lord Grenville, which prophesied that tolerating a blasphemous and seditious press would invite an English reprise of the French Revolution (506-7).

15. Robert Hole, *Pulpits, Politics, and Public Order,* pp. 178-79.

16. For an account of the Evangelical position on blasphemy, see Ursula Henriques, *Religious Toleration in England, 1787-1833* (Toronto: University of Toronto Press, 1961), pp. 206-59.

17. Sidmouth oversaw these efforts vigilantly. The Home Secretary's Circular of 1817 stepped up the efforts to control blasphemy by authorizing local magistrates to arrest publishers and booksellers on nothing more than the suspicion of libel. The Home Office offered financial support for the trials of blasphemers as well, and upon merely hearing of the publication in 1818 of *Christianity Unveiled* (a translation of Holbach), Sidmouth offered to disburse funds from the Treasury to pay for the prosecution (see Wickwar, pp. 70, 113).

18. Joel H. Wiener, *Radicalism and Freethought in Nineteenth-Century Britain: The Life of Richard Carlile* (Westport, Conn.: Greenwood Press, 1983), p. 34.

19. Edward Royle, *Radical Politics 1790-1900: Religion and Unbelief* (London: Longman, 1971), p. 30; Wickwar, p. 102; Wiener, pp. 47-48.

20. In 1819 Murray brought Hone's forgery, *Don Juan, Canto the Third* to Byron's attention. Byron's reference to the "false Don Juans" in a letter to Murrary (29 October 1819) indicates that the latter had informed him about Hone's publication of a forgery (*BLJ* VI, 236).

21. Dated July 1821, the issue appeared in October; Byron finished *Cain* September 10. See Hill Shine and Helen Chadwick Shine, *The Quarterly Review under Gifford: Identification of Contributors, 1809-1824* (Chapel Hill: University of North Carolina Press, 1949), p. 74. I am indebted to Donald H. Reiman for directing me to this source.

22. *Quarterly Review,* 25 (1821), 348, 363, 362.

23. For satanic representations of Napoleon, see F. J. Maccunn, *The Contemporary English View of Napoleon* (London: G. Bell, 1914), pp. 302, 336, 402-3, 429; see also A. M. Broadley, *Napoleon in Caricature: 1795-1821,* 2 vols. (London: John Lane, 1911) I, 6-10, 234-39.

24. "The Substance of a Speech . . . ," *Quarterly Review,* 22 (1820), 492-560 (511); hereafter cited parenthetically in the text.

25. In the poem quoted by Wickwar (p. 80), Satan tours London and visits his "Radical Friends," the first of

whom is Carlile, "by his blasphemous pile / Man's laws and God's laws defying."

26. *Quarterly Review,* 23 (1820), 225.

27. Byron said that the accusation, "being interpreted, means that I worship the devil" (*The Works of Lord Byron: Letters and Journals,* ed. Rowland E. Prothero, 6 vols. [London: John Murray, 1898-1901], V, 563).

28. Robert Southey, *A Vision of Judgment,* in *Poetical Works* (London: Longman, 1850), p. 776; hereafter cited parenthetically.

29. The only study of *Cain* which considers intertextual relationships between the play and the work of Richard Carlile is Stephen L. Goldstein, "Byron's *Cain* and the Painites," *Studies in Romanticism,* 14 (Fall 1975), 391-410. Goldstein's focus is restricted to the affinities between Byron's use of controversial scientific thought in *Cain* and the political deployments of the same kinds of ideas in the pages of *The Republican.*

30. In part II of *The Age of Reason* Paine characterizes the alliance of church and state as follows: "It has been the scheme of the Christian church, and of all the other invented systems of religion, to hold man in ignorance of the Creator, as it is of government to hold him in ignorance of his rights. The systems of the one are as false as those of the other, and are calculated for mutual support" (*Complete Writings,* IV, 190-91).

31. See, for example, Carlile's article asserting that the Christian mythology was invented to play on human fears of invisible powers; tyrants and priests used these "captivating engines of ignorance and superstition" to establish themselves as the only beings capable of averting the wrath of the divine powers (*The Republican,* 1.7 [8 October 1819], 107). Beginning in early 1820 (*The Republican,* 2.9 [17 March 1820], 299ff.), Carlile produced his most sustained piece of anti-Christian writing, an exhaustive reply to the Reverend Thomas Horne's pamphlet "Deism Refuted"; Carlile goes systematically through the Bible, beginning with a sentence-by-sentence refutation of the creation myth of Genesis in the light of modern science. (*The Republican* is hereafter cited parenthetically.)

32. *The Letters of Percy Bysshe Shelley,* ed. Frederick L. Jones, 2 vols. (Oxford: Clarendon Press, 1964), II, 143.

33. The approximate date of this essay has been convincingly established by Stuart Curran and Joseph Anthony Wittreich, Jr., in "The Dating of Shelley's 'On the Devil, and Devils,'" *Keats-Shelley Journal,* 21-22 (1972-1973), 83-94. They suggest that Carlile was at least on Shelley's mind as he wrote this essay

(92). Butler argues that its date is 1820, and that the opening is a reply to Heber's attack in the *Quarterly Review* on Byron's "Manicheism" ("Romantic Manicheism," 23-24).

34. "On the Devil, and Devils," in *The Complete Works of Percy Bysshe Shelley* (Julian Edition), ed. Roger Ingpen and Walter E. Peck, 10 vols. (New York: Charles Scribner's Sons, 1926-1930), VII, 92; hereafter cited parenthetically as "Julian."

35. In the essay, Shelley remarks that had Milton not provided the arguments of his Devil the "shelter of any dramatic order, [they] would have been answered by the most conclusive of syllogisms—persecution" (Julian, VII, 91).

36. Charles Robinson, *Shelley and Byron: The Snake and Eagle Wreathed in Fight* (Baltimore: Johns Hopkins University Press, 1976), pp. 192-93. Contemporaries were convinced that Shelley's hand was in the work, Robinson observes, noting also that Byron was anxious to deny it and claim his originality and independence of Shelley's atheism (pp. 196-97).

37. To the Evangelical, James Kennedy, Byron asserted that "the history of the creation and the fall is, by many doctors of the Church, believed to be a mythos, or at least an allegory" (*Conversations on Religion with Lord Byron . . .* [London, John Murray, 1830], p. 140). In Canto XV of *Don Juan,* he articulates the function of religious myth in terms which approximate the infidel position as expounded in Shelley's letter to the *Examiner*: "'Tis wonderful what fable will not do! / 'Tis said it makes reality more bearable" (lines 708-9; *Works,* V, 614).

38. "It is useless to tell one *not* to *reason* but to *believe*—you might as well tell a man not to *wake* but *sleep*—and then to *bully* with torments!" ("Detached Thoughts," *BLJ* IX, 45). In his "Letter to Lord Ellenborough," Shelley argues that "Belief is an involuntary operation of the mind" (Julian, V, 285). This conviction was an assumption broadly shared among infidels, as Ursula Henriques notes (*Religious Toleration in England,* p. 241).

39. Wickwar discusses the Whig response to the Six Acts (pp. 141-52).

40. *Byron: A Poet Before His Public,* p. 155.

41. *The Romantics Reviewed,* part B, II, 770. Byron may also have wished to test the Trinity Act of 1813, a flawed attempt to provide toleration for Unitarians: in 1817 John Wright was prosecuted for blasphemy because he denied the Trinity and the Atonement (Henriques, *Religious Toleration in England,* p. 209). Wickwar suggests that Carlile republished Paine to test the Act (p. 73).

42. Donald Thomas, *A Long Time Burning: A History of Literary Censorship in England* (London: Routledge and Kegan Paul, 1969), p. 207.

43. Steffan chronicles these events in *Lord Byron's Cain,* pp. 13-18.

44. Even here, Byron's disarming manner slips back into provocation: invoking the authority of Watson is not only meant to be outrageous (the irreligious Lord Byron allying himself with the Bishop of Llandaff) but ironic as well, since Byron suspected Watson did not take the Bible seriously (see Kennedy, *Conversations on Religion,* p. 140).

45. William Dodd is representative, insisting that the New Testament scheme of Redemption depends on this reading of Genesis (*A Commentary on the Books of the Old and New Testament* [London: R. Davis, 1770], signature "E"). Even Pierre Bayle, supposed by many to be Byron's mentor in skeptical exegesis of the Bible, cites several "Fathers" who deny the identity of Satan and the serpent, only to condemn this "absurd" distinction. He then explicitly sides with "the most true Opinion, that *Eve* was seduced by the Devil concealed under the Body of a Serpent" (*The Dictionary Historical and Critical of Mr. Peter Bayle,* trans. anon., 6 vols. [London: Knapton, 1734-1738; repr. Garland, 1984], II, 851-52). Byron did have some authority for detaching the serpent from Satan; to James Kennedy he cited Thomas Scott's commentary, but Byron was probably confusing Scott, who reads Genesis 3 in traditional terms, with Adam Clarke (Kennedy, *Conversations,* p. 140). For an account of Clarke's controversial interpretation of Genesis, see John Rogerson, *Old Testament Criticism in the Nineteenth Century: England and Germany* (London: Society for Promoting Christian Knowledge, 1984), pp. 180-82. To Medwin, Byron cited Warburton as yet another authority (*Conversations of Lord Byron,* ed. Ernest J. Lovell, Jr. [Princeton: Princeton University Press, 1966], p. 212). (I am indebted to Bubba for the reference from William Dodd.)

46. I am not trying to establish Byron's religious position, but merely his perspective on scripture. While Byron does affirm that the human condition is radically imperfect, *Cain* undermines the mythic bases for the dogmas of Original Sin, Atonement, and Redemption: the play does not countenance the scriptural event of the Fall.

47. For Byron's denials that he intended blasphemy, see his letters to Murray of 3 November 1821 (*BLJ* IX, 53-54) and 8 February 1822 (*BLJ* IX, 103-5); see also his letters to Moore of 4 March 1822 (*BLJ* IX, 118-19) and 8 March 1822 (*BLJ* IX, 122-23).

48. The satanic figures in the heroic poems of Byron's day (for example, those of Southey and Moore) operate within conventional theological frameworks. Other works displaying satanic hero-villains, like Schiller's *Die Rauber* (1781) and Radcliffe's *The Italian* (1797) do not in the long run challenge established values, as Jerome McGann observes (*Don Juan in Context,* p. 30). Nor were Byron's early satanic heroes perceived as ideologically threatening; the reviewers generally found them titillating. Milton's Satan himself was no longer a controversial figure. The argument that his speeches subverted the reader's religion had been effectively silenced by Johnson in his *Life of Milton* (1779-1781) (see *Milton 1732-1801,* ed. John T. Shawcross [New York: Barnes and Noble, 1972], p. 299).

49. See the reviews in the *Evangelical Magazine* (*The Romantics Reviewed,* part B, II, 999), *Literary Gazette* (part B, IV, 1431), and *Monthly Magazine* (part B, IV, 1687).

50. David Eggenschwiler, "Byron's *Cain* and the Anti-mythological Myth," *Modern Language Quarterly,* 37.4 (December 1976), 324-38 (329).

51. Thomas Paine, *The Age of Reason* (*Complete Writings,* IV, 31).

52. The thesis of *The Divine Legation of Moses,* which refuses to affirm a doctrine of immortality in the Old Testament, is that Moses was not ignorant of the idea; that he declined to teach postmortal reward and punishments proves that the Jews were under a special Providence. See *The Divine Legation of Moses,* 4 vols. (1738-1765; repr. New York: Garland, 1978), IV, 316-62.

53. See, for example, the reviews in the *Investigator* (*The Romantics Reviewed,* part B, III, 1189), *Literary Gazette* (part B, IV, 1431), and *Manchester Iris* (part B, IV, 1635).

54. *Shelley: Poetical Works,* ed. Thomas Hutchinson, rev. G. M. Matthews (1905; London: Oxford University Press, 1970), p. 45 (line 347), p. 46 (lines 373-78).

55. William D. Brewer, "The Diabolical Discourse of Byron and Shelley," 58-59.

56. *Queen Mab,* Canto VII, lines 83-275 (*Poetical works,* ed. Hutchinson, pp. 788-92); hereafter cited parenthetically.

57. Byron's principal debt to Bayle is his skeptical demonstration that rationalistic theology cannot reconcile the co-existence of evil with an omnipotent and benevolent God; this problem can be resolved only through faith and revelation. Short of this last resort, Bayle says clearly, the Manichean objection to monotheism is unanswerable. It is this train of thought, developed most fully in his article titled "Paulicians," which Byron drew upon to develop Lucifer's Gnostic refutation of Christian theodicy (*Dictionary,* IV, 512-28). Byron appears to have borrowed from Bayle principally to introduce into his play a layer of respectable irreligion, the tradition of skepticism extending from Bayle through Voltaire and Gibbon (See Howard Robinson, *Bayle the Skeptic* [New York: Co-

lumbia University Press, 1931], pp. 253-65). This skeptical perspective Byron offers as a sophisticated form of infidelism, perhaps as an alternative to the vulgarian mode of Carlile.

58. Marilyn Butler, "Myth and Mythmaking," 7-8; and "Romantic Manicheism," 16-18.

59. Lucifer's denunciation of the Atonement would have recalled for contemporary readers Paine's anecdote in *The Age of Reason*; upon hearing at the age of seven a sermon on the Atonement, Paine saw that the doctrine made "God Almighty act like a passionate man, that killed his son, when he could not revenge himself any other way" (*Complete Writings,* IV, 64-65).

60. *Religious Toleration in England,* p. 241.

61. These thinkers were willing to extend backward in time and expand into ages the first "days" of Creation, so long as the Creation of man remained a very recent event. Thus men like William Buckland had sanitized the implications of Cuvier's research. For an account of the pious uses to which Cuvier's work was put, see Charles Gillispie, *Genesis and Geology* (New York: Harper, 1951), pp. 101-15 and Francis C. Haber, *The Age of the World: Moses to Darwin* (Baltimore: Johns Hopkins University Press, 1959), pp. 191-203. Leroy E. Page shows that Cuvier's work did excite controversy, among more secular-minded geologists who affirmed a deluge had occurred but refused to identify it with the biblical flood ("Diluvianism and its Critics in Great Britain in the Early Nineteenth Century," in *Toward A History of Geology,* ed. Cecil J. Schneer [Cambridge: M.I.T. Press, 1969], 257-71).

62. See Goldstein, "Byron's *Cain* and the Painites," 396-97.

63. See Thorslev, *The Byronic Hero,* p. 181; McGann, *Fiery Dust,* pp. 255-62; and Cantor, pp. 148-55.

64. This is the view persuasively argued by Wolf Z. Hirst in "Byron's Revisionary Struggle with the Bible," in *Byron, the Bible, and Religion,* ed. Wolf Z. Hirst (Newark: University of Delaware Press, 1991), 77-100 (89-95).

65. See, for example, his argument that the deconstruction of the myth of Satan spells the end of the myth of God (*The Republican,* 6.16 [13 September 1822], 489-90); see also Joseph Swann's blasphemous remarks (which earned him a conviction) on Genesis 3—that the Devil defeated God by telling Eve the truth (*The Republican,* 6.21 [18 October 1822], 654).

66. Marilyn Butler, *Romantics, Rebels and Reactionaries: English Literature and its Background 1760-1830* (Oxford: Oxford University Press, 1981), p. 146.

LUCIFERIAN DISCOURSE IN EUROPEAN LITERATURE

Nicolae Babuts (essay date 1981)

SOURCE: "Hugo's *La fin de Satan*: The Identity Shift," in *Symposium,* Vol. 35, No. 2, Summer, 1981, pp. 91-101.

[*In the following essay, Babuts analyzes Victor Hugo's imaginative identification with the demonic protagonist of his* La fin de Satan.]

Many critics approach *La Fin de Satan* with the growing realization that there are striking similarities between Satan and the poet, and that the original aspects of the myth can be seen as a sublimation of Hugo's predicament in exile. Baudouin points out the kinship between "sa fille bien-aimée Léopoldine" and the angel Liberté.[1] Reinforcing this point of view, Zumthor calls Léopoldine "médiatrice."[2] Grant and Denommé propose similar perspectives, though the former moderates the scope of the biographical approach by urging that the resanctification of Hugo's Satan "be viewed in the sequence of imagery that the poet had developed."[3] Comparing images Milner finds that Satan's solitude resembles Hugo's own in the poem "Ô Gouffre!"[4] I propose to show that Hugo's capacity to form bonds of identity with the fallen archangel has its beginnings in the act of meditation, and that it is part of a prevailing creative behavior in which the poet assumes the identity of the protagonist.

The identity shift ranges far. It is present in "Saison des Semailles" (1865), for example, a poem which is not structurally related to *La Fin de Satan*. In studying the way Hugo identified himself with the sower, Ward speaks of a relationship that was carefully worked out in successive drafts.[5] It also runs deep. In Gaudon's view, the convict Jean Tréjean of *Les Misères* (1846) is both "l'image du poète visionnaire" and "la préfiguration de Satan."[6] Albouy is struck by the same affinity and believes that the convict is a forerunner of Satan.[7] Hugo's continuing interest in a character whose role could be defined further through its avatars and new identities is a mark of the extraordinary consistency of his creative drive.

Influenced by several converging factors, the drive reached a crucial stage in 1854, with the composition of "Satan dans la nuit," and "Et nox facta est." These two sections represent the nucleogenesis of his spiritual cosmology. Milner is even more specific, arguing that Satan's initial cry "je l'aime" is "le point de départ, la cellule-mère de toute l'œuvre" (II, 367).

In a letter to Mme de Girardin, Hugo hints at the changes that are taking place: "[Paul Meurice] vous a-t-il dit que tout un système quasi cosmogonique, par moi couvé et à moitié écrit depuis vingt ans, avait été confirmé par la table avec des élargissements magnifiques? Nous vivons dans un horizon mystérieux qui change la perspective de l'exil."[8]

Hugo's initiation to spiritualism began in September 1853. By 1854 the full impact of his commerce with the table became apparent. It would be hard to overestimate the significance of the new perspective. 1854 is an "année terrible,"[9] a year of fear, darkness, and revelations of the invisible that take form in "Horror" (March), "Dolor" (March), "Pleurs dans la nuit" (April), "Inferi" (June), and "Ce que dit la Bouche d'Ombre" (October). It is also the year of *La Fin de Satan*: "Satan dans la nuit" (January), "Et nox facta est" (March), and other fragments. Ultimately it may prove unnecessary to decide whether the table functioned as a catalyst or echoed what Hugo's creative powers would have produced any way after years of experimentation both on the technical and the visionary levels. It is clear, however, that the burst of visionary activity coincides in 1854 with the peak of Hugo's interest in spiritualism. Both the belief in, and the practices of the table, geared as they were towards the abolition of barriers between the two levels of existence—between the human reality and the cosmic sphere—facilitated creation of his cosmological system. Now in exile, he undertook to face the invisible with even greater determination than in the past.

The remarkable fact about *La Fin de Satan* is that, in it, the poet establishes links with the past reveries at the very moment when he makes his most important visionary and stylistic advances. One link can be seen in a degree of thematic and lexical similarity with poems like "Puits de l'Inde!" (1839) and "Ô Gouffre!" (September 1853). And there are others. Studying textual resemblances between "La Pente de la rêverie" and *Les Misères,* and similarities between *La Fin de Satan* and *Les Misères,* Gaudon shows that the early draft (1846) of Hugo's great novel *Les Misérables* (1860-62) represents "une étape importante dans la conquête que fait Hugo de son univers" (pp. 149-50). Defining Jean Valjean's universe of damnation and the structure of redemption in the novel, Albouy reaches similar conclusions (pp. 299-303). We can go a step further. Additional textual evidence and Hugo's own testimony are incontrovertible proof that the pattern of Satan's response to his fall and exile is fundamentally related to the dynamics of descent and exploration of "La Pente de la rêverie." The affinity between the 1830 poem and the divisions of *La Fin de Satan,* written in 1854, is even more striking than the similarities to *Les Misères.* The 1846 passage appears as an intermediate, and perhaps tentative, stage.

Both the exploratory advance of "La Pente de la rêverie" and the progression of the fall in "Et nox facta est" are accompanied by an increase in darkness and the disappearance of all forms:

> Bientôt autour de moi les ténèbres s'accrurent,
> L'horizon se perdit, les formes disparurent . . .
>
> ("La Pente")[10]

Les ténèbres sans bruit croissaient dans le néant.

("Et nox," III)[11]

L'abîme s'effacait. Rien n'avait plus de forme.

("Et nox," IV)

Each protagonist feels reality slipping away from his grip and becoming vague: "Tout devenait douteux et vague" ("La Pente"), and the abyss is "Pareil au brouillard vague" ("Et nox," IV). And again: "Tout fuyait" ("La Pente") and "tout à présent le fuyait" ("Et nox," II). The two shiver in their solitude: "le frisson me prit. J'étais seul" ("La Pente") and "l'Archange alors frémit; Satan eut le frisson" ("Et nox," V). Stretching the verbal resources of his art to the limit, Hugo employs some of the same words as before, but more often in order to strengthen key reactions. Images and fragments of the earlier vision must have been preserved by memory and associated with certain words, which were by now part of the poet's command of the language. Inevitably,[12] the analogous visionary reality to be interpreted galvanized them into action, and this lexical instrumentation in turn increased the bond potential between the two responses. Firmly anchored at the center of Hugo's personality, the mnemonic factor regulated the economy of the creative drive. The following passages illustrate three stages in the development of the poet's relationship with the protagonist. In the first, the poet himself recounts the conclusion of the visionary experience; in the second (this is the passage quoted by Gaudon) Jean Valjean has reached a tentative decision not to give himself up and meditates; in the third, Satan brings his monologue to a close:

> Oh! cette double mer du temps et de l'espace
> Où le navire humain toujours passe et repasse,
> Je voulus la sonder, je voulus en toucher
> Le sable, y regarder, y fouiller, y chercher,
> Pour vous en rapporter quelque richesse étrange,
> Et dire si son lit est de roche ou de fange.
> Mon esprit plongea donc sous ce flot inconnu,
> Au profond de l'abîme il nagea seul et nu,
> Toujours de l'ineffable allant à l'invisible . . .
> Soudain il s'en revint avec un cri terrible,
> Ébloui, haletant, stupide, épouvanté,
> Car il avait au fond trouvé l'éternité.
>
> ("La Pente de la rêverie")

On ne trouve les diamants que dans les ténèbres de la terre; on ne trouve les vérités que dans les profondeurs de la pensée. Il lui semblait qu'après être descendu dans ces profondeurs, après avoir longtemps tâtonné au plus noir de ces ténèbres, il venait enfin de trouver un de ces diamants, une de ces vérités, et qu'il la tenait dans sa main; et il s'éblouissait à la regarder.

("Une tempête sous un crâne")[13]

> Oh! je monte et descends et remonte sans cesse,
> De la cr.éaction flaunt le subterrane;
> Le bas est de l'acier, le haut est de l'airain,
> A jamais, à jamais, à jamais! Je frissonne,
> Et je cherche et je crie et j'appelle. Personne!
> Et, furieux, tremblant, désespéré, banni,
> Frappant des pieds, des mains et du front l'infini,
> Ainsi qu'un moucheron heurte une vitre sombre,

A l'immensité morne arrachant des pans d'ombre,
Seul, sans trouver d'issue et sans voir de clarté,
Je tâte dans la nuit ce mur, l'éternité.

("Satan dans la nuit," XII)

All three texts are organized around the structure of descent, exploration, and final discovery. The probing of the unknown depths—"abîme," "profondeurs de la pensée," "souterrain"—is defined by similar verbs: "fouiller," "chercher," and "tâtonner." All three protagonists desire to touch or to hold what they have discovered. And the resemblances between the first and the third go deeper. Both the poet and Satan begin with the same exclamation and end with the word "éternité." We detect the same movement, an alternation of passing and repassing or climbing and descending, the same pace, punctuated by a repetition of adjectives and past participles, and the same rhythm or "danse intérieure," as Jean Prévost would call it. The difference—and stressing it reinforces my argument—is the metaphoric field, that is, not only the semantic connotations and visual nuances of a specific context, but also the tension of the original creative process. Roughly translated the tension appears to be a function of the dramatic or structural conflict. Yet the creative urgency may differ even in the treatment of the same drama by the same mind. Because the metaphoric field encompasses all levels of meaning, two structurally similar images are not necessarily interchangeable in the sense of meaning. There is, of course, a good deal of tension in "La Pente de la rêverie," especially at the moment of the "cri terrible,"[14] and in the prose passage, where it is generated by the moral problem Jean Valjean (Jean Tréjean) is facing. However, neither in strength nor in quality can it be compared to that of the exile poem. In 1830 the poet acts like a tourist, curious enough to want to know if the beach is made of rock or mud, and conscientious enough to bring back "quelque richesse étrange," somewhat in the manner of Baudelaire's travelers, gathering something beautiful for their "brothers" at home; in 1846 the visionary convict—perhaps the child in him—is fascinated by the diamond-truth he holds in his hand like a rare find; in 1854 Hugo's whole personality is involved. His efforts preceding the discovery are no idle curiosity, no possessive instinct, but necessity to find a way out. This is steel and bronze, and he is the caged archangel brought to the response level of a midge. In January 1854, paralleling this urgency, Hugo intervened in behalf of Tapner, in a vain attempt to save the life of the condemned Guernesey murderer. So preoccupied was he with Tapner's possible pardon that during the séance of 29 January 1854, he put the question to the spirit: "Peux-tu me dire si l'homme de Guernesey sera sauvé?"[15] The question may have functioned as a springboard to the 1860 epic ending in which Satan is indeed forgiven.

The more we measure the strength of the creative pressure in *La Fin de Satan,* and therefore the distance between 1830 and 1854, the more difficult the similarity appears to brush aside. If, considering Hugo's verbal genius, we discard—as we logically must—the idea of intentional borrowing, we are left with an apparent puzzle. Yet the answer is not far to seek. The undeniable evolution of the structure of visionary descent does not rule out the affinity between the various stages, just as this affinity cannot preempt the uniqueness of each poem. The pattern had been in the making for a long time, evolving, while the lexical and visionary instruments were being perfected. Hugo himself confirms this view in a declaration of major significance made during the séance of 19 September 1854:

Les êtres qui habitent l'invisible et qui voient la pensée dans nos cerveaux savent que, depuis vingt-cinq ans environ je m'occupe des questions que la table soulève et approfondit. Dans plus d'une occasion, la table m'a parlé de ce travail; l'Ombre du Sépulcre m'a engagé à le terminer. Dans ce travail, et il est évident qu'on le connaît là-haut, dans ce travail de vingt-cinq années, j'avais trouvé par la seule méditation plusieurs des résultats qui composent aujourd'hui la révélation de la table, j'avais vu distinctement et affirmé quelques-uns de ces résultats sublimes, j'en avais entrevu d'autres, qui restaient dans mon esprit à l'état de linéaments confus. . . . Aujourd'hui, les choses que j'avais vues en entier, la table les confirme, et les demi-choses, elle les complète.[16]

The chronology takes us back to within a few months of the date of "La Pente de la rêverie," 28 May 1830. Since Hugo says "about twenty-five years," there is no discrepancy. The early meditation stands to the revelations of the table in a relation of the partial to the whole, of the incomplete to the complete, of the vaguely intuited to the clearly understood. Some of the revelations had been barely apprehended earlier; others had been wholly and distinctly seen and had simply to be confirmed by the table. This is precisely the relation between the two poems. "J'avais trouvé par la seule méditation. . . ." These words postulate the identity of the content of the visions and prove that Hugo's justly praised[17] mythopoeic powers have their origin in the earlier "rêverie," in the hallucinatory quality of his meditation. On the lexical level the obsessive character of the twenty-five-year drive is translated into a piling of "frissonner," "descend," "sonde," "pâlissant," "spirale," "brume," "brouillard," and other key words associated with the exploration of the invisible. On the metaphoric level, it results in a distortion of reality that foreshadows at times Rimbaldian daring, and at others surrealist experimentation. Hugo's testimony corroborates the stylistic evidence that 1854 represents a stage of even greater visionary advances than those of 1830.[18] In 1854 the command of the language, the momentum of the drive, the state of mind, and the logic of the exile events were all favorable to the composition of the apocalyptic poems.[19] They were also decisive factors in the abolition of the identity boundaries between the poet and the fallen archangel.

A new lucidity guided the creative process. Satan's banishment conceived by the mind of the seer and Hugo's exile in reality coalesced and became one experience. Hugo thus negotiated the rite of passage to the angelic condition by means of the mythic union with the banished archangel. Once the necessary elements were positioned in a final imaginary configuration, the identity fusion had to be consummated through a displacement in time. To become archangel, the poet had to adopt the bold gambit of the doctrine of incarnation, to sacrifice chronological accuracy by going back beyond the beginning of life on this earth:

> Avant d'être sur cette terre,
> Je sens que jadis j'ai plané;
> J'étais l'archange solitaire,
> Et mon malheur, c'est d'être né.

> ("A celle qui est voilée," *Les Contemplations*)

Hugo speaks in his own name in this poem dated January 1854. The date is the same as that of "Satan dans la nuit," and Albouy found several stanzas of the poem in the manuscript of *La Fin de Satan*.[20] He believes, however, that the stanza quoted here may have been added to the poem later that year. At any rate, it must have been written sometime between January 1854 (the date at the end of the published poem) and 11 January 1855 (the date on the manuscript), and probably within a few months after the following lines in which Satan speaks: "Jadis, ce jour levant, cette lueur candide, / C'était moi.—Moi!—J'étais l'archange au front splendide" ("Satan dans la nuit," I). The tone of the first statement is somewhat more subdued; but the voice modulates the same awareness of the protagonist's former preeminence and his present plight. The angelic experience pivots on the word "jadis" and rises in a nostalgia for the lost edenic grace. In the mythical space of *La Fin de Satan,* Léopoldine's promise to her father, "Tu redeviendras ange ayant été martyr" ("Claire"), acquires a significance that could not have been foreseen in 1846, at Claire's death. We may go one step further: In the perspective adopted here, it is hard to imagine a clear statement of Hugo's archangel nature before 1854. In 1846 the angelic condition is still defined by the opposition between "Léopoldine-ange" and "le génie-aigle."[21] It is only in 1854 that, having obtained knowledge of the cosmic sphere, Hugo is able to postulate the idea of the archangel-seers. Clearly foreshadowed by the "mage effaré" of "Ibo" (1854), the concept will soon be developed into a coherent doctrine of incarnation in "Les Mages" (1855), and in *William Shakespeare* (1863), where Hugo will devote a whole chapter to the men of genius, to these "âmes cosmiques," full of the dream of a former existence.

With justifiable confidence Albouy notes that "the most perfect model" of this category of men is Hugo himself.[22] In 1874, still in possession of the dream and under attack from a multitude of "pygmies," a rabble, Hugo responds with this monologue:

> Toi qui jadis planais archange, et qu'une loi
> Met sur la terre, au fond des visions funèbres,
> Prisonnier dans la cage énorme des ténèbres,
> Toi, l'aigle échevelé de l'ombre, le banni
> Tombé d'un infini dans un autre infini,
> Du zénith dans l'abîme et du ciel dans ton âme . . .
> Rongé du noir regret du firmament vermeil . . .

> (*Toute la lyre,* V, xxxvi)[23]

The similarity between this poem and *La Fin de Satan* is so striking that Riffaterre offers it as a challenge to the reader, being sure that the latter will identify the speaker as Satan.[24] The reason is obvious: a network of images highly appropriate to Satan's condition "hors de la terre," like "banni tombé," "l'ombre," "abîme," and "regret du firmament vermeil." Yet no passage could define better the poet's human pride and the bitter pill of injustice he had to swallow. As in the last two quotations, the word "jadis" informs and directs the flow of images. The identity shift is so complete that in recapitulating a specific event common to both destinies, the poet no longer needs to separate the vision of the seer from the experience of the man. What has happened is that by now the capacity to put on different identity masks has become a specific ability, which Hugo can easily recognize. In a note to the *Toute la lyre* poem, he writes: "Après avoir écrit ces vers, je me souviens tout à coup de vers que j'ai écrits il y a cinquante ans, censés adressés à Lord Byron, et en réalité adressés à moi-même, et se terminant par: Pensif, tu regardes ailleurs . . ." (p. 380).[25]

Half a century earlier, by his own estimation, the identity shift enabled Hugo to transfer the dedication to another poet. And because this was done at the beginning, he can now come back and assign it to the real dedicatee. The process is thus reversible. It is essential then to see that in the 1874 poem, as in the Byron dedication, Hugo can re-cross the identity boundaries without penalty because he first abolished Customs. Obviously he is conscious of it. He can speak now in his own name, using images suitable to the condition of the fallen archangel, because once he soared, fell, and was imprisoned with the archangel, because he was the archangel.

One may distinguish three basic identity gears or positions: Hugo the man, Hugo the seer, and Hugo the protagonist. In "La Pente de la rêverie," "Puits de l'Inde!" and "Ce que dit la Bouche d'Ombre," for example, freedom is granted to the poet as seer, but is confined to the act of triggering the mechanism of "rêverie." The seer is free to choose to enter or not to enter—to his friends Hugo says "stay away" and to others "enter if you dare"—but once he has committed himself, severe limitations are imposed on his freedom. He becomes protagonist and no longer has control over his visions. The suddenly violent encounter with the specter at the beginning of "Ce que dit la Bouche d'Ombre" may come to mind. At times even the protagonist's response to the given revelations seems regulated, if not determined, by a superior power. Rather than stand with God in a relationship of character to character, Satan appears to be an actor in a play directed by the divine will. And it is clear that in "Et nox facta est," Satan corresponds to the protagonist of "La Pente de la rêverie," and that the structural equivalent of the seer, the initiator of "La Pente," is not Satan but "le penseur" reintroduced at the end of Section IX.

The need to make this distinction and to label the exploratory character of the poem clearly—the terms are identical with those in "La Pente de la rêverie," "creuser," "fouiller," "sonder"—explains why Hugo added this passage, separating it by an asterisk from a section that appears complete without it. Somewhat surprised to see it, Gaudon writes: "un étrange paragraphe vient inexplicablement transformer le mouvement de la chute du damné en une méditation sur le poète-visionnaire" (p. 158). However, the separation is consistent with the dynamics of "rêverie," the source of the identity shift; it marks the transition to the spiritual dimension of reality. While in most exploratory poems the beginning hinges on this transition, in "Et nox facta est" Hugo adopts a new strategy and begins well within the cosmic space, and therefore the spiritual. He then simply tacks an explanatory passage at the end.

The analysis undertaken above should not be construed as an attempt to identify Satan and Hugo the man. The two become one only in the role of a protagonist, only on the level of myth. The distinction is useful in other cases of identity shift as well. One can imagine the glee with which Hugo's detractors must have greeted his matter-of-fact statement: "Écoutez. Je suis Jean. J'ai vu des choses sombres." Yet, whether we take it that John speaks in Hugo's words, or that Hugo assumes John's identity, the startling aspect of the assertion comes from its suddenness, its lack of transition. The seer and protagonist roles collapse into one.

In *La Fin de Satan* the process of identification involved a particularly strong convergence of personal attitudes, creative experience, and habits of language. When "le grand banni" asks in a burst of resentment, "Croit-il pas que j'irai sangloter à sa porte?" ("Et nox," III), the image of Satan at the gates of heaven brings to mind its corollary: Hugo at the doors of Napoléon le petit. While the parallelism cannot be pushed to its logical consequences, it can be pressed into service to suggest that Hugo's involvement in the creative process was deep and all embracing. And if, as most critics agree, his experience weighs rather heavily in the balance, it is not surprising that at the end Satan is forgiven. Nor is it hard to understand that the angel Liberté acts as a mediator.

The table simply reinforced Hugo's belief that his long drive towards the invisible was no accident. Léopoldine's drowning, an accident by any standard, had already become part of the fabric of necessity, part of "the price the poet had to pay for his visionary powers."[26] The myth of the fallen archangel and the doctrine of incarnation supplied the coordinates Hugo needed to relate his experience to a vaster universal dynamics.

It may be that he believed his own destiny could be affected by the new cosmological order he was about to impose on the spiritual world. As the myth ceased to be an outside pattern and became part of the inner struggle, the identity shift afforded a degree of leverage in his attempt to influence the outcome of the redemptive process. And to the extent that the fall into the lower darkness began to parallel the descent on the Piranesian stairs of "le gouffre intérieur," the cosmic sphere began to reflect the unconscious. The psychoanalytical approach remains outside the scope of this article; but it may be useful to note that the shift to the role of protagonist entailed both fear and a loss of control. Thus the initial voluntary character of the visionary descent resolves itself into a tension between the seer's hope to give direction to his spiritual quest and the protagonist's fear of the nightmarish visions, fear of the unknown. In the end the exile in the depths revealed that hell is absence of divine love and pointed out the way to the angelic condition. Man can climb from darkness to light. Discovery is more than passive knowledge: it is a dangerous enterprise in which the seer becomes protagonist to act upon, and within, the very visions granted to him.

Notes

1. Charles Baudouin, *Psychanalyse de Victor Hugo* (1943; rpt. Paris: Armand Colin, 1972), p. 293.

2. Paul Zumthor, *Victor Hugo poète de Satan* (Paris: Robert Laffont, 1946), p. 224.

3. Richard B. Grant, *The Perilous Quest, Image, Myth, and Prophecy in the Narratives of Victor Hugo* (Durham, N.C.: Duke U. Press, 1968), p. 152. See also Robert T. Denommé, *Nineteenth-Century French Romantic Poets* (Carbondale & Edwardsville: Southern Illinois University Press, 1969), p. 120.

4. Max Milner, *Le Diable dans la littérature française* (Paris: Corti, 1960), II, 372.

5. Patricia A. Ward, "Victor Hugo's Creative Process in 'Saison des Semailles,'" *FS* [*French Studies*], 26 (Oct. 1972), 421.

6. Jean Gaudon, "Je ne sais quel jour de soupirail . . . ," in *Centenaire des Misérables 1862-1962. Hommage à Victor Hugo* (Actes du Colloque du Centre de Philologie et de Littératures Romanes de la Faculté des Lettres de Strasbourg. Strasbourg: La Faculté des Lettres, 1962), p. 158.

7. Pierre Albouy, *La Création mythologique chez Victor Hugo* (Paris: Corti, 1963), p. 299.

8. The date: 4 January 1855. See Hugo's *Correspondance*, II (Paris: Albin Michel, 1950), 205. Quoted by Bettina Knapp, "Victor Hugo: "What the Mouth of Darkness Says,'" *ECr* [*Essays in Criticism*], 16 (1976), 178.

9. For this expression and for a view of the importance of 1854 see Jean-Bertrand Barrère, *La Fantaisie de Victor Hugo, 1852-1855* (Paris: Corti, 1960), pp. 64-65 and p. 70. See also Maurice Levaillant, *La Crise mystique de Victor Hugo, 1843-1856* (Paris: Corti, 1954), p. 66.

10. Hugo, *Œuvres poétiques*, I, ed. Pierre Albouy (Paris: Gallimard, 1964), 773. All quotations from "La Pente de la rêverie" are taken from this edition.

11. Hugo, *La Légende des siècles, La Fin de Satan, Dieu,* ed. Jacques Truchet (Paris: Gallimard, 1950), p. 769. Subsequent references are to this edition.

12. A similar point of view is suggested by Milner, who writes: "C'est tout naturellement que les mêmes images lui viennent pour exprimer l'angoisse de Satan et la sienne" (II, 371).

13. Hugo, *Les Misérables,* ed. Maurice Allem, Pléiade (Paris: Gallimard, 1951), p. 242. Quoted by Gaudon, p. 155.

14. Victor Brombert links the terror of the poet to the risk of madness. See "Victor Hugo, la prison et l'espace," *RSH* [*Revue des Sciences Humaines*], 117 (1965), 78. The same text is available in English. See Brombert, *The Romantic Prison* (Princeton: Princeton U. Press, 1978), p. 118.

15. Levaillant, *La Crise,* p. 104.

16. *Ce que disent les tables parlantes,* ed. Jean Gaudon (Paris: J.-J. Pauvert, 1963), p. 54. Quoted by Levaillant, p. 190.

17. It is refreshing to read Herbert J. Hunt's praise: "Satan's entry into his domain is magnificently portrayed in *Et nox facta est.*" *The Epic in Nineteenth-Century France* (Oxford: Blackwell, 1941), p. 307.

18. Impressed with Hugo's achievement in "La Pente de la rêverie," critics treat 1830 as a new beginning in his creative development. Baudelaire was the first to see the extraordinary character of this poem. In "Réflexions sur quelques-uns de mes contemporains" (1861), he wrote: "Cependant qui ne se souvient de *La Pente de la rêverie,* déjà si vieille de date? Une grande partie de ses œuvres [Hugo's] récentes semble le développement aussi régulier qu'énorme de la faculté qui a présidé á la géneration de ce poeme enivrant." Pléiade ed. (1961), p. 709. For the vocabulary of "La Pente" see J.-B. Barrère, *Hugo, L'Homme et l'œuvre* (Paris: Hatier, Boivin, 1952), p. 75. Others seeing the poem as an adumbration of Hugo's later style are John P. Houston, *The Demonic Imagination, Style and Theme in French Romantic Poetry* (Baton Rouge: Louisiana State U. Press, 1969), p. 29, and Grant, pp. 126-27. Zumthor does not mention "La Pente" but believes that most of the ideas and images of *La Fin de Satan* had been borrowed "from a capital of visions and dreams accumulated since 1848 or even 1830" (p. 243).

19. This is also Levaillant's view. See *La Crise,* p. 66.

20. Pierre Albouy, ed., Victor Hugo, *Œuvres poétiques,* II, (Paris: Gallimard, 1967) 1636-37.

21. In lines which are as moving as they are revealing, Léopoldine's voice explains:

> Mon père, Dieu . . . Nous donne . . .
>
> Des ailes à tous deux, mais quel mystère étrange!

> À toi des ailes d'aigle, à moi des ailes d'ange!
>
> Tu deviens grand, illustre et puissant; moi je meurs.
>
> ("Voix entendue la nuit")

Dated 1846. See Albouy, ed., II, 841, and his notes, p. 1698.

22. *La Création,* p. 207. See also Albouy, ed., II, 1657-58, n. 1.

23. *Toute la lyre,* vol. XIII of *Œuvres complètes* (Paris: A. Michel, 1935), p. 66.

24. Michael Riffaterre, *Essais de stylistique structurale* (Paris: Flammarion, 1971), pp. 209-210.

25. The line mentioned is actually line 12 of "Dédain" (*Les Feuilles d'automne*).

26. See Albouy's perceptive comments in his ed., II, 1539, n. 1.

Marilyn Georgas (essay date 1982)

SOURCE: "Dickens, Defoe, the Devil and the Dedlocks: The 'Faust Motif' in *Bleak House*," in *Dickens Studies Annual,* Vol. 10, 1982, pp. 23-44.

[*In the following essay, Georgas claims that Mr. Tulkinghorn in Charles Dickens's novel* Bleak House *is a devil figure and the symbolic embodiment of absolute evil.*]

While Dickens' *Bleak House* is greatly admired, the character of Mr. Tulkinghorn has posed a serious problem for most readers. Studies of *Bleak House* have focused rather exclusively on Chancery and the law as the novel's symbolic center, and on the story of Jarndyce and Jarndyce as its significant plot. Such studies may regard Mr. Tulkinghorn as one of the more notably characterized lawyers in the novel, but since he is not related to Jarndyce and Jarndyce, he and his pursuit of Lady Dedlock are regarded as irrelevant to the main business of the novel. Moreover, his persecution of Lady Dedlock is seen as insufficiently motivated for the Tulkinghorn-Dedlock plot to be credible as an entity. Tulkinghorn's so-called "purposeless malignance"[1] becomes a major weakness of the novel. There are, of course, successful characters in literature who may be described as figures of motiveless evil, most notably Iago; but as Grahame Smith sees it, Iago is a "poetic presentation of absolute evil, and as such is imbued with a more than personal force," while Tulkinghorn is simply "a realistic figure whose delineation is impaired by his lack of motivation." Smith thinks that there can be no "saving explanation" for the story of Lady Dedlock and Mr. Tulkinghorn.[2]

A few critics have found explanations for Tulkinghorn which leave them satisfied with his role. Eugene Quirk, for example, finds Tulkinghorn sufficiently motivated to be fully effective as a literal, realistic character. Though he does not deal with the Tulkinghorn-Dedlock plot in relation to the novel as a whole, Quirk argues convincingly that the desire for revenge on the fashionable world, to whom he is a mere retainer, is Tulkinghorn's driving motive, a motive sufficient to make his role in the novel credible.[3] Joseph I. Fradin, on the other hand, disregards the significance of motivation entirely. He likens Tulkinghorn's role to that of a witch in a fairy tale, and says simply that a witch with credible, human motivation would cease to be a witch. Fradin is exceptional and illuminating in arguing a super-personal identity for Tulkinghorn— Tulkinghorn is, finally a "monstrous embodiment of the will to power,"[4] yet his interpretation denies any effectiveness to Tulkinghorn at the literal level.

Tulkinghorn is, I think, believable enough as a proud, resentful, crafty, malicious old man who hounds Lady Dedlock because in getting at her he is getting at the aristocratic circle of whom he is subtly but viciously resentful. But he is much more than this. It is the purpose of this study to make clear that Tulkinghorn is imbued with a "more than personal force," that he is not just a malicious old lawyer, credible or otherwise, but that he is a vision of absolute evil, and as such, is drawn deliberately and carefully as a devil figure. He is, therefore, more than flat embodiment of a single form of evil; he subsumes all the forms that evil may take. In recognizing Tulkinghorn's super-personal identity, we shall gain a new concept of his pursuit of Lady Dedlock and shall come to recognize the central importance to the novel of that pursuit.

It will be necessary first to demonstrate that Tulkinghorn is drawn as a fully-developed archetypal devil figure, and then to define the Tulkinghorn-Dedlock relationship in terms of the patterns which that identity dictates. This will enable us in turn to recognize the artistic implications and intentions of this relationship. Various literary and folklore materials with which Dickens was familiar will be the main sources by which my arguments are established. In addition, a few secondary works will be cited.

I

First it is necessary to show that Tulkinghorn is a devil figure. Most helpful in doing so is Defoe's *Political History of the Devil*. While this book was largely a repository of familiar ideas about the devil and probably provided Dickens with little actual devil lore that he did not already know about,[5] its organization, its intense and opinionated style, and its lively digressions made it a unique reading experience. Dickens' enthusiasm for the work is revealed in a letter written to Forster on November 3, 1837, in which he exclaimed of it, "What a capital thing it is! I bought it for a couple of shillings yesterday morning, and have been quite absorbed in it ever since."[6] The work is helpful for the purposes of this study in defining a specific quantity of material with which we can be sure Dickens was familiar. Another encyclopedic source of concepts about the devil and his workings among mankind with

which Dickens, along with most literate Victorians, was familiar, was, of course, *Paradise Lost*. These two works, along with Maximilian Rudwin's *The Devil in Legend and Literature*, will be the main sources used in this section.

In his first appearance in the novel, Tulkinghorn is three times in notably close succession called by the epithet "the old gentleman," which is one of the more than fifty traditional epithets for the devil incorporating the adjective "old" listed by Maximilian Rudwin.[7] Throughout the novel Tulkinghorn is called by this and other such epithets—"the old scholar,"[8] for example, and "the old man" (xxxiii, 416). The name "Tulkinghorn" echoes another common tag, "Old Horny," as well as evoking an image of the devil's traditional hornedness. Also it echoes the Scottish epithet "muckled-horned Dee'l," mentioned by Defoe.[9] Late in the novel, he is more often called the "enemy" (as in lv, 666), another familiar epithet.

The "old gentleman" Tulkinghorn's black clothing calls to mind the traditional folklore devil, who always wore black, but the emphasis on the dullness of Tulkinghorn's clothes (as in xxix, 358), their constant description as "irresponsive to any glancing light" (ii, 13-14), suggests the Miltonic Satan, whose "luster" is "visibly impaired"; who along with his horde, has "lost all transcendent brightness," and has now only a "faded splendor wan."[10]

Defoe tells of the devil's unusual powers and liberties of moving about both "upon the surface of this earth, as well as in the compass of the atmosphere" (200). Tulkinghorn is imaged in this tradition. He seems simply to "melt" from one place to another (xlii, 514), to "drop into" his room at Chesney Wold, to "appear" ten minutes before dinner (xii, 146). As for habitat, he seems happy only when he goes to his wine-cellar, a dark underground location analogous to the "bowels of the earth" where the prince of darkness reigns. In his conferences with Lady Dedlock he usually seeks the proximity of the fireplace (as xii, 149), and the vicinity of his apartment in Lincoln's Inn Fields is described as an "oven made by the hot pavements and hot buildings" (xlii, 514).

The dominant description of Tulkinghorn, as an old gentleman always in a black suit and a knotted necktie and accepted into the best drawing rooms, suggests a figure in total contrast to the commonplace medieval devil. The medieval devil was thought of as cloven-hoofed, deformed, or otherwise malignant-looking. He was thought to change himself into animal forms as a principal means of deluding and capturing souls, and was thought also to work particularly through jugglers, puppet shows, magicians and the like, since occasions for the activities of these groups were sure to draw crowds. The devil, therefore, was connected particularly with the atmosphere of the fair. But Defoe says that as the world grew wiser, the devil had to become subtle and sophisticated. He was "obliged to lay by his puppet shows and his tumblers . . . his mountebanking and quacking," and to take on the "grand manner" (355). In *Bleak House*, the Smallweed family are drawn pointedly from the older tradition, being imaged frequently as a family of spiders and monkeys, and stylized much like figures from a puppet show at a fair. In fact, Bartholomew's Fair is directly suggested by the grandson's name, Bart, and the granddaughter is named Judy. Grandfather Smallweed is like Punch in his abuse of his wife and offspring, though he has none of Punch's charm.

Tulkinghorn, on the other hand, is drawn largely from the image of the latter-day Satan, with his dignity and his courtly manners, his proper black suit and necktie. There are details, however, which link him to the older tradition, or to the "old school," a relationship which Dickens frequently enforces by calling Tulkinghorn a gentleman "of the old school" (as in ii, 14, xi, 129). Several images relate Tulkinghorn to conjuring, such as the one in which Sir Leicester is described as being to Tulkinghorn as "the coin of the conjuror's trick" (ii, 13). Tulkinghorn's name is close to being "tusk" and "horn," both of which words link him to the predatory animal. A few times he is imaged directly with animal images—likened to "a larger species of rook" (xii, 146) at one time, for example, and called "an Oyster of the old school" (x, 119) at another. And incongrously, his bow is always "clumsy" (xlviii, 575). In such ways as these, the "old gentleman's" alter ego is kept before us.

Just as description identifies Tulkinghorn with the devil-figure of folklore and literature, so also do his dominant character traits. No trait is more frequently referred to than his identity as a repository of secrets, which he carries "in every limb of his body, and every crease of his dress" (xii, 147). The love of secrets is regarded by Defoe as a major characteristic of the devil, who exercises "indefatigable vigilance" (154) in his task of discovering frauds and revealing secrets (260). He excells at finding the one weak place at which even the best man is susceptible (157). Once he possesses a victim, he proceeds to reveal his victim's secret sins.[11] This, of course, is an accurate description of Tulkinghorn's relationship to Lady Dedlock.

Hatred and suspicion of women in general is a trait universally attributed to the devil,[12] and is one of the most overtly-drawn traits of Tulkinghorn. This trait helps to account for his pursuit of Lady Dedlock, but, as Quirk demonstrates, his desire for control over Lady Dedlock finally grows out of his bitter resentment of the fashionable world in which Lady Dedlock reigns supreme. He despises this "splendour of which he is a distant beam" (xxix, 357). His malignance toward Lady Dedlock is a means to reach and gain power over Sir Leicester, the real seat of the power to which he must be subservient.[13]

Here Tulkinghorn is in a position much like Milton's Satan in relationship to heaven. He is in an eternally secondary position and knows that he is doomed to be so, yet will neither accept his position nor change his ways, but instead responds with envy, hatred and defiance. From Satan's hatred springs "So deep a malice, to confound the race / Of mankind in one root" (*PL*, ii, 382-383), and in

going after Sir Leicester, Tulkinghorn is exhibiting the same plan. But he is in no position to wage open war; like Satan, Tulkinghorn must work "in close design, by fraud or guile" (*PL*, i, 645-646). Thus the obsessive love of secrets, and thus the "imperturbable" countenance so frequently noted (xxxiv, 429; xl, 494). Satan, too, "each perturbation smoothed with outward calm" (*PL*, iv, 120).

Tulkinghorn's pitiless pursuit of Lady Dedlock as a means of revenging himself upon her circle, especially upon Sir Leicester, its center, projects a situation and motivation similar to Satan's relationship to Adam and Eve. Through Adam and Eve, Satan would injure God. Sir Leicester stands, however, both as Adam, the husband to be injured, and as God, in this microcosmic universe which, in turn, stands as Paradise or as a heavenly firmament to Tulkinghorn. While the story of Adam and Eve is the prototypical account of Satan's ensnaring man by the use of woman as his agent, this propensity for making relentless and pitiless use of women as tools for effecting a larger evil is a standard part of devil lore.[14]

Tulkinghorn is marked by one other essential diabolical trait—he is the victim of despair. This trait is revealed mainly in one extended passage. One evening when Tulkinghorn, alone as always in his apartment, is drinking some of his fine old wine and pondering his secrets, he spares a thought to "that one bachelor friend of his, a man of the same mould and a lawyer too, who lived the same kind of life until he was seventy-five years old, and then, suddenly conceiving (as it is supposed) an impression that it was too monotonous, gave his gold watch to his hairdresser one summer evening and walked leisurely home to the Temple, and hanged himself" (xxii, 273). This friend is, of course, a mirror image of Tulkinghorn, whose old-fashioned necktie, always "loosely twisted" about his neck (xlviii, 572), suddenly takes on a special significance with its suggestion of suicide. Tulkinghorn is cut off from love, has no sympathy for women and marriage, does not even have a hairdresser as far as we know; and he is forever cut off from full status in the class which he moves in and envies since one can only enter it by birth or marriage. Such ultimate despair is, of course, Satan's destiny.

Defoe explains that Satan is filled with "horrible resolutions of revenge" against mankind, and that the impossibility of executing those resolutions creates "a hell in his own breast" (188) and leaves despair "the reigning passion of his mind" (192). Milton too draws at length the despair of Satan, who knows that he cannot defeat God, yet despairs of peace, "For who can think submission?" (*PL*, i, 661). Tulkinghorn, then, is not just another lawyer in this novel. He is a devil-figure.

Tulkinghorn's role in the novel consists solely of his pursuit of Lady Dedlock and the activities necessary for entrapping her, and, as has been pointed out, to question his role is to question hers, as well as to question the point of their presence in the novel. When Tulkinghorn is recognized as a devil-figure, and Lady Dedlock identified as the object of a stylized diabolical pursuit, we have a new perspective from which to examine her role.

II

In order to understand Lady Dedlock's role, we need first to review a bit further Dickens' frame of reference in relation to literary and folklore versions of the devil. Dickens was, of course, familair with the Faust legend. This story, fixed in English tradition by Marlowe's version, enjoyed fresh vitality in Dickens' day as a result of Goethe's treatment, with its new "redeemable" Faust, popularized in England largely through Abraham Hayward's prose translation, published first in 1833, and reprinted in 1847 and 1855, and through P. J. Bailey's extravagant verse recreation *Festus*, first published in 1839, and by 1854, in its fifth edition.[15] The Faust story is itself a version of the basic medieval and Renaissance morality plot, familiar to Dickens from many sources—from morality plays such as "Infans et Mundus," for example, which, in his edition of *Dodsley's Old Plays* as "Child and the World," he owned at least as early as 1844; and from the plight of the Red Cross Knight in Book One of Spenser's *Faerie Queene,* and of Christian in Bunyan's *Pilgrim's Progress,* two further works which were among his books by 1844.[16] Each of these three works had its prideful sinner, each its devil figure, and each, of course, its good angel.

In the configuration of characters that we considered in the discussion of Tulkinghorn above, Lady Dedlock was shown to be related in some respects to Eve. In general, she is understandable in terms of immediate Victorian religious concepts—she is proud and worldly, she harbors an unrepented sin, suffers terrors of conscience and has few or no redeeming "signs of election" (xxxvi, 450-452). But Lady Dedlock is imaged most fully in terms and patterns which relate her to medieval and Renaissance literary works in which the protagonist suffers from the deadly sin of sloth. Sloth, it should be recalled, presupposed pride. It was pride, the substitution of one's own will for God's will, which made one susceptible to sloth, which in turn caused one to become susceptible to the other deadly sins. Sloth amounted to the loss of joy in the things of the spirit, and was regarded as the inevitable gateway to worldliness; for the slothful sinner, losing joy in the things of the spirit, sought compensation in the only other source available to him, the pleasures of the world, and he took increasing pride in worldly triumphs as he left spiritual aspirations behind. But he gradually came to realize the hollowness of his worldly triumph yet was so stricken with guilt that he felt himself past all hope of salvation. From here came the tendency to despair. Early literary treatments of this cycle are characterized by a climactic episode in which the protagonist meets his adversary, the devil or a devil figure, in personified form. For the Infans in "Child and the World," for example, the adversary is Wanhope; for the Red Cross Knight and Bunyan's Christian, it is a personification of despair.

The cycle that I have just sketched will be referred to as the morality plot in the discussion below. The Faust story will be regarded as a specialized version of the morality plot which is distinguished by most or all of the following characteristics: (1) a deliberate pact with the devil made within the action or clearly implied as antecedent action; (2) a second pact made within the action; (3) the devil figure as a central character throughout the main action, as opposed to his appearance as an allegorical figure in a single climactic episode; (4) a time span of twenty to twenty-four years indicated as the length of the protagonist's wrong-doing before the devil comes for payment; (5) a configuration of characters that conspicuously duplicates the basic characters of the Faust legend.

Lady Dedlock is imaged from the beginning of *Bleak House* as "bored, frigid, and weary of soul." In her first major appearance in the novel, we are told that on the previous Sunday, in Paris, Lady Dedlock, "in the desolation of Boredom and the clutch of Giant Despair, almost hated her own maid for being in spirits" (xii, 139). The detail that this was her state on Sunday emphasizes the absence of comfort to her of spiritual practices, the basic symptom of sloth, and the reference to the Giant Despair provides clear linkage to *Pilgrim's Progress*. Sundays at Chesney Wold too, it should be noted, have already been singled out as joyless days (ii, 11).

Revelation of antecedent action lets us know that the young Honoria Barbary, now Lady Dedlock, had fallen in love with a Captain Hawdon in her youth, had borne his child out of wedlock while he was at sea, had been told by a bigoted sister that the child was dead, and had despaired of Hawdon's return, there having been a report that he had drowned. We are told nothing of her immediate reaction to these events, but are shown that without too much delay she went very deliberately after other stakes—wealth, position, and power, pursuing them with "beauty, pride, ambition, insolent resolve, and sense enough to portion out a legion of fine ladies" in the race for Sir Leicester Dedlock's favor (ii, 12). Honoria, then, had abandoned her commitment to her heart's honest desire for love, for physical fulfillment, for a child, and had gone after worldly values, values which she has pursued with dazzling success by the time that we meet her. This sketch suggests that Lady Dedlock had in a sense sold herself to the devil, and as the antecedent action is further revealed and the present played out, we see that Dickens definitely intended us to draw the parallel for he shaped the relationship of Tulkinghorn and Lady Dedlock with marked similarities to the traditional relationship of Mephistopheles and Faustus.

First of all, we should notice that the name "Mister Tulkinghorn" echoes precisely the syllabic cadence of "Mephistopheles" and duplicates the stressed consonants as well, giving a sound similarity that seems a deliberate suggestion of the parallel intended between the two characters. Not so conclusive in themselves perhaps, but certainly of significance in conjunction with "Mister Tulkinghorn" are the Dedlocks' names. "Honoria" is a close phonetic counterpart, perhaps as close as one could find among female names, for Goethe's Faust's first name in English, "Henry." And one can hardly avoid thinking of Mr. Tulkinghorn's patron Sir Leicester as Lucifer at times, a substitute which Dickens even suggests through Mr. Boythorn (ix, 108). (The sense in which Sir Leicester serves as Lucifer will be discussed further below.) Dating in the novel, moreover, can be worked out very specifically to indicate that exactly twenty-four years, the most typical length of time for a bond with the devil, and the time allowed in Marlowe's version of the legend, elapse between the time that Lady Dedlock dedicated herself to worldly pursuits and the time when the devil claims dominion (xlviii, 580-583). Esther was "almost fourteen" (iii, 20) when her godmother died, and it was immediately thereafter that she went to Greenleaf, where she passed "six happy, quiet years" (iii, 26) before Richard and Ada came into her life. When she first met Richard and Ada, then, she was twenty or very close to it, Richard "not more than nineteen, if quite so much," but two years older than Ada. This made Ada right at seventeen, Richard right at nineteen, and Esther right at twenty, establishing Esther as three years older than Ada. As Lady Dedlock nears exposure, we find Ada having her twenty-first birthday (i, 600), making Esther twenty-four. This is just after Tulkinghorn, shortly after claiming Lady Dedlock, has been killed and just as suspicion begins to go to Lady Dedlock, therefore just before she strips away all that she had sold herself for—sumptuous apparel, wealth, position, and power in society. Her powers are abandoned as ineffectual after a clearly-defined twenty-four year period of reign for which she has paid with an ever-increasing despair and frigidity.

The present action of the novel deals only with the climactic years of the protagonist's power, when the allotted time for her reign is running low and an agent of the devil is on hand to collect. Though Tulkinghorn, like Marlowe's Mephistopheles, abhors marriage and tells Lady Dedlock that he is as much against her marriage now as he was when it first occurred (xli, 512), he is not shown to have been a participant in the original diabolical efforts at procurement of Lady Dedlock's soul, but only as following his own nature, and in so doing operating in the larger scheme of destruction and malice as the agent who is now on hand to claim the devil's due.

We first meet Lady Dedlock at the time that Esther is about twenty and Lady Dedlock many years into her reign in the world of fashion. The reader knows of Lady Dedlock's weary enthrallment to the Giant Despair, yet what the world sees is her constant movement about in England and abroad (ii, 11-12; xii, 139). When we first hear of her, she has just returned from her town house to Chesney Wold previous to going to Paris; and after the trip to Paris, which brought her no joy, we hear of her intensified movement in England and abroad (xvi, 195), a version of the terrestrial wanderings that typified Faustus's years of power, just as the secret conflict and discontent characterized him. A difference however is that Marlowe's Faustus really enjoyed his pleasure, at least at times when it "conquered sweet despair." Lady Dedlock enjoys nothing except for the rural girl Rosa, with whom she finds some moments of release. This redemptive interest in Rosa echoes the relationship of Goethe's Faustus to the rural girl Margaret, and is a point to which we shall return.

While despondent within, however, Lady Dedlock continues to reign over a shrine of followers who worship her beauty, title and wealth. The scenes of Lady Dedlock's continued reign, particularly the scene in chapter twelve, suggest in their pomp the Vanity Fair scene from *Pilgrim's Progress,* yet even more notably link Lady Dedlock to Lucifera and her reign in the House of Pride in Book One of *The Faerie Queene.* In these scenes, Sir Leicester is in a sense the devil to Lady Dedlock. His name reminds one of "Lucifer," and it is he who has the limp, from gout, that recalls the cloven foot of the devil. In his insensitivity to change and in his giving Lady Dedlock those prizes for which she sells her honest self, he is Lucifer. She is his Lady Lucifera, occupying a "gaudy platform" (xli, 512) where troops of visitors come into her presence as to a shrine (xii, 143-145).[17]

It is in chapter twelve, at the height of her power yet bored and despairing, that Lady Dedlock first notices the rural girl Rosa and asks her age (xii, 141). She ponders Rosa's answer, "nineteen," which the reader will subsequently realize is the approximate age of her own daughter. Lady Dedlock's relationship to Rosa will culminate in her breaking a "second pact" with the devil-figure Tulkinghorn. The motif of the "second pact" is common to Faust literature,[18] familiar to most of us from the last act of Marlowe's *Dr. Faustus,* where after the old man evokes a surge of repentance in Faustus, Faustus promptly rallies to Mephistopheles' threats and offers his blood again to reconfirm his former vows to Lucifer.

Throughout the novel, Lady Dedlock has felt increasingly Tulkinghorn's power over her. His menace culminates in chapter forty in his telling the story of her past, in a thinly-disguised form, to the entire fashionable circle gathered at Chesney Wold. In the next chapter it is later that same night. Lady Dedlock goes to Tulkinghorn's room and announces her plan to leave at once and her willingness to sign any sort of paper or release that Tulkinghorn wishes in order to spare her husband trouble "in obtaining his release" (xli, 509), presumably in achieving a legal separation which she assumes he would want when the truth came out. Tulkinghorn blocks her intention to leave by his demands for a new bargain, a second pact, if she is not to be exposed, and Sir Leicester, as a result, "driven out of his wits, or laid upon a death-bed," the family reputation and credit ruined (xli, 511-513). Tulkinghorn stipulates that as long as she continues her life exactly as before, "holding its pains at [his] pleasure, day by day" (xli, 512), she can be assured that he will forewarn her before he exposes her, should he decide to do so. Repeatedly he asserts that his only concern is for Sir Leicester. Even as he tortures Lady Dedlock in this scene, he is struck with admiration for her (xli, 508), reminding one of Satan's suspended admiration for Eve in the midst of his ruining her (*PL,* ix, 463-465).

Lady Dedlock is subdued by Tulkinghorn's casuistry. In Despaire's confrontation with the Red Cross Knight in the ninth canto of Book One of *The Faerie Queene,* Despaire uses "guilt" and "justice" as the loaded terms to bring the Knight to the point of final despair, at which time Una steps forth to remind him of love and mercy. In this scene, Lady Dedlock lacks the vision to challenge Tulkinghorn's sophistical arguments, which define Sir Leicester's good solely in terms of worldly values, "reputation" and "credit." She seems not to perceive that her lord the aged husband has sufficient love and mercy to render him forgiving, though there is reason to think that she has too much pride to accept a lesser position in his or any other eyes even it if were offered (xxxvi, 451).

The morality plot aspects of the scene—the desperation of the blind sinner and the bounteous mercy of her "lord," are emphasized when Dickens closes the chapter by describing Lady Dedlock's desperate frenzy after she returns to her room and then juxtaposing an account of Sir Leicester, close by in his own room, dreaming a dream which marks him as the very emblem of mercy. In the previous chapter he had expressed the utmost contempt and dread at the outcome of an election in which "his people" had elected an ironmaster to parliament, but at the end of this chapter, we are shown Sir Leicester "pardoning the repentant country in a magnificently condescending dream" (xli, 513).

In the confrontation scene between Lady Dedlock and Esther in chapter xxvi (450-452), Esther, in the role of "good angel," had urged her mother to take hope and to tell Mr. Jarndyce of the problem, that is, to confess and repent. Lady Dedlock was blind to the possibilities of hope and faith in that scene just as she was blind to the possibilities of mercy during the "second pact" scene just discussed. Yet in the final analysis, Lady Dedlock, unlike Marlowe's Faustus, who always backs down in his tentative defiance of the devil, breaks her agreement with Mr. Tulkinghorn. And it is not until the scene of that defiance and the confrontation with Tulkinghorn that follows it that the sounding out of Lady Dedlock's soul is complete.

In the defiance scene (xlviii, 567-582), Lady Dedlock announces in the presence of Sir Leicester and Tulkinghorn, as well as Rouncewell the ironmaster, that she wants Rosa put out because of her foolish attachment to Wat Rouncewell. Arrogantly, she indicates that if the girl may be so stupid as to let such an attachment intrude upon her advantages as a member of the house of Dedlock, she wants the girl out of her house. Sir Leicester's capacity for understanding and compassion are emphasized in this scene as he questions Lady Dedlock's ultimatum and defends Rosa. Tulkinghorn looms "bigger and blacker" than ever before Lady Dedlock throughout the scene, but he must repress his reaction in the presence of others. As for Lady Dedlock, only icy haughtiness is apparent, but the reader understands that Lady Dedlock dismisses Rosa from the household in order to protect the girl's chances for a good marriage from being spoiled if it is discovered that

she lives under the patronage of a "ruined" woman. If Rosa separates herself from such a woman, her honor will be intact when that woman is exposed.

This dismissal of Rosa, of course, is an act not typical of Lady Dedlock's life as it has been and to which Tulkinghorn has constrained her. Thus she has broken the second pact. It is not long before Tulkinghorn finds opportunity to confront Lady Dedlock alone. There is a new "indefinable freedom" in Tulkinghorn's manner with Lady Dedlock now that she is, in his opinion, totally in his power (xlviii, 580). His manner suggests to the reader, however, an overreaching ambition, the flaw which led to his counterpart Satan's downfall. Tulkinghorn tells her that she can count on no warning from him now, that he will do as he pleases when he pleases; she simply must wait helplessly. In the very midst of his gloating torture of her—he even indulges in a "slight smile"—he continues to wonder at her control and composure, and to puzzle at her behavior. "*She* cannot be spared," he thinks, "Why should she spare others?" (xlviii, 581-82).

Though Tulkinghorn seems not to recognize that he has lost his prey, it has been made apparent to the reader that Lady Dedlock is not finally of the devil's party. The very fact that she has disobeyed the conditions of Tulkinghorn's agreement has shown us that she is throwing off the devil's rule over her life. And in breaking the agreement, she is sacrificing herself for Rosa and thereby performing a redemptive act, which allows us to assume that she dies in a state of grace, like Goethe's Faust. Her death occurs shortly after this last interview with Mr. Tulkinghorn. She has clad herself in poor apparel and headed for the burial place of Captain Hawdon. Pride and slothful passiveness are gone as she casts herself upon the gate of the cemetery in a final effort to reach his grave. Stripped of her sumptuous apparel, without regard for the world's opinion, she dies trying to reach all that remains of that which in her youth, as again now, evoked and defined her best, truest self.

Within the symbolic structure of the novel, the murder of Tulkinghorn after his triumphant interview with Lady Dedlock, hence at the moment of his highest presumption, seems appropriate. And there are various traditions which include the death of the devil, notable among which is the Punch and Judy story. This story invariably ends with the death of the devil, at which the crowd cheers, though they know full well that the devil will be alive and well for the next performance. Defoe summarizes the common conceptions that the devil acts through agents, of which there is a never-ending supply (207-208). The devil acting through Tulkinghorn as agent has been defeated in his efforts totally to secure Lady Dedlock and thereby torment and destroy Sir Leicester, but we know that the devil will find other agents and other prey. Lady Dedlock, however, dies reunited with her original self and Sir Leicester's last coherent breaths express love for his lady and an impassioned hope for her return; his last days are comforted by honoring her memory and by other ties of affection reflected in George Rouncewell's devotion to him. Tulking-horn did not destroy his spirit.

Like the typical medieval morality play, the morality plot of *Bleak House* indicates that it is never too late for redemption, that no person is steeped too deeply in pride and sin to reverse his course. Lady Dedlock's is not a very abundant or glorious redemption—she could have had so much more if she had only thrown herself upon her lord's gracious mercy. Yet she would have been violating her character just as surely as Marlowe's Faustus would have had he repented at the last hour. She was never as fully gratified by her sin as Faustus, and she was projected into it through a grievous experience, not merely through a spontaneous desire for power. For these reasons, the possibility of salvation remains present in her characterization to a greater extent than in Faustus'. But a full, melodramatic reconciliation with her husband and her long-lost daughter would require an unbelievable reversal of character on her part, and would give, I think, a falsified vision of human possibility and likelihood. Lady Dedlock dies a tortured spirit, barely resisting outright suicide, but she had hold of a sufficient shred of honesty, truth and repentance for one to feel that heaven can forgive her. No more; no less.

III

While Lady Dedlock's character and her relationship to Tulkinghorn have been defined largely in terms of medieval and Renaissance literature and of Goethe's version of the Faust legend, it is in Defoe that one finds a possible source. The most unusual feature of Dickens' use of the "Faust motif" is his use of a female figure in the Faust role. In E. M. Smeed's bibliography of literary treatments of the Faust theme, there is only one title indicating a female Faust figure, *Die Grafin Faustine,* by Ida Grafin Von Hahn-Hahn, a German work first published in 1841.[19] By 1845, two English translations had been published in London, but if Dickens had heard of or read this novel, he would have found only a romanticized character type, with none of the Faust legend's machinery. The book's heroine is a beautiful, gifted poetess who marries her ideal lover and has a beautiful and perfect little son, yet because of her craving for the infinite withdraws to a contemplative order of nuns and dies young.[20] Arnold's brief "To Fausta," published in 1849, makes no use of the legend. These works, could, however, have provided some suggestion for the female Faust figure. Certainly Dickens' own inventive powers were sufficient to suggest the possibility of the role reversal—he suggests the possibility of a female Othello through a comment by Bucket to Mrs. Snagsby when Mrs. Snagsby is in a jealous fit against Guster (lix, 708). But one finds in Defoe, a work with which we are sure that Dickens was familiar, a passage strongly suggestive of the possibility of a female Faust figure, and of one drawn remarkably along the lines of Lady Dedlock.

Heretofore in this study I have not claimed any influence by Defoe, whose *History of the Devil,* as I have pointed out, was largely a repository of familiar lore. In this instance there is no unique information. But Defoe's juxta-position of traditional materials with his own speculations and disgressions forms a possible source. As to whether the passage struck a conscious creative response at Dickens' first reading in 1837 or in a subsequent reading, I will not conjecture. I simply wish to point out the fact that this passage, with which we are sure that Dickens was familiar, provides marked suggestion of the characterization and role that Dickens gives to Lady Dedlock. The passage consists of chapter seven and the beginning of chapter eight in *The History of the Devil.*

In the seventh chapter (258-288), Defoe is largely discussing the devil's methods. In pointing out that the devil works at recruiting his agents and his victims, Defoe suggests one of those methods, achieving intimacy with his intended object, as he comments, "No doubt the Devil and Dr. Faustus were very intimate . . . ; no doubt the Devil showed himself in the glass to that fair lady who looked in it to see where to place her patches" (261). A bit farther along he asserts that "hoop-petticoats" are one of the devil's favorite disguises (271), and spends the remainder of the chapter on the devil's particular liking for the "fine lady" (277) and for ladies of "a fine face, a divine shape and a heavenly aspect" (287) as means for his disguise.

The next chapter, chapter eight (289-309), proceeds to the topic of pacts with the devil. Defoe refers to Dr. Faustus's bargain as well as to other folklore versions of such pacts as he dispenses the relevant lore. Toward the later part of the commentary, he remarks:

> I might, before I quit this point, seriously reflect here upon our *beau monde,* viz., the gay part of mankind especially those of the times we live in, who walk about in a composure and tranquility inexpressible, and yet, as we all know, must certainly have all sold themselves to the Devil, for the power of acting the foolishest things with the greater applause.

> (304)

In the progression of Defoe's narrative that I have just summarized, we have the juxtaposition of an image of the devil and Faustus with an image of the devil and a fashionable woman in the context of a discussion of the devil's methods of securing souls. Then follows as extended discussion of a role that reverses conventional identities, the devil as a woman, rather than a man; then comes a discussion of the *beau monde* as participants in pacts with the devil. The possibility of a female figure from the *beau monde* bargaining with the devil is strongly suggested in this passage. The passage provides, I think, a likely source of Dickens' conception of the character of Lady Dedlock, reigning light of the "beau monde" (xii, 138), yet in bondage to the devil, to whom she has sold her soul for applause.

We have seen a rich synthesis of traditional literary and folklore materials in Dickens' creation of Tulkinghorn and Lady Dedlock and their relationship. Recognizing that this relationship was shaped with features which make it overtly parallel with the Faust legend adds greatly to our understanding of the meaning and intention of this plot. But the story exists as part of a much larger whole, and only in functioning significantly within the whole can it be judged as artistically effective in the final analysis. It is time now to consider what further meaning is given to the novel by the explication that has been provided in this study.

IV

After one recognizes the thorough development of the Tulkinghorn-Dedlock plot as a Faustian morality plot, one realizes that numerous other plots in the book share conspicuously some of the same characteristics. Nemo is referred to in his neighborhood as one who has "sold himself to the Enemy" (x, 124), and his story, revealed largely through a conversation between Mr. George and Small-weed (xxi, 269-270), reveals that he had definitely been an early candidate for despair, already in the clutches of gamblers and usurers when he went on the sea journey during which he went overboard, "whether intentionally or accidentally, I don't know," Mr. George reports. It becomes apparent in this conversation that Hawdon deliberately let the rumor of his drowning stand to avoid vicious creditors, presumably never even attempting to communicate with Honoria after his return. At one point in the novel, the omniscient narrator comments that the devil is "a more designing, callous, and intolerable devil when he sticks a pin in his shirt-front, calls himself a gentleman, backs a card or colour, plays a game or so of billiards, and knows a little about bills and promissory notes, than in any other form he wears" (xxvi, 324). It was to the devil in this guise that Captain Hawdon had sold himself, at the same time drawing the young Honoria Barbary into an intimacy that jeopardized her well being.[21] Some twenty years later, we find him as Nemo, a derelict opium addict, his only possibly redeeming features his kindness to Jo during this last phase of his life and his treasuring to the end of Honoria's letters. At the scene of his death is the devil figure Tulkinghorn, along with Krook and his cat, who suggest a folklore devil and his familiar.

Trooper George's approximately twenty years of vagrancy culminate in his being at the mercy of Smallweed's "friend in the city" whose name "begins with a D," and who will "have his bond" (xxi, 266-267). This "friend in the city," a "slow-torturing" kind of "old man" (xlvii, 566) and none other that Tulkinghorn himself, offers George a second pact of sorts which George is forced to accept (xxxiv, 429). George, after further suffering, is finally allowed full repentance and is restored as nearly as he can be to the family, friends and values of his youth.

It is Richard Carstone's story that provides the fullest and most significant parallel to the Tulkinghorn-Dedlock plot. This is a poignantly telescoped version of the plot, for Richard's whole life lasted little over twenty years. It is as if he was born into the devil's clutches. He never had any

sense of purpose or "calling" in his entire life. In his plot, we have in Richard the errant sinner, in Esther, the good angel, in Ada, the redemptive love, and in Vholes, the devil figure on hand to snatch Richard's soul at the appropriate time.[22] Richard's suffering is portrayed physiologically, in passages that remind on of the Red Cross Knight's preliminary despondency and debility when he was imprisoned by the giant Orgoglio,[23] while Lady Dedlock's, as we have seen, is imaged psychologically, as is predominantly the case with the Red Cross Knight during his encounter with Despaire. Richard had not the strength to wage the battle required of an acceptable fictional protagonist. Lady Dedlock did. Richard is allowed repentance and reconciliation with family and friends before death. Lady Dedlock is not.

Gridley's case largely parallels Richard's, as does Miss Flite's. And there is more. But by now it has become apparent that the Faust motif and devil lore in general provide a unifying principle of the novel. In making the Faustian morality plot a virtual "master plot" of his novel, Dickens confirms his sense of this plot's authenticity as a basic pattern of human experience.

V

Having seen that the Tulkinghorn-Dedlock plot exists among numerous parallel plots, it remains for us to consider this plot's relationship to other principal motifs of the novel. As has been pointed out, most studies of *Bleak House* focus on the forces of Chancery and the law as the major symbolization of evil in the novel and as the major instrument for creating hell on earth—Richard Carstone's hell, for example, and the hell of Tom-all-Alone's and the hellish plight of Jo, all of which take place within the sanction of the law, not to mention the church. Yet Jarndyce and Jarndyce has no real significance in Lady Dedlock's life, and her pursuer is bent on personal revenge, not involved in a Chancery activity. Still, she as much as any victim of Chancery is in a hell, and Tulkinghorn is her chief tormentor. And he is a principal actor in a number of the novel's plots. Views regarding Chancery as the sole significant symbol of evil in the novel are, therefore, highly incomplete.

Chancery is surely one of the most potent and suggestive of artistic symbols of evil and its workings among mankind. The Lord Chancellor, his counterpart Krook, and all the descending ranks of lawyers convey a sense of the hopeless and stupid folly of the whole legal process and of the hopelessness of assigning blame within the network of a complex institution, perhaps within life itself. But Tulkinghorn defines evil as it works within the human personality and he defines it comprehensively. His characterization provides some significant contrasts with the other agents of evil in the novel. These agents, mostly the legal corps and their satellites, partake in varying degrees of Tulkinghorn's faults. They are guileful, secretive, and lacking in feeling or pity for others. But there are sharp differences. Even the Smallweeds, for example, have a family life, and a sort of give-and-take involvement with each other. And the repulsive Vholes has made some sort of personal contact in his life, for he has daughters as well as a father in the Vale of Taunton with whom he shares his life. This group is also motivated by greed; they enjoy the money they get, even if, as with Smallweed, only in a miserly way. Suddenly greed for money, which is tangible and can bring pleasure, seems healthy compared to the pure hatred and envy and spite that motivate Tulkinghorn. Tulkinghorn is a comprehensive personification of ultimate evil. Other characters are evil insofar as they partake of his nature. Lady Dedlock participates in his nature in her repression of her honest emotion and self and in her dedication to pursuits that give her position and power over others.

In Tulkinghorn and his pursuit of Lady Dedlock we are getting another view of evil, a view just as essential to the meaning of *Bleak House* as the more noted view symbolized by Chancery and its appendages. Lady Dedlock's suffering and vulnerability to the powers of evil are created not by legal problems, but by personal or spiritual problems—a sense of her own falseness, sinfulness and exemption from salvation. Given money, and power—all that Chancery suppliants yearn for and think would assure their happiness—Lady Dedlock is nevertheless the most miserable and desperate of souls. We see in Lady Dedlock that despair, waste, grief and misery are problems of the spirit; that evil and the susceptibility to evil are in the spirit, not in the external circumstances of life. Her story suggests that had Richard, Miss Flite, and Gridley achieved the wealth of which they dreamed, their spiritual peace and happiness might not have been any greater. The plot of Lady Dedlock insists on the tragic dimension of human suffering, its root within the human spirit, its final inevitability as a part of the human condition, as a result of human nature itself.

This vision is expressed in various ways in the novel; for example, in the contrast between Tom Jarndyce and John Jarndyce. Given the same circumstances, Tom was vulnerable to erosion of the spirit by the false promises of Chancery, as was Richard; John was not. Tom committed suicide and John survived as a productive, if limited, human being. But the central contrast is that between Lady Dedlock and Esther. Lady Dedlock was vulnerable to spiritual erosion in the face of personal and emotional deprivation. Esther was not. The novel, then, does not merely indict the presence of evil; it confronts and portrays the mystery of human susceptibility to evil.

In conclusion, I want to point out some implications of my reading in relation to the structure of the novel. Dickens' use of dual narrators has often been criticized, labelled a sign that Dickens was divided in artistic purpose or lacking in an adequate technique to encompass the breadth of his vision. And the character of Esther has been criticized as too much a personfication of self-sacrifice and devotion to duty to hold our serious attention. These criticisms have

been variously made and variously answered. My reading provides a few further bases for rebuttal.

Recognizing Tulkinghorn as the personification of the evil that dominates in the omnisciently-narrated part of the novel provides a counterpart character to Esther as the personification of compassion, selflessness, and devotion to duty who dominates the parts of the book which she narrates. Chancery, an abstraction, does not appropriately balance with her in a good versus evil juxtaposition. Nor is Krook, a grotesque and in many ways pitiable emblem of evil, an appropriate counterpart. But Tulkinghorn is. He and Esther each function effectively at a literal level, but each also functions essentially as a symbolic extremity. Just as she is the touchstone for good in the novel, he is the touchstone for evil. Each is delineated by an image pattern that suggests his or her extremity as a character. Light imagery predominates in her world just as it is present in her name, while hellish imagery—fogs, mists, blackness, shadows and ominous animals—predominates in his, and is suggested in his name. In recognizing this organization into two worlds, each epitomized by a character who functions as the dominant principle of that world, we must recognize an organization related in concept to Milton's *Paradise Lost*. Like Milton, Dickens has given us two worlds, forever at war, both having to be traversed by every mortal in his earthly life, each taking its toll in various ways and to various extents. Lady Dedlock, I assert, is the protagonist of the novel; it is she who traverses most thoroughly before our eyes the landscapes of both worlds. It is she who is subject both to the good angel and the bad angel. Recognizing her plight as a treatment of the great epic struggle between good and evil brings into new focus the design of this remarkably complex novel and surely marks it as one of the most comprehensive of all such treatments.

Notes

1. Edgar Johnson's phrase, *Charles Dickens: His Tragedy and Triumph,* 2 vols. (New York: Simon and Schuster, 1952), II, 765. Johnson's entire discussion, 762-782, especially 762 and 765, reflects the position being described. For earlier statements of the complaint, see E. B. Lupton, *Dickens the Immortal* (Kansas City: A. Fowler, 1923), p. 61, and David Cecil, *Early Victorian Novelists* (Indianapolis: Bobbs-Merrill, 1935), pp 48-49. For a recent statement see Michael Wilkins. "Dickens's Portrayal of the Dedlocks," *The Dickensian,* 72 (1976), 71.

2. Grahame Smith, *Dickens, Money and Society* (Berkeley and Los Angeles: University of California Press, 1968), pp. 125, 129. Two recent studies defend Lady Dedlock's story on the basis of its significance to Esther's story, but neither considers the role of Tulkinghorn in her story. These are Geoffrey Thurley in *Dickens' Mythology* (New York: St. Martin's Press, 1976), pp. 172-202, and H. M. Daleski in *Dickens and the Art of Analogy* (New York: Schocken

Books, 1970), pp. 156-190. Thurley discusses Tulkinghorn briefly, pp. 193-195, but only as another of the novel's lawyers, and Daleski gives no attention directly to Tulkinghorn. Daleski does, however, challenge the excessive attention to the Chancery plot and the "fog imagery" as the main clues to the novel's meaning, especially pp. 157, 159.

3. Eugene F. Quick, "Tulkinghorn's Buried Life: A Study of Character in *Bleak House*," *JEGP* [*Journal of English and German Philology*], 72 (1972), 526-535, Quick also notices other studies that have attempted to define a significant role for Tulkinghorn and points out their shortcomings, 527 and note. See Fred Kaplan, *Dickens and Mesmerism* (Princeton: Princeton University Press, 1975), pp. 201-203, for an interesting defense of Tulkinghorn. Kaplan's discussion is largely theoretical, concerned with the ultimate causes of human commitment to good or evil more than with immediate, humanly perceptible causes.

4. Joseph I. Fradin, "Will and Society in *Bleak House*," *PMLA* [*Publications. Modern Language Association of America*] 81 (1966), pp. 102-104.

5. See Lauriat Lane, Jr., "The Devil in *Oliver Twist*," *The Dickensian*, 52 (1956), 132-136, on the commonplace nature of Defoe's devil lore. In this article, Lane challenges the argument of Marie Hamilton Law, "The Indebtedness of *Oliver Twist* to Defoe's *History of the Devil*," *PMLA*, 40 (1925), 892-897, that Defoe influenced Dickens' conception of Fagin as a devil figure. These two studies provide the only discussion of Defoe's relation to Dickens that I have seen.

6. *The Letters of Charles Dickens, 1820-1839*, ed. Madeline House and Graham Storey (Oxford: The Clarendon Press, 1969), I, 328. (Pilgrim Edition, referred to hereafter as Pilgrim *Letters*).

7. Maximilian Rudwin, *The Devil in Legend and Literature* (1931; rpt., LaSalle, Ill.: The Open Court Publishing Co., 1959), p. 32.

8. *Bleak House*, ed. George Ford and Sylvère Monod (New York: W. W. Norton and Co., Inc., 1977), ch. xi, p. 129. Subsequent references to this edition will be given parenthetically within the text, showing the chapter number followed by the page number.

9. *The Political History of the Devil*, Vol. X of *The Novels and Miscellaneous Works of Daniel Defoe* (1840; rpt., New York: AMS Press, 1973), p. 17. Subsequent references to this edition will be given parenthetically within the text, showing Defoe's name followed by the page number, unless otherwise indicated.

10. *Paradise Lost*, Book I, line 86 and Book IV, lines 850 and 870. All subsequent references to *Paradise Lost* will be given parenthetically within the text, showing the initial *PL* followed by the Book number and then the line number.

11. Rudwin, p. 138.

12. Rudwin, pp. 225-226.

13. Quirk, especially 531-532, demonstrates this motivation effectively.

14. Rudwin, pp. 266-269.

15. There were by mid-century various stage versions of the legend, both dramatic and musical. See *BMC*, "Faust (Johann), Dr.," subheading "Dramatization." See Pilgrim *Letters*, ed. Madeline House and Graham Storey (Oxford: The Clarendon Press, 1969), II, 334, and note, for Dickens' plans to see such a dramatization, William Leman Rede's *The Devil and Dr. Faustus*. Rede's version (Cumberland's British Theater, No. 367) turns the legend into an undistinguished melodrama.

16. To identify Dickens' editions of these works as well as of Defoe's *Political History of the Devil* and of *Paradise Lost* owned in 1844, see the inventory of books made in 1844, in Pilgrim *Letters*, ed. Kathleen Tillotson, IV, 711-726. To identify editions of these works owned at the time of his death, see J. H. Stonehouse, ed., *Catologue of the Library of Dickens from Gadshill* (Picadilly: Fountain Press, 1935). These lists do not show an edition of Marlowe's or Goethe's drama. Both show an edition of R. H. Horne's verse drama *The Death of Marlowe* (n. p., 1839). *German Novelists*, edited by Thomas Roscoe (London: H. Colburn, 1826), included in both lists, contained in Vol. I a German folk version, "Doctor Faustus," translated by Roscoe.

17. See *The Faerie Queene*, Book one, Canto iv, especially stanzas 4 and 14, for similarities in imagery.

18. E. M. Smeed, *The Fortunes of Faust* (Cambridge: Cambridge University Press, 1952), pp. 9, 20.

19. J. W. Smeed, *Faust in Literature* (New York: Oxford University Press, 1975), pp. 262-271.

20. One translation was by "A. E. I.," the other by "H. N. S." I used the latter (London: H. G. Clarke and Co., 1844).

21. Edgar Johnson, II, 765, assumes that Honoria had refused Hawdon because she was ambitious for aristocratic rank. I find no reason to assume this, while the passage that I am citing does give reason to assume his desertion of Honoria.

22. Thurley (note 2 above), p. 109, defines the quality of Richard's pride when he comments that it is "the refusal to take life as it is, without special privilege, that destroys Richard Carstone."

23. *The Faerie Queene*, Book One, Canto VIII. stanzas 38-43.

Robert Godwin-Jones (essay date 1983)

SOURCE: "Where the Devil Leads: Peasant Superstitions in George Sand's *Petite Fadette* and Droste-Hülshoff's *Judenbuche*," in *Neohelicon*, Vol. 10, No. 1, 1983, pp. 221-38.

[*In the following essay, Godwin-Jones details peasant superstitions related to the Devil in representative works by George Sand and Annette von Droste-Hülshoff.*]

Both George Sand and Annette von Droste-Hülshoff belonged to aristocratic families who owned landed estates. Each spent the majority of her youth in the country and remained firmly attached to the particular region in which she was brought up, Sand in Berry, Droste in Westphalia. Both women ultimately rejected the lure of the cities, the centers of literary culture, preferring to reside at their country estates. This love of their native regions is reflected in the best-known works of each woman. Yet the reflection in each case is radically different. This is a result of diametrically opposed intellectual backgrounds and socio-political beliefs.

Sand, an ardent admirer of Rousseau, was essentially a child of the Enlightenment. She believed in the natural goodness of man and placed great faith in the efficacy of human reason. Sand was very much influenced by the utopian socialism popular in France in the first half of the century.[1] Like her mentor, Pierre Leroux, Sand believed in the coming of a future golden age in which all property would be collectively owned and where absolute equality would reign. She saw her fiction as a means of working towards this dream.[2] Indeed, Sand went further than just writing about social solidarity. When the 1848 revolution broke out, Sand went to Paris to help the revolutionaries, going so far as to call for the use of force if the national elections did not return a majority of socialists.[3]

Droste's intellectual roots lie in German romanticism. Like the Romantics, Droste rejected the notion that the world can be logically explained and human actions rationally guided. As is typical of writers of late Romanticism, Droste was a firm conservative in her social and political views and emphatically rejected the abolition of the class structure. Her letters as well as her poetry offer an explicit statement of this view.[4] Droste felt that all literature should have "einen klar bettimmten religiösen Nutzen".[5] The serious moral message Droste felt her writing should incorporate was all the more important in an age which, she believed, lay "unter einem schweren Fluch."[6] Droste saw the future with considerable apprehension; she felt she was living in an increasingly irresponsible and menacing world.

These contrasting intellectual backgrounds resulted in a very different treatment of one important aspect of both writers' fiction, the portrayal of peasant superstitions.[7] In two of their works superstitions and supernatural occurrences play a major role in shaping the narrative structure and in determining the direction in which the protagonist develops. These are *La petite Fadette* (1848), the third in the series of short novels Sand grouped together under the title *Les Veillées du chanvreur,* and *Die Judenbuche* (1842), Droste's best-known work and one of the outstanding examples of the nineteenth-century novella. A comparative study of this one aspect of the two works yields important insights into the ways in which the two women integrated aspects of peasant culture into their fiction. At the same time, the different role which superstition plays in their two works points to fundamental aspects of the author's opposing social and political beliefs.

I

Sand's *Petite Fadette* is narrated by a peasant, a fact which plays a determining role in the way superstitions are portrayed in the novel. The narrator, himself an organic part of the peasant culture he is depicting, accepts without question many of the beliefs whose validity an outsider would doubt. Thus the faith in the village wise women—at once midwives, healers and soothsayers—is presented as a matter of course. These figures, la mère Fadet, la mère Sagette and la Baigneuse de Clavières, play a major role in shaping the peasant's tale; their prophecies provide the basic thematic structure of the novel, namely the development of the Barbeau twins' relationship to each other and to Fadette. That Sylvinet falls in love with Fadette, for example, is a fulfillment of a prophecy of la Baigneuse de Clavières. La Baigneuse also predicts that Sylvinet will only ever love this one woman, a prophecy which is also fulfilled.

Other of the wise women's prophecies, however, do not prove as accurate. Central to the unfolding of the plot, for example, is the curse which, according to la mère Sagette, hangs over the lives of all twins. Twice this superstition, that one twin must perish for the other to thrive, seems on the verge of fulfillment by Sylvinet's death. Sylvinet becomes critically ill after his twin has fallen in love with Fadette. Yet with the help of Fadette's healing powers, he eventually recovers. Once again, near the end of the novel, Sylvinet appears to be sacrificing himself for Landry's welfare when he becomes a soldier, hoping for death in battle rather than the fate of loving the same woman as his brother. Yet, contrary to the dictates of the curse, Sylvinet lives to become a high-ranking army officer while Landry prospers as a farmer. The course of events seems at first to confirm the wise woman's prophecy yet, ultimately, that prediction is proven wrong. That Sand has her narrator tell his tale in such a way that the prophecy seems about to be fulfilled is natural due to the peasant narrator's own belief in the village soothsayers and their superstitions. At the same time, the sudden turn of events which disproves the superstition provides for a dramatic effect.[8]

The ambiguity in the portrayal of the wise women's prophecies is echoed in that of the supernatural occurrences evoked in the novel, most notably in the important events surrounding the "feu follet" (will-o'-the wisp). In its initial appearance, as Landry is trying to make his way over a stream, the light is presented in a manner which leaves no doubt as to its supernatural character: "C'était vraiment une vilaine chose à voir. Tantôt il [le feu follet] filait comme un martin-pêcheur, et tantôt il disparaissait tout à fait. Et, d'autres fois, il devenait gros comme la tête d'un bœuf, et tout aussitôt menu comme un œil de chat; et il accourait auprès de Landry, tournait autour de lui si vite, qu'il en était ébloui."[9] The narrator views the light as a mysterious and evil phenomenon, intent on pursuing any chance passerby. This is, he tells us, common knowledge: "On sait qu'il [le follet] s'obstine à courir après ceux qui courent et qu'il se met en travers de leur chemin jusqu'à ce qu'il les ait rendus fous et fait tomber dans quelque mauvaise passe" (p. 107). Yet at the end of this episode, the narrator offers a quite different explanation of the strange light: "Comme ils [Landry et Fadette] marchaient vite tous les deux et qu'ils ouvraient un courant d'air au feu follet, ils étaient toujours suivis de ce météore, comme l'appelle le maître d'école de chez nous, qui en sait long sur cette chose-là, et qui assure qu'on n'en doit avoir nulle crainte" (p. 109). Here we encounter a rational explanation for what had seemed a supernatural occurrence, offered, it should be noted, only when the episode is over and attributed to the local schoolmaster, someone outside the peasant community.

Sand initially wants the reader to believe that the will-o'-the-wisp is unearthly and inexplicable. It is important for the development of the episode that we suspend our disbelief, since this reading of the episode spotlights all the more dramatically Fadette's apparent connection with the supernatural world. Yet once the will-o'-the-wisp has served its purpose, Sand changes our perspective on the scene, interjecting the schoolmaster's rational view of the strange play of lights. This kind of sudden turnabout is an important element in Sand's fictional strategy, and of course the eventual rational explanation is in keeping with Sand's faith in reason as the only true means of perceiving reality.

In contrast to Sand's peasant narrator, Droste's *Judenbuche* is written in impersonal third-person narration. The narrator makes every effort to distance himself from the story he is telling, claiming at several points that he is retelling a true story without any additions or assumptions on his part. He is careful not to reveal any more than an outside observer could have witnessed and refrains from interpreting the events he chronicles. Indeed, he goes so far as to withhold the solution of the murder of Brandes the forester, since, he explains, the courts were never able to determine the murderer's identity. Sensing the disappointment of the reader in not discovering the solution of the case, which had been discussed at considerable length in the text, the narrator justifies himself by calling attention to his devotion to accurate reporting: "Es würde in einer erdichteten Geschichte unrecht sein, die Neugier des Lesers so zu täuschen. Aber dies hat sich wirklich zugetragen; ich kann nichts davon oder dazu tun."[10] The narrator's refusal to give clear-cut answers to some of the crucial questions in *Die Judenbuche* has led to a great deal of

speculation by critics as to what actually does happen in the story and how the reader should fill in the missing information.[11]

In his depiction of peasant superstitions, the narrator, in keeping with his desire for objectivity, is careful to avoid any comment on their validity. The reports of old Mergel's resurrection as a ghost, for example, are related in a matter-of-fact tone with no attempts at rationalizing the apparitions: "Der alte Mergel war das Gespenst des Brederholzes geworden; einen Betrunkenen führte er als Irrlicht bei einem Haar in den Zellerklok (Teich); die Hirtenknaben, wenn sie nachts bei ihren Feuern kauerten und die Eulen in den Gründen schrien, hörten zuweilen in abgebrochenen Tönen ganz deutlich dazwischen sein 'Hör mal an, feins Liseken', und ein unprivilegierter Holzbauer, der unter der breiten Eiche eingeschlafen und dem es darüber Nacht geworden war, hatte beim Erwachen sein geschwollenes blaues Gesicht durch die Zweige lauschen sehen" (p. 890). No explanation for these events is ever offered by the narrator. A later apparent manifestation of Mergel's spirit is found to be false, but is, in itself, a portent of evil: the noise of beating sticks and the cry of pain thought by Herr von S.'s servants to be the ghost, were in reality the sounds of the murder of Aaron, the moneylender.

The objective narrative stance of *Die Judenbuche* is a crucial element in the treatment of the most important nonrational occurrence in the work, that surrounding the "Judenbuche." The Jews, frustrated in their efforts to find Aaron's murderer, buy the beech tree under which the murder was committed and carve into it an inscription in Hebrew. The meaning of the inscription is not divulged until twenty-eight years later when a man identified as Friedrich Mergel is found hanged in the tree, apparently a victim of suicide. After the dead man has been identified, the narrator concludes the novella with these words: "Dies hat sich nach allen Hauptumständen wirklich so begeben im September des Jahres 1789. Die hebräische Schrift an dem Baum heisst: 'Wenn du dich diesem Orte nahest, so wird es dir ergehen, wie du mir getan hast'" (p. 936). Thus the narrator makes no comment on the apparent fulfillment of the curse, claiming simply to have told a true story.

Due to the narrator's insistence on revealing only externally observable events, many questions remain at the end of the novella. Was the man who is found hanging in the tree Friedrich Mergel, as Herr von S. says, or is he Johannes Niemand as he himself had claimed? What was it that drew the victim to the beech tree? Was it simply remorse, or some hidden power emanating from the Jews' inscription? Droste's refusal to offer any rational explanation for the unusual chain of events invites the reader to view them as occurrences which defy logic and reason. In the absence of any more rational explanation, and in light of the prominence of the Hebrew curse in the concluding line of the novella, it seems justified to assume that the victim was Friedrich and that his fate was somehow connected to the inscription cut into the tree.[12]

In *Die Judenbuche,* as demonstrated by Friedrich's death, events beyond the pale of reason determine the direction in which the plot is resolved. The "Judenbuche" along with the other unexplained events in the story exert a powerful influence on the lives of the characters and thereby provide the essential framework of the novella. In *La petite Fadette,* too, superstitions, especially in the form of the wise women's prophecies, seem to provide the basic structure of the narrative. Yet in Sand's novel, this is not carried through consistently. Some of the prophecies are fulfilled, while others are "red herrings", false leads which the author later exploits for melodramatic effect.

Supernatural occurrences in *Die Judenbuche* are not rationalized away. The narrator does not offer any coherent, logical perspective from which to view, for example, the irrational events surrounding the "Judenbuche". In *La petite Fadette,* on the other hand, the reader is given alternative ways of perceiving the seemingly supernatural events. The reader's perspective on the will-o'-the-wisp, for instance, ranges from the narrator's and the peasant community's unquestioned belief in its supernatural character to the school teacher's conviction that it is a natural phenomenon, scientifically explainable. Whereas a degree of uncertainty and confusion is present in Droste's narrative due to the sparsity of information the narrator makes available to the reader, doubt and ambiguity are present in Sand's novel due to an overabundance of information. Our lack of knowledge in *Die Judenbuche* makes the course of events seem all the more inexplicable while the different angles from which the bizarre occurrences are illuminated in *La petite Fadette* show the reader, at least after the fact, that they need not be considered supernatural. This contrasting illumination of supernatural events is a clear reflection of Sand and Droste's opposing *Weltanschauungen*. For Sand, the world is capable of being rationally explained; we need only penetrate beyond the deceptive outward manifestations of reality. For Droste, there is no possibility of arriving at an understanding of truth; all that results from our efforts to do so is chaos and confusion.

II

In both works, the protagonist undergoes a considerable transformation in the course of the narrative. In each case these changes are directly related to beliefs concerning the devil. From her first appearance in Sand's novel, Fadette is depicted as a sorceress who derives her powers from Satan. Upon their initial meeting in the novel, Fadette knows without being told that Landry is looking for his brother. During this meeting she appears to conjure up a storm, which suddenly appears overhead, as if on command; the narrator comments: "[Landry] ne s'était avisé de l'orage qu'au moment où la petite Fadette lui avait annoncé; et tout aussitôt, son jupon s'était enflé; ses vilains cheveux noirs sortant de sa coiffe, qu'elle avait toujours mal attachée, et quintant sur son oreille, s'étaient dressés comme des crins" (p. 80). With her black hair standing on end and her skirt puffed out by the wind, Fadette projects the image of a witch. The narrator seems to concur with this view when he comments, after Landry has found Sylvinet through Fadette's help: "Landry fut si aise qu'il

commença par remercier le bon Dieu dans son cœur, sans songer à lui demander pardon d'avoir eu recours à la science du diable pour avoir ce bonheur-là" (p. 83). A similar tone is struck later when Fadette once again helps Landry with her mysterious powers when he is confronted by the will-'o-the-wisp while trying to cross a stream: "Landry n'était guère plus à son aise dans la société de la petite sorcière que dans celle du follet. Cependant, comme il aimait mieux voir le diable sous l'apparence d'un être de sa propre espèce que sous celle d'un feu si sournois et si fugace, il ne fit pas de résistance" (p. 108). Landry is not alone in his view of Fadette; everyone in the village is in agreement that she is in league with the Evil One. They are quick to find, for example, the reason for Fadette's attendance at church: it is simply a ploy "pour mieux cacher son jeu avec le diable" (p. 124). Again and again in the novel, Fadette is depicted as a sorceress, a witch, a disciple of the devil.

Yet by the end of the novel, Fadette has undergone a startling transformation. From an ugly and dirty mischief-maker, she becomes a well-behaved and beautiful young lady. Even more surprising than the change in her appearance and behavior is the sudden turnabout in her character. Through Landry's conversation with Fadette it becomes clear that she is not in consort with the devil, but is simply a victim of social prejudice and has at times gone along with the image of sorceress in order to wreak revenge for the suffering others have inflicted on her. Rather than being an incarnation of evil, Fadette turns out to be among the most pious of the villagers. She instructs Landry in the meaning of prayer, stays longer after church to say additional prayers and is called "une parfaite chrétienne" (p. 238) by a nun whom Fadette helps in aiding the poor and infirm. Fadette may even be, as Landry says, "trop chrétien" (p. 186), for in explaining her Christianity and in disclaiming any supernatural powers, she goes so far as to deny the very existence of the devil: "Il n'y qu'un esprit et il est bon, car c'est celui de Dieu. Lucifer est de l'invention de monsieur le curé" (p. 185). Fadette is transformed before the reader's eyes from a worshiper of Satan into an incarnation of goodness and piety. Indeed, when she cures Sylvinet near the end of the novel, she addresses him in terms reminiscent of those of Christ: "Je vas sortir, et vous vous lèverez, Sylvain, car vous n'avez plus la fièvre" (p. 263). Sylvinet is instantly able to rise and is henceforth cured of his illness.

The transformation of Fadette is signaled in the text by a change in the use and the meaning of the word "diable". Until Landry falls in love with her and begins to see her true character, the word is used literally in reference to Fadette, indicating her intimate knowledge of the Satanic arts. After Landry first kisses Fadette, however, he thinks of her afterwards as "cette diablesse" (p. 152), used here not as a description of her diabolical nature, but as a term of endearment. When Fadette and Landry meet for their secret rendez-vous in a deserted pigeon house, the narrator comments: "le diable eût été fin s'il eût été surprendre là les entretiens de ces jeunes amoureux" (p. 193). The devil is no longer associated with Fadette, but is viewed as an intrusive, outside party. When Fadette is said to have, in her conversation with le père Barbeau near the end of the novel, "un esprit du diable" (p. 233), the term devil has lost its connotation as the embodiment of evil and has come simply to refer to a charmingly mischievous person.

In order for Fadette's transformation not to appear completely unexpected and arbitrary, the narrator had been careful all along to offer alternative ways of viewing Fadette's apparently devilish acts. Fadette's reading of Landry's mind when he is searching for Sylvinet could be explained, he says, by Fadette having overheard Landry ask her mother for information concerning his brother's whereabouts. That a storm suddenly appears as if by Fadette's command could be explained, the narrator tells us, by the fact that Landry was searching so intently for his brother that he was unaware of the gradual and natural approach of the storm. Fadette's supernatural healing powers the narrator, after her transformation, explains as a natural gift of God: "[Fadette] découvrait et devinait, comme qui invente, les vertus que le bon Dieu a mises dans certaines herbes et dans certaines manières de les employer. Elle n'était point sorcière pour cela, elle avait raison de s'en défendre; mais elle avait l'esprit qui observe, qui fait des comparaisons, des remarques, des essais, et cela c'est un don de la nature, on ne peut pas le nier" (pp. 189-90). Nature is in Sand's novel not a diabolical force used by Fadette to harm her enemies, but rather a force for good, particularly if wielded by someone, like Fadette, possessing a special sympathy with nature.

Fadette does not undergo so much a change in character as she does a demystification. Her initial appearance in the novel as a sorceress was deceptive; she was using her "witchcraft" as a mask. Friedrich Mergel, in *Die Judenbuche,* does on the other hand undergo a change in character. His transformation, in contrast to that of Fadette, is from good to evil, from innocence to guilt. The unveiling of the true Fadette was brought about through the influence of Landry's love. Friedrich's corruption is accomplished primarily through the pernicious influence of his uncle, a surrogate Satan.

Friedrich, in his boyhood role as shepherd, exudes an aura of pastoral innocence, simplicity and Christian virtue. When he is nine, however, a dramatic event transforms his dreamy piety into what, as other critics have shown, becomes an important aspect of his world view, namely the fear of the devil.[13] When his father does not return from a wedding celebration one winter's evening, Friedrich and his mother retire to bed and bolt the door. Yet Friedrich thinks he hears a knocking on the door and asks his mother what would happen if his father were to come home; thereupon the following exchange ensues: "'Den hält der Teufel fest genug!'—'Wo ist der Teufel, Mutter?'—'Wart, du Unrast! er steht vor der Tür und will dich holen, wenn du nicht ruhig bist!'" (p. 887). The mother's reference to the devil is of course simply an attempt to frighten Friedrich into silence. Yet for Friedrich, this conversation becomes indelibly stamped on his mind, for just as "Friedrich dachte an den Teufel, wie der wohl aussehen möge" (p. 888), people from the village arrive at the cabin, telling his mother that her husband has been found dead in the "Brederholz."

As if in answer to Friedrich's day-dreaming about the appearance of the devil, the next episode in the novella introduces Friedrich's demonic uncle: "Simon Semmler war ein kleiner, unruhiger, magerer Mann mit vor dem Kopf liegenden Fischaugen und überhaupt einem Gesicht wie ein Hecht, ein unheimlicher Geselle . . . der gern einen aufgeklärten Kopf vorgestellt hätte und statt dessen für einen fatalen, Händel suchenden Kerl galt" (pp. 890-91). In addition to his sinister looks and character, Simon also has fiery red hair and when he walks away with Friedrich, the tail of his red coat follows after him "wie Feuerflammen" (p. 893). The depiction of Simon as an incarnation of Satan, together with Friedrich's terrified fascination with the devil, assure Simon a strong influence over his nephew.

Initially, Friedrich and Simon, both in appearance and character, are worlds apart. Yet there is a strong bond between uncle and nephew, strengthened by Friedrich's almost hypnotic obedience to Simon. From the beginning, there are hints that their family tie will grow into a stronger, and more sinister, relationship: "So hatte er [Simon] ziemlich das Aussehen eines feurigen Mannes, der unter dem gestohlenen Sacke büsst; Friedrich ihm nach, fein und schlank für sein Alter, mit zarten, fast edlen Zügen . . . Dennoch war eine grosse Familienähnlichkeit beider nicht zu verkennen, und wie Friedrich so langsam seinen Führer nachtrat, die Blicke fest auf denselben geheftet, der ihm gerade durch das Seltsame seiner Erscheinung anzog, erinnerte er unwillkürlich an jemand, der in einem Zauberspiegel das Bild seiner Zukunft mit verstörter Aufmerksamkeit betrachtet" (p. 893). The contrast between the two, despite the family resemblance, is at this point striking—Simon with his distorted features and look of a hardened criminal and Friedrich with his gentle, almost noble appearance and quiet melancholy. And yet in looking at the two, one has the impression of seeing the same person at different stages in his life, thus foreshadowing the transformation Friedrich will undergo and the direction in which he develops.

Simon, true to his role as a devilish corruptor, in his first conversation alone with Friedrich quizzes the boy on his religious practices and expresses satisfaction upon hearing that Friedrich does not like to pray. In this same conversation Simon uses terror to assure his control over Friedrich. He shows the boy the tree under which his father was found dead, saying "hier haben Ohm Franz und der Hülsmeyer deinen Vater gefunden, als er in der Betrunkenheit ohne Busse und Ölung zum Teufel gefahren war" (p. 895). Simon's references to the devil and to the absurdity of Christian practices, added to his uncanny appearance, cause him to take on more and more in Friedrich's eyes a Satanic aura and serve to maintain his despotic control over the boy.

Under the influence of his uncle, Friedrich undergoes a great change in character: He loses his dreaminess, and begins to pay more attention to what others think of him. In the process, he becomes proud and vain. Simon's influence is particularly great in determining the moral and ethical regression in Friedrich. This is above all evident in one central episode. Friedrich suspects Simon of complicity in the murder of Brandes and intends early one Sunday to slip out of Simon's house to go confess to the village priest. Just as Friedrich is about to leave, Simon appears. His sudden appearance seems uncanny: "Er [Friedrich] warf die Augen umher und fuhr zusammen; in der Kammertür stand Simon, fast ungekleidet; seine dürre Gestalt, sein ungekämmtes, wirres Haar und die vom Mondschein verursachte Blässe des Gesichts gaben ihm ein schauerlich verändertes Aussehen" (p. 912). This mysterious appearance, as if Simon had suddenly been conjured up from the bowels of the earth, causes Friedrich to freeze with terror. Simon is able to dissuade Friedrich from going to confession, thus leading him further down the path of perdition.

From this and other incidents, it is clear that Simon is intent on corrupting Friedrich: "Wer zweifelt daran, dass Simon alles tat, seinen Adoptivsohn dieselben Wege zu leisten, die er selber ging. Und in Friedrich lagen Eigenschaften, die dies nur zu sehr erleichterten" (p. 913). Simon is only too successful: Friedrich turns wild and irresponsible and neglects his mother completely. His appearance now contrasts sharply with his character: "Er war äusserlich ordentlich, nüchtern, anscheinend treuherzig, aber listig, prahlerisch und oft ein Mensch, an dem niemand Freude haben konnte, am wenigstens seine Mutter, und der dennoch durch seine gefürchtete Tücke ein gewisses Übergewicht im Dorfe erlangt hatte" (p. 914). He comes to resemble his evil uncle more and more and when at a wedding dance Friedrich's head bobs up and down "wie ein Hecht" (p. 916), the same comparison which was originally used to describe Simon's appearance, it is a signal that the transformation has been completed. Soon afterwards Friedrich apparently kills the Jewish moneylender, thus following in the footsteps of his uncle who was at least partially responsible for the murder of Brandes.

Beliefs surrounding the devil play a major role in determining the character of both Fadette and Friedrich Mergel, yet they develop in diametrically-opposed directions. It is simply social prejudice which causes Fadette to be viewed as a sorceress and this misconception is dispelled upon a more enlightened examination of her character. In Sand's novel, superstition is overcome by reason. In *Die Judenbuche,* on the other hand, supernatural occurrences are never rationally explained; the devil, working through Simon, and the curse of the Jews seem to determine Friedrich's final fate. Here, superstition proves stronger than reason. The opposing directions in which the superstitions and the supernatural events of the two works point are a reflection of the wide gulf separating the utopian socialist Sand and the late romantic Droste. For Sand, reason was a positive force for change. In her desire to show the way to a new, classless society, Sand was intent on demonstrating the injustice of social prejudice. She believed that in portraying sympathetically a figure from a low social stratum who is exposed to blatantly unjust treatment by those above her socially and economically, the reader's own sense of justice would awaken in him a feeling of solidarity with the downtrodden in society.[14] Droste, on the other hand, was very distrustful of the individual's reliance in his own powers of reasoning. As demonstrated in *Die Judenbuche,* logic and rational analysis cannot explain how human lives are structured. In Droste's view, the world was traveling down the path to perdition because of an overreliance on human sagacity and on man's ability to control his own destiny.

III

In Sand's novel, the major superstitious belief, that involving Fadette as a sorceress, is false. Not only is Fadette not associated with the devil, the very existence of the devil is denied. This is in keeping with Sand's own belief that Satan did not exist.[15] That Fadette, who closely imitates in her actions the life of Christ, is taken for a witch, is a comment on the blindness and injustice of the author's age. In Droste's work, however, the reader is left in doubt concerning the reality of the supernatural events in the story. This confusion mirrors Droste's own religious uncertainty. Although, in contrast to Sand, an orthodox Catholic, she nonetheless underwent serious religious doubts, evidenced above all in her poetry.[16] Whether or not Droste herself was convinced of the existence of Satan, it is clear in *Die Judenbuche* that some evil power is at work. Simon's association with the devil is never discounted and his evil influence over Friedrich is only too real.

In *Die Judenbuche,* evil lurks everywhere. Nature itself is hostile to man, as demonstrated by the "Brederholz" and the "Judenbuche", both of which are connected in a causal way with the deaths of several characters. This is far removed from the positive role nature plays in *La petite Fadette.* The forest, for example, both provides a *locus amoenus* for Landry and Fadette, and supplies the materials which Fadette uses for her healing potions. Rather than being a place of evil and death, the woods for Sand's characters represent a life-giving force.

In *La petite Fadette* and *Die Judenbuche* the narrative stance used relieves the author of the necessity of commenting directly on the inexplicable occurrences she portrays. The limited vision of the two narrators permits their respective authors to remain in the background. The reader is more likely to accept the major role superstitions and supernatural events play in each novel, and to suspend his disbelief, if the stories are told in a way which bypasses a discussion of their validity. It is natural for Sand's peasant narrator not to question the truth of the beliefs he shares, and Droste's chronicler is too concerned with giving an exact rendition of the story as he knows it to deny the validity of the seemingly supernatural occurrences. If the reader sensed in the narrative the presence of the author, in each case a highly-educated and sophisticated noble-woman, he would be less willing to accept the superstition as anything more than local color; he would have to expect that at some point the author would clearly demonstrate the falsity of the peasants' beliefs. It is only through the use of an objective, distanced type of narrative that Sand and Droste are able to allow superstition to play a major role in their works.

At the same time, this kind of narration was necessary in order to allow superstitions to play the kind of pivotal role they do in *Die Judenbuche* and *La petite Fadette*. Sand's novel had to be narrated by a peasant in order for the belief in peasant superstitions to be convincing. The peasant narrator conveys his own faith in the peasant superstitions to the reader. It is essential to Sand's narrative strategy that the reader accept the superstitions and supernatural events, at least at first, at face value. This is particularly true in the case of Fadette's characterization as a sorceress; in her initial depiction of Fadette, Sand is setting up the reader for the dramatic reversal to come later in the novel. In this way, Sand hoped, the reader would, upon seeing Fadette's true nature, be shocked into a recognition of his prejudiced view towards the whole social class which Fadette represents.

Droste, on the other hand, did not want to have the superstitions or the diabolical nature of her characters explained away. This might well have happened with a narrator who, as the reader might reasonably expect, offered his own comments and interpretations of the unusual course of events in the novella. Droste's narrator does not give a natural, logical explanation for the mysterious occurrences or unsolved murders, and the ambiguity and doubt which result invite the reader to accept the possibility that the superstitions portrayed hold at least some measure of validity. This serves to underscore Droste's attack on the individual's faith in reason as a guide to understanding human existence.

Although they differ greatly in the role which they assign peasant superstitions, both Sand and Droste grant them a central place in their works. For each woman, these traditional beliefs offered a way of incorporating her own social and political convictions into her fiction without seeming to preach to the reader. At the same time, the broad role given superstitious beliefs and supernatural occurrences in *La petite Fadette* and *Die Judenbuche* was the essential factor in determining the narrative strategy and character portrayal of the two works. Thus the two women used the same framework on which to construct their fiction. Yet due to their divergent views on social change, this resulted in two works which in their fundamental message point in diametrically opposed directions.

Notes

1. For a treatment of the social and political views of George Sand see Lucien Buis, *Les Théories sociales de George Sand* (Paris: A. Pedone, 1910); Jean Lar-nac, *George Sand Revolutionnaire* (Paris: Editions Hier et Aujourd'hui, 1947); David Owen Evans, *Social Romanticism in France, 1830-1848* (Oxford: Oxford University Press, 1951).

2. See prefaces to her rustic and socialist novels and also her letters, notably her profession of faith to Leroux in a letter to Charles Poncy in her *Correspondance* (Paris: Garnier, 1969,) VI, 68.

3. For a complete discussion of Sand's role in the 1848 revolution, see Larnac's study.

4. See for example, such poems as "Halt fest," "Mein Beruf" and "Instinkt." For a discussion of Droste's social, political and philosophical beliefs, see Dominique Iehl, *Le Monde religieux et poétique d'Annette von Droste-Hülshoff* (Paris: Marcel Didier, 1965); Ronald Schneider, *Annette von Droste-Hülshoff* (Stuttgart: Metzler, 1977) and Walter Silz, "Problems of 'Weltanschauung' in the Works of Annette von Droste Hülshoff," *PMLA* [*Publications. Modern Language Association of America*], 64 (1949), pp. 678-700.

5. Cited in Schneider, p. 15.

6. *Die Briefe von Annette von Droste-Hülshoff* (Jena: Eugen Diederich, 1944), ed. Karl Kemminghausen, II, 448.

7. Superstitions play an important role in Sand's *La Mare au Diable* (1845) and *Jeanne* (1844) and in Droste's *Bilder aus Westfalen* (1848), which contains a regular catalogue of Westphalian peasant superstitions.

8. Sand made frequent use of such melodramatic reversals; see in particular *Le Meunier d'Angibault* (1845) and *Le Compagnon du tour de France* (1840).

9. George Sand, *La petite Fadette* (Paris: Garnier, 1958), ed. Pierre Salomon and Jean Mallion, p. 106. All Sand citations are from this edition.

10. Annette von Droste-Hülshoff, *Sämtliche Werke* (München: Carl Hanser Verlag, 1966), p. 912. All Droste citations are from this edition.

11. See, for example, James McGlathery's survey of critical interpretations in "Fear of Perdition in Droste-Hülshoff's *Judenbuche*." *Lebendige Form. Interpretationen zur deutschen Literatur* (München: Wilhelm Fink Verlag, 1970), pp. 229-30.

12. To idenfify the victim as Johannes Niemand, as some critics have done, is an improbable solution due to his minor role in the story. The principal theme of the work is the gradual degeneration of Friedrich, who is unquestionably the central focus of attention throughout the novella. The idea that Friedrich would commit murder is consistent with his pattern of development up to that point. Moreover, we have no reason to doubt Herr von S. when he identifies the victim as Friedrich, since the rich landowner has previously proven himself to be a paragon of reason and good sense.

13. See McGlathery's essay.

14. For more on Sand's views on this question see Robert Godwin-Jones, "The Representation of Economic Reality in George Sand's Rural Novels," *Studies in the Literary Imagination,* 12, No. 2 (1979) pp. 58-60.

15. See Sand, p. XVIII.

16. See Heinrich Henel, "Annette von Droste-Hülshoff: Erzählstil und Wirklichkeit." *Festschrift für Bernhard Blume,* ed. Egon Schwarz et al. (Göttingen: Vandenhoeck und Ruprecht, 1967), pp. 165-67.

Kevin Corrigan (essay date 1986)

SOURCE: "Ivan's Devil in *The Brothers Karamazov* in the Light of a Traditional Platonic View of Evil," in *Forum for Modern Language Studies,* Vol. XXII, No. 1, January, 1986, pp. 1-9.

[*In the following essay, Corrigan highlights parallels between the devil of Ivan's dream in Feodor Dostoevsky's* The Brothers Karamazov *and Plato's philosophical conception of evil.*]

In striking contrast to the dramatic power of the Mephistopheles of Goethe or Marlowe and the Satan of Milton or Dante is the devil who appears to Ivan Karamazov. On the threshold of the twentieth century, the devil is depicted as a down-at-heel gentleman, a sponger, a shirker, agreeable enough, but really a bore and a rascal. He would appear, therefore, to be the very antithesis of our conceptions of demonic power. Furthermore, a central dilemma of both the introductory portrayal and the conversation, a dilemma which is never resolved, is the status of the devil's existence: is he the creation of Ivan's sickness, a mere figment of the imagination? Is he ultimately Ivan himself? It might seem to the inattentive reader that not only is Dostoevsky's devil a very undramatic, pedantic bore who adds little or nothing to the novel or to our understanding of Ivan, but also from the logic of the passage he has no real existence, since he is simply a part of Ivan's hallucination.[1] Such a reading would be terribly mistaken. But it is also a mistake to think that this portrayal of the devil lacks its own dramatic power or that it is the antithesis of traditional views of evil. In this article I shall argue that Ivan's devil is the more powerful because Dostoevsky, consciously or unconsciously, includes fundamental elements of a traditional view of evil which originates in Plato, is developed in later Platonism, notably that of Plotinus (third century A.D.), and from there passes to St Augustine. In this tradition evil is non-being, yet it possesses a terrible subreality of its own. Dostoevsky's knowledge of Plato could have come from two different sources. Grossman's catalogue of Dostoevsky's library reveals that he possessed at least two books on Plato, one of which was a close account of the Platonic dialogues.[2] Moreover, it is known that Dostoevsky and Solovyev became friends in 1873 and that the

latter had a strong influence upon Dostoevsky's reworking of *The Brothers Karamazov.*[3] It is also known that in 1878 Dostoevsky attended Solovyev's lectures on God-Manhood which included a study of Plato and later Greek philosophy.[4] Some influence, therefore, is not altogether out of the question, whether from the pagan or the Christian sides of the tradition. However, I do not wish to press detailed correspondences so much as to present what seems to me to be a natural affinity between Dostoevsky and Plato because it helps to shed extra light upon many of the seemingly inconsequential details of this profound and powerful passage.

It must be made clear at the outset that Plato does not have a systematic theory of evil or of matter. Aristotle was the first to develop a concept of matter as such and Plotinus first identified matter and evil and explored the consequences of this. However, it can be said that for Plato[5] the material principle is both positive and negative. The material principle is the Receptacle of becoming, the room, or space, in which all things come to be.[6] On the other hand, it is only grasped by a "sort of bastard reasoning", it is a phantasm, a lie, an illusion, a dream, the image reflected in it clings to "existence on pain of not existing at all".[7] It is malleable, flexible, ready to assume any appearance, but it cannot itself be changed.[8] Furthermore, it is recalcitrant, the seat of the irrational and a kind of non-being.[9] In sum, it is the negative presence of something which does not properly exist as well as a necessary element in the composition of the visible universe.

In Dostoevsky's initial description[10] the devil is portrayed in terms of an opposition between appearance and reality, wealth and poverty: he appears at first to be what on closer inspection he is not. He is a gentleman,[11] but no longer young; he wears a brown coat, cut by a good tailor, but rather threadbare; his linen is such as is worn by smart gentlemen, but on closer inspection "rather dirty and the wide scarf very threadbare" etc. Like the Platonic Receptacle, the devil bears a semblance of reality which proves at a second glance to be without substance. The Receptacle is a principle of false appearance. One can never say of the things which appear in it that they *are,* for they have no permanent reality.

The devil is described as a "has-been" and as "behind the fashion", perhaps owing to poverty. There is the strong suspicion that he is merely dressing the part or dressed up for the occasion. Related to this is the fact that after being well-to-do, he is now a sponger (*prizival' šik*) who travels from house to house living off his friends. In Plato's *Symposium,* and in the later tradition, the material principle is characteristically viewed as poverty or as a beggar only able to live off the life of the reality above it; and since it remains unchanged by what is given to it, whatever clothing it puts on is only a show which proves on analysis to be extraneous to it.[12] Thus, even the fact that Dostoevsky's devil is behind the fashion indicates that he is behind, or below, form, a substratum to an appearance which is false. As a "has-been" (*byvšij*), he even falls below the level of time.

Dostoevsky next describes the devil as an agreeable character, a decent fellow in the specific sense that he is ready to assume any role (dinner, cards, etc.): "agreeable and ready to assume any amiable expression that occasion should demand" (*gotovaja, sudja po obstojatel' slvam, na vsjakoe ljubeznoe vyraženie*). But this is qualified in an important way. The reality of his agreeableness is not one of trust or liking, for he is "most decidedly averse from carrying out any commissions forced upon" him. These two features are perhaps the most salient features of the Platonic Receptacle: firstly, that it is ready to assume any and every appearance, and secondly, that it remains not only impervious to all the appearances it assumes, but actually resistant in some way to the power of the form upon it.[13]

Impassivity and recalcitrance are also suggested by the description of the devil as a solitary bachelor or widower, that is, the material principle either in itself or in its relation to creation. Matter, or Poverty, is traditionally solitary, one and the same despite all appearances. But even in his relation to other things the devil is destitute. On the hypothesis that he is a widower (i.e., that he has *lost* his wife), his children, *if* he has any, are brought up in "a faraway province" (*gde-to daleko*) by their aunts (i.e., as the only females of the passage, souls); and in his present company he is naturally ashamed of them. This distance between the devil and creation is further emphasised at the end of the description. The devil has no watch (i.e. time), but he does carry a lorgnette. He cannot come into direct contact with reality, but always requires some medium.

Two further points must be made. Firstly, the devil has evidently at one time been received in good and fashionable society and has once had good connections, which, Dostoevsky notes, he still preserves. Here the fall of Lucifer is, of course, suggested. But in the late Platonic tradition, a similar fall happens to matter. In Plotinus, matter, like Lucifer, is cast out of the spiritual world to become the eternal darkness of ultimate matter, which is below the level of the physical world.[14] In Plato the Receptacle is represented as existing before the generation of the physical world and Plato expresses how it maintains its old connections by saying that it now "partakes in some very puzzling way of the intelligible".[15]

Secondly, in the light of these correspondences it seems possible to press a few details of this passage a little further. Plato's Receptacle, like Ivan's devil is seen "as in a dream".[16] It is the *seat* of all becoming and in a famous simile it is likened to the gold out of which things are made.[17] In later Platonism matter-evil is the source of all weakness, moral and physical, the source of madness.[18]

Ivan's nightmare starts in his sickness, his delirium, and his attention is first delimited by the space of his own room: "sitting down, he began looking around him, as though trying to discern something" (p.745). Then it becomes fixed on one place, the *sofa*, a receptacle or seat, if ever there was, upon which the devil will materialise.[19] At the conclusion of the description, the devil's "massive gold ring" is given some prominence. The cheap opal stone set in it only serves to epitomise the essential poverty of the gaudy appearance.

It would seem, therefore, that the description of the devil as a down-at-heel gentleman and a hanger-on is (among other things) a profoundly apt and accurate transformation of the ancient pagan positive-negative material principle. According to this conception the devil is a *subordinate* evil. A certain "banality" must, therefore, attach to him. But in the subsequent conversation, although the devil retains his vulgarity to the end, we begin to realise more and more deeply the horror of what is actually happening.

What relation does the devil bear to Ivan? Is he a part of Ivan's imagination/sickness or is he independent? It is important to recognise that the devil is *both* dependent and independent, for this is where the horror of the situation resides.

A central dramatic pivot of the conversation is Ivan's belief/disbelief, which remains unresolved:

> "Confess you believe, well, a ten-thousandth part."
>
> "Not for a moment!" Ivan replied curiously. "I'd like to believe in you, though," he replied strangely.
>
> (p.759)

A psychological ambiguity is also preserved in the subsequent Alyosha scene, where Ivan *acts* as though he believes, then insists that the devil is only himself, but belies this identity by recounting to Alyosha, as the devil's words, words which we know the devil did not say.[20] What becomes clearer, as the episode proceeds, is that this unresolved opposition between belief and disbelief[21] is deliberate, for just as the devil cannot know that God exists,[22] since he falls below the level of such knowledge, so Ivan cannot believe in the devil *simpliciter*, since the devil is not an object of belief. He is a proper object neither of perception nor of belief, but the object of a diseased imagination or fantastic, dreamlike perception. This situation bears an affinity to the Platonic Receptacle which is expressly stated to be the object neither of perception nor of belief, but a fantastic semblance of reality, able to be grasped not by the mind as such, but only by a "sort of bastard reasoning".[23]

In Dostoevsky, therefore, we are locked from the start into a situation in which there is no possibility of any certainty, rest or resolution and which, in its devastatingly quiet and insistent way, bears all the marks of hell. Although the devil is non-being and from a level of "existence" lower than Ivan or Smerdyakov (the "*bastard*" brother); although he is dependent upon Ivan (i.e. he is "a lie, an illness, a phantasm"[24] [*ty Lož bolezn' moja, ty prizrak*] who enters through Ivan's sickness and repeats his thoughts), he is also independent, for he is a problem which cannot be resolved by Ivan himself or by anyone else. And when the devil says things which, it would seem, Ivan could not have known, whether or not this is in fact the case, the suggestion is made that the devil is not simply restricted to Ivan, but is ultimately of wider scope. At the same time, on the level of reality he is only Ivan's nightmare:

> "Though I'm your hallucination, yet, as in a nightmare, I say original things which had not entered your head before, so that I don't repeat your thoughts at all, and yet I'm only your nightmare and nothing more".

> (p.752)

The character of this independence-in-dependence emerges with greater force during the course of the conversation.

Firstly, the devil waits for Ivan to start the conversation, but it is he himself who actually initiates it:

> Ivan was resentfully silent and would not begin the conversation. His visitor waited and sat exactly like a hanger-on who had just come down from his room to keep his host company at tea, but who was discreetly silent in view of the fact that his host was preoccupied and thinking of something, knitting his brows; he was, however, ready to engage in any polite conversation as soon as his host began it. Suddenly a worried look passed over his face.
>
> "I say", he addressed Ivan, "just to remind you . . ."

> (pp.747-748)

This apparently trivial detail is important because it reveals that the devil is the actual *cause* of Ivan's full sinking to that level of non-reality. Similarly in Plato it is Poverty who initiates the proceedings; in Plotinus the soul is not evil in itself, but in its co-operation with the *initiating presence* of matter-evil the soul descends to matter and can become evil.[25] Here too, then, in Dostoevsky it is an important detail that the presence of the devil, and his access to a past event ("I say, just to remind you"), is the proximate cause of the conversation.

Secondly, the devil is a principle of false appearance and a dream or nightmare. Ivan thinks that during the conversation he wrapped a towel around his head (pp.748-749), but in the next chapter we discover that he was in fact deluded: the towel has not been touched. Do we regard this episode (and that of the glass Ivan thinks he has thrown) as simply due to Ivan's sickness or is there more to it? Again, it is important to recognise that it is both the product of Ivan's sickness and yet goes beyond this, for in the universe of discourse relevant to Ivan's conversation with the devil it is expressly stated that Ivan wrapped the towel around his head:

> Ivan went into the corner of the room, took a towel and did as he said, and with a wet towel on his head began walking up and down the room.

> (p.749)

The most profound explanation for this, I propose, is that on a plane of existence in such proximity to the devil even normal physical actions cease to have the reality they usu-

ally possess. This seems to be remarkably akin to the ancient theory, first fully stated by Plotinus, that evil has the power to transform and corrupt both morally and physically whatever looks towards it. For Plotinus evil is an absence which, at a more fundamental level, is realised to be a presence of a totally negative and unique sort.[26] A similar conception stands at the heart of Dostoevsky's vision. We begin to realise that the devil remains both passive and impervious throughout the conversation to all of Ivan's feelings and even to Ivan's terrible abuse. But in a much more sinister fashion he gradually *takes over* the whole conversation until his is the only voice and Ivan, in great torment, fruitlessly stops his ears. This "sponger", therefore, is flexible, malleable and passive (traditional Graeco-Roman attributes of matter), but he is not changed thereby. Rather, he exercises a totally negative power within his apparent agreeableness and the cul-de-sac thereby created is surely one of the great horrors of this passage. At the end of the conversation the only reality capable of stopping the vulgar, but deadly, persistence of the devil's voice is the physical knocking on the door of the *angelic* Alyosha. At this, the devil disappears, but Ivan is still bound by invisible fetters. Only when the sound gets louder does he re-emerge properly onto the physical level.

Finally, it is worth examining a few elements in the devil's view of himself. Perhaps the most conspicuous is his claim that he is "the only man in the universe who loves truth and sincerely desires good" (p.761), as also that it is his deepest wish to become a sixteen-stone market woman and light candles to the Lord (p.751), the devil's mocking way of referring to the lowest creature in the scale of nature. It is one of the most traditional attributes of the material principle that it loves or desires form. For Plotinus, interpreting Plato's *Timaeus* on the Receptacle, matter *always* desires form because it can never grasp form. Matter is utter destitution and like an excluded lover, she desires to become form, but can only lie alongside it.[27] Even the lowest creature is, therefore, in this sense beyond evil's grasp.

Evil assumes a certain spurious reality (cf. "my life on earth does assume some sort of reality" [p.750], "what can I be *on earth* except a sponger?" [p.749]), but there is no creativity in this. Like Ivan, the devil "suffers from" the fantastic and, therefore loves "earthly realism", which for him takes the form of geometrical shapes (in Plato's *Timaeus* geometrical shapes are invested in matter by the Demiurge); but he lives here as in a dream and he can only treat earthly reality in a *superstitious* way:

> "I adopt all your habits here" (*Ja zdes'vse vasi privyčki prinimaju*).

> (p.751)

Even in the adoption of form, then, there is no freedom or creativity of movement, simply a strait-jacket. Since he is also Ivan's illness and the source of all weakness, it befits his superstitious nature, and especially his derisive humour, that he should also be the hypochondriac *par excellence*:

"How can you expect me to philosophise when the whole of my right side is numb and I'm moaning and groaning. I've consulted all sorts of doctors etc."

(p.753)

The most important of the devil's claims is that he is necessary to the composition of the physical universe ("For what, I thought at that instant, would have happened after my 'hosannah'? Everything in the world would at once have been extinguished and no events would have happened after that" [p.762]) and the slightly different point that he is the "indispensable minus" (p.762), the principle of the negativity (p.755).

It must be emphasised that these explicit philosophical aspects of the devil's role are the butt of his derisive mockery:

"My best feelings, gratitude, for instance, are *formally* (*formal'no*) denied me simply because of my social position."

"Getting philosophical again, are you?" Ivan snarled.

(p.754)

However, it is characteristic of Platonism that the material principle, which is the seat of irrational movement and the source of a kind of brute necessity in the world, should also be included in the generation of the physical universe. When the devil mockingly (but straightforwardly too) itemises his philosophical role, we hear an echo of this ancient conception: without criticism there would be nothing but "hosannah"; the devil did not create the world and he is not responsible; he is the principle of negation and demands annihilation for himself, but, he complains, "they made me contribute to the section of criticism" and so he "serves with a heavy heart so that there should be events and performs what is irrational by order" (p.755). Human beings suffer and live, whilst the devil suffers, but does not live. He is just an *x* in an indeterminate equation. Here again we touch upon the Platonic-Aristotelian conception of matter or the substratum: matter is an everlasting phantom that cannot be known or named ("I am a sort of phantom who has lost all the beginnings and ends and who has even forgotten what his name is" [p.755]), it is pure indeterminacy, an ultimate unknowable *x* posited in the analysis of physical objects.[28] Even the devil's description of hell (a sort of retarded reflection of earth: "All our chaps there are in a muddle, and all because of your science . . . Everything you have, we've got too" [p.756]) bears a distant echo of Plato's description of the chaotic material principle which functions, in the absence of God, like a distorted mirror.[29]

In conclusion, I propose that there is a real parallel between Dostoevsky's portrayal of the devil in Ivan's dream and what may be described as a traditional Platonic view of evil. Perhaps this is hardly surprising. Plato, like Dostoevsky, unrelentingly confronted the brute fact of evil and its consequences in his *Dialogues,* and even went so far as to envisage in his *Laws* the possibility of an evil World Soul responsible for all recalcitrant or evil movements in the universe. For both thinkers (and also for Plotinus) evil could not be simple *privatio boni* (privation of good) but demanded more fundamental investigation. The power of Dostoevsky's portrayal is certainly enhanced by his ability to hold all these different, often contradictory, elements together in his mind at once and to transform them into his own new vision of the terrible "actualness" of non-being. Most important of all, I believe, is the realisation that this pathetic, but impassive, sponger, although dependent upon the complex psychology of Ivan himself, is also independently powerful in his own right in a manner which never makes him more than he can be, but which strips his impoverished victim of his rational and even of his physical powers. In Smerdyakov we see the "bastard" consequences of Ivan's reasoning. In Ivan's dream we glimpse the horror of the ultimate ground to which these "bastard" consequences tend.[30]

Notes

1. On this see Berdyaev, N., *Dostoevsky* (trans. D. Attwater), London: Sheed and Ward, pp. 109, 10; Simmons, E J., *Dostoevsky. The Making of a Novelist,* New York: Random House (Vintage Books), 1962, p.354; Curle, R., *Characters of Dostoevsky,* London, 1950; Terras, V., *A Karamazov Companion,* Wisconsin: University of Wisconsin Press, 1981, p.93. These critics tend to treat Ivan's devil as simply his "double" (Simmons), "other self" Terras) or personified symbol of inner evil (Berdyaev). I think this to be a mistake or at least superficial. I shall argue here that the horror of this meeting with the devil consists largely in the realisation that the devil is *both* Ivan's double-dream-phantasm *and* the devil. Both of these poles, phantasm and actuality, are locked into this situation and it seems important to recognise them together as inseparable.

2. Grossman, L. P., *Seminar on Dostoevsky,* England: Prideaux Press, 1972, p.29, catalogue number 59 (*Plato in the Presentation of Clifton Collins,* translated into Russian by Rezener) and p.36, cat.no.120 (Pisarev, D. I., *Sochinenia* chapter on Plato).

3. See Zenkovsky, V. V., "Dostoevsky's Religious and Philosophical Views" in *Dostoevsky: A Collection of Critical Essays,* ed. R. Wellek, New Jersey: Prentice-Hall, 1962, p.139 n.14.

4. Mochulsky, K., *Vladimir Solovyev: Žizn'i učenie,* Paris, YMCA, 1951, pp.94-95. On Solovyev's love for Plato and Plotinus see also p.117.

5. All quotations from Plato's *Timaeus* will be from the translation of F. M. Cornford, *Plato's Cosmology,* London: Routledge & Kegan Paul, 1937 (Reprint 1971), unless otherwise specified. The Greek text used is *Platonis Opera,* ed. J. Burnet, 5 vols., Oxford: Clarendon, 1946. Quotations from Plotinus will be from *Plotinus,* ed. & trans. A. H. Armstrong, 3 vols., London: Loeb Classical Library, 1966-1967. References to Plotinus (e.g., II, 4 [12], 10, 2) are to

be interpreted as follows: the Roman numeral denotes the Ennead, the first Arabic number the treatise, the number in square brackets the chronological number of the treatise, the fourth number the chapter and the final number the line.

6. *Timaeus* 52 A8 - B1.

7. Ibid. 52 B2 - C5; *Republic* 382 A. For Plotinus matter is an illegitimate phantasm (II, 4[12], 10, 7-9). When the soul tries to think matter it thinks it as a "dim thing dimly and a dark thing darkly, and it thinks it without thinking" (II, 4[12], 10, 30-31).

8. *Timaeus* 50 D2 - 51 B2.

9. Ibid. 52 D - 53 C; Artistotle, *Physics* 192 A 14-16.

10. See *The Brothers Karamazov*, trans. D. Magarshack, vol. 2, Penguin Books, 1958 (Reprint 1972), pp.743-747. All subsequent references to this initial description of the devil are from these pages, and all English quotations are from this edition. The Russian text consulted throughout is *Polnoe sobranie sočinenii*, red. V. G. Bazanov, vol. 15, Leningrad: Bauka, 1976, pp.69-85.

11. For the satire of this description see Terras, op.cit. (see Note 1), p.386, n.294 and p.387, n.302.

12. *Symposium* 203 B4 - C1. Plotinus III, 6[26], 14, 5-25; I, 8[51], 14, 35-50. Since Plato lacks a systematic concept of matter it is anachronistic to say that Poverty is clearly depicted as the antithesis of the divine nature and as the personification of the "mortal nature". R. G. Bury (*The Symposium of Plato*), edited with introduction, critical notes and commentary, Cambridge 1969, Introduction p.xl) writes: "We must conclude . . . that as Poros (Plenty) is the source of the divine side of the nature of Eros, so Penia (Poverty) is the source of the anti-divine side . . . We are justified in identifying this anti-divine side with mortality." And in a note he adds (p.xli): "So Plotinus is not far astray when he equates Penia (poverty) with hule, matter, potency."

13. *Timaeus* 50 D - 51 A; 52 D - E.

14. II, 5[25], 4-5.

15. *Timaeus* 51 A.

16. Ibid. 52 B-C. This is the translation of F. M. Cornford (*Plato's Cosmology*, London, Kegan & Paul, 1952 [Third Impression], p.192). In this passage Plato indicates how we become aware of the Receptacle. It is apprehended without the senses by a bastard form of reasoning. It is hardly an object of belief. Finally, "This indeed, is that which we look upon as in a dream." Although the dreamlike psychological experience is real enough, the apprehension itself is clearly below the level of ordinary experience and of normal perception.

17. Ibid., 50 A - B.

18. See Plotinus, I, 8[51] passim.

19. Cf. Plotinus I, 8[51], 14, 44-48: "This is the fall of the soul, to come . . . to matter and to become weak, because all its powers do not come into action; matter hinders them from coming by occupying the place which soul holds and producing a kind of cramped condition, and making evil what it has got hold of by a sort of theft. . . ."

20. *The Brothers Karamazov,* pp.767-770.

21. On Ivan's sickness and Dostoevsky's striving for absolute precision in his representation of psychological states, see K. Mochulsky, *Dostoevsky. His Life and Work* (trans. M. A. Miniham), Princeton: University Press, 1967, p.594.

22. The devil (naturally enough) does not *know* if God *or Satan* exists (see the bottom of p.755 and top of p.756). The ambiguous "I" of the present situation is all he can assent to.

23. *Timaeus* 52 B.

24. *The Brothers Karamazov,* p.749.

25. Plato, *Symposium* 203 B - C; Plotinus, I, 8[51], 14.

26. See II, 4[12]; I, 8[51] and III, 6[262], 6-19 *passim.*

27. Plato, *Symposium* 203 B - C; Aristotle, *Physics* 192 A 16-25. Cf. Plotinus, II, 4[12], 16; VI,5[23], 10,2-9.

28. Cf. Aristotle, *Metaphysics* Z 3, 1029 A 11-26.

29. *Timaeus* 52 D - 53 B.

30. I would like to thank Yuri Glazov and Elena Glazov-Corrigan for their help with the Russian text of Dostoevsky and for their suggestions.

Adam Weiner (essay date 1998)

SOURCE: "The Evils of *Dead Souls,*" in *By Authors Possessed: The Demonic Novel in Russia,* Northwestern University Press, 1998, pp. 57-92.

[*In the following excerpt, Weiner describes the demonological elements of Nikolai Gogol's novel* Dead Souls *and their relationship to the novelist's authorial persona.*]

SOBAKEVICH, PLIUSHKIN, AND DEMONIC ISOLATION

The Devil acquired national characteristics in this first great Russian demonic novel [*Dead Souls*] through Gogol's creative use of two religious demonologies that antedate the christianization of Rus, but endured in legend and literature until Gogol's day and beyond. These are the Slavonic myth involving the pagan devil Koshchei the Deathless (Koshchei Bessmertnyi) and Bogomilism's heretical dualist cosmogony. By invoking the Koshchei myth Gogol's narrator invites us to piece together the elements of a pagan-folk demonology that are scattered throughout the novel and that mainly implicate Sobakevich, Pliushkin, and the narrator. The narrator's comment that "there are yet many remnants of paganism in the Slavonic nature" (6:229), like many of his seemingly frivolous, casual, or ironic evaluations, in fact indicates a central theme of *Dead Souls*: the demonism of a pagan outlook in the Christian age. Sobakevich, Pliushkin, and the narrator are the figures that best convey Gogol's anxiety of remaining spiritually pagan regardless of his knowledge of the Christian ideal; this is, from the Christian vantage point, the equivalent of destroying one's eternal soul. By examining the principle of the dead, or more precisely the *deadened*, soul, I shall address the narrator's terror of falling into the pagan-demonic condition of soullessness—a terror, by the way, that bears upon the ultimate significance of the novel's title and central theme.

The myth of Koshchei serves as a model for demonic behavior through much of *Dead Souls*. The allusion to Koshchei occurs in Gogol's wonderful description of Sobakevich's postprandial repose. "It was as though this body were completely devoid of soul or rather, he had a soul, but by no means where it ought to be; rather, like the deathless Koshchei's, it was somewhere beyond the mountains and enclosed in such a shell that whatever stirred at the bottom of it made no impression whatsoever on the surface" (6:101). In the Russian magic tale, Koshchei kidnaps the hero Tsarevich's bride, and the Tsarevich must discover the location of the demon's soul in order to kill him, winning back his bride. The captive bride pleads with her captor to confess the location of his soul, and the slow-witted demon finally consents, admitting that it is beyond the mountains, buried under an oak, concentrically enclosed within an egg, a duck, a hare, and a box.[1]

The narrator's characterization of Sobakevich prompts us to contemplate the novel's structure in the light of this myth of the pagan demon. By doing so, we use the magic tale to establish some significant allegorical equivalencies. By dint of this allegory, Chichikov emerges as a kind of tsarevich who must secure the demon Sobakevich's soul: of course, the cunning Sobakevich seems to outwit him by delivering up the "souls" of (that is, the deeds to) his serfs (and dead ones at that), while his own soul remains safely buried or submerged. Sobakevich's kinship with Koshchei is confirmed by the fact that his physical aspect is grossly developed to the detriment of the spiritual: Chichikov's reflection that Sobakevich resembles a tree trunk, hewn by nature with a few rude ax swings, suggests the oak under which the demon's soul is buried in the myth. At the same time, Chichikov himself is somehow implicated in Sobakevich's demonism; indeed, he is explicitly likened to Sobakevich immediately before his arrival at the latter's estate, when Nozdrev—a character whose words have a strange authority in the novel—abuses Chichikov as "an absolute Sobakevich, such a scoundrel!" (6:82). Likewise, the Koshchei allegory, which ties the novel's main theme of soullessness to demonism, implicates many of the central heroes in a state of pagan evil.

One finds other pieces of the Koshchei puzzle distributed pell-mell throughout the pages of *Dead Souls*. Chichikov's downfall, his figurative death, is linked to the governor's daughter, whose *egg*-like head first enthralls him, significantly, at the end of the Sobakevich chapter. The image of the soul encased appears in many variants: Chichikov's case containing the deeds for "dead souls" is a conspicuous example.[2] Like Koshchei's, Chichikov's doom, or soul, is multiply enclosed: it lies not only within an "egg" (the governor's daughter) but also a "box" (Korobochka). The relevance of Korobochka's name, meaning "small box," to the allegory emerges when Chichikov exclaims that Korobochka has "done him in" with her thickheadedness, "Ah, she's done me in, the accursed old woman!"[3] This ejaculation provokes the narrator to describe Chichikov's box, thus connecting Korobochka with the box as two locations of his ruin. Korobochka's arrival in town, which expedites Chichikov's downfall, depicts Madame "Little Box" in a carriage that the lyrical narrator turns into a "fat-cheeked, swollen watermelon" (6:176). Hence, a box within an oval—the inverse of the oval-within-a-box of the Koshchei tale. Moreover, the oval of the watermelon is depicted in terms of human physiognomy, so that it recalls the other ovular face of the novel: that of the governor's daughter. Here is an instance of what T. E. Little describes as Gogol's delight "in the rearrangement of objects and concepts to conform with a private relish for topsy turvy-dom."[4] The hare and duck, which further envelop the demon's soul in the Koshchei tale, have more subtle counterparts in the novel. Nozdrev, despite his brother-in-law's incredulity, claims to have caught a hare (*rusak*) by its hind legs on his estate—a boast that is characteristic of the narrative "Nozdrevism" that, as we shall soon see, is the common link between Nozdrev and the narrator. In the absence of an actual duck in the text, this Nozdrev-like narrator, the *gogol'*-bird-author himself, becomes the final piece of the puzzle.

Koshchei, then, is one of the demonic identities the novel establishes as a measure for Chichikov's actions and potentials. Unlike Koshchei, Chichikov does not abduct and enslave a maiden, but his potential for such a deed is humorously explored in the wave of gossip that also proposes his resemblance to the legendary Captain Kopeikin and to Antichrist. Gogol's two pleasant gossiping ladies come to the conclusion that the dead souls are merely a screen to cover Chichikov's real intent of kidnapping the governor's daughter. They even consider for a moment the possibility that he had similar plans for Korobochka—or that "he's after the old woman!"—though this latter idea is dismissed as too fanciful.[5] When the officials and their wives split into groups to try to make some sense of Chichikov, the narrator characterizes the men's camp, which focuses on the dead souls as the real issue, as "the more hare-brained," implying that the women's interest in the kidnapping corresponds more closely to Chichikov's actual goals.[6] The fact that Chichikov has no intention whatsoever of kidnapping any maidens on a literal level does not alter the development in the transcendental truths revealed through the allegory of the pagan myth. The next phase of the myth is the death of the demon.

Even if we discount Chichikov's fall from the townfolk's good graces and his flight as a symbolic death at best, an actual death does result from the fatal encounter between demon (Chichikov) and maiden (the governor's daughter / Korobochka). In the ensuing chaos, the prosecutor dies of fright; in so doing, he provides the most suggestive, and at the same time comic, example of the Koshcheian principle of buried soul:

> it became apparent that the prosecutor was but a soul-less corpse. Only then was it learnt with regret that the deceased had indeed been endowed with a soul, which out of modesty he had never shown. And meanwhile the manifestation of death was as terrible in a small man as in a great one: the man who had but recently been walking, moving about, playing whist, signing various papers and who was often seen, with his thick brows and his winking eye, among the officials, now lay stretched out on the table; his left eye winked no more, but one eyebrow was still raised in a sort of in-terrogating way. What the dead man wanted to know, why he died or why he had lived—God only knows.
>
> (6:210)

In his life, the prosecutor, as a "sky-smudger"—to use Pereverzev's celebrated term for a Gogolian Everyman[7]—cultivated the mundane to such a degree that a fatal schism rent him asunder. The result is that his spiritual faculty be-comes entirely divorced from his physical. His soul, like Sobakevich's and Chichikov's, had grown heavy and re-sistant to Christian transfiguration, so he has locked the most essential part of himself away in a Koshcheian box, and only his dense eyebrows and winking eye offer evi-dence that he ever existed.[8]

Chichikov's awareness of this problem is one of the fac-tors that lift him in the final chapter closer to the narrator hovering above the world of *Dead Souls*: "Well, and so much for the prosecutor! He lived and lived, and then he died! And they will say in the papers that he died to the regret of his staff and all mankind, a respected citizen, a rare father, a model husband . . . but if one were to look into the matter, it would turn out that all there was to you were your bushy eyebrows" (6:219-20). By intimating the absurdity and tragedy of soulless living, Chichikov seems to offer hope for future spiritual growth. At the same time, his failure to abstract the prosecutor's exclusively corpo-real life to a universal principle—which in particular ap-plies to himself, the failure, in short, to be a good reader of life—heralds his immanent peripety.[9] Chichikov, as is shown by his laughably intense scrutiny of a theater poster he picks up on the street, is a thorough and careful reader, but he reads things that cannot develop his puny spiritual life. His servant Petrusha, in contrast, reads religious lit-erature as well as anything else that comes his way, but without his master's diligent scrutiny—unburdened, in fact, by even the slightest comprehension of the texts pass-ing before his eyes. Satire mocks vice in fictional charac-

ters with the hope that we will root that vice from our-selves, and the narrator's admonitions that readers study the text and apply its lessons to their own lives make use of this satirical principle: "And who among you who are full of Christian meekness—not in public, but in silence, alone, in a moment of solitary communion with yourself—will direct this difficult query deep into the recesses of your own soul: 'And is there not something of Chichikov within me?' That's hardly likely!" (6:245).

The myth of Koshchei the Deathless is the novel's model for the universal and inevitable peripety of death, and is thus a warning not only for hero and reader, but for the narrator as well. The demon's contempt for death is instru-mental in bringing it about. The paradoxical mortality of the "deathless" devil is the central motif of the myth and is perhaps as puzzling as Gogol's motif of "dead souls." Chichikov, by hinting "even at the Last Judgment" in his verbal drubbing of the town smiths, brings a healthy dose of authorial irony down on his own head, but the theme of retribution has implications not only for Chichikov. Gogol uses the Koshchei myth to characterize the human soul's thralldom to the evil pagan cult of physicality, and thus entwines the novel's main themes of soullessness and de-monism. Gogol invokes pagan myth in *Dead Souls* to ex-plore a concept of great personal anxiety to him: the sub-mersion of the Christian soul in an elemental physicality and the accompanying demonic isolation. If we sometimes see the narrator himself engaged through his heroes in a desperate struggle with this form of evil, it is hardly a cause for surprise; Gogol later confessed in *An Author's Confession* and "Four Letters Apropos of *Dead Souls*" to having poured his own demons and vices into his heroes in an attempt to purge himself of those monsters:[10]

> a combination of all the possible abominations [*ga-dostei*], a bit of each one, was contained within me. . . . [God] also populated my soul with several good qualities at my birth; but the best one . . . was the *de-sire to be better*. I never loved my evil [*durnykh*] quali-ties . . . by a higher power of miraculous suggestion a desire intensified within me to rid myself of them. . . . I began to allot to my heroes, above and beyond their inherent filth, my own personal dross [*drian'iu*].[11]

Gogol pretends to present the metamorphosis of Christians into pagan demons through their obsession with individual "fervors" (*zadory, strastishki*), but behind both So-bakevich's gluttony and Pliushkin's miserdom abides an obsessive, "pagan" delight in the world that Gogol's own materialism savored but that his Christian dualism demon-ized.

If the narrator implicitly connects himself with So-bakevich's pagan soullessness, then he is explicit in in-criminating himself with Pliushkin's evil. Following hard on the heels of the Sobakevich chapter, the Pliushkin chap-ter is quite concrete in depicting its subject's metamorpho-sis from man to demon. Since the "fervor" of interest in this chapter is miserliness, the narrator presents that vice as the engine of Pliushkin's perversion from goodness;

however, by reading with care, we can discern that Pliushkin, like Sobakevich, symbolizes a return to the evils of primordial, pre-Christian Slavdom. The narrator takes us from Pliushkin's present hoard of stolen junk to a time when "he was merely a frugal landowner" (6:117) in order to trace his metamorphosis from an "industrious spider" (6:118) to "not a man but a devil"[12]—a transformation paralleled by that of his estate from an "agricultural spider web" to a full-blown hell. The death of his wife made him, "like all widowers, more suspicious and stingier" (6:118). And his degradation further intensifies when he curses first his elder daughter for eloping, and then his son for joining the army against his wishes. But when his younger daughter dies, he is alone in the world. His feelings, which were never very pronounced anyway, "grew shallower by the minute." Once surrounded by loved ones, Pliushkin now plunges into evil isolation. Where there had once been a man there is now a pagan devil.[13] This is the state in which Chichikov encounters Pliushkin.

But it was Gogol's fervent hope that the state of evil epitomized by Pliushkin need not be permanent. So when Chichikov asks Pliushkin whether he has any acquaintance who could act as proxy in the sale of his dead souls, something human, as distinct from pagan nature, stirs deep within him. Gogol's metaphor for describing this stirring merits scrutiny.

> And suddenly a kind of ray of warm light flashed in this wooden [*dereviannom*] face, expressing not so much a feeling as a sort of pale reflection of one, a phenomenon resembling the unexpected appearance of a drowning man on the surface of the water which produces a joyful cry in the crowd on the bank. But in vain do his rejoicing brothers and sisters throw a rope from the shore, waiting for another glimpse of his back or arms, exhausted with the struggle—the appearance was his last. Everything is mute, and the still surface of the silent element [*bezotvetnoi stikhii*] is more terrible and void than before. So Pliushkin's face, after the fleeting feeling had passed over it, became more senseless and petty than ever [*eshche beschuvstvennei i eshche poshlee*].
>
> (6:126)

Dead Souls thus distinguishes feeling man from unfeeling nature. When man loses the feelings that hold him apart from and above the elements, he becomes "wooden," and is lost to the goodness of Creation, even as he enters senselessly into the thick of that Creation. Woodenness has two important senses in the metamorphosis described.

Pliushkin's woodenness stresses his retreat from Christianity back to a pagan past, and his name, meaning "ivy," confirms this sense by suggesting nature's reclaiming of the gains of Christian culture. The description of Pliushkin's estate serves as an example of just how nature encroaches upon what was once human, while at the same time indicating the nature of the metamorphosis through which Pliushkin has become "a demon." For if Sobakevich resembles Koshchei, then Pliushkin is a *leshii*, the Slavonic

wood demon resembling the trees among which he lives. Besides Sobakevich and Pliushkin's common link to nature—both are "wooden" or treelike—their spiritual makeup is nearly identical: the human soul has plunged so deep below its corporeal shell that it resists the positive Christian metamorphosis of transfiguration, activating instead the negative transformation of man into demon. The submersion metaphor, which in Sobakevich's case explicitly alludes to a Koshcheian essence, cannot but do the same with Pliushkin, whose chapter is in immediate proximity to Sobakevich's. Like Sobakevich's soul, Pliushkin's is buried or submerged somewhere, whether in his bags of gold, or at the bottom of the sea with the soul of Koshchei the Deathless. In an earlier draft of this passage, Gogol had explored the process by which Pliushkin's feelings become more petty (*poshlye*) with time until finally, "none of himself remains within him": "But when you try to get at his soul, it no longer exists. A piece of petrified wood [*Okremenevshii kusok*] and a man [now] wholly transformed into a terrible Pliushkin" (6:692). I believe that the Bogomil creation legends discussed earlier supplied Gogol with the imagery for Pliushkin's downward metamorphosis, particularly in the draft text: both passages involve a demonic figure sinking under water and resurfacing, and both make use of the image of flint, an emblem of the opacity, hardness, and heaviness of the soul that closes itself off from transfiguration. Such an ossified soul is a dead soul, the processes of ossification and mortification being nearly identical. Mochul'skii has properly described the crucial relationship in Gogol's thinking between death and evil: "From childhood, Gogol experienced cosmic evil as the beginning of mortification and death."[14]

The second sense of "woodenness" is the process of petrifaction that renders Sobakevich and Pliushkin no more than statues or idols, figures hewn from tree trunks with an ax. In Ovidian metamorphosis (and Dante's related notion of *contrappasso,* or retributive justice), a god often punishes human vice by giving the offender a form appropriate to the transgression. For his worship of graven images (in this case, money), Pliushkin is appropriately transformed into one. Sobakevich and Pliushkin are the pagan deities—and thus Christian demons—of *Dead Souls'* world. According to a well-known essay of Roman Jakobson's, the Orthodox Church was especially vehement in condemning sculpture "as pagan or diabolic vice": "On Russian soil, sculpture was closely associated with whatever was unchristian, even Anti-christian."[15] Gogol himself, in his essay "Sculpture, Painting, and Music," had clearly conveyed the pagan connotations of sculpture just before he began the composition of *Dead Souls*: "Sculpture was born along with the clearly shaped pagan world; it expressed that world—and died along with it. Vain was the desire to depict through sculpture the lofty phenomena of Christianity, for sculpture departed from Christianity as much as paganism itself did."[16] In both essay and novel, Gogol ties the theme of pagan sculpture to Mammonish worship of the material world, a worship Christianity views as a return to paganism. It is interesting that, having denied sculpture the capacity to express the Christian worldview, Gogol uses the figure of sculpture in works like *Dead Souls* and *Taras Bul'ba*. Must we then conclude that such fictions are not meant to convey the lofty phenomena of Christianity, that they sooner convey the base phenomena of paganism, exuding anti-Christian attitudes? So much is suggested not only by the heroes of works written in the *Dead Souls* period, but by the authorial persona as well.

In "Holy Sunday" (*Svetloe voskresenie*), the concluding piece of *Selected Passages,* Gogol offers Orthodoxy as the antidote to the type of metamorphosis that Pliushkin undergoes in *Dead Souls.* "Holy Sunday" paints a picture of the "devil of pride" as the chief demon of the nineteenth century, through whose promptings people "break the first and holiest commandments of Christ several times a day" (8:415). It is pride that prevents the demons inhabiting Russia from reclaiming their humanity, and the result is a terrible metamorphosis by which the entire face of the earth has been made to reflect a condition that cannot fail to recall Pliushkin's demonism. Here all of the terms of Pliushkin's metamorphosis into a demon are present: drowning, petrifaction, and idolatry:[17]

> If only one could so desire, if only one could coerce oneself to do this, to cling to this [day] as a drowning man clings to a board [*dosku*]! God knows, perhaps for this sole desire, a ladder is ready to drop down from the heavens to us and a hand ready to extend itself to us, to help us soar up that ladder.
>
> But the man of the nineteenth century does not wish to spend even one day in such a fashion! And the earth already burns with an incomprehensible anguish; life becomes ever more callous [*cherstvei i cherstvei*]; things become pettier and shallower [*mel'chaet i meleet*], and only a solitary, gigantic image of boredom [*ispolinskii obraz skuki*] rises up in plain sight, attaining a more immeasurable height with every passing day. All is empty [*glukho*], and the grave yawns everywhere. Oh, God! It becomes desolate and terrible in your world!
>
> (8:416)

Gogol's description of Pliushkinism gone wild had such ghostly appeal that Dostoevsky would echo its tonality in his fiction.[18] Gogol sought truth in his Russia and world, but everywhere found only his own frozen reflection. During the early 1840s especially, he was frightened by the deadness he saw within and without. "I know all about you: how you are reputed to be alive and yet are dead. Wake up; revive what little you have left: it is dying fast" (Rev. 3:2): the words of Saint John the Divine could serve as epigraph to *Dead Souls.* And if there is no direct reference to this verse of Revelation in the novel itself, then there is in Gogol's notebooks drafts, which assert that Chichikov had forgotten "that he had reached that fateful age in life when a person becomes ever lazier, when it becomes necessary to awaken him, to awaken him so that he does not fall asleep forever" (6:691). If we turn to the relevant passage in Revelation, we see that it immediately follows a contrast between true Christians and the pagans whom Christ will destroy (Rev. 2:27-28). The biblical

source amplifies the novel's equation of spiritual mortification with pagan demonism, while at the same time adding to the urgency of Gogol's message: Russia must awaken spiritually and purge itself of what the narrator calls residual paganism. Gogol's poetic eye, which was perhaps oversusceptible to pathetic fallacy, saw a confirmation of his own internal spiritual emptiness in external Russia.

It is tempting to conclude that the haunting lyricism of the passages describing spiritual emptiness could not be based on anything but Gogol's personal experience of paganism and its petrifying effect on the Christian soul. And this notion is borne out well by Gogol's correspondence. After publishing *Dead Souls,* gripped by excruciating religious despair and disenchantment in Russia, Gogol traveled to Jerusalem to pray at the Lord's Sepulcher. It seemed to him that his prayers were ineffectual, and his description of his mortified spiritual life at the height of this crisis reminds us again of Pliushkin's plight: "My . . . prayers were not even capable of escaping from my breast, much less of soaring up, and never yet before had my hard-heartedness, callousness and woodenness appeared to me so palpably."[19] In another letter (5 February 1839) Gogol had used the same terms to remind his friend Danilevskii that they must not let the "petrifying forces" of passing time bury their "live impressions," covering them in "bark . . . so thick that they [live impressions] will never break through to the surface." To Gogol, Christianity was often a losing battle against nature's ever-encroaching demonic forces, which vulgarize feelings and encrust the soul, hardening it against the saving grace of transfiguration. Gogol's well-known anxiety of being buried alive reflects the more literal aspect of his fear of being submersed in pagan nature. Ultimately these images of submersion, interment, or encrustation reflect a spiritual alienation that terrified Gogol.

The task of this part of this chapter has been to examine demonic isolation as an internal state. The return to pagan physicality results from the soul's stubborn opposition to God's transfiguring light. Such a soul hardens and sinks so deep into the body that the material life reigns supreme. In this sense, Sobakevich, Pliushkin, and the narrator conjure up the shades of such Western devils as Marlowe's Mephistopheles or Milton's Satan, carrying hell within them wherever they go as a spiritual condition. Physically and spiritually spurning Christian Creation, the narrator is eternally composing his own demonic society as an alternative. Sartre's observation on the "relationship between Evil and poetry," and indeed on the poetry that "goes so far as to take Evil," bears directly upon the narrator's image in Gogol's great "poem":

> And he who damns himself acquires a solitude which is a feeble image of the great solitude of the truly free man. In a certain sense he creates. In a universe where each element sacrifices itself in order to converge in the greatness of the whole, he brings out the singularity, that is to say the rebelliousness of a fragment or a detail. Thus something appears which did not exist be-

fore, which nothing can efface and which was in no way prepared by worldly materialism. It becomes a work of luxury, gratuitous and unpredictable.[20]

The narrator's rebellion casts him into an isolation, or exile, that seems more than he can bear. He responds by creating the "work of luxury, gratuitous and unpredictable" that is the narration of *Dead Souls*; herein lies his attempt to fill the void of his self-imposed exile from godly Creation. However, this creative urge, our next subject, will not provide an escape from the demonism of isolation; the narrator's creativeness evokes less a divine than a diabolical genius.

OVERCOMING ISOLATION: FROM ZAMANILOVKA TO NOZDREVISM

The narrator explores Nozdrevism as a potential antidote to the slow, inexorable metamorphosis into the demonic fauna or flora of Gogol's pagan Russia. Unable or unwilling to appreciate divine Creation in his alienation, the narrator of *Dead Souls* turns to his own creativity, and the novel itself emerges as his attempt to fill the abyss with his demonic constructs.[21] If Sobakevich and Pliushkin are designed to carry the narrator's sense of demonic alienation or submersion, then Nozdrev is a vessel for the Satanic creative impulse with which the narrator staves off this pagan void.[22] It is Nozdrev's wild verbal creativity that most clearly sets him apart. In his brilliant *Gogol and the Devil*, Merezhkovskii makes a compelling argument that I believe applies to Nozdrev: Merezhkovskii shows Khlestakov to be the devil Gogol concealed in *The Inspector General*,[23] and since Gogol repeatedly likened himself to Khlestakov, Merezhkovskii concludes that Gogol came to view himself as the Devil, expressing his own demonism through his hero Khlestakov. There is much evidence to substantiate Merezhkovskii's theory, including Gogol's confession of having cast out his personal demons in the form of his literary heroes. Nozdrev's direct descendancy from Khlestakov is so clear that those who accept Merezhkovskii's thesis, as I do, must see a reflection of Gogol in Nozdrev as well. Nozdrev occupies a privileged position in the narrative structure of the novel. His broadcasting of Chichikov's offer to buy dead souls at the governor's ball accelerates Chichikov's downfall. He is the only character who refuses to transfer his souls to Chichikov, instead yelling, "You'll get nothing from me but a bald-headed devil." His abusive characterizations of Chichikov— "you're a sharper, a nasty chimney-sweep"—as well as his insistence that he deserves to be hanged, seem backed by some higher authority.[24]

Nozdrev is the bearer of the Khlestakovian spirit in *Dead Souls*; like his precursor, Nozdrev flaunts the poetics of the inspired lie and brings about revelation through nonsense. Consider Nozdrev's interrogation by the town officials into the matter of Chichikov's origins.

> This was decisively a man for whom there were no doubts whatsoever. . . . He answered all of their questions without any hesitation, declaring that Chichikov

had bought several thousand rubles' worth of dead souls and that he himself had sold him some because he saw no reason not to; to the question of whether Chichikov was not a spy trying to uncover something, Nozdrev answered that he was a spy and that even at the school they attended together Chichikov was known as a squealer and that for this reason his schoolmates, including Nozdrev, had roughed him up a bit, so that 240 leeches had to be applied to his temples alone— that is, he had wanted to say 40, but the 200 somehow narrated [*skazalos'*] their way in of their own accord.

(6:208)

Nozdrev's fabrication evokes the narration of *Dead Souls*; they both represent a hyperbolism that has grown from a rhetorical device to an end in itself. The poetic formula underlying such hyperbole is suggested by Nozdrev's 240 leeches: one begins with the most absurd exaggeration conceivable, and proceeds to multiply it by six. It is interesting that, while seeming to reveal the origin of one evil, the elusive demonism of Chichikov, Nozdrev in fact allows us a glimpse into the workings of quite another.

The connection between Nozdrev's fantastic lying and the narration itself is important because it indicates a central element of Christianity's way of demonizing competing doctrines: the myth-making impulse itself comes to be seen as evil in a world that sanctifies the Christian creation myth as Truth. This is why Gogol's activation of the myth of the Satanic *gogol'* is so crucial to understanding the narrative demonism of the novel. The *gogol'*-author, like Nozdrev, is taken in by his own fictions and at some point ceases to understand where the lifeless world created by his narration ends—and where God's Creation begins. At the start of chapter 7, the narrator's unexpected dissertation on the two kinds of authorship confirms the sense of creative crisis that imbues *Dead Souls*. This discussion of novel writing also helps elucidate the narrational situation, the imaginative space where the narrator's creation takes place. According to the narrator's typology of writers, happy is the author "who soars high above all of the other geniuses of the world," for "there is no equal to him in strength—he is God!" (6:134). "But," continues the narrator, "another destiny belongs to the writer who has dared to summon up . . . the entire terrible and astounding mire of trifles that bog down our lives, all the depths of cold, fractured, daily characters with which our earthly, at times bitter and wearisome, road writhes." Needless to say, this second, "unhappy" author is of the Gogolian sort. While the "happy" writer ascends to the divine heights, the Gogolian writer descends into the cold, murky abyss. The metaphor again recalls the Bogomil *gogol'* plunging to the sea bottom to find the rude, raw material of his creation. The narrator continues, complaining that the unsympathetic reading public will brand "the cherished creations" of the unhappy (*gogol'*-like) writer "contemptible and base" and "will assign him a scornful corner in the pantheon of writers who insult humanity, will ascribe to him the qualities of the heroes he himself has depicted, will deny him his heart, and his soul, and the divine flame of talent" (6:134). By now, the passage has become a litany of Gogol's direst fears concerning the demonic quality of his own authorship, a reflection of his fear that his audience will ascribe to him the soullessness of his creatures and deny his talent is divine.

In order better to comprehend the narrator's "unhappy writer," this representation of Gogol's mature authorial persona, let us turn to Manilov, who oddly combines Sobakevich's soullessness with Nozdrev's urge to fabricate.[25] It will be noted, first of all, that, as he persuades Chichikov to pay him a visit, Manilov tells a Nozdrev-like lie, claiming that his estate lies within a short fifteen versts of town: as Chichikov later learns, Manilovka is in fact at least thirty versts distant. It is then appropriate that Chichikov, upon asking for directions at the fifteen-verst marker, mispronounces the estate's name, Manilovka, as "Zamanilovka," a humorous derivation from the verb "zamanit'" 'to entice, lure, entrap.'[26] The narrator continues this wordplay, stating that "Manilovka could lure [*zamanit'*] few with its location" (6:22) and that Manilov himself "smiled enticingly [*zamanchivo*]" (6:24). Chichikov in fact finally finds himself at Zamanilovka sooner than Manilovka. Manilov's estate is located at an eerily distant remove from society, in total isolation. And from the void of this "Zamanilovka" emanates an endless procession of ephemeral images: Manilov devotes his life to the invention of a phantasmagorical world, populated by touching friendships, pleasant conversations, houses of such enormous proportions that one might see remote Moscow from their belvederes, nonexistent bridges across nonexistent rivers, and so on (6:39). Manilov, as it turns out, has lured Chichikov to his estate in order that Chichikov share in these visions: "But you know," Manilov tempts Chichikov, "how fine indeed it would be to live together, under a single roof, or in the shade of an elm to philosophize about something, to delve deeply" (6:38). Manilov's delving into the spiritual void, his perpetual creation there of one grotesquerie after another, once more resembles the creative method of the "unhappy" *gogol'*-writer and the narration itself. The term "Zamanilovka" helps us to envisage the imaginative landscape in which such a creation occurs. As Manilov lures Chichikov from town to his distant, isolated, barren estate, the authorial persona "entices" readers from belief in Creation into a belief in its distorted representation.

The tour Nozdrev entices Chichikov to take of his estate further elucidates the device of narrative Zamanilovka. Having dragged Chichikov across what seems an endless, muddy mire to arrive at the very boundary of his realm, Nozdrev launches into a characteristically ridiculous lie: "'Here is the border!' said Nozdrev. 'All that you see on this side, it's all mine, and even on the other side'" (6:74). Nozdrev attempts to convince Chichikov through the force of his "fictions" that there is in fact no border separating what is his from what is not, that all the world is his own estate, or his "chertova propast'" (literally, "devil's abyss"; figuratively, "great quantity of things"), as he elsewhere refers to his property (6:81). Having likewise lured us into his fictional world, the *gogol'*-writer attempts to bilk us

into believing that the fiction is fact, that the Russia of *Dead Souls* is God's Russia, Gogolian fabrication—divine Creation. Readers are seduced into the Gogolian void and urged to believe that this "devil's abyss" is the creative center of the entire cosmos, and not the backwaters of the artist's mind. Thus, the narrator, in describing the void of his and Chichikov's road, is torn between the Gogolian extremes of nothing and everything: starting with the statement that "there is nothing, and one is on the road again," the narrator quickly slips into Nozdrev's idiom and claims as his literary estate the entire world, the "measureless fields on the one side and on the other" (6:220).

The opening of chapter 6 of *Dead Souls* is a lucid illustration of the alternating urges of demonic isolation and demonic creation. The narrator begins by bemoaning his fading capacity to find artistic inspiration in the surrounding world. His lament about the advent of old age and its petrifying effect on the human soul contains the very terms that later in the chapter, in a passage we have already examined, are to describe the hardening process in Pliushkin.

> Now I ride up to each unfamiliar village and indifferently glance at its vulgar outer image; nothing comforts my gaze, which has grown cold, nothing seems funny, and that which in former years would have awakened a living movement in my face, laughter and ceaseless speech now slips past, while my lips maintain an apathetic silence. Oh my youth! Oh my fresh years![27]

But having expressed the Gogolian fear of death by submersion, the narrator belies himself by producing one of the most strikingly vivid descriptive passages ever encountered in a novel: the famous description of Pliushkin's estate.[28] By virtue of the verbal canvas he paints, the narrator demonstrates that the minutia of life can yet awaken ceaseless wonder and speech in him. In the process, he continues to entice the reader along his endless road to another Zamanilovka, another devil's abyss. However, the narrator will concede in the final pages of *Dead Souls* that his novelistic emanations, like the creations of the Satanic *gogol'*, lack the breath of divine life that separates them from God's biblical Creation: "the book is dead beside the living word!" (6:223). Gogol himself perceived the morbid quality that Rozanov was later to fault in his works, and the novel conveys this authorial perception through the dichotomy of spiritual deadening and demonic creation. Gogol's creatures, like their author, were doomed to wander endlessly and alone throughout what Nabokov aptly called Gogol's "own distorted and dreadful and devilish image of the world."[29] . . .

Notes

1. References to Afanas'ev's collection of folk tales are to tale or note number and to page number; thus, the reference (156:286) is for tale 156, page 286. In some variants of the magic tale, it is the demon's soul, in others his death, that is the object of the hero's quest. The tale's implicit equation of "death" and "soul," by the way, resonates well with the title of Gogol's

novel. The devil's death/soul may also be found in an egg on the sea floor (93a:491), which implicates more Pliushkin, perhaps, than Sobakevich.

2. Siniavskii (*V teni Gogolia*) suggests that Gogol's model for Chichikov's double-tiered box is the double drawers of the Ukrainian folk puppet theater (*vertep*). *V teni Gogolia,* vol. 2 of *Sobranie sochinenii v dvukh tomakh,* ed. N. S. Kochareva (Moscow: Start, 1992).

3. "Ekh umorila kak, prokliataia starukha!" 6:56.

4. T. E. Little, "Dead Souls," in *Knaves and Swindlers: Essays on the Picaresque Novel in Europe,* ed. Christine Whitbourn (London: Oxford University Press, 1974), 126.

5. "za starukhu prinialsia," 6:185, 183.

6. "samaia bestolkovaia," 6:191.

7. V. F. Pereverzev, *Tvorchestvo Gogolia,* in *Gogol', Dostoevskii: Issledovaniia* (Moscow: Sovetskii pisatel', 1982), 40-186.

8. The synecdoche here points to the fundamental Gogolian principle that a person living independently of the concerns of the spirit is as grotesquely demonic as are his independently living body parts—whether someone's nose ("The Nose"), leg ("The Story of How Ivan Ivanovich Quarreled with Ivan Nikiforovich") or eyebrows ("Nos," 1835; "Povest' o tom, kak possorilsia Ivan Ivanovich s Ivanom Nikiforovichem," 1835). The diabolical essence of the Gogolian synecdoche is best revealed in "Nevskii Prospect": "some devil or other splintered the entire world into a myriad of various fragments and these fragments senselessly, meaninglessly mixed together the ladies' gleaming shoulders and black frock-coats" (3:24). See [Robert A. Maguire] on the basic Orthodoxy of Gogol's treatment of the evil of fragmentation: "he follows the mind of his Church in regarding 'individuality' as pernicious, even depicting it in his fiction as fragmentation, disorder, chaos, isolation, and death. These are also the images many Orthodox theologians use to describe the wages of sin" (*Exploring Gogol* [Stanford: Stanford University Press, 1994] 87).

9. In *The Inspector General,* [Revizor, 1836] Gogol illustrates for readers and audiences the mechanics of the fall through pride. Artemii Filippovich's children are named Nikolai, Ivan, Elizaveta, Mar'ia, and Perepetuia (4:64). The unexpected appearance of Perepetuia, whose name derives from *peripeteia*—a sudden change of circumstances or sudden fall, as in a tragedy—foreshadows the mayor's plummet from the heights of "vysokogo poleta, chort poberi!" (a lofty flight, the Devil take it! 4:81) to the depths of "svinye rozhi" (pig snouts; 4:93). The demonism behind this fall is accented by the diction.

10. *Avtorskaia ispoved'* (1847). *Chetyre pis'ma po povodu Mertvykh dush* (1847).

11. Emphasis in original (8:294).

12. "bes, a ne chelovek" (6:119).

13. The kind of "minor-epic" narration used in describing Pliushkin's metamorphosis is rare in *Dead Souls* in that, while similar transformations have evidently occurred with nearly all of the other characters, we usually see only postmetamorphic shapes—the objects, animals, and demons that populate the novel's pages. Nonetheless the germs of such metamorphoses are ubiquitous in *Dead Souls,* as in much of Gogol's work up until 1842: a peasant becomes a samovar, officials—flies, the Sobakevichs—a gourd and a cucumber. As Gippius points out, Gogol's revision of the second volume of *Dead Souls,* consisted of a disciplining on a stylistic level, a "toning down" of the early hyperbolic, caricaturish style to one that is more "realistic" and descriptive: Petukh goes from being a watermelon to being *like* one as he passes from one draft to the next, and Kochkarev's triangle-face, his pressed hair, nose, lips, and chin, are excised in the later version (*Gogol* [ed. and trans. Robert A. Maguire (Durham: Duke University, Press, 1989] 171). In his revisions of "The Portrait" and "St. John's Eve" Gogol had likewise mitigated the demonic elements, modifying the style from fantastic to merely heavily laden with a symbolic demonic potential. By the second volume of *Dead Souls,* Gogol seems to have decided that the demonic metamorphosis was an impossible vehicle for conveying positive types.

14. [Mochul'skii] *Dukhovnyi put' Gogolia* [Paris, 1934], 96.

15. "The Statue in Pushkin's Poetic Mythology," in *Language in Literature,* ed. Krystyna Pomorska and Stephen Rudy (Cambridge: Belknap Press of Harvard University Press, 1987), 362 and 363.

16. "Skul'ptura, zhivopis' i muzyka" (1835) (8:10).

17. In the following passage, this Gogolian "petrifaction" is conveyed particularly by the words *doska* (board), *cherstvei* (more hardened), and *glukho* (hollow).

18. The close of "A Gentle Creature" ("Krotkaia," 1876), for instance, presents a vision of a universe murdered by Dostoevskian *kosnost'* (inertia)—a concept very similar to Gogol's petrifaction: "Inertia! Oh, nature! . . . They say that the sun gives life to the universe. When the sun comes up, study it—is it not a corpse? All is dead, and corpses are everywhere. There are only people, and about them silence—that's the earth!" (24:35).

19. "beschuvstvennost', cherstvost' i dereviannost'"; letter to A. P. Tolstoy of 25 April 1848.

20. In Georges Bataille, *Literature and Evil,* trans. Alastair Hamilton (London: Marion Boyars, 1990), 36.

21. Mochul'skii's description of Gogol's spiritual conflict of the early 1840s helps explain what in the writer himself could have been translated into such a narrator in *Dead Souls*: "Towards 1842 Gogol begins to have doubts about his status as the chosen. When the moments of mystical ecstasy would pass, his conviction in his path to holiness grew weak; he would see his 'dark side': sinfulness, 'spiritual hardness.' The author of *Dead Souls* sensed the principle of evil and death in his own soul. And here is where the stubborn and meticulous search for shortcomings and vices begins. Gogol looms over his soul, as if over a dark abyss whose bottom is seething with terrible monsters unknown even to him" (*Dukhovnyi put' Gogolia* 63).

22. It should be pointed out that Gogol criticism has understood Nozdrev in other ways as well. Commentators have typically associated him with the folkish traditions of the puppet-show (vertep) bully or the carnival buffoon (*shut*). V. F. Pereverzev (*Tvorchestvo Gogolia* 140-41) fits him into his quirky typology as the epitome of the "active sky-smudger" (*aktivynyi nebokoptitel'*). Nozdrev is a complex character who combines the traits of Gogol's previous characters, such as Pirogov, Khlestakov, and Kovalev.

23. For some reason, Merezhkovskii goes on to state that Gogol did not dare go so far as to see a reflection of Chichikov in himself ("Gogol" 99). Although Gogol may have identified more with certain other characters (Nozdrev and Khlestakov, for instance), Merezhkovskii offers no evidence for such a distinction. It is plausible that Gogol invented Chichikov, too, as an incarnation of some aspect of himself.

24. 6:82, 79, 172.

25. The narrator characterizes Manilov as a man so spiritually dull and empty that he does not even entertain any absurd little pastimes or fervors.

26. 6:22. The verb *zamanivat'/zamanit'* has the connotation of luring by deception or trickery in contradistinction to the verb *manit'*, which signifies a more neutral attracting.

27. 6:111. In the novel's final chapter, the narrator will again return to this theme of the solitude that comes with age and with the deadening of the soul: "It is unfitting for the author, who has been a grown man for a long time already, who has been trained by a severe inner life and the refreshing sobriety of solitude, to forget himself like a youth" (6:273).

28. For a somewhat different reading of this passage, see Maguire, who argues that the narrator relinquishes control of the story here to Chichikov, from whose vantage we see the garden (*Exploring Gogol* 231).

29. [Vladimir Nabokov,] *Nikolai Gogol,* [New York: New Directions, 1944] 122.

FURTHER READING

Criticism

Butler, Marilyn. "Romantic Manichaeism: Shelley's 'On the Devil, and Devils' and Byron's Mythological Dramas." In *The Sun Is God: Painting, Literature and Mythology in the Nineteenth Century,* edited by J. B. Bullen, pp. 13-37. Oxford: Clarendon Press, 1989.
    Analyzes the religious and mythological claims of the two nineteenth-century poets, Lord Byron and Percy Bysshe Shelley, most frequently associated with Satanism in the popular mind.

de Montluzin, Emily Lorraine. "Southey's 'Satanic School' Remarks: An Old Charge for a New Offender." In *Keats-Shelley Journal* 21-22 (1972-73): 29-33.
    Observes that many of Robert Southey's attacks on Byron as head of the socalled *"Satanic School"* of poetry were actually redactions of claims Southey made against another poet, Thomas Moore.

Dudek, Andrzej. "The Devil in 19th Century Russian Poetry." In *Slavia Orientalis* XLI, No. 1 (1992): 19-26.
    Maintains that Russian poetry of the nineteenth century, unlike fiction of the period, generally equates demonism with Romantic self-expression rather than some moral or social evil.

Gottlieb, Elaine. "Singer and Hawthorne: A Prevalence of Satan." In *Southern Review* 8 (Spring 1972): 359-70.
    Contrasts representations of Satan in the fiction of Nathaniel Hawthorne and Isaac Bashevis Singer.

Granger, Byrd Howell. "Devil Lore in 'The Raven.'" In *Poe Studies* 5, No. 2 (December 1972): 53-54.
    Explicates Edgar Allan Poe's poem "The Raven" by considering the bird's folkloric reputation as "the Devil's bird."

Hollinger, Karen. "'Young Goodman Brown': Hawthorne's 'Devil in Manuscript': A Rebuttal." In *Studies in Short Fiction* 19, No. 4 (Fall 1982): 381-84.
    Refutes the claim of James L. Williamson's 1981 article that the narrator of Nathaniel Hawthorne's short story "Young Goodman Brown" is in some manner a representation of Satan.

Merezhkovsky, Dmitry. "Gogol and the Devil." In *Gogol from the Twentieth Century: Eleven Essays,* edited by Robert A. Maguire, pp. 57-102. Princeton, N.J.: Princeton University Press, 1974.
    Enumerates the numerous qualities of the Devil—including his status as a literal denial of God and the infinite—found in the pages of Nikolai Gogol's novel *Dead Souls.*

Praz, Mario. "The Metamorphoses of Satan." In *The Romantic Agony,* translated by Angus Davidson, pp. 51-91. New York: Meridian Books, 1956.

Illustrates changes in the poetic representation of Satan from John Milton's influential description of the fallen angel in *Paradise Lost* to characters in Lord Byron's verse dramas.

Putney, Christopher. *Russian Devils and Diabolic Conditionality in Nikolai Gogol's* Evenings on a Farm near Dikanka. New York: Peter Lang, 1999, 250 p.
    Studies the origins of the Devil in Medieval folklore, theology, and literature and analyzes Gogol's varied use of this personification of evil in his fiction.

Stevenson, Warren. "Wordsworth's 'Satanism.'" In *Wordsworth Circle* 15, No. 2 (Spring 1984): 82-84.
    Traces some echoes of the Miltonic Satan of *Paradise Lost* in William Wordsworth's *The Prelude*.

Terras, Victor. "Turgenev and the Devil in *The Brothers Karamazov*." *Canadian-American Slavic Studies* VI, No. 2 (Summer 1972): 265-71.
    Views Ivan Karamazov's devil in Feodor Doestoevsky's novel as an incarnation of the prototypical Russian atheist.

Science in Nineteenth-Century Literature

The nineteenth century was a period of many advances in the field of science and medicine. Society placed a great deal of emphasis on the empirical understanding imparted by the use of scientific methodology, and leading periodicals printed essays and treatises on scientific and medical theories of the time, thus imparting this knowledge to the general public.

INTRODUCTION

One of the most important influences of the Romantic movement was its belief in the authority of nature over social conventions. For the Romantic poets and philosophers, nature represented a moral and physical sanctuary for self-expression and imaginative invention. In contrast, scientific advancement and the public's increased interest in science during the Victorian era led to the replacement of the seemingly transcendental power of nature with the new and more authoritative discourse of science. Science itself was imbued with romance, and imaginative ideas and scientific fact often interacted with each other. Authors such as T. S. Eliot and G. H. Lewes were well versed in contemporary scientific theory, and they enjoyed differentiating truth from superstition, ardently pursuing scientific accuracy in their writing and theory.

A significant landmark in this shift of focus from the power of nature to the power of science occurred in the 1830s, when Charles Lyell proposed his Uniformitarian theory, which stated that changes in the earth's surface had occurred gradually over millions of years. Despite vehement attacks by creationists—those who believed in the literal truth of the Bible's version of the origin of the earth and its inhabitants—most nineteenth-century intellectuals accepted the idea of evolution by the 1850s. By 1860, when Charles Darwin issued *Origin of the Species,* the authoritative text on evolutionary theory, many scholars, scientists, and writers were already incorporating this and other contemporary scientific theories into their work and writings. Although nature was no longer perceived as a quasi-divine force, the study of nature nonetheless provided an understanding of the meaning and value of human life. This was a time of great public participation in these discoveries—Victorians were interested in acquiring this new knowledge and attended numerous lectures on scientific subjects. Scientists like William Tyndall and Thomas Huxley enjoyed the same recognition and popularity as such novelists as George Eliot and Charles Dickens.

In addition to advances in theory, the nineteenth century also witnessed an explosion in technology, promising abundance and a good life for all. Science itself held out the tempting prospect that it was possible to discover the truth about the universe and human life, and there was a strong belief in the perfectibility of humans, whose continual progress from the ancestral ape toward celestial entities was seen as a realistic outcome of evolution. The writing of the time explored these possibilities, and many works of literature focused on the promise that science would reveal all mysteries. Victorians were fascinated by the possibility of revealed secrets and this preoccupation was most obviously demonstrated in their focus on the field of medical science. In an essay discussing George Eliot's *The Lifted Veil* Kate Flint examines this very issue, characterizing Eliot's text as an intervention in this arena.

While the literature of the time explored scientific theory and knowledge, some also satirized nineteenth-century science, most notably the works of such authors as Mark Twain. Science's critics focused on the debate over the inherent superiority of scientific study over other forms of knowledge, and philosophers such as Huxley—known for popularizing scientific thought—became special targets for the era's satirists. The prevailing belief that the natural world could, via empirical dissection, be completely understood, as well as the belief that scientific revelation was the highest possible form of intellectual insight were both parodied by many authors of the time; this was, in fact, a recurrent theme in the writings of both Emily Dickinson and Percy Bysshe Shelley. While scientists stressed the value of objective observation and inductive reasoning, other theories of social Darwinism stressed man's inevitable future progress towards a higher evolutionary status. These and other ideas about the finite and essentially mechanistic nature of the universe were strongly influential in the literature of the time, leading many contemporary authors to respond to these ideas in their prose and poetry.

The nineteenth century witnessed the emergence of various disciplines of study, some of which encroached on intellectual territory previously dominated by literature. In the past, the task of representing and dissecting society had been seen as the purview of novelists, writers, and poets. With the emergence of such disciplines as sociology and anthropology, though, the various anxieties, premises, and social formations typically explored in literature were increasingly being scrutinized as part of a formal branch of science. Many writers, including Herman Melville, Henry James, and Theodore Dreiser, responded to this phenomenon in their writings. In an essay that explores these simultaneous developments, Susan Mizruchi states that the study of the rise of sociology in terms of contemporary novels helps to greatly enhance our understanding of the imaginative aspects of this new nineteenth-century discipline. Earlier writers, such as Wordsworth, Coleridge, Whitman, and Thoreau, had also found themselves deeply enmeshed in the changes scientific discoveries brought upon their work. With the advent of science, the literature of nature that these authors were best known for also underwent many changes. In this new Age of Science, when the general public became increasingly fascinated with the emerging and fast-changing disciplines of astronomy, geology, geography, and chemistry, a new space was opened for writers who could interpret these ideas for a popular audience. Yet, at the same time that the vibrant and connective powers of science were bringing an understanding of the whole of nature to humans, many writers also felt that there was much about the new disciplines that would alienate and leave behind those who could not keep pace with the increasingly inaccessible nature of its discourse. These conflicts were seen in many works written at this time, especially in the works of authors who themselves were deeply engaged with science.

Not surprisingly, the rise and influence of scientific study had the most profound affect on the place of poetry in society. For the Romantics, poetry served to uplift and edify, and the poet occupied a central place in the interpretation of the divine and natural forces that made up the universe. The advent of empirical ideas, many of which stressed methodology and objective reporting over imagination and inspiration, caused many writers and intellectuals to question the role and value of poetry in contemporary society. The works of Darwin and others were challenging the spiritual values that had previously been the domain of poetry, and many scientists forecast the demise of poetry altogether since scientists were considered the logical replacements of poets as interpreters of universal ideals. While some argued the superiority of one discipline over the other, many poets seized this opportunity to integrate new scientific knowledge into their writing. This, coupled with numerous other societal changes involving such issues as economic welfare, commercialism, and women's rights, led many contemporary poets to experiment extensively with both content and form in the verse they were producing. In the United States, the optimistic nineteenth-century belief in the perfectibility of humankind was soon replaced by a crisis of faith following the Civil War—people questioned their faith in innate goodness, and many of the early benefits of technological advances were increasingly offset by disadvantages and risks. There was an increasing disparity between the rich and poor, and technology seemed to be undermining the country's early sense of unity and goodwill. Eventually, the conflicts and issues raised by scientific theories that had left people in doubt of the existence of a divine creator led to a need for reconciliation between science, religion, and the human imagination, forcing the birth of a poetry that would help explain how evolution might coexist with religious explanations of creation and human nature.

REPRESENTATIVE WORKS

Charles Darwin

On the Origin of the Species by Means of Natural Selection, or The Preservation of Favoured Races in the Struggle for Life (non-fiction) 1860

Emily Dickinson

Poems by Emily Dickinson (poetry) 1890

George Eliot

The Lifted Veil (novel) 1859

Middlemarch (novel) 1871

Thomas Hardy

Far From the Madding Crowd (novel) 1874

A Laodicean: A Novel (novel) 1881

Two on a Tower: A Romance (novel) 1882

Edgar Allan Poe

"Ligeia" (short story) 1838

The Raven and Other Poems (poetry) 1845

Percy Bysshe Shelley

Queen Mab: A Philosophic Poem, with Notes (poetry) 1813

A Defence of Poetry (essay) 1820

Adonais: An Elegy on the Death of John Keats, Author of Endymion, Hyperion, Etc. (poetry) 1821

Alfred Tennyson

In Memoriam (poetry) 1850

Henry David Thoreau

Walden, or Life in the Woods (non-fiction) 1854

OVERVIEWS AND GENERAL STUDIES

William Brackett (essay date 1879)

SOURCE: "Modern Science in its Relationship to Literature," in *Popular Science Monthly,* Vol. 15, June, 1879, pp. 166-78.

[*In the following essay, Brackett discusses the relationship between science and literature in the nineteenth century, claiming that new avenues in literature were limited and science offered the opportunity to achieve notoriety while exploring a new and vital topic.*]

The innovations made by science upon other modes of thought and study within the last half century are without a parallel in the history of human progress. It has swept away many of our most cherished convictions, hoary with the dust of ages, and left others in their places entirely irreconcilable with them. Marching on with the might and majesty of a conqueror, it has spread dismay in the ranks of opposing forces, and caused a complete abdication in its favor of many of those who were most hostile to it. Nor has it taken the field in an aggressive or bellicose spirit. On the contrary, almost all its conquests have been made without any design of inspiring opposition or terror, and while engaged in pursuits that of all others require for their prosecution the most pacific and philosophic temper.

It might be easily shown by the comparison, were this essential to my design, that in the three great departments of human study, namely, those of science, religion, and literature, the cultivators of science have always shown a disposition to be more tolerant of opposition and more lenient toward their enemies than those engaged in either of the other pursuits. It might be shown that religious controversies, and the animosities engendered by them, hold the first rank in the scale of bitterness. Next come those of a literary nature, which, in the last century, were scarcely less implacable; while, with few exceptions, the great problems that have engaged the attention of scientists have been singularly free from heated and acrimonious discussion.

Much of this serene treatment of scientific subjects is due, no doubt, to their peculiar nature. In a given investigation the truth must, sooner or later, come to the light. Either the investigation will have to be abandoned altogether, because it is found to be beyond the province of the human understanding, or the problem will eventually be solved. In either event, long-continued doubt and uncertainty can not hang over the result. Hence few will venture, if so disposed, to cast ridicule upon efforts which may be crowned with success, and which may in the end expose the scoffers to similar reproaches.

Besides, the study of science, which is the study of nature, engages the mind in the study and contemplation of truth; and, as has been well said, "Truth is without passion." The little asperities, therefore, which ruffle other controversial natures, find scarcely any lodgment in the breast of him who searches after experimental truth. And such would be the effect produced upon the students of theology and literature were their conclusions capable of verification like those of the scientist. But, dealing for the most part with abstract subjects which in the nature of things can not be subjected to rigid mathematical tests, they find themselves afloat upon a wide sea of conjecture, in which faith and imagination are almost the only guides.

At this triumphant entry and career of Science upon the stage of modern thought, Religion is the only power that has as yet sounded the note of alarm, or assumed any very hostile attitude. Nor could she well do otherwise, because,

one by one, she has seen her adherents falling away from her, and joining the ranks of her ostensible adversary, and, one by one, she has seen some of the fairest portions of her territory invaded, and either falling a prey to anarchy and dissolution, or rudely wrested from her. In vain she has cried out for help, or tried to throw up barriers against this invasion. The sapping and mining process has nevertheless gone on; so that, if in the next half century the progress of science shall make as great inroads upon the prevailing popular belief as it has made within the last, it is safe to predict that only a moiety of it will be left, or, what is more probable, it will be changed into something more consonant with the new scientific discoveries, and with what is called "the spirit of the age."

If the changes thus following in the wake of physical discovery have been so marked and significant upon one of the interesting branches of human knowledge to which allusion has been made, how has it fared with the other, which, if not so widespread in its influences, can not nevertheless be affected in its character or career without producing results of the greatest consequence? Has literature as well as religion felt the wand of the mighty magician? and is it likely, in the future, to be retarded in its growth, crippled in its strength, or to any extent diverted from its purpose by this onward and sweeping march of science? These are questions of so much importance that the candid consideration of them can not be without its interest if not without its profit.

The commonwealth of literature embraces many states and distinct divisions, of which only those are particularly referred to in these pages that are usually comprehended under the title of polite or elegant literature, including works of the imagination, such as poetry and fiction, as well as authentic narratives, set off, as in history, with the graces of polished composition. Limited to even this description, literature has performed such an important part in administering to the instruction and delight of the world, that we could not afford to see it banished, even though a more efficient teacher should occupy its place. Nor can such a fate now in reality overtake it. Even should the number of its votaries ever be diminished, or should it ever fall into hands too feeble to sustain it, we would still have access to the ancient well-springs of its power, whose waters, though incapable of extension, can yet never run dry. It is a consolation to know that, though it may be impossible to add anything of sterling value to what has already been written, the great works of literary genius, treasured up in so many different languages, can never be taken away from us, and that their influence survives the manifold changes that happen to society in so many other respects.

Now, if it be true—that complaint of Labruyère—that "we are come into the world too late to produce anything new, that nature and life are preoccupied, and that description and sentiment have been long exhausted"; if it be true that literary labor, in times past, has spent itself in producing those wonderful creations which, by the common consent of mankind, stand as the highest models of composition and the highest types of literary excellence, then we must conclude that literature has reached its climax and fulfilled its mission, and that consequently there is no reason to regret its decadence. Better employ the measure of strength and talent with which we are endowed in exploring new lands and cultivating new soils than waste them in a field that is already gleaned of its harvests and exhausted of its fertility. To such a gloomy view of the present condition and future prospects of literature many men of sound judgment are unwilling to subscribe. And yet it seems to me, if they carefully consider the subject, especially in connection with the new direction which has been given of late years to the studies and aspirations of the noblest minds, they must see good reason for modifying their judgment. Let us examine it for a few moments with respect to two of the departments of letters that are regarded among scholars at least with the highest esteem and veneration of any—I mean poetry and history.

Those who are most familiar with the poetry of different countries, and of ancient and modern times, must admit the remarkable resemblance and repetition to be found in it. Under the garb perhaps of a new diction, in one poet, will be found lurking the identical idea expressed by another. As Emerson says: "The originals are not original. There is imitation, model and suggestion, to the very archangels, if we knew their history. The first book tyrannizes over the second. Read Tasso, and you think of Virgil; read Virgil, and you think of Homer; and Milton forces you to reflect how narrow are the limits of human invention." And as Dryden somewhere says about the modern poets, "You may track them in the snow of the ancients." Even the imagery and what is called the "machinery" of poetry repeat themselves in different ages, in the pages of different writers. The only difference is in the language—the thought remains a constant quantity, being stereotyped and reproduced to suit the emergency.

Now, this perpetual recurrence of the same idea among different poets is often stigmatized as plagiarism. But such a charge is not necessary, and is, I believe, in the majority of cases, entirely without foundation. A man gifted, or who imagines himself gifted, with the power of composing verses, and who has read with care and attention the great masters of the art, will insensibly reproduce many of their best thoughts. Yet such a man is not a plagiarist. He is, at the worst, only an imitator, and an unconscious imitator at that. And for this reason, if not for the one Aristotle gave, poetry may be called emphatically an "imitative art." But there is a still higher reason why one poet should become, as it were, the echo of another; and that is to be found in the nature and limitations of the human mind itself.

The maxim, *Poeta nascitur non fit,* is the true expression and interpretation of the law which governs the poetical order of intellects. At rare intervals, Nature has sent into the world a few souls endowed with the largest possible measure of ideality and poetical power. Their number may be counted upon one's ten fingers. Inspired with song, this

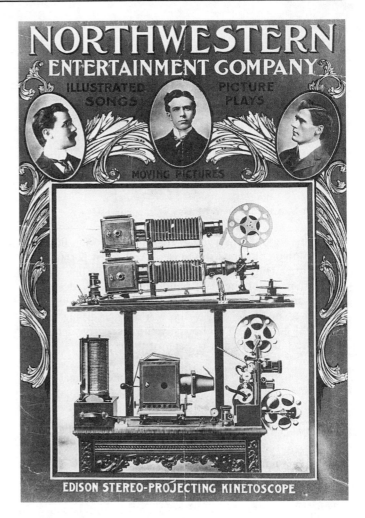

Advertisement for Thomas Edison's invention, the Stereo-Projecting Kinetoscope.

gifted few can not choose but sing. They are the leaders of the choir; while all the rest are but subordinates, obeying the heaven-born impulse given to them by the muses' elect. As well might the mocking-bird essay the highest and sweetest notes of the nightingale, or the fledgling try the eagle's flight, as one of the non-elect aspire to reach the heavenly harmony of these natural minstrels and apostles of song. Such men as Homer, and Dante, and Shakespeare, constitute the grand natural hierarchy of genius, to which inferior minds instinctively pay homage, and before which they "pale their ineffectual fires." These are the great central lights of poetry, while all the rest are the little miniature worlds revolving around them, and really borrowing from them all their effulgence. Hence we ought not to be surprised to find nothing in the lesser luminaries which the greater do not contain. It is in the order of nature, which it were vain to attempt either to resist or reverse.

Thus the task being almost hopeless of trying to achieve any lasting distinction or success in a field already preoccupied, and incapable of further profitable cultivation, many of the most gifted intellects, in our day, are diverted from it by the greater prospect of reward held out by science, whose territory is vastly more extensive as well as prolific. It were easy to name more than one man eminent in science, whose natural gifts would qualify him to shine in the lists of poetry, and yet who has wisely chosen the path leading to higher honor and remuneration. Hugh Miller might have stood high among the Scottish bards, had he devoted himself to the muses with the same ardor and enthusiasm with which he grappled some of the profoundest questions in geology; and with how much more of justice might that line of Pope—

How sweet an Ovid Murray was our boast!—

have been applied to Tyndall than to Lord Mansfield, had Tyndall also cultivated the muses! And yet it is safe to say that neither Hugh Miller nor Tyndall, by rivaling some of the first poets of the day, would have acquired as much honor, and, what is of far more importance, would have been of as much service to the world, as in filling so worthily and performing so honestly the respective spheres of scientific labor assigned to each of them.

Besides opening up such an avenue to men of real genius, the pursuit of science, when properly understood, is far more attractive and more in harmony with their tastes than can possibly be the cultivation of an art already touched by the hand of decay, and passing into the limbo of faded and effete systems. In the pursuit of science we go in quest of natural laws that there is every reason for believing are almost innumerable and inexhaustible; in poetry, the search is for phantoms of the imagination which, ten to one, have already flitted across other minds and been appropriated by them. In science, we search for the real, oftentimes more wonderful and beautiful than the most splendid visions; in poetry we search for the ideal, which, if it be new, now almost impossible, fails to command admiration, unless it be set before us in the most pleasing colors, and in a style of the highest finish. This elaborate toilet being unnecessary, though admissible to some extent in the treatment of scientific subjects, more range is given to the reason and less to the discursive faculties. And herein lies one of the chief advantages of the scientific method. While giving sufficient rein to the imagination to keep it in healthy exercise, it makes use of the reflective and perceptive powers in an eminent degree. Hence it engenders the greatest strength and breadth of the intellect; and it is no exaggeration to say that, if all other methods were abandoned, the study of science alone is capable of raising the mind to the loftiest possible standard of development.

Sooner or later educational institutions must take notice of this fact, and give it the heed its vast importance deserves. It seems impossible that a few narrow-minded patrons and disciples of the old system, watching at the gates, should much longer shut out from our seminaries of learning that great herald of freedom, of reform, and of progress, panoplied in the armor of truth, who has already dethroned so many idols of the forum, the pulpit, and the market-place, and who stands ready, on entering these seminaries, to perform a similar lustration. And nothing needs it more. Palsied almost by a *régime* which administers public instruction on pretty much the same plan upon which wars are conducted in some of the countries of the Old World—that is, without adopting either the new discipline or the new arms which have enabled other countries to achieve victories—our system of public schools is sinking into decrepitude and decay for want of a new stimulus. Give it this in the shape of lessons in modern science, in all its freedom and amplitude, and it will be infused with new life. Give it this, and the education of our youth will be something more and something higher than injecting into the mind several new languages, to the sad neglect of the mother tongue, and loading the memory with a useless mass of rules, and definitions, and other abstract forms, which are forgotten as soon as the student enters upon the stage of practical life.

But to return from what may seem a digression. The influence exerted by the march of modern science upon history and historical composition is even more direct and decided than its influence upon poetry. Dealing with the actions of man either in his individual or collective capacity, even the best historians have been in the habit, until within a few years past, of regarding them as the result either of self-directed will or of special providences. Consequently their pages are filled with the marvels wrought by heroes and conquerors, particularly those who were regarded as the especial favorites of Heaven. No margin has been left in these pages for the operation of general laws, guiding and controlling human conduct. And it is only within a recent period that the theory has been formulated that the progress of society is not to be attributed to the casual disturbances made by powerful individuals, or to the ascription of supernatural means, but wholly to the force of laws working out their results without the interference of either divine or human agency. This contribution, or rather new direction to history, constituting by far its most essential feature and element, we owe to science. A few great minds, chief among whom may be mentioned Comte in France and Herbert Spencer in Great Britain, taking their stand upon the recognized principles and harmonies prevailing in the material universe, have transferred this grand conception of law and order amid apparent discordances into the sphere of human societies. Here, as well as in the material universe, the relations existing between different communities, and between the individual members of each, are relations due to the interaction of natural forces; and here, as well as in the material universe, the changes that have been wrought out by these forces are changes analogous to those we see exhibited in the consolidation of the crust of the earth, and in the genesis and growth of the solar and stellar systems—changes, that is to say, from a state of homogeneity to greater and greater complexity and apparent elaboration of detail.

Now, this evident leaning of historians, in common with almost every other class of writers, at the present day, toward the theory of evolution, is so great, and so much is expected of them on account of this theory, that if they were practically to disregard it, in writing history, they would be almost left without readers. I might go further, and say that the tendency to connect the facts of history with the overruling operations of law is fast breaking down the barriers which separate our views of the government of the material world from those we hold concerning the affairs of man; so that it is safe to predict that the time is not far distant when, in a philosophical point of view, no very perceptible difference will be seen between the forces which control the conduct and career of nations and those which preside over the movements and revolutions of planets.

In view of this overshadowing influence, it were useless to touch upon the minor disturbances which science is producing upon history. It may almost be described as the grand motive power, which, in our day, is dragging the car of history along with it, as it drags all the rest in the train of literature. Whether they are the luxurious palace-cars, like poetry and history, furnished with all the elegance which man's inventive genius has been accumulating for centuries, and which only the richly-endowed may enter, or whether they are the plainer passenger-cars, like fiction and eloquence, filled with a group of motley characters, of greater or less pretensions and importance, and tricked out in a variety of costumes—they are all whirled along over the same road, obedient to the impulse given them by the mighty machine which stands, or rather flies, at the head of the train.

The highest aim of science is to discover the truths of nature. Literature, aspiring to something similar to this, recognizes the highest merit of literary composition in what is called its "truth to nature." In delineations of character, in descriptions of scenery, in the skillful weaving together of the component parts of a play or a novel, in the birth of sentiment, or in the happy turn given to an expression, what we most admire is the writer's adherence to certain rules or standards that have the closest conformity with what we observe in the internal or external worlds. From what we perceive in ourselves or in things around us, we derive the measure and gauge of all literary excellence. True, our own perceptions are trained and quickened by the thoughts and perceptions of others; so that what we read or hear aids us in correcting, enlarging, or refining our literary judgments. But we must be able to combine empirical tests with subjective analysis, before the intellectual process can be completed which authorizes us to determine whether any given production reaches that highest grade of excellence implied in its being "true to nature." But what, it may be asked, does this truth to nature actually consist in? Is it necessary that the author should set before us something that really exists?—something to be seen in nature, like a tree or a waterfall? Do we require of him an absolute verity? So far from this, it is only necessary that he should not shock us with anything that, at first sight, is repugnant to our tastes or feelings—anything that bears on its face the marks of falsehood or extrava-

gance. Within these limits, a "counterfeit presentment" is as good as the original. All that the most fastidious reader can ask in an author is a certain similitude to nature. He never looks for anything more than what is called *vraisemblance* or plausibility. What *seems* to be true satisfies him as well as what *is* true.

How opposite to this the mental discipline and research required of the scientist! No illusions or half-truths can ever satisfy *his* mind. Engaged in prolonged labors to find out the laws of natural phenomena, he counts nothing as gained so long as these remain undiscovered. One after another chimeras vanish from his mind; theories are tried, only to be discarded, if found not to fit in with facts; verifications from many opposite quarters are applied to test the value of a given hypothesis; and, if, after all, any of them are seen to be at variance with it, the hypothesis is abandoned, though it may have been cherished with all the ardor of a first and only affection.

That the semblance of truth answers the purpose of almost every kind of literature, as well as the reality, and thus places it in marked contrast with the rigid requirements of science, is further manifest from this, that we often see two propositions or apothegms, entirely repugnant to each other, equally applauded by the multitude, and maintaining a place and a good character in current literature; while of two rival theories or doctrines in science, either both are sooner or later rejected, or they become reconciled, or one is finally substantiated. Every one's reading, if at all extensive, will readily suggest illustrations of the truth of this remark. A few of these inconsistencies or contradictions in literature may not be out of place here. First, we will compare what is said by two distinguished philosophers upon the subject of anger. "To be moved by passion," says Marcus Aurelius, "is not manly, but mildness and gentleness, as they are more agreeable to human nature; so, also, are they more manly; and he who professes these qualities possesses strength, nerve, and courage—and not the man who is subject to fits of passion and discontent. For in the same degree in which a man's mind is nearer to freedom from all passion, in the same degree also is it nearer to strength. And as the sense of pain is a characteristic of weakness, so also is anger. For he who yields to pain and he who yields to anger are both wounded, and both submit." On the other hand, Bacon: "To seek to extinguish anger utterly is but a bravery of the Stoics. We have better oracles. . . . In refraining from anger, it is the best remedy to win time, and to make a man's self believe that the opportunity of his revenge is not yet come; but that he foresees a time for it, and so to still himself, in the mean time, and reserve it." Next, hear what two others of the same guild have to advise us concerning knowledge: "It is a vanity to waste our days in the blind pursuit of knowledge; it is but attending a little longer, and we shall enjoy that by instinct and infusion which we endeavor at here by labor and inquisition. It is better to sit down in a modest ignorance, and rest contented with the natural blessings of our own reason, than buy the uncertain knowledge of this life with sweat and vexation, which death gives every fool gratis" (Sir Thomas Browne). "No way has been found for making heroism easy even for the scholar. Labor, iron labor, is for him. . . . There is so much to be done that we ought to begin quickly to bestir ourselves. This day-labor of ours, we confess, has hitherto a certain emblematic air, like the annual plowing and sowing of the Emperor of China. Let us make it an honest sweat" (Emerson). Who shall decide when doctors disagree? Once more, look at what Herbert Spencer calls the "great-man theory" in history. He and Macaulay and Buckle, on one side, are as wide apart as the poles of the earth from Carlyle and Emerson, on the other, concerning this theory. Hear Carlyle first: "We can not look, however imperfectly, upon a great man without gaining something by him. He is the living light-fountain, which it is good and pleasant to be near—the light which enlightens, which has enlightened, the darkness of the world; and this not as a kindled lamp only, but rather as a natural luminary, shining by the gift of Heaven." To the same effect, Emerson: "Literary history, and all history, is a record of the power of minorities, and of minorities of one. . . . The importance of the one person who has truth over nations who have it not is because power obeys reality and not appearance, according to quality and not quantity. How much more are men than nations! . . . So that, wherever a true man appears, everything usually reckoned great dwarfs itself. He is the only great event; and it is easy to lift him into a mythological person."

On the other side, hear Macaulay: "Those who have read history with discrimination know the fallacy of those panegyrics and invectives which represent individuals as effecting great moral and intellectual revolutions, subverting established systems, and impressing a new character on the age. The difference between one man and another is by no means so great as the superstitious crowd supposes. . . . The sun illuminates the hills while it is still below the horizon; and truth is discovered by the highest minds a little before it becomes manifest to the multitude. This is the extent of their superiority. They are the first to catch and reflect a light which, without their assistance, must, in a short time, be visible to those who lie far beneath them." And here is what Herbert Spencer offers on the same side: "The origin of the great man is natural; and, immediately he is thus recognized, he must be classed with all other phenomena in the society that gave him birth as a product of its antecedents. Along with the whole generation of which he forms a minute part, along with its institutions, language, knowledge, manners, and its multitudinous arts and appliances, he is a resultant of an enormous aggregate of causes that have been operating for ages. . . . If it be a fact that the great man may modify his nation in its structure and actions, it is also a fact that there must have been those antecedent modifications constituting national progress before he could be evolved. Before he can make his society, his society must make him; so that all those changes, of which he is the proximate imitator, have their chief causes in the generations which gave him birth. If there is to be anything like a real explanation of these changes, it must be sought in that aggregate of conditions out of which both he and they have arisen."

And so on through the literature of all nations, from the earliest times down to the present day, it abounds in antagonism of sentiment. And when two or more authors happen to agree, others will be found who will refute their positions, and convict them of mistakes; so as almost to justify that saying of Voltaire, that "the history of human opinion is scarcely anything more than the history of human error." More than this: not only will these various disagreements be discovered among different authors, but different passages in the same author will show a similar want of harmony, and, what is a greater wonder and anomaly still, the same passage, which will not want for admirers on account of its beauty and the justice and accuracy of the sentiments it expresses, will sometimes find just as many, even though its meaning be entirely reversed. Take the commencement of one of Emerson's latest essays, called "Resources," to illustrate what I mean. I place side by side with the original affirmative propositions their negatives:

> "Men are made up of potences. We are magnets in an iron globe. We have keys to all doors. We are all inventors, each sailing out on a voyage of discovery, guided each by a private chart, of which there is no duplicate," etc.

> Men are made up of impotences. We are magnets in a wooden globe. We have keys to no doors. Scarcely any are inventors, sailing out on a voyage of discovery. Scarcely any are guided by a private chart, of which there is no duplicate, etc.

Or take this passage from one of Dr. Johnson's essays: "It seems to be the fate of man to seek all his consolations in futurity. The time present is seldom able to fill desire or imagination with immediate enjoyment, and we are forced to supply its deficiencies by recollection or anticipation. . . . Thus every period of life is obliged to borrow its happiness from time to come. In youth we have nothing past to entertain us, and in age we derive little from retrospect but hopeless sorrow." If there are persons to be found who will subscribe to these views, there are more who will adopt the contrary, as thus: It seems to be the fate of man to seek all his consolations in the present. The future is seldom able to fill desire or imagination with sufficient enjoyment, and hence we are forced to supply its deficiencies with that which is immediate. . . . Thus every period of life is obliged to borrow its happiness from the present moment, etc.

Now, as I have before hinted, there is no chance for such contradictions in science; or, if they ever occur, their existence, from the very nature of the pursuit, can not be of permanent duration. There is no such thing as imaginary laws controlling phenomena. Nature abhors a fallacy or a fiction more than a vacuum; and though for a stated period the true cause of a given phenomenon may be hidden from view, owing to the imperfect means or the imperfect intelligence employed to unravel it, and thus a fictitious origin be assigned for it, yet in course of time the error is sure to be detected and the truth to be revealed. Thus it was with the astronomical system of Ptolemy. Up to the time of Copernicus the learned world as well as the illiterate were led to believe that the sun and all the rest of the heavenly bodies revolved around the earth, as the center of the entire system. Yet, as soon as the error was exploded, and the truth demonstrated, there was a universal rejection of the one and a universal recognition of the other. So, at a later period, when the true theory of ethereal undulations, as applied to light, fought its way against much opposition into popular belief, the old theory of emanations was dropped, never to be again taken up.

Nevertheless, from what has been said, it must not be inferred that what are called coincidences of thought never occur among scientists. On the contrary, these are so common as to give license for believing in the existence of a law, akin to that of evolution if not a part of it, by virtue of which, in the progress of knowledge, certain new truths dawn upon the world, receiving expression simultaneously from more than one mind. Given the age which is ripe for any discovery, and it breaks out in many different quarters of the globe at the same moment. Men seem to be watching for it, and, like a meteor glancing across the heavens, it is witnessed by several observers from many points of the compass. Take, for example, the great law of natural selection, as applicable to man's origin—it was discovered simultaneously in England by Darwin and Wallace; while in Germany, at the same time, Haeckel had promulgated a similar theory; and in France, in a preceding age, Lamarck had laid the foundation for it in the most unmistakable manner.

But it is only in this single point of occasional coincidence or identity that the leading thoughts of science take on a certain likeness with those of literature. The analogy ends with the admission that each of these thoughts may have rival paternities. Beyond this the difference becomes manifest; and it consists in this: While the utterances of different literatures may seem to be original, this is often owing to a variation in their phraseology, an examination of which will show them to be identical; and, in addition to this, there is no criterion by which their truth can be tested. But in science, while different claims may be made for originality of discovery, each truth stands out in bold relief, is distinct and well defined, and, after it has been submitted to all the various verifications of which it is susceptible, it no longer admits of any doubt and becomes a part of the common stock of human knowledge, possessing, as nearly as possible, the attributes of positive, absolute, and immutable truth.

Owing to the endless tautologies of literature, it requires little discernment to see that it must be approaching a crisis in, if not a completion of, its destiny. Traveling in the same old circle, and treating us perpetually to the same round of entertainment without change or variety, it must gradually cease to interest, and eventually die a natural death. With no new oil to fill its lamps, steeped in a kind of Stygian darkness of its own creation, one may well exclaim with Othello:

> I know not where is that Promethean heat
> That can its light relume.

And that this would have been a natural result if modern science had not come to the rescue at the right moment, and furnished its proper share of this "Promethean heat," admits of scarcely a doubt, especially in view of the fact that the most successful cultivators of letters in modern times are found resorting, for their choicest inspiration, to the new fountains thus opened to use. Notably among poets such men as Tennyson, among historians such men as Buckle, and among critics such men as Taine, have availed themselves of these helps to their genius; while by differentiating the condition of man, in some of the most important particulars, science has so wrought upon his character and destiny as to render it possible for such splendid intellects as Goethe, Dickens, and Victor Hugo to say something original of him. For, if you strip their pages of what may be called their scientific coloring, if you take away what directly or indirectly may be traced to the magic web which science has woven all through the affairs of modern life, you strip them of much of their witchery and of most of their originality.

Now, without going into particulars, we may say generally that the way in which science has wrought this great reform and revolution in literature has been by widening our survey of both man and nature. From a being of comparative insignificance, ruled by the rod of a tyrant, or made the sport of demons, and whose views of things were bounded by the narrowest horizon, she has transformed man into a being of the highest order of which we have any knowledge, having risen to it by the operation of laws that have been shaping his destiny for ages. Step by step his powers have been unfolding and the range of his vision enlarging, until he has been able to find some clew to his origin, and some interpretation of natural laws that before were a mystery to him. By the aid of what may be considered a sort of "second sight," namely, instruments of his own invention, he has been enabled to explore the remotest bounds of creation, and thus literally open to himself a new heaven and a new earth. With the telescope he has reached the most distant of planets, with the spectroscope he has discovered many of their constituent elements, and with the microscope he has penetrated into the secrets of the minutest forms of insect life. Through molecular physics and the grand modern triumph of evolution, both in its relation to man and the totality of nature, he has brought near to him many of the outlying provinces of human knowledge, and poured upon them a flood of light.

To the investigation of principles has succeeded the application of useful inventions. Theories have almost invariably germinated into practical science. From the study of mathematics, physics, chemistry, and geology, industries have been developed which have made the commonest dwelling of modern times a palace and the poorest cities a miracle of magnificence, compared with those of the past.

And all of this material advancement has been attended by a corresponding diffusion of knowledge and awakening of intellectual activity, so that the merest tyro in knowledge, at the present day, surpasses in intellectual acquisitions all that the most successful scholar of Greece and Rome could boast of, even though he had mastered all the learning of antiquity. More marvelous still, the latest expression of psychological science forces upon us the conviction that the mental faculties themselves, in harmony with the results of evolution everywhere else, are brought within its grasp, that they are thus enlarged in their capacity, and made equal to the task of furnishing through the revolving ages disclosures of the almost limitless secrets of the material world, and of the agency which brought it into being.

Here then, finally, we may look for the only avenue of escape from the doom with which literature was threatened—a doom not unlike that which settled over the Empire of Dullness as painted by the poet. In that picture the whole assembled concourse of wits and critics are represented as falling into a profound slumber, while listening to the sleepy literary performances of one or two of their heroes. Nor did *they* ever rise out of this lethargy. Fortunately, the comparison ends here. For while, without doubt, the same leaden slumber was fast settling over the prostrate form of modern Literature, the mighty enchantress, modern Science, touched it at the propitious moment with her potent rod, and woke into new life its exhausted and dying energies.

John Burroughs (essay date 1888)

SOURCE: "Science and the Poets," in *Cosmopolitan,* Vol. 5, No. 2, April, 1888, pp. 127-30.

[*In the following essay, Burroughs looks at nineteenth-century literary figures, including Keats, Tennyson, Emerson, and Carlyle, to assess the extent to which these writers were influenced by science.*]

It is interesting to note to what extent the leading literary men of our country and time have been influenced by science, or have availed themselves of its results. A great many of them not at all, it would seem. Among our own writers Bryant, Irving, Hawthorne, Longfellow, Whittier, show little or no trace of the influence of science. The later English poets, Arnold, Swinburne, Rossetti, do not appear to have profited by science. There is no science in Rossetti, unless it be a kind of dark, forbidden science, or science in league with sorcery. Rossetti's muse seems to have been drugged with an opiate that worked inversely and made it morbidly wakeful instead of somnolent. The air of his "House of Life" is close, and smells not merely of midnight oil, but of things much more noxious and suspicious.

Byron, Shelley, Keats, Landor, seem to have owed little or nothing directly to science; Coleridge and Wordsworth probably more, though with them the debt was inconsiderable. Wordsworth's great ode shows no trace of scientific knowledge. Yet Wordsworth was certainly an interested observer of the scientific progress of his age, and was the first to indicate the conditions under which the poet could avail himself of the results of physical science. "The Poet," he says, "writes under one restriction only, namely, that of the necessity of giving immediate pleasure to a human Being possessed of that information which may be expected from him, not as a lawyer, a physician, a mariner, an astronomer, or a natural philosopher, but as a Man." "The knowledge both of the Poet and the Man of Science," he again says, "is pleasure; but the knowledge of the one cleaves to us as a necessary part of our existence, our natural and unalienable inheritance; the other as a personal and individual acquisition, slow to come to us, and by no habitual and direct sympathy connecting us with our fellow beings." In reaching his conclusion, he finally says: "The remotest discoveries of the Chemist, the Botanist, or Mineralogist, will be as proper objects of the Poet's art as any upon which it can be employed, if the time should ever come when these things shall be familiar to us, and the relations under which they are contemplated by the followers of these respective sciences shall be manifestly and palpably material to us as enjoying and suffering beings. If the time should ever come when what is now called Science, thus familiarized to men, shall be ready to put on, as it were, a form of flesh and blood, the Poet will lend this divine spirit to aid the transfiguration, and will welcome the Being thus produced as a dear and genuine inmate of the household of man." To clothe science with flesh and blood, to breathe into it the breath of life, is a creative work which only the Poet can do. Several of the younger poets, both in this country and in England, have made essays in this direction, but with indifferent success. It is still science when they have done with it, and not poetry. The transfiguration of which Wordsworth speaks is not perfect. The inorganic has not clearly become the organic. Charles DeKay has some good touches, but still the rock is too near the surface. The poetic covering of vegetable mold is too scanty. More successful, but still rather too literal, are several passages in Mr. Nichols' "Monte Rosa." A passage beginning on page 9,

> "Of what was doing on earth
> Ere man had come to see,"

is good science and pretty good poetry.

> And that unlettered time slipped on,
> Saw tropic climes invade the polar rings,
> The polar cold lay waste the tropic marge;
> Saw monster beasts emerge in ooze and air,
> And run their race and stow their bones in clay;
> Saw the bright gold bedew the elder rocks,
> And all the gems grow crystal in their caves;
> Saw plant wax quick, and stir to moving worm,
> And worm move upward, reaching toward the brute;
> Saw brute by habit fit himself with brain,
> And startle earth with wondrous progeny;

Saw all of these, and still saw no true man,
For man was not, or still so rarely was,
That as a little child his thoughts were weak,
Weak and forgetful and of nothing worth,
And Nature stormed along her changeful ways
Unheeded, undescribed, the while man slept
Infolded in his germ, or with fierce brutes,
Himself but brutal, waged a pigmy war,
Unclad as they, and with them housed in caves,
Nor knew that sea retired or mountain rose."

Whether the science in this and similar passages, with which Mr. Nichols' epic abounds, has met with a change of heart and become pure poetry, may be questioned. There is a more complete absorption of science and the emotional reproduction of it in Whitman, as there is also in Tennyson. "In Memoriam" is full of science winged with passion.

Tennyson owes a larger debt to physical science than any other current English poet, Browning the largest debt to legerdemain or the science of jugglery. Occasionally Tennyson puts wings to a fact of science very successfully, as in his "The Dragon Fly":

"To-day I saw the dragon fly
Come from the wells where he did lie.
An inner impulse rent the veil
Of his old husk; from head to tail
Came out clear plates of sapphire mail.

"He dried his wings; like gauze they grew;
Through crofts and pastures wet with dew
A living flash of light he flew."

Keats' touches are often accurate enough for science, and free and pictorial enough for poetry.

"Here are sweet peas, on tiptoe for a flight;
With wings of gentle flush o'er delicate white,
And taper fingers catching at all things,
To bind them all about with tiny rings."

Or this by a "streamlet's rushy banks":

"Where swarms of minnows show their little heads,
Staying their wavy bodies 'gainst the streams,
To taste the luxury of sunny beams
Temper'd with coolness, how they ever wrestle
With their own sweet delight, and ever nestle
Their silver bellies on the pebbly sand!"

Only a naturalist can fully appreciate Keats' owl—"the downy owl," as the quills and feathers of this bird are literally tipped with down, making it soft to the hand and silent in its flight.

On the other hand, it takes a poet to fully appreciate Linnæus' marriage of the planets and his naming of the calyx the *thalamus,* or bridal chamber; and the eorolla, the tapestry of it.

The two eminent poets of our own language whose attitude toward science is the most welcome and receptive are undoubtedly Emerson and Whitman, the former especially. No other imaginative writer seems to have been so stimulated and aroused by the astounding discoveries of physics. There was something in the boldness of science, in its surprises, its paradoxes, its affinities, its attractions and repulsions, its circles, its compensations, its positive and negative, its each in all, its all in each, its subtle ethics, its modulations, its perpetuity and conservation of forces, its spires and invisible germs in the air, its electricity, its mysteries, its metamorphoses, its perception of the unity, the oneness of nature, etc.,—there was something in all these things that was peculiarly impressive to Emerson. They were in the direction of his own thinking; they were like his own startling affirmations. He was constantly seeking and searching out the same things in the realm of ideas and of morals. In his laboratory you shall witness wonderful combinations, surprising affinities, unexpected relations of opposites, threads and ties unthought of.

Emerson went through the cabinet of the scientist as one goes through a book-stall to find an odd volume to complete a set; or through a collection of pictures, looking for a companion piece. He took what suited him, what he had use for at home. He was a provident bee exploring all fields for honey, and he could distill the nectar from the most unlikely sources. Science, for its own sake, he perhaps cared little for, and on one occasion refers rather disdainfully to "this *post-mortem* science." Astrology, he says, interests us more, "for it tied man to the system. Instead of an isolated beggar, the farthest star felt him, and he felt the star." "The human heart concerns us more than the peering into microscopes, and is larger than can be measured by the pompous figures of the astronomer." But where he could turn science over and read a moral on the other side, then he valued it—then the bud became a leaf on a flower instead of a thorn.

While in London in 1848 he heard Faraday lecture in the Royal Institute on *dia,* or cross magnetism, and Emerson instantly caught at the idea as applicable in metaphysics. "Dia-magnetism," he says, "is a law of *mind* to the full extent of Faraday's idea; namely, that every mind has a new compass, a new north, a new direction of its own, differing in genius and aim from every other mind." In chemistry, in botany, in physiology, in geology, in mechanics, he found keys to unlock his enigmas. No matter from what source the hint came, he was quick to take it. The stress and urge of expression with him was very great, and he would fuse and recast the most stubborn material. There is hardly a fundamental principle of science that he has not turned to ideal uses. "The law of nature is alternation for evermore. Each electrical state super-induces the opposite." "The systole and diastole of the heart are not without their analogy in the ebb and flow of love," and so on. In "spiritual laws" he gives a happy turn to the law of gravitation:

"Let us draw a lesson from nature, which always works by short ways. When the fruit is ripe it falls. When the fruit is dispatched, the leaf falls. The circuit of the waters is mere falling. The walking of man and all animals is a falling forward. All our manual labor and works of strength, as prying, splitting, digging, rowing, and so forth, are done by dint of continual falling, and the globe, earth, moon, comet, sun, star, fall for ever and ever."

He is an evolutionist, not upon actual proof like Darwin, but upon poetic insight. "Man," he says, "carries the world in his head, the whole astronomy and chemistry suspended in a thought. Because the history of nature is charactered in his brain, therefore is he the prophet and discoverer of her secrets. Every known fact in natural science was divined by the presentiment of somebody before it was actually verified." Thus that stupendous result of modern experimental science, that heat is only a mode of motion, was long before (in 1844) a fact in Emerson's idealism. "A little heat, that is a little motion, is all that differences the bald, dazzling white and deadly poles of the earth from the prolific tropical climates. All changes pass without violence, by reason of the two cardinal conditions of boundless space and boundless time. Geology has initiated us into the secularity of nature, and taught us to disuse our dame-school measure and exchange our Mosaic and Ptolemaic schemes for her large style. We knew nothing rightly for want of perspective. Now we learn what patient periods must round themselves before the rock is formed, then before the rock is broken, and the first lichen race has disintegrated the thinnest external plate into soil, and opened the door for the remote flora, fauna, ceres and pomonas to come in. How far off yet is the trilobite! how far the quadruped! how inconceivably remote is man! All duly arrive, and then race after race of men. It is a long way from granite to the oyster; farther yet to Plato and the preaching of the immortality of the soul. Yet all must come assurely as the atom has two sides."

Indeed most of Emerson's writings, including his poems, seem curiously to imply science, as if he had all these bold deductions and discoveries under his feet, and was determined to match them in the ideal. He has taken courage from her revelations. He would show another side to nature equally wonderful. Such men as Tyndall confess their obligation to him. His optics, his electricity, his spectrum analysis, his chemical affinity, his perpetual forces, his dynamics, his litmus tests, his germs in the air, etc., are more wonderful than theirs. How much he makes of circles, of polarity, of attraction and repulsion, of natural selection, of

> "the famous might that lurks
> In reaction and recoil,
> Makes flame to freeze, and ice to boil."

He is the astronomer and philosopher of the moral sentiment. He is full of the surprises and paradoxes, the subtle relations and affinities, the great in the little, the far in the near, the sublime in the mean, that science has disclosed in the world about us. He would find a more powerful fulminant than has yet been discovered. He likes to see two harmless elements come together with a concussion that

will shake the roof. It is not so much for material that Emerson is indebted to science, as for courage, example, inspiration.

When he used scientific material he fertilized it with his own spirit. This the true poet will always do when he goes to this field. Hard pan will not grow corn; meteoric dust will not nourish melons. The poet adds something to the hard facts of science that is like vegetable mold to the soil, like the contributions of animal and vegetable life, and of the rains, the dews, the snows.

Carlyle's debt to science is much less obvious than that of Emerson. He was not the intellectual miser, the gleaner and hoarder of ideas for their own sake, that Emerson was, but the prophet and spokesman of personal qualities, the creator and celebrator of heroes. So far as science ignored or belittled man, or the ethical quality in man, and rests with a mere mechanical conception of the universe, he was its enemy. Individuality alone interested him. Not the descent of the species, but the ascent of personal attributes, was the problem that attracted him. He was unfriendly to the doctrine of physical evolution, yet his conception of natural selection and the survival of the fittest as applied to history, is as radical as Darwin's. He had studied astronomy to some purpose. The fragment left among his papers called "Spiritual Optics," and published by Froude in his life of him, shows what a profound interpretation and application he had given to the cardinal astronomical facts. His sense of the reign of law, his commanding perception of the justice and rectitude inherent in things, of the reality of the ideal, of the subordination of the lesser to the greater, the tyranny of mass, power, etc., have evidently all been deepened and intensified by his absorption of the main principles of this department of physical science. What disturbed him especially was any appearance of chaos, anarchy, insubordination; he wanted to see men governed and duly obedient to the stronger force, as if the orbs of heaven were his standard. He seemed always to see man and human life in their sidereal relations, against a background of immensity, depth beyond depth, terror beyond terror, splendor above splendor, surrounding them. Indeed, without the light thrown upon the universe by the revelations of astronomy, Carlyle would probably never have broken from the Calvinistic creed of his fathers. By a kind of sure instinct he spurned all that phase of science which results in such an interpretation of the universe as is embodied in the works of Spencer—works which, whatever their value, are so utterly barren to the literary and artistic mind.

The inquisitions of science, the vivisections, the violent, tortuous, disrupting processes are not always profitable. Wherein nature answers the easiest, cheerfulest, directest, we find our deepest interest; where science just anti pates the natural sense, as it were, or shows itself a little quicker witted than our slow faculties, as in the discovery of the circulation of the blood. The real wonder is that mankind should not always have known and believed it, because circulation is the law of nature. Everything circulates, or finally comes back to its starting point. Stagnation is death. The sphericity of the earth, too—how could we ever believe anything else? Does not the whole system of things center into balls; every form in nature strive to be spherical? The sphere is the infinity of form, that in which all specific form is merged and lost, or into which it escapes or gets transformed. The doctrine of the correlation and conservation of forces is pointed to by the laws of the mind. The poets have always said it, and all men have felt it: why await scientific proof? The spectroscope has revealed the universality of chemistry, that the farthermost star, as compared with our earth, is bone of her bone and flesh of her flesh. This is a poetic truth as well as a scientific, and is valuable to all men, because the germ of it always lay in their minds. It is a comfort to know for a certainty that these elements are cosmic; that matter is the same, and spirit, or law, the same everywhere, and that if we were to visit the remotest worlds, we would not find the men rooted to the ground and the trees walking about, but life on the same terms as here. The main facts of natural history also lie in the main direction of our natural faculties, and are proper and welcome to all men. So much of botany, so much of biology, so much of geology, of chemistry, of natural philosophy, as lies within the sphere of legitimate observation, or within the *plane* of man's natural knowledge, is capable of being absorbed by literature, and heightened to new significance.

Thomas E. Mayne (essay date 1894)

SOURCE: "Science in Song," in *The Westminster Review,* Vol. 141, No. 6, 1894, pp. 668-74.

[*In the following essay, Mayne discusses how poetry and science are more similar than different in that they both seek truth. Likewise, Mayne claims that the best way to popularize scientific knowledge is to put it into verse.*]

It was once fashionable to say that poetry and truth were composed of such antagonistic qualities that by no process of fusion in the crucible of genius could they be got to mix. Coleridge gave his opinion that science and poetry were for ever irreconcilable. Edgar Poe insisted on the same fallacy. Other and lesser poets and versifiers caught up the strain for the purpose of demonstrating how eternally separated they were. But, as matter of fact, science is but another name for truth, which is generally applied to tangible or substantial things. Where, then, is the line to be drawn between objective and subjective truth? The truths of philosophy were allowed to be compatible with the genius of the Muses, for Shakespeare and Wordsworth had placed that question beyond dispute; but science, considered in its narrower technical sense, was excluded from the domain of true poetry. Yet this arose merely from a superficial appreciation of the question. Shakespeare had intuitions on matters of science which have been but lately confirmed. Wordsworth had considerable botanical knowledge. Shelley was imbued with a spirit of exact science:

"How sweet a scene will earth become!
Of purest spirits, a pure dwelling-place,
Symphonious with the planetary spheres;
When man, with changeless Nature coalescing,
Will undertake regeneration's work,
When its ungenial poles no longer point
    To the red and baleful sun
    That faintly twinkles there."

Thus writes Shelley in his famous youthful poem, explaining in a note that the earth in its present state of obliquity points to the north polar star, but that this obliquity tends gradually to diminish until the equator will, it is thought, at some time coincide with the ecliptic. So much for the irreconcilableness of poetry and science. It is conceivable that the poet, embodying the state of learning of his age, will likewise embody its mistakes and misapprehensions. Thus Shakespeare, speaking of toothache as "a humour or a worm," was not speaking a scientific truth, but represented the conception of his times on this matter. Shakespeare had the eye of a scientist, and was careful and minute in recording what he saw. Who does not remember his observations on the preference shown by that "guest of summer, the temple-haunting martlet," for situations where the air is mild and delicate? Who cannot see his minuteness of description in the "mole, cinque-spotted like the crimson drops i' the bottom of a cowslip," on the pure breast of Imogen? If Shakespeare had not known the value of a scientific accuracy, he would not be so fresh and acceptable to us now after the lapse of three hundred years. But, though art and civilisation progress with ever accelerated momentum, we cannot get beyond truth, which is by nature eternal.

If properly considered, poetry must itself be a kind of truth, if it be poetry at all. Unless it represents truly the different states and emotions of the mind, the most melodious phrasing will fail to make its way into our affections. The heart will not be convinced by the exquisite charming of the mere artist in words, charm he never so wisely. We look instinctively for the soul of poetry—which is simply that quality we now so grossly personify—the spirit of truth dwelling inwardly. Much of the so-called poetry of the hour we feel to be devoid of this necessary verisimilitude, this closeness to physical and moral facts. It is often as entrancingly musical as Apollo's lyre, the tone rich, and the melody various and complicated; there is the sweet and nimble variation rung upon the theme, the gradual swell and *accelerando,* the modulated air, the lagging *rallentando* and languid fall; they are all there in simple words. We seem to have achieved almost a complete mastery of the *technique* of word music. Some of the productions of the modern muse might as well be labelled "fugue," "symphony," or "caprice," so near has the art of phrase-making approached to that of the instrumentalist. But if we look for a moral purpose in these compositions, or, indeed, a purpose of any kind, however perverse, we too often find it lacking, and are forced to pronounce them false to Nature and to right art—which is also sacred to truth—and to confess that they fall strictly under the category of the abnormal and the monstrous.

It is feared by some that science in song would mean only a worthless science and an enfeebled verse. But this objection is greatly more apparent than real. Tennyson, being the latest representative poet, is more imbued with a spirit of pure science than any other. Never, to our thinking, does he sing so sweetly as in his prefigurations of the truths discovered by science. The Pleiades likened to "a swarm of golden fire-flies, tangled in a silver braid," is a familiar instance. And this, for which modern science seems alone responsible, is not verse hampered by science, but science lending its inspiration to verse:

> "We sleep, and wake and sleep, but all things move;
> The sun flies forward to his brother sun;
> The dark earth follows, wheeled in her ellipse,
> And human things returning on themselves,
> Move onward, leading up the golden year."

The profoundest discoveries of science might be dealt with and simplified by poetry. It falls strictly within the poet's province to stimulate the scientist in his noble work for the benefit of the race. With his grand words let him encourage the searcher for truth to

> "Rift the hills, and roll the waters, flash the lightnings,
>   weigh the sun."

Science is that wisdom which is justified in all its works. Slowly it tends to gather all that is best to itself. It borrows the soul from religion, the mind from philosophy, the long-suffering from charity, and, that it may captivate the world and win it to itself, it must also have the sweet voice of poetry. The benefit is not all on the one side. The best poetry is better of the sure guidance of science, though in the airiest regions. Even the winds are bound by law, and thought itself cannot penetrate beyond the jurisdiction of strict necessity.

The popular conception of science, as a mere materialistic study of phenomena, is gradually disappearing before the herculean efforts of men of the stamp of Professor Huxley. It begins to dawn upon the public mind that Tyndall, Darwin, Pasteur, and others, are leading, not towards a chaos of bestial anarchy, but upwards to order and good-will and right-doing. Science has crawled before it walked, but later it has developed wings and built itself a habitation on the heights. It dares to pass that mysterious gulf which separates matter from mind and boldly deals with the larger problems of man's spiritual nature. It becomes fitting, therefore, that it should unite with poetry which readily mingles with what is highest in the mental sphere. The great poet yet to come, who is to be in some measure representative of his age, will require to be broadly versed in the broad knowledge of science. Society is growing scientific down to the lowest stratum. Our workmen are conning eagerly what scientific lore comes, through free libraries or the purveyors of cheap literature, within their reach. It is becoming a recognised fact that reforms have been hitherto generally attempted in an inverted way. We must begin with the physical improvement of the people, and let a clearer spiritual life grow out of bettered material

surroundings. The best way to raise men who live the life of swine, amidst poverty and dirt, is to make an observance of sanitary laws a step in their spiritual advancement. A sound house and some home comforts should precede demands for a strict rectitude of character. A system of main drainage may be as effective as the most elaborate ecclesiastical system extant in socially and morally benefiting the working-classes. The intellect also should be trained, so that men, when oppressed by the tyranny of circumstance, may have some sort of mental stay to fall back upon. With the poor, when their days are not filled with action either good or bad, their lives become a blank and utter vacancy. A well-furnished mind gives its owner a capacity for resting neutral, which may be of infinite value to him. The assertion, which is sometimes made, that intellectual culture is in no way a check on the mind's natural tendency to evil, is simply untrue. When all has been said on the matter, virtue is an acquired quality not inherent in mankind, and it should be in every way strengthened and stimulated, otherwise it may fail the individual at any moment.

The most effectual way of popularising scientific knowledge, and so widening and elevating men's minds, of banishing degrading superstitions, of teaching men to live to their higher intuitions, of fitting the mind of the mass for the reception of the brightest religious conceptions, is to wed science and verse together, if possible, with genius to consecrate the tie.

Almost all of Emerson's poetry is of a thoroughly scientific character. Though not admitted into that sacred arcanum where dwell the elect sons of melody, yet his verse, like his prose, possesses that electric quality of running through nerves and fibres, and eliciting a thrilling response from the natural magnetism of the mind. He is like a battery always charged, and cannot be touched without a free absorption of the nervous force. His was the pleasant creed that

> "The world was built in order
>   And the atoms march in tune;
> Rhyme the pipe and Time the warder,
>   Cannot forget the sun, the moon.
> Orb and atom forth they prance,
>   When they hear from far the rune;
> None so backward in the troop,
>   When the music and the dance
>   Reach his place and circumstance,
> But knows the sun-creating sound,
> And, though a pyramid, will bound."

It was his choice to sing

> "Of tendency through endless ages,
> Of star-dust and star-pilgrimages,
> Of rounded worlds, of space and time,
> Of the old flood's subsiding slime,
> Of chemic matter, force, and form,
> Of poles and powers, cold, wet, and warm."

He, at least, has shown that the subject of science need not introduce a single discordant note in poetry. The principles of gravitation, of attraction and repulsion, are tuneful to him. Geology, hard and dry, becomes musical like the statue of Memnon at sunrise. The orbs were musical in their courses in Shakespeare's imagination; there is no reason why they should not be so to us. Let them be so; let poetry make our exacter knowledge full of sweetness to sense and ear. Let the atoms march in tune, and the pyramids bound with the light-creating music which true genius in poesy produces.

Emerson is sometimes somewhat cold, but always musical, in a clear flute-like fashion. His bold individualism is expressed in language at once deeply scientific and poetical. Cosmos was an unceasing harmony sounding in his ears with the steady rhythm of law. All goes fairly and well in the world as a whole:

> "The journeying atoms,
>   Primordial wholes,
> Firmly draw, firmly drive,
>   By their animate poles.
>
> "Sea, earth, air, sound, silence,
>   Plant, quadruped, bird,
> By one music enchanted,
>   One deity stirred—
>
> "Each other adorning,
>   Accompany still;
> Night veileth the morning,
>   The vapour the hill."

But a greater than Emerson has united the best of both science and poetry in one indissoluble bond. Goethe is the great reconciler; he has mingled history, philosophy, science, and fable into one integral whole of wondrous beauty. He is the miracle-working alchemist who transmutes the baser earth-metals into a pure golden residue of wisdom. Goethe seems to have searched into every known art and science to find where truth was hidden, and he gave the world the result through the purifying and beautifying medium of poetry.

If I may be pardoned for again reverting to Tennyson, I would point out how instinct with the spirit of science is his latest great poem, the variously estimated *Locksley Hall Sixty Years After.* Tennyson—petted and spoiled child of fortune as he was—yet managed to keep abreast of the later developments of the times, and marked the steps of progress in his declining days with the eager appreciation of youth. His last great poem seems—if one may venture to say it—his greatest. It is the most original, the most in accordance with modern ideas, and in ways the most imaginative of all he wrote. It is as musical as the earlier poem of which it is a sequel, but comes more face to face with vital and insisting facts. The early poem is the outpouring of an individual disappointment and impatience, the later merges into the mass of sorrows burdening the world, is instinct with a larger passion of humanity. It contains the noblest utterance of scientific truth in the language.

> "Forward, backward, backward, forward, in the immeasurable sea,
> Sway'd by vaster ebbs and flows than can be known to you or me.
>
> "All the suns—are these but symbols of innumerable man,
> Man or mind that sees a shadow of the planner in the plan?
>
> "Is there evil but on earth? or pain in every peopled sphere?
> Well, be grateful for the sounding watchword "Evolution" here,
>
> "Evolution ever climbing after some ideal good,
> And Reversion ever dragging Evolution in the mud.
>   . . . . .
>
> "While the silent Heavens roll and Suns along their fiery way,
> All the planets whirling round them, flash a million miles a day.
>
> "Many an æon moulded earth before her highest man was born,
> Many an æon, too, may pass when earth is manless and forlorn.
>
> "Earth so huge and yet so bounded—pools of salt and plots of land—
> Shallow skin of green and azure—chains of mountains, grains of sand!
>
> "Only That which made us meant us to be higher by-and-by,
> Set the spheres of all the boundless heavens within the human eye,
>
> "Sent the shadow of Himself, the boundless, thro' the human soul;
> Boundless inward, in the atom, boundless outward, in the whole."

Susan Mizruchi (essay date 1991)

SOURCE: "Fiction and the Science of Society," in *The Columbia History of the American Novel,* edited by Emory Elliott, Columbia University Press, 1991, pp. 189-215.

[In the following essay, Mizruchi examines the emergence of the science of sociology in the nineteenth century and discusses the ways in which the concerns of this new science corresponded to the concerns of contemporary novelists.]

In *The Incorporation of America* (1982), Alan Trachtenberg describes the significance of the White City as symbol, its ability to transform the diverse and conflicted America of 1893 into an image of national unity. White City was a study in managed pluralism: organized into twenty departments and two hundred twenty-five divisions, contained within one overarching "symmetrical order . . . each building and each vista serving as an image of the whole." The choice of White City as the main design for the Chicago World's Columbian Exposition of 1893 was suggestive at the most fundamental level. As Herman Melville knew, the color white is a negation of the various rays of the color spectrum. It reflects but it does not absorb. One indication of White City's strategy for managing diversity was its presentation of certain cultures. Instead of being invited (like other constituencies) to portray their experiences in the nation's history, African Americans and Native Americans were presumed to be represented by an exhibit on primitive populations throughout the world. This ambition—unity without absorption, harmony through denial—is no doubt one reason why Frederick Douglass renamed the fair "white sepulchre."

It seems appropriate in retrospect that just one year earlier the city's foremost educational facility, the University of Chicago, had instituted one of the country's first sociology departments. Of all the social science disciplines developing at this time, sociology was most driven by the vision of social interdependence and unity that inspired the architects of White City. For the early sociologists, knowing society meant knowing the social whole. Other social scientists—economists, psychologists, political scientists, anthropologists—saw social reality piecemeal, through the narrow lens of their specialization. Sociology was unique in its aim to combine these disparate specialties into one integral discipline. This methodological imperative was matched by a theory that saw an unprecedented affinity of human consciousness and interests throughout modern life. In the landmark essay in which he declares "the scope of sociology" to be the organization of the "human sciences into a system of reciprocally reinforcing reports," Albion Small characterizes society as a "realm of circuits of reciprocal influence between individuals and groups." In keeping with the strategies of White City, Small's image is achieved at the cost of an evolutionary sleight of hand. What Small calls at one point, for example, that "serious scientific problem, the status of the coloured race in the United States," is subsumed in the image of "the last native of Central Africa . . . whom we inoculate with a desire for whiskey add[ing] an increment to the demand for our distillery products and effect[ing] the internal revenue of the United States."

Small's vision of human reciprocity, his description of alien populations that can be "innoculated" into a worldwide web of social and economic interest, was framed in a society fragmented by a bewildering heterogeneity of interests. This late nineteenth-century landscape of social change included: unprecedented immigration rates, especially from Southern and Eastern Europe; escalating capital-labor conflict; challenges to traditional women's roles that brought increasing numbers of women into an embattled labor force; rapid urbanization and industrialization; the rise of trusts; and the ever-intensifying problem of race relations. Like any discursive field, sociology was

an attempt to tell a certain kind of story about a particular historical reality. The burden of American sociology at its moment of origin was to reinscribe a conflicted and potentially explosive social reality as a terrain of consensus and integration.

The dedication to knowing the social whole that gripped an emerging sociological discipline is readily seen as consistent with the ambitions of contemporaneous American novelists. What is less often recognized are their various involvements (direct and indirect) with the anxieties, premises, and methods of this new science of society. The response of writers such as Herman Melville, Henry James, Gertrude Stein, Theodore Dreiser, to the formulation of a science that professionalized the main business of novelists—social observation, description of human types and types of interaction, the classification of these types—is an untold story whose narration provides a critical index to the social engagement of American novels. At the same time, to explore the rise of sociology in terms of contemporary novels is to enhance our understanding of the imaginative aspects of this new science.

The most vivid link between sociological and novelistic writings of the period is their shared interest in a language of social types. From Max Weber's "Protestant Ethic" (1905) to Theodore Dreiser's "An American Tragedy" (1925), from W. E. B. Du Bois's "Philadelphia Negro" (1899) to Henry James's "American Heiress" (1903), sociologists and novelists sought uniform types for mediating a vast and heterogeneous modern society. While literary authors have always been drawn to type categories, the typological methods employed by American novelists of this period have a particular historical resonance. They were formulated in response to the same pressing social landscape that gave rise to a modern discipline based on typological method. Type categories invested individuals and social phenomena with the semblance of predictability and control. They were key tools in turn-of-the-century efforts to circumscribe an ever-expanding society—to clarify, order, and label the social world. Types also served to promote and exclude different forms of social being. As Ian Hacking suggests in the essay "Making Up People," "numerous kinds of human beings and human acts came into being hand in hand with our invention of the categories labelling them." This interest in the varieties and limits of human action points to another central concern of the era: the question of individualism. American sociologists and novelists were at the forefront of changing conceptions of the individual. Their use of type categories was part of their struggle to mediate the divide between social determination and individuality in support of an ideal that was basic to American values, as well as essential to capitalist development.

What did it mean to *know* society for the first formulators of social science? For Adam Ferguson, whose *Essay on the History of Civil Society* (1767) is generally recognized as a key forerunner of sociological analysis, knowing society involved viewing it as a totality: describing its interrelated institutions, classifying its various parts, identifying its stages of development. Ferguson stressed empirical method; social study must be based on scientific observation, rather than on speculation. If sociological beginnings are detectable in the work of Ferguson, it was late eighteenth-century France that gave the emerging field a sense of urgency and purpose. Vitalized and christened in an era of revolution, sociology pointed toward a permanent condition of post-revolution. The Enlightenment values that had inspired revolution were now rechanneled into the shaping of a stabilizing social science.

The institutional origins of American sociology lie in the 1850 founding of a Board of Aliens Commission by the State of Massachusetts, whose charge was "to superintend the execution of all laws in relation to the introduction of aliens in the Commonwealth." From the ranks of this organization, the American Social Science Association was founded in 1865. The motto of the association, "Ne Quid Nimis" (Everything in Moderation), and a representative sample of papers from the association's journal ("Pauperism in New York City"; "The Emmigration of Colored Citizens from the Southern States"; "Immigration and Nervous Diseases"; "Immigration and Crime") suggest its anxiety about immigrants and internal marginals.

American sociology was shaped by specific social and political pressures, as well as by strong international influences. At the point of its emergence it was also substantially supported by Christian reform organizations, as evidenced by the abundance of articles on Christian sociology in the early years of *The American Journal of Sociology*. The links between sociology and Christianity are consistent with the fact that many of the first American sociologists had close ties to the ministry.

American sociology in this period was often broken down into three interrelated clusters of inquiry: (1) attention to society's *static* dimensions, which addressed the question of social stability: how does society manage to preserve the status quo? (2) attention to society's *evolutionary* dimensions, which addressed the question of change: how did society come to be as it is and what might we predict about its future? (3) attention to society's *technologic* dimensions, which addressed the question of control: what actions can be taken to improve society and ensure a better future? Running through each of these lines of exploration was the ongoing struggle with the subject of individualism. As Albion Small observed, "Today's sociology is still struggling with the preposterous initial fact of the individual. He is the only possible social unit, and he is no longer a thinkable possibility. He is the only real presence, and he is never present." Sociology's emphasis on social determination, its insistence that human consciousness was formed and existed in interaction alone, seemed to undermine an American tradition of individualism. But in fact the task of "reconstructing individualism" was a continuing preoccupation. Thus, for static analyses the question was: how could individuals be fit into the existing social system? For evolutionary analyses the question was: how

do individual differences come about; are they products of inheritance or environment? For technologic analyses the question was: can education and scientific knowledge equip certain individuals with special powers for social betterment? In what follows I will discuss these three clusters of sociological analysis by way of specific American novels. I consider in turn Herman Melville and realism, Henry James and naturalism, and W. E. B. Du Bois, Gertrude Stein, and experimentalism. This genealogy moves from writers whose major concerns coincided with those of social science, to writers who absorbed social science into their very techniques. The works of Stein and Du Bois, I argue, were overburdened with social scientific methods, which compromised their aesthetic power but made them ideal registers of the ties between sociology and literature in this period.

The overriding concern of Herman Melville's novella *Billy Budd, Sailor* (written from 1886 to 1891) is social transformation: how to channel the revolutionary energies of the late eighteenth century into the industrial work of the nineteenth century. As a work written in the turbulent closing decades of nineteenth-century America, and set in a climactic moment of revolution and consolidation at the beginning of the "modern" era, *Billy Budd* parallels the situation of late nineteenth-century sociology, a discipline that draws upon founding principles framed in the same revolutionary Europe.

Riding the nervous British seas of 1797, haunted by British Jacobinism, Revolutionary France, and mutinies that year at Nore and Spithead, authorities aboard the *Bellipotent* are consumed with the problem of social order. Like the early European sociologists who were fresh from the experience of social revolt, Captain Vere and his officers fear lower-class uprising. Described as one whose "settled convictions were as a dike against those invading waters of novel opinion social, political and otherwise, which carried away as in a torrent no few minds in those days," Captain Vere knows the reparative powers of a careful and consistent empiricism. The *Bellipotent* operates through an elaborate network of watching and cataloging: methods of social description and typecasting that keep everyone on board, especially potentially disruptive elements of the sea commonalty, identified and ordered. The power to label and interpret the world around him is critical to Captain Vere's rule.

A key instance of typecasting is the parable of the black sailor at Liverpool that opens the novella. Transformed kaleidoscopically from an ideal to a sacrificial type, the black sailor foreshadows the experiences of Billy Budd. As a handsome cynosure, the black sailor elicits the "spontaneous homage" of his fellow sailors, a moment of collective tribute that is threatening in its ability to "arrest" the normal affairs of the Liverpool wharf. In keeping with this threat, another type, which casts the sailor as the sculptured bull of the Assyrian priests, emerges with a kind of grim necessity at the close of the passage. Now an object of sacrifice within an order of nature and ritual, the black sailor is neutralized. This double echo from the past (a mid-eighteenth-century moment that recalls an ancient rite) points to a simpler era when societies cohered by means of a common conscience reinforced by violence. It also registers the traces of primitivism still lurking in modern forms of social control.

Like the black sailor, Billy Budd is marked early on as an outstanding specimen, capable of inspiring his fellow sailors in unpredictable ways. Had Billy not killed Claggart, Captain Vere would have had to find some other reason for his demise. The necessity of his sacrifice, in other words, seems built into the situation from the beginning: a nervous ship in a time of mutiny and revolution, a handsome sailor who inspires collective pride, his execution. Typing Billy as the "Angel of God" who "must hang," Vere transforms Billy into a visual emblem of his power. Billy's execution is a spectacle that confirms Vere's ability to contain collective sentiments.

The link between typecasting and social control brings us to contemporary sociological theories on social types. In *Social Control* (1901), E. A. Ross argued that a heterogeneous mass society like modern America required deliberate strategies for ensuring social obedience. He advocated the promotion of social models, ideal types, which society "induces its members to adopt as their guide." Based on the principle of self-regulation, what Ross called "bind-[ing] from within," Ross's types left the individual "with the illusion of self-direction even at the moment he martyrizes himself for the ideal we have sedulously impressed upon him." "The fact of control," Ross continues, "is in good sooth, no gospel to be preached abroad . . . the wise sociologist . . . will not tell the street Arab, or the Elmira inmate how he is managed." Ross's use of types for the purposes of social control had its analogue in various disciplines of this era. According to philosopher Josiah Royce, the value of an ideal type lay in its ability to instill a feeling of subordination to a unified whole. The loyal individual, he suggested in *The Philosophy of Loyalty* (1908), embodied the ideal union of individual identity and social commitment. "You can be loyal," he wrote, "only to a tie that binds you and others into some sort of unity . . . the cause to which loyalty devotes itself has always this union of the personal and the seemingly super-individual about it." For the William James of *The Varieties of Religious Experience* (1902) as well, the sign of the healthy religious type is his or her "sense of integration" in a benevolent social whole.

Like these social philosophers, Captain Vere seeks more than Billy's compliance; he needs Billy to believe in his sacrifice, as socially necessary and beneficial. After typing him "fated boy," Vere takes various measures (their "closeted interview," for example) to ensure that Billy embrace his fate. Billy's declaration at the point of execution, "God bless Captain Vere," signals the success of Vere's methods.

Perhaps an even deeper threat to Captain Vere's methods of social control is his master-at-arms, John Claggart. As one who eludes classification, described at one point as an "uncatalogued creature of the deep," Claggart seems uniquely resistant to Vere's authority. Yet Claggart is ultimately as tied to Vere's system as Billy through his burning desire to rise in the ship's hierarchy. Both Billy and Claggart represent to authorities like Captain Vere the hope that the dream of vertical mobility, through success in Claggart's case or martyrdom in Billy's, can be counted on to offset lateral threats of collective identification. It is this hope that underlies sociological reconceptions of individuality. In an exemplary formulation, Albion Small moves from the observation that "individuals are different," to the claim that "the associated state [Small's phrase for society] is a process of making them different." As he explains further in adopting what he calls "the genetic view," the social process is "a progressive production of more and more dissimilar men." Though he intends another meaning of "genetic," Small's use of the term here foregrounds the sense that the modern liberal state has become an active producer of human types. For Small, social processes conspire to produce uniformly related selves, whose functional attributes can be neatly fit into the social system. Unsolicited differences—of race, ethnicity, political or religious belief—that threaten the status quo are subsumed by produced differences that support it. In the creation of type categories that provided model individuals capable of succeeding in modern society, sociologists were responding to contemporary anxieties about the erosion of individual initiative. At the same time they were controlling perceptions of human possibility.

An assumption governing the sociological use of types, which Captain Vere shares, is that the maker of these classifying terms is himself a neutral analyst. For Captain Vere, neutrality is part of being a professional. Off duty, Vere "never garnished unprofessional talk with nautical terms," a sign of the strict division in his mind between public office and private life. Vere's personal discretion is matched by a professional objectivity that brings him to substitute an "imperial code" for the claims of "private conscience." Vere's call for the suppression of instinct confirms a late nineteenth-century ethic of professionalism. Like its other key tropes, this professional ethic aligns the novella with a literary realist movement that coincided with Melville's final decade: the years when he was working in the New York Custom House and writing *Billy Budd*.

The novels of William Dean Howells, Stephen Crane, Henry James, Mark Twain, the paintings of Thomas Eakins, picture the frozen status quo worlds dreamed of by the rulers of the *Bellipotent*. In realism, social conflict is shifted to the borders of scenes or swiftly quelled. The worlds of realism are controlled by vigilance: the vulnerable visibility of the poor, the empowered visibility of professional elites, the invisibility of the rich. In an analysis of publicity in this period, Philip Fisher considers Thomas Eakins's *The Gross Clinic* as an instance of professional transcendence: the modern expert as God. Eakins's representation of the master surgeon at work presupposes the surgeon's power to select the moments when he is publicly seen. This moment is balanced by access to a privileged invisibility, which Fisher locates in the self-enclosed homes designed by Frank Lloyd Wright, homes that ensure the absolute immunity of their inhabitants from outward detection. While the public images of professional elites were carefully circumscribed, society's *most* powerful were invisible altogether. Eric Hobsbawm describes the increasing obscurity of governing elites in the late nineteenth-century era of mass democratization: "When the men who governed really wanted to say what they meant, they had henceforth to do so in the obscurity of the corridors of power." This is corroborated by Henry James's analysis of that pivotal political figure, "the boss," who operates in a shell of oblivion, his "political role" at once "so effaced, but so universal."

In the case of the lower classes, this situation was inverted: their lives, at work and at home, were increasingly exposed to public scrutiny in this period. The introduction of production methods systematizing industrial work led to greater vigilance in the factories. The activity of social reformers, increasingly devoted to the domestic lives of the poor and the immigrant, led to greater surveillance at home. The impact of these reformers was mixed: while their obvious goal was improvement, they also participated in a more ominous campaign to know and manage a potentially dangerous underclass. Social scientists adopted a more remote attitude, but their relationships to the impoverished lives they cataloged from a greater remove were equally ambiguous. Liberal sociology mainly identified with the sober middle class, and kept the poor and the wealthy (whose interests they nevertheless implicitly supported) at a distance. The main concern of realist literature as well was the conventional and the middle class. A notable example of realism's occasional forays into the world of the poor is Henry James's *In the Cage,* his only work narrated from the perspective of a lower-class character.

The protagonist of this 1895 novella is a featureless telegraph operator, whose one distinctive trait is a classically overactive Jamesian imagination. The telegraph operator spends her days serving the wealthy who have grown addicted to a new technology that facilitates the rapid conduct of their (usually extramarital) affairs. To her customers, she is no more significant than the machine that relays their messages. Indeed, the novella ingeniously inverts its titular metaphor that casts the telegraph operator as a caged zoo animal. While she does work in a cage, it is her customers rather than she who are exposed to view. "It had occurred to her early," the novella begins, "that in her position—that of a young person spending, in framed and wired confinement, the life of a guinea-pig or a magpie—she should know a great many persons without their recognizing the acquaintance." The story's plot centers on her effort to exploit this circumstance of being hidden but ever vigilant. Scrutinizing their faces like a detective, she assumes a fantastic intimacy with her customers, a knowledge of their every desire and scheme. Thus the predictable lower classes become the predictors of the upper

class. By investing his telegraph operator with the story's main imaginative value, James identifies her as an artist of sorts. And through this character, James presents the Jamesian artist as a predatory dissector of the wealthy. Ultimately, however, James foils the visual powers of the telegraph operator, restoring realism's usual hierarchy of vigilance. The telegraph operator is foiled because she attempts to enter into the lives of her subjects. By trying to realize her visual intimacy, she violates the boundary of vigilance. Empirical control over others requires distance.

As one of the gentile poor, James's telegraph operator fulfills Emile Durkheim's theory of anomie. Defined in his classic study *Suicide,* anomie (literally, "without norms") is a condition of rootlessness bordering on self-annihilation that occurs when human desires are raised beyond their realistic life expectations. According to this theory, hopeless poverty is a protection against suicide. But unqualified desire leads to disorientation and worse. It is appropriate, therefore, that the novella's final scene pictures the telegraph operator standing before a bridge while a policeman eyes her suspiciously. The policeman is an externalization of the control the telegraph operator no longer exercises over herself.

The telegraph operator is an anomaly in James's realist canon, not only because she is poor, but also because she doesn't police herself. Rather than an internal plane for the individual's struggle and eventual reconciliation with social law (as in the case of a typical Jamesian heroine like Isabel Archer), the imagination of the telegraph operator is a plane of transgression. The task of regulating one's imagination, of internalizing external forms of vigilance, is a key activity of realist fiction. Realism emphasizes selective incorporation, its primary reflex is establishing borders. This is reflected in the claustrophobic atmospheres of realist works, which feel uniformly cramped whether depicting the interior spaces of Henry James or the battlefields of Stephen Crane. The scene of Stephen Crane's "The Open Boat" (1897) can be taken as paradigmatic. The challenge for the story's characters is maintaining the integrity of their craft ("no bigger than a bathtub," the narrator snaps with characteristic cruelty) against an encroaching ocean. The homely similes, which seem to crowd the characters as much as the ocean (the captain is like a father "soothing his children," the seaweed is like "carpets"), are there not only to taunt the characters by reminding them of the habitual protections they lack but to represent their inevitable restitution. Moreover, these similes are products of the characters' imaginations; the narrator is merely miming their familiarization of the threatening landscape. Like the wobbling boat that serves as its controlling metaphor, the story is concerned with what can be taken in, and what must be kept out, in order to ensure sanity and social stability. No matter how vast and wild its territory, realism concentrates on the most local mechanisms for stabilizing the social world—human perceptions and categories.

The central features of realism—the trope of vigilance, the emphasis on internalization, and the focus on individual over collective experience—come together in the most distinctive aspect of realist fiction—its view of character as type. The type supplies an immediately identifiable public persona, a boundary around the self. But it also acknowledges some residual aspects of personality that are inexpressible to others and perhaps even unknown to the individual. In the essay "How Is Society Possible?" Georg Simmel refers to the "non-social imponderables"—temperament, fate, etc.—those features that lend "a certain nuance" to an individual but do not fundamentally change his "relevant social category." This makes the self potentially limitless in idiosyncratic terms, but poses a limit on what individuals can be in social terms. In keeping with this, Stephen Crane's "Oiler," "Westerner," "Cook," and "Gambler," as well as Henry James's "Heiress" and "Dilettante," are individuals limited by function. But the idiosyncratic freedoms allotted James's more central characters are finally inconsequential in terms of plot. They are not allowed to stand in the way of their social function. Thus, Isabel Archer, the "intelligent but presumptuous girl . . . affronting [her] destiny," for all her expansiveness, is fundamentally a type, and is so conceived by her fellow characters.

The typing of realist characters counters a threat that continually pressures the realist text: the threat of collective identification. The concept of type provides a view of self-sufficient, uniformly related individuals, whose collective existence is a matter not of choice or identity but of interdependence. Society promotes differences among its members so that they may be profitably related. This ideology of interdependence was set against the forms of spontaneous association that from the late eighteenth-century era of revolution to the late nineteenth-century era of expansion social observers most feared.

The novels of Henry James may appear to have little in common with naturalism. But in fact the issue of social evolution is a dominant concern of James's fiction, especially the fiction of the major phase. Poised on the edge of a new century, imposing its titular category of adolescence on society as well as on women, *The Awkward Age* (1899) is an exemplary case of this deepening concern. What are the differences among cultural rites for socializing women? how do those of modern society compare to those of primitive society? are there elements of barbarism in modern culture?—these are the questions the novel addresses. Like Thorstein Veblen's *The Theory of the Leisure Class* (published the same year), which ruthlessly cataloged the primitive offenses of modern elites, James's satire on the British ruling class focuses on their treatment of women. The marriage market of James's modern London looks surprisingly like the barter systems of primitive societies described by contemporary social theorists such as Herbert Spencer and J. F. McLennan (whose *Primitive Marriage* James owned and almost certainly read).

In her essay "The Traffic in Women," Gayle Rubin discusses the ominous constancy of women's treatment from primitive to modern times. "Women are given in marriage, taken in battle, exchanged for favors, sent as tribute, traded, bought, and sold. Far from being confined to the 'primitive' world, these practices seem only to become more pronounced and commercialized in more 'civilized' societies." From its opening pages, *The Awkward Age* is explicit about the commodification of women in the modern era. It seems to go out of its way to press the similarities between primitive and modern societies. For the novel's upper class shares a critical affinity with the primitive populations described by the era's sociologists: their demise is at hand. The novel's elite offers little hope for generational continuity. Its female protagonist, Nanda Brookenham, is described at one point as just the kind to preside over "a fine old English family" of "half-a-dozen." The projected size of Nanda's family is statistically precise: four was the minimum number of offspring specified by population experts of this era for a stock to maintain itself. The novel's end, however, pictures Nanda's retreat to the country as the ward of a man three times her age, her prospects for marriage and family ruined. James's portrait of an upper class in decline, stripped of its reproductive powers, is consistent with the perceptions of other social observers of his day.

James's seedy upper class helps to shed light on social taxonomies of the era, where elites appeared in catalogs of "special classes" requiring scientific scrutiny. In a 1900 essay on social types published simultaneously in Durkheim's *L'Année Sociologique* and excerpted in *The American Journal of Sociology,* S. R. Steinmetz cites the variety of social characters about whom too little is known. "There are great entomological studies for the study of insects," he observes, "but we do not give ourselves any trouble to know the people around us." Among these unknowns, he cites the "primitive populations" "rapidly disappearing." He includes as well what he calls "special classes of the population": "prostitutes, the criminal and dangerous classes . . . wandering artists, nobles, millionaires." The obvious mystery on this list is social elites ("nobles, millionaires"). Why would its members require scientific attention? What does it share with these other groups? Each of these groups is marginal to the interdependent community of socialized selves described by Albion Small. At the same time, each helps to define the boundaries of that functional society by its very marginal relationship to it. As our observations so far have suggested, James's social circle has most in common with the "disappearing" "primitive peoples."

Yet why would primitives and nobles require scientific scrutiny? Primitives and nobles need to be managed intellectually because they contradict the narrative of evolutionary progress favored by social analysts of the era. Primitives threaten the thesis of evolutionary uniformity that ascribes a fundamental similarity to the development of all peoples. Primitives are defined as vestiges of a previous evolutionary stage, with little promise of meeting the demands of evolutionary progress, and their rapid decline is predicted. As a supposedly superior class that is regressing, nobles are living contradictions of the evolutionary thesis. Degenerate rather than vital, incapable of transmitting their valuable traits, they are defined as a social excrescence, a class that has been living off the fruits of others' labor for too long.

James's attentions to the place of his bourgeois and aristocratic characters on the evolutionary scale goes to the heart of a fictional enterprise usually considered alien to his fiction, naturalism. By exposing the barbaric propensities of civilized society, James revises the dominant nineteenth-century narrative of evolutionary progress. If James pictures a reservoir of social superiority that cannot sustain itself, Frank Norris and Theodore Dreiser explore a self-destructive sphere of social difference, the world of the lower class and the immigrant.

Naturalist literature provided an analytical yet voyeuristic view into the low life. Both senses of this perspective—the detached and the compulsive—are important. Even when naturalist narrators betray overt hostility (a naturalist trademark) toward their precivilized characters, there is still room for identification with them. For turn-of-the-century readers, immersed in ideas of progress, naturalism provided the experience of looking into an evolutionary mirror. Readers could see themselves at an earlier historical moment: barbaric, unconscious, twisted. Thus naturalist characters incited an antagonism that might easily be internalized, illuminating one's own carefully hidden savagery. The difference of naturalist characters, then, was a difference that had to be reckoned with. As Michel Foucault has observed, prior to the seventeenth century every species was identified in and of itself, by a certain mark that it bore *independent* of all other species. But from the seventeenth century onward, identity was established in relation to all other possible identities. By the nineteenth century, difference was understood in terms of a larger conviction about the cohesiveness and unity of the social organism. Naturalist literature solved the problem of how to accommodate the alien and brutal with a normative reading of human progress in accordance with that of Herbert Spencer. At its most extreme, naturalist characters threw into relief the progress of "normal" Americans.

The worlds of Frank Norris, in *Vandover and the Brute* (1914) and *McTeague* (1899) in particular, are worlds of extreme naturalism. *McTeague* features inbred, sterile, and insane characters—the wasted undesirables who are better left to die out. Immobilized oddities (Old Grannis and Miss Baker), distorted gold worshipers (Maria Macapa, Zerkow, and Trina McTeague), brutes (McTeague and Marcus Schouler), these are human types who fail at everything: love, business, mere survival. Nor is it accidental that these characters have strange-sounding names. *McTeague*'s abnormals were the immigrant and worker populations, whose features when seen up close justified their domination. Norris's fundamental contempt for his characters is exemplified by the novel's ending, where McTeague survives a monumental desert struggle against Marcus Schouler only to find himself handcuffed to the dead body. What the perverse underworld of *McTeague* shares

with the hypercivilized community of *The Awkward Age* is the incapacity for self-generation.

The works of Theodore Dreiser offer a different perspective on naturalism by highlighting a modern capitalist social order that has subsumed the natural. In contrast to Norris's degenerate (and eminently expendable) social types, Dreiser's fiction features functional types who become dysfunctional. A register of the differences between Norris's and Dreiser's naturalism is their metaphorical use of newspapers. Norris's characters don't read newspapers (it's not clear that they can even read); rather they are the stuff of newspapers. Dreiser's characters, in contrast, are guided by them. Far from Norris's sites of extremity, newspapers in Dreiser are repositories of human possibility to be imitated. In Dreiser newspapers are a paradoxical medium both craved and feared. To be an object of publicity is an ideal state. Yet publicity can also mean that one is a victim or a casualty. Dreiser's fictions are themselves like newspapers, representing the unlikely but accessible circumstances that elude the majority. Consider, for example, Clyde Griffiths, the everyman who becomes the dastardly object of awed crowds as he enters prison, or Hurstwood, who begins *Sister Carrie* (1900) as a generic businessman and ends as a pathetic object of urban voyeurs in a panhandler's line. Publicity is also the lot of Sister Carrie in her acting stardom, but it is the nature of a "star" to fall as well as rise. As they fall, Dreiser's characters become spectacles, illustrating the potential decline of anyone in the risk-driven society of capitalism. The vicissitudes of modern capitalism as portrayed in Dreiser's works put barbarism always within our reach.

Thus, where Norris's naturalism tends to corroborate a social evolutionary scheme, Dreiser's naturalism, by showing how such a scheme justifies and entrenches a man-made social system, tends to challenge it. Dreiser is interested in social science and capitalism as interpenetrating ideologies. He is at once more committed to and reflective about social scientific analysis. Like contemporary social scientists, he is drawn to the situations and individuals that repeat in modern life: the social fall or rise, the sexual conquest, the double-dealing, the "American Tragedy," the ambitious youth, the coquette, the female innocent, the fast-talking city slicker. This cataloging impulse, however, defines the limit of Dreiser's fascination with American capitalism. Likewise, Dreiser parts ways with the passive vision of Social Darwinism, including its instrumental version. In shadow types like the Captain of *Sister Carrie,* who opposes the sentimental idealism of the supposed hero, Ames, in portraits of immobile worlds dominated by rhetorics of social mobility (*An American Tragedy* [1925]), Dreiser reveals the prevailing social theory of his era to be the ideological handmaid to a basically unjust capitalist system. Dreiser's resistance to the naturalist assumptions embedded in liberal social theory brings us to the final set of literary examples to be considered: two writers who first embraced the practical potential of social science, and ended up more critical of its assumptions than any of the authors so far discussed. Yet however critical they became, W. E. B. Du Bois and Gertrude Stein remained attached to social science in ways that informed the works that are of concern to the history of the novel—*The Souls of Black Folk* (1903) and *The Making of Americans* (1906-8).

W. E. B. Du Bois and Gertrude Stein share the position of social marginals, as well as the experience of social scientific training. Both were also self-exiles from American society: Du Bois settled in Ghana at the end of his life, Stein moved to Paris before she was thirty. Perhaps the most significant similarity is that both studied with William James and were heavily influenced by his pragmatist social science.

For Du Bois and Stein, typecasting was not an inevitable process but a political activity. Both saw the damaging effects of typecasting on their respective social groups and believed that greater control over their group's representation would extend its social possibility. They sought out the role of the expert cataloger of modern social life as a means of remedy and instruction.

As two writers who were personally implicated in questions of social difference and drawn to the promise of liberal social science, Du Bois and Stein represent powerful confrontations with the central intellectual concerns of their era: the seductive potential of categories and types, the social scientific conflation of knowledge and uniformity, individualism versus collectivism as competing ideals, the role of literature in relation to social science. They are distinctive, and crucial to our exploration, in having recognized the pivotal role that social science played in the modern era. While they were critical of this role, they also pursued it. This ambivalence toward the posture of social scientific expertise is built into the narrative personae of their two major novelistic works.

Of all the literary authors discussed so far, Du Bois is unique in actively combining sociological and literary methods. As a student of history and sociology at Harvard in the 1890s (with two years of study in Germany), Du Bois was drawn to the potential of this new discipline for arbitrating the problem of race in America. He more often found, however, that sociology was a symptom of the problem rather than a solution to it. Even the most enlightened of sociologists, W. I. Thomas, in a 1904 article, "The Psychology of Race-Prejudice" (*American Journal of Sociology*), came perilously close to calling racial prejudice inherent. And F. H. Giddings's concept of "the consciousness of kind," which held that the sense of community inevitably diminished with the increase of racial and ethnic differences, was used to justify turn-of-the century schemes for the deportation of African Americans.

Du Bois's earliest training was in history and economics, culminating in his dissertation *The Suppression of the African Slave-Trade 1638-1870* (1896). The book's bias is historicist, that is, Du Bois focuses on the historical genesis of slavery in order to redress the condition of African Americans in his contemporary society. Like *Billy Budd, Suppression* is most drawn to the closing decades of the eighteenth century: Melville's post-Revolutionary era of consolidation matches Du Bois's post-Revolutionary America, the moment of enlightenment that managed to entrench the most oppressive of slave systems. "There never was a time in the history of America," wrote Du Bois, "when the system had a slighter economic, political, and moral justification than in 1787, and yet with this real, existent, growing evil before their eyes, a bargain largely of dollars and cents was allowed to open the highway that led straight to the Civil War." By delineating the economic considerations that consistently overshadowed the moral question of slavery, *Suppression* embodies the weight of historical memory that tempered Du Bois's faith in social instrumentalism. Any program of social action had to contend with the historical process that had created and still informed African American possibility.

Given Du Bois's career-long interest in the theoretical problem of racial difference and its relationship to conceptions of social evolution, it seems appropriate that his entry into social science was through history. Du Bois's historical approach is consistent with the methods of the era's classic sociological theorists, for whom sociological analysis required a broad command of different cultures as well as historical periods. Like Spencer, Durkheim, and Weber, Du Bois is interested in the transformation of societies, as well as in the persistence of certain ideas and habits over time. Du Bois differs from these analysts in attending to the ways in which social evolution occurs and also fails to occur as a consequence of deliberate social policy. Du Bois likewise departs from an essentially static evolutionary script (favored by Spencer and Durkheim) that projects a normative pattern of development and evaluates all populations according to that pattern. The culmination of Du Bois's training as a social scientist was his classic anatomy of African American society in Philadelphia.

The central drama of *The Philadelphia Negro* (1899) lies in Du Bois's effort to strike a balance between assessing the collective condition of Philadelphia's African Americans and distinguishing the various strata of that community, with their different relationships to American norms and values. His study contains the seeds of his growing dissatisfaction with social science while it lays the groundwork for the problem that would plague his career: how could a commitment to a collective African American destiny be accommodated to the promise of individual assimilation and progress dividing that collectivity? Sociological theories of stratification together with his continuing absorption in Spencerian ideas formed the unsettling core of Du Bois's method. His turn away from sociology following *The Philadelphia Negro* may have had as much to do with the ways in which it magnified an emerging contradiction in his own thought as with the limitations he saw in the discipline itself. In practicing sociology, he adopted the dominant sociological trajectory of his era: the supplanting of basically conservative, essentialist notions about human potential with a liberal ideal that emphasized assimilation and training. This new ideal, however, retained a fundamental tie to the essentialist view, in upholding a belief in "the survival of the fittest." The superior elements of any social group, went the argument, would inevitably rise and prosper. Given this sociological climate, it is not surprising that an outgrowth of Du Bois's Philadelphia study was his first conceptualization of "the talented tenth," an attempt to distinguish the best "strata" of the African American race.

Du Bois's adaptation of these sociological principles for African American Philadelphia was timely, given a prevailing racial ideology of two nations, one white, one black, that relentlessly homogenized African Americans. Against this biological fiat of racial homogeneity, Du Bois set another biological fiat implicitly condoned by social science, which emphasized inherent differences of talent within each group. Du Bois thus used Social Darwinist ideas to challenge a prevailing racial ideology.

The irony is that his struggle against a white conspiracy that intentionally muffles African American achievements was mirrored by the response to his book. Through the reception (or more accurately, nonreception) of *The Philadelphia Negro* by the sociological profession—which took over half a century to confer its "classic" status—Du Bois experienced firsthand the limits upon all African Americans. Du Bois's failure to gain a hearing as a sociologist signaled the failed promise of the discipline's liberal assumptions. In declaring his next major study, *The Souls of Black Folk* (1903), a work of "faith and passion," he seemed to be deliberately distancing himself from the rational agenda of *The Philadelphia Negro*.

In *The Souls of Black Folk*, Du Bois undertakes the imaginative reconstruction of the territory he covered in his sociological classic. His desire to gain control over the representation of African Americans will not be accomplished through the straitjacket of sociological method, he implies, but requires a more literary technique. If *Philadelphia* undertakes the work of social description, *Souls* undertakes the work of social change. *Philadelphia* selects among preexisting African American types assigned by the dominant society, while *Souls* surveys all the available African American types and, finding them wanting, begins to recover the powers of self-identification for African Americans themselves.

The two books are best seen as companion pieces, which need to be read together in order to understand their deepest implications. The striving Philadelphian bent on self-improvement joins the collectivity of African American souls. The insistence of *Souls* on plurality suggests Du Bois's new attitude toward the liberal individualism of sociology—it has never represented a true possibility for African Americans. *Souls* dismisses the claim that African Americans are individuals, the "fittest" capable of assimilating and rising like any "immigrant" group. What was deplored in *Philadelphia*, the "tendency on the part of the community to consider the Negroes as comprising one practically homogeneous mass," is embraced in *Souls*. The homogenizing of African Americans is transformed into an enabling device; African Americans become a self-identified and therefore empowered collectivity. *Souls* explodes some other powerful sociological myths as well. The trajectory of *Philadelphia* is from South to North, as the book charts the making of a modern African American populace, a narrative of liberal progress that pictures the race's "fittest" rising to the top. *Souls,* however, moves from North to South, thus implying that African Americans must come to terms with the roots of their experience in America, by returning to "the scene of the crime," as it were. The static evolutionary reading of African American history in *Philadelphia*—history in the sociological vein as a grand narrative that explains the present via the past—is replaced by history as *bricolage*. *Souls* is *annales* history: an amalgam of tales, songs, mythologies, critiques, autobiography, elegy. Its concern is not progress measured in terms of the dominant society but the shaping of collective identity.

Souls seems in every way opposed to its social scientific predecessor, yet in fact Du Bois never strays very far from an implicitly sociological agenda. His achievement is that he manages at once to criticize and to revitalize the new science of society. *Souls* is filled with critical references to "the cold statistician," the "sociologists who gleefully count" African American "bastards" and "prostitutes," "the car window sociologist . . . who seeks to understand and know the South by devoting the few leisure hours of a holiday trip to unravelling the snarl of centuries."

Du Bois's answer to these limitations is the aestheticizing of sociology. The sociological method of typecasting becomes exploratory, experimental. Far from merely typologizing, *Souls* elaborates a theory of types. For what is the color line but the penultimate type or boundary demarcating the limit of African American possibility? The book is a sustained effort to extend the boundary around the African American self. Du Bois devotes each chapter to elaborating a different unrealized potential: the African American as failed transmitter of a generational legacy (chapter 11, on the death of his son); the African American as failed educator (chapter 4, on his teaching career in Tennessee); the African American as failed spiritual leader (chapter 12, on Alexander Crummel). These promising but unfulfilled types are played off against the degraded types of the dominant society. The book is thus a dialectic of typological categories, and Du Bois's major insight is that the African American self internalizes them all. Thus the "warring" within that derives from this "double-consciousness": "looking at one's self through the eyes of others . . . measuring one's soul by the tape of a world that looks on in amused contempt and pity." The African American self is alienated from both versions of self: the type of the white society, and the inner soul with which it conflicts.

But as Du Bois suggests, this condition of double-consciousness is also basic to the practice of sociology. As a discipline that enacts the dilemma of being subject and object simultaneously, whose practitioners are inevitably the objects of their own investigations, sociology epitomizes the circumstances of the African American soul. Because contemporary sociology failed to come to terms with this paradox, it could not realize the promise it held out to Du Bois.

By conceptualizing a different kind of social science founded upon a critique of capitalism, as well as an awareness of its own perilous objectivity, Du Bois pointed the way toward a critical social theory that would not be fully articulated until the rise of the Frankfurt School thirty years later. This perspective, formulated by Theodor Adorno and Max Horkheimer, among others, rejected orthodox social science, the American version in particular, as an apology for capitalism. They adopted in its place a theory based on the method of negative dialectics, critical of all reigning forms of analysis, and directed toward fundamental social change. For W. E. B. Du Bois, as well as for Adorno and Horkheimer, a social theory without this commitment was unworthy of the name.

Du Bois's ventures in literature after *Souls* had limited results. His first full-fledged novel, *The Quest of the Silver Fleece* (1911), has all the trappings of socialist realism, with its cast of dark and light characters: the idealized African American hero and heroine, Bles and Zora; the weak and selfish whites, most of them monstrous vessels of capitalist greed; the weak African Americans who succumb to the evil temptations of capitalism. It is telling that however ambivalent Du Bois was toward the sociology of his day, he never equaled the powerful blend of literary and sociological imaginings he achieved in *Souls*.

"Mostly no one knowing me can like it that I love it that everyone is a kind of men and women, that always I am looking and comparing and classifying them, always I am seeing their repeating." So writes Gertrude Stein in *The Making of Americans,* expressing her era's simultaneous attraction and resistance to social categorization. Her own most obvious response is parody. The lists of human types that pervade Stein's "great American novel" are often absurd. One such list runs to: "being one liking swimming, being one tired of ocean bathing before they have really been in more than twice in a season." But despite such parodic attitudes, she was deeply committed to the enterprise of knowing human kinds. How did Stein come to be a maker of lists? What brought her to desire a unified knowledge of America? A clue to these questions lies in her pursuit of social science.

Stein's advanced education began at Harvard in the 1890s, where she studied mainly psychology, and ended at Johns Hopkins at the turn of the century, where she studied brain anatomy. Both of these educational experiences suggest provocative sources for *The Making of Americans*. Stein's Harvard research (which was published as "Cultivated Motor Automatism: A Study of Character in Its Relation to Attention," in *The Psychological Review,* 1898) was based on experiments with Harvard and Radcliffe students. It ad-

dressed the question of how automatic behavior can be cultivated in human subjects; how can subjects be made to internalize suggested actions as their own habits? Among the issues that Stein's experiment takes up is the question of gender difference: is there a consistent opposition between male and female responses to suggested action? Another is the problem of change: once learned, how can subjects be induced to abandon old actions and adopt new ones? Stein's research produced its own catalog of human types. Type I, "girls . . . found naturally in literature courses" and men bound for law, is "nervous, high-strung, very imaginative." Type II, "blond and pale," is "distinctly phlegmatic," a general "New England" type that is repressed and self-conscious. The parallels between Stein's research and the ideas of William James are revealing. James describes habit, in the famous essay of that name, as "the enormous fly-wheel of society, its most precious conservative agent. . . . It also prevents the hardest and most repulsive walks of life from being deserted by those brought up to tread therein." With this observation, James links the intricate psychology of habit to larger mechanisms of organization and control. And this points to the larger arena Stein will create for her psychological studies in *The Making of Americans.*

At Johns Hopkins Medical School, where she went on the advice of James, Stein sought even more objective knowledge of human minds. Garland Allen, a historian of biology, has characterized the dominant tradition at Hopkins during this period as "descriptive naturalist." This involved an emphasis on morphology—the study and classification of form—which assumed the underlying unity of diverse organisms. Among the techniques taught was the construction of family trees and phylogenies, which identified a single common ancestor as the progenitor of modern lines.

Stein's developing interest in typology culminated in her preoccupation with the work of Otto Weininger, the German psychologist, whose book *Sex and Character* (1906) inspired her during her writing of *The Making of Americans.* A precursor to Nazi ideology, Weininger's book offered a system of characterology, whose main purpose seemed to be the identification of human types that threatened the deterioration of nations. However rigidly schematic Weininger's ideas, he was willing to accept ambiguity, by admitting that some despised characteristics were present to varying degrees in all human types. Significantly, in light of Stein's Jewish-lesbian identity, the two main sources of degeneracy in Weininger's system were Jews and women. The extent of feminine possibility for Weininger was prostitute, mother, servant, saint, and masculine woman. Jews occupied a unique position in Weininger's typology since Jewish traits were confined to the race alone. They therefore provide an opportunity for the in-depth study of degeneracy.

What is so obviously startling about Stein's adoption of Weininger's ideas, which she claimed expressed "her own thoughts exactly," was that it required the complete suppression of her own identity. Indeed, she seems to have identified so fully with Weininger that she sometimes referred to his system as her own. As she wrote in her notebook, "That thing of mine of sex and mind and character all coming together seems to work absolutely." Stein's engagement with Weininger points to an important feature of *The Making of Americans*. Stein's representation of her own subjective processes, her use of herself as an object of study, was a means of self-distancing. Stein's spectacular detachment fulfills Georg Simmel's sociological prescription for aesthetics, from *The Philosophy of Money*: "The basic principle of art was to bring us closer to things by placing them at a distance from us." It also reveals what is perhaps the most elitist aspect of Stein's vision: that other human beings are to her objects, with readily identifiable "bottom beings," while Stein's own identity is endlessly elusive and revisable.

The Making of Americans is an effort to bring us closer to the various mythologies of American culture, by analytically detaching ourselves from them. American minds, the book's narrative suggests, are thickets of repetition: filled with a finite set of stories, plans, opinions. Stay with one for a certain length of time and you begin to hear the repetitions, to note patterns, which hold the clue to that individual's "bottom being." This white noise exists in our minds apart from the practical thoughts that impel our action. When we sit back to reflect on ourselves, or to present ourselves to others, we become aware of the fog of repetition in which we are always enveloped. If this is true on an individual level, it is also true of nations. Perhaps more than any other American writer, Stein is devoted to the idea of a national mind. For Stein this national mind, like the repetitions that reveal individual being, comes alive through cliché, parable, all the little stories that form the mental tissue of American life. Another name for this mental tissue is ideology, and Stein aims to crack the enormous web of images and ideals that go into the making of Americans.

The central creation of Stein's novel is the great American writer. Stein claims supreme authority for writers. Stories are powerful. They exploit, indeed they create, the appetite for fantasy that is essential to any successful nation.

Yet how are we to take Stein's emphasis, starting with the title, on the production side of American culture? As a catalog of the seemingly infinite number of American types, Stein's book can be understood as celebrating the sheer activity of production. This is consistent with the spirit of her gargantuan 925-page book. It seems to contradict, however, her continual undermining of human reproduction and hereditary transmission. What Stein is suggesting is that this patriarchal model is becoming obsolete, the concept of fathering is losing ground to another kind of manufacture. Progress, as Stein defines it, involves the displacement of traditional forms of production by a modern capitalist ideal of production, with which the monumentally productive writer implicitly identifies. At the same time, Stein's American writer has become an active producer of selves, in the sociological vein. To this end,

the novel begins with a sputtering, fantastically abbreviated patriarchal plea for the maintenance of tradition. And the remainder of the book can be read as a rebuttal of this two-line dictum.

The patriarchal figure who threatens to dominate the book is David Hersland, who closely resembles Stein's own father Daniel. In contrast to the other fathers, this immigrant who made good fulfills a very liberal, very modern American pattern. He had "gone west to make his fortune . . . he was big and abundant and full of new ways of thinking." An Emersonian type, "he was as big as all the world about him . . . the world was all him, and there was no difference in it in him . . . there were no separations of him or from him, and the whole world he lived in always lived inside him." David Hersland is the representative of the misguided dream of human transparency and uniformity. And in a sense Stein's whole book is an assault on this dream. The world, Stein argues, does not conform to the domineering unities of this patriarch. And yet the real action of her book involves not so much his discrediting as his rebirth in the form of the great American novelist. Stein's own penchant for knowing the social world, for cataloging its various parts, derives from this figure. Every restriction of this desire, every assertion that society resists knowledge and codification, is balanced by a reaffirmation of the desire to know. Though Stein readily admits that any such effort is bound to be a process of self codification, she also recognizes this as a truth too dark to accept.

In one of the book's most brilliant passages, Stein records our stubborn inability to accept this darkness. She describes "being with someone who has always been walking with you, and you always have been feeling that one was seeing everything with you and you feel then that they are seeing that thing the way you are seeing it and then you go sometime with that one to a doctor to have that one have their eyes examined and then you find that things you are seeing, you are writing completely only for one and that is yourself then and to every other one it is a different thing. . . . You know it then yes but you do not really know it as a continuous knowing in you for then in living always you are feeling that someone else is understanding, feeling seeing something the way you are feeling, seeing, understanding that thing."

This passage is paradigmatic of Stein's vision. It reflects her preoccupation with the very processes by which human beings process knowledge, a subject as visceral as the function of the retina. Harking back to her interest in anatomy and automatic action, the passage reveals her conviction that predispositions, ideas, myths, once absorbed, are as stubborn as biology. This does not make Stein a biological determinist. Rather she imaged ideology in physical terms as a reminder of its power. The passage is most striking in its awareness of the limits of awareness. You can know this "truth," about the limits of knowing, she says, you can look it square in the face, but it won't change your fundamental need to know. It won't alter the presumptuous habits that form the basis of American liberalism—that society and its members are transparent, that they are just like us.

The Making of Americans brings us full circle in our analysis, back to Ian Hacking's sense of "Making Up People." For Stein, as for Hacking, to classify is to invent; describing is a creative activity. Typological description involves not only the invention of human beings but the invention of language. "So I found myself getting deeper and deeper into the idea of describing really describing every individual that could exist," Stein writes in "The Gradual Making of The Making of Americans" (1934-35), "while I was doing all this all unconsciously at the same time a matter of tenses and sentences came to fascinate me." Stein's experimental language, this passage suggests, comes directly out of her addiction to social scientific methods of description. Her understanding of social scientific method reveals its fundamentally aesthetic aspects. While it locks others into typological schemes, it frees the typologist for acts of invention.

Stein's America, a turn-of-the-century scene of immigration, scientific discovery, economic expansion, looming sexual liberation, offers an open field for the making of Americans. The typological thinking of this era reveals a moment when the concerns of American novelists were vividly aligned with those of more scientific social analysts. In keeping with the other novelists we have discussed, Stein's sustained meditations on typological thinking remind us that literature tends to absorb contemporary ideologies. But they also remind us that literature can give us insight into social categories—the historical pressures that shape them, the human beings they affect—and, in so doing, may provide a source of resistance as well as a source of understanding and critique.

Allene Cooper (essay date 1994)

SOURCE: "Science and the Reception of Poetry in Postbellum American Journals," in *American Periodicals*, Vol. 4, 1994, pp. 24-46.

[*In the following essay, Cooper traces the influence of the scientific theories of evolution and determinism on nineteenth-century poetry, explaining that the period was one of extensive experimentation in the subject matter and form of verse.*]

In 1870, the editor of *Putnam's Magazine* wrote an essay titled "Poetry Not Dead" (*P* 5 4/70 505).[1] In it, he argued against claims that our society no longer had any use for poetry that strives to uplift and edify. Notwithstanding his defense, the sentimental poetry he aspired to save for the most part died and was replaced in the twentieth century by a more skeptical, less unified and moralistic verse. Our literary histories seem to assert by relative indifference to the postbellum period that this new poetry sprang unheralded and fully developed in the 1890s.[2] But research into

the popular and literary journals of the postbellum years reveals that the new poetry grew out of and developed in response to natural forces and tensions long before the turn of the century.

The subject matter of that 1870 essay in *Putnam's* was the threat of the scientific revolution against poetry. Scientific discoveries endangered both the office and the subject matter of verse, and the imminent death of sentimentalist verse was a topic of great concern to poetry lovers throughout the early years following the Civil War. *Putnam's* author felt impelled to argue that "it is nonsense to say that industrial and scientific activity excludes the artistic and kills poetry. No one branch of true human culture impedes another." Fourteen years later *The Century Magazine* still echoed *Putnam's* concern and hope: "The age of poetry is not past; there is nothing in culture or science antagonistic to it. The old he [the poet] has and all the new" (*CE* 27 4/84 820).[3] Nearly 100 years of criticism, mostly unfriendly to both sentimentalism and historicism, has obscured the journalistic battle to save uplifting poetry that is recorded in the journals of the period. Because literary scholars in the early part of the twentieth century labeled the period following the Civil War as univocally genteel, few Americanists have cared to explore the conditions under which poetry was reborn for the 20th century.[4] But without re-examining the reception poetry received and without understanding what contemporary writers perceived as the challenges poetry faced, we cannot hope to understand the forces and tensions that shaped the poetry of that period and thus the roots of our own.

The popular and literary journal entries of the period reveal that many cultural issues, such as economic welfare, commercialism, women's rights, and mass education influenced poetry, and they show that it was a time of extensive experimentation in the subject matter and form of verse. Moreover, the poetry reviews reveal that it was also an era of critical distress and debate about whether poetry had a future at all. Objectively reporting and analytically defining the world, science seemed to be displacing explanations for human existence less observable such as could be obtained by means of poetry and religion.

The influence of scientific theories of evolution and determinism on fiction has been examined by modern scholars.[5] But although for the most part poetry has been neglected in this regard, it, too, felt the effects of the scientific revolution. The works of Darwin and Spencer challenged the spiritual values that had been the very domain of poetry. Scientists forecast the eventual extinction of verse altogether. In the years following the Civil War, poetry reviews became a forum where the issue was debated as reviewers expressed their fears that poets were losing their place as interpreters of universal ideals. Some literary editors argued that poetry was superior to science. Others conceded that it might not be superior, but at least poets could adapt by integrating the new knowledge that science provided. That poetry had to change seemed clear to those outside the circle of stalwart defenders of the literary tradition of moral sentiment.[6]

While many poets were experimenting outside that tradition, for most popular poets and readers, sentimentality had continued essential up to the time of the Civil War. This tradition was based primarily on seventeenth- and eighteenth-century notions of a moral sentiment that equated ethical and aesthetic values for poetry. Even the noted "American Renaissance" of the Massachusetts romantics did little to alter the course of an already strong popular current whose ethical purpose originated in a belief in the basic goodness and eventual perfection of humankind.[7] Poets and readers for over a century had aimed at sharing bonds of sympathy that grew out of innate moral sensitivity. Walter Jackson Bate reports in his *From Classic to Romantic* (1946) that sentimental aesthetic concepts began as early as the seventeenth-century when proponents of *je ne sais quoi* aesthetics argued that to account for what is pleasing in art one must appeal to a faculty other than reason. Adherents of sentimentalism claimed that "Taste" has an inexplicable emotional base rather than a rational one. Lord Shaftesbury, for example, had argued that the employment of benevolent feelings constitutes both "taste" in the aesthetic realm and "moral sense" in the ethical realm.

Fred Kaplan, in his *Sacred Tears: Sentimentality in Victorian Literature,* reasons that the twentieth century misunderstands Victorian literature because we are "misled by a common vocabulary into assuming that the words meant then what they do now" (5). Kaplan examines the influence of moral sentiment on the fiction of Dickens and Thackeray and finds that Victorian doctrines of sentimentality proposed "to defend human nature from further devaluation" incited by Puritan Calvinism, deterministic theories, and philosophic realism. Citing the intellectual contributions of Lord Shaftesbury, Francis Hutcheson, Adam Smith, and David Hume, Kaplan outlines the Victorian "belief that human beings are innately good, that the source of evil is malignant social conditioning, and that the spontaneous, uninhibited expression of the natural feelings . . . is admirable and the basis for successful human relationships" (7).

Poetry's office was to express elevated values and to inspire behavior consonant with highest ideals of familial devotion and ethical social conduct.[8] Sentimentalists found merit in art that would bring poet and reader together sympathetically, that would "move," "elevate," and "teach" readers to live by the expression of their "inner sense," their innately endowed emotions, and so improve the condition of humanity (*SM* 11 11/72 627).[9]

As the English-speaking world responded to the many changes of the nineteenth century, poets held even more tightly to past traditions. Jay Martin in his description of the transformation of American culture during the nineteenth century uses Freud's idea of "psychic withdrawal" to account for American writers' retreat to eighteenth-century notions of order (13). This same need to give shape to a seemingly chaotic world increased poets' reliance on established forms and moral themes.

SCIENCE THREATENS IMAGINATIVE INTERPRETATION

For nineteenth-century believers in the perfectibility of humankind and the benevolent nature of the universe of which humanity is a part, optimism and cheerfulness were intrinsic to healthy moral poetry. But by the end of the Civil War readers had suffered a crisis of faith in innate goodness. Growing disparity between rich and poor, increasing populations in crowded cities, escalating prejudice against immigrants, and encroaching technology tended to uproot a sense of unity and goodwill that many had believed was necessary to the American experiment (Martin 1-11). The advances of the scientific movement encouraged as much as any of these factors the disillusion of nineteenth-century mind. Certainly the wide publicity of *On the Origin of Species* (1859) during the Civil War contributed to nearly a universal disenchantment with notions that humanity, although perhaps depraved, is at least of prominence in a divine plan. In this early treatise, Darwin shocked many with his conclusion that natural selection rather than divine guidance determined the evolution of living beings. His *Descent of Man, and Selection in Relation to Sex* appeared in 1871, further eroding belief in the moral perfectibility of humankind by claiming evidence that humans descended from beings with ape-like characteristics.

The immediate threat to poetry made by science, however, was its insistence that analytic thought and observation were superior to imagination and inspiration. Poets claimed the ability to exercise the sympathetic and imaginative faculties in such a way that allowed them to understand feelings associated with situations they may not have experienced themselves but which might be important to readers. The sentimental poet's goal had been to express these moral feelings so that readers would be similarly moved.

Scientific discoveries not only conflicted with traditional cultural definitions of the human race, which were the material of poetry, but the reliance on objective observation challenged both imaginative invention and the interpretive purpose for writing. *The Dial,* a conservative, Midwest journal begun in 1880, noted with alarm that some scientists predicted that ultimately, as society evolved, there would be no need either for the imaginative faculty nor for its child—poetry. Poetry would die—just as other useless capabilities have—as humankind learned to use analysis and observation to explain the world. In a review of Lanier's *Science of English Verse, The Dial's* founder and editor, Francis F. Browne, disconcertedly reported that the president of the American Association of Science had prophesied the continual "decline" of poetry since as modern civilization evolved it would become increasingly "averse to the cultivation of the imagination" (*D* 1 7/80 55-8).[10] Scientists, recorded Browne in dismay, believe that, as the English statesman Macaulay put it, ". . . it is only among nations emerging from barbarism that we are to look for the . . . development of poetic taste." "[These] poetic skeptics," *The Dial* went on, "plainly deny that the future is to have any poetry except those fragments which it may be able to preserve from a less civilized and more imaginative past." When scientific investigations came to define the world, the need for mythic explanations of the universe and humankind's relationships to it would be eliminated. When the scientist, as recorder of natural events, gained followers, the poet/seer would no longer need to exist.

Religiously oriented journals, such as *Catholic World,* argued in angry response that poetic inspiration was a spiritual process, and that the "fallen" state of contemporary art and poetry was a direct result of the influence of "Comte and the positive philosophy" (*CW* 12 10/70 98; 35 4/82 138). Less sure of direct divine inspiration for poetry, most popular journals continued to defend human imagination. *Scribner's,* for example, agreed with *Catholic World* that science was not superior to art. But in one of his "Topics of the Times" essays, editor Josiah Gilbert Holland argued that poetry was only "indirectly . . . dependent upon the spiritual world for its inspirations and its materials" (*S* 22 9/81 786-7).[11] Instead, *Scribner's* argued, poetry could be superior to the dogmas both of science societies and of religious sects. The human faculty of imagination, by itself, interprets the world.[12]

Intensely moral yet fiercely nonsectarian, J. G. Holland claimed that human imagination could eventually be the force that would "reconcile science and religion." For while neither supernatural nor material inspiration had sufficiently explained humanity, its moral inclinations, or the universal truths evident in experience, the divine gift of human imagination could do so. The imagination, wrote *Scribner's'* reviewer in explanation, "demands illimitable space, illimitable time, illimitable freedom of invention, release from bondage to the material and real, and liberty to explore the spiritual and the ideal." The poet, maintained *Scribner's,* "arrives at his conclusions by a process unknown . . . and . . . superior to science." The journal insisted that while poetic inspiration is free from religious imperatives, it is also superior to scientific analysis. The journal asserted that intuition is not the child of reason. "Vision is not born of logic, and poetry never has been an outgrowth of science, and it is safe to say that it never will be."

Moreover, *Scribner's* claimed, agreeing with *Catholic World,* that observation is not a superior way of knowing. Since science "deals with matter" and denies "the existence of mind independent of matter," it is obviously inferior to poetry. And since "[Science] refuses to recognize the existence of such a thing as imagination" and instead "interferes with [the] liberty" of the imagination, science "is a foe to poetry and a curse to literature" (*S* 22 9/81 786-7).

Scribner's, ascribing to imagination the highest of human powers and duties, called on poetry to rise above the fray, "to attack questions as old as humanity, [to harmonize] the conflicting answers . . . which hitherto given by religion and science are alike unsatisfactory" (*S* 11 1/76 446), to

"depict man neither in the wrong old way, as the center of all things, nor in the wrong new way, as sufficient in his own strength" (*S* 5 3/73 651). Still acting as seer, the poet would rise above the logic of science and the dogma of religion ultimately to define and describe the human soul.

SCIENTISTS AND POETS TRY TO ADAPT TO EACH OTHER

Eventually, a new poetry was to emerge from the arguments about scientific observation, religious inspiration, and human imagination, but meanwhile the relationship between science and poetry seems to have been on the minds of a lot of journal contributors besides literary editors. Some scientific writers and poets disregarded arguments about which was superior and focused, instead, on combining the two in a variety of ways. A few scientists tried their hands at writing poetry and some poets, on their part, tried to be more objective.

Some scientists undertook to harmonize poetry and science by including poems in the scientific papers they submitted to the journals. The highly successful middle-class and middle-of-the-road journal, *Harper's,* for example, published a piece called "Poetry and Philosophy of Indian Summer," in which the unidentified science writer interspersed lines of poetry to embellish his discourse on North America's "fifth season" (*H* 48 12/73 89-98). First, the author, quite possibly Spencer F. Baird, secretary of the Smithsonian Institution and *Harper's* science editor for a time, would write in technical detail and then insert a poem that might move readers from fact to imaginative contemplation of the subject. For instance, at one point, the author explains the Indian Summer phenomenon as "earth's passage in November . . . through or beneath the great meteor stratum" and the retardation of "the refrigeration by the meteors returning to her a portion of the heat which they themselves receive from the sun." Thereafter follows a line from Longfellow: "The great sun / Looked with the eye of love upon the golden vapors around him." Which description of Indian summer best pleased readers can only be imagined.

Another scientist announced his technical discoveries in verse. *The Critic* reviewed his work with humor, however, and without quoting from his *Science in Song,* noted:

> It is a sufficient commentary on the fact that science *per se* is not adapted to poetry, however easily it may adapt itself to rhyme, that the author has had to provide twenty-two pages of notes to explain one hundred and eight pages of rhymed scientific facts.

> (*CR* 67 4/11/85 171)

The *North American Review* criticized still another would-be scientist/poet who tried to "follow" the "debated line between science and religion." The poet attempted to prove that logic, not imagination, could drive the invention and organization of poetry. The reviewer quotes the following lines as embodying the author's "logical" theme:

"We may not hope to read / Nor comprehend the whole. . . ." Addressing the "Voice of Nature," the author amplifies that theme:

> Tell us of a force, behind
> Nature's force, supreme, alone;
> Tell us of a larger mind
> Than the partial power we own;
> Tell us of a Being wholly
> Wise and great and just and holy;—

But the reviewer, possibly editor Henry Adams, wrote without hope for the success of such poetry, "Perhaps the reader, like the critic, will feel an uncomfortable doubt whether this is, as poetry or as logic, quite satisfactory. . . . [H]e follows the train of reasoning at the cost of the poetic sentiment" (*NAR* 120 4/75 440).

At the same time, while some scientists tried to use poetry for their own ends, others called poets to task for their inaccuracies and lack of knowledge about nature. *The Atlantic Monthly: A Magazine of Literature, Science, Art and Politics,* which had added the word "Science" to its subtitle in 1865, for example, ran an article called "The Poets' Birds," written by ornithologist Philip Robinson.[13] In it, Robinson lamented that "poetry is hardly . . . satisfactory when it shows an unnecessary disregard of scientific facts." He argued that most poets irresponsibly misrepresented the character and habits of the birds they used in their imagery. He asserted contemptuously that while poets claim

> . . . that they are the chief ministers and high priests of Nature . . . [and are] in exceptional communion with her, . . . the bards are not only inadequately informed as to the ordinary objects in nature, but curiously unfair towards those which they profess to understand.

(*A* 49 6/82 780-88)

Robinson was especially offended that poets contradicted themselves while ascribing human characteristics to birds. "That which is grand in eagles," cited the author, "is wicked in hawks. The latter are always 'rending' something, or 'ravening,' or 'gorged'," wrote the author, while the same natural behavior by eagles was described by poets as noble and honorable. It upset Robinson that the blameless raven, "taunted with its conduct towards Noah," was also "robbed of the credit of nourishing Elijah." He found it ridiculous to describe a bird as "solitary," "dark and foul," "greedy," or "obscene." In addition, he claimed the owl is unjustly depicted as "silent," hoarse," "moody," "grim," "boding," "moping," "complaining," "ghastly," "dire." Thus, Robinson took nature's "interpreters" to task and argued that their "ignorance" has put them "out of sympathy with Nature."

By arguing that poets were not only incorrect but irresponsible, Robinson defied sentimentalist claims that poets had a heightened understanding of nature. His argument had come in response to a previous essay in *Scribner's* whose editor had boasted that "poets are usually the best natural-

ists; not only because they are alert and impressionable, but because a true poet is more or less *en rapport* with nature" (*S* 19 12/79 285-95). The author had conceded that "it is curious to note how our singers sometimes trip in their dealings with her," making the violet come "early as it does in England," or putting blue eggs in a hummingbird's nest. In addition, the journal had admitted that Bayard Taylor mistook the American starling for the English lark and that Longfellow inaccurately put the blue-bird in the elm when it more characteristically would be as Lowell wrote, 'shifting his light load of song / From post to post along the cheerless fence.'" And Bryant "was certainly drawing largely upon his imagination," for his facts about the yellow violet, acknowledged the journalist, since it is not true that

> Of all her train, the hands of Spring
> First plant thee in the watery mold;
> And I have seen thee blossoming
> Beside the snow-bank's edges cold.

But *Scribner's'* editors excused these inaccuracies. They argued that natural objects were merely the materials with which the poet worked. The journal insisted that "The poetic interpretation of nature, which has come to be a convenient phrase, is, of course, a myth, or is to be read the other way. It is the soul the poet interprets, not nature" (*S* 19 12/79 285-95). For sentimentalists, nature was merely the vehicle that aided the interpretation of the incomprehensible soul. That interpretation required the inspiration of a true poet. In fact, wrote *Scribner's'* editor, advocating the supremacy of humanity over the material world, "There is nothing in nature but what the beholder supplies. . . . Nature is a dead clod until you have breathed upon it with your genius. You commune with your own soul, not with woods or waters."

Scribner's maintained that poets had license to be unscientific. The journal praised Whitman's "Out of the Cradle Endlessly Rocking," as an example of a poem that while "not at all ornithological," is still "altogether poetical." In *Scribner's'* sentimental view, Whitman and other poets who responded with human emotion to nature were quite within their office in interpreting the souls of humankind.

By 1885, editors of *The Critic,* Jeanette and Joseph Gilder, though they objected to "putting mere facts into rhyme," and were loath to give up Wordsworth, for example, whether or not he be faithful in his descriptions, were agreeing with scientists and other journalists that poets could be more accurate and still appeal to the poetic spirit. They applauded Tennyson, for instance, for the "perfect truth of every botanic and geological allusion" (*CR* 4/11/85).

And there were poets, not so ardent as *Scribner's'* editor in the belief in poetry's lofty role, who consciously tried to accommodate nature verse to objectivism. A comparison of one of their nature "word paintings" to a poem written by *Scribner's'* Holland demonstrates the difference between what the sentimentalists believed poetry should do and one of the directions the new poetry would take.

A number of new poets made no attempt to unite writer and reader in hope-filled pathos or to interpret and explain human yearnings, and for them no subject was considered inherently unpoetic.[14] Robert Weeks's poems, such as "Sunset," "Another Snow Shower in April," "A Hill-Top," attempt to describe a scene without sentiment, without moral. A friendly reviewer for *The Atlantic* remarked in discussing "A Hill-Top" that it is "as if some American student of the French school had painted it for you; and the poem has no more explicit thought than many a French landscape has; you put into it whatever sentiment you will" (*A* 39 1/77 91).[15]

> A Hill-Top
>
> Little more than a rock nearly bare,
> Rough with lichens gray-green, and a line
> Of pale-yellow grass, here and there,
> A few daisies, a tree, and a vine.
>
> But the woodbine's aglow and a stream
> Like a cloud that the sun setting fires,
> And star-like the still daisies gleam,
> And flame-like the cedar aspires.
>
> (35)

In Weeks's poem, the scene is painted for its own sake and for the emotion such a scene might invoke if it were observed in nature. The contrast between verses is left for the reader to note just as a person looking at such a hill might be awed by the change in the simple objects set aglow by the setting sun.

In contrast is a section from J. G. Holland's *Kathrina*. Holland, in addition to editing *Scribner's*, also wrote some of the most popular sentimental poetry of the period. His *Kathrina* was second in sales only to *Hiawatha*. His poetry exemplifies the interpretive character to which sentimentalist poets aspired. When the heroine of Holland's book-length narrative dies, the narrator exclaims:

> I sought the window, to relieve the pain
> Of long suppressed emotion. In the East,
> Tinged with the golden dawn, the morning star
> Was blazing in its glory, while beneath,
> The slender moon, at its last rising, hung,
> Paling and dying in the growing light,
> And passing with that leading up to heaven.
> My daughter stood beside her mother's bed,
> But I had better vision of the scene
> In the sweet symbol God had hung for me
> Upon the sky.
>
> Swiftly the dawn advanced,
> And higher rose, and still more faintly shone,
> The star-led moon. Then, as it faded out,
> Quenched by prevailing day, I heard one sigh—
> A sigh so charged with pathos of deep joy,
> And peace ineffable, that memory
> Can never lose the sound; and all was past!
>
> (Holland 315)

In Holland's poems nature mirrors and symbolizes human emotion, and as sentimentalist, the author does not hesitate to direct the reader's sympathies to God's reassurances in the universe.

The most appropriate subject for poetry, contended the journal Holland edited, was not "the mere treatment of Nature" (*S* 4 3/72 637):

> Is a tree, or a pond, or a mulleinstalk . . . so high a theme that a poet or a painter shall be justified in disregarding those larger, graver, sweeter themes, the interests of men and women? . . . Man is himself the highest Nature.

But while *Scribner's* held on to the view that objectivist poets writing about "Moss," "Weeds," "A Bat," or a "Box" gave "importance . . . to trivial or repulsive subjects" (*S* 3 12/71 253), *The Atlantic,* on the other hand, praised the objective poems for their lack of moral didacticism and objective accuracy.

In addition to the word-painters already mentioned, other poets, too, hoped to reconcile the apparent disparity between poetry and science. Sidney Lanier's analysis of poetic form is well documented. In its review of his *Science of English Verse, The Dial* indicated the direction of scientific structuralism that some twentieth-century literary analyses would take. Its editor, Browne, wrote:

> The advance of modern science is thus curiously made, not to abrogate poetry, but to aid and interpret it; for the poetry of the future, according to Mr. Lanier, is itself to be a science, and is to be constructed and investigated in strict accordance with scientific methods.
>
> (*D* 7/80 56)

Although Browne believed that Lanier's scientific investigations of the pleasure brought by rhyme and rhythm had "nothing to do" with the sentiment of a poem, he believed it a "new and novel field of inquiry."

Browne was confident that scientists and poets could get along. After all, he wrote, "In their higher forms, poetic genius and scientific genius seem akin; and from both poets and scientific men have come sentiments of mutual recognition and dependence" (*D* 7/80 56). Browne recognized John Tyndall as a friend to poetry in the science camp. British physicist and professor at the Royal Institution, London, Tyndall, reported Browne,

> declares that science comes not as the antagonist of poetry, but as its ally . . . and he speaks hopefully of the coming time 'when Poetry shall take her younger sister Science by the hand and lead her forward with the joy of a bacchanal.'

But what direction could poetry take? Perhaps, poets, rather than using scientific methods to construct or analyze poetry, could modify the traditional role from one of interpreting the human soul to one of re-interpreting the objective world subjectively. Browne cited Mr. Stopford Brooke,

Irish poet, who expressed hope that "to write on the universal ideas of science, through the emotions which they excite, will be part of the work of future poets of nature" (*D* 7/80 56). *The Dial* also referred readers to John Campbell Shairp, who held the chair of poetry at Oxford, as one artist and critic who believed poetry could exist alongside science. Quoting Shairp, *The Dial* wrote that "while Science gives to Poetry new regions to work upon, Poetry repays the debt by familiarizing and humanizing what Science has discovered."

Only a few admitted attempts at "humanizing" the discoveries of science surfaced in the journals of the time. And these failed in most reviewers' judgment. Bayard Taylor, for example, wrote a long dramatic poem which *Scribner's,* just two months after Taylor's death, soberly called "nothing less than the evolution of human thought from the age of classical antiquity up to the present time, and somewhat beyond" (*S* 17 2/79 602). Allegorical characters represented the forces "that have been active in human history, advancing or retarding the onward march of man." *Scribner's* could not recommend Taylor's *Prince Deukalian* to the public "however much of talent or genius it may exhibit," said Holland in a "Topics of the Time" essay, because "it occupies an atmosphere quite too highly rarified for the common breathing, and deals with personages, or conceptions of personages, mainly beyond the reach of human sympathies" (*S* 17 3/79 755). In his efforts to demonstrate how scientific theories could explain the human condition, Taylor wrote for the "cultured" few, and *Scribner's* explained, "the reading world wants men and women to deal with, moved by the common passions of humanity, and not gods and imaginary personages representing histories, institutions and ideas."[16]

In another experiment at applying human values to the discoveries of science, William B. Wright tried to describe the life and consciousness of a body of water as if it had characteristics of a human soul. Wright's reviewer explained that the poem was not intended to be allegorical. Instead "taking the Brook as his subject, [the author attributes] to it the emotion and the vicissitudes which man undergoes, . . . endowing [the brook] with consciousness, [he] seeks to enter into that consciousness and express its working" (*S* 53/73 650). But, wrote the reviewer, Wright's purpose and also his difficulty lay in his determination to treat the brook as a living conscious being and to imbue it with a subjectivity an object simply doesn't have. At least to *Scribner's* reviewer, *The Brook* failed because the consciousness of a stream of water was untenable as a poetic subject.

Consistently loyal to its sentimental creed, *Scribner's* stalwartly objected to poets who forgot that while "physical science deals with the outward object alone, . . . poetry has to do with the object *plus* the soul of man" (*S* 15 1/78 440-1). By thus refusing to abandon the human soul as poetry's rightful primary subject, *Scribner's* no doubt influenced the most important legacy poetry was to leave to twentieth-century writers. Whether referring to popular song lyrics or serious verse, describing and explaining human responses to life's conditions remains one of the chief offices of poetry today.

POETRY OF HOPE IN DOUBT

Scientific theories had left postbellum readers in doubt as to the existence of a divine creator. Darwinian notions bred an uncertainty as to the divine potential of humankind. The formidable task of reconciling science, religion, and human imagination required more powerful poetry than the new idea-less word-pictures. It required a poetry responsible for explaining how discoveries such as evolution and the process of selection might co-exist with religious explanations of the creation, of human nature, and of human potential.

Edward J. Harding, writing for *The Critic,* observed that "the spread of [the] modern scientific ideas" of Darwin and Spencer had caused "a difference in spirit," a change "of atmosphere," and a "doubt and hesitation," (*CR* 5/17/84 229-30). He claimed that "[d]isillusion has quenched our cheer." *The North American Review* reported that science had left humanity with "a depressing sense of the infinities" (*NAR* 138 6/84 601).[17] If poetry were to continue to explain the strivings of the human soul, it would have to consider a new disillusioned human spirit.

Poets dealt with this new spirit by writing verse that *The New Eclectic Magazine* (later *Southern Magazine*) called "The Modern Poetry of Doubt." The magazine recorded that the new poetry had "interwoven . . . [into a] tone of utter desolation a thread of manly and solemn conviction that 'there is more faith in honest doubt,' than in all the creeds" (*NE* 7/6/70 490-3). This modern poetry, maintained the author, expresses

> the almost unspeakable fear that we may be left alone with that [utterly careless] Nature . . . in that process of selection which science has so triumphantly established, but which only a poet can picture to us in all its terror.

But, wrote the author, the "higher poets of our day" seemed to be in consensus in expressing a "frank and sad confession of Doubt with an undertone of Faith."

This undertone of faith marked much postbellum poetry and its reviews. Retaining the optimism of moral sentimentalism, journals registered approval of poetry which, while it addressed the uncertainty of the age, acted to assure readers that there were those who still had hope in the future for humanity on this earth and in a world to come.

A reader wrote to *The Critic* asserting that "surging in from every side" was a multitude of poetic voices that acknowledged this hope in uncertainty. In addition to Arnold's work, the reader observed that the poems of Frederic Myers, for example, are exquisite in expression, tremulous with a passion of eager faith and love, yet thrilled throughout with the wail of one who knows and suffers from the doubt, the pain, the longing for perfect knowledge with which the Time-Spirit urges his followers.

(*CR* 6/7/84 265-7)

The author noted a "skepticism qualified by a yearning of hope" in the postbellum poetic community and a "loving doubt and longing for knowledge and perfect faith" that seemed to mark the age on both sides of the Atlantic.

The contributor noted that a "discontent," an "exposition of . . . longing," a "gloom-spirit," was evident in the "countless sweet, sad, earnest, voices [that] well up on every side." Listing such poets as Arnold, Clough, Blanco White, and George Eliot, the author praised lines such as

> Is it so, O Christ in heaven, that whichever way we go,
> Walls of darkness must surround us, things we would but cannot know?
> That the Infinite must bound us, as a temple veil unrent,
> While the Finite ever wearies, so that none attain content.
>
> (Sarah Williams)

> Yet up through heaven's deep blue we yearn and seek
> Some answer to the vast and awful doubt;
> The golden letters gleam—our eyes are weak
> We cannot spell them out.
>
> (G. Herbert Sass)

> How e'er thou turn'st wrong Earth! still Love's in sight,
> For we are taller than the breadth of night.
>
> (Sidney Lanier)

The note of faith mixed with sadness expressed by these poets, the author maintained, continued in a line from Shelley to Arnold and Clough. Another of the poets cited by *The Critic*'s reader was Christopher Pearse Cranch, whose work Stedman later included in *The Library of American Literature* (vol. 7 221-4). Stedman selected Cranch's "If Death Be Final" (1887), a poem that demonstrates the despair prompted by scientific notions of a life "without a [divine] purpose or a form":

> If death be final, what is life, with all
> Its lavish promises, its thwarted aims,
> Its lost ideals, its dishonored claims,
> Its uncompleted growth? A prison wall,
> Whose heartless stones but echo back our call;
> An epitaph recording but our names;
> A puppet-stage where joys and griefs and shames
> Furnish a demon jester's carnival;
> A plan without a purpose or a form;
> A roofless temple; an unfinished tale.
> And men like madrepores through calm and storm

> Toil, die to build a branch of fossil frail,
> And add from all their dreams, thoughts, acts, belief,
> A few more inches to a coral-reef.

Other lines by Cranch defy the sentimental creed that humanity shares a bond of innate feelings, that the human condition can be improved through joint expression of noble emotions. He wrote in 1844 that "We are spirits clad in veils . . . All our deep communion fails / To remove the shadowy screen." He continues:

> Heart to heart was never known;
> Mind with mind did never meet;

For Cranch, there was some hope. But it was based neither on a sentimental belief in an innate moral sense nor on a scientific trust of physical perceptions. He, and perhaps other "hope in doubt" poets, anticipated a unity different from that embraced by Western sentimentalism:

> Only when our souls are fed
> By the Fount which gave them birth,
> And by inspiration led,
> Which they never drew from earth,
>
> We, like parted drops of rain
> Swelling till they meet and run,
> Shall be all absorbed again,
> Melting, flowing into one.

The Atlantic had, like *The Critic,* recognized this "hope-in-doubt animating very many earnest thinkers, or dreamers, about the divine" (*A* 29 6/72 750). The journal cited Bayard Taylor's *Masque of the Gods,* where Christ is included as an equal member with all the gods of the pagan world. Although the poem might "not be perfectly satisfactory to the average churchgoer," admitted the reviewer, it has a "devout and reverent spirit," and "a deep sense of majesty."

In Taylor's poem, the gods

> reason together of what they are and have been, with a misgiving (very comfortable to humanity similarly perplexed) as to their own origin, and an avowed sense of somewhat yet more supernal. They wonder if man, who has adored, did not also make them.

"A Voice from Space" interrupts the gods' discussion and validates the legitimacy of each of them. Then Man, who has acted the part of the Chorus throughout the poem, cries in reverent awe:

> We hearken to the words
> We cannot understand. If we look up
> Beyond the shining form wherein Thy Love
> Made holiest revelation, we must shade
> Our eyes beneath the broadening wing of Doubt,
> To save us from Thy splendor. All we learn
> From delving in the marrow of the earth,
> From scattering thought among the timeless stars,
> From slow-deciphered hieroglyphs of power

In chemic forces, planetary paths,
Or primal cells whence all Thy worlds are born,
But lifts Thee higher, seats Thee more august,
Till Thou art grown so vast and wonderful,
We dare not name Thee, scarce dare pray to Thee.

Reviewers commended poems like this because the authors admitted new ideas while reinforcing traditional faith in a hereafter by "foreshadow[ing] an existence unhampered by the accidents of time and undeluded by the senses" (*NAR* 124 3/77 252). Evolution and the accidents of natural selection could be explained as part of a creator's plan. Human spirit could still be thought of existing apart from the sensible finite mutable world. *The Unitarian Review and Religious Magazine,* for example, praised William Leighton's "Change," which fostered this soft evolution (*U* 114/79 345).[18] Writing that Leighton's work "in many places" rises "to poetic fervor and loftiness," its reviewer noted that though the poet reminds us that "we too are atoms in the grasp and grind of 'Change,'" he also has several 'cheerful' thoughts, such as this from the preface: The poet is '[s]ure of an eternal government / Above all change, and rests in calm content.'"

Much work remains to be done in locating and documenting the "many earnest thinkers," such as Leighton, the "countless sweet, sad, earnest, voices" that reacted to science and objective inquiry referred to in these reviews. But meanwhile, we can witness the recorded tension of the poets' struggle with the implications of scientific theories in the period's journals.

Among the many power and cultural shifts that took place in the Western world in the last half of the 19th Century, the change from almost universal acceptance of an innate, divine sentiment as a moral guide to the near total reliance on scientific investigation was perhaps the most far-reaching. In 1881, just months before the deaths of Emerson and Longfellow, Stedman summarized the history of "Poetry in America" in a two-part article for *Scribner's* (*S* 2 10/81 540-550, 816-828). These essays later appeared as foundation chapters in his book, *Poets of America* (1895). In them, he lists influences that had recently improved the environment for poets in America: moral and emotional conflicts preceding the war which "stimulated poetic ardor," the beginning of monetary reward for writers, the encouragement by publishers for poetic endeavors, and the interest in native authors with the rise of journalism (550). All of these, he wrote, were aids that came at a moment when poetry would have become unable to "bear up against" the "scientific restraint" that newly burdened American verse. So important to American literature was the scientific movement that Stedman considered its rise marked the end of the first epoch of American poetry. A few years later, in 1885, in an essay entitled "The Twilight of the Poets," he wrote that although the "iconoclasm" of science had forced poets "to adjust," they had kept pace "so that each new wonder leads to greater things" (*CE* 30 9/85 798). To express his trust in a successful transition in American poetry, Stedman avowed, "If my bark sink, 'tis to another sea."

While poetry reviewers of nearly every critical persuasion avidly sought a future poetry that would continue to reflect our culture's feelings about the human condition, a clear perception of what poetry could or should do in relation to science and religion was not determined during the early years following the war. The poetry that did emerge has indeed become more objective and less didactic, but it also has remained concerned with emotional issues. For, rather than seeking to objectify our experiences, twentieth-century poetry reflects an emotional conflict with increasing forces of objectification. Roy Harvey Pearce has witnessed this conflict. He writes that modern American poetry has been characteristic of an age "torn asunder by its own increasingly depersonalized, mechanized, bureaucratized power" (253). Modern poets confronting issues begun in the scientific revolution of the nineteenth century, writes Pearce, "cannot finally commit themselves to American life, for it will furnish them neither the means nor the substance to sustain themselves as authentic, whole persons." The disillusionment and cynicism of American culture as reflected in some of the poetry of the last half of the nineteenth century and in our own century grew in part out of the persistent threat on the human heart posed by science. It is in the journals of the period that evidence of this threat is recorded.

Notes

1. Parke Godwin took the editorship of *Putnam's* over from Edmund Clarence Stedman in April 1870.

2. See Kindilien's "Introduction" for the idea that the '90s were unusual. For notable exceptions to the indifference shown the postbellum poets, see the works of Cary, Dickason, and Scholnick (1977).

3. The statement was made in an essay called "Sidney Lanier, Poet." The author was William Hayes Ward.

4. Douglas Wilson records that Santayana identified the genteel tradition with a female sensibility (13). Postbellum poetry was to him passive, decorous, delicate and even senile. Building on this evaluation of the period Vernon Parrington labeled it timid and uncreative (17); Sinclair Lewis claimed that American letters exemplified a divorce of intellectual life from authenticism and reality (18), and Leo Marx complained that rather than "solid reality" the period's literature was an "ecstatic dream" (19).

5. See, for example, Arthur E. Jones, Jr.'s *Darwinism and Its Relationship to Realism and Naturalism in American Fiction, 1860-1900* and Bert Bender's "The Teeth of Desire: *The Awakening and The Descent of Man.*"

6. For essays on the imminence of the change, see Walt Whitman *NAR* 133 1/81 195-210; James Herbert Morse *CR* 1/10/85 169-79; Edmund Clarence Stedman *CE* 30 9/85 786-800.

7. Witness the popularity of the Fireside poets even as late as mid-twentieth century.

8. My dissertation documents the various voices of sentimentalist reader desire recorded in the periodicals of the postbellum years.

9. *Southern Magazine* was edited by William Hand Browne and was the official journal of the Southern Historical Society. The quotation appeared in a review of J. G. Holland's *The Marble Prophesy.*

10. Browne may have been referring to Lewis H. Morgan, anthropologist and authority on the Iroquois, who was president of the American Association for the Advancement of Science in 1880.

11. For a good description of *Scribner's* as a journal that "positioned itself squarely in the center of American civil religion, but removed from a position above the unseemly doctrinal battles that were being waged all around it," see Robert J. Scholnick's article in the first number of *American Periodicals*. Unless otherwise noted, we must assume that Josiah Gilbert Holland, editor of *Scribner's* is the author of reviews quoted here. For more on Holland's life, poetry, and influence, see Plunkett (1894), Peckham (1940), and Scholnick (1986).

12. Howells joined others who questioned the future of poetry, and he insisted that the novel was better suited to describing real life. Scholnick documents this argument under the heading "The Battle of Genres" (104-7). The facility with which fiction adapted to describing life is amply recorded in literary history. See, for example, Robert Falk's "The Rise of Realism," Cowie's *The Rise of the American Novel,* and *The Columbia History of the American Novel.*

13. Thomas Bailey Aldrich had taken over the editorship of *The Atlantic* from William Dean Howells in February of 1881.

14. In another paper, I illustrate the varieties of word-paintings that developed out of attempts to bypass discourse and objectify emotion.

15. The reviewer was William Dean Howells, editor of *The Atlantic* from August 1871-January 1881.

16. Very little evidence exists in the reviews that the social Darwinism that inspired some fiction of the period affected poets. In 1885, however, a reviewer wrote of a poem called "Glenaveril," in which an individual severed at birth from his family showed that "antenatal tendencies and inherited instincts are stronger than all after effects of circumstance and education" (*CR* 89 9/12/85 131). Other forms of postbellum realism have sources other than the scientific revolution and so I have not included them in this discussion. Poetry that depicted real-life scenes or that encouraged social reform is discussed in my paper on aesthetic realism and in my dissertation, however. Another related form of nineteenth-century poetry is women's "poetry of woe," which originated more from dissatisfaction with women's roles and from graveyard sentiments than from scientific influences. It deserves more attention than is possible in this paper. Cheryl Walker begins an investigation of women's realistic poetry in her essay "Nineteenth-Century Women Poets and Realism."

17. The editor of *The North American Review* from 1877-1889 was Allen Thorndike Rice. The quotation appears in an essay about Whitman written by Walker Kennedy.

18. The editors of *The Unitarian Review* from 1875-1879 were John Hopkins Morison and Henry H. Barber.

Works Cited

Bate, Walter Jackson. *From Classic To Romantic: Premises of Taste in Eighteenth-Century England.* New York: Harper & Brothers, 1946.

Bender, Bert. "The Teeth of Desire: *The Awakening and The Descent of Man.*" *American Literature* 63 (September 1991): 459-73.

Cary, Richard. *The Genteel Tradition in America, 1850-1875.* Diss. Cornell U, 1952.

Columbia History of the American Novel. Ed. Emory Elliott. New York: Columbia UP, 1991.

Cooper, Allene. "*Vers de Société* and the Philosophy of Moral Sentiment in Postbellum America." *Studies in American Humor* 6 (1988): 52-60.

———. *Postbellum American Poetry and Reader Desire.* Diss. Arizona State U, 1991.

Cowie, Alexander. *The Rise of the American Novel.* New York: American Book Co., 1948.

Dickason, David Howard. *The Daring Young Men: The Story of the American Pre-Raphaelites.* New York: B. Blom, 1970.

Falk, Robert. "The Rise of Realism." *Transitions in American Literature.* Ed. Harry H. Clark. Durham: Duke UP, 1945.

John, Arthur. *The Best Years of the* Century*: Richard Watson Gilder,* Scribner's Monthly, *and* The Century Magazine, *1870-1909.* Urbana: U of Illinois P, 1981.

Jones, Arthur E., Jr. *Darwinism and Its Relationship to Realism and Naturalism in American Fiction, 1860-1900.* Madison, NJ: Drew University, 1950.

Kaplan, Fred. *Sacred Tears: Sentimentality in Victorian Literature.* Princeton: Princeton UP, 1987.

Kindilien, Carlin T. *American Poetry in the Eighteen Nineties.* Providence: Brown UP, 1956.

Martin, Jay. *Harvests of Change: American Literature 1865-1914.* Englewood Cliffs: Prentice-Hall, 1967.

Mott, Frank Luther. *A History of American Magazines.* 5 Vols. Cambridge: Harvard UP, 1970.

Pearce, Roy Harvey. *The Continuity of American Poetry.* Princeton: Princeton UP, 1961.

Peckham, Harry Houston. *Josiah Gilbert Holland in Relation to His Times.* Philadelphia: U of Pennsylvania P, 1940.

Plunkett, H. M. *Josiah Gilbert Holland.* New York: Charles Scribner's Sons, 1894.

Scholnick, Robert J. *Edmund Clarence Stedman.* Boston: Twayne Publishers, 1977.

———. "J. G. Holland and the 'Religion of Civilization' in Mid-Nineteenth-Century America." *American Studies* 27 (1986): 55-79.

———. "*Scribner's Monthly* and the 'Pictorial Representation of Life and Truth' in Post-Civil War America." *American Periodicals* 1 (1991): 46-69.

Stedman, Edmund Clarence. *Poets of America.* Boston: Houghton, Mifflin, 1895.

Stedman, Edmund Clarence, and Ellen Mackay Hutchinson. *Library of American Literature from the Earliest Settlement to the Present time.* 11 vols. New York: William Evarts Benjamin, 1894.

Walker, Cheryl. "Nineteenth-Century Women Poets and Realism." *American Literary Realism* 23 (Spring 1990): 25-41.

Who Was Who in American History: Science and Technology. Chicago: Marquis, 1976.

Wilson, Douglas L., ed. *The Genteel Tradition: Nine Essays by George Santayana.* Cambridge: Harvard UP, 1967.

ABBREVIATION GUIDE

A: *Atlantic Monthly A Magazine of Literature, Science, Art and Politics*

CE: *The Century Illustrated Monthly Magazine*

CR: *The Critic and Good Literature*

CW: *The Catholic World: A Monthly Magazine of General Literature and Science*

D: *The Dial: A Monthly Review and Index of Current Literature*

H: *Harper's New Monthly Magazine*

NAR: *North American Review*

NE: *New Eclectic*

P: *Putnam's Magazine: Original Papers on Literature, Science, Art, and National Interests*

S: *Scribner's Monthly, an Illustrated Magazine for the People*

SM: *Southern Magazine*

U: *Unitarian Review and Religious Magazine*

Laura Dassow Walls (essay date 1998)

SOURCE: "Science and the Shaping of Nineteenth-Century American Nature Literature," in *Literature of Nature: An International Sourcebook,* edited by Patrick D. Murphy, Fitzroy Dearborn Publishers, 1998, pp. 18-25.

[*In the following essay, Walls finds that the rise of nature literature is related to the hardening distinctions between science and literature, an issue that was of great significance to intellectuals in the nineteenth century.*]

Nineteenth-century science both created and constrained the possibilities for nature literature, making their relationship an uneasy one throughout the century. This was the Age of Science, as intellectuals then and since have styled it, and the general fascination with the emerging and rapidly changing sciences of astronomy, geology, the "new" geography, biology, chemistry, physics, anthropology and psychology opened a space for those writers, whether scientific or popular, who could interpret science for a popular audience and explain what the dazzling advances meant for "modern" life. The dynamic and increasingly connective power of science seemed to promise that the whole of nature was at last coming under the grasp of the human mind, validating ancient intuitions of the holistic interconnections of the universe, and yet, much about science seemed alienating to those left behind by its increasingly esoteric character.

Romantic literary artists who were deeply engaged with science—Wordsworth, Coleridge, Carlyle, Ruskin; Emerson, Thoreau, Poe, Whitman—also found themselves registering fierce protests against it. William Wordsworth imagined the Poet and the Man of Science walking side by side, the Poet "carrying sensation into the midst of the objects of the Science itself" (pp. 606-607); yet in his poem "The Tables Turned," he famously objected that "Our meddling intellect / Mis-shapes the beauteous forms of things; / —We murder to dissect" (pp. 130-131). Henry David Thoreau found in science a way to love nature, yet lamented the "inhumanity of science" that "tempted" him to kill a rare snake to ascertain its species: "I feel that this is not the means of acquiring true knowledge" (*Journal,* VI:311). Walt Whitman wrote that the true use of poetry would be "to give ultimate vivification" to science, and he stuffed his notebooks with science news—yet in a well-known poem he turned his back on the "charts and diagrams" of the "learned astronomer" to look up "in perfect silence at the stars" (pp. 564, 271).

Criticisms of science such as these have suggested to influential critics such as Alfred North Whitehead and M. H. Abrams that Romantic writers fundamentally rejected the mechanistic and soul-deadening rule of science in favor of the integrative power of organic nature, but this view tends to project twentieth-century divisions and fears onto the past. In fact, European and American Romantics drew on the power of the dynamic new sciences to correct and extend the philosophy of the Enlightenment. Among both educated and popular audiences, literary and scientific cultures interpenetrated each other well beyond midcentury, although disciplinary barriers arose between them as tensions mounted.

Indeed, it was the very hardening of the distinction between science and literature that gave rise to nature literature. For instance, William Bartram's *Travels* is read today both as a contribution to American science and as a landmark of early American nature writing. By midcentury, however, the professionalization of science was relegating the naturalist to amateur status, and increasing specialization was weakening the generalist's claim to scientific authority. In particular, the laboratory-based and reductionist biologist, intent on physiological processes rather than whole organisms, elbowed aside the field-based and holistic natural historian. In the United States, this contest was played out over the 15 years following the arrival in 1846 of the Swiss glaciologist and zoologist Louis Agassiz, who from his position at Harvard reorganized American science according to European professional standards. These were also, as it happened, Thoreau's most productive years. As opposed to Bartram, Thoreau has only recently begun to receive sustained attention as a contributor to American science.

The very withdrawal of the professional scientific specialist from the world of the educated lay reader opened a new space for writers like Thoreau and John Burroughs, who were willing to engage a broader audience through common experience of nature and to provide the wide-ranging philosophical syntheses that scientific precision discouraged. By century's end, journalism had largely taken over the task of translating science to a mass audience, but as late as the 1870s science writers were often themselves working scientists. Charles Lyell, Alexander von Humboldt, and Louis Agassiz all shared their vision with an educated public who attended their lectures, read their articles, and turned their books into scientific best sellers. And while amateur natural historians were screened out of the newly formed scientific societies, anyone from novice to professional could play a symbiotic role as field-collector and correspondent for the scientific centers. Louis Agassiz and Asa Gray at Harvard and Spencer F. Baird at the Smithsonian Institution all relied on an enormous network of specimen collectors who were often themselves competent local authorities in zoology and botany. Finally, a proliferation of textbooks and handbooks like those of Elmira Lincoln Phelps and Asa Gray encouraged the study of natural history, especially botany, as a genteel and healthful pursuit for young people and women. This trend may have "feminized" nature study, but it also granted women new access to fields traditionally reserved for men. By century's end, scientific amateurs had not disappeared at all, but rather, had formed their own local associations and networks, filling the social space opened, then abandoned, by science. In short, as science withdrew from common experience, both popular science and nature writing emerged to fill the gap between science and popular culture.

Throughout the nineteenth century, the scientific method was developed, regularized, instituted and coordinated through advanced university education (as at Harvard, Yale, and Johns Hopkins); through scientific societies like the American Association for the Advancement of Science (founded in 1847) and the National Academy of Sciences (established by an act of Congress in 1863); through aggressive government funding; and through ever-more-specialized science journals. The resulting methodological polarization resulted in a familiar distinction. Where stringent disciplinary training valued scientific distance and objectivity, the nature writer celebrated connections and sympathy with one's fellow creatures. Where the scientist presided over a sterile laboratory, the nature writer immersed himself in the raw experience of wild nature. Despite this dichotomy, tensions existed within science itself, and dilemmas shaped nineteenth-century nature literature in diverse and even conflicting ways.

Four interrelated issues suggest the mixed and complex legacy conferred by natural science to its popularizers and interpreters. First, was knowledge of nature best gained by a trained professional elite, or through democratic participation by all concerned? Second, was truth about nature best reached through a priori reasoning and tested under controlled laboratory conditions, or through lived experience in unpredictable wild nature? Third, was science a natural ally of religion, or did science need to distance itself from faith—and vice versa? Indeed, was nature really a morally meaningful and designed creation, or had natural systems somehow organized themselves in a contingent and alien universe? Finally, was "nature" separable from human purpose, making it available for spiritual aid and material exploitation? Or, were natural processes bound inextricably with human purpose, catching both in an ecological web that wove mind and nature together?

Each of these four issues takes up one facet of a single interrelated complex. Individual practitioners can seldom be neatly categorized. Consider for example the first question raised above: was science elitist or democratic? Louis Agassiz (who was lionized wherever he travelled) argued that scientific truth "must be woven into the common life of the world," and he attempted through his popular lectures, books, and articles to open his insights to the common reader. Yet he agonized that the steep "threshold" of scientific discipline cut science off from common understanding: "Nature does not open her sanctuary without exacting due penance from her votaries" (pp. 42, 297). Despite his ideals, his own science became a priesthood open only to the select few, those talented students, like Samuel H. Scudder and Nathaniel Shaler, who survived his strict training to mature into the next generation's scientific leaders. Thoreau was for a time one of Agassiz's specimen collectors, but he gained his own scientific training not in the scientific centers but through the informal networks that supported them: books and articles, lectures, personal contacts, and in Thoreau's case, association with the Boston Society of Natural History, which was then still an active research institution but would soon be converted to a museum and educational center. Thoreau attempted to weave science into common life by forging a natural science that would be participatory and radically democratic. In "The Succession of Forest Trees," Thoreau not only advanced a scientific theory but appealed directly to landowners, suggesting they learn scientific principles in order to better manage their forest land. Thoreau's experiment was cut off by his untimely death, but the direction he was taking can be seen in *Faith in a Seed,* which finally makes available some of his long-unpublished manuscripts.

Only two years after Thoreau's death, George Perkins Marsh independently offered a vision of participatory and democratic natural science quite similar to Thoreau's in his popular book *Man and Nature.* Yet Marsh did so not as a practicing scientist but as an avowed amateur, inviting his readers to become not mere observers of nature but activists who contributed to a common stock of knowledge. In contrast to Agassiz's "sanctuary," the study Marsh recommended "allows its votaries to occupy themselves with such broad and general views as are attainable by every person of culture," without years of special study. To wait for the "slow and sure progress of exact science," he argued, was to condemn the earth, "our dwelling," to certain destruction. Marsh urged his lay readers to contribute to an informed national policy of enlightened management of nature (pp. 17, 52). Of the three—Agassiz the professional scientist, Thoreau the passionate practitioner, Marsh the dedicated hobbyist—only Thoreau is typically called a "nature writer," yet all three saw themselves contributing both to the love and understanding of nature, and to the shared social and cultural enterprise of science. Despite his intentions, Agassiz's practice cut science off from the experience of the nature enthusiast, and Marsh's advocacy led not to literary contemplation but to government policy. It was Thoreau who tried to join all three.

Second, was scientific truth best reached through a priori reasoning or through experience in nature? For all his desire to bring science to the people, Agassiz also believed that knowledge was best reached through a priori reasoning and tested under highly controlled conditions. Part of his legacy was a pedagogy of intense observation of the isolated natural object with the goal of achieving the ultimate insight into the object's true nature, literally its "idea" in the mind of God—since to Agassiz, all objects in nature were thoughts of God materialized. This idea, associated with German *Naturphilosophie,* offered a powerfully integrative view that dominated pre-Darwinian biology. Emerson, for instance, had long been attracted to it through his reading in Goethe, Schelling, Oken, and others. Agassiz also brought to America certain European ideals: "Truth" was achieved through a strenuous discipline that demanded the student remove himself from the common confusions of daily life to that carefully prepared theater of knowledge, the scientific laboratory. Agassiz and his students were enormously influential in the development of institutionalized American science, which insists upon a rigorous and exclusive course of university-based training through which the student learns to see with the eye of the scientist.

What, then, of the observer who, by preference or circumstance, lacks access to such specialized and centralized training? Agassiz's own mentor, Alexander von Humboldt, promoted another model that was also tremendously influential in the United States. Living nature, like human history, said Humboldt, was too full of "accidental individualities" and "variations" for knowledge of it to be "based only on a rational foundation, that is to say, of being deduced from ideas alone" (*Cosmos,* I: 49-50). One must physically immerse oneself in wild nature, become an explorer who gathers observations, notes, and specimens from the widest possible field and who opens himself to all nature's influences. Only then, when drenched in lived experience, can one begin to speculate and connect what has been seen, smelled, and felt into the patterns that might indicate natural laws. Humboldt was a key figure in integrating the expanse of wild nature with the emerging cultural institutions of professional, middle-class, modern science. He helped organize the international networks of scientific societies, linking far-flung collectors with scientific centers, and his example served as a model for the exploring expeditions, such as those of John Charles Frémont and John Wesley Powell, that mapped the American West. Popular American culture saw him as the global explorer who connected a young American republic with the wider world, our "second Columbus" who had discovered America for science.

Humboldt's practice and writings advocated a proto-ecological view in which man and nature were fully integrated. In the preface to the first volume of *Cosmos,* Humboldt announced that the higher aim of his studies had been "to comprehend the phenomena of physical objects in their general connection, and to represent nature as one great whole, moved and animated by internal forces" (p. vii). Indeed, by century's end Humboldt's comprehensive science, dubbed the "new geography," had evolved into (and been wholly absorbed by) a new scientific specialty—"ecology." His own primary experience of wild nature had been gained during his five-year exploration of South and Central America, from 1799-1804, and translations of his popular books—*Personal Narrative, Views of Nature,* and *Cosmos*—captured the imaginations of Thoreau, John Muir, and the artist Frederic Church. They each read and idolized Humboldt, and each sought in his own way to recreate the Humboldtian venture in which the love of wild nature led first to the desire for knowledge, then to an ethic of freedom and an aesthetics of science expressed in literature and art.

Third, were science and religion allies or rivals? More than anyone else, Charles Darwin had absorbed and developed the rich scientific possibilities of Humboldt's theories. Ironically, Humboldt's optimistic view of natural forces in dynamic harmony was dismissed by the same generation that accepted Darwin, in a contest that at last definitively split science from religion. Darwin had inherited a tradition that saw nature as God's divine creation and science as the reasoned understanding of God's great design. This belief, "natural theology," which had ani-

Charles Darwin (1809-1882).

though Humboldt's Enlightenment-based cosmic ecology had made no mention of God, his emphasis on natural harmony allowed his work to be taken up by natural theologians. Darwin's *Origin of Species* on the other hand gave tremendous authority to the suppressed view that natural systems had somehow organized themselves, and that human beings, instead of being embraced and reflected by a separate and morally correspondent universe, were the product of uncaring and amoral natural forces. The shock of Darwinian ideas finally succeeded in driving science and religion into separate spheres, with the result that science would govern natural knowledge and religion would guide spiritual belief. Here, too, in the gap opened by the hardening of barriers, nature writers like Muir and Burroughs would continue to insist on the continuities between humanity and nature, and on the regenerative possibilities of their differences. As Burroughs put it, "If Nature planned and invented as man does, she would attain to mere unity and simplicity. It is her blind, prodigal, haphazard methods that result in her endless diversity" (p. 99). Burroughs's new natural theology was both higher and wilder than the old:

> This is the way of the Infinite—to multiply endlessly, to give a free rein to the physical forces and let them struggle with one another for the stable equilibrium to which they never, as a whole, attain; to give the same free rein to the organic forces and let their various forms struggle with one another for the unstable equilibrium which is the secret of their life.

(p. 100)

Burroughs rides serenely above the turbulent waves of post-Darwinian science, mediating between scientific truth and human life by offering a spiritual interpretation of the Darwinian sublime.

Fourth, were man and nature separate, or bound together by the very process of perception? In *Nature,* a landmark for American nature literature as well as the popularization of science, Ralph Waldo Emerson erected a scale of uses for nature, from commodity to spirit, assuming in the traditional natural theological manner that nature was a separate creation of God intended for the use and service of Man. "Nature," wrote Emerson, "is thoroughly mediate. It is made to serve. . . . One after another, his victorious thought comes up with and reduces all things, until the world becomes, at last, only a realized will,—the double of the man" (p. 28). This vision of an ultimately humanized nature accords well with the nineteenth century's rapid technological development and widening scientific understanding: poetry, science, and technology were coordinate ways of accomplishing the Emersonian goal of taking nature into the mind. Yet Emerson resisted not only the utilitarian callousness of such a view, but the Cartesian divorce of mind and matter that underwrote it. The new science that so attracted Emerson celebrated not division and categorization but dynamic and organizing process, including the mysterious but powerful process of knowledge: "Nature is the incarnation of a thought, and turns to a thought again, as ice becomes water and gas. The world

mated Gilbert White's classic *Natural History of Selborne,* accounts for the young Darwin's otherwise puzzling decision to become a clergyman. Until the opportunity for global exploration turned him in a more secular direction, Darwin had planned to follow the honored Anglican tradition popularized by White. He would become the parson-naturalist whose explorations of parish nature showed forth the beauty and ingenuity of God's creation. Until well past midcentury, science was generally understood to be the ally, not the rival, of religion, particularly in America. In the decades before Darwin, most of America's scientists—Benjamin Silliman, Louis Agassiz, Asa Gray, Joseph Henry—were deeply religious men.

The certainty that nature is not only a carefully designed creation but also morally meaningful continues to underwrite the spiritual element in American nature writing; to the older Anglican tradition, American writers and intellectuals like Thomas Jefferson, the poet Philip Freneau, Ralph Waldo Emerson and Walt Whitman added the special conviction that America's Destiny was uniquely bound to the vast spiritual and material resources of the North American continent.

As the fate of Enlightenment deists like Tom Paine suggests, the post-Revolutionary United States had little use for European "materialists" who replaced God with Natural Law and excluded divine explanation from science. Al-is mind precipitated, and the volatile essence is forever escaping again into the state of free thought" (p. 555). Nature as "fate" becomes the raw material of thought as "freedom," and the dynamic antagonism of these two poles generates the process of human life. Ultimately thought cannot be separated from material nature; the mind knows itself only as it penetrates matter, and fate and freedom slide into each other in what Emerson calls a "web of relation" in which the planet is not made, but "makes itself," and life is not directed from above, but is "self-directed" (pp. 961-962). Nineteenth-century science bore within it both fields of possibility: dualistic exploitation as well as ecological interrelation; deterministic law given from above as well as self-organizing freedom rising up from below.

Nature literature inherits both extremes and, as in Emerson, weaves contradictions together into a tangled complex not easily broken into neat analytical categories. And yet, it is possible to distinguish two complementary and internally coherent strategies for understanding nature, based on the preference given to rational or empirical modes of reasoning. Both modes believed in nature as one great, interconnected whole, although "rational" modes began by assuming, as did Coleridge, Emerson, and Agassiz, that the universe, as a designed whole, could be grasped through an a priori process of reason whereby the mind of man would mirror or follow the mind of God. Since such insight demanded either disciplinary training or intuitive genius, it was available only to a select few, and the truths those few disseminated to the many would show forth the harmony of the Creation with the purposes and laws of the Creator. Human beings were installed as rulers or stewards of a nature intended for human use—although as Marsh warned, our independent power over nature was a uniquely dangerous force, to be countered only by an increase in knowledge.

The "empirical" mode began by asserting, like Humboldt, Thoreau, and William James, that the universe was not designed but self-generating, hence infinite, open-ended and unpredictable. Such a universe could be known only through experience, not thought, hence detailed knowledge of nature in all its manifestations must be sought firsthand, and connected by the perceiving mind into patterns and hence into descriptive laws. All humankind participates in this on-going and all-inclusive endeavor, either by helping to gather and consolidate knowledge or by absorbing and applying knowledge for the advancement of humanity.

This is not to say that those who favor one mode cannot borrow from the other. A "rational holist" can, as Goethe and Agassiz did, work with delicately nuanced empirical details; an "empirical holist" can, as Asa Gray and John Muir did, be convinced that empirical details ultimately proclaim a divinely designed universe. From the two modes arise two quite different concepts of nature. From the "rational" mode arises the ideal of wilderness as a separate and primal domain from which all contaminating

traces of humanity have been erased, an Edenic Garden preserving a pure, eternal, and harmonious Creation before the Fall, offering emotional and spiritual release from the confusion and pollution of human society. From the "empirical" mode arises the concept of ecology, wherein nature is not a bounded place but an ongoing creative process, not wilderness but Thoreau's regenerative "wildness"—a dynamic interaction of energy and matter that ultimately involves not only all the sciences but all the ways in which mind and nature interpenetrate and create each other. Both concepts are of tremendous importance to twentieth century thought. The wilderness ethic, which values "pristine and unspoiled" nature purified of human contamination, and an ecological ethic, which acknowledges the human as part of the living process of nature, both arose from longstanding but quite different scientific traditions that were contesting for dominance in the nineteenth century, and both derive emotional power from their redemptive aesthetics of nature.

It was the eruption of Darwin's ideas that shifted the balance. Natural scientists now tended to postulate not the loving, designed and morally significant universe of natural theology, but the indifferent, contingent and amoral universe of Darwinism. As the gap opened by scientific professionalization and specialization widened into an abyss, nature literature sought to heal the wound by reminding its readers of the many ways human beings are intimately connected with nature, a part of—not alienated from—the sublime whole. In a sense, the very success of nature writers such as John Muir, John Burroughs, and Ernest Thompson Seton marks the finality of the split between science and literature. Canonical literary artists, such as "naturalists" Stephen Crane, Frank Norris and Jack London, reiterated humanity's alienation from a harsh and indifferent nature. As Crane wrote in his autobiographical story, "The Open Boat":

> When it occurs to a man that nature does not regard him as important, and that she feels she would not maim the universe by disposing of him, he at first wishes to throw bricks at the temple, and he hates deeply the fact that there are no bricks and no temples. . . . A high cold star on a winter's night is the word he feels that she says to him. Thereafter he knows the pathos of his situation.
>
> (pp. 84-85)

In contrast to Crane's existential dread, the unperturbed loyalty of the "naturalists" to the scientific viewpoint and to the older popular and didactic tradition still marks them as non-literary. At century's end, nature writers continued to provide links to and understandings with the sciences, but if this had seemed daring and innovative, even oppositional, in the age of Emerson and Thoreau, now in the twentieth century the nature writer's persistent attachment to natural science was dismissed as old-fashioned and nostalgic. Those who continued to believe in nature created a new and separate genre in effect, and only now is nature literature vying to be integrated, once again, into the literary canon.

Selected Works and Further Reading

Abrams, M. H., *The Mirror and the Lamp: Romantic Theory and the Critical Tradition,* New York: Oxford University Press, 1953; London: Oxford University Press, 1971

Agassiz, Louis, *Methods of Study in Natural History,* Boston: Ticknor and Fields, 1863

Bartram, William, *Travels Through North & South Carolina, Georgia, East & West Florida, the Cherokee Country, the Extensive Territories of the Muscogulges, or Creek Confederacy, and the Country of the Chactaws,* Philadelphia and London: James and Johnson, 1791; also published as *The Travels of William Bartram,* edited by Mark Van Doren, New York: Macy-Masius, 1928

Botting, Douglas, *Humboldt and the Cosmos,* New York: Harper & Row, 1973; London: Sphere, 1973

Bramwell, Anna, *Ecology in the 20th Century: A History,* New Haven, Connecticut: Yale University Press, 1989

Burroughs, John, *Accepting the Universe,* Boston: Houghton Mifflin, 1920; London: Constable, 1920

Coleridge, Samuel Taylor, *Hints Towards the Formation of a More Comprehensive Theory of Life,* London: John Churchill, 1848; also published in *Miscellanies, Aesthetic and Literary, to Which Is Added the Theory of Life,* edited by T. Ashe, London: George Bell, 1885

Crane, Stephen, *Tales of Adventure: The Works of Stephen Crane,* vol. 5, Charlottesville: University Press of Virginia, 1970

Daniels, George H., *Science in American Society: A Social History,* New York: Knopf, 1971

Darwin, Charles, *On the Origin of Species: A Facsimile of the First Edition,* edited by Ernst Mayr, Cambridge, Massachusetts: Harvard University Press, 1964

Emerson, Ralph Waldo, *The Early Lectures of Ralph Waldo Emerson,* vol. 1, edited by Stephen E. Whicher and Robert E. Spiller, Cambridge, Massachusetts: Harvard University Press, 1966

————, *Essays and Lectures,* New York: Library of America, 1983; Cambridge: Press Syndicate of the University of Cambridge, 1983

Frémont, John Charles, *Report of the Exploring Expedition to the Rocky Mountains in the Year 1842, and to Oregon and North California in the Years 1843-44,* Washington, D.C.: Gales and Seaton, 1845; also published as *Narrative of the Exploring Expedition to the Rocky Mountains in the Year 1842, and to Oregon and North California in the Years 1843-44,* London: Wiley and Putnam, 1846

Goethe, Johann Wolfgang von, *Goethe's Botanical Writings,* translated by Bertha Mueller, Honolulu: University Press of Hawaii, 1952

Goldstein, Daniel, "'Yours for Science': The Smithsonian Institution's Correspondents and the Shape of Scientific Community in Nineteenth-Century America," *Isis* 85:4 (December 1994), pp. 572-599

Gray, Asa, *The Botanical Text-Book,* New York: Wiley & Putnam, 1842

Humboldt, Alexander von, *Aspects of Nature, in Different Lands and Different Climates; with Scientific Elucidations,* translated by Elizabeth Sabine, London: Longman, Brown, Green, and Longmans and J. Murray, 1849; reprinted, Philadelphia: Lea and Blanchard, 1983

————, *Cosmos, a Sketch of a Physical Description of the Universe,* 5 vols., translated by E. C. Otté et al., London: H. G. Bohn, 1848-1858; New York: Harper and Brothers, 1850-1870

————, *Personal Narrative of Travels to the Equinoctial Regions of the New Continent During the Years 1799-1804,* translated by Helen M. Williams, London: Longman, Hurst, Rees, Orme, & Brown, 1814; also published as *Personal Narrative,* translated by Jason Wilson, New York and London: Penguin, 1995

James, William, *A Pluralistic Universe,* New York: Longmans, Green, 1909; also published in *Writings 1902-1910,* New York: Literary Classics of the United States, 1987

Keeney, Elizabeth, *The Botanizers: Amateur Scientists in Nineteenth-Century America,* Chapel Hill: University of North Carolina Press, 1992

Lyell, Charles, *Principles of Geology,* London: J. Murray, 1830; reprinted, Chicago: University of Chicago Press, 1990

Marsh, George Perkins, *Man and Nature,* New York: Scribner's, 1864; reprinted, edited by David Lowenthal, Cambridge, Massachusetts: Belknap Press of Harvard University Press, 1965

Muir, John, *The Yosemite,* New York: Century, 1912; reprinted, Garden City, New York: Doubleday, 1962

Novak, Barbara, *Nature and Culture: American Landscape and Painting, 1825-1875,* New York: Oxford University Press, 1980; London: Thames and Hudson, 1980

Phelps, Elmira Lincoln, *Familiar Lectures on Botany,* New York: H. and F. J. Huntington, 1829

Powell, John Wesley, *The Exploration of the Colorado River and Its Canyons,* 1895; New York: Dover, 1961

Seton, Ernest Thompson, *The Arctic Prairies,* New York: Scribner's, 1911; London: Constable, 1912

Smith, Jonathan, *Fact and Feeling: Baconian Science and the Nineteenth-Century Literary Imagination,* Madison: University of Wisconsin Press, 1994

Thoreau, Henry David, *Faith in a Seed: The Dispersion of Seeds and Other Late Natural History Writings,* edited by Bradley P. Dean, Washington, D.C.: Island/Shearwater, 1993

————, *The Journal of Henry D. Thoreau,* 14 vols., edited by Bradford Torrey and Francis Allen, Boston: Houghton Mifflin, 1906; reprinted, 2 vols., New York: Dover, 1962

————, *The Natural History Essays,* edited by Robert Sattelmeyer, Salt Lake City, Utah: Peregrine Smith, 1980

Walls, Laura Dassow, *Seeing New Worlds: Henry David Thoreau and Nineteenth-Century Natural Science,* Madison: University of Wisconsin Press, 1995

————, "Textbooks and Texts from the Brooks: Inventing Scientific Authority in America," *American Quarterly* 49:1 (March 1997), pp. 1-25

White, Gilbert, *The Natural History of Selborne,* New York: Harper & Brothers, 1788; London: T. Bensley for B. White, 1789

Whitehead, Alfred North, *Science and the Modern World,* New York: New American Library, 1925; Cambridge: Cambridge University Press, 1926

Whitman, Walt, *Leaves of Grass: Comprehensive Reader's Edition,* edited by Harold W. Blodgett and Sculley Bradley, New York: New York University Press, 1965

Wordsworth, William, *William Wordsworth,* edited by Stephen Gill, New York and Oxford: Oxford University Press, 1984

Worster, Donald, *Nature's Economy,* San Francisco: Sierra Club, 1977; Cambridge: Cambridge University Press, 1985

William Morgan (essay date 1999)

SOURCE: "Universal Aspirations: Social Theory and American Literary Culture," in *Modern Fiction Studies,* Vol. 45, No. 4, Winter, 1999, pp. 1012-18.

[*In the following essay, Morgan reviews two 1998 texts dealing with the effects of modernization and globalization on late-nineteenth-century intellectuals, commenting on the resonating power of questions raised by social theorists at the turn of century.*]

In *Middlemarch* (1871), George Eliot portrays nineteenth-century intellectuals as victims of the totalizing ambitions of their vocations. Causabon, a theologian, strives to codify the "Key to All Mythologies" and Lydgate, a doctor and medical researcher, seeks the "primitive tissue" from which bodily organs develop. In the desacralized world of the novel, God is displaced by vain specialists whose scientific fantasies of recuperated wholeness and biological unity drive them to premature deaths. Conversely, Eliot's sole personification of cosmopolitan acceptance is the slight Will Ladislaw. A dilettante whose touristic perspective enables him to enjoy the amalgamation of cultures in Rome, Ladislaw becomes an oddly idealized figure in the text, one that critics of Eliot's realism continue to distrust. Ladislaw supposedly rescues Dorothea Brooke from both Causabon's archaic sensibility and the miscellaneousness of Rome that cause her breakdown. But in spite of his receptivity to her dreams of reshaping subjectivity and society, he remains an uncertain figure for a redemptive global subjectivity.

Although neither Susan Mizruchi's *The Science of Sacrifice* nor Thomas Peyser's *Utopia & Cosmopolis* refers directly to *Middlemarch,* these studies recuperate the scholarly ambitions and uncertain responses to modernization and globalization suggested by Eliot. Taken together, they demonstrate how forcefully social theorists at the turn of the twentieth century reshaped the cultural imaginary and how their search for universal answers to the questions generated by collective experience still resonates today. A much better scholar than Causabon, Mizruchi masterfully synthesizes the work of theologians, social scientists, and literary intellectuals who sought transhistorical answers to their own crises of social transition. In addition, while placing American utopianism and literary realism into a global context, Peyser offers an elegant survey of the various renovating visions of society available at the turn of the twentieth century.

The late nineteenth century emerges as an intellectual hothouse in Mizruchi's account of its socioscientific culture, a culture profoundly interdisciplinary, profoundly scarred by racism and cultural imperialism, but vigorously thoughtful and thought-provoking. *The Science of Sacrifice* gives its readers an unparalleled introduction to abstruse materials, immersing them in the treasures of the arcane. While discussing Arthur Stanley's obscure bibliogeographical tome *Sinai and Palestine* (1865), for instance, Mizruchi quotes Stanley's imaginative recuperation of the nose of the Egyptian Sphinx. The Sphinx is fictively reanimated as a sacrificial voluptuary, its "gigantic nostrils" having been burned out like a cocaine addict's from "gorging on the smoke" of sacrificial offerings. The aim of *The Science of Sacrifice* itself is to recover, and re-evaluate in relation to canonical literary texts, sacrificial narratives like this one. The book's argument, like Causabon's "Key," is that "sacrifice is not only necessary to modern Western society, it is basic; it makes society what it is."

Mizruchi aspires to demonstrate a near total knowledge of her interdisciplinary subject. Chapter 1 lays out the vast dimensions of her transatlantic archive. It also defines the rhetoric, thematics, and aesthetics of sacrifice through comparative analysis of the works of social theorists and literary realists. The rhetoric of sacrifice is shown to be central to justifying inequalities, managing heterogeneity, and maintaining social control in turn-of-the-century America. Immigrants, women, racial minorities, and the working classes are depicted as the favored sacrificial victims of our culture. The logic of compensation undergirding capitalism is exposed as sacrificial, and stories of the fall, replete with sacrificial longings, are replayed in the era's literature. Sacrifice for Mizruchi is what the economy is for Marx, the unconscious for Freud, and power (virtually) for Foucault. It is foundational to her understanding of modern society.

Herman Melville, Henry James, and W. E. B. Du Bois are the canonical authors whose sacrificial insights make them the heart of this study. The "sacrificial designs" of Melville's *Billy Budd* (1891), his theological interests, and his work as a customs house inspector serve as the starting point for chapter 2. Reading outward from the religious and sociological comparativism of *Typee* (1846) and *Moby-Dick* (1850), Mizruchi demonstrates that early social science itself was deeply indebted to nineteenth-century theological criticism and religious comparativism. In addition, in Mizruchi's analysis of the sacrificial drama of *Billy Budd,* Vere, driven by his mania for control, emerges as a functional sociologist; Claggart is read as a resentful immigrant who suffers from the "disease of modernism"; and Billy, who willingly complies in his own oblation, reveals a deep connection between Melville and Schopenhauer, as well as Melville's subtle understanding of the ambiguity and mystery of sacrifice.

Chapter 3 gives new prominence to *The Awkward Age* (1899) in the corpus of James because of its detailed evocation of the sacrificial rites governing "historical as well as biological transition." Mizruchi deftly illustrates the socioscientific significance of key Jamesian collectivities and character types: the aristocratic kinship group; the urbane, wealthy priest of civilization; the female innocent who is sacrificed; the perversely selfish, oddly likable matriarch; and the repressed, desirable homosexual man. In addition to unveiling James's sociological imagination, Mizruchi explores the professional discourses about female reproductivity, maternalism, homosexuality, and charity in England and America at the turn of the last century. Most often leading into a "fantastic web of detail," her take on the novel adds up to a remarkably learned account of James's place in the period.

The discussion of the postbellum decline of sympathy in the United States in chapter 4 is one of the book's most compelling. Casting *The Souls of Black Folk* (1903) as a "border text" that fills in the margins between literature and sociology, Mizruchi develops Du Bois's keen awareness of sympathy's occasional rather than evolutionary character. She demonstrates her provocative claim that "if sympathy contributed to the liberation of Blacks during the [Civil W]ar, it contributed to their lynching afterward," by illustrating how various sociologists defined sympathy as a circumscribed, merely intratribal faculty, not a universal one. Lynching irresistibly emerges as the logical culmination of the study, and Du Bois, for his penetrating insight into society's sacrificial logic, also emerges as the book's hero. His *The Philadelphia Negro* (1899) reveals the sacrificial heart of white civilization, its desire for scapegoats and need of martyrs. Mizruchi goes on to suggest that African American literature in general is peculiarly perceptive about sacrifice, citing from works by Charles Chesnutt, Ralph Ellison, and Toni Morrison.

Whereas Mizruchi argues that the drive of social theory toward universalism results in its rediscovery of sacrifice, Peyser, in *Utopia & Cosmopolis,* sees the era's universalizing impulse arising from and contributing to its incipient globalization. Two versions of historicism, Mizruchi's shows the sociological imagination returning endlessly to the past; Peyser's recaptures its creative excitement about the future. Moreover, the cosmopolitanism of Mizruchi's archive is thematized in *Utopia & Cosmopolis.* Peyser's work concerns the enthusiasms and dangers emerging as creatively destructive responses to the integration of "the world as a whole." He argues that "utopia and cosmopolis both promise the advent of a universality standing at the end of history; both announce the culmination of a modern will to simultaneous expansion and integration."

According to Peyser, the core insights of globalization theory are available in turn-of-the-century utopian and realist fiction. Although this literature has usually been understood within a national context, he shows that it has a global currency. The emerging possibilities of social reorganization, the developing conditions of "cosmopolitan decenteredness," and the threats associated with racial and cultural amalgamation become the primary themes of *Utopia & Cosmopolis.* The book is structured dialectically, and its largest dialectic contrasts "utopian alternatives and cosmopolitan realities." As it tarries back and forth between "dreams of unity" and "forms of multiplicity," the book offers a cogent examination of the attenuation of the modern self brought on by the "longing for cosmopolitan universality."

Peyser achieves a compact synthesis of his momentous topic by reading closely a few primary texts. In chapter 1 ("The World a Department Store"), he explicates Edward Bellamy's idiosyncratic celebration in *Looking Backward* (1888) of the evaporation of the self into a consumerist, collective utopia. Theoretically rigorous, Peyser avoids the free-floating claims of a less careful theorist. Sophisticated continental theory is made to seem germane through careful literary interpretations and selective historical citations. For instance, when showing that Bellamy prophetically believed, with Horkheimer and Adorno, that "the 'culture industry' is fatal to individual autonomy," Peyser qualifies an easy homology with the subtler insight that "what they deplore he actively seeks." Peyser also skillfully contextualizes Bellamy's idealization of the department store. He relates it to Zola's sense of department stores replacing churches, the Nazis' fear that department stores would become sites for consumer cosmopolitanism, and advertisements from the 1890s suggesting that Macy's red star, with all its totalitarian implications, might serve as a symbol for national solidarity.

As Peyser's other main example of utopianism, Charlotte Perkins Gilman's *Herland* (1915) also exhibits a totalizing drive toward unity and a desire "to rationalize existence." This chapter falls short, however, because it spends too much time fighting off Gilman's feminist defenders only to make the familiar argument that imperialist longings and racism are constitutive to her social thought. Gail Bederman's *Manliness and Civilization* (1995) covers the same ground, while placing Gilman into the discourse of "civilization" and retaining a fuller sense of her feminism. But even in this chapter, Peyser's formulations remain crisp, his style graceful and often sly. For instance, while revealing the tribal utopianism of *Herland,* he deems Gilman's white, female enclave an "imperial ghetto." According to Peyser, Bellamy and Gilman, in antithetical ways, sought to radicalize the totalitarian tendencies of their age toward self- and social control, toward an entirely systematized (and therefore utopian) civilization.

By contrast, William Dean Howells and Henry James, eschewing ideological closure, are shown to be searching for satisfying metaphors of cosmopolitanism. Chapter 3 catches the qualifications and complications that make Howells's fiction by turns playful, humane, and tedious. Revising Amy Kaplan's understanding of Howellsian realism as containing and managing social change, Peyser shows that Howells's *A Hazard of New Fortunes* (1891) exemplifies the author's uncertain cosmopolitanism. Set in the emerging postnational space of New York City, the novel suggests both Howells's Habermasian fantasy of a democratic "culture of conservation" and his fear of "unresolvable conflicts of value" in a society riddled by foreign tongues and alien pressures. Simultaneously sensing the loss of his national subject (Peyser makes much of Lindau's assertion that "Dere *iss* no Ameriga anymore") and developing a modernist's suspicion of the relation between language and "reality," Howells retreats from the realism of *Hazard* to the smaller canvasses of leisure-class utopianism in the Altrurian romances (1894-1907). Here, a tragicomic playfulness enables him to continue writing in the face of political pessimism. With "the detached eye of anthropological analysis," Howells resigns himself to representing the experiences of anomie and disembeddedness that the era's more vigilant advocates of control staved off.

The book's final chapter, despite its predictability in casting James as a hero, is dazzling. In his reading of the imperializing aesthetic of *The Golden Bowl* (1904), Peyser shows how James fashions a more compelling style of cosmopolitanism than either Howells or Eliot. The museum serves throughout this chapter as a model for how transactions are conducted between colonial and colonized cultures; curators and live specimens metaphorically interact as if society is an exhibition. Peyser convincingly likens the expansive "connoisseurship" (what he calls the "exemplary multiculturalism") valued in the novel to the scientific objectivity of the imperial gaze outlined by several advocates of U.S. imperialism. James, however, is hardly just another jingoist. Instead of cultural imperialism as it is normally grasped, his model of empire ultimately suggests "the dissolving of the self in[to] the other" and the abandonment of "center . . . and periphery." As the Jamesian self is untethered from nation and race and becomes free-floating, "elasticity" and "multiplicity" figure the new "synthesis" the author aspires toward. Peyser's revaluation of James's cosmopolitanism consequently leaves open the possibility for something at the end of history other than a wasteland of quotations and amalgamations. A creative reader and an inspired critic, Peyser concludes his study with the openness of a promise, as if posing the question: who is to say that things might not be otherwise?

MAJOR FIGURES

Fred D. White (essay date 1992)

SOURCE: "'Sweet Skepticism of the Heart': Science in the Poetry of Emily Dickinson," in *College Literature*, Vol. 19, No. 1, February, 1992, pp. 121-28.

[*In the following essay, White discusses the impact of science on Dickinson's poetry, speculating that the poet used her writing to explore the negative effects of the scientific impulse to uncover every secret of nature.*]

Few poets in the twentieth century, let alone the nineteenth, have incorporated scientific concepts into their work as purposively and effectively as Emily Dickinson.[1] She possessed an amazingly comprehensive scientific and technical vocabulary.[2] More than 200 of her poems touch on scientific themes (see Appendix); she draws on most of the sciences, from physical sciences such as physics, astronomy, chemistry, and geology, to biological sciences such as botany, physiology, medicine, and even psychology, to science in general (the largest category), plus mathematics and applied science or technology.

Why did Dickinson devote such attention to science? We know that she studied the subject in school, apparently with considerable enthusiasm. Writing to Abiah Root from Mount Holyoke Seminary in January 1848, Dickinson expresses her enthusiasm for "'Silliman's Chemistry' & Cutler's Physiology" (*L* 20)[3]; shortly thereafter she writes to her brother Austin that his last letter found her "all engrossed in the history of Sulphuric Acid!!!!!" (*L* 22)—a humorous exclamation, to be sure, but in view of Mary Lyon's stringent curriculum, probably factual nonetheless. Even earlier, at Amherst Academy, Dickinson had almost certainly fallen under the spell of the naturalist and Christian mystic Edward Hitchcock, who taught geology at the college (later he became its president) and who believed that close study of nature was a way of coming to know God.[4]

One must also consider the widespread scientific and technological developments that were taking place during Dickinson's childhood and adolescence in the 1830s and 40s. To cite a few examples: Joseph Henry discovered electromagnetic induction and electromotive force, the Massachusetts inventor Samuel Guthrie discovered chloroform, and John Bull established the first steam railway in the United States, all in 1831; Samuel Morse invented the telegraph in 1832 (it was put to commercial use in 1844); in the same year, cadaver dissection was legalized in Massachusetts; Henry Fox Talbot and Louis Daguerre invented photography in 1839; Crawford Long used ether in surgery in 1842; a new planet—Neptune—was discovered in 1846; and the American Association for the Advancement of Science was established in 1848. During the same period Johannes Müller (1801-58) and Gustav Fechner (1801-87) were pioneering the science of psychology.

As someone whose "Business is Circumference," as she proclaimed in her fourth letter to Thomas Wentworth Higginson (L 268), Dickinson must have regarded science as a basis for testing the outer boundaries of human understanding and experience. On the one hand science was transforming the world around her in astonishing ways, sending locomotives charging into the New England garden like Boanerges in "I like to see it lap the Miles" (*P* 585),[5] or sending lightning "singing . . . with Insulators . . . upon the Ropes—above our Head— / Continual— with the News" (*P* 630). On the other hand science was fast becoming civilization's new Holy Grail in the quest for certainty, and seemed to be undermining the validity of religious and aesthetic modes of knowing.

Understandably, many poets expressed alarm at this development. John Donne had been among the first: "[The] new Philosophy calls all in doubt / The Element of fire is quite put out," he laments in "The First Anniversary" in 1611— the year after Galileo's momentous astronomical discoveries (lines 205-06). Romantics such as John Keats and Edgar Allan Poe echoed the sentiment. "Do not all charms fly / At the mere touch of cold philosophy?" Keats wonders in "Lamia" (229-30). Poe portrays science preying upon the poet's heart as a vulture "whose wings are dull realities," ("Sonnet: To Science" 4).

Dickinson's attitude toward science is subtler than this, even though she may superficially resemble Donne, Keats, and Poe in a few of her poems. In one of them, the speaker tells us that the secrets of nature are everywhere revealed, to be plucked like berries—but it is important to resist the plucking because "It's finer—not to know— / If Summer were *an Axiom* / What sorcery had *Snow*?" (*P* 191). The point is that those phenomenological secrets—the "facts" of science—are meaningless by themselves. Unlike Donne and the others, Dickinson is suggesting that it is the scientistic impulse, not the scientific, that is monstrous in its negation of the human spirit. She makes this even more explicit in *P* 70: "I pull a flower from the woods— / A monster with a glass / Computes the stamens in a breath— / And has her in a 'class'!"

The epistemological dilemma—the struggle between certainty and uncertainty—is central to Dickinson's poetic vision. She uses poetry to perform, in effect, experiments in language, her counterpart to scientific experiments, which she accepted as equally valid efforts for apprehending essential Truth.[6] "Experiment" becomes an emblem of human daring, a venturing out to the limits of experience:

> Experiment to me
> Is everyone I meet
> If it contain a Kernel?
> The Figure of a Nut
>
> Presents upon a Tree
> Equally plausibly
> But Meat within, is requisite
> To squirrels and to Me.

(*P* 1073)[7]

Moreover, a great many of Dickinson's poems are set up virtually as mathematical equations—or as Sharon Cameron describes them, "metonymic equations" that "serve as links between the poet's interior world and the external phenomenon taking place" (27). These poems typically follow (sometimes in the negative) the paradigms X <is> Y, X <has> Y, or X <does> Y. For example: "'Nature' <is> what we see" (*P* 668); "It<'s> like the Light— / A fashionless Delight—" (*P* 297—one of the "riddle poems" in which the solution is found at the end, just as in a mathematical equation); "It <was not> death, for I stood up" (*P* 510); "The Heart <has> narrow Banks" (*P* 928); "A wounded deer <leaps> highest" (*P* 165). Other "equation" poems are framed as hypotheses: "If you were coming in the Fall, / I'd brush the summer by" (*P* 511).

Dickinson's poetic equations perform the opposite function to that of their scientific counterparts: they are designed to heighten mysteries, not solve them. They work to counteract scientific reductionism, which tempts us into thinking that science can present reality whole and undistorted. Cameron (27) offers an especially fascinating example: *P* 967. In this poem Dickinson establishes two equations regarding pain that ironically contradict each other:

> Pain—expands the Time—
> Ages coil within
> The minute Circumference
> Of a single Brain—
>
> Pain contracts—the Time—
> Occupied with Shot
> Gammuts of Eternities
> Are as they were not—

Unlike Ralph Waldo Emerson, in whose universe the soul of the individual flows like a tributary into the cosmic soul, and for whom reading deeply in the book of nature brings us to a transcendent understanding of and harmony with the cosmos, Dickinson points to an insurmountable gulf between our finite selves and the infinite cosmos. Emerson writes that "the lover of nature is he whose inward and outward senses are still truly adjusted to each other" (189) and that "Nature conspires with spirit to emancipate us" (209), but Dickinson cannot accept the possibility that one can be emancipated by nature. Instead, she squarely confronts the gulf, painfully aware that crossing it, even if it could be done, would constitute death. For Dickinson the essence of life *is* its finitude, its "fording the mystery" while "the rendezvous of Light" remains in the unreachable distance (*P* 1564). In another poem (301) she dismisses with aloof indifference any attempts at drawing conclusions about life's ultimate purpose—or purposelessness:

> I reason, Earth is short—
> And Anguish—absolute—
> And many hurt,
> But, what of that?

I reason, we could die—
The best Vitality
Cannot excel Decay,
But, what of that?

I reason, that in Heaven—
Somehow, it will be even—
Some new Equation, given—
But, what of that?

Why even try to transcend our human perceptions of nature? Any attempt to solve the equation of life pulls one out of life's circumference, out of experience. Indeed, whatever is experienced—and that includes empirical science—remakes nature in human terms. Human existence limits "finite infinity" (*P* 1695), not only according to our sensory capacities for pleasure, pain, anguish, or transport, but also according to our own individual life experiences, as she demonstrates in *P* 285: "The Robin's my Criterion for Tune— / Because I grow—where Robins do— / But, were I Cuckoo born— / I'd swear by him—."

Just as William Wordsworth, in his Preface to *Lyrical Ballads,* calls for an infusion of sensations "into the midst of the objects of . . . science itself" (456), Dickinson wants to experience nature with her entire being, not with her intellect alone. She wants the magic and the beauty of nature to be at one with her own nature. Positivist science "murders to dissect"; and Dickinson clearly echoes the Wordsworthian admonition when she writes in *P* 108, "Surgeons must be very careful / When they take the knife! / Underneath their fine incisions / Stirs the culprit—Life!" There is an ironic undertone here: no matter how exacting the surgeons' incisions, "life" will always elude them— and yet the body, along with the entire phenomenal universe, is intimately linked to the deepest mysteries of existence. What we observe scientifically, taxonomically, can suddenly blaze forth as a thing of beauty whose essence is intuited, groped for, but never grasped. To put it another way: science itself enables us to transcend science. "Split the Lark—and you'll find the Music" (*P* 861); observe the moon, and like the speaker in the following poem, we might well see it as

. . . a Head—a Guillotine
Slid carelessly away—
Did independent, Amber—
Sustain her in the sky—

Or like a Stemless Flower—
Upheld in rolling Air
By finer Gravitations—
Than bind Philosopher . . .

The privilege to scrutinize
Was scarce upon my Eyes
When with a Silver practise
She vaulted out of Gaze—

And next—I met her on a Cloud—
Myself too far below

To follow her superior Road
Or its advantage—Blue—

(*P* 629)

The moon is one of those "finished creatures" (*P* 954; see note 4) indifferent to human concerns—which is precisely why Dickinson tries to grasp her with such extravagant metaphors. The poet, through her creative perception, captures the moon in a way the astronomer never could.[8]

Dickinson wishes to make the scientific angle of vision, complete with scientific and technical language, amplify rather than reduce the mystery of what is being dwelt upon—because this way of seeing is being used to describe *human* attributes.[9] Thus "Hope is a strange invention— / A Patent of the Heart—" (*P* 1392), and Faustian scientists will one day "find the Cube of the Rainbow" (in other words, explain away the rainbow's magic and beauty—but only to discover such knowledge to be a grotesque distortion, a "cubing," of the rainbow's essential reality). What is more, "the Arc of a Lover's conjecture / Eludes the finding out" (*P* 1484). Without any philosophizing, Dickinson brilliantly allows the scientific concepts—inventions, patents, cubes, arcs—to demonstrate their own limitations.

What science achieves for Dickinson, then, is a clearer sense of what human beings can and cannot know. Indeed, the more deeply we probe that "arc" of love, the deeper the mystery will become. Unlike Nathaniel Hawthorne's Aylmer in "The Birthmark," Dickinson acknowledges the inaccessibility of ultimate reality. She is free to do with human circumference what she will, given her purely human resources; and so language takes primacy over phenomena.[10] Science is at the mercy of language—language as it radiates from the poet's creative vision, triumphant *because* of its limitations. Beyond circumference lies an inhuman reality. Far better to "dwell in Possibility— / A fairer House than Prose—," a universe in which the poet reigns supreme over her creation, celebrating "The spreading wide my narrow Hands / To gather Paradise—" (*P* 657). Once acclimated to this interior universe, the reader begins to notice that the poet is indeed the analogue of the scientist.

Dickinson's poetic experiments, then, inevitably result in clashes between intellect and heart—and of course they neither can be nor should be resolved. After all, she reminds us, "Wonder—is not precisely Knowing / And not precisely Knowing not— / A beautiful but bleak condition / He has not lived who has not felt—" (*P* 1331). Not only emotion-based wonder, but intellect-based skepticism—the driving force of scientific inquiry—is essential to being fully alive:

Sweet Skepticism of the Heart—
That knows—and does not know—
And tosses like a Fleet of Balm
Affronted by the snow—
Invites and then retards the Truth
Lest Certainty be sere

> Compared with the delicious throe
> Of transport filled with Fear—
>
> (*P* 1413)

Certainty is no prize; it brings no transport, no experience of either joy or dread, but a shutting down of vital life forces of continual discovery and movement. In one of her most powerful poems, Dickinson makes her premise startlingly clear:

> This World is not Conclusion.
> A Species stands beyond—
> Invisible, as Music—
> But positive, as Sound—
> It beckons, and it baffles—
> Philosophy—don't know
> And through a Riddle, at the last—
> Sagacity, must go—
> To guess it, puzzles scholars—
> To gain it, Men have borne
> Contempt of Generations
> And Crucifixion, shown—
> Faith slips—and laughs, and rallies—
> Blushes, if any see—
> Plucks at a twig of Evidence—
> And asks a Vane, the way—
> Much Gesture, from the Pulpit—
> Strong Hallelujahs, roll—
> Narcotics cannot still the Tooth
> That nibbles at the soul—
>
> (*P* 501)

We struggle to find closure, plucking at any "twig of Evidence" that comes our way, but closure eludes us, and not even narcotics can quell our need to keep on searching. That, of course, is what life is all about for Dickinson. The "nibbling at the soul," the "sweet skepticism of the heart," is what keeps one moving ahead: "A doubt . . . / Assists the staggering Mind" (*P* 859). Indeed, doubt begins to resemble faith in Dickinson's universe—the kind of faith that leads one to hold off "conclusion" in order to experience the intangible without the skeptic's need to keep on searching for more evidence: "'Faith' is a fine invention / When Gentlemen can *see*— / But *Microscopes* are prudent / In an Emergency" (*P* 185). To speak of the importance of "seeing" in the context of faith suggests the follies of believing without understanding or even wanting to understand. In that case, it is better to see with microscopes than to be sightless with faith; for microscopes, those preeminent icons of positivist science, ironically will reveal new wonders, give even more evidence that "this world is not Conclusion."

APPENDIX: DICKINSON'S SCIENCE POEMS

The following tabulation is meant to give a general overview of the range and frequency of Dickinson's poems that invoke a scientific concept, either to illuminate that concept or to give insight into a nonscientific concept by way of analogy. Poems that employ generic terms alone ("stars," "flowers") are not considered. Poems invoking more than one scientific discipline are categorized under the science that seems dominant, or that is treated first. *P* 1753, for example, focuses upon a psychological theme (and has been so classified), although chemical metaphors are used. No poem appears under more than one heading.

Science in general: 2, 3, 41, 70, 89, 97, 100, 101, 122, 168, 185, 191, 285, 290, 301, 327, 351, 415, 420, 433, 443, 501, 534, 600, 668, 780, 782, 812, 835, 836, 859, 860, 861, 883, 970, 972, 1071, 1073, 1077, 1084, 1116, 1129, 1163, 1170, 1202, 1228, 1229, 1247, 1329, 1331, 1373, 1386, 1389, 1400, 1411, 1413, 1417, 1431, 1434, 1455, 1482, 1603, 1770

Biology: 354, 986, 1099, 1101, 1128, 1138, 1244, 1371, 1387, 1405, 1448, 1475, 1524, 1575, 1685

Botany: 66, 128, 142, 173, 180, 314, 811, 978, 1047, 1058, 1080, 1082, 1097, 1241, 1288, 1298, 1422, 1424, 1508, 1716, 1744

Chemistry: 422, 689, 838, 854, 954, 1063

Geology: 128, 175, 245, 320, 356, 601, 1146, 1302, 1677, 1705, 1748

Mathematics: 69, 88, 125, 257, 269, 545, 728, 769, 798, 802, 928, 1158, 1184, 1295, 1484

Medicine and physiology: 108, 177, 396, 559, 786, 1261, 1270, 1274

Physics and astronomy: 6, 240, 287, 378, 429, 591, 611, 629, 700, 851, 889, 906, 909, 958, 985, 997, 1057, 1106, 1276, 1286, 1315, 1336, 1408, 1419, 1581, 1605, 1638, 1672

Psychology: 165, 241, 252, 264, 280, 281, 301, 341, 348, 419, 532, 556, 650, 689, 733, 744, 894, 937, 967, 998, 1046, 1054, 1299, 1333, 1355, 1453, 1598, 1714, 1717, 1737, 1753

Technology: 187, 365, 585, 630, 789, 983, 1142, 1392, 1630

Notes

1. An earlier version of this paper was presented at the Society for Literature and Science Annual Conference, Albany, New York, October 1988.

2. William Howard has determined that out of the 770 words Dickinson uses from specialized disciplines (law, military science, the natural sciences, agriculture, philology, and so on), 328 are drawn from the natural sciences and technology (230).

3. All citations of Dickinson's letters [*L*] refer to *The Letters of Emily Dickinson*, edited by Thomas H. Johnson and Theodora Ward. Likewise, citations of Dickinson's poems [*P*] are taken from the variorum *Poems*, edited by Johnson.

4. According to Richard B. Sewall, Hitchcock "set the educational tone for the whole [Amherst] community [and] . . . inspired a whole generation with a love of nature that combined a sense of its sublimity with an accurate knowledge of its parts and processes" (342-

43). Hitchcock delivered his lectures at the college in 1845 (as well as 1847-49), and "hence [they were] open to students in Amherst Academy during Emily's years there" (344). A few of Dickinson's poems have a distinct Hitchcockian flavor, such as the following, which alludes to the law of conservation of energy, brilliantly making it work as a counter-metaphor for life's fragmented relationships: "The Chemical conviction / That Nought be lost / Enable in Disaster / My fractured Trust / The faces of the Atoms / If I shall see / How more the Finished Creatures / Departed me!" (*P* 954). Jack L. Capps notes, too, that Dickinson drew upon Hitchcock's *Elementary Geology* (1840) for place names, especially names and sites of volcanoes (106).

5. When the railroad reached Amherst in 1852, Dickinson shared the town's excitement. "Nobody *believes* it yet," she writes to Susan Gilbert; "it seems like a fairy tale, a most *miraculous* event in the lives of us all" (*L* 72).

6. Johnson states (with reference to *P* 835, "Nature and God—I neither knew"), "God, man, and nature [Dickinson] sharply differentiates. Nature cannot be explained any more easily than God can be explained, but both can be personified" (184). Dickinson made her point most succinctly when she wrote to Higginson, "Nature is a Haunted House—but Art—a house that tries to be haunted" (*L* 459A).

7. See also *P* 1770: "Experiment escorts us last— / His pungent company / Will not allow an Axiom / An Opportunity."

8. W. T. Jones would extend this assertion to typify poetry in general: "A poem," Jones writes, "is . . . the pursuit of perceiving beyond the capacities of common sense[:] . . . the attempt to render some *affect* precisely, not to designate some *fact* precisely" (197; emphasis mine). That is, "affect" is the counterpart of "fact" in the context of ultimate reality. Joanne Feit Diehl makes a similar point; according to her, Dickinson "perform[s] a solipsistic usurpation of nature in which the imagination assumes complete control. Repeatedly Dickinson makes the distinction between the poem over which she exercises power and the natural world which retains its unpredictability" (50). Likewise, "The objective reality attains its fullest meaning in the vision of the artist," asserts Inder Nath Kher (40). Kher refers here to *P* 451, "The Outer—from the Inner," but the assertion can apply to Dickinson's intent in most of her science poetry.

9. According to Daniel J. Orsini, Dickinson anchors "her transcendent vision upon concrete verifiable data" (60); science serves to validate her spiritual ideals, even though they may appear contrary to them on another level.

10. Cristanne Miller sees Dickinson's distortions of grammar and syntax as examples of her desire "to make [language] less instead of more natural" (153).

Works Cited

Cameron, Sharon. *Lyric Time: Dickinson and the Limits of Genre.* Baltimore: Johns Hopkins UP, 1979.

Capps, Jack L. *Emily Dickinson's Reading, 1836-1886.* Cambridge: Harvard UP, 1966.

Dickinson, Emily. *The Complete Poems of Emily Dickinson.* 3 vols. Ed. Thomas H. Johnson. Cambridge: Belknap (Harvard UP), 1955.

———. *The Letters of Emily Dickinson.* 3 vols. Ed. Thomas H. Johnson and Theodora Ward. Cambridge: Belknap (Harvard UP), 1958.

Diehl, Joanne Feit. *Dickinson and the Romantic Imagination.* Princeton: Princeton UP, 1981.

Emerson, Ralph Waldo. *Nature.* 1836. *Selected Writings of Ralph Waldo Emerson.* Ed. William H. Gilman. New York: New American Library, 1965. 186-223.

Howard, William. "Emily Dickinson's Poetic Vocabulary." *PMLA* 72 (March 1957): 225-48.

Johnson, Thomas H. *Emily Dickinson: An Interpretive Biography.* Cambridge: Belknap (Harvard UP), 1955.

Jones, W. T. *The Sciences and the Humanities: Conflict and Resolution.* Berkeley: U of California P, 1967.

Kher, Inder Nath. *The Landscape of Absence: Emily Dickinson's Poetry.* New Haven: Yale UP, 1974.

Miller, Cristanne. *Emily Dickinson: A Poet's Grammar.* Cambridge: Harvard UP, 1987.

Orsini, Daniel J. "Emily Dickinson and the Romantic Use of Science." *Massachusetts Studies in English* 7.4/8.1 (1981): 57-69.

Sewall, Richard B. *The Life of Emily Dickinson.* 2 vols. New York: Farrar, 1974.

Wordsworth, William. Preface to the Second Edition of *Lyrical Ballads.* 1800. *Selected Poems and Prefaces.* Ed. Jack Stillinger. Boston: Houghton, 1965. 445-64.

Beverly A. Hume (essay date 1995)

SOURCE: "The Madness of Art and Science in Poe's 'Ligeia,'" in *Essays in Arts and Sciences,* Vol. 24, October, 1995, pp. 21-32.

[In the following essay, Hume analyses Poe's "Ligeia" as a synthesis of mythology and science.]

In a September 1839 letter to Philip Cooke, Edgar Allan Poe expressed his view that "Ligeia" was "intended to convey an idea of truth to the narrator" (*Letters* 118). Although numerous critics have offered theories about what this "truth" might be, they all tend to treat Poe's narrator either as a romantic artist or madman, diminishing his scientific ruminations in this tale. However, a close reading of this narrator's "scientific" speculations in relation to his treatment of the mythological dimensions of Ligeia reveal that he is, as D. H. Lawrence first suggested in *Studies in Classic American Literature,* as much a mad scien-tist as an artist in his investigation of Ligeia's phenomenal return from the dead. More, this narrator develops, however unsystematically, a "theory" about human nature that both forces the issue of his authorial sanity and draws into question the mythological meaning and relationship of the "Lady Ligeia" to both his literary and scientific Western heritage.

"Ligeia" is a tale of the narrator's "remembrance" of his wife Ligeia and also of his speculation about the significance of her return from the dead in relation to his understanding of both physical and metaphysical reality. Almost immediately, he tells the reader that his memory has been made "feeble through much suffering." Except for his memories of Ligeia, however, he has been "buried in studies of a nature more than all else adapted to deaden impressions of the outward world" (110). Such sentiments suggest that Ligeia is, at present, dead and that the meaning of her death is one which extends beyond the narrator's bizarre conclusion about her brief return and strange symbiosis with his second wife, Rowena. That is, the narrator early reveals that he is attempting both to reconstruct a phenomenal event and to piece together, in as credible terms as possible, one of the "many incomprehensible anomalies of the science of mind" (113) with which he claims familiarity. The precise nature of his present "suffering" or the kind of studies in which he is obsessively "buried" is unclear, but they have clearly failed to bring him any more than a dull understanding of the complex nature of reality and of the natural world. His vague memory of Ligeia and her phenomenal return from the dead (however temporary) promises him that there is still something more to be learned about the natural world, something beyond his immediate comprehension, something that he is on the "verge" of remembering—and does, indeed, seem vaguely to apprehend at the end of his narrative.

Although no summary can do justice to Poe's (or to his narrator's) complex narrative, it is, I think, safe to say that it details an unnamed narrator's discovery of the meaning of what he believes to be his first wife's, Ligeia's, struggle against death and her subsequent return from the dead and "possession" of his second wife, Rowena. Poe was not a consciously feminist author, but the symbolic intricacies of this plot have not only invited recent feminist or gender criticism, but also provoked gender-related speculations from among Poe's earliest critics, including the above-noted Lawrence who not only first drew attention to the vampire motif in "Ligeia" but used it to examine the disconcertingly "scientific" attitude of Poe's narrator. Although Lawrence was concerned principally with describing the narrator's (and Poe's) diseased sexuality, he aptly perceived Poe's "science" as central to an understanding of the vampire motif in this tale. Subsequent critics, however, have tended to focus more on this latter motif in "Ligeia" than on the narrator's quasi-scientific detailing.

Yet such detailing in "Ligeia" is crucial, I will demonstrate in this essay, to an understanding not only of the implied vampirism in the story but also of the narrator's fantastic synthesis of mythology and science—a synthesis which like most fantastic literature remains precariously balanced between "the hesitation experienced by a [narrator] who knows only natural laws" and the existence of an "apparently supernatural event" (Todorov 29). The narrator takes great pains to detail and rationally comprehend the nature of Ligeia's various transformations in his narrative, but those transformations are directly related to her mythological stature. Although Ligeia has been variously compared by critics to Eve, to a siren, to a vampire, to a romantic or a linguistic icon, to a transcendent being or symbol, and to a nightmarish illusion,[1] none have considered the relationship of two ancient, mythological deities mentioned in the text (the "misty-winged Astophet" and the "grim Azreal," *Ligeia* 111, 115) not only to Ligeia but also to the narrator's "science." However, these mythic creatures are central to an understanding of both the narrator's romanticism and scientism.

Whereas "Azrael" is the Angel of Death in Moslem and Jewish legend, "Astophet" is not the actual name of a deity but seems, as David Galloway points out, to refer both to "Ashtoreth, the Phoenician and Egyptian goddess [of love and fertility] and Tophet, a version of hell associated in the Old Testament with the Egyptian worship of Moloch" (528). Ligeia is also indirectly associated with mythological realms through her actual name which is identical to one of the sirens in Milton's *Comus* and one of the dryads in Book IV of Virgil's *Georgics.* Simultaneously, she is allusively associated by Poe's narrator to the legendary Greek "daughters of Delos," with the "Houri of the Turk," with the celestial "twin stars" (or sons) of the legendary Leda, and with the feminine "tribe of the valley of Nourjahad" created by Frances Sheridan in her 1767 Oriental romance, *The History of Nourjahad* (*Ligeia* 111-112). Through such mythological allusions, Ligeia becomes aligned not only with death and with demonism but also with legendary and literary femininity, with both feminine mortality and immortality.

The narrator's allusions have not only produced numerous critical conjectures about Ligeia's relation to various mythological and metaphoric figures, but have encouraged many critics to regard the narrator as essentially a humanist, albeit a mad one. Ligeia is, as the narrator says, an unknown, perhaps unknowable, being whose presence he recalls only as a series of complex correspondences and analogies. Although he does not think he can fully comprehend her mystery, I would like to suggest that it is indirectly related to yet another mythological deity with whom Ligeia is indirectly associated—that is, to Lilith, the mythic Hebriac figure who was one of Ashtoreth's most well-known variants in the nineteenth century and also the first wife to the Biblical Adam, mother to countless demons, consort to God, and a creature who maintained a steadfast place in vampire lore and in Greek, Egyptian, Babylonian, Assyrian and Roman mythologies.[2] Indeed, one of Ligeia's most definite aspects in the narrator's remembrance resides in "the delicate outlines of [her] nose" which possesses a "perfection" that he has seen "nowhere but in the graceful medallions of the Hebrews" (111).

Yet if Ligeia is a mythic creature who bears a resemblance to immortal demonic variants such as Ashtoreth and Lilith, what makes her "fantastic" is the narrator's belief that she is simultaneously an actual, mortal, living (or once-living) woman. As some critics have noted, both Rowena and Ligeia are comparable to the dark and fair-haired women of western literary tradition and convention. As such, they can be relatively easily aligned with Poe's own western literary (and patriarchal) heritage. However, here the alignment ends, for Poe's narrator posits Ligeia, not Rowena (or, to put it in the implied mythological terms of the text, Lilith not Eve) as the true maternal figure of that heritage. Unlike Ligeia, Rowena is not only a mortal woman but also an afterthought to the narrator (who barely describes her and then with contempt); as Joan Dayan observes, Poe "did not [even] add the description of 'the fair-haired, the blue-eyed' Rowena until the 1845 version of 'Ligeia'" (189).

In contrast, Ligeia's "immense knowledge" and refined complexity is, in the narrator's view, part of "a wisdom too divinely precious not to be forbidden" (115). The narrator's fascination with Ligeia's "forbidden" knowledge, Jules Zanger suggests, reveals that he regards her as a kind of malignant Eve—not only as a mythic woman who tempts this Adamic narrator to his destruction but also as a "metaphor for original sin, and, by extension, for carnality" (537). If she is an alter "Eve," however, Ligeia would seem to be a combination of both Lilith and Eve, for the narrator's description of her aligns her not only with she-demons from various religious traditions, including the Judeo-Christian one from which both Lilith and Eve rise but also with a vampire tradition with which Lilith (and not Eve) is most often associated (*Man, Myth, and Magic* 292-3).[3]

Ligeia's complex, quasi-demonic nature is strangely clarified by the narrator's quasi-scientific interest in it, an interest which transforms Poe's narrative, I believe, into one of his most unusual science-fantasies. Although the narrator's evident familiarity with mythology and philosophy, along with his highly allusive narrative and "vision" of Ligeia, reveals his partial knowledge of art and literature, his scientific perspective has been too often understated. For example, most critics regard the allusion to Joseph Glanvill, an English philosopher associated with spiritualism and the occult, as one which was probably contrived by Poe (since it has never been found in Glanvill's writings) to enhance the supernatural or fantastic quality in the narrative. Certainly, this allusion does enhance that quality, particularly in light of Glanvill's stated belief in witches in *A Philosophical Endeavor towards the Defense of the Being of Witches and Apparitions* (1666).

However, Glanvill was also a philosophical skeptic engaged, as was popularly depicted in then-contemporary journals and as Poe most likely knew, with understanding man before the Fall or at that time when he had "knowledge of things in their true, immediate and necessary causes" in relation to man after the Fall, the present time, when he is unable to any longer know "the hidden things of Nature . . . the first springs and wheels that set the rest agoing" (*Scepsis Scientifica* 15). For Glanvill, as for Poe's narrator in "Ligeia," the senses are deceptive and one's knowledge of the world is, to some degree, necessarily uncertain. Although Poe's quotation from Glanvill has not been found in Glanvill's writings, it is consistent with Glanvill's skepticism and philosophical uncertainty and with his perception of God's will and vast and purposeful presence. This quotation is also strangely consistent with Glanvill's then-popularized interest in Hebrew cabalism and the possibility of spiritual manifestations of the soul's immortality. However, where Poe's narrator differs markedly from Glanvill is in his experiential perception of Ligeia and her "will."

In detailing Ligeia's strangeness, Poe's narrator seems, as Lawrence was first to observe, as much a scientist as a romantic writer. When, for example, the narrator attempts to describe Ligeia, he says that he "examined" her, carefully observing "the contour of the lofty and pale forehead" and her cadaverous and "ivory" skin and "raven-black . . . tresses" (111). Although he states that their relation is probably best understood as a romantic one, he feels compelled to add that her vampirish yet strangely spiritual eyes are hypnotic and compelling "orbs" for which there are "no models in the remotely antique" (113). These eyes, he continues, contain a hidden mystery, one which he apprehends in "the commonest objects in the universe," in "certain sounds from stringed music," and in Glanvill's "sentiments" about the mysterious power of the will (113)—words which, in the context of what has come before, not only allude to Ligeia's bewitching demeanor and, possibly, to Glanvill's version of religious truth but also to her relation to the "commonest objects in the universe"—in a "rapidly growing vine"; in "a moth, a butterfly, a chrysalis, a stream of running water"; in "the ocean; in the falling of a meteor"; in "the glances of unusually aged people" or in "one or two stars in heaven"—those that are "double and changeable" (113). What these "common objects" all suggest to the narrator is that her eyes are connected to *natural* growth, to *natural* transformation or change, to the *natural* process of aging.

Two other cryptic, but notable, allusions are made to scientific thinkers in "Ligeia": to Democritus and to Francis Bacon. Although these allusions are brief, even dismissive, they shed some additional light not only on the narrator's reading interests but also on his "scientific" perspective in coming to terms with what he thinks Ligeia is. He alludes first to Democritus. Democritus was one of the first men to pose a "materialist philosophy of nature," a philosophy in which he explored the possibility that "all substance consists of atoms, that is, of indivisible and imperceptively small particles" and that "the finest, smoothest, and most agile atoms constitute the substance of mind" and that therefore human perception can be explained "as an emanation of tiny copies of sensible things (*eidola*), which, through their impact upon the atoms of mind, leave impressions responsible for the facts of memory" (*Philosophy* 91). The other allusion is to Francis Bacon, most well-known in Poe's time (and ours) for his utilization and development of the scientific process of inductive reasoning, of apprehending a general law from observed details of specific data. Poe's narrator approaches the mystery of Ligeia inductively, moving from his specific observations of all that he has witnessed (or can recall witnessing) toward the general "law of the will" presumably proposed by Glanvill and cited several times in his narrative, once even by Ligeia before she dies.

Poe's narrator attempts to reconstruct Ligeia not only by dissecting her down to the last nerve ending but also by recalling those specific details about her which he has been unable to remember about her. In so doing, he hopes to understand the relation of her mortal (or immortal?) will to the most common, but evolving or transforming, objects in the natural world and the universe. Described by some critics as the narrator's transcendentalist tendencies, such detailing instead suggests that the narrator is attempting to use inductive reasoning in order to understand not only Ligeia but also the universal principle or law which he suspects that her nature embodies. Although New England transcendentalists also incorporated inductive reasoning into their philosophical treatises and strategies, they did not do so with the uncertainties, hesitations, and general sense of exploratory dread communicated by Poe's narrator in "Ligeia." Unlike the New England transcendentalists, this narrator does not really want to discover the truth about Ligeia's transcendent aspect; rather, he feels driven by his need to know the "truth" that her existence reveals.

To this narrator, Ligeia has come to represent more than a mere mortal woman or literary artifact; she has transformed before his close and rational scrutiny into a feminine entity who exists beyond human realms and history. Writing about Ligeia's return from the grave (an event which has already happened and which may or may not have been temporary), his narrative offers his attempt to reconcile his vision of her essentially inhuman and vampirish nature with his sense that she is far more than this—an entity "*upon the very verge* of [his] remembrance" (113). Despite Ligeia's vampirish qualities, the narrator "senses" she is no typical vampire. For Ligeia not only appeals, according to the narrator, to a "Divine Father" before her demise, but she is more knowledgeable than all other mortal men and women and does not have a clearly evil nature.[4]

Before he met Ligeia, the narrator recalls, he had only a limited knowledge of metaphysics. Indeed, he can only recall with admiration Ligeia's complex knowledge, the "most abstruse of the boasted erudition of the academy" since she is a woman who has "traversed, and successfully, all the wide areas of the moral, physical, and math-ematical science" (114). She becomes his guide "through the chaotic world of metaphysical speculation" with which he is evidently unfamiliar, despite his familiarity with myth and romance and his considerable knowledge of "medical reading" (124). The narrator, then, is a limited Renaissance man, one who has dabbled in philosophy, literature, science, and medicine, but only with the entrance of Ligeia does he begin seriously to contemplate metaphysics. Although Poe's interest in Newtonian science, in earlier Greek cosmogonic and atomic theories, and in scientific materialism is critically common knowledge, "Ligeia" suggests, albeit erratically, that there may be some mystery beyond such ancient and then-contemporary science, some unifying principle which will finally prove them all inadequate.

Although the "principle" is intricately related to Ligeia's femininity, it is involved, more broadly, with what can be loosely classified as her "biology." Biology in Poe's nineteenth-century America was, as William Coleman suggests, a science that was still being "introduced" (1), a science in the process of being integrated with other nineteenth-century sciences. Primarily concerned with defining the question of what "life" was, scientists interested in biological issues were still generally immersed in the debate between scientific "vitalism" (or the idea that there were two sets of natural laws, one for the living and the other for the dead or inanimate universe) and scientific "mechanism" (in which the inanimate universe and organic life were viewed as part of a complex machine).

In "Ligeia," this debate takes on a curious, new form. Poe's narrator is principally fascinated with what he calls the nature of the human will and with the role it plays in both the life and death process. In his portrait of Ligeia, he offers a strange brew of both vitalistic and mechanistic thought in which he implies that the individual "will" is both part of a larger, cosmic, mechanistic design and simultaneously individual, vital, and *separate* from that design. In his search for the "truth" about Ligeia, he raises questions not only about the relation between the living and the dead but also about the nature of the "sentience" or conscious *will* of the individual in relation to the physical body, to natural laws, and, ultimately, to the universe. Ligeia's willful and biological defiance of death offers the narrator, among other things, a possible (and extraordinary) insight into the relation between vitalistic and mechanistic explanations of human biology—most significantly in relation to where blood comes from and where it goes.

William Harvey's seventeenth-century theory about the circulation of blood through the heart "was accepted by biologists generally" and remains an accepted early contribution to modern biology (Asimov 25). But this "mechanistic" theory that "the blood in the veins could travel in only one direction, toward the heart" and that veins and arteries were intricately related to the whole organic body opposed earlier vitalistic assumptions that both animate and inanimate forces were at work in the blood's circulation and were mutually exclusive. In short, Harvey's theory "opened a battle between [the] two opposing views of [mechanism] and [vitalism]" (Asimov 25) that was not yet resolved in Poe's early nineteenth century. In "Ligeia," the question of where blood comes from and where it goes arguably extends *beyond* the human body. For the free-floating "ruby colored fluid"—symbolically reminiscent of blood—that Poe's narrator holds responsible for Rowena's death and final transformation into Ligeia offers a new source of speculation for him (125). Although blood is central to biological existence, this strange blood transfusion between Ligeia and Rowena suggests that it may be connected to an even larger organic whole (perhaps the universe itself) and can exist (as it evidently does in the dead Ligeia) in some altered form or stasis after death. More, the narrator implicitly speculates whether such personal yet simultaneously cosmic "blood" can be transferred, at will, from one body into another living organism (in this case, Rowena), even altering an existing biological creation. With both amazement and terror, Poe's narrator not only watches Rowena go through her final, convulsive death seizures after the "ruby colored fluid" is dropped into her cup but also actually *"grow taller since her malady"* (125). The transfer of blood from victim to victimizer is, as Poe knew, seminal to the vampire tale, but in "Ligeia," he uses this motif to intensify the ambiguity and complexity of the narrator's quasi-scientific understanding of this phenomena.

Is this narrator a madman? Numerous critics have suggested that the "ruby colored fluid" the narrator imagines he sees "fall in the goblet" is poison (125) and that either Ligeia commits a supernaturally vicious act against Rowena or that the narrator himself is Rowena's murderer, and a mad one at that. Most of Poe's other critics have tended to follow the narrator's suggestion that the source of this illusion or hallucination may be related to his excessive consumption of opium after Ligeia's death; in this view, the narrator becomes more a man who is attempting to use language to reconstruct not only a phenomenal event, but Ligeia herself. I believe, however, that the "scientific" nature of his inquiry and detailing about this event also raises for him another alternative: the possibility that he has actually witnessed the transference of Ligeia's "universal" blood and consciousness into another biological organism, into Rowena. At the same time, all three views—Ligeia's supernatural demonism, the narrator's madness, and the possible, phenomenal existence of such a "ruby colored fluid"—remain possibilities in the narrative, hence its "fantastic" suspension between the natural and supernatural, the scientific and the mythological, the literal and the allegorical.

If, for example, this narrator is a madman who has murdered Rowena, it is also likely that he has murdered Ligeia. Both women die, in fact, in markedly similar manners—mysteriously and suddenly. Ligeia abruptly "grew ill," the narrator says, whereas Rowena was "attacked with sudden illness" (115, 120). Both also have convulsions and resist death. Ligeia has "convulsive writhings" and a "fierceness of resistance to death" (115), whereas Rowena's frame is

"racked" by the disorder as she struggles wildly against it (121). However, *if* this narrator has murdered one or both women, the question remains: why? In works such as "The Black Cat" or "The Tell-Tale Heart," Poe's mad narrators re-veal their motives, however bizarre, for murder, but what motivates the narrator of "Ligeia" toward madness and murder? If such a character were to murder these two women, is it possible that he would do so as an "experiment," one designed to satiate his desire not so much to possess a woman but rather to *know,* to understand, what he perceives (madly or otherwise) as the essential organic unity, or "Oneness" as Poe's later narrator in *Eureka* classifies it, of the universe? It is, in terms of his narrative, quite possible.

Offering a retrospective analysis of his situation, in fact, the narrator of "Ligeia" describes, in clearly distraught terms, what he, as a man with no initial interest in metaphysics but only in the natural sciences, did not think possible in either the natural world or in the universe—but what he, as a man, now thinks may be true. In the previously mentioned September 1839 letter to Philip Cooke, Poe observed that he should have revised his story to reveal that "Ligeia (who had only succeeded in so much as to convey an idea of truth to the narrator) should be at length entombed as Rowena—the bodily alterations having gradually faded away" (*Letters* 118). However, no such transformation took place, though Poe revised "Ligeia" in 1845 and wrote to Cooke again in 1846 to say that the story had been "much improved" (*Letters* 348). These "improvements" included not only the terse, stereotypical description of Rowena as the "fair" feminine counterpart to the "dark" Ligeia but also the introduction of Ligeia's poem, "The Conqueror Worm," which had been published earlier and separately in *Graham's Magazine* in 1843.

What such revisions suggest is that Poe did not want only to create, as some critics have speculated, an opium-addicted madman or murderer in "Ligeia"; rather, they suggest that he wanted to convey, as he told Cooke, "an idea of truth to the narrator," an idea that might drive his narrator to madness or murder, but would, in any case, prevent him from ever being restored to his former sense of normalcy or reality. Poe wanted not only to illustrate further the typological connection between the "dark" Ligeia and the "fair" Rowena but also to make both Ligeia's mythic stature and her indictment of "Man" pronounced. The inclusion of "The Conqueror Worm" intensifies the reader's sense that Ligeia's struggle is not only biologic, but mythic—one between the gendered angels, gods, and demons of a sentient universe.[5]

In both the 1838 version and in the 1845 version, Ligeia does not reveal either her origins or her paternal name to the narrator; she possesses more wisdom than any mortal man or woman the narrator has known; and she loves the narrator (he claims) with excessive, aggressive, and extraordinary feminine passion. The 1845 poem, however, offers the reader Ligeia's nightmarish vision of a grotesquely phallic "Conqueror Worm" who consumes "Mimes" and whom she links to the "tragedy, Man" (116-117) in what seems to be, as Leland Person suggests, a "pointed reference" to gender vic-timization (22). When Ligeia appeals to a paternal figure ("God! O Divine Father!"), she also asks, "[S]hall this Conqueror be not once conquered? Are we not part and parcel in Thee?" (117). She expects to be given both divine guidance and sanctioning with such a request. Ligeia asks not merely to survive the "Conqueror Worm" of "death" and this "tragedy, Man," but to conquer it, to defeat it, and to do so through her connection to a "Divine Father."

The "truth," then, that Ligeia seems to represent to Poe's narrator (and perhaps even to Poe) is that she, as an immortally feminine demon, is in conflict with an equally immortal and patriarchal god and universe. Although Poe never specifically cites the Lilith legend in his statements about Ligeia, his narrator's allusions to Biblical and classical mythology suggest that Poe intended, at least in part, to create in his narrator's portrait of Ligeia an exaggerated synthesis of popularized female vampires and ancient, albeit sinister, female fertility "goddesses"—mythic "sisters" such as the narrator's invented "Ashtophet" or her sister goddesses Ashtoreth, Astarte, and Lilith who (whether Poe consciously realized this or not) have similar mythic origins (Graves and Patai 68-9).

If Ligeia is a fictive variant (or at least an equivalent she-demon and fertility goddess) to figures such as Lilith, then it seems that Poe envisioned in his Ligeia a mystery which he felt that only an undefined narrator with broad scientific and humanistic knowledge might "examine" and understand. Such a narrator might also speculate, as he does, on the relation of the living to the dead (the organic world to inanimate matter), and, finally, on the relation of man (and woman) to a complex reality and universe. Could the existence of a being like Ligeia (a mortal woman with more complex knowledge than generally imagined possible) drive such a man to murder, to delusion, to mad-ness? Could Ligeia actually be "real"? Could there be a "mortal" woman who, through the vagaries of her knowledge and her will, might temporarily return from the grave, take temporary possession of Rowena's body, and then die again—leaving him in his current mental state? The reader can never "know," given the complex nature of this narrative, a narrative suspended as it is between "truth" and "madness." This narrator's unique correlation of interrelated but abstract ideas about mythological female deities and the nature of the universe serves to intensify the ambivalent effect Poe desired and make his narrative one in which the supernatural and the natural remain equally plausible "realities."

Along with the mythic allusions already discussed, the narrator's response to Ligeia's "death" reinforces her stature both as a demonic goddess and as a mortal woman. After Ligeia's death, the narrator transforms his home into a gothic nightmare, as he becomes a "bounden slave in the trammels of opium" and soon finds little difference be-

tween his home and his opium hallucinations (118). Interestingly, his transformed home, aside from being, as the narrator says, arabesque and grotesque, also becomes a suggestively mythic realm in which pagan and civilized religious artifacts and images run rampant, creating "bedlam patterns" (118). For example, the narrator has "grotesque specimens of a semi-Gothic, semi-Druidical device"—evidently some mysterious remnant from that ancient and mysterious Celtic priesthood. Further, he decorates his chambers with ritualistic or representative artifacts from Eastern religious traditions—with a "huge censer" of Arabian design for burning incense; with ottomans and "golden candelabras of Eastern figure"; with a "bridal couch—of an Indian model"; and with "a gigantic sarcophagus of black granite . . . from the tombs of [ancient Egyptian] kings" (118-119).

More, all these ritualistic or religious artifacts are enclosed by a "heavy and massive-looking tapestry," which was "spotted all over, at irregular intervals, with arabesque figures," bizarre but undefined "ghastly forms" which he simultaneously associates with "the superstitions of the Norman" (or paganistic Vikings) and "the guilty slumbers of the [Christian] monk" (120). Finally, the "phantasmagoric effect" of these figures is "vastly heightened by the artificial introduction of a strong current of wind behind the draperies—giving a hideous and uneasy animation to the whole" (121). Although this wind is artificial, it is eventually this same wind which signals Ligeia's startling, if not sinister, return and possession of the innocent Rowena. A sister to the female demon or wind spirit "Lilitu" as much as is Lilith (Graves and Patai 68), Ligeia *belongs* in this room which, to all appearances, has been arranged by this semi-conscious male narrator to reveal his—or "Man's"—complicity in her creation. Oriental or Eastern imagery, then, is fused with Judeo-Christian and pagan imagery in this narrator's disturbed imagination, offering further reference to the mixed patriarchal heritages from which female literary doubles such as Ligeia and Rowena are born.

As a participant in a patriarchal tradition that romantically envisions denigrated and submissive Eve-like creatures such as Rowena, the narrator guarantees that Ligeia, her mythic (and less consciously known) counterpart, will not only return, but do so with a vengeance. More, in terms of the universe that he has now come to apprehend (and perhaps even fear) as an essentially mechanistic but paradoxically "sentient" (and vital) one which *can* embody fantastic beings like Ligeia, such an "apocalypse"—both secular and immortal—becomes inevitable. Like Ligeia, the universe is not "dead"—not an object that can be studied and dissected; rather, it is, the narrator now realizes with both awe and terror, an organic, sentient creature which has, as much as Ligeia, a will and transformative capability of its own. He thus thinks he discovers, with similar horror and awe, that there is no such thing as biological "death"—in either the conventional or scientific sense of the term.

The forbidden knowledge which Poe's narrator gains may be vaguely related to sexual knowledge, but it does not have, as G. R. Thompson and other critics have speculated, a strictly "vampirish quality" (186). Rather, it involves the narrator's conscious recognition that before the mythological (and Western) Fall from the Garden, Ligeia and Rowena were one woman but that after it, they were "divided": one into the vampirish, immortal and all-knowing fantastic creature that is Ligeia, the other into the mortal, submissive and denigrated female counterpart, the Eve-like Rowena, the mother of all mortal women, for whom he feels unqualified contempt. When Ligeia assumes Rowena's body and identity, it does not matter, as Poe told Philip Cooke, whether Ligeia remains dominant, or Rowena comes briefly back to life, then dies. Poe's primary interest was, as he said, in revealing the "idea of truth" that their strange symbiosis brings, however temporarily, to his narrator's (and perhaps his own) conscious and tormented awareness. It is the disturbing "truth" that these volatile feminine doubles, one immortal and the other mortal, ultimately share the same divine or universal nature and simultaneously bear an intimate but forgotten (and near incommunicable) relationship to the "truth" and the unrealized complexity of his own nature and existence.

Notes

1. See, for example, Joseph Andriano "Archetypal Projection in 'Ligeia': A Post-Jungian Reading," *Poe Studies* 19 (1986): 27-31; Maurice J. Bennett "'The Madness of Art': Poe's 'Ligeia' as Metafiction," *Poe Studies* 14 (1981): 1-6; Ronald Bieganoski "The Self-Consuming Narrator in Poe's 'Ligeia' and 'Usher,'" *American Literature,* No. 2 (1988): 175-198; Joan Dayan "The Intelligibility of Ligeia" in *Fables of Mind: An Inquiry Into Poe's Fiction* (New York and Oxford: Oxford University Press, 1987): 179-192; James W. Gargano, "Poe's 'Ligeia': Dream and Destruction," *College English* 23 (1962): 335-42; Clark Griffith "Poe's 'Ligeia' and the English Romantics," *University of Toronto Quarterly* 24 (1954): 8-25; Daryl E. Jones, "Poe's Siren: Character and Meaning in 'Ligeia,'" *Studies in Short Fiction* Vol. 20, No. 1 (1983): 33-37; D. H. Lawrence, "Edgar Allan Poe" in *Studies in Classic American Literature* (New York: Doubleday & Co., Inc., 1953): 73-92; G. R. Thompson "Proper Evidence of Madness: American Gothic and the Interpretation of 'Ligeia,'" *ESQ: A Journal of the American Renaissance* 18 (1972): 30-49; and Jules Zanger "Poe and the Theme of Forbidden Knowledge," *American Literature* 49 (1978): 533-542.

2. The primary text consulted on Lilith's Hebraic heritage was Raphael Patai's definitive text *The Hebrew Goddess.* Patai summarizes Lilith's significance to this heritage: "The main features of Lilith's mythical biography first appear in Sumerian culture about the middle of the 3rd millennium B.C.E. What she meant for the Biblical Hebrews can only be surmised, but by the Talmudic period (2nd-5th centuries C.E.) she was a fully developed evil she-demon and during the Kabbalistic age she rose to the high position of

queenly consort at God's side" (221). Complementing this text is Patai's co-authored work with Robert Graves, *Hebrew Myths: The Book of Genesis,* a text which supplements Patai's examination of Lilith's relation to later vampire lore and to earlier mythic counterparts in Greek, Egyptian, Babylonian, Assyrian, and Roman mythology.

3. Although none of Poe's named sources for "Ligeia" indicate that he consciously had Lilith in mind, literary references to Ashtoreth and Astarte, demonic feminine goddesses who are variations on Lilith, were common in Poe's nineteenth century. Feminine demons such as Lilith, Graves and Patai observe, "not only are characteristic of civilizations where women are treated as chattel [and] . . . must adopt the recumbent posture during intercourse which Lilith refused" (69), but are characteristic of all living patriarchal religious traditions such as Christianity, Judaism, Hinduism, Buddhism, and Islam where women have "as a normal rule . . . been expected to play a role, religious and social, second to that of men" (*Abingdon Dictionary* 806).

4. Vampire lore typically depicts the vampire as one alienated from God; the vampire is a walking corpse, not a spirit, and is typically associated with Christian demonology, hence its fear of the crucifix (which can kill it), the name of God, holy water, and pious Christians generally (*Man, Myth, and Magic* 11, 292-295).

5. In Kabbalistic tradition, "Lilith's greatest triumph and the high point in her career came with the destruction of the Jerusalem Temple" (Patai 249), for when this happened, Lilith became God's concubine, replacing the Matronit, the "spouse of God" (Patai 152). This usurpation will not end until the apocalyptic "coming of the Messiah" at which time Lilith will cease to exist (Patai 250). Because of his vision of Ligeia, Poe's narrator seemingly experiences a similar, albeit personal, apocalypse.

Works Cited

Asimov, Isaac. *A Short History of Biology.* Garden City, New York: Natural History Press, 1964.

The Abingdon Dictionary of Living Religions. Ed. Keith Crim. Nashville: Abingdon Press, 1981.

Coleman, William. *Biology in the Nineteenth Century: Problems of Form, Function and Transformation.* London, New York, and Melbourne: Cambridge University Press, 1977.

Dayan, Joan. *Fables of Mind: An Inquiry Into Poe's Fiction.* New York and Oxford: Oxford University Press, 1987.

Dictionary of Philosophy, Ed. Dagobert D. Runes. Totowa, N.J.: Rowman and Allanheld, 1984.

Galloway, David. "Notes." *The Fall of the House of Usher and Other Writings.* Ed. David Galloway. New York: Penguin, 1986.

Glanvill, Joseph. *Scepsis Scientifica or, Confest ignorance, the way to science; in an essay of the vanity of dogmatizing and confident opinion.* Ed. John Owen. London. Rpt. of 1665 edition, London: Kegan Paul, Trench & Co., 1885.

Graves, Robert and Raphael Patai. *Hebrew Myths. The Book of Genesis.* New York: McGraw-Hill Book Company, 1966.

Herndon, Jerry.

Howard, Brad.

Lawrence, D. H. "Edgar Allan Poe." *Studies in Classic American Literature.* New York: Doubleday & Co., Inc. 1953: 73-92.

Man, Myth, and Magic. The Illustrated Encyclopedia of Mythology, Religion, and the Unknown. Vols. 1, 6, 11. Ed. Richard Cavendish. New York, London, Toronto: Cavendish, 1989.

Patai, Raphael. *The Hebrew Goddess.* 3rd ed. Detroit: Wayne State University Press, 1990.

Person, Leland Jr. *Aesthetic Headaches.* Athens: University of Georgia Press, 1989.

Poe, Edgar Allen. *The Letters of Edgar Allan Poe.* Ed. John W. Ostrom. Cambridge: Harvard University Press, 1948.

———. "Ligeia." *The Fall of the House of Usher and Other Writings.* Ed. David Galloway. New York: Penguin, 1986.

Thompson, G. R. *Poe's Fiction: Romantic Irony in the Gothic Tales.* Madison: University of Wisconsin Press, 1973.

Todorov, Tzvetan. *The Fantastic: A Structural Approach to a Literary Genre.* Trans. Richard Howard. Ithaca: Cornell University Press, 1975.

Zanger, Jules. "Poe and the Theme of Forbidden Knowledge." *American Literature.* Vol. 49. 1979: 533-542.

Kate Flint (essay date 1997)

SOURCE: "Blood, Bodies, and *The Lifted Veil*," in *Nineteenth-Century Literature*, Vol. 51, No. 4, March, 1997, pp. 455-73.

[*In the following essay, Flint examines George Eliot's* The Lifted Veil *as a text representative of the developing contemporary debate about the relationship between physiology and psychology.*]

On 17 March 1878 Edith Simcox paid a visit to George Eliot and her companion, George Lewes. Simcox recorded their conversation in her *Autobiography*: "I asked about the Lifted Veil. Lewes . . . asked what I thought of it. I was embarrassed and said—as he did—that it was not at all like her other writings, wherefrom she differed; she said it was 'schauderhaft' [horrible, ghastly] was it, and I [said] yes; but I was put out by things that I didn't quite know what to do with."[1] *The Lifted Veil,* written in the early months of 1859 and first published in *Blackwood's Magazine* in June of that year, has long been a work that critics have not known quite what to do with. It has been seen as a Tale of Mystery and Imagination, in the style of Edgar Allan Poe; a short novel dealing with moral problems; an early example of the sensation fiction that was to become so popular in England during the 1860s. It has stimulated questions concerning the part it plays in George Eliot's career as a writer—particularly in relation to the fact that in this work she conspicuously and deliberately adopts a first-person male persona.[2] The relationship between gender and knowledge—important, as we shall see, to a reading of the tale in the context of medical science—is raised by the implications of the title itself. Veils are inescapably associated with eroticism, exoticism, and fetishism. To lift the veil is to peep at the forbidden, to access taboo knowledge; to occupy, by connotation, a masculine position.[3] This is not to say, of course, that one relishes what one finds; this is the message of Shelley's sonnet where he advises one *not* to shed one's illusions: "Lift not the painted veil which those who live / Call life."[4] The horrors of looking, voluntarily or involuntarily, "behind the veil" inform the novella. Latimer, the narrator, does not welcome his unbidden powers of prevision; moreover, the fascination exerted on him by the Water-Nixie, Bertha, is in great measure due to the fact that hers is the only mind he cannot read: "my oasis of mystery in the dreary desert of knowledge."[5] George Eliot's story is, among other things, a dramatization of the folly of pursuing Woman on the grounds that she represents a mysterious Other.

In more formal terms *The Lifted Veil* provokes conjectures about the operations of fiction. Composed at a time when George Eliot was developing her theories concerning realism, the story bends laws of probability in order to investigate questions that are implicit throughout many of her later novels: what would happen if we could lift what Latimer calls "the curtain of the future" (p. 4)?[6] If we could foresee the consequences of our actions, would we act differently? If sympathy toward others is a desirable thing, is it only possible to express this sympathy when we do not know as much as it would be possible to know about the other person? To what extent does personality color perception? All these questions tend toward a wider issue: if we could have more strongly developed powers of vision, if we could lay bare the future and the thoughts of others, as a physiologist can lay bare the hidden workings of the mysteriously veiled human body, would we choose to accept such powers?

This question goes beyond a poser for fiction. It is inseparably linked to a developing contemporary debate about the relationship between physiology and psychology. The Victorians were fascinated by the possibility, the necessity, of making things visible. Nowhere was this more true than in the sphere of medical science. This fascination evolved out of the work of Enlightenment scientists, who developed, as Barbara Stafford has put it,

> proper and improper rituals for scanning, touching, cutting, deforming, abstracting, generating, conceiving, marking, staining, enlarging, reducing, imagining, and sensing. Constituting visual styles or manners of behavior, these procedures provided right or wrong sensory and intellectual strategies for "opening" recalcitrant materials and otherwise impenetrable substances. Normal or abnormal processes and modes for proceeding could assure one, or not, of getting a glimpse into secretive physiognomies. Body tropes thus provided critical clues for how insight might be gained into the interior of any concealed territory.[7]

The task of the medical clinic, as Michel Foucault wrote in *The Birth of the Clinic*, was "no longer . . . simply to read the visible; it has to discover its secrets."[8] The secrets of the body are complicated in their concealment, however, since they are apparently contained in two types of systems. On the one hand there is blood, muscle, bone, organs; on the other, the complex workings of the mind. For much of the nineteenth century the workings of body and mind were commonly believed to be inseparable.[9] However, such assumptions did not pass unquestioned, and it is my contention that *The Lifted Veil* may usefully be read as an intervention in this scientific arena. Notably informed by contemporary science, it implicitly poses the question as to whether identical hypotheses and modes of investigation are indeed suitable when it comes to understanding the workings of the mind and of the body.

In writing *The Lifted Veil* George Eliot, unlike a physiologist, is unhampered by laws of corporeal possibility. The novella provides a controlled space in which she can set up her own experiment, asking "what if?" At the same time, as we shall see, she carefully ties in to contemporary science the blood transfusion episode, the most ghoulish and incredible of all the scenes in the story—incredible since others than Latimer are witness to it, and thus it cannot be accounted for by hallucinatory peculiarities and coincidence. The novella's interrogations of the limits of positivism are dependent for their importance and credibility on this very definite scientific grounding.

Edith Simcox, like many subsequent critics, may have felt that *The Lifted Veil* was something of a cuckoo in George Eliot's fictional nest. In the autobiographical passage quoted above Simcox records Lewes's contribution to the discussion that she and the novelist were having: "He Oh, but the moral is plain enough—it is only an exaggeration of what happens—the one-sided knowing of things in relation to the self—not whole knowledge because 'tout comprehendre est tout pardonner'" (*George Eliot Letters,* IX, 220). It is notable that Lewes felt that he *could* comment so confidently upon the text's import—even if his explanation may not be crystal clear to us—since his own connection to *The Lifted Veil* and its themes is a crucial one. For George Eliot's novella would have been impossible without Lewes's physiological researches, and in many respects her work should explicitly be seen as a dialogue with them.

Many of the critical problems posed around *The Lifted Veil* center on the quality of prevision. Yet prevision is not in itself a particularly strange characteristic. A term used, indeed, to describe visionary experience, it also has its function as a term within scientific and sociological investigation. Praising Auguste Comte in the final chapter of *A Biographical History of Philosophy,* which he published in 1845-46, Lewes maintained firmly that "the positive Method is the only Method . . . on which truth can be found is easily proved: on it alone can *prevision* of phenomena depend. Prevision is the characteristic and the test of knowledge. If you can predict certain results and they occur as you predicted, then are you assured that your knowledge is correct."[10] Prevision may be a goal not just of philosophical endeavor but of physiology. The more we know about the constitution of the body and the relations of its various parts, the more accurately will we be able to understand its functioning and diagnose and treat its disorders. The importance of the body and its indicative manifestations runs through *The Lifted Veil.* Latimer characterizes himself—once his affliction of penetrating, unbidden, into the mental processes of others becomes habitual—as suffering not so much from a mental aberration as from "the stamp of a morbid organisation, framed for passive suffering" (p. 20). He does not describe his strange "diseased participation in other peoples' consciousness" (p. 26) in supernatural terms but complains that it results from experiencing "the lot of a being finely organised for pain, but with hardly any fibres that responded to pleasure" (p. 36); he compares it, in language prefiguring the passage in chapter 20 of *Middlemarch* that contemplates the pain of having too keen a vision of human life, to "a preternaturally heightened sense of hearing, making audible to one a roar of sound where others find perfect stillness" (p. 26). Throughout *The Lifted Veil* (as indeed throughout all of George Eliot's subsequent fictions) the workings of the body are inseparably bound in with the emotions: thus Latimer looks back to the fading of what little happiness he has known in his marriage "as a man might look back on the last pains in a paralysed limb" (p. 47). Latimer's narrative gains credibility from the fact that he, schooled in science, confidently employs medical vocabulary not just in the examples cited but as he gives the specifics of three deaths: his brother's, through "a concussion of the brain" (p. 41); Mrs. Archer's (peritonitis); and his own foreseen demise, from angina pectoris. Moreover, George Eliot, via Latimer, drops a strong hint that not only are bodies important in their own right but that our comprehension of their workings may be analogous to our interpretation of texts: "We learn *words* by rote, but not their meaning; *that* must be paid for with our life-blood, and printed in the subtle fibres of our nerves" (p. 52). *The Lifted Veil,* in its very construction, is based on a paradigm of morbid anatomy: a narrative that keeps pace, to quote Lawrence Rothfield writing of George Eliot in a different context, with "the temporality of the body, its organic growth and decay, its duration of illness, its descent toward death, its complicated finitude: the narrative, in short, of a pathological organicism."[11]

The speculative, imaginative, fiction-creating mind, with its capacity for prevision, has the ability to travel backward and forward in time. But the human body has no such ability, and nor, suggests George Eliot through Latimer, can our deep-seated responses adjust themselves according to rational knowledge about the one thing that is certain, not speculative, about our futures: "Our impulses, our spiritual activities, no more adjust themselves to the idea of their future nullity, than the beating of our heart, or the irritability of our muscles" (p. 44). This language takes us straight into physiology, and the implications of the relation of *The Lifted Veil* to contemporary medical science, with its interest in the connections between mental and physical activity.

The importance of conventional medical science in relation to *The Lifted Veil* has hitherto been passed over in favor of more tendentious forms of inquiry. Beryl Gray has usefully illuminated some of the ways in which George Eliot's novella relates to practices that lay on the very borders of acceptable science in the 1840s and 1850s, particularly mesmerism, animal magnetism, and clairvoyance.[12] "Indications of claire-voyance witnessed by a competent observer," George Eliot wrote in a 22 April 1852 letter to George Combe, "are of thrilling interest and give me a restless desire to get at more extensive and satisfactory evidence" (*George Eliot Letters,* VIII, 45). She had become familiar with such highly topical subjects in the 1840s through her friendship with Charles and Arthur Bray. In 1851 Charles Bray had introduced her to Combe, the Edinburgh phrenologist, with whom she corresponded until her relationship with Lewes put an end to the connection.

In *The Lifted Veil* phrenology seems an effective diagnostic tool. Mr. Letherall, a friend of Latimer's father, takes the "small head" of the boy "between his large hands, and pressed it here and there in an exploratory, suspicious manner—then placed each of his great thumbs on my temples" (p. 6), before detecting supposed deficiencies and excesses of sensibility and prescribing a course of scientific, classificatory education that ran counter to the young Latimer's natural inclination toward unpractical literary pursuits—but this education effects no conspicuous change in his innate disposition. Through Combe, George Eliot became alerted to the work of William Gregory, Professor of Chemistry at Edinburgh University. As Gray has noted, in his *Letters to a Candid Inquirer, on Animal Magnetism* (1851) Gregory writes of the experiences of one of his patients, "Mr. D.," who became clairvoyant when in deep mesmeric sleep, developing the capacity to describe accurately places he had never seen, such as Cologne, and people he had never met—in a manner very like that in which Latimer intensely visualizes Prague before he has traveled there.[13] Moreover, Professor Gregory believed strongly in the possibility of "sympathetic clairvoyance," the ability both to read the thoughts of others and to see into the future, for: "If past occurrences leave a trace behind them, may not 'coming events cast a shadow before?'" (p. 159). *The Lifted Veil* undoubtedly owes a

good deal to George Eliot's interest in the moral and metaphysical questions raised by such quasi-scientific investigations and speculations. But the relationship between *The Lifted Veil* and more mainstream science is much closer than has previously been recognized, and the main agency of that closeness is G. H. Lewes.

The most sensational scene in *The Lifted Veil* occurs near the end when the doctor, Meunier, performs an experiment on Bertha's maid and companion, Mrs. Archer. This is not a scene that critics have dwelt on with any comfort—if, indeed, they have chosen to confront it at all. "The blood transfusion incident is a piece of tawdry melodrama, a grotesque and infelicitous flaw, a *fiction,*" writes Terry Eagleton, stating further that "we can't believe it; and yet of course we must, for this is a 'realist' tale, and within those conventions what Latimer as observer says goes. It *must* have happened—Bertha must therefore be guilty— and yet, somehow, it didn't" (p. 58). Eagleton wriggles out of this problem by suggesting that here we have nothing less than the theoretical problem of realist fiction to ponder upon: how do we know that what Latimer writes is "truth"? How do we account for Latimer's previsionary powers having failed him with regard to his wife, except by recourse to an explanation that reads into his specific situation a paradigm for the fact that all narrative fiction must pretend "not to know," to some extent, in order to function *as* a narrative?[14]

Other critics are less subtle than Eagleton but no less dismissive. Judith Wilt, seeing the novella as a mid-nineteenth-century staging post between *Frankenstein* and *Dracula,* labels the transfusion "the most splendidly Gothic scene of all."[15] A "lurid scene," Mary Jacobus calls it.[16] Beryl Gray passes hastily over it in her "Afterword" to the Virago edition, after having initially termed it a "ghoulish, quasi-scientific resurrection from the dead": "On the surface, the transfusion of Dr. Meunier's own blood straight into the neck vein of the corpse does seem preposterously melodramatic, but it is described quite perfunctorily. The narrative drives on towards the climax, which is not the momentary success of the operation, but the shock of the posthumous release of Mrs. Archer's malice."[17] And even in the article where she concentrates on George Eliot and science in relation to this novella, Gray writes of the author's "unorthodox means" and remarks that the operation emulates "that remarkable efficiency displayed by many a Gothic doctor when coping with macabre apparatus" ("Pseudoscience," p. 420). Jennifer Uglow and U. C. Knoepflmacher perhaps come nearest to offering satisfactory remarks about the episode. Uglow writes that the culminating scene of the novel is one that serves to contradict the wish of Latimer's father and of his teacher, Dr. Letherall, "to correct the boy's over-sensitivity by a dose of scientific education. . . . by a nice twist of the plot, George Eliot shows that they were wrong to see science as devoid of imagination, for in the end, through the activities of Meunier, it will be used to break the barriers of normal reality in the most terrifying way."[18] And Knoepflmacher, in a thoughtful chapter on *The Lifted Veil,* notes that Meunier's response functions as a comment on the limitations of pathological investigations and that this points forward to George Eliot's later fiction: "'life for that moment ceased to be a scientific problem for him,' as it will be for that other physician in Middlemarch who must adjust his scientific view of woman."[19]

Yet this blood transfusion is no melodramatic invention on the author's part: it is very much in keeping with the theme of medical investigation and questioning that has been raised by Latimer's own condition. Indeed, rather than being sensationalist and improbable, Meunier's experiment is directly linked to contemporary physiology. When Latimer introduces Meunier in his story as a young man with whom he became friendly in Geneva, he lets us know that he describes him under a pseudonym: "I shall call him Charles Meunier; his real surname—an English one, for he was of English extraction—having since become celebrated. He was an orphan, who lived on a miserable pittance while he pursued the medical studies for which he had a special genius" (p. 9). George Eliot had, it would appear, a particular prototype in mind for Meunier. Born in Mauritius in 1817, Charles-Edouard Brown-Séquard was the son of a French mother and of a captain in the American merchant marine who died before his child was born.[20] Sometime before the end of 1838 the family's friends clubbed together to send this academically promising boy from Mauritius to Paris, where he quickly passed his baccalaureate and enrolled in the École de Médecine. He had notably little money to live on and seems to have been something of a social outsider at the time. By 1846 he had begun his experiments in blood transfusion, using the bodies of animals who were on the point of death.

Two of his experiments are of particular interest. In June 1851 Brown-Séquard "was provided with the decapitated corpse of a healthy young murderer of twenty, freshly guillotined" at eight in the morning. By nine p.m. the muscles had lost their irritability (the irritability of muscles figuring in George Eliot's terminology in *The Lifted Veil* concerning the instinctual movements of the body). "Brown-Séquard had two medical friends, Dr. Bonnefin and Dr. Deslauriers, draw half a liter of blood from his own arm. They defibrinated the blood [that is, rid it of the properties that cause clotting] . . . by beating and strained out the clots through linen." This blood, "at 19°, a temperature considerably below normal body temperature, was slowly injected into the radial artery" of the corpse's arm "over a period of ten minutes and allowed to flow out of veins which had been opened. In about 45 minutes at least twelve separate muscles had once more become irritable," or responsive to sensation, again (Olmsted, pp. 41-42).

Later the same year Brown-Séquard attempted an experiment on a dog suffering from peritonitis—the same ailment from which Mrs. Archer expires. He waited until all movement had stopped, the dog had emptied itself of fecal matter and urine, its pupils had dilated, and he could no longer hear the heart beat. At this point he made a transfusion of blood from another, live dog into the right carotid artery. The first sign of temporary recovery was the recommencement of the heart-beat, and then, albeit aided at first by artificial respiration, the dog began to breathe again, and eventually "all the main functions of animal and organic life returned to it. Although feeble, the animal raised itself on its forepaws and wagged its tail when stroked." Four or five hours later it died: "I almost said, died *again*." Brown-Séquard wrote up this experiment in an article of 1858, "Research into the possibility of temporarily bringing back to life individuals dying from illness," which appeared in his own newly launched magazine, *Journal de la Physiologie de l'homme et des animaux,* available to Lewes at the time he was putting together *The Physiology of Common Life* (1859), and hence also potentially familiar to George Eliot. Brown-Séquard concluded his account with a speculation:

> Would it be possible to extrapolate from these experiments some consequences relating to the combined application of transfusion, artificial respiration and the blood-letting of the jugular, to the human dying from inflammatory, or other, ailments? It is evident that, in the vast majority of cases, it would be useless, if not cruel, to keep from death, for what would have to be a very short length of time, an individual of our species whose irreparable physical injuries condemned them to die. But one could have cases in which it mattered that understanding, speech, the faculties of the senses and voluntary movement were given back to the suffering patient. For, the facts mentioned in this study, in showing that *all functions of animal life can be reestablished for several hours in animals in which their agony had already almost completely ensured that death had taken place,* make it extremely probable that the intellectual faculties, the faculties of the senses, speech, etc., may be re-established, for several hours, in those sick people who have just lost the use of their faculties.[21]

Such methods were to provoke speculation in other medical researchers, notably in France (and as a sidenote, it is worth noting that the transfusion scene itself in *The Lifted Veil* evidently stimulated French artistic imagination: a painting depicting it, *La Transfusion du Sang,* by H. É. Blanchon, was hung in the French Salon in 1879).[22] A. Vulpian, in his *Leçons sur la physiologie générale et comparée du système nerveux faites au muséum d'histoire naturelle* (1866), recounts yet another of Brown-Séquard's experiments, in which he transfused blood into the neck arteries of a decapitated dog. After several minutes the muscles of the eye and the face showed that "brain functions had been reestablished." "Perhaps," continues Vulpian, "I might be taxed with temerity in putting forward the idea that this experiment might be successful with a Man. If a physiologist tried this experiment on the head of an executed criminal, a few moments after death, he would perhaps be witness to a great and terrifying spectacle. Perhaps he could give back its brain functions to this head, and reanimate the eyes and the facial muscles, movements which, in Man, are provoked by the passions and by the thoughts of which the brain is the seat."[23] Such an idea was taken up by S. Weir Mitchell, medical practitioner and writer of a substantial amount of sensationalist, sometimes comic, and habitually gruesome fiction, in his 1870 short story for the *Atlantic Monthly,* "Was He Dead?"[24] This tale contains a certain amount of discussion between medical men about the way in which blood transfusion raises questions relating to individual identity, and a recitation of experiments that have been carried out on men and dogs in the past, before the men carry theory into practice and transfuse blood into the corpse of a recently hanged man, a known criminal who, revivified in this way, confesses to the murder of an elderly woman for which an innocent young man has already been hanged.

George Eliot, however, has already seized on the imaginative possibilities of such a resurrection. She would certainly have been familiar with Brown-Séquard's work. Although she and Lewes were in Germany when Brown-Séquard gave his series of six lectures on the Physiology and Pathology of the Nervous System at the Royal College of Surgeons in May 1858, Lewes cites the *Journal de la Physiologie* (which he had in his own library) at some length in his chapter on "The Structure and Uses of our Blood" in *The Physiology of Common Life.* Moreover, at the time *The Lifted Veil* was published, Brown-Séquard had not only lectured in London but had conducted a fashionable Harley Street practice: *Blackwood's* readership might well have recognized something of his identity in Meunier.

The Physiology of Common Life came out in 1859, the same year as *The Lifted Veil.* Lewes's interest in the relationship of the life of the mind with that of the body had, as we shall see, a good deal in common with the broad preoccupations of George Eliot's novella. Although disclaiming that blood may be any more significant in its vital properties that any other part of the human organism, Lewes records the beliefs of those who have thought otherwise, including William Harvey, who first developed a theory of the blood's circulation. In *The Physiology of Common Life* Lewes quotes from Harvey's *Anatomical Exercitations concerning the Generation of Living Creatures* (1653): "Life consists in the blood (as we read in Holy Scripture), because in it the Life and Soule do first dawn and last set. . . . The blood is the genital part, the fountain of Life, *primum vivens, ultimum moriens.*"[25] And Lewes himself attributes considerable vital force to this fluid, describing its circulation through the body as "a mighty river of life . . . the mysterious centre of chemical and vital actions as wonderful as they are indispensable, soliciting our attention no less by the many problems offered to speculative ingenuity, than by the important practical conclusions to which our ideas respecting the Blood necessarily lead" (*Physiology,* I, 239). It is striking that Latimer's affliction of prevision is described by George Eliot in terms that are highly similar to those in which Lewes writes of the circulation of blood. Latimer asks whether the reader is "unable to imagine this double consciousness at work within me, flowing on like two parallel streams which never mingle their waters and blend into a

common hue?" (p. 32). This closely echoes the passage in *The Physiology of Common Life* that describes the circulation of the blood in highly suggestive terms:

> If for a moment we could with the bodily eye see into the frame of man, as with the microscope we see into the transparent frames of some simpler animals, what a spectacle would be *unveiled*! Through one complex system of vessels we should see a leaping torrent of blood, carried into the depths and over the surfaces of all the organs, with amazing rapidity, and carried from the depths and surfaces through another system of vessels, back again to the heart: yet in spite of the countless channels and the crowded complexity of the tissues, nowhere should we detect any confusion, nowhere any failure. Such a spectacle as this is *unveiled* to the mental eye alone, and we cannot contemplate it, even in thought, without a thrill.

> (I, 271; emphasis added)

Yet the "uninterrupted throbbing stream" of life (I, 241), to quote Lewes again, is itself not unmitigatingly positive in its associations. Blood also carries with it the connotations of a pollutant, and hence its representation carries with it a range of superstitions and taboos. These are briefly alluded to when Latimer refers to the Faust myth: "It is an old story, that men sell themselves to the tempter, and sign a bond with their blood, because it is only to take effect at a distant day" (*The Lifted Veil,* p. 31). As Lewes reminds us, "by some the Blood is regarded as the source of all diseases" (*Physiology,* I, 239). It bears associations of violence, wounds, and the shedding of waste products. Furthermore, it differs from the other major category of pollutant, the excremental, precisely because of something that is latent in those lines from Harvey: its relationship to sexual difference. For blood not only flows through each living being's veins, but it also is shed by the menstruating woman. The threat it presents in this connection has been summarized by Julia Kristeva in *Powers of Horror:* she differentiates blood from "excrement and its equivalents (decay, infection, disease, corpse, etc.)," which "stand for the danger to identity that comes from without: the ego threatened by the non-ego, society threatened by its outside, life by death. Menstrual blood, on the contrary, stands for the danger issuing from within the identity (social or sexual)."[26] Blood is troublesome because it belongs to the category that Kristeva designates as the abject: for her it is "not lack of cleanliness or health that causes abjection but what disturbs identity, system, order. What does not respect borders, positions, rules" (p. 4).

Blood transfusions, especially when they are between a man and a woman, as in *The Lifted Veil,* provide a powerful image for this disturbing challenging of symbolic as well as physical boundaries. Medical writings, moreover, helped to sexualize the practice of blood transfusion, since it was most commonly carried out on women who were about to give birth or who had just given birth. It was recommended, too, that men rather than women supply the vital fluid, since they were less liable to faint.[27] This challenging of boundaries is most famously played upon in

Bram Stoker's *Dracula* (1897). In that novel the implications of blood transfusions are unmistakably sexualized. Dr. Seward writes in his diary, after his blood has first been used to reanimate Lucy's white, wan body, that "it was with a feeling of personal pride that I could see a faint tinge of colour steal back into the pallid cheeks and lips. No man knows till he experiences it, what it is to feel his own life-blood drawn away into the veins of the woman he loves."[28] There is an illicit thrill involved in this exchange of fluids: Professor Van Helsing reminds Seward not to breathe a word about the transfusion to Lucy's fiancé, Arthur, since it would engender jealousy. In this context one might usefully recall the remark made by Ernest Jones in his 1931 study *On the Nightmare* that "in the unconscious mind blood is commonly an equivalent for semen."[29] Moreover, as Elisabeth Bronfen has pointed out, the "artificial reanimation" that takes place in *Dracula* "is also a representation of paternal birthgiving ('a feeling of personal pride'), pitched against natural decay, and implicitly against the maternal function."[30]

In *The Lifted Veil* the mingling of bodily fluids in Mrs. Archer's body, ensuring her temporary resurrection, reveals her intense hatred for Bertha. "The scene," as Mary Jacobus puts it, "presents as self-evident the proposition that women are murderously commonplate, morally debased, loving neither men nor each other, but only themselves; and that this essential, unredeemably carnal feminine nature persists even beyond death—residing in the body itself" (*Reading Woman*, p. 269). But the transfusion leads to more than this. Mrs. Archer's words are not so much inward looking as oracular, pointing an accusing finger at Bertha, pronouncing the authoritative evidence for her mistress's murderous intentions toward Latimer. The intake of *male* blood, through the combined power of Meunier's body and profession (for class as well as gender boundaries are traversed in this transfusion), gives Mrs. Archer new power to speak. This is something that may be related back to the way in which this text functions as an experiment, among other things, in George Eliot's awareness of the complications involved in a woman author writing with masculine authority—whether one takes "masculine" in the sense of personal identity or dominant discourse.

Yet in the long run a pathologized reading of *The Lifted Veil* invites interpreting the novella not just in the light of experiments in transfusion and, by extension, the way in which making the inner voice public may involve entering a masculine world: the work may also usefully be placed back in the context of *The Physiology of Common Life* as a whole, which entails more than looking at the physical and figurative broaching of gender boundaries, even if the gendering of knowledge may still be at stake. Lewes's text, like George Eliot's story, is concerned with the relationship of the normal and the abnormal, the connections between mind and brain and between cerebral activity and physical functions. George Eliot shows not just in this novella but in subsequent writings that it is essential to acknowledge, as Lewes does in his physiological and psy-

chological works, the interrelations of mental and physical processes. But this does not mean that one should seek to be able to subject aspects of the mind's operations to detailed scientific scrutiny in order to unveil them. Latimer's "superadded consciousness" is in many ways a dramatization of the desire voiced by Lewes: "If for a moment we could with the bodily eye see into the frame of man." But the experiment does not necessarily yield wondrous results, even if the promise of just such a revelatory experience is what any imaginative novelist holds out. Rather, through Latimer's unveiling of others' thoughts, George Eliot suggests that the experience might be a tawdry rather than a miraculous one; instead of providing a welcome, miraculous revelation:

> it urged on me the trivial experience of indifferent people, became an intense pain and grief when it seemed to be opening to me the souls of those who were in a close relation to me—when the rational talk, the graceful attentions, the wittily-turned phrases, and the kindly deeds, which used to make the web of their characters, were seen as if thrust asunder by a microscopic vision, that showed all the intermediate frivolities, all the suppressed egoism, all the struggling chaos of puerilities, meanness, vague capricious memories, and indolent make-shift thoughts, from which human words and deeds emerge like leaflets covering a fermenting heap.
>
> (pp. 19-20)

The weaknesses of Latimer's brother's character, for example, may be read not through ordinary behaviorial gestures, "but in all their naked skinless complication" (p. 21).

In the chapter in *The Physiology of Common Life* entitled "Feeling and Thinking" Lewes makes it extremely clear that he regards his own task as a physiologist as essentially different from that of the psychologist. While mind and body are for him in constant interplay, "our science does not pretend to cope with the mysteries of [the psychologist's]" (II, 3). In going along with this, as she does, George Eliot is tacitly contesting the orthodoxy of her time that a woman's mental processes may be explained by the functions of her body. Lewes continues by noting that although the mysteries of the mind's workings will most probably forever remain unsolved, the labors of physiologists have in the meantime "made it possible that there should be at least a science of those vital phenomena connected with the Nervous System; and 'thus,' to use the fine expression of Professor Huxley, 'from the region of disorderly mystery, which is the domain of ignorance, another vast province has been added to science, the realm of *orderly mystery*'" (*Physiology*, II, 3-4). Yet it is important that this sense of mystery is acknowledged. It is as orderly mystery, *The Lifted Veil* suggests, that the workings of the minds of others are perhaps best preserved. This is consonant, in fact, with George Eliot's views concerning other contemporary scientific developments. Following the publication of *On the Origin of Species* later that same year, on 5 December 1859 she wrote to Barbara Bodichon that "to me the Development theory and all other explanations of processes by which things came to be, produce a feeble impression compared with the mystery that lies under the processes" (*George Eliot Letters,* III, 227).

In *The Lifted Veil* George Eliot implicitly questions the idea that mental processes may most usefully be understood by examining a conjectured continuous relationship between mind and body. In so doing she conspicuously interrogates the positivistic implications and desires of contemporary physiological science. Moreover, in arguing that we perhaps would not want to see where we might be able to see—if science would allow us to—George Eliot's novella challenges that often-assumed Victorian drive toward making things visible. By establishing the precise scientific context of *The Lifted Veil* and demonstrating George Eliot's knowledge of contemporary medical debate, we can see this work as a deliberate questioning of the desirability of specularity. Rendering "the invisible visible by imagination,"[31] she suggests, is far more valuable as a tool for understanding the human mind than is lifting aside the fleshly veil and looking within with the bodily eye.

Notes

1. Edith Simcox, quoted in *The George Eliot Letters,* ed. Gordon S. Haight, 9 vols. (New Haven: Yale Univ. Press, 1954-78), IX, 220.

2. See Carroll Viera, "'The Lifted Veil' and George Eliot's Early Aesthetic," *Studies in English Literature, 1500-1900,* 24 (1984), 749-67; and Sandra M. Gilbert and Susan Gubar, *The Madwoman in the Attic: The Woman Writer and the Nineteenth-Century Literary Imagination* (New Haven: Yale Univ. Press, 1979), pp. 443-77.

3. For a full discussion of the implications of veil imagery, see Gilbert and Gubar's chapter; see also Eve Kosofsky Sedgwick, "The Character in the Veil: Imagery of the Surface in the Gothic Novel," *PMLA,* 96 (1981), 255-70.

4. Percy Bysshe Shelley, "Sonnet, 'Lift not the painted veil . . . ,'" in *Poetical Works,* ed. Thomas Hutchinson, new ed. corrected by G. M. Matthews (New York: Oxford Univ. Press, 1978), p. 569.

5. George Eliot, *The Lifted Veil* (London: Virago, 1985), p. 26. Further references are to this edition and appear in the text.

6. See Gillian Beer, "Myth and the Single Consciousness: *Middlemarch* and *The Lifted Veil,*" in *This Particular Web: Essays on "Middlemarch,"* ed. Ian Adam (Toronto: Univ. of Toronto Press, 1975), pp. 91-115; and Terry Eagleton, "Power and Knowledge in 'The Lifted Veil,'" *Literature & History,* 9 (1983), 52-61.

7. Barbara Maria Stafford, *Body Criticism: Imaging the Unseen in Enlightenment Art and Medicine* (Cambridge, Mass.: MIT Press, 1991), p. 17.

8. *The Birth of the Clinic: An Archaeology of Medical Perception,* trans. A. M. Sheridan Smith (New York: Pantheon, 1973), p. 120.

9. See Robert M. Young, *Mind, Brain, and Adaptation in the Nineteenth Century: Cerebral Localization and Its Biological Context from Gall to Ferrier* (Oxford: Clarendon Press, 1970).

10. G. H. Lewes, *A Biographical History of Philosophy,* 4 vols. (London: Charles Knight, 1845-46), IV, 256.

11. Lawrence Rothfield, *Vital Signs: Medical Realism in Nineteenth-Century Fiction* (Princeton: Princeton Univ. Press, 1992), p. 106.

12. See B. M. Gray, "Pseudoscience and George Eliot's 'The Lifted Veil,'" *Nineteenth-Century Fiction,* 36 (1982), 407-23.

13. See William Gregory, *Letters to a Candid Inquirer, on Animal Magnetism* (London: Taylor, Walton, and Maberly, 1851), pp. 425-40.

14. This is, of course, no more than an application of the meditation on Latimer's part that George Eliot inserts into the text: "So absolute is our soul's need of something hidden and uncertain for the maintenance of that doubt and hope and effort which are the breath of its life, that if the whole future were laid bare to us beyond to-day, the interest of all mankind would be bent on the hours that lie between; we should pant after the uncertainties of our one morning and our one afternoon; we should rush fiercely to the Exchange for our last possibility of speculation, of success, of disappointment; we should have a glut of political prophets foretelling a crisis or a no-crisis within the only twenty-four hours left open to prophecy. Conceive the condition of the human mind if all propositions whatsoever were self-evident except one, which was to become self-evident at the close of the summer's day, but in the meantime might be the subject of question, of hypothesis, of debate. Art and philosophy, literature and science, would fasten like bees on that one proposition which had the honey of probability in it, and be the more eager because their enjoyment would end with sunset" (pp. 43-44).

15. *Ghosts of the Gothic: Austen, Eliot, and Lawrence* (Princeton: Princeton Univ. Press, 1980), p. 185.

16. *Reading Woman: Essays in Feminist Criticism* (New York: Columbia Univ. Press, 1986), p. 269.

17. Gray, "Afterword" to *The Lifted Veil,* pp. 69, 87.

18. Jennifer Uglow, *George Eliot* (London: Virago, 1987), p. 118.

19. U. C. Knoepflmacher, *George Eliot's Early Novels: The Limits of Realism* (Berkeley and Los Angeles: Univ. of California Press, 1968), p. 148.

20. For biographical details, see J.M.D. Olmsted, *Charles-Édouard Brown-Séquard: A Nineteenth Cen-*

tury Neurologist and Endocrinologist (Baltimore: Johns Hopkins Press, 1946).

21. E. Brown-Séquard, "Recherches sur la possibilité de rappeler temporairement à la vie des individus mourant de maladie," *Journal de la Physiologie de l'homme et des animaux,* 1 (1858), 672 (my translation).

22. George Eliot, who had been told of this work by Emilia Pattison, commented in a 12 June 1879 letter to William Blackwood: "I call this amusing—I ought rather to have said typical of the relation my books generally have with the French mind" (*George Eliot Letters,* VII, 165).

23. A. Vulpian, *Leçons sur la Physiologie générale et comparée du système nerveux faites au muséum d'histoire naturelle* (Paris: G. Baillière, 1866), p. 460 (my translation).

24. See [S. Weir Mitchell], "Was He Dead?" *Atlantic Monthly,* 25 (1870), 86-102. I am most grateful to Lucy Bending for drawing this story to my attention.

25. George Henry Lewes, *The Physiology of Common Life,* 2 vols. (Edinburgh and London: William Blackwood, 1859) I, 254.

26. Julia Kristeva, *Powers of Horror: An Essay on Abjection,* trans. Leon S. Roudiez (New York: Columbia Univ. Press, 1982), p. 71.

27. See Charles Egerton Jennings, *Transfusion: Its History, Indications, and Modes of Application* (London: Baillière, Tindall, and Cox, 1883), pp. 3, 22, 35.

28. Bram Stoker, *Dracula,* ed. A. N. Wilson (New York: Oxford Univ. Press, 1983), p. 128.

29. *On the Nightmare* (London: The Hogarth Press and the Institute of Psycho-analysis, 1931), p. 110.

30. *Over Her Dead Body: Death, Femininity, and the Aesthetic* (Manchester: Manchester Univ. Press, 1992), p. 317.

31. This phrase is in fact Lewes's, from an essay of 1865, demonstrating still further the two-way circulation of ideas in this personal and intellectual partnership (see "Imagination," in *The Principles of Success in Literature,* ed. T. Sharper Knowlson [London: Walter Scott, 1898], p. 55).

Ted Underwood (essay date 1997)

SOURCE: "The Science in Shelley's Theory of Poetry," in *Modern Language Quarterly,* Vol. 58, No. 3, September, 1997, pp. 298-321.

[*In the following essay, Underwood evaluates Shelley's engagement with contemporary debates on science and natural philosophy, remarking on the connections between his scientific studies and poetic theories.*]

Awareness of Percy Shelley's interest in science has had surprisingly little effect on criticism of his poetry. Romanticists have known since the publication of Carl Grabo's *Newton among Poets* that many of Shelley's images were modeled on the science of his time.[1] But when critics offer extended readings of his works, they generally choose to view those connections as something to note briefly and set aside. Some still feel, with C. M. Bowra, that "scientific speculations" are "not very relevant" to studies of Shelley, because "he transforms them to suit his own system. They concern, in his view, not matter but spirit."[2]

The skeptical idealism of most of Shelley's works is beyond dispute, but it need not imply an inversion of contemporary scientific ideas. Shelley's skeptical bracketing of matter was influenced by thinkers like William Drummond, who followed Newton's first rule of reasoning: Introduce no more hypothetical causes than are necessary to explain observed phenomena.[3] Drummond and Shelley used that principle to reject the logical necessity of matter itself, to be sure, but in so doing they followed a path set by British natural philosophers. Joseph Priestley and James Hutton had already invoked Newton's rule to dispose of inert, solid matter as a superfluous hypothesis.[4]

The ontological distinction between materialism and idealism is not, however, the most serious obstacle to understanding the importance of science in Shelley's thought. Recent historical critics of Shelley tend not to insist on ontology as firmly as Bowra did, but they reproduce the same separation of science and poetry as a literary-historical distinction between Enlightenment and romanticism. For instance, Shelley's acquaintance with Enlightenment science is said to have been mediated through mesmerism and occult tradition, so that "all science tended to become for Shelley 'occult science.'"[5] Explicitly or implicitly it is assumed that the scientific imagery in his works ceased, after *Queen Mab* (1813), to have any connection to mainstream scientific discourse. The reason for the assumption is not ontological but disciplinary: it allows critics to retain the period boundaries that organize literary study, as well as the more important distinction between cultural criticism and the history of science.

Early-twentieth-century critics like Grabo were interested in Shelley's science because they saw the truth of his ideas about the natural world as an index to the prophetic character, and truth, of his poetry (197). Thus Grabo concentrated chiefly on the aspects of Shelley's science that seemed to have been confirmed by subsequent research. More recently, historical critics of Shelley have sought to examine science simply as a facet of romantic culture.[6] But the subjects contemporary critics choose to write about suggest that they have reversed Grabo's criterion rather than set it aside. Romanticists now concentrate primarily on scientific discourses that, like mesmerism and physiognomy, are no longer used by anyone to guide interaction with the world. Such discourses are no less "scientific" than chemistry—the term *pseudoscience* has no place in historical study—but since they are now quite dead, they lend themselves to being read as culture and nothing but culture.[7] There is no remainder of life in physiognomy to hint that its determining factors may not be exhausted by cultural criticism.

Scientific texts that have living descendants, on the other hand, seem disqualified from critical consideration. Hutton's theory of "subterraneous fire" and Lavoisier's oxygen theory of combustion were at least as controversial and as fascinating to contemporaries as mesmerism, but in recent criticism references to Mesmer vastly outnumber references to Lavoisier. Romanticists too often adhere in practice to a distinction between science and pseudoscience that they have rightly discarded in principle; they seem unwilling to believe that texts can be at once falsifiable claims about the world and important cultural productions. It thus becomes necessary to assert that Shelley's scientific ideas have undergone a thorough transmutation. If "all science tended to become for Shelley 'occult science,'" the scientific ideas in his writing can be read as a discourse whose cultural status few will now doubt and can be thereby re-created as a safe object for literary study. Scientific ideas are, in effect, converted into literature by the cultural critic, if not (as Bowra had demanded) by the poet.

This view of literary history may seem to accord with Shelley's own aesthetic theory. His "Defence of Poetry," for instance, tells us that poetry "transmutes all that it touches, and every form moving within the radiance of its presence is changed by wondrous sympathy to an incarnation of the spirit which it breathes."[8] But for Shelley, the radiance of poetry is an aspect of all perception; never fully present in a written poem, it "is that which comprehends all science and that to which all science must be referred" (293). Romanticists have turned Shelley's figure of a transmuting light to different ends by using it as a theory of the historical relation between poetic and other discourses. Implying that poems alter the mere knowledge they encounter into a form of being or a form of power, this theory of literary history excludes scientific ideas from serious critical consideration. Yet Shelley's figure for poetic transmutation—a radiance that reveals the world only by reproducing the world as an incarnation of its own power—was itself drawn from the science of his time.

Shelley's engagement with natural philosophy was long and continuous, but the connections between his scientific reading and his poetic theory can be seen at their most condensed in late poems, including the "Hymn of Apollo" and "Epipsychidion," that develop figures subsequently used in the "Defence of Poetry." In these texts Shelley relied on scientific ideas about sunlight to develop a figural logic that represents poetry neither simply as mimesis nor simply as inspiration but as a light that pervades all things and reveals them by reproducing them within itself. To say that his theory of poetry was "modeled" on science would understate the connection. It developed out of natural philosophy (and philosophical poetry) in a way that makes it impossible to say where scientific reasoning ends and po-

etic reasoning begins. The "Defence of Poetry" implies a union of perception, pleasure, and creative power, but so did the science on which it was based. Shelley did not treat the scientific ideas he borrowed as mere conceits or invert them so as to reach a different conclusion. He changed them mainly by using figural reasoning to foreground consequences that scientists, and other poets, had left implicit.

APOLLO AND THE CHEMISTRY OF LIGHT

When early-nineteenth-century poets suggest that a lifelike power may inhabit, roll through, or brood over the apparently inanimate world, it is not often helpful to ask whether the poem is about, say, the recent discovery of galvanism. Such a mode of reading is unnecessarily limiting, not because it links poetry with science but because it underestimates the complexity of scientific writing in the period by treating it as a discourse that simply made new entities available for discussion. Experiments and philosophical texts were not deictic gestures but interventions in an ongoing debate over the boundaries between a variety of phenomena. Are light and heat identical, or does light produce heat only in certain kinds of matter? How many kinds of electric fluid are there? Is electric fluid condensed light? Rarely are the speculations in early-nineteenth-century poems assignably "about" electricity, galvanism, or light, whose boundaries were in flux. Any of them could serve as the starting point for a philosophical poem. But poets, like natural philosophers, were chiefly fascinated by the horizon of possibility where those entities might begin to converge.

So it is important to pay attention not just to the discovery of new phenomena but to the history of practicable connections between them. Light was hardly a new discovery, like galvanism, but it was nevertheless one of the most important vehicles for this sort of connection. Isaac Newton had suggested, in the "queries" added to the second English edition of his *Opticks* (1717), that a single elastic ether might account for gravity, for animal motion, and for the refraction of rays of light.[9] Whereas the *Opticks* maintained a distinction between the etheric medium and light, eighteenth-century reception of Newton's hypothesis tended to conflate this medium with elemental fire, electricity, and light itself, rather like the Stoic and alchemical traditions that had shaped Newton's early thought about the ether.[10]

In the 1770s chemical experiments on plants began to suggest a further connection, between light and the power of thought. After finding that plants could restore the air "vitiated" by animal respiration, Priestley reasoned that they absorbed "phlogiston," elemental fire, from the air. When animals ate plants, the phlogiston was converted into electric fluid by the brain.[11] Priestley already suspected that light was also a form of phlogiston (1:280); Jan Ingenhousz decisively connected this physiological argument to the sun by showing that plants purified air only when exposed to sunlight.[12] Though he disagreed with Priestley about phlogiston, Antoine Lavoisier accepted the connection between light and consciousness: "Organization, sensation, spontaneous motion, and all the operations of life, only exist . . . in places exposed to the influence of light. . . . By means of light, the benevolence of the Deity hath filled the surface of the earth with organization, sensation, and intelligence. The fable of Promotheus [*sic*] might perhaps be considered as giving a hint of this philosophical truth, which had even presented itself to the knowledge of the ancients."[13]

Lavoisier was not the first to perceive echoes of Greek myth in recent philosophy. The new chemistry of light fascinated writers because it seemed to ratify allegorical traditions (both classical and Christian) that made the sun a figure for God. Late-eighteenth-century poets reworked those traditions, however, by literalizing the allegory. Light became not an image of God's benevolent mind but itself a sort of benevolence or Godlike mind. In 1779, the same year Ingenhousz published *Experiments upon Vegetables,* Lady Anne Miller asked the visitors to her villa at Batheaston to contribute poems on the sun. One of them, S. J. Pratt ("Courtney Melmoth"), wrote an "Ode to the Sun" that combines natural philosophy with Greek myth.

> By thee our tender garlands grow,
> Our laurels shoot, our mirtles blow;
> By thee our Priestess forms her bower,
> Invoking still thy genial power.
>
> Thine, Phoebus, is the sparkling *thought*,
>   The radiant *verse,* the glowing *strain,*
> From thee is *inspiration* caught,
>   And thine the *sunshine* of the brain.[14]

It had long been recognized that the sun fostered the growth of plants, if only by warming the soil; likewise, an allegorical association between the sun and poetry, mediated by Apollo, was nothing new. What is new in Pratt's ode is that these claims are conjoined as parallel. The sun seems to endow minds with "sparkling thought" in the same way that it grows vegetation. The insistent adjectives—"sparkling," "radiant," "glowing"—make "thought" and "verse" into luminous substances like light or electric fluid; the power in the poet and the "genial power" growing the poet's laurel wreath are the same.

Other poets of sensibility, like Anna Seward, similarly used solar imagery to justify a merging of genial and intellectual power, which unite in the sun's "life-enkindling light" as they do in poetry.[15] Seward's recurring metaphor for poetic power, "the Sun of Genius" (2:135; see also 1:12, 2:347, 3:67, 3:338, 3:371), was not an empty flourish. The sun became the chief figure for genius in the poetry of sensibility for reasons at once poetic and philosophical: the premise that light was also an animating "electric fire" made it possible to represent animation and enthusiasm as forms of enlightenment.[16] Mary Robinson's "Ode to Genius," for instance, begins by addressing genius as an illuminating power, a "SUN" providing a "lustrous stream of mental sight." But the poem indicates that the light of genius is also a source of inward animation:

> I've seen thee, through the soul diffuse
> Th' electric fire that fills the Muse!
> When o'er the poet's breast
> Thou fling'st thy sunny vest.[17]

The philosophical premise on which Robinson implicitly relies, that electricity and sunlight are interconvertible, allowed late-eighteenth-century poets to represent the "Sun of Genius" as a power that animated things precisely by enlightening them.

At least one British chemist shared the poets' interest in this figure. Humphry Davy (1778-1829) wrote a number of youthful poems that trace the energy of genius as it descends from its source in the sun.[18] In 1799 he tried to give the same idea a systematic chemical form. Davy updated Priestley's hypothesis that phlogiston was extracted in the brain to make it consistent with Lavoisier's oxygen theory: sunlight combines chemically with oxygen; the light can be liberated as fire, or (when oxygen is inhaled by animals) it can be extracted by the brain, where it becomes the material basis of "perception" and "pleasure."[19] The sun, itself a "reservoir" of consciousness, is centrally located to diffuse perception and pleasure throughout the solar system: "Thus will the laws of gravitation, as well as the chemical laws, be considered as subservient to one grand end, PERCEPTION. Reasoning thus, it will not appear impossible that one law alone may govern and act upon matter: an energy of mutation, impressed by the will of the Deity, a law which might be called the law of animation, tending to produce the greatest possible sum of perception, the greatest possible sum of happiness" ("An Essay," 85). For Davy, the chemistry of sunlight thus supports the same sort of connection between happiness and perception, animation and enlightenment, that the figure of the sun supported in the poems by Seward and Robinson.

Although there is no evidence that Shelley read Davy's 1799 essay, he encountered similar ideas through other reading and through friends. In 1812 he met Thomas Love Peacock; the two remained correspondents for the rest of Shelley's life. Also in 1812, as it happens, Peacock published an ode titled "The Spirit of Fire," in which he continues the philosophical tradition identifying consciousness with light. To do so without the earnest and omniscient perspective that had characterized late-eighteenth-century philosophical odes, Peacock mediated natural philosophy playfully through Zoroastrian mythology.[20] "The spirit of fire" is identified both as a god dwelling in a specific Persian temple and as the power of all light and fire. Speaking in the first person, it takes credit for life, for poetic inspiration, and for consciousness itself:

> In nascent beauty robed, the grateful earth
> Hailed my primordial power with loud acclaim,
>   That gave her countless tribes of being birth,
> And strung with motion man's commanding frame,
> And kindled in his mind my own empyreal flame.[21]

Both in its use of mythology and in its boastful, divine, and rather masculinist first-person speaker,[22] "The Spirit of

Fire" provides a likely model for Shelley's "Hymn of Apollo." It also marks an intermediate stage in the treatment of the subject: although Peacock (like Shelley) personifies the spirit of fire, he does not think about natural philosophy carefully enough to develop the figure's full implications.

THE SUN'S TRANSFORMING POWER: SHELLEY'S "HYMN OF APOLLO"

The "Hymn of Apollo" (1820) is one of a pair of poems that Percy Shelley contributed to Mary Shelley's play *Midas,* based in turn on a story from Ovid's *Metamorphoses.* Apollo and Pan are engaged in a singing contest that the hill god Tmolus will judge. After both deities sing, Tmolus gives the prize to Apollo, but the mortal king Midas remarks that he prefers Pan's singing. Apollo, displeased, gives Midas the ears of an ass. In Ovid, the king's preference for Pan is a sign of uncouth, rustic judgment, but readers of Mary Shelley's play are left to guess whose hymn is really superior. In fact the playwright balances the scales: Pan plausibly claims that Tmolus has a vested interest in preferring the sun god Apollo:

> Old Grey-beard, you say false! you think by this
> To win Apollo and his sultry beams
> To thaw your snowy head, and to renew
> The worn out soil of your bare, ugly hill![23]

The songs themselves illuminate opposed and complementary aspects of being, so that a final choice between them is neither possible nor necessary. Earl Wasserman aptly calls Pan's hymn a celebration of "lived experience."[24] But in describing Apollo as "the mind's ideal and abstract powers"—or, worse, as "absolute subjectivity" (49, 55)—Wasserman too hastily humanizes the sun god to make the singing contest dramatize opposing possibilities of specifically human existence. The opposition is on a rather larger scale. Apollo's power, of which the mind is a portion, extends beyond human capacities; it can, for instance, renew the "worn out soil" of a "bare, ugly hill." Apollo's "Hymn" differs from Pan's in speaking not about Apollo's perception but only about his actions and effects. His power brings the world to consciousness, both as light and as poetry, without being itself a subjectivity or a point of view.

In the first and second stanzas of his "Hymn" Apollo is personified as sun god. In the second stanza a complex metaphor, at once visual and abstractly erotic, expresses the sun's immediate presence in the world he illumines:

> Then I arise, and climbing Heaven's blue dome,
>   I walk over the mountains and the waves,
> Leaving my robe upon the ocean foam;
>   My footsteps pave the clouds with fire; the caves
> Are filled with my bright presence, and the air
> Leaves the green Earth to my embraces bare.[25]

The sun has left his "robe upon the ocean foam," and his nakedness finds an answering nakedness in "the green Earth." The sun's disrobing evokes the blazing image of the solar disk as it rises in the sky and leaves the softer colors of dawn behind. But it also expresses an unveiling of power that fills and partly constitutes transparent space. Even the caves of earth "are filled with my bright presence." Writing "bright presence" rather than "light" allows the poem to forget temporarily that the sun is a distant body sending out rays, in order to represent him as omnipresent and directly active throughout the spacious world. The sun does not pass through the air; rather, the air's transparency is a nakedness that leaves the earth "bare" to the sun's "embraces."

But the poem's forgetfulness serves a larger design. The solar omnipresence first represented as a mutual nakedness recurs in the fourth stanza, paradoxically, as clothing. Transforming things into incarnations of himself by robing them in his light, the sun reveals them in the only possible way. Optical mediation of the world, then, is inseparable from visual immediacy.

> I feed the clouds, the rainbows and the flowers
>   With their aethereal colours; the moon's globe
> And the pure stars in their eternal bowers
>   Are cinctured with my power as with a robe;
> Whatever lamps on Earth or Heaven may shine
> Are portions of one power, which is mine.

Since the theory of poetry Shelley developed in the following year also depends on the figure of a power that "transmutes all that it touches" by clothing things in its own light, it is worth looking at the passage in some detail.

In writing "I feed the clouds, the rainbows and the flowers / With their aethereal colours," Shelley chooses examples that show (as "feed" implies) that the sun's light not only reveals but constitutes color. The first two examples draw on the Newtonian idea that all colors are latent in sunlight and become visible when separated. Separation through refraction creates the rainbow. Clouds acquire their colors, according to Newton, through selective reflection: particles of different sizes (in themselves transparent) reflect different colors of sunlight.[26]

In referring to "flowers," Shelley may be drawing on the same Newtonian idea and merely pointing out that the color of flowers is itself reflected sunlight. But the rest of the stanza suggests that he is alluding to a more recent hypothesis: the sun's light endows all living things with color through its chemical action. After Ingenhousz discovered that plants carried out chemical reactions when exposed to sunlight, a number of writers, including the self-taught scientific lecturer Adam Walker (1731-1821), concluded that the color, fragrance, and combustibility of plants were effects of the sunlight or "elemental fire" stored in them.[27] Shelley heard Walker's lectures at Syon House and again at Eton.[28] Davy, a more widely respected source, also attributed the color in plants and animals to sunlight and stated specifically that "flowers owe the variety of their hues to the influence of the solar beams" in *Elements of Chemical Philosophy,* which Percy Shelley owned and read with Mary late in 1816.[29]

Paired with Shelley's knowledge of Newton, such photo-chemical ideas fully justify Apollo's claim that the sun feeds the earth with color. Not that Shelley is writing "about" science; he is allowing Apollo to speak in a way that contemporary readers would have understood as a playful allusion to natural philosophy, but both author and reader remain free to interpret Apollo's claims as a description of the unity of visual experience.

That unity, however, is directly modeled on the scientific claim, most strikingly expressed in the stanza's concluding couplet, that visual phenomena are constituted by sunlight: "Whatever lamps on Earth or Heaven may shine / Are portions of one power, which is mine." The lamps of heaven are easily explained: Shelley would have known that the moon and planets were seen by reflected sunlight and also that the fixed stars were bodies like our sun, producing light by the same (unknown, but probably chemical) processes.[30] Apollo's claim about "lamps on Earth" is more interesting, because it shows how natural philosophy continued to underwrite the romantic merging of perception and pleasure, vision and animation. We have seen that it was a commonplace of late-eighteenth-century natural philosophy "that it is the light of the sun which is here stored up in the substance of vegetable bodies, as fixed light, or phlogiston, the principle of fire."[31] Walker's lectures filled Shelley with enthusiasm specifically for "the element of *fire*."[32] By the 1810s Lavoisier's oxygen theory of combustion had supplanted theories of phlogiston and elemental fire, but the hypothesis that all inflammable compounds were produced by sunlight survived.[33] Shelley's readers would have been likely to agree that sunlight and "lamps on Earth" were literally "portions of one power."

But we need not take "lamps on Earth" to refer merely to visual illumination. Apollo has already claimed responsibility for moral "light" in the third stanza, and the poem ends with a reference to the "light" of poetry:

> I am the eye with which the Universe
>   Beholds itself and knows itself divine;
> All harmony of instrument or verse,
>   All prophecy, all medicine is mine,
>   All light of art or nature;—to my song
> Victory and praise in its own right belong.

Apollo's is both a visible power and a power of the mind; it encompasses "all light of art or nature."[34] Yet Apollo is more than a figure for knowledge or perception. The universe does not just "know itself" through him; at once revealed and transfigured by his power, it "knows itself divine." Apollo is less a subjectivity than a power that reveals the world by animating it.

Shelley himself may well have understood the union of visible, intellectual, and poetic light in idealist terms. In a world where "nothing exists but as it is perceived," there is simply no reason to draw a rigid distinction between sunlight and poetry; both can be understood as aspects of a greater power that constitutes all perception.[35] But the union of sunlight and poetry represented by Apollo was in no way dependent on Shelley's idealism. Writers like Davy, Seward, and Pratt had already used the chemistry of light to link the sun's vegetative power and "the sunshine of the brain." Peacock, Shelley's close friend, had made similar claims in a poem whose boastful first-person speaker provided a likely model for Apollo. Peacock's notes show that he meant to imply the material identity of light, elemental fire, and "nervous fluid" (259). But the line dividing "materialism" from "idealism" in this tradition is thin, since both Peacock and Shelley understand the "empyreal flame" provided by the sun not merely as the basis of consciousness but as consciousness itself.

What distinguishes Shelley's "Hymn of Apollo" from earlier treatments of the theme is not its idealist ontology but its skepticism, which surfaces in Apollo's remark that the moral effect of his light lasts only "until diminished by the reign of Night." The stress on transience suggests not that night has an alternative moral claim to make but that the absolute illumination represented by Apollo is always qualified, always fading, in the temporal realm of human experience. The "Hymn of Pan," an emblem of that realm, emphasizes this limitation by dwelling on twilight:

> Liquid Peneus was flowing,
>   And all dark Tempe lay
> In Pelion's shadow, outgrowing
>   The light of the dying day,
>   Speeded by my sweet pipings.
>
> (*Poetical Works*, 613)

Present participles—"flowing," "outgrowing," and "dying"—emphasize that twilight is not a moment but a process. The sun enters the mutable world only as a "shadow" or as something already "dying." The same veiled and fading sun appears in many of Shelley's earlier poems, especially "The Sunset" (1816), where the figure similarly underlines the limitation of mortal knowledge. The skepticism of the "Hymn of Pan" is balanced, however, against the omnipresent power of the "Hymn of Apollo," and neither poem entirely cancels the other. Nor are power and skepticism folded into each other here as in some of Shelley's earlier poems. Apollo is not a "secret Strength" as in "Mont Blanc" (1816), nor is he, like Demogorgon, "ungazed upon and shapeless," darting rays of gloom.[36] He is a principle that animates and transfigures the world to make perception possible, without himself being perceived.

SOLAR IMAGERY AND SHELLEY'S THEORY OF POETRY, 1820-1821

Other poems written in 1820, including the brief lyric "Liberty," continue to experiment with the same set of scientific ideas about the sun. But the main development of Shelley's solar imagery between the "Hymn of Apollo" and the "Defence of Poetry" takes place in "Epipsychidion," addressed to an auditor named Emily who is consistently characterized as an "Incarnation of the Sun" (*Poetical Works*, 419). The solar metaphor underlines the speaker's central erotic claim: "Ah me! / I am not thine: I am a part of *thee*" (51-2). Like Apollo, Emily penetrates, animates, and transfigures both the world and the mind. That Shelley assigns this role indifferently to male and female figures is not especially liberating: Apollo, one should recall, is more a power than a perspective, and Emily acquires his power but not his abstractly first-person voice. "Epipsychidion" does nothing, in short, to rise above the masculinism inherent in the conventional representation of woman as muse. It is nevertheless an important stage in the development of Shelley's theory of poetry, because it begins to bring his scientific conception of poetry as a transforming light into connection with more familiar tropes of aesthetic theory:

> Thou Wonder, and thou Beauty, and thou Terror!
> Thou Harmony of Nature's art! Thou Mirror
> In whom, as in the splendour of the Sun,
> All shapes look glorious which thou gazest on!
>
> (29-32)

The analogy between mirror, sun, and eye has resisted explication; commentators who do not ignore it usually remark that confusion itself is the only referent. John F. Slater finds that the poem's subsequent reference to "'dim words that obscure' attests to a clear understanding of its own maneuvers."[37] For Wasserman, similarly, "the indeterminacy of Emily's nature" points to "man's paradoxical condition" (427).

Having discussed the scientific rationale of Shelley's solar imagery, we see that the passage is not incoherent. It is obscure, but largely because Shelley is working with a figural shorthand borrowed from earlier poems. We have seen that in the "Hymn of Apollo" the sun is "the eye with which the Universe / Beholds itself and knows itself divine." In the "Ode to Heaven" (1819) Shelley referred to the sun as a mirror: "that Power which is the glass / Wherein man his nature sees" (*Poetical Works,* 576). In "Epipsychidion" the metaphors of sun-as-eye and sun-as-mirror fuse into a new and more complex image:

> Thou Mirror
> In whom, as in the splendour of the Sun,
> All shapes look glorious which thou gazest on!

Critics usually assume that the "mirror" of the sun's splendor belongs to the earth, which reflects the sun's light, and find the image inconsistent with the metaphor of the sun as a gazing eye or lamp. But as in Shelley's "Hymn of Apollo," where all things that the sun colors become "portions" of its power, all things that the sun shines on here are reproduced as portions of its "splendour" and in that sense become portions of the sun itself. The mirror is not the earth at all but the sun, which reproduces things "within" itself in a more glorious form. Simultaneously the world is brought to consciousness, and thus the sun can be understood not only as a mirror and a lamp but as an eye. Shelley's knowledge of natural philosophy allows him to reconcile traditionally incompatible figures for aesthetic production in the single figure of the sun.

Shelley's "Defence of Poetry" (March 1821), written immediately after "Epipsychidion" (January-February 1821),

is shaped by the same solar imagery in ways not usually recognized. Shelley had planned the "Defence" as a letter to the editor of *Ollier's Literary Miscellany,* in which Peacock's "Four Ages of Poetry" had appeared. He soon found that "the subject . . . requires more words than I expected" and composed a freestanding essay,[38] but the first draft of the letter to Charles Ollier shows how the solar imagery he had elaborated in the "Hymn of Apollo" and "Epipsychidion" entered into his conception of the "Defence." After a long, wry summary of Peacock's repudiation of poetry, the argument turns around: "These are indeed high objects, [*& I pledge myself to worship Themis rather than Apollo if . . . if it could be found that . . .*]" (Letters, 2:273).[39] The draft then breaks off and begins again; the mention of Apollo has brought solar imagery to mind: "So dark a paradox as to . . . absorb the brightest rays of mind which fall upon it. . . . He would extinguish Imagination which is the Sun of life, & grope his way by the cold & uncertain & borrowed light of the Moon which he calls Reason,—stumbling over the interlunar chasm of time where she deserts us, and an owl, rather than an eagle, stare with dazzled eyes on the watery orb which is the Queen of his pale Heaven" (*Letters,* 2:273).

The passage circles around a single analogy: imagination is to life what the sun is to the visible world. In framing it as an argument, Shelley tries to base his rhetorical point on the absurdity of an attempt to extinguish the sun in favor of the moon, reason. The strategy continues with the mock-outraged remark "[*I hope soon to see . . . a Treatise against the light of the Sun in . . . one of your columns*]" a few lines later, but not very successfully. Either the letter-to-the-editor form is uncongenial—Shelley makes an awkward curmudgeon—or Shelley is handicapped by the necessity of introducing humor to palliate what is, after all, an attack on a friend. In the final version he wisely drops all direct reference to Peacock, and the mock outrage gives way to a measured analytic tone; consequently, Shelley no longer needs the machinery of suns and moons and owls and eagles. But the underlying analogy—poetry is to life what the sun is to the visible world—remains central.

In the "Defence" poetry is repeatedly compared to light (*Prose,* 276, 280, 282, 286, 294); more important, its light is represented as both laying bare and reclothing the world. In the "Hymn of Apollo" the sun's "bright presence" at once reveals the world and reproduces it as a portion of its own power; in the "Defence," similarly, "poetry lifts the veil from the hidden beauty of the world and makes familiar objects be as if they were not familiar; it reproduces all that it represents, and the impersonations clothed in its Elysian light stand thenceforward in the minds of those who have once contemplated them as memorials of that gentle and exalted content which extends itself over all thoughts and actions with which it coexists" (*Prose,* 282). This sentence's two halves, although connected by a semicolon, appear to make two very different claims. Poetry unveils the world, but it does so by impersonating the world and reproducing it in a newly clothed form. The business of taking clothes off by putting them on has puzzled commentators ever since M. H. Abrams concluded that it exposes "a combination of Platonism and of psychological empiricism, and of the mimetic and expressive point of view."[40] The solution to the paradox lies not in Plato or in Hume, however, but in ideas about the sun that Shelley drew from natural philosophy and invoked in the "Hymn of Apollo" and "Epipsychidion."[41] Shelley models his claims for poetry on his claims for the sun, whose light reveals things in their nakedness by clothing them "with my power as with a robe." This figural logic does much to explain the peculiarly Shelleyan conflation of mimetic and expressive theories throughout the "Defence."

The general project of combining such theories was not new. Any theory of the imagination as a synthetic power implies that the mind's own activity complements perception so as to color, assimilate, or recreate the things perceived. But the "Defence" extends the idea to argue that the harmonious order thus established (which Shelley calls poetry) actually makes perception itself—and, indeed, all knowledge—possible. Poetry "is at once the center and circumference of knowledge. . . . It is the perfect and consummate surface and bloom of all things" (*Prose*, 293).[42] The nearest equivalent to this merging of imagination and perception is the comparison that Coleridge draws in the thirteenth chapter of the *Biographia Literaria* between the "secondary imagination," a conscious and synthetic power, and the primary imagination, "the living Power and prime Agent of all human Perception, and . . . a repetition in the finite mind of the eternal act of creation in the infinite I AM."[43]

But Coleridge, as a Christian, can compare the creative act of a finite mind to perception understood as the creative act of an infinite mind. Shelley, who abjured a creative God, finds it much more difficult to make a convincing link between perception and imagination. His main intellectual proposition, that poetry, in defamiliarizing the world, "unveils" it and reveals it anew, serves a larger figural argument: "Poetry turns all things to loveliness. . . . It transmutes all that it touches, and every form moving within the radiance of its presence is changed by wondrous sympathy to an incarnation of the spirit which it breathes; its secret alchemy turns to potable gold the poisonous waters which flow from death through life; it strips the veil of familiarity from the world and lays bare the naked and sleeping beauty, which is the spirit of its forms" (295). In one long sentence the claim that poetry transmutes things into incarnations of itself strangely metamorphoses into the apparently contradictory claim that poetry "lays bare the naked and sleeping beauty" of the world. But Shelley needs both halves of the paradox. If poetry were merely a transmuting power, it might be understood to disguise the world rather than to reveal it. If it merely defamiliarized the world and laid it bare, it might permit clear perception, but it could not be described as "the perfect and consummate surface and bloom of all things." What Shelley implies, therefore, is that poetry reveals things by transmuting them into itself.

This paradox is borrowed from the solar logic that Shelley developed in "Epipsychidion" and the "Hymn of Apollo," and traces of the original metaphor can still be detected. "The radiance of its presence," for instance, echoes Apollo's "bright presence," which transformed all things into portions of one power as poetry does here. Furthermore, "potable gold" alludes to the description of the sun in book 3 of *Paradise Lost*. There the sun's "arch-chemic" power, compared to that of the philosopher's stone, makes rivers on the sun's surface run "potable gold" (3.608-9). Shelley's reference to a "secret alchemy" underlines the aptness of the allusion: poetry for Shelley, like the sun for Milton, is a transmuting power. But the allusion serves theoretical ends determined by the chemical and poetic discourse of Shelley's own time; nothing in the alchemical tradition suggested that the sun revealed the world *by* transmuting it. Shelley's insistence on the inseparability of the two processes develops out of his own poetic engagement with natural philosophy; it can be traced most immediately not to alchemy but to late-eighteenth-century chemists' and poets' fascination with the sun's ability simultaneously to animate and to enlighten.[44]

For Shelley, however, the transfiguration effected by poetry is fleeting and imperfect. The tension between solar imagery and skepticism in the pairing of the "Hymn of Apollo" with the "Hymn of Pan" reappears in the "Defence" as a tension between the claims that poetry is "the perfect and consummate surface and bloom of all things" and that it is an "unapprehended inspiration" (297). Just as Apollo's light is always already "dying" by the time it enters the realm of Pan, "the mind in creation is as a fading coal," so that "the most glorious poetry that has been communicated to the world is probably a feeble shadow of the original conceptions of the poet" (294).

Eloquently summarizing the skeptical implications of this famous simile, Angela Leighton remarks that Shelley "refuses to affirm Poetry as an abiding presence."[45] His skepticism about the ability of mortal faculties to apprehend poetry coexists, however, with a description of poetry as a light that reveals and transfigures the world. Poetry is not perceptible but is itself the power enabling perception. Poetry cannot be apprehended, but to be apprehended, the world must be re-created as a portion of poetry's power. Shelley constructed this paradoxical figure in poems, such as the "Hymn of Apollo" and "Epipsychidion," that rely heavily on natural philosophy for their ideas and imagery. His skepticism constantly undermines any attempt to represent poetic power as something immanent in the natural world. Nonetheless, he draws on natural philosophy for the connection between mimetic knowledge and expressive power.

This realization does not stand Shelley's "Defence" on its head but only clears away layers of anachronism that prevent modern readers from understanding it. To be sure, Shelley defends poetry against Peacock's idolatry of reason. But Shelley and other early-nineteenth-century writers understood natural science as a product of the synthetic imagination, which compares and combines, not solely as a product of reason.[46] Shelley did not set out in the "Defence" to attack scientific modes of knowledge or to distinguish them from poetry; rather, he hoped to incorporate scientific knowledge into poetry to show that it "is that which comprehends all science and that to which all science must be referred" (293). The encompassing gesture may be arrogant, but it needs to be criticized on philosophical rather than historical grounds. Since Shelley defines poetry as a power enabling all knowledge, the historical connection to science explored in this essay does not necessarily undermine his theory. He could quite consistently reply that the scientific ideas he borrowed were already informed by poetic imagination.

The case is different with theories of literary history that echo Shelley by modeling the relation between poetry and other discourses, or between romanticism and Enlightenment, on his account of the relation between perception and the world. As I have noted, Shelley's critics commonly play down the importance of natural science by arguing, in effect, that his writing "transmutes all that it touches." Science can enter only by being reproduced as a portion of a power called "poetry" in older versions of this argument and "romanticism" in more recent versions. Whereas Shelley's definition of poetry encompassed other discourses, twentieth-century critics have used his metaphor of transmutation to create a sharp boundary between poetry and falsifiable knowledge. But the construction of Shelley's metaphor itself shows that the boundary is not at all sharp. The photochemistry in late-eighteenth-century poems and philosophical essays already linked enlightenment with animation, and perception with happiness; it underwent changes in becoming a theory of poetry, but it did not need to be transubstantiated.

Notes

1. Grabo, *A Newton among Poets: Shelley's Use of Science in "Prometheus Unbound"* (Chapel Hill: University of North Carolina Press, 1930). Also useful is Peter Butter, *Shelley's Idols of the Cave,* Language and Literature, 7 (Edinburgh: Edinburgh University Press, 1954).

2. Bowra, *The Romantic Imagination,* Charles Eliot Norton Lectures (Cambridge, Mass.: Harvard University Press, 1949), 120. See also the dismissal of "scientific allegorizing" in Harold Bloom, *Shelley's Mythmaking* (Ithaca, N.Y.: Cornell University Press, 1969), 119.

3. The indebtedness of Shelley's skepticism to empirical philosophy was first explained by C. E. Pulos, *The Deep Truth: A Study of Shelley's Scepticism* (Lincoln: University of Nebraska Press, 1954). The connection to Newtonian tradition is particularly clear in Drummond, *Academical Questions* (1805; Ann Arbor, Mich.: University Microfilms, 1971), 201-4.

4. "Power and action is [*sic*] all that, in strict reasoning, can be concluded as really subsisting. . . . But be-

sides those powers, there is supposed, in the one theory, a thing with volume and figure, which the other theory does not require, and which in the science of metaphysics may be demonstrated not to exist, as a thing external or independent of our mind" (Hutton, *Dissertations on Different Subjects in Natural Philosophy* [Edinburgh: Strahan, 1792], 412-3).

5. Andrew J. Welburn, *Power and Self-Consciousness in the Poetry of Shelley* (New York: St. Martin's, 1986), 69. Welburn rightly argues that scientific ideas have in Shelley a "constant association with the sense of hidden reality" (69). To explain the association through the influence of mesmerism, however, he has to override biographical testimony that Shelley knew little about mesmerism before late 1820 (81). The "association with the sense of hidden reality" is, rather, present in mainstream science itself.

6. Thus Nigel Leask properly attacks the distinction between science and pseudoscience as a useless one ("Shelley's 'Magnetic Ladies': Romantic Mesmerism and the Politics of the Body," in *Beyond Romanticism: New Approaches to Texts and Contexts, 1780-1832,* ed. Stephen Copley and John Whale [London: Routledge, 1992], 53-4).

7. In this essay I use "science" as a name for a collection of discourses that were collectively called "natural philosophy" in the late eighteenth century and that came to be called "sciences" in the early nineteenth century.

8. "A Defence of Poetry," in *Shelley's Prose; or, The Trumpet of a Prophecy,* ed. David Lee Clark (London: Fourth Estate, 1988), 295.

9. Newton, *Opticks; or, A Treatise of the Reflections, Refractions, Inflections, and Colours of Light* (New York: Dover, 1952), 348-54.

10. See I. Bernard Cohen, *Franklin and Newton: An Inquiry into Speculative Newtonian Experimental Science and Franklin's Work in Electricity as an Example Thereof,* Memoirs of the American Philosophical Society, 43 (Philadelphia: American Philosophical Society, 1956), 232, 254. For a representative midcentury work identifying the ether with electricity and light, and naming the sun as the fountain of all three, see Richard Lovett, *Philosophical Essays* (Worcester: Lewis; London: J. Johnson, 1766), 232-40. In an early alchemical text Newton speculates that the ether might act simply as a vehicle for "the body of light" and describes it as "Natures universall agent, her secret fire, the onely ferment and principle of all vegetation" ("Of Natures Obvious Laws and Processes in Vegetation," in *The Janus Faces of Genius: The Role of Alchemy in Newton's Thought,* by Betty Jo Teeter Dobbs [Cambridge: Cambridge University Press, 1991], 264-5).

11. Priestley, *Experiments and Observations on Different Kinds of Air,* 3 vols. (London: J. Johnson, 1774-7), 1:277-80.

12. Ingenhousz, *Experiments upon Vegetables* (London: P. Elmsley, 1779), 28-30.

13. Lavoisier, *Elements of Chemistry,* trans. Robert Kerr (1790; rpt. New York: Dover, 1965), 184.

14. Pratt, *Miscellanies,* 4 vols. (London: T. Becket, 1785), 2:67.

15. Seward, as it happens, was one of Lady Miller's contributors ("Ode to the Sun" [1779], in *The Poetical Works of Anna Seward,* ed. Walter Scott, 3 vols. [Edinburgh: J. Ballantyne, 1810], 2:49).

16. Jerome McGann has recently drawn attention to the way light, "lustre," and "glowing" warmth function in Mary Robinson's verse as emblems of sensibility and enlightenment at once ("Mary Robinson and the Myth of Sappho," *Modern Language Quarterly* 56 [1995]: 60-3). I propose that the imagery of light can be doubly charged in this manner because of the eighteenth-century scientific belief that light, electric fire, and life are aspects of a single power that both illuminates and animates.

17. Robinson, "Ode to Genius," in *Poems,* 2 vols. (London: J. Evans, 1791-3), 2:126.

18. "The Life of the Spinosist," Humphry Davy Papers, Royal Institution, London, notebook 13c 7-10. An unreliable version is reprinted in Clement Carlyon, *Early Years and Late Reflections,* 4 vols. (London: Whittaker, 1858), 1:234-5.

19. "An Essay on Light, Heat, and the Combinations of Light," in *The Collected Works of Humphry Davy,* ed. John Davy, 9 vols. (London: Smith, Elder, 1839), 2:82-5.

20. The reasons for the early-nineteenth-century antipathy to the anonymous third-person voice fall outside the scope of this article. The classic treatment of the question is M. H. Abrams, "Structure and Style in the Greater Romantic Lyric," in *From Sensibility to Romanticism: Essays Presented to Frederick A. Pottle,* ed. Frederick W. Hilles and Harold Bloom (New York: Oxford University Press, 1965), 527-60. Paul Magnusson's recent analysis of Coleridge's poetic development in the 1790s suggests that the fundamental reason for the antipathy may be political ("The Shaping of 'Fears in Solitude,'" in *Coleridge's Theory of Imagination Today,* ed. Christine Gallant, Georgia State Literary Studies, 4 [New York: AMS Press, 1989], 200, 209).

21. Peacock, "The Spirit of Fire," in *Works,* ed. H. F. B. Brett-Smith and C. E. Jones, 10 vols. (London: Constable, 1927), 6:250-1.

22. Sunlight was not consistently identified as a male principle in late-eighteenth-century poetry. Davy, for instance, compares the sun's influence on the infant mind to the "orbed beauty" and "living rill" of a maternal breast ("Spinosist," 9).

23. Mary Shelley, *Midas,* in *"Proserpine" and "Midas,"* ed. A. Koszul (London: Humphrey Milford, 1922), 55.

24. Wasserman, *Shelley: A Critical Reading* (Baltimore, Md.: Johns Hopkins University Press, 1971), 49.

25. Shelley, *Poetical Works,* ed. Thomas Hutchinson (London: Oxford University Press, 1967), 612.

26. Particle size has this effect because light goes through "fits of easy reflection and easy transmission" (Newton, 281-5).

27. Walker, *A System of Familiar Philosophy in Twelve Lectures,* 2 vols. (London: Printed for the author, 1802), 2:101-3.

28. Andrew Amos, "Shelley and His Contemporaries at Eton," *Athenaeum,* 15 April 1848, 390. The connection between Walker and Shelley's poetry is also discussed in Butter (n. 1 above), 136, 140-8.

29. Davy, *Elements of Chemical Philosophy* (London: J. Johnson, 1812), 213; Mary Shelley, *Journal,* ed. F. L. Jones (Norman: University of Oklahoma Press, 1947), 67.

30. *British Encyclopedia; or, Dictionary of the Arts and Sciences* (London: Longman, Hurst, Rees, 1809-11), s.v. "astronomy."

31. James Hutton, *A Dissertation on the Philosophy of Light, Heat, and Fire* (Edinburgh: Cadell, 1794), 323.

32. Amos reported that Shelley began to call him, "after attending Walker's lectures," and "*Apurist*; indicating classically thereby one who did not appreciate properly the element of *fire*" (390). Shelley's well-known electrical experiments and his interest in "the element of fire" were two expressions of a single fascination. Walker had explicitly argued that electricity was fire in an elemental form (1:2).

33. The *British Encyclopedia,* s.v. "light," for instance, continued to speculate that "the light afforded by ignited bodies" may "have been previously imbibed by them" (see also Davy, *Elements,* 213).

34. A description of the sun as the "world's eye" can be found in both Ovid and Milton, but not with this implication. See Ovid, *Metamorphoses,* trans. Rolfe Humphries (Bloomington: Indiana University Press, 1955), 4.226-8; and Milton, *Paradise Lost,* ed. Scott Elledge (New York: Norton, 1975), 5.171-2.

35. Shelley, "On Life," in *Prose* (n. 8 above), 174.

36. Shelley, *Prometheus Unbound,* 2.4.5, in *Poetical Works,* 236.

37. Slater, "Self-Concealment and Self-Revelation in Shelley's 'Epipsychidion,'" *Papers on Language and Literature* 11 (1975): 285.

38. *The Letters of Percy Bysshe Shelley,* ed. Frederick L. Jones, 2 vols. (Oxford: Oxford University Press, 1964), 2:271.

39. Shelley's cancellations are given in square brackets and italics.

40. Abrams, "Shelley and Romantic Platonism," in *The Mirror and the Lamp: Romantic Theory and the Critical Tradition* (New York: Norton, 1958), 130.

41. Platonic critics of Shelley are rarer than they used to be, so I will condense to a footnote an argument that might once have taken up a whole essay. Shelley, who was steeped in Plato, may well have found encouragement for his use of solar imagery in the sixth book of the *Republic*. But the paradoxical figures with which he elaborates poetry's mode of action cannot be Platonically explained. For Shelley, the objects of knowledge do not "participate" in poetry; rather, poetry transforms them into incarnations of its own power by impersonating them. The idea that representation heightens beauty and truth is positively anti-Platonic; the new valorization of appearances derives from British empiricism, mediated here mainly by optics and photochemistry. For Plato, the sun endows the eyes with the power of sight (*Republic,* trans. Benjamin Jowett, 5 vols. [London: Oxford University Press, 1931], 3:208-10); for Shelley, poetry clothes the world with light, and only through that luminous impersonation can the world conceivably come to consciousness.

42. Wordsworth wrote that "Poetry . . . is the impassioned expression which is in the countenance of all science" ("Preface to Lyrical Ballads" [1802], in *Lyrical Ballads and Other Poems, 1797-1800,* ed. James Butler and Karen Green, in *The Cornell Wordsworth,* ed. Stephen Parrish [Ithaca, N.Y.: Cornell University Press, 1992], 752-3). Shelley raises the stakes by assuming, in effect, that "the impassioned expression" makes the "countenance" itself possible, and his optical metaphor justifies the assumption.

43. Coleridge, *Biographia Literaria,* ed. James Engell and W. Jackson Bate, vol. 7 in *Collected Works,* ed. Kathleen Coburn (Princeton, N.J.: Princeton University Press, 1983), 1:304.

44. The alchemical connection between the sun and a transmuting power latent in matter influenced Newton's concept of the ether (n. 10 above) and in that sense did help shape the chemical discourse on which Shelley relies.

45. Leighton, *Shelley and the Sublime: An Interpretation of the Major Poems* (Cambridge: Cambridge University Press, 1984), 45-7.

46. See Harry White, "Shelley's Defence of Science," *Studies in Romanticism* 16 (1977): 319-30.

Beverly A. Hume (essay date 1997)

SOURCE: "Twain's Satire on Scientists: *Three Thousand Years Among the Microbes,*" in *Essays in Arts and Sciences,* Vol. 26, October, 1997, pp. 71-84.

[*In the following essay, Hume characterizes* Three Thousand Years Among the Microbes *as one of Twain's few satiric attacks on the scientific ideologies of his time.*]

Despite the fact that Mark Twain's *Three Thousand Years Among the Microbes* is as substantial a work as other late literary fragments such as the *Mysterious Stranger Manuscripts,* critics have come to regard *Microbes* as one of Mark Twain's lesser late fragmentary writings which, as Virginia Starret summarizes in the 1993 *Mark Twain Encyclopedia,* is "a noteworthy, albeit minor, indicator of Twain's persistent grappling with mammoth questions concerning the nature of existence" and, along with "other dark writings of Twain's later years" remains "an oddity" that has been "relegated to the background of Twain scholarship" (736). Yet this fragment is arguably one of Twain's mort important late works, for despite its unfinished status, it offers the author's only pronounced satirical attack on scientific ideologies he is more often credited with embracing than mocking in his final years: that is, the scientific positivism and mechanistic determinism embraced by various nineteenth-century American scientists who continued to believe either in the Newtonian scientific world view or in some form of biological or social Darwinism with regards to man's evolution, progress, and nature.

When critics mention the humorous texture of *Microbes* in their discussion of Twain's late works, it is usually described as burlesque, darkly or grotesquely humorous, or farcical—but not satiric. Although some deal with specific satiric targets—such as Benjamin Franklin, Christian Science, or the barbarism of humankind generally—most seem tacitly to agree with William MacNaughton's general conclusion that the satiric impetus of this work is "eminently forgettable, because it has neither satiric focus nor sting, only a series of random observations about pride, greed, Christian Science, the American love of titles, currency reform, medical butcheries during the Spanish-American War, stock watering, and so on" (202). Conversely, when the work is taken more seriously by critics, it is done so within the context of Twain's intensifying mechanistic determinism or more general speculative cynicism about the meaning of human existence.[1]

Because of the peculiar content and structure of *Microbes,* its significance as a satire directed against nineteenth-century science and scientists needs to be understood, first, in relation to its narrative framing. The primary narrative is introduced by two "Prefaces" from Twain who claims to be the "translator" of this work written "By A Microbe" who initially identifies himself as "B.b. Bkshop" (161). The first "Preface" defines *Microbes* as a "History," one Twain claims he believes is "true" since its author "was conscientiously trying to state bare facts, unembellished by fancy" (161). In the second "Preface," Twain adds the brief editorial comment that he attempted to reform this microbic narrator's writing, "but gave it up" since it "amounted to putting evening dress on a stevedore and making him stand up in the college and lecture" (162). This narrator's prose, Twain continues, is "elegant, but cold and unsympathetic. In fact, corpsy," while his style is "loose and wandering and garrulous and self-contented beyond anything I have ever encountered before" and his "grammar breaks the heart" (162). Such a narrative frame not only draws the narrator's credibility and competence sharply into focus, but is intensified by the narrator's opening statement and brief explanation as to how he became a microbe: "The magician's experiment miscarried, because of the impossibility of getting pure and honest drugs in those days, and the rest was that he transformed me into a cholera-germ when he was trying to turn me into a bird" (163).

With this abrupt and absurd beginning, the narrator haphazardly constructs his "History," claiming early on to have once been a human paleontologist with the middle name of "Huxley" (199) and also to have retained his human memory. Thus, he says he can "observe the germs from their own point of view" and, at the same time, "observe them from a human being's point of view" (163). He claims, also, to be intrigued by what he perceives, despite the time differential between the lifespan of microbes and men (3000 years microbe time is approximately three weeks human time), their essentially analogous situation. Finally, this microbic narrator reveals his determination to gather "facts" and to deal with these "facts" as only a human-turned-microbic scientist can and with the positivistic assumption that they will lead humankind (if not microbekind) to a higher understanding. More specifically, these facts, he claims, will pertain not only to the "History" of his former human world, but also to his new microbic environment—the body of a "hoary and moldering old-bald-headed tramp named Blitzowski" (164). The narrative that follows is, as Twain has already warned, "loose and wandering and garrulous," but this is due principally to the fact that the satiric object of this narrative, as the "Prefaces" and early characterization of the narrator indicate, is the human-paleontologist-turned-microbic-scientist narrator.

This microbic narrator prefers, he says, to be called "Huck," an abbreviation of his former human middle name, "Huxley," and this preference, as John Tuckey suggests, reveals a relation between this narrator and Clemens' earlier Huck Finn.[2] There are, in fact, a few similarities between Huck Finn's role (as narrator) and that of Twain's microbic narrator who I will call, for the sake of clarity, Huck Huxley. Both Hucks are in a diseased body, both are boyish and naive but clever narrators who inadvertently reveal the absurdity of their situations through Twain's manipulation of their narratives, both lie in order to survive in their respective worlds, and both often seem victims of circumstance or training. Here, however, the similarities abruptly end. For Huck Finn, a character in a realistic novel, is an uneducated antebellum Southern boy who inadvertently finds himself transformed into a criminal after he helps a slave escape, whereas Huck Huxley, a character in a quasi-allegorical fantasy, is presumably an educated adult, a scientist, who inadvertently finds himself transformed into a microbe due both to human error and an unlikely experiment. Unlike Huck Finn, moreover, Huck Huxley claims to be committed to understanding, as

Thomas Henry Huxley (1827-1895).

a microbic scientist, the new universe he inhabits and, ultimately, to serve both as its primary educator and historian.

Instead of regarding this narrator as a transformed Huck Finn, then, I think it more productive to consider the possibility that the choice of the name "Huxley" was deliberate on Twain's part. Although he did not specifically cite *Microbes,* Hyatt Waggoner was the first (and only) critic to argue that T. H. Huxley, a British biologist most well-known in Twain's time for his public promotion of Darwin's ideas about evolution, had a pronounced influence on Twain's later writings. In fact, after surveying various scientific influences, Waggoner concludes, "It is to [T. H.] Huxley, with his full development of the implications of Darwinism, that we must turn for the closest parallel between science and Mark Twain's thought" (366). Waggoner summarizes that those parallels lay in Huxley's tendency to stress or emphasize the "fleeting, shifting, impermanence of life," the "reign of strict causality throughout the whole universe," "the amount of pain and suffering that is inevitable in the struggle for life," "the antithesis between natural processes and man's morals," and "the struggle for existence—[or] nature as 'red in tooth and claw'" (366). According to Waggoner, these "doctrines are central to the thought of Mark Twain" (366), and although he does not deal with them in relation to *Mi-*

crobes, the absurd circumstances of Huck Huxley's narration consistently undermine such ideas when they do, on occasion, surface.

In his lectures and writings that attempted to popularize Darwinian and other then-contemporary scientific ideas, T. H. Huxley did tend to oversimplify the relation between science and knowledge, as, for example, when he asserts in such essays as "Technical Education" (1877) or "A Liberal Education and Where To Find It" (1868) not only that the scientist and the technologist are intellectually advanced over other educators since they deal in "tangible facts" (*Technical* 407), but also that "education is the instruction of the [scientific] laws of Nature" and should therefore also "embrace a training in the law and practice of obedience to the moral laws of Nature" (*Liberal* 88). At the same time, however, that Huxley posited such positivistic assertions about the inherent superiority of scientific to other forms of knowledge, he criticized one of the foremost scientific positivists of the century, August Comte, for his "aloof and authoritarian pronouncements" on various intellectual disciplines, making it pointedly clear in his 1866 essay, 'On the Advisableness of Improving Natural Knowledge,' that it "was the speculative and visionary ends of scientific research he valued most highly" (Paradis 76). In this essay and in others, Huxley took direct issue with Comte's three stages of history (theological, metaphysical, and positivistic or scientific) as being "reductive," even though his "own ideas about a progression toward a condition where natural knowledge would 'become co-extensive with the range of knowledge' were similar in tone to Comte's" (Paradis 81). Outspoken, flamboyant, complex, contradictory, aggressively interested in restructuring educational systems to fully embrace scientific methodology and knowledge, and well-known for his popularization of scientific thought in Twain's late nineteenth-century America, Huxley, as a satiric target, may have been irresistible to Twain since he was a complicated, but clearly representative man of nineteenth-century science.

I am not suggesting that T. H. Huxley is the sole object of Twain's satire in *Microbes,* but rather that Twain uses his name symbolically to represent those late nineteenth-century scientists who, like Huxley, popularized science, were markedly influenced by Darwinian thought, possessed earlier Newtonian and Baconian perceptions that the natural world could, through empirical dissection, be fully understood, and tended toward scientific positivism or the view that scientific insight was the highest form of intellectual insight humanly attainable. Twain may also have satirized Huxley as a form of self-satire since Twain may have felt empathetic toward Huxley not only because both men were strongly influenced by their reading of Darwin, but also because Huxley was such a colorful and outspoken popularizer of Darwin's theories about natural selection and human evolution, both in Europe and in America. Popularly labelled "Darwin's Bulldog," Huxley was so strongly persuaded by Darwin's thought in the mid-nineteenth century that he not only turned from the study

of physiology to paleontology early in his career, publishing "38 paleontological papers" by 1871 (Geison 439), but also openly clashed with the church, "attacking Bishop Samuel Wilberforce in a celebrated exchange in 1860 at the British Association meeting in Oxford when he declared that he would rather be descended from an ape than a bishop" (*Cambridge Dictionary* 752). Huxley was also outspoken in his support of integrating science into the educational curriculum in *Evolution and Ethics* (1893), the book with which Twain is said to have been most familiar. *Evolution and Ethics* does, along with Huxley's *Science and Education,* published six years later, include numerous essays stressing the need to integrate scientific training, regarding both the factual and moral "laws" of Nature, into the moral education of children ("Science and Morals," 1886).

In *Microbes,* Twain's Huck Huxley claims to have been a paleontologist before his transformation, displays a strong and consistent aversion toward religious orthodoxy generally (including the then-developing Christian Science orthodoxy of Mary Baker Eddy), frequently posits a Newtonian view of a mechanistic universe or a Darwinian view of the "evolution" of human or microbekind, asserts that facts, logical and empirical reasoning, and scientific insight lead, as Bacon maintained, to the purest form of knowledge, and, along with teaching his microbic students interdisciplinary courses on "Applied Theology, Theological Arithmetic, and Metaphysical Dilutions" (262), remains inordinately preoccupied with developing an "Institute of Applied Morals" (275) for young microbes.

Twain uses this curiously-named narrator, I believe, to make three broad indictments not only against a symbolic T. H. Huxley, but also against nineteenth-century scientists generally: 1) against the damaging quasi-religious theoretical postulates of science and social science, particularly those related to biological or social evolution, Newtonian mechanism, Baconian empiricism, and scientific positivism; 2) against the arrogance, vanity, boyishness, intellectual limitations, greed, and general frailty to which such scientists are no more or less subject than others of their species; and 3) against the absurdly detached and ultimately self-interested morality of much nineteenth-century scientific discourse. Although Twain's comic exaggeration in this narrative sometimes moves into the realm of the burlesque (or even grotesque when he describes, for example, the delights of microbic cannibalism), they consistently create the impression of a satirist's attack on something unjust, harmful, malignant. Because of Twain's volatile and exaggerative prose style, he has often been perceived as a humorist who, as Beidler suggests, writes a "kind of satire we would call 'burlesque'" and thus engages in a kind of "incidental satire" (655). However, Twain's "style" in *Microbes* is his microbic narrator's "style," and its erratic, if not chaotic, quality serves more as a commentary on the latter than the former and, in essence, forms the main part of the satiric impetus of the text.[3]

Before and after he wrote *Microbes,* Twain offered, as many critics have suggested, contradictory impressions about the value and nature of scientific inquiry. However, none of these earlier works draw the impact of such inquiry as radically into question as does *Microbes.* Part of August Comte's positivist legacy to the history of science (particularly nineteenth-century science) was not only the assumption that ideas are constantly being governed and overturned by ideas, but that no ideas have been as important as scientific ones. *Microbes* not only questions such an assumption, but modifies it to suggest, finally, that no ideas may have been as insignificant to human progress as scientific ones.

Besides reading Huxley and Darwin, Twain was relatively well-versed in popularized scientific thought since he "surely read," as Cummings demonstrates, journalistic tributes to science not only in the *Galaxy* (for which he wrote), but also in "eastern journals" where "he saw the word *science* everywhere written, like the name of a god, and science itself credited with enormous powers" (5). It is now critically common knowledge, too, that Twain was, like Huxley, deeply impressed by Darwin's ideas, most notably *The Descent of Man* which he read and reacted to with "extensive marginal notes" and underlining "shortly after its publication in 1871" (Cummings 33). Cummings and others have also convincingly argued that from Twain's reading of the Newtonian world view in Thomas Paine's *Age of Reason,* of Darwin's *Descent of Man,* of numerous other then-contemporary texts on science, and of various popular journals, Twain had a reasonably impressive understanding of then-contemporary scientific thought.[4] Twain appears to have been most familiar with general nineteenth-century scientific ideas which stressed the value of objective observation and of inductive reasoning; with theories about the finite and essentially mechanistic or materialistic nature of the universe; with the significance of geologic time and man's relative insignificance to it; with Darwin's theories of the descent of man through the process of natural selection; and other varieties of social Darwinism, including that of Twain's well-known contemporary, Herbert Spencer, who stressed man's inevitable future progress toward a higher evolutionary status.[5]

The application of such ideas by Twain's narrator in *Microbes,* however, reveals only humankind's, microbekind's, and, finally, his own absurdity. Additionally, Twain has his narrator quite unwittingly give his fellow microbic scientists suggestively allusive names. Two of the most outspoken scientists in the narrative, "Ben Franklin" and "Lem Gulliver," are readily associated not only with eighteenth-century Enlightenment ideas about the inherent superiority of science and the Newtonian world view, but also with satiric fiction. Also, Huck Huxley calls the microbic scientist who most clearly sympathizes with him "Louis XIV"—a microbe whose human counterpart was not only a patron to the Enlightenment satirist, Moliere, but also a tyrant well-known for his war-like regime and rapacious appetites. Huck Huxley refers to such scientific colleagues as "the boys" throughout most of his narrative, and they

do seem more boyish than mature, particularly since they have the added human-like failings of egotism, vanity, competitiveness, and greed. Also, the narrator exposes their ignorance about the true nature of their universe (not a real universe, as they imagine, but merely the body of a drunken bum), and he also exposes the arrogance and brutality inherent in their clinical detachment toward suffering, war, and the degraded nature of the class system. "Evolution," Huck Huxley observes at one point with unconscious irony, "is a mighty doctrine: nothing can ever remove it from its firm base, nothing dissolve it, but evolution" (200). The scientific theory of evolution, conceived in the mind of man, is true only in relation to that mind which, as this narrative consistently implies, is not only microbic, but brutish, even among those who imagine themselves to be sophisticated, enlightened, refined intellectuals.

This microbic narrator's "History" does possess, as Twain warns and as critics have duly noted, tremendous transitional gaps, and the narrator's memory, because of his transformation from man to microbe, is "loose and wandering." How can man (such a narrative structure continuously and implicitly asks) trace the development of his evolving consciousness if changes in it have been as radical as Darwinian ideas suggest? Is this not an implicitly absurd enterprise, or at least as absurd as what Huck Huxley describes, at one point, as the "Giddyite religion" of some microbes? The "Giddyite religion" that Huck Huxley details (and to which his microbic secretary, "Catherine of Aragon," subscribes) mocks the Christian Science religion which Twain mocked in other writings of this period. In *Microbes,* however, this religion is described by the narrator as one which promotes the idea of another kind of evolution, a "transforming" or "votalizing" process by which the flesh transforms into the highest form-spirit (220). The narrator knows, he says, that the Giddyite religion is delusional and foolish, but hesitates to make this pronouncement to Catherine because he has just been laughed at by "the boys," the other germ scientists, for telling them about his former human world, something they regard as factually, "scientifically," impossible and accept only as a poetic vision. He does not laugh at Catherine, however, because he "had seen a certainty of mine dubbed a delusion and laughed at by a couple of able minds—minds trained to search and examine the phenomena of Nature, and segregate fact from fancy, truth from illusion, and pronounce final judgment . . ." (22). The question is not asked, but is implicitly posed by this comparison: Is science, like Christian Science, merely a new kind of delusional religion?

What *Microbes* reveals is that Huck Huxley's training and knowledge may finally be as naive and limiting as any other kind of presumed knowledge, including that gained through mystical vision. Like Twain's earlier Huck Finn, whose racist training informed part of his social response to Jim, Huck Huxley's scientific training partially prevents him from understanding the ironic implications of the relation of his situation to that of the founder of a new (and, he thinks, improbable) religion. Worse, despite such partial insights, he persists in his faith in science. Offering, for example, a "lofty and impassioned tribute to the real nobility of Science and her devotees," Huck Huxley classifies "the domain of Science" as a "republic" where microbic scientists "democratically" reject any truth which cannot be scientifically proven. Just as Huck Finn fails to recognize the absurdity and depravity of Jim's treatment by antebellum Southern society as a slave, Twain's microbic Huck Huxley fails to recognize the absurdity of his belief—as both a microbe and a former human—in the superiority of scientific inquiry, method, and discourse.

Microbes stands apart from other of Twain's late writings primarily because even as it embodies sentiments from his other dark writings on social Darwinism, cosmic mechanism, and the damned human race generally, it is penned by a professed scientist who imagines himself to be the most enlightened germ of his time. All of the narrator's intellectually loose meanderings are essentially self-referential, for *Microbes* finally seems directed primarily against those cynical and nihilistic ruminations about human heredity, conditioning, and training that plagued Twain throughout his career, and increasingly during his final years. Twain's self-contented, microbic narrator may, for some examples, believe that "pus and civilization" are "substantially the same thing" (167); that "Twain" was an agriculturalist who was "finally hanged, many thought unjustly" because he "had once chopped down a cherry tree" and would "not tell a lie" (though it was eventually revealed that he not only shot a man "in five places" but had "already killed dozens of persons of every sex," 184); that "evolution is the law of policies: Darwin said it, Socrates endorsed it, Cuvier proved it and established it for all time in his paper on 'The Survival of the Fittest'" (195); or that "the scientist is not permitted to exhibit surprise, eagerness, emotion, he must be carefully of his trade-dignity—it is the law" (203), and so on. Yes, Twain's microbic scientist may believe such distorted facts as "objective" data—but does Twain? "No" would seem the obvious answer—not only because Huck Huxley's failing human memory is responsible for creating such bizarre truths, but also because of the conclusion in which this increasingly confused narrator attempts to manipulate his microbic colleagues in a gold prospecting enterprise in one of Blitzowski's molars in order, he zealously claims, to save his project, the "Institute of Applied Morals," from being corrupted.

In *Microbes,* the microbic narrator continuously suggests that humans and microbes are victims of their cultural training and biases. In the realistic context of *The Adventures of Huckleberry Finn,* such a suggestion is partially viable, but in the exaggerative, quasi-allegorical, and bizarre world of *Microbes,* the suggestion that microbes are victims of training or cultural bias becomes, along with the theorist who posits it, ludicrous. Twain's microbic narrator has not, as he imagines, recorded "History," but rather revealed that his radically transformed (or devolved) consciousness cannot finally make sense either of his human

or his microbic worlds. In *Microbes,* finally, Mark Twain mockingly and self-mockingly examines what may once have been his own faith in nineteenth-century scientific inquiry and scientists. Even though Twain did not complete the admittedly bizarre narrative of *Three Thousand Years Among the Microbes* before his death and did not resolve, in his lifetime, the riddle of what it means to be human, he did, as what survives of the *Microbes* manuscript attests, aggressively consider the possibility that then-contemporary science might actually hinder him in such a quest.

Notes

1. John Tuckey suggests, for example, that in writing *Microbes,* Twain was "returning to a view of the human situation that had been in his thoughts since" August 1884 "when he noted on a draft of *The Adventures of Huckleberry Finn*: 'I think we are only the microscopic trichina concealed in the blood of some vast creature's veins, and it is that vast creature whom God concerns Himself about and not us'" (xv), while Susan Gillman argues that *Microbes* is one of Twain's late "dream writings" which explores late nineteenth-century ideas about "cosmic consciousness" that were then being furthered by William James, Frederic Myers and others affiliated with the London Society for Psychical Research (172-6), and Kathleen Walsh asserts that Twain "is fascinated with the arbitrariness of time and with the potentiality of science to transform our world into one which we are no longer certain of comprehending" (27). See, also, discussions of the deterministic implications of Twain's late writings in Sherwood Cummings book on Twain and science, John Tuckey's "Twain's Later Dialogue: The 'Me' and the Machine," and Stanley Poole's "In Search of the Missing Link: Mark Twain and Darwinism."

2. "B.b Bkship," Tuckey also observes, "appears to be a coding of 'Blankenship,' the last name of the Hannibal boy who served as a real-life model for Huckleberry Finn." Thus "Huck Bkshp, who exists within Blitzowski," in Tuckey's view, becomes, as described in Twain's "note of August 1884" (cited in Note 1), a germ "'concealed in the blood of some vast creature's veins' . . . a Huckian germ adrift in the Mississippi-like veins of a cosmic Pap Finn!" (xvii). For Tuckey, this reinforces the idea that Twain became a more cynical writer and in *Microbes* is returning to an idea he had only earlier flirted with in *The Adventures of Huckleberry Finn.*

3. Although James Cox suggests that exaggeration is the "characterizing style of the Twain persona who shapes all of Clemens' humor" (22), the narrator of *Microbes* differs from other of Twain's narrators not only because he generally does not perceive of himself as exaggerative, or in Huck Finn's terms, a liar, but also because his intensifying confusion—and his chaotic style—arguably makes him the only of Twain's "mad" narrators. Because of the volatile na-

ture of his comedic style and his use of exaggerative "low" comedy or burlesque, Twain has always posed interpretive difficulties for critics attempting to come to terms with the meaning of his humor. Yet most agree that it is from Twain's hyperbolic propensities and manipulation of language that his most significant comedic episodes surface, or erupt. See also, for representative general interpretive responses about Twain's complex but volatile comedic strategies, David E. E. Sloane's *Mark Twain as a Literary Comedian,* Bruce Michelson's *Mark Twain on the Loose,* or David B. Kesterson's "The Literary Comedians and the Language of Humor."

4. In addition to Cummings' assessment of Twain's reading of Darwin, Paine, and Herbert Spencer on Twain's understanding of natural selection, biologic and social Darwinism, and the Newtonian world view, see also Alan Gribben's overview of Twain's readings in the sciences and social sciences in the *Mark Twain Encyclopedia* and *Mark Twain's Library: A Reconstruction.*

5. Bowler also points out that "Spencer's evolutionary ethics eliminated morality as it traditionally had been understood. Confronted with a behavior choice, the individual must not decide what to do in terms of any absolute standard of right and wrong [but] . . . must simply decide the most effective way of conforming to his particular society, which will ensure his own happiness and contribute to general progress" (227). The narrator of *Microbes* expresses this type of amorphous, yet certain "morality," particularly as he concludes his narrative with the judgment that microbes can only progress if one applies a relativistic morality to both social or personal conduct. Although Darwin was often misunderstood by social Darwinists like Herbert Spencer, the "striking resemblance," science-historian John Greene points out, "between these two types of speculation was more than coincidental, for, given the condition of gradual progress from a primitive condition whether of man or of the earth, the problem was to explain the assumed development by means of a few judiciously selected principles supported by an assortment of judiciously selected facts" (61). Twain's narrator is similarly selective, though clearly injudicious and arguably insane by the end of his narrative.

Works Cited

Beidler, Philip D. "Satire." *Mark Twain Encyclopedia.* New York: Garland Publishing, 1993, 665.

Bowler, Peter J. *Evolution. The History of an Idea.* Berkeley: University of California Press, 1984.

Cambridge Biographical Dictionary. Ed. Magnus Magnusson, K. B. E. Cambridge: Cambridge University Press, 1990.

Clemens, Samuel L. *Three Thousand Years Among the Microbes. The Devil's Race-Track: Mark Twain's Great Dark*

Writings. Ed. John S. Tuckey. Berkeley: University of California Press, 1980.

Cummings, Sherwood. *Mark Twain and Science: Adventures of a Mind.* Baton Rouge: Louisiana State University Press, 1988.

Geison, Gerald L. "T. H. Huxley." *Encyclopedia of World Biography.* Volume 5. McGraw-Hill Book Company/International Publications: New York et al, 1973, 438-9.

Gillman, Susan. *Dark Twins. Imposture and Identity in Mark Twain's America.* Chicago and London: University of Chicago Press, 1989.

Greene, John C. *Science, Ideology, and World View. Essays in the History of Evolutionary Ideas.* Berkeley: University of California Press, 1981.

Gribben, Alan. *Mark Twain's Library: A Reconstruction.* 2 volumes. Boston: G. K. Hall, 1980.

———. "Reading." *Mark Twain Encyclopedia.* New York: Garland Publishing, 1993, 619-20.

Huxley, T. H. "A Liberal Education and Where to Find It." *Science and Education. Collected Essays.* Volume III. Rpt. 1893 London: MacMillan and Co. text. New York: George Olms Verlag Hidesheim, 1970, 76-110.

———. "Science and Culture." *Science and Education. Collected Essays.* Volume III. Rpts. 1893 London: MacMillan and Co. text. New York: George Olms Verlag Hidesheim, 1970, 134-159.

———. "Science and Morals." *Evolution and Ethics. Collected Essays.* Volume IX. Rpts. 1893 London: MacMillan and Co. text. New York: George Olms Verlag Hidesheim, 1970, 117-146.

———. "Technical Education." *Science and Education. Collected Essays.* Volume III. Rpts. 1893 London: MacMillan and Co. text. New York: George Olms Verlag Hidesheim, 1970, 404-426.

Kesterson, David B. "The Literary Comedians and the Language of Humor." *Studies in American Humor,* 1982, 44-51.

MacNaughton, William. *Mark Twain's Last Years As a Writer.* Columbia, Mo.: University of Missouri Press, 1979.

Michelson, Bruce. *Mark Twain on the Loose: A Comic Writer and the American Self.* Amherst: University of Massachusetts Press, 1995.

Paradis, James G. *T. H. Huxley: Man's Place in Nature.* Lincoln: University of Nebraska Press, 1978.

Poole, Stan. "In Search of the Missing Link: Mark Twain and Darwinism." *Studies in American Fiction* 13 (1985), 201-215.

Sloane, David E. E. *Mark Twain as a Literary Comedian.* Baton Rouge: Louisiana State University Press, 1979.

Starrett, Virginia. "Three Thousand Years Among the Microbes." *Mark Twain Encyclopedia.* New York: Garland Publishing, 1993, 734-6.

Tuckey, John S. "Introduction." *The Devil's Race-Track: Mark Twain's Great Dark Writings.* Ed. John S. Tuckey. Berkeley: University of California Press, 1980, ix-xx.

―――. "Twain's Later Dialogue: The 'Me' and the Machine." *American Literature* XLI (1970), ix-xx.

Waggoner, Hyatt H. "Science in the Thought of Mark Twain." *American Literature* VIII (1937), 357-70.

Walsh, Kathleen, "Rude Awakenings and Swift Recoveries: The Problem of Reality in Mark Twain's 'The Great Dark' and 'Three Thousand Years Among the Microbes.'" *American Literary Realism 1870-1910* (1988), 19-28.

Patricia O'Neill (essay date 1997)

SOURCE: "Victorian Lucretius: Tennyson and the Problem of Scientific Romanticism," in *Writing and Victorianism,* edited by J. B. Bullen, Longman, 1997, pp. 104-19.

[*In the following essay, O'Neill offers an analysis of Tennyson's poetry, explaining that his synthesis of the romantic and scientific helped define the Victorian response to the muddied waters stirred by scientific discovery.*]

One of the most important influences of the Romantic movement in literature was its belief in the authority of nature over social conventions. Guiding and mediating individual thoughts and feelings, the processes and objects of nature inspired poets such as Wordsworth, Keats and Shelley with an organic sense of the unity of being. In contrast to the oppressive forms of an increasingly industrial society, nature represented a moral if not physical sanctuary for self-expression and imaginative invention. But the seemingly transcendental power of nature in Romantic poetry was undermined by the new and more authoritative discourse of Victorian science.

By the 1830s, Charles Lyell's uniformitarian theory that changes in the earth's surface had occurred gradually over millions of years reduced human consciousness to geological insignificance. Despite continued attacks by creationists—those who believed in the literal truth of the Bible—by the 1850s, most intellectuals had accepted the idea of evolution. Nature for the Victorians, therefore, was no longer a quasi-divinity or a moral arbiter between the individual and the conditions of his/her society. In Tennyson's famous phrase, nature had become 'red in tooth and claw', an arbiter only of survival, and neither the reflection of nor an analogy for a beneficent power or sympathetic universe.

Nevertheless, the spell of Romantic ideology—from the idea of the natural rights of man to a confidence in the quest for knowledge of nature—was passed on to the next generation of writers and thinkers. For Victorian scientists in particular, study of the physical laws of nature provided new understanding of the meaning and value of human life. Eventually, a newly professionalized generation of scientists assumed the mantle of cultural sages as well as the authority of experts in specialized fields of knowledge.

Even a cursory reading of Charles Darwin's *Voyage of the Beagle* (1842) or Thomas Henry Huxley's and John Tyndall's many essays for a general audience reveals how far Victorian scientists shared the Romantics' enthusiasm for the individual quest for the secrets of nature. Huxley and Tyndall in particular developed a style of explanation that appealed to a poetic sense of personal adventure. In their representation of science, Truth was wrested from an indifferent universe and an authoritarian culture by the lonely heroism of a few inexhaustible men. Thus as late as 1894, Huxley quoted Tennyson's 'Ulysses' (1833) to inspire his Oxford audience with the unrelenting struggle of science against superstition.[1] Likewise, Tyndall recalled how reciting the lines of Athena, goddess of wisdom, from Tennyson's 'Oenone' (1830) had refreshed him as he pursued his scientific work.[2] Such integration of science and poetry in the orientation of Victorian scientists was reflected as well in their appreciation of the imaginative aspects of scientific reasoning.

Here, for example, is the last paragraph of Tyndall's 1864 essay on 'Alpine Sculpture'. He is comparing the catastrophist theory of fracture to the uniformitarian theory of erosion in order to explain what he calls the 'fantastic form' of the Alps:

> There is a grandeur in the secular integration of small effects implied by the theory of erosion almost superior to that involved in the idea of a cataclysm. Think of the ages which must have been consumed in the execution of this colossal sculpture. . . . In the falling of a rock from a mountain-head, in the shoot of an avalanche, in the plunge of a cataract, we often see more impressive illustrations of the power of gravity than in the motions of the stars. When the intellect has to intervene, and calculation is necessary to the building up of the conception, the expansion of the feelings ceases to be proportional to the magnitude of the phenomena.[3]

Although he writes in the passive voice of scientific discourse, Tyndall's concern is for something more than scientific facts. In his emphatically 'secular' analysis of the formation of the mountains, Tyndall exults in the immediacy of the physical forces at work. The sensation of 'grandeur' is greater for Tyndall in the study of geological rather than cosmological forces precisely because we can better 'sense' the shoot of the avalanche and the plunge of a cataract than the motions of the stars. Small effects in nature may thus generate more feelings and ultimately more understanding for the force we call gravity than the mathematical calculations of astronomers.

Such a concern for the sensuous details and imaginative appeal of science reflects Tyndall's sympathy with the Romantic poet's task to humanize the experience of nature. Although Tyndall's first concern as the successor to Michael Faraday was to promote experiments to ascertain the physical laws of nature, his collected essays show how much his philosophy of nature was inspired by poets and writers such as Goethe, Emerson, Carlyle and Tennyson, among others. For Victorians interested in acquiring knowledge and willing to attend evening lectures, scientists like Tyndall and Huxley came to enjoy the same popularity as contemporary novelists such as Charles Dickens and George Eliot and poets like Tennyson and Robert Browning. Science in the nineteenth century thus took its place among other cultural discourses competing for the minds and hearts of the Victorian public.

Because of his cultural centrality as Queen Victoria's Poet Laureate, Tennyson exemplifies the poetic response to what might be called scientific romanticism in Victorian culture. For Tennyson, Victorian culture was marked by contradictory historical tendencies. On the one hand, his contemporaries longed nostalgically for a time of cultural uniformity. On the other hand, they faced an urgent and complex reality of disparate social forces. To the extent that science represented a revolutionary break with clerical authority, it provided a rallying point for ambitious young men of otherwise diverse political and intellectual sensibilities. Because of Tennyson's education at Cambridge among some of the leading natural philosophers of his day, he respected the facts of scientific discovery and was well-read in a number of scientific fields. In his poetry, however, Tennyson sought what his contemporary, the poet-critic Matthew Arnold, called 'intellectual deliverance'.[4]

Deeply suspicious of the Romantic mystique of individualism and moral heterodoxy, Tennyson doubted that the scientific quest would sustain the emotional and spiritual hopes of humankind. Employing the same Romantic imagery, themes and ideological orientation as his contemporaries in science, Tennyson's poetry represents instead the dangers of a materialist philosophy for individual and social well-being. Moreover, despite his friendships with scientists like Tyndall, Tennyson increasingly used his dramatis personae to prove that traditional social authority and religious beliefs are no less compelling for an ethical society than the 'natural' laws touted by Victorian scientists.

Tennyson's most important work—*In Memoriam* (1850)—is an elegy for Arthur Hallam, Tennyson's school friend, who died at the age of twenty-three in a shipwreck. In mourning the loss of his friend, Tennyson could rely neither on a traditional faith in God's will nor on the poetic tradition of pastoral elegy. Along with his contemporaries, Tennyson required something more than a figurative or symbolic allusion to the cycles of death and rebirth in nature. Throughout his poem, Tennyson rehearses the arguments for and against the idea of an afterlife and the existence of an immortal soul; however, his desire for such assurances is thwarted by his understanding of natural history. Having read widely in the works of geologists and evolutionary theorists, Tennyson reflects on the discrepancies between biblical accounts of God's care for each individual soul and scientific accounts of the profligacy of nature.

> The wish, that of the living whole
> 　No life may fail beyond the grave,
> 　Derives it not from what we have
> The likest God within the soul?
>
> Are God and Nature then at strife,
> 　That Nature lends such evil dreams?
> 　So careful of the type she seems,
> So careless of the single life,
>
> 　　　. . . . .
>
> 'So careful of the type'? but no,
> 　From scarped cliff and quarried stone
> 　She cries, 'A thousand types are gone;
> I care for nothing, all shall go.
>
> 　　　　　　　(55. 1-8; 56. 1-4)

In recounting the history of organic life, Tennyson recognizes the insignificance of any individual creature, and, indeed, the actual extinction of entire species. Against such a futile view of life, Tennyson juxtaposes a 'larger hope' in both God's love and his own devotion to his friend's memory. This personal solution to the problem of immortality gains a wider significance in the rest of the poem as Tennyson mythologizes Arthur Hallam as a figure of more significance than the individual man. Increasingly, he is part of a spiritual reality whose influence is felt by Tennyson with the same ritual certainty and grace as a Christian feels for Christ at Christmas time.

More importantly, Tennyson had found some scientific reassurance for his belief in the soul's immortality. Before he published his poem Tennyson had been deeply impressed by reading Robert Chambers's *Vestiges of the Natural History of Creation* (1846). Although many scientists criticized Chambers's methods, his theory of development was later acknowledged by Darwin to have anticipated the main tenets of evolutionary theory. For Tennyson, Chambers showed the way to reconcile scientific knowledge with religious faith. By imagining God as the force behind evolution, Chambers and Tennyson projected humankind as representing the highest stage in an ongoing evolution of ever more perfect beings.

> Contemplate all this work of Time,
> 　The giant labouring in his youth;
> 　Nor dream of human love and truth,
> As dying Nature's earth and lime;
>
> But trust that those we call the dead
> 　Are breathers of an ampler day
> 　For ever nobler ends. They say
> The solid earth whereon we tread
>
> In tracts of fluent heat began,
> 　And grew to seeming-random forms,
> 　The seeming prey of cyclic storms,
> Till at last arose the man;
>
> 　　　　　　　(118. 1-12)

While Tennyson accepts the geologists' sense of tremendous change over long periods of time, yet the appearance of rational beings gives meaning to the otherwise 'seeming-random forms' of nature. With humanity, agency enters the scheme of things. Humankind, unlike the rest of nature, has a will and thus, for Tennyson, is capable of affecting the course of evolutionary history.

> Arise and fly
> The reeling Faun, the sensual feast;
>   Move upward, working out the beast,
> And let the ape and tiger die.
>
>   (118. 25-8)

Both knowledge and feeling unite in humankind to suggest the progressive movement of life towards a higher state of being. Thus at the end of *In Memoriam* Tennyson celebrates the wedding of his sister and anticipates the future in which

> No longer half-akin to brute,
>   For all we thought and loved and did,
>   And hoped, and suffer'd, is but seed
> Of what in them is flower and fruit;
>
> Whereof the man, that with me trod
>   This planet, was a noble type
>   Appearing ere the times were ripe,
> That friend of mine who lives in God,
>
> That God, which ever lives and loves,
>   One God, one law, one element,
>   And one far-off divine event,
> To which the whole creation moves.
>
>   (Epilogue. 133-44)

No longer the immediate creator of each individual soul, God remains as the guarantor of the goodness of creation which in this version of evolutionary theory embraces a divine teleology—the divine event which authorizes and justifies humankind's existence and advancement.

Having resolved his own crisis of faith and through his poem offered solace to many Victorians, including the recently widowed Queen Victoria, Tennyson pursued the problems of religious doubt and social alienation in poems as different as 'The Lotus Eaters' and his epic work *Idylls of the King.* According to Tennyson scholars such as Herbert F. Tucker, Tennyson's poetry was at once traditional and original. While inheriting the subjective orientation of his Romantic predecessors, he developed a classical interpretation of the Romantic quest, and thereby gave it a new respectability and social framework.[5] In effect, while Tennyson pursued the Romantics' concern for the fate of individual characters, he also adapted to his position as Poet Laureate—gained in 1850 after the publication of *In Memoriam*—by subverting the stance of the solitary genius, one of the hallmarks of Romantic ideology.

As a member of the Metaphysical Society (1869-79), Tennyson listened to the ongoing discussions of intellectuals, clergymen and scientists concerning the philosophical and social significance of scientific method. His only contribu-

tion to the Society's monthly discussions was an inaugural poem, 'The Higher Pantheism', which suggests that divinity is immanent in nature and is beyond human comprehension. Mirroring and reversing the significance of such distinctions between knowledge of nature and faith in God, Huxley coined for himself the term 'agnostic' to mean one who knows nothing of the supernatural. Yet despite their differences, Tennyson remained attentive to the empirical details of scientific theory, and Huxley acknowledged Tennyson as the only poet since Lucretius to understand the drift of modern science.[6] Concern about the materialist tendencies of Victorian science, however, continued as a source of controversy amongst members of the Metaphysical Society. In response, both Tennyson and Tyndall considered the problem historically be reinterpreting the life and work of the Roman poet-philosopher Lucretius.

Tennyson had read *De Rerum Natura,* a long philosophical poem, in which the second-century poet explains the origins of the universe and the physical basis of life. According to Frank Turner, commentaries on Lucretius until the 1860s had focused on his merits as a poet. Tennyson's poem helped to renew interest in his ideas, which Tyndall and others agreed had anticipated many of the principles of physical science.[7] As a philosopher, Lucretius followed the materialist views of the Greek philosophers, principally Epicurus and Democritus. He posited that nothing comes from nothing, that everything in the world is composed of atoms, and that natural processes proceed without the interference or intervention of the gods. In paying poetic homage to a classical predecessor, Tennyson acknowledged his own role as a poet-interpreter of the laws of nature for his own time. What Tennyson's dramatic interpretation of Lucretius focuses on, however, is not his theories of nature but a legendary account of Lucretius's madness and suicide. In so doing, Tennyson's dramatic monologue 'Lucretius' (1868) explores the dangerous aspects of the scientific quest itself.

The poem is framed by a narrative which tells how Lucretius's neglected wife secretly administered a love potion to her husband. Under the influence of the potion, Lucretius loses confidence in his ability to reason or to pursue the moral life of philosophy that he has enjoyed. Lucretius describes his fears and confusion by recounting three of his dreams. In the first, the poet dreams of the disintegration of the world into its primal atomic matter. The details of this passage and others come from *De Rerum Natura* and were written in consultation with Tyndall, who delighted in Tennyson's poetic representation of physical processes. As always, Tennyson took pains to describe natural phenomena with scientific accuracy. In 'Lucretius', moreover, Tennyson's interpretation of the Roman poet's atomic theories allowed him to consider the effects of a materialist philosophy on a pre-Christian consciousness and so avoid any obvious partisanship or heresy among the advocates of Victorian science or religion.

While Tennyson's Lucretius is startled by the apocalyptic aspect of his first dream, he owns the dream as part of his own construction of the world. But he is horrified by the second and third dreams in which naked dancing girls and the breasts of Helen of Troy suggest a repressed bestial nature that he has not experienced in himself before. Despite his disbelief in the gods, Lucretius appeals to Venus and falls back on conventional superstitions to explain and alleviate his condition until, realizing the contradictoriness of his arguments, he acknowledges his confusion and despairs. If the gods are as careless of his woes as his philosophy has suggested, then Lucretius sees no reason why he should not kill himself.

> O ye Gods,
> I know you careless, yet, behold to you
> From childly wont and ancient use I call—
> I thought I lived securely as yourselves—
> No lewdness, narrowing envy, monkey-spite,
> No madness of ambition, avarice, none:
>
> . . . . .
>
> But now it seems some unseen monster lays
> His vast and filthy hands upon my will,
>
> . . . . .
>
> Why should I, beastlike as I find myself,
> Not manlike end myself?
>
> (207-12; 219-20; 231-2)

Like a noble Roman, Lucretius decides to die rather than indulge the sexual fantasies and brutish sensations that threaten to overwhelm him. The natural philosophy that had sustained the tranquillity of his reason and the sublimity of his poetry now provides a vision of the consequences of his death.

> And therefore now
> Let her, that is the womb and tomb of all,
> Great Nature, take, and forcing apart
> Those blind beginnings that have made me man,
> Dash them anew together at her will
> Through all her cycles—
>
> . . . . .
>
> And even his bones long laid within the grave,
> The very sides of the grave itself shall pass,
> Vanishing, atom and void, atom and void,
> Into the unseen for ever—
>
> (242-7; 255-8)

Having foregone the possibility of immortality, even for his poetry, Lucretius stabs himself. The poem ends with his wife's return and sorrow. To her cries, Lucretius answers enigmatically, 'Care not thou! / Thy duty? What is duty? Fare thee well!'

For Victorian readers of 'Lucretius', the discrepancy between the circumstances (the administering of a love potion) and the motives (his fear of insanity and possible dishonour) of his death allowed two very different interpretations of the poem. Some thought the poem was meant as an interpretation of Lucretius's character and his personal tragedy. Others thought Tennyson intended ironic

commentary on contemporary science. In any case, the brooding brilliance of Lucretius's language places him among other doomed Romantic questers such as Byron's Manfred and Shelley's poet in *Alastor.*

If Tennyson's Lucretius exemplifies the Romantic spirit, however, he also raises questions about the intellectual authority of Romantic or Lucretian philosophy, and indirectly, all materialist philosophies, for the suicide is the result of the speaker's misunderstanding of his physical and mental condition. His despair suggests the inadequacy of his power to perceive the underlying causes of his illness. A less solipsistic man or more platonic philosopher might have avoided such a fate. Nevertheless, as Tyndall was to point out, it is the unhealthiness of Lucretius's brain that is the effective cause of his illness, rather than any inherent flaw in his character or philosophy. Thus Tennyson's poem provided ammunition for both materialist and idealist interpretations of the relations of body and mind.

Tyndall's 1874 address to the British Association for the Advancement of Science also draws on the philosophy of Lucretius in order to offer a defence of science and scientific method. Tyndall begins his argument by taking a historical approach to the quest for knowledge of natural phenomena and the origin of things. Unlike Tennyson, Tyndall emphasizes the heroic nature of the scientific quest: 'Far in the depths of history we find men of exceptional power differentiating themselves from the crowd, rejecting these anthropomorphic notions, and seeking to connect natural phenomena with their physical principles.[8] Privileging those thinkers who relied on observation and reflection to explain physical principles, Tyndall develops a genealogy of philosophers up to Lucretius.

He then proposes a debate between materialist and idealist points of view by imagining a dialogue between a follower of Lucretius and a follower of Bishop Butler, whose 'Analogy of Religion' had provided the main arguments for natural theology in the early part of the nineteenth century. Tyndall's conclusion to the debate acknowledges the inadequacy of both approaches: science cannot explain how inorganic atoms acquire consciousness; religion cannot explain the existence of consciousness apart from its physical manifestations through the brain and nervous system. But in his subsequent remarks on the development of evolutionary theory, Darwin's argument for natural selection, and Herbert Spencer's philosophical insight into the necessary interactions of organism and environment, Tyndall reiterates the lesson of Lucretius: 'Divorced from matter, where is life to be found? Whatever our *faith* may say, our *knowledge* shows them to be indissolubly joined. Every meal we eat, and every cup we drink, illustrates the mysterious control of Mind by Matter.'

Having made his case for a scientific materialism, however, Tyndall concedes that there is a parallelism without contact between the development of the nervous system and the phenomena of sensation and thought: 'man the *object* is separated by an impassable gulf from man the *subject*'. Moreover, Tyndall allows that human feelings, including love and religious feelings, are also of ancient origin and must be recognized as adding to the poetry and dignity of humanity. Scientists themselves, as Tyndall acknowledges, often derive their enthusiasm and moral force from ultrascientific sources. Thus for Tyndall, science is not divorced from literature or culture.

Science, nevertheless, provides in Tyndall's view 'a surer check to any intellectual or spiritual tyranny', and for this reason Tyndall not only defends the materialist principles of Lucretius but enjoins a scientific approach to all questions of knowledge, to 'wrest', as he says, 'from theology the entire domain of cosmological theory'. His lecture ends with a vision of the human mind in quest after the 'Mystery from which it has emerged, seeking so to fashion it as to give unity to thought and faith' without prejudice or fixity of conception, as the most noble exercise of the 'creative faculties of man'. Such a view, while undermining the authority of religion and any static view of science, reinforced a Romantic attitude towards the imagination as an autonomous faculty whose 'unrestricted' exercise was a moral and emotional necessity for a scientific culture.

For defenders of religious faith, Tyndall's defence of Lucretius's classical materialism showed the inability of modern science to distinguish between the superstitions of the past and the enlightened faith of modern religion. By associating Lucretius's philosophy with modern scientific theory, Tyndall gave his opponents the opportunity to dismiss or belittle the results of modern experiment and empirical research. For scientists, the point of Tyndall's argument remained the individual's right to discern the 'truth' of nature and extrapolate its consequences for human life regardless of religious orthodoxy.[9]

For Tennyson, the importance of Lucretius extended beyond the metaphysical or methodological squabbles of clerics and scientists. The ending of his 'Lucretius', which he revised after its initial publication, raises a question of great concern for Victorian readers. In Lucretius's dismissal of his wife's regret that she had failed in her duty to him and in his rejection of duty itself apart from self-judgement, Lucretius reflects his ignorance of the ethical consequences of his intellectual and poetical endeavours. By introducing the question of duty in such a context, Tennyson challenged the implied heroism of the scientific quest from the point of view of culture and social responsibility, but did not resolve it. For his part, Tyndall conceded only the possibility that each age 'must be held free to fashion the mystery in accordance with its own needs' through the individual's 'creative' rather than 'knowing' faculties without any expectation of ultimate resolution. The polarization of science and religion and of knowledge and feeling in Tyndall's speech reflected the seriously divided consciousness of many Victorians. After several personal conversations with Tyndall at his home in Farringford, Tennyson returned to the question of duty and the ethical requirement of any quest for knowledge. In 'The

Ancient Sage' (1885), however, Tennyson uses the speaker to describe his own deeply felt beliefs and to challenge directly the Romantic rhetoric of an advocate for a materialist approach to life.

The form of 'The Ancient Sage' allows the reader to juxtapose two voices and perspectives. One perspective is that of the ancient sage, a philosopher like the Chinese Lao-tze whose work and life Tennyson had been reading; the other is a youth whose attitude towards life is limited to his understanding of natural phenomenon. Instead of representing two speakers, however, Tennyson represents the sage reading and commenting upon a poem written by the youth who has followed him. Here are the opening lines of the youth's poem:

> How far thro' all the bloom and brake
>   That nightingale is heard!
> What power but the bird's could make
>   This music in the bird?
> How summer-bright are yonder skies,
>   And earth as fair a hue!
> And yet what sign of aught that lies
>   Behind the green and blue?
> But man today is fancy's fool
>   As man hath ever been.
> The nameless Power, or Powers that rule
>   Were never heard or seen.
>
>   (19-30)

The youth alludes to Keats's 'Ode to a Nightingale', but, unlike Keats, he insists on the empirical nature of the bird and remains staunchly critical of any transcendental spirit in the bird's song or in nature generally. The sage responds to the youth's agnostic attitude by offering two examples, personal to Tennyson, of his own experience of a 'nameless Power'. The first he describes as a 'passion for the past', a pantheistic connectedness to a world which even in his youth had seemed already remote.

> A breath, a whisper—some divine farewell—
> Desolate sweetness—far and far away—
> What had he loved, what had he lost, the boy?
> I know not, and I speak of what has been.
>
>   (225-8)

It is not the memory of a particular beloved, but of his once passionate response to life that justifies the sage's resistance to the youth's call for dissipation in a life of wine and laughter.

The sage's second example of a non-material force, a trance-like state that comes from the chanting of his own name, again shifts concern away from the empirical experience of self towards a recognition of a spiritual realm. Yet, unlike some of Tennyson's other poems and notably *In Memoriam*, this poem does not posit an evolutionary teleology or make a counter-argument. Both the youth's poem and the sage's responses remain logically consistent in their expression of faith and doubt until the sage gives up the verbal battle and suggests a course of action. The sage's advice to the youth is 'Let be thy wail, and help thy fellow-men' (258). By urging ethical action, Tennyson sidesteps the opposition between materialist and idealist philosophies. For the ancient sage who lives 'a thousand summers ere the time of Christ' creates consensus on a practical level by reminding the Romantic youth and the scientifically attuned reader that the traditional wisdom of the past remains relevant to modern concerns regardless of scientific advances.

The last twenty-five lines of the poem list the sage's moral instructions for a life that will lead beyond 'the hot swamp of voluptuousness' to 'the Mount of Blessing'. Ultimately, the prospect from such heights as the ethical life may allow the youth to attain spiritual promise rather than a biological or even social horizon. Pointing still higher than human vision can comprehend, the sage exhorts the youth to 'see / the high-heaven dawn of more than mortal day / Strike on the Mount of Vision' (283-4). If the sage's last words, 'So, farewell', strike a less triumphant note than the 'one far-off divine event' projected in the finale of *In Memoriam,* we might suppose that the elderly Tennyson had come to admit the tenuousness of the visionary gleam. Instead, the simple leave-taking throws moral responsibility back on the youth or reader of the poem. It is understandable, then, that scientists like Tyndall either missed Tennyson's implied critique of their position or understood Tennyson to be agreeing with them.

Tyndall was especially pleased with 'The Ancient Sage' since it include themes he had discussed with Tennyson personally. In his contribution to Hallam Tennyson's memoir of his father, Tyndall rejects the idea that the youth is criticized in the poem and offers his own interpretation:

> I would here remark, once for all, that the passages read from the young man's scroll, far from being the language of a libertine—so far from being a 'death song for the Ghouls'—are of a quality which no libertine or associate of Ghouls could possibly have produced. Supreme beauty and delicacy of language are not consistent with foul companionship.[10]

Tyndall points to Tennyson's language as a truer indication of the poet's intentions than the overt criticisms of the sage. Perhaps Tyndall appreciated the young man's boldness in trying to undermine the sage's complaisant desire to 'cleave ever to the sunnier side of doubt' (68).

Like Huxley's debates with Arnold on the relations of science and literature, Tyndall's interpretation of Tennyson's 'The Ancient Sage' points to the new manner in which many Victorians were viewing the social role of literature. Tyndall appreciated the music and grandeur of Tennyson's poetry in the same way that he appreciated the fantastic forms of the Alps: as a secular and undogmatic form of religion, separate from science and knowledge of nature. In an 'Address to Students', Tyndall explains that

> the hopes and terrors which influenced our fathers are passing away, and our trust henceforth must rest on the innate strength of man's moral nature. And here, I think, the poet will have a great part to play in the future culture of the world. To him . . . we have a right to look for that heightening and brightening of life which so many of us need. . . . Void of offense to science, he may freely deal with conceptions which science shuns, and become the illustrator and interpreter of that Power which as 'Jehovah, Jove, or Lord,' has hitherto filled and strengthened the human heart.[11]

Despite their different methods and beliefs, both Tennyson and Tyndall sought authority for their points of view by appealing to traditions, either scientific or literary, to link the present to the past, and both the poet and the scientist believed in a moral imperative behind their different quests for knowledge and meaning in human life. If Tyndall remained a figure of Romantic will for Tennyson, his understanding of Tennyson's poem and of the poet's role in society offer us another way of looking at literary history.

The dangers of scientific romanticism resided for Tennyson in the kind of social and moral chaos that might occur if the limits of human understanding were breached and made to serve the interests of a particular point of view. That is why in response to the youth's scepticism, expressed metaphorically through images of night and day, shadow and light, the sage stops the play of words and answers in a formal tone:

> No night no day!—I touch thy world again—
> No ill no good! such counter-terms, my son,
> Are border-races, holding, each its own
> By endless war: but night enough is there
> In yon dark city:
>
> (249-53)

Tennyson is not interested in refuting the discoveries of science, but in pointing out the limitations of all forms of human knowledge. As he contemplated the darkened state of most of humanity, the claims of both scientists and theologians seemed merely 'border-races'. Like many other Victorian intellectuals, Tennyson feared the breakdown of traditional authority among ordinary men and women. By appropriating the language of Romanticism in his poetry, Tennyson was able to circumscribe its ideological appeal, and by giving the voice of science its due within a carefully constructed narrative or dramatic context, Tennyson effectively mediated its impact for his Victorian readers. Such mediation depended upon Tennyson's sense of continuity with literary tradition as well as his interpretation of the relations of literature to other kinds of social discourse. Tennyson's characterizations of scientific romanticism demonstrated to his readers that the individual is subject *to* nature, rather than existing either as an agent of infinite possibilities or as a being entirely determined by natural law. By developing new forms of poetry to express conventional morality, Tennyson appealed to his readers' desire for social coherence amidst the utterly changed circumstances of Victorian religious beliefs. For contemporary readers, understanding the interchange of scientific and literary discourses in the writings of Victorian poets and scientists alike reveals the struggle for cultural authority that underlines the richness and polemical brilliance of Tennyson's best works.

Notes

1. Thomas Henry Huxley, 'Evolution and Ethics', in *Evolution and Ethics and Other Essays* (New York, 1904).

2. John Tyndall, 'A Glimpse of Farringford, 1858; and "The Ancient Sage," 1885' in *Alfred Lord Tennyson: A Memoir by his Son* (New York, 1897), II, pp. 469-78.

3. John Tyndall, 'Alpine Sculpture', in *Hours of Exercise in the Alps* (New York, 1897), p. 251.

4. Matthew Arnold, 'On the Modern Element in Literature', in *Matthew Arnold: Selected Prose*, ed. P. J. Keating (New York and Harmondsworth, 1970).

5. Herbert F. Tucker, *Tennyson and the Doom of Romanticism* (Cambridge, Mass., 1988).

6. *The Life and Letters of Thomas Henry Huxley,* ed. Leonard Huxley (New York, 1900), II, p. 338.

7. Frank M. Turner, 'Lucretius Among the Victorians', *Victorian Studies,* 16 (March 1973), p. 330.

8. John Tyndall, 'The Belfast Address', in *Fragments of Science: A Series of Detached Essays, Addresses, and Reviews* (New York, 1892), II, pp. 135-201.

9. Turner, 'Lucretius Among the Victorians', pp. 336-48.

10. Tyndall, 'A Glimpse of Farringford', p. 477.

11. John Tyndall, 'An Address to Students', in *Fragments of Science,* II, p. 99.

Eric Wilson (essay date 1998)

SOURCE: "Dickinson's Chemistry of Death," in *American Transcendental Quarterly,* Vol. 12, No. 1, March, 1998, pp. 27-43.

[*In the following essay, Wilson examines Dickinson's poems concerning death, noting that while the poet's attitude toward the power of the scientific method is generally favorable, she rejects the validity of scientific conclusions about death's mysteries.*]

In 1877, in the autumn of her life, Emily Dickinson, drawing from her internal spring, reminisced about connections among science, death, and language in a letter to Thomas Higginson: "When Flowers annually died and I was a child, I used to read Dr. Hitchcock's Book on the Flowers of North America. This comforted their Absence—assuring me they lived" (*L* 2:573).[1] Dickinson here refers to the *Catalogue of Plants Growing Without Cultivation in the Vicinity of Amherst College* (1829) of Edward Hitchcock,

the scientist and theologian who brought modern science to Amherst during his tenure as president of Amherst College (1845-54) and who likely opened young Emily's eyes to the wonders of science through a series of textbooks, treatises, and lectures during and shortly after her time at Amherst Academy (Sewall 342-47). Dickinson, like her scientific mentor Hitchcock, reveled in exploring ostensibly intractable mysteries, like death, with science. It seems that she garnered from Hitchcock's *Catalogue,* for instance, the reassuring scientific law that the wilting flowers of fall would be again vibrant in spring; perhaps the very language of science, like that of poetry, distilled eternal qualities from the destructions of time, saving for the faithful patterns that persist, shreds of security in a riddling world.

Yet, for Dickinson, always the fly buzzes, the certain slant of light oppresses: the "[w]orld is not conclusion." She could not find in science, as could the optimistic natural theologian Hitchcock, unquestionable solutions to mysteries, to the ultimate mystery: death. In *Religion of Geology* (1851), read by Emily's brother Austin and almost certainly by her, Hitchcock invokes chemistry, particularly the law of conversation of matter, to solve the riddle of death. With this science, he affirms the validity of Biblical theories of the future destruction of the world and of the resurrection of the body after death. According to Hitchcock, when God destroys the world, the solid substance of the earth will be consumed, while its particles will remain; likewise, the resurrected body will be identical to the earthly one in proportion and structure but not in constitution because when the body decomposes, its elements "are scattered all over earth and enter into new combinations." "Thus science," Hitchcock asserts, "instead of proving [Biblical] statements to be erroneous, only enables us more correctly to understand them" (*Religion* 7-8; qtd. in Sewall 346-47n). As Richard B. Sewall notes, Dickinson responds to this optimism with her own ironic slant:

> The Chemical Conviction
> That Nought be lost
> Enable in Disaster
> My fractured Trust
> The Faces of the Atoms
> If I shall see
> How more the Finished Creatures
> Departed me!
>
> (qtd. in Sewall 346n)

What on the surface appears to be a celebration of the efficacy of chemistry in solving death's riddle is underneath an indictment of the hubris of science. The "Chemical Conviction" is both a belief in chemistry and a coconviction of it; chemistry, it seems, both "enables" and, through a pun, "unables" her trust; though she may see the "Atoms," the basic particles, of the departed, she also knows that they are "Adams," deprived of the Tree of Life, condemned to suffer with the mystery of death.

Dickinson, avatar of Janus, takes a double stance toward Hitchcock's brand of science in several poems on her most persistent subject, death: she approves the power of scientific method for exploring the corpse while undercutting the validity of scientific conclusions about the enigmas of dying. Emphasizing the utility of the unbiased gaze, her poems indeed constitute scientific experiments—empirical, clear-eyed observations of the intricacies of physical, mental, spiritual worlds supported by tentative conclusions. Indeed, as Joanne Feit Diehl observes, Dickinson writes "quest poems" that test the boundaries of knowledge, practicing in her verse a scientific rigor, what Glauco Cambon would term a "radical inquiry" (161; 125). However, her verses uncover the limits of the very science she endorses. While she uses chemical terminology—like "dissolution," "sublimation," and "distillation"—to account for death, she simultaneously reveals the limits of this scientific vocabulary, finding it efficacious in sounding the mystery of the corpse but inadequate to brighten its deepest reaches. While death may be no more than chemical sublimation, it remains sublime. In practicing this chemistry of death, this "Science of the Grave" (#539), Dickinson both participates in and critiques the Hitchcockian scientific optimism of her age; for her, science, like Virgil for Dante, leads the poet through the labyrinth to the door of the temple but must there stop short, leaving the pilgrim to encounter the ambiguous sublime alone.

MICROSCOPES

While she was by no means a scientist, Dickinson was always favorably disposed toward methods of scientific inquiry. Her endorsement of scientific seeing as a way of avoiding dogma is memorably expressed in #185: while "'Faith' is a fine invention," "Microscopes are prudent / In an Emergency," in situations where specimens—like the poet's beloved birds, flowers, stones, or her loved and feared death—actually emerge in their full being. In one of the few accounts of Dickinson's use of science, Daniel J. Orsini observes that while "Dickinson well understood the flaws inherent in the scientific and empirical approach to otherworldly experience," "one of her chief strengths as a writer—a feature largely ignored by her critics—remains her daring and original use of science" (57). Indeed, William Howard has illustrated that Dickinson drew considerably from a stock of scientific terms in her poems, using 328 words "generally found only in scientific or academic discourse" (230). While others, like Jack Capps and Rebecca Patterson, have nodded to Dickinson's interest in science (105-06, 189-91; 110-113), Sewall in considering her relationship to Hitchcock has done the most justice to the poet as scientist.

Scientific terminology likely got into her poetry by way of Hitchcock. According to Sewall, Hitchcock could not have failed to exert a profound influence on the young poet.[2] As President of Amherst College, Hitchcock pushed his scientific agenda not only on the students in the college, but also on those in the nearby Amherst Academy where Dickinson was a student. Adept in geology, chemistry, astronomy, and botany, the versatile Hitchcock, in lectures Emily likely attended, in textbooks and books she almost certainly read, would have introduced students in Amherst to striking parallels between scientific fact and religious doctrine, demonstrating, for instance, in *Religious Lectures on Peculiar Phenomena in the Four Seasons* (1850) how the sun, after an ice storm, sparkles through ice like the jewels in Revelation and how the glories of sublunar spring emblematize those of the Christian Resurrection. Sewall conjectures that Hitchcock, as the "living embodiment" of the positive values of the Academy, "open[ed] [the young Dickinson's] eyes, [gave] her a discipline, and set her studies in the largest possible frame of reference" (34748; 354).

Hitchcock served as a leader of a popular movement in American Protestantism in the 1840s and 50s: natural theology, the effort to make religion a branch of science and/or science an outgrowth of religion. What George H. Daniels coins "The Reign of Bacon" in the first part of the nineteenth century encouraged enthusiastic belief in objective knowledge gained through induction.[3] Curiously, this welter of inductive, scientific activity bred in Protestant theologians not doubt but faith, faith that the senses could provide evidence for God's laws (63-85). Discoveries in all sciences suggested to theologians that universal laws existed in nature; these laws must, they thought, presuppose a lawgiver, God. Science did not work against religion but validated it, revealing and illuminating God's grandeur (Bozeman 80-81; Bruce 122). In the middle of the century, theological curricula nationwide began to incorporate science, hoping to fulfill the 1853 prediction of Hitchcock, officially Professor of Natural Theology at Amherst College: "[E]ntire harmony will be the final result of all researches in religion and philosophy" ("Relations" 191-92; qtd. in Daniels 52). The *Religion of Geology* stands as a valiant attempt to marry faith and fact. The book enthusiastically calls for colleges to instruct natural theology in their seminaries and takes for its ambitious subject the development "of relations between geology and religion." He proposes that "scientific discoveries furnish another means of [the Bible's] correct interpretation, where it describes natural phenomena" and throughout the book draws on most every science to analyze scriptural passages (*Religion* xii-1; 5). In another work, the above-mentioned *Religious Lectures,* Hitchcock takes nature for his text, showing how natural processes are "evidences" for heavenly ones; spring time and the metamorphosis of insects, for example, "evidence," respectively, the final and individual Resurrection. Justifying his methods, he asserts "The manner in which I have endeavored to defend the scripture doctrine of the resurrection of the body, by an appeal to certain principles of chemistry and biology seems to me quite conclusive" (34, 43; qtd. in Hovenkamp 42). For Hitchcock, the natural theologian combines the highest ideals of precision and piety: "He is a man who loves Nature, and with untiring industry endeavors to penetrate her mysteries. With a mind too large for narrow views, too generous and frank for distorting prejudice, and too pure to be the slave of appetite and passion, he calmly surveys the phenomena of nature, to learn from thence the great plan of the universe as it lay originally in the divine mind" ("Relations" 191-92; qtd. in Daniels 52).

While Dickinson may have learned the wonders of the physical world from Hitchcock and his sort of science, she was far from a natural theologian; her basic attitude toward him and his science was double, simultaneously approving and skeptical. While at times she seems fascinated by his work, weaving it into the fabric of her poems, borrowing his ideas and images, at other times she critiques the scientific tendencies he endorsed. Still other times, she simultaneously celebrates and deflates the science of which Hitchcock was a representative, invoking chemical vocabulary to account for death, while at the same time showing the inadequacy of these terms.

In several poems, early and late, Dickinson draws on Hitchcock for ideas and images. In #1063, an 1865 poem, for example, she again alludes to Hitchcock's use of the conversation of matter: a "Chemist" might be able to "disclose" into what "Carbonates" a cremated "Departed Creature" has been converted. In #100, written in 1859, she likely invokes his *Religion of Geology,* in which he extols the virtues of comparative anatomy, which enables the scientist to reconstruct the eating and behavioral habits of an animal from only a small part of the skeleton (Religion 78). Dickinson, perhaps ironically, carries this methodology over to the seasons: just as "'Comparative Anatomy,'" the "Savants" of "science" say, can make a "single bone" "unfold" the "secret" of an animal, so the "prospective" eye can from the "meekest" winter flower reconstruct roses, lilies, and "countless Butterfly." As late as 1881, as Sewall notes (346n), she enters into debates in geology over whether the earth originated from a great fire or a great flood (#1599). While Hutton espoused "Vulcanism," holding that the earth was of an igneous origin, his rival Abraham Gottlob Werner maintained "Neptunism," believing that the planet had an aqueous origin (Hovenkamp 121-22). According to George H. Daniels, Hitchcock began his career as a Wernerian, but as he grew older moved far enough away from the Neptunists to "adopt a theory of a central fire" (12). In a series of articles, lectures, and in his *Religion of Geology,* Hitchcock speculates on the earth's origin, attempting, of course, to reconcile geology with Genesis. Dickinson clearly draws on these theories in #1599, ostensibly siding with the Neptunists. She supposes that "Though the great Waters sleep," we "cannot doubt" "[t]hat they are still the Deep." "No vacillating God," she conjectures,

> "[i]gnited this Abode / To put it out."

Other poems, however, take issue with the presuppositions of Hitchcock's natural theology. In #1241, from 1872, Dickinson, as Sewall again notes (355n), seems to pose a clear challenge to his scientific optimism. Comparing the setting sun to a vast, sublime flower, she asserts that the "Scientist of Faith" cannot account for such natural phenomena: the "Flora unimpeachable" is beyond "Time's Analysis," a "Revelation" not to be "detained" by "theses"

of the scientist. Other poems take this tone, finding the scientist's reductions of revelation to ratio troubling: "Saints, with ravished slate and pencil," cannot "Solve our April Day" (#65); "It's very mean of Science / To go and interfere" with nature by reducing phenomena to one name (#70); this visible "World" studied by scientists is "not Conclusion"—"A Species stands beyond" that "beckons" and "baffles" "Philosophy" (#501); it's foolish for scientists to think that if they "Split the Lark" in dissection, they will "find the Music" (#861).

Dickinson, in her unwillingness to reduce the abundance and mystery of nature to mere chemical or geological process, was in a sense more scientific than Hitchcock and the natural theologians. While the natural theologians may have been more adept in the individual sciences than Dickinson, they remained rigid, almost scholastic, in method, reducing the physical world to dogma, while she, a sort of skeptical Baconian, dwelt forever in "Possibility" (#657), refusing to minimize enigma in homage to idols. As the following discussion of her double use of science in facing death shows, she worked to keep her inductions as free from presuppositions as possible. Because she is more rigorous than the likes of Hitchcock, she pushes science to its limits, hiring it as the most able guide into "'Undiscovered Continent[s]'" (#832), where it finds its strengths and weaknesses exposed.

CORPSES

In an autumn, 1882 letter, Dickinson reported that the death of her mother was both "benumbing" and "electric" (L 3: 752). This paradoxical sensibility details the characteristic duplicity with which Dickinson approaches death: with despair and ecstasy, fear and fascination, with a sense of terror and beauty. While this paradoxical sensibility perhaps inspired her to invoke the explanations of science to clear up tensions and contradictions, it also likely kept her from reducing the difficulties of death to mere chemistry. Indeed, she did approach death with an inductive, scientific rigor. As Joanne Feit Diehl remarks, Dickinson's poems "anticipate, observe, and follow the movements of the dying. This concentration on final moments is Dickinson's protest against the inviolate silence of death" (165). In her verse, according to Thomas H. Johnson, she "viewed death from every possible angle" (203); her gaze on death, as Thomas W. Ford observes, was part of her quest to embrace the concrete, to sound the deepest mysteries of finite existence (13). What motion is to Newton, what space and time are to Einstein, death is to Dickinson.

Her "gaze" on death is scientific, empirical: focused, intense, patient, she examines the morphology of death before, during, and after its strike. Death, for her, becomes a form of living, a site of possible revelation of the meaning of life. In #1633, for example, she approaches another's death like a surgeon, wanting to illuminate its mystery at the very point of expiration.

> Still own thee—still thou art
> What surgeons call alive

Though slipping—slipping I perceive
To thy reportless Grave
Which question shall I clutch
What answer wrest from thee
Before thou dost exude away
In the recalless sea?

Indeed, as we shall see, Dickinson constantly explores the darkness of death in hopes of understanding bright life, what it means to walk among the living. In this approach toward death, she unconsciously participates in what Michel Foucault has shown to be one of the major scientific breakthroughs of the nineteenth century. A new episteme, or structure of knowledge, emerged at the beginning of the century when scientists began to uncover the mystery of life by opening up corpses. According to Foucault, in the pioneering anatomo-clinical work of Xavier Bichat (1771-1802), the darkness of death becomes the light of life. Bichat claims in Anatomie generale (1801):

> For twenty years, from morning to night, you have taken notes at patients' bedsides on affections of the heart, the lungs and the gastric viscera, and all is confusion for you in the symptoms which, refusing to yield up their meaning, offer you a succession of incoherent phenomena. Open up a few corpses: you will dissipate at once the darkness that observation alone could not dissipate
>
> (xcix; qtd. in Foucault 146)

Drawing on Bichat, Foucault observes that by dissecting corpses, doctors for the first time could "see and analyze organic dependencies and pathological sequences"; exploring the decomposing cadaver, scientists could "[burst] upon the wonders of genesis." Paradoxically, for early nineteenth-century pathological anatomists, "[t]hat which hides and envelops, the curtain of night over truth . . . is life; and death, on the contrary, opens up to the light of day the black coffer of the body." In construing death as the ultimate object of study, this new medicine changed the way people relate to their own death, transforming it into an intense form of life. Life becomes a realm of ignorance; death, of knowledge. Poets and artists like Baudelaire and Delacroix (and, of course, Dickinson, though Foucault does not mention her) participate in the scientific "Gaze" on death: "The Gaze that envelops, caresses, details, atomizes the most individual flesh and enumerates its secret bites in that fixed, attentive, rather dilated gaze which, from the height of death, has already condemned life." Suddenly, in the scientific perception of death, the individual faces his own finitude, singles himself out of the mass, escapes from "a monotonous, average life": in the early nineteenth century, "[d]eath left its old tragic heaven and became the lyrical core of man: his invisible truth, his visible secret" (144, 166, 171, 172).

Though almost certainly Dickinson did not read Bichat, she vigorously participates in this new episteme. While indeed the methods and findings of the Bichat-inspired "Paris school" of pathological anatomy that flourished from 1800 to 1840 profoundly influenced antebellum American medi-

cine (Shyrock 124-30), it is unlikely that Dickinson was acutely aware of such developments. Indeed, Millicent Todd Bingham reports that medicine in Dickinson's Amherst remained rather primitive, with bloodletting a "favorite remedy" (176-78). Still, like her scientific contemporaries in Europe and America, Dickinson attempts to analyze death clinically, tries to reduce it to chemical process, often referring to it as "dissolution"; yet, she finds that always a residue remains beyond analysis, that while science effectively reveals the mysteries of death in their full light, it cannot solve them.

DISSOLUTION

She perhaps picked up the equation of death with "dissolution" from her beloved Sir Thomas Browne's *Hydriotaphia* (268, 269, 270), but she also saw it emphasized in Edward Hitchcock's *Religion of Geology*. In a chapter sure to have caught Dickinson's eye, "Death a Universal Law of Organic Beings on this Globe from the Beginning," Hitchcock draws on findings in comparative anatomy—a science, like pathological anatomy, whose conclusions on life are dependent on analyzing the structures of the dead—to prove that "in such a system as exists in the world, this universal decay and dissolution are indispensable." Scientifically speaking, death must have occurred on the planet before Adam fell; the facts suggest that dissolution is "an essential feature of the present system of organized nature; it must have entered into the plan of the creation in the divine mind originally." With his characteristic optimism, Hitchcock sets out to prove that death is "a benevolent provision," part of the "present system of the world," the best "infinite wisdom and benevolence could devise" (*Religion* 77, 79, 85).

While Dickinson's gaze on "dissolution" is scientific, she is unwilling or unable to view it in such confident and optimistic light. In fact, Dickinson, forever the purveyor of paradox, plays on the duplicity of "dissolution": as she learned from her cherished "Lexicon," the word, deriving from the Latin dis (apart) + solvere (to release, to loosen), describes the processes by which solids are decomposed into parts or dissolved into liquids as well as an excessive freedom, a lack of restraint; the word denotes then both extinction and releasement, disintegration and loosening.[4] Is dissolution the chemical process by which the body breaks apart into its constituent parts, or is! it is a releasing, a loosening of solidity into some spiritual ether? Is death as dissolution the finality of decomposition or the possibility of freedom? Dickinson mediates on the intricacies of the science of dissolution:

The Province of the Saved
Should be the Art—To save
Through Skill obtained in Themselves
The Science of the Grave
No Man can understand
But he that hath endured
The Dissolution—in Himself
That Man—be qualified
To qualify Despair

To Those who failing new
Mistake Defeat for Death—Each time
Till acclimated—to—

　　　　　　　　　　　　　　　　　　(#539)

Those who have "endured" some sort of "dissolution" and have observed its distinguishing characteristics are "scientists" whose conclusions can help others distinguish between mere despair and actual death. These "dissolved" scientists are paradoxically both "dead," decomposed, and "saved," "qualified" as experts with valuable knowledge. In several other poems Dickinson calls death, either literal or figurative, "dissolution" or a "dissolving"; in each, the term cannot be reduced to one meaning but is a site of paradox. For example, in #236, she wonders if death "dissolves" one into "nothing" or "more" and in #976, death is "a Dialogue between / The Spirit and the Dust," a site of "dissolution" of the body into dust and loosening of the body into spirit. Other poems that equate some form of death and dissolution are #243, #370, #548, #560, #628, #721, #817, #928, #1774. In each, the word, ostensibly one of scientific precision, loosens the poem into mystery. Aptly, the variants for the term "revolving" in Dickinson's famous "hummingbird" poem recommend Dickinson's synonyms for "dissolving"; in her mind, it seems that connections existed among "revolving," "dissolving," "dissembling," and "renewing." Each of these words might be used by Dickinson to detail death. Does death as dissolution benumb with finality or electrify with knowledge? Is dissolution ending or beginning? A riddle or renewal? Darkness or light? Is death decomposition of knowing, the "incognito" (#114), "the only Secret" (#153), or is it a loosening, a release, into "Vitality" (#816), an "unveil-[ing]" (#1732)?

SUBLIMATION

For Dickinson, death is a powerful source of the sublime, a site of knowledge and bewilderment, gain and loss, power and annihilation, beauty and terror. She equates dissolution and the sublime in an 1862 poem likely incited by the Civil War. She confesses that "It feels a shame to be Alive / When Men so brave—are dead." These brave men pay a great price—their lives—in fighting for liberty.

　　　The price is great—Sublimely paid
　　　Do we desenze—a Thing
　　　That lives—like Dollars—must be piled
　　　Before we may obtain?
　　　Are we that wait—sufficient worth
　　　That such Enormous Pearl
　　　As life—dissolved by—for Us
　　　In Battle's—horrid Bowl?
　　　It may beta Renown to live
　　　I think the Men who die
　　　Those unsustained—Saviors
　　　Present Divinity

　　　　　　　　　　　　　　　　　　(#444)

The dissolution of the soldiers is sublime: paradoxically, they are decomposed into food for the maw of death in battle's "horrid Bowl" while they are simultaneously transformed into divinity. The terror of death is the ecstasy of transfiguration. Other inversions support this sublime contradiction: living civilians, those "that wait," are not worth the soldierly dead; the "unsustained" are "Saviors"; the "Renown" of living is inferior to the "Divinity" of the dying. In another dirge to martyrdom, Dickinson pays homage to the "sublime deportment" of those who died for the good of the many (#295). In #310 she surmises that the "Marble Disc[s]," the tombstones, created by death are of a "Sublimer sort" than ordinary speech. "Conjecture" about what happens to the dead after expiration "Grapples with a Theme stubborn as Sublime" (#1221).

Equating death with the sublime, Dickinson's clinical gaze has revealed another chemical process: sublimation. Dissolution is sublimation, the chemical conversion of matter directly from a solid to a gas, the alchemical transformation of matter into spirit. Indeed, Dickinson's "Lexicon," the 1844 Webster's *American Dictionary of the English Language,* offers entries for "sublime" as the grand and lofty and as the process of sublimation. Chemistry and alchemy are easily conflated with aesthetics: just as sublimation is a transmutation of solid into gas, matter into spirit, essence into quintessence, so the sublime engenders sudden transport from one state to a radically different one, moving the beholder from the ordinary to the extraordinary, the familiar to the unfamiliar. The dissolving corpse is converted into something else, as Dickinson knew from Hitchcock's account of the conservation of energy, the basis of her "Chemical Conviction." Is there ground for believing that chemical breakdown is preparation for transfiguration into a higher state, a spiritual realm? The "Science of the Grave" has led to this possibility. Yet, the new datum concerning dissolution reveals a further mystery, bringing the chemical to trial. "Sublime" and "sublimation" originate from an antithetical root: sub, meaning both "up to" or "under," and limen, signifying "threshold" or "boundary." While the "sublime" and "sublimation" could point to a conversion from below "up to" a threshold—an ascension to the lofty—they could also refer to a change from above to "under" a boundary—a descending into an abyss (Twitchell 2-3). This correspondence both increases apprehension and deepens mystery. On the one hand, we learn that the decomposition/loosening of dissolution is a conversion; on the other, we are bewildered by the conversion's result. Is dissolution a rising or a sinking? A movement toward spirit or matter? The very form of the word "sublime" supports its contradictory content; "sublimation," like "dissolution," directs a bright, scientific beam on the mystery of death only to darken it further.

Dickinson's chemistry of the grave suggests that scientific inquiry confuses as much as it clarifies when it takes on subjects such as death. Chemical accounts of death do not secure and rationalize it; on the contrary, they reveal the very impossibility of corralling the intricacies of sublime death into brightly lighted cabinets. Science is useful insofar as it reveals the limits of objectivity, showing where sublimation ends and the sublime begins.

DISTILLATION

What conclusions is the scientist of the grave to draw from this "radical inquiry" into death? Chemistry seems to hide facts as quickly as it uncovers them. The hypothesis "Death is dissolution" proved useful for uncovering the complexities of death and suggesting the further hypothesis that "dissolution is sublimation," which on one hand clarified dissolution into conversion and on the other unearthed the mysteries of conversion. Can the scientist discern any laws, any causal relationships, any formulas, from these findings?

Dickinson does not confirm a conclusion, but surmises yet another hypothesis, suggesting that death, like the world, is not "conclusion." The best the scientist can do in the face of death is turn scientific poet, retaining chemical skills while living in mystery. The result of scientific method is not conclusion, but the poet's "distillation."

> This was a Poet—it is That
> Distills amazing sense
> From ordinary Meanings
> And Attar so immense
> From the familiar species
> That Perished by the DoorWe wonder it was not Ourselves
> Arrested it—before—
>
> (#448)

The poet fastens her scientific gaze on the "familiar species / That perished by the Door" to reveal their sublimity, their "amazing sense." The method is chemical: "distillation" refers to the process of heating substances in order to refine them, to separate or extract the core of them. For instance, through distillation, the perfumer extracts the "Attar," the essential oil or fragrance, the perfume, from the petals of flowers. The poet's gaze is the heat refining ordinary facts, like death, into extraordinary senses; the poem is the distillate, the essence. Her examinations of corpses show death to be "amazing" exhilarating and bewildering and "immense"—boundless and terrifying. Her rendering of these mysteries in language perfumes them, sweetens the odor of decay, houses them in a flowered coffin. She sweats in the laboratory, the examining room, to produce for the world the multifoliate rose, riddling intricacy condensed into a temporary pattern of petals. As Dickinson presented Thomas Higginson with two lilies as her mysterious "introduction," so the poet introduces to her readers the sublime distilled in floral words.

Dickinson does not, because she cannot, solve the mysteries unearthed by her research, but presents them in a form that stimulates readers to meditate mystery on their own. These forms are not merely synecdoches, but sites of what E. Miller Budick calls, borrowing from Martin Foss, "infinite process," "whereby one realm, vital and forceful in itself, is viewed in relation to another realm, equally valid, and whereby the two realms are not collapsed into a symbol which in stabilizing and fixing meaning also reduces it" (222; 14-18). Dickinson's distillations relate the realms of life and death, science and religion, hypothesis and conclusion, chemistry and spirituality, the ordinary and the extraordinary, never equating the two or reducing one to the other, but using one to explore the other, as the scientist uses the dissected corpse to sound the depths of life. These mutual explorations yield the dynamic, shifting, contradictory results of her poetic experiments. Under her gaze, chemical reductions dissolve into spiritual mysteries; spiritual mysteries are best viewed through chemistry. Dissolution is decomposition and transcendence; sublimation, the sublime.

Her distillations cast readers in her scientific role. Her verses are scientific reports that recreate her experiments, placing readers before the corpse. Just as she stands awed before the sublime dissolutions her scientific scrutiny has revealed, so readers, after engaging her riddling poems, abide in bewilderment, galvanized by the sublime. As the corpse is to the poet, so the poem is to readers. In distilling her sublime vision into sublime verses, she turns readers into scientists of the grave, engaging them to test hypotheses on the mysteries of death, to find the wonders and limits of science.

CHEMISTRY OF DEATH

Dickinson's famous poem "I heard a Fly buzz—when I died" (#465) distills her chemistry of death, presenting death, after close scientific inspection, as a sublime mystery for readers to contemplate. Patient and examiner, object and subject, are occupied by the same speaker in this poem. The dying patient is on the table detailing her symptoms, attempting, in a clinical fashion, to understand what happens during the process of dying. Those in the room, whose eyes are "wrung" "dry," are viewing the examination at one remove, likewise straining to understand death. The poem dramatizes the scientific method of poet and readers: the dying person observing her demise represents Dickinson the poet scientifically exploring death; the attending mourners depict readers inspecting one of Dickinson's scientific reports, one of her poems, on death. As Dickinson is to death, as the speaker is to her own dying, as the mourners are to the expiring speaker, so readers are to this poem.

The poem, famously in past tense, the speaker coming to us from the other side of the grave, opens with a highly specific catalogue of sensations occurring during death.

> I heard a Fly buzz—when I died
> The Stillness in the Room
> Was like the Stillness in the Air
> Between the Heaves of Storm

The stanza contains startling juxtapositions: between a housefly and the moment of death, stillness and buzzing. These curious contiguities are reinforced by the paradoxical "Heaves." The pregnant, twice-used "Stillness," a limen between two worlds, divides "Heaves of Storm," presumably life and death. These "heaves" could be uplifting and buoyant, as the word means the act of raising or lifting with great power; or, they might be destructive, jarring, the term also signifying the act of displacing forcefully. Is the stillness the instant before transcendence or catastrophe? Loosening or decomposition? Does the buzzing "Fly" anticipate carrion or ascension? Is death a grand mystery, a moment of transformation, or an ordinary event, no more special than the common housefly? The speaker and readers are clearly in the realm of dissolution and sublimation, facing at the same time the lofty and the abysmal.

The next stanza moves outward to attendants and readers.

> The Eyes around—had wrung them dry
> And Breaths were gathering firm
> For the last Onset—when the King
> Be witnessed—in the Room

All are consumed by the gaze, their eyes dry from observing and crying, straining, like the speaker and the readers, to understand the impending death. Has their watching yielded apprehension that allows them to cease crying, their eyes now dry? Or has it left them thirsty for sustenance? They, like the speaker, entertain the possibility that death is grand, lofty, royal: they wait for the "King." He is expected to follow the "Onset," either an assault or a beginning. Is he warlike, coming to wreak destruction after the dying person has been assaulted? Or is he benevolent, come to escort her to begin her blissful afterlife?

The poem returns to the speaker, who reports on how she will "distill" her experiences.

> I willed my Keepsakes—Signed away
> What portion of me be
> Assignable—and then it was
> There interposed a Fly

Her will is a written document that lives after her; it is a distillation of her life; it is this poem, the scientific "conclusion" about her death. She has extracted the "amazing senses" of her life, those "Keepsakes"—memories, things—that can be detailed in language, that are "Assignable," fit to be marked with signs. The mourners and readers benefit from this will/poem; it provides them with an account of death from one already dead, a journal of a mysterious journey on which they must one day embark. The poem, though, is not a simple synecdoche for her life, a part corresponding to the whole—the fly interposes, comes between word and meaning, symbol and symbolized. Within the drama of the poem, the speaker and mourners are irritated during the will-signing ceremony by the buzzing of a fly—static, as it were, hindering clear communication. The fictional mourners must wonder—what does this mean about death, that a fly would bother such a serious moment? Readers of the poem, too, are agitated by the riddle of the fly: is the buzzing an irritation that demeans this moment customarily thought to be so significant or is it a charge of energy—an electric hum—that hopefully betokens life, suggesting that life goes on, on this world and elsewhere? The speaker's distillation is a sublime dissolution, an "infinite process" in which two

realms—life and death, the sacred and the profane, the visible and the invisible—endlessly vitalize one another.

In the final stanza, the speaker continues to explore the ambiguous energy of the fly.

> With Blue—uncertain stumbling Buzz
> Between the light—and me
> And then the Windows failed—and then
> I could not see to see

The agitation of the fly, beautiful and bungling, spills into this stanza. The fly, like "dissolution" and "sublimation," simultaneously contains positive and negative poles. Without intending to close off other interpretations to this mysterious poem, we wonder: is the fly a "blue" messenger sent by a caring God to buzz a dirge to her dying, or is it a harbinger of nature's, and the world's, indifference to individual death? Just as the fly interposed between part and whole, word and meaning, here it comes between the speaker and light: does it block the speaker from or bridge her to the light—a lamp, the sun, earthly life, or the face of God? The failing "Windows" encompass binaries as well. They could be a sign of the speaker's "failed" vision as she is fading away, no longer able to see the physical world around her. This possibility would constitute a rather horrible end, her final moment stolen by a household pest. Conversely, the windows, not the speaker, could be failing, suggesting a revelatory moment in which this world passes away and a new heaven and earth emerge. In this case, she would no longer "see to see" the visible world because it is dissolving to reveal an invisible one. Her death is either, to use the words describing suffering and death in Shakespeare's *King Lear,* an "image of that horror"—a meaningless death in an indifferent world or the "promised end"—a revelation, suffering rewarded (5.3.264-65).

This poem is chemical. The poet's study of death has revealed that it is indeed structured by the chemical processes of "dissolution" and "sublimation." She has "distilled" the "results" of this study into this brief poem, her will, which forces readers to examine the intricacies of death as she does, to become scientists of the grave. Dickinson has donated her corpus to science so her readers can feel the electricity of death that galvanizes life.

Elsewhere, Dickinson memorably recalls Odysseus's deception of the Cyclops, casting herself and her readers as the Greek hero, the first scientist of the western world: "I'm Nobody! Who are you? / Are you Nobody—Too? / Then there's a pair of us!" Insatiably curious, always transgressing boundaries (for which Dante condemns him), Odysseus wanders onto the island of the Cyclops for no other reason than to gather data about the inhabitants of the island. He repeatedly does this throughout the Odyssey, risking much for the sake of knowledge of the unknown. In the case of his excursion into Polyphemos' domain, faced with the riddle of the one-eyed monster, he must contrive a trick of his own in order to return to the safety of his familiar ship. Odysseus, like Dickinson, a female version of the Greek hero, is a type of the bold scientist, hazarding secure conclusions by pushing beyond the maps of cool reason, revealing the wonders and limits of scientific inquiry. Returning from the riddles of the unmapped—of death, of the monstrous—both leave riddles behind, offering us the opportunity to experience what they have: the sublime dissolving of safe solutions, the conviction of the chemical. Standing before her poetic puzzles, we become decomposed to be released, nobody to become all.

Notes

1. I shall cite letters and poems within the text, designating letters with L, followed by volume and page, and poems by providing the poem numbers used by Thomas H. Johnson in his edition of Dickinson's poems. The letters are from *The Letters of Emily Dickinson* and the poems from *The Complete Poems of Emily Dickinson.*

2. Millicent Todd Bingham, in *Emily Dickinson's Home; Letters and Life of Edward Dickinson and His Family,* 103-111, also explores Hitchcock's presence in Amherst and the Dickinson family, but not nearly as specifically as Sewall does. For further information on Dickinson's reading of Hitchcock, see Carlton Lowenberg, *Emily Dickinson's Textbooks,* 57-60

3. For a similar account of Bacon's influence in America, see also Theodore Dwight Bozeman, *Protestants in an Age of Science: The Baconian Ideal and Antebellum American Religious Thought,* 3-31;52-60.

4. As Carlton Lowenberg notes in *Emily Dickinson's Textbooks,* scholars cannot agree on which edition of Webster's *American Dictionary of the English Language* Dickinson used for her "Lexicon"; generally they choose between the 1841 and 1844 editions. The 1844 edition, published by Harper and Brothers in New York (the Dickinsons owned the same edition published by J. S. and C. Adams in Amherst), offers these definitions for the transitive verb form of "dissolve," meanings that clearly bear the word's primary semantic paradox—to disintegrate or annihilate and to loosen or release: "1. To melt; to liquefy; to convert from a solid or a fixed state to a fluid state by means of heat or moisture. 2. To disunite; to break; to separate. 3. To loose; to disunite. 4. To loose the ties or bonds of any thing; to destroy any connected system. 5. To loose; to break. 6. To break up; to cause to separate; to put an end to. 7. To clear; to solve; to remove; to dissipate, or to explain. 8. To break; to destroy. 9. To loosen or relax; to make languid. 10. To waste away; to consume; to cause to vanquish or perish. To annul; to rescind." Germane definitions for the intransitive verb form are "To melt away in pleasure; to become soft or languid"; "To waste away; to perish; to be decomposed."

Works Cited

Bichat, Xavier. *Anatomie generale.* Paris, 1801.

Bingham, Millicent Todd. *Emily Dickinson's Home: Letters and Life of Edward Dickinson and His Family.* New York: Harper and Brothers, 1955.

Bozeman, Theodore Dwight. *Protestants in an Age of Science: The Baconian Ideal and Antebellum American Religious Thought.* Chapel Hill: U of North Carolina P, 1977.

Browne, Sir Thomas. *Hydriotaphia, urn-burial; or, A discourse of the sepulchral urns lately found in Norfolk. The Major Works.* Ed. and Intro. C. A. Patrides. New York: Penguin, 1977.

Bruce, Robert V. *The Launching of Modern American Science 1846-1876.* New York: Knopf, 1987.

Budick, EX Miller. "The Dangers of the Living Word: Aspects of Dickinson's Epistemology, Cosmology, and Symbolism." *ESQ* 29:4 (1983).

Cambon, Glauco. "Emily Dickinson and the Crisis of Self-Reliance." *Transcendentalism and Its Legacy.* Ed. Myron Simon and Thornton H. Parsons. Ann Arbor, Michigan: U of Michigan P, 1969.

Capps, Jack. *Emily Dickinson's Reading: 1836–1886.* Cambridge, Massachusetts: Harvard UP, 1966.

Dickinson, Emily. *The Complete Poems of Emily Dickinson.* Ed. Thomas H. Johnson. Cambridge, Massachusetts: The Belknap Press of Harvard UP, 1955.

———. *The Letters of Emily Dickinson.* Ed. Thomas H. Johnson and Theodora Ward. Cambridge, Massachusetts: The Belknap Press of Harvard UP, 1958.

Diehl, Joanne Feit. *Dickinson and the Romantic Imagination.* Princeton: Princeton UP, 1981.

Ford, Thomas W. *Heaven Beguiles the Tired: Death in the Poetry of Emily Dickinson.* University: U of Alabama P, 1966.

Foss, Martin. *Symbol and Metaphor in Experience.* Princeton, New Jersey: Princeton UP, 1949.

Foucault, Michel. *The Birth of the Clinic: An Archaeology of Medical Perception.* Trans. A. M. Sheridan Smith. New York: Vintage, 1973.

Hitchcock, Edward. "The Relations and Mutual Duties Between the Philosopher and the Theologian." *Bibliotecha Sacra* 10 (1853).

———. *The Religion of Geology and Its Connected Sciences.* Boston: Phillips, Sampson, and Co., 1851.

———. *Religious Lectures on Peculiar Phenomena in the Four Seasons* (Amherst: J. S. and C. Adams, 1850).

Hovenkamp, Herbert. *Science and Religion in America 1800-1860.* Philadelphia: U of Pennsylvania P, 1978.

Howard, William. "Emily Dickinson's Poetic Vocabulary." *Publications of the Modern Language Association* 72 (1957).

Johnson, Thomas H. *Emily Dickinson: An Interpretive Biography.* Cambridge, Massachusetts: Harvard UP, 1955.

Lowenberg, Carlton. *Emily Dickinson's Textbooks.* Eds. Territa A. Lowenberg and Carla L. Brown. Lafayette, California, 1986.

Orsini, Daniel J. "Emily Dickinson and the Romantic Use of Science." *Massachusetts Studies in English* 7:4/8:1 (1981).

Patterson, Rebecca. *Emily Dickinson's Imagery.* Amherst: U of Massachusetts P, 1979.

Sewall, Richard B. *The Life of Emily Dickinson.* Cambridge: Harvard UP, 1974.

Shyrock, Richard Harrison. *Medicine and Society in America, 1660–1860.* New York: New York UP, 1960.

Twitchell, Paul. *Romantic Horizons: Aspects of the Sublime in English Poetry and Painting,* 1770–1850. Columbia, Missouri: U of Missouri P, 1983.

Clare Pettitt (essay date 1998)

SOURCE: "'Cousin Holman's Dresser': Science, Social Change, and the Pathologized Female in Gaskell's 'Cousin Phillis,'" in *Nineteenth-Century Literature,* Vol. 52, No. 4, March, 1998, pp. 471-89.

[*In the following essay, Pettitt uses "Cousin Phillis" to probe Elizabeth Gaskell's views of science and contemporary scientific culture.*]

Gaskell completed her novel *Sylvia's Lovers,* the "tiresome book" that had taken her three years to write, in January 1863.[1] It is a novel in which will and desire seem impotent over the development of narrative and history, and, despite the fact that no scientists appear in its pages, there is evidence within the very narrative structure of *Sylvia's Lovers* that Gaskell is engaging with scientific discourses and the much-discussed theories of unconscious development that were current in the 1860s.[2] It is impossible that Gaskell, living through the 1850s and 1860s in Unitarian, middle-class Manchester, related by marriage to Charles Darwin, and in contact with many of the leading scientists of her age, could have ignored a rapidly developing scientific culture.[3] As Arnold Thackray has pointed out, for the Mancunian middle class in the nineteenth century, science "offered a coherent explanatory scheme for the unprecedented, change-orientated society in which [social reformers] found themselves unavoidably if willingly cast in leading roles."[4]

Nevertheless, disentangling Gaskell's view—or rather views—of science is a confusing process that seems at first to yield only contradictions. "Not scientific nor mechanical" was Gaskell's own emphatic assessment of herself in a September 1851 letter to her friend Anne Robson in which she describes a trip to the Great Exhibition in

that year (*Letters,* p. 159). Yet I argue that while Gaskell energetically rejected any simplistic notion of science as a "coherent explanatory scheme," throughout her work she inscribes and reinscribes versions of "scientific progress," repeatedly attempting to find a scientific paradigm for social change that is genuinely capable of expressing and ordering her desire for social transformation. I also argue that, when scientific paradigms break down in Gaskell's fiction, the failures are projected onto the feminine subject. The female occupies a double space in Gaskell's narrative that renders her both hero and victim: both "bound by another's rules" (in Gaskell's words)[5] and simultaneously representative of the power to transform those rules. That the developing scientific culture and the gender-divided culture of "separate spheres" are ideologically linked in Gaskell's work becomes very clear in her last two works of fiction, the novella "Cousin Phillis" and the unfinished novel *Wives and Daughters: An Everyday Story.* In these last narratives, as she had done in her earlier work, Gaskell again takes up figurations of the scientist in an attempt to conflate human agency and change, while using the female as the site upon which change is ultimately projected.

Gaskell wrote "Cousin Phillis" directly after *Sylvia's Lovers,* throughout the autumn and winter of 1863, and the novella appeared in parts in the *Cornhill* between November 1863 and February 1864.[6] At first reading, the work seems to mark a complete departure from *Sylvia's Lovers.* A. W. Ward describes it as a "simple tale" of "homely charm,"[7] and indeed Gaskell seems to have restored the control of nature to man; there is nothing of the wild landscape or treacherous sea of *Sylvia's Lovers* in the cultivated garden and farm where most of the action of "Cousin Phillis" takes place. Even the surrounding countryside is described as "very wild and pretty."[8] Gaskell has changed the scale, and the very brevity and intimacy of the novella form supports the theme of her story; for "Cousin Phillis" is about looking closely, about attention to detail. The initial impression is that the wide, created universe has been circumscribed and shrunk into the garden of Hope Farm: "there was a low wall round it, with an iron railing on the top of the wall, and two great gates between pillars crowned with stone balls for a state entrance" (p. 265). This is a place where order and privacy prevail, at least superficially. Yet there are four scientists in "Cousin Phillis." Every male character in the story, with the exception of the farm-laborer Timothy Cooper and the ministers, is to some degree a man of science. After her bleak examination of Darwinian theory in *Sylvia's Lovers,* with "Cousin Phillis" Gaskell returns to the scientific paradigm of mechanics and heavy industry that she had used before in both *Mary Barton* and *North and South.*

Gaskell's friend Catherine Winkworth gives an account in an 18 March 1856 letter to Emily Shaen of a visit to Mr. Nasmyth's Patricroft works made by a party comprising herself, Selina Winkworth, Gaskell, and her eldest daughter, Marianne. Leaping up to explain the workings of some piece of machinery, Nasmyth "illustrated with impromptu diagrams drawn on the wall alternately with a piece of white chalk and a sooty forefinger."[9] Jenny Uglow notices the transposition of this incident into "Cousin Phillis" (see Uglow, p. 544), when the irrepressibly scientific Mr. Manning, an inventor and the narrator's father, uses the same method of illustration:

> I saw my father taking a straight burning stick out of the fire, and, after waiting for a minute, and examining the charred end to see if it was fitted for his purpose, he went to the hard-wood dresser, scoured to the last pitch of whiteness and cleanliness, and began drawing with the stick; the best substitute for chalk or charcoal within his reach, for his pocket-book pencil was not strong or bold enough for his purpose. When he had done, he began to explain his new model of a turnip-cutting machine to the minister, who had been watching him in silence all the time. Cousin Holman had, in the meantime, taken a duster out of a drawer, and, under pretence of being as much interested as her husband in the drawing, was secretly trying on an outside mark how easily it would come off, and whether it would leave her dresser as white as before.
>
> ("Cousin Phillis," p. 289)

The similarity of the accounts is undeniable, but Gaskell transposes the inscription from a factory wall to a hard-wood dresser in the kitchen of the Holmans' farmhouse. The comfortable small comedy of Cousin Holman's surreptitious attempts to assess the damage to her dresser frames the scene with the recognizable referents of domestic comedy. But in fact Cousin Holman's dresser will never be as white as before. Gaskell chooses to represent the nineteenth-century "march of progress" in terms of intimate material changes that penetrate the most traditional of homes. Scientific innovation crosses classes and creeds and threatens traditional boundaries, just like the railway lines that Holdsworth is laying over "the shaking, uncertain ground" (p. 263). And while celebrating the potential of scientific change, Gaskell also struggles to incorporate, or at least to include, its effects on individual lives in her inventories of the small details of human existence.

"Through Mr Manning Gaskell shows that the older, simpler order can co-exist with industrial progress," claims Uglow (p. 544). Mr. Manning does, indeed, seem to be presented as the "good scientist," but he does not belong to an "older, simpler order"; rather he belongs to the discourse of self-help to which Gaskell returns after her bleak evocation in *Sylvia's Lovers* of a world devoid of will. The "older, simpler order" of science is as much of a myth as the "natural" sexual innocence of women. Yet in "Cousin Phillis" Gaskell seems able to engage aggressively only with the latter myth. She transfers all her potentially radical questions about change onto a central female character while leaving the more problematic questions of class and technological and social change unresolved.

Manning is an example of the hero-victim inventor of nineteenth-century self-help literature. He is introduced leaving Paul at his new lodgings in Eltham, when he is reported to have delivered "a few plain precepts" to his son (p. 259). Gaskell's emphasis, in all of the sporadic descriptive glimpses of Manning, is on his rejection of superfluity, verbal or financial:

> He was a mechanic by trade, but he had some inventive genius, and a great deal of perseverance, and had devised several valuable improvements in railway machinery. He did not do this for profit, though, as was reasonable, what came in the natural course of things was acceptable; he worked out his ideas, because, as he said, "until he could put them into shape, they plagued him by night and by day."
>
> (p. 259)

The scattered clues that the reader is given about Manning—in a narrative from which he is largely absent—can be reconstructed into a variation on a familiar self-help invention narrative. Typically, perseverance is privileged over genius, of which Manning only possess "some." Unlike Jem Wilson's "crank, or somewhat" in *Mary Barton*,[10] though, Manning's inventions are not only in the form of "devised . . . improvements" to machinery already in existence. He is also the creator of Manning's Patent Winch: "It was in the *Gazette*," boasts Paul; "It was patented. I thought every one had heard of Manning's patent winch" (p. 276). During the narrative, too, Manning is busy designing "Manning's driving wheel" (p. 287). Yet despite this, Manning is no radical genius likely to change the world at one stroke. Gaskell insists on the Holmans' ignorance of his great innovation in shunting, and later in the book, when Holdsworth is about to leave suddenly for Canada, she inserts a significant parenthesis as he receives the letter of commission: "'It is from Greathed the engineer' (Greathed was well known in those days; he is dead now, and his name half-forgotten)" (p. 313). These small details seem to indicate that Gaskell is anxious to dispel any suspicion that Manning may be in possession of power. She seems equally anxious to indicate the gradualism of his transformation into a rich man. It is stressed that Manning does not invent for money but rather because he is "called" to do it as a Romantic vocation. Even when his ideas are capitalized by the rich Mr. Ellison ("who lives in King Street? why, he drives his carriage!" [p. 290]), Gaskell stresses that profit is "a long way off, anyhow" (p. 290). And, indeed, when Paul subsequently makes a visit home to Birmingham he finds no evidence of sudden social transformation: "There was no display of increased wealth in our modest household" (p. 306). In fact, the social position of Mr. Manning is not shown to change at all in the course of the narrative, although the reader is told that it has changed substantially. At the start of the novel it is noted, carefully, that Paul's situation as a clerk to a railway engineer is "rather above his [father's] in life" (p. 259)—which is that of a mechanic—so Manning's partnership with Ellison represents a significant social leap.

Yet while Gaskell so cautiously plays down Manning's growing fame and fortune, she allows other, contradictory evidence to accrue. For instance, Holdsworth, in paying homage to the older man, shows Paul his "ungrudging ad-miration of his *great mechanical genius*" (p. 293; empha-sis added), and Holdsworth is reported to have spoken of Manning "often . . . as having the same kind of genius for mechanical invention as that of George Stephenson" (p. 287). While Holdsworth seems to see a greatness of genius in Manning that makes him a powerful figure, he also gives an account of Manning's life that fits it per-fectly for the pages of Samuel Smiles's *Self-Help* (1859):

> "Here's a Birmingham workman, self-educated, one may say—having never associated with stimulating minds, or had what advantages travel and contact with the world may be supposed to afford—working out his own thoughts into steel and iron, making a scientific name for himself—a fortune, if it pleases him to work for money—and keeping his singleness of heart, his perfect simplicity of manner."
>
> (p. 294)

Money here, and in such other "industrial success litera-ture,"[11] is the unstable signifier. When Gaskell repeatedly and emphatically represents Manning as not interested in "money," the word stands in place of "social power." The "Birmingham workman" could have as much money as he liked, and as quickly as he liked, if this would not affect his social position. But, inevitably, it would. Gaskell finds herself in something of an ideological bind here: she needs to reward Manning as a good and virtuous working-class man, yet she also needs to control the social change that such a reward necessarily entails, because her fear of working-class power remains active. Her solution is to limit his access to the text, creating a sense of his presence by narrativizing his absence with contradictory evidence of his social mobility and of his simultaneously staying in precisely the same place as before.[12]

As an independent center of value in "Cousin Phillis," Manning is not successful because, like Job Legh and Jem Wilson, he suffers from being the unstable creation of a discourse other than that of the narrative that contains him. All of these characters are, in a word, stereotypes. They are the hero-victim inventors of self-help literature, and al-though Gaskell attempts to deploy them within her narra-tives as agents of change, they are unable to perform the symbolic work that she intends for them, disabled as they are by the essential contradiction in their construction. To say, as Uglow does, that "through Mr Manning Gaskell shows that the older, simpler order can co-exist with in-dustrial progress" makes the strange assumption that an "order" of scientists like Manning existed as somehow separate and that it antedated "industrial progress." In fact, men like James Nasmyth and George Stephenson were the agents of "industrial progress." Similarly, the implication that "older" and "simpler" are adjectives that sit logically together is another assumption founded on the very myth of progressive development that Gaskell attacks elsewhere in her work. Yet Uglow's is precisely the reading that the text of "Cousin Phillis" is very carefully constructed to produce. Through Manning, I would argue, Gaskell at-tempts to invent an "older, simpler order" and thus sepa-rates the "Birmingham workman" from the processes of "industrial progress" and, furthermore, separates "indus-trial progress" from its inevitable corollary, social change.[13]

The two principal scientists in "Cousin Phillis," Manning and Holdsworth, dramatize Gaskell's own conflicting views of science and its social roles. Holdsworth is not a hero-victim; he is a new type in Gaskell's fiction, and he represents a move toward the representation of a "real" so-cial and scientific "new type," the professional scientist. In "Cousin Phillis" Holdsworth appears as the Romantic Sci-entist. Not only is he the flippant focus of the romantic plot, but Gaskell also heaps him with all the accoutre-ments of the "romantic hero." He is undeniably "exotic": "he had travelled on the Continent, and wore mustachios and whiskers of a somewhat foreign fashion" (p. 261); he is "young, handsome, keen, well-dressed" (p. 287); he speaks fluent Italian and has "a long soft drawl" (p. 287); and Phillis initially thinks him "very like a foreigner" (p. 300). He is also slightly dangerous: the two good dissent-ing ladies of the pastry shop that Paul lodges above disap-proved of him (p. 262), and he gives Phillis a copy of *I Promessi Sposi,* a novel that would probably not be ap-proved of by her father, who feels that Holdsworth's com-pany "is like dram-drinking" (p. 305). All of these vital credentials for the stereotypical romantic hero are supplied by Gaskell over and above the adulation that Holdsworth is afforded by the adolescent Paul, who immediately grants him "the position of hero in my boyish mind" (p. 261). The narrator insists on this "hero-worship" (p. 283), re-flecting on "his empire over me" (p. 293) and noticing that Holdsworth similarly exerts an "unconscious hold" (p. 305) over the Holman family.

Holdsworth, in contrast to Manning, is an educated and well-read scientist, a southerner and a "gentleman." He re-fers to "my heaps of scientific books" (p. 294), but he is far from bookish—"He had no notion of doing or saying things without a purpose" (p. 265)—and is not interested in anything that is "merely narrative, without leading to action" (p. 287). He tells Paul that "'Activity and readi-ness go a long way in our profession'" (p. 314), a maxim that seems to mirror Minister Holman's injunction to Paul: "'Whatsoever thine hand findeth to do, do it with all thy might'" (p. 330).[14] But Holdsworth's is a restless and pro-miscuous purpose, looking for work in the global capitalist marketplace, whereas Minister Holman looks for his du-ties within the boundaries of his "circumscribed life" (p. 326). Although it is not clear whether Hope Farm is run for subsistence only, none of the characters is ever seen going to market. The Holmans seem to live within a closed and self-sufficient economy where "there was plenty all around in which the humblest labourer was made to share" (p. 333).[15] Holdsworth, by contrast, inhabits the free mar-ket, and his restlessness and opportunism belong to the competitive world of industrial capitalism. He represents for Gaskell the dangerous and disruptive power of science and industry that potentially unsettles and disturbs such enclosed self-sufficiency. His sudden absences—first from his job, in the "dark overshadowed dale" (p. 294) where he contracts the low fever, and then his final departure to Canada—extend the world of the novella suddenly, so that Hope Farm no longer seems quite so entirely a microcosm. Holdsworth's letters bring "a whiff of foreign atmosphere into [Minister Holman's] circumscribed life" (p. 326)—a connection is formed between Hope Farm and the macrocosm. Holdsworth, unlike Manning, represents science and industrial progress as change. Old stories will necessarily be interrupted: the romantic hero will suddenly leave for Canada, never to return.

In comparison with Manning, Holdsworth is frenetically mobile, but his is not a social mobility. Gaskell is at pains to make clear in the passage in which Holdsworth and Manning meet that Holdsworth is a "gentleman":

> my father, . . . his hands, blackened beyond the power of soap and water by years of labour in the foundry; speaking a strong Northern dialect, while Mr Holdsworth had a long soft drawl in his voice, as many of the Southerners have, and was reckoned in Eltham to give himself airs.
>
> (p. 287)

The fact that Manning was a mechanic in the works where Holdsworth served his engineering apprenticeship makes their "mutual regard" (p. 287) suspect. Manning is figured as the classless inventor who can joke with the gentleman, Holdsworth, about other gentlemen wearing gloves for dirty mechanical work. While this passage could be read uncritically as a celebration of the democratizing power of science, it can also be read as a transparent middle-class fantasy of class reconciliation and cooperation.

Manning is supposed to be consulting Holdsworth about his driving wheel and the offer he has been made of a partnership. This attempt to bring the two scientists together is convincing neither as social realism nor in terms of the representations that Gaskell is using. A vast gulf yawns between the social positions of a mechanic and a gentleman-apprentice. Such a relationship between a young and foppish professional and a middle-aged laborer is unlikely enough; that it could function with no class friction at all seems preposterous. The other problem is representational. Because Gaskell has drawn on the hero-victim inventor myth for her representation of Manning, he cannot authentically enter systems of exchange and the capitalist market. Holdsworth, although no less a stereotype, represents exchange value and is, perhaps excessively, "transferable." The two men cannot communicate, as they are created in different genres, and it is perhaps significant that their conversation is not represented but rather is reported by Paul.

Holdsworth tries to explain Minister Holman's scientific ability as hereditary—"it's evidently good blood" (p. 294)—but Paul "knocks a pretty theory on the head" (p. 294) by pointing out that Minister Holman is not related to his father by blood but by marriage. Thus Gaskell calls into question the basis of scientific ability: it seems to be spread arbitrarily and widely among the male characters in

"Cousin Phillis." "I have fewer books than leisure to read them, and I have a prodigious big appetite," remarks the Minister, when he asks Paul to help him with the technical words in "a volume of stiff mechanics" (p. 277). Later he asks Paul to recommend "any simple book on dynamics that I could put in my pocket, and study a little at leisure times in the day" (p. 278). The Minister appears to be engaged in a program of rigorous self-help, which in some ways allies him to the representation of Manning: Gaskell tells us that the two men "seemed to come together by instinct" (p. 288). If Manning seems more substantial in the company of Minister Holman than in the company of Holdsworth, it is because both Hope Farm and Manning himself are represented by Gaskell as outside of the social and capitalist world. The drawing on the dresser of the turnip-cutting machine represents the pure value of the turnip-cutting machine, not its potential exchange value. Minister Holman insists on pure representation, and like Manning he eschews superfluity, as is shown when Holdsworth remarks that he enjoys talking to the Minister: "really it is very wholesome exercise, this trying to make one's words represent one's thoughts" (p. 303). Holdsworth's usual mode of speech, with its "random assertions and exaggerated expressions . . . merely looking to [his words'] effect on others" (p. 303), reveals his attitude to meaning as detachable and manipulable and, with his propensity to "talk a subject up," constitutes further evidence of his adaptation to a commercial environment.

The fourth scientist in "Cousin Phillis" is, of course, Paul Manning, the narrator. The reader hears little about Paul's own scientific ambitions, although the few details given indicate that he is conscientious: "I really had taken an interest in my work; nor would Mr Holdsworth, indeed, have kept me in his employment if I had not given my mind as well as my time to it" (p. 275). His father remarks: "Thou'rt not great shakes, I know, in th' inventing line" (p. 290); the impression is that Paul is steady and unexceptional, and by finally marrying Miss Ellison he guarantees both his own professional future and the patrimony of the Manning name. Paul's work is largely that of an interpreter: he explains technical words to Minister Holman, and Phillis's interest in his railway work makes him "take more pains in using clear expressions" (p. 276). The novella is ostensibly concerned with the process of Paul's coming of age, both intellectually and sexually, but his centrality to his bildungsroman is challenged by his function as narrator, as the interpreter of other, obscure signs.

The scene in which Manning draws the turnip-cutting machine on the dresser, along with the one in which Paul espies "the three. I counted their heads, joined together in an eager group over Holdsworth's theodolite" (p. 308), both use science as the focus of an unorthodox grouping. The heads "joined together" are temporarily united by scientific enthusiasm. Yet there is a jarring note in these scenes of scientific community. Gaskell may fantasize that classes are reconciled over the theodolite, the turnip-cutter, or in Manning's friendship with Holdsworth, but she projects elsewhere all of the potential for disruption and damage that science also threatens: as in her earlier work, the female once again becomes the problematic site of transformation.

Looking at Manning's drawing of the turnip-cutting machine, Phillis is "leaning over and listening greedily, . . . sucking in information" (p. 289), and although her head is one of the three "joined together" over the theodolite, Paul says that "she had hardly time to greet me, so desirous was she to hear some answer to *her father's question*" (p. 308; emphasis added). Science is male, and exclusively so, and Phillis can only gratify her appetite for scientific knowledge by eavesdropping on male conversations. Unlike Sylvia, she is hungry for "masculine news" (p. 294), but like Sylvia she has no control over her own "feminine" story. In her portrayal of Phillis, Gaskell is doing two things at once. On one hand she is engaging more explicitly than ever in the debate surrounding the social position and education of women, which was being exhaustively conducted in the periodical press in the late 1850s and 1860s. On the other hand she is using the representation of Phillis to resolve some of the ideological problems produced in the text by her portrayal of science and technological change.

An article in the *English Woman's Journal* in 1858, pleading for more educational opportunities and jobs for women, states: "Let woman put her shoulder to the slowly revolving wheel of progression, and she need not fear to be left behind, nor to be refused the countenance of her fellow-worker, man."[16] Certainly, Phillis is trying to put her shoulder to the wheel, but she is constantly repelled by a culture of male exclusivity. Although Gaskell kept herself assiduously separate from the "strong-minded women" campaigning for women's rights in the 1860s, there is evidence in her letters that indicates a private admiration for their work and, indeed, personal acquaintance with a few of them.[17] However little she engaged with the organized radical opposition to "the established opinions of the world," Gaskell must have been aware of what those opinions consisted. Here, for instance, is W. R. Greg discussing womankind in his well-known 1850 article "Prostitution" in the *Westminster Review*:

> for . . . the desire scarcely exists in a definite and conscious form, till they *have* fallen. In this point there is a radical and essential difference between the sexes. . . . In men, in general, the sexual desire is inherent and spontaneous, and belongs to the condition of puberty. In the other sex, the desire is dormant, if not nonexistent, till excited; always till excited by undue familiarities. . . .[18]

This is precisely the view of feminine passivity, here sexual but in Gaskell both sexual and intellectual, that she attacks in "Cousin Phillis." It seems, too, to be Minister Holman's view: when he accuses Paul of "put[ting] such thoughts into the child's head . . . spoil[ing] her peaceful maidenhood" (p. 345), he assumes that Phillis is "dormant" (in Greg's phrase), just as Holdsworth likens her to the sleeping beauty: "I shall come back like a prince from

Canada, and waken her to my love" (p. 315). It is only Paul and Phillis who "knew that the truth was different" (p. 345).

Realist writing depends on leaving clues or fragments from which the reader can reconstruct an entirety of meaning. "Cousin Phillis" is a detective novel, but it is a pathologized detective novel in which the detective is also the criminal. Paul certainly transgresses when he tells Phillis that Holdsworth loves her, but he is also the anxious detector of signs by which he—along with the reader—attempts to piece together the possible state of Phillis's invisible inner life. The signs are almost entirely somatic rather than psychological or verbal. Phillis's body becomes a theater where all of the activity and emotion that is denied free expression displays itself.

The somatic figuring of Phillis is pervasive in the narrative. Her "large, quiet eyes" and "white skin" (p. 266) are disturbed by Holdsworth's arrival; and at their introduction she is "blushing a little," "flushed," and "in a blushing hurry" (pp. 298-99). Later her eyes are "glad and bright," and a word from Holdsworth "called out her blushes" (p. 309); when Holdsworth draws her portrait "her colour came and went, her breath quickened" (p. 311). After Holdsworth's departure, Paul notices Phillis's "face white and set, her dry eyes"; she is "as pale as could be" and "looking so pale and weary" (pp. 317-18); and when she hears Paul read out a letter from Holdsworth, Paul notices "two spots of brilliant colour on the cheeks that had been so pale before" (p. 319). At chapel on Christmas day the gossips talk about the possibility of Phillis dying of "a decline" (p. 320); Paul sees that "her grey eyes looked hollow and sad; her complexion was of a dead white" (p. 320); in the kitchen he hears "a noise which made me pause and listen—a sob, an unmistakable, irrepressible sob" (p. 321). The pause, indicated here by a dash on the page, dramatizes Paul's detective activity and implicates the reader as witness. This is the climax of the mystery for Paul, the detective, although not of course for the reader, who has been patiently assembling not only the clues about Phillis's state of mind but also those that indicate that Paul's own inexperience makes him an unreliable narrator. The vital clue for Paul is the book containing Holdsworth's margin notes: "Could that be it? Could that be the cause of her white looks, her weary eyes, her wasted figure, her struggling sobs?" (p. 322). This is a clue that reveals Phillis's inner life to Paul "like a flash of lightning on a dark night" (p. 322), yet Phillis continues to express nothing verbally, and it is only through somatic symptoms that Paul reads her happiness when he tells her that Holdsworth loves her: "Her eyes, glittering with tears as they were, expressed an almost heavenly happiness" (p. 324). Part Four opens with "the chapel-gossips complimenting cousin Holman on her daughter's blooming looks" (p. 325), and Paul notes that Phillis's "state of vivid happiness this summer was markedly different to the peaceful serenity of former days" (p. 329). After Paul tells Phillis of Holdsworth's marriage to Lucille Ventadour, her parents continue to read Phillis's symptoms as purely physical, and her mother interprets her show of temper as a reaction to the stormy weather. It is the servant, Betty, who reads the truth of the symptoms: "you've likely never heared of a fever-flush. . . . What makes her come in panting and ready to drop into that chair" (p. 336). When Holdsworth's letter arrives with the public announcement of his marriage, "her face was brilliantly flushed; her eyes were dry and glittering" (p. 339). Paul reports the pathological signs of Phillis's reaction in minute detail:

> But once my eyes fell upon her hands, concealed under the table, and I could see the passionate, convulsive manner in which she laced and interlaced her fingers perpetually, wringing them together from time to time, wringing till the compressed flesh became perfectly white. . . . I wondered that others did not read these signs as clearly as I did.
>
> (p. 342)

After Phillis confesses her love for Holdsworth to her father, Paul notes Minister Holman's failure to notice Phillis's symptoms: "her beautiful eyes dilated with a painful, tortured expression. He went on, without noticing the look on her face; he did not see it, I am sure" (p. 346). Then comes the collapse, which throws both Minister Holman and Paul into silence—"I pointed to the quivering of the muscles round her mouth" (p. 347)—and the subsequent brain fever.

I have quoted at such length because I think Gaskell's portrayal of Phillis almost exclusively through somatic symptoms is quite extraordinary. She achieves two things by this sustained treatment of Phillis's repressed subjectivity. First, by pathologizing her heroine within her narrative Gaskell demonstrates radically and effectively the pressure under which women are placed by the lack of permitted expressions of subjectivity. Phillis says very little in the novella, and less and less as it proceeds. "I loved him, father!" (p. 346) is the first expression of her selfhood that she is permitted, and it is figured as transgressive nevertheless. Thus Gaskell uses her representation of Phillis to illustrate the pathologization of women by a midnineteenth-century society that, literally, makes them ill.

The second achievement of this sustained pathologization of Phillis relates to the male community of scientists. All of them, despite their remarkable scientific gifts, fail Phillis in various ways. Holdsworth fails her by underestimating her and by allowing himself to ignore the pain that he knows he has caused her by lazily relying on the "established opinions" that characterize women as passive sleeping beauties. Minister Holman fails repeatedly and obstinately to read his daughter's symptoms as signs of an independent subjectivity. Manning "reads" Phillis only in terms of another woman—"poor Molly," who pined away for love of him many years before—or as a potential wife for Paul. He reinforces the "established opinions" that militate against female subjectivity when he assures Paul that marriage and children would cure Phillis of Latin and Greek (p. 292). Paul himself, although he reads Phillis almost obsessively closely, does not always read her correctly. And he fails her most disastrously when, albeit in an effort to comfort her, he misjudges the effect and miscalculates the risk of telling her about Holdsworth's "love" for her.

Their science has failed all of them in diagnosing Phillis as a subject. Science, for Gaskell, still does not fit life sufficiently enough to be useful. The men examine and understand the mechanisms of turnip-cutters, drive wheels, winches, and railway tracks in minute detail, but the hidden mechanisms of the woman who sits beside them receive no attention, even when she seriously begins to show dysfunction. Paul is the exception, of course, but his attempted reading of Phillis leads him to an act that ultimately causes more pain. He knows the facts and he sees the symptoms, but he fails to infer adequately Phillis's inner life from them. His naive assumption is that Phillis can be "mended" by the information he gives her.

The whole plot of "Cousin Phillis" can be reconstructed from its appearance on Phillis's body. The novella, with its physical and somatic dramatization for the reader of the business of diagnosis, of paying close attention to signs, is a supremely realist narrative. Phillis's body becomes the site of radical transformations, projected by Gaskell away from the scientific-industrial plot. Catherine Belsey remarks that illness in nineteenth-century realist fiction is used as a strategy to express "the problem of change it symbolises."[19] Certainly the problem of social change seems to be symbolized through Phillis. That science and the scientific man have disrupted her story and caused her pain and suffering is manifestly present in the novella in a way that the pain of class friction and social change are not. And Phillis's resolution to adjust to that change is offered as the resolution of the narrative as a whole: "She blushed a little as she faltered out her wish for change of thought and scene" (p. 354). At last Phillis speaks, and makes a demand. It is true that she also blushes, but only "a little." "Her wish for change" carries the ideological burden of the story, and that she chooses to go to Manning for her change is perhaps less significant than that she chooses to go to urban, industrial Birmingham.[20] Her final, paradoxical remark—"Then—we will go back to the peace of the old days. I know we shall; I can, and I will!" (p. 354)—demonstrates the irreversible change that has taken place in Phillis; "the peace of the old days" depended on her willlessness. Now that she has spoken herself into subjectivity, the peace of the old days will never return.

In "Cousin Phillis" Gaskell substitutes Phillis's pain for the pain of class division, social change, and the new science. By presenting a fantasized class reconciliation, particularly through the representation of the relationship between Holdsworth and Manning, the text disguises and evades confrontation of actual class tensions. But, by closely reading Phillis's extraordinarily detailed somatic symptoms, the reader is able to reconstruct the repressed narrative of pain underlying the story—a powerful pain that breaks beyond the conventions of the romantic plot in order to reflect Gaskell's own troubled response to rapid social change and the iniquitous divisions between both classes and sexes that, she seems to suggest, can be numbered among its results.

Notes

1. Gaskell's daughter Meta, in a 19 December 1862 letter to Effie Wedgwood, described her mother "writing 10 pages a day of the tiresome book that is really 'a story without an end'" (quoted in Jenny Uglow, *Elizabeth Gaskell: A Habit of Stories* [London: Faber and Faber, 1993], p. 503).

2. Both Uglow in *Elizabeth Gaskell,* chapter 24, and Kate Flint, in *Elizabeth Gaskell* (Plymouth: Northcote House, 1995), chapter 6, discuss the Darwinian structure of *Sylvia's Lovers.* Although no actual evidence exists of Gaskell's ever having read Darwin's *On the Origin of Species,* she could not have failed to have been aware of the furor over its publication in 1859, moving as she did in intellectual and unorthodox circles, and she was certainly aware of the sister-scandal over the publication of *Essays and Reviews,* which appeared only three months afterward. She writes to Charles Eliot Norton in April 1861: "Everybody was talking about America, & 'Essays and Reviews'" (letter to Charles Eliot Norton, 16 April 1861, in *The Letters of Mrs. Gaskell,* ed. J.A.V. Chapple and Arthur Pollard [Cambridge, Mass.: Harvard Univ. Press, 1967], p. 646). As Benjamin Jowett and Mark Pattison, two of the seven theologians who contributed to *Essays and Reviews,* were friends of the Gaskells, "everybody" presumably includes herself.

3. Scientists of the Gaskells' acquaintance included James Nasmyth, the inventor of the steam hammer; Joseph Paxton, the designer of the Crystal Palace; William Fairbairn, inventor of the riveting machine; George Allman, Professor of Zoology at Edinburgh University; Lord Francis Egerton, patron of Manchester science; Benjamin Brodie, Professor of Chemistry at Oxford; the physicist James Joule; and the chemists James Allan, Edward Schunk, and Henry Roscoe (see Uglow, pp. 559-60).

4. "Natural Knowledge in Cultural Context: The Manchester Model," *American Historical Review,* 79 (1974), 682.

5. Letter to Catherine Winkworth, 29 November 1848, in *Letters,* p. 64. "Mrs J. J. Tayler is shocked at such a subject of conversation [Scott's *Kenilworth*] on a *Sunday,*—so there I am in a scrape,—well! it can't be helped, I am myself and nobody else, and can't be bound by another's rules" (pp. 63-64).

6. Jenny Uglow has suggested that Gaskell's portrayal of Minister Holman's shock at his daughter's confession of her love for Holdsworth owes something to Gaskell's own state of mind at the time of writing "Cousin Phillis," as news reached her in March 1863 of the sudden engagement of her daughter Florence to a young barrister and "scientific" young man, Charles Crompton (see Uglow, p. 538).

7. "Introduction" to *Cousin Phillis,* ed. Ward, vol. 7 of *The Works of Mrs. Gaskell, Knutsford Edition* (London: Smith, Elder and Co., 1906; rpt. New York: AMS Press, 1972), pp. xiii and xvii.

8. Elizabeth Gaskell, "Cousin Phillis," in *Cousin Phillis and Other Tales,* ed. Angus Easson (New York: Oxford Univ. Press, 1981), p. 261. Further references to this work are to this edition and appear in the text.

9. Quoted in Uglow, pp. 667-68, n. 18.

10. Elizabeth Gaskell, *Mary Barton,* ed. Edgar Wright (New York: Oxford Univ. Press, 1987), pp. 165-66.

11. The phrase is Patrick Brantlinger's, in *The Spirit of Reform: British Literature and Politics, 1832–1867* (Cambridge, Mass.: Harvard Univ. Press, 1977), p. 120.

12. Uglow argues convincingly that Manning is based on Gaskell's acquaintance James Nasmyth, giving as evidence the Patricroft works visit and an anecdote apparently told by Nasmyth about gentleman-apprentices wearing gloves, which appears as a shared joke between Holdsworth and Manning in "Cousin Phillis" (see p. 287; see Uglow, chapter 25). If this is the case, I think it is only important insofar as it exacerbates Gaskell's problems with the representation of Manning. In *The Machinery Question and the Making of Political Economy, 1815–1848* (Cambridge: Cambridge Univ. Press, 1980) Maxine Berg writes: "By the 1820s and 1830s James Nasmyth, James Fox, Matthew Murray, Sharp, Roberts & Co., Hicks, Hargreaves & Co., Fairbairn and Lillie, and Joseph Whitworth were directing large-scale machine shops, foundries and engine factories in the Midlands and the North" (pp. 153-54). Nasmyth was clearly a rich industrialist, while Manning is represented as simultaneously successful and poor.

13. The intentionality of this process of representation is perhaps not entirely clear from my reading. I am not suggesting that Gaskell intended to write the working classes out of any share in industrial progress and, therefore, social change. I am rather attempting to argue that Gaskell, once she decides to deploy the good and worthy stereotype of Mr. Manning, is locked into a discourse that inevitably produces this outcome.

14. This was a popular maxim in the nineteenth century. William Bell Scott had used it shortly before "Cousin Phillis" as the motto for his picture *Iron and Coal,* painted 1856–61, one of his "Scenes from Border History," a series of public paintings that celebrate industrial progress on Tyneside. Information from the Witt Library, London University.

15. We hear a great deal about the farm's produce in "Cousin Phillis": Phillis reads Virgil while paring

apples, she and Holdsworth first meet in the kitchen garden where she is picking peas, she tells Paul that her basket of eggs contains potatoes, and she entertains Holdsworth with "home-made bread, and newly-churned butter" (p. 299). This, I think, reinforces the sense of self-sufficiency that Holdsworth disrupts.

16. Anon., "Female Education in the Middle Classes," *English Woman's Journal,* 1 (1858), 227.

17. The most prominent was the "Langham Place" group of campaigners for women's rights. In 1857 Barbara Leigh Smith Bodichon and Bessie Rayner Parkes, who were both Unitarians, established what became the *English Woman's Review.* The *Review* shared its Langham Place offices with The Society for Promoting the Employment of Women, founded in 1859 and run by Jessie Boucherett. Barbara Bodichon went on to become one of the founders of Girton College, Cambridge in the 1870s. Gaskell grudgingly admits, in a 5 April 1860 letter to Charles Eliot Norton, some admiration for Barbara Bodichon, although she seems to find it necessary to explain Bodichon's radicalism by her illegitimacy: "She is—I think in consequence of her birth, a strong fighter against the established opinions of the world,—which always goes against my—what shall I call it?—*taste*—(that is not the word,) but I can't help admiring her noble bravery, and respecting—while I don't personally *like* her" (*Letters,* p. 607). Gaskell also seems to have been acquainted with Bessie Parkes, who, in a 25 October 1859 letter to Marianne Gaskell, she reports is coming to tea and "to 'want my judgment' on something or other"—if her tone is somewhat irritable she explains later in the same letter that "callers swallow up all my days" (*Letters,* pp. 902, 903). Gaskell's friend Harriet Martineau contributed an article to the debate: "Female Industry" appeared in the *Edinburgh Review,* 109 (1859), 293-336.

18. [W. R. Greg], "Prostitution," *Westminster Review,* 53 (1850), 456-57. Greg adds: "We do not mean to say that uneasiness may not be felt—that health may not sometimes suffer; but there is no consciousness of the cause" (p. 457).

19. *Critical Practice* (London: Methuen, 1980), p. 74.

20. The published ending was not the one that Gaskell originally intended, as is revealed by two unpublished letters from Gaskell to George Smith, 10 December 1863, MS. Acc. 6713, 2/4, National Library of Scotland, reprinted in J. A. V. Chapple, "Elizabeth Gaskell: Two Unpublished Letters to George Smith," *Etudes Anglaises,* 33 (1980), 183-87. In the originally intended ending, Paul, married, returns years later to find Heathbridge struck by typhus, "and comes across Phillis using Holdsworth's old sketches to help her drain the marshy land." She is running her father's farm and has adopted two orphaned children, but she has never married. This putative ending could be read conventionally as a fable of loyalty to the memory of true love, or it could be read more radically as a male-less fantasy of female reproductive and productive self-sufficiency.

Linda C. Brigham (essay date 1999)

SOURCE: "Disciplinary Hybridity in Shelley's *Adonais,*" in *Mosaic,* Vol. 32, No. 3, September, 1999, pp. 21-39.

[*In the following essay, Brigham studies Shelley's* Adonais *as an interdisciplinary poem that incorporates scientific literature with traditional poetry.*]

Research programs in science studies—as well as more general programs in women's studies and cultural studies—have for the past two decades testified to a dissatisfaction with traditional disciplinary boundaries in the academy. At the same time, negative reactions to these interdisciplinary forays, most notoriously in Paul Gross's and Norman Levitt's *Higher Superstition* (1994), indicate the intense significance of such boundaries from the standpoint of many scientists. Included on Gross's and Levitt's enemies list is anthropologist of science Bruno Latour who has analyzed the nearly imperturbable cultural architecture supporting the ideal of scientific purity, that is, the conception of science as purged of cultural bias, a condition built into our very notion of science. Latour sees disciplinary purity as part of the deep structure of modernity, built into the pulse of modern common sense. But he points out more emphatically that this purity comes under increasing pressure from the mixture of disciplinary activities that constitutes everyday life, despite the effacement of this mixture from the way that we consider either science on the one hand, or the humanities on the other.

Latour is significant among interdisciplinary advocates because he communicates the simultaneous power of assumptions maintaining disciplinary purity and the quotidian frequency of disciplinary crossover, of disciplinary hybridity. This approach to modern culture as double-visioned, although it depicts science as a social practice rather than the accumulation of truths about reality (a perspective eliciting the wrath of *Higher Superstition*), also properly emphasizes the extraordinarily agile intransigence of seemingly contradictory activities. As Latour sees it, the ideal of scientific objectivity, and more generally, the purifying processes of modernity itself, is too deeply rooted in the way we think for us simply to imagine ourselves out of them. If we are to alter modern disciplinary formation, we must understand modernity as a capacity to live two lives without combining them, to think in disciplinarily purified terms and yet act in terms of disciplinary hybridity at the same moment. Hybridity is hidden in plain sight, in the very extremity of disciplinarity.

In a similar way, I will argue, Romantic poet Percy Bysshe Shelley came closest to an interdisciplinary poetry—a scientific literature in the fullest oxymoronic sense—from *within* poetry, specifically in one of his most hyperbolically literary works, his elegy on John Keats, *Adonais* (1821). My focus on this poem derives in part from the fact that it *is* an elegy, that is, that it treats death, the site of the most extreme divergence between scientific and humanistic understanding. In this essay, I will first elaborate Latour's notion of disciplinarity, introduce some recent interdisciplinary developments from within science that might contribute to undermining modernity's double vision, and then present a deliberately anachronistic reading of *Adonais,* a reading, I argue, that takes up the spirit of Shelley's struggle in the poem to overcome the modern disciplinary categories by which he was imprisoned. My interpretation is anachronistic insofar as it is a reading that could not have existed for Shelley himself. *Adonais,* however, invites this interpretive license: Shelley incites us to assemble new cultural formations where human and natural significance can be thought together, a synthesis of what we now call science and the humanities.

Possibly only now can we read *Adonais* as "anti-modern," because we live in the twilight of modernity, and linger on the verge of a "posthumanism." The fact that such phrases have meaning in the humanities but as yet no scientific value, testifies to a barrier uncrossed. True interdisciplinary thought remains impossible, and attempts at it unearth only a fractured logic. In *We Have Never Been Modern,* Latour sketches an example of such fracture in the peculiar asymmetry found in the definition of "modern":

> Modernity is often defined in terms of humanism, either as a way of saluting the birth of "man" or as a way of announcing his death. But this habit itself is modern, because it remains asymmetrical. It overlooks the simultaneous birth of "nonhumanity"—things, or objects, or beasts—and the equally strange beginning of a crossed-out God, relegated to the sidelines.
>
> (13)

Modernity simultaneously gave birth to both the humanities and science. This birth of science is so momentous as to have relegated God to the sidelines, yet the idea of modernity as a rupture, a historical concept, is completely excluded from science. Scientific law continues to be seen as timeless, universal; it is about what is and has always been—that is, about nature. Latour goes on to claim that if one does manage to see the term "modern" in its full scope, encompassing *both* science and the humanities, then "one ceases to be modern" (13).

The centrality of birth and death to Latour's humanistic definition of modernity is apt. Scientist and clergy may attend both, yet have nothing to say to each other as professionals, or both hygiene and faith would falter. The archetypal modern scientist Victor Frankenstein consulted not bibles or poetry but chemistry texts and decaying flesh in his obsessive quest for the secrets of life and death. Moreover, given Frankenstein's failure to transmit the technique for reanimating a corpse to the scientific community at large, the term "immortality" has also definitively been

sidelined to the humanities, like the term "modern": immortality is a figural or mythical state, the product of fame, hope, or faith. It would seem, conversely, that *Adonais* lies securely in this high-cultural domain, purified of any pretensions to scientific fact, just as science in Latour's view must be purified of culture (10). But suppose it is possible, given a dawning interdisciplinarity, to read Shelley's elegy in the same way one might read Victor Frankenstein's textbooks? Suppose a poem can present scientific truths about death that cannot quite be called figurative, that is, are not confined to the category of literature, but operate under a new category of a double-visioned humane science?

To summarize, modern science studies the natural world. But to do so, as Latour presents it, that world must be purged of subjects, of social presuppositions and beliefs, of ideological purposes, of tendentious rhetoric. This purgation is essential to science, even though scientific practice is also social practice and goes on as a hybrid of nature and culture. At this point, therefore, I want to depart from Latour and sketch the process of disciplinary purification in a different context: the context of disciplinary autonomy as conceived by sociologist Niklas Luhmann. Noting that some degree of autonomy is the condition of both disciplinary and personal identity, Luhmann defines modernity as the fragmentation of society into autonomous subsystems—one of which is science. Luhmann bases his notion of autonomy on a concept developed in science, specifically in biological studies of cognition: the concept of "autopoiesis."

Developed by biologist Humberto Maturana and cognitive psychologist Francisco Varela, autopoiesis, literally "self-making," is a powerful abstraction defining the individuation of an entity from its environment. Autopoietic entities have a "self," that is, operate as a consistent system whose systematicity distinguishes it from an environment. This self consists of a process, not of an extrinsic state of affairs; this process, moreover, is specifically a process of self-reference. The autopoietic entity maintains a self/environment distinction by making this distinction—self *as* not-environment—a criterion for ongoing distinctions. As Luhmann puts it, "the system makes the difference between system and environment and copies that difference in the system to be able to use it as a distinction" ("Why" 172-73). Such a process is highly abstract, and has been taken beyond Maturana and Varela's original context to describe phenomena such as the conservation of form in a crystal, the maintenance of a subjective sense of personal identity, or, in Luhmann's usage, the autonomy of social institutions.

In any case, autopoiesis cuts across the modern divide by hybridizing subject and object, human and non-human categories. It locates a notion of self at the heart of science, in recursive processes describing a wide range of things. Thus if we accept Luhmann's application of autopoiesis to institutions, then both pure science and pure art—or in this case, an autonomous sphere of literature—can be redefined as products of a reiterative self-making whose autonomy must dissolve if the process of continual self-reinscription stops. Modern disciplines collapse if they fail continually to distinguish themselves from other disciplines. If we were to anticipate what might be called a non- or post-modern vocabulary, as yet non-existent, we might say such disciplines "die"—without the traditional metaphorical resonance of the phrase. They *really* die like we all die. In any case, the concept of autopoiesis as deeply interdisciplinary suggests that the key to both modernity and its undoing lies in the concept of "self"—and this is what *Adonais* takes up.

Adonais has often been read in ways that ordinary usage deems "interdisciplinary," usually as a philosophical poem. As two insightful readers of Shelley, Stuart Curran and William A. Ulmer, observe, this criticism typically divides into two camps, one stressing skepticism, the other some form of Platonic transcendentalism; one apocalyptic, desperate and uncertain, the other optimistic and assertively stable. These opposed perspectives are aptly exemplified in Shelley scholarship respectively by C. E. Pulos and James A. Notopoulos. Also drawing upon resources in philosophy is Earl Wasserman who, however, equally enlists early anthropology of myth, the classical literary tradition, and even the science of Shelley's day. In his masterful and influential reading of *Adonais*, Wasserman characterizes the movement of the elegy as a kind of organic development, a development which, he emphasizes, "*is* dramatic in a manner somewhat akin to embryological growth, for it passes through discrete stages that superficially bear little resemblance to its final form and yet in which that final form organically inheres" (471). Wasserman, and later Donald H. Reiman, describes the development of *Adonais* as proceeding in three sections, related quasi-dialectically. This multifaceted, dialectical organicism, moreover, sounds like an appropriate viewpoint from which to tackle what Wasserman asserts as the elegy's consistent underlying questions, crucial questions for organic life: "What is death? and, therefore, What is the ultimate reality?" (469).

Yet Wasserman's very erudition, the exemplary erudition of a thorough scholarly acquaintance with a wide range of territories in the humanities, is one element that keeps us from seeing his explication of the elegy's answer to these questions as anything but humanistic answers to problems expressed in humanistic terms. Shelley's use of pre-modern legend and classical texts seem only to reinforce the elegy's disciplinary identity as literature, as a meaning-affirming fiction, but not as concerned with the facts of life and death. Wasserman's study was written in 1971, and more recent deconstructionist readings foster an inkling of such a limitation. In these views, the project of restoring *Adonais* to a critical tradition that found it inconsistent and fragmented forms only one more iteration of the course of the elegiac genre itself, which restores the dead through a rhetorical immortality; this restorative function can operate only with the self-enclosure of language from its own material dissemination. Thus Ulmer writes that Shelley's "displacement of immortality as literary tra-

dition undergoes a further displacement which refers tradition to rhetoric, so that questions of poetic history defer to the question of a poetics of history. . . . In *Adonais*, history's collapse illustrates a figural logic and testifies to a deathliness inherent in poetic representation" (4).

We might draw out Ulmer's observation to hypothesize that this deathliness—figuratively meant as the dissolution of reality into reality-effects, as effects of rhetoric—suggests that the truth about death can come only from a domain that can no longer speak of it in a humane way: from science. Deconstruction can be a means of exposing the asymmetries created by the split between science and the humanities, but to see it as a kind of skepticism only domesticates it for the humanities, and leaves its potential to cross the domains of science and the humanities largely untapped. Like autopoiesis, deconstruction is able to theorize self as process rather than presence, so that if the "deathliness" that Ulmer finds in *Adonais* is the product of a thoroughly deconstructive reading, that "deathliness" should resonate in both science and the humanities, in the realm of non-subjects as well as in the domain of subjects—eliding the barrier between the two.

Shelley's notion of subjectivity has biological leanings that anticipate the hybridity of autopoiesis. In *On Life* (1819), Shelley argues that the distinction between entity and environment is a matter of point of view, a kind of self-observation; reiterated, this self-observation, or self-processing, becomes a mechanical habit, naturalizing the self-other distinction that it creates:

> Those who are subject to the state called reverie feel as if their nature were dissolved into the surrounding universe, or as if the surrounding universe were absorbed into their being. They are conscious of no distinction. And these are states which precede or accompany or follow an unusually intense and vivid apprehension of life. As men grow up, this power commonly decays, and they become mechanical and habitual agents. Their feelings and their reasonings are the combined result of a multitude of entangled thoughts, of a series of what are called impressions, planted by reiteration.
>
> (477)

The recursive process of identity maintenance consists of the continual conversion of the constructedness of the border between entity and environment into a habitual sense of self, of feelings and reasonings into properties by a process of "reiteration," a process that differentiates self, its memories, its cares, from the world at large. The subject, in Luhmann's words, "copies that difference in the system to be able to use it as a distinction" ("Why" 172-73); likewise, Shelley's self copies its reiterated impressions into criteria that distinguish it from environment, narrowing the possibilities of future distinctions.

This process is not necessarily pernicious in Shelley's view, even if it promotes the illusion of a substantial self. In *A Defence of Poetry* (1821), Shelley relates conservation of a self/other distinction to pleasure, and in turn to poetics. Of the many self/environment distinctions it is possible to instantiate, some are more pleasurable than others. However, given conditions of constant change, the pleasure of such relations soon decays. Poets have an expanded capacity to represent a particular order of the environment (and implicitly define *as* environment) that from which "highest delight" results, and to transform it into poetry which in turn "gathers a sort of reduplication from that community" (481-82). In other words, poets render a gratifying form of the environment as reiterable representations, a creative act that simultaneously defines what is and is not self—and these distinctions come to be reiterated by other selves. Shelley famously describes the relationship of expression to environment as "vitally metaphorical," a metaphorical phrase itself, possessing a double movement. It both instantiates and cross-fertilizes a distinction between tenor and vehicle. In its highest "vital" form, metaphor is the pulse of life itself, like the breath, inhaling unity and exhaling separation. But the vital, breathed word, becoming habitual through reiteration, produces a decay of the "vitally metaphorical" relationship between expression and object; language "marks the before unapprehended relations of things, and perpetuates their apprehension, until the words which represent them, become through time signs for portions or classes of thoughts," with the eventual result that (unless poets come to the rescue) "language will be dead to all the nobler purposes of human intercourse" (482).

This continual conversion of impressions to expressions, and subsequently to self-attributed feelings and reasons, might also be described as the continual dissemination of tenors into vehicles, of meaning into means. Things, signs of other things, gain identity in their own right, and lose the capacity to signify the larger dynamism of which they are effects. This decay conceals the initial equivocality of self and environment that occasions the creativity of distinction-making. Modern disciplinary categories, especially the segregation of the truths of nature from human truths, come to seem natural, pre-given. In a deep sense, then, Shelley's complaint in both *On Life* and *A Defence* is about modernity, about the way that an original unity of expression and practical apprehension become segregated at a particular historical juncture. Culture's own structures become self-validating technologies whose perpetuation is maintained by a process analogous to the maintenance of the illusion of self.

Adonais, as an elegy, reflects on the literary tradition that generated it in a manner similar to the way that *On Life* reflects on selfhood and *A Defence of Poetry* reflects on poetic production in general. While a full treatment of literary antecedents is beyond the scope of this essay, the way in which *Adonais* assimilates Keats's poetry provides an exemplary case for Shelley's experiment in merging notions of literary immortality with biological mortality, a merger that means a radical reconstitution of selfhood along autopoietic lines. Early in the poem, Shelley performs a kind of absorption of Keats by figuring Keats's own poetic figures:

> . . . one, with soft enamoured breath,
> Rekindled all the fading melodies,
> With which, like flowers that mock the corse beneath,
> He had adorned and hid the coming bulk of death.
>
> (15-18)

Shelley does not quote Keats here, but metaphorizes quotation (and other forms of intertextuality) as a beautiful parasitism. Keats, the dead host, feeds Shelley's verses with his body. A. W. Heffernan's brilliant discussion of the complex interpersonal and professional implications of this consumption needs to be balanced by the larger disciplinary perspective in which Shelley profits from Keats's death. If we were no longer modern, we might see that Keats is incorporated into Shelley's elegy in the same way food is incorporated into the body, and in this "literal" way he *becomes* the body of the poem. Shelley's conventional employment of flowers in the passage as a figure for rhetoricity does not, contrary to a prevalent critical view, signify an impotent and unoriginal phase of the poem; instead, their conventionality highlights *Adonais*'s assimilation of Keats into a yet-to-be-realized cultural vision that can itself assimilate poetic tradition, an assimilation that in turn extends to *Adonais* itself.

This absorption of Keats by Shelley, though, remains troubled by the very death of individual identity that it marks. The new Shelley-as-Keats (or Shelley-having-eaten-Keats) continues to worry about its own distinction from Keats-as-dead, Keats-as-food. As the poem re-represents Keats's death in the stanzas that follow, it portrays the world's fecund vitality as a catastrophic contrast to the dead poet's body. Flowers "mock the corse beneath"; their vibrancy only underscores Adonais's mortality. The shock of death figured in this shock of contrast continues; flowers are once again rejected in stanza 16:

> Grief made the young Spring wild, and she threw
>   down
> Her kindling buds, as if she Autumn were,
> Or they dead leaves; since her delight is flown
> For whom should she have waked the sullen year?
> To Phoebus was not Hyacinth so dear
> Nor to himself Narcissus, as to both
> Thou Adonais. . . .
>
> (136-43)

Yet in the process of rejection, the narrator mentions the flowers into which legendary mortals were preservatively transformed by Venus. The antithesis of flowers to the dead drifts into the suggestion—although at this moment, still dormant, as Spring halts her course—of flowers as continuations of the dead. Contrast, in other words, spreads out in time as transformation; it is unable to freeze its grief, to freeze the identity that it maintains by mourning and that Keats maintains by being mourned. This asymmetry of synchronic and diachronic identity-processes foreshadows the potential for a new synthesis. It also refers to an old one. The myths from which the poem draws combine references to the natural processes with symbolic reflections on mortality. The botanical incarnations of Hyacinth and Narcissus are, besides figures, the products of organic metamorphosis, a metamorphosis due to fire (Phoebus) in the case of Hyacinth and water in the case of Narcissus. This synthesis marks a premodern sensibility that successfully hybridizes nature and the human, and it provides consolation, if not compensation, for the insufficiencies of a merely "literary" account of death.

This premodern metamorphosis seems in some ways more compatible with biology than it does with the humanistic tradition into which it has been incorporated. The biological products of the corpse continue to interrupt the process of getting the dead buried. This suggestion of a modern metamorphic relation between flowers and the dead develops in stanza 20, after Spring has presumably continued on her way, succeeded by the full cycle of seasons:

> The leprous corpse touched by this spirit tender
> Exhales itself in flowers of gentle breath;
> Like incarnations of the stars, when splendour
> Is changed to fragrance, they illumine death
> And mock the merry worm that wakes beneath. . . .
>
> (172-76)

The corpse mirrors the transformations of Hyacinth and Narcissus on the level of biology, and flowers mock the "corse" no longer, but the worms who, in their metonymic association with decay, now form the counterpart to the mockery of stanza 2. It is true that this triumph is short lived; stanza 21 follows lamenting the inadequacy of nature's brand of immortality: "Alas! that all we loved of him should be, / But for our grief, as if it had not been, / And grief itself be mortal . . ." (181-83). Although presenting a powerful truth about things, biology continues to elide the personhood of Keats; modernity splits body and soul. However, once again, as in stanza 16, stanza 20 has introduced in its unstressed metaphors the basis for later transformation, as Jerrold Hogle has discussed (304). The complicated tension between premodern and modern, and between science and the humanities, energizes a move to a higher level of complexity. The basis for these metaphors are not similitudes between discrete objects, but similitudes between the productive processes of objects, the active "soul" of objects. The stanza coheres around an analogy between emanations: flowers produce fragrance as stars produce light.

This analogy of the activities of flowers and stars as a simile of processes anticipates the elegy's conclusion, where the stars become the narrator's destiny as he is borne "Darkly, fearfully afar" from the graveside at which the elegy opens. For Wasserman, these stars imply transcendence and triumph; more skeptical critics find a subversion of transcendentalism in the darkness and fear. But according to the pattern established early in the poem, instead of either confirming or undercutting hope or faith, the poem continually returns to the problem that hope and faith can be rendered only figuratively, barricaded in humanistic literature—as "spiritual truths" segregated from nature. The drive to find what life and death "are," apart

from this segregation, lies subtly beneath the elegy's tortuous exposition. And indeed there exists another trajectory in the poem that complicates the transition from flowers to stars with a recovery of decay itself, an equivocation of life and death that struggles to *include* natural transformation as *other* than figure, as other than spiritual or symbolic reconciliation. Within *Adonais* the worm constitutes a suppressed but consistently present alternative to the initial constellation of images that makes flowers a basis for connotatively positive, literarily conventional development. The worm functions as a double as well as a contrast to the flowers, requiring a dual perspective that, in the spirit of science, suspends reading the binary of parasite and host figuratively, humanistically, with their pathetic resonance—even while the poem cannot but express such a resonance. Although the "worm" seldom appears literally in the poem, the dominion of the worm structures the personifications of the whole first third of the elegy; it reigns where "Death feeds" (27), where the sky comprises a "charnel-roof" (60), and "Invisible corruption waits" and "eternal Hunger sits" (67, 69). All of these emblems of decay counterpose but also copy the transitory "feeding" of the mourners on memories of Adonais, on his more rarified existence in his poetic products.

As the poem proceeds, the conflictual element in the relation between flowers and worms climaxes in Shelley's metaphor for the critical agon that he insisted caused Keats's death, the slanderous review of *Endymion* that Shelley attributed to Robert Southey, a belief held against evidence from a number of Shelley's own sources, as Kenneth Cameron has shown. In stanza 36 the narrator blasts the reviewer: "What deaf and viperous murderer could crown / Life's early cup with such a draught of woe? / The nameless worm would now itself disown . . . (317-19). The reviewer wrought the initially invisible decay in Keats's body that culminated in his death from tuberculosis, and thus gave birth to the "merry worm" that devours Adonais's corpse. Yet it is also true that Southey provides the carrion on which Shelley's elegy feeds in order to recover Keats from the bad odor of reputational decay and exhale him in flowers, and at last in the splendor of the stars. So Shelley, in his castigation of Southey, does not "purify" literary history from its destructive predators, but problematizes its purity further by a parasitic mode of poetic composition, by a hybridization, corresponding to Shelley's own parasitism of Keats.

In essence, Shelley's employment of Southey on the side of the worms is not simply a contrast to the positive metamorphosis from corpse to flower to star, but an alternative reiteration of the equivocality of the individual in transformative processes. Following on the heels of the narrator's castigation of the reviewers, the poem embarks on its last movement, taking the narrator beyond the earth and its inhabitants. Here the worm appears again, its biological activity becoming the vehicle for a metaphor about recalcitrant human expectations: "Cold hopes swarm like worms within our living clay" (351). Thoughts unmetamorphically stuck in reified identities rot the spirit from within.

And "hope," a sentiment valued by the humanities, but irrelevant, even destructive, to science, cannot accept the complicity of worms with life that science is free to declare; as worms erode the integrity of the body, hope, based on the purifying premises of the modern organization of the disciplines, undermines that purity by secretly proliferating hybrids, again rotting the spirit from within—literally. This double rot in *Adonais,* embodied both in the corpse and in the dissolution of the narrator's grief, finally permits the narrator to "mock the merry worm"—not death, but categories that separate literary and scientific value.

Elsewhere in Shelley's writing of the period the worm has been a metaphor for production as well as decay. Shelley himself had been mocked as a worm, a topic about which he made merry in his 1820 poem, *The Letter to Maria Gisborne.* In the opening of the *Letter,* the narrator describes himself as a writer blighted by accusations of moral turpitude, as "a thing whom moralists call worm . . ." (5); instead of rejecting the epithet, or, as in *Adonais,* returning it to its source, the *Letter* transforms the worm into a producer of delicate beauty: a silk worm, who

> Sit[s] spinning still round this decaying form,
> From the fine threads of rare and subtle thought—
> No net of words in garish colours wrought
> To catch the idle buzzers of the day—
> But a soft cell, where when that fades away,
> Memory may clothe in wings my living name
> And feed it with the asphodels of fame,
> Which in those hearts which must remember me
> Grow, making love an immortality.
>
> (6-14)

The worm's products, Shelley's poetry, called both "winding sheet and cradle" (4), in a sense hide the poet from "the coming bulk of death" just as Adonais's songs hid him (stanza 2). But like Keats's poetry in *Adonais,* the chrysalis in the *Letter* works by autopoietic transformation: spun out of the worm's own substance, the ideas that clothe it and separate it from the world become the basis for its internal transformation, providing it with the wings that again reunite it with the world. At a higher level of abstraction, matter and meaning, the winged moth and poetic reputation, not only support each other but arise out of a single imaginative process—a process that builds sequentially, by autopoietic reiteration, into a new unselved self. And as a consequence of this transformation of selfhood, Shelley's moth can function as both the vehicle of the poem and its tenor; the poem can talk of nature and of humans.

So the alternatives of worm and flower that appear to structure a conventional opposition in *Adonais,* both as metaphors themselves and as the chains of metaphors that build upon them, do not function as antitheses or as complements. They work instead as hybrids; their multiple associations and dynamics perplex the modern schism between science and the humanities on which the provenance of literary history depends. The disciplinary schism reflects, in turn, the self-creating split between entity and environment; indeed, modern disciplinary segregation is crucial to modern subjective identity. Reflecting the tendentiousness of identity formations, the poem's various contexts—premodern literary/scientific, modern literary, and modern scientific—fail to resolve. From deep within the boundaries of humanistic discourse, *Adonais* unsettles the boundaries that create it, producing a longing for more synthetic truths.

By the end of the Regency decade, Shelley had long left behind the kind of interdisciplinarity employed in *Queen Mab* (1813), where literary pronouncements are supported and reinforced by "facts" described in the extensive prose notes. *Queen Mab* employs science to amplify a purportedly aesthetic unification of historical and political positions, but the relationship of the disciplines remains crude, the discursive and institutional barriers between them substantially uninterrogated. Yet as much as the mature Shelley may have scorned his early work, interdisciplinarity itself remained important to him. Shelley's friendship with Henry Reveley, the engineer son of Maria Gisborne, provides strong evidence not only for Shelley's continued interest in "practical" knowledge, but also for his concern over the relationship between science and imagination. Shelley's friendship with Reveley was, among other things, a form of interdisciplinary exchange.

Daniel Stempel, in discussing *Prometheus Unbound* (1820), emphasizes the importance of the motor—specifically, Reveley's steam engine—as an emblem of Shelley's efforts to combine science and poetry. Stempel examines the details of Shelley's relation with Reveley as evidence for the poet's realization that competition between practical knowledge and literature was a serious disciplinary issue, and that mere complementarity did not go deep enough to address it. Reveley's steam engine, Stempel explains, like all motors, including language, runs on difference, capitalizing on local instability (112). This difference—in the motor's case, the pressure differential that gives steam its explosive impact in a confined space, which in turn depends on the thermal difference of fire and water—is harnessed to create another difference, an alteration of state. In the motor, the state of a piston alters, and this alteration, in turn, changes the position of Reveley's model steamboat. Overall, the difference between the elemental components of the motor become translated into a difference in the relationship of the whole object to its environment. Reveley's engine models Shelley's notion of metaphor and its growth from local, specific interactions into a cultural body of knowledge; the motor works like a grammatological machine, a package of controlled and patterned dynamics maintaining itself as a unit on the surface of the unmarked sea.

In *The Letter to Maria Gisborne,* written at the height of Shelley's interest in Reveley, the narrator recites a litany of technology in the second stanza—"Great screws, and cones, and wheels, and grooved blocks" (52), and halts his list with what seems to be an expression of resigned bafflement: "disentangle them who may" (97), he says of the mathematical scribbles surrounding him; but he then suddenly reverses his role and changes from onlooker to pedagogue, trying to explain

> . . . a most inexplicable thing,
> With lead in the middle—I'm conjecturing
> How to make Henry understand; but no—.

(100-02)

The "inexplicable thing" is a pencil, a tool common to science and *belles lettres*. It is clear from his letters that Shelley had been trying to encourage Reveley's writing, and viewed their disciplinary distinction as an opportunity for exchange, a partnership that would compose an interdisciplinary engine itself:

> [M]y motive in soliciting your correspondence, and that flowing from your own mind and clothed in your own words, is that you may begin to accustom to discipline yourself to the only practise of life in which you appear deficient. . . . Do not think me arrogant. There are subjects of the highest importance in which you are far better qualified to instruct me, than I am qualified to instruct you in this subject—.

(*Letters* 2:131-32)

Yet Shelley's attitude toward the motor and the practical science it represents is ambivalent; his tone throughout the poetic *Letter* is satiric. In the third stanza, the narrator wraps up his technological litany with a metaphor for poetic composition; he becomes a "weird archimage":

> Plotting dark spells, and devilish enginery,
> The self-impelling steam-wheels of the mind
> Which pump up oaths from clergymen, and grind
> The gentle spirit of our meek reviews
> Into a powder foam of salt abuse. . . .

(109-11)

In this way he returns once again to the critics who lambasted his decadence. As with the worm imagery, Shelley here disrupts identities by figuring them as the product of point of view, of what constitutes environment and what entity. He figures his own literary production as a machine that moves across history by creating a kind of contained ethical turbulence. Shelley, however, also soon gives this up as mere metaphoric play, and ends by subordinating both science and poetry to his personal grief over an absent friend, Maria:

> How could one worth your friendship heed the war
> Of worms?—the shriek of the world's carrion jays,
> Their censure, or their wonder, or their praise?
>
> You are not here. . . .

(129-32)

Shelley's metaphoric engine fails, just as the complementarity of science and poetry failed aesthetically in *Queen Mab*; in this case, however, it is not because of a naive un-

derestimation of the barriers to a hybrid sensibility but more likely because of the failure of either technology or poetry to rise above the "war of worms" and grapple with the reality of human absence—or, as in *Adonais*, death—those realities that seem both too affecting for science and too real for literature.

Other letters from Shelley also indicate that his flagging faith in the efficacy of poetry affected his own sense of identity. He himself experienced the way that being cast as a poet circumscribed his abilities. In 1819, writing to Thomas Love Peacock, he laments,

> I consider Poetry very subordinate to moral & political science, & if I were well, certainly I should aspire to the latter; for I can conceive a great work, embodying the discoveries of all ages, & harmonizing the contending creeds by which mankind have been ruled."

(*Letters* 2:71)

A similar sense of frustration becomes the rationale for his ill-fated pursuit of a post abroad for the East India Company in 1821, strongly stated in his expression of disappointment that Peacock failed to support his application.

To conclude, then, let me turn to the last third of *Adonais,* where Shelley faces head-on the "war of worms" that he left behind in *The Letter to Maria Gisborne* and tried to escape in his own vocation. In order to win the war of worms, the poet must return to the wound that segregates the disciplines, and mend both science and poetry with some synthetic discourse of truth. Scientific observations play a significant role toward the end of the poem, as Wasserman has already noted. The final third of the poem exploits the conclusions of astronomers who assert a distinction between the "reality" of the heavenly bodies and their earthly appearances, and as supporting evidence Wasserman cites Shelley's note to *Queen Mab*: "Beyond our atmosphere the sun would appear as a rayless orb of fire in the midst of a black concave . . ." (483). The moist atmosphere accounts for colors, and the softness of light we experience on earth. Wasserman explains the famous shattering of the "dome of many-coloured glass" (462) as the acquisition of a unity visible only from a cosmic perspective; color appears only to an earthbound eye; from the heavens, all light is a white radiance. Death is the end of illusion, asserts Wasserman, "shattering the many colored dome of the sky" (485).

Still, Wasserman subordinates this astronomical material to a symbolic, literary, and figurative purpose. He asserts that Shelley effects a "metempsychosis" of Keats-Adonais into Vesper, invoking the intertext of the poem's epigraph from Plato, designating Vesper as only a "phase" of Venus, the sensible component of an eternal essence (478). So it is unclear that this account presents any real interdisciplinary advance beyond *Queen Mab*; "facts" remain subordinated to "symbols." And literature continues to employ, to use Stempel's words, "an elaborate self-deception pieced together from old myths and strained metaphors" (111). Peacock was even more biting in *The Four Ages of Poetry* (1820): "While the historian and the philosopher are advancing in, and accelerating, the progress of knowledge, the poet is wallowing in the rubbish of departed ignorance, and raking up the ashes of dead savages to find gewgaws and rattles for the grown babies of the age" (128).

Even leaving science aside, the final series of stanzas in *Adonais* offers a problematic mixture. In plotting the posthumous destination of Adonais, the poem intertwines the subject of literary immortality with personal immortality—already, perhaps, straining propriety. But the issue of mortality is further strained: the last stanzas raise a deeply personal loss; they include a jarring though indirect allusion to the recent death of Shelley's infant son, William—like Keats, buried in Rome. To express reflections on such an intimate tragedy with the heavily formal language of the elegy, an elegy that, moreover, reflects on Shelley's own literary reputation, threatens the already tense relations between rhetoricity and sincerity, a tension that led Samuel Johnson to deplore the elegy as a self-aggrandizing performance at the expense of grief.

Yet, if an elegy is "really" to be about death, it must handle all these forms of death. That *Adonais*'s bid to do so has been missed, and that such an omission follows from disciplinary segregation, is indicated by Wasserman's reading of the significance of "ephemera" in the poem. Wasserman claims that Urania's description of the production and destruction of "each ephemeral insect" in stanza 29 is ironic:

> "The sun comes forth, and many reptiles spawn;
> He sets, and each ephemeral insect then
> Is gathered into death without a dawn,
> And the immortal stars awake again. . . ."
>
> (253-56)

Urania, Wasserman implies, does not mean to suggest that reality is *really* as mutable, as ephemeral, as the appearances described here. It only seems so to a naive and limited psyche for whom the stars appear and disappear with the rising of the sun, when in fact these alterations are illusions produced by the intensity of the sun's light. But what about the insects? Ephemera in *Adonais* are throughout more deeply interwoven into the fabric of the poem. As often noted, ephemerality constitutes both the object and the subject of mourning: the apparent ephemerality of life finds its echo in the transience of grief that only a stubborn and deliberate melancholy would prolong. Ephemerality also describes the physical status of the mourners themselves as Shelley figures them: like echoes of Keats's poetry, they are so completely transitory as to fade "with no stain / . . . like a cloud which had outwept its rain" (89-90). Far from reducing ephemerality to "mere appearance," the poem works to revalue ephemerality, particularly the ephemerality of self-hood, a revaluing that has the potential to speak in a unified language about both the non-human and the human world, and about both things and signs.

By altering the domain of subjects significant to it, *Adonais* resituates death beyond conventional elegiac death. This, in turn, works towards a hopeful synthesis of the resonance of life and death in literature with its resonance in other areas, particularly in natural science. Shelley's invocation of literary figures in the last part of the poem, in contrast to the opening stanzas, subtly shifts the domain of literature itself. While early in the poem Milton appears as a source of power and inspiration because of his monumental literary influence, in the last section lesser poets, Chatterton, Sydney, and Lucan, who, like Keats and like "ephemeral insects," died young, arise, and "Oblivion as they rose shrank like a thing reproved" (405). Yet this does not mean that Shelley valued these poets above Milton; instead, it implies that the poem's conception of immortality is not literary. At first glance, Shelley seems simply to invoke an alternative literary canon by means of what Foucault has led us to term the "author-function," the use of names to index important fictional writing. The author-function controls the circulation and interpretation of literary discourse by attributing such writings to a person, as records of thoughts belonging to subjects, with no necessary relation to objects. This attribution functions to distinguish literary truth-value from that of documents that concern the "real world." But Shelley is actually countering the work of the author-function by exposing the false investment in names that such authority offers. Stanza 44 continues the list of Chatterton, Sydney, and Lucan with "many more, whose names on earth are dark . . ." (406). Reversing Foucault's author-function, author-names aim not to elicit a literary response to literary claims, but instead are attempts to use names to stand for responses—sentiments, memories, reflections—as kinds of things, as events, no longer confined by a segregating culture from "reality."

This interpretation has the consequence that it belittles the earthly achievement that the humanities have called "immortality." But rather than read this shift as evidence of Shelley's pessimism, we might view it as gesturing towards an unselving of achievement, particularly literary achievement, the kind of language most associated with an "author," a reified self. The poem suggests that literary history ultimately fails to immortalize not only Keats and the composer of *Adonais,* but everyone else, including Shelley's son William. For the price of his son, along with the host of non-human others that have no purchase in humanistic discourse, Shelley would have us exchange his fame, at least within the frame of the poem. He vindicates transitory products of individuation because of, rather than despite, their swift decay, and grants equal standing to worms, flowers, stars, Southey, Keats—and William—by refusing the veil of purification, as Latour would call it, that segregates the kinds of truths we attempt to believe. If we moderns work to read Shelley's late work as interdisciplinary in the deep sense described by Latour, we might be able to arrive at a consolation for our own hybridity, and face what an ever more anemic humanist tradition suppresses.

Works Cited

Cameron, Kenneth Neill. "Shelley vs. Southey: New Light on an Old Quarrel." *PMLA* 57 (1942): 489-512.

Curran, Stuart. "Adonais in Context." *Shelley Revalued: Essays from the Gregynog Conference.* Ed. Kelvin Everest. Leicester: Leicester UP, 1983. 165-82.

Gross, Paul R., and Norman Levitt. *Higher Superstition: The Academic Left and its Quarrel with Science.* Baltimore: Johns Hopkins UP, 1994.

Heffernan, A. W. "*Adonais*: Shelley's Consumption of Keats." *Studies in Romanticism* 23 (1984): 295-315.

Hogle, Jerrold E. *Shelley's Process: Radical Transference and the Development of His Major Works.* New York: Oxford UP, 1988.

Latour, Bruno. *We Have Never Been Modern.* Trans. Catherine Porter. Cambridge: Harvard UP, 1993.

Luhmann, Niklas. "Why Does Society Describe Itself as Postmodern?" *Cultural Critique* 30 (1995): 171-86.

Maturana, Humberto A., and Francisco. J. Varela. *Autopoiesis and Cognition: The Realization of the Living.* Boston: Reidel, 1980.

Notopoulos, James A. *The Platonism of Shelley.* Durham: Duke UP, 1949.

Peacock, Thomas Love. *Memoirs of Shelley and other Essays and Reviews.* Ed. Howard Mills. London: Hart-Davis, 1970.

Pulos, C.E. *The Deep Truth: A Study of Shelley's Scepticism.* Lincoln: U of Nebraska P, 1954.

Reiman, Donald H. *Percy Bysshe Shelley.* Updated ed. Boston: Twayne, 1990.

Shelley, Percy Bysshe. *The Letters of Percy Bysshe Shelley.* Ed. Frederick L. Jones. 2 vols. Oxford: Clarendon, 1964.

———. *Shelley's Poetry and Prose.* Ed. Donald H. Reiman and Sharon B. Powers. New York: Norton, 1977.

Stempel, Daniel. "'A Rude Idealism': Models of Nature and History in Shelley's *Prometheus Unbound.*" *Contexts: The Interdisciplinary Study of Literature.* Ed. John J. Teunissen. Special Issue of *Mosaic* 21. 2-3 (1988): 105-21.

Ulmer, William A. "*Adonais* and the Death of Poetry." *Studies in Romanticism* 32 (1993): 425-51.

Wasserman, Earl R. *Shelley: A Critical Reading.* Baltimore: Johns Hopkins UP, 1971.

Robert Schweik (essay date 1999)

SOURCE: "The influence of religion, science, and philosophy on Hardy's writings," in *The Cambridge Companion to Thomas Hardy,* edited by Dale Kramer, Cambridge University Press, 1999, pp. 54-72.

[*In the following essay, Schweik outlines the influence of contemporary religious, scientific, and philosophic thought on Thomas Hardy's writings.*]

A consideration of the influence of contemporary religion, science, and philosophy on Hardy's writings requires some prefatory cautions. First, such influences often overlap, and identification of how they affected Hardy's work must sometimes be no more than a tentative pointing to diverse and complex sets of possible sources whose precise influence cannot be determined. Thus in *Far from the Madding Crowd* Gabriel Oak intervenes to protect Bathsheba's ricks from fire and storm, uses his knowledge to save her sheep, and in other ways acts consistently with the biblical teaching that man was given the responsibility of exercising dominion over nature. At the same time, Oak's conduct is congruent with Thomas Henry Huxley's argument in *Man's Place in Nature* that it is mankind's ethical responsibility to control a morally indifferent environment. However, Oak's actions are even more remarkably consistent with details of the philosophical analysis of man's moral relationship to the natural world in John Stuart Mill's essay "Nature"—though its date of publication makes that influence only barely possible.[1] In this and many other such cases, questions of which, and to what degree, one or more possible sources—"religious," "scientific," or "philosophical"—might have affected what Hardy wrote cannot be resolved with any certainty.

It must be emphasized, too, that Hardy was intellectually very much his own man. He was a voracious reader, widely inquisitive, but usually skeptical and hesitant to embrace wholeheartedly any of the various systems of ideas current in his day. Furthermore—as Hardy many times insisted—the views he did incorporate in his texts were unsystematic and inconsistent "impressions," often the utterances of various *personae* in specific dramatic situations. In short, elements of contemporary thought in Hardy's works tend to be embedded in a densely intricate web of imaginative connections and qualifications so complex that a consideration of them can hope only partly to illuminate the manifold ways they may have influenced his writings.

RELIGION

When Hardy was an architect's apprentice in Dorchester, a dispute with a fellow apprentice and the sons of a Baptist minister on the subject of infant baptism prompted him to more intense study of the Bible and to further inquiry into Anglican doctrine on pedobaptism. Hardy's autobiographical account of his decision to "stick to his own side" (*LW,* pp. 33-34) reveals something of the diverse ways religion could influence his writing. The character of the minister in *A Laodicean* Hardy patterned after the Baptist minister (*LW,* p. 35); his rendering of the issue of baptism in that novel stems partly from his youthful experience but also from later research (*PN,* pp. 180-83); and the phrasing he quoted in his autobiography, "stick to his own side," echoed a phrase from *Far from the Madding Crowd* in a scene where the rustics engage in a memorably comic discussion of differences between Anglicans and Nonconformists (*FMC,* xlii, p. 296)—a scene which itself was probably in part inspired by Hardy's amused recollection of his own youthful decision.

But Hardy's representations of religion were most profoundly influenced by his loss of faith in Christian dogma. He described himself as "among the earliest acclaimers of *The Origin of Species*" (*LW*, p. 158) and recorded that he was "impressed" by *Essays and Reviews* (*LW*, p. 37); one can only guess at what other intellectual and emotional experiences at that time might have contributed to the erosion of his religious beliefs. He had considered the possibility of a career as a clergyman, and as late as 1865, out of deference to his mentor, Horace Moule, wished he could be convinced by the arguments in John Henry Newman's *Apologia*. But Hardy found he could not (*LW*, pp. 50-51), and in that same year he rejected further clerical aspirations, explaining that "he could hardly take the step with honour while holding the views that on examination he found himself to hold" (*LW*, p. 53). By 1888, when a clergyman asked him how to reconcile the absolute goodness and non-limitation of God with the horrors of human existence, Hardy referred him to the life of Darwin and the works of Herbert Spencer and "other agnostics" for a "provisional view of the universe" (*LW*, p. 214). Ten years later, in his poem "Nature's Questioning," he had his speaker respond to Nature's puzzled speculations on the origins of the universe with a flat, "No answerer I . . ." (*CPW*, I, pp. 86-87)—a reply that characterized one strain of Hardy's own religious views throughout much of his career.

Yet although Hardy became an agnostic, he remained emotionally involved with the Church: many of his writings dramatize aspects of the pernicious influence of religious doctrines or the ineffectuality of institutional Christianity, but he could also evoke a wistful sense of the loss of an earlier, simpler faith, or affirm the lasting value of Christian Charity. In short, one thing that sets Hardy apart from many of his contemporaries was his capacity to hold the wide variety of "impressions" of religion that inform his writings.

One manifestation of the way Christianity remained a persistent influence on Hardy's writings is that his fiction is saturated with biblical allusions. Critics have disagreed on how effectively Hardy used them, as commentaries on his references to Satan reveal,[2] but scriptural and other religious allusions in Hardy's fiction are distributed unevenly, and in some novels they form patterns that obviously play important roles. In *Far from the Madding Crowd*, for example, many Old and New Testament references enhance the ambiance of timeless antiquity which is one of that novel's most important aesthetic features. For *The Mayor of Casterbridge*, on the other hand, Hardy employed allusions to the biblical story of Saul and David as a major structural element in rendering its plot and character relationships.[3] And in *Tess* and *Jude*, where he was particularly concerned with the inimical relationship of religious mores to human lives, scriptural references repeatedly appear in contexts which suggest that Christianity is a pervasive hindrance to the fulfillment of human aspiration.

Hardy's writings also abound with pejorative characterizations of Christian clergy and other representatives of the Church, as well as with dramatizations of the harmful consequences of Christian teaching: one thinks, for example, of the fanatical text-painter in *Tess*, or of the snobbish and foolishly conventional Felix and Cuthbert Clare, who are ironically called "unimpeachable models" of clergymen (*T*, xxv, p. 162). But Hardy's presentations of representatives of Christianity and his renderings of the impact of Christian belief on both individual characters and on society generally were remarkably diverse and nuanced. In the novels, he tended to treat clergymen and Christianity with increasing hostility. Maybold in *Under the Greenwood Tree* is mildly parsimonious and class-conscious, but Swancourt in *A Pair of Blue Eyes* is a social snob whose prejudices do more serious harm. Hardy's revisions reveal that over the course of time he was increasingly critical of Bishop Helmsdale of *Two on a Tower*,[4] and part of the plot of that novel turns on the cruel choices imposed on the heroine by intolerant Christian attitudes toward human sexuality. By the time he came to write *Tess* and *Jude*, Hardy was even more explicit in dramatizing the way Christian teachings had widespread malign human consequences.

An even more various treatment of the limitations of clerics and Christianity is notable in his short stories and poems. "The Son's Veto," for example, depicts how a clerical education shaped a clergyman's cruel treatment of his mother, while "A Tragedy of Two Ambitions" delineates the plight of brothers who realize that to succeed in the Church of England they must above all be gentlemen rather than scholars or preachers. In Hardy's poems there is the well-meaning but bumbling clergyman of "The Curate's Kindness," the hypocritical preacher of "In Church," the credulous fool of "In the Days of Crinoline," the dully indifferent Mr. Dowe of "An East-End Curate," the disenchanted Parson Thirdly in "Channel Firing," the narrow-minded priest of "The Inscription," the misguided vicar in "The Choirmaster's Burial," and that sincere (but therefore unpromoted) clergyman of "Whispered at the Church-opening." In short, although one generalization which can be made about Hardy's writings is that many involve the limitations of Christian clergy as well as the personal and social harm done by organized Christianity, the ways Hardy handled those themes could scarcely be more diverse.

On the other hand, Hardy from time to time portrayed Christianity as a transient and ineffectual creed based on dubious legends no longer believed. As early as *Far from the Madding Crowd* he had his narrator remark on the durable usefulness of the great shearing-barn as compared to the worn-out purposes of church and castle (*FMC*, xxii, p. 150); similarly, in *Tess* he contrasted the endurance of an ancient abbey mill to the abbey itself which "had perished, creeds being transient" (*T*, xxxv, p. 230). And in *The Dynasts* the Spirit of the Years refers to Christianity as "a local cult" scarcely recognized because it had changed so much (Part First, I, vi, lines 1-12; *CPW*, IV, pp. 53-54). In some poems—e.g., "A Christmas Ghost-Story," "A Drizzling Easter Morning," and "Christmas: 1924"—Hardy rings emotional changes on the theme of Christianity's in-effectualness; in others he fancifully images god as variously flawed—forgetful in "God Forgotten," absent-minded in "By the Earth's Corpse," and error-prone in "I Met a Man." In still others, like "Panthera," he provides secular accounts of biblical stories in the manner of those higher critics who persuaded the speaker of "The Respectable Burgher on 'The Higher Criticism'" to abandon scripture and turn, instead, to "that moderate man Voltaire" (*CPW*, I, pp. 198-99).

There were, however, aspects of Christianity and the Church Hardy treated more positively. Given the testimony in his autobiography of the sincerity he admired in the Baptist minister Frederick Perkins, it is not surprising that some of his more sincere fictional clergymen—Raunham in *Desperate Remedies*, Thirdly in *Far from the Madding Crowd*, Woodwell in *A Laodicean*, Torkingham in *Two on a Tower*, and even old Mr. Clare in *Tess*—are portrayed with greater sympathy. Furthermore, particularly in his earlier fiction, Hardy frequently exploited references to Christian values as a means of influencing reader attitudes toward both character and moral situation. *Far from the Madding Crowd* provides a variety of examples. There Hardy used the revelation that Troy's claim of regular church attendance was false to impugn his character (*FMC*, xxix, p. 204), and he had Bathsheba, in her agitated suspicion of the possibility of Troy's infidelity, see Oak humbly at his evening prayers and be chastened by his calm piety (xliii, p. 306). Near the conclusion of the novel, he used quotations from Newman's "Lead Kindly Light" to underscore Bathsheba's sense of her waywardness (lvi, pp. 402-03) and defined the strength of Oak's and Bathsheba's love by an allusion to the Song of Solomon (lvi, p. 409). Then, too, there are poems like "Afternoon Service at Mellstock," "The Impercipient," "The Darkling Thrush," and "The Oxen" which in their very different ways all convey some sense of regret for a faith now no longer possible. Even in his most anti-Christian novel, *Jude*, Hardy had both Sue and Jude agree with *Corinthians* that "Charity seeketh not her own" (*J*, VI, iv, p. 382), and the speaker of his poem "Surview" also affirms St. Paul's teaching on Charity (*CPW*, II, p. 485).

As late as 1922, Hardy asserted the need for "an alliance between religion, which must be retained unless the world is to perish, and complete rationality, which must come" (*CPW*, II, p. 325). But when he occasionally voiced some dream of a reformed Church, he spoke of it only as dedicated to "the promotion of that virtuous living on which all honest men are agreed" and "reverence & love for the ethical ideal" (*Letters* 1, p. 136 and 3, p. 5 [the latter a quotation from Thomas Huxley]). Not surprisingly, then, in his literary works Hardy did not advance any substitute for the religious faith he had lost. He comically deflated Paula Power's determination at the end of *A Laodicean* to live according to Matthew Arnold's vague formula of "imaginative reason," and, in a far more serious novel, *Tess*, the ultimate norms he invoked involve diverse and conflicting ethical perspectives which at best suggest that

human moral worth cannot be reduced to some formula.[5] As David J. DeLaura has persuasively argued in analyses of *The Return of the Native, Tess,* and *Jude*, Hardy tended to undercut contemporary optimistic views of achieving some "modern" blend of pagan Hellenic and neo-Christian religion: his treatments of such characters as Clym, Angel, and Sue dramatize in various ways their failures to live by such ideals—and suggest that neither Christianity nor any substitute creed ultimately avails human beings trapped in a blind and morally indifferent universe.[6]

SCIENCE

Certainly Hardy's readings in the scientific thought of his day strengthened his sense that the supernaturalism of theological doctrines was an outdated relic hindering development of more rational views of the world. In a letter to Edward Clodd of 17 January 1897, for example, he bitterly complained of "the arrest of light & reason by theology" (*Letters* 2, p. 143). Nevertheless, on the whole, the "light and reason" of science tended not to brighten but to darken Hardy's view of the human condition.

ASTRONOMY AND PHYSICS

In his poem "Afterwards," Hardy described himself as having an eye for the "mysteries" of the "full-starred heavens" (*CPW*, II, p. 308); yet his was for the most part an eye keen for artistic effects rather than for science, and often Hardy's references to astronomical phenomena are of a distinctly romantic kind. In "The Comet at Yell'ham," for example, the comet serves primarily as a device for making the poetic point that by the time it returns, "its strange swift shine / Will fall on Yell'ham; but not then / On face of mine or thine" (*CPW*, I, p. 189).

Two on a Tower, however, was, at least in intention, different, for Hardy described it as having been undertaken specifically "to make science, not the mere padding of a romance, but the actual vehicle of romance" (*Letters* 1, p. 110). Although he owned a copy of Richard A. Proctor's *Essays in Astronomy*, and a few notes in his *Literary Notebooks* show that he also read other of Proctor's popular expositions of astronomy, it is clear that in preparing to write *Two on a Tower* he took pains to more thoroughly familiarize himself not only with practical details—his research included a visit to Greenwich Observatory—but with the larger implications of current ideas in astronomy and physics. As a consequence, whatever artistic deficiencies that novel may be judged to have—including often clumsy uses of astronomical imagery—it is strikingly indicative of what impact the astronomy of Hardy's day had upon his vision of the human predicament. Among the scientific developments that lie behind *Two on a Tower* are Sir William Herschel's discovery that nebulae are clusters of stars at unimaginably immense distances from the earth and his conclusion that those stars, including the sun, must in time burn themselves out—a conclusion later compellingly confirmed by the research of Lord Kelvin, who in 1851 formulated the second law of thermodynamics. It is a vision of the ultimate consequence of Kelvin's theory of entropy in the universe that Hardy evoked in the words of his "votary of science," Swithin St. Cleeve:

> "And to add a new weirdness to what the sky possesses in its size and formlessness, there is involved the quality of decay. For all the wonder of these everlasting stars, eternal spheres, and what not, they are not everlasting, they are not eternal; they burn out like candles . . . The senses may become terrified by plunging among them . . . Imagine them all extinguished, and your mind feeling its way through a heaven of total darkness, occasionally striking against the black invisible cinders of those stars."

(TT, iv, pp. 34-35)

Thereafter, Hardy would occasionally return to such grim prophecies of the future. Some time after 1900 he pasted a cutting in his "Literary Notebooks" of a review which dwelled on Ernst Haeckel's description of the unimportance of man on an unimportant planet doomed to grow cold and lifeless (*LN* 2, pp. 98-101). Hardy incorporated that troubling image in some of his poems: "In Vision I Roamed," for example, dramatizes a wandering by "footless traverse through ghast heights of sky" in a universe "trackless, distant, drear" (*CPW,* I, pp. 10-11), while in "Genitrix Laesa" Hardy's speaker sees no point in curing Nature's ills when "all is sinking / To dissolubility" (*CPW,* III, p. 89).

But the ideas of Herschel, Kelvin, and Haeckel were rooted in eighteenth-century Newtonian physics, and one sign of Hardy's wide-ranging curiosity is that, having lived on into the twentieth century and encountered a radically new physics, he began to ponder its non-Newtonian implications: that time and space are relative to the speed of the motion of an observer, and that time itself is a "fourth dimension." He took notes on popular expositions of Einstein's theories (*LN* 2, pp. 228-29), bought an edition of *Relativity: The Special and the General Theory: A Popular Exposition,* and, in a letter to J. Ellis McTaggart, 31 December 1919, observed that, after Einstein, "the universe seems to be getting too comic for words" (*Letters* 5, p. 353). Predictably, Hardy's readings influenced his poetry. In "A Dream Question" of 1909, for example, Hardy had one of his many imagined gods remark that "A fourth dimension, say the guides, / To matter is conceivable" (*CPW,* I, p. 317). But by the time he published *Human Shows* in 1925, he had absorbed enough of popular expositions of Einstein's theories to subordinate them more fully to his poetic purposes: thus, in "The Absolute Explains" he imaginatively transformed Einstein's "Fourth Dimension" from a concept in physics to a place where, comfortably, love, song, and glad experience are all "unhurt by age" (*CPW,* III, p. 70, line 45), while the speaker of a companion poem, "So, Time," is consoled by the idea that time is "nought / But a thought / Without reality" (*CPW,* III, p. 72). There is, however, less consolation in *Winter Words,* where, in a drinking song, Hardy had his speaker resignedly toast the way man's apparent importance in the universe had diminished from Thales to Einstein (*CPW,* III, pp. 247-50).

ARCHAEOLOGY

In an "interview" on Stonehenge Hardy wrote for the *Daily Chronicle,* he had thoughtful suggestions for abating its erosion (*PW,* pp. 196-200), and his account of a dig at Maumbury Ring combines evocations of the excitement of its finds with carefully precise details about the excavated site (*PW,* pp. 225-31). It was no doubt partly that interest in archaeology which led him in 1881 to become a member of the Dorset Natural History and Antiquarian Field Club—an organization he imaginatively transformed into the "Wessex Field and Antiquarian Club" whose members narrate the stories of *A Group of Noble Dames.* In 1884, in the course of reading a paper for the Club on "Some Romano-British Relics Found at Max Gate, Dorchester" (*PW,* pp. 191-95), Hardy made a disparaging allusion to a Dorset antiquary, Edward Cunnington, whom he ironically dubbed a "local Schliemann." It is almost certainly his awareness of Cunnington's combination of archaeological incompetence and lack of integrity that lies behind Hardy's short story "A Tryst at an Ancient Earthwork," in which an unscrupulous local antiquary illegally digs at an archaeological site and steals a gold statuette of Mercury.

But it was above all Hardy's imaginative setting of the hopes and fears of the living against archaeological records of the indifferent passage of time that is the most moving consequence of his interest in archaeology. Tess's capture at Stonehenge is certainly his most poignantly effective use of that kind of setting, but only one of many such. Hardy's Wessex landscapes are studded with prehistoric burial cairns: most memorably the "Rainbarrow" of *The Return of the Native,* but also the barrows he compared to the many-breasted Diana of Ephesus that appear in *The Mayor of Casterbridge* (*MC,* xlv, p. 330), in *Tess* (*T,* xlii, p. 273), and, again, in his poem "By the Barrows" (*CPW,* I, p. 317). The inhabitants of Hardy's Casterbridge live against a backdrop of skeletal reminders that ancient Romans before them also once "loved, laughed, and fought, hailed their friends, drank their toasts / At their meeting-times here"("After the Fair"; *CPW,* I, p. 295), and the even more ancient prehistoric originators of Maumbury Ring "mock the chime / Of . . . Christian time / From its hollows of chalk and loam"("Her Death and After"; *CPW,* I, p. 54, lines 78-80).

In short, just as contemporary astronomy and physics influenced Hardy's imaginative perception of man's trivial physical position in the stellar universe, so his writings reveal a similar preoccupation with the way human aspirations are dwarfed in the vast dimensions of archaeological time. It is worth remembering, then—given the optimistic tone of Darwin's conclusion to *The Origin of Species* and Huxley's visions of prospects for the possibility of human progress—that the sometimes grimmer image of the human condition notable in Hardy's writing was at least in part rooted in discoveries so compelling as the inexorable implications of the second law of thermodynamics and so poignant as those manifold reminders in his Wessex landscape of how fleeting human hopes and desires appear in the long passage of mankind's time on earth.

BIOLOGICAL EVOLUTION

Nevertheless, Hardy's letters and notebooks make clear that he had the deepest respect for Darwin and Huxley as representatives of the best scientific thought of his day. It is possible that Darwin's views on heredity (along with those of August Weismann, Herbert Spencer, and William Galton) may have influenced Hardy's treatment of heredity in *The Well-Beloved*,[7] but the chief impact of evolutionary theory on Hardy's writing is notable in two other ways. First, it prompted him to set images of human life against the backdrop of geologic and evolutionary time—a time he would emphasize was incomparably longer than man's archaeological traces. In *The Return of the Native*, for example, his memorable evocation of the timelessness of Egdon Heath ends with a comment on how even its slight irregularities "remained as the very finger-touches of the last geological change" (*RN*, I, i, p. 6), and in *A Pair of Blue Eyes*, when Knight is suspended on the face of a cliff and staring into the eyes of a fossilized Trilobite, Hardy conveyed the immense lapse of evolutionary time that "closed up like a fan" before his eyes by providing a retrospective account, replete with technical terminology, of evolution from man back to that fossil (*PBE*, xxii, pp. 209-10). In his poetry, too, he exploited geology for similar purposes: in "The Clasped Skeletons," for example, an imaginative meditation on the long dead lovers found in a barrow dated about 1800 BC turns on the idea that, in the vast scale of geologic time, they might have been buried only yesterday (*CPW*, III, pp. 209-11).

But Hardy's insights into the implications of evolutionary theory also influenced some attitudes toward human moral responsibility that emerged in his later writings. As Hardy saw it, "The discovery of the law of evolution . . . shifted the centre of altruism from humanity to the whole conscious world collectively" (*LW*, p. 373)—a view relatable to those powerful scenes in which Tess mercifully kills wounded game birds (*T*, xli, p. 271) and Jude does the same for a suffering pig (*J*, I, x, p. 64). Similar attitudes underlie such poems as "The Puzzled Game Birds" and "Compassion: An Ode." But Hardy's sense of mankind's new responsibility toward animals also troubled him: in a letter to Frederic Harrison he expressed doubt that humans would accept the new moral duty thrust upon them (*Letters* 3, pp. 230-31), and in "Afterwards" he characterized himself as one who "strove that . . . innocent creatures should come to no harm," but did so in vain (*CPW*, II, p. 308).

However, it was the plight of mankind trapped in a universe oblivious to human feelings and ethical aspirations that not only most powerfully moved Hardy but also set him apart from many of his contemporaries who saw some "grandeur" or "progress" in evolutionary change. To one such optimist, he pointedly stressed that "nature is *unmoral*" (*Letters* 3, p. 231), and in his autobiography recorded a note to the effect that "emotions have no place in a world of defect, and it is a cruel injustice that they should have developed in it" (*LW*, p. 153). Hardy took up related themes in his poetry: his "Before Life and After," for ex-

ample, includes the affirmation that before the evolution of consciousness "all went well" (*CPW*, I, p. 333). But it was in his novels that he most plangently rendered the condition of those who futilely aspire to happiness, or fruitlessly strive to achieve ethical ideals, or struggle with painful feelings of moral obligation in a universe otherwise indifferent to such aspirations and feelings. Of his earlier fiction, *The Return of the Native* most distinctly embodies those concerns. Hardy's characterization of Clym Yeobright as bearing evidence "that ideal physical beauty is incompatible with growth of fellow-feeling and a full sense of the coil of things" (*RN*, II, vi, p. 138); his dramatization of Eustacia Vye's frustrated longings for hopeless ideals; his authorial observations on how that "old-fashioned revelling in the general situation grows less and less possible as we uncover the defects of natural laws, and see the quandary that man is in by their operation" (*RN*, III, i, p. 169)—all convey the alienation of thinking and feeling humans in a universe indifferent to human ideals and sensitivities.

In a notebook entry of 1876, Hardy copied the following from an article by Theodore Watts: "Science tells us that, in the struggle for life, the surviving organism is not necessarily that which is absolutely the best in an ideal sense, though it must be that which is most in harmony with surrounding conditions" (*LN*, I, p. 40). The human predicament in those "surrotions" is no more profoundly explored than in *The Woodlanders*, Hardy's most Darwinian novel in the emphasis he placed on the bleak struggle for survival in a woodland setting where "the lichen ate the vigour of the stalk, and the ivy slowly strangled to death the promising sapling" (vii, p. 53). In this context, Hardy's Grace Melbury, Giles Winterborne, Mr. Melbury, and Mrs. Charmond are out of harmony with their surroundings: all rack themselves with futile questions of conscience that, in the end, yield no satisfactory results, while the two characters who do manage to find some "harmony" with an environment indifferent to human moral concerns do so at terrible cost—either by renouncing common human desire, as does Marty South, or by selfishly satisfying desire with no regard for others, as does Edred Fitzpiers. In Hardy's vision of the universe of *The Woodlanders*, there appear to be no acceptable moral choices. *Tess* and *Jude* provide similarly bleak views of the human predicament. In *Jude*, for example, the sensitive and aspiring Jude and Sue are ultimately crushed, while the coarse Arabella and unscrupulous Vilbert are well enough adapted to succeed in satisfying their lower aims.

It was, then, of the consequences of human evolution that Hardy was often particularly pessimistic; in his autobiography, for example, he recorded a note of April, 1889: "A woeful fact—that the human race is too extremely developed for its corporeal conditions, the nerves being evolved to an activity abnormal in such an environment . . . This planet does not supply the materials for happiness to higher existences" (*LW*, p. 227). That view Hardy gave most explicit expression to in *Jude*, where he echoed his own ideas in Sue's distraught imagining that "at the framing of the terrestrial conditions there seemed never to have been contemplated such a development of emotional perceptiveness among the creatures subject to those conditions as that reached by thinking and educated humanity" (*J,* VI, iii, p. 361).

PHILOSOPHY

While pondering a world which contemporary science increasingly revealed to be indifferent to human feelings and values, Hardy was also reading widely in and about the works of contemporary philosophers, many of whom were responding to that same world view. To the ideas of some—such as Nietzsche and Bergson—he was so hostile (see *Letters* 5, pp. 50-51, 78-79, and 6, p. 259) that any influence they may have had on his writings could only be negative. But in others Hardy found support for his agnosticism, possible alternatives to the supernaturalism of Christian ethics, and various theories of what forces in an uncaring universe might account for the human predicament and conceivably effect its amelioration. Of those writers who most notably influenced Hardy, the chief were Leslie Stephen, François Fourier, Herbert Spencer, John Stuart Mill, Ludwig Feuerbach, Auguste Comte, Arthur Schopenhauer, and Eduard von Hartmann.

FOUR GENERAL INFLUENCES: STEPHEN, FOURIER, SPENCER, AND MILL

Hardy stated that the editor and philosopher Leslie Stephen had a stronger influence on him than that of any other of his contemporaries, and "The Schreckhorn," a sonnet celebrating Stephen's personal qualities, testifies to Hardy's respect for him. That they could share a wide-ranging curiosity about philosophical questions is suggested from Hardy's account of how Stephen called upon him to witness his signature on a renunciation of holy orders—after which they talked of "theologies decayed and defunct, the origin of things, the constitution of matter, the unreality of time, and kindred subjects" (*LW,* pp. 108-09). Throughout the rest of his life Hardy cherished the agnostic Stephen's friendship (*LW,* pp. 188), and no doubt his fiction and poetry owe much to the intellectual support Hardy found in such an impressive father-figure.

What influences François Fourier's ideas may have had on Hardy's writings were also of an indefinite kind. In 1863 Hardy was enough impressed to sketch—and thereafter preserve—an elaborate diagram of ideas in Fourier's *The Passions of the Human Soul,* a work he had obviously studied carefully.[8] It is possible that Fourier's view that much of human suffering stemmed from conflicts between intellect and passion, resulting often from Christianity's teachings about marriage, may have influenced some major themes that appear in Hardy's fiction—particularly his hostile portrayal of Christian views on marriage in *The Woodlanders, Tess,* and, especially, *Jude,* which Hardy described as dramatizing the "deadly war waged between flesh and spirit" (*J,* Preface, p. xxxv).

Contemporary scientific evidences that man was infinitesimal in the vastness of the universe no doubt made Hardy more receptive to philosophical views that challenged conventional perception of space and time. It is not surprising, then, that he declared Herbert Spencer's *First Principles* sometimes acted "as a sort of patent expander when I had been particularly narrowed down by the events of life" (*Letters* 2, pp. 24-25), for one of Spencer's major arguments was that space and time were incomprehensible. In fact, the question, "What are Space and Time?" with which Spencer opened chapter 3 of his *First Principles*[9] is probably one source (Kant, of course, could be another) of the line, *"What are Space and Time? A fancy!"* in *The Dynasts* (Part Third, I, iii, line 84; *CPW,* V, p. 25). It was in Spencer's writings, too, that Hardy came across the suggestion that there might not be any comprehension underlying the universe (*Letters* 3, p. 244)—an idea that may have influenced his conception of an unconscious Will in *The Dynasts.*

A similar kind of influence is notable in Hardy's response to J. S. Mill. Hardy claimed that in the 1860s he knew Mill's *On Liberty* "almost by heart" (*LW,* p. 355), and, in fact, in *Jude* he had Sue Bridehead quote from one of Mill's arguments for liberty of thought (*J,* IV, iii, p. 234). Certainly Mill's confident secular individualism, like Stephen's and Spencer's agnosticism, encouraged Hardy in the independent pursuit of his own world view. Then, too, some of the ideas Mill developed in his "Theism"—e.g., that there is no need to postulate a beginning to matter and force in the universe and that consciousness may arise from unconscious causes—might have influenced Hardy's conception in *The Dynasts* of the Immanent Will becoming conscious—though Hardy claimed the latter idea as his own (*Letters* 3, p. 255).

FEUERBACH AND COMTE

The effects of the thought of both Ludwig Feuerbach and Auguste Comte on Hardy's writings are possible to identify with somewhat greater specificity. Feuerbach's idea that the Christian god is the product of man's need to imagine perfection was twice summarized by Hardy in the phrase, "God is the product of man": once in a notebook (*LN* 2, p. 166) and again in a letter to Edward Clodd (*Letters* 3, p. 244). In *The Return of the Native,* the narrator's comment that humans always make a "generous endeavour to construct a hypothesis that shall not degrade a first cause" (*RN,* VI, i, p. 387) may owe something to Feuerbach's influence, but there are poems in *Satires of Circumstance* which almost certainly do. In "A Plaint to Man," for example, one of Hardy's imagined gods asks, "Wherefore, O Man, did there come to you / The unhappy need of creating me[?]" (*CPW,* II, p. 33); in "God's Funeral," the speaker inquires, "Whence came it we were tempted to create / One whom we can no longer keep alive?" (*CPW,* II, p. 35, lines 23-24); and in "Aquae Sulis" the Christian god chides the British goddess of the waters of Bath with the words, "You know not by what frail thread we equally hang; / It is said we are images both—twitched by people's desires" (*CPW,* II, p. 91).

Far more complex influences on Hardy's thought may be traced to the writings of August Comte and his Positivist followers. Hardy marked some passages in the 1865 translation of Comte's *A General View of Positivism* given to him by Horace Moule, and his autobiography includes references to his reading Comte in 1870 and again in 1873 (*LW*, pp. 79, 100); furthermore, his notebooks and letters from 1876 onward show that he read in a *System of Positive Polity* as well as in works by such Positivists as Edward Spencer Beesley, John Morley, Cotter Morrison, and Frederic Harrison. He certainly agreed with Comte's aim to promote human altruism—which he saw as equatable with the Christian "Love your Neighbour as Yourself" (*LW*, p. 235)—and he acknowledged that "no person of serious thought in these times could be said to stand aloof from Positivist teaching & ideals" (*Letters* 3, p. 53). In his autobiography, he added that if Comte had included Christ in his calendar, it would have made Positivism palatable to people who know it "to contain the germs of a true system" (*LW*, pp. 150-51).

Yet, for all that, Hardy's word *germs* is indicative of the qualified response he took to Comte. For example, in his *Social Dynamics*, Comte described human progress as a "looped orbit," sometimes going backward by way of gathering strength to spring forward again. Hardy's imagination was obviously caught by that metaphor: in one of his notebooks he diagramed it (*LN* 1, p. 76); later he incorporated it in his "Candour in English Fiction," and, again, in his "Apology" of 1922 (*PW*, pp. 126-27, 57-58). But, in that same "Apology," he criticized the Positivists' optimistic view of progress (*PW*, p. 53).

Nevertheless, other influences of Positivist thought can be detected both in Hardy's fiction and in his poetry. For example, Clym Yeobright's "relatively advanced" ideas, based on Parisian "ethical systems popular at the time" (*RN*, III, ii, p. 174), prompted one reviewer to see him as "touched with the asceticism of a certain positivistic school."[10] At least one of Hardy's contemporaries also saw Positivism in *Tess*. In fact, in that novel Hardy probably did adapt notes he made of Comte's division of mankind's "theological" stage into "fetishistic," "polytheistic," and "monotheistic" parts (*LN* 1, pp. 67, 73-74, 77-78): Tess, Hardy's narrator remarks, is afflicted by "fetishistic fear" (*T*, iii, p. 28) and her rhapsody to nature is described as "a Fetichistic [*sic*] utterance in a Monotheistic setting" (xvi, p. 109). Then, too, the book Angel Clare describes as promoting a moral "system of philosophy" (xviii, p. 120), and the "ethical system without any dogma" he accepts (xlvii, p. 319), both call to mind Comte's *System of Positive Polity*. Furthermore, in 1887 Hardy had taken notes from the Positivist Cotter Morrison's *The Service of Man*, including his argument that primitive religions had no connection with morals (*LN* 1, p. 190)—an argument which Tess repeats to Alec when she tries to "tell him that he had mixed . . . two matters, theology and morals, which in the primitive days of mankind had been quite distinct" (*T*, xlvii, p. 320).[11] It was probably such particulars, as well as the final change in Clym from moral rigidity to sympathy and love for Tess, that prompted Frederic Harrison's comment to Hardy that *Tess* reads "like a Positivist allegory."[12]

Comte also argued that poets must promote altruism and "adequately portray the new man in his relation to the new God."[13] Some poems of Hardy's appear to have been influenced by that conception. His "A Plaint to Man," for example, with its theme that humanity must depend on its resources alone for the promotion of an altruistic "loving-kindness" (*CPW*, II, p. 34) sounds very Positivist, as do poems like "The Graveyard of Dead Creeds," "God's Funeral," and "The Sick Battle-God," all of which express some hope for the emergence of altruism in humanity.

Schopenhauer and von Hartmann

What is striking about the impact on Hardy of Stephen, Fourier, Spencer, Mill, Feuerbach, and Comte is that, for the most part, they influenced him by the ways they served as role-models for his repudiation of religious belief, or offered some explanation of Christianity's attraction, or provided an alternative to Christian ethics and values. But, as notes he took on various philosophers ranging in time from Baruch Spinoza to William Clifford reveal, Hardy was also interested in more abstract questions about the nature of what fundamental force or forces might underlie the universe. Of these, his writings were most notably influenced by the central ideas of Arthur Schopenhauer and Eduard von Hartmann, in addition to such concepts as Herbert Spencer's suggestion that there may be no ultimate comprehension in the universe and John Stuart Mill's observation that consciousness may arise from unconscious causes.

In 1907 Hardy undertook to explain to a correspondent that the "philosophy of life" he utilized in *The Dynasts* was a "generalized form of what the thinking world had gradually come to adopt." According to Hardy, its chief features were three: (1) that there is an unconscious and impersonal "urging force" that is immanent in the universe; (2) that man's individual will is subservient to that Immanent Will, but "whenever it happens that all the rest of the Great Will is in equilibrium the minute portion called one person's will is free"; and (3) that the Unconscious Will is "growing aware of Itself . . . & ultimately, it is to be hoped, sympathetic" (*Letters* 3, p. 255). Variations on such unsystematic and generalized "impressions" dramatized by Hardy in *The Dynasts* and elsewhere were no doubt in part influenced by the writings of Schopenhauer and von Hartmann.

Hardy's reported comments on Schopenhauer's influence are contradictory: by one account, he denied being influenced at all (Millgate, *Biography*, p. 199); by another, he asserted that his "philosophy" was "a development from Schopenhauer through later philosophers."[14] The latter is more likely. Hardy owned translations of *The World as Will and Idea* (1896) and *On the Four-fold Root of the Principle of Sufficient Reason* (1889)—in which (among others) he marked a passage asserting that "a *will* must be attributed to all that is lifeless."[15] In 1891 he made extensive notebook entries from Schopenhauer's *Studies in Pessimism*, including one emphasizing that "unless *suffering* is the direct & immediate object of life, our existence must entirely fail of its aim" (*LN* 2, p. 28). Furthermore, some time before 1888 Hardy consulted the *Encyclopaedia Britannica* to take a note on Schopenhauer's pessimistic view of the will to live (*LN* 1, p. 203), and later, no doubt to help clarify Schopenhauer's confusing prose, he turned to *Chambers's Encyclopaedia,* from which he took a note on Schopenhauer's idea of "the unconscious, automatic, or reasonless Will" (*LN* 2, p. 107).

Nevertheless, Schopenhauer's influence on Hardy's writings appears to be limited. His reference in *Tess* to the extremeness of Mr. Clare's "renunciative philosophy which had cousinship with that of Schopenhauer and Leopardi" (*T,* xxv, p. 161), for example, expresses no more than the popular image of Schopenhauer's pessimistic advocacy of renunciation of life—a view which may also have influenced a passage in *Jude* about "the coming universal wish not to live" (*J,* vi, ii, p. 355). Similarly, the concept of an unknowing immanent "Will" in the universe that figures in "He Wonders About Himself," in the "Fore Scene" of *The Dynasts,* and in later spirit choruses, may reflect Hardy's note-taking from *On the Four-fold Root of the Principle of Sufficient Reason,* or from *Chambers's Encyclopaedia,* or from other expositions of Schopenhauer's thought. But, in fact, little Hardy wrote compels attribution to Schopenhauer of influence beyond the level of generality characteristic of popular summaries of his pessimism and of his concept of "Will" as a force underlying the phenomena of the universe.

Specific instances of the influence of Eduard von Hartmann's ideas on Hardy reveal how radically he would modify them. For example, in the late 1890s Hardy took a note on Hartmann's view of the "infallible purposive . . . activity" of an "unconscious clairvoyant" intelligence; he headed that note, "God as *super*-conscious," and followed it with an excerpted quotation from Hartmann: "We shall . . . designate this intell[i]g[ence], superior to all consc[iousness], at once unconsc[ious] & super-conscious" (*LN* 2, p. 111). To this Hardy added "'? processive" above von Hartmann's "purposive," and then jotted his observation, "very obscure." Later, Hardy imported a version of that "very obscure" passage into the mouth of the Spirit of the Years in *The Dynasts,* but again changed the word *purposive* to *processive*—a term which conveys a concept markedly different from von Hartmann's:

> *In that immense unweeting Mind is shown*
> One far above forethinking; prócessive,
> Rapt, superconscious; a Clairvoyancy
> That knows not what It knows . . .

> (Part First, v, iv; lines 184-87; *CPW,* iv, p. 137)

Hence, although Hardy no doubt partly agreed with von Hartmann's concept of the Will as Unconscious, even when almost quoting him he freely made changes that radically altered von Hartmann's views.[16]

What can be said with greatest certainty is that Hardy's readings of and about Schopenhauer and von Hartmann

confirmed some ideas he had arrived at independently or that he might earlier have derived from Mill, Spencer, Huxley, and others. Schopenhauer did probably suggest to Hardy the name *Will* for that underlying force in the universe about which he had long ruminated (though Hardy freely used many other names as well), and, by his theory of the "Unconscious," von Hartmann no doubt reinforced what Hardy himself had already conceived—that such a force could be as uncomprehending as those "purblind Doomsters" in his "Hap" (*CPW,* 1, p. 10). It is likely, too, that Hardy took from von Hartmann the word *immanent* for his "Immanent Will"; at least the translator of the edition Hardy used more than once speaks of the Will as an "immanent cause."[17] Beyond that, even the most careful efforts to make point-for-point comparisons of what Hardy wrote with Schopenhauer's and von Hartmann's thought are bound to be highly speculative.[18]

But, finally, it is important to note that, as Hardy judged them, Schopenhauer and von Hartmann took a supercilious view of the forlorn hope which (with some lapses) he clung to for an amelioration of the human condition (see "Apology," *Late Lyrics and Earlier* [1922]; *CPW,* II, p. 325). Furthermore they differed greatly from Hardy in the attitudes they adopted toward the human condition. Just as Schopenhauer's claim to take a detached view of life was foreign to Hardy's engaged concern for the suffering of humankind and higher animals, so was von Hartmann's celebration of an Unconscious evolving at the expense of untold human pain. In the end, neither they, nor any other intellectual influences, altered Hardy's conviction, conveyed often both in his poetry and his prose, that human aspiration, human feeling, and human hope, however dwarfed in the cosmic scale of things, were nevertheless more important than all the rest.

Notes

1. For a consideration of such possible influences on *FMC,* see G. Glen Wickens, "Literature and Science: Hardy's Response to Mill, Huxley and Darwin," *Mosaic: A Journal for the Interdisciplinary Study of Literature,* 14/3 (1981), 63-79.

2. See, for example, J. O. Bailey, "Hardy's Mephistophelian Visitants," *PMLA,* 61 (1946), 1146-84; Frank B. Pinion, "Mephistopheles, Satan, and Cigars," *Thomas Hardy: Art and Thought* (Totowa, N.J.: Rowman and Littlefield, 1977), pp. 57-66; Marilyn Stall Fontane, "The Devil in *Tess,*" *Thomas Hardy Society Review,* 1 (1982), 250-54; and Timothy Hands, *Thomas Hardy: Distracted Preacher? Hardy's Religious Biography and its Influence on his Novels* (New York: St. Martin's Press, 1989), pp. 59-60 and 120-21.

3. Julian Moynihan, "*The Mayor of Casterbridge* and the Old Testament's First Book of Samuel: A Study of Some Literary Relationships," *PMLA,* 71 (1956), 118-30.

4. Simon Gatrell, *Hardy the Creator: A Textual Biography* (Oxford: Clarendon Press, 1988), pp. 193-98.

5. See Robert Schweik, "Theme, Character, and Perspective in Hardy's *The Return of the Native*," *Philological Quarterly*, 41 (1962), 554-57, and Bernard J. Paris, "'A Confusion of Many Standards': Conflicting Value Systems in *Tess of the d'Urbervilles*," *Nineteenth-Century Fiction*, 24 (1969), 57-79.

6. David J. DeLaura, "'The Ache of Modernism' in Hardy's Later Novels," *ELH*, 34 (1967), 380-99.

7. See J. B. Bullen's "Hardy's *The Well-Beloved*, Sex, and Theories of Germ Plasm," in *A Spacious Vision: Essays on Hardy*, ed. Phillip V. Mallett and Ronald P. Draper (Newmill, Cornwall: Patten Press, 1994), pp. 79-88.

8. For an analysis of Hardy's diagram, see Lennart A. Björk's *Psychological Vision and Social Criticism in the Novels of Thomas Hardy* (Stockholm: Almqvist & Wiksell International, 1987), pp. 38-42.

9. Herbert Spencer, *First Principles* (1862; New York: The DeWitt Revolving Fund, 1958), p. 60.

10. Robert Gittings, *Thomas Hardy's Later Years* (Boston: Little, Brown and Co., 1978), p. 9.

11. Tess's speech may also have been influenced by the ideas of John Aldington Symonds; see Björk, *Psychological Vision*, pp. 131-32.

12. Letter from Frederic Harrison of 19 December 1891, Dorset County Museum.

13. Auguste Comte, *A General View of Positivism*, trans. by J. H. Bridges (1831; London: Trübner, 1865), p. 252.

14. Helen Garwood, *Thomas Hardy: An Illustration of the Philosophy of Schopenhauer* (Philadelphia: John C. Winston Co., 1911), pp. 10-11.

15. Carl Weber, "Hardy's Copy of Schopenhauer," *Colby Library Quarterly*, 4/12 (November, 1957), p. 223.

16. An instance of how freely Hardy would deviate from von Hartmann's ideas is notable in William Archer's "Real Conversations. Conversation I. With Mr. Thomas Hardy," *The Critic*, 38 (April 1901), p. 316.

17. See, for example, Eduard von Hartmann, *The Philosophy of the Unconscious: Speculative Results According to the Inductive Method of Physical Science*, trans. by William Chatterton Coupland, 3 vols. (1869; London: Kegan Paul, Trench, Trübner, 1893), 1, p. 69.

18. Examples of such analyses may be found in J. O. Bailey's *Thomas Hardy and the Cosmic Mind: A New Reading of The Dynasts* (Chapel Hill: University of North Carolina Press, 1956), and Walter F. Wright's *The Shaping of "The Dynasts"* (Lincoln: University of Nebraska Press, 1967).

Further Reading

Beer, Gillian. *Darwin's Plots: Evolutionary Narrative in Darwin, George Eliot and Nineteenth-Century Fiction*. London: Routledge & Kegan Paul, 1983.

Collins, Deborah L. *Thomas Hardy and His God: A Liturgy of Unbelief*. London and Basingstoke: Macmillan, 1990.

Gilmour, Robin. *The Victorian Period: The Intellectual and Cultural Context of English Literature, 1830–1890*. London: Longman, 1993.

Jedrzejewski, Jan. *Thomas Hardy and the Church*. London and Basingstoke: Macmillan, 1996.

Orel, Harold. *The Unknown Thomas Hardy: Lesser-Known Aspects of Hardy's Life and Career*. Brighton, Sussex: The Harvester Press, 1987.

Paradis, James and Thomas Postlewait, eds. *Victorian Science and Victorian Values: Literary Perspectives*. New York: The New York Academy of Sciences, 1981.

Rutland, William R. *Thomas Hardy: A Study of His Writings and Their Background*. Oxford: Blackwell, 1938.

Abbreviations for texts cited

CPW: Complete Poetical Works, ed. Samuel Hynes

FMC: Far from the Madding Crowd

J: Jude the Obscure

L: A Laodicean

MC: The Mayor of Casterbridge

PBE: A Pair of Blue Eyes

RN: The Return of the Native

T: Tess of the d'Urbervilles

TM: The Trumpet-Major

TT: Two on a Tower

UGT: Under the Greenwood Tree

Abbreviations for other primary works and scholarly works

Letters 1-7: The Collected Letters of Thomas Hardy, ed. Richard Little Purdy and Michael Millgate (Oxford: Clarendon Press, 1978-88), in seven volumes.

LN 1-2: The Literary Notebooks of Thomas Hardy, ed. Lennart A. Björk (London: Macmillan, 1985), 2 vols. (Partially published, Göteborg, Sweden: Acta Universitatis Gothoburgensis, 1974.)

LW: The Life and Work of Thomas Hardy by Thomas Hardy, ed. Michael Millgate (London: Macmillan, 1985). See Millgate's essay in this volume for the history of Hardy's autobiography, originally published under the name of his second wife and accepted as a biography for three decades. The original two volumes (1928, 1930) and the one-volume edition (1962; corrected edition, 1972) are often cited in scholarship.

PN: The Personal Notebooks of Thomas Hardy, ed. Richard H. Taylor (London and Basingstoke: Macmillan, 1979).

PW: Thomas Hardy's Personal Writings: Prefaces, Literary Opinions, Reminiscences, ed. Harold Orel (London and Basingstoke: Macmillan, 1966).

SOCIOPOLITICAL CONCERNS

Laura Dassow Walls (essay date 1995)

SOURCE: "A Plurality of Worlds," in *Seeing New Worlds: Henry David Thoreau and Nineteenth-Century Nature Science,* University of Wisconsin Press, 1995, pp. 167-211.

[*In the following excerpt, Walls surveys nineteenth-century theories about the plurality of worlds in the context of several notable non-fiction works of the time.*]

> We might try our lives by a thousand simple tests; as, for instance, that the same sun which ripens my beans illumines at once a system of earths like ours. If I had remembered this it would have prevented some mistakes.
>
> —Henry David Thoreau, *Walden*

One of the controversies that enlivened scientific discourse of the 1840s and 1850s concerned the possible plurality of worlds. Was earth unique, or was there, as Thoreau fancied in *Walden,* "a system of earths like ours"? The controversy turned on integrating the findings of the new science of geology with the older science of astronomy, or deep time with vast space. Both sciences suggested that a great deal of the universe had nothing whatsoever to do with human beings. Did this mean that the universe was an infinitude of waste and chaos, within which the earth alone gave sanctuary to life and intelligence—God's one special creation, his Garden? Yes, argued the redoubtable Whewell, in *The Plurality of Worlds* (1853).[1] But how, argued others, could this poor, flawed planet truly be God's single creation? There had to be other, finer worlds in the heavens. To doubt their existence denigrated God, implying His power did not extend across all time and space. Or, proposed still others, had God's law simply, from the first moment of Creation, set in motion the progressive evolution of matter into life, here on earth and everywhere in the heavens? This was the position taken by Robert Chambers in his popular book *The Vestiges of Creation* (1844), the book Whewell was targeting. Chambers had proposed only "a blind process governed solely by mechanical necessity."[2] Thus Thoreau's allusion to Chambers' theory points toward the deepening divides which were already tearing natural theology apart, well before 1859 and Darwin's *Origin of Species.*

Thoreau was already moving beyond the terms set by traditional natural theology, in his sanguine acceptance (at least much of the time) of a cosmos in which man was only a small part. The real point of the plurality of worlds debate was, of course, not life on the stars but life on earth. Were all those extraneous other beings beyond the circle of humanity truly waste and chaos? Or did they evidence the power of life to form worlds other than ours? Thoreau found the latter prospect exhilarating:

> The stars are the apexes of what wonderful triangles! What distant and different beings in the various mansions of the universe are contemplating the same one at the same moment! Nature and human life are as various as our several constitutions. Who shall say what prospect life offers to another? Could a greater miracle take place than for us to look through each other's eyes for an instant?
>
> (WA 10)

As he concludes: "there are as many ways as there can be drawn radii from one center" (11). Though he centered vision on the constitutional magic of the self, the self that initiated the world didn't always circumscribe it. In the long meditation ending with his declaration that "The whole world is an America—a *New World,*" Thoreau explores such a vision: "The poet says the proper study of mankind is man—I say study to forget all that—take wider views of the universe—That is the egotism of the race." One has only to get up at midnight to find the whole civilized world, that "gigantic institution" of mankind, slumbering. "Man is but the place where I stand & the prospect (thence) hence is infinite. it [*sic*] is not a chamber of mirrors which reflect me—when I reflect myself—I find that there is other than me" (4:418-20; 4/2/52).

One consequence of his penchant for turning the mirror inside out, imagining the other *as* other yet with eyes like himself, was his political conviction that no man has the right to pursue his pleasure on the back of another. In science, this principle has the effect of breaking down the subject/object dualism that lay at the heart of scientific acts of knowing. Instead, to Thoreau, each object could be the subject of its *own* knowing: "If I had remembered this it would have prevented some mistakes" (WA 10). If we could remember that the eyes of every object are also gazing back at the subject, we could live in not one but *many* worlds—"aye, in all the worlds of the ages" (10). By contrast, to render nature either symbolically or (f)actually instrumental—to ride on nature's back like Emerson's Savior on the meekly receiving ass—one must sever the possibility of nature's answering back by insisting, like Coleridge, that it is not a living and self-generating system but a collection of dead objects, available for animation by our own needs and desires. But Thoreau's reciprocal and interactive process of knowledge breaks down the subject/object duality altogether, and strikes down the notion of "objective" science at its root:

> There is no such thing as pure *objective* observation. Your observation, to be interesting, *i.e.* to be significant, must be *subjective.* The sum of what the writer of whatever class has to report is simply some human ex-

perience, whether he be poet or philosopher or man of science. The man of most science is the man most alive, whose life is the greatest event.

(VI:236-37; 5/6/54; emphasis in original)

Across the shared ground of language, science is fundamentally the same as poetry and philosophy: none can do more, or less, than report human "experience," and all three will live, or not, according to the fullness of life brought to bear on them. The goal, then, is to *live,* to experience:

It makes no odds into what seeming deserts the poet is born. Though all his neighbors pronounce it a Sahara, it will be a paradise to him; for the desert which we see is the result of the barrenness of our experience. No mere willful activity whatever, whether in writing verses or collecting statistics, will produce true poetry or science.

(VI:237)

All a man can do, Thoreau concludes, is "tell the story of his love," and if he is fortunate he will remain forever in love, keeping "coldness"—*lack* of relation—from reaching the heart.

Not one's external circumstances, but the condition of one's mind and heart, will turn fact into truth, the Sahara into Paradise. But how does one cultivate such a faculty, if "mere willful activity" is inadequate? It takes a pose of sublime, transcendental confidence to condemn "method" and "willful activity." Thoreau, like any successful artist or scientist, must rely on both, and yet he must agonize that such reliance signifies his loss of the health and wholeness from which natural inspiration was to spring as a spontaneous function. It could not be achieved willfully, any more than Calvinist grace, by dint of intellectual effort or knowledge.[3] The need to labor at it signified malfunction, loss, disease, one's fall from harmony with the whole, out of alignment with the flow. And so were set the poles of work and spontaneity which drew Thoreau into creative effort, yielding the twin strategies of knowledge or "intentionality," and ignorance or "seeing with the side of the eye," which worked together in what I have called Thoreau's "epistemology of contact."

INTENTIONS OF THE EYE

In Humboldt, seeing is both partial and total: partial, in the place-bound, limited view given to the researcher who is in actual contact with nature; total in the way such partial views combine and interconnect to create the grand view, the mountaintop perspective that integrates the multitude of details into a coherent whole. The eagle-eyed view from the alpine or celestial heights transmutes into the totalizing God vision of the scientist, scaling the heights while the rest of us go on with our lives down in the warm valleys:

Mathematical truths stand aloof from the warm life of man—the mere cold and unfleshed skeletons of truth.

Perhaps the whole body of what is now called moral or ethical truth may have once existed as abstract science, and have been only gradually won over to humanity.— Have gradually subsided from the intellect into the heart.

In Thoreau's 1840 meditation, abstract law from on high descends like Christ to assume human form, even as God's absolute truth must put on the garments of the affections. As he continues:

The eye that can appreciate the naked and absolute beauty of a scientific truth, is far rarer than that which discerns moral beauty. Men demand that the truth be clothed in the warm colors of life—and wear a flesh and blood dress. They do not love the absolute truth, but the partial, because it fits and measures them and their commodities best—but let them remember that notwithstanding these delinquencies in practice—Science still exists as the sealer of weights and measures.

(1:196-97; 11/12/40)

And yet Thoreau ends with a warning. Cold and abstract law from on high "seals" the measure of our lives—science the stern lawgiver. Does science consist of the abstracted, "unfleshed," "skeletal" commandments that delivered from the mountaintop seal our human fate? Or the collective sum of all the bustling confusion that extends from the top of the mountain, to its foot, to the horizon and beyond, into infinity? The latter might seem fuller, richer, warmer, more descriptively responsive to reality "on the ground," but the former offers a tremendous advantage: power. "Holistic explanation bears a sort of mirror image relationship to reductionism," notes the biologist Richard Lewontin.[4] Reductionism does not diminish the field of vision, but expands it beyond the horizon, beyond to all possible horizons. In its chamber of mirrors, it sees itself everywhere, never anywhere new.

Thoreau's problem was to retain the power yet see something other than his own reflection, to look into the infinite from the place where he stands and yet see a connected and meaningful whole. Science, like poetry, is made possible by "putting an interval between"—the saving interval which allows abstraction and composition. This interval separates life from the writing: the fish in the brook from the specimen in the book or the laboratory jar; the experience in the field from the collocation of results in the report; the man on the street from the cadaver on the slab. The interval makes the creative act possible, but also makes it partial, fitting truth to our commodities. However, it has become part of the powerful fiction of science that such willful activity is not partial and selective, but total; that truth exists not out in the fragmented and imperfect world but in the vacuum of the laboratory, which is so carefully constructed and sealed precisely to enable the facts to speak the truth.[5] Hence science is not fictive, accomplished by a human community, but transcendent, absolute, and "objective."

But Thoreau's working experience convinced him that no fact could exist in a vacuum; or, that all facts become visible to us only when we know what it is we seek, in which case we must, as Darwin noted, have some theory or concept that will make a fact "significant." The theory might be, for example, that all facts can be catalogued and stored away: Thoreau notices that books are usually written "willfully," or "as parts of a system, to supply a want real or imagined. Books of natural history aim commonly to be hasty schedules, or inventories of God's property, by some clerk"—and so conduct to ignorance not knowledge (WK 97-98). But that there must *be* a theory or system was unavoidable. For instance, moved by spring's return to theorize that the year is a circle, Thoreau concludes that learning the iterations of the natural system might guide him into calling forth something novel:

> Why should just these sights & sounds accompany our life? Why should I hear the chattering of blackbirds—why smell the skunk each year? I would fain explore the mysterious relation between myself & these things. I would at least know what these things unavoidably are— —make a chart of our life—know how its shores trend—that butterflies reappear & when—know why just this circle of creatures completes the world. Can I not by expectation affect the revolutions of nature—make a day to bring forth something new?
>
> (4:468; 4/18/52)

Under his theory that the universe formed a "complete" and closed circle, Thoreau was determined to observe all possible causes and coincidences, but he quickly found himself hard put. Over the next few weeks he tried to keep up with the totality of spring's onset, but by mid-May he was losing track. On the nineteenth he complained that since the fourteenth there had been too much to observe; the next day, he despaired that there were just too many birds arriving and plants leafing: "I must observe it again next year." Or perhaps he could get a jump start on the spring, by catching it twice in the *same* year: "It is worth the while," he decided three days later, "to go a little south to anticipate nature at home" (IV:65-69; 5/19-5/23/52). A few weeks later he envisioned a complementary strategy, a strategic withdrawal:

> Nature is reported not by him who goes forth consciously as an observer, but in the fullness of life. To such a one she rushes to make her report. To the full heart she is all but a figure of speech. This is my year of observation. . . . You are a little bewildered by the variety of objects. There must be a certain meagreness of details and nakedness for wide views.
>
> (IV:174; 7/2/52)

It became evident to him that the plenitude of nature must be edited, even for the most (Whitmanically) inclusive observer. Indeed, the eye edits automatically, Thoreau has noticed, just by choosing what to see or not see. One of his earliest narratives records how he *chose* to see an arrowhead, and lo, there it was at his feet (1:8-9; 10/29/37). This limitation, then, can be cultivated into a strength, if one educates oneself in the art of "anticipation," or "expectation." One can call forth something new, as when by sheer force of expectation he became the first to locate a rare or unknown plant. Yet even so, not all one's callings are answered: "We soon get through with Nature. She excites an expectation which she cannot satisfy. The merest child which has rambled into a copsewood dreams of a wilderness so wild and strange and inexhaustible as Nature can never show him." He expects *more*—more than every year the same old dead suckers floating on the river. Coleridgean dejection seizes him: "In me is the sucker that I see. No wholly extraneous object can compel me to recognize it. I am guilty of suckers" (VI:293-94; 5/23/54). If nature lives "in his life alone," no fact exists independently of his consciousness, and he is the guilty perpetrator of all the evil he sees.

But fortunately such exhaustion and its consequent guilt were rare; Thoreau's solipsistic moods tended not to be productive ones, for he needed the energizing assurance that nature was rushing to him to make her report. More typical of the late years was his steady refinement of "anticipation" into a principle he named "intentionality of the eye":

> It requires a different intention of the eye in the same locality to see different plants, as, for example, *Juncaceæ* and *Gramineæ* even; *i.e.,* I find that when I am looking for the former, I do not see the latter in their midst. How much more, then, it requires different intentions of the eye and of the mind to attend to different departments of knowledge! How differently the poet and the naturalist look at objects!
>
> (XI:153; 9/9/58)

The counter-intuitiveness of this notion delighted him: "A man sees only what concerns him. A botanist absorbed in the pursuit of grasses does not distinguish the grandest pasture oaks. He as it were tramples down oaks unwittingly in his walk" (XI:153). Earlier he had written that it was "impossible for the same person to see things from the poet's point of view and that of the man of science," though even there he permitted the poet to have science as his "second love" (4:356; 2/18/52). But, importantly, with "intentionality," both the poet's and the naturalist's vision could be available to the *same* person, if that person could learn to refocus his intention not just from rushes and grasses to oaks, but from one discipline to the other: from "poet/naturalist" to "poet-naturalist." After all, there are "manifold visions in the direction of every object" (WK 48).

Thoreau suggested the possibility of such manifold vision two months later: the distance that counted was finally not between poet and naturalist, but between them both together and the "mass of men" who are uninterested in, say, lichens, and could hardly imagine them as "sympathizing companions":

> It is remarkable how little any but a lichenist will observe on the bark of trees. The mass of men have but the vaguest and most indefinite notion of mosses, as a sort of shreds and fringes, and the world in which the

lichenist dwells is much further from theirs than one side of this earth from the other. . . . Each phase of nature, while not invisible, is yet not too distinct and obtrusive. It is there to be found when we look for it, but not demanding our attention. It is like a silent but sympathizing companion. . . .

(XI:296; 11/8/58)

The poet's love has matured into a form of "attention," alert but undemanding, and steeped in the kind of knowledge that makes such acute responsiveness possible. This form of attention became a key tool of scientific research once Thoreau had mastered both the method and a scientific theory, as we shall see shortly in discussing *The Dispersion of Seeds*. Such insights put Thoreau in the vanguard of scientific theorists of his day. John Herschel and William Whewell (whom Thoreau apparently did not read) had been at work since the 1830s formulating the "scientific method," or that powerful heuristic whereby feedback loops between theory and fact (or call and response?) advance our state of knowledge about the physical universe. Both Herschel and Whewell recognized how fundamentally contingent this process is: we can never be certain, though we can be provisionally sure, since our theories have led us to make only appropriate discoveries. Thoreau, using his poet's lens, put it differently: "The hunter may be said to invent his game, as Neptune did the horse, and Ceres corn" (XIII:140; 2/12/60).

The problem with such a powerful heuristic is that it can eliminate any possibility which you fail to "anticipate." Even just looking too hard will cost: "the more you look the less you observe," Thoreau observes; "Go not to the object; let it come to you." What he needs, he decides, "is not to look at all, but a true sauntering of the eye" (IV:351; 9/13/52), a sidelong vision that will invite the unbidden. In the midst of the fatigue that brought on his call for "a little Lethe!" Thoreau admonished himself that "Man cannot afford to be a naturalist, to look at Nature directly, but only with the side of his eye. He must look through and beyond her. . . . I feel that I am dissipated by so many observations. I should be the magnet in the midst of all this dust and filings" (V:45; 3/23/53). Such an insight is the necessary counterbalance to forms of attention. Thoreau even finds that the occasional distraction is actually productive. After a session of surveying, he was again reminded

of the advantage to the poet, and philosopher, and naturalist, and whomsoever, of pursuing from time to time some other business than his chosen one,—seeing with the side of the eye. The poet will so get visions which no deliberate abandonment can secure. The philosopher is so forced to recognize principles which long study might not detect. And the naturalist even will stumble upon some new and unexpected flower or animal.

(VIII:314; 4/28/56)

Experience taught him that even the walk that seemed "profitless and a failure" was "on the point of being a success, for then you are in that subdued and knocking mood to which Nature never fails to open" (XIII:111; 1/27/60).

As he also said, to be lost is the beginning of being found, for "not till we are lost do we begin to realize where we are, and the infinite extent of our relations" (V:64; 3/29/53; cf. WA 171).

These twinned and mutually generating strategies, intentionality and side-of-the-eye, parallel and support the dialectic that runs through Thoreau's work between knowledge and ignorance: Learn science, he has advised; then forget it. Live at home like a traveler. Knowledge guides the eye, but limits it to what it already knows; ignorance informed by knowledge defamiliarizes the known and prepares the mind for the novel, the unanticipatable. Thoreau is establishing, in effect, a way to let chaos sneak into the system, the order and arrangement created by the mind; or, a way to build disorder and incompleteness into the fabric of orderly structures. In some of his last and richest writing on this matter, he makes clear that the goal of this process is not some flawless mirror of nature, a perfect representation in words, but an altogether new entity, a *new* fact in nature:

It is only when we forget all our learning that we begin to know. . . . To conceive of it with a total apprehension I must for the thousandth time approach it as something totally strange. If you would make acquaintance with the ferns you must forget your botany. . . . You must be aware that *no thing* is what you have taken it to be. . . . You have got to be in a different state from common. Your greatest success will be simply to perceive that such things are, and you will have no communication to make to the Royal Society.

(XII:371; 10/4/59)

To succeed in perceiving that "such things are" is to use science to go beyond it, make some form of communication of no interest to the Royal Society—for one to be redeemed by ferns, he adds, takes a different method than the Aristotelian. He enlarged on this idea, so reminiscent of the late poems of Wallace Stevens, one year later: the truest description (or representation) of an object is the sight of the thing itself, which no scientific description, or representation, can replace. Perhaps, then, the "unconsidered expressions of our delight" are nearer to absolute truth, in their "unconscious affirmations" of existence—Stevens' "pure being." Scientific description sees "mechanically," giving us nothing new, but only an object "mechanically daguerreotyped on our eyes, but a true description growing out [of] the perception and appreciation of it is itself a new fact, never to be daguerreotyped, indicating the highest quality of the plant,—its relation to man . . ." (XIV:117-18; 10/13/60). The closer we are to the object itself, the more completely we can shed the measured or scientific account: we are not distracted from the thing itself to the system or arrangement, our hierarchy of "captains" and "lieutenants"—though this is, as a society, what we reward. Instead, Thoreau conceived someone (himself, surely) "Who describes the most familiar object with a zest and vividness of imagery as if he saw it for the first time, the novelty consisting not in the strangeness of the object, but in the new and clearer perception of it"

(XIV:120). His meditations were taking him not just into the ecology of nature, but into an apperception of the ecology of mind. "My thought is a part of the meaning of the world . . ." (IV:410). A thought becomes itself a "new fact," entering the economy of the system and altering it—or as he wrote in 1842, "I dont [*sic*] know how much I assist in the economy of nature when I declare a fact—Is it not an important part in the history of the flow that I tell my friend where I found it—" (1:383; 3/20/42). Or as he wondered in 1840, "Do not thoughts and men's lives enrich the earth and change the aspect of things as much as a new growth of wood?" (1:147; 7/3/40).

Through his initial engagement with all the particulars of his environment Thoreau learned how to *see* "new worlds," and he learned that in seeing—in the eye's intention, or the eye's side vision—he did not just see but *created* his world, even as he was created by it. Doing this required the sustained energy and attention that he called, simply, being "awake": "Morning is when I am awake and there is a dawn in me," as he wrote in *Walden*; "To be awake is to be alive." We must learn to "reawaken" ourselves "by an infinite expectation of the dawn," and so we can elevate our lives "by a conscious endeavor," carving and painting "the very atmosphere and medium through which we look, which morally we can do" (WA 90). So *Walden* became his experiment in the making of life, in exploring just how far "The universe constantly and obediently *answers* to our conceptions . . ." (97; emphasis added). When, toward the end of the book, Thoreau asks, "Why do precisely these objects which we behold make a world?"—Why is man neighbored by "just these species of animals . . . ?" (225), we recognize this as the familiar Adamic theme: the heroically innocent American sweeping the world clean for a new beginning, baptizing it anew in the purified waters of the cleansed consciousness.[6] But for Thoreau, for all its world-making power the consciousness can never be cleansed; what makes his writing so interesting is his discovery, which he is too scrupulous to ignore, that preexisting ideas always control the mind, that this tendency finally is not wrong but inevitable, and should be not denied but educated. Nor can the world ever be swept clean, for we are "neighbored" by other consciousnesses than our own. The pull of these twin resistances—the structures of our own perception, knowledge, and ideology, which organize our vision, and the fantastic complexity of an external world that may answer to us but always keeps something in reserve—generated in Thoreau a dialectical understanding which convinced him that none of our "worlds" are wholly new; all are imbricated with traces of their origins. Yet in the poet-naturalist's consilience or "leaping together" of the opposites of mind and nature, something new *is* made, what for Thoreau is the greatest wonder of all: a wholly new fact in nature.

If we call that "new fact" a work of art, none of this seems surprising; Coleridge and T. S. Eliot have taught us to think of art as something "new" that arises organically out of the "old" to reshape, by some small or great degree, the entirety of human culture. Of course the canonical Tho-

reau can be read comfortably in this fashion: he is a distinctly "individual" talent within the American "tradition." But instead of reabsorbing Thoreau's works into literary tradition, where the "ideal order" they modify hovers above the material facts of social history, science, and technology, I would like to ask how Thoreau's "new world" ramified into *science*. The poet-naturalist's visions, in Thoreau, are precisely the kind of fact which assists in the "economy of nature," since the poet's task is to yoke material and spiritual, and thereby show the infinite interrelatedness of both realms. So, for instance, at Walden Pond the ecological system of Middlesex County was taken up by Thoreau's own linguistic system, merged with the resources of American literature as *Walden,* and added to language as a new concept, "Walden"; thus contributing a new fact to the economy of Concord, the United States, and "nature" both local and global. So long as it was just a body of water in eastern Massachusetts, no one could encounter it unless he or she were also in eastern Massachusetts; but Thoreau went out, inscribed the pond onto paper, and returned with an inscription with which he hoped to win over allies who would believe in his new facts/truths. Until Thoreau translated "the pond" (or any of his observed and collected facts) onto paper, he could not possibly mobilize it (or them) on his behalf, to persuade others. That is, what gave his writing its persuasive power was, as Matthiessen first noted, its specificity. He grounded his metaphors in facts of his experience, which he rendered into facts of our experience, thereby mustering us (if we accede) to his side.

This interpretation attempts to read Thoreau's endeavors through Bruno Latour's account of the process of science. According to Latour, the distinctive pattern of Western science has been the sustained and collective construction of networks or pathways of agreed-upon "facts," through the process of going "out," collecting and inscribing things to render them "mobile," and bringing them back to central locations where they, and calculations about them, can be assembled, presented, and compared.[7] What made Humboldtian science so attractive and powerful in this particular half century in America was its ability to provide the methodology necessary for success in exactly this endeavor, in its exploratory and network-building phase—literally providing a way to "*see new* things."[8] Recall, for instance, that the expeditions whose reports Thoreau read—such as John Charles Frémont's—were directed toward selecting railroad routes, to expanding the networks of material transmission; and some of this insight worked its way into Thoreau's evocations of the Fitchburg Line. As the network expanded, the effort was increasingly collective—as was, for instance, Agassiz's collecting network, in which Thoreau so memorably participated. Thoreau assisted in mobilizing things—literally packing turtles into boxes—for another's use, transmitting them to Harvard, thereby helping to establish Harvard as New England's own "center of calculation."

The power of the methodology was quickly obvious to Thoreau, but having theories of his own, he wished to be his *own* center, not to collect for another's. He cast himself, like the heroic Humboldt, as both his own explorer and the man at the center of his own calculations; like Humboldt, gathering the inscriptions of others (through his notebooks), generating his own (in his personal collections and his *Journal*), and with them crafting the cosmos. Thoreau applied the scientific methodology he was learning to "higher" ends: not the nationalistic appropriation of territory, or the improved commodification of nature into resources, or the transport of products to market centers, but the establishment of the vital importance of those more volatile elements of experience which could not be carried on the tracks of commodification. This meant rousing people to "awaken" and transform their condition from commodified and alienated isolates to communally responsive individuals. In effect, he rejected his position on the network in order to construct a counternetwork. But science is above all social. The individual scientist who is isolated and without allies ceases to be an effective scientist; if he persists, he will be labeled a crank—or, perhaps, a poet. By refusing to be a cooperative and subordinate worker on another's scientific network, Thoreau sought to develop, using similar methodology, a scientific network of his own—an anarchist science to match his anarchist politics. This was his weakness, in that it cut him off from institutional science and limited what he could do, as well as what he would be perceived as doing.[9] It also was his strength, for in adopting so powerful a model to his own purposes he achieved an eloquence and persuasive power that enabled his work to survive, and ultimately to influence the cultural network in ways that outflanked American institutional science.

Neither poetry nor science alone seemed adequate to Thoreau. Ungrounded poetry was slipshod and callow, and the "mass of men," uneducated in science, were liable to the dangerous ignorance of those who had never learned how to see. Even what they *did* know, however vital and rich in relational understanding, could not be shared because it was limited to their isolated experience. On the other hand, science, though calculated to be public, was thereby shorn of that very vitality:

> Science does not embody all that men know—only what is for men of science. The Woodman tells me how he caught trout in a box trap—how he made his troughs for maple sap of pine logs—& the spouts of sumack or white ash which have a large pith. [He can relate his facts to human life][10]

> The knowledge of an unlearned man is living & luxuriant like a forest—but covered with mosses & lichens and for the most part inaccessible & going to waste— the knowledge of the man of science is like timber collected in yards for public works which stub supports a green sprout here & there—but even this is liable to dry rot.

> (3:174; 1/7/51)

Thoreau tried to join the "Woodman" and the "man of science" into something new: literary science, perhaps; not literature-and-science but science seen as literature, in its fictive constructions of the world, and literature seen as science, in its operational effectiveness in the world. Thoreau's consilience of an Emersonian insistence on higher or spiritual ends with a Humboldtian, worldly empiricism resulted in not just a new "fact" or a new literary work but an experimental new genre, conceptually avant-garde even in our own time.

Perhaps there could be some science, Thoreau implies, which is *not* suffering from "dry rot." The object of such science would be not the "husk," the specimen pickled and preserved and shipped to Boston alongside apples, huckleberries, and timber. The "effluence" such science cannot perceive and so leaves behind is still out there in the field, in the strong but evanescent relationships between the scientific observer and the subjects of his investigations, and in the interactions among the subjects themselves. The lesson of Thoreau's science would be not division and sterility, which confirmed the mournful descent Thoreau feared into the "evil days." It was instead the lesson of renewal and continuance. For all that was gone, his science taught Thoreau how much yet remained in the beauty, abundance, and complexity of the animal and plant life around Concord. The hills the woodcutters laid bare were instantly reclothed with huckleberries. Nature had long ago anticipated and provided for such an emergency, healing the scar and compensating for the loss with fruits the forest could not produce; so "Nature rewards with unexpected fruits the hand that lays her waste" (NHE 227-28). What was more, the forest "laid waste" around Walden in the early 1850s was growing back. Creation, Thoreau was convinced—even before reading Darwin's *Origin of Species* (1859)—was going on at every moment and all around him. If the evil days *were* coming, perhaps a new kind of science could even fend them off. In the late 1850s, Thoreau turned his investigations to a systematic study of regeneration. The fact that thus flowered into the most compelling truth of all was, at last, the seed; and it was to the dispersion and growth of seeds that Thoreau turned, in the studies of his final years.

WORLDS WITHOUT END: *THE DISPERSION OF SEEDS*

One of the enabling assumptions of Coleridgean and of Emersonian romanticism was that matter in itself lacks the power to "organize." That power, which makes dead matter alive or "organic," comes from above nature—"supernatural"—as spirit which circulates through matter, imbreathes or "animates" it, making it body forth the thoughts of the Creator. The creator as poet or hero or scientist bodies forth his own thoughts in alignment with the creative spirit that subtends and circulates through all: command through obedience. To the mind that shapes the universe in solitary splendor belongs the triumphs of the spirit, and the burden of despair, for the creative transformation of the universe into mind begins and ends with the originating self. Thus "intentionality of the eye" organizes the chaos of the universe into meaning, in a momentously powerful technology of control; the power of that control is generated by the force of contending opposites which initiate and sustain its grand progressive dialectic. The polar opposites describe between them the field as a whole, in its totality; the universe is closed and secured against change, even as it is haunted by the irrational chaos it has constructed itself against.

The system seems impermeable, except for one lurking suspicion voiced in Kant but quickly suppressed: what if matter organizes *itself*? What if living nature does not require the power of preexisting mind—whether divine or human—to lift it from chaos, but creates its own quite independent order, forming and building it from within according to its own purposes? If it was not created *for* us, or for anyone, but just is? For one thing, the singleness of a nature ultimately unified by the one and only one would be interrupted, deflected into a vision of the universe more like Humboldt's "rich luxuriance of living nature and the mingled web of free and restricted natural forces" (*Cosmos* I:79). For another, man would be deflected from the organizing center to somewhere on the side—indeed, there would be no clear center, only a shifting one responsive to one perspective or another. Humboldt organized his *Cosmos* to emphasize this point: he deliberately began his narrative with the stars, worlds beyond earth, to displace not just man but all things terrestrial from our illusory center. "Here, therefore, we do not proceed from the subjective point of view of human interests. The terrestrial must be treated only as a part, subject to the whole. The view of nature ought to be grand and free, uninfluenced by motives of proximity, social sympathy, or relative utility" (*Cosmos* I:83).

As Thoreau stood on the sandbank of the Deep Cut, admiring the thawing forms that flowed down its sides, he could look in both directions. The released energy of the earth flowed into the forms of life:

> Innumerable little streams overlap and interlace one with another, exhibiting a sort of hybrid product, which obeys half way the law of currents, and half way that of vegetation. As it flows it takes the forms of sappy leaves or vines, making heaps of pulpy sprays a foot or more in depth, and resembling, as you look down on them, the laciniated lobed and imbricated thalluses of some lichens; or you are reminded of coral, of leopards' paws or birds' feet, of brains or lungs or bowels, and excrements of all kinds.

(WA 305)

The animation is a direct creation of the sun, as he can see; the shaded bank will remain "inert," while on the sunny bank the luxuriant foliage forms are "springing into existence." It is as if he were in "the laboratory of the Artist who made the world and me," who was "with excess of energy strewing his fresh designs about."[11] Here near the "vitals of the globe" he can see "in the very sands an anticipation of the vegetable leaf. No wonder that the earth expresses itself outwardly in leaves, it so labors with the idea inwardly. The atoms have already learned this law,

and are pregnant by it" (306). The law is the law of the leaf, in an insight recalling his Goethean ghost leaves from twelve years before: "Even ice begins with delicate crystal leaves" (307); "The Maker of this earth but patented a leaf" (308). The flowing sand forms into fingers and blood vessels, arteries that "glance like lightning" from stage to stage before being swallowed up into the deltoid fan at their base. Thoreau imagines the human body expanding and flowing into these rivers of life, boundaries dissolving, matter yielding to the flow of energy, poetry, life:

> The earth is not a mere fragment of dead history, stratum upon stratum like the leaves of a book, to be studied by geologists and antiquaries chiefly, but living poetry like the leaves of a tree, which precede flowers and fruit,—not a fossil earth, but a living earth; compared with whose great central life all animal and vegetable life is merely parasitic.

We—the earth, ourselves, our institutions—are "plastic like clay in the hands of the potter" (309).[12]

In the midst of this ecstatic vision—a Thoreauvian answer to Emerson's transparent eyeball—Thoreau sounds one small note of sharp-eyed difference: "It is wonderful how rapidly yet perfectly the sand organizes itself as it flows, using the best material its mass affords to form the sharp edges of its channel" (307). The flowing sand is organized by the single law of the leaf, but somehow it also crafts itself as it descends, selecting material with which to turn the boundaries of its forms as it translates itself from form to form, and finally to the rippled stasis at Thoreau's feet.

In the workshop of nature, central law was organizing raw matter into the forms of life—yet perhaps even raw matter had some power to "organize itself" as it was carried to its Maker's end. In the sandbank passage, earth's poetry was articulated in Thoreau's poetry, as his mind took the sandbank up into spirit and rendered its truth. This was a distinct and highly particularized phenomenon, readily linked with one of the oldest patterns in Thoreau's thought, and he made the most of it. Meanwhile in his *Journal* other, newer patterns were emerging—and matter itself became an acute problem, as the *Journal* amassed itself around his daily practice of studying, walking, and writing. Apart from the value of the *Journal* as an accumulating timescape of experience in the land, coherent by virtue of its totality, smaller patterns were emerging and clustering around phenomena less conducive to literary convention's single convergent law: continuance, rather than narrative closure; boundary breakdowns, as wild nature rooted itself in the street gutter and domestic productions ran wild; new boundary formations, as leaves didn't flow but ripened and fell like fruit. Such observations cued Thoreau into acts of attention which, instead of spiraling him up and beyond the material world, lured him ever more deeply into it.[13]

It had all started with that call to vigilance: if you wait for something to attract your attention, "you are not interested at all about it, and probably will never see it" (DI 127). Nature may call, but you will never hear it until you at-

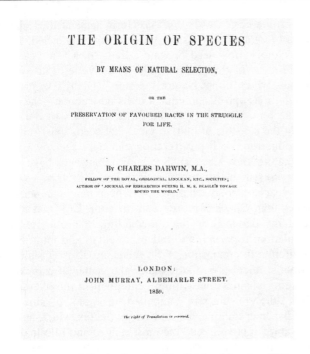

Title page of Charles Darwin's The Origin of Species, *1860.*

tend, until you *look* for a thing instead of waiting for it. It amazed Thoreau how many things had been so little attended to. And once he was looking with intent, he found himself a practitioner of science: observation led to question, question to theory, theory to new observation. It was a self-conscious process, as when Thoreau noticed how the plumes of the pitch pines were gnawed off every fall. Mere noticing was not enough: "I resolved last fall to look into the matter." Accordingly, one night, he thinks it over, and reasons that squirrels must gnaw off the twigs "to come at the cones, and also to make them more portable. I had no sooner thought this out than I as good as knew it." He returns to the forest, looks for twigs, observes the signs they have indeed been cut off, carried away, and collected together by squirrels for ease of transport, consumption, and storage. "Thus, my theory was confirmed by observation" (28-29).

It's a simple case, but that's what makes it typical of Thoreau: though so obvious, no one had ever thought to look before. It "called" but no one heard. Thoreau's emerging questions are exactly of this type: the obvious, mundane, and trivial, so easily and always dismissed as "*little* things" (NHE 211). Such as: why do just *these* plants and animals live exactly *here*? Such a question—the distribution of local inhabitants, their relations to past inhabitants—had started Charles Darwin "patiently accumulating and reflecting on all sorts of facts which could possibly have any bearing on it": result, the origin of *Origin of Species* (1). While Darwin had ranged widely, Thoreau used the centering device of Concord, relating everything to "our village" and using labels of human ownership: Lee's Cliff, Beck Stow's Swamp. The more global your question, the more local must be your address. Thoreau's question became, not what unifying law governed the distribution of

life, but how do plants and animals distribute themselves across the landscape? It was a Humboldtian, a Kantian, move: we cannot address the law or system until we understand what the components are and how they interact.

Darwin's attention had been directed by unexpected changes in space, while Thoreau's was directed by unanticipated changes in time: he observed patterns of growth shifting. The landscape exhibited a history of change that, unlike geological change, he could observe within his lifetime. A favorite blackberry field imperceptibly metamorphosed into a pitch pine wood—which perhaps he would "survey and lot off for a wood auction, and see the choppers at their work" (DI 33). An open grassy field east of the Deep Cut turned into "Thrush Alley," a favorite walk in deep pinewood where he hears the wood thrush sing in the shade (34). In his experience, human action (including his) was a regular part of the process of change. In *Walden* he had mourned that since he left its shores "the woodchoppers have still farther laid them waste," ending his rambles through the woods and silencing his Muse: "How can you expect the birds to sing when their groves are cut down?" (192). But two paragraphs later the destruction lays the conditions for hope: "where a forest was cut down last winter another is springing up by its shore as lustily as ever" (193). In the millennial narrative, earth is coming to an end, the land is "laid waste," Apocalypse darkens the sky. But, as Thoreau marvels over and over in the 1850s, the world didn't end, couldn't be coming to an end. Nature refused the Christian narrative, incorporated destruction into continual regeneration. A white birch springs up in the gutter on main street, and Thoreau sees how quickly the forest "would prevail here again if the village were deserted" (45). His attention turns to what comes *after,* even after ripeness and fruition: dispersal, circulation, renewal. Not death, but "succession." The *agent* of succession becomes the key, a material metaphor, matter which fables before his eyes: the seed. "As time elapses and the resources from which our forests have been supplied fail, we too shall of necessity be more and more convinced of the significance of the seed" (DI 23-24).

As Thoreau admitted in a letter of 1856, "I am drawing a rather long bow."[14] It would take years of dedicated labor before he could have much to show. But by 1860, he was forming the mass of writing around a series of clusters, and beginning to draft his answer to what would come after *Walden*. At his death he left 631 pages of manuscript on "Wild Fruits," thousands of pages of notes, and a 354-page first draft for a book with the working title *The Dispersion of Seeds*. Unpublished for generations, this manuscript now forms the bulk of the "new" Thoreau volume, *Faith in a Seed*—a significant addition to the Thoreau canon, and one which makes clearer and more accessible the nature of Thoreau's natural history studies.[15]

In these studies, the dynamic principle that drives nature remains the same, but the singular center is dispersed and distributed across multiple lines of connection. "Law" has given way to pattern. In *Walden* Thoreau parodied the philosopher as lawgiver: the pompous "Hermit" advises the

"Poet" where to dig for fish bait, "for I have found the increase of fair bait to be very nearly as the squares of the distances" (224). Compare the hard-earned observation Thoreau makes in *Dispersion*: "I have many times measured the direct distance on a snowy field from the outmost pine seed to the nearest pine to windward, and found it equal to the breadth of the widest pasture" (27). The measure of a pine seed's blown distance over snow gives the measure of maximum pasture width: pasture size is not random but the result of the interaction, in real space, between a tree, its seed, the snow field, and the wind—all made commensurate by Thoreau's act of measure, which relates or makes relative the apparently arbitrary. Measurement has in this case related two networks—tree distance, or surface topography, and the distance a pine seed can blow when it has the snow on which to "sled" (27). Helped along like this, a pine seed can perhaps travel many miles from its source, and pines be spread from Concord to the far end of the continent. Why is this important? This small fact points to the multitude of networks that interconnect everything in nature (including man). The basic question is "how the seed is transported from where it grows to where it is planted," and the principle "agents" are wind, water, and animals (24). There is no longer just the one network, but as many networks as the combined ingenuity of these four elements can devise—not all roads lead to Boston. Their combinations will account for the nature and distribution of life on the face of the earth.

The plant universe divides in two—not a polar dualism this time, but a distributional distinction, along the uniting factor of transport. Some seeds, such as pine, birch, and maple, have built-in wings and fly and plant themselves. Other seeds are heavy and lack wings, and so borrow the wings or feet of animals and are planted by them. Cherries, for instance, lack vegetable wings, so "Nature has impelled the thrush tribe to take them into their bills and fly away with them; and they are winged in another sense, and more effectually than the seed of pines, for these are carried even against the wind" (68). As this suggests, these two classes correlate with two general patterns of dispersal and growth: windblown seeds form distinct, confined patches or stands, as the seeds were blown altogether; planted seeds form irregularly bounded woods of varying size and purity (163). Blown seeds are distributed everywhere, but spring up only if conditions are favorable (28); heavier, planted seeds encounter certain constraints (they go only where the animals go), but also certain advantages (animals often put them exactly where they want to be).

A million seeds blow everywhere so that one may grow. Such fecundity proves nature's economy is not economical but spendthrift, extravagant: "apparently only one in a million gets to be a shrub or tree. Nevertheless, that suffices; and Nature's purpose is completely answered" (61). This is a sign of health: "I love to see that Nature is so rife with life that myriads can be afforded to be sacrificed and suffered to prey on one another," Thoreau had written in *Walden* (318). "You must try a thousand themes before you find the right one—as nature makes a thousand acorns

to get one oak" (4:41; 9/4/51). He is agog at the calculations of catastrophe if such vitality were unleashed. If every white willow seed became a tree, "in a few years the entire mass of the planet would be converted into willow woods, which is not Nature's design" (DI 61). In nature's design, mass profusion entails mass destruction—the more of the one, the more of the other, as Darwin detailed. From the sensible utilitarian view that seeds exist only for reproduction, such proliferation can only seem wasteful. But nature knows better: "She knows that seeds have many other uses than to reproduce their kind. If every acorn of this year's crop is destroyed, or the pines bear no seed, never fear. She has more years to come" (37). Nature's economy depends on the snowballing of production and circulation: to spend is to indebt, to entail and interlink, to proliferate in connections.[16] So seeds are also for squirrels, redpolls, mice, jays, foxes—each the center of a universe, pursuing business, unwittingly complicit in the overall design: "the consumer is compelled to be at the same time the disperser and planter, and this is the tax which he pays to Nature" (114). Even "the most ragged and idle loafer or beggar may be of some use in the economy of Nature, if he will only keep moving" (97). Just keep circulating. The three basic agents of transport multiply exponentially: wind from all directions and at all speeds, water from dew to torrent, steam to snow; every living being crossing paths across every inch of ground at every height, creating a vast hum of activity just below the level of our hearing. The interpenetration of plant and animal worlds continues into Thoreau's metaphors: cherries grow thrush wings, birch seeds are "tiny brown butterflies" (42), maple seeds are veined "like green moths" (50), pitch pine seeds blow like schools of brown, "deep-bellied" fish (25).

Out of this "blooming, buzzing confusion" emerge patterns that reveal a deeper structure. Birches often grow in parallel lines, because a spring freshet carried the seeds and deposited them along its edge, or the seeds lodged "in the parallel waving hollows of the snow" (44). Elms border streams since that is where green rafts of the seeds have lodged (54), and willows cluster on muddy banks because the seed down forms a white scum on the water in which the seeds germinate, and which deposits the seedlings on bare mud as the water level drops (62). Clumps of maples, elms, or ash grow around rocks in river meadows because the rock "first detained the floating seed, protected the young trees, and now preserves the very soil in which they grow" (55). Maple seeds will not spring up in the grass of a bare pasture, but plow the ground and the seeds which land there can catch and germinate; and so a plowed field can suddenly turn into a maple wood (52). Similarly, "lay bare any spot in our woods, however sandy, by a railroad cutting for instance," or where frost keeps other trees out, and a willow or poplar will "plant itself there" (59). Their downy seeds, like those of milkweed, settle into hollows "where there is a lull of the wind" (59); causeways, fence lines, and embankments catch the seed and so grow natural willow hedges along their length (60). The river shores of the barren northern prairies are populated by willows and aspens—the very trees that are the first to spring up on burnt lands:

> It is remarkable that just those trees whose seeds are the finest and lightest should be the most widely dispersed—the pioneers among trees, as it were, especially in more northern and barren regions . . . while the heavy-seeded trees for which they may prepare the way are comparatively slow to spread themselves.
>
> (58)

So, for instance, though birch and alder are closely allied and their seeds are similar, the tiny brown winged birch seeds float high and spread everywhere, for "how many hundreds of miles" (43)—even to the far north, where a burned evergreen wood will spring up in a birch forest "as if by magic" (46). Alder seeds, however, are not winged but flattened, larger and heavier: "There is, of course, less need that they be winged, since they grow along streams or in wet places, whither their seeds may be floated in freshets; but the birches, though they have a wide range, grow chiefly in dry soil, often on the tops of dry hills" (48-49). Seed form correlates directly with plant habitat. Thoreau evidences the only alder that grows high on mountains: it alone "has winged seeds, apparently in order that the seeds may be spread from one ravine to another and also attain to higher levels" (49).

Everywhere Thoreau looks, he learns to read such relationships between seed form, plant habitat, growth patterns, and geographical distribution: each creates the other. In April 1856, George Hubbard remarked of some pines that "if they were cut down oaks would spring up, and sure enough," Thoreau confirms, across the road where Loring had just cut down his white pines, the ground was covered with oaks (VIII:315; 4/28/56). He has his theory in place within days. A few weeks later, when he was doing some surveying for John Hosmer, the old man "who had been buying and selling woodlots all his life" asked Thoreau if he could tell "how it happened that when a pine wood was cut down an oak one commonly sprang up, and vice versa" (VIII:363; 6/3/56; DI 104). It so happened by then that he *could,* and his answer became the heart of "The Succession of Forest Trees" and from there, *Dispersion of Seeds*: because of the interaction of winged seeds and heavy seeds and nuts. The wind conveys winged pine seeds into hardwoods and onto open lands, where, as he slowly proves to his satisfaction, the seedlings survive far better than under the dense shade of their own kind. Meanwhile "the squirrels and other animals are conveying the seeds of oaks and walnuts into the pine woods, and thus a rotation of crops is kept up" (DI 106). The ramifications fill many pages of his nascent book, as he develops this fundamental insight into the key that unlocks the history of the mixed and patchwork forests and fields around Concord.[17] "Thus you can unroll the rotten papyrus on which the history of the Concord forest is written" (169).

As Thoreau teases the patterns into meaning, he realizes how careless and wasteful his neighbors and their ances-

tors have been, through sheer ignorance. "Our woodlots, of course, have a history, and we may often recover it for a hundred years back, though we *do* not. . . . Yet if we attended more to the history of our woodlots, we should manage them more wisely" (164). In normal usage, as pitch pines seed into open pastures, they are bushwhacked and cattle are turned out to graze on the land. Both cows and bushwhacking break down the pines, until in fifteen or twenty years, having "suffered terribly," they stubbornly push themselves above the farmer's head, finally commanding his astonished attention as trees, whereupon he drives out the cattle, fences in the trees, and declares it a woodlot—having nearly ruined it in the meantime. "What shall we say to that management that halts between two courses? Does neither this nor that but botches both?" (171-72). So in New England "we have thus both poor pastures and poor forests," while in Old England, where resources are dearer, they have taken "great pains to learn how to create forests" (172).

Thoreau's admonition bears on one of the themes of the book: that American self-involvement has bankrupted the land. There is no pure nature created gloriously apart from the American to supply him with an endless fountain of resources—be they material, aesthetic, or spiritual. We blithely assume that when one forest is cut, another will "as a matter of course" spring up, and so, "never troubling ourselves about the succession," we don't anticipate the time when succession will fail and we shall have to learn the connection of seeds with trees (23). Instead of a nature pure, boundless, and Edenic, Thoreau proposes a nature thoroughly hybrid, limited, and postlapsarian: he who has truly *seen* the new world has seen that no world is truly new or belongs to us alone. Nature that is endlessly new is also endlessly old, imbricated with past lives and ages; Europeans who came to the "New World" were folded into American nature just like the Indians they displaced, who also burned and cultivated the land, creating a hybrid landscape that mixes nature's design with layers of human purpose, the nature of the oak and pine forest with "the necessities or whims of John and Sally and Jonas, to whom it has descended" (170). In *this* new world, knowledge is neither the evil nor the power, but the lifeline to survival. Chestnut timber, for example, is disappearing so rapidly "that there is danger, if we do not take unusual care, that this tree will become extinct here" (126). If only we understood that chestnuts do not come from God or out of nowhere but from chestnut seeds, we could replant chestnut forests. Nor is the problem confined to a single species: "The noblest trees, and those which it took the longest to produce, and which are the longest lived—as chestnuts, hickories, and oaks—are the first to become extinct under our present system and are the hardest to reproduce, and their place is taken by pines and birches, of feebler growth than the primitive pines and birches, for want of a change of soil" (130-31). We do not command, but *survive,* by obeying nature.

Accordingly, Thoreau's mission to educate is urgent, and his advice is specific. Forests must be of diverse kinds, planted in alternating bands and incorporating "countless trees in every stage of growth" (131-32), or they will not thrive.[18] Nature has a design and it is not ours—but we are having to learn it the hard way. Just as the English planters, through "very extensive and thorough experiments," have learned that the *only* way to raise oaks is by planting them under pines! And they had the audacity to declare this their "discovery," and to lay down as a principle that in cultivation art and design must regulate every step, with "'nothing whatever, or, at least, as little as possible, left to unassisted nature'" (125). Take another simple, practical problem: how to store nuts over the winter. On January 10, Thoreau buys some nuts at the store, and collects some from under the leaf mold in the forest. Over half the store nuts are spoiled; the natural nuts are every one wholesome. "Nature knows how to pack them best. They were still plump and tender"—and ready to sprout in the spring. "Would it not be well to consult with Nature in the outset?—for she is the most extensive and experienced planter of us all, not excepting the dukes of Athol" (134).

It all seems like reasonable, sound, practical Yankee advice. But Thoreau is after more than a practical handbook to resource management. Why insist so repeatedly and firmly that every plant comes from a *seed*? It would occur to few of today's readers to argue with him, but it did occur to no less a one than Horace Greeley, who published Thoreau's "Succession of Forest Trees" in the *New York Weekly Tribune* on October 8, 1860, then wrote Thoreau a letter challenging him to reconcile his theory that trees are never generated spontaneously with the fact that after fire devastates pine forest, "up springs a new and thick growth of White Birch—a tree not before known there." Greeley printed his letter, and Thoreau's reply, on February 2, 1861.[19] Thoreau framed his argument in *Dispersion* to answer just such objections. Why, for instance, if fireweed is so spontaneously generated, is it "not so produced in Europe as well as in America? Of course, the Canada thistle is spontaneously generated just as much, yet why was it not generated here until the seed had come from Europe?" (89).[20]

His insistence on the material agency of the seed made Thoreau one of Darwin's earliest and strongest allies. Even before the publication of *Origin of Species,* Thoreau was working along lines that can only be described as Darwinian.[21] The first and fundamental move toward Darwin's theory of evolution was to reject as "erroneous" the view "which most naturalists entertain, and which I formerly entertained—namely, that each species has been independently created" (*Origin* 6). Separate creation had solved the obvious problems resulting from the assertion that all life had radiated from one central point—problems like those to which Thoreau pointed in his discussion of fireweed and thistle—and did so in congruence with the dominant belief in a dead nature that had to be willed into life from outside. But Thoreau's emerging vision was of a living nature that willed *itself,* and so relied on material networks of circulation and exchange to proliferate and spread—as it did, to all parts of the globe.

The principle of life did not skip and flow independent of matter, but was transmitted by matter—through seeds: "A seed, which is a plant or tree in embryo, which has the principle of growth, of life, in it, is more important in my eyes, and in the economy of Nature, than the diamond of Kohinoor" (XIV:334; 3/22/61). "Life" became, not fragile and dependent, but sturdy and independent—profligate, stubborn, tenacious, like the willow whose twigs broke off at the least touch into Thoreau's boat, and which he pitied for being "made so brittle." Then he learned the twigs will sprout, so are "shed like seeds which float away and plant themselves in the first bank on which they lodge." Where he had once pitied the tree, "now I admired its invulnerability" (DI 63). Tradition was in error. Experience with living reality showed him the willow tree was not the symbol of sorrow and despairing love, but "an emblem of triumphant love and sympathy with all Nature. It may droop, it is so lithe, but it never weeps" (64).

The seed was an efficient explanatory principle, but it also gave Thoreau the tough, wily, independent, and astonishingly beautiful nature that could be, like a human friend, separate enough to show him mystery, yet close enough to involve him as partner and companion, in "sympathy" and even love. The seed gave Thoreau the principle of connection, of present with past and future, of all the globe with the common and local inhabitants of Concord, the designs of men with the design of nature. To Thoreau, the seed as material cause, the "little strokes" that *raise* great oaks (36-37), was still more magical than the false "magic" of spontaneous generation. The sense of the marvelous permeates his writing, and flashes into moments of joy and admiration. He finds the year's newest pitch pine seedling in a pasture, and wonders at the infant tree:

> It was, as it were, a little green star with many rays, half an inch in diameter, lifted an inch and a half above the ground on a slender stem. What a feeble beginning for so long-lived a tree! By the next year it will be a star of greater magnitude, and in a few years, if not disturbed, these seedlings will alter the face of Nature here.
>
> (27)

Not only do the mechanisms delight him, but he is moved by the way such an interwebbed nature anticipates itself, opposites interpenetrating to create beauty. The "strong, prickly, and pitchy chest" of the pitch pine cone contains about a hundred seeds in pairs. A membrane or "wing" clasps each seed "like a caged bird holding the seed in its bill and waiting till it shall be released that it may fly away with and plant it. / For already some rumor of the wind has penetrated to this cell, and preparation has been made to meet and use it." Thoreau marvels further: "This wing is so independent of the seed that you can take the latter out and spring it in again, as you do a watch crystal" (25). The wonder and delight in such precision echo Paley, except in Thoreau there is no sense that the wondrous contrivances bespeak the power and ingenuity of the Contriver, but rather the astonishing achievement wrought by the cooperation of independent agents all using each other to accomplish their ends, in a harmonious universe presided over by nature's wise design. The veined mothlike wing of the maple is essential to that design, for if the seed is to reproduce under favorable conditions, nature "must also secure it those favorable conditions" (XIV:334; 3/22/61). So the wing develops even when

> the seed is abortive—Nature being, you would say, more sure to provide the means of transporting the seed than to provide the seed to be transported. In other words, a beautiful thin sack is woven around the seed, with a handle to it such as the wind can take hold of, and it is then committed to the wind, expressly that it may transport the seed and extend the range of the species.
>
> (DI 50)

Entire worlds "spring" from the tiniest seed. Thoreau calculates the seed of the earth, were it proportional to that of the willow, "would have been equal to a globe less than two and a half miles in diameter, which might lie on about one-tenth the surface of this town" (67).

In this new order, every phenomenon in nature has a cause or connective principle. Knowing the language allowed Thoreau to understand new sentences, as for instance when he notices that sugar maples retain some of their seed so late, and "suspect[s] that their distribution may be somewhat aided by the snow" (52). Given chains of connection like this, Thoreau has a world that "springs" into meaning, and a meaning that can be read in the real world. Things are joined together not by penetration, dissolution, etherealization, by the flow of spirit precipitating into shadow forms, but by contact, a chain of contacts, multiple chains, creating an order in which man is neither ruler nor intruder but incorporated into the "economy" as casually as the beggar-tick burr borrows a pant-leg to hitchhike into town, or as the oak seedlings, coiled and ready to spring into being as a forest, borrow the material needs of the woodlot owner who logs and sells the pine trees.

Only our self-centered view has prevented us from seeing all this. Intrigued with a blue butterfly, for instance, Thoreau grumbles that the only insects of which science takes account are those that are noxious or injurious to vegetation: "Though God may have pronounced his work good, we ask, 'Is it not poisonous?'" (XII:170-71; 5/1/59). "How little observed are the fruits we do not use! How few attend to the ripening and dispersion of the white-pine seed" (DI 34). Since this is not a simple world in which we are lawgivers, but a complex world we cannot predict, we pay it the less attention:

> When lately the comet was hovering in our northwest horizon, the thistledown received the greater share of my attention. . . . Astronomers can calculate the orbit of that thistledown called the comet, conveying its nucleus, which may not be so solid as a thistle seed, somewhither; but what astronomer can calculate the orbit of your thistledown and tell where it will deposit its precious freight at last? It may still be travelling when you are sleeping.
>
> (87)

While we have been asleep, the whole world has been traveling around us.

The single thistledown, as it rises from Thoreau's hand hundreds of feet into the air "and then passes out of sight eastward" (87), becomes, briefly, a world, one that soon passes beyond his sight. In this plural universe there are new worlds everywhere, concealed only by our ignorance—the ignorance that regards squirrels as "vermin," when it would be "more civilized as well as humane" to honor them in an annual ceremony as the planters of our forests (130). So Thoreau spends some time thinking about a squirrel world: how they "strip and spoil the tree" (but perhaps the trimming is to the tree's benefit?). How they gather in their own October harvest just like the farmer, and even more "sedulously" (39-40). There is a squirrel mind, and squirrel knowledge—"But he does not have to think what he knows" (32). These other beings are utterly at home in their worlds, in a way that Thoreau finds heroic, and endlessly fascinating. He creates moments of intersection and watches them turn away from him, pursuing their own direction, like the milkweed seed he launches which "rises slowly and uncertainly at first," until it catches the strong north wind and is born off, "till at fifty rods off and one hundred feet above the earth, steering south—I lose sight of it" (93).

Not that their worlds are always easy. Thoreau digs up oak and hickory seedlings and learns to his surprise that frail seedlings conceal thick, vigorous roots, "lusty oaken carrots" (117-18). Examination reveals the stubs of old shoots, repeated attempts to lift a tree into a hostile world; one little hickory seedlings turns out to have been "at *least* eleven years old" (138). Their perseverance earns Thoreau's respect:

> There are those who write the lives of what they call *self-educated* men, and celebrate the *pursuit* of knowledge under difficulties. It will be very suggestive to such novices just to go and dig up a dozen seedling oaks and hickories, read their biographies, and see what they here contend with.
>
> (142)

Many of their difficulties are caused by the farmers who are so careless of "little" things and material causes. "The history of a woodlot is often, if not commonly, here a history of cross-purposes, of steady and consistent endeavor on the part of Nature, of interference and blundering with a glimmering of intelligence at the eleventh hour on the part of the proprietor" (170). Thoreau ends his draft with a story of a landowner who logged his pinewood in the winter of 1859. Thoreau stopped by the following October to "see how the little oaks" were doing. To his "surprise and chagrin," the field had been burned over and planted with winter rye: "What a fool! Here Nature had got everything ready for this emergency, kept them ready for many years—oaks half a dozen years old with fusiform roots full charged and tops already pointing skyward, only waiting to be touched off by the sun—and he thought he knew better. . . ." And so, instead of "an oak wood at once," he will get from his woodlot a bare field, "pine-sick" and shriven of oaks. "So he trifles with Nature," harumphs her closest student (172-73).

One of Darwin's operant principles was "Nature non facit saltum"—there are no gaps in nature. This was an old saw in natural history, one which had aided Lyell's gradualist geology, had driven Jefferson to seek for mastodons in inland North America, and Goethe to seek in the leaf the principle for all vegetable life. But Darwin's question was new: "Why, on the theory of Creation, should this be so? Why should all the parts and organs of many independent beings, each supposed to have been separately created for its proper place in nature, be so invariably linked together by graduated steps?" (*Origin* 194). His answer was that all organisms are related by descent—not metaphorically or metaphysically, but by actual, physical, lineal descent. To communicate this idea, Darwin borrowed an old figure of language and literalized it:

> As buds give rise by growth to fresh buds, and these if vigorous, branch out and overtop on all sides many a feebler branch, so by generation I believe it has been with the great Tree of Life, which fills with its dead and broken branches the crust of the earth, and covers the surface with its ever branching and beautiful ramifications.
>
> (130)

By the "Tree of Life," all living beings are related through common ancestry. But Darwin's nature doesn't really look like a noble tree. It looks more like a tangled bank:

> It is interesting to contemplate an entangled bank, clothed with many plants of many kinds, with birds singing on the bushes, with various insects flitting about, and with worms crawling through the damp earth, and to reflect that these elaborately constructed forms, so different from each other, and dependent on each other in so complex a manner, have all been produced by laws acting around us.
>
> (489)

The laws are simple and discoverable by anyone. Darwin's great argument builds through the careful wrangling of commonplace and familiar facts, such as the variability of domestic dogs and pigeons; the family resemblance of child to parent; fecundity in a world where so few can survive. Given the plain and commonplace, Darwin like a good traveler defamiliarizes it, then with surefooted steps leads the reader through this strange new landscape to the inescapable and extraordinary conclusion: life created itself. Its own power responds to the force of circumstances by proliferating, in an unbroken chain, into all the beings in and on the earth.[22] Darwin closed his book by proclaiming the beauty of his vision, even as he dreaded the way it would be received:

> There is grandeur in this view of life, with its several powers, having been originally breathed into a few forms or into one; and that, whilst this planet has gone

cycling on according to the fixed law of gravity, from so simple a beginning endless forms most beautiful and most wonderful have been, and are being, evolved.

(Origin 490)

Thoreau had already intuited something like Darwin's Tree of Life in the *Walden* sandbank passage, where the descending sand mixes, proliferates, and transforms itself into all the forms of life, in a continuous, unbroken flow. Yet the pre-Darwinian evolutionary ideas on which Thoreau's vision drew were not physical but *meta*physical: Life assumed and discarded form after form, in its upward yearning to reach man and return to God. What shocked nineteenth-century readers was not Darwin's theory of evolution (already an old idea), but his assertion that the old *metaphor* of evolution was the literal truth. A continuous chain of physical contact linked every single organic form. Thus our classifications express true genealogies: "community of descent is the hidden bond which naturalists have been unconsciously seeking, and not some unknown plan of creation, or the enunciation of general propositions, or the mere putting together and separating objects more or less alike" (*Origin* 420). In Thoreau's terms: there was *always* a seed. Make *that* a fact of your understanding, and the whole world would "spring" into being. For Thoreau, the metaphor of the seed had to be a "radical" metaphor, had to be fully spiritual and fully material, simultaneously. In literalizing the metaphor of the seed, Thoreau paralleled Darwin's move in literalizing the metaphoric Tree of Life: both created communities of descent. Thoreau saw science as metaphor; Darwin saw metaphor as science. Having exposed the metaphorical nature of science, they both go on to insist that the metaphor is real after all. Darwin alludes to Goethe: "Naturalists frequently speak of the skull as formed of metamorphosed vertebræ; . . . [and] the stamens and pistils of flowers as metamorphosed leaves"; however, they use such language "only in a metaphorical sense. . . . On my view these terms may be used literally" (438-39). Gillian Beer points out that "in the process of Darwin's thought, one movement is constantly repeated: the impulse to substantiate metaphor and particularly to find a real place in the natural order for older mythological expressions."[23] As Thoreau would put it, to so state facts that they may be mythological. If only we truly understood it, the material world would fabulate, and the truly fabulous would exist in fact. Thus would the whole world signify.

Thoreau read *On the Origin of Species* within weeks of its publication in London on November 24, 1859.[24] By February 1860 he was copying extracts from it into his notebooks, and he spent the next several months expanding his research in directions inspired by Darwin. "Never had Thoreau been so captivated by a project," notes William Howarth.[25] That September he distilled his researches into "The Succession of Forest Trees" for public presentation, and for the next two months he worked daily on gathering still more new material and expanding the "Succession" lecture into *The Dispersion of Seeds*. The work was slowed by the cold he contracted on December 3, 1860, after a day spent counting tree rings in the rain. From that point on his health steadily deteriorated until his death on May 6, 1862; yet even during the journey he took to Minnesota from May to July in 1861, in hopes of regaining his health, he was taking notes that expanded the field of his observations to the northern plains.[26] All this time he was juggling work on *Dispersion* with "Wild Fruits," the enormous project which had been ongoing through the late 1850s and toward which he was amassing, from March 1860 to January 1862, over 750 pages of lists and charts correlating his years of minute seasonal observations into a "Kalendar" of Concord. Exactly how these various projects were related or what might have come of them is unclear, and given the state of the manuscripts, may always remain so. It is more clear that his reading of Darwin changed the tenor of his work, giving it a context, a direction, and a dynamic focus that were taking Thoreau beyond old-fashioned seasonal chronology and rank-and-file natural history. The revolution that Humboldt had started, Darwin was completing.

The *Dispersion* manuscript several times alludes to Darwin on technical matters, but only once discusses more theoretical questions, in a passage musing on ponds; while Darwin needed to account for the origin of species on ocean islands, Thoreau's concern lay in the immigration of species to inland waters. The immediate problem was to account for the lilies and the fish (pouts and pickerel) that had appeared seemingly out of nowhere in Sleepy Hollow Cemetery's newly dug pond. Thoreau, directly applying Darwin, asserts the fish "had undoubtedly come up from the river, slight and shallow as the connexion is," while the lily seeds had been conveyed "by fishes, reptiles, or birds which feed on them" (DI 100-101). Thus he can assert: "If you dig a pond anywhere in our fields you will soon have not only waterfowl, reptiles, and fishes in it, but also the usual water plants, as lilies and so on. You will no sooner have got your pond dug than nature will begin to stock it" (100). Yet he continues to pursue the question: then how did *Pontederia* and spatterdock get to "the little pool at the south end of Beck Stow's," which *lacks* a stream? Perhaps carried by reptiles and birds—but the real question is broader: "*Indeed,* we might as well ask how they got anywhere, for all the pools and fields have been stocked thus, and we are not to suppose as many new creations as pools." How, then, did *any* plant get anywhere? By the same process:

> I think that we are warranted only in supposing that the former was stocked in the same way as the latter and that there was not a sudden new creation, at least since the first. Yet I have no doubt that peculiarities more or less considerable have thus been gradually produced in the lilies thus planted in various pools, in consequence of their various conditions, though they all came originally from one seed.

(DI 101; cf. XIV:146-47; 10/18/60)

Thoreau is running Darwin's theory—descent of all life from a single "seed," speciated by variation across isolated populations—through his own observations and conclu-

sions, and finding them perfectly congruent. Darwin provided the theoretical framework toward which Thoreau had been groping, and confirmed Thoreau's intuitive vision of the world: "We find ourselves in a world that is already planted, but is also still being planted as at first" (101). What he learned of the living lilies at Beck Stow's would be just as true of any fossil lilies geologists might unearth: the newest connects with the oldest, and the old is ever new: "The development theory implies a greater vital force in nature, because it is more flexible and accommodating, and equivalent to a sort of constant new creation" (102). Thoreau concludes the discussion by quoting one of Darwin's experiments in which Darwin allowed every seed in three tablespoons of pond mud, collected in February, to germinate and grow. At the end of six months "the plants were of many kinds and were altogether 537 in number; and yet the viscid mud was all contained in a breakfast cup!" (DI 102; *Origin* 386-87).

Darwin had designed this experiment to show how a bit of mud on the foot or beak of a waterbird could convey seeds across great distances, over land or water. As Thoreau said, given the seed, the next question was "how the seed is transported from where it grows to where it is planted" (DI 24). Darwin conducted many investigations of this kind, for he believed such questions were some of the most important, and least well understood, in contemporary natural science:

> No one ought to feel surprise at much remaining as yet unexplained in regard to the origin of species and varieties, if he makes due allowance for our profound ignorance in regard to the mutual relations of all the beings which live around us. Who can explain why one species ranges widely and is very numerous, and why another allied species has a narrow range and is rare? Yet these relations are of the highest importance, for they determine the present welfare, and, as I believe, the future success and modification of every inhabitant of this world.
>
> (*Origin* 6)

Questions regarding "the mutual relations of all the beings which live around us" had already preoccupied Thoreau for nearly a decade. He was deeply engaged in meticulous and broad-ranging field research devoted to addressing some of the most vexing, most important, and least comprehended questions of his time (and of ours): the causes of speciation, patterns of distribution and migration, habitat separation, the phenomena of coevolution. These form the center of Darwin's work and writing, a fact overshadowed by the consensus that equates Darwin's name only with the brutal struggle to survive. The consensus overshadowed as well the true method and intent of Thoreau's late work—what Emerson famously called his "broken task."

Stephen Jay Gould, considering the puzzle of Humboldt's eclipse, finds the most telling cause in Darwin's *Origin*—in a painful irony, the student superannuated the teacher, only a few months after Humboldt's death in 1859. Why? In the darker post-Darwinian view, Humboldtian higher harmony became "a scene of competition and struggle." Humboldt's confidence in universal progress became opportunistic local adaptation with no intrinsic upward direction, and Humboldt's multiple harmonious forces became random internal forces in precarious balance with the caprices of environmental change.[27] Yet Darwin's own language of "checks" and "struggle" regularly transmutes into visions of sublime nature. As his discussion verged on Thoreau's own field, Darwin emphasized not Thoreauvian creation, cooperation, or exchange, but the order generated by so "many different checks" that must come into play in the life of any species. But what an extraordinary order this becomes:

> When we look at the plants and bushes clothing an entangled bank, we are tempted to attribute their proportional numbers and kinds to what we call chance. But how false a view is this! Every one has heard that when an American forest is cut down, a very different vegetation springs up. . . .

Yet the second-growth forests growing on ancient Indian burial mounds display the same "beautiful diversity" as the virgin forests:

> What a struggle between the several kinds of trees must here have gone on during long centuries, each annually scattering its seeds by the thousand; what war between insect and insect—between insects, snails, and other animals with birds and beasts of prey—all striving to increase, and all feeding on each other or on the trees or their seeds and seedlings, or on the other plants. . . . Throw up a handful of feathers, and all must fall to the ground according to definite laws; but how simple is this problem compared to the action and reaction of the innumerable plants and animals which have determined, in the course of centuries, the proportional numbers and kinds of trees now growing on the old Indian ruins!

> (*Origin* 74-75)

Darwin's language of war and defeat sounds glum enough next to Thoreau's language of triumph, joy, and renewal, but even Darwin is swept away by a vision of the beauty and complexity created by the vying forces of life. Conversely, Thoreau does admit the presence of death, from the war of nature in *Walden*'s battle of the ants, to asides about struggling hickories, or the puzzling loss of so many acorns to frost (XIV:149). But in the unending cycle of destruction and renewal, Thoreau refuses death as nature's ultimate truth, instead throwing his rhetorical and imaginative weight into images of vitality. Death, in a move reminiscent of Whitman and Wallace Stevens, is only the necessary mother of beauty.

As Gould himself acknowledges, the bleakness of the Darwinian worldview was not shared by Darwin himself, who accepted that "Nature simply is what she is; nature does not exist for our delectation, our moral instruction or our pleasure."[28] Indeed, *Origin,* especially in its unbridled first edition, brims with life and wonder. Despite the regular in-

tonements of "the war of nature . . . famine and death" (490), its metaphoric and emotional heart is Darwin's awe before the world's beauty. He reiterates, typically, "I can see no limit to this power, in slowly and beautifully adapting each form to the most complex relations of life" (469). The lesson Darwin himself carries away is a sublime confidence:

> As all the living forms of life are the lineal descendants of those which lived long before the Silurian epoch, we may feel certain that the ordinary succession by generation has never once been broken, and that no cataclysm has desolated the whole world. Hence we may look with some confidence to a secure future of equally inappreciable length.

> (489)

Thoreau launches his thoughts after the milkweed seed that has sailed aloft and is "steering south":

> Thus, from generation to generation it goes bounding over lakes and woods and mountains. . . . I am interested in the fate or success of every such venture which the autumn sends forth. And for this end these silken streamers have been perfecting themselves all summer, snugly packed in this light chest, a perfect adaptation to this end—a prophecy not only of the fall, but of future springs. Who could believe in prophecies of Daniel or of Miller that the world would end this summer, while one milkweed with faith matured its seeds?

> (DI 93)

For Thoreau, nature's manifold views held no room for apocalyptic visions.

Where Darwin saw war and the feeding of all upon all, Thoreau detailed cooperation, collusion, a community bound together by exchange and prospering through extravagance and excess. Thoreau read nature, even Darwin's nature, through Humboldtian eyes. To speculate: is it possible, just conceivable, that had Thoreau lived he could have offered to his time a thoroughly up-to-date and Darwinian view of nature that might have defied the canonical determinism that cut Darwin's joy to its own grim and dualistic measure? Could Thoreau, in some slight degree, have complicated the accelerating rupture that drove the chill and competitive world of "Darwinian" nature apart from the warm and womanly hearth of the humanists and artists?

Speculations aside, Thoreau did enter upon a campaign to inform and enlighten the public in general, and the masters of the land in particular. If the forests he loved were being bound over by ignorance to loss and depletion, he could intervene and educate, teach others how to read the history of the forests. The end would be community action for the improvement of all, just as he recommended in the essay salvaged from "Wild Fruits" as "Huckleberries." What to do with the farmer fool who ruins his land? "That he should call himself an agriculturalist! He needs to have a guardian placed over him. . . . Forest wardens should be appointed by the town—overseers of poor husbandmen" (DI 173). Thus concludes his long-unpublished first draft: this Thoreau would have fathered the United States Forest Service, in the Department of Agriculture!²⁹

Though the idea died with him, he did succeed in presenting publicly the "first fruit" of his researches, and if dispersion be any measure, he had embarked in a most promising way: "Succession" had the widest circulation of any essay within Thoreau's lifetime.³⁰ This is significant, for the situation he faced in writing and presenting "The Succession of Forest Trees" had specific social demands which were new to Thoreau, and which put him in an anomalous position. He who had exiled himself so grandly from the social network of Agassiz and American science now needed to reconnect with it, for this was the network of knowledge and power, and Thoreau wanted his new knowledge to acquire the power to change the face of nature in America—like his little pitch pine stars—beginning like them with the battered pastures of Concord. Thoreau had to present himself believably as a scientist, or else stand by and watch his forests die.

THE TRANSCENDENTALIST AT THE CATTLE SHOW:
THOREAU'S IRONIC SCIENCE

In Thoreau's new science, ironies abound: nothing is as it seems. Pine forests are really oak forests. Willow, from time immemorial the symbol of sorrow, is really the emblem of triumph and joy. The "downy atoms" of willow seed, "which strike your cheek without your being conscious of it, may come to be pollards five feet in diameter" (DI 57). When his neighbor expressed a wish for a quantity of birches, Thoreau dropped by and extracted "one hundred birch trees" from his pocket (47). On a rainy day in September 1860, during the annual cattle show, when Thoreau stood in the Concord Town Hall before the assembled membership of the Middlesex Agricultural Society to present a "serious scientific subject," he knew many in his audience thought of him rather as the town crank, an eccentric, a poet, even a woods burner.³¹ In a moment steeped in ironies, not the least is that the text in which he most artfully negotiated the difficult passage between poetry and science has fallen between them into obscurity.

Thoreau opened his lecture by squaring off directly against the disciplinary expectations of his immediate audience: "Every man is entitled to come to Cattle-Show, even a transcendentalist. . . ." Just how is the transcendental poet and peripatetic town surveyor to address the substantial landowning citizens of the Middlesex Agricultural Society? Thoreau began by deflecting their mutual awkwardness through a strained joke at his own expense. He recalls to his audience another festival regular, that "weak-minded and whimsical fellow" who for a cane carries a crooked stick, when, we all know, "a straight stick makes the best cane. . . . Or why choose a man to do plain work who is distinguished for his oddity?" Perhaps, he jests disarmingly, his audience thinks they have made the same mistake. Yet he then gently and firmly turns the joke on

them: it is *he* who knows the straight path in the woods, who has "several times shown the proprietor the shortest way out of his woodlot" (NHE 72-73). Having thus established his own authority as the local land surveyor (with "title" to speak, if not to property), Thoreau invites their attention to "a purely scientific subject": namely, why is it "that when a pine wood was cut down an oak one commonly sprang up, and *vice versa*" (73). Slowly and carefully, Thoreau unpacks and pieces together his answer: wind conveys pine seeds into the hardwoods and open land, while squirrels, jays, and other animals convey hardwood seeds into the pinewoods. The seedlings of neither will mature in the shade of the other, but cut the woods, and the seedlings, there but unseen all along, will spring up into their own.

As far as Thoreau's science-minded audience was concerned, their speaker negotiated the divide successfully. For all his witticisms, Thoreau took the occasion seriously and delivered a solid lecture. The society's president, ex-governor of Massachusetts George S. Boutwell, concluded the event by congratulating the audience on hearing an address "so plain and practical, and at the same time showing such close and careful study of natural phenomena."³² So Thoreau's immediate, science-inclined audience agreed that Thoreau's representation of the forest would count as science: they reprinted it as such and even today it is so acknowledged. Accordingly, when it was reprinted in the *Eighth Annual Report of the Massachusetts Board of Agriculture,* the literary frame was deleted,³³ turning Thoreau's work into a serious scientific paper with throwaway literary asides. The deletions helped stabilize this text *as* science, making it legible within the context of other scientific reports.

It has proven more difficult for literary critics to integrate this essay into the context of other literary works. The science tends to be bracketed as "just" science, stabilizing the lecture as a serious literary essay with throwaway scientific asides, which however dominate to such a degree that they distract from the great domain of *imaginative* truth. Howarth remarks, "Ironically, [Thoreau's] contribution to succession theory was ignored by scientists for almost a century, and many later readers have assumed that this 'purely scientific subject' . . . has little value as literature." John Hildebidle, in the midst of careful consideration of "The Succession of Forest Trees" and of *The Dispersion of Seeds,* finds the coexistence in "Succession" of Thoreau the "moralist" and Thoreau the "observer" to be "rather stale and unprofitable"; "Whatever its virtues as science, the lecture as art is something of a disappointment." Joan Burbick, who gives this essay a serious and thoughtful reading, sees it as a failure in "the synthesis of natural causes and of imaginative associations." The seed, Thoreau's most (so to speak) pregnant metaphor of all, is in her words "demetaphorized into a natural cause." The seed is "redefined" as limited and material until the end of the essay, when Thoreau adds "a countermanding postscript" that reassigns the seed to the realm of imaginative, not material cause: "separate systems for the two realms," precisely what Thoreau is trying to avoid.³⁴

The essay's dubious status, and Thoreau's own dubious tone in the opening, suggest in small scale the problems this larger project faced: how to make a single, hybrid text coherent to readers with double vision? To make his most radical metaphor viable in *both* realms? If Thoreau failed, it may be because his first priority seemed the more urgent: to convince his audience to listen to him, to accept science from a transcendentalist. Sitting before him in the lecture audience were the very people who manipulated the forests he so loved, and in whose decisions he could hope to intervene. Their expectations of "science" demanded from Thoreau the role of neutral and modest expert, delivering objective scientific truth, and though he might, instead, have read them a poem, that would have sacrificed the occasion to a principle in which he disbelieved, that discourse was merely discourse. That is, this was not a relativistic space of mere words, in which any words would have sufficed; Thoreau, caring deeply about forests, needed words that would influence how his neighbors would construct, literally not just literarily, the forested land which they owned and exploited. Thus he was concerned, as he wrote to Blake, with getting "more precision & authority" into the work that would lead to his 1860 lecture.[35] Facing this powerful constraint, Thoreau disciplined himself as a scientist, and addressed them with authoritative empirical data and precise cause-and-effect explanations.

But Thoreau's larger task was to intervene in the "deadening" discourse of science, and to demonstrate an alternative mode which nevertheless would be successful *as* science—successful, that is, in generating agreement among a particular and powerful community who would then accept and integrate his statements as "fact." This second task might explain why this essay is, after all, such an odd specimen of "scientific" writing, full of jokes and wordplay, asides and parables. One could assume that Thoreau simply didn't know how to reproduce the well-established genre of the scientific paper, or that he simply couldn't help himself and must leaven his text with humor, producing a science so sugarcoated even a transcendentalist could deliver it. I would like, instead, to ask how this essay would look if we take his words seriously, as if he meant what he said.

How is the power of scientific discourse constructed? Through conventions of discourse which Thoreau deliberately attempts to disrupt by employing two techniques, "feedbacking" and "inversion."[36] The first convention of scientific discourse requires that the author suppress her "personal" view and eliminate any suggestion of a connection between the author and the object of study. This convention had already been in place for over 150 years, and as a regular reader of science writing, Thoreau was not only familiar with it but regularly chafed at it: "Ah what a poor dry compilation is the Annual of Scientific Discovery. I trust that observations are made during the year which are not chronicled there" (3:354; 8/5/51). In "feedbacking," the author attempts to disrupt the putative "objectivity" by visibly reconnecting object and subject, em-

phasizing rather than suppressing her own presence both in the text and in the process of science. Second, the construction of objectivity assumes that the object gives rise to its own representation; it "speaks for itself," and the author is but the transparent channel of truth. "Inversion" disrupts this coupling by reversing it, insisting that it is the representation which precedes and gives rise to the object: we see what we look for. As we have seen, Thoreau was familiar with this principle, calling it the "intentionality of the eye" whereby our knowledge constructs its supporting facts, and basing on it his major critique of conventional scientific practice. By employing these two techniques, Thoreau ran the risk of defining his work as not scientific at all, but wholly literary, undercutting the effectiveness of his critique even before it achieved a hearing.

"Feedbacking" focuses on the role of the putative "discoverer," in this case Thoreau himself. In "objective" science, this role would be that of transparent intermediary between the scientist's object and ourselves, the readers and witnesses. The act of discovery being essentially passive, anyone, the story goes, could have stumbled across it; I just happened to be the one, and I merely convey my finding to you. The narrating "I/eye" we expect in scientific rhetoric claims merely to record what is there all along for anyone to see, staying rhetorically out of sight, suppressing any sense of its own agency—for, recall, there has been no agency. The very power of this view rests on this premise: command by obedience. But if objectivity is undercut, one can no longer claim simply to channel the docile body of the discovered to its interested onlookers, nor posit oneself as the passive vehicle of intelligence, pure, unmarked, invisible, neutral, and uncontaminating. Feedbacking, therefore, disrupts this fictive role by foregrounding agency. The discover/scientist/author will emphasize rather than suppress individual presence, action, and circumstance, through the use of what Steve Woolgar calls "modalizers" which "draw attention to the existence and role of an agent in the constitution of a fact or factual statement."[37] Or even more dramatically, the author may put in a sudden and unexpected appearance—not an easy thing to do, I've noticed—revealing the convention that has kept her "silent."

I suggest this is precisely what Thoreau does. Throughout "Succession" he insists on foregrounding his own role as an agent, both in the field and at the podium; furthermore, all the other operative elements are active agents as well, co-producers of both the forest and of his own process of discovery. Each one of his major narratives of deduction, quest, and discovery is framed by his actions and local circumstances. For example, an observation of a squirrel "planting" a hickory nut begins, "On the 24th of September, in 1857, as I was paddling down the Assabet, in this town, I saw a red squirrel run along the bank under some herbage, with something large in its mouth" (78-79). The passive, agentless statement is here nowhere to be found; his statements are all active: "I saw," "I approached," "Digging there, I found," "I walked," "I selected." Nor is Thoreau the only one actively engaged about his business.

He is surrounded by equally active entities, who are as aware of *his* presence as he of theirs: "One of the principal agents in this planting, the red squirrels, were all the while curiously inspecting me, while I was inspecting their plantation" (80). He must even compete with these "agents" for specimens: "The jays scream and the red squirrels scold while you are clubbing and shaking the chestnut trees, for they are there on the same errand, and two of a trade never agree" (82). The squirrels cast down the green chestnut burrs, "and I used to think, sometimes, that they were cast at me" (83). He mocks the English foresters who were "discovering" the secret of cultivating oaks: "but they appear not to have discovered that it was discovered before, and that they are merely adopting the method of Nature, which she long ago made patent to all. She is all the while planting the oaks amid the pines without our knowledge," and so our woodchoppers cut down the pines and "rescue an oak forest, at which we wonder as if it had dropped from the skies" (82). But of course it didn't—the absurdity of his image adds the backstroke to the edge of Thoreau's argument. The oak forest was *produced,* by the actions of pines and cones and winged pine seeds, wind, sun, shade, oaks, acorns, squirrels and jays and mice, the woodlot proprietors, the watchful town surveyor, the woodchoppers and their axes, the Middlesex Agricultural Society, British agriculturalists, "Nature" herself.

The essay thus demonstrates a number of feedbacking techniques for disrupting the illusion of an invisible omniscient "I" whose all-seeing "eye" has laid bare the truth of the universe. The first is, instead of gliding smoothly and silently down the halls of discovery, to make lots of narrative noise. This essay, as already noted, opens with a strained and extended joke. It bumps along through extravagant assertions ("that I can tell,—it is no mystery to me"), asides ("As I have said . . ."), circumlocutions ("I think that I may venture to say . . ."), and gratuitous remarks ("The ground looks like a platform before a grocery, where the gossips of the village sit to crack nuts and less savory jokes" [86]), to a hyperbolic fable about a squash. We are never suffered to forget that this essay is being voiced by a single idiosyncratic personality.

The second is to reassert the fictive character of the narrative by inserting long rhetorical flights, which should be totally unacceptable in a "factual" context. Thus, from a straightforward description of a pine seed, Thoreau leaps by way of its ingenious construction to a conceit about the "patent office at the seat of government of the universe" which oversees such things (75). He returns to this notion at the essay's close, expanding it to suggest the millennial potential of a seed, and of a patent office that distributed such seeds (91). Such transcendental interruptions elaborate on that distinctive authorial voice, which refuses to operate invisibly but instead ostentatiously takes control to remind us who is speaking, and in what context.

The third is to reiterate the active agency, at every level, of the author who is constructing this narrative. After announcing that he, alone, has the answer to the "mystery," Thoreau takes us collectively by the elbow: "*Let me* lead *you* back into *your* wood-lots again" (74; emphasis added). Having insisted on being his listeners' guide, he reminds them regularly that *he* is the one doing the leading, walking, deducing, seeing, probing, connecting. It is he who fashions the myriad data, and links them into a story designed for the consumption of his particular audience, namely, the legal owners of the woods in question, who are also his employers, those who in some sense "own" him—or not, any more than they "own" the squirrels and jays who also inhabit and make their living from the wood-lots, just as, when you come down to it, the proprietors themselves do, in cutting and marketing the timber. Thoreau foregrounds his own agency in constructing this convoluted tale, and in so doing, acts as the solvent dissolving the boundaries between all the other elements, which are also revealed as actors, agents in their own right, co-producers of the story Thoreau is seen to be fashioning.

Thus the fourth technique is to emphasize the voices of all the other participants, from proprietors who question, to jays who scold, to scientists who make competing claims. Thoreau treats all the participants in his narrative as actors, "agents." This is not a passive and docile field subject to his manipulations, or a rational cosmos revealed by his God vision, or even a world evoked into meaning by his Adamic power of naming. The various actors here not only question and scold, but hide, and hide evidence, from him; they collect, disseminate, and plant, carry, bury, swallow, design, fly, choke and overshadow, spring up, thrive, die. Thoreau's world here is a very busy place, and Thoreau lets us see just how hard he must work to compose a coherent story out of its confusion.

Both Thoreau and Woolgar discuss "intentionality," or "inversion," in the context of "discovery," wherein, according to the ideology of representation, the object was there all along and the discoverer more or less manages to stumble across it. Thoreau focuses on our propensity to *miss* what we stumble across routinely—as he writes in 1842 in "Natural History of Massachusetts," "it is much easier to discover than to see when the cover is off. . . . We must look a long time before we can see" (NHE 29). Here he illustrates the principle by revealing all the unseen oak seedlings living in a particularly dense pine grove: "Standing on the edge of this grove and looking through it . . . you would have said that there was not a hardwood tree in it, young or old. But on looking carefully along over its floor I *discovered,* though it was not till my eye had got used to the search," that the forest floor was scattered regularly with little oaks, from three to twelve inches high (80; emphasis added). That is, once he knew what to look for, Thoreau knew, first, to seek out a particular kind of forest; and once there, he taught his eyes to see what no one had ever seen, but had been there all along. Once one knows what to look for, one finds it.

"Discovery" defines something both novel and significant. Previously, the oak seedlings were neither; once constructed otherwise, they leapt into view. The discovery of America by Columbus was a social process, beginning with an orientation and setting out, ending with consolidation and assertion. The process is successful when it is socially acknowledged: we agree (or did until recently) that it was Columbus who "discovered" America, not the Vikings—and certainly not the "Indians" (an object of discovery can hardly discover itself!).[38] Thoreau's point is that the "cover" is always "off"; the act or process of discovery constructs the unseen into the seeable, and then finds and declares it for all to see, just as he was doing in his Middlesex Agricultural Society lecture. Two months later he added shrewdly in his *Journal*, "How is any scientific discovery made? Why, the discoverer takes it into his head first. He must all but see it" (XIV:267; 11/25/60).

If discovery proceeds by making visible those objects in the natural world that cooperate with our knowledge, the *narrative* of discovery is constructed by separating nature from knowledge, fact from truth, and insisting that instead of being complexly intertwined they are wholly independent. This dualism allows the inversion by which the now "freestanding" fact is imagined to have given rise to the hypothesis or document, and the preceding steps are denied, minimized, or simply forgotten.[39] Once we imagine that the fact or object gave rise to our knowledge, we can point back to the object we now imagine as independent and uncontaminated, as the unanswerable legitimation of what we have decided is the essential and incontrovertible truth. Thoreau provides an example: everyone knew that seeds lay dormant in the ground for many years. So when an old pine grove was cut and oak trees sprang up, that fact proved what everybody knew, that for generations acorns had lain dormant under the pines. The strength of the social work that constructed this circle of "knowledge" could be measured by the resistance which Thoreau met when he sought to offer an alternative explanation. It did take some degree of effort to show that acorns do not preserve their vitality for very long, but the acorns cooperated nicely with Thoreau: he could show that by November virtually every acorn left on the ground had either "sprouted or decayed" (88).[40] Obviously there could be no dormant survivors. He intervened in what "everybody knew" by showing them what *he* knew (and that, incidentally, the acorns themselves—who should know, after all—were on *his* side).

Thoreau's larger claim, that the forests and fields of Concord were the fleeting expression of an interactive system of innumerable agents acting across various paths of contact, even yet meets with a degree of resistance; for it assumes that "phenomena" are, as he put it, *not* independent of us but related to us, and that our knowledge can exist only in that shifting field *between* ourselves and our "objects." What Thoreau was arguing against was the "ideology of representation," as Woolgar calls it, which objectifies the world as thing, then asserts that what is out there can be correctly, i.e., objectively, seen. Lapses are due to contamination or failure which can, at least in theory, be corrected to yield accurate vision: "The fire of scientific scrutiny burns away from the idea—the hypothesis or the theory—the stain of its origin."[41] But Thoreau's point is that no vision can be simply accurate. As he writes, "There is no such thing as pure *objective* observation." All observation is necessarily "*subjective*" (VI:236). To the problem of representation, he proposes the solution of relational knowing:

> I think that the man of science makes this mistake, and the mass of mankind along with him: that you should coolly give your chief attention to the phenomenon which excites you as something independent on [*sic*] you, and not as it is related to you. The important fact is its effect on me. . . . With regard to such objects, I find that it is not they themselves (with which the men of science deal) that concern me; the point of interest is somewhere *between* me and them (*i.e.* the objects). . . .

(X:164-65; 11/5/57)[42]

"Between" subject and object: that is, in their conjunction or relationship, which denies that "objective" knowing is even possible, let alone desirable. Science eliminates that very point of interest: "You would say," he grumbles, "that the scientific bodies were terribly put to it for objects and subjects. A dead specimen of an animal, if it is only well preserved in alcohol, is just as good for science as a living one preserved in its native element" (XI:360; 11/30/58). Thoreau criticizes science repeatedly for its lack of "relation," to us and to its objects—for its presumption, as George Levine says, "that to observe a thing carefully, one must not care about it." Self-annihilation is necessary to protect science from the consequences of knowledge and so authenticate it.[43]

No science will ever preserve a forest in alcohol. Thoreau's sarcasm and dismay turn on his crucial paradox of independence and relational knowing: everything is sovereign, therefore nothing is passive and docile, "subject" to our "objective" knowing. Or, everything is related, therefore nothing hangs on us and our designs alone. We cannot impose, only invite. So in his complex moral vision, knowledge is authenticated not by protection from, but by exposure to, its consequences: we should believe him because he *does* care, not because he doesn't. In Thoreau's alternative science, authority comes from individual involvement and experience. What is more, we should care too, because we are all similarly involved, implicated. As our designs tangle with those of willows and squirrels and oaks and beggar-ticks, we all become co-producers of Concord, and by extension, the "environment" around us, wherever we are.[44] Hence we can no longer rationalize treating oaks and pines as just a commodity, of value only as we can insert them into our social-economic system. Thoreau's essay becomes a prescient plea for what later readers would call environmentally based consciousness and action.

Within various registers—from dormant acorns to village religious dogma to the conquest of Mexico and the American institution of slavery—Thoreau worries about the way a posteriori rationalization operates to make advocacy appear "objective," a social construction appear "natural" and inevitable. As Woolgar puns, such a construction becomes a thing, a *res* which "*resists*" our efforts to deconstruct it.[45] Against this form of social resistance Thoreau throws up a form of counterresistance: "things," objects, which refuse to be passively manipulated into our constructions, but actively "*resist*" us; we can, if we wish, imagine that acorns lie dormant, but they resist, and sprout or rot despite us. (Or as Latour puts it: "reality as the latin word *res* indicates, is what *resists*").[46] We may dismiss squirrels, jays, thrushes, and mice as inconsequential, even as vermin, but they too resist and go about planting and shaping our forests. They perform in effect their wild woodland version of "civil disobedience"—or as Thoreau's original title had it, "*Re*sistance to Civil Government."

Among these various acts of resistance and cooperation, Thoreau fabricates a narrative out of his own actions, which include not only looking and counting (239 pitch pine cone cores in one pile alone! [84]) but surveying the land for its proprietor's economic use, during the course of which he too is inspected and even scolded. By foregrounding all this Thoreau is advertising the status of his representation *as* a representation, not some clairvoyant reading of the truth of the universe. That is, the nature of representation itself is an issue here, and his critique is meant on principle. Yet Thoreau is faced with the problem of mounting "an adequate and effective resistance in a situation where adequacy and effectiveness are defined by the ideology (representation) under critique."[47] Thoreau does attempt to reconstitute the moral order of representation, by disputing the role of science as "the sealer of weights and measures," sole arbiter of what "counts." That is, he, a poet and a transcendentalist, "counts" too—as do the other participants, two-, four-, and non-legged altogether. There are many measures; they should all be welcome at the cattle show.

But representation which reflexively interrogates the status of representation is defined by the ideology of representation as poetic or literary. So when Thoreau mounts a critique of representation by offering an alternate story and an alternative means of representation, one which acknowledges its status as storytelling, his critique, meant as principled, runs the risk of being sidelined as marginal to the great domain of scientific truth. If science offers "the" representation of the woods, has not the poet merely offered a secondary one, forming at best a kind of supplement? Is this not after all a quirky and marginal text, neither mainstream science nor very good literature? Clearly this essay rejects the assumptions encoded in such a statement, asking instead that we attempt to recover Thoreau's writing in all its extravagant intertextuality. His attempt to remake science was more broadly an attempt to interlace the separating domains of science, society, and poetry at exactly the historical point when the three were precipitating out of a common culture into specialized disciplines. In other words, Thoreau was not just pioneering a "discovery" or a

new scientific concept. He was arguing for a new concept of science, a nonmodern science in which the subject and object are not split into separate and independent entities but caught mutually in a web of relationship. He shows us how we might continue to make science, while recalling all the while that it is finally *ourselves making* science.

Thoreau closes his essay by releasing the metaphor that has been lurking just below the surface of his prose, concealed in plain sight like his little sheltered oak seedlings coiled under the pines, waiting to "spring up":

> Though I do not believe that a plant will spring up where no seed has been, I have great faith in a seed,—a, to me, equally mysterious origin for it. Convince me that you have a seed there, and I am prepared to expect wonders

—or the millennium and the reign of justice, even, "when the Patent Office, or Government, begins to distribute, and the people to plant, the seeds of these things" (91). Then he tells us an odd story about turning loose in a corner of his garden a "brace of terriers," six squash seeds (dispersed to him straight from the Patent Office). A little hoeing and manuring, and "*abracadabra presto-chango* . . . lo! true to the label, they found for me 310 pounds of *poitrine jaune grosse* there, where it never was known to be, nor was before." Why, look at the squash my seeds have discovered! Thoreau chortles, mocking the tag-phrase magic of spontaneous generation. Not only that: "But I have more hounds of the same breed. . . . Other seeds I have which will find other things in that corner of my garden, in like fashion, almost any fruit you wish . . ." (91-92). Other seeds in an imaginary garden, indeed: the seed-hounds of a thought will point us to a discovery—the discovery of oak trees where you would have said there were none, of a community where you would have said were only trees, of literary coproduction where you would have said was only a lone naturalist in the woods. The two orders, material and imaginary, do not fall away from but interpenetrate and define each other.

Truly, interdisciplinarity is (as Stanley Fish's title has it) "so very hard to do"—but perhaps not quite impossible. It requires multiple and simultaneous acknowledgment of manifold factors and perspectives, keeping material and imaginary realms in focus at once in a kind of material semiosis, both letting a representation stand and querying the doubleness of its stance. Thoreau is dazzled by the magic of this simultaneity: that a representation could so unfailingly find its object, in a universe so infinitely undiscovered. Nature always answers to our conceptions. Given such seeds as this, "the corner of my garden is an inexhaustible treasure-chest. Here you can dig, not gold, but the value which gold merely *represents* . . ." (92; emphasis added). Yet, he concludes, even in the presence of such a garden, the fertile source of infinite representations, men still prefer the sterile trickery of isolated and perpetual self-production: "Yet farmers' sons will stare by the hour to see a juggler draw ribbons from his throat, though he tells them it is all deception." Disciplines too seem to prefer this magic trick of producing themselves endlessly out of themselves.

This is why I find so sad Thoreau's choice of a closing statement: "Surely, men love darkness rather than light" (92). Given the seed, the earth, and the mind, he asks us to hope for more than sterile self-production, yet stands already in the anticipation of being misunderstood. In the work most deeply influenced by Darwin, Thoreau like Darwin had to defend his vision, had to assert the wonder and beauty of the merely material, the "little *things*" that were seeds: "I have great faith in a seed,—a, to me, equally mysterious origin for it. Convince me that you have a seed there, and I am prepared to expect wonders. . . ." The "mysterious origin" of a seed is, of course, another seed: the most prosaic of magic. Just as Darwin's "Tree of Life" fills the earth and covers its surface "with its ever branching and beautiful ramifications," so does Thoreau's seed, if only his hearers will attend:

> Other seeds I have which will find other things in that corner of my garden, in like fashion, almost any fruit you wish, every year for ages, until the crop more than fills the whole garden. You have but little more to do than throw your cap up for entertainment these American days. Yet farmers' sons will stare by the hour to see a juggler draw ribbons from his throat, though he tells them it is all deception.

Against the sterile deception of endless self-reproduction, the carnival trickery of "spontaneous generation," Thoreau interposes the chain of real connection, of real causes and their astounding effects. Yet he closes without optimism: "Surely, men love darkness rather than light" (92). Time and again in his late essays Thoreau effectively says "Yes!" in thunder until compelled to say "No."

Thoreau's closing reference to his "garden" links this essay to his other cross-grained and hybrid seeds—"Autumnal Tints," "Wild Apples," "Huckleberries"—in which the garden, *his* garden, is the wild. Not some faraway Eden, but here under our noses, in our living vision: "These are *my* China-asters, *my* late garden-flowers. . . . Only look at what is to be seen, and you will have garden enough, without deepening the soil in your yard. We have only to elevate our view a little, to see the whole forest as a garden" (NHE 172). This "garden" will be not a warehouse of resources for translation into the networks and centers of commerce, but an ultimate value in itself—that which "gold merely represents." Because it is no one's and everyone's it is "ours" for the *seeing,* offering us a kind of abundance not consumed with use. He who "shoots at beauty," who has "dreamed of it, so that he can *anticipate* it," then, indeed, "flushes it at every step, shoots double and on the wing, with both barrels, even in corn-fields." Nor will his desire ever fail him: "If he lives, and his game spirit increases, heaven and earth shall fail him sooner than game" (NHE 175-76).

To our quiet desperation, nature offers spiritual bounty and abundance: a profusion of berries, abandoned apples, for-

ests full of acorns and chestnuts, "Slight and innocent savors which relate us to Nature, make us her guests, and entitle us to her regard and protection" (NHE 241). Here is the weight behind his oft-quoted line from "Walking": "in Wildness is the preservation of the World" (NHE 112). Against the coming of the evil days, in which men who love darkness better than light run after carnival tricks and the husks of experience, Thoreau invokes the real redeemer: Nature wild and unappropriated, the muck that will fertilize our withered fields, Chaos that does not just burrow through but abolishes altogether the "dead dry life of society," engendering each new Cosmos. At the close of *Walden,* cosmos emerges not from the sterile frost of winter but from that thawing, dissolving, flowing, self-organizing chaos of spring, even to sacrifice and destruction and the rain of flesh and blood. We should not forget that Thoreau built his Eden not only on cooperation and community but on waste and excess, vultures, carrion, and decay. His Eden will incorporate the Fall: it is a paradise erected on transgression.

Notes

1. The book was published anonymously in 1853, but its authorship was an open secret; a new edition, with a sixty-page supplement in which Whewell answered his critics, was published in 1856. For the American edition, see *The Plurality of Worlds,* introduction by Edward Hitchcock (Boston: Gould and Lincoln, 1856).

2. See Brooke 272. Chambers' evolutionary natural theology was echoed by Robert Hunt, in his *Poetry of Science* (312-13), which Thoreau also read in the early 1850s.

3. Hildebidle 99: "There is always in Thoreau a strong element of the notion (heretical, for a native of Puritan New England) that insight, and along with it redemption, are earned."

4. Lewontin, Rose, and Kamin, *Not in Our Genes* 280.

5. Behind this account lies the landmark study by Steven Shapin and Simon Schaffer, *The Leviathan and the Air Pump* (1985).

6. Lewis 25-26.

7. See Latour, *Science in Action* chap.6; "Drawing Things Together."

8. Ibid. 225.

9. Robert Sattelmeyer, "Introduction," NHE xxi.

10. Added in pencil; see *Journal* 3:611.

11. Robert Sattelmeyer notes that this single passage "was the product of several years of observation and evolution in his thought"; see "Remaking of *Walden*" 442. As William Rossi notes, one of the key revisions was altering "studio of the artist" to "*laboratory* of the Artist," reflecting Thoreau's stubborn insistence that imaginative and scientific truths were

fused. See Rossi, "'Laboratory of the Artist'" 200; Sattelmeyer, "Remaking of *Walden*" 443.

12. Compare the words of an anonymous reviewer who seized on Whewell's *Plurality of Worlds* to reproach "Nature worshippers": "'you are . . . worshipping ye know not what. The stars are *not* worlds, they are mere chaotic masses. Nature is not such a finished rounded thing as you dream, much less is it God; it is only a crude process, not a perfected result, far less a living cause. This Universe, glorious as it looks to *man's* imagination, is not infinite, is not beautiful even: it is but clay in the hands of an Almighty Potter.'" *Eclectic Review* 7 (1854): 527-28. Quoted in Brooke 282 n. 381. Clearly the metaphor can be molded to various ends.

13. See Robert E. Abrams 250: Thoreau's sense of immediacy "deepens, complicates, and turns problematic during his travels into it; it does not recede back into the lost, immutable authority of some unwarped primordial world."

14. Quoted in Richardson, *Henry David Thoreau* 344; Howarth, *Book of Concord* 123. The letter was to Calvin H. Greene; CO 425-26.

15. On the tangle of late manuscripts and the character of the seasonal charts, see Richardson, *Henry David Thoreau* 381-82, and "Thoreau's Broken Task" 3; also Howarth, *Book of Concord*.

16. See Grusin.

17. The process is of course somewhat more complicated in its details: squirrels transport pine seeds in the cones, for instance. Thoreau was working out an exhaustive range of qualifications and permutations. For an account of Thoreau's forest studies, see Stoller 71-107. As Stoller points out, the only new element in Thoreau's studies, as Thoreau himself understood, was seed dispersion; "the other essential components" had been described in 1846 by George B. Emerson (a distant cousin of Waldo's), in *A report on the trees and shrubs growing naturally in the forest of Massachusetts,* a book which Thoreau relied on throughout the 1850s. See also Kehr; Whitford; and Whitney and Davis. According to Whitney and Davis, in 1850 the percentage of wooded land in Concord was at its lowest point in history: 10.5 percent. Currently it is about 50 percent.

18. Nearly 150 years later, monoculture and even-age stands are resulting in declining production, and the "new forestry" is discovering the guidelines Thoreau outlined in his unpublished manuscripts.

19. Brad Dean, ed., in Thoreau, *Faith in a Seed* 228.

20. On March 22, 1961, Thoreau in his *Journal* takes up the quarrel with "a writer in the *Tribune*," who insists that cherry trees must be spontaneously generated; evidently the debate was still lively. See XIV:331-34.

21. See also Richardson, "Thoreau's Broken Task"; Richardson notes Thoreau's "curt dismissal" of Agassiz's special creationism in June 1858, well before Thoreau read Darwin. See *Journal* X:467-68. As Ki-chung Kim noted, "in his time insistence on naturalistic explanations was little short of revolutionary" (129).

22. On Darwin's "plain man" argument, see Cannon, "Darwin's Vision" 162. A modern biologist would hardly phrase Darwin's theory this way, so as a corrective I offer a more standard definition of Darwinian evolution: "adaptive change as the result primarily of natural selection operating over long periods on the small variations present in plant and animal populations" (Bynum et al. 132). Darwin seldom used the word "evolution," preferring the more exact phrase "descent with modification."

23. Beer 80. As Gillian Beer says, this should be understood as "part of a profound imaginative longing shared by a great number of [Darwin's] contemporaries. . . . The palpable, the particular, became not only evidence, but ideal." Conversely, ideas would "find their truest form in substance" (42, 49). For Darwin's Tree of Life metaphor from this perspective, see Beer 93. See also George Levine's discussion of Darwinian metaphor in *Darwin and the Novelists* 109-10.

24. On January 1, 1860, Asa Gray's brother-in-law, Charles Brace, arrived in Concord with a copy of Darwin's *Origin of Species,* and he joined Thoreau and Bronson Alcott for dinner with Frank Sanborn, at which they discussed the book; Thoreau borrowed a copy. See Harding, *Days* 429; Borst 550. In his journal for 1860, Emerson records an interesting exchange with Thoreau: when he told Thoreau of Agassiz's scorn of Darwin, Thoreau replied: "If [Agassiz] sees two thrushes so alike that they bother the ornithologist to discriminate them, he insists they are . . . two species; but if he see Humboldt & Fred. Cogswell, he insists that they come from one ancestor" (JMN 14:350). Cogswell was "'a kindly, under-witted inmate of Concord Almshouse'" (*Journal* IX:270).

25. Howarth, *Book of Concord* 198.

26. Horace Mann, Jr., who accompanied Thoreau on this journey, was already on the rise in what would have been a major career in botany. Tragically, he died seven years later, at twenty-four, of tuberculosis. See Richardson, *Henry David Thoreau* 387.

27. Gould, "Church, Humboldt, and Darwin" 104.

28. Ibid. 104, 106-7.

29. For Thoreau and the history of forest management practices, see Kehr 32-33.

30. Harding lists at least five separate publications or long summaries of it (*Days* 439-40).

31. During a fishing trip in April 1844, Thoreau and Edward Hoar had lit a cooking fire that burned out of control, destroying over three hundred acres; the epithet followed Thoreau for years. See Howarth, *Book of Concord* 34.

32. Harding, *Days* 438.

33. Ibid. 439. The deletions, which are acknowledged, consist of the opening three paragraphs and the closing three paragraphs, with no editing of the body of the text; the ostensible purpose may have been to save space.

34. Howarth, *Book of Concord* 195; Hildebidle 68; Burbick 129-30.

35. Richardson, *Henry David Thoreau* 343-44; CO 423-24.

36. I am borrowing the methodology here from the "strong programme" of SSK, the sociology of scientific knowledge, and the specific terminology from Steve Woolgar, *Science, the Very Idea.* For an outstanding treatment of the rhetoric of science, which deftly joins and separates the discourses of science and literature, see David Locke, *Science as Writing.*

37. Woolgar 71.

38. Ibid. 58-61. For a non-SSK discussion of the rhetoric of discovery, see Pratt 202-4. Another aspect of this argument concerns Thomas Kuhn's concept of the scientific paradigm, which creates the very rules that make scientific facts "seeable," or the mechanism by which, in Thoreau's terms, the scientist makes his discovery by "taking it into his head first." Thoreau's identification of anomalies like the oak seedlings suggests that he is working outside "normal science," and until the paradigm was adjusted to include the anomalies so important to Thoreau, his new fact would seem "not quite a scientific fact at all." Thus part of the urgency of Thoreau's rhetoric is in his desire to persuade the scientist "to see nature in a different way." See Kuhn 52-53; also 64-65.

39. Woolgar 68-69.

40. On this notion of agents, or in Latour's terms "actants," "cooperating" with the investigator, see Latour, *Science in Action,* esp. Chap. 2, "Laboratories" (63-100).

41. David Locke 17.

42. According to Richardson, the probable target here is Louis Agassiz (*Henry David Thoreau* 362).

43. Levine, *Darwin and the Novelists* 212, 214.

44. For another, extended version of the argument that organisms actively produce their environment, see Lewontin, *Biology as Ideology,* particularly the final chapter, "Science as Social Action" (105-23).

45. Woolgar 59-60.

46. Latour, *Science in Action* 93. This would be, I believe, a Thoreauvian reply to the dilemma raised by Walter Benn Michaels, in "*Walden*'s False Bottoms" (420): in a world where interpretation is constantly undercutting its own foundation, where will one find principles for action? Yes, uncertainty is built in everywhere; therefore the one thing that cannot be doubted is the paradox that material reality is utterly independent of us and utterly susceptible to our least decisions. Thoreau rewrites Emerson: We must treat nature as if it were real; perhaps it is.

47. Woolgar 105. Steve Woolgar anticipates this will be the problem for the next generation of the social studies of science, and I would add that it is also currently a problem for interdisciplinary criticism: in its vulnerability, it needs all the more to assert clairvoyance; yet in its ideology, it is all the less able to do so.

Abbreviations

Works by Henry David Thoreau

CC: *Cape Cod*

CO: *Correspondence*

CP: *Collected Poems*

DI: *Dispersion of Seeds* (in *Faith in a Seed*)

EE: *Early Essays*

FB: *Thoreau's Fact Book*

LN: *Thoreau's Literary Notebook*

MW: *Maine Woods*

NHE: *Natural History Essays*

RP: *Reform Papers*

WA: *Walden*

WK: *A Week on the Concord and Merrimack Rivers*

Works by Ralph Waldo Emerson

CW: *Collected Works*

JMN: *Journals and Miscellaneous Notebooks*

David Knight (essay date 1997)

SOURCE: "Thomas Henry Huxley and Philosophy of Science," in *Thomas Henry Huxley's Place in Science and Letters,* edited by Alan P. Barr, University of Georgia Press, 1997, pp. 51-66.

[*In the following essay, Knight appraises Thomas Henry Huxley's influence on the study and popularity of science in the nineteenth century.*]

Huxley was a bold, accessible, and above all controversial writer, at his best defending a friend or attacking an enemy—a David in constant search of Goliaths, if we may use the kind of biblical imagery in which he delighted. Like Aristotle, another keen student of living organisms, Huxley developed his positions in argument with others, living or dead. Unlike Aristotle, he is not much cited in philosophical writings today. Charles Darwin was "Philos" to his shipmates on HMS *Beagle,* and like him and like Michael Faraday, Huxley saw himself as a natural philosopher. The new word "scientist" had been coined in his childhood, by analogy with "artist," but it was not popular in the nineteenth century; it implied narrowness, whereas Huxley and others were determined to develop and promote a worldview, like the ancient Ionians.

We do not, by contrast, find in Darwin or in Faraday much explicit discussion of what we would call philosophy of science; they both had new ways of looking at the world, involving natural selection and fields of force, and had to promote these to win acceptance among the scientific community of their day. But they did not have to explore the nature of scientific thinking and practice itself, in the way that Huxley did in his various conflicts—in which he was at first the outsider challenging the Establishment, like Galileo breaking into the patronage system, and then the champion of underdogs when he had himself rather surprisingly risen to the pinnacle of the scientific world. While interested in, and interesting on, philosophy, Huxley may best be seen not as a philosopher, but as a sage like Carlyle or Ruskin.

Huxley's writing on philosophy of science is thus mostly found in his more popular writings, especially where he described scientific method. This was something that often came up in the context of teaching science in Huxley's generation. It seemed that the method of science might be separated from the mass of detail involved in learning any particular science, and that this method should be of very wide applicability, and hence great educational importance. Huxley's views (like those of most nineteenth-century Britons) were what we might broadly call Baconian: for him, science was an open-minded search for truth, in contrast to dogmatic tradition, especially that represented by the Roman Catholic Church—the great bugbear for John Tyndall and others of Huxley's circle, as well as for British men of science more generally. It is in controversy then, and on education, that we shall meet Huxley philosophizing: but we shall also want to see how far his method is actually exemplified in his research, because he was a practitioner generalizing from his own experience and that of those he admired. His greatest pupil, Michael Foster, wrote that after 1860 Huxley "to a large extent deserted scientific research and forsook the joys which it might bring to himself, in order that he might secure for others that full freedom of inquiry which is the necessary condition for the advance of natural knowledge" (qtd. in Lodge 36). This "full freedom of inquiry," which became for Huxley agnosticism, is thus the first key to his thinking.

Huxley was, like Bacon, particularly good at aphorisms (what we might call soundbites); his widow edited a little book of his "reflections." One announces that, "Agnosticism, in fact, is not a creed but a method." It was not just for intellectuals, but for everyone. Henrietta Huxley reminds us also of the working men, "whose cause my husband so ardently espoused" (*Aphorisms and Reflections* 35, vi). Agnosticism for Huxley was as old as Socrates, and was the basis of science, while science was more a creed to live by than something to philosophize about (see Lightman 14). It would thus empower working men or schoolchildren. It was not, like religions, mysterious; its pursuit did not require an elite priesthood; as common sense, it was democratic and accessible: all of us constantly generalize and reason back to causes. In the natural history sciences common sense seemed a plausible guide, but when Huxley confronted mathematical physicists he found himself out of his depth. We can best examine his philosophy of science by seeing him interact with the ideas of Auguste Comte, René Descartes, David Hume, and A. J. Balfour: and then, because his philosophizing acquired authority from his scientific position, we shall look at his practice—what he did as well as what he said.

Darwin, like others of his generation, had been much impressed by Sir John Herschel's *Preliminary Discourse* of 1830, which set out a sophisticated Baconianism, with examples from the physical sciences. Herschel, the son of a great astronomer, was a most distinguished all-round man of science who had just failed to be elected (as a Reform candidate) President of the Royal Society. One might have expected that Huxley would also have taken up Herschel, but he does not seem to use him much. His references are to John Stuart Mill, whose *System of Logic* (1843) owed much to Herschel, and then back to David Hume. Mill's great adversary was William Whewell, Master of Trinity College, Cambridge (see Fisch; Fisch & Schaffer; Yeo), whose vision of science had strongly Kantian elements. For Whewell, the intuitive leap of reason that meant getting the right end of the stick, the appropriate fundamental idea, different in different sciences, was crucial—any science consisted of facts ordered by theory. Huxley had Kantian interests too, notably in epistemology and ethics, but on science his pronouncements put him squarely in Mill's empiricist camp; thus in 1854 he explained that "Science is not, as many would seem to suppose, a modification of the black art, suited to the tastes of the nineteenth century, and flourishing mainly in consequence of the decay of the Inquisition. Science is, I believe, nothing but *trained and organized common sense,* differing from the latter only as a veteran may differ from a raw recruit" ([*Collected Essays*; hereafter cited as *CE*] 3:45-46). He was opposed to any idea of a hierarchy of sciences, in which physicists would look down indulgently upon those engaged in the less exacting discipline of the more descriptive sciences.

REACTION TO COMTE

In his fascinating new study of Richard Owen, Nicolaas Rupke describes Huxley as a positivist, indeed as one of "the three musketeers of positivism," with Herbert Spencer and G. H. Lewes (Rupke 205). This is surely mistaken, because even in the early 1850s Huxley felt it necessary to distance himself from Auguste Comte, whose *Cours de Philosophie Positive* had begun to appear in 1830. An English version was prepared in 1853 by Harriet Martineau, a friend of Charles Darwin's brother, Erasmus, and positivism became very popular in the nineteenth century. Comte's notion that knowledge, in the race and the individual alike, begins theologically, passes into a metaphysical phase, and then (with time and education) into its final, positive, and scientific stage, was taken up into a kind of scientism. This provoked counterattacks; just as Charles Darwin needed to distance himself from "gutter evolutionists" (see Desmond and Moore), so Huxley kept his agnosticism distinct from vulgar atheism and its connections with immorality, as exemplified in the seamy life of John Chapman of the *Westminster Review* (Haight 81). Huxley had to demonstrate, as he did in his life and in his writing, that agnosticism was the route to truth, responsibility, and respectability. Edward James Mortimer Collins (1827-76), a schoolmaster turned professional writer, in his poem "The Positivists" provides a good clue to the dangers Huxley's reputation faced.

> Life and the Universe show Spontaneity;
> Down with ridiculous notions of Deity!
> Churches and creeds are all lost in the mists;
> Truth must be sought with the Positivists.
>
> Wise are their teachers beyond all comparison,
> Comte, Huxley, Tyndall, Mill, Morley, and Harrison;
> Who will adventure to enter the lists,
> With such a squadron of Positivists?
>
> Social arrangements are awful miscarriages;
> Cause of all crime is our system of marriages;
> Poets with sonnets, and lovers with trysts,
> Kindle the ire of the Positivists.
>
> Husbands and wives should be all one community,
> Exquisite freedom with absolute unity;
> Wedding rings worse are than manacled wrists,—
> Such is the creed of the Positivists.
>
> There was an APE in the days that were earlier;
> Centuries passed and his hair became curlier;
> Centuries more gave a thumb to his wrist,—
> Then he was MAN—and a Positivist.
>
> If you are pious, (mild form of insanity,)
> Bow down and worship the mass of humanity.
> Other religions are buried in mists;
> We're our own gods, say the Positivists.

> (qtd. in Watson 240)

These were not propositions to which Huxley wished to assent, and just as he dissented vigorously from the evolutionary doctrines set out in *Vestiges* (1844), so he attacked Comte; those who think rather like us are often most provoking. In particular, he saw in Comte (as in *Vestiges*) poor science: dogma, inaccuracies, inconsistencies, misinterpretations, and hasty generalizations. As Huxley remarked bluntly: "M. Comte, as his manner is, contradicts himself two pages further on, but that will hardly relieve him from the responsibility of such a paragraph as the above" (*CE* 3:49n). This was with reference to Comte's remark that the biological sciences were concerned with observation rather than experiment (and thus probably ranked below physics); its context was Huxley's urging, in 1854, the educational value of the natural history sciences.

In 1863, in a famous series of lectures to working men, Huxley argued again for the unity of sciences, believing that the man of science thought just as the man of sense would do: and he explicitly referred to Mill the empiricist "those who wish to study fully the doctrines of which I have endeavoured to give some rough-and-ready illustrations" (*CE* 2:363, 376n). There was nothing mysterious in "Baconian philosophy" or scientific method. Everyone could appreciate it, and perhaps join in.

By 1863 Huxley had already emerged as Darwin's bulldog, notably at the British Association for the Advancement of Science in 1860. Defending a wide-ranging theory like evolution by natural selection might seem to involve abandoning inductivism, and Huxley's reputation in science was as a formidable expert, with no time for genial amateurs who might, like Bishop Wilberforce, propose "common sense" ideas at scientific meetings (see Barton). But although he accepted the need for hypotheses in science, Huxley never found Darwin's deductive pattern of thought congenial. His empiricism thus looked to outsiders like positivism, and in 1868 in a lecture in Edinburgh he returned to the task of distancing himself from Comte. Not long before, the Archbishop of York had in the same city identified Huxley's agnostic "New Philosophy" with positivism. Huxley would have none of it: "In so far as my study of what specially characterises the Positive Philosophy has led me, I find therein little or nothing of any scientific value, and a great deal which is as thoroughly antagonistic to the very essence of science as anything in ultramontane Catholicism. In fact, M. Comte's philosophy in practice might be compendiously described as Catholicism minus Christianity" (*CE* 1:156). This statement provoked an outcry, though Comte's "Religion of Humanity" might seem to us to fit this designation rather well. Huxley was pleased with it, and in 1869 set about defending himself against a critic, Richard Congreve, translator of Comte's *Catechism* where the calendar and doctrines of positivism are set out.

Whether against his old adversary Richard Owen the anatomist *(Man's Place)* or later against St. George Mivart (*CE* 2:125-50). Huxley was prepared to absorb his opponents' learning in order to defeat them on their own ground. Now, he picked out Comte's failures to see what was best in the science of his own day: his approval of phrenology (the science of the bumps) and dismissal of psychology, his description of Georges Cuvier as "brilliant but superficial" (*Lay Sermons* 155). Next, he attacked the whole notion of the "three states" as being neither self-consistent nor empirically true; "the positive state has more or less co-existed with the theological, from the dawn of human intelligence" (158). Anyone who had watched a child would know that Comte's schema was false; and the word "positive" was anyway "in every way objectionable" (161n). He believed that the "last and greatest of all speculative problems" was "Does human nature possess any free, volitional, or truly anthropomorphic element, or is it only the cunningest of all Nature's clocks? Some, among whom I count myself, think that the battle will for ever remain a drawn one, and that, for all practical purposes, this result is as good as anthropomorphism winning the day" (164). In short, we shall never reach Comte's positive stage.

Comte's taxonomy of the sciences was also faulty for Huxley, who emphasized unity rather than hierarchy but who also saw how scientific progress inevitably undermines any such arrangement. He pointed to the "dogmatism and narrowness" with which Comte discussed doctrines he disliked, and his "meddling systematization and regulation" (*Lay Sermons* 170). Comte was a prescriptive philosopher of science, laying down rules for good science, whereas Huxley was a man of science hoping to generalize from his experience and that of others to produce a descriptive philosophy based upon excellent practice. Comte, moreover, hoped to found a spiritual power exercising enormous influence over temporal affairs; this, to Huxley, smacked of Roman Catholicism. Whatever Collins may have supposed in writing his poem, Comteans like Congreve and Frederic Harrison in Britain knew that Huxley was not really one of them.

FRANCE AND GERMANY

For over two hundred years, Cartesian dogmatizing had been set against cautious Baconian advance, or plodding, as its critics preferred to see it, and Huxley's remarks about Comte seem to be part of the long-running Anglo-French wars. Again like most of his British contemporaries, Huxley himself was an admirer of Germany, where he saw research and intellectual life given due emphasis. He had found his great hero in Karl von Baer, the embryologist; and whereas Darwinism made rapid headway in Germany (see Kelly), it never did in France. When Huxley was born, Paris had been the world's scientific capital; by 1860 it was so no longer. We can see Huxley's distrust of centralized, dogmatic and now provincial French science in his review of two reviews of the *Origin of Species,* one German (by an opponent Huxley considered worthy of respect) but the other by M. J. P. Flourens, Permanent Secretary of the French Academy of Sciences and an eminent physiologist (see Crosland).

Flourens received the sort of treatment Huxley gave Owen or Wilberforce: "while displaying a painful weakness of logic and shallowness of information," Huxley complained, he "assumes a tone of authority, which always touches upon the ludicrous, and sometimes passes the limits of good breeding" (*CE* 2:98). England was fortunate in being denied the "blessings of an Academy" if it meant dogmatism; and Flourens, "missing the substance and grasping at a shadow[, is] . . . blind to the admirable exposition . . . which Mr Darwin has given." He had "utterly failed to comprehend the first principles of the doctrine which he assails so rudely," and used language so "preposterous" that it simply gave away his ignorance, especially of embryology (104-6). Lucky Britons had never had academies to tell people what to think, like the French under the ancien regime. The Royal Society's motto, "Nullius in verba" [Take nothing on authority], aptly expresses Huxley's deepest convictions: while happy to expound a worldview, he would have been pained at the idea that he was promulgating a paradigm, or dogmatic normal science, which would have been counter to his agnosticism.

Unsympathetic as he was to the vanity of dogmatizing, Huxley was impressed by Descartes. In a talk of 1870 he traced from him two strands (*CE* 1:166-98). One is exemplified in the Critical Idealism of Immanuel Kant, an "idealism which refuses to make any assertions, either positive or negative, as to what lies beyond consciousness" (2:178). The other strand leads towards materialism, and here Huxley has another go at the Roman Catholics: "The Cardinals are at the Ecumenical Council [Vatican 1], still at their old business of trying to stop the movement of the world" (2:180), just as in Galileo's and Descartes's time. Descartes is thus a great precursor, leading "by way of Berkeley and Hume, to Kant and Idealism" and also, "by way of De La Mettrie and Priestley, to modern physiology and Materialism" (2:190). Huxley was happy to go with materialists as far as Descartes's path might lead them. He concluded with a description of the "Extrachristian" world in which he lived "a good deal," trying to distinguish truth from falsehood as Descartes had done (2:195). Huxley hoped that, unlike the Inquisition of the seventeenth century, the Christianity of his time would not seem to future generations to have recognized leading thinkers of the day simply as "objects of vilification."

DAVID HUME AND SKEPTICISM

The doubting Descartes was thus attractive to Huxley, for whom science had to be an agnostic enterprise, but his real philosophical hero was the skeptical empiricist Hume. He even wrote a book about him, which tells us as much about its author as its subject. His excuse for writing, he said, "must be an ineradicable tendency to make things clear" (*CE* 6:51-52). Psychology was Huxley's, and he believed Hume's, route into philosophy. It differed from physical sciences only in its subject matter, and not in its method; and the essential prerequisite to philosophy was the application of scientific method to less abstruse subjects: "The laboratory is the fore-court of the temple of philosophy" (6:61). Huxley's Hume had recognized that philosophy was based on psychology, meaning experiment in moral subjects, and that all science has to start with hypotheses, to be tested and criticized until only the "exact verbal expression remains" and the scaffolding has gone (6:65). "Mitigated skepticism" was his recipe for keeping down dogmatism and superstition alike (6:67-68). Hume's physiological speculations (about animal spirits) Huxley updated as, "The key to the comprehension of mental operations lies in the study of the molecular changes of the nervous apparatus by which they are originated. . . . Operations of the mind are functions of the brain" (6:94). Huxley's favorite science of physiology was thus the basis for psychology and philosophy, and while this might indeed be materialism, Huxley believed it was compatible with the purest idealism.

Huxley explored Hume's account of miracles, deciding that while experience leads us to a firm belief in order, and demands very strong evidence indeed for breaches of it, we could never really say that an event exceeded the power of natural causes (*CE* 6:153-55). This kind of robust thinking goes with the practice of science: blank misgivings about the rule of law would lead to dropping out, which Huxley would never want to do. The book includes challenges to the clergy. Indeed, by his later years, Huxley, the "unconquerable champion and literary swordsman" had become a Goliath rather than a David, though he was never a philistine (Freeman 170). He points out that belief in necessity and determinism is as much a feature of Jonathan Edwards and other orthodox Calvinist divines as of freethinkers like Hume. When Huxley published the book in 1878, Hume was in the news; he had not usually been seen as a canonical philosopher, but there had been an edition of his writings in 1874-75, and T. H. Green of Balliol College had engaged with it in his enterprise of bringing German philosophy to Britain. Huxley brought Hume into the scientific tradition, as a great empiricist rather than just as a paradoxical thinker.

BACON AND BALFOUR

Examining Huxley's philosophy of science in his practice, we begin with his attitude to Darwin's idea of development with modification, through natural selection. Mario di Gregorio explored the differences between Darwin and Huxley: whereas Darwin saw the unifying value of his theory, for Huxley it remained a hypothesis because a change of one species into another, no longer interfertile with it, had not yet been demonstrated. It is striking how in his textbook *The Crayfish,* only the last 10 percent of the book is concerned with its evolutionary history. Its anatomy and physiology, and its use as a "type" of invertebrate in his course, are given prominence; the final section, on its evolution, is presented as though it were an optional extra, for those who wanted to wrestle with such questions. This went well with the Baconian tone of much older textbooks, such as William Nicholson's on chemistry, where he "formed the determination of confining the theory, for the most part, to the ends of chapters" (vii).

Huxley's view that science was organized common sense echoed Davy's earlier statement about applied science (Knight, *Davy* 44). Many physical scientists since Galileo had, however, admired those prepared to defy common sense when experiment and mathematical reasoning indicated that it was right to do so (Banks 77-86). They had

indeed expected that science and common sense would be at odds (see Wolpert). In 1879 A. J. Balfour, later prime minister, president of the British Association for the Advancement of Science, and the man who declared Palestine a homeland for the Jewish people, published *A Defence of Philosophic Doubt.* Through his brother-in-law, Lord Rayleigh, who had followed James Clerk Maxwell as Cavendish Professor of Physics at Cambridge, Balfour was well informed about science. His thesis was that all knowledge rested upon belief (Knight, "Balfour"); and his later philosophical writings, as he became more famous, attracted more attention to this message. The crisis in physics at the turn of the century seemed to support his view that science could not be separated from metaphysical doctrines: beliefs about causation, space and time, matter and energy, changed as classical physics was abandoned. The new beliefs were once again in defiance of common sense.

Balfour's skepticism placed religion and science on the same footing. Following the *via negativa* of Henry Mansel (1859), who had proposed a kind of Christian agnosticism (see Lightman ch. 2), such doubters outraged Huxley for whom Christians' deviations from what he saw as the fully orthodox position seemed an intolerable evasion: "[doubt as] 'the first and most essential step towards being a sound believing Christian,' though adopted and largely acted upon by many a champion of orthodoxy in these days, is questionable in taste, if it is meant as a jest, and more than questionable in morality, if it is to be taken in earnest. To pretend that you believe any doctrine for no better reason than that you doubt everything else, would be dishonest, if it were not preposterous" (*CE* 6:173n). This is rather the tone of one who believes that his clothes have been stolen by the opposition while he had been happily swimming in the ebbing sea of faith.

At the very end of Huxley's life, in 1895, Balfour published his *Foundations of Belief,* with a strong and witty attack upon what he saw as the dogmatic "scientific naturalism" of Huxley and his associates, which left no room for beauty or for morality. Huxley felt that he must reply, writing and revising a review on his deathbed. He wrote a spirited letter (full of contempt for inappropriate authority) to one of his daughters about it: "I think the cavalry charge in this month's *Nineteenth [Century]* will amuse you. The heavy artillery and the bayonets will be brought into play next month. Dean Stanley told me he thought being made a bishop destroyed a man's moral courage. I am inclined to think that the practice of the methods of political leaders destroys their intellect for all serious purposes" (*Life* 2:421). He added in a note to the editor that he was "rather pleased with the thing myself, so it is probably not very good!" He was thus outwardly in excellent form to the end, drawing upon Hume not for a deep skepticism like Balfour's, but for a critical empiricism.

HUXLEY'S METHOD IN PRACTICE

Unlike his French contemporary Claude Bernard, whose *Introduction to the Study of Experimental Medicine* (1865)

MONKEYANA.

AM. I
A
MAN AND
A
BROTHER?

Aᴍ I satyr or man?
Pray tell me who can,
And settle my place in the scale.
A man in ape's shape,
An anthropoid ape,
Or monkey deprived of his tail?

Editorial cartoon appearing in Punch *magazine.*

is a classic work on method, Huxley never wrote anything like a book on philosophy of science. *The Crayfish* was a textbook, where controversy and wit would be inappropriate; and it is in his more popular writings that we find his contentious remarks about science, its power, and its method. *Man's Place in Nature,* where we see serious comparative anatomy attractively presented, is midway between a monograph and a popularization (di Gregorio pt. 2). The idea that we should, to remove all prejudice, imagine ourselves scientific Saturnians, is an amusing way of making the Baconian point that we all have preconceptions or "idols" from whose pervasive influence we must escape. Science in *Man's Place* is indeed presented as superior common sense, in accordance with Huxley's characteristic views. Its subject and its style made it of wide interest; our relationship with the apes, and our common ancestry with them, is an exciting topic about which there were and are different strongly held opinions.

Other publications were more austere. Huxley had written up his researches on marine invertebrates done during his voyage as a surgeon on board HMS *Rattlesnake* in Australian waters. After various delays, which were not Huxley's

fault, they were published in a handsome format but addressed to experts. The plates, engraved rather than lithographed (which would have been cheaper), are delicately and attractively done from drawings by Huxley; all science, but especially natural history, depends on both visual and ordinary language. The work is primarily descriptive: "a scientific classification is, after all, nothing more than a convenient mode of expressing the facts and laws established by the morphologist" (*Oceanic Hydrozoa* 20). Huxley pointed out a "general law of structure" among the Hydrozoa and "extended the generalization" from some to the whole group—an idea others adopted and confirmed (1). In classifying, Huxley had relied heavily on embryology: "the Hydrozoon travels for a certain distance along the same great highway of development as the higher animal, before it turns off to follow the road which leads to its special destination" (2). This did not mean that at this stage Huxley believed in what we call evolution; the book is in fact an excellent example of inductive science, with cautious generalizing following careful observation and wide reading. Making his way in science, he always needed to be very sure of his ground in order to maintain his reputation.

Relationships among groups of animals remained Huxley's concern, especially as he shadowed Owen (Rupke 71). In 1867-68 he explored the relationships between the reptiles and the birds, looking notably at dinosaurs (see Desmond 124-31), because the Pterodactyls were not particularly close to birds. By now, he could begin a Royal Institution lecture with the declaration "Those who hold the doctrine of Evolution (and I am one of them)" ([*The Scientific Memoirs of Thomas Henry Huxley*; hereafter cited as *SM*] 3:303). He demonstrated how the newly discovered fossils *Archaeopteryx,* clearly a bird, and the small dinosaur *Compsognathus longipes,* helped link two groups that most people had considered to be very far apart; lizards and tortoises do not seem very like sparrows or eagles, and dinosaurs had been perceived as creeping like alligators rather than running on their hind legs like rheas.

Thus bold in lectures not only to working men but also to the elite audience at the Royal Institution, he was still the careful inductivist in more formal writings, though by now self-confident. His paper on the classification of birds begins: "The members of the class Aves so nearly approach the Reptilia in all the essential and fundamental points of their structure, that the phrase 'Birds are greatly modified Reptiles' would hardly be an exaggerated expression of the closeness of that resemblance" (*SM* 3:238). Starting with illustrations of their skulls, he draws a family tree for the birds, with the *Ratitae* or struthious birds (the ostrich kind) as a group near the bottom, and considers carefully the geographical distribution of the various families. But in the formal papers there is not the enthusiasm for Darwinian theory that informs the contemporary Royal Institution lecture on the same subject. In his scientific practice, Huxley remained the Baconian inductive reasoner, separating the generalizations from the hypotheses, which were necessarily at the back (or even at the front) of his mind. His kind of science was far from what was going on in physics. He had begun as an explorer, and as an intellectual explorer he continued, if we may adopt a comparison from the new physics gaining momentum as Huxley died.

Thus J. J. Thomson, Rayleigh's successor at Cambridge, distinguished two sorts of scientists, comparing William Crookes's work on cathode rays with his own: "In his investigations he was like an explorer in an unknown country, examining everything that seemed of interest, rather than a traveller wishing to reach some particular place, and regarding the intervening country as something to be rushed through as quickly as possible" (*Recollections* 379). Crookes, a contemporary of Huxley's, described and demonstrated new and strange phenomena; Thomson had a counterintuitive theory of unobservable corpuscles (later called electrons) to test. Crookes's science was not far from Huxley's organized common sense; Thomson's cast of mind was deductive like Darwin's. With the triumphs of physics and of biochemistry, philosophy of science in the twentieth century has generally focused upon the traveler rather than the explorer in these voyages through strange seas of thought, and plumped for a hypothetico-deductive method.

Actually engaged in research, Huxley in his writing and his practice exemplified a view of science and its method that was close to the general view of his day, as propounded by Herschel and Mill. His originality was shown in his science, and not in his philosophy of science. When expressing and defending his general view of the world, he was altogether bolder, and his writings are most alive when he propagates his scientific naturalism.

Thomson's successor, Ernest Rutherford, is alleged to have said that there were two kinds of science, physics and stamp collecting. Our conception of physics as the fundamental science goes back to Huxley's contemporary Hermann Helmholtz (see Cahan), whose trajectory from medicine led him through physiology to physics. Physics became the key to power and influence in the scientific establishment. Huxley, against Helmholtz's friend William Thomson, Lord Kelvin, had stuck out for the autonomy of biology and geology (W. Thomson 6-127); but physicists' defiance of common sense has in the end carried the day, in the tradition of Galileo and Descartes rather than Bacon.

We certainly need Huxleys today to promote a critical and informed understanding of science as an exciting and imaginative activity based on freedom of inquiry. It may be that science has now become the kind of dogmatic system Huxley would have hated and that the time has come again for his Humean (and humane) skeptical empiricism. Mitigated skepticism is probably the right spirit in which laypeople especially should approach science and its claims. Similarly, organized common sense (in the form of public health, for example, or intermediate technology) may be much more valuable for solving humanity's prob-

lems than more high-flying science. Above all, Huxley's stand against inappropriate authority is always worth imitating. His staunch moral commitment is also something we could learn from. For him, science was to improve our lives at all levels. Faraday was portrayed as a saint. Nobody thought Huxley a saint, but in becoming a sage he showed how to move from knowledge to wisdom. Not all sages have practiced what they preached; on the whole, Huxley did.

Works Cited

Balfour, Arthur J. *A Defence of Philosophic Doubt.* London: Macmillan, 1879.

———. *The Foundations of Belief.* 2d ed. London: Longmans Green, 1895.

Banks, Rex E. R., et al., eds. *Sir Joseph Banks: A Global Perspective.* London: Royal Botanic Garden, Kew, 1994.

Barton, Ruth. "An Influential Set of Chaps: The X-Club and Royal Society Politics, 1864-1885." *British Journal for the History of Science* 23 (1990): 53-81.

Cahan, David, ed. *Hermann von Helmholtz and the Foundations of Nineteenth-Century Science.* Berkeley: U of California P, 1993.

Comte, Auguste. *The Catechism of Positive Religion.* 3d ed. Trans. R. Congreve. London: Kegan Paul, Trench, Trubner, 1891.

———. *The Positive Philosophy.* Trans. H. Martineau. London: John Chapman, 1853.

Crosland, Maurice P. *Science Under Control: The French Academy of Sciences, 1795-1914.* Cambridge: Cambridge UP, 1992.

Desmond, Adrian. *Archetypes and Ancestors: Palaeontology in Victorian London, 1850-1875.* Chicago: U of Chicago P, 1984.

Desmond, Adrian, and James Moore. *Darwin.* London: Michael Joseph, 1991.

di Gregorio, Mario A. *T. H. Huxley's Place in Natural Science.* New Haven: Yale UP, 1984.

Fisch, Menachim. *William Whewell, Philosopher of Science.* Oxford: Oxford UP, 1991.

Fisch, Menachim, and Simon Schaffer, eds. *William Whewell: A Composite Portrait.* Oxford: Oxford UP, 1991.

Freeman, Richard B. *Charles Darwin: A Companion.* Folkestone: Dawson, 1978.

Haight, Gordon S. *George Eliot: A Biography.* Oxford: Clarendon Press, 1968.

Herschel, John F. W. *A Preliminary Discourse on the Study of Natural Philosophy.* 1830. Intro. M. Partridge. N.Y.: Johnson, 1966.

Huxley, Leonard. *Life and Letters of Thomas H. Huxley.* 2 vols. N.Y.: Appleton, 1901.

Huxley, Thomas H. *Aphorisms and Reflections*. Ed. Henrietta A. Huxley. London: Macmillan, 1907.

———. *Collected Essays*. 9 vols. 1894. N.Y.: Greenwood Press, 1968.

———. *The Crayfish: An Introduction to the Study of Zoology*. London: Kegan Paul, 1880.

———. *Lay Sermons, Addresses, and Reviews*. 6th ed. London: Macmillan, 1877.

———. *The Oceanic Hydrozoa*. London: Ray Society, 1859.

———. *The Scientific Memoirs of Thomas Henry Huxley*. Ed. Michael Foster and E. Ray Lankester. 4 vols. plus supplement. London: Macmillan, 1898-1903.

Kelly, Alfred. *The Descent of Darwin: The Popularization of Darwinism in Germany, 1860-1914*. Chapel Hill: U of NCP, 1981.

Knight, David. "Arthur James Balfour (1848-1930), Scientism and Scepticism." *Durham University Journal*, 87 (1995): 23-30.

———. *A Companion to the Physical Sciences*. London: Routledge, 1989.

———. *Humphry Davy: Science and Power*. Oxford: Blackwell, 1992.

Lightman, Bernard. *The Origins of Agnosticism: Victorian Unbelief and the Limits of Knowledge*. Baltimore: Johns Hopkins UP, 1987.

Lodge, Oliver, ed. *Huxley Memorial Lectures*. Birmingham, Eng.: Cornish Brothers, 1914.

Mansel, Henry L. *The Limits of Religious Thought*. 4th ed. London: Murray, 1859.

Nicholson, William. *The First Principles of Chemistry*. 3d ed. London: Robinson, 1796.

Owen, Richard. *The Hunterian Lectures in Comparative Anatomy, 1837*. Ed. P. R. Stone. London: Natural History Museum, 1992.

Rupke, Nicolaas A. *Richard Owen: Victorian Naturalist*. New Haven: Yale UP, 1994.

Thomson, Joseph J. *Recollections and Reflections*. London: Nelson, 1936.

Thomson, William. *Popular Lectures and Addresses*. Vol. 2. London: Macmillan, 1894.

Watson, J. Richard, ed. *Everyman's Book of Victorian Verse*. London: Dent, 1982.

Wolpert, Lewis. *The Unnatural Nature of Science*. London: Faber & Faber, 1992.

Yeo, Richard. *Defining Science: William Whewell, Natural Knowledge, and Public Debate in Early Victorian Britain*. Cambridge: Cambridge UP, 1993.

FURTHER READING

Criticism

Berger, Michael. "Henry David Thoreau's Science in *The Dispersion of Seeds*." *Annals of Science*, 53 (1996): 381-97.
> A discussion of *The Dispersion of Seeds* as evidence of Thoreau's pioneering role in the history of ecology.

Cowlishaw, Brian. "'A Warning to the Curious': Victorian Science and the Awful Unconscious in M. R. James's Ghost Stories."*The Victorian Newsletter*, 94 (Fall 1998): 36-42.
> Theorizes that James's stories are representative of Victorian assumptions regarding history, evolution, and human civilization.

Early, Julie English. "Unescorted in Africa: Victorian Women Ethnographers Toiling in the Fields of Sensational Science." *Journal of American Culture*, 18, No. 4 (Winter 1995): 67-75.
> Examines the state of ethnographic study in the late nineteenth-century, focusing on two women travelers of the era, May French Sheldon and Mary Kingsley.

Hardack, Richard. "'Infinitely Repellent Orbs': Visions of the Self in the American Renaissance." *Languages of Visuality: Crossings between Art, Science, Politics, and Literature*, edited by Beate Allert. Detroit: Wayne State University Press, pp. 89-110.
> An analysis of political pantheism in nineteenth-century America, focusing on the works of Emerson and Melville and their respective versions of the self.

Gemme, Paola. "Rewriting the Indian Tale: Science, Politics, and the Evolution of Ann S. Stephens's Indian Romances." *Prospects: An Annual Journal of American Cultural Studies*, 19 (1994): 375-87.
> Attributes the changes in Stephens' representations of Native Americans over time to the concurrently changing scientific discourse on racial difference.

Haack, Susan. "Between Science and Conversationalism." *Philosophy and Literature* 20, No. 2 (October 1996): 455-74.
> Traces the relationship between philosophy, science, and literature.

Henry, Freeman G. "Anti-Darwinism in France: Science and the Myth of Nation." *Nineteenth Century French Studies* 27, No. 3-4 (Spring-Summer 1999): 290-304.

An analysis of the French scientific response and resistance to Darwin's theories.

Myers, William. "Evolution and Progress: Herbert Spencer, Thomas Hardy, and Amartya Sen." *The Presence of Persons: Essays on Literature, Science, and Philosophy in the Nineteenth Century.* Aldershot: Ashgate, 1998, pp. 36-48.

Examines various theories regarding evolutionary progress put forth in Sen's 1992 lecture and situates the discussion within the context of the writings of Herbert Spencer and Thomas Hardy.

Rose, Anita. "Elizabeth Burgoyne Corbett's *New Amazonia*: Gender Equity, Science, Utopia." *English Literature in Transition (1880-1920)* 40, No. 1 (1997): 6-20.

Discussion of the cultural authority enjoyed by scientific discourse in the nineteenth century.

Uno, Hiroko. "'Chemical Conviction': Dickinson, Hitchcock, and the Poetry of Science." *The Emily Dickinson Journal* 7, No. 2 (1998): 95-111.

An essay detailing the impact of Edward Hitchcock's scientific thinking on the writings of Emily Dickinson, focusing on Dickinson's struggle to cope with science's threat to her faith.

Wells, Susan. "Women Write Science: The Case of Hannah Longshore." *College English* 58, No. 2 (February 1996): 176-91.

Explores the writings of nineteenth-century women who practiced medicine, focusing on the writings of Hannah Longshore.

How to Use This Index

The main references

> **Calvino, Italo**
> 1923-1985 .... CLC **5, 8, 11, 22, 33, 39,**
> **73; SSC 3**

list all author entries in the following Gale Literary Criticism series:

BLC = *Black Literature Criticism*
CLC = *Contemporary Literary Criticism*
CLR = *Children's Literature Review*
CMLC = *Classical and Medieval Literature Criticism*
DA = *DISCovering Authors*
DAB = *DISCovering Authors: British*
DAC = *DISCovering Authors: Canadian*
DAM = *DISCovering Authors: Modules*
      DRAM: *Dramatists Module;* **MST:** *Most-Studied Authors Module;*
      MULT: *Multicultural Authors Module;* **NOV:** *Novelists Module;*
      POET: *Poets Module;* **POP:** *Popular Fiction and Genre Authors Module*
DC = *Drama Criticism*
HLC = *Hispanic Literature Criticism*
LC = *Literature Criticism from 1400 to 1800*
NCLC = *Nineteenth-Century Literature Criticism*
NNAL = *Native North American Literature*
PC = *Poetry Criticism*
SSC = *Short Story Criticism*
TCLC = *Twentieth-Century Literary Criticism*
WLC = *World Literature Criticism, 1500 to the Present*

The cross-references

> See also CANR 23; CA 85-88;
> obituary CA116

list all author entries in the following Gale biographical and literary sources:

AAYA = *Authors & Artists for Young Adults*
AITN = *Authors in the News*
BEST = *Bestsellers*
BW = *Black Writers*
CA = *Contemporary Authors*
CAAS = *Contemporary Authors Autobiography Series*
CABS = *Contemporary Authors Bibliographical Series*
CANR = *Contemporary Authors New Revision Series*
CAP = *Contemporary Authors Permanent Series*
CDALB = *Concise Dictionary of American Literary Biography*
CDBLB = *Concise Dictionary of British Literary Biography*
DLB = *Dictionary of Literary Biography*
DLBD = *Dictionary of Literary Biography Documentary Series*
DLBY = *Dictionary of Literary Biography Yearbook*
HW = *Hispanic Writers*
JRDA = *Junior DISCovering Authors*
MAICYA = *Major Authors and Illustrators for Children and Young Adults*
MTCW = *Major 20th-Century Writers*
SAAS = *Something about the Author Autobiography Series*
SATA = *Something about the Author*
YABC = *Yesterday's Authors of Books for Children*

Literary Criticism Series
Cumulative Author Index

Amiel, Henri Frederic 1821-1881 .... **NCLC 4**

Amis, Kingsley (William)
1922-1995 ...... **CLC 1, 2, 3, 5, 8, 13, 40, 44, 129; DA; DAB; DAC; DAM MST, NOV**
See also AITN 2; BRWS 2; CA 9-12R; 150; CANR 8, 28, 54; CDBLB 1945-1960; CN; CP; DA3; DLB 15, 27, 100, 139; DLBY 96; HGG; INT CANR-8; MTCW 1, 2; SFW

Amis, Martin (Louis) 1949- .... **CLC 4, 9, 38, 62, 101**
See also BEST 90:3; BRWS 4; CA 65-68; CANR 8, 27, 54, 73, 95; CN; DA3; DLB 14, 194; INT CANR-27; MTCW 1

Ammons, A(rchie) R(andolph)
1926-2001 ...... **CLC 2, 3, 5, 8, 9, 25, 57, 108; DAM POET; PC 16**
See also AITN 1; CA 9-12R; CANR 6, 36, 51, 73; CP; CSW; DLB 5, 165; MTCW 1, 2

Amo, Tauraatua i
See Adams, Henry (Brooks)

Amory, Thomas 1691(?)-1788 .... **LC 48**

Anand, Mulk Raj 1905- .. **CLC 23, 93; DAM NOV**
See also CA 65-68; CANR 32, 64; CN; MTCW 1, 2; RGSF

Anatol
See Schnitzler, Arthur

Anaximander c. 611B.C.-c. 546B.C. .... **CMLC 22**

Anaya, Rudolfo A(lfonso) 1937- ...... **CLC 23; DAM MULT, NOV; HLC 1**
See also AAYA 20; CA 45-48; CAAS 4; CANR 1, 32, 51; CN; DLB 82, 206; HW 1; MTCW 1, 2; NFS 12

Andersen, Hans Christian
1805-1875 .... **NCLC 7, 79; DA; DAB; DAC; DAM MST, POP; SSC 6; WLC**
See also CLR 6; DA3; MAICYA; RGSF; RGWL; SATA 100; YABC 1

Anderson, C. Farley
See Mencken, H(enry) L(ouis); Nathan, George Jean

Anderson, Jessica (Margaret) Queale
1916- .... **CLC 37**
See also CA 9-12R; CANR 4, 62; CN

Anderson, Jon (Victor) 1940- . **CLC 9; DAM POET**
See also CA 25-28R; CANR 20

Anderson, Lindsay (Gordon)
1923-1994 .... **CLC 20**
See also CA 125; 128; 146; CANR 77

Anderson, Maxwell 1888-1959 .... **TCLC 2; DAM DRAM**
See also CA 105; 152; DLB 7, 228; MTCW 2; RGAL

Anderson, Poul (William)
1926-2001 .... **CLC 15**
See also AAYA 5, 34; CA 1-4R, 181; CAAE 181; CAAS 2; CANR 2, 15, 34, 64; CLR 58; DLB 8; FANT; INT CANR-15; MTCW 1, 2; SATA 90; SATA-Brief 39; SATA-Essay 106; SCFW 2; SFW

Anderson, Robert (Woodruff)
1917- .... **CLC 23; DAM DRAM**
See also AITN 1; CA 21-24R; CANR 32; DLB 7

Anderson, Sherwood 1876-1941 ..... **TCLC 1, 10, 24; DA; DAB; DAC; DAM MST, NOV; SSC 1, 46; WLC**
See also AAYA 30; CA 104; 121; CANR 61; CDALB 1917-1929; DA3; DLB 4, 9, 86; DLBD 1; GLL 2; MTCW 1, 2; NFS 4; RGAL; RGSF; SSFS 4,10,11

Andier, Pierre
See Desnos, Robert

Andouard
See Giraudoux, Jean(-Hippolyte)

Andrade, Carlos Drummond de ..... **CLC 18**
See also Drummond de Andrade, Carlos

Andrade, Mário de 1893-1945 .... **TCLC 43**

Andreae, Johann V(alentin)
1586-1654 .... **LC 32**
See also DLB 164

Andreas-Salome, Lou 1861-1937 ... **TCLC 56**
See also CA 178; DLB 66

Andress, Lesley
See Sanders, Lawrence

Andrewes, Lancelot 1555-1626 .... **LC 5**
See also DLB 151, 172

Andrews, Cicily Fairfield
See West, Rebecca

Andrews, Elton V.
See Pohl, Frederik

Andreyev, Leonid (Nikolaevich)
1871-1919 .... **TCLC 3**
See also CA 104; 185

Andrić, Ivo 1892-1975 .... **CLC 8; SSC 36**
See also CA 81-84; 57-60; CANR 43, 60; DLB 147; MTCW 1

Androvar
See Prado (Calvo), Pedro

Angelique, Pierre
See Bataille, Georges

Angell, Roger 1920- .... **CLC 26**
See also CA 57-60; CANR 13, 44, 70; DLB 171, 185

Angelou, Maya 1928- ... **CLC 12, 35, 64, 77; BLC 1; DA; DAB; DAC; DAM MST, MULT, POET, POP; PC 32; WLCS**
See also AAYA 7, 20; AMWS 4; BW 2, 3; CA 65-68; CANR 19, 42, 65; CDALBS; CLR 53; CP; CPW; CSW; CWP; DA3; DLB 38; MTCW 1, 2; NCFS 2; NFS 2; PFS 2, 3; RGAL; SATA 49; YAW

Anna Comnena 1083-1153 .... **CMLC 25**

Annensky, Innokenty (Fyodorovich)
1856-1909 .... **TCLC 14**
See also CA 110; 155

Annunzio, Gabriele d'
See D'Annunzio, Gabriele

Anodos
See Coleridge, Mary E(lizabeth)

Anon, Charles Robert
See Pessoa, Fernando (Ant

Anouilh, Jean (Marie Lucien Pierre)
1910-1987 .... **CLC 1, 3, 8, 13, 40, 50; DAM DRAM; DC 8**
See also CA 17-20R; 123; CANR 32; DFS 9, 10; EW; GFL 1789 to the Present; MTCW 1, 2; RGWL

Anthony, Florence
See Ai

Anthony, John
See Ciardi, John (Anthony)

Anthony, Peter
See Shaffer, Anthony (Joshua); Shaffer, Peter (Levin)

Anthony, Piers 1934- .... **CLC 35; DAM POP**
See also AAYA 11; CA 21-24R; CANR 28, 56, 73; CPW; DLB 8; FANT; MTCW 1, 2; SAAS 22; SATA 84; SFW; YAW

Anthony, Susan B(rownell)
1820-1906 .... **TCLC 84**
See also FW

Antoine, Marc
See Proust, (Valentin-Louis-George-Eug

Antoninus, Brother
See Everson, William (Oliver)

Antoninus, Marcus Aurelius
121-180 .... **CMLC 45**

Antonioni, Michelangelo 1912- .... **CLC 20, 144**
See also CA 73-76; CANR 45, 77

Antschel, Paul 1920-1970
See Celan, Paul
See also CA 85-88; CANR 33, 61; MTCW 1

Anwar, Chairil 1922-1949 .... **TCLC 22**
See also CA 121

Anzaldúa, Gloria (Evanjelina) 1942-
See also CA 175; CSW; CWP; DLB 122; FW; HLCS 1

Apess, William 1798-1839(?) .... **NCLC 73; DAM MULT**
See also DLB 175; NNAL

Apollinaire, Guillaume 1880-1918 .. **TCLC 3, 8, 51; DAM POET; PC 7**
See also CA 152; GFL 1789 to the Present; MTCW 1; RGWL; WP

Appelfeld, Aharon 1932- ... **CLC 23, 47; SSC 42**
See also CA 112; 133; CANR 86; CWW 2; RGSF

Apple, Max (Isaac) 1941- .... **CLC 9, 33**
See also CA 81-84; CANR 19, 54; DLB 130

Appleman, Philip (Dean) 1926- .... **CLC 51**
See also CA 13-16R; CAAS 18; CANR 6, 29, 56

Appleton, Lawrence
See Lovecraft, H(oward) P(hillips)

Apteryx
See Eliot, T(homas) S(tearns)

Apuleius, (Lucius Madaurensis)
125(?)-175(?) .... **CMLC 1**
See also DLB 211

Aquin, Hubert 1929-1977 .... **CLC 15**
See also CA 105; DLB 53

Aquinas, Thomas 1224(?)-1274 ..... **CMLC 33**
See also DLB 115

Aragon, Louis 1897-1982 .. **CLC 3, 22; DAM NOV, POET**
See also CA 69-72; 108; CANR 28, 71; DLB 72; GFL 1789 to the Present; GLL 2; MTCW 1, 2; RGWL

Arany, Janos 1817-1882 .... **NCLC 34**

Aranyos, Kakay 1847-1910
See Mikszath, Kalman

Arbuthnot, John 1667-1735 .... **LC 1**
See also DLB 101

Archer, Herbert Winslow
See Mencken, H(enry) L(ouis)

Archer, Jeffrey (Howard) 1940- ...... **CLC 28; DAM POP**
See also AAYA 16; BEST 89:3; CA 77-80; CANR 22, 52, 95; CPW; DA3; INT CANR-22

Archer, Jules 1915- .... **CLC 12**
See also CA 9-12R; CANR 6, 69; SAAS 5; SATA 4, 85

Archer, Lee
See Ellison, Harlan (Jay)

Archilochus c. 7th cent. B.C.- .... **CMLC 44**
See also DLB 176

Arden, John 1930- .... **CLC 6, 13, 15; DAM DRAM**
See also BRWS 2; CA 13-16R; CAAS 4; CANR 31, 65, 67; CBD; CD; DFS 9; DLB 13; MTCW 1

Arenas, Reinaldo 1943-1990 . **CLC 41; DAM MULT; HLC 1**
See also CA 124; 128; 133; CANR 73; DLB 145; GLL 2; HW 1; MTCW 1; RGSF

Arendt, Hannah 1906-1975 .... **CLC 66, 98**
See also CA 17-20R; 61-64; CANR 26, 60; DLB 242; MTCW 1, 2

Aretino, Pietro 1492-1556 .... **LC 12**
See also RGWL

Arghezi, Tudor .... **CLC 80**
See also Theodorescu, Ion N.
See also CA 167; DLB 220

Blixen, Karen (Christentze Dinesen)
1885-1962
See Dinesen, Isak
See also CA 25-28; CANR 22, 50; CAP 2;
DA3; MTCW 1, 2; NCFS 2; SATA 44

Bloch, Robert (Albert) 1917-1994 .... **CLC 33**
See also AAYA 29; CA 5-8R, 179; 146;
CAAE 179; CAAS 20; CANR 5, 78;
DA3; DLB 44; HGG; INT CANR-5;
MTCW 1; SATA 12; SATA-Obit 82; SFW

Blok, Alexander (Alexandrovich)
1880-1921 .... **TCLC 5; PC 21**
See also CA 104; 183

Blom, Jan
See Breytenbach, Breyten

Bloom, Harold 1930- .... **CLC 24, 103**
See also CA 13-16R; CANR 39, 75, 92;
DLB 67; MTCW 1; RGAL

Bloomfield, Aurelius
See Bourne, Randolph S(illiman)

Blount, Roy (Alton), Jr. 1941- .... **CLC 38**
See also CA 53-56; CANR 10, 28, 61;
CSW; INT CANR-28; MTCW 1, 2

Bloy, Léon 1846-1917 .... **TCLC 22**
See also CA 121; 183; DLB 123; GFL 1789
to the Present

Blume, Judy (Sussman) 1938- .. **CLC 12, 30;**
DAM NOV, POP
See also AAYA 3, 26; CA 29-32R; CANR
13, 37, 66; CLR 2, 15, 69; CPW; DA3;
DLB 52; JRDA; MAICYA; MTCW 1, 2;
SATA 2, 31, 79; YAW

Blunden, Edmund (Charles)
1896-1974 .... **CLC 2, 56**
See also CA 17-18; 45-48; CANR 54; CAP
2; DLB 20, 100, 155; MTCW 1

Bly, Robert (Elwood) 1926- .... **CLC 1, 2, 5,**
10, 15, 38, 128; DAM POET
See also AMWS 4; CA 5-8R; CANR 41,
73; CP; DA3; DLB 5; MTCW 1, 2

Boas, Franz 1858-1942 .... **TCLC 56**
See also CA 115; 181

Bobette
See Simenon, Georges (Jacques Christian)

Boccaccio, Giovanni 1313-1375 ... **CMLC 13;**
SSC 10
See also RGSF; RGWL

Bochco, Steven 1943- .... **CLC 35**
See also CA 124; 138

Bodel, Jean 1167(?)-1210 .... **CMLC 28**

Bodenheim, Maxwell 1892-1954 .... **TCLC 44**
See also CA 110; 187; DLB 9, 45; RGAL

Bodker, Cecil 1927- .... **CLC 21**
See also CA 73-76; CANR 13, 44; CLR 23;
MAICYA; SATA 14

Boell, Heinrich (Theodor)
1917-1985 ..... **CLC 2, 3, 6, 9, 11, 15, 27,**
32, 72; DA; DAB; DAC; DAM MST,
NOV; SSC 23; WLC
See also Böll, Heinrich
See also CA 21-24R; 116; CANR 24; DA3;
DLB 69; DLBY 85; MTCW 1, 2

Boerne, Alfred
See Doeblin, Alfred

Boethius 480(?)-(?) .... **CMLC 15**
See also DLB 115; RGEL

Boff, Leonardo (Genezio Darci)
1938- .... **CLC 70; DAM MULT; HLC 1**
See also CA 150; HW 2

Bogan, Louise 1897-1970 .... **CLC 4, 39, 46,**
93; DAM POET; PC 12
See also AMWS 3; CA 73-76; 25-28R;
CANR 33, 82; DLB 45, 169; MTCW 1,
2; RGAL

Bogarde, Dirk
See Van Den Bogarde, Derek Jules Gaspard
Ulric Niven

Bogosian, Eric 1953- .... **CLC 45, 141**
See also CA 138; CAD; CD

Bograd, Larry 1953- .... **CLC 35**
See also CA 93-96; CANR 57; SAAS 21;
SATA 33, 89

Boiardo, Matteo Maria 1441-1494 .... **LC 6**

Boileau-Despréaux, Nicolas 1636-1711 . **LC 3**
See also GFL Beginnings to 1789; RGWL

Bojer, Johan 1872-1959 .... **TCLC 64**
See also CA 189

Bok, Edward W. 1863-1930 .... **TCLC 101**
See also DLB 91; DLBD 16

Boland, Eavan (Aisling) 1944- .. **CLC 40, 67,**
113; DAM POET
See also BRWS 5; CA 143; CANR 61; CP;
CWP; DLB 40; FW; MTCW 2; PFS 12

Böll, Heinrich
See Boell, Heinrich (Theodor)
See also RGSF; RGWL

Bolt, Lee
See Faust, Frederick (Schiller)

Bolt, Robert (Oxton) 1924-1995 ...... **CLC 14;**
DAM DRAM
See also CA 17-20R; 147; CANR 35, 67;
CBD; DFS 2; DLB 13, 233; MTCW 1

Bombal, María Luisa 1910-1980 ...... **SSC 37;**
HLCS 1
See also CA 127; CANR 72; HW 1

Bombet, Louis-Alexandre-Cesar
See Stendhal

Bomkauf
See Kaufman, Bob (Garnell)

Bonaventura .... **NCLC 35**
See also DLB 90

Bond, Edward 1934- .... **CLC 4, 6, 13, 23;**
DAM DRAM
See also BRWS 1; CA 25-28R; CANR 38,
67; CBD; CD; DFS 3,8; DLB 13; MTCW
1

Bonham, Frank 1914-1989 .... **CLC 12**
See also AAYA 1; CA 9-12R; CANR 4, 36;
JRDA; MAICYA; SAAS 3; SATA 1, 49;
SATA-Obit 62; TCWW 2; YAW

Bonnefoy, Yves 1923- .. **CLC 9, 15, 58; DAM**
MST, POET
See also CA 85-88; CANR 33, 75, 97;
CWW 2; GFL 1789 to the Present; MTCW
1, 2

Bontemps, Arna(ud Wendell)
1902-1973 ..... **CLC 1, 18; BLC 1; DAM**
MULT, NOV, POET
See also BW 1; CA 1-4R; 41-44R; CANR
4, 35; CLR 6; CWRI; DA3; DLB 48, 51;
JRDA; MAICYA; MTCW 1, 2; SATA 2,
44; SATA-Obit 24

Booth, Martin 1944- .... **CLC 13**
See also CA 93-96; CAAE 188; CAAS 2;
CANR 92

Booth, Philip 1925- .... **CLC 23**
See also CA 5-8R; CANR 5, 88; CP; DLBY
82

Booth, Wayne C(layson) 1921- .... **CLC 24**
See also CA 1-4R; CAAS 5; CANR 3, 43;
DLB 67

Borchert, Wolfgang 1921-1947 .... **TCLC 5**
See also CA 104; 188; DLB 69, 124

Borel, Pétrus 1809-1859 .... **NCLC 41**
See also GFL 1789 to the Present

Borges, Jorge Luis 1899-1986 ... **CLC 1, 2, 3,**
4, 6, 8, 9, 10, 13, 19, 44, 48, 83; DA;
DAB; DAC; DAM MST, MULT; HLC
1; PC 22, 32; SSC 4, 41; WLC
See also AAYA 26; CA 21-24R; CANR 19,
33, 75; DA3; DLB 113; DLBY 86; DNFS
1,2; HW 1, 2; MTCW 1, 2; RGSF;
RGWL; SFW; SSFS 4,9; TCLC 109

Borowski, Tadeusz 1922-1951 .... **TCLC 9**
See also CA 106; 154; RGSF

Borrow, George (Henry)
1803-1881 .... **NCLC 9**
See also DLB 21, 55, 166

Bosch (Gavino), Juan 1909-
See also CA 151; DAM MST, MULT; DLB
145; HLCS 1; HW 1, 2

Bosman, Herman Charles
1905-1951 .... **TCLC 49**
See also Malan, Herman
See also CA 160; DLB 225; RGSF

Bosschere, Jean de 1878(?)-1953 ... **TCLC 19**
See also CA 115; 186

Boswell, James 1740-1795 ...... **LC 4, 50; DA;**
DAB; DAC; DAM MST; WLC
See also CDBLB 1660-1789; DLB 104, 142

Bottomley, Gordon 1874-1948 ..... **TCLC 107**
See also CA 120; DLB 10

Bottoms, David 1949- .... **CLC 53**
See also CA 105; CANR 22; CSW; DLB
120; DLBY 83

Boucicault, Dion 1820-1890 .... **NCLC 41**

Boucolon, Maryse
See Cond

Bourget, Paul (Charles Joseph)
1852-1935 .... **TCLC 12**
See also CA 107; DLB 123; GFL 1789 to
the Present

Bourjaily, Vance (Nye) 1922- .... **CLC 8, 62**
See also CA 1-4R; CAAS 1; CANR 2, 72;
CN; DLB 2, 143

Bourne, Randolph S(illiman)
1886-1918 .... **TCLC 16**
See also Aurelius
See also CA 117; 155; DLB 63

Bova, Ben(jamin William) 1932- ...... **CLC 45**
See also AAYA 16; CA 5-8R; CAAS 18;
CANR 11, 56, 94; CLR 3; DLBY 81; INT
CANR-11; MAICYA; MTCW 1; SATA 6,
68; SFW

Bowen, Elizabeth (Dorothea Cole)
1899-1973 . **CLC 1, 3, 6, 11, 15, 22, 118;**
DAM NOV; SSC 3, 28
See also BRWS 2; CA 17-18; 41-44R;
CANR 35; CAP 2; CDBLB 1945-1960;
DA3; DLB 15, 162; FW; HGG; MTCW
1, 2; SSFS 5

Bowering, George 1935- .... **CLC 15, 47**
See also CA 21-24R; CAAS 16; CANR 10;
DLB 53

Bowering, Marilyn R(uthe) 1949- .... **CLC 32**
See also CA 101; CANR 49; CP; CWP

Bowers, Edgar 1924-2000 .... **CLC 9**
See also CA 5-8R; 188; CANR 24; CP;
CSW; DLB 5

Bowie, David .... **CLC 17**
See also Jones, David Robert

Bowles, Jane (Sydney) 1917-1973 ..... **CLC 3,**
68
See also CA 19-20; 41-44R; CAP 2

Bowles, Paul (Frederick) 1910-1999 . **CLC 1,**
2, 19, 53; SSC 3
See also AMWS 4; CA 1-4R; 186; CAAS
1; CANR 1, 19, 50, 75; CN; DA3; DLB
5, 6; MTCW 1, 2

Box, Edgar
See Vidal, Gore
See also GLL 1

Boyd, Nancy
See Millay, Edna St. Vincent
See also GLL 1

Boyd, Thomas (Alexander)
1898-1935 .... **TCLC 111**
See also CA 111; 183; DLB 9; DLBD 16

Boyd, William 1952- .... **CLC 28, 53, 70**
See also CA 114; 120; CANR 51, 71; CN;
DLB 231

Boyle, Kay 1902-1992 .... **CLC 1, 5, 19, 58,**
121; SSC 5
See also CA 13-16R; 140; CAAS 1; CANR
29, 61; DLB 4, 9, 48, 86; DLBY 93;
MTCW 1, 2; RGAL; RGSF; SSFS 10

Bullins, Ed 1935- .... **CLC 1, 5, 7; BLC 1; DAM DRAM, MULT; DC 6**
See also BW 2, 3; CA 49-52; CAAS 16; CAD; CANR 24, 46, 73; CD; DLB 7, 38; MTCW 1, 2; RGAL

Bulwer-Lytton, Edward (George Earle Lytton) 1803-1873 .... **NCLC 1, 45**
See also DLB 21; SFW

Bunin, Ivan Alexeyevich 1870-1953 .... **TCLC 6; SSC 5**
See also CA 104

Bunting, Basil 1900-1985 ..... **CLC 10, 39, 47; DAM POET**
See also CA 53-56; 115; CANR 7; DLB 20; RGEL

Bunuel, Luis 1900-1983 .. **CLC 16, 80; DAM MULT; HLC 1**
See also CA 101; 110; CANR 32, 77; HW 1

Bunyan, John 1628-1688 ... **LC 4; DA; DAB; DAC; DAM MST; WLC**
See also CDBLB 1660-1789; DLB 39; RGEL

Buravsky, Alexandr .... **CLC 59**

Burckhardt, Jacob (Christoph) 1818-1897 .... **NCLC 49**

Burford, Eleanor
See Hibbert, Eleanor Alice Burford

Burgess, Anthony . **CLC 1, 2, 4, 5, 8, 10, 13, 15, 22, 40, 62, 81, 94; DAB**
See also Wilson, John (Anthony) Burgess
See also AAYA 25; AITN 1; BRWS 1; CD-BLB 1960 to Present; DLB 14, 194; DLBY 98; MTCW 1; RGEL; RHW; SFW; YAW

Burke, Edmund 1729(?)-1797 .... **LC 7, 36; DA; DAB; DAC; DAM MST; WLC**
See also DA3; DLB 104; RGEL

Burke, Kenneth (Duva) 1897-1993 ... **CLC 2, 24**
See also CA 5-8R; 143; CANR 39, 74; DLB 45, 63; MTCW 1, 2

Burke, Leda
See Garnett, David

Burke, Ralph
See Silverberg, Robert

Burke, Thomas 1886-1945 .... **TCLC 63**
See also CA 113; 155; CMW; DLB 197

Burney, Fanny 1752-1840 .... **NCLC 12, 54**
See also BRWS 3; DLB 39; RGEL

Burney, Frances
See Burney, Fanny

Burns, Robert 1759-1796 . **LC 3, 29, 40; DA; DAB; DAC; DAM MST, POET; PC 6; WLC**
See also CDBLB 1789-1832; DA3; DLB 109; RGEL

Burns, Tex
See L'Amour, Louis (Dearborn)
See also TCWW 2

Burnshaw, Stanley 1906- .... **CLC 3, 13, 44**
See also CA 9-12R; CP; DLB 48; DLBY 97

Burr, Anne 1937- .... **CLC 6**
See also CA 25-28R

Burroughs, Edgar Rice 1875-1950 . **TCLC 2, 32; DAM NOV**
See also AAYA 11; CA 104; 132; DA3; DLB 8; FANT; MTCW 1, 2; RGAL; SATA 41; SFW; YAW

Burroughs, William S(eward) 1914-1997 .. **CLC 1, 2, 5, 15, 22, 42, 75, 109; DA; DAB; DAC; DAM MST, NOV, POP; WLC**
See also Lee, William; Lee, Willy
See also AITN 2; AMWS 3; CA 9-12R; 160; CANR 20, 52; CN; CPW; DA3; DLB 2, 8, 16, 152; DLBY 81, 97; HGG; MTCW 1, 2; SFW

Burton, SirRichard F(rancis) 1821-1890 .... **NCLC 42**
See also DLB 55, 166, 184

Busch, Frederick 1941- .... **CLC 7, 10, 18, 47**
See also CA 33-36R; CAAS 1; CANR 45, 73, 92; CN; DLB 6

Bush, Ronald 1946- .... **CLC 34**
See also CA 136

Bustos, F(rancisco)
See Borges, Jorge Luis

Bustos Domecq, H(onorio)
See Bioy Casares, Adolfo; Borges, Jorge Luis

Butler, Octavia E(stelle) 1947- .... **CLC 38, 121; BLCS; DAM MULT, POP**
See also AAYA 18; AFAW 2; BW 2, 3; CA 73-76; CANR 12, 24, 38, 73; CLR 65; CPW; DA3; DLB 33; MTCW 1, 2; NFS 8; SATA 84; SFW; SSFS 6; YAW

Butler, Robert Olen, (Jr.) 1945- ...... **CLC 81; DAM POP**
See also CA 112; CANR 66; CSW; DLB 173; INT 112; MTCW 1; SSFS 11

Butler, Samuel 1612-1680 .... **LC 16, 43**
See also DLB 101, 126

Butler, Samuel 1835-1902 . **TCLC 1, 33; DA; DAB; DAC; DAM MST, NOV; WLC**
See also BRWS 2; CA 143; CDBLB 1890-1914; DA3; DLB 18, 57, 174; SFW

Butler, Walter C.
See Faust, Frederick (Schiller)

Butor, Michel (Marie François) 1926- .... **CLC 1, 3, 8, 11, 15**
See also CA 9-12R; CANR 33, 66; DLB 83; EW; GFL 1789 to the Present; MTCW 1, 2

Butts, Mary 1890(?)-1937 .... **TCLC 77**
See also CA 148

Buzo, Alexander (John) 1944- .... **CLC 61**
See also CA 97-100; CANR 17, 39, 69; CD

Buzzati, Dino 1906-1972 .... **CLC 36**
See also CA 160; 33-36R; DLB 177; RGWL; SFW

Byars, Betsy (Cromer) 1928- .... **CLC 35**
See also AAYA 19; CA 33-36R, 183; CAAE 183; CANR 18, 36, 57; CLR 1, 16; DLB 52; INT CANR-18; JRDA; MAICYA; MTCW 1; SAAS 1; SATA 4, 46, 80; SATA-Essay 108; YAW

Byatt, A(ntonia) S(usan Drabble) 1936- ...... **CLC 19, 65, 136; DAM NOV, POP**
See also BRWS 4; CA 13-16R; CANR 13, 33, 50, 75, 96; DA3; DLB 14, 194; MTCW 1, 2; RHW

Byrne, David 1952- .... **CLC 26**
See also CA 127

Byrne, John Keyes 1926-
See Leonard, Hugh
See also CA 102; CANR 78; CD; DFS 13; INT 102

Byron, George Gordon (Noel) 1788-1824 .... **NCLC 2, 12; DA; DAB; DAC; DAM MST, POET; PC 16; WLC**
See also Lord Byron
See also CDBLB 1789-1832; DA3; DLB 96, 110; PFS 1

Byron, Robert 1905-1941 .... **TCLC 67**
See also CA 160; DLB 195

C. 3. 3.
See Wilde, Oscar (Fingal O'Flahertie Wills)

Caballero, Fernan 1796-1877 .... **NCLC 10**

Cabell, Branch
See Cabell, James Branch

Cabell, James Branch 1879-1958 .... **TCLC 6**
See also CA 105; 152; DLB 9, 78; FANT; MTCW 1; RGAL

Cabeza de Vaca, Alvar Nunez 1490-1557(?) .... **LC 61**

Cable, George Washington 1844-1925 .... **TCLC 4; SSC 4**
See also CA 104; 155; DLB 12, 74; DLBD 13; RGAL

Cabral de Melo Neto, João 1920-1999 .... **CLC 76; DAM MULT**
See also CA 151

Cabrera Infante, G(uillermo) 1929- . **CLC 5, 25, 45, 120; DAM MULT; HLC 1; SSC 39**
See also CA 85-88; CANR 29, 65; DA3; DLB 113; HW 1, 2; MTCW 1, 2

Cade, Toni
See Bambara, Toni Cade

Cadmus and Harmonia
See Buchan, John

Caedmon fl. 658-680 .... **CMLC 7**
See also DLB 146

Caeiro, Alberto
See Pessoa, Fernando (Ant

Cage, John (Milton, Jr.) 1912-1992 . **CLC 41**
See also CA 13-16R; 169; CANR 9, 78; DLB 193; INT CANR-9

Cahan, Abraham 1860-1951 .... **TCLC 71**
See also CA 108; 154; DLB 9, 25, 28; RGAL

Cain, G.
See Cabrera Infante, G(uillermo)

Cain, Guillermo
See Cabrera Infante, G(uillermo)

Cain, James M(allahan) 1892-1977 .. **CLC 3, 11, 28**
See also AITN 1; CA 17-20R; 73-76; CANR 8, 34, 61; CMW; DLB 226; MTCW 1

Caine, Hall 1853-1931 .... **TCLC 97**
See also RHW

Caine, Mark
See Raphael, Frederic (Michael)

Calasso, Roberto 1941- .... **CLC 81**
See also CA 143; CANR 89

Calderón de la Barca, Pedro 1600-1681 .... **LC 23; DC 3; HLCS 1**

Caldwell, Erskine (Preston) 1903-1987 .. **CLC 1, 8, 14, 50, 60; DAM NOV; SSC 19**
See also AITN 1; CA 1-4R; 121; CAAS 1; CANR 2, 33; DA3; DLB 9, 86; MTCW 1, 2

Caldwell, (Janet Miriam) Taylor (Holland) 1900-1985 .. **CLC 2, 28, 39; DAM NOV, POP**
See also CA 5-8R; 116; CANR 5; DA3; DLBD 17; RHW

Calhoun, John Caldwell 1782-1850 .... **NCLC 15**
See also DLB 3

Calisher, Hortense 1911- ..... **CLC 2, 4, 8, 38, 134; DAM NOV; SSC 15**
See also CA 1-4R; CANR 1, 22, 67; CN; DA3; DLB 2; INT CANR-22; MTCW 1, 2; RGAL; RGSF

Callaghan, Morley Edward 1903-1990 ...... **CLC 3, 14, 41, 65; DAC; DAM MST**
See also CA 9-12R; 132; CANR 33, 73; DLB 68; MTCW 1, 2

Callimachus c. 305B.C.- .... **CMLC 18**
See also DLB 176; RGEL

Calvin, Jean
See Calvin, John
See also GFL Beginnings to 1789

Calvin, John 1509-1564 .... **LC 37**
See also Calvin, Jean

Cassiodorus, Flavius Magnus c. 490(?)-c. 583(?) .... **CMLC 43**

Cassirer, Ernst 1874-1945 .... **TCLC 61**
See also CA 157

Cassity, (Allen) Turner 1929- .... **CLC 6, 42**
See also CA 17-20R; CAAS 8; CANR 11; CSW; DLB 105

Castaneda, Carlos (Cesar Aranha) 1931(?)-1998 .... **CLC 12, 119**
See also CA 25-28R; CANR 32, 66; HW 1; MTCW 1

Castedo, Elena 1937- .... **CLC 65**
See also CA 132

Castedo-Ellerman, Elena
See Castedo, Elena

Castellanos, Rosario 1925-1974 .... **CLC 66; DAM MULT; HLC 1; SSC 39**
See also CA 131; 53-56; CANR 58; DLB 113; FW; HW 1; MTCW 1; RGSF; RGWL

Castelvetro, Lodovico 1505-1571 .... **LC 12**

Castiglione, Baldassare 1478-1529 .... **LC 12**

Castiglione, Baldesar
See Castiglione, Baldassare

Castle, Robert
See Hamilton, Edmond

Castro (Ruz), Fidel 1926(?)-
See also CA 110; 129; CANR 81; DAM MULT; HLC 1; HW 2

Castro, Guillen de 1569-1631 .... **LC 19**

Castro, Rosalia de 1837-1885 ... **NCLC 3, 78; DAM MULT**

Cather, Willa
See Cather, Willa Sibert
See also NFS 2; RGAL; RGSF; RHW; TCWW 2

Cather, Willa Sibert 1873-1947 ...... **TCLC 1, 11, 31, 99; DA; DAB; DAC; DAM MST, NOV; SSC 2; WLC**
See also Cather, Willa
See also AAYA 24; CA 104; 128; CDALB 1865-1917; DA3; DLB 9, 54, 78; DLBD 1; MTCW 1, 2; SATA 30; SSFS 2,7

Catherine, Saint 1347-1380 .... **CMLC 27**

Cato, Marcus Porcius 234B.C.-149B.C. .... **CMLC 21**
See also DLB 211

Catton, (Charles) Bruce 1899-1978 . **CLC 35**
See also AITN 1; CA 5-8R; 81-84; CANR 7, 74; DLB 17; SATA 2; SATA-Obit 24

Catullus c. 84B.C.- .... **CMLC 18**
See also DLB 211; RGEL

Cauldwell, Frank
See King, Francis (Henry)

Caunitz, William J. 1933-1996 .... **CLC 34**
See also BEST 89:3; CA 125; 130; 152; CANR 73; INT 130

Causley, Charles (Stanley) 1917- .... **CLC 7**
See also CA 9-12R; CANR 5, 35, 94; CLR 30; CWRI; DLB 27; MTCW 1; SATA 3, 66

Caute, (John) David 1936- .... **CLC 29; DAM NOV**
See also CA 1-4R; CAAS 4; CANR 1, 33, 64; CBD; CD; CN; DLB 14, 231

Cavafy, C(onstantine) P(eter) ... **TCLC 2, 7; DAM POET**
See also Kavafis, Konstantinos Petrou
See also CA 148; DA3; MTCW 1

Cavallo, Evelyn
See Spark, Muriel (Sarah)

Cavanna, Betty .... **CLC 12**
See also Harrison, Elizabeth Cavanna
See also JRDA; MAICYA; SAAS 4; SATA 1, 30

Cavendish, Margaret Lucas 1623-1673 .... **LC 30**
See also DLB 131

Caxton, William 1421(?)-1491(?) .... **LC 17**
See also DLB 170

Cayer, D. M.
See Duffy, Maureen

Cayrol, Jean 1911- .... **CLC 11**
See also CA 89-92; DLB 83

Cela, Camilo José 1916- .... **CLC 4, 13, 59, 122; DAM MULT; HLC 1**
See also BEST 90:2; CA 21-24R; CAAS 10; CANR 21, 32, 76; DLBY 89; HW 1; MTCW 1, 2

Celan, Paul .... **CLC 10, 19, 53, 82; PC 10**
See also Antschel, Paul
See also DLB 69; RGWL

Céline, Louis-Ferdinand .. **CLC 1, 3, 4, 7, 9, 15, 47, 124**
See also Destouches, Louis-Ferdinand
See also DLB 72; GFL 1789 to the Present; RGWL

Cellini, Benvenuto 1500-1571 .... **LC 7**

Cendrars, Blaise .... **CLC 18, 106**
See also Sauser-Hall, Frederic
See also GFL 1789 to the Present; RGWL; WP

Centlivre, Susanna 1669(?)-1723 .... **LC 65**
See also DLB 84

Cernuda (y Bidón), Luis 1902-1963 .... **CLC 54; DAM POET**
See also CA 131; 89-92; DLB 134; GLL 1; HW 1

Cervantes, Lorna Dee 1954- .... **PC 35**
See also CA 131; CANR 80; CWP; DLB 82; HLCS 1; HW 1

Cervantes (Saavedra), Miguel de 1547-1616 .. **LC 6, 23; DA; DAB; DAC; DAM MST, NOV; SSC 12; WLC**
See also NFS 8

Césaire, Aimé (Fernand) 1913- . **CLC 19, 32, 112; BLC 1; DAM MULT, POET; PC 25**
See also BW 2, 3; CA 65-68; CANR 24, 43, 81; DA3; GFL 1789 to the Present; MTCW 1, 2; WP

Chabon, Michael 1963- .... **CLC 55**
See also CA 139; CANR 57, 96

Chabrol, Claude 1930- .... **CLC 16**
See also CA 110

Challans, Mary 1905-1983
See Renault, Mary
See also CA 81-84; 111; CANR 74; DA3; MTCW 2; SATA 23; SATA-Obit 36

Challis, George
See Faust, Frederick (Schiller)
See also TCWW 2

Chambers, Aidan 1934- .... **CLC 35**
See also AAYA 27; CA 25-28R; CANR 12, 31, 58; JRDA; MAICYA; SAAS 12; SATA 1, 69, 108; YAW

Chambers, James 1948-
See Cliff, Jimmy
See also CA 124

Chambers, Jessie
See Lawrence, D(avid) H(erbert Richards)
See also GLL 1

Chambers, Robert W(illiam) 1865-1933 .... **TCLC 41**
See also CA 165; DLB 202; HGG; SATA 107

Chamisso, Adelbert von 1781-1838 .... **NCLC 82**
See also DLB 90; RGWL

Chandler, Raymond (Thornton) 1888-1959 .... **TCLC 1, 7; SSC 23**
See also AAYA 25; AMWS 4; CA 104; 129; CANR 60; CDALB 1929-1941; CMW; DA3; DLB 226; DLBD 6; MTCW 1, 2

Chang, Eileen 1921-1995 .... **SSC 28**
See also CA 166; CWW 2

Chang, Jung 1952- .... **CLC 71**
See also CA 142

Chang Ai-Ling
See Chang, Eileen

Channing, William Ellery 1780-1842 .... **NCLC 17**
See also DLB 1, 59, 235; RGAL

Chao, Patricia 1955- .... **CLC 119**
See also CA 163

Chaplin, Charles Spencer 1889-1977 .... **CLC 16**
See also Chaplin, Charlie
See also CA 81-84; 73-76

Chaplin, Charlie
See Chaplin, Charles Spencer
See also DLB 44

Chapman, George 1559(?)-1634 .... **LC 22; DAM DRAM**
See also DLB 62, 121; RGEL

Chapman, Graham 1941-1989 .... **CLC 21**
See also Monty Python
See also CA 116; 129; CANR 35, 95

Chapman, John Jay 1862-1933 .... **TCLC 7**
See also CA 104

Chapman, Lee
See Bradley, Marion Zimmer
See also GLL 1

Chapman, Walker
See Silverberg, Robert

Chappell, Fred (Davis) 1936- ..... **CLC 40, 78**
See also CA 5-8R; CAAS 4; CANR 8, 33, 67; CN; CP; CSW; DLB 6, 105; HGG

Char, René(-Émile) 1907-1988 .... **CLC 9, 11, 14, 55; DAM POET**
See also CA 13-16R; 124; CANR 32; GFL 1789 to the Present; MTCW 1, 2; RGWL

Charby, Jay
See Ellison, Harlan (Jay)

Chardin, Pierre Teilhard de
See Teilhard de Chardin, (Marie Joseph) Pierre

Charlemagne 742-814 .... **CMLC 37**

Charles I 1600-1649 .... **LC 13**

Charriere, Isabelle de 1740-1805 .. **NCLC 66**

Chartier, Emile-Auguste
See Alain

Charyn, Jerome 1937- .... **CLC 5, 8, 18**
See also CA 5-8R; CAAS 1; CANR 7, 61; CMW; CN; DLBY 83; MTCW 1

Chase, Adam
See Marlowe, Stephen

Chase, Mary (Coyle) 1907-1981 .... **DC 1**
See also CA 77-80; 105; CAD; CWD; DFS 11; DLB 228; SATA 17; SATA-Obit 29

Chase, Mary Ellen 1887-1973 .... **CLC 2**
See also CA 13-16; 41-44R; CAP 1; SATA 10

Chase, Nicholas
See Hyde, Anthony
See also CCA 1

Chateaubriand, François René de 1768-1848 .... **NCLC 3**
See also DLB 119; EW; GFL 1789 to the Present; RGWL

Chatterje, Sarat Chandra 1876-1936(?)
See Chatterji, Saratchandra
See also CA 109

Chatterji, Bankim Chandra 1838-1894 .... **NCLC 19**

Chatterji, Saratchandra .... **TCLC 13**
See also Chatterje, Sarat Chandra
See also CA 186

Chatterton, Thomas 1752-1770 ..... **LC 3, 54; DAM POET**
See also DLB 109; RGEL

Chatwin, (Charles) Bruce 1940-1989 . **CLC 28, 57, 59; DAM POP**
See also AAYA 4; BEST 90:1; BRWS 4; CA 85-88; 127; CPW; DLB 194, 204

Chaucer, Daniel
See Ford, Ford Madox
See also RHW

Chaucer, Geoffrey 1340(?)-1400 .. **LC 17, 56; DA; DAB; DAC; DAM MST, POET; PC 19; WLCS**
See also CDBLB Before 1660; DA3; DLB 146; RGEL

Chavez, Denise (Elia) 1948-
See also CA 131; CANR 56, 81; DAM MULT; DLB 122; FW; HLC 1; HW 1, 2; MTCW 2

Chaviaras, Strates 1935-
See Haviaras, Stratis
See also CA 105

Chayefsky, Paddy .... **CLC 23**
See also Chayefsky, Sidney
See also CAD; DLB 7, 44; DLBY 81; RGAL

Chayefsky, Sidney 1923-1981
See Chayefsky, Paddy
See also CA 9-12R; 104; CANR 18; DAM DRAM

Chedid, Andree 1920- .... **CLC 47**
See also CA 145; CANR 95

Cheever, John 1912-1982 ..... **CLC 3, 7, 8, 11, 15, 25, 64; DA; DAB; DAC; DAM MST, NOV, POP; SSC 1, 38; WLC**
See also AMWS 1; CA 5-8R; 106; CABS 1; CANR 5, 27, 76; CDALB 1941-1968; CPW; DA3; DLB 2, 102, 227; DLBY 80, 82; INT CANR-5; MTCW 1, 2; RGAL; RGSF; SSFS 2

Cheever, Susan 1943- .... **CLC 18, 48**
See also CA 103; CANR 27, 51, 92; DLBY 82; INT CANR-27

Chekhonte, Antosha
See Chekhov, Anton (Pavlovich)

Chekhov, Anton (Pavlovich)
1860-1904 .... **TCLC 3, 10, 31, 55, 96; DA; DAB; DAC; DAM DRAM, MST; DC 9; SSC 2, 28, 41; WLC**
See also CA 104; 124; DA3; DFS 1, 5, 10, 12; SATA 90; SSFS 5

Cheney, Lynne V. 1941- .... **CLC 70**
See also CA 89-92; CANR 58

Chernyshevsky, Nikolay Gavrilovich
1828-1889 .... **NCLC 1**
See also DLB 238

Cherry, Carolyn Janice 1942-
See Cherryh, C. J.
See also CA 65-68; CANR 10; FANT; SFW; YAW

Cherryh, C. J. .... **CLC 35**
See also Cherry, Carolyn Janice
See also AAYA 24; DLBY 80; SATA 93

Chesnutt, Charles W(addell)
1858-1932 .. **TCLC 5, 39; BLC 1; DAM MULT; SSC 7**
See also AFAW 1, 2; BW 1, 3; CA 106; 125; CANR 76; DLB 12, 50, 78; MTCW 1, 2; SSFS 11

Chester, Alfred 1929(?)-1971 .... **CLC 49**
See also CA 33-36R; DLB 130

Chesterton, G(ilbert) K(eith)
1874-1936 . **TCLC 1, 6, 64; DAM NOV, POET; PC 28; SSC 1, 46**
See also CA 104; 132; CANR 73; CDBLB 1914-1945; CMW; DLB 10, 19, 34, 70, 98, 149, 178; FANT; MTCW 1, 2; SATA 27

Chiang, Pin-chin 1904-1986
See Ding Ling
See also CA 118

Ch'ien Chung-shu 1910- .... **CLC 22**
See also CA 130; CANR 73; MTCW 1, 2

Chikamatsu Monzaemon 1653-1724 ... **LC 66**

Child, L. Maria
See Child, Lydia Maria

Child, Lydia Maria 1802-1880 .. **NCLC 6, 73**
See also DLB 1, 74; RGAL; SATA 67

Child, Mrs.
See Child, Lydia Maria

Child, Philip 1898-1978 .... **CLC 19, 68**
See also CA 13-14; CAP 1; RHW; SATA 47

Childers, (Robert) Erskine
1870-1922 .... **TCLC 65**
See also CA 113; 153; DLB 70

Childress, Alice 1920-1994 .. **CLC 12, 15, 86, 96; BLC 1; DAM DRAM, MULT, NOV; DC 4**
See also AAYA 8; BW 2, 3; CA 45-48; 146; CAD; CANR 3, 27, 50, 74; CLR 14; CWD; DA3; DFS 2,8; DLB 7, 38; JRDA; MAICYA; MTCW 1, 2; RGAL; SATA 7, 48, 81; YAW

Chin, Frank (Chew, Jr.) 1940- ...... **CLC 135; DAM MULT; DC 7**
See also CA 33-36R; CANR 71; CD; DLB 206

Chislett, (Margaret) Anne 1943- ...... **CLC 34**
See also CA 151

Chitty, Thomas Willes 1926- .... **CLC 11**
See Hinde, Thomas
See also CA 5-8R; CN

Chivers, Thomas Holley
1809-1858 .... **NCLC 49**
See also DLB 3; RGAL

Choi, Susan .... **CLC 119**

Chomette, Rene Lucien 1898-1981
See Clair, Rene
See also CA 103

Chomsky, (Avram) Noam 1928- ..... **CLC 132**
See also CA 17-20R; CANR 28, 62; DA3; MTCW 1, 2

Chopin, Kate . **TCLC 5, 14; DA; DAB; SSC 8; WLCS**
See also Chopin, Katherine
See also AAYA 33; AMWS 1; CDALB 1865-1917; DLB 12, 78; NFS 3; RGAL; RGSF; SSFS 2

Chopin, Katherine 1851-1904
See Chopin, Kate
See also CA 104; 122; DAC; DAM MST, NOV; DA3; FW

Chrétien de Troyes c. 12th cent. - . **CMLC 10**
See also DLB 208

Christie
See Ichikawa, Kon

Christie, Agatha (Mary Clarissa)
1890-1976 .... **CLC 1, 6, 8, 12, 39, 48, 110; DAB; DAC; DAM NOV**
See also AAYA 9; AITN 1, 2; BRWS 2; CA 17-20R; 61-64; CANR 10, 37; CDBLB 1914-1945; CMW; CPW; DA3; DFS 2; DLB 13, 77; MTCW 1, 2; NFS 8; RHW; SATA 36; YAW

Christie, (Ann) Philippa
See Pearce, Philippa
See also CA 5-8R; CANR 4; CWRI; FANT

Christine de Pizan 1365(?)-1431(?) .... **LC 9**
See also DLB 208; RGWL

Chubb, Elmer
See Masters, Edgar Lee

Chulkov, Mikhail Dmitrievich
1743-1792 .... **LC 2**
See also DLB 150

Churchill, Caryl 1938- .... **CLC 31, 55; DC 5**
See also BRWS 4; CA 102; CANR 22, 46; CBD; CWD; DFS 12; DLB 13; FW; MTCW 1; RGEL

Churchill, Charles 1731-1764 .... **LC 3**
See also DLB 109; RGEL

Chute, Carolyn 1947- .... **CLC 39**
See also CA 123

Ciardi, John (Anthony) 1916-1986 . **CLC 10, 40, 44, 129; DAM POET**
See also CA 5-8R; 118; CAAS 2; CANR 5, 33; CLR 19; CWRI; DLB 5; DLBY 86; INT CANR-5; MAICYA; MTCW 1, 2; SAAS 26; SATA 1, 65; SATA-Obit 46

Cibber, Colley 1671-1757 .... **LC 66**
See also DLB 84; RGEL

Cicero, Marcus Tullius
106B.C.-43B.C. .... **CMLC 3**
See also DLB 211

Cimino, Michael 1943- .... **CLC 16**
See also CA 105

Cioran, E(mil) M. 1911-1995 .... **CLC 64**
See also CA 25-28R; 149; CANR 91; DLB 220

Cisneros, Sandra 1954- . **CLC 69, 118; DAM MULT; HLC 1; SSC 32**
See also AAYA 9; AMWS 7; CA 131; CANR 64; CWP; DA3; DLB 122, 152; FW; HW 1, 2; MTCW 2; NFS 2; RGAL; RGSF; SSFS 3; YAW

Cixous, Hélène 1937- .... **CLC 92**
See also CA 126; CANR 55; CWW 2; DLB 83, 242; FW; MTCW 1, 2

Clair, Rene .... **CLC 20**
See also Chomette, Rene Lucien

Clampitt, Amy 1920-1994 .... **CLC 32; PC 19**
See also CA 110; 146; CANR 29, 79; DLB 105

Clancy, Thomas L., Jr. 1947-
See Clancy, Tom
See also CA 125; 131; CANR 62; CPW; DA3; DLB 227; INT 131; MTCW 1, 2

Clancy, Tom .... **CLC 45, 112; DAM NOV, POP**
See also Clancy, Thomas L., Jr.
See also AAYA 9; BEST 89:1, 90:1; CMW; MTCW 2

Clare, John 1793-1864 ... **NCLC 9, 86; DAB; DAM POET; PC 23**
See also DLB 55, 96; RGEL

Clarin
See Alas (y Urena), Leopoldo (Enrique Garcia)

Clark, Al C.
See Goines, Donald

Clark, (Robert) Brian 1932- .... **CLC 29**
See also CA 41-44R; CANR 67; CBD; CD

Clark, Curt
See Westlake, Donald E(dwin)

Clark, Eleanor 1913-1996 .... **CLC 5, 19**
See also CA 9-12R; 151; CANR 41; CN; DLB 6

Clark, J. P.
See Clark Bekedermo, J(ohnson) P(epper)
See also DLB 117

Clark, John Pepper
See Clark Bekedermo, J(ohnson) P(epper)
See also CD; CP

Clark, M. R.
See Clark, Mavis Thorpe

Clark, Mavis Thorpe 1909- .... **CLC 12**
See also CA 57-60; CANR 8, 37; CLR 30; CWRI; MAICYA; SAAS 5; SATA 8, 74

Clark, Walter Van Tilburg
1909-1971 .... **CLC 28**
See also CA 9-12R; 33-36R; CANR 63; DLB 9, 206; SATA 8

Clark Bekedermo, J(ohnson) P(epper)
1935- .. **CLC 38; BLC 1; DAM DRAM, MULT; DC 5**
See also Clark, J. P.; Clark, John Pepper
See also BW 1; CA 65-68; CANR 16, 72; DFS 13; MTCW 1

Dahl, Roald 1916-1990 ...... **CLC 1, 6, 18, 79;**
DAB; DAC; DAM MST, NOV, POP
See also AAYA 15; BRWS 4; CA 1-4R; 133;
CANR 6, 32, 37, 62; CLR 1, 7, 41; CPW;
DA3; DLB 139; HGG; JRDA; MAICYA;
MTCW 1, 2; RGSF; SATA 1, 26, 73;
SATA-Obit 65; SSFS 4; YAW

Dahlberg, Edward 1900-1977 .. **CLC 1, 7, 14**
See also CA 9-12R; 69-72; CANR 31, 62;
DLB 48; MTCW 1; RGAL

Daitch, Susan 1954- .... **CLC 103**
See also CA 161

Dale, Colin .... **TCLC 18**
See also Lawrence, T(homas) E(dward)

Dale, George E.
See Asimov, Isaac

Dalton, Roque 1935-1975
See also HLCS 1; HW 2

Daly, Elizabeth 1878-1967 .... **CLC 52**
See also CA 23-24; 25-28R; CANR 60;
CAP 2; CMW

Daly, Maureen 1921-1983 .... **CLC 17**
See also AAYA 5; CANR 37, 83; JRDA;
MAICYA; SAAS 1; SATA 2; YAW

Damas, Leon-Gontran 1912-1978 .... **CLC 84**
See also BW 1; CA 125; 73-76

Dana, Richard Henry Sr.
1787-1879 .... **NCLC 53**

Daniel, Samuel 1562(?)-1619 .... **LC 24**
See also DLB 62; RGEL

Daniels, Brett
See Adler, Renata

Dannay, Frederic 1905-1982 . **CLC 11; DAM**
POP
See also Queen, Ellery
See also CA 1-4R; 107; CANR 1, 39;
CMW; DLB 137; MTCW 1

D'Annunzio, Gabriele 1863-1938 ... **TCLC 6,**
40
See also CA 104; 155

Danois, N. le
See Gourmont, Remy(-Marie-Charles) de

Dante 1265-1321 .... **CMLC 3, 18, 39; DA;**
DAB; DAC; DAM MST, POET; PC
21; WLCS
See also Alighieri, Dante
See also DA3; EFS 1

d'Antibes, Germain
See Simenon, Georges (Jacques Christian)

Danticat, Edwidge 1969- .... **CLC 94, 139**
See also AAYA 29; CA 152; CANR 73;
DNFS 1; MTCW 1; SSFS 1; YAW

Danvers, Dennis 1947- .... **CLC 70**

Danziger, Paula 1944- .... **CLC 21**
See also AAYA 4, 36; CA 112; 115; CANR
37; CLR 20; JRDA; MAICYA; SATA 36,
63, 102; SATA-Brief 30; YAW

Da Ponte, Lorenzo 1749-1838 .... **NCLC 50**

Darío, Rubén 1867-1916 .... **TCLC 4; DAM**
MULT; HLC 1; PC 15
See also CA 131; CANR 81; HW 1, 2;
MTCW 1, 2

Darley, George 1795-1846 .... **NCLC 2**
See also DLB 96; RGEL

Darrow, Clarence (Seward)
1857-1938 .... **TCLC 81**
See also CA 164

Darwin, Charles 1809-1882 .... **NCLC 57**
See also DLB 57, 166; RGEL

Daryush, Elizabeth 1887-1977 ...... **CLC 6, 19**
See also CA 49-52; CANR 3, 81; DLB 20

Dasgupta, Surendranath
1887-1952 .... **TCLC 81**
See also CA 157

Dashwood, Edmee Elizabeth Monica de la
Pasture 1890-1943
See Delafield, E. M.
See also CA 119; 154

Daudet, (Louis Marie) Alphonse
1840-1897 .... **NCLC 1**
See also DLB 123; GFL 1789 to the Present;
RGSF

Daumal, Rene 1908-1944 .... **TCLC 14**
See also CA 114

Davenant, William 1606-1668 .... **LC 13**
See also DLB 58, 126

Davenport, Guy (Mattison, Jr.)
1927- .... **CLC 6, 14, 38; SSC 16**
See also CA 33-36R; CANR 23, 73; CN;
CSW; DLB 130

Davidson, Avram (James) 1923-1993
See Queen, Ellery
See also CA 101; 171; CANR 26; DLB 8;
FANT; SFW

Davidson, Donald (Grady)
1893-1968 .... **CLC 2, 13, 19**
See also CA 5-8R; 25-28R; CANR 4, 84;
DLB 45

Davidson, Hugh
See Hamilton, Edmond

Davidson, John 1857-1909 .... **TCLC 24**
See also CA 118; DLB 19

Davidson, Sara 1943- .... **CLC 9**
See also CA 81-84; CANR 44, 68; DLB
185

Davie, Donald (Alfred) 1922-1995 .... **CLC 5,**
8, 10, 31; PC 29
See also BRWS 6; CA 1-4R; 149; CAAS 3;
CANR 1, 44; CP; DLB 27; MTCW 1;
RGEL

Davies, Ray(mond Douglas) 1944- ... **CLC 21**
See also CA 116; 146; CANR 92

Davies, Rhys 1901-1978 .... **CLC 23**
See also CA 9-12R; 81-84; CANR 4, DLB
139, 191

Davies, (William) Robertson
1913-1995 .... **CLC 2, 7, 13, 25, 42, 75,**
91; DA; DAB; DAC; DAM MST, NOV,
POP; WLC
See also Marchbanks, Samuel
See also BEST 89:2; CA 33-36R; 150;
CANR 17, 42; CN; CPW; DA3; DLB 68;
HGG; INT CANR-17; MTCW 1, 2

Davies, Walter C.
See Kornbluth, C(yril) M.

Davies, William Henry 1871-1940 ... **TCLC 5**
See also CA 104; 179; DLB 19, 174

Da Vinci, Leonardo 1452-1519 ..... **LC 12, 57,**
60
See also AAYA 40

Davis, Angela (Yvonne) 1944- .... **CLC 77;**
DAM MULT
See also BW 2, 3; CA 57-60; CANR 10,
81; CSW; DA3; FW

Davis, B. Lynch
See Bioy Casares, Adolfo; Borges, Jorge
Luis

Davis, B. Lynch
See Bioy Casares, Adolfo

Davis, Gordon
See Hunt, E(verette) Howard, (Jr.)

Davis, H(arold) L(enoir) 1896-1960 . **CLC 49**
See also CA 178; 89-92; DLB 9, 206; SATA
114

Davis, Rebecca (Blaine) Harding
1831-1910 .... **TCLC 6; SSC 38**
See also CA 104; 179; DLB 74, 239; FW

Davis, Richard Harding
1864-1916 .... **TCLC 24**
See also CA 114; 179; DLB 12, 23, 78, 79,
189; DLBD 13; RGAL

Davison, Frank Dalby 1893-1970 ..... **CLC 15**
See also CA 116

Davison, Lawrence H.
See Lawrence, D(avid) H(erbert Richards)

Davison, Peter (Hubert) 1928- .... **CLC 28**
See also CA 9-12R; CAAS 4; CANR 3, 43,
84; CP; DLB 5

Davys, Mary 1674-1732 .... **LC 1, 46**
See also DLB 39

Dawson, Fielding 1930- .... **CLC 6**
See also CA 85-88; DLB 130

Dawson, Peter
See Faust, Frederick (Schiller)
See also TCWW 2, 2

Day, Clarence (Shepard, Jr.)
1874-1935 .... **TCLC 25**
See also CA 108; DLB 11

Day, Thomas 1748-1789 .... **LC 1**
See also DLB 39; YABC 1

Day Lewis, C(ecil) 1904-1972 . **CLC 1, 6, 10;**
DAM POET; PC 11
See also Blake, Nicholas
See also BRWS 3; CA 13-16; 33-36R;
CANR 34; CAP 1; CWRI; DLB 15, 20;
MTCW 1, 2

Dazai Osamu .... **TCLC 11; SSC 41**
See also Tsushima, Shuji
See also CA 164; DLB 182; MJW

de Andrade, Carlos Drummond
See Drummond de Andrade, Carlos

Deane, Norman
See Creasey, John

Deane, Seamus (Francis) 1940- ...... **CLC 122**
See also CA 118; CANR 42

de Beauvoir, Simone (Lucie Ernestine Marie
Bertrand)
See Beauvoir, Simone (Lucie Ernestine
Marie Bertrand) de

de Beer, P.
See Bosman, Herman Charles

de Brissac, Malcolm
See Dickinson, Peter (Malcolm)

de Campos, Alvaro
See Pessoa, Fernando (Ant

de Chardin, Pierre Teilhard
See Teilhard de Chardin, (Marie Joseph)
Pierre

Dee, John 1527-1608 .... **LC 20**

Deer, Sandra 1940- .... **CLC 45**
See also CA 186

De Ferrari, Gabriella 1941- .... **CLC 65**
See also CA 146

Defoe, Daniel 1660(?)-1731 ..... **LC 1, 42; DA;**
DAB; DAC; DAM MST, NOV; WLC
See also AAYA 27; CDBLB 1660-1789;
CLR 61; DA3; DLB 39, 95, 101; JRDA;
MAICYA; NFS 9; RGEL; SATA 22

de Gourmont, Remy(-Marie-Charles)
See Gourmont, Remy(-Marie-Charles) de

de Hartog, Jan 1914- .... **CLC 19**
See also CA 1-4R; CANR 1; DFS 12

de Hostos, E. M.
See Hostos (y Bonilla), Eugenio Maria de

de Hostos, Eugenio M.
See Hostos (y Bonilla), Eugenio Maria de

Deighton, Len .... **CLC 4, 7, 22, 46**
See also Deighton, Leonard Cyril
See also AAYA 6; BEST 89:2; CDBLB
1960 to Present; CMW; CN; CPW; DLB
87

Deighton, Leonard Cyril 1929-
See Deighton, Len
See also CA 9-12R; CANR 19, 33, 68;
DAM NOV, POP; DA3; MTCW 1, 2

Dekker, Thomas 1572(?)-1632 . **LC 22; DAM**
DRAM; DC 12
See also CDBLB Before 1660; DLB 62,
172; RGEL

Delafield, E. M. .... **TCLC 61**
See also Dashwood, Edmee Elizabeth
Monica de la Pasture
See also DLB 34; RHW

de la Mare, Walter (John)
1873-1956 ..... TCLC 4, 53; DAB; DAC;
DAM MST, POET; SSC 14; WLC
See also CA 163; CDBLB 1914-1945; CLR
23; CWRI; DA3; DLB 162; HGG; MTCW
1; SATA 16

Delaney, Franey
See O'Hara, John (Henry)

Delaney, Shelagh 1939- .... CLC 29; DAM
DRAM
See also CA 17-20R; CANR 30, 67; CBD;
CD; CDBLB 1960 to Present; CWD; DFS
7; DLB 13; MTCW 1

Delany, Martin Robinson
1812-1885 .... NCLC 93
See also DLB 50; RGAL

Delany, Mary (Granville Pendarves)
1700-1788 .... LC 12

Delany, Samuel R(ay), Jr. 1942- . CLC 8, 14,
38, 141; BLC 1; DAM MULT
See also AAYA 24; AFAW 2; BW 2, 3; CA
81-84; CANR 27, 43; DLB 8, 33; MTCW
1, 2

De La Ramée, (Marie) Louise 1839-1908
See Ouida
See also SATA 20

de la Roche, Mazo 1879-1961 .... CLC 14
See also CA 85-88; CANR 30; DLB 68;
RHW; SATA 64

De La Salle, Innocent
See Hartmann, Sadakichi

Delbanco, Nicholas (Franklin)
1942- .... CLC 6, 13
See also CA 17-20R; CAAE 189; CAAS 2;
CANR 29, 55; DLB 6, 234

del Castillo, Michel 1933- .... CLC 38
See also CA 109; CANR 77

Deledda, Grazia (Cosima)
1875(?)-1936 .... TCLC 23
See also CA 123

Delgado, Abelardo (Lalo) B(arrientos) 1930-
See also CA 131; CAAS 15; CANR 90;
DAM MST, MULT; DLB 82; HLC 1; HW
1, 2

Delibes, Miguel .... CLC 8, 18
See also Delibes Setien, Miguel

Delibes Setien, Miguel 1920-
See Delibes, Miguel
See also CA 45-48; CANR 1, 32; HW 1;
MTCW 1

DeLillo, Don 1936- ..... CLC 8, 10, 13, 27, 39,
54, 76, 143; DAM NOV, POP
See also AMWS 6; BEST 89:1; CA 81-84;
CANR 21, 76, 92; CN; CPW; DA3; DLB
6, 173; MTCW 1, 2; RGAL

de Lisser, H. G.
See De Lisser, H(erbert) G(eorge)
See also DLB 117

De Lisser, H(erbert) G(eorge)
1878-1944 .... TCLC 12
See also de Lisser, H. G.
See also BW 2; CA 109; 152

Deloney, Thomas 1543(?)-1600 .... LC 41
See also DLB 167; RGEL

Deloria, Vine (Victor), Jr. 1933- ...... CLC 21,
122; DAM MULT
See also CA 53-56; CANR 5, 20, 48; DLB
175; MTCW 1; NNAL; SATA 21

Del Vecchio, John M(ichael) 1947- .. CLC 29
See also CA 110; DLBD 9

de Man, Paul (Adolph Michel)
1919-1983 .... CLC 55
See also CA 128; 111; CANR 61; DLB 67;
MTCW 1, 2

DeMarinis, Rick 1934- .... CLC 54
See also CA 57-60, 184; CAAE 184; CAAS
24; CANR 9, 25, 50

Dembry, R. Emmet
See Murfree, Mary Noailles

Demby, William 1922- .... CLC 53; BLC 1;
DAM MULT
See also BW 1, 3; CA 81-84; CANR 81;
DLB 33

de Menton, Francisco
See Chin, Frank (Chew, Jr.)

Demetrius of Phalerum c.
307B.C.- .... CMLC 34

Demijohn, Thom
See Disch, Thomas M(ichael)

Deming, Richard 1915-1983
See Queen, Ellery
See also CA 9-12R; CANR 3, 94; SATA 24

de Montherlant, Henry (Milon)
See Montherlant, Henry (Milon) de

Demosthenes 384B.C.- .... CMLC 13
See also DLB 176; RGEL

de Natale, Francine
See Malzberg, Barry N(athaniel)

de Navarre, Marguerite 1492-1549 ..... LC 61
See also Marguerite de Navarre

Denby, Edwin (Orr) 1903-1983 .... CLC 48
See also CA 138; 110

Denis, Julio
See Cort

Denmark, Harrison
See Zelazny, Roger (Joseph)

Dennis, John 1658-1734 .... LC 11
See also DLB 101; RGEL

Dennis, Nigel (Forbes) 1912-1989 ...... CLC 8
See also CA 25-28R; 129; DLB 13, 15, 233;
MTCW 1

Dent, Lester 1904(?)-1959 .... TCLC 72
See also CA 112; 161; CMW; SFW

De Palma, Brian (Russell) 1940- ...... CLC 20
See also CA 109

De Quincey, Thomas 1785-1859 ..... NCLC 4,
87
See also CDBLB 1789-1832; DLB 110, 144

Deren, Eleanora 1917(?)-1961
See Deren, Maya
See also CA 111

Deren, Maya .... CLC 16, 102
See also Deren, Eleanora

Derleth, August (William)
1909-1971 .... CLC 31
See also CA 1-4R; 29-32R; CANR 4;
CMW; DLB 9; DLBD 17; HGG; SATA 5

Der Nister 1884-1950 .... TCLC 56

de Routisie, Albert
See Aragon, Louis

Derrida, Jacques 1930- .... CLC 24, 87
See also CA 124; 127; CANR 76, 98; DLB
242; MTCW 1

Derry Down Derry
See Lear, Edward

Dersonnes, Jacques
See Simenon, Georges (Jacques Christian)

Desai, Anita 1937- ..... CLC 19, 37, 97; DAB;
DAM NOV
See also BRWS 5; CA 81-84; CANR 33,
53, 95; CN; CWRI; DA3; DNFS 2; FW;
MTCW 1, 2; SATA 63

Desai, Kiran 1971- .... CLC 119
See also CA 171

de Saint-Luc, Jean
See Glassco, John

de Saint Roman, Arnaud
See Aragon, Louis

Desbordes-Valmore, Marceline
1786-1859 .... NCLC 97
See also DLB 217

Descartes, René 1596-1650 .... LC 20, 35
See also GFL Beginnings to 1789

De Sica, Vittorio 1901(?)-1974 .... CLC 20
See also CA 117

Desnos, Robert 1900-1945 .... TCLC 22
See also CA 121; 151

Destouches, Louis-Ferdinand
1894-1961 .... CLC 9, 15
See also Céline, Louis-Ferdinand
See also CA 85-88; CANR 28; MTCW 1

de Tolignac, Gaston
See Griffith, D(avid Lewelyn) W(ark)

Deutsch, Babette 1895-1982 .... CLC 18
See also CA 1-4R; 108; CANR 4, 79; DLB
45; SATA 1; SATA-Obit 33

Devenant, William 1606-1649 .... LC 13

Devkota, Laxmiprasad 1909-1959 . TCLC 23
See also CA 123

De Voto, Bernard (Augustine)
1897-1955 .... TCLC 29
See also CA 113; 160; DLB 9

De Vries, Peter 1910-1993 .... CLC 1, 2, 3, 7,
10, 28, 46; DAM NOV
See also CA 17-20R; 142; CANR 41; DLB
6; DLBY 82; MTCW 1, 2

Dewey, John 1859-1952 .... TCLC 95
See also CA 114; 170; RGAL

Dexter, John
See Bradley, Marion Zimmer
See also GLL 1

Dexter, Martin
See Faust, Frederick (Schiller)
See also TCWW 2

Dexter, Pete 1943- .. CLC 34, 55; DAM POP
See also BEST 89:2; CA 127; 131; CPW;
INT 131; MTCW 1

Diamano, Silmang
See Senghor, L

Diamond, Neil 1941- .... CLC 30
See also CA 108

Diaz del Castillo, Bernal 1496-1584 .. LC 31;
HLCS 1

di Bassetto, Corno
See Shaw, George Bernard

Dick, Philip K(indred) 1928-1982 ... CLC 10,
30, 72; DAM NOV, POP
See also AAYA 24; CA 49-52; 106; CANR
2, 16; CPW; DA3; DLB 8; MTCW 1, 2;
NFS 5; SFW

Dickens, Charles (John Huffam)
1812-1870 .... NCLC 3, 8, 18, 26, 37, 50,
86; DA; DAB; DAC; DAM MST, NOV;
SSC 17; WLC
See also AAYA 23; CDBLB 1832-1890;
CMW; DA3; DLB 21, 55, 70, 159, 166;
HGG; JRDA; MAICYA; NFS 4, 5, 10;
SATA 15

Dickey, James (Lafayette)
1923-1997 .... CLC 1, 2, 4, 7, 10, 15, 47,
109; DAM NOV, POET, POP
See also AITN 1, 2; AMWS 4; CA 9-12R;
156; CABS 2; CANR 10, 48, 61; CDALB
1968-1988; CP; CPW; CSW; DA3; DLB
5, 193; DLBD 7; DLBY 82, 93, 96, 97,
98; INT CANR-10; MTCW 1, 2; NFS 9;
PFS 6, 11

Dickey, William 1928-1994 .... CLC 3, 28
See also CA 9-12R; 145; CANR 24, 79;
DLB 5

Dickinson, Charles 1951- .... CLC 49
See also CA 128

Dickinson, Emily (Elizabeth)
1830-1886 ..... NCLC 21, 77; DA; DAB;
DAC; DAM MST, POET; PC 1; WLC
See also AAYA 22; CDALB 1865-1917;
DA3; DLB 1; PFS 1, 2, 3, 4, 5, 6, 8, 10,
11; SATA 29

Dickinson, Peter (Malcolm) 1927- .. CLC 12,
35
See also AAYA 9; CA 41-44R; CANR 31,
58, 88; CLR 29; CMW; DLB 87, 161;
JRDA; MAICYA; SATA 5, 62, 95; SFW;
YAW

Dickson, Carr
See Carr, John Dickson

Dickson, Carter
See Carr, John Dickson

Diderot, Denis 1713-1784 .... **LC 26**
See also GFL Beginnings to 1789; RGWL

Didion, Joan 1934- .... **CLC 1, 3, 8, 14, 32, 129; DAM NOV**
See also AITN 1; AMWS 4; CA 5-8R; CANR 14, 52, 76; CDALB 1968-1988; CN; DA3; DLB 2, 173, 185; DLBY 81, 86; MTCW 1, 2; NFS 3; RGAL; TCWW 2

Dietrich, Robert
See Hunt, E(verette) Howard, (Jr.)

Difusa, Pati
See Almodovar, Pedro

Dillard, Annie 1945- .. **CLC 9, 60, 115; DAM NOV**
See also AAYA 6; AMWS 6; CA 49-52; CANR 3, 43, 62, 90; DA3; DLBY 80; MTCW 1, 2; NCFS 1; RGAL; SATA 10

Dillard, R(ichard) H(enry) W(ilde) 1937- .... **CLC 5**
See also CA 21-24R; CAAS 7; CANR 10; CP; CSW; DLB 5

Dillon, Eilis 1920-1994 .... **CLC 17**
See also CA 9-12R, 182; 147; CAAE 182; CAAS 3; CANR 4, 38, 78; CLR 26; MAICYA; SATA 2, 74; SATA-Essay 105; SATA-Obit 83; YAW

Dimont, Penelope
See Mortimer, Penelope (Ruth)

Dinesen, Isak .... **CLC 10, 29, 95; SSC 7**
See also Blixen, Karen (Christentze Dinesen)
See also FW; HGG; MTCW 1; NFS 9; RGSF; RGWL; SSFS 6

Ding Ling .... **CLC 68**
See also Chiang, Pin-chin

Diphusa, Patty
See Almodovar, Pedro

Disch, Thomas M(ichael) 1940- ... **CLC 7, 36**
See also AAYA 17; CA 21-24R; CAAS 4; CANR 17, 36, 54, 89; CLR 18; CP; DA3; DLB 8; HGG; MAICYA; MTCW 1, 2; SAAS 15; SATA 92; SFW

Disch, Tom
See Disch, Thomas M(ichael)

d'Isly, Georges
See Simenon, Georges (Jacques Christian)

Disraeli, Benjamin 1804-1881 ... **NCLC 2, 39, 79**
See also DLB 21, 55

Ditcum, Steve
See Crumb, R(obert)

Dixon, Paige
See Corcoran, Barbara

Dixon, Stephen 1936- .... **CLC 52; SSC 16**
See also CA 89-92; CANR 17, 40, 54, 91; CN; DLB 130

Doak, Annie
See Dillard, Annie

Dobell, Sydney Thompson 1824-1874 .... **NCLC 43**
See also DLB 32

Döblin, Alfred .... **TCLC 13**
See also Doeblin, Alfred

Dobrolyubov, Nikolai Alexandrovich 1836-1861 .... **NCLC 5**

Dobson, Austin 1840-1921 .... **TCLC 79**
See also DLB 35; 144

Dobyns, Stephen 1941- .... **CLC 37**
See also CA 45-48; CANR 2, 18; CMW; CP

Doctorow, E(dgar) L(aurence) 1931- .... **CLC 6, 11, 15, 18, 37, 44, 65, 113; DAM NOV, POP**
See also AAYA 22; AITN 2; AMWS 4; BEST 89:3; CA 45-48; CANR 2, 33, 51, 76, 97; CDALB 1968-1988; CN; CPW; DA3; DLB 2, 28, 173; DLBY 80; MTCW 1, 2; NFS 6; RHW

Dodgson, Charles Lutwidge 1832-1898
See Carroll, Lewis
See also CLR 2; DA; DAB; DAC; DAM MST, NOV, POET; DA3; MAICYA; SATA 100; YABC 2

Dodson, Owen (Vincent) 1914-1983 .... **CLC 79; BLC 1; DAM MULT**
See also BW 1; CA 65-68; 110; CANR 24; DLB 76

Doeblin, Alfred 1878-1957 .... **TCLC 13**
See also Döblin, Alfred
See also CA 110; 141; DLB 66

Doerr, Harriet 1910- .... **CLC 34**
See also CA 117; 122; CANR 47; INT 122

Domecq, H(onorio Bustos)
See Bioy Casares, Adolfo

Domecq, H(onorio) Bustos
See Bioy Casares, Adolfo; Borges, Jorge Luis

Domini, Rey
See Lorde, Audre (Geraldine)
See also GLL 1

Dominique
See Proust, (Valentin-Louis-George-Eug

Don, A
See Stephen, SirLeslie

Donaldson, Stephen R(eeder) 1947- .... **CLC 46, 138; DAM POP**
See also AAYA 36; CA 89-92; CANR 13, 55; CPW; FANT; INT CANR-13; SATA 121; SFW

Donleavy, J(ames) P(atrick) 1926- .... **CLC 1, 4, 6, 10, 45**
See also AITN 2; CA 9-12R; CANR 24, 49, 62, 80; CD; CN; DLB 6, 173; INT CANR-24; MTCW 1, 2

Donne, John 1572-1631 .... **LC 10, 24; DA; DAB; DAC; DAM MST, POET; PC 1; WLC**
See also CDBLB Before 1660; DLB 121, 151; PFS 2,11; RGEL

Donnell, David 1939(?)- .... **CLC 34**

Donoghue, P. S.
See Hunt, E(verette) Howard, (Jr.)

Donoso (Yañez), José 1924-1996 ... **CLC 4, 8, 11, 32, 99; DAM MULT; HLC 1; SSC 34**
See also CA 81-84; 155; CANR 32, 73; DLB 113; HW 1, 2; MTCW 1, 2

Donovan, John 1928-1992 .... **CLC 35**
See also AAYA 20; CA 97-100; 137; CLR 3; MAICYA; SATA 72; SATA-Brief 29; YAW

Don Roberto
See Cunninghame Graham, Robert (Gallnigad) Bontine

Doolittle, Hilda 1886-1961 . **CLC 3, 8, 14, 31, 34, 73; DA; DAC; DAM MST, POET; PC 5; WLC**
See also H. D.
See also AMWS 1; CA 97-100; CANR 35; DLB 4, 45; FW; GLL 1; MTCW 1, 2; PFS 6; RGAL

Dorfman, Ariel 1942- ...... **CLC 48, 77; DAM MULT; HLC 1**
See also CA 124; 130; CANR 67, 70; CWW 2; DFS 4; HW 1, 2; INT 130

Dorn, Edward (Merton) 1929-1999 .... **CLC 10, 18**
See also CA 93-96; 187; CANR 42, 79; CP; DLB 5; INT 93-96

Dor-Ner, Zvi .... **CLC 70**

Dorris, Michael (Anthony) 1945-1997 .... **CLC 109; DAM MULT, NOV**
See also AAYA 20; BEST 90:1; CA 102; 157; CANR 19, 46, 75; CLR 58; DA3; DLB 175; MTCW 2; NFS 3; NNAL; SATA 75; SATA-Obit 94; TCWW 2; YAW

Dorris, Michael A.
See Dorris, Michael (Anthony)

Dorsan, Luc
See Simenon, Georges (Jacques Christian)

Dorsange, Jean
See Simenon, Georges (Jacques Christian)

Dos Passos, John (Roderigo) 1896-1970 ... **CLC 1, 4, 8, 11, 15, 25, 34, 82; DA; DAB; DAC; DAM MST, NOV; WLC**
See also AMW; CA 1-4R; 29-32R; CANR 3; CDALB 1929-1941; DA3; DLB 4, 9; DLBD 1, 15; DLBY 96; MTCW 1, 2; RGAL

Dossage, Jean
See Simenon, Georges (Jacques Christian)

Dostoevsky, Fedor Mikhailovich 1821-1881 . **NCLC 2, 7, 21, 33, 43; DA; DAB; DAC; DAM MST, NOV; SSC 2, 33, 44; WLC**
See also AAYA 40; DA3; DLB 238; NFS 3, 8; SSFS 8

Doughty, Charles M(ontagu) 1843-1926 .... **TCLC 27**
See also CA 115; 178; DLB 19, 57, 174

Douglas, Ellen .... **CLC 73**
See also Haxton, Josephine Ayres; Williamson, Ellen Douglas
See also CN; CSW

Douglas, Gavin 1475(?)-1522 .... **LC 20**
See also DLB 132; RGEL

Douglas, George
See Brown, George Douglas
See also RGEL

Douglas, Keith (Castellain) 1920-1944 .... **TCLC 40**
See also CA 160; DLB 27

Douglas, Leonard
See Bradbury, Ray (Douglas)

Douglas, Michael
See Crichton, (John) Michael

Douglas, (George) Norman 1868-1952 .... **TCLC 68**
See also CA 119; 157; DLB 34, 195

Douglas, William
See Brown, George Douglas

Douglass, Frederick 1817(?)-1895 .. **NCLC 7, 55; BLC 1; DA; DAC; DAM MST, MULT; WLC**
See also AMWS 3; CDALB 1640-1865; DA3; DLB 1, 43, 50, 79; FW; NCFS 2; RGAL; SATA 29

Dourado, (Waldomiro Freitas) Autran 1926- .... **CLC 23, 60**
See also CA 25-28R; 179; CANR 34, 81; DLB 145; HW 2

Dourado, Waldomiro Autran
See Dourado, (Waldomiro Freitas) Autran
See also CA 179

Dove, Rita (Frances) 1952- .... **CLC 50, 81; BLCS; DAM MULT, POET; PC 6**
See also AMWS 4; BW 2; CA 109; CAAS 19; CANR 27, 42, 68, 76, 97; CDALBS; CP; CSW; CWP; DA3; DLB 120; MTCW 1; PFS 1

Doveglion
See Villa, Jose Garcia

Dowell, Coleman 1925-1985 .... **CLC 60**
See also CA 25-28R; 117; CANR 10; DLB 130; GLL 2

Dowson, Ernest (Christopher) 1867-1900 .... **TCLC 4**
See also CA 105; 150; DLB 19, 135

Doyle, A. Conan
See Doyle, Arthur Conan

Dwight, Timothy 1752-1817 .... **NCLC 13**
See also DLB 37; RGAL

Dworkin, Andrea 1946- .... **CLC 43, 123**
See also CA 77-80; CAAS 21; CANR 16, 39, 76, 96; FW; GLL 1; INT CANR-16; MTCW 1, 2

Dwyer, Deanna
See Koontz, Dean R(ay)

Dwyer, K. R.
See Koontz, Dean R(ay)

Dwyer, Thomas A. 1923- .... **CLC 114**
See also CA 115

Dybek, Stuart 1942- .... **CLC 114**
See also CA 97-100; CANR 39; DLB 130

Dye, Richard
See De Voto, Bernard (Augustine)

Dylan, Bob 1941- .... **CLC 3, 4, 6, 12, 77**
See also CA 41-44R; CP; DLB 16

Dyson, John 1943- .... **CLC 70**
See also CA 144

E. V. L.
See Lucas, E(dward) V(errall)

Eagleton, Terence (Francis) 1943- .. **CLC 63, 132**
See also CA 57-60; CANR 7, 23, 68; DLB 242; MTCW 1, 2

Eagleton, Terry
See Eagleton, Terence (Francis)

Early, Jack
See Scoppettone, Sandra
See also GLL 1

East, Michael
See West, Morris L(anglo)

Eastaway, Edward
See Thomas, (Philip) Edward

Eastlake, William (Derry)
1917-1997 .... **CLC 8**
See also CA 5-8R; 158; CAAS 1; CANR 5, 63; CN; DLB 6, 206; INT CANR-5; TCWW 2

Eastman, Charles A(lexander)
1858-1939 .... **TCLC 55; DAM MULT**
See also CA 179; CANR 91; DLB 175; NNAL; YABC 1

Eberhart, Richard (Ghormley)
1904- .. **CLC 3, 11, 19, 56; DAM POET**
See also CA 1-4R; CANR 2; CDALB 1941-1968; CP; DLB 48; MTCW 1

Eberstadt, Fernanda 1960- .... **CLC 39**
See also CA 136; CANR 69

Echegaray (y Eizaguirre), Jose (Maria Waldo) 1832-1916 .... **TCLC 4; HLCS 1**
See also CA 104; CANR 32; HW 1; MTCW 1

Echeverria, (Jose) Esteban (Antonino)
1805-1851 .... **NCLC 18**

Echo
See Proust, (Valentin-Louis-George-Eug

Eckert, Allan W. 1931- .... **CLC 17**
See also AAYA 18; CA 13-16R; CANR 14, 45; INT CANR-14; SAAS 21; SATA 29, 91; SATA-Brief 27

Eckhart, Meister 1260(?)-1327(?) ... **CMLC 9**
See also DLB 115

Eckmar, F. R.
See de Hartog, Jan

Eco, Umberto 1932- .... **CLC 28, 60, 142; DAM NOV, POP**
See also BEST 90:1; CA 77-80; CANR 12, 33, 55; CPW; CWW 2; DA3; DLB 196, 242; MTCW 1, 2

Eddison, E(ric) R(ucker)
1882-1945 .... **TCLC 15**
See also CA 109; 156; FANT; SFW

Eddy, Mary (Ann Morse) Baker
1821-1910 .... **TCLC 71**
See also CA 113; 174

Edel, (Joseph) Leon 1907-1997 .. **CLC 29, 34**
See also CA 1-4R; 161; CANR 1, 22; DLB 103; INT CANR-22

Eden, Emily 1797-1869 .... **NCLC 10**

Edgar, David 1948- .. **CLC 42; DAM DRAM**
See also CA 57-60; CANR 12, 61; CBD; CD; DLB 13, 233; MTCW 1

Edgerton, Clyde (Carlyle) 1944- ...... **CLC 39**
See also AAYA 17; CA 118; 134; CANR 64; CSW; INT 134; YAW

Edgeworth, Maria 1768-1849 .... **NCLC 1, 51**
See also BRWS 3; DLB 116, 159, 163; FW; RGEL; SATA 21

Edmonds, Paul
See Kuttner, Henry

Edmonds, Walter D(umaux)
1903-1998 .... **CLC 35**
See also CA 5-8R; CANR 2; CWRI; DLB 9; MAICYA; RHW; SAAS 4; SATA 1, 27; SATA-Obit 99

Edmondson, Wallace
See Ellison, Harlan (Jay)

Edson, Russell .... **CLC 13**
See also CA 33-36R

Edwards, Bronwen Elizabeth
See Rose, Wendy

Edwards, G(erald) B(asil)
1899-1976 .... **CLC 25**
See also CA 110

Edwards, Gus 1939- .... **CLC 43**
See also CA 108; INT 108

Edwards, Jonathan 1703-1758 .... **LC 7, 54; DA; DAC; DAM MST**
See also DLB 24; RGAL

Efron, Marina Ivanovna Tsvetaeva
See Tsvetaeva (Efron), Marina (Ivanovna)

Ehle, John (Marsden, Jr.) 1925- ...... **CLC 27**
See also CA 9-12R; CSW

Ehrenbourg, Ilya (Grigoryevich)
See Ehrenburg, Ilya (Grigoryevich)

Ehrenburg, Ilya (Grigoryevich)
1891-1967 .... **CLC 18, 34, 62**
See also CA 102; 25-28R

Ehrenburg, Ilyo (Grigoryevich)
See Ehrenburg, Ilya (Grigoryevich)

Ehrenreich, Barbara 1941- .... **CLC 110**
See also BEST 90:4; CA 73-76; CANR 16, 37, 62; FW; MTCW 1, 2

Eich, Guenter 1907-1972 .... **CLC 15**
See also Eich, Günter
See also CA 111; 93-96; DLB 69, 124

Eich, Günter
See Eich, Guenter
See also RGWL

Eichendorff, Joseph 1788-1857 .... **NCLC 8**
See also DLB 90

Eigner, Larry .... **CLC 9**
See also Eigner, Laurence (Joel)
See also CAAS 23; DLB 5

Eigner, Laurence (Joel) 1927-1996
See Eigner, Larry
See also CA 9-12R; 151; CANR 6, 84; CP; DLB 193

Einstein, Albert 1879-1955 .... **TCLC 65**
See also CA 121; 133; MTCW 1, 2

Eiseley, Loren Corey 1907-1977 .... **CLC 7**
See also AAYA 5; CA 1-4R; 73-76; CANR 6; DLBD 17

Eisenstadt, Jill 1963- .... **CLC 50**
See also CA 140

Eisenstein, Sergei (Mikhailovich)
1898-1948 .... **TCLC 57**
See also CA 114; 149

Eisner, Simon
See Kornbluth, C(yril) M.

Ekeloef, (Bengt) Gunnar
1907-1968 ... **CLC 27; DAM POET; PC 23**
See also CA 123; 25-28R

Ekelöf, (Bengt) Gunnar
See Ekeloef, (Bengt) Gunnar

Ekelund, Vilhelm 1880-1949 .... **TCLC 75**
See also CA 189

Ekwensi, C. O. D.
See Ekwensi, Cyprian (Odiatu Duaka)

Ekwensi, Cyprian (Odiatu Duaka)
1921- ...... **CLC 4; BLC 1; DAM MULT**
See also BW 2, 3; CA 29-32R; CANR 18, 42, 74; CN; CWRI; DLB 117; MTCW 1, 2; SATA 66

Elaine .... **TCLC 18**
See also Leverson, Ada

El Crummo
See Crumb, R(obert)

Elder, Lonne III 1931-1996 .... **DC 8**
See also BLC 1; BW 1, 3; CA 81-84; 152; CAD; CANR 25; DAM MULT; DLB 7, 38, 44

Eleanor of Aquitaine 1122-1204 ... **CMLC 39**

Elia
See Lamb, Charles

Eliade, Mircea 1907-1986 .... **CLC 19**
See also CA 65-68; 119; CANR 30, 62; DLB 220; MTCW 1; SFW

Eliot, A. D.
See Jewett, (Theodora) Sarah Orne

Eliot, Alice
See Jewett, (Theodora) Sarah Orne

Eliot, Dan
See Silverberg, Robert

Eliot, George 1819-1880 ...... **NCLC 4, 13, 23, 41, 49, 89; DA; DAB; DAC; DAM MST, NOV; PC 20; WLC**
See also CDBLB 1832-1890; CN; CPW; DA3; DLB 21, 35, 55; RGEL; RGSF; SSFS 8

Eliot, John 1604-1690 .... **LC 5**
See also DLB 24

Eliot, T(homas) S(tearns)
1888-1965 ...... **CLC 1, 2, 3, 6, 9, 10, 13, 15, 24, 34, 41, 55, 57, 113; DA; DAB; DAC; DAM DRAM, MST, POET; PC 5, 31; WLC**
See also AAYA 28; CA 5-8R; 25-28R; CANR 41; CDALB 1929-1941; DA3; DFS 4, 13; DLB 7, 10, 45, 63; DLBY 88; MTCW 1, 2; PFS 1, 7

Elizabeth 1866-1941 .... **TCLC 41**

Elkin, Stanley L(awrence)
1930-1995 .. **CLC 4, 6, 9, 14, 27, 51, 91; DAM NOV, POP; SSC 12**
See also AMWS 6; CA 9-12R; 148; CANR 8, 46; CN; CPW; DLB 2, 28; DLBY 80; INT CANR-8; MTCW 1, 2

Elledge, Scott .... **CLC 34**

Elliot, Don
See Silverberg, Robert

Elliott, Don
See Silverberg, Robert

Elliott, George P(aul) 1918-1980 .... **CLC 2**
See also CA 1-4R; 97-100; CANR 2

Elliott, Janice 1931-1995 .... **CLC 47**
See also CA 13-16R; CANR 8, 29, 84; CN; DLB 14; SATA 119

Elliott, Sumner Locke 1917-1991 ..... **CLC 38**
See also CA 5-8R; 134; CANR 2, 21

Elliott, William
See Bradbury, Ray (Douglas)

Ellis, A. E. .... **CLC 7**

Ellis, Alice Thomas .... **CLC 40**
See also Haycraft, Anna (Margaret)
See also DLB 194; MTCW 1

Fair, Ronald L. 1932- .... **CLC 18**
  See also BW 1; CA 69-72; CANR 25; DLB 33

Fairbairn, Roger
  See Carr, John Dickson

Fairbairns, Zoe (Ann) 1948- .... **CLC 32**
  See also CA 103; CANR 21, 85; CN

Fairman, Paul W. 1916-1977
  See Queen, Ellery
  See also CA 114; SFW

Falco, Gian
  See Papini, Giovanni

Falconer, James
  See Kirkup, James

Falconer, Kenneth
  See Kornbluth, C(yril) M.

Falkland, Samuel
  See Heijermans, Herman

Fallaci, Oriana 1930- .... **CLC 11, 110**
  See also CA 77-80; CANR 15, 58; FW; MTCW 1

Faludi, Susan 1959- .... **CLC 140**
  See also CA 138; FW; MTCW 1

Faludy, George 1913- .... **CLC 42**
  See also CA 21-24R

Faludy, Gyoergy
  See Faludy, George

Fanon, Frantz 1925-1961 ... **CLC 74; BLC 2; DAM MULT**
  See also BW 1; CA 116; 89-92

Fanshawe, Ann 1625-1680 .... **LC 11**

Fante, John (Thomas) 1911-1983 .... **CLC 60**
  See also CA 69-72; 109; CANR 23; DLB 130; DLBY 83

Farah, Nuruddin 1945- ... **CLC 53, 137; BLC 2; DAM MULT**
  See also BW 2, 3; CA 106; CANR 81; CN; DLB 125

Fargue, Leon-Paul 1876(?)-1947 .... **TCLC 11**
  See also CA 109

Farigoule, Louis
  See Romains, Jules

Farina, Richard 1936(?)-1966 .... **CLC 9**
  See also CA 81-84; 25-28R

Farley, Walter (Lorimer)
  1915-1989 .... **CLC 17**
  See also CA 17-20R; CANR 8, 29, 84; DLB 22; JRDA; MAICYA; SATA 2, 43; YAW

Farmer, Philip Jose 1918- .... **CLC 1, 19**
  See also AAYA 28; CA 1-4R; CANR 4, 35; DLB 8; MTCW 1; SATA 93; SFW

Farquhar, George 1677-1707 ... **LC 21; DAM DRAM**
  See also DLB 84; RGEL

Farrell, J(ames) G(ordon)
  1935-1979 .... **CLC 6**
  See also CA 73-76; 89-92; CANR 36; DLB 14; MTCW 1; RHW

Farrell, James T(homas) 1904-1979 . **CLC 1, 4, 8, 11, 66; SSC 28**
  See also CA 5-8R; 89-92; CANR 9, 61; DLB 4, 9, 86; DLBD 2; MTCW 1, 2

Farrell, Warren (Thomas) 1943- .... **CLC 70**
  See also CA 146

Farren, Richard J.
  See Betjeman, John

Farren, Richard M.
  See Betjeman, John

Fassbinder, Rainer Werner
  1946-1982 .... **CLC 20**
  See also CA 93-96; 106; CANR 31

Fast, Howard (Melvin) 1914- .. **CLC 23, 131; DAM NOV**
  See also AAYA 16; CA 1-4R, 181; CAAE 181; CAAS 18; CANR 1, 33, 54, 75, 98; CMW; CN; CPW; DLB 9; INT CANR-33; MTCW 1; RHW; SATA 7; SATA-Essay 107; TCWW 2; YAW

Faulcon, Robert
  See Holdstock, Robert P.

Faulkner, William (Cuthbert)
  1897-1962 .... **CLC 1, 3, 6, 8, 9, 11, 14, 18, 28, 52, 68; DA; DAB; DAC; DAM MST, NOV; SSC 1, 35, 42; WLC**
  See also AAYA 7; CA 81-84; CANR 33; CDALB 1929-1941; DA3; DLB 9, 11, 44, 102; DLBD 2; DLBY 86, 97; MTCW 1, 2; NFS 4, 8; SSFS 2, 5, 6, 12

Fauset, Jessie Redmon
  1882(?)-1961 .... **CLC 19, 54; BLC 2; DAM MULT**
  See also AFAW 2; BW 1; CA 109; CANR 83; DLB 51; FW

Faust, Frederick (Schiller)
  1892-1944(?) .... **TCLC 49; DAM POP**
  See also Austin, Frank; Brand, Max; Challis, George; Dawson, Peter; Dexter, Martin; Evans, Evan; Frederick, John; Frost, Frederick; Manning, David; Silver, Nicholas
  See also CA 108; 152

Faust, Irvin 1924- .... **CLC 8**
  See also CA 33-36R; CANR 28, 67; CN; DLB 2, 28; DLBY 80

Fawkes, Guy
  See Benchley, Robert (Charles)

Fearing, Kenneth (Flexner)
  1902-1961 .... **CLC 51**
  See also CA 93-96; CANR 59; CMW; DLB 9

Fecamps, Elise
  See Creasey, John

Federman, Raymond 1928- .... **CLC 6, 47**
  See also CA 17-20R; CAAS 8; CANR 10, 43, 83; CN; DLBY 80

Federspiel, J(uerg) F. 1931- .... **CLC 42**
  See also CA 146

Feiffer, Jules (Ralph) 1929- ..... **CLC 2, 8, 64; DAM DRAM**
  See also AAYA 3; CA 17-20R; CAD; CANR 30, 59; CD; DLB 7, 44; INT CANR-30; MTCW 1; SATA 8, 61, 111

Feige, Hermann Albert Otto Maximilian
  See Traven, B.

Feinberg, David B. 1956-1994 .... **CLC 59**
  See also CA 135; 147

Feinstein, Elaine 1930- .... **CLC 36**
  See also CA 69-72; CAAS 1; CANR 31, 68; CN; CP; CWP; DLB 14, 40; MTCW 1

Feke, Gilbert David .... **CLC 65**

Feldman, Irving (Mordecai) 1928- ..... **CLC 7**
  See also CA 1-4R; CANR 1; CP; DLB 169

Felix-Tchicaya, Gerald
  See Tchicaya, Gerald Felix

Fellini, Federico 1920-1993 .... **CLC 16, 85**
  See also CA 65-68; 143; CANR 33

Felsen, Henry Gregor 1916-1995 ..... **CLC 17**
  See also CA 1-4R; 180; CANR 1; SAAS 2; SATA 1

Felski, Rita .... **CLC 65**

Fenno, Jack
  See Calisher, Hortense

Fenollosa, Ernest (Francisco)
  1853-1908 .... **TCLC 91**

Fenton, James Martin 1949- .... **CLC 32**
  See also CA 102; CP; DLB 40; PFS 11

Ferber, Edna 1887-1968 .... **CLC 18, 93**
  See also AITN 1; CA 5-8R; 25-28R; CANR 68; DLB 9, 28, 86; MTCW 1, 2; RGAL; RHW; SATA 7; TCWW 2

Ferdowsi, Abu'l Qāsem 940-1020 . **CMLC 43**

Ferguson, Helen
  See Kavan, Anna

Ferguson, Niall 1964- .... **CLC 134**
  See also CA 190

Ferguson, Samuel 1810-1886 .... **NCLC 33**
  See also DLB 32

Fergusson, Robert 1750-1774 .... **LC 29**
  See also DLB 109; RGEL

Ferling, Lawrence
  See Ferlinghetti, Lawrence (Monsanto)

Ferlinghetti, Lawrence (Monsanto)
  1919(?)- .... **CLC 2, 6, 10, 27, 111; DAM POET; PC 1**
  See also CA 5-8R; CANR 3, 41, 73; CDALB 1941-1968; CP; DA3; DLB 5, 16; MTCW 1, 2

Fern, Fanny
  See Parton, Sara Payson Willis

Fernandez, Vicente Garcia Huidobro
  See Huidobro Fernandez, Vicente Garcia

Fernandez-Armesto, Felipe .... **CLC 70**

Fernandez de Lizardi, Jose Joaquin
  See Lizardi, Jose Joaquin Fernandez de

Ferre, Rosario 1942- ...... **CLC 139; HLCS 1; SSC 36**
  See also CA 131; CANR 55, 81; CWW 2; DLB 145; HW 1, 2; MTCW 1

Ferrer, Gabriel (Francisco Victor) Miro
  See Miro (Ferrer), Gabriel (Francisco Victor)

Ferrier, Susan (Edmonstone)
  1782-1854 .... **NCLC 8**
  See also DLB 116

Ferrigno, Robert 1948(?)- .... **CLC 65**
  See also CA 140

Ferron, Jacques 1921-1985 .... **CLC 94; DAC**
  See also CA 117; 129; CCA 1; DLB 60

Feuchtwanger, Lion 1884-1958 .... **TCLC 3**
  See also CA 104; 187; DLB 66

Feuillet, Octave 1821-1890 .... **NCLC 45**
  See also DLB 192

Feydeau, Georges (Léon Jules Marie)
  1862-1921 .... **TCLC 22; DAM DRAM**
  See also CA 113; 152; CANR 84; DLB 192; EW; GFL 1789 to the Present; RGWL

Fichte, Johann Gottlieb
  1762-1814 .... **NCLC 62**
  See also DLB 90

Ficino, Marsilio 1433-1499 .... **LC 12**

Fiedeler, Hans
  See Doeblin, Alfred

Fiedler, Leslie A(aron) 1917- .. **CLC 4, 13, 24**
  See also CA 9-12R; CANR 7, 63; CN; DLB 28, 67; MTCW 1, 2

Field, Andrew 1938- .... **CLC 44**
  See also CA 97-100; CANR 25

Field, Eugene 1850-1895 .... **NCLC 3**
  See also DLB 23, 42, 140; DLBD 13; MAICYA; RGAL; SATA 16

Field, Gans T.
  See Wellman, Manly Wade

Field, Michael 1915-1971 .... **TCLC 43**
  See also CA 29-32R

Field, Peter
  See Hobson, Laura Z(ametkin)
  See also TCWW 2

Fielding, Helen 1959(?)- .... **CLC 146**
  See also CA 172; DLB 231

Fielding, Henry 1707-1754 ..... **LC 1, 46; DA; DAB; DAC; DAM DRAM, MST, NOV; WLC**
  See also CDBLB 1660-1789; DA3; DLB 39, 84, 101; RGEL

Fielding, Sarah 1710-1768 .... **LC 1, 44**
  See also DLB 39; RGEL

Fields, W. C. 1880-1946 .... **TCLC 80**
  See also DLB 44

Fierstein, Harvey (Forbes) 1954- .... **CLC 33; DAM DRAM, POP**
  See also CA 123; 129; CAD; CD; CPW; DA3; DFS 6; GLL

Fourier, Charles 1772-1837 .... **NCLC 51**
Fournier, Henri Alban 1886-1914
   See Alain-Fournier
   See also CA 104; 179
Fournier, Pierre 1916- .... **CLC 11**
   See Gascar, Pierre
   See also CA 89-92; CANR 16, 40
Fowles, John (Philip) 1926- .. **CLC 1, 2, 3, 4,**
   6, 9, 10, 15, 33, 87; DAB; DAC; DAM
   MST; SSC 33
   See also BRWS 1; CA 5-8R; CANR 25, 71;
   CDBLB 1960 to Present; CN; DA3; DLB
   14, 139, 207; HGG; MTCW 1, 2; RHW;
   SATA 22
Fox, Paula 1923- .... **CLC 2, 8, 121**
   See also AAYA 3, 37; CA 73-76; CANR
   20, 36, 62; CLR 1, 44; DLB 52; JRDA;
   MAICYA; MTCW 1; NFS 12; SATA 17,
   60, 120; YAW
Fox, William Price (Jr.) 1926- .... **CLC 22**
   See also CA 17-20R; CAAS 19; CANR 11;
   CSW; DLB 2; DLBY 81
Foxe, John 1517(?)-1587 .... **LC 14**
   See also DLB 132
Frame, Janet .. **CLC 2, 3, 6, 22, 66, 96; SSC**
   29
   See also Clutha, Janet Paterson Frame
   See also CN; CWP; RGSF
France, Anatole .... **TCLC 9**
   See also Thibault, Jacques Anatole François
   See also DLB 123; GFL 1789 to the Present;
   MTCW 1; RGWL
Francis, Claude .... **CLC 50**
Francis, Dick 1920- .... **CLC 2, 22, 42, 102;**
   DAM POP
   See also AAYA 5, 21; BEST 89:3; CA 5-8R;
   CANR 9, 42, 68; CDBLB 1960 to Present;
   CMW; CN; DA3; DLB 87; INT CANR-9;
   MTCW 1, 2
Francis, Robert (Churchill)
   1901-1987 .... **CLC 15; PC 34**
   See also CA 1-4R; 123; CANR 1; PFS 12
Frank, Anne(lies Marie)
   1929-1945 . **TCLC 17; DA; DAB; DAC;**
   DAM MST; WLC
   See also AAYA 12; CA 113; 133; CANR
   68; DA3; MTCW 1, 2; NCFS 2; SATA
   87; SATA Brief 42; YAW
Frank, Bruno 1887-1945 .... **TCLC 81**
   See also CA 189; DLB 118
Frank, Elizabeth 1945- .... **CLC 39**
   See also CA 121; 126; CANR 78; INT 126
Frankl, Viktor E(mil) 1905-1997 ...... **CLC 93**
   See also CA 65-68; 161
Franklin, Benjamin
   See Ha
Franklin, Benjamin 1706-1790 .. **LC 25; DA;**
   DAB; DAC; DAM MST; WLCS
   See also CDALB 1640-1865; DA3; DLB
   24, 43, 73
Franklin, (Stella Maria Sarah) Miles
   (Lampe) 1879-1954 .... **TCLC 7**
   See also CA 104; 164; DLB 230; FW;
   MTCW 2
Fraser, (Lady)Antonia (Pakenham)
   1932- .... **CLC 32, 107**
   See also CA 85-88; CANR 44, 65; CMW;
   MTCW 1, 2; SATA-Brief 32
Fraser, George MacDonald 1925- ...... **CLC 7**
   See also CA 45-48, 180; CAAE 180; CANR
   2, 48, 74; MTCW 1; RHW
Fraser, Sylvia 1935- .... **CLC 64**
   See also CA 45-48; CANR 1, 16, 60; CCA
   1
Frayn, Michael 1933- .... **CLC 3, 7, 31, 47;**
   DAM DRAM, NOV
   See also CA 5-8R; CANR 30, 69; CBD;
   CD; CN; DLB 13, 14, 194; FANT; MTCW
   1, 2; SFW

Fraze, Candida (Merrill) 1945- .... **CLC 50**
   See also CA 126
Frazer, Andrew
   See Marlowe, Stephen
Frazer, J(ames) G(eorge)
   1854-1941 .... **TCLC 32**
   See also BRWS 3; CA 118
Frazer, Robert Caine
   See Creasey, John
Frazer, Sir James George
   See Frazer, J(ames) G(eorge)
Frazier, Charles 1950- .... **CLC 109**
   See also AAYA 34; CA 161; CSW
Frazier, Ian 1951- .... **CLC 46**
   See also CA 130; CANR 54, 93
Frederic, Harold 1856-1898 .... **NCLC 10**
   See also DLB 12, 23; DLBD 13; RGAL
Frederick, John
   See Faust, Frederick (Schiller)
   See also TCWW 2
Frederick the Great 1712-1786 .... **LC 14**
Fredro, Aleksander 1793-1876 .... **NCLC 8**
Freeling, Nicolas 1927- .... **CLC 38**
   See also CA 49-52; CAAS 12; CANR 1,
   17, 50, 84; CMW; CN; DLB 87
Freeman, Douglas Southall
   1886-1953 .... **TCLC 11**
   See also CA 109; DLB 17; DLBD 17
Freeman, Judith 1946- .... **CLC 55**
   See also CA 148
Freeman, Mary E(leanor) Wilkins
   1852-1930 .... **TCLC 9; SSC 1**
   See also CA 106; 177; DLB 12, 78, 221;
   FW; HGG; SSFS 4, 8
Freeman, R(ichard) Austin
   1862-1943 .... **TCLC 21**
   See also CA 113; CANR 84; CMW; DLB
   70
French, Albert 1943- .... **CLC 86**
   See also BW 3; CA 167
French, Marilyn 1929- .... **CLC 10, 18, 60;**
   DAM DRAM, NOV, POP
   See also CA 69-72; CANR 3, 31; CN;
   CPW; FW; INT CANR-31; MTCW 1, 2
French, Paul
   See Asimov, Isaac
Freneau, Philip Morin 1752-1832 ... **NCLC 1**
   See also AMWS 2; DLB 37, 43
Freud, Sigmund 1856-1939 .... **TCLC 52**
   See also CA 115; 133; CANR 69; MTCW
   1, 2
Friedan, Betty (Naomi) 1921- .... **CLC 74**
   See also CA 65-68; CANR 18, 45, 74; FW;
   MTCW 1, 2
Friedlander, Saul 1932- .... **CLC 90**
   See also CA 117; 130; CANR 72
Friedman, B(ernard) H(arper)
   1926- .... **CLC 7**
   See also CA 1-4R; CANR 3, 48
Friedman, Bruce Jay 1930- ...... **CLC 3, 5, 56**
   See also CA 9-12R; CAD; CANR 25, 52;
   CD; CN; DLB 2, 28; INT CANR-25
Friel, Brian 1929- .... **CLC 5, 42, 59, 115; DC**
   8
   See also BRWS 5; CA 21-24R; CANR 33,
   69; CBD; CD; DFS 11; DLB 13; MTCW
   1; RGEL
Friis-Baastad, Babbis Ellinor
   1921-1970 .... **CLC 12**
   See also CA 17-20R; 134; SATA 7
Frisch, Max (Rudolf) 1911-1991 ... **CLC 3, 9,**
   14, 18, 32, 44; DAM DRAM, NOV
   See also CA 85-88; 134; CANR 32, 74;
   DLB 69, 124; MTCW 1, 2
Fromentin, Eugène (Samuel Auguste)
   1820-1876 .... **NCLC 10**
   See also DLB 123; GFL 1789 to the Present

Frost, Frederick
   See Faust, Frederick (Schiller)
   See also TCWW 2
Frost, Robert (Lee) 1874-1963 .. **CLC 1, 3, 4,**
   9, 10, 13, 15, 26, 34, 44; DA; DAB;
   DAC; DAM MST, POET; PC 1; WLC
   See also AAYA 21; CA 89-92; CANR 33;
   CDALB 1917-1929; CLR 67; DA3; DLB
   54; DLBD 7; MTCW 1, 2; PFS 1, 2, 3, 4,
   5, 6, 7, 10; SATA 14
Froude, James Anthony
   1818-1894 .... **NCLC 43**
   See also DLB 18, 57, 144
Froy, Herald
   See Waterhouse, Keith (Spencer)
Fry, Christopher 1907- .... **CLC 2, 10, 14;**
   DAM DRAM
   See also BRWS 3; CA 17-20R; CAAS 23;
   CANR 9, 30, 74; CBD; CD; CP; DLB 13;
   MTCW 1, 2; RGEL; SATA 66
Frye, (Herman) Northrop
   1912-1991 .... **CLC 24, 70**
   See also CA 5-8R; 133; CANR 8, 37; DLB
   67, 68; MTCW 1, 2
Fuchs, Daniel 1909-1993 .... **CLC 8, 22**
   See also CA 81-84; 142; CAAS 5; CANR
   40; DLB 9, 26, 28; DLBY 93
Fuchs, Daniel 1934- .... **CLC 34**
   See also CA 37-40R; CANR 14, 48
Fuentes, Carlos 1928- .. **CLC 3, 8, 10, 13, 22,**
   41, 60, 113; DA; DAB; DAC; DAM
   MST, MULT, NOV; HLC 1; SSC 24;
   WLC
   See also AAYA 4; AITN 2; CA 69-72;
   CANR 10, 32, 68; CWW 2; DA3; DLB
   113; DNFS 2; HW 1, 2; MTCW 1, 2; NFS
   8; RGSF; RGWL
Fuentes, Gregorio Lopez y
   See Lopez y Fuentes, Gregorio
Fuertes, Gloria 1918-1998 .... **PC 27**
   See also CA 178, 180; DLB 108; HW 2;
   SATA 115
Fugard, (Harold) Athol 1932- . **CLC 5, 9, 14,**
   25, 40, 80; DAM DRAM; DC 3
   See also AAYA 17; CA 85-88; CANR 32,
   54; CD; DFS 3, 6, 10; DLB 225; DNFS
   1, 2; MTCW 1
Fugard, Sheila 1932- .... **CLC 48**
   See also CA 125
Fukuyama, Francis 1952- .... **CLC 131**
   See also CA 140; CANR 72
Fuller, Charles (H., Jr.) 1939- .... **CLC 25;**
   BLC 2; DAM DRAM, MULT; DC 1
   See also BW 2; CA 108; 112; CAD; CANR
   87; CD; DFS 8; DLB 38; INT CA-112;
   MTCW 1
Fuller, Henry Blake 1857-1929 .... **TCLC 103**
   See also CA 108; 177; DLB 12; RGAL
Fuller, John (Leopold) 1937- .... **CLC 62**
   See also CA 21-24R; CANR 9, 44; CP;
   DLB 40
Fuller, Margaret
   See Ossoli, Sarah Margaret (Fuller marchesa
   d')
   See also AMWS 2
Fuller, Roy (Broadbent) 1912-1991 ... **CLC 4,**
   28
   See also CA 5-8R; 135; CAAS 10; CANR
   53, 83; CWRI; DLB 15, 20; SATA 87
Fuller, Sarah Margaret
   See Ossoli, Sarah Margaret (Fuller marchesa
   d')
Fulton, Alice 1952- .... **CLC 52**
   See also CA 116; CANR 57, 88; CP; CWP;
   DLB 193
Furphy, Joseph 1843-1912 .... **TCLC 25**
   See also CA 163; DLB 230; RGEL
Fuson, Robert H(enderson) 1927- .... **CLC 70**
   See also CA 89-92

Gellhorn, Martha (Ellis)
1908-1998 .... **CLC 14, 60**
See also CA 77-80; 164; CANR 44; CN;
DLBY 82, 98

Genet, Jean 1910-1986 .. **CLC 1, 2, 5, 10, 14,
44, 46; DAM DRAM**
See also CA 13-16R; CANR 18; DA3; DFS
10; DLB 72; DLBY 86; GFL 1789 to the
Present; GLL 1; MTCW 1, 2; RGWL

Gent, Peter 1942- .... **CLC 29**
See also AITN 1; CA 89-92; DLBY 82

Gentile, Giovanni 1875-1944 .... **TCLC 96**
See also CA 119

Gentlewoman in New England, A
See Bradstreet, Anne

Gentlewoman in Those Parts, A
See Bradstreet, Anne

Geoffrey of Monmouth c.
1100-1155 .... **CMLC 44**
See also DLB 146

George, Jean Craighead 1919- .... **CLC 35**
See also AAYA 8; CA 5-8R; CANR 25;
CLR 1; DLB 52; JRDA; MAICYA; SATA
2, 68; YAW

George, Stefan (Anton) 1868-1933 . **TCLC 2,
14**
See also CA 104

Georges, Georges Martin
See Simenon, Georges (Jacques Christian)

Gerhardi, William Alexander
See Gerhardie, William Alexander

Gerhardie, William Alexander
1895-1977 .... **CLC 5**
See also CA 25-28R; 73-76; CANR 18;
DLB 36

Gerstler, Amy 1956- .... **CLC 70**
See also CA 146

Gertler, T. .... **CLC 134**
See also CA 116; 121

Ghalib .... **NCLC 39, 78**
See also Ghālib, Asadullāh Khān

Ghālib, Asadullāh Khān 1797-1869
See Ghalib
See also DAM POET

Ghelderode, Michel de 1898-1962 ..... **CLC 6,
11; DAM DRAM; DC 15**
See CA 85-88; CANR 40, 77

Ghiselin, Brewster 1903- .... **CLC 23**
See also CA 13-16R; CAAS 10; CANR 13;
CP

Ghose, Aurabinda 1872-1950 .... **TCLC 63**
See also CA 163

Ghose, Zulfikar 1935- .... **CLC 42**
See also CA 65-68; CANR 67; CN; CP

Ghosh, Amitav 1956- .... **CLC 44**
See also CA 147; CANR 80; CN

Giacosa, Giuseppe 1847-1906 .... **TCLC 7**
See also CA 104

Gibb, Lee
See Waterhouse, Keith (Spencer)

Gibbon, Lewis Grassic .... **TCLC 4**
See also Mitchell, James Leslie

Gibbons, Kaye 1960- .... **CLC 50, 88, 145;
DAM POP**
See also AAYA 34; CA 151; CANR 75;
CSW; DA3; MTCW 1; NFS 3; RGAL;
SATA 117

Gibran, Kahlil 1883-1931 .... **TCLC 1, 9;
DAM POET, POP; PC 9**
See also CA 104; 150; DA3; MTCW 2

Gibran, Khalil
See Gibran, Kahlil

Gibson, William 1914- .. **CLC 23; DA; DAB;
DAC; DAM DRAM, MST**
See also CA 9-12R; CAD; CANR 9, 42,
75; CD; CN; CPW; DFS 2; DLB 7;
MTCW 1; SATA 66; SCFW 2; SFW;
YAW

Gibson, William (Ford) 1948- ... **CLC 39, 63;
DAM POP**
See also AAYA 12; CA 126; 133; CANR
52, 90; DA3; MTCW 1

Gide, André (Paul Guillaume)
1869-1951 . **TCLC 5, 12, 36; DA; DAB;
DAC; DAM MST, NOV; SSC 13; WLC**
See also CA 104; 124; DA3; DLB 65; EW;
GFL 1789 to the Present; MTCW 1, 2;
RGSF; RGWL

Gifford, Barry (Colby) 1946- .... **CLC 34**
See also CA 65-68; CANR 9, 30, 40, 90

Gilbert, Frank
See De Voto, Bernard (Augustine)

Gilbert, W(illiam) S(chwenck)
1836-1911 .... **TCLC 3; DAM DRAM,
POET**
See also CA 104; 173; SATA 36

Gilbreth, Frank B., Jr. 1911-2001 .... **CLC 17**
See also CA 9-12R; SATA 2

Gilchrist, Ellen 1935- .... **CLC 34, 48, 143;
DAM POP; SSC 14**
See also CA 113; 116; CANR 41, 61; CN;
CPW; CSW; DLB 130; MTCW 1, 2;
RGAL; RGSF; SSFS 9

Giles, Molly 1942 .... **CLC 39**
See also CA 126; CANR 98

Gill, Eric 1882-1940 .... **TCLC 85**

Gill, Patrick
See Creasey, John

Gillette, Douglas .... **CLC 70**

Gilliam, Terry (Vance) 1940- .... **CLC 21, 141**
See also Monty Python
See also AAYA 19; CA 108; 113; CANR
35; INT 113

Gillian, Jerry
See Gilliam, Terry (Vance)

Gilliatt, Penelope (Ann Douglass)
1932-1993 .... **CLC 2, 10, 13, 53**
See also AITN 2; CA 13-16R; 141; CANR
49; DLB 14

Gilman, Charlotte (Anna) Perkins (Stetson)
1860-1935 .... **TCLC 9, 37; SSC 13**
See also CA 106; 150; DLB 221; FW;
HGG; MTCW 1; SFW; SSFS 1

Gilmour, David 1949- .... **CLC 35**
See also CA 138; 147

Gilpin, William 1724-1804 .... **NCLC 30**

Gilray, J. D.
See Mencken, H(enry) L(ouis)

Gilroy, Frank D(aniel) 1925- .... **CLC 2**
See also CA 81-84; CAD; CANR 32, 64,
86; CD; DLB 7

Gilstrap, John 1957(?)- .... **CLC 99**
See also CA 160

Ginsberg, Allen 1926-1997 .... **CLC 1, 2, 3, 4,
6, 13, 36, 69, 109; DA; DAB; DAC;
DAM MST, POET; PC 4; WLC**
See also AAYA 33; AITN 1; AMWS 2; CA
1-4R; 157; CANR 2, 41, 63, 95; CDALB
1941-1968; CP; DA3; DLB 5, 16, 169;
GLL 1; MTCW 1, 2; PFS 5; RGAL

Ginzburg, Eugenia .... **CLC 59**

Ginzburg, Natalia 1916-1991 .... **CLC 5, 11,
54, 70**
See also CA 85-88; 135; CANR 33; DLB
177; MTCW 1, 2; RGWL

Giono, Jean 1895-1970 .... **CLC 4, 11**
See also CA 45-48; 29-32R; CANR 2, 35;
DLB 72; GFL 1789 to the Present; MTCW
1; RGWL

Giovanni, Nikki 1943- .... **CLC 2, 4, 19, 64,
117; BLC 2; DA; DAB; DAC; DAM
MST, MULT, POET; PC 19; WLCS**
See also AAYA 22; AITN 1; BW 2, 3; CA
29-32R; CAAS 6; CANR 18, 41, 60, 91;
CDALBS; CLR 6; CP; CSW; CWP;
CWRI; DA3; DLB 5, 41; INT CANR-18;
MAICYA; MTCW 1, 2; RGAL; SATA 24,
107; YAW

Giovene, Andrea 1904- .... **CLC 7**
See also CA 85-88

Gippius, Zinaida (Nikolayevna) 1869-1945
See Hippius, Zinaida
See also CA 106

Giraudoux, Jean(-Hippolyte)
1882-1944 .... **TCLC 2, 7; DAM DRAM**
See also CA 104; DLB 65; EW; GFL 1789
to the Present; RGWL

Gironella, José María 1917-1991 ..... **CLC 11**
See also CA 101

Gissing, George (Robert)
1857-1903 .... **TCLC 3, 24, 47; SSC 37**
See also CA 105; 167; DLB 18, 135, 184

Giurlani, Aldo
See Palazzeschi, Aldo

Gladkov, Fyodor (Vasilyevich)
1883-1958 .... **TCLC 27**
See also CA 170

Glanville, Brian (Lester) 1931- .... **CLC 6**
See also CA 5-8R; CAAS 9; CANR 3, 70;
CN; DLB 15, 139; SATA 42

Glasgow, Ellen (Anderson Gholson)
1873-1945 .... **TCLC 2, 7; SSC 34**
See also CA 104; 164; DLB 9, 12; MTCW
2; RHW; SSFS 9

Glaspell, Susan 1882(?)-1948 . **TCLC 55; DC
10; SSC 41**
See also AMWS 3; CA 110; 154; DFS 8;
DLB 7, 9, 78, 228; RGAL; SSFS 3;
TCWW 2; YABC 2

Glassco, John 1909-1981 .... **CLC 9**
See also CA 13-16R; 102; CANR 15; DLB
68

Glasscock, Amnesia
See Steinbeck, John (Ernst)

Glasser, Ronald J. 1940(?)- .... **CLC 37**

Glassman, Joyce
See Johnson, Joyce

Glendinning, Victoria 1937- .... **CLC 50**
See also CA 120; 127; CANR 59, 89; DLB
155

Glissant, Edouard 1928- . **CLC 10, 68; DAM
MULT**
See also CA 153; CWW 2

Gloag, Julian 1930- .... **CLC 40**
See also AITN 1; CA 65-68; CANR 10, 70;
CN

Glowacki, Aleksander
See Prus, Boleslaw

Glück, Louise (Elisabeth) 1943- .. **CLC 7, 22,
44, 81; DAM POET; PC 16**
See also AMWS 5; CA 33-36R; CANR 40,
69; CP; CWP; DA3; DLB 5; MTCW 2;
PFS 5

Glyn, Elinor 1864-1943 .... **TCLC 72**
See also DLB 153; RHW

Gobineau, Joseph-Arthur
1816-1882 .... **NCLC 17**
See also DLB 123; GFL 1789 to the Present

Godard, Jean-Luc 1930- .... **CLC 20**
See also CA 93-96

Godden, (Margaret) Rumer
1907-1998 .... **CLC 53**
See also AAYA 6; CA 5-8R; 172; CANR 4,
27, 36, 55, 80; CLR 20; CN; CWRI; DLB
161; MAICYA; RHW; SAAS 12; SATA
3, 36; SATA-Obit 109

Godoy Alcayaga, Lucila
1899-1957 .... **TCLC 2; DAM MULT;
HLC 2; PC 32**
See also Mistral, Gabriela
See also BW 2; CA 104; 131; CANR 81;
DNFS 1; HW 1, 2; MTCW 1, 2

Godwin, Gail (Kathleen) 1937- ..... **CLC 5, 8,
22, 31, 69, 125; DAM POP**
See also CA 29-32R; CANR 15, 43, 69;
CN; CPW; CSW; DA3; DLB 6, 234; INT
CANR-15; MTCW 1, 2

Heredia, Jose Maria 1803-1839
See also HLCS 2

Hergesheimer, Joseph 1880-1954 ... **TCLC 11**
See also CA 109; DLB 102, 9; RGAL

Herlihy, James Leo 1927-1993 .... **CLC 6**
See also CA 1-4R; 143; CAD; CANR 2

Hermogenes fl. c. 175- .... **CMLC 6**

Hernández, José 1834-1886 .... **NCLC 17**

Herodotus c. 484B.C.-c. 420B.C. .. **CMLC 17**
See also DLB 176; RGWL

Herrick, Robert 1591-1674 .... **LC 13; DA; DAB; DAC; DAM MST, POP; PC 9**
See also DLB 126; RGAL; RGEL

Herring, Guilles
See Somerville, Edith

Herriot, James .... **CLC 12; DAM POP**
See also Wight, James Alfred
See also AAYA 1; CA 148; CANR 40; MTCW 2; SATA 86

Herris, Violet
See Hunt, Violet

Herrmann, Dorothy 1941- .... **CLC 44**
See also CA 107

Herrmann, Taffy
See Herrmann, Dorothy

Hersey, John (Richard) 1914-1993 .... **CLC 1, 2, 7, 9, 40, 81, 97; DAM POP**
See also AAYA 29; CA 17-20R; 140; CANR 33; CDALBS; CPW; DLB 6, 185; MTCW 1, 2; SATA 25; SATA-Obit 76

Herzen, Aleksandr Ivanovich 1812-1870 .... **NCLC 10, 61**

Herzl, Theodor 1860-1904 .... **TCLC 36**
See also CA 168

Herzog, Werner 1942- .... **CLC 16**
See also CA 89-92

Hesiod c. 8th cent. B.C.- .... **CMLC 5**
See also DLB 176; RGWL

Hesse, Hermann 1877-1962 ... **CLC 1, 2, 3, 6, 11, 17, 25, 69; DA; DAB; DAC; DAM MST, NOV; SSC 9; WLC**
See also CA 17-18; CAP 2; DA3; DLB 66; MTCW 1, 2; NFS 6; RGWL; SATA 50

Hewes, Cady
See De Voto, Bernard (Augustine)

Heyen, William 1940- .... **CLC 13, 18**
See also CA 33-36R; CAAS 9; CANR 98; CP; DLB 5

Heyerdahl, Thor 1914- .... **CLC 26**
See also CA 5-8R; CANR 5, 22, 66, 73; MTCW 1, 2; SATA 2, 52

Heym, Georg (Theodor Franz Arthur) 1887-1912 .... **TCLC 9**
See also CA 106; 181

Heym, Stefan 1913- .... **CLC 41**
See also CA 9-12R; CANR 4; CWW 2; DLB 69

Heyse, Paul (Johann Ludwig von) 1830-1914 .... **TCLC 8**
See also CA 104; DLB 129

Heyward, (Edwin) DuBose 1885-1940 .... **TCLC 59**
See also CA 108; 157; DLB 7, 9, 45; SATA 21

Heywood, John 1497-1580 .... **LC 65**
See also RGEL

Hibbert, Eleanor Alice Burford 1906-1993 .... **CLC 7; DAM POP**
See also BEST 90:4; CA 17-20R; 140; CANR 9, 28, 59; CMW; CPW; MTCW 2; RHW; SATA 2; SATA-Obit 74

Hichens, Robert (Smythe) 1864-1950 .... **TCLC 64**
See also CA 162; DLB 153; HGG; RHW

Higgins, George V(incent) 1939-1999 .... **CLC 4, 7, 10, 18**
See also CA 77-80; 186; CAAS 5; CANR 17, 51, 89, 96; CMW; CN; DLB 2; DLBY 81, 98; INT CANR-17; MTCW 1

Higginson, Thomas Wentworth 1823-1911 .... **TCLC 36**
See also CA 162; DLB 1, 64

Higgonet, Margaret ed. .... **CLC 65**

Highet, Helen
See MacInnes, Helen (Clark)

Highsmith, (Mary) Patricia 1921-1995 .... **CLC 2, 4, 14, 42, 102; DAM NOV, POP**
See also Morgan, Claire
See also BRWS 5; CA 1-4R; 147; CANR 1, 20, 48, 62; CMW; CPW; DA3; MTCW 1, 2

Highwater, Jamake (Mamake) 1942(?)-2001 .... **CLC 12**
See also AAYA 7; CA 65-68; CAAS 7; CANR 10, 34, 84; CLR 17; CWRI; DLB 52; DLBY 85; JRDA; MAICYA; SATA 32, 69; SATA-Brief 30

Highway, Tomson 1951- .... **CLC 92; DAC; DAM MULT**
See also CA 151; CANR 75; CCA 1; CD; DFS 2; MTCW 2; NNAL

Hijuelos, Oscar 1951- .... **CLC 65; DAM MULT, POP; HLC 1**
See also AAYA 25; AMWS 8; BEST 90:1; CA 123; CANR 50, 75; CPW; DA3; DLB 145; HW 1, 2; MTCW 2; RGAL

Hikmet, Nazim 1902(?)-1963 .... **CLC 40**
See also CA 141; 93-96

Hildegard von Bingen 1098-1179 . **CMLC 20**
See also DLB 148

Hildesheimer, Wolfgang 1916-1991 .. **CLC 49**
See also CA 101; 135; DLB 69, 124

Hill, Geoffrey (William) 1932- ...... **CLC 5, 8, 18, 45; DAM POET**
See also BRWS 5; CA 81-84; CANR 21, 89; CDBLB 1960 to Present; CP; DLB 40; MTCW 1

Hill, George Roy 1921- .... **CLC 26**
See also CA 110; 122

Hill, John
See Koontz, Dean R(ay)

Hill, Susan (Elizabeth) 1942- .... **CLC 4, 113; DAB; DAM MST, NOV**
See also CA 33-36R; CANR 29, 69; CN; DLB 14, 139; HGG; MTCW 1; RHW

Hillard, Asa G. III .... **CLC 70**

Hillerman, Tony 1925- . **CLC 62; DAM POP**
See also AAYA 40; BEST 89:1; CA 29-32R; CANR 21, 42, 65, 97; CMW; CPW; DA3; DLB 206; RGAL; SATA 6; TCWW 2; YAW

Hillesum, Etty 1914-1943 .... **TCLC 49**
See also CA 137

Hilliard, Noel (Harvey) 1929-1996 ... **CLC 15**
See also CA 9-12R; CANR 7, 69; CN

Hillis, Rick 1956- .... **CLC 66**
See also CA 134

Hilton, James 1900-1954 .... **TCLC 21**
See also CA 108; 169; DLB 34, 77; FANT; SATA 34

Himes, Chester (Bomar) 1909-1984 .. **CLC 2, 4, 7, 18, 58, 108; BLC 2; DAM MULT**
See also AFAW 2; BW 2; CA 25-28R; 114; CANR 22, 89; CMW; DLB 2, 76, 143, 226; MTCW 1, 2

Hinde, Thomas .... **CLC 6, 11**
See also Chitty, Thomas Willes

Hine, (William) Daryl 1936- .... **CLC 15**
See also CA 1-4R; CAAS 15; CANR 1, 20; CP; DLB 60

Hinkson, Katharine Tynan
See Tynan, Katharine

Hinojosa(-Smith), Rolando (R.) 1929-
See also CA 131; CAAS 16; CANR 62; DAM MULT; DLB 82; HLC 1; HW 1, 2; MTCW 2

Hinton, S(usan) E(loise) 1950- .... **CLC 30, 111; DA; DAB; DAC; DAM MST, NOV**
See also AAYA 2, 33; CA 81-84; CANR 32, 62, 92; CDALBS; CLR 3, 23; CPW; DA3; JRDA; MAICYA; MTCW 1, 2; NFS 5, 9; SATA 19, 58, 115; YAW

Hippius, Zinaida .... **TCLC 9**
See also Gippius, Zinaida (Nikolayevna)

Hiraoka, Kimitake 1925-1970
See Mishima, Yukio
See also CA 97-100; 29-32R; DAM DRAM; DA3; MTCW 1, 2; SSFS 12

Hirsch, E(ric) D(onald), Jr. 1928- .... **CLC 79**
See also CA 25-28R; CANR 27, 51; DLB 67; INT CANR-27; MTCW 1

Hirsch, Edward 1950- .... **CLC 31, 50**
See also CA 104; CANR 20, 42; CP; DLB 120

Hitchcock, Alfred (Joseph) 1899-1980 .... **CLC 16**
See also AAYA 22; CA 159; 97-100, SATA 27; SATA-Obit 24

Hitler, Adolf 1889-1945 .... **TCLC 53**
See also CA 117; 147

Hoagland, Edward 1932- .... **CLC 28**
See also CA 1-4R; CANR 2, 31, 57; CN; DLB 6; SATA 51; TCWW 2

Hoban, Russell (Conwell) 1925- . **CLC 7, 25; DAM NOV**
See also CA 5-8R; CANR 23, 37, 66; CLR 3, 69; CN; CWRI; DLB 52; FANT; MAICYA; MTCW 1, 2; SATA 1, 40, 78; SFW

Hobbes, Thomas 1588-1679 .... **LC 36**
See also DLB 151; RGEL

Hobbs, Perry
See Blackmur, R(ichard) P(almer)

Hobson, Laura Z(ametkin) 1900-1986 .... **CLC 7, 25**
See also Field, Peter
See also CA 17-20R; 118; CANR 55; DLB 28; SATA 52

Hoch, Edward D(entinger) 1930-
See Queen, Ellery
See also CA 29-32R; CANR 11, 27, 51, 97; CMW; SFW

Hochhuth, Rolf 1931- .. **CLC 4, 11, 18; DAM DRAM**
See also CA 5-8R; CANR 33, 75; CWW 2; DLB 124; MTCW 1, 2

Hochman, Sandra 1936- .... **CLC 3, 8**
See also CA 5-8R; DLB 5

Hochwaelder, Fritz 1911-1986 .... **CLC 36; DAM DRAM**
See also Hochwälder, Fritz
See also CA 29-32R; 120; CANR 42; MTCW 1

Hochwälder, Fritz
See Hochwaelder, Fritz

Hocking, Mary (Eunice) 1921- .... **CLC 13**
See also CA 101; CANR 18, 40

Hodgins, Jack 1938- .... **CLC 23**
See also CA 93-96; CN; DLB 60

Hodgson, William Hope 1877(?)-1918 .... **TCLC 13**
See also CA 111; 164; CMW; DLB 70, 153, 156, 178; HGG; MTCW 2; SFW

Hoeg, Peter 1957- .... **CLC 95**
See also CA 151; CANR 75; CMW; DA3; MTCW 2

Hoffman, Alice 1952- ... **CLC 51; DAM NOV**
See also AAYA 37; CA 77-80; CANR 34, 66; CN; CPW; MTCW 1, 2

Hoffman, Daniel (Gerard) 1923- . **CLC 6, 13, 23**
See also CA 1-4R; CANR 4; CP; DLB 5

Hoffman, Stanley 1944- .... **CLC 5**
See also CA 77-80

Kelman, James 1946- .... **CLC 58, 86**
　　See also BRWS 5; CA 148; CANR 85; CN;
　　DLB 194; RGSF

Kemal, Yashar 1923- .... **CLC 14, 29**
　　See also CA 89-92; CANR 44; CWW 2

Kemble, Fanny 1809-1893 .... **NCLC 18**
　　See also DLB 32

Kemelman, Harry 1908-1996 .... **CLC 2**
　　See also AITN 1; CA 9-12R; 155; CANR 6,
　　71; CMW; DLB 28

Kempe, Margery 1373(?)-1440(?) ... **LC 6, 56**
　　See also DLB 146; RGEL

Kempis, Thomas a 1380-1471 .... **LC 11**

Kendall, Henry 1839-1882 .... **NCLC 12**
　　See also DLB 230

Keneally, Thomas (Michael) 1935- ... **CLC 5,
　　8, 10, 14, 19, 27, 43, 117; DAM NOV**
　　See also BRWS 4; CA 85-88; CANR 10,
　　50, 74; CN; CPW; DA3; MTCW 1, 2;
　　RHW

Kennedy, Adrienne (Lita) 1931- ..... **CLC 66;
　　BLC 2; DAM MULT; DC 5**
　　See also AFAW 2; BW 2, 3; CA 103; CAAS
　　20; CABS 3; CANR 26, 53, 82; CD; DFS
　　9; DLB 38; FW

Kennedy, John Pendleton
　　1795-1870 .... **NCLC 2**
　　See also DLB 3; RGAL

Kennedy, Joseph Charles 1929-
　　See Kennedy, X. J.
　　See also CA 1-4R; CANR 4, 30, 40; CP;
　　CWRI; SATA 14, 86

Kennedy, William 1928- .. **CLC 6, 28, 34, 53;
　　DAM NOV**
　　See also AAYA 1; AMWS 7; CA 85-88;
　　CANR 14, 31, 76; DA3; DLB 143; DLBY
　　85; INT CANR-31; MTCW 1, 2; SATA
　　57

Kennedy, X. J. .... **CLC 8, 42**
　　See also Kennedy, Joseph Charles
　　See also CAAS 9; CLR 27; DLB 5; SAAS
　　22

Kenny, Maurice (Francis) 1929- ..... **CLC 87;
　　DAM MULT**
　　See also CA 144; CAAS 22; DLB 175;
　　NNAL

Kent, Kelvin
　　See Kuttner, Henry

Kenton, Maxwell
　　See Southern, Terry

Kenyon, Robert O.
　　See Kuttner, Henry

Kepler, Johannes 1571-1630 .... **LC 45**

Kerouac, Jack ..... **CLC 1, 2, 3, 5, 14, 29, 61**
　　See also Kerouac, Jean-Louis Lebris de
　　See also AAYA 25; AMWS 3; CDALB
　　1941-1968; DLB 2, 16; DLBD 3; DLBY
　　95; GLL 1; MTCW 2; NFS 8; RGAL

Kerouac, Jean-Louis Lebris de 1922-1969
　　See Kerouac, Jack
　　See also AITN 1; CA 5-8R; 25-28R; CANR
　　26, 54, 95; CPW; DA; DAB; DAC; DAM
　　MST, NOV, POET, POP; DA3; MTCW 1,
　　2; WLC

Kerr, Jean 1923- .... **CLC 22**
　　See also CA 5-8R; CANR 7; INT CANR-7

Kerr, M. E. .... **CLC 12, 35**
　　See also Meaker, Marijane (Agnes)
　　See also AAYA 2, 23; CLR 29; SAAS 1

Kerr, Robert .... **CLC 55**

Kerrigan, (Thomas) Anthony 1918- .. **CLC 4,
　　6**
　　See also CA 49-52; CAAS 11; CANR 4

Kerry, Lois
　　See Duncan, Lois

Kesey, Ken (Elton) 1935- ..... **CLC 1, 3, 6, 11,
　　46, 64; DA; DAB; DAC; DAM MST,
　　NOV, POP; WLC**
　　See also AAYA 25; CA 1-4R; CANR 22,
　　38, 66; CDALB 1968-1988; CN; CPW;
　　DA3; DLB 2, 16, 206; MTCW 1, 2; NFS
　　2; SATA 66; YAW

Kesselring, Joseph (Otto)
　　1902-1967 .... **CLC 45; DAM DRAM,
　　MST**
　　See also CA 150

Kessler, Jascha (Frederick) 1929- ...... **CLC 4**
　　See also CA 17-20R; CANR 8, 48

Kettelkamp, Larry (Dale) 1933- .... **CLC 12**
　　See also CA 29-32R; CANR 16; SAAS 3;
　　SATA 2

Key, Ellen (Karolina Sofia)
　　1849-1926 .... **TCLC 65**

Keyber, Conny
　　See Fielding, Henry

Keyes, Daniel 1927- ...... **CLC 80; DA; DAC;
　　DAM MST, NOV**
　　See also AAYA 23; CA 17-20R, 181; CAAE
　　181; CANR 10, 26, 54, 74; DA3; MTCW
　　2; NFS 2; SATA 37; SFW

Keynes, John Maynard
　　1883-1946 .... **TCLC 64**
　　See also CA 114; 162, 163; DLBD 10;
　　MTCW 2

Khanshendel, Chiron
　　See Rose, Wendy

Khayyam, Omar 1048-1131 .... **CMLC 11;
　　DAM POET; PC 8**
　　See also DA3; RGWL

Kherdian, David 1931- .... **CLC 6, 9**
　　See also CA 21-24R; CAAS 2; CANR 39,
　　78; CLR 24; JRDA; MAICYA; SATA 16,
　　74

Khlebnikov, Velimir .... **TCLC 20**
　　See also Khlebnikov, Viktor Vladimirovich
　　See also RGWL

Khlebnikov, Viktor Vladimirovich 1885-1922
　　See Khlebnikov, Velimir
　　See also CA 117

Khodasevich, Vladislav (Felitsianovich)
　　1886-1939 .... **TCLC 15**
　　See also CA 115

Kielland, Alexander Lange
　　1849-1906 .... **TCLC 5**
　　See also CA 104

Kiely, Benedict 1919- .... **CLC 23, 43**
　　See also CA 1-4R; CANR 2, 84; CN; DLB
　　15

Kienzle, William X(avier) 1928- ..... **CLC 25;
　　DAM POP**
　　See also CA 93-96; CAAS 1; CANR 9, 31,
　　59; CMW; DA3; INT CANR-31; MTCW
　　1, 2

Kierkegaard, Soren 1813-1855 ..... **NCLC 34,
　　78**

Kieslowski, Krzysztof 1941-1996 .... **CLC 120**
　　See also CA 147; 151

Killens, John Oliver 1916-1987 .... **CLC 10**
　　See also BW 2; CA 77-80; 123; CAAS 2;
　　CANR 26; DLB 33

Killigrew, Anne 1660-1685 .... **LC 4**
　　See also DLB 131

Killigrew, Thomas 1612-1683 .... **LC 57**
　　See also DLB 58; RGEL

Kim
　　See Simenon, Georges (Jacques Christian)

Kincaid, Jamaica 1949- ..... **CLC 43, 68, 137;
　　BLC 2; DAM MULT, NOV**
　　See also AAYA 13; AFAW 2; AMWS 7; BW
　　2, 3; CA 125; CANR 47, 59, 95;
　　CDALBS; CLR 63; CN; DA3; DLB 157,
　　227; DNFS 1; FW; MTCW 2; NCFS 1;
　　NFS 3; SSFS 5, 7; YAW

King, Francis (Henry) 1923- .... **CLC 8, 53,
　　145; DAM NOV**
　　See also CA 1-4R; CANR 1, 33, 86; CN;
　　DLB 15, 139; MTCW 1

King, Kennedy
　　See Brown, George Douglas

King, Martin Luther, Jr.
　　1929-1968 .... **CLC 83; BLC 2; DA;
　　DAB; DAC; DAM MST, MULT;
　　WLCS**
　　See also BW 2, 3; CA 25-28; CANR 27,
　　44; CAP 2; DA3; MTCW 1, 2; SATA 14

King, Stephen (Edwin) 1947- .... **CLC 12, 26,
　　37, 61, 113; DAM NOV, POP; SSC 17**
　　See also AAYA 1, 17; AMWS 5; BEST
　　90:1; CA 61-64; CANR 1, 30, 52, 76;
　　CPW; DA3; DLB 143; DLBY 80; HGG;
　　JRDA; MTCW 1, 2; SATA 9, 55; WYAS
　　1; YAW

King, Steve
　　See King, Stephen (Edwin)

King, Thomas 1943- ... **CLC 89; DAC; DAM
　　MULT**
　　See also CA 144; CANR 95; CCA 1; CN;
　　DLB 175; NNAL; SATA 96

Kingman, Lee .... **CLC 17**
　　See also Natti, (Mary) Lee
　　See also SAAS 3; SATA 1, 67

Kingsley, Charles 1819-1875 .... **NCLC 35**
　　See also DLB 21, 32, 163, 190; FANT;
　　RGEL; YABC 2

Kingsley, Sidney 1906-1995 .... **CLC 44**
　　See also CA 85-88; 147; CAD; DLB 7;
　　RGAL

Kingsolver, Barbara 1955- .... **CLC 55, 81,
　　130; DAM POP**
　　See also AAYA 15; AMWS 7; CA 129, 134,
　　CANR 60, 96; CDALBS; CPW; CSW;
　　DA3; DLB 206; INT CA-134; MTCW 2;
　　NFS 5, 10, 12; RGAL

Kingston, Maxine (Ting Ting) Hong
　　1940- .... **CLC 12, 19, 58, 121; DAM
　　MULT, NOV; WLCS**
　　See also AAYA 8; CA 69-72; CANR 13,
　　38, 74, 87; CDALBS; CN; DA3; DLB
　　173, 212; DLBY 80; FW; INT CANR-13;
　　MTCW 1, 2; NFS 6; SATA 53; SSFS 3

Kinnell, Galway 1927- ..... **CLC 1, 2, 3, 5, 13,
　　29, 129; PC 26**
　　See also AMWS 3; CA 9-12R; CANR 10,
　　34, 66; CP; DLB 5; DLBY 87; INT
　　CANR-34; MTCW 1, 2; PFS 9; RGAL

Kinsella, Thomas 1928- ..... **CLC 4, 19, 138**
　　See also BRWS 5; CA 17-20R; CANR 15;
　　CP; DLB 27; MTCW 1, 2; RGEL

Kinsella, W(illiam) P(atrick) 1935- . **CLC 27,
　　43; DAC; DAM NOV, POP**
　　See also AAYA 7; CA 97-100; CAAS 7;
　　CANR 21, 35, 66, 75; CN; CPW; FANT;
　　INT CANR-21; MTCW 1, 2

Kinsey, Alfred C(harles)
　　1894-1956 .... **TCLC 91**
　　See also CA 115; 170; MTCW 2

Kipling, (Joseph) Rudyard
　　1865-1936 .... **TCLC 8, 17; DA; DAB;
　　DAC; DAM MST, POET; PC 3; SSC
　　5; WLC**
　　See also AAYA 32; CA 105; 120; CANR
　　33; CDBLB 1890-1914; CLR 39, 65;
　　CWRI; DA3; DLB 19, 34, 141, 156;
　　FANT; MAICYA; MTCW 1, 2; SATA
　　100; SFW; SSFS 8; YABC 2

Kirkland, Caroline M. 1801-1864 . **NCLC 85**
　　See also DLB 3, 73, 74; DLBD 13

Kirkup, James 1918- .... **CLC 1**
　　See also CA 1-4R; CAAS 4; CANR 2; DLB
　　27; SATA 12

Kirkwood, James 1930(?)-1989 .... **CLC 9**
　　See also AITN 2; CA 1-4R; 128; CANR 6,
　　40; GLL 2

Kumin, Maxine (Winokur) 1925- ..... **CLC 5, 13, 28; DAM POET; PC 15**
See also AITN 2; AMWS 4; CA 1-4R; CAAS 8; CANR 1, 21, 69; CP; CWP; DA3; DLB 5; MTCW 1, 2; SATA 12

Kundera, Milan 1929- . **CLC 4, 9, 19, 32, 68, 115, 135; DAM NOV; SSC 24**
See also AAYA 2; CA 85-88; CANR 19, 52, 74; CWW 2; DA3; DLB 232; MTCW 1, 2; RGSF; SSFS 10

Kunene, Mazisi (Raymond) 1930- ... **CLC 85**
See also BW 1, 3; CA 125; CANR 81; DLB 117

Kung, Hans .... **CLC 130**
See also Kueng, Hans

Kunikida, Doppo 1869(?)-1908 ...... **TCLC 99**
See also DLB 180

Kunitz, Stanley (Jasspon) 1905- .. **CLC 6, 11, 14; PC 19**
See also AMWS 3; CA 41-44R; CANR 26, 57, 98; CP; DA3; DLB 48; INT CANR-26; MTCW 1, 2; PFS 11

Kunze, Reiner 1933- .... **CLC 10**
See also CA 93-96; CWW 2; DLB 75

Kuprin, Aleksander Ivanovich
1870-1938 .... **TCLC 5**
See also CA 104; 182

Kureishi, Hanif 1954(?)- .... **CLC 64, 135**
See also CA 139; CBD; CD; CN; DLB 194; GLL 2; IDFW 4

Kurosawa, Akira 1910-1998 .... **CLC 16, 119; DAM MULT**
See also AAYA 11; CA 101; 170; CANR 46

Kushner, Tony 1957(?)- .... **CLC 81; DAM DRAM; DC 10**
See also CA 144; CAD; CANR 74; CD; DA3; DFS 5; DLB 228; GLL 1; MTCW 2; RGAL

Kuttner, Henry 1915-1958 .... **TCLC 10**
See also CA 107; 157; DLB 8; FANT; SFW

Kuzma, Greg 1944- .... **CLC 7**
See also CA 33-36R; CANR 70

Kuzmin, Mikhail 1872(?)-1936 ...... **TCLC 40**
See also CA 170

Kyd, Thomas 1558-1594 .... **LC 22; DAM DRAM; DC 3**
See also DLB 62

Kyprianos, Iossif
See Samarakis, Antonis

La Bruyère, Jean de 1645-1696 .... **LC 17**
See also GFL Beginnings to 1789

Lacan, Jacques (Marie Emile)
1901-1981 .... **CLC 75**
See also CA 121; 104

Laclos, Pierre Ambroise François
1741-1803 .... **NCLC 4, 87**
See also EW; GFL Beginnings to 1789; RGWL

Lacolere, Francois
See Aragon, Louis

La Colere, Francois
See Aragon, Louis

La Deshabilleuse
See Simenon, Georges (Jacques Christian)

Lady Gregory
See Gregory, Isabella Augusta (Persse)

Lady of Quality, A
See Bagnold, Enid

La Fayette, Marie-(Madelaine Pioche de la Vergne) 1634-1693 .... **LC 2**
See also GFL Beginnings to 1789; RGWL

Lafayette, Rene
See Hubbard, L(afayette) Ron(ald)

La Fontaine, Jean de 1621-1695 .... **LC 50**
See also GFL Beginnings to 1789; MAICYA; RGWL; SATA 18

Laforgue, Jules 1860-1887 . **NCLC 5, 53; PC 14; SSC 20**
See also GFL 1789 to the Present; RGWL

Lagerkvist, Paer (Fabian)
1891-1974 ...... **CLC 7, 10, 13, 54; DAM DRAM, NOV**
See also Lagerkvist, Pär
See also CA 85-88; 49-52; DA3; MTCW 1, 2

Lagerkvist, Pär .... **SSC 12**
See also Lagerkvist, Paer (Fabian)
See also MTCW 2

Lagerloef, Selma (Ottiliana Lovisa)
1858-1940 .... **TCLC 4, 36**
See also Lagerlof, Selma (Ottiliana Lovisa)
See also CA 108; MTCW 2; SATA 15

Lagerlof, Selma (Ottiliana Lovisa)
See Lagerloef, Selma (Ottiliana Lovisa)
See also CLR 7; SATA 15

La Guma, (Justin) Alex(ander)
1925-1985 .... **CLC 19; BLCS; DAM NOV**
See also BW 1, 3; CA 49-52; 118; CANR 25, 81; DLB 117, 225; MTCW 1, 2

Laidlaw, A. K.
See Grieve, C(hristopher) M(urray)

Lainez, Manuel Mujica
See Mujica Lainez, Manuel
See also HW 1

Laing, R(onald) D(avid) 1927-1989 . **CLC 95**
See also CA 107; 129; CANR 34; MTCW 1

Lamartine, Alphonse (Marie Louis Prat) de 1790-1869 . **NCLC 11; DAM POET; PC 16**
See also GFL 1789 to the Present; RGWL

Lamb, Charles 1775-1834 ..... **NCLC 10; DA; DAB; DAC; DAM MST; WLC**
See also CDBLB 1789-1832; DLB 93, 107, 163; RGEL; SATA 17

Lamb, Lady Caroline 1785-1828 ... **NCLC 38**
See also DLB 116

Lamming, George (William) 1927- ... **CLC 2, 4, 66, 144; BLC 2; DAM MULT**
See also BW 2, 3; CA 85-88; CANR 26, 76; DLB 125; MTCW 1, 2

L'Amour, Louis (Dearborn)
1908-1988 ...... **CLC 25, 55; DAM NOV, POP**
See also Burns, Tex; Mayo, Jim
See also AAYA 16; AITN 2; BEST 89:2; CA 1-4R; 125; CANR 3, 25, 40; CPW; DA3; DLB 206; DLBY 80; MTCW 1, 2

Lampedusa, Giuseppe (Tomasi) di
.... **TCLC 13**
See also Tomasi di Lampedusa, Giuseppe
See also CA 164; DLB 177; MTCW 2

Lampman, Archibald 1861-1899 ... **NCLC 25**
See also DLB 92; RGEL

Lancaster, Bruce 1896-1963 .... **CLC 36**
See also CA 9-10; CANR 70; CAP 1; SATA 9

Lanchester, John .... **CLC 99**

Landau, Mark Alexandrovich
See Aldanov, Mark (Alexandrovich)

Landau-Aldanov, Mark Alexandrovich
See Aldanov, Mark (Alexandrovich)

Landis, Jerry
See Simon, Paul (Frederick)

Landis, John 1950- .... **CLC 26**
See also CA 112; 122

Landolfi, Tommaso 1908-1979 .... **CLC 11, 49**
See also CA 127; 117; DLB 177

Landon, Letitia Elizabeth
1802-1838 .... **NCLC 15**
See also DLB 96

Landor, Walter Savage
1775-1864 .... **NCLC 14**
See also DLB 93, 107

Landwirth, Heinz 1927-
See Lind, Jakov
See also CA 9-12R; CANR 7

Lane, Patrick 1939- ... **CLC 25; DAM POET**
See also CA 97-100; CANR 54; CP; DLB 53; INT 97-100

Lang, Andrew 1844-1912 .... **TCLC 16**
See also CA 114; 137; CANR 85; DLB 98, 141, 184; FANT; MAICYA; RGEL; SATA 16

Lang, Fritz 1890-1976 .... **CLC 20, 103**
See also CA 77-80; 69-72; CANR 30

Lange, John
See Crichton, (John) Michael

Langer, Elinor 1939- .... **CLC 34**
See also CA 121

Langland, William 1332(?)-1400(?) ... **LC 19; DA; DAB; DAC; DAM MST, POET**
See also DLB 146; RGEL

Langstaff, Launcelot
See Irving, Washington

Lanier, Sidney 1842-1881 ..... **NCLC 6; DAM POET**
See also AMWS 1; DLB 64; DLBD 13; MAICYA; RGAL; SATA 18

Lanyer, Aemilia 1569-1645 .... **LC 10, 30**
See also DLB 121

Lao-Tzu
See Lao Tzu

Lao Tzu fl. 6046th cent. B.C.-490 ... **CMLC 7**

Lapine, James (Elliot) 1949- .... **CLC 39**
See also CA 123; 130; CANR 54; INT 130

Larbaud, Valery (Nicolas)
1881-1957 .... **TCLC 9**
See also CA 106; 152; GFL 1789 to the Present

Lardner, Ring
See Lardner, Ring(gold) W(ilmer)
See also RGAL; RGSF

Lardner, Ring W., Jr.
See Lardner, Ring(gold) W(ilmer)

Lardner, Ring(gold) W(ilmer)
1885-1933 .... **TCLC 2, 14; SSC 32**
See also Lardner, Ring
See also CA 104; 131; CDALB 1917-1929; DLB 11, 25, 86, 171; DLBD 16; MTCW 1, 2

Laredo, Betty
See Codrescu, Andrei

Larkin, Maia
See Wojciechowska, Maia (Teresa)

Larkin, Philip (Arthur) 1922-1985 ... **CLC 3, 5, 8, 9, 13, 18, 33, 39, 64; DAB; DAM MST, POET; PC 21**
See also BRWS 1; CA 5-8R; 117; CANR 24, 62; CDBLB 1960 to Present; DA3; DLB 27; MTCW 1, 2; PFS 3, 4, 12

Larra (y Sanchez de Castro), Mariano Jose de 1809-1837 .... **NCLC 17**

Larsen, Eric 1941- .... **CLC 55**
See also CA 132

Larsen, Nella 1893-1963 .... **CLC 37; BLC 2; DAM MULT**
See also AFAW 1, 2; BW 1; CA 125; CANR 83; DLB 51; FW

Larson, Charles R(aymond) 1938- ... **CLC 31**
See also CA 53-56; CANR 4

Larson, Jonathan 1961-1996 .... **CLC 99**
See also AAYA 28; CA 156

Las Casas, Bartolome de 1474-1566 ... **LC 31**

Lasch, Christopher 1932-1994 .... **CLC 102**
See also CA 73-76; 144; CANR 25; MTCW 1, 2

Lasker-Schueler, Else 1869-1945 ... **TCLC 57**
See also CA 183; DLB 66, 124

Laski, Harold J(oseph) 1893-1950 . **TCLC 79**
See also CA 188'

Latham, Jean Lee 1902-1995 .... **CLC 12**
See also AITN 1; CA 5-8R; CANR 7, 84; CLR 50; MAICYA; SATA 2, 68; YAW

Lowry, (Clarence) Malcolm
1909-1957 .... **TCLC 6, 40; SSC 31**
See also BRWS 3; CA 105; 131; CANR 62;
CDBLB 1945-1960; DLB 15; MTCW 1,
2

Lowry, Mina Gertrude 1882-1966
See Loy, Mina
See also CA 113

Loxsmith, John
See Brunner, John (Kilian Houston)

Loy, Mina ..... **CLC 28; DAM POET; PC 16**
See also Lowry, Mina Gertrude
See also DLB 4, 54

Loyson-Bridet
See Schwob, Marcel (Mayer Andr

Lucan 39- .... **CMLC 33**
See also DLB 211; EFS 2; RGEL

Lucas, Craig 1951- .... **CLC 64**
See also CA 137; CAD; CANR 71; CD;
GLL 2

Lucas, E(dward) V(errall)
1868-1938 .... **TCLC 73**
See also CA 176; DLB 98, 149, 153; SATA
20

Lucas, George 1944- .... **CLC 16**
See also AAYA 1, 23; CA 77-80; CANR
30; SATA 56

Lucas, Hans
See Godard, Jean-Luc

Lucas, Victoria
See Plath, Sylvia

Lucian c. 125- .... **CMLC 32**
See also DLB 176; RGEL

Ludlam, Charles 1943-1987 .... **CLC 46, 50**
See also CA 85-88; 122; CAD; CANR 72,
86

Ludlum, Robert 1927-2001 .... **CLC 22, 43;
DAM NOV, POP**
See also AAYA 10; BEST 89:1, 90:3; CA
33-36R; CANR 25, 41, 68; CMW; CPW;
DA3; DLBY 82; MTCW 1, 2

Ludwig, Ken .... **CLC 60**
See also CAD

Ludwig, Otto 1813-1865 .... **NCLC 4**
See also DLB 129

Lugones, Leopoldo 1874-1938 ...... **TCLC 15;
HLCS 2**
See also CA 116; 131; HW 1

Lu Hsun .... **TCLC 3; SSC 20**
See also Shu-Jen, Chou

Lukacs, George .... **CLC 24**
See also Lukács, György (Szegeny von)

Lukács, György (Szegeny von) 1885-1971
See Lukacs, George
See also CA 101; 29-32R; CANR 62; DLB
242; MTCW 2

Luke, Peter (Ambrose Cyprian)
1919-1995 .... **CLC 38**
See also CA 81-84; 147; CANR 72; CBD;
CD; DLB 13

Lunar, Dennis
See Mungo, Raymond

Lurie, Alison 1926- .... **CLC 4, 5, 18, 39**
See also CA 1-4R; CANR 2, 17, 50, 88;
CN; DLB 2; MTCW 1; SATA 46, 112

Lustig, Arnost 1926- .... **CLC 56**
See also AAYA 3; CA 69-72; CANR 47;
CWW 2; DLB 232; SATA 56

Luther, Martin 1483-1546 .... **LC 9, 37**
See also DLB 179; RGWL

Luxemburg, Rosa 1870(?)-1919 ..... **TCLC 63**
See also CA 118

Luzi, Mario 1914- .... **CLC 13**
See also CA 61-64; CANR 9, 70; CWW 2;
DLB 128

L'vov, Arkady .... **CLC 59**

Lyly, John 1554(?)-1606 .... **LC 41; DAM
DRAM; DC 7**
See also DLB 62, 167; RGEL

L'Ymagier
See Gourmont, Remy(-Marie-Charles) de

Lynch, David (K.) 1946- .... **CLC 66**
See also CA 124; 129

Lynch, James
See Andreyev, Leonid (Nikolaevich)

Lyndsay, SirDavid 1485-1555 .... **LC 20**

Lynn, Kenneth S(chuyler)
1923-2001 .... **CLC 50**
See also CA 1-4R; CANR 3, 27, 65

Lynx
See West, Rebecca

Lyons, Marcus
See Blish, James (Benjamin)

Lyotard, Jean-François
1924-1998 .... **TCLC 103**
See also DLB 242

Lyre, Pinchbeck
See Sassoon, Siegfried (Lorraine)

Lytle, Andrew (Nelson) 1902-1995 ... **CLC 22**
See also CA 9-12R; 150; CANR 70; CN;
CSW; DLB 6; DLBY 95; RHW

Lyttelton, George 1709-1773 .... **LC 10**

Lytton of Knebworth
See Bulwer-Lytton, Edward (George Earle
Lytton)

Maas, Peter 1929- .... **CLC 29**
See also CA 93-96; INT 93-96; MTCW 2

Macaulay, Catherine 1731-1791 .... **LC 64**
See also DLB 104

Macaulay, (Emilie) Rose
1881(?)-1958 .... **TCLC 7, 44**
See also CA 104; DLB 36; RHW

Macaulay, Thomas Babington
1800-1859 .... **NCLC 42**
See also CDBLB 1832-1890; DLB 32, 55

MacBeth, George (Mann)
1932-1992 .... **CLC 2, 5, 9**
See also CA 25-28R; 136; CANR 61, 66;
DLB 40; MTCW 1; PFS 8; SATA 4;
SATA-Obit 70

MacCaig, Norman (Alexander)
1910-1996 .... **CLC 36; DAB; DAM
POET**
See also BRWS 6; CA 9-12R; CANR 3, 34;
CP; DLB 27

MacCarthy, Sir(Charles Otto) Desmond
1877-1952 .... **TCLC 36**
See also CA 167

MacDiarmid, Hugh .... **CLC 2, 4, 11, 19, 63;
PC 9**
See also Grieve, C(hristopher) M(urray)
See also CDBLB 1945-1960; DLB 20

MacDonald, Anson
See Heinlein, Robert A(nson)

Macdonald, Cynthia 1928- .... **CLC 13, 19**
See also CA 49-52; CANR 4, 44; DLB 105

MacDonald, George 1824-1905 .... **TCLC 9**
See also CA 106; 137; CANR 80; CLR 67;
DLB 18, 163, 178; FANT; MAICYA;
SATA 33, 100; SFW

Macdonald, John
See Millar, Kenneth

MacDonald, John D(ann)
1916-1986 .. **CLC 3, 27, 44; DAM NOV,
POP**
See also CA 1-4R; 121; CANR 1, 19, 60;
CMW; CPW; DLB 8; DLBY 86; MTCW
1, 2; SFW

Macdonald, John Ross
See Millar, Kenneth

Macdonald, Ross ..... **CLC 1, 2, 3, 14, 34, 41**
See also Millar, Kenneth
See also AMWS 4; DLBD 6; RGAL

MacDougal, John
See Blish, James (Benjamin)

MacDougal, John
See Blish, James (Benjamin)

MacEwen, Gwendolyn (Margaret)
1941-1987 .... **CLC 13, 55**
See also CA 9-12R; 124; CANR 7, 22; DLB
53; SATA 50; SATA-Obit 55

Macha, Karel Hynek 1810-1846 .... **NCLC 46**

Machado (y Ruiz), Antonio
1875-1939 .... **TCLC 3**
See also CA 104; 174; DLB 108; HW 2

Machado de Assis, Joaquim Maria
1839-1908 ..... **TCLC 10; BLC 2; HLCS
2; SSC 24**
See also CA 107; 153; CANR 91

Machen, Arthur .... **TCLC 4; SSC 20**
See also Jones, Arthur Llewellyn
See also CA 179; DLB 36, 156, 178

Machiavelli, Niccolò 1469-1527 ..... **LC 8, 36;
DA; DAB; DAC; DAM MST; WLCS**
See also NFS 9; RGWL

MacInnes, Colin 1914-1976 .... **CLC 4, 23**
See also CA 69-72; 65-68; CANR 21; DLB
14; MTCW 1, 2; RHW

MacInnes, Helen (Clark)
1907-1985 .... **CLC 27, 39; DAM POP**
See also CA 1-4R; 117; CANR 1, 28, 58;
CMW; CPW; DLB 87; MTCW 1, 2;
SATA 22; SATA-Obit 44

Mackenzie, Compton (Edward Montague)
1883-1972 .... **CLC 18**
See also CA 21-22; 37-40R; CAP 2; DLB
34, 100

Mackenzie, Henry 1745-1831 .... **NCLC 41**
See also DLB 39; RGEL

Mackintosh, Elizabeth 1896(?)-1952
See Tey, Josephine
See also CA 110; CMW

MacLaren, James
See Grieve, C(hristopher) M(urray)

Mac Laverty, Bernard 1942- .... **CLC 31**
See also CA 116; 118; CANR 43, 88; CN;
INT CA-118

MacLean, Alistair (Stuart)
1922(?)-1987 .. **CLC 3, 13, 50, 63; DAM
POP**
See also CA 57-60; 121; CANR 28, 61;
CMW; CPW; MTCW 1; SATA 23; SATA-
Obit 50; TCWW 2

Maclean, Norman (Fitzroy)
1902-1990 .... **CLC 78; DAM POP; SSC
13**
See also CA 102; 132; CANR 49; CPW;
DLB 206; TCWW 2

MacLeish, Archibald 1892-1982 ... **CLC 3, 8,
14, 68; DAM POET**
See also CA 9-12R; 106; CAD; CANR 33,
63; CDALBS; DLB 4, 7, 45; DLBY 82;
MTCW 1, 2; PFS 5; RGAL

MacLennan, (John) Hugh
1907-1990 . **CLC 2, 14, 92; DAC; DAM
MST**
See also CA 5-8R; 142; CANR 33; DLB
68; MTCW 1, 2

MacLeod, Alistair 1936- .... **CLC 56; DAC;
DAM MST**
See also CA 123; CCA 1; DLB 60; MTCW
2; RGSF

Macleod, Fiona
See Sharp, William
See also RGEL

MacNeice, (Frederick) Louis
1907-1963 .... **CLC 1, 4, 10, 53; DAB;
DAM POET**
See also CA 85-88; CANR 61; DLB 10, 20;
MTCW 1, 2

MacNeill, Dand
See Fraser, George MacDonald

Macpherson, James 1736-1796 .... **LC 29**
See also Ossian
See also DLB 109; RGEL

Macpherson, (Jean) Jay 1931- .... **CLC 14**
See also CA 5-8R; CANR 90; CP; CWP;
DLB 53
MacShane, Frank 1927-1999 .... **CLC 39**
See also CA 9-12R; 186; CANR 3, 33; DLB
111
Macumber, Mari
See Sandoz, Mari(e Susette)
Madach, Imre 1823-1864 .... **NCLC 19**
Madden, (Jerry) David 1933- .... **CLC 5, 15**
See also CA 1-4R; CAAS 3; CANR 4, 45;
CN; CSW; DLB 6; MTCW 1
Maddern, Al(an)
See Ellison, Harlan (Jay)
Madhubuti, Haki R. 1942- . **CLC 6, 73; BLC
2; DAM MULT, POET; PC 5**
See also Lee, Don L.
See also BW 2, 3; CA 73-76; CANR 24,
51, 73; CP; CSW; DLB 5, 41; DLBD 8;
MTCW 2; RGAL
Maepenn, Hugh
See Kuttner, Henry
Maepenn, K. H.
See Kuttner, Henry
Maeterlinck, Maurice 1862-1949 ... **TCLC 3;
DAM DRAM**
See also CA 104; 136; CANR 80; DLB 192;
GFL 1789 to the Present; RGWL; SATA
66
Maginn, William 1794-1842 .... **NCLC 8**
See also DLB 110, 159
Mahapatra, Jayanta 1928- .... **CLC 33; DAM
MULT**
See also CA 73-76; CAAS 9; CANR 15,
33, 66, 87; CP
Mahfouz, Naguïb (Abdel Azïz Al-Sabilgi)
1911(?)-
See Mahf
See also BEST 89:2; CA 128; CANR 55;
CWW 2; DAM NOV; DA3; MTCW 1, 2;
SSFS 9
Mahfûz, Najïb (Abdel Azïz al-Sabilgi)
.... **CLC 52, 55**
See also Mahfouz, Naguïb (Abdel Azïz Al-
Sabilgi)
See also DLBY 88
Mahon, Derek 1941- .... **CLC 27**
See also BRWS 6; CA 113; 128; CANR 88;
CP; DLB 40
Maiakovskii, Vladimir
See Mayakovski, Vladimir (Vladimirovich)
Mailer, Norman 1923- ... **CLC 1, 2, 3, 4, 5, 8,
11, 14, 28, 39, 74, 111; DA; DAB;
DAC; DAM MST, NOV, POP**
See also AAYA 31; AITN 2; CA 9-12R;
CABS 1; CANR 28, 74, 77; CDALB
1968-1988; CN; CPW; DA3; DLB 2, 16,
28, 185; DLBD 3; DLBY 80, 83; MTCW
1, 2; NFS 10; RGAL
Maillet, Antonine 1929- ... **CLC 54, 118; DAC**
See also CA 115; 120; CANR 46, 74, 77;
CCA 1; CWW 2; DLB 60; INT 120;
MTCW 2
Mais, Roger 1905-1955 .... **TCLC 8**
See also BW 1, 3; CA 105; 124; CANR 82;
DLB 125; MTCW 1; RGEL
Maistre, Joseph 1753-1821 .... **NCLC 37**
See also GFL 1789 to the Present
Maitland, Frederic William
1850-1906 .... **TCLC 65**
Maitland, Sara (Louise) 1950- .... **CLC 49**
See also CA 69-72; CANR 13, 59; FW
Major, Clarence 1936- . **CLC 3, 19, 48; BLC
2; DAM MULT**
See also AFAW 2; BW 2, 3; CA 21-24R;
CAAS 6; CANR 13, 25, 53, 82; CN; CP;
CSW; DLB 33

Major, Kevin (Gerald) 1949- . **CLC 26; DAC**
See also AAYA 16; CA 97-100; CANR 21,
38; CLR 11; DLB 60; INT CANR-21;
JRDA; MAICYA; SATA 32, 82; YAW
Maki, James
See Ozu, Yasujiro
Malabaila, Damiano
See Levi, Primo
Malamud, Bernard 1914-1986 .. **CLC 1, 2, 3,
5, 8, 9, 11, 18, 27, 44, 78, 85; DA;
DAB; DAC; DAM MST, NOV, POP;
SSC 15; WLC**
See also AAYA 16; AMWS 1; CA 5-8R;
118; CABS 1; CANR 28, 62; CDALB
1941-1968; CPW; DA3; DLB 2, 28, 152;
DLBY 80, 86; MTCW 1, 2; NFS 4, 9;
RGAL; RGSF; SSFS 8
Malan, Herman
See Bosman, Herman Charles; Bosman,
Herman Charles
Malaparte, Curzio 1898-1957 .... **TCLC 52**
Malcolm, Dan
See Silverberg, Robert
Malcolm X .... **CLC 82, 117; BLC 2; WLCS**
See also Little, Malcolm
Malherbe, François de 1555-1628 .... **LC 5**
See also GFL Beginnings to 1789
Mallarmé, Stéphane 1842-1898 ...... **NCLC 4,
41; DAM POET; PC 4**
See also GFL 1789 to the Present; RGWL
Mallet-Joris, Françoise 1930- .... **CLC 11**
See also CA 65-68; CANR 17; DLB 83;
GFL 1789 to the Present
Malley, Ern
See McAuley, James Phillip
Mallowan, Agatha Christie
See Christie, Agatha (Mary Clarissa)
Maloff, Saul 1922- .... **CLC 5**
See also CA 33-36R
Malone, Louis
See MacNeice, (Frederick) Louis
Malone, Michael (Christopher)
1942- .... **CLC 43**
See also CA 77-80; CANR 14, 32, 57
Malory, Thomas 1410(?)-1471(?) .... **LC 11;
DA; DAB; DAC; DAM MST; WLCS**
See also CDBLB Before 1660; DLB 146;
EFS 2; SATA 59; SATA-Brief 33
Malouf, (George Joseph) David
1934- .... **CLC 28, 86**
See also CA 124; CANR 50, 76; CN; CP;
MTCW 2
Malraux, (Georges-)André
1901-1976 .... **CLC 1, 4, 9, 13, 15, 57;
DAM NOV**
See also CA 21-22; 69-72; CANR 34, 58;
CAP 2; DA3; DLB 72; EW; GFL 1789 to
the Present; MTCW 1, 2; RGWL
Malzberg, Barry N(athaniel) 1939- ... **CLC 7**
See also CA 61-64; CAAS 4; CANR 16;
CMW; DLB 8; SFW
Mamet, David (Alan) 1947- .. **CLC 9, 15, 34,
46, 91; DAM DRAM; DC 4**
See also AAYA 3; CA 81-84; CABS 3;
CANR 15, 41, 67, 72; CD; DA3; DFS 2,
3, 6, 12; DLB 7; IDFW 4; MTCW 1, 2
Mamoulian, Rouben (Zachary)
1897-1987 .... **CLC 16**
See also CA 25-28R; 124; CANR 85
Mandelshtam, Osip
See Mandelstam, Osip (Emilievich)
Mandelstam, Osip (Emilievich)
1891(?)-1943(?) .... **TCLC 2, 6; PC 14**
See also Mandelshtam, Osip
See also CA 104; 150; MTCW 2
Mander, (Mary) Jane 1877-1949 ... **TCLC 31**
See also CA 162; RGEL
Mandeville, John fl. 1350- .... **CMLC 19**
See also DLB 146

Mandiargues, Andre Pieyre de .... **CLC 41**
See also Pieyre de Mandiargues, André
See also DLB 83
Mandrake, Ethel Belle
See Thurman, Wallace (Henry)
Mangan, James Clarence
1803-1849 .... **NCLC 27**
Maniere, J.-E.
See Giraudoux, Jean(-Hippolyte)
Mankiewicz, Herman (Jacob)
1897-1953 .... **TCLC 85**
See also CA 120; 169; DLB 26; IDFW 3
Manley, (Mary) Delariviere
1672(?)-1724 .... **LC 1, 42**
See also DLB 39, 80
Mann, Abel
See Creasey, John
Mann, Emily 1952- .... **DC 7**
See also CA 130; CAD; CANR 55; CD;
CWD
Mann, (Luiz) Heinrich 1871-1950 ... **TCLC 9**
See also CA 106; 164, 181; DLB 66, 118;
EW; RGWL
Mann, (Paul) Thomas 1875-1955 ... **TCLC 2,
8, 14, 21, 35, 44, 60; DA; DAB; DAC;
DAM MST, NOV; SSC 5; WLC**
See also CA 104; 128; DA3; DLB 66; GLL
1; MTCW 1, 2; SSFS 4, 9
Mannheim, Karl 1893-1947 .... **TCLC 65**
Manning, David
See Faust, Frederick (Schiller)
See also TCWW 2
Manning, Frederic 1887(?)-1935 ... **TCLC 25**
See also CA 124
Manning, Olivia 1915-1980 .... **CLC 5, 19**
See also CA 5-8R; 101; CANR 29; FW;
MTCW 1
Mano, D. Keith 1942- .... **CLC 2, 10**
See also CA 25-28R; CAAS 6; CANR 26,
57; DLB 6
Mansfield, Katherine .... **TCLC 2, 8, 39;
DAB; SSC 9, 23, 38; WLC**
See also Beauchamp, Kathleen Mansfield
See also DLB 162; FW; GLL 1; RGEL;
RGSF; SSFS 2,8,10,11
Manso, Peter 1940- .... **CLC 39**
See also CA 29-32R; CANR 44
Mantecon, Juan Jimenez
See Jim
Mantel, Hilary (Mary) 1952- .... **CLC 144**
See also CA 125; CANR 54; CN; RHW
Manton, Peter
See Creasey, John
Man Without a Spleen, A
See Chekhov, Anton (Pavlovich)
Manzoni, Alessandro 1785-1873 ... **NCLC 29,
98**
See also RGWL
Map, Walter 1140-1209 .... **CMLC 32**
Mapu, Abraham (ben Jekutiel)
1808-1867 .... **NCLC 18**
Mara, Sally
See Queneau, Raymond
Marat, Jean Paul 1743-1793 .... **LC 10**
Marcel, Gabriel Honore 1889-1973 . **CLC 15**
See also CA 102; 45-48; MTCW 1, 2
March, William 1893-1954 .... **TCLC 96**
Marchbanks, Samuel
See Davies, (William) Robertson
See also CCA 1
Marchi, Giacomo
See Bassani, Giorgio
Marcus Aurelius
See Antoninus, Marcus Aurelius
Marguerite
See de Navarre, Marguerite

McKuen, Rod 1933- .... **CLC 1, 3**
See also AITN 1; CA 41-44R; CANR 40

McLoughlin, R. B.
See Mencken, H(enry) L(ouis)

McLuhan, (Herbert) Marshall
1911-1980 .... **CLC 37, 83**
See also CA 9-12R; 102; CANR 12, 34, 61;
DLB 88; INT CANR-12; MTCW 1, 2

McMillan, Terry (L.) 1951- .... **CLC 50, 61,**
112; BLCS; DAM MULT, NOV, POP
See also AAYA 21; BW 2, 3; CA 140;
CANR 60; CPW; DA3; MTCW 2; YAW

McMurtry, Larry (Jeff) 1936- .. **CLC 2, 3, 7,**
11, 27, 44, 127; DAM NOV, POP
See also AAYA 15; AITN 2; AMWS 5;
BEST 89:2; CA 5-8R; CANR 19, 43, 64;
CDALB 1968-1988; CN; CPW; CSW;
DA3; DLB 2, 143; DLBY 80, 87; MTCW
1, 2; TCWW 2

McNally, T. M. 1961- .... **CLC 82**

McNally, Terrence 1939- ... **CLC 4, 7, 41, 91;**
DAM DRAM
See also CA 45-48; CAD; CANR 2, 56; CD;
DA3; DLB 7; GLL 1; MTCW 2

McNamer, Deirdre 1950- .... **CLC 70**

McNeal, Tom .... **CLC 119**

McNeile, Herman Cyril 1888-1937
See Sapper
See also CA 184; CMW; DLB 77

McNickle, (William) D'Arcy
1904-1977 .... **CLC 89; DAM MULT**
See also CA 9-12R; 85-88; CANR 5, 45;
DLB 175, 212; NNAL; SATA-Obit 22

McPhee, John (Angus) 1931- .... **CLC 36**
See also AMWS 3; BEST 90:1; CA 65-68;
CANR 20, 46, 64, 69; CPW; DLB 185;
MTCW 1, 2

McPherson, James Alan 1943- .. **CLC 19, 77;**
BLCS
See also BW 1, 3; CA 25-28R; CAAS 17;
CANR 24, 74; CN; CSW; DLB 38;
MTCW 1, 2; RGAL; RGSF

McPherson, William (Alexander)
1933- .... **CLC 34**
See also CA 69-72; CANR 28; INT
CANR-28

McTaggart, J. McT. Ellis
See McTaggart, John McTaggart Ellis

McTaggart, John McTaggart Ellis
1866-1925 .... **TCLC 105**
See also CA 120

Mead, George Herbert 1873-1958 . **TCLC 89**

Mead, Margaret 1901-1978 .... **CLC 37**
See also AITN 1; CA 1-4R; 81-84; CANR
4; DA3; FW; MTCW 1, 2; SATA-Obit 20

Meaker, Marijane (Agnes) 1927-
See Kerr, M. E.
See also CA 107; CANR 37, 63; INT 107;
JRDA; MAICYA; MTCW 1; SATA 20,
61, 99; SATA-Essay 111; YAW

Medoff, Mark (Howard) 1940- ... **CLC 6, 23;**
DAM DRAM
See also AITN 1; CA 53-56; CAD; CANR
5; CD; DFS 4; DLB 7; INT CANR-5

Medvedev, P. N.
See Bakhtin, Mikhail Mikhailovich

Meged, Aharon
See Megged, Aharon

Meged, Aron
See Megged, Aharon

Megged, Aharon 1920- .... **CLC 9**
See also CA 49-52; CAAS 13; CANR 1

Mehta, Ved (Parkash) 1934- .... **CLC 37**
See also CA 1-4R; CANR 2, 23, 69; MTCW
1

Melanter
See Blackmore, R(ichard) D(oddridge)

Melies, Georges 1861-1938 .... **TCLC 81**

Melikow, Loris
See Hofmannsthal, Hugo von

Melmoth, Sebastian
See Wilde, Oscar (Fingal O'Flahertie Wills)

Meltzer, Milton 1915- .... **CLC 26**
See also AAYA 8; CA 13-16R; CANR 38,
92; CLR 13; DLB 61; JRDA; MAICYA;
SAAS 1; SATA 1, 50, 80; YAW

Melville, Herman 1819-1891 ..... **NCLC 3, 12,**
29, 45, 49, 91, 93; DA; DAB; DAC;
DAM MST, NOV; SSC 1, 17, 46; WLC
See also AAYA 25; CDALB 1640-1865;
DA3; DLB 3, 74; NFS 7, 9; RGAL;
RGSF; SATA 59; SSFS 3

Membreno, Alejandro .... **CLC 59**

Menander c. 342B.C.- .... **CMLC 9; DAM**
DRAM; DC 3
See also DLB 176; RGEL

Menchú, Rigoberta 1959-
See also CA 175; DNFS 1; HLCS 2

Mencken, H(enry) L(ouis)
1880-1956 .... **TCLC 13**
See also CA 105; 125; CDALB 1917-1929;
DLB 11, 29, 63, 137, 222; MTCW 1, 2

Mendelsohn, Jane 1965- .... **CLC 99**
See also CA 154; CANR 94

Mercer, David 1928-1980 .... **CLC 5; DAM**
DRAM
See also CA 9-12R; 102; CANR 23; CBD;
DLB 13; MTCW 1; RGEL

Merchant, Paul
See Ellison, Harlan (Jay)

Meredith, George 1828-1909 .. **TCLC 17, 43;**
DAM POET
See also CA 117; 153; CANR 80; CDBLB
1832-1890; DLB 18, 35, 57, 159; RGEL

Meredith, William (Morris) 1919- .... **CLC 4,**
13, 22, 55; DAM POET; PC 28
See also CA 9-12R; CAAS 14; CANR 6,
40; CP; DLB 5

Merezhkovsky, Dmitry Sergeyevich
1865-1941 .... **TCLC 29**
See also CA 169

Mérimée, Prosper 1803-1870 ... **NCLC 6, 65;**
SSC 7
See also DLB 119, 192; GFL 1789 to the
Present; RGSF; RGWL; SSFS 8

Merkin, Daphne 1954- .... **CLC 44**
See also CA 123

Merlin, Arthur
See Blish, James (Benjamin)

Merrill, James (Ingram) 1926-1995 .. **CLC 2,**
3, 6, 8, 13, 18, 34, 91; DAM POET; PC
28
See also AMWS 3; CA 13-16R; 147; CANR
10, 49, 63; DA3; DLB 5, 165; DLBY 85;
INT CANR-10; MTCW 1, 2

Merriman, Alex
See Silverberg, Robert

Merriman, Brian 1747-1805 .... **NCLC 70**

Merritt, E. B.
See Waddington, Miriam

Merton, Thomas 1915-1968 ..... **CLC 1, 3, 11,**
34, 83; PC 10
See also AMWS 8; CA 5-8R; 25-28R;
CANR 22, 53; DA3; DLB 48; DLBY 81;
MTCW 1, 2

Merwin, W(illiam) S(tanley) 1927- ... **CLC 1,**
2, 3, 5, 8, 13, 18, 45, 88; DAM POET
See also AMWS 3; CA 13-16R; CANR 15,
51; CP; DA3; DLB 5, 169; INT CANR-
15; MTCW 1, 2; PFS 5

Metcalf, John 1938- .... **CLC 37; SSC 43**
See also CA 113; CN; DLB 60; RGSF

Metcalf, Suzanne
See Baum, L(yman) Frank

Mew, Charlotte (Mary) 1870-1928 .. **TCLC 8**
See also CA 105; 189; DLB 19, 135

Mewshaw, Michael 1943- .... **CLC 9**
See also CA 53-56; CANR 7, 47; DLBY 80

Meyer, Conrad Ferdinand
1825-1905 .... **NCLC 81**
See also DLB 129; RGWL

Meyer, Gustav 1868-1932
See Meyrink, Gustav
See also CA 117; 190

Meyer, June
See Jordan, June
See also GLL 2

Meyer, Lynn
See Slavitt, David R(ytman)

Meyers, Jeffrey 1939- .... **CLC 39**
See also CA 73-76; CAAE 186; CANR 54;
DLB 111

Meynell, Alice (Christina Gertrude
Thompson) 1847-1922 .... **TCLC 6**
See also CA 104; 177; DLB 19, 98

Meyrink, Gustav .... **TCLC 21**
See also Meyer, Gustav
See also DLB 81

Michaels, Leonard 1933- .... **CLC 6, 25; SSC**
16
See also CA 61-64; CANR 21, 62; CN;
DLB 130; MTCW 1

Michaux, Henri 1899-1984 .... **CLC 8, 19**
See also CA 85-88; 114; GFL 1789 to the
Present; RGWL

Micheaux, Oscar (Devereaux)
1884-1951 .... **TCLC 76**
See also BW 3; CA 174; DLB 50; TCWW
2

Michelangelo 1475-1564 .... **LC 12**

Michelet, Jules 1798-1874 .... **NCLC 31**
See also GFL 1789 to the Present

Michels, Robert 1876-1936 .... **TCLC 88**

Michener, James A(lbert)
1907(?)-1997 .... **CLC 1, 5, 11, 29, 60,**
109; DAM NOV, POP
See also AAYA 27; AITN 1; BEST 90:1;
CA 5-8R; 161; CANR 21, 45, 68; CN;
CPW; DA3; DLB 6; MTCW 1, 2; RHW

Mickiewicz, Adam 1798-1855 .. **NCLC 3, 101**
See also RGWL

Middleton, Christopher 1926- .... **CLC 13**
See also CA 13-16R; CANR 29, 54; DLB
40

Middleton, Richard (Barham)
1882-1911 .... **TCLC 56**
See also CA 187; DLB 156; HGG

Middleton, Stanley 1919- .... **CLC 7, 38**
See also CA 25-28R; CAAS 23; CANR 21,
46, 81; CN; DLB 14

Middleton, Thomas 1580-1627 .... **LC 33;**
DAM DRAM, MST; DC 5
See also DLB 58; RGEL

Migueis, Jose Rodrigues 1901- .... **CLC 10**

Mikszath, Kalman 1847-1910 .... **TCLC 31**
See also CA 170

Miles, Jack .... **CLC 100**

Miles, Josephine (Louise)
1911-1985 .. **CLC 1, 2, 14, 34, 39; DAM**
POET
See also CA 1-4R; 116; CANR 2, 55; DLB
48

Militant
See Sandburg, Carl (August)

Mill, John Stuart 1806-1873 .... **NCLC 11, 58**
See also CDBLB 1832-1890; DLB 55, 190;
FW 1

Millar, Kenneth 1915-1983 ... **CLC 14; DAM**
POP
See also Macdonald, Ross
See also CA 9-12R; 110; CANR 16, 63;
CMW; CPW; DA3; DLB 2, 226; DLBD
6; DLBY 83; MTCW 1, 2

Millay, E. Vincent
See Millay, Edna St. Vincent

Millay, Edna St. Vincent
1892-1950 .... **TCLC 4, 49; DA; DAB; DAC; DAM MST, POET; PC 6; WLCS**
See also Boyd, Nancy
See also CA 104; 130; CDALB 1917-1929; DA3; DLB 45; MTCW 1, 2; PFS 3; RGAL

Miller, Arthur 1915- ...... **CLC 1, 2, 6, 10, 15, 26, 47, 78; DA; DAB; DAC; DAM DRAM, MST; DC 1; WLC**
See also AAYA 15; AITN 1; CA 1-4R; CABS 3; CAD; CANR 2, 30, 54, 76; CD; CDALB 1941-1968; DA3; DFS 1,3; DLB 7; MTCW 1, 2; RGAL; WYAS 1

Miller, Henry (Valentine)
1891-1980 .... **CLC 1, 2, 4, 9, 14, 43, 84; DA; DAB; DAC; DAM MST, NOV; WLC**
See also CA 9-12R; 97-100; CANR 33, 64; CDALB 1929-1941; DA3; DLB 4, 9; DLBY 80; MTCW 1, 2

Miller, Jason 1939(?)-2001 .... **CLC 2**
See also AITN 1; CA 73-76; CAD; DFS 12; DLB 7

Miller, Sue 1943- .... **CLC 44; DAM POP**
See also BEST 90:3; CA 139; CANR 59, 91; DA3; DLB 143

Miller, Walter M(ichael, Jr.)
1923-1996 .... **CLC 4, 30**
See also CA 85-88; DLB 8; SFW

Millett, Kate 1934- .... **CLC 67**
See also AITN 1; CA 73-76; CANR 32, 53, 76; DA3; FW; GLL 1; MTCW 1, 2

Millhauser, Steven (Lewis) 1943- .... **CLC 21, 54, 109**
See also CA 110; 111; CANR 63; CN; DA3; DLB 2; FANT; INT 111; MTCW 2

Millin, Sarah Gertrude 1889-1968 ... **CLC 49**
See also CA 102; 93-96; DLB 225

Milne, A(lan) A(lexander)
1882-1956 ..... **TCLC 6, 88; DAB; DAC; DAM MST**
See also CA 104; 133; CLR 1, 26; CMW; CWRI; DA3; DLB 10, 77, 100, 160; FANT; MAICYA; MTCW 1, 2; SATA 100; YABC 1

Milner, Ron(ald) 1938- .... **CLC 56; BLC 3; DAM MULT**
See also AITN 1; BW 1; CA 73-76; CAD; CANR 24, 81; CD; DLB 38; MTCW 1

Milnes, Richard Monckton
1809-1885 .... **NCLC 61**
See also DLB 32, 184

Milosz, Czeslaw 1911- ...... **CLC 5, 11, 22, 31, 56, 82; DAM MST, POET; PC 8; WLCS**
See also CA 81-84; CANR 23, 51, 91; CWW 2; DA3; MTCW 1, 2

Milton, John 1608-1674 .... **LC 9, 43; DA; DAB; DAC; DAM MST, POET; PC 19, 29; WLC**
See also CDBLB 1660-1789; DA3; DLB 131, 151; EFS 1; PFS 3; RGEL

Min, Anchee 1957- .... **CLC 86**
See also CA 146; CANR 94

Minehaha, Cornelius
See Wedekind, (Benjamin) Frank(lin)

Miner, Valerie 1947- .... **CLC 40**
See also CA 97-100; CANR 59; FW; GLL 2

Minimo, Duca
See D'Annunzio, Gabriele

Minot, Susan 1956- .... **CLC 44**
See also AMWS 6; CA 134; CN

Minus, Ed 1938- .... **CLC 39**
See also CA 185

Miranda, Javier
See Bioy Casares, Adolfo
See also CWW 2

Miranda, Javier
See Bioy Casares, Adolfo

Mirbeau, Octave 1848-1917 .... **TCLC 55**
See also DLB 123, 192; GFL 1789 to the Present

Miro (Ferrer), Gabriel (Francisco Victor)
1879-1930 .... **TCLC 5**
See also CA 104; 185

Misharin, Alexandr .... **CLC 59**

Mishima, Yukio ... **CLC 2, 4, 6, 9, 27; DC 1; SSC 4**
See also Hiraoka, Kimitake
See also DLB 182; GLL 1; MTCW 2; SSFS 5

Mistral, Frédéric 1830-1914 .... **TCLC 51**
See also CA 122; GFL 1789 to the Present

Mistral, Gabriela
See Godoy Alcayaga, Lucila
See also RGWL

Mistry, Rohinton 1952- .... **CLC 71; DAC**
See also CA 141; CANR 86; CCA 1; CN; SSFS 6

Mitchell, Clyde
See Ellison, Harlan (Jay); Silverberg, Robert

Mitchell, James Leslie 1901-1935
See Gibbon, Lewis Grassic
See also CA 104; 188; DLB 15

Mitchell, Joni 1943- .... **CLC 12**
See also CA 112; CCA 1

Mitchell, Joseph (Quincy)
1908-1996 .... **CLC 98**
See also CA 77-80; 152; CANR 69; CN; CSW; DLB 185; DLBY 96

Mitchell, Margaret (Munnerlyn)
1900-1949 . **TCLC 11; DAM NOV, POP**
See also AAYA 23; CA 109; 125; CANR 55, 94; CDALBS; DA3; DLB 9; MTCW 1, 2; NFS 9; RHW; WYAS 1; YAW

Mitchell, Peggy
See Mitchell, Margaret (Munnerlyn)

Mitchell, S(ilas) Weir 1829-1914 .... **TCLC 36**
See also CA 165; DLB 202

Mitchell, W(illiam) O(rmond)
1914-1998 .. **CLC 25; DAC; DAM MST**
See also CA 77-80; 165; CANR 15, 43; CN; DLB 88

Mitchell, William 1879-1936 .... **TCLC 81**

Mitford, Mary Russell 1787-1855 ... **NCLC 4**
See also DLB 110, 116

Mitford, Nancy 1904-1973 .... **CLC 44**
See also CA 9-12R; DLB 191

Miyamoto, (Chujo) Yuriko
1899-1951 .... **TCLC 37**
See also CA 170, 174; DLB 180

Miyazawa, Kenji 1896-1933 .... **TCLC 76**
See also CA 157

Mizoguchi, Kenji 1898-1956 .... **TCLC 72**
See also CA 167

Mo, Timothy (Peter) 1950(?)- ... **CLC 46, 134**
See also CA 117; CN; DLB 194; MTCW 1

Modarressi, Taghi (M.) 1931-1997 ... **CLC 44**
See also CA 121; 134; INT 134

Modiano, Patrick (Jean) 1945- .... **CLC 18**
See also CA 85-88; CANR 17, 40; CWW 2; DLB 83

Moerck, Paal
See Roelvaag, O(le) E(dvart)

Mofolo, Thomas (Mokopu)
1875(?)-1948 .. **TCLC 22; BLC 3; DAM MULT**
See also CA 121; 153; CANR 83; DLB 225; MTCW 2

Mohr, Nicholasa 1938- .... **CLC 12; DAM MULT; HLC 2**
See also AAYA 8; CA 49-52; CANR 1, 32, 64; CLR 22; DLB 145; HW 1, 2; JRDA; RGAL; SAAS 8; SATA 8, 97; SATA-Essay 113; YAW

Mojtabai, A(nn) G(race) 1938- ..... **CLC 5, 9, 15, 29**
See also CA 85-88; CANR 88

Molière 1622-1673 .... **LC 10, 28, 64; DA; DAB; DAC; DAM DRAM, MST; DC 13; WLC**
See also DA3; DFS 13; GFL Beginnings to 1789

Molin, Charles
See Mayne, William (James Carter)

Molina, Tirso de 1580(?)-1648 .... **DC 13**
See also Tirso de Molina
See also HLCS 2

Molnár, Ferenc 1878-1952 .. **TCLC 20; DAM DRAM**
See also CA 109; 153; CANR 83; DLB 215; RGWL

Momaday, N(avarre) Scott 1934- ...... **CLC 2, 19, 85, 95; DA; DAB; DAC; DAM MST, MULT, NOV, POP; PC 25; WLCS**
See also AAYA 11; AMWS 4; CA 25-28R; CANR 14, 34, 68; CDALBS; CN; CPW; DA3; DLB 143, 175; INT CANR-14; MTCW 1, 2; NFS 10; NNAL; PFS 2, 11; SATA 48; SATA-Brief 30; YAW

Monette, Paul 1945-1995 .... **CLC 82**
See also CA 139; 147; CN; GLL 1

Monroe, Harriet 1860-1936 .... **TCLC 12**
See also CA 109; DLB 54, 91

Monroe, Lyle
See Heinlein, Robert A(nson)

Montagu, Elizabeth 1720-1800 .... **NCLC 7**
See also FW

Montagu, Mary (Pierrepont) Wortley
1689-1762 .... **LC 9, 57; PC 16**
See also DLB 95, 101

Montagu, W. H.
See Coleridge, Samuel Taylor

Montague, John (Patrick) 1929- .... **CLC 13, 46**
See also CA 9-12R; CANR 9, 69; CP; DLB 40; MTCW 1; PFS 12

Montaigne, Michel (Eyquem) de
1533-1592 .... **LC 8; DA; DAB; DAC; DAM MST; WLC**
See also EW; GFL Beginnings to 1789; RGWL

Montale, Eugenio 1896-1981 ... **CLC 7, 9, 18; PC 13**
See also CA 17-20R; 104; CANR 30; DLB 114; MTCW 1; RGWL

Montesquieu, Charles-Louis de Secondat
1689-1755 .... **LC 7**
See also GFL Beginnings to 1789

Montessori, Maria 1870-1952 ...... **TCLC 103**
See also CA 115; 147

Montgomery, (Robert) Bruce 1921(?)-1978
See Crispin, Edmund
See also CA 179; 104; CMW

Montgomery, L(ucy) M(aud)
1874-1942 .... **TCLC 51; DAC; DAM MST**
See also AAYA 12; CA 108; 137; CLR 8; DA3; DLB 92; DLBD 14; JRDA; MAICYA; MTCW 2; SATA 100; YABC 1

Montgomery, Marion H., Jr. 1925- .... **CLC 7**
See also AITN 1; CA 1-4R; CANR 3, 48; CSW; DLB 6

Montgomery, Max
See Davenport, Guy (Mattison, Jr.)

Montherlant, Henry (Milon) de
1896-1972 ..... **CLC 8, 19; DAM DRAM**
See also CA 85-88; 37-40R; DLB 72; EW; GFL 1789 to the Present; MTCW 1

Monty Python
See Chapman, Graham; Cleese, John (Marwood); Gilliam, Terry (Vance); Idle, Eric; Jones, Terence Graham Parry; Palin, Michael (Edward)
See also AAYA 7

Moodie, Susanna (Strickland)
1803-1885 .... **NCLC 14**
See also DLB 99

Moody, William Vaughan
1869-1910 .... **TCLC 105**
See also CA 110; 178; DLB 7, 54

Mooney, Edward 1951-
See Mooney, Ted
See also CA 130

Mooney, Ted .... **CLC 25**
See also Mooney, Edward

Moorcock, Michael (John) 1939- ...... **CLC 5, 27, 58**
See also Bradbury, Edward P.
See also AAYA 26; CA 45-48; CAAS 5; CANR 2, 17, 38, 64; CN; DLB 14, 231; FANT; MTCW 1, 2; SATA 93; SFW

Moore, Brian 1921-1999 ... **CLC 1, 3, 5, 7, 8, 19, 32, 90; DAB; DAC; DAM MST**
See also Bryan, Michael
See also CA 1-4R; 174; CANR 1, 25, 42, 63; CCA 1; CN; FANT; MTCW 1, 2; RGEL

Moore, Edward
See Muir, Edwin
See also RGEL

Moore, G. E. 1873-1958 .... **TCLC 89**

Moore, George Augustus
1852-1933 .... **TCLC 7; SSC 19**
See also CA 104; 177; DLB 10, 18, 57, 135

Moore, Lorrie .... **CLC 39, 45, 68**
See also Moore, Marie Lorena
See also DLB 234

Moore, Marianne (Craig)
1887-1972 .... **CLC 1, 2, 4, 8, 10, 13, 19, 47; DA; DAB; DAC; DAM MST, POET; PC 4; WLCS**
See also CA 1-4R; 33-36R; CANR 3, 61; CDALB 1929-1941; DA3; DLB 45; DLBD 7; MTCW 1, 2; SATA 20

Moore, Marie Lorena 1957-
See Moore, Lorrie
See also CA 116; CANR 39, 83; CN; DLB 234

Moore, Thomas 1779-1852 .... **NCLC 6**
See also DLB 96, 144; RGEL

Moorhouse, Frank 1938- .... **SSC 40**
See also CA 118; CANR 92; CN; RGSF

Mora, Pat(ricia) 1942-
See also CA 129; CANR 57, 81; CLR 58; DAM MULT; DLB 209; HLC 2; HW 1, 2; SATA 92

Moraga, Cherrie 1952- .... **CLC 126; DAM MULT**
See also CA 131; CANR 66; DLB 82; FW; GLL 1; HW 1, 2

Morand, Paul 1888-1976 .... **CLC 41; SSC 22**
See also CA 184; 69-72; DLB 65

Morante, Elsa 1918-1985 .... **CLC 8, 47**
See also CA 85-88; 117; CANR 35; DLB 177; MTCW 1, 2; RGWL

Moravia, Alberto .... **CLC 2, 7, 11, 27, 46; SSC 26**
See also Pincherle, Alberto
See also DLB 177; MTCW 2; RGSF; RGWL

More, Hannah 1745-1833 .... **NCLC 27**
See also DLB 107, 109, 116, 158; RGEL

More, Henry 1614-1687 .... **LC 9**
See also DLB 126

More, Sir Thomas 1478-1535 .... **LC 10, 32**

Moréas, Jean .... **TCLC 18**
See also Papadiamantopoulos, Johannes
See also GFL 1789 to the Present

Morgan, Berry 1919- .... **CLC 6**
See also CA 49-52; DLB 6

Morgan, Claire
See Highsmith, (Mary) Patricia
See also GLL 1

Morgan, Edwin (George) 1920- .... **CLC 31**
See also CA 5-8R; CANR 3, 43, 90; CP; DLB 27

Morgan, (George) Frederick 1922- .. **CLC 23**
See also CA 17-20R; CANR 21; CP

Morgan, Harriet
See Mencken, H(enry) L(ouis)

Morgan, Jane
See Cooper, James Fenimore

Morgan, Janet 1945- .... **CLC 39**
See also CA 65-68

Morgan, Lady 1776(?)-1859 .... **NCLC 29**
See also DLB 116, 158; RGEL

Morgan, Robin (Evonne) 1941- .... **CLC 2**
See also CA 69-72; CANR 29, 68; FW; MTCW 1; SATA 80

Morgan, Scott
See Kuttner, Henry

Morgan, Seth 1949(?)-1990 .... **CLC 65**
See also CA 185; 132

Morgenstern, Christian (Otto Josef Wolfgang) 1871-1914 .... **TCLC 8**
See also CA 105

Morgenstern, S.
See Goldman, William (W.)

Mori, Rintaro
See Mori Ogai
See also CA 110

Moricz, Zsigmond 1879-1942 .... **TCLC 33**
See also CA 165

Mörike, Eduard (Friedrich)
1804-1875 .... **NCLC 10**
See also DLB 133

Mori Ogai 1862-1922 .... **TCLC 14**
See also CA 164; DLB 180

Moritz, Karl Philipp 1756-1793 .... **LC 2**
See also DLB 94

Morland, Peter Henry
See Faust, Frederick (Schiller)

Morley, Christopher (Darlington)
1890-1957 .... **TCLC 87**
See also CA 112; DLB 9

Morren, Theophil
See Hofmannsthal, Hugo von

Morris, Bill 1952- .... **CLC 76**

Morris, Julian
See West, Morris L(anglo)

Morris, Steveland Judkins 1950(?)-
See Wonder, Stevie
See also CA 111

Morris, William 1834-1896 .... **NCLC 4**
See also CDBLB 1832-1890; DLB 18, 35, 57, 156, 178, 184; FANT; SFW

Morris, Wright 1910-1998 .. **CLC 1, 3, 7, 18, 37**
See also CA 9-12R; 167; CANR 21, 81; CN; DLB 2, 206; DLBY 81; MTCW 1, 2; RGAL; TCLC 107; TCWW 2

Morrison, Arthur 1863-1945 .... **TCLC 72; SSC 40**
See also CA 120; 157; CMW; DLB 70, 135, 197; RGEL

Morrison, Chloe Anthony Wofford
See Morrison, Toni

Morrison, James Douglas 1943-1971
See Morrison, Jim
See also CA 73-76; CANR 40

Morrison, Jim .... **CLC 17**
See also Morrison, James Douglas

Morrison, Toni 1931- . **CLC 4, 10, 22, 55, 81, 87; BLC 3; DA; DAB; DAC; DAM MST, MULT, NOV, POP**
See also AAYA 1, 22; AFAW 1, 2; AMWS 3; BW 2, 3; CA 29-32R; CANR 27, 42, 67; CDALB 1968-1988; CN; CPW; DA3; DLB 6, 33, 143; DLBY 81; FW; MTCW 1, 2; NFS 1, 6, 8; RGAL; RHW; SATA 57; SSFS 5; YAW

Morrison, Van 1945- .... **CLC 21**
See also CA 116; 168

Morrissy, Mary 1958- .... **CLC 99**

Mortimer, John (Clifford) 1923- ..... **CLC 28, 43; DAM DRAM, POP**
See also CA 13-16R; CANR 21, 69; CD; CDBLB 1960 to Present; CMW; CN; CPW; DA3; DLB 13; INT CANR-21; MTCW 1, 2

Mortimer, Penelope (Ruth)
1918-1999 .... **CLC 5**
See also CA 57-60; 187; CANR 45, 88; CN

Morton, Anthony
See Creasey, John

Mosca, Gaetano 1858-1941 .... **TCLC 75**

Mosher, Howard Frank 1943- .... **CLC 62**
See also CA 139; CANR 65

Mosley, Nicholas 1923- .... **CLC 43, 70**
See also CA 69-72; CANR 41, 60; CN; DLB 14, 207

Mosley, Walter 1952- .... **CLC 97; BLCS; DAM MULT, POP**
See also AAYA 17; BW 2; CA 142; CANR 57, 92; CMW; CPW; DA3; MTCW 2

Moss, Howard 1922-1987 ...... **CLC 7, 14, 45, 50; DAM POET**
See also CA 1-4R; 123; CANR 1, 44; DLB 5

Mossgiel, Rab
See Burns, Robert

Motion, Andrew (Peter) 1952- .... **CLC 47**
See also CA 146; CANR 90; CP; DLB 40

Motley, Willard (Francis)
1912-1965 .... **CLC 18**
See also BW 1; CA 117; 106; CANR 88; DLB 76, 143

Motoori, Norinaga 1730-1801 .... **NCLC 45**

Mott, Michael (Charles Alston)
1930- .... **CLC 15, 34**
See also CA 5-8R; CAAS 7; CANR 7, 29

Mountain Wolf Woman 1884-1960 .. **CLC 92**
See also CA 144; CANR 90; NNAL

Moure, Erin 1955- .... **CLC 88**
See also CA 113; CP; CWP; DLB 60

Mowat, Farley (McGill) 1921- .... **CLC 26; DAC; DAM MST**
See also AAYA 1; CA 1-4R; CANR 4, 24, 42, 68; CLR 20; CPW; DLB 68; INT CANR-24; JRDA; MAICYA; MTCW 1, 2; SATA 3, 55; YAW

Mowatt, Anna Cora 1819-1870 ..... **NCLC 74**
See also RGAL

Moyers, Bill 1934- .... **CLC 74**
See also AITN 2; CA 61-64; CANR 31, 52

Mphahlele, Es'kia
See Mphahlele, Ezekiel
See also DLB 125, 225; RGSF; SSFS 11

Mphahlele, Ezekiel 1919- .... **CLC 25, 133; BLC 3; DAM MULT**
See also Mphahlele, Es'kia
See also BW 2, 3; CA 81-84; CANR 26, 76; CN; DA3; DLB 225; MTCW 2; SATA 119

Mqhayi, S(amuel) E(dward) K(rune Loliwe) 1875-1945 ...... **TCLC 25; BLC 3; DAM MULT**
See also CA 153; CANR 87

Mrozek, Slawomir 1930- .... **CLC 3, 13**
See also CA 13-16R; CAAS 10; CANR 29; CWW 2; DLB 232; MTCW 1

Newby, P(ercy) H(oward)
1918-1997 .... **CLC 2, 13; DAM NOV**
See also CA 5-8R; 161; CANR 32, 67; CN;
DLB 15; MTCW 1
Newcastle
See Cavendish, Margaret Lucas
Newlove, Donald 1928- .... **CLC 6**
See also CA 29-32R; CANR 25
Newlove, John (Herbert) 1938- .... **CLC 14**
See also CA 21-24R; CANR 9, 25; CP
Newman, Charles 1938- .... **CLC 2, 8**
See also CA 21-24R; CANR 84; CN
Newman, Edwin (Harold) 1919- ...... **CLC 14**
See also AITN 1; CA 69-72; CANR 5
Newman, John Henry 1801-1890 . **NCLC 38, 99**
See also DLB 18, 32, 55; RGEL
Newton, (Sir)Isaac 1642-1727 .... **LC 35, 52**
Newton, Suzanne 1936- .... **CLC 35**
See also CA 41-44R; CANR 14; JRDA;
SATA 5, 77
New York Dept. of Ed. .... **CLC 70**
Nexo, Martin Andersen
1869-1954 .... **TCLC 43**
See also DLB 214
Nezval, Vitezslav 1900-1958 .... **TCLC 44**
See also CA 123
Ng, Fae Myenne 1957(?)- .... **CLC 81**
See also CA 146
Ngema, Mbongeni 1955- .... **CLC 57**
See also BW 2; CA 143; CANR 84; CD
Ngugi, James T(hiong'o) .... **CLC 3, 7, 13**
See also Ngugi wa Thiong'o
Ngugi wa Thiong'o 1938- .. **CLC 36; BLC 3; DAM MULT, NOV**
See also Ngugi, James T(hiong'o)
See also BW 2; CA 81-84; CANR 27, 58;
DLB 125; DNFS 2; MTCW 1, 2
Nichol, B(arrie) P(hillip) 1944-1988 . **CLC 18**
See also CA 53-56; DLB 53; SATA 66
Nichols, John (Treadwell) 1940- ...... **CLC 38**
See also CA 9-12R; CAAE 190; CAAS 2;
CANR 6, 70; DLBY 82; TCWW 2
Nichols, Leigh
See Koontz, Dean R(ay)
Nichols, Peter (Richard) 1927- .... **CLC 5, 36, 65**
See also CA 104; CANR 33, 86; CBD; CD;
DLB 13; MTCW 1
Nicholson, Linda ed. .... **CLC 65**
Ní Chuilleanáin, Eiléan 1942- .... **PC 34**
See also CA 126; CANR 53, 83; CP; CWP;
DLB 40
Nicolas, F. R. E.
See Freeling, Nicolas
Niedecker, Lorine 1903-1970 ..... **CLC 10, 42; DAM POET**
See also CA 25-28; CAP 2; DLB 48
Nietzsche, Friedrich (Wilhelm)
1844-1900 .... **TCLC 10, 18, 55**
See also CA 107; 121; DLB 129
Nievo, Ippolito 1831-1861 .... **NCLC 22**
Nightingale, Anne Redmon 1943-
See Redmon, Anne
See also CA 103
Nightingale, Florence 1820-1910 ... **TCLC 85**
See also CA 188; DLB 166
Nik. T. O.
See Annensky, Innokenty (Fyodorovich)
Nin, Anaïs 1903-1977 ..... **CLC 1, 4, 8, 11, 14, 60, 127; DAM NOV, POP; SSC 10**
See also AITN 2; CA 13-16R; 69-72;
CANR 22, 53; DLB 2, 4, 152; GLL 2;
MTCW 1, 2; RGAL
Nishida, Kitaro 1870-1945 .... **TCLC 83**
Nishiwaki, Junzaburō 1894-1982 .... **PC 15**
See also CA 107; MJW

Nissenson, Hugh 1933- .... **CLC 4, 9**
See also CA 17-20R; CANR 27; CN; DLB
28
Niven, Larry .... **CLC 8**
See also Niven, Laurence Van Cott
See also AAYA 27; DLB 8; SCFW 2
Niven, Laurence Van Cott 1938-
See Niven, Larry
See also CA 21-24R; CAAS 12; CANR 14,
44, 66; CPW; DAM POP; MTCW 1, 2;
SATA 95; SFW
Nixon, Agnes Eckhardt 1927- .... **CLC 21**
See also CA 110
Nizan, Paul 1905-1940 .... **TCLC 40**
See also CA 161; DLB 72; GFL 1789 to the
Present
Nkosi, Lewis 1936- ... **CLC 45; BLC 3; DAM MULT**
See also BW 1, 3; CA 65-68; CANR 27,
81; CBD; CD; DLB 157, 225
Nodier, (Jean) Charles (Emmanuel)
1780-1844 .... **NCLC 19**
See also DLB 119; GFL 1789 to the Present
Noguchi, Yone 1875-1947 .... **TCLC 80**
Nolan, Christopher 1965- .... **CLC 58**
See also CA 111; CANR 88
Noon, Jeff 1957- .... **CLC 91**
See also CA 148; CANR 83; SFW
Norden, Charles
See Durrell, Lawrence (George)
Nordhoff, Charles (Bernard)
1887-1947 .... **TCLC 23**
See also CA 108; DLB 9; RHW 1; SATA
23
Norfolk, Lawrence 1963- .... **CLC 76**
See also CA 144; CANR 85; CN
Norman, Marsha 1947- .... **CLC 28; DAM DRAM; DC 8**
See also CA 105; CABS 3; CAD; CANR
41; CD; CSW; CWD; DFS 2; DLBY 84;
FW
Normyx
See Douglas, (George) Norman
Norris, Frank .... **SSC 28**
See also Norris, (Benjamin) Frank(lin, Jr.)
See also CDALB 1865-1917; DLB 12, 71,
186; RGAL; TCWW 2
Norris, (Benjamin) Frank(lin, Jr.)
1870-1902 .... **TCLC 24**
See also Norris, Frank
See also CA 110; 160; NFS 12
Norris, Leslie 1921- .... **CLC 14**
See also CA 11-12; CANR 14; CAP 1; CP;
DLB 27
North, Andrew
See Norton, Andre
North, Anthony
See Koontz, Dean R(ay)
North, Captain George
See Stevenson, Robert Louis (Balfour)
North, Milou
See Erdrich, Louise
Northrup, B. A.
See Hubbard, L(afayette) Ron(ald)
North Staffs
See Hulme, T(homas) E(rnest)
Norton, Alice Mary
See Norton, Andre
See also MAICYA; SATA 1, 43
Norton, Andre 1912- .... **CLC 12**
See also Norton, Alice Mary
See also AAYA 14; CA 1-4R; CANR 68;
CLR 50; DLB 8, 52; JRDA; MTCW 1;
SATA 91; YAW
Norton, Caroline 1808-1877 .... **NCLC 47**
See also DLB 21, 159, 199

Norway, Nevil Shute 1899-1960
See Shute, Nevil
See also CA 102; 93-96; CANR 85; MTCW
2; RHW; SFW
Norwid, Cyprian Kamil
1821-1883 .... **NCLC 17**
Nosille, Nabrah
See Ellison, Harlan (Jay)
Nossack, Hans Erich 1901-1978 .... **CLC 6**
See also CA 93-96; 85-88; DLB 69
Nostradamus 1503-1566 .... **LC 27**
Nosu, Chuji
See Ozu, Yasujiro
Notenburg, Eleanora (Genrikhovna) von
See Guro, Elena
Nova, Craig 1945- .... **CLC 7, 31**
See also CA 45-48; CANR 2, 53
Novak, Joseph
See Kosinski, Jerzy (Nikodem)
Novalis 1772-1801 .... **NCLC 13**
See also DLB 90; RGEL
Novis, Emile
See Weil, Simone (Adolphine)
Nowlan, Alden (Albert) 1933-1983 . **CLC 15; DAC; DAM MST**
See also CA 9-12R; CANR 5; DLB 53; PFS
12
Noyes, Alfred 1880-1958 ...... **TCLC 7; PC 27**
See also CA 104; 188; DLB 20; FANT; PFS
4; RGEL
Nunn, Kem .... **CLC 34**
See also CA 159
Nwapa, Flora 1931-1993 .... **CLC 133; BLCS**
See also BW 2; CA 143; CANR 83; CWRI;
DLB 125
Nye, Robert 1939- **CLC 13, 42; DAM NOV**
See also CA 33-36R; CANR 29, 67; CN;
CP; CWRI; DLB 14; FANT; HGG;
MTCW 1; RHW; SATA 6
Nyro, Laura 1947-1997 .... **CLC 17**
Oates, Joyce Carol 1938- .. **CLC 1, 2, 3, 6, 9, 11, 15, 19, 33, 52, 108, 134; DA; DAB; DAC; DAM MST, NOV, POP; SSC 6; WLC**
See also AAYA 15; AITN 1; AMWS 2;
BEST 89:2; CA 5-8R; CANR 25, 45, 74;
CDALB 1968-1988; CN; CP; CPW;
CWP; DA3; DLB 2, 5, 130; DLBY 81;
FW; HGG; INT CANR-25; MTCW 1, 2;
NFS 8; RGAL; RGSF; SSFS 1, 8
O'Brien, Darcy 1939-1998 .... **CLC 11**
See also CA 21-24R; 167; CANR 8, 59
O'Brien, E. G.
See Clarke, Arthur C(harles)
O'Brien, Edna 1936- ... **CLC 3, 5, 8, 13, 36, 65, 116; DAM NOV; SSC 10**
See also CA 1-4R; CANR 6, 41, 65; CD-
BLB 1960 to Present; CN; DA3; DLB 14,
231; FW; MTCW 1, 2; RGSF
O'Brien, Fitz-James 1828-1862 ..... **NCLC 21**
See also DLB 74; RGAL
O'Brien, Flann .... **CLC 1, 4, 5, 7, 10, 47**
See also O Nuallain, Brian
See also BRWS 2; DLB 231
O'Brien, Richard 1942- .... **CLC 17**
See also CA 124
O'Brien, (William) Tim(othy) 1946- . **CLC 7, 19, 40, 103; DAM POP**
See also AAYA 16; CA 85-88; CANR 40,
58; CDALBS; CN; CPW; DA3; DLB 152;
DLBD 9; DLBY 80; MTCW 2
Obstfelder, Sigbjoern 1866-1900 .... **TCLC 23**
See also CA 123
O'Casey, Sean 1880-1964 .... **CLC 1, 5, 9, 11, 15, 88; DAB; DAC; DAM DRAM, MST; DC 12; WLCS**
See also CA 89-92; CANR 62; CBD; CD-
BLB 1914-1945; DA3; DLB 10; MTCW
1, 2

Ovid 43B.C.- .. CMLC 7; DAM POET; PC 2
    See also DA3; DLB 211; RGEL
Owen, Hugh
    See Faust, Frederick (Schiller)
Owen, Wilfred (Edward Salter)
    1893-1918 .... TCLC 5, 27; DA; DAB;
    DAC; DAM MST, POET; PC 19; WLC
    See also CA 104; 141; CDBLB 1914-1945;
    DLB 20; MTCW 2; PFS 10
Owens, Rochelle 1936- .... CLC 8
    See also CA 17-20R; CAAS 2; CAD;
    CANR 39; CD; CP; CWD; CWP
Oz, Amos 1939- ...... CLC 5, 8, 11, 27, 33, 54;
    DAM NOV
    See also CA 53-56; CANR 27, 47, 65;
    CWW 2; MTCW 1, 2; RGSF
Ozick, Cynthia 1928- .... CLC 3, 7, 28, 62;
    DAM NOV, POP; SSC 15
    See also AMWS 5; BEST 90:1; CA 17-20R;
    CANR 23, 58; CN; CPW; DA3; DLB 28,
    152; DLBY 82; INT CANR-23; MTCW
    1, 2; RGAL; RGSF; SSFS 3, 12
Ozu, Yasujiro 1903-1963 .... CLC 16
    See also CA 112
Pacheco, C.
    See Pessoa, Fernando (Ant
Pacheco, José Emilio 1939-
    See also CA 111; 131; CANR 65; DAM
    MULT; HLC 2; HW 1, 2
Pa Chin .... CLC 18
    See also Li Fei-kan
Pack, Robert 1929- .... CLC 13
    See also CA 1-4R; CANR 3, 44, 82; CP;
    DLB 5; SATA 118
Padgett, Lewis
    See Kuttner, Henry
Padilla (Lorenzo), Heberto
    1932-2000 .... CLC 38
    See also AITN 1; CA 123; 131; 189; HW 1
Page, Jimmy 1944- .... CLC 12
Page, Louise 1955- .... CLC 40
    See also CA 140; CANR 76; CBD; CD;
    CWD; DLB 233
Page, P(atricia) K(athleen) 1916- ...... CLC 7,
    18; DAC; DAM MST; PC 12
    See also Cape, Judith
    See also CA 53-56; CANR 4, 22, 65; CP;
    DLB 68; MTCW 1
Page, Stanton
    See Fuller, Henry Blake
Page, Stanton
    See Fuller, Henry Blake
Page, Thomas Nelson 1853-1922 .... SSC 23
    See also CA 118; 177; DLB 12, 78; DLBD
    13; RGAL
Pagels, Elaine Hiesey 1943- .... CLC 104
    See also CA 45-48; CANR 2, 24, 51; FW
Paget, Violet 1856-1935
    See Lee, Vernon
    See also CA 104; 166; GLL 1; HGG
Paget-Lowe, Henry
    See Lovecraft, H(oward) P(hillips)
Paglia, Camille (Anna) 1947- .... CLC 68
    See also CA 140; CANR 72; CPW; FW;
    GLL 2; MTCW 2
Paige, Richard
    See Koontz, Dean R(ay)
Paine, Thomas 1737-1809 .... NCLC 62
    See also AMWS 1; CDALB 1640-1865;
    DLB 31, 43, 73, 158; RGAL; RGEL
Pakenham, Antonia
    See Fraser, (Lady)Antonia (Pakenham)
Palamas, Kostes 1859-1943 .... TCLC 5
    See also CA 105; 190; RGWL
Palazzeschi, Aldo 1885-1974 .... CLC 11
    See also CA 89-92; 53-56; DLB 114
Pales Matos, Luis 1898-1959
    See also HLCS 2; HW 1

Paley, Grace 1922- .... CLC 4, 6, 37, 140;
    DAM POP; SSC 8
    See also AMWS 6; CA 25-28R; CANR 13,
    46, 74; CN; CPW; DA3; DLB 28; FW;
    INT CANR-13; MTCW 1, 2; RGAL;
    RGSF; SSFS 3
Palin, Michael (Edward) 1943- .... CLC 21
    See also Monty Python
    See also CA 107; CANR 35; SATA 67
Palliser, Charles 1947- .... CLC 65
    See also CA 136; CANR 76; CN
Palma, Ricardo 1833-1919 .... TCLC 29
    See also CA 168
Pancake, Breece Dexter 1952-1979
    See Pancake, Breece D'J
    See also CA 123; 109
Pancake, Breece D'J .... CLC 29
    See also Pancake, Breece Dexter
    See also DLB 130
Panchenko, Nikolai .... CLC 59
Pankhurst, Emmeline (Goulden)
    1858-1928 .... TCLC 100
    See also CA 116; FW
Panko, Rudy
    See Gogol, Nikolai (Vasilyevich)
Papadiamantis, Alexandros
    1851-1911 .... TCLC 29
    See also CA 168
Papadiamantopoulos, Johannes 1856-1910
    See Mor
    See also CA 117
Papini, Giovanni 1881-1956 .... TCLC 22
    See also CA 121; 180
Paracelsus 1493-1541 .... LC 14
    See also DLB 179
Parasol, Peter
    See Stevens, Wallace
Pardo Bazán, Emilia 1851-1921 .... SSC 30
    See also FW
Pareto, Vilfredo 1848-1923 .... TCLC 69
    See also CA 175
Paretsky, Sara 1947- .. CLC 135; DAM POP
    See also AAYA 30; BEST 90:3; CA 125;
    129; CANR 59, 95; CMW; CPW; DA3;
    INT 129; RGAL
Parfenie, Maria
    See Codrescu, Andrei
Parini, Jay (Lee) 1948- .... CLC 54, 133
    See also CA 97-100; CAAS 16; CANR 32,
    87
Park, Jordan
    See Kornbluth, C(yril) M.; Pohl, Frederik
Park, Robert E(zra) 1864-1944 ..... TCLC 73
    See also CA 122; 165
Parker, Bert
    See Ellison, Harlan (Jay)
Parker, Dorothy (Rothschild)
    1893-1967 .... CLC 15, 68; DAM POET;
    PC 28; SSC 2
    See also CA 19-20; 25-28R; CAP 2; DA3;
    DLB 11, 45, 86; MTCW 1, 2
Parker, Robert B(rown) 1932- .... CLC 27;
    DAM NOV, POP
    See also AAYA 28; BEST 89:4; CA 49-52;
    CANR 1, 26, 52, 89; CMW; CPW; INT
    CANR-26; MTCW 1
Parkin, Frank 1940- .... CLC 43
    See also CA 147
Parkman, Francis, Jr. 1823-1893 .. NCLC 12
    See also AMWS 2; DLB 1, 30, 186, 235
Parks, Gordon (Alexander Buchanan)
    1912- .... CLC 1, 16; BLC 3; DAM
    MULT
    See also AAYA 36; AITN 2; BW 2, 3; CA
    41-44R; CANR 26, 66; DA3; DLB 33;
    MTCW 2; SATA 8, 108
Parmenides c. 515B.C.-c.
    450B.C. .... CMLC 22
    See also DLB 176

Parnell, Thomas 1679-1718 .... LC 3
    See also DLB 94; RGEL
Parra, Nicanor 1914- ...... CLC 2, 102; DAM
    MULT; HLC 2
    See also CA 85-88; CANR 32; CWW 2;
    HW 1; MTCW 1
Parra Sanojo, Ana Teresa de la 1890-1936
    See also HLCS 2
Parrish, Mary Frances
    See Fisher, M(ary) F(rances) K(ennedy)
Parshchikov, Aleksei .... CLC 59
Parson
    See Coleridge, Samuel Taylor
Parson Lot
    See Kingsley, Charles
Parton, Sara Payson Willis
    1811-1872 .... NCLC 86
    See also DLB 43, 74, 239
Partridge, Anthony
    See Oppenheim, E(dward) Phillips
Pascal, Blaise 1623-1662 .... LC 35
    See also GFL Beginnings to 1789; RGWL
Pascoli, Giovanni 1855-1912 .... TCLC 45
    See also CA 170
Pasolini, Pier Paolo 1922-1975 .. CLC 20, 37,
    106; PC 17
    See also CA 93-96; 61-64; CANR 63; DLB
    128, 177; MTCW 1; RGWL
Pasquini
    See Silone, Ignazio
Pastan, Linda (Olenik) 1932- .... CLC 27;
    DAM POET
    See also CA 61-64; CANR 18, 40, 61; CP;
    CSW; CWP; DLB 5; PFS 8
Pasternak, Boris (Leonidovich)
    1890-1960 .... CLC 7, 10, 18, 63; DA;
    DAB; DAC; DAM MST, NOV, POET;
    PC 6; SSC 31; WLC
    See also CA 127; 116; DA3; MTCW 1, 2
Patchen, Kenneth 1911-1972 .. CLC 1, 2, 18;
    DAM POET
    See also CA 1-4R; 33-36R; CANR 3, 35;
    DLB 16, 48; MTCW 1; RGAL
Pater, Walter (Horatio) 1839-1894 . NCLC 7,
    90
    See also CDBLB 1832-1890; DLB 57, 156
Paterson, A(ndrew) B(arton)
    1864-1941 .... TCLC 32
    See also CA 155; DLB 230; SATA 97
Paterson, Katherine (Womeldorf)
    1932- .... CLC 12, 30
    See also AAYA 1, 31; CA 21-24R; CANR
    28, 59; CLR 7, 50; CWRI; DLB 52;
    JRDA; MAICYA; MTCW 1; SATA 13,
    53, 92; YAW
Patmore, Coventry Kersey Dighton
    1823-1896 .... NCLC 9
    See also DLB 35, 98
Paton, Alan (Stewart) 1903-1988 ...... CLC 4,
    10, 25, 55, 106; DA; DAB; DAC; DAM
    MST, NOV; WLC
    See also AAYA 26; BRWS 2; CA 13-16;
    125; CANR 22; CAP 1; DA3; DLB 225;
    DLBD 17; MTCW 1, 2; NFS 3, 12; SATA
    11; SATA-Obit 56
Paton Walsh, Gillian 1937- .... CLC 35
    See also Walsh, Jill Paton
    See also AAYA 11; CANR 38, 83; CLR 2,
    65; DLB 161; JRDA; MAICYA; SAAS 3;
    SATA 4, 72, 109; YAW
Paton Walsh, Jill
    See Paton Walsh, Gillian
Patton, George S(mith), Jr.
    1885-1945 .... TCLC 79
    See also CA 189
Paulding, James Kirke 1778-1860 ... NCLC 2
    See also DLB 3, 59, 74; RGAL

Paulin, Thomas Neilson 1949-
See Paulin, Tom
See also CA 123; 128; CANR 98; CP
Paulin, Tom .... **CLC 37**
See also Paulin, Thomas Neilson
See also DLB 40
Pausanias c. 1st cent. - .... **CMLC 36**
Paustovsky, Konstantin (Georgievich)
1892-1968 .... **CLC 40**
See also CA 93-96; 25-28R
Pavese, Cesare 1908-1950 .. **TCLC 3; PC 13; SSC 19**
See also CA 104; 169; DLB 128, 177; RGSF; RGWL
Pavic, Milorad 1929- .... **CLC 60**
See also CA 136; CWW 2; DLB 181
Pavlov, Ivan Petrovich 1849-1936 . **TCLC 91**
See also CA 118; 180
Payne, Alan
See Jakes, John (William)
Paz, Gil
See Lugones, Leopoldo
Paz, Octavio 1914-1998 . **CLC 3, 4, 6, 10, 19, 51, 65, 119; DA; DAB; DAC; DAM MST, MULT, POET; HLC 2; PC 1; WLC**
See also CA 73-76; 165; CANR 32, 65; CWW 2; DA3; DLBY 90, 98; DNFS 1; HW 1, 2; MTCW 1, 2; RGWL
p'Bitek, Okot 1931-1982 .... **CLC 96; BLC 3; DAM MULT**
See also BW 2, 3; CA 124; 107; CANR 82; DLB 125; MTCW 1, 2
Peacock, Molly 1947- .... **CLC 60**
See also CA 103; CAAS 21; CANR 52, 84; CP; CWP; DLB 120
Peacock, Thomas Love
1785-1866 .... **NCLC 22**
See also DLB 96, 116; RGEL; RGSF
Peake, Mervyn 1911-1968 .... **CLC 7, 54**
See also CA 5-8R; 25-28R; CANR 3; DLB 15, 160; FANT; MTCW 1; SATA 23; SFW
Pearce, Philippa .... **CLC 21**
See also Christie, (Ann) Philippa
See also CLR 9; DLB 161; MAICYA; SATA 1, 67
Pearl, Eric
See Elman, Richard (Martin)
Pearson, T(homas) R(eid) 1956- .... **CLC 39**
See also CA 120; 130; CANR 97; CSW; INT 130
Peck, Dale 1967- .... **CLC 81**
See also CA 146; CANR 72; GLL 2
Peck, John 1941- .... **CLC 3**
See also CA 49-52; CANR 3; CP
Peck, Richard (Wayne) 1934- .... **CLC 21**
See also AAYA 1, 24; CA 85-88; CANR 19, 38; CLR 15; INT CANR-19; JRDA; MAICYA; SAAS 2; SATA 18, 55, 97; SATA-Essay 110; YAW
Peck, Robert Newton 1928- .... **CLC 17; DA; DAC; DAM MST**
See also AAYA 3; CA 81-84, 182; CAAE 182; CANR 31, 63; CLR 45; JRDA; MAICYA; SAAS 1; SATA 21, 62, 111; SATA-Essay 108; YAW
Peckinpah, (David) Sam(uel)
1925-1984 .... **CLC 20**
See also CA 109; 114; CANR 82
Pedersen, Knut 1859-1952
See Hamsun, Knut
See also CA 104; 119; CANR 63; MTCW 1, 2
Peeslake, Gaffer
See Durrell, Lawrence (George)
Péguy, Charles Pierre 1873-1914 ... **TCLC 10**
See also CA 107; GFL 1789 to the Present

Peirce, Charles Sanders
1839-1914 .... **TCLC 81**
Pellicer, Carlos 1900(?)-1977
See also CA 153; 69-72; HLCS 2; HW 1
Pena, Ramon del Valle y
See Valle-Incl
Pendennis, Arthur Esquir
See Thackeray, William Makepeace
Penn, William 1644-1718 .... **LC 25**
See also DLB 24
PEPECE
See Prado (Calvo), Pedro
Pepys, Samuel 1633-1703 ..... **LC 11, 58; DA; DAB; DAC; DAM MST; WLC**
See also CDBLB 1660-1789; DA3; DLB 101; RGEL
Percy, Thomas 1729-1811 .... **NCLC 95**
See also DLB 104
Percy, Walker 1916-1990 .... **CLC 2, 3, 6, 8, 14, 18, 47, 65; DAM NOV, POP**
See also AMWS 3; CA 1-4R; 131; CANR 1, 23, 64; CPW; CSW; DA3; DLB 2; DLBY 80, 90; MTCW 1, 2; RGAL
Percy, William Alexander
1885-1942 .... **TCLC 84**
See also CA 163; MTCW 2
Perec, Georges 1936-1982 .... **CLC 56, 116**
See also CA 141; DLB 83; GFL 1789 to the Present
Pereda (y Sanchez de Porrua), Jose Maria de 1833-1906 .... **TCLC 16**
See also CA 117
Pereda y Porrua, Jose Maria de
See Pereda (y Sanchez de Porrua), Jose Maria de
Peregoy, George Weems
See Mencken, H(enry) L(ouis)
Perelman, S(idney) J(oseph)
1904-1979 .. **CLC 3, 5, 9, 15, 23, 44, 49; DAM DRAM; SSC 32**
See also AITN 1, 2; CA 73-76; 89-92; CANR 18; DLB 11, 44; MTCW 1, 2
Péret, Benjamin 1899-1959 .... **TCLC 20; PC 33**
See also CA 117; 186; GFL 1789 to the Present
Peretz, Isaac Loeb 1851(?)-1915 ... **TCLC 16; SSC 26**
See also CA 109
Peretz, Yitzkhok Leibush
See Peretz, Isaac Loeb
Pérez Galdós, Benito 1843-1920 ... **TCLC 27; HLCS 2**
See also CA 125; 153; HW 1
Peri Rossi, Cristina 1941-
See also CA 131; CANR 59, 81; DLB 145; HLCS 2; HW 1, 2
Perlata
See P
Perloff, Marjorie G(abrielle)
1931- .... **CLC 137**
See also CA 57-60; CANR 7, 22, 49
Perrault, Charles 1628-1703 ... **LC 3, 52; DC 12**
See also GFL Beginnings to 1789; MAICYA; RGWL; SATA 25
Perry, Anne 1938- .... **CLC 126**
See also CA 101; CANR 22, 50, 84; CMW; CN; CPW
Perry, Brighton
See Sherwood, Robert E(mmet)
Perse, St.-John
See Leger, (Marie-Rene Auguste) Alexis Saint-Leger
Perutz, Leo(pold) 1882-1957 .... **TCLC 60**
See also CA 147; DLB 81
Peseenz, Tulio F.
See Lopez y Fuentes, Gregorio

Pesetsky, Bette 1932- .... **CLC 28**
See also CA 133; DLB 130
Peshkov, Alexei Maximovich 1868-1936
See Gorky, Maxim
See also CA 105; 141; CANR 83; DA; DAC; DAM DRAM, MST, NOV; MTCW 2
Pessoa, Fernando (António Nogueira)
1898-1935 .... **TCLC 27; DAM MULT; HLC 2; PC 20**
See also CA 125; 183
Peterkin, Julia Mood 1880-1961 ...... **CLC 31**
See also CA 102; DLB 9
Peters, Joan K(aren) 1945- .... **CLC 39**
See also CA 158
Peters, Robert L(ouis) 1924- .... **CLC 7**
See also CA 13-16R; CAAS 8; CP; DLB 105
Petofi, Sándor 1823-1849 .... **NCLC 21**
Petrakis, Harry Mark 1923- .... **CLC 3**
See also CA 9-12R; CANR 4, 30, 85; CN
Petrarch 1304-1374 .... **CMLC 20; DAM POET; PC 8**
See also DA3; RGEL
Petronius c. 20- .... **CMLC 34**
See also DLB 211; RGWL
Petrov, Evgeny .... **TCLC 21**
See also Kataev, Evgeny Petrovich
Petry, Ann (Lane) 1908-1997 ... **CLC 1, 7, 18**
See also AFAW 1, 2; BW 1, 3; CA 5-8R; 157; CAAS 6; CANR 4, 46; CLR 12; CN; DLB 76; JRDA; MAICYA; MTCW 1; SATA 5; SATA-Obit 94
Petursson, Halligrimur 1614-1674 .... **LC 8**
Peychinovich
See Vazov, Ivan (Minchov)
Phaedrus c. 15B.C.-c. 50 .... **CMLC 25**
See also DLB 211
Philips, Katherine 1632-1664 .... **LC 30**
See also DLB 131
Philipson, Morris H. 1926- .... **CLC 53**
See also CA 1-4R; CANR 4
Phillips, Caryl 1958- . **CLC 96; BLCS; DAM MULT**
See also BRWS 5; BW 2; CA 141; CANR 63; CBD; CD; CN; DA3; DLB 157; MTCW 2
Phillips, David Graham
1867-1911 .... **TCLC 44**
See also CA 108; 176; DLB 9, 12; RGAL
Phillips, Jack
See Sandburg, Carl (August)
Phillips, Jayne Anne 1952- .... **CLC 15, 33, 139; SSC 16**
See also CA 101; CANR 24, 50, 96; CN; CSW; DLBY 80; INT CANR-24; MTCW 1, 2; RGAL; RGSF; SSFS 4
Phillips, Richard
See Dick, Philip K(indred)
Phillips, Robert (Schaeffer) 1938- .... **CLC 28**
See also CA 17-20R; CAAS 13; CANR 8; DLB 105
Phillips, Ward
See Lovecraft, H(oward) P(hillips)
Piccolo, Lucio 1901-1969 .... **CLC 13**
See also CA 97-100; DLB 114
Pickthall, Marjorie L(owry) C(hristie)
1883-1922 .... **TCLC 21**
See also CA 107; DLB 92
Pico della Mirandola, Giovanni
1463-1494 .... **LC 15**
Piercy, Marge 1936- .... **CLC 3, 6, 14, 18, 27, 62, 128; PC 29**
See also CA 21-24R; CAAE 187; CAAS 1; CANR 13, 43, 66; CN; CP; CWP; DLB 120, 227; FW; MTCW 1, 2; PFS 9; SFW
Piers, Robert
See Anthony, Piers

Pieyre de Mandiargues, André 1909-1991
  See Mandiargues, Andre Pieyre de
  See also CA 103; 136; CANR 22, 82; GFL
  1789 to the Present
Pilnyak, Boris .... **TCLC 23**
  See also Vogau, Boris Andreyevich
Pincherle, Alberto 1907-1990 .... **CLC 11, 18;**
  DAM NOV
  See also Moravia, Alberto
  See also CA 25-28R; 132; CANR 33, 63;
  MTCW 1
Pinckney, Darryl 1953- .... **CLC 76**
  See also BW 2, 3; CA 143; CANR 79
Pindar 518B.C.- .... **CMLC 12; PC 19**
  See also DLB 176; RGEL
Pineda, Cecile 1942- .... **CLC 39**
  See also CA 118; DLB 209
Pinero, Arthur Wing 1855-1934 ... **TCLC 32;**
  DAM DRAM
  See also CA 110; 153; DLB 10
Piñero, Miguel (Antonio Gomez)
  1946-1988 .... **CLC 4, 55**
  See also CA 61-64; 125; CAD; CANR 29,
  90; HW 1
Pinget, Robert 1919-1997 .... **CLC 7, 13, 37**
  See also CA 85-88; 160; CWW 2; DLB 83;
  GFL 1789 to the Present
Pink Floyd
  See Barrett, (Roger) Syd; Gilmour, David;
  Mason, Nick; Waters, Roger; Wright, Rick
Pinkney, Edward 1802-1828 .... **NCLC 31**
Pinkwater, Daniel Manus 1941- .... **CLC 35**
  See also Pinkwater, Manus
  See also AAYA 1; CA 29-32R; CANR 12,
  38, 89; CLR 4; CSW; FANT; JRDA;
  MAICYA; SAAS 3; SATA 46, 76, 114;
  SFW; YAW
Pinkwater, Manus
  See Pinkwater, Daniel Manus
  See also SATA 8
Pinsky, Robert 1940- .... **CLC 9, 19, 38, 94,**
  121; DAM POET; PC 27
  See also AMWS 6; CA 29-32R; CAAS 4;
  CANR 58, 97; CP; DA3; DLBY 82, 98;
  MTCW 2; RGAL
Pinta, Harold
  See Pinter, Harold
Pinter, Harold 1930- .. **CLC 1, 3, 6, 9, 11, 15,**
  27, 58, 73; DA; DAB; DAC; DAM
  DRAM, MST; DC 15; WLC
  See also BRWS 1; CA 5-8R; CANR 33, 65;
  CBD; CD; CDBLB 1960 to Present; DA3;
  DFS 3, 5, 7; DLB 13; IDFW 3, 4; MTCW
  1, 2; RGAL
Piozzi, Hester Lynch (Thrale)
  1741-1821 .... **NCLC 57**
  See also DLB 104, 142
Pirandello, Luigi 1867-1936 ...... **TCLC 4, 29;**
  DA; DAB; DAC; DAM DRAM, MST;
  DC 5; SSC 22; WLC
  See also CA 104; 153; DA3; DFS 4, 9;
  MTCW 2; RGSF; RGWL
Pirsig, Robert M(aynard) 1928- ... **CLC 4, 6,**
  73; DAM POP
  See also CA 53-56; CANR 42, 74; CPW 1;
  DA3; MTCW 1, 2; SATA 39
Pisarev, Dmitry Ivanovich
  1840-1868 .... **NCLC 25**
Pix, Mary (Griffith) 1666-1709 .... **LC 8**
  See also DLB 80
Pixérécourt, (René Charles) Guilbert de
  1773-1844 .... **NCLC 39**
  See also DLB 192; GFL 1789 to the Present
Plaatje, Sol(omon) T(shekisho)
  1878-1932 .... **TCLC 73; BLCS**
  See also BW 2, 3; CA 141; CANR 79; DLB
  225
Plaidy, Jean
  See Hibbert, Eleanor Alice Burford

Planché, James Robinson
  1796-1880 .... **NCLC 42**
Plant, Robert 1948- .... **CLC 12**
Plante, David (Robert) 1940- ...... **CLC 7, 23,**
  38; DAM NOV
  See also CA 37-40R; CANR 12, 36, 58, 82;
  CN; DLBY 83; INT CANR-12; MTCW 1
Plath, Sylvia 1932-1963 ..... **CLC 1, 2, 3, 5, 9,**
  11, 14, 17, 50, 51, 62, 111; DA; DAB;
  DAC; DAM MST, POET; PC 1; WLC
  See also AAYA 13; AMWS 1; CA 19-20;
  CANR 34; CAP 2; CDALB 1941-1968;
  DA3; DLB 5, 6, 152; FW; MTCW 1, 2;
  NFS 1; PFS 1; RGAL; SATA 96; YAW
Plato c. 428B.C.-347B.C. .... **CMLC 8; DA;**
  DAB; DAC; DAM MST; WLCS
  See also DA3; DLB 176; RGWL
Platonov, Andrei
  See Klimentov, Andrei Platonovich
Platt, Kin 1911- .... **CLC 26**
  See also AAYA 11; CA 17-20R; CANR 11;
  JRDA; SAAS 17; SATA 21, 86
Plautus c. 254B.C.-c. 184B.C. ...... **CMLC 24;**
  DC 6
  See also DLB 211; RGWL
Plick et Plock
  See Simenon, Georges (Jacques Christian)
Plieksans, Janis
  See Rainis, Janis
  See also CA 170; DLB 220
Plimpton, George (Ames) 1927- .... **CLC 36**
  See also AITN 1; CA 21-24R; CANR 32,
  70; DLB 185, 241; MTCW 1, 2; SATA 10
Pliny the Elder c. 23-79 .... **CMLC 23**
  See also DLB 211
Plomer, William Charles Franklin
  1903-1973 .... **CLC 4, 8**
  See also CA 21-22; CANR 34; CAP 2; DLB
  20, 162, 191, 225; MTCW 1; SATA 24
Plotinus 204-270 .... **CMLC 46**
  See also DLB 176
Plowman, Piers
  See Kavanagh, Patrick (Joseph)
Plum, J.
  See Wodehouse, P(elham) G(renville)
Plumly, Stanley (Ross) 1939- .... **CLC 33**
  See also CA 108; 110; CANR 97; CP; DLB
  5, 193; INT 110
Plumpe, Friedrich Wilhelm
  1888-1931 .... **TCLC 53**
  See also CA 112
Po Chu-i 772-846 .... **CMLC 24**
Poe, Edgar Allan 1809-1849 ..... **NCLC 1, 16,**
  55, 78, 94, 97; DA; DAB; DAC; DAM
  MST, POET; PC 1; SSC 1, 22, 34, 35;
  WLC
  See also AAYA 14; CDALB 1640-1865;
  CMW; DA3; DLB 3, 59, 73, 74; HGG;
  PFS 1, 3, 9; RGAL; RGSF; SATA 23;
  SFW; SSFS 2, 4, 7, 8
Poet of Titchfield Street, The
  See Pound, Ezra (Weston Loomis)
Pohl, Frederik 1919- .... **CLC 18; SSC 25**
  See also AAYA 24; CA 61-64; CAAE 188;
  CAAS 1; CANR 11, 37, 81; CN; DLB 8;
  INT CANR-11; MTCW 1, 2; SATA 24;
  SCFW 2; SFW
Poirier, Louis 1910-
  See Gracq, Julien
  See also CA 122; 126; CWW 2
Poitier, Sidney 1927- .... **CLC 26**
  See also BW 1; CA 117; CANR 94
Polanski, Roman 1933- .... **CLC 16**
  See also CA 77-80
Poliakoff, Stephen 1952- .... **CLC 38**
  See also CA 106; CBD; CD; DLB 13

Police, The
  See Copeland, Stewart (Armstrong); Sum-
  mers, Andrew James; Sumner, Gordon
  Matthew
Polidori, John William 1795-1821 . **NCLC 51**
  See also DLB 116; HGG
Pollitt, Katha 1949- .... **CLC 28, 122**
  See also CA 120; 122; CANR 66; MTCW
  1, 2
Pollock, (Mary) Sharon 1936- .... **CLC 50;**
  DAC; DAM DRAM, MST
  See also CA 141; DLB 60
Polo, Marco 1254-1324 .... **CMLC 15**
Polonsky, Abraham (Lincoln)
  1910-1999 .... **CLC 92**
  See also CA 104; 187; DLB 26; INT 104
Polybius c. 200B.C.-c. 118B.C. ...... **CMLC 17**
  See also DLB 176; RGWL
Pomerance, Bernard 1940- ... **CLC 13; DAM**
  DRAM
  See also CA 101; CAD; CANR 49; CD;
  DFS 9
Ponge, Francis 1899-1988 . **CLC 6, 18; DAM**
  POET
  See also CA 85-88; 126; CANR 40, 86;
  GFL 1789 to the Present; RGWL
Poniatowska, Elena 1933- ... **CLC 140; DAM**
  MULT; HLC 2
  See also CA 101; CANR 32, 66; DLB 113;
  HW 1, 2
Pontoppidan, Henrik 1857-1943 .... **TCLC 29**
  See also CA 170
Poole, Josephine .... **CLC 17**
  See also Helyar, Jane Penelope Josephine
  See also SAAS 2; SATA 5
Popa, Vasko 1922-1991 .... **CLC 19**
  See also CA 112; 148; DLB 181; RGWL
Pope, Alexander 1688-1744 ...... **LC 3, 58, 60,**
  64; DA; DAB; DAC; DAM MST,
  POET; PC 26; WLC
  See also CDBLB 1660-1789; DA3; DLB
  95, 101; PFS 12; RGEL
Popov, Yevgeny .... **CLC 59**
Porter, Connie (Rose) 1959(?)- .... **CLC 70**
  See also BW 2, 3; CA 142; CANR 90;
  SATA 81
Porter, Gene(va Grace) Stratton .. **TCLC 21**
  See also Stratton-Porter, Gene(va Grace)
  See also CA 112; CWRI; RHW
Porter, Katherine Anne 1890-1980 ... **CLC 1,**
  3, 7, 10, 13, 15, 27, 101; DA; DAB;
  DAC; DAM MST, NOV; SSC 4, 31, 43
  See also AITN 2; CA 1-4R; 101; CANR 1,
  65; CDALBS; DA3; DLB 4, 9, 102;
  DLBD 12; DLBY 80; MTCW 1, 2;
  RGAL; RGSF; SATA 39; SATA-Obit 23;
  SSFS 1,8,11
Porter, Peter (Neville Frederick)
  1929- .... **CLC 5, 13, 33**
  See also CA 85-88; CP; DLB 40
Porter, William Sydney 1862-1910
  See Henry, O.
  See also CA 104; 131; CDALB 1865-1917;
  DA; DAB; DAC; DAM MST; DA3; DLB
  12, 78, 79; MTCW 1, 2; YABC 2
Portillo (y Pacheco), Jose Lopez
  See Lopez Portillo (y Pacheco), Jose
Portillo Trambley, Estela 1927-1998
  See Trambley, Estela Portillo
  See also CANR 32; DAM MULT; DLB
  209; HLC 2; HW 1
Posse, Abel .... **CLC 70**
Post, Melville Davisson
  1869-1930 .... **TCLC 39**
  See also CA 110; CMW

Rivera, Tomás 1935-1984
See also CA 49-52; CANR 32; DLB 82;
HLCS 2; HW 1; TCWW 2
Rivers, Conrad Kent 1933-1968 .... **CLC 1**
See also BW 1; CA 85-88; DLB 41
Rivers, Elfrida
See Bradley, Marion Zimmer
See also GLL 1
Riverside, John
See Heinlein, Robert A(nson)
Rizal, Jose 1861-1896 .... **NCLC 27**
Roa Bastos, Augusto (Antonio)
1917- .... **CLC 45; DAM MULT; HLC 2**
See also CA 131; DLB 113; HW 1
Robbe-Grillet, Alain 1922- .... **CLC 1, 2, 4, 6,**
8, 10, 14, 43, 128
See also CA 9-12R; CANR 33, 65; DLB
83; GFL 1789 to the Present; IDFW 4;
MTCW 1, 2; RGWL
Robbins, Harold 1916-1997 .... **CLC 5; DAM**
NOV
See also CA 73-76; 162; CANR 26, 54;
DA3; MTCW 1, 2
Robbins, Thomas Eugene 1936-
See Robbins, Tom
See also CA 81-84; CANR 29, 59, 95; CN;
CPW; CSW; DAM NOV, POP; DA3;
MTCW 1, 2
Robbins, Tom .... **CLC 9, 32, 64**
See also Robbins, Thomas Eugene
See also AAYA 32; BEST 90:3; DLBY 80;
MTCW 2
Robbins, Trina 1938- .... **CLC 21**
See also CA 128
Roberts, Charles G(eorge) D(ouglas)
1860-1943 .... **TCLC 8**
See also CA 105; 188; CLR 33; CWRI;
DLB 92; SATA 88; SATA-Brief 29
Roberts, Elizabeth Madox
1886-1941 .... **TCLC 68**
See also CA 111; 166; CWRI; DLB 9, 54,
102; RGAL; RHW; SATA 33; SATA-Brief
27
Roberts, Kate 1891-1985 .... **CLC 15**
See also CA 107; 116
Roberts, Keith (John Kingston)
1935-2000 .... **CLC 14**
See also CA 25-28R; CANR 46; SFW
Roberts, Kenneth (Lewis)
1885-1957 .... **TCLC 23**
See also CA 109; DLB 9; RHW
Roberts, Michele (Brigitte) 1949- ..... **CLC 48**
See also CA 115; CANR 58; CN; DLB 231;
FW
Robertson, Ellis
See Ellison, Harlan (Jay); Silverberg, Robert
Robertson, Thomas William
1829-1871 .... **NCLC 35; DAM DRAM**
See also Robertson, Tom
Robertson, Tom
See Robertson, Thomas William
See also RGEL
Robeson, Kenneth
See Dent, Lester
Robinson, Edwin Arlington
1869-1935 ..... **TCLC 5, 101; DA; DAC;**
DAM MST, POET; PC 1, 35
See also CA 104; 133; CDALB 1865-1917;
DLB 54; MTCW 1, 2; PFS 4; RGAL
Robinson, Henry Crabb
1775-1867 .... **NCLC 15**
See also DLB 107
Robinson, Jill 1936- .... **CLC 10**
See also CA 102; INT 102
Robinson, Kim Stanley 1952- .... **CLC 34**
See also AAYA 26; CA 126; CN; SATA 109;
SFW

Robinson, Lloyd
See Silverberg, Robert
Robinson, Marilynne 1944- .... **CLC 25**
See also CA 116; CANR 80; CN; DLB 206
Robinson, Smokey .... **CLC 21**
See also Robinson, William, Jr.
Robinson, William, Jr. 1940-
See Robinson, Smokey
See also CA 116
Robison, Mary 1949- .... **CLC 42, 98**
See also CA 113; 116; CANR 87; CN; DLB
130; INT 116; RGSF
Rod, Edouard 1857-1910 .... **TCLC 52**
Roddenberry, Eugene Wesley 1921-1991
See Roddenberry, Gene
See also CA 110; 135; CANR 37; SATA 45;
SATA-Obit 69
Roddenberry, Gene .... **CLC 17**
See also Roddenberry, Eugene Wesley
See also AAYA 5; SATA-Obit 69
Rodgers, Mary 1931- .... **CLC 12**
See also CA 49-52; CANR 8, 55, 90; CLR
20; CWRI; INT CANR-8; JRDA; MAI-
CYA; SATA 8
Rodgers, W(illiam) R(obert)
1909-1969 .... **CLC 7**
See also CA 85-88; DLB 20
Rodman, Eric
See Silverberg, Robert
Rodman, Howard 1920(?)-1985 .... **CLC 65**
See also CA 118
Rodman, Maia
See Wojciechowska, Maia (Teresa)
Rodo, Jose Enrique 1871(?)-1917
See also CA 178; HLCS 2; HW 2
Rodolph, Utto
See Ouologuem, Yambo
Rodriguez, Claudio 1934-1999 .... **CLC 10**
See also CA 188; DLB 134
Rodriguez, Richard 1944-
See also CA 110; CANR 66; DAM MULT;
DLB 82; HLC 2; HW 1, 2
Roelvaag, O(le) E(dvart)
1876-1931 .... **TCLC 17**
See also Rølvaag, O(le) E(dvart)
See also CA 117; 171; DLB 9
Roethke, Theodore (Huebner)
1908-1963 .... **CLC 1, 3, 8, 11, 19, 46,**
101; DAM POET; PC 15
See also CA 81-84; CABS 2; CDALB 1941-
1968; DA3; DLB 5, 206; MTCW 1, 2;
PFS 3
Rogers, Samuel 1763-1855 .... **NCLC 69**
See also DLB 93; RGEL
Rogers, Thomas Hunton 1927- .... **CLC 57**
See also CA 89-92; INT 89-92
Rogers, Will(iam Penn Adair)
1879-1935 ... **TCLC 8, 71; DAM MULT**
See also CA 105; 144; DA3; DLB 11;
MTCW 2; NNAL
Rogin, Gilbert 1929- .... **CLC 18**
See also CA 65-68; CANR 15
Rohan, Koda
See Koda Shigeyuki
Rohlfs, Anna Katharine Green
See Green, Anna Katharine
Rohmer, Eric .... **CLC 16**
See also Scherer, Jean-Marie Maurice
Rohmer, Sax .... **TCLC 28**
See also Ward, Arthur Henry Sarsfield
See also DLB 70
Roiphe, Anne (Richardson) 1935- .. **CLC 3, 9**
See also CA 89-92; CANR 45, 73; DLBY
80; INT 89-92
Rojas, Fernando de 1475-1541 .... **LC 23;**
HLCS 1
See also RGWL

Rojas, Gonzalo 1917-
See also HLCS 2; HW 2
Rojas, Gonzalo 1917-
See also CA 178; HLCS 2
Rolfe, Frederick (William Serafino Austin
Lewis Mary) 1860-1913 .... **TCLC 12**
See also Corvo, Baron
See also CA 107; DLB 34, 156; RGEL
Rolland, Romain 1866-1944 .... **TCLC 23**
See also CA 118; DLB 65; GFL 1789 to the
Present; RGWL
Rolle, Richard c. 1300-c. 1349 ...... **CMLC 21**
See also DLB 146; RGEL
Rølvaag, O(le) E(dvart)
See Roelvaag, O(le) E(dvart)
See also DLB 212; NFS 5
Romain Arnaud, Saint
See Aragon, Louis
Romains, Jules 1885-1972 .... **CLC 7**
See also CA 85-88; CANR 34; DLB 65;
GFL 1789 to the Present; MTCW 1
Romero, Jose Ruben 1890-1952 .... **TCLC 14**
See also CA 114; 131; HW 1
Ronsard, Pierre de 1524-1585 . **LC 6, 54; PC**
11
See also GFL Beginnings to 1789; RGWL
Rooke, Leon 1934- . **CLC 25, 34; DAM POP**
See also CA 25-28R; CANR 23, 53; CCA
1; CPW
Roosevelt, Franklin Delano
1882-1945 .... **TCLC 93**
See also CA 116; 173
Roosevelt, Theodore 1858-1919 ..... **TCLC 69**
See also CA 115; 170; DLB 47, 186
Roper, William 1498-1578 .... **LC 10**
Roquelaure, A. N.
See Rice, Anne
Rosa, Joao Guimaraes 1908-1967 ... **CLC 23;**
HLCS 1
See also CA 89-92; DLB 113
Rose, Wendy 1948- .. **CLC 85; DAM MULT;**
PC 13
See also CA 53-56; CANR 5, 51; CWP;
DLB 175; NNAL; RGAL; SATA 12
Rosen, R. D.
See Rosen, Richard (Dean)
Rosen, Richard (Dean) 1949- .... **CLC 39**
See also CA 77-80; CANR 62; CMW; INT
CANR-30
Rosenberg, Isaac 1890-1918 .... **TCLC 12**
See also CA 107; 188; DLB 20; RGEL
Rosenblatt, Joe .... **CLC 15**
See also Rosenblatt, Joseph
Rosenblatt, Joseph 1933-
See Rosenblatt, Joe
See also CA 89-92; CP; INT 89-92
Rosenfeld, Samuel
See Tzara, Tristan
Rosenstock, Sami
See Tzara, Tristan
Rosenstock, Samuel
See Tzara, Tristan
Rosenthal, M(acha) L(ouis)
1917-1996 .... **CLC 28**
See also CA 1-4R; 152; CAAS 6; CANR 4,
51; CP; DLB 5; SATA 59
Ross, Barnaby
See Dannay, Frederic
Ross, Bernard L.
See Follett, Ken(neth Martin)
Ross, J. H.
See Lawrence, T(homas) E(dward)
Ross, John Hume
See Lawrence, T(homas) E(dward)
Ross, Martin 1862-1915
See Martin, Violet Florence
See also DLB 135; GLL 2; RGEL; RGSF

Ross, (James) Sinclair 1908-1996 ... **CLC 13; DAC; DAM MST; SSC 24**
See also CA 73-76; CANR 81; CN; DLB 88; TCWW 2

Rossetti, Christina (Georgina) 1830-1894 . **NCLC 2, 50, 66; DA; DAB; DAC; DAM MST, POET; PC 7; WLC**
See also BRW; DA3; DLB 35, 163, 240; MAICYA; PFS 10; RGEL; SATA 20; WCH

Rossetti, Dante Gabriel 1828-1882 . **NCLC 4, 77; DA; DAB; DAC; DAM MST, POET; WLC**
See also CDBLB 1832-1890; DLB 35; RGEL

Rossner, Judith (Perelman) 1935- . **CLC 6, 9, 29**
See also AITN 2; BEST 90:3; CA 17-20R; CANR 18, 51, 73; CN; DLB 6; INT CANR-18; MTCW 1, 2

Rostand, Edmond (Eugene Alexis) 1868-1918 .... **TCLC 6, 37; DA; DAB; DAC; DAM DRAM, MST; DC 10**
See also CA 104; 126; DA3; DFS 1; DLB 192; MTCW 1

Roth, Henry 1906-1995 ..... **CLC 2, 6, 11, 104**
See also CA 11-12; 149; CANR 38, 63; CAP 1; CN; DA3; DLB 28; MTCW 1, 2; RGAL

Roth, (Moses) Joseph 1894-1939 ... **TCLC 33**
See also CA 160; DLB 85

Roth, Philip (Milton) 1933- ... **CLC 1, 2, 3, 4, 6, 9, 15, 22, 31, 47, 66, 86, 119; DA; DAB; DAC; DAM MST, NOV, POP; SSC 26; WLC**
See also AMWS 3; BEST 90:3; CA 1-4R; CANR 1, 22, 36, 55, 89; CDALB 1968-1988; CN; CPW 1; DA3; DLB 2, 28, 173; DLBY 82; MTCW 1, 2; SSFS 12

Rothenberg, Jerome 1931- .... **CLC 6, 57**
See also CA 45-48; CANR 1; CP; DLB 5, 193

Rotter, Pat ed. .... **CLC 65**

Roumain, Jacques (Jean Baptiste) 1907-1944 ...... **TCLC 19; BLC 3; DAM MULT**
See also BW 1; CA 117; 125

Rourke, Constance (Mayfield) 1885-1941 .... **TCLC 12**
See also CA 107; YABC 1

Rousseau, Jean-Baptiste 1671-1741 ...... **LC 9**

Rousseau, Jean-Jacques 1712-1778 .... **LC 14, 36; DA; DAB; DAC; DAM MST; WLC**
See also DA3; EW; GFL Beginnings to 1789; RGWL

Roussel, Raymond 1877-1933 .... **TCLC 20**
See also CA 117; GFL 1789 to the Present

Rovit, Earl (Herbert) 1927- .... **CLC 7**
See also CA 5-8R; CANR 12

Rowe, Elizabeth Singer 1674-1737 ..... **LC 44**
See also DLB 39, 95

Rowe, Nicholas 1674-1718 .... **LC 8**
See also DLB 84; RGEL

Rowlandson, Mary 1637(?)-1678 .... **LC 66**
See also DLB 24, 200; RGAL

Rowley, Ames Dorrance
See Lovecraft, H(oward) P(hillips)

Rowling, J(oanne) K. 1966(?)- .... **CLC 137**
See also AAYA 34; CA 173; CLR 66; SATA 109

Rowson, Susanna Haswell 1762(?)-1824 .... **NCLC 5, 69**
See also DLB 37, 200

Roy, Arundhati 1960(?)- .... **CLC 109**
See also CA 163; CANR 90; DLBY 97

Roy, Gabrielle 1909-1983 .... **CLC 10, 14; DAB; DAC; DAM MST**
See also CA 53-56; 110; CANR 5, 61; CCA 1; DLB 68; MTCW 1; RGWL; SATA 104

Royko, Mike 1932-1997 .... **CLC 109**
See also CA 89-92; 157; CANR 26; CPW

Rozanov, Vassili 1856-1919 .... **TCLC 104**

Rozewicz, Tadeusz 1921- ..... **CLC 9, 23, 139; DAM POET**
See also CA 108; CANR 36, 66; CWW 2; DA3; DLB 232; MTCW 1, 2

Ruark, Gibbons 1941- .... **CLC 3**
See also CA 33-36R; CAAS 23; CANR 14, 31, 57; DLB 120

Rubens, Bernice (Ruth) 1923- ... **CLC 19, 31**
See also CA 25-28R; CANR 33, 65; CN; DLB 14, 207; MTCW 1

Rubin, Harold
See Robbins, Harold

Rudkin, (James) David 1936- .... **CLC 14**
See also CA 89-92; CBD; CD; DLB 13

Rudnik, Raphael 1933- .... **CLC 7**
See also CA 29-32R

Ruffian, M.
See Ha

Ruiz, Jose Martinez .... **CLC 11**
See also Martinez Ruiz, Jose

Rukeyser, Muriel 1913-1980 . **CLC 6, 10, 15, 27; DAM POET; PC 12**
See also AMWS 6; CA 5-8R; 93-96; CANR 26, 60; DA3; DLB 48; FW; GLL 2; MTCW 1, 2; PFS 10; RGAL; SATA-Obit 22

Rule, Jane (Vance) 1931- .... **CLC 27**
See also CA 25-28R; CAAS 18; CANR 12, 87; CN; DLB 60; FW

Rulfo, Juan 1918-1986 ...... **CLC 8, 80; DAM MULT; HLC 2; SSC 25**
See also CA 85-88; 118; CANR 26; DLB 113; HW 1, 2; MTCW 1, 2; RGSF; RGWL

Rumi, Jalal al-Din 1207-1273 .... **CMLC 20**

Runeberg, Johan 1804-1877 .... **NCLC 41**

Runyon, (Alfred) Damon 1884(?)-1946 .... **TCLC 10**
See also CA 107; 165; DLB 11, 86, 171; MTCW 2

Rush, Norman 1933- .... **CLC 44**
See also CA 121; 126; INT 126

Rushdie, (Ahmed) Salman 1947- .... **CLC 23, 31, 55, 100; DAB; DAC; DAM MST, NOV, POP; WLCS**
See also BEST 89:3; BRWS 4; CA 108; 111; CANR 33, 56; CN; CPW 1; DA3; DLB 194; FANT; INT CA-111; MTCW 1, 2

Rushforth, Peter (Scott) 1945- .... **CLC 19**
See also CA 101

Ruskin, John 1819-1900 .... **TCLC 63**
See also CA 114; 129; CDBLB 1832-1890; DLB 55, 163, 190; RGEL; SATA 24

Russ, Joanna 1937- .... **CLC 15**
See also CA 5-28R; CANR 11, 31, 65; CN; DLB 8; FW; GLL 1; MTCW 1; SCFW 2; SFW

Russell, George William 1867-1935
See Baker, Jean H.
See also CA 104; 153; CDBLB 1890-1914; DAM POET; RGEL

Russell, Jeffrey Burton 1934- .... **CLC 70**
See also CA 25-28R; CANR 11, 28, 52

Russell, (Henry) Ken(neth Alfred) 1927- .... **CLC 16**
See also CA 105

Russell, William Martin 1947- .... **CLC 60**
See also CA 164; DLB 233

Rutherford, Mark .... **TCLC 25**
See also White, William Hale
See also DLB 18; RGEL

Ruyslinck, Ward .... **CLC 14**
See also Belser, Reimond Karel Maria de

Ryan, Cornelius (John) 1920-1974 ..... **CLC 7**
See also CA 69-72; 53-56; CANR 38

Ryan, Michael 1946- .... **CLC 65**
See also CA 49-52; DLBY 82

Ryan, Tim
See Dent, Lester

Rybakov, Anatoli (Naumovich) 1911-1998 .... **CLC 23, 53**
See also CA 126; 135; 172; SATA 79; SATA-Obit 108

Ryder, Jonathan
See Ludlum, Robert

Ryga, George 1932-1987 .... **CLC 14; DAC; DAM MST**
See also CA 101; 124; CANR 43, 90; CCA 1; DLB 60

S. H.
See Hartmann, Sadakichi

S. S.
See Sassoon, Siegfried (Lorraine)

Saba, Umberto 1883-1957 .... **TCLC 33**
See also CA 144; CANR 79; DLB 114; RGWL

Sabatini, Rafael 1875-1950 .... **TCLC 47**
See also CA 162; RHW

Sabato, Ernesto (R.) 1911- .... **CLC 10, 23; DAM MULT; HLC 2**
See also CA 97-100; CANR 32, 65; DLB 145; HW 1, 2; MTCW 1, 2

Sa-Carniero, Mario de 1890-1916 . **TCLC 83**

Sacastru, Martin
See Bioy Casares, Adolfo
See also CWW 2

Sacastru, Martin
See Bioy Casares, Adolfo

Sacher-Masoch, Leopold von 1836(?)-1895 .... **NCLC 31**

Sachs, Marilyn (Stickle) 1927- .... **CLC 35**
See also AAYA 2; CA 17-20R; CANR 13, 47; CLR 2; JRDA; MAICYA; SAAS 2; SATA 3, 68; SATA-Essay 110; YAW

Sachs, Nelly 1891-1970 .... **CLC 14, 98**
See also CA 17-18; 25-28R; CANR 87; CAP 2; MTCW 2; RGWL

Sackler, Howard (Oliver) 1929-1982 .... **CLC 14**
See also CA 61-64; 108; CAD; CANR 30; DLB 7

Sacks, Oliver (Wolf) 1933- .... **CLC 67**
See also CA 53-56; CANR 28, 50, 76; CPW; DA3; INT CANR-28; MTCW 1, 2

Sadakichi
See Hartmann, Sadakichi

Sade, Donatien Alphonse François 1740-1814 .... **NCLC 3, 47**
See also EW; GFL Beginnings to 1789; RGWL

Sadoff, Ira 1945- .... **CLC 9**
See also CA 53-56; CANR 5, 21; DLB 120

Saetone
See Camus, Albert

Safire, William 1929- .... **CLC 10**
See also CA 17-20R; CANR 31, 54, 91

Sagan, Carl (Edward) 1934-1996 .... **CLC 30, 112**
See also AAYA 2; CA 25-28R; 155; CANR 11, 36, 74; CPW; DA3; MTCW 1, 2; SATA 58; SATA-Obit 94

Sagan, Françoise .... **CLC 3, 6, 9, 17, 36**
See also Quoirez, Françoise
See also CWW 2; DLB 83; GFL 1789 to the Present; MTCW 2

Sahgal, Nayantara (Pandit) 1927- .... **CLC 41**
See also CA 9-12R; CANR 11, 88; CN

Said, Edward W. 1935- .... **CLC 123**
See also CA 21-24R; CANR 45, 74; DLB 67; MTCW 2

Saint, H(arry) F. 1941- .... **CLC 50**
See also CA 127

St. Aubin de Teran, Lisa 1953-
See Teran, Lisa St. Aubin de
See also CA 118; 126; CN; INT 126

Saint Birgitta of Sweden c.
1303-1373 .... **CMLC 24**

Sainte-Beuve, Charles Augustin
1804-1869 .... **NCLC 5**
See also EW; GFL 1789 to the Present

**Saint-Exupéry, Antoine (Jean Baptiste
Marie Roger)** de 1900-1944 .... **TCLC 2,
56; DAM NOV; WLC**
See also CA 108; 132; CLR 10; DA3; DLB
72; EW; GFL 1789 to the Present; MAI-
CYA; MTCW 1, 2; RGWL; SATA 20

St. John, David
See Hunt, E(verette) Howard, (Jr.)

Saint-John Perse
See Leger, (Marie-Rene Auguste) Alexis
Saint-Leger
See also GFL 1789 to the Present; RGWL

Saintsbury, George (Edward Bateman)
1845-1933 .... **TCLC 31**
See also CA 160; DLB 57, 149

Sait Faik .... **TCLC 23**
See also Abasiyanik, Sait Faik

Saki .... **TCLC 3; SSC 12**
See also Munro, H(ector) H(ugh)
See also BRWS 6; MTCW 2; RGEL; SSFS
1

Sala, George Augustus 1828-1895 . **NCLC 46**

Saladin 1138-1193 .... **CMLC 38**

Salama, Hannu 1936- .... **CLC 18**

Salamanca, J(ack) R(ichard) 1922- .. **CLC 4,
15**
See also CA 25-28R

Salas, Floyd Francis 1931-
See also CA 119, CAAS 27; CANR 44, 75,
93; DAM MULT; DLB 82; HLC 2; HW
1, 2; MTCW 2

Sale, J. Kirkpatrick
See Sale, Kirkpatrick

Sale, Kirkpatrick 1937- .... **CLC 68**
See also CA 13-16R; CANR 10

Salinas, Luis Omar 1937- ..... **CLC 90; DAM
MULT; HLC 2**
See also CA 131; CANR 81; DLB 82; HW
1, 2

Salinas (y Serrano), Pedro
1891(?)-1951 .... **TCLC 17**
See also CA 117; DLB 134

Salinger, J(erome) D(avid) 1919- .. **CLC 1, 3,
8, 12, 55, 56, 138; DA; DAB; DAC;
DAM MST, NOV, POP; SSC 2, 28;
WLC**
See also AAYA 2, 36; CA 5-8R; CANR 39;
CDALB 1941-1968; CLR 18; CN; CPW
1; DA3; DLB 2, 102, 173; MAICYA;
MTCW 1, 2; NFS 1; SATA 67; YAW

Salisbury, John
See Caute, (John) David

Salter, James 1925- .... **CLC 7, 52, 59**
See also CA 73-76; DLB 130

Saltus, Edgar (Everton) 1855-1921 . **TCLC 8**
See also CA 105; DLB 202

Saltykov, Mikhail Evgrafovich
1826-1889 .... **NCLC 16**
See also DLB 238;

Samarakis, Antonis 1919- .... **CLC 5**
See also CA 25-28R; CAAS 16; CANR 36

Sanchez, Florencio 1875-1910 .... **TCLC 37**
See also CA 153; HW 1

Sanchez, Luis Rafael 1936- .... **CLC 23**
See also CA 128; DLB 145; HW 1

Sanchez, Sonia 1934- .... **CLC 5, 116; BLC 3;
DAM MULT; PC 9**
See also BW 2, 3; CA 33-36R; CANR 24,
49, 74; CLR 18; CP; CSW; CWP; DA3;
DLB 41; DLBD 8; MAICYA; MTCW 1,
2; SATA 22

Sand, George 1804-1876 ..... **NCLC 2, 42, 57;
DA; DAB; DAC; DAM MST, NOV;
WLC**
See also DA3; DLB 119, 192; FW; GFL
1789 to the Present; RGWL

Sandburg, Carl (August) 1878-1967 . **CLC 1,
4, 10, 15, 35; DA; DAB; DAC; DAM
MST, POET; PC 2; WLC**
See also AAYA 24; CA 5-8R; 25-28R;
CANR 35; CDALB 1865-1917; CLR 67;
DA3; DLB 17, 54; MAICYA; MTCW 1,
2; PFS 3, 6, 12; SATA 8

Sandburg, Charles
See Sandburg, Carl (August)

Sandburg, Charles A.
See Sandburg, Carl (August)

Sanders, (James) Ed(ward) 1939- ... **CLC 53;
DAM POET**
See also CA 13-16R; CAAS 21; CANR 13,
44, 78; CP; DLB 16

Sanders, Lawrence 1920-1998 .... **CLC 41;
DAM POP**
See also BEST 89:4; CA 81-84; 165; CANR
33, 62; CMW; CPW; DA3; MTCW 1

Sanders, Noah
See Blount, Roy (Alton), Jr.

Sanders, Winston P.
See Anderson, Poul (William)

Sandoz, Mari(e Susette) 1900-1966 .. **CLC 28**
See also CA 1-4R; 25-28R; CANR 17, 64;
DLB 9, 212; MTCW 1, 2; SATA 5;
TCWW 2

Saner, Reg(inald Anthony) 1931- .... **CLC 9**
See also CA 65-68; CP

Sankara 788-820 .... **CMLC 32**

Sannazaro, Jacopo 1456(?)-1530 .... **LC 8**
See also RGWL

Sansom, William 1912-1976 .... **CLC 2, 6;
DAM NOV; SSC 21**
See also CA 5-8R; 65-68; CANR 42; DLB
139; MTCW 1; RGEL; RGSF

Santayana, George 1863-1952 .... **TCLC 40**
See also CA 115; DLB 54, 71; DLBD 13;
RGAL

Santiago, Danny .... **CLC 33**
See also James, Daniel (Lewis)
See also DLB 122

Santmyer, Helen Hooven
1895-1986 .... **CLC 33**
See also CA 1-4R; 118; CANR 15, 33;
DLBY 84; MTCW 1; RHW

Santoka, Taneda 1882-1940 .... **TCLC 72**

Santos, Bienvenido N(uqui)
1911-1996 .... **CLC 22; DAM MULT**
See also CA 101; 151; CANR 19, 46

Sapir, Edward 1884-1939 .... **TCLC 108**
See also DLB 92

Sapper .... **TCLC 44**
See also McNeile, Herman Cyril

Sapphire
See Sapphire, Brenda

Sapphire, Brenda 1950- .... **CLC 99**

Sappho fl. 6256th cent. B.C.- .... **CMLC 3;
DAM POET; PC 5**
See also DA3; DLB 176; RGEL

Saramago, José 1922- ..... **CLC 119; HLCS 1**
See also CA 153; CANR 96

Sarduy, Severo 1937-1993 .... **CLC 6, 97;
HLCS 1**
See also CA 89-92; 142; CANR 58, 81;
CWW 2; DLB 113; HW 1, 2

Sargeson, Frank 1903-1982 .... **CLC 31**
See also CA 25-28R; 106; CANR 38, 79;
GLL 2; RGEL; RGSF

Sarmiento, Domingo Faustino 1811-1888
See also HLCS 2

Sarmiento, Felix Ruben Garcia
See Dar

Saro-Wiwa, Ken(ule Beeson)
1941-1995 .... **CLC 114**
See also BW 2; CA 142; 150; CANR 60;
DLB 157

Saroyan, William 1908-1981 ... **CLC 1, 8, 10,
29, 34, 56; DA; DAB; DAC; DAM
DRAM, MST, NOV; SSC 21; WLC**
See also CA 5-8R; 103; CAD; CANR 30;
CDALBS; DA3; DLB 7, 9, 86; DLBY 81;
MTCW 1, 2; RGAL; RGSF; SATA 23;
SATA-Obit 24

Sarraute, Nathalie 1900-1999 .... **CLC 1, 2, 4,
8, 10, 31, 80**
See also CA 9-12R; 187; CANR 23, 66;
CWW 2; DLB 83; GFL 1789 to the
Present; MTCW 1, 2; RGWL

Sarton, (Eleanor) May 1912-1995 ..... **CLC 4,
14, 49, 91; DAM POET**
See also AMWS 8; CA 1-4R; 149; CANR
1, 34, 55; CN; CP; DLB 48; DLBY 81;
FW; INT CANR-34; MTCW 1, 2; SATA
36; SATA-Obit 86

Sartre, Jean-Paul 1905-1980 . **CLC 1, 4, 7, 9,
13, 18, 24, 44, 50, 52; DA; DAB; DAC;
DAM DRAM, MST, NOV; DC 3; SSC
32; WLC**
See also CA 9-12R; 97-100; CANR 21;
DA3; DFS 5; DLB 72; GFL 1789 to the
Present; MTCW 1, 2; RGSF; RGWL;
SSFS 9

Sassoon, Siegfried (Lorraine)
1886-1967 .... **CLC 36, 130; DAB; DAM
MST, NOV, POET; PC 12**
See also BRW; CA 104; 25-28R; CANR
36; DLB 20, 191; DLBD 18; MTCW 1,
2; PAB; RGEL

Satterfield, Charles
See Pohl, Frederik

Satyremont
See P

Saul, John (W. III) 1942- ...... **CLC 46; DAM
NOV, POP**
See also AAYA 10; BEST 90:4; CA 81-84;
CANR 16, 40, 81; CPW; HGG; SATA 98

Saunders, Caleb
See Heinlein, Robert A(nson)

Saura (Atares), Carlos 1932-1998 .... **CLC 20**
See also CA 114; 131; CANR 79; HW 1

Sauser-Hall, Frederic 1887-1961 ...... **CLC 18**
See also Cendrars, Blaise
See also CA 102; 93-96; CANR 36, 62;
MTCW 1

Saussure, Ferdinand de
1857-1913 .... **TCLC 49**

Savage, Catharine
See Brosman, Catharine Savage

Savage, Thomas 1915- .... **CLC 40**
See also CA 126; 132; CAAS 15; CN; INT
132; TCWW 2

Savan, Glenn (?)- .... **CLC 50**

Sayers, Dorothy L(eigh)
1893-1957 .... **TCLC 2, 15; DAM POP**
See also BRWS 3; CA 104; 119; CANR 60;
CDBLB 1914-1945; CMW; DLB 10, 36,
77, 100; MTCW 1, 2; RGEL; SSFS 12

Sayers, Valerie 1952- .... **CLC 50, 122**
See also CA 134; CANR 61; CSW

Sayles, John (Thomas) 1950- . **CLC 7, 10, 14**
See also CA 57-60; CANR 41, 84; DLB 44

Scammell, Michael 1935- .... **CLC 34**
See also CA 156

Scannell, Vernon 1922- .... **CLC 49**
See also CA 5-8R; CANR 8, 24, 57; CP;
CWRI; DLB 27; SATA 59

Scarlett, Susan
See Streatfeild, (Mary) Noel

Scarron 1847-1910
See Mikszath, Kalman

Sender, Ramón (José) 1902-1982 ...... **CLC 8; DAM MULT; HLC 2**
  See also CA 5-8R; 105; CANR 8; HW 1; MTCW 1

Seneca, Lucius Annaeus c. 4B.C.-c. 65 .... **CMLC 6; DAM DRAM; DC 5**
  See also DLB 211

Senghor, Léopold Sédar 1906- .... **CLC 54, 130; BLC 3; DAM MULT, POET; PC 25**
  See also BW 2; CA 116; 125; CANR 47, 74; DNFS 2; GFL 1789 to the Present; MTCW 1, 2

Senna, Danzy 1970- .... **CLC 119**
  See also CA 169

Serling, (Edward) Rod(man) 1924-1975 .... **CLC 30**
  See also AAYA 14; AITN 1; CA 162; 57-60; DLB 26; SFW

Serna, Ramon Gomez de la
  See Gomez de la Serna, Ramon

Serpieres
  See Guillevic, (Eugene)

Service, Robert
  See Service, Robert W(illiam)
  See also DAB; DLB 92

Service, Robert W(illiam) 1874(?)-1958 .... **TCLC 15; DA; DAC; DAM MST, POET; WLC**
  See also Service, Robert
  See also CA 115; 140; CANR 84; PFS 10; RGEL; SATA 20

Seth, Vikram 1952- .... **CLC 43, 90; DAM MULT**
  See also CA 121; 127; CANR 50, 74; CN; CP; DA3; DLB 120; INT 127; MTCW 2

Seton, Cynthia Propper 1926-1982 .. **CLC 27**
  See also CA 5-8R; 108; CANR 7

Seton, Ernest (Evan) Thompson 1860-1946 .... **TCLC 31**
  See also CA 109; CLR 59; DLB 92; DLBD 13; JRDA; SATA 18

Seton-Thompson, Ernest
  See Seton, Ernest (Evan) Thompson

Settle, Mary Lee 1918- .... **CLC 19, 61**
  See also CA 89-92; CAAS 1; CANR 44, 87; CN; CSW; DLB 6; INT 89-92

Seuphor, Michel
  See Arp, Jean

Sévigné, Marie (de Rabutin-Chantal) 1626-1696 .... **LC 11**
  See also GFL Beginnings to 1789

Sewall, Samuel 1652-1730 .... **LC 38**
  See also DLB 24; RGAL

Sexton, Anne (Harvey) 1928-1974 ..... **CLC 2, 4, 6, 8, 10, 15, 53, 123; DA; DAB; DAC; DAM MST, POET; PC 2; WLC**
  See also AMWS 2; CA 1-4R; 53-56; CABS 2; CANR 3, 36; CDALB 1941-1968; DA3; DLB 5, 169; FW; MTCW 1, 2; PFS 4; SATA 10

Shaara, Jeff 1952- .... **CLC 119**
  See also CA 163

Shaara, Michael (Joseph, Jr.) 1929-1988 .... **CLC 15; DAM POP**
  See also AITN 1; CA 102; 125; CANR 52, 85; DLBY 83

Shackleton, C. C.
  See Aldiss, Brian W(ilson)

Shacochis, Bob .... **CLC 39**
  See also Shacochis, Robert G.

Shacochis, Robert G. 1951-
  See Shacochis, Bob
  See also CA 119; 124; INT 124

Shaffer, Anthony (Joshua) 1926- ..... **CLC 19; DAM DRAM**
  See also CA 110; 116; CBD; CD; DFS 13; DLB 13

Shaffer, Peter (Levin) 1926- .. **CLC 5, 14, 18, 37, 60; DAB; DAM DRAM, MST; DC 7**
  See also BRWS 1; CA 25-28R; CANR 25, 47, 74; CBD; CD; CDBLB 1960 to Present; DA3; DFS 5, 13; DLB 13, 233; MTCW 1, 2; RGEL

Shakey, Bernard
  See Young, Neil

Shalamov, Varlam (Tikhonovich) 1907(?)-1982 .... **CLC 18**
  See also CA 129; 105

Shamlu, Ahmad 1925-2000 .... **CLC 10**
  See also CWW 2

Shammas, Anton 1951- .... **CLC 55**

Shandling, Arline
  See Berriault, Gina

Shange, Ntozake 1948- .... **CLC 8, 25, 38, 74, 126; BLC 3; DAM DRAM, MULT; DC 3**
  See also AAYA 9; AFAW 1, 2; BW 2; CA 85-88; CABS 3; CAD; CANR 27, 48, 74; CD; CP; CWD; CWP; DA3; DFS 2, 11; DLB 38; FW; MTCW 1, 2; NFS 11; RGAL; YAW

Shanley, John Patrick 1950- .... **CLC 75**
  See also CA 128; 133; CAD; CANR 83; CD

Shapcott, Thomas W(illiam) 1935- .. **CLC 38**
  See also CA 69-72; CANR 49, 83; CP

Shapiro, Jane .... **CLC 76**

Shapiro, Karl (Jay) 1913-2000 ...... **CLC 4, 8, 15, 53; PC 25**
  See also AMWS 2; CA 1-4R; 188; CAAS 6; CANR 1, 36, 66; CP; DLB 48; MTCW 1, 2; PFS 3

Sharp, William 1855-1905 .... **TCLC 39**
  See also Macleod, Fiona
  See also CA 160; DLB 156; RGEL

Sharpe, Thomas Ridley 1928-
  See Sharpe, Tom
  See also CA 114; 122; CANR 85; CN; DLB 231; INT 122

Sharpe, Tom .... **CLC 36**
  See also Sharpe, Thomas Ridley
  See also DLB 14

Shatrov, Mikhail .... **CLC 59**

Shaw, Bernard
  See Shaw, George Bernard
  See also BW 1; MTCW 2

Shaw, G. Bernard
  See Shaw, George Bernard

Shaw, George Bernard 1856-1950 .. **TCLC 3, 9, 21, 45; DA; DAB; DAC; DAM DRAM, MST; WLC**
  See also Shaw, Bernard
  See also CA 104; 128; CDBLB 1914-1945; DA3; DFS 1, 3, 6, 11; DLB 10, 57, 190; MTCW 1, 2

Shaw, Henry Wheeler 1818-1885 .. **NCLC 15**
  See also DLB 11; RGAL

Shaw, Irwin 1913-1984 .... **CLC 7, 23, 34; DAM DRAM, POP**
  See also AITN 1; CA 13-16R; 112; CANR 21; CDALB 1941-1968; CPW; DLB 6, 102; DLBY 84; MTCW 1, 21

Shaw, Robert 1927-1978 .... **CLC 5**
  See also AITN 1; CA 1-4R; 81-84; CANR 4; DLB 13, 14

Shaw, T. E.
  See Lawrence, T(homas) E(dward)

Shawn, Wallace 1943- .... **CLC 41**
  See also CA 112; CAD; CD

Shea, Lisa 1953- .... **CLC 86**
  See also CA 147

Sheed, Wilfrid (John Joseph) 1930- . **CLC 2, 4, 10, 53**
  See also CA 65-68; CANR 30, 66; CN; DLB 6; MTCW 1, 2

Sheldon, Alice Hastings Bradley 1915(?)-1987
  See Tiptree, James, Jr.
  See also CA 108; 122; CANR 34; INT 108; MTCW 1

Sheldon, John
  See Bloch, Robert (Albert)

Sheldon, Walter J(ames) 1917-1996
  See Queen, Ellery
  See also AITN 1; CA 25-28R; CANR 10

Shelley, Mary Wollstonecraft (Godwin) 1797-1851 ..... **NCLC 14, 59; DA; DAB; DAC; DAM MST, NOV; WLC**
  See also AAYA 20; BRW; BRWS 3; CD-BLB 1789-1832; DA3; DLB 110, 116, 159, 178; HGG; NFS 1; RGEL; SATA 29; SCFW; SFW

Shelley, Percy Bysshe 1792-1822 .. **NCLC 18, 93; DA; DAB; DAC; DAM MST, POET; PC 14; WLC**
  See also CDBLB 1789-1832; DA3; DLB 96, 110, 158; PAB; PFS 2; RGEL; WP

Shepard, Jim 1956- .... **CLC 36**
  See also CA 137; CANR 59; SATA 90

Shepard, Lucius 1947- .... **CLC 34**
  See also CA 128; 141; CANR 81; HGG; SCFW 2; SFW

Shepard, Sam 1943- .... **CLC 4, 6, 17, 34, 41, 44; DAM DRAM; DC 5**
  See also AAYA 1; AMWS 3; CA 69-72; CABS 3; CAD; CANR 22; CD; DA3; DFS 3, 6, 7; DLB 7, 212; IDFW 3, 4; MTCW 1, 2; RGAL

Shepherd, Michael
  See Ludlum, Robert

Sherburne, Zoa (Lillian Morin) 1912-1995 .... **CLC 30**
  See also AAYA 13; CA 1-4R; 176; CANR 3, 37; MAICYA; SAAS 18; SATA 3; YAW

Sheridan, Frances 1724-1766 .... **LC 7**
  See also DLB 39, 84

Sheridan, Richard Brinsley 1751-1816 .... **NCLC 5, 91; DA; DAB; DAC; DAM DRAM, MST; DC 1; WLC**
  See also CDBLB 1660-1789; DFS 4; DLB 89; RGEL

Sherman, Jonathan Marc .... **CLC 55**

Sherman, Martin 1941(?)- .... **CLC 19**
  See also CA 116; 123; CANR 86

Sherwin, Judith Johnson
  See Johnson, Judith (Emlyn)
  See also CANR 85; CP; CWP

Sherwood, Frances 1940- .... **CLC 81**
  See also CA 146

Sherwood, Robert E(mmet) 1896-1955 .... **TCLC 3; DAM DRAM**
  See also CA 104; 153; CANR 86; DFS 11; DLB 7, 26; IDFW 4

Shestov, Lev 1866-1938 .... **TCLC 56**

Shevchenko, Taras 1814-1861 .... **NCLC 54**

Shiel, M(atthew) P(hipps) 1865-1947 .... **TCLC 8**
  See also Holmes, Gordon
  See also CA 106; 160; DLB 153; HGG; MTCW 2; SFW

Shields, Carol 1935- .... **CLC 91, 113; DAC**
  See also AMWS 7; CA 81-84; CANR 51, 74, 98; CCA 1; CN; CPW; DA3; MTCW 2

Shields, David 1956- .... **CLC 97**
  See also CA 124; CANR 48

Shiga, Naoya 1883-1971 ..... **CLC 33; SSC 23**
  See also CA 101; 33-36R; DLB 180; MJW

Shikibu, Murasaki c. 978- .... **CMLC 1**
  See also EFS 2; RGWL

Sjoewall, Maj 1935- .... **CLC 7**
  See also Sjowall, Maj
  See also CA 65-68; CANR 73
Sjowall, Maj
  See Sjoewall, Maj
  See also CMW 1
Skelton, John 1460-1529 .... **PC 25**
  See also RGEL
Skelton, Robin 1925-1997 .... **CLC 13**
  See also Zuk, Georges
  See also AITN 2; CA 5-8R; 160; CAAS 5;
  CANR 28, 89; CCA 1; CP; DLB 27, 53
Skolimowski, Jerzy 1938- .... **CLC 20**
  See also CA 128
Skram, Amalie (Bertha)
  1847-1905 .... **TCLC 25**
  See also CA 165
Skvorecky, Josef (Vaclav) 1924- ...... **CLC 15,
  39, 69; DAC; DAM NOV**
  See also CA 61-64; CAAS 1; CANR 10,
  34, 63; DA3; DLB 232; MTCW 1, 2
Slade, Bernard .... **CLC 11, 46**
  See also Newbound, Bernard Slade
  See also CAAS 9; CCA 1; DLB 53
Slaughter, Carolyn 1946- .... **CLC 56**
  See also CA 85-88; CANR 85; CN
Slaughter, Frank G(ill) 1908-2001 ... **CLC 29**
  See also AITN 2; CA 5-8R; CANR 5, 85;
  INT CANR-5; RHW
Slavitt, David R(ytman) 1935- ..... **CLC 5, 14**
  See also CA 21-24R; CAAS 3; CANR 41,
  83; CP; DLB 5, 6
Slesinger, Tess 1905-1945 .... **TCLC 10**
  See also CA 107; DLB 102
Slessor, Kenneth 1901-1971 .... **CLC 14**
  See also CA 102; 89-92; RGEL
Slowacki, Juliusz 1809-1849 .... **NCLC 15**
Smart, Christopher 1722-1771 .. **LC 3; DAM
  POET; PC 13**
  See also DLB 109; RGEL
Smart, Elizabeth 1913-1986 .... **CLC 54**
  See also CA 81-84; 118; DLB 88
Smiley, Jane (Graves) 1949- ...... **CLC 53, 76,
  144; DAM POP**
  See also AMWS 6; CA 104; CANR 30, 50,
  74, 96; CN; CPW 1; DA3; DLB 227, 234;
  INT CANR-30
Smith, A(rthur) J(ames) M(arshall)
  1902-1980 .... **CLC 15; DAC**
  See also CA 1-4R; 102; CANR 4; DLB 88;
  RGEL
Smith, Adam 1723-1790 .... **LC 36**
  See also DLB 104; RGEL
Smith, Alexander 1829-1867 .... **NCLC 59**
  See also DLB 32, 55
Smith, Anna Deavere 1950- .... **CLC 86**
  See also CA 133; CD; DFS 2
Smith, Betty (Wehner) 1896-1972 .... **CLC 19**
  See also CA 5-8R; 33-36R; DLBY 82;
  SATA 6
Smith, Charlotte (Turner)
  1749-1806 .... **NCLC 23**
  See also DLB 39, 109; RGEL
Smith, Clark Ashton 1893-1961 .... **CLC 43**
  See also CA 143; CANR 81; FANT; HGG;
  MTCW 2; SFW
Smith, Dave .... **CLC 22, 42**
  See also Smith, David (Jeddie)
  See also CAAS 7; DLB 5
Smith, David (Jeddie) 1942-
  See Smith, Dave
  See also CA 49-52; CANR 1, 59; CP; CSW;
  DAM POET
Smith, Florence Margaret 1902-1971
  See Smith, Stevie
  See also CA 17-18; 29-32R; CANR 35;
  CAP 2; DAM POET; MTCW 1, 2

Smith, Iain Crichton 1928-1998 .... **CLC 64**
  See also CA 21-24R; 171; CN; CP; DLB
  40, 139; RGSF
Smith, John 1580(?)-1631 .... **LC 9**
  See also DLB 24, 30
Smith, Johnston
  See Crane, Stephen (Townley)
Smith, Joseph, Jr. 1805-1844 .... **NCLC 53**
Smith, Lee 1944- .... **CLC 25, 73**
  See also CA 114; 119; CANR 46; CSW;
  DLB 143; DLBY 83; INT CA-119
Smith, Martin
  See Smith, Martin Cruz
Smith, Martin Cruz 1942- .... **CLC 25; DAM
  MULT, POP**
  See also BEST 89:4; CA 85-88; CANR 6,
  23, 43, 65; CMW; CPW; HGG; INT
  CANR-23; MTCW 2; NNAL; RGAL
Smith, Mary-Ann Tirone 1944- .... **CLC 39**
  See also CA 118; 136
Smith, Patti 1946- .... **CLC 12**
  See also CA 93-96; CANR 63
Smith, Pauline (Urmson)
  1882-1959 .... **TCLC 25**
  See also DLB 225
Smith, Rosamond
  See Oates, Joyce Carol
Smith, Sheila Kaye
  See Kaye-Smith, Sheila
Smith, Stevie .... **CLC 3, 8, 25, 44; PC 12**
  See also Smith, Florence Margaret
  See also BRWS 2; DLB 20; MTCW 2; PFS
  3; RGEL
Smith, Wilbur (Addison) 1933- .... **CLC 33**
  See also CA 13-16R; CANR 7, 46, 66;
  CPW; MTCW 1, 2
Smith, William Jay 1918- .... **CLC 6**
  See also CA 5-8R; CANR 44; CP; CSW;
  CWRI; DLB 5; MAICYA; SAAS 22;
  SATA 2, 68
Smith, Woodrow Wilson
  See Kuttner, Henry
Smolenskin, Peretz 1842-1885 .... **NCLC 30**
Smollett, Tobias (George) 1721-1771 ... **LC 2,
  46**
  See also BRW; CDBLB 1660-1789; DLB
  39, 104; RGEL
Snodgrass, W(illiam) D(e Witt)
  1926- .... **CLC 2, 6, 10, 18, 68; DAM
  POET**
  See also CA 1-4R; CANR 6, 36, 65, 85;
  CP; DLB 5; MTCW 1, 2
Snow, C(harles) P(ercy) 1905-1980 ... **CLC 1,
  4, 6, 9, 13, 19; DAM NOV**
  See also CA 5-8R; 101; CANR 28; CDBLB
  1945-1960; DLB 15, 77; DLBD 17;
  MTCW 1, 2; RGEL
Snow, Frances Compton
  See Adams, Henry (Brooks)
Snyder, Gary (Sherman) 1930- . **CLC 1, 2, 5,
  9, 32, 120; DAM POET; PC 21**
  See also AMWS 8; CA 17-20R; CANR 30,
  60; CP; DA3; DLB 5, 16, 165, 212;
  MTCW 2; PFS 9
Snyder, Zilpha Keatley 1927- .... **CLC 17**
  See also AAYA 15; CA 9-12R; CANR 38;
  CLR 31; JRDA; MAICYA; SAAS 2;
  SATA 1, 28, 75, 110; SATA-Essay 112;
  YAW
Soares, Bernardo
  See Pessoa, Fernando (Ant
Sobh, A.
  See Shamlu, Ahmad
Sobol, Joshua .... **CLC 60**
  See also CWW 2
Socrates 470B.C.-399B.C. .... **CMLC 27**
Söderberg, Hjalmar 1869-1941 ...... **TCLC 39**
Södergran, Edith (Irene)
  See Soedergran, Edith (Irene)

Soedergran, Edith (Irene)
  1892-1923 .... **TCLC 31**
  See also Södergran, Edith (Irene)
Softly, Edgar
  See Lovecraft, H(oward) P(hillips)
Softly, Edward
  See Lovecraft, H(oward) P(hillips)
Sokolov, Raymond 1941- .... **CLC 7**
  See also CA 85-88
Sokolov, Sasha .... **CLC 59**
Solo, Jay
  See Ellison, Harlan (Jay)
Sologub, Fyodor .... **TCLC 9**
  See also Teternikov, Fyodor Kuzmich
Solomons, Ikey Esquir
  See Thackeray, William Makepeace
Solomos, Dionysios 1798-1857 .... **NCLC 15**
Solwoska, Mara
  See French, Marilyn
Solzhenitsyn, Aleksandr I(sayevich)
  1918- .. **CLC 1, 2, 4, 7, 9, 10, 18, 26, 34,
  78, 134; DA; DAB; DAC; DAM MST,
  NOV; SSC 32; WLC**
  See also AITN 1; CA 69-72; CANR 40, 65;
  DA3; MTCW 1, 2; NFS 6; SSFS 9
Somers, Jane
  See Lessing, Doris (May)
Somerville, Edith 1858-1949 .... **TCLC 51**
  See also DLB 135; RGEL; RGSF
Somerville & Ross
  See Martin, Violet Florence; Somerville,
  Edith
Sommer, Scott 1951- .... **CLC 25**
  See also CA 106
Sondheim, Stephen (Joshua) 1930- . **CLC 30,
  39; DAM DRAM**
  See also AAYA 11; CA 103; CANR 47, 67
Song, Cathy 1955- .... **PC 21**
  See also CA 154; CWP; DLB 169; FW; PFS
  5
Sontag, Susan 1933- .... **CLC 1, 2, 10, 13, 31,
  105; DAM POP**
  See also AMWS 3; CA 17-20R; CANR 25,
  51, 74, 97; CN; CPW; DA3; DLB 2, 67;
  MTCW 1, 2; RGAL; RHW; SSFS 10
Sophocles 496(?)B.C.-(?)B.C. . **CMLC 2; DA;
  DAB; DAC; DAM DRAM, MST; DC
  1; WLCS**
  See also DA3; DFS 1,4,8; DLB 176; RGEL
Sordello 1189-1269 .... **CMLC 15**
Sorel, Georges 1847-1922 .... **TCLC 91**
  See also CA 118; 188
Sorel, Julia
  See Drexler, Rosalyn
Sorokin, Vladimir .... **CLC 59**
Sorrentino, Gilbert 1929- .. **CLC 3, 7, 14, 22,
  40**
  See also CA 77-80; CANR 14, 33; CN; CP;
  DLB 5, 173; DLBY 80; INT CANR-14
Soto, Gary 1952- .... **CLC 32, 80; DAM
  MULT; HLC 2; PC 28**
  See also AAYA 10, 37; CA 119; 125; CANR
  50, 74; CLR 38; CP; DLB 82; HW 1, 2;
  INT 125; JRDA; MTCW 2; PFS 7;
  RGAL; SATA 80, 120; YAW
Soupault, Philippe 1897-1990 .... **CLC 68**
  See also CA 116; 147; 131; GFL 1789 to
  the Present
Souster, (Holmes) Raymond 1921- .... **CLC 5,
  14; DAC; DAM POET**
  See also CA 13-16R; CAAS 14; CANR 13,
  29, 53; CP; DA3; DLB 88; RGEL; SATA
  63
Southern, Terry 1924(?)-1995 .... **CLC 7**
  See also CA 1-4R; 150; CANR 1, 55; CN;
  DLB 2; IDFW 3, 4
Southey, Robert 1774-1843 .... **NCLC 8, 97**
  See also DLB 93, 107, 142; RGEL; SATA
  54

Summers, Hollis (Spurgeon, Jr.)
1916- .... **CLC 10**
See also CA 5-8R; CANR 3; DLB 6

Summers, (Alphonsus Joseph-Mary
Augustus) Montague
1880-1948 .... **TCLC 16**
See also CA 118; 163

Sumner, Gordon Matthew .... **CLC 26**
See also Sting

Surtees, Robert Smith 1805-1864 .. **NCLC 14**
See also DLB 21; RGEL

Susann, Jacqueline 1921-1974 .... **CLC 3**
See also AITN 1; CA 65-68; 53-56; MTCW
1, 2

Su Shi
See Su Shih
See also RGWL

Su Shih 1036-1101 .... **CMLC 15**
See also Su Shi

Suskind, Patrick
See Sueskind, Patrick
See also CA 145; CWW 2

Sutcliff, Rosemary 1920-1992 .... **CLC 26;**
DAB; DAC; DAM MST, POP
See also AAYA 10; CA 5-8R; 139; CANR
37; CLR 1, 37; CPW; JRDA; MAICYA;
RHW; SATA 6, 44, 78; SATA-Obit 73;
YAW

Sutro, Alfred 1863-1933 .... **TCLC 6**
See also CA 105; 185; DLB 10; RGEL

Sutton, Henry
See Slavitt, David R(ytman)

Suzuki, D. T.
See Suzuki, Daisetz Teitaro

Suzuki, Daisetz T.
See Suzuki, Daisetz Teitaro

Suzuki, Daisetz Teitaro
1870-1966 .... **TCLC 109**
See also CA 121; 111; MTCW 1, 2

Suzuki, Teitaro
See Suzuki, Daisetz Teitaro

Svevo, Italo .... **TCLC 2, 35; SSC 25**
See also Schmitz, Aron Hector
See also RGWL

Swados, Elizabeth (A.) 1951- .... **CLC 12**
See also CA 97-100; CANR 49; INT 97-
100

Swados, Harvey 1920-1972 .... **CLC 5**
See also CA 5-8R; 37-40R; CANR 6; DLB
2

Swan, Gladys 1934- .... **CLC 69**
See also CA 101; CANR 17, 39

Swanson, Logan
See Matheson, Richard Burton

Swarthout, Glendon (Fred)
1918-1992 .... **CLC 35**
See also CA 1-4R; 139; CANR 1, 47; SATA
26; TCWW 2; YAW

Sweet, Sarah C.
See Jewett, (Theodora) Sarah Orne

Swenson, May 1919-1989 ...... **CLC 4, 14, 61,**
106; DA; DAB; DAC; DAM MST,
POET; PC 14
See also AMWS 4; CA 5-8R; 130; CANR
36, 61; DLB 5; GLL 2; MTCW 1, 2;
SATA 15

Swift, Augustus
See Lovecraft, H(oward) P(hillips)

Swift, Graham (Colin) 1949- ...... **CLC 41, 88**
See also BRWS 5; CA 117; 122; CANR 46,
71; CN; DLB 194; MTCW 2

Swift, Jonathan 1667-1745 ..... **LC 1, 42; DA;**
DAB; DAC; DAM MST, NOV, POET;
PC 9; WLC
See also CDBLB 1660-1789; CLR 53;
DA3; DLB 39, 95, 101; NFS 6; RGEL;
SATA 19

Swinburne, Algernon Charles
1837-1909 .... **TCLC 8, 36; DA; DAB;**
DAC; DAM MST, POET; PC 24; WLC
See also CA 105; 140; CDBLB 1832-1890;
DA3; DLB 35, 57; PAB; RGEL

Swinfen, Ann .... **CLC 34**

Swinnerton, Frank Arthur
1884-1982 .... **CLC 31**
See also CA 108; DLB 34

Swithen, John
See King, Stephen (Edwin)

Sylvia
See Ashton-Warner, Sylvia (Constance)

Symmes, Robert Edward
See Duncan, Robert (Edward)

Symonds, John Addington
1840-1893 .... **NCLC 34**
See also DLB 57, 144

Symons, Arthur 1865-1945 .... **TCLC 11**
See also CA 107; 189; DLB 19, 57, 149;
RGEL

Symons, Julian (Gustave)
1912-1994 .... **CLC 2, 14, 32**
See also CA 49-52; 147; CAAS 3; CANR
3, 33, 59; CMW; DLB 87, 155; DLBY
92; MTCW 1

Synge, (Edmund) J(ohn) M(illington)
1871-1909 . **TCLC 6, 37; DAM DRAM;**
DC 2
See also BRW; CA 104; 141; CDBLB 1890-
1914; DLB 10, 19; RGEL

Syruc, J.
See Milosz, Czeslaw

Szirtes, George 1948- .... **CLC 46**
See also CA 109; CANR 27, 61; CP

Szymborska, Wislawa 1923- .... **CLC 99**
See also CA 154; CANR 91; CWP; CWW
2; DA3; DLB 232; DLBY 96; MTCW 2

T. O., Nik
See Annensky, Innokenty (Fyodorovich)

Tabori, George 1914- .... **CLC 19**
See also CA 49-52; CANR 4, 69; CBD; CD

Tagore, Rabindranath 1861-1941 ... **TCLC 3,**
53; DAM DRAM, POET; PC 8
See also CA 104; 120; DA3; MTCW 1, 2;
RGEL; RGSF; RGWL

Taine, Hippolyte Adolphe
1828-1893 .... **NCLC 15**
See also EW; GFL 1789 to the Present

Talese, Gay 1932- .... **CLC 37**
See also AITN 1; CA 1-4R; CANR 9, 58;
DLB 185; INT CANR-9; MTCW 1, 2

Tallent, Elizabeth (Ann) 1954- .... **CLC 45**
See also CA 117; CANR 72; DLB 130

Tally, Ted 1952- .... **CLC 42**
See also CA 120; 124; CAD; CD; INT 124

Talvik, Heiti 1904-1947 .... **TCLC 87**

Tamayo y Baus, Manuel
1829-1898 .... **NCLC 1**

Tammsaare, A(nton) H(ansen)
1878-1940 .... **TCLC 27**
See also CA 164; DLB 220

Tam'si, Tchicaya U
See Tchicaya, Gerald Felix

Tan, Amy (Ruth) 1952- . **CLC 59, 120; DAM**
MULT, NOV, POP
See also AAYA 9; BEST 89:3; CA 136;
CANR 54; CDALBS; CN; CPW 1; DA3;
DLB 173; FW; MTCW 2; NFS 1; SATA
75; SSFS 9; YAW

Tandem, Felix
See Spitteler, Carl (Friedrich Georg)

Tanizaki, Jun'ichirō 1886-1965 ... **CLC 8, 14,**
28; SSC 21
See also CA 93-96; 25-28R; DLB 180;
MJW; MTCW 2; RGSF; RGWL

Tanner, William
See Amis, Kingsley (William)

Tao Lao
See Storni, Alfonsina

Tarantino, Quentin (Jerome)
1963- .... **CLC 125**
See also CA 171

Tarassoff, Lev
See Troyat, Henri

Tarbell, Ida M(inerva) 1857-1944 . **TCLC 40**
See also CA 122; 181; DLB 47

Tarkington, (Newton) Booth
1869-1946 .... **TCLC 9**
See also CA 110; 143; CWRI; DLB 9, 102;
MTCW 2; SATA 17

Tarkovsky, Andrei (Arsenyevich)
1932-1986 .... **CLC 75**
See also CA 127

Tartt, Donna 1964(?)- .... **CLC 76**
See also CA 142

Tasso, Torquato 1544-1595 .... **LC 5**
See also EFS 2; RGWL

Tate, (John Orley) Allen 1899-1979 .. **CLC 2,**
4, 6, 9, 11, 14, 24
See also CA 5-8R; 85-88; CANR 32; DLB
4, 45, 63; DLBD 17; MTCW 1, 2; RHW

Tate, Ellalice
See Hibbert, Eleanor Alice Burford

Tate, James (Vincent) 1943- ..... **CLC 2, 6, 25**
See also CA 21-24R; CANR 29, 57; CP;
DLB 5, 169; PFS 10

Tauler, Johannes c. 1300-1361 ...... **CMLC 37**
See also DLB 179

Tavel, Ronald 1940- .... **CLC 6**
See also CA 21-24R; CAD; CANR 33; CD

Taviani, Paolo 1931- .... **CLC 70**
See also CA 153

Taylor, Bayard 1825-1878 .... **NCLC 89**
See also DLB 3, 189; RGAL

Taylor, C(ecil) P(hilip) 1929-1981 .... **CLC 27**
See also CA 25-28R; 105; CANR 47; CBD

Taylor, Edward 1642(?)-1729 ..... **LC 11; DA;**
DAB; DAC; DAM MST, POET
See also DLB 24; RGAL

Taylor, Eleanor Ross 1920- .... **CLC 5**
See also CA 81-84; CANR 70

Taylor, Elizabeth 1932-1975 ..... **CLC 2, 4, 29**
See also CA 13-16R; CANR 9, 70; DLB
139; MTCW 1; RGEL; SATA 13

Taylor, Frederick Winslow
1856-1915 .... **TCLC 76**
See also CA 188

Taylor, Henry (Splawn) 1942- .... **CLC 44**
See also CA 33-36R; CAAS 7; CANR 31;
CP; DLB 5; PFS 10

Taylor, Kamala (Purnaiya) 1924-
See Markandaya, Kamala
See also CA 77-80; CN

Taylor, Mildred D(elois) 1943- .... **CLC 21**
See also AAYA 10; BW 1; CA 85-88;
CANR 25; CLR 9, 59; CSW; DLB 52;
JRDA; MAICYA; SAAS 5; SATA 15, 70;
YAW

Taylor, Peter (Hillsman) 1917-1994 .. **CLC 1,**
4, 18, 37, 44, 50, 71; SSC 10
See also AMWS 5; CA 13-16R; 147; CANR
9, 50; CSW; DLBY 81, 94; INT CANR-9;
MTCW 1, 2; SSFS 9

Taylor, Robert Lewis 1912-1998 .... **CLC 14**
See also CA 1-4R; 170; CANR 3, 64; SATA
10

Tchekhov, Anton
See Chekhov, Anton (Pavlovich)

Tchicaya, Gerald Felix 1931-1988 .. **CLC 101**
See also CA 129; 125; CANR 81

Tchicaya U Tam'si
See Tchicaya, Gerald Felix

Teasdale, Sara 1884-1933 .... **TCLC 4; PC 31**
See also CA 104; 163; DLB 45; GLL 1;
RGAL; SATA 32

Tuohy, John Francis 1925-
See Tuohy, Frank
See also CA 5-8R; 178; CANR 3, 47; CN

Turco, Lewis (Putnam) 1934- ..... **CLC 11, 63**
See also CA 13-16R; CAAS 22; CANR 24, 51; CP; DLBY 84

Turgenev, Ivan 1818-1883 .... **NCLC 21, 37; DA; DAB; DAC; DAM MST, NOV; DC 7; SSC 7; WLC**
See also DFS 6; DLB 238; RGSF; RGWL

Turgot, Anne-Robert-Jacques
1727-1781 .... **LC 26**

Turner, Frederick 1943- .... **CLC 48**
See also CA 73-76; CAAS 10; CANR 12, 30, 56; DLB 40

Tutu, Desmond M(pilo) 1931- .... **CLC 80; BLC 3; DAM MULT**
See also BW 1, 3; CA 125; CANR 67, 81

Tutuola, Amos 1920-1997 ...... **CLC 5, 14, 29; BLC 3; DAM MULT**
See also BW 2, 3; CA 9-12R; 159; CANR 27, 66; CN; DA3; DLB 125; DNFS 2; MTCW 1, 2; RGEL

Twain, Mark .... **TCLC 6, 12, 19, 36, 48, 59; SSC 34; WLC**
See also Clemens, Samuel Langhorne
See also AAYA 20; CLR 58, 60, 66; DLB 11, 12, 23, 64, 74; FANT; NFS 1, 6; RGAL; RGSF; SFW; SSFS 1, 7; YAW

Tyler, Anne 1941- .. **CLC 7, 11, 18, 28, 44, 59, 103; DAM NOV, POP**
See also AAYA 18; AMWS 4; BEST 89:1; CA 9-12R; CANR 11, 33, 53; CDALBS; CN; CPW; CSW; DLB 6, 143; DLBY 82; MTCW 1, 2; NFS 2, 7, 10; RGAL; SATA 7, 90; YAW

Tyler, Royall 1757-1826 .... **NCLC 3**
See also DLB 37; RGAL

Tynan, Katharine 1861-1931 .... **TCLC 3**
See also CA 104; 167; DLB 153, 240; FW

Tyutchev, Fyodor 1803-1873 .... **NCLC 34**

Tzara, Tristan 1896-1963 ...... **CLC 47; DAM POET; PC 27**
See also CA 153; 89-92; MTCW 2

Uhry, Alfred 1936- .. **CLC 55; DAM DRAM, POP**
See also CA 127; 133; CAD; CD; CSW; DA3; DFS 11; INT 133

Ulf, Haerved
See Strindberg, (Johan) August

Ulf, Harved
See Strindberg, (Johan) August

Ulibarrí, Sabine R(eyes) 1919- .... **CLC 83; DAM MULT; HLCS 2**
See also CA 131; CANR 81; DLB 82; HW 1, 2

Unamuno (y Jugo), Miguel de
1864-1936 ..... **TCLC 2, 9; DAM MULT, NOV; HLC 2; SSC 11**
See also CA 104; 131; CANR 81; DLB 108; HW 1, 2; MTCW 1, 2

Undercliffe, Errol
See Campbell, (John) Ramsey

Underwood, Miles
See Glassco, John

Undset, Sigrid 1882-1949 .... **TCLC 3; DA; DAB; DAC; DAM MST, NOV; WLC**
See also CA 104; 129; DA3; FW; MTCW 1, 2; RGWL

Ungaretti, Giuseppe 1888-1970 ... **CLC 7, 11, 15**
See also CA 19-20; 25-28R; CAP 2; DLB 114; RGWL

Unger, Douglas 1952- .... **CLC 34**
See also CA 130; CANR 94

Unsworth, Barry (Forster) 1930- .... **CLC 76, 127**
See also CA 25-28R; CANR 30, 54; CN; DLB 194

Updike, John (Hoyer) 1932- . **CLC 1, 2, 3, 5, 7, 9, 13, 15, 23, 34, 43, 70, 139; DA; DAB; DAC; DAM MST, NOV, POET, POP; SSC 13, 27; WLC**
See also AAYA 36; CA 1-4R; CABS 1; CANR 4, 33, 51, 94; CDALB 1968-1988; CN; CP; CPW 1; DA3; DLB 2, 5, 143, 227; DLBD 3; DLBY 80, 82, 97; HGG; MTCW 1, 2; NFS 12; SSFS 3

Upshaw, Margaret Mitchell
See Mitchell, Margaret (Munnerlyn)

Upton, Mark
See Sanders, Lawrence

Upward, Allen 1863-1926 .... **TCLC 85**
See also CA 117; 187; DLB 36

Urdang, Constance (Henriette)
1922-1996 .... **CLC 47**
See also CA 21-24R; CANR 9, 24; CP; CWP

Uriel, Henry
See Faust, Frederick (Schiller)

Uris, Leon (Marcus) 1924- .... **CLC 7, 32; DAM NOV, POP**
See also AITN 1, 2; BEST 89:2; CA 1-4R; CANR 1, 40, 65; CN; CPW 1; DA3; MTCW 1, 2; SATA 49

Urista, Alberto H. 1947- .... **PC 34**
See also Alurista
See also CA 45-48, 182; CANR 2, 32; HLCS 1; HW 1

Urmuz
See Codrescu, Andrei

Urquhart, Guy
See McAlmon, Robert (Menzies)

Urquhart, Jane 1949- .... **CLC 90; DAC**
See also CA 113; CANR 32, 68; CCA 1

Usigli, Rodolfo 1905-1979
See also CA 131; HLCS 1; HW 1

Ustinov, Peter (Alexander) 1921- .... **CLC 1**
See also AITN 1; CA 13-16R; CANR 25, 51; CBD; CD; DLB 13; MTCW 2

U Tam'si, Gerald Felix Tchicaya
See Tchicaya, Gerald Felix

U Tam'si, Tchicaya
See Tchicaya, Gerald Felix

Vachss, Andrew (Henry) 1942- .... **CLC 106**
See also CA 118; CANR 44, 95; CMW

Vachss, Andrew H.
See Vachss, Andrew (Henry)

Vaculik, Ludvik 1926- .... **CLC 7**
See also CA 53-56; CANR 72; CWW 2; DLB 232

Vaihinger, Hans 1852-1933 .... **TCLC 71**
See also CA 116; 166

Valdez, Luis (Miguel) 1940- .. **CLC 84; DAM MULT; DC 10; HLC 2**
See also CA 101; CAD; CANR 32, 81; CD; DFS 5; DLB 122; HW 1

Valenzuela, Luisa 1938- .... **CLC 31, 104; DAM MULT; HLCS 2; SSC 14**
See also CA 101; CANR 32, 65; CWW 2; DLB 113; FW; HW 1, 2; RGSF

Valera y Alcala-Galiano, Juan
1824-1905 .... **TCLC 10**
See also CA 106

Valéry, (Ambroise) Paul (Toussaint Jules)
1871-1945 ... **TCLC 4, 15; DAM POET; PC 9**
See also CA 104; 122; DA3; EW; GFL 1789 to the Present; MTCW 1, 2; RGWL

Valle-Inclán, Ramón (Maria) del
1866-1936 .... **TCLC 5; DAM MULT; HLC 2**
See also CA 106; 153; CANR 80; DLB 134; HW 2

Vallejo, Antonio Buero
See Buero Vallejo, Antonio

Vallejo, César (Abraham)
1892-1938 .. **TCLC 3, 56; DAM MULT; HLC 2**
See also CA 105; 153; HW 1

Vallès, Jules 1832-1885 .... **NCLC 71**
See also DLB 123; GFL 1789 to the Present

Vallette, Marguerite Eymery
1860-1953 .... **TCLC 67**
See also CA 182; DLB 123, 192

Valle Y Pena, Ramon del
See Valle-Incl

Van Ash, Cay 1918- .... **CLC 34**

Vanbrugh, Sir John 1664-1726 . **LC 21; DAM DRAM**
See also DLB 80; IDTP; RGEL

Van Campen, Karl
See Campbell, John W(ood, Jr.)

Vance, Gerald
See Silverberg, Robert

Vance, Jack .... **CLC 35**
See also Vance, John Holbrook
See also DLB 8; SCFW 2

Vance, John Holbrook 1916-
See Queen, Ellery; Vance, Jack
See also CA 29-32R; CANR 17, 65; CMW; FANT; MTCW 1; SFW

Van Den Bogarde, Derek Jules Gaspard
Ulric Niven 1921-1999 .... **CLC 14**
See also CA 77-80; 179; DLB 19

Vandenburgh, Jane .... **CLC 59**
See also CA 168

Vanderhaeghe, Guy 1951- .... **CLC 41**
See also CA 113; CANR 72

van der Post, Laurens (Jan)
1906-1996 .... **CLC 5**
See also AFW; CA 5-8R; 155; CANR 35; CN; DLB 204; RGEL

van de Wetering, Janwillem 1931- ... **CLC 47**
See also CA 49-52; CANR 4, 62, 90; CMW

Van Dine, S. S. .... **TCLC 23**
See also Wright, Willard Huntington

Van Doren, Carl (Clinton)
1885-1950 .... **TCLC 18**
See also CA 111; 168

Van Doren, Mark 1894-1972 .... **CLC 6, 10**
See also CA 1-4R; 37-40R; CANR 3; DLB 45; MTCW 1, 2

Van Druten, John (William)
1901-1957 .... **TCLC 2**
See also CA 104; 161; DLB 10

Van Duyn, Mona (Jane) 1921- ...... **CLC 3, 7, 63, 116; DAM POET**
See also CA 9-12R; CANR 7, 38, 60; CP; CWP; DLB 5

Van Dyne, Edith
See Baum, L(yman) Frank

van Itallie, Jean-Claude 1936- .... **CLC 3**
See also CA 45-48; CAAS 2; CAD; CANR 1, 48; CD; DLB 7

van Ostaijen, Paul 1896-1928 .... **TCLC 33**
See also CA 163

Van Peebles, Melvin 1932- .... **CLC 2, 20; DAM MULT**
See also BW 2, 3; CA 85-88; CANR 27, 67, 82

van Schendel, Arthur(-Francois-Émile)
1874-1946 .... **TCLC 56**

Vansittart, Peter 1920- .... **CLC 42**
See also CA 1-4R; CANR 3, 49, 90; CN; RHW

Van Vechten, Carl 1880-1964 .... **CLC 33**
See also AMWS 2; CA 183; 89-92; DLB 4, 9, 51

van Vogt, A(lfred) E(lton) 1912-2000 . **CLC 1**
See also CA 21-24R; 190; CANR 28; DLB 8; SATA 14; SFW

Varda, Agnes 1928- .... **CLC 16**
See also CA 116; 122

Wahloo, Per 1926-1975 .... **CLC 7**
See also CA 61-64; CANR 73; CMW 1

Wahloo, Peter
See Wahloo, Per

Wain, John (Barrington) 1925-1994 . **CLC 2, 11, 15, 46**
See also CA 5-8R; 145; CAAS 4; CANR 23, 54; CDBLB 1960 to Present; DLB 15, 27, 139, 155; MTCW 1, 2

Wajda, Andrzej 1926- .... **CLC 16**
See also CA 102

Wakefield, Dan 1932- .... **CLC 7**
See also CA 21-24R; CAAS 7; CN

Wakoski, Diane 1937- ...... **CLC 2, 4, 7, 9, 11, 40; DAM POET; PC 15**
See also CA 13-16R; CAAS 1; CANR 9, 60; CP; CWP; DLB 5; INT CANR-9; MTCW 2

Wakoski-Sherbell, Diane
See Wakoski, Diane

Walcott, Derek (Alton) 1930- .... **CLC 2, 4, 9, 14, 25, 42, 67, 76; BLC 3; DAB; DAC; DAM MST, MULT, POET; DC 7**
See also BW 2; CA 89-92; CANR 26, 47, 75, 80; CBD; CD; CP; DA3; DLB 117; DLBY 81; DNFS 1; EFS 1; MTCW 1, 2; PFS 6; RGEL

Waldman, Anne (Lesley) 1945- .... **CLC 7**
See also CA 37-40R; CAAS 17; CANR 34, 69; CP; CWP; DLB 16

Waldo, E. Hunter
See Sturgeon, Theodore (Hamilton)

Waldo, Edward Hamilton
See Sturgeon, Theodore (Hamilton)

Walker, Alice (Malsenior) 1944- ... **CLC 5, 6, 9, 19, 27, 46, 58, 103; BLC 3; DA; DAB; DAC; DAM MST, MULT, NOV, POET, POP; PC 30; SSC 5; WLCS**
See also AAYA 3, 33; AFAW 1, 2; AMWS 3; BEST 89:4; BW 2, 3; CA 37-40R; CANR 9, 27, 49, 66, 82; CDALB 1968-1988; CN; CPW; CSW; DA3; DLB 6, 33, 143; FW; INT CANR-27; MTCW 1, 2; NFS 5; SATA 31; SSFS 2, 11; YAW

Walker, David Harry 1911-1992 ...... **CLC 14**
See also CA 1-4R; 137; CANR 1; CWRI; SATA 8; SATA-Obit 71

Walker, Edward Joseph 1934-
See Walker, Ted
See also CA 21-24R; CANR 12, 28, 53; CP

Walker, George F. 1947- . **CLC 44, 61; DAB; DAC; DAM MST**
See also CA 103; CANR 21, 43, 59; CD; DLB 60

Walker, Joseph A. 1935- .... **CLC 19; DAM DRAM, MST**
See also BW 1, 3; CA 89-92; CAD; CANR 26; CD; DFS 12; DLB 38

Walker, Margaret (Abigail) 1915-1998 .... **CLC 1, 6; BLC; DAM MULT; PC 20**
See also AFAW 1, 2; BW 2, 3; CA 73-76; 172; CANR 26, 54, 76; CN; CP; CSW; DLB 76, 152; FW; MTCW 1, 2; RHW

Walker, Ted .... **CLC 13**
See also Walker, Edward Joseph
See also DLB 40

Wallace, David Foster 1962- ..... **CLC 50, 114**
See also CA 132; CANR 59; DA3; MTCW 2

Wallace, Dexter
See Masters, Edgar Lee

Wallace, (Richard Horatio) Edgar 1875-1932 .... **TCLC 57**
See also CA 115; CMW; DLB 70; RGEL

Wallace, Irving 1916-1990 .... **CLC 7, 13; DAM NOV, POP**
See also AITN 1; CA 1-4R; 132; CAAS 1; CANR 1, 27; CPW; INT CANR-27; MTCW 1, 2

Wallant, Edward Lewis 1926-1962 ... **CLC 5, 10**
See also CA 1-4R; CANR 22; DLB 2, 28, 143; MTCW 1, 2; RGAL

Wallas, Graham 1858-1932 .... **TCLC 91**

Walley, Byron
See Card, Orson Scott

Walpole, Horace 1717-1797 .... **LC 49**
See also DLB 39, 104; HGG; RGEL

Walpole, Hugh (Seymour) 1884-1941 .... **TCLC 5**
See also CA 104; 165; DLB 34; HGG; MTCW 2; RGEL; RHW

Walser, Martin 1927- .... **CLC 27**
See also CA 57-60; CANR 8, 46; CWW 2; DLB 75, 124

Walser, Robert 1878-1956 .... **TCLC 18; SSC 20**
See also CA 118; 165; DLB 66

Walsh, Gillian Paton
See Paton Walsh, Gillian

Walsh, Jill Paton .... **CLC 35**
See also Paton Walsh, Gillian
See also CLR 2, 65

Walter, Villiam Christian
See Andersen, Hans Christian

Wambaugh, Joseph (Aloysius, Jr.) 1937- .... **CLC 3, 18; DAM NOV, POP**
See also AITN 1; BEST 89:3; CA 33-36R; CANR 42, 65; CMW; CPW 1; DA3; DLB 6; DLBY 83; MTCW 1, 2

Wang Wei 699(?)-761(?) .... **PC 18**

Ward, Arthur Henry Sarsfield 1883-1959
See Rohmer, Sax
See also CA 108; 173; CMW; HGG

Ward, Douglas Turner 1930- .... **CLC 19**
See also BW 1; CA 81-84; CAD; CANR 27; CD; DLB 7, 38

Ward, E. D.
See Lucas, E(dward) V(errall)

Ward, Mrs.Humphry 1851-1920
See Ward, Mary Augusta
See also RGEL

Ward, Mary Augusta 1851-1920 ... **TCLC 55**
See also Ward, Mrs.Humphry
See also DLB 18

Ward, Peter
See Faust, Frederick (Schiller)

Warhol, Andy 1928(?)-1987 .... **CLC 20**
See also AAYA 12; BEST 89:4; CA 89-92; 121; CANR 34

Warner, Francis (Robert le Plastrier) 1937- .... **CLC 14**
See also CA 53-56; CANR 11

Warner, Marina 1946- .... **CLC 59**
See also CA 65-68; CANR 21, 55; CN; DLB 194

Warner, Rex (Ernest) 1905-1986 ...... **CLC 45**
See also CA 89-92; 119; DLB 15; RGEL; RHW

Warner, Susan (Bogert) 1819-1885 .... **NCLC 31**
See also DLB 3, 42, 239

Warner, Sylvia (Constance) Ashton
See Ashton-Warner, Sylvia (Constance)

Warner, Sylvia Townsend 1893-1978 .... **CLC 7, 19; SSC 23**
See also CA 61-64; 77-80; CANR 16, 60; DLB 34, 139; FANT; FW; MTCW 1, 2; RGEL; RGSF; RHW

Warren, Mercy Otis 1728-1814 ..... **NCLC 13**
See also DLB 31, 200

Warren, Robert Penn 1905-1989 .. **CLC 1, 4, 6, 8, 10, 13, 18, 39, 53, 59; DA; DAB; DAC; DAM MST, NOV, POET; SSC 4; WLC**
See also AITN 1; CA 13-16R; 129; CANR 10, 47; CDALB 1968-1988; DA3; DLB 2, 48, 152; DLBY 80, 89; INT CANR-10; MTCW 1, 2; RGAL; RGSF; RHW; SATA 46; SATA-Obit 63; SSFS 8

Warshofsky, Isaac
See Singer, Isaac Bashevis

Warton, Thomas 1728-1790 ..... **LC 15; DAM POET**
See also DLB 104, 109; RGEL

Waruk, Kona
See Harris, (Theodore) Wilson

Warung, Price .... **TCLC 45**
See also Astley, William
See also RGEL

Warwick, Jarvis
See Garner, Hugh
See also CCA 1

Washington, Alex
See Harris, Mark

Washington, Booker T(aliaferro) 1856-1915 ...... **TCLC 10; BLC 3; DAM MULT**
See also BW 1; CA 114; 125; DA3; SATA 28

Washington, George 1732-1799 .... **LC 25**
See also DLB 31

Wassermann, (Karl) Jakob 1873-1934 .... **TCLC 6**
See also CA 104; 163; DLB 66

Wasserstein, Wendy 1950- .. **CLC 32, 59, 90; DAM DRAM; DC 4**
See also CA 121; 129; CABS 3; CAD; CANR 53, 75; CD; CWD; DA3; DFS 5; DLB 228; FW; INT 129; MTCW 2; SATA 94

Waterhouse, Keith (Spencer) 1929- . **CLC 47**
See also CA 5-8R; CANR 38, 67; CBD; CN; DLB 13, 15; MTCW 1, 2

Waters, Frank (Joseph) 1902-1995 .. **CLC 88**
See also CA 5-8R; 149; CAAS 13; CANR 3, 18, 63; DLB 212; DLBY 86; TCWW 2

Waters, Mary C. .... **CLC 70**

Waters, Roger 1944- .... **CLC 35**

Watkins, Frances Ellen
See Harper, Frances Ellen Watkins

Watkins, Gerrold
See Malzberg, Barry N(athaniel)

Watkins, Gloria Jean 1952(?)-
See hooks, bell
See also BW 2; CA 143; CANR 87; MTCW 2; SATA 115

Watkins, Paul 1964- .... **CLC 55**
See also CA 132; CANR 62, 98

Watkins, Vernon Phillips 1906-1967 .... **CLC 43**
See also CA 9-10; 25-28R; CAP 1; DLB 20; RGEL

Watson, Irving S.
See Mencken, H(enry) L(ouis)

Watson, John H.
See Farmer, Philip Jose

Watson, Richard F.
See Silverberg, Robert

Waugh, Auberon (Alexander) 1939-2001 .... **CLC 7**
See also CA 45-48; CANR 6, 22, 92; DLB 14, 194

Waugh, Evelyn (Arthur St. John) 1903-1966 .. **CLC 1, 3, 8, 13, 19, 27, 44, 107; DA; DAB; DAC; DAM MST, NOV, POP; SSC 41; WLC**
See also CA 85-88; 25-28R; CANR 22; CD-BLB 1914-1945; DA3; DLB 15, 162, 195; MTCW 1, 2

Wheelock, John Hall 1886-1978 .... **CLC 14**
See also CA 13-16R; 77-80; CANR 14;
DLB 45
White, Babington
See Braddon, Mary Elizabeth
White, E(lwyn) B(rooks)
1899-1985 . **CLC 10, 34, 39; DAM POP**
See also AITN 2; AMWS 1; CA 13-16R;
116; CANR 16, 37; CDALBS; CLR 1, 21;
CPW; DA3; DLB 11, 22; FANT; MAI-
CYA; MTCW 1, 2; SATA 2, 29, 100;
SATA-Obit 44
White, Edmund (Valentine III)
1940- .... **CLC 27, 110; DAM POP**
See also AAYA 7; CA 45-48; CANR 3, 19,
36, 62; CN; DA3; DLB 227; MTCW 1, 2
White, Patrick (Victor Martindale)
1912-1990 ...... **CLC 3, 4, 5, 7, 9, 18, 65,
69; SSC 39**
See also BRWS 1; CA 81-84; 132; CANR
43; MTCW 1; RHW
White, Phyllis Dorothy James 1920-
See James, P. D.
See also CA 21-24R; CANR 17, 43, 65;
CMW; CN; CPW; DAM POP; DA3;
MTCW 1, 2
White, T(erence) H(anbury)
1906-1964 .... **CLC 30**
See also AAYA 22; CA 73-76; CANR 37;
DLB 160; FANT; JRDA; MAICYA;
RGEL; SATA 12; SUFW; YAW
White, Terence de Vere 1912-1994 ... **CLC 49**
See also CA 49-52; 145; CANR 3
White, Walter
See White, Walter F(rancis)
See also BLC; DAM MULT
White, Walter F(rancis)
1893-1955 .... **TCLC 15**
See also White, Walter
See also BW 1; CA 115; 124; DLB 51
White, William Hale 1831-1913
See Rutherford, Mark
See also CA 121; 189
Whitehead, Alfred North
1861-1947 .... **TCLC 97**
See also CA 117; 165; DLB 100
Whitehead, E(dward) A(nthony)
1933- .... **CLC 5**
See also CA 65-68; CANR 58; CD
Whitemore, Hugh (John) 1936- .... **CLC 37**
See also CA 132; CANR 77; CBD; CD;
INT CA-132
Whitman, Sarah Helen (Power)
1803-1878 .... **NCLC 19**
See also DLB 1
Whitman, Walt(er) 1819-1892 .. **NCLC 4, 31,
81; DA; DAB; DAC; DAM MST,
POET; PC 3; WLC**
See also CDALB 1640-1865; DA3; DLB 3,
64, 224; PFS 2, 3; SATA 20; WYAS 1
Whitney, Phyllis A(yame) 1903- ...... **CLC 42;
DAM POP**
See also AAYA 36; AITN 2; BEST 90:3;
CA 1-4R; CANR 3, 25, 38, 60; CLR 59;
CMW; CPW; DA3; JRDA; MAICYA;
MTCW 2; RHW; SATA 1, 30; YAW
Whittemore, (Edward) Reed (Jr.)
1919- .... **CLC 4**
See also CA 9-12R; CAAS 8; CANR 4; CP;
DLB 5
Whittier, John Greenleaf
1807-1892 .... **NCLC 8, 59**
See also AMWS 1; DLB 1; RGAL
Whittlebot, Hernia
See Coward, No
Wicker, Thomas Grey 1926-
See Wicker, Tom
See also CA 65-68; CANR 21, 46

Wicker, Tom .... **CLC 7**
See also Wicker, Thomas Grey
Wideman, John Edgar 1941- ...... **CLC 5, 34,
36, 67, 122; BLC 3; DAM MULT**
See also AFAW 1, 2; BW 2, 3; CA 85-88;
CANR 14, 42, 67; CN; DLB 33, 143;
MTCW 2; RGAL; RGSF; SSFS 6, 12
Wiebe, Rudy (Henry) 1934- .. **CLC 6, 11, 14,
138; DAC; DAM MST**
See also CA 37-40R; CANR 42, 67; CN;
DLB 60; RHW
Wieland, Christoph Martin
1733-1813 .... **NCLC 17**
See also DLB 97; RGWL
Wiene, Robert 1881-1938 .... **TCLC 56**
Wieners, John 1934- .... **CLC 7**
See also CA 13-16R; CP; DLB 16
Wiesel, Elie(zer) 1928- .... **CLC 3, 5, 11, 37;
DA; DAB; DAC; DAM MST, NOV;
WLCS**
See also AAYA 7; AITN 1; CA 5-8R; CAAS
4; CANR 8, 40, 65; CDALBS; DA3; DLB
83; DLBY 87; INT CANR-8; MTCW 1,
2; NFS 4; SATA 56; YAW
Wiggins, Marianne 1947- .... **CLC 57**
See also BEST 89:3; CA 130; CANR 60
Wiggs, Susan .... **CLC 70**
Wight, James Alfred 1916-1995
See Herriot, James
See also CA 77-80; CPW; SATA 55; SATA-
Brief 44; YAW
Wilbur, Richard (Purdy) 1921- ..... **CLC 3, 6,
9, 14, 53, 110; DA; DAB; DAC; DAM
MST, POET**
See also AMWS 3; CA 1-4R; CABS 2;
CANR 2, 29, 76, 93; CDALBS; CP; DLB
5, 169; INT CANR-29; MTCW 1, 2; PFS
11, 12; SATA 9, 108
Wild, Peter 1940- .... **CLC 14**
See also CA 37-40R; CP; DLB 5
Wilde, Oscar (Fingal O'Flahertie Wills)
1854(?)-1900 .... **TCLC 1, 8, 23, 41; DA;
DAB; DAC; DAM DRAM, MST, NOV;
SSC 11; WLC**
See also CA 104; 119; CDBLB 1890-1914;
DA3; DFS 4, 8, 9; DLB 10, 19, 34, 57,
141, 156, 190; FANT; SATA 24; SSFS 7
Wilder, Billy .... **CLC 20**
See also Wilder, Samuel
See also DLB 26
Wilder, Samuel 1906-
See Wilder, Billy
See also CA 89-92
Wilder, Stephen
See Marlowe, Stephen
Wilder, Thornton (Niven)
1897-1975 .. **CLC 1, 5, 6, 10, 15, 35, 82;
DA; DAB; DAC; DAM DRAM, MST,
NOV; DC 1; WLC**
See also AAYA 29; AITN 2; CA 13-16R;
61-64; CANR 40; CDALBS; DA3; DFS
1, 4; DLB 4, 7, 9, 228; DLBY 97; MTCW
1, 2; RHW; WYAS 1
Wilding, Michael 1942- .... **CLC 73**
See also CA 104; CANR 24, 49; CN; RGSF
Wiley, Richard 1944- .... **CLC 44**
See also CA 121; 129; CANR 71
Wilhelm, Kate .... **CLC 7**
See also Wilhelm, Katie (Gertrude)
See also AAYA 20; CAAS 5; DLB 8; INT
CANR-17; SCFW 2
Wilhelm, Katie (Gertrude) 1928-
See Wilhelm, Kate
See also CA 37-40R; CANR 17, 36, 60, 94;
MTCW 1; SFW
Wilkins, Mary
See Freeman, Mary E(leanor) Wilkins

Willard, Nancy 1936- .... **CLC 7, 37**
See also CA 89-92; CANR 10, 39, 68; CLR
5; CWP; CWRI; DLB 5, 52; FANT; MAI-
CYA; MTCW 1; SATA 37, 71; SATA-
Brief 30
William of Ockham 1290-1349 ..... **CMLC 32**
Williams, Ben Ames 1889-1953 ..... **TCLC 89**
See also CA 183; DLB 102
Williams, C(harles) K(enneth)
1936- .... **CLC 33, 56; DAM POET**
See also CA 37-40R; CAAS 26; CANR 57;
CP; DLB 5
Williams, Charles
See Collier, James L(incoln)
Williams, Charles (Walter Stansby)
1886-1945 .... **TCLC 1, 11**
See also CA 104; 163; DLB 100, 153;
FANT; RGEL; SUFW
Williams, (George) Emlyn
1905-1987 .... **CLC 15; DAM DRAM**
See also CA 104; 123; CANR 36; DLB 10,
77; MTCW 1
Williams, Hank 1923-1953 .... **TCLC 81**
Williams, Hugo 1942- .... **CLC 42**
See also CA 17-20R; CANR 45; CP; DLB
40
Williams, J. Walker
See Wodehouse, P(elham) G(renville)
Williams, John A(lfred) 1925- ..... **CLC 5, 13;
BLC 3; DAM MULT**
See also AFAW 2; BW 2, 3; CA 53-56;
CAAS 3; CANR 6, 26, 51; CN; CSW;
DLB 2, 33; INT CANR-6; SFW
Williams, Jonathan (Chamberlain)
1929- .... **CLC 13**
See also CA 9-12R; CAAS 12; CANR 8;
CP; DLB 5
Williams, Joy 1944- .... **CLC 31**
See also CA 41-44R; CANR 22, 48, 97
Williams, Norman 1952- .... **CLC 39**
See also CA 118
Williams, Sherley Anne 1944-1999 . **CLC 89;
BLC 3; DAM MULT, POET**
See also AFAW 2; BW 2, 3; CA 73-76; 185;
CANR 25, 82; DLB 41; INT CANR-25;
SATA 78; SATA-Obit 116
Williams, Shirley
See Williams, Sherley Anne
Williams, Tennessee 1914-1983 . **CLC 1, 2, 5,
7, 8, 11, 15, 19, 30, 39, 45, 71, 111; DA;
DAB; DAC; DAM DRAM, MST; DC
4; WLC**
See also AAYA 31; AITN 1, 2; CA 5-8R;
108; CABS 3; CAD; CANR 31; CDALB
1941-1968; DA3; DFS 1,3,7,12; DLB 7;
DLBD 4; DLBY 83; GLL 1; MTCW 1, 2;
RGAL
Williams, Thomas (Alonzo)
1926-1990 .... **CLC 14**
See also CA 1-4R; 132; CANR 2
Williams, William C.
See Williams, William Carlos
Williams, William Carlos
1883-1963 .... **CLC 1, 2, 5, 9, 13, 22, 42,
67; DA; DAB; DAC; DAM MST,
POET; PC 7; SSC 31**
See also CA 89-92; CANR 34; CDALB
1917-1929; DA3; DLB 4, 16, 54, 86;
MTCW 1, 2; PFS 1, 6, 11; RGAL; RGSF
Williamson, David (Keith) 1942- .... **CLC 56**
See also CA 103; CANR 41; CD
Williamson, Ellen Douglas 1905-1984
See Douglas, Ellen
See also CA 17-20R; 114; CANR 39
Williamson, Jack .... **CLC 29**
See also Williamson, John Stewart
See also CAAS 8; DLB 8; SCFW 2

Williamson, John Stewart 1908-
See Williamson, Jack
See also CA 17-20R; CANR 23, 70; SFW

Willie, Frederick
See Lovecraft, H(oward) P(hillips)

Willingham, Calder (Baynard, Jr.)
1922-1995 .... **CLC 5, 51**
See also CA 5-8R; 147; CANR 3; CSW;
DLB 2, 44; IDFW 3; MTCW 1

Willis, Charles
See Clarke, Arthur C(harles)

Willy
See Colette, (Sidonie-Gabrielle)

Willy, Colette
See Colette, (Sidonie-Gabrielle)
See also GLL 1

Wilson, A(ndrew) N(orman) 1950- .. **CLC 33**
See also BRWS 6; CA 112; 122; CN; DLB
14, 155, 194; MTCW 2

Wilson, Angus (Frank Johnstone)
1913-1991 . **CLC 2, 3, 5, 25, 34; SSC 21**
See also BRWS 1; CA 5-8R; 134; CANR
21; DLB 15, 139, 155; MTCW 1, 2

Wilson, August 1945- ... **CLC 39, 50, 63, 118;
BLC 3; DA; DAB; DAC; DAM
DRAM, MST, MULT; DC 2; WLCS**
See also AAYA 16; AFAW 2; AMWS 8; BW
2, 3; CA 115; 122; CAD; CANR 42, 54,
76; CD; DA3; DFS 3,7; DLB 228; MTCW
1, 2; RGAL

Wilson, Brian 1942- .... **CLC 12**

Wilson, Colin 1931- .... **CLC 3, 14**
See also CA 1-4R; CAAS 5; CANR 1, 22,
33, 77; CMW; CN; DLB 14, 194; HGG;
MTCW 1; SFW

Wilson, Dirk
See Pohl, Frederik

Wilson, Edmund 1895-1972 .. **CLC 1, 2, 3, 8,
24**
See also CA 1-4R; 37-40R; CANR 1, 46;
DLB 63; MTCW 1, 2; RGAL

Wilson, Ethel Davis (Bryant)
1888(?)-1980 .... **CLC 13; DAC; DAM
POET**
See also CA 102; DLB 68; MTCW 1;
RGEL

Wilson, Harriet E. Adams
1827(?)-1863(?) .... **NCLC 78; BLC 3;
DAM MULT**
See also DLB 50

Wilson, John 1785-1854 .... **NCLC 5**

Wilson, John (Anthony) Burgess 1917-1993
See Burgess, Anthony
See also CA 1-4R; 143; CANR 2, 46; DAC;
DAM NOV; DA3; MTCW 1, 2

Wilson, Lanford 1937- .... **CLC 7, 14, 36;
DAM DRAM**
See also CA 17-20R; CABS 3; CAD; CANR
45, 96; CD; DFS 4, 9, 12; DLB 7

Wilson, Robert M. 1944- .... **CLC 7, 9**
See also CA 49-52; CAD; CANR 2, 41; CD;
MTCW 1

Wilson, Robert McLiam 1964- .... **CLC 59**
See also CA 132

Wilson, Sloan 1920- .... **CLC 32**
See also CA 1-4R; CANR 1, 44; CN

Wilson, Snoo 1948- .... **CLC 33**
See also CA 69-72; CBD; CD

Wilson, William S(mith) 1932- .... **CLC 49**
See also CA 81-84

Wilson, (Thomas) Woodrow
1856-1924 .... **TCLC 79**
See also CA 166; DLB 47

Wilson and Warnke eds. .... **CLC 65**

Winchilsea, Anne (Kingsmill) Finch
1661-1720
See Finch, Anne

Windham, Basil
See Wodehouse, P(elham) G(renville)

Wingrove, David (John) 1954- .... **CLC 68**
See also CA 133; SFW

Winnemucca, Sarah 1844-1891 .... **NCLC 79;
DAM MULT**
See also DLB 175; NNAL

Winstanley, Gerrard 1609-1676 .... **LC 52**

Wintergreen, Jane
See Duncan, Sara Jeannette

Winters, Janet Lewis .... **CLC 41**
See Lewis, Janet
See also DLBY 87

Winters, (Arthur) Yvor 1900-1968 .... **CLC 4,
8, 32**
See also AMWS 2; CA 11-12; 25-28R; CAP
1; DLB 48; MTCW 1

Winterson, Jeanette 1959- .... **CLC 64; DAM
POP**
See also BRWS 4; CA 136; CANR 58; CN;
CPW; DA3; DLB 207; FANT; FW; GLL
1; MTCW 2; RHW

Winthrop, John 1588-1649 .... **LC 31**
See also DLB 24, 30

Wirth, Louis 1897-1952 .... **TCLC 92**

Wiseman, Frederick 1930- .... **CLC 20**
See also CA 159

Wister, Owen 1860-1938 .... **TCLC 21**
See also CA 108; 162; DLB 9, 78, 186;
RGAL; SATA 62; TCWW 2

Witkacy
See Witkiewicz, Stanislaw Ignacy

Witkiewicz, Stanislaw Ignacy
1885-1939 .... **TCLC 8**
See also CA 105; 162; DLB 215; SFW

Wittgenstein, Ludwig (Josef Johann)
1889-1951 .... **TCLC 59**
See also CA 113; 164; MTCW 2

Wittig, Monique 1935(?)- .... **CLC 22**
See also CA 116; 135; CWW; DLB 83;
FW; GLL 1

Wittlin, Jozef 1896-1976 .... **CLC 25**
See also CA 49-52; 65-68; CANR 3

Wodehouse, P(elham) G(renville)
1881-1975 .... **CLC 1, 2, 5, 10, 22; DAB;
DAC; DAM NOV; SSC 2**
See also AITN 2; BRWS 3; CA 45-48; 57-
60; CANR 3, 33; CDBLB 1914-1945;
CPW 1; DA3; DLB 34, 162; MTCW 1, 2;
RGEL; RGSF; SATA 22; SSFS 10; TCLC
108

Woiwode, L.
See Woiwode, Larry (Alfred)

Woiwode, Larry (Alfred) 1941- ... **CLC 6, 10**
See also CA 73-76; CANR 16, 94; CN;
DLB 6; INT CANR-16

Wojciechowska, Maia (Teresa)
1927- .... **CLC 26**
See also AAYA 8; CA 9-12R, 183; CAAE
183; CANR 4, 41; CLR 1; JRDA; MAI-
CYA; SAAS 1; SATA 1, 28, 83; SATA-
Essay 104; YAW

Wojtyla, Karol
See John Paul II, Pope

Wolf, Christa 1929- .... **CLC 14, 29, 58**
See also CA 85-88; CANR 45; CWW 2;
DLB 75; FW; MTCW 1; RGWL

Wolfe, Gene (Rodman) 1931- .... **CLC 25;
DAM POP**
See also AAYA 35; CA 57-60; CAAS 9;
CANR 6, 32, 60; CPW; DLB 8; FANT;
MTCW 2; SATA 118; SCFW 2; SFW

Wolfe, George C. 1954- .... **CLC 49; BLCS**
See also CA 149; CAD; CD

Wolfe, Thomas (Clayton)
1900-1938 ...... **TCLC 4, 13, 29, 61; DA;
DAB; DAC; DAM MST, NOV; SSC
33; WLC**
See also CA 104; 132; CDALB 1929-1941;
DA3; DLB 9, 102; DLBD 2, 16; DLBY
85, 97; MTCW 1, 2

Wolfe, Thomas Kennerly, Jr. 1930-
See Wolfe, Tom
See also CA 13-16R; CANR 9, 33, 70;
DAM POP; DA3; DLB 185; INT
CANR-9; MTCW 1, 2

Wolfe, Tom .... **CLC 1, 2, 9, 15, 35, 51**
See also Wolfe, Thomas Kennerly, Jr.
See also AAYA 8; AITN 2; AMWS 3; BEST
89:1; CN; CPW; CSW; DLB 152; RGAL

Wolff, Geoffrey (Ansell) 1937- .... **CLC 41**
See also CA 29-32R; CANR 29, 43, 78

Wolff, Sonia
See Levitin, Sonia (Wolff)

Wolff, Tobias (Jonathan Ansell)
1945- .... **CLC 39, 64**
See also AAYA 16; AMWS 7; BEST 90:2;
CA 114; 117; CAAS 22; CANR 54, 76,
96; CN; CSW; DA3; DLB 130; INT CA-
117; MTCW 2; SSFS 4,11

Wolfram von Eschenbach c. 1170-c.
1220 .... **CMLC 5**
See also Eschenbach, Wolfram von
See also DLB 138

Wolitzer, Hilma 1930- .... **CLC 17**
See also CA 65-68; CANR 18, 40; INT
CANR-18; SATA 31; YAW

Wollstonecraft, Mary 1759-1797 ..... **LC 5, 50**
See also BRWS 3; CDBLB 1789-1832;
DLB 39, 104, 158; FW; RGEL

Wonder, Stevie .... **CLC 12**
See also Morris, Steveland Judkins

Wong, Jade Snow 1922- .... **CLC 17**
See also CA 109; CANR 91; SATA 112

Woodberry, George Edward
1855-1930 .... **TCLC 73**
See also CA 165; DLB 71, 103

Woodcott, Keith
See Brunner, John (Kilian Houston)

Woodruff, Robert W.
See Mencken, H(enry) L(ouis)

Woolf, (Adeline) Virginia
1882-1941 .. **TCLC 1, 5, 20, 43, 56, 101;
DA; DAB; DAC; DAM MST, NOV;
SSC 7; WLC**
See also Woolf, Virginia Adeline
See also CA 104; 130; CANR 64; CDBLB
1914-1945; DA3; DLB 36, 100, 162;
DLBD 10; FW; MTCW 1; NCFS 2; NFS
8, 12; SSFS 4, 12

Woolf, Virginia Adeline
See Woolf, (Adeline) Virginia
See also MTCW 2

Woollcott, Alexander (Humphreys)
1887-1943 .... **TCLC 5**
See also CA 105; 161; DLB 29

Woolrich, Cornell .... **CLC 77**
See also Hopley-Woolrich, Cornell George

Woolson, Constance Fenimore
1840-1894 .... **NCLC 82**
See also DLB 12, 74, 189, 221; RGAL

Wordsworth, Dorothy 1771-1855 .. **NCLC 25**
See also DLB 107

Wordsworth, William 1770-1850 .. **NCLC 12,
38; DA; DAB; DAC; DAM MST,
POET; PC 4; WLC**
See also CDBLB 1789-1832; DA3; DLB
93, 107; PFS 2; RGEL

Wotton, SirHenry 1568-1639 .... **LC 68**
See also DLB 121; RGEL

Wouk, Herman 1915- ... **CLC 1, 9, 38; DAM
NOV, POP**
See also CA 5-8R; CANR 6, 33, 67;
CDALBS; CN; CPW; DA3; DLBY 82;
INT CANR-6; MTCW 1, 2; NFS 7

Wright, Charles (Penzel, Jr.) 1935- .. **CLC 6,
13, 28, 119, 146**
See also AMWS 5; CA 29-32R; CAAS 7;
CANR 23, 36, 62, 88; CP; DLB 165;
DLBY 82; MTCW 1, 2; PFS 10

Literary Criticism Series
Cumulative Topic Index

This index lists all topic entries in Gale's *Classical and Medieval Literature Criticism,
Contemporary Literary Criticism, Literature Criticism from 1400 to 1800, Nineteenth-Century
Literature Criticism,* and *Twentieth-Century Literary Criticism.*

Topic Index

Topic Index

Topic Index

NCLC Cumulative Nationality Index

Nationality Index

ISBN 0-7876-4555-9

90000

9 780787 645557